CHI '92
Conference Proceedings

ACM Conference on Human Factors in Computing Systems

STRIKING A BALANCE

May 3–7, 1992

Monterey, California

Edited By

Penny Bauersfeld,

John Bennett, and Gene Lynch

Sample Citation Information:
...In proceedings of CHI, 1992 (Monterey, California, May 3-May 7, 1992) ACM, New York, 1992. pp. 23-35

Ordering Information

Nonmembers
Nonmember orders placed within the U.S. should be directed to:

Addison-Wesley Publishing Company
Order Department
Jacob Way
Reading, MA 01867
Tel: 1-800-447-2226

Addison-Wesley will pay postage and handling on orders accompanied by check. Credit card orders may be placed by mail or by calling the Addison-Wesley Customer Service Department at the same number.

Please include the Addison-Wesley ISBN number with your order:

A-W ISBN 0-201-53344-X

Nonmember orders from outside the U.S. should be addressed as noted below:

Latin America and Asia:
Addison-Wesley Publishing Company Inc.
Reading, MA 01867, U.S.A.
TEL: 617-944-3700;
Cable: ADIWES READING;
Telex: 94-9416

Canada: Addison-Wesley
Publishing (Canada) Ltd.
36 Prince Andrew Place
Don Mills, Ontario M3C2T8, Canada
Tel: 416-447-5101

Australia and New Zealand:
Addison-Wesley Publishing Company
6 Byfield Street
North Ryde, N.S.W. 2113
Australia
Tel: 888-2733;
Cable: ADIWES SYDNEY;
Telex: AA71919

United Kingdom, Republic of Ireland, Africa (excluding North Africa) and South Africa:
Addison-Wesley Publishers Ltd.
Finchampstead Road
Wokingham
Berkshire RG11 2NZ, England
Cable: ADIWES Wokingham;
Telex: 846136

Continental Europe, the Near East, Middle East, and North Africa:
Addison-Wesley Publishing Company
De Lairesstraat, 90
1071 PJ Amsterdam
The Netherlands
Tel: 020 76 40-44
Cable: ADIWES AMSTERDAM
Telex: 844-14046

ACM Members
A limited number of copies are available at the ACM member discount. Send order with payment to:

ACM Order Department
P.O. Box 64145
Baltimore, MD 21264

ACM will pay postage and handling on orders accompanied by check.

Credit card orders only:
1-800-342-6626

Customer service, or credit card orders from Alaska, Maryland, and outside the U.S.: 301-528-4261.

Credit card orders may also be placed by mail.

Please include your ACM member number and the ACM Order number with your order.

ACM Order Number: 608921
Soft Cover ACM ISBN: 0-89791-513-5
Series Hard Cover ACM ISBN: 0-89791-514-3

Contents

TUESDAY 2:00 - 3:30 pm

Papers: Text and Hypertext

Session Chair: Robin Jeffries, *Hewlett-Packard Laboratories*

Papers: Studies of Media Supported Collaboration

Session Chair: Hiroshi Ishii, *NTT Human Interface Laboratories*

Laboratory Overviews: Graphics

Session Chair: Gitte Lindgaard, *Telecom Australia*

Panel: Anthropomorphism: From Eliza to Terminator 2

Demonstration: User Interface Management Systems I

Session Chair: Lorna A. Zorman, *USC Information Sciences Institute*

TABLE OF CONTENTS

Panel: Designing Collaborative, Knowledge-Building Environments for Tomorrow's Schools 427

Organizer: Anne Nicol Thomas, *Children Using Technology*
Panelists:

    Jim Pellegrino, *Vanderbilt University*
    Peter Rowley, *Ontario Institute for Studies in Education*
    Marlene Scardamalia, *Ontario Institute for Studies in Education*
    Elliot Soloway, *University of Michigan*
    Jim Webb, *Huron Public School*

Demonstration: Analysis Tools/Multimedia Help

Session Chair: Steven Feiner, *Columbia University*

WEDNESDAY 5:30 - 7:00 pm

Special Panel: Sci-Fi at CHI: Cyberpunk Novelists Predict Future User Interfaces 435

Organizer: Aaron Marcus, *Aaron Marcus & Associates*
Participants:

    Rudy Rucker *Author, Mathematician*
    Bruce Sterling, *Author*
    Vernor Vinge, *Author, San Diego State University*
Discussant: Donald Norman, *University of California, San Diego*

THURSDAY 8:30 - 10:00 am

Papers: Participatory Design

Session Chair: William W. Gaver, *Rank Xerox EuroPARC*

Papers: Case Studies - Methods for Developing Systems Using Application Packages

Session Chair: Brian Shackel, *HUSAT Research Institute, Loughborough University of Technology*

Papers: Understanding and Supporting the Design Process

Session Chair: John Karat, *IBM T. J. Watson Research Center*

Panel: Collaborating in the World of Interactive Media 517

Organizer: Michael Arent, *Apple Computer, Inc.*
Panelists:

    Donna Cohen, *Warner New Media*
    Mike Mills, *Apple Computer, Inc.*
    Chris Krueger, *Arborescence*
    Wendy Richmond, *WGBH*

Welcome to CHI '92!

1992 finds CHI at something of a crossroads. It has now been ten years since the Gaithersberg Conference on Human Factors in Computer Systems that led to CHI, and, in many ways, our field is flourishing as never before. Our fundamental point — that considerations of the fit between people and computer systems must play a fundamental role in the design and implementation of those systems — has been accepted in almost all parts of the computing industry. CEOs of major computer and electronics companies now talk regularly of the importance of understanding user needs and of producing good interfaces. The integration of computing and the arts is inspiring new and exciting forms of human expression. HCI research — and researchers — continue to gain prominence in a wide range of academic disciplines. And the market for ideas in this field continues to expand, with ever-larger journals and conferences. In our case, CHI '92 received a record number of technical program submissions, and set a new record for conference attendance. Clearly, we are playing a central role in defining how the world views computing — which, at this point in the 20th century, means that we are having a major impact on the world.

So what's the downside? With growth comes change, and we need to learn how to manage this change. We must find the synergy that comes from the disciplines that make up CHI, without being overwhelmed by the alternate views of HCI that these disciplines provide. We must find the right blend of theory, practice, and innovation to drive the work on specific topics, without losing track of how these advances fit into the global picture of HCI. We must find a way to manage our growth, so that we gain the advantages of size and benefit from the new ideas that are brought to our discipline without becoming overwhelmed by the greater numbers. In short, we must strike a balance between the often contradictory directions the different aspects of our field might individually go, and find a way to move forward to a richer and more profound understanding of HCI.

CHI is the one place where we can do this. We can all come together here, share our ideas with old friends and new acquaintances, and leave with new perspectives on our work and ourselves. There is probably something in this volume that's not quite your cup of tea — at least, there will be if we on the conference committee have done our job. That's the price of a wide-ranging conference like CHI, where all the different aspects of the community are running with a full head of steam, daring you to look in on their work and understand what's going on. CHI '92 will have succeeded if there's something in these proceedings that challenges and surprises you, and makes you rethink an idea that you thought you had figured out a long time ago. We consider this success because CHI should not be a relaxing conference, but an intellectual tempest that stirs up the field, opens up new possibilities, and maybe even raises more questions than it answers. Grab on, and enjoy the ride.

Jim Miller & John "Scooter" Morris

WELCOME

Welcome from ACM/SIGCHI

On behalf of the Executive Committee of Association for Computing Machinery's (ACM) Special Interest Group on Computer & Human Interaction (ACM/SIGCHI), welcome to CHI '92, the annual conference on Human Computer Interaction (HCI). Each conference provides a new opportunity to improve the tried and true, to explore the new and different, and above all to learn from the experience. This year is no exception: we think you'll find this to be one of the most innovative and high quality conferences yet. The CHI conference is undoubtedly the most visible activity of SIGCHI, but we do much more:

SIGCHI sponsors other conferences, such as Computer Supported Cooperative Work, Hypertext, and User Interface Software and Technology.

We support workshops on special topics and in special places.

Members receive the CHI conference proceedings (and often the proceedings of the other supported conferences) as well as a respected quarterly Bulletin.

To support HCI education, the Curriculum Development Committee has just completed a landmark work on HCI curriculum.

We financially support the Ohio State Online Bibliography of HCI material (free to all via the Internet).

We track the information about HCI academic programs at the graduate and undergraduate levels.

We are also currently exploring the creation of a Transactions on HCI and a User Interface Magazine.

What is all this about? SIGCHI is a worldwide group of volunteers who share an interest in the many facets of HCI. The fact that SIGCHI is the fastest-growing Special Interest Group in ACM, and has a growing number of local chapters, is evidence that the field of HCI is receiving greater and greater attention. As computers are embedded in more and more of our everyday objects, the concomitant demands for monitoring, managing and controlling increase the need for HCI research, development and informed use.

This conference is a wonderful opportunity to meet and exchange views, formally and informally, not only on the design of products but also on the processes and the organizational, legislative and legal climate that shape design and use. The conference is also a good time to explore taking a more active role in SIGCHI either on the local or central level. You can do this by contacting us at the society booth and by attending the SIGCHI Open Business meeting.

On behalf of ACM/SIGCHI, we congratulate the conference committee and all the volunteers for a job well done. The conference program is first class and Monterey is a beautiful setting. The conference chairs and their committees have done a superb job of providing all of us with the opportunity to enjoy both. Welcome to CHI '92!

Austin Henderson, Co-Chair
Peter Polson, Co-Chair
ACM/SIGCHI

Conference Committee

Conference Co-Chairs
James R. Miller
Hewlett-Packard Laboratories

John "Scooter" Morris
Genentech, Inc.

Advisor
Don Patterson
Lawrence Livermore National Laboratories

Audio-Visual
Kevin Schofield, Chair
Microsoft Corp.

Childcare
Robin Jeffries, Chair
Hewlett-Packard Laboratories

Computing Support
Mark L. Miller, Chair
Apple Computer, Inc.

European Coordinator
Michael Tauber
University Paderborn

Executive Administrator
Carol Klyver
Foundations of Excellence

Industry Liaison
Charles Grantham
University of San Francisco

Interactive Experience
Alan Wexelblat, Chair
Electric Blue Lighting and Art

Maddy Brower-Janse
Philips IPO

Abbe Don
In Context

Kim Fairchild
National University of Singapore

Vivienne Begg
Xerox Corporation

Bob Root
Bellcore

Interactive Performance
Craig Hubley
Craig Hubley Associates

Abbe Don
In Context

Mark Petrakis
Cobra Lounge Melt-o-Media, pARTyScience

Beth Wenzel
NASA Ames

Local Arrangements
Michael Zyda, Chair
Naval Postgraduate School

Merchandising
Dan Norton-Middaugh, Co-Chair
Ginger Brewer Associates

Betsy Norton-Middaugh, Co-Chair
Interling Software

Pacific Rim Coordinator
Gen Suzuki
NTT Human Interface Laboratories

Publications
Penny Bauersfeld, Chair
Human Interface Design Consultant

Bruce "Tog" Tognazzini
Apple Computer, Inc

Publicity
Beth Adelson, Co-Chair
Rutgers University

Rosemary Wick, Co-Chair
Center for Economic Conversion

Registration
Steve Anderson, Chair
Lawrence Livermore National Laboratories

Student Volunteers
Jarrett Rosenberg, Chair
Sun Microsystems, Inc.

Kevin Mullet, Associate Chair
Sun Microsystems, Inc.

Treasurer
David Mischel
Genentech, Inc.

Tutorials
Tom Hewett, Chair
Drexel University

Terry Bleser
Washington, D.C.

Margaret Christensen
Drexel University

Tom Carey
University of Guelph

Wendy Kellogg
IBM T.J. Watson Research Center

Karen Kvavik
Karen Kvavik & Associates

Lorraine Normore
Chemical Abstracts Service

Michael Wilson
Rutherford Appleton Lab

ACM Liaison
Diane Darrow
ACM

SIGGRAPH Liaison
Branko Gerovac
Digital Equipment Corporation

TECHNICAL PROGRAM

Technical Program Co-Chairs
Gene Lynch
Tektronix, Inc.

John Bennett
IBM Almaden Research Center

Demonstrations
Jon Schlossberg, Co-Chair
Lockheed Artificial Intelligence Center

Joe Sullivan, Co-Chair
Lockheed Artificial Intelligence Center

Linda Cook
Linda Cook & Associates

Allen Cypher
Apple Computer, Inc.

Doug Dankel
University of Florida

Steven Feiner
Columbia University

Gale Martin,
Neural Net Lab, MCC

Jean McKendree
NYNEX Science & Technology, Inc.

Mark Musen
Stanford University School of Medicine

Bob Remington
Lockheed Missiles&Space Company

Sharon Walter
Griffiss AFB

CONFERENCE COMMITTEE

Doctoral Consortium
James Foley, Chair
Georgia Institute of Technology

Lin Brown
Sun Microsystems, Inc.

Gerhard Fischer
University of Colorado

Michael Harrison
University of York

David Kieras
University of Michigan

Laboratory Overviews
Jakob Nielsen, Chair
Bellcore

Laura De Young
Independence Technologies, Inc.

Beverly Harrison
University of Toronto

Anker Helms Jørgensen
Copenhagen University

Mike King
U S WEST Advanced Technologies

Gitte Lindgaard
*Telecom Australia Research
Laboratories*

Shogo Nishida
Mitsubishi Electric Corporation

Panels Committee
Stephanie M. Doane, Chair
University of Illinois

George Englebeck, Associate Chair
U S WEST Advanced Technologies

Mark Altom
AT&T Bell Laboratories

Arnold Lund
Ameritech Services, Inc.

S. Joy Mountford
Apple Computer, Inc.

Wayne Zachary
CHI Systems, Inc.

Papers
Ruven Brooks, Chair
*Schlumberger Laboratory for
Computer Science*

Papers: Subcommittee Chairs
John Carroll
IBM T.J. Watson Research Center

Bill Curtis
Carnegie Mellon University

Susan Dray
IDS Financial Services

John Gould
IBM T.J. Watson Research Center

Robert J. K. Jacob
Naval Research Laboratory

Robin Jeffries
Hewlett-Packard Laboratories

Clayton Lewis
University of Colorado

Dan Olsen, Jr.
Brigham Young University

Judith Olson
University of Michigan

Peter Polson
University of Colorado

Pamela Samuelson
University of Pittsburgh

Sylvia Sheppard
NASA Goddard Space Center

Papers: Full Members
Beth Adelson
Rutgers University
Robert Allen
Bellcore

Michael Atwood
NYNEX Science & Technology

Randolph Bias
IBM Austin

Meera Blattner
University of California, Davis

Sara Bly
Xerox PARC

Hans Brunner
U S WEST Advanced Technologies

Stuart Card
Xerox PARC

Tom Carey
University of Guelph

George Furnas
Bellcore

William W. Gaver
Rank Xerox EuroPARC

Jonathan Grudin
University of California, Irvine

Raymonde Guindon
Stanford University

William Hefley
Carnegie Mellon University

Austin Henderson
Xerox PARC

Ralph Hill
Bellcore

William Hill
Bellcore

Erik Hollnagel
Computer Resources International

Scott Hudson
University of Arizona

Hiroshi Ishii
NTT Human Interface Laboratories

Bonnie John
Carnegie Mellon University

Peter Johnson
University of London

Clare-Marie Karat
IBM T.J. Watson Research Center

John Karat
IBM T.J. Watson Research Center

Irvin Katz
Educational Testing Service

David Kieras
University of Michigan

Andreas Lemke
GMD Institute for IPSI

Wendy MacKay
Rank Xerox EuroPARC

Jock Mackinlay
Xerox PARC

Allan MacLean
Rank Xerox EuroPARC

Marilyn Mantei
University of Toronto

Jean McKendree
NYNEX Science & Technology, Inc.

Tom Moher
*University of Illinois, Chicago
Circle*

Thomas Moran
Xerox PARC

S. Joy Mountford
Apple Computer, Inc.

Bonnie A. Nardi
Hewlett-Packard Laboratories

Robert Neches
USC / Information Sciences Institute

Jakob Nielsen
Bellcore

Gary Olson
University of Michigan

Randy Pausch
University of Virginia

Catherine Plaisant
University of Maryland

Phyllis Reisner
IBM

Teresa Roberts
U S WEST Advanced Technologies

George Robertson
Xerox PARC

Scott Robertson
Rutgers University

Jarrett Rosenberg
Sun Microsystems

Mary Beth Rosson
IBM T.J. Watson Research Center

Chris Schmandt
MIT Media Lab

John Sibert
George Washington University

Kevin Singley
IBM T.J. Watson Research Center

Elliot Soloway
University of Michigan

Gen Suzuki
NTT Human Interface Lab

John Tang
Sun Microsystems, Inc.

Michael Tauber
University Paderborn

Bruce Tognazzini
Apple Computer, Inc.

Thea Turner
NYNEX Science & Technology, Inc.

Jacob Ukelson
IBM T.J. Watson Research Center

Gerrit van der Veer
Vrije Universiteit

Ted White
Twente University of Technology

Juergen Ziegler
Fraunhofer Institute IAO

Papers: Corresponding Members
Bengt Ahlström
FOA

Philip Barnard
MRC Applied Psychology Unit

Andre Bisseret
INRIA

Tom Bosser
Psychologisches Institut

William Buxton
University of Toronto

Richard Catrambone
Georgia Institute of Technology

Ellis Cohen
Open Software Foundation

Dennis Egan
Bellcore

Kate Ehrlich
Sun Microsystems, Inc.

Steven Feiner
Columbia University

Steve Fickas
University of Oregon

Michael Good
Digital Equipment Corporation

Wayne Gray
Fordham University

Mark Green
University of Alberta

Saul Greenberg
University of Calgary

Andrew Howes
MRC Applied Psychology Unit

Reinhard Keil-Slawik
Technische Universitaet Berlin

Muneo Kitajima
University of Colorado

Mark Lansdale
Loughborough University of Technology

Mark Linton
Silicon Graphics, Inc.

John Long
University of London

Hans Marmolin
UI Design AB

Michael J. Muller
Bellcore

Dianne Murray
University of Surrey

Richard Pew
BBN Laboratories

Ken Pier
Xerox PARC
Peter Piroli
University of California, Berkeley

Jim Rhyne
IBM T.J. Watson Research Center

John Richards
IBM T.J. Watson Research Center

Susan Rudman
U S WEST Advanced Technologies

Robert Spence
Imperial College

Jacques Theureau

William Verplank
IDEO

Catherine Wolf
IBM T.J. Watson Research Center

Patricia Wright
MRC Applied Psychology Unit

Richard Young
MRC Applied Psychology Unit

Papers: Additional Reviews
James Alexander
U S WEST Advanced Technologies

Richard Anderson
Pacific Bell / Human Factors

Ron Baecker
University of Toronto

John Bennett
IBM Almaden Research Center

Deborah Boehm-Davis
George Mason University

Susan Bovair
Georgia Institute of Technology

John Bowers
University of Manchester

Douglas Brems
AT&T Bell Laboratories

Mike Burns
AT&T Bell Laboratories

Jeff Conklin
MCC

Stephanie Doane
University of Illinois

Gerhard Fischer
University of Colorado

James Foley
Georgia Institute of Technology

T. R. G. Green
MRC Applied Psychology Unit

H. Rex Hartson
Virginia Polytechnic Institute & State University

David Hill
University of Calgary

Deborah Hix
Virginia Polytechnic Institute & State University

Karen Holtzblatt
Digital Equipment Corp.

Gene Lynch
Tektronix, Inc.

I. Scott MacKenzie
University of Toronto

Jane Malin
NASA Johnson Space Center

Aaron Marcus
Aaron Marcus & Associates

Catherine Marshall
U S WEST Advanced Technologies

Gurminder Singh
National University of Singapore

Yngve Sundblad
KTH

Pedro Szekely
USC/Information Sciences Institute

Jim Thomas
Battelle Pacific Northwest Lab

Brad Vander Zanden
University of Tennessee

Steve Whittaker
Hewlett-Packard Laboratories

Kristina Woolsey
Apple Computer, Inc.

Posters and Short Talks
Dennis Wixon, Chair
Digital Equipment Corporation

Betsy Comstock, Associate Chair
Digital Equipment Corporation

Michael Atwood
NYNEX Science & Technology, Inc.

Arlene Aucella
AFA Design Consultants

Elizabeth Bayle
User Interface Design

Minette Beabes
Digital Equipment Corporation

Walter Bender
Massachusetts Institute of Technology

Deborah Boehm-Davis
George Mason University

Stephen Boies
IBM T.J. Watson Research Center

Christine V. Bullen
MIT Sloan School
Kate Ehrlich
Sun Microsystems, Inc.

Jay Elkerton
Philips Laboratories

Danielle Fafchamps
Hewlett-Packard Laboratories

William W. Gaver
Rank Xerox EuroPARC

Saul Greenberg
University of Calgary

Alfred Kobsa
University of Konstanz

Thomas K. Landauer
Bellcore

J. Bryan Lewis
IBM T.J. Watson Research Center

Jerry Lohse
University of Michigan

Deborah Mayhew
Deborah Mayhew & Associates

Michael Muller
Bellcore

Randy Pausch
University of Virginia

Richard Pew
BBN, Inc.

Pam Samuelson
University of Pittsburgh

Dominique L. Scapin
INRIA

Mathias Schneider-Hufschmidt
Siemens AG

Dan Shapiro
University of Lancaster

Wanda Smith
Hewlett-Packard Corporation

Gerd Szwillus
University Paderborn

Manfred Tscheligi
University of Vienna

Alonso Vera
Carnegie Mellon University

Jan Walker
Digital Equipment Corporation

Suzanne Watzman
Watzman Information Design

Ellen White
Bellcore

Catherine Wolf
IBM T.J. Watson Research Center

SIGs and Workshops
John Karat, Chair
IBM T.J. Watson Research Center

Tom Dayton
Bellcore

Wayne Gray
Fordham University

William Hefley
Carnegie Mellon University

Michael Muller
Bellcore

Linda Tetzlaff
IBM T.J. Watson Research Center

Videos
Brad A. Myers, Chair
Carnegie Mellon University

Ken Pier
Xerox PARC

Angela Lucas
Logica Cambridge Limited

David Canfield Smith
Apple Computer, Inc.

William L. Verplank
IDEO

Jim Alexander
U S WEST Advanced Technologies

Professional Services
Administrator/Production Consultant
Carol Klyver
Foundations of Excellence

Audio/Visual Consultant
Chris Folck
Photo and Sound

Conference Management
Paul Henning
Conference and Logistics Consultants

Design Consultant/Production
Gayle Mahoney

Printing Services
Todd McCartney
Trademark Graphics

Photography
Ira Kahn

Cooperating Societies

CHI '92 is sponsored by the Association for
Computing Machinery's Special Interest Group on
Computer and Human Interaction (ACM/SIGCHI)
in cooperation with:

ACM/SIGCAPH

ACM/SIGGRAPH

ACM/SIGOIS

Austrian Computer Society (OCG)

Committee for Human Interface Society
of Instrument and Control Engineers
(SICE-HI)

Cognitive Science Society

The Division of Applied Experimental
and Engineering Psychologists of the
American Psychological Association
(division 21 OF APA)

Dutch Computer Society (NGI)

European Association of Cognitive
Ergonomics (EACE)

Gesellschaft für Informatik (GI)

Human Computer Interaction Specialists
Group of the British Computer Society
(BCS-HCI)

Human Factors Society (HFS)

Human Factors Society, Europe Chapter

IEEE Computer Society Technical
Committee on Computer and Display
Ergonomics

International Network of the IUPsyS on
Man-Computer Interaction Research
(MACINTER)

Italian Association for Artificial
Intelligence (AIIA)

Schweizer Informatiker Gesellschaft (SI)

Software Psychology Society

COOPERATING SOCIETIES

Appreciation

The annual CHI Conference is dependent upon the efforts of volunteers. CHI '92 expresses appreciation to the following organizations for their significant support of CHI '92 volunteers:

Apple Computer, Inc.

Drexel University

Genentech, Inc.

Hewlett-Packard

IBM

Lawrence Livermore National Laboratory

Microsoft Corporation

Schlumberger Laboratories for Computer Science

Tektronix, Inc.

Xerox

CHI '92 also recognizes the contributions of the following organizations in support of active conference volunteers:

Bellcore

Carnegie Mellon University

Center for Economic Conversion

Digital Equipment Corporation

Electric Blue Lighting and Art

Georgia Institute of Technology

Lockheed Artificial Intelligence Center

Naval Postgraduate School

NTT Human Interface Laboratories

Rutgers University

Sun Microsystems, Inc.

University of Illinois

University Paderborn

University of San Francisco

Special Acknowledgements

Putting together a CHI conference is a team effort, and all of the members of the committee worked together to make CHI '92 a reality. Much of the work is done by volunteers from our field (all of the people in the various committee lists have volunteered their time) and CHI '92 could not have happened without their efforts. This year we also had the assistance of several professionals whose efforts went well beyond their remuneration. We would like to acknowledge the efforts of: Carol Klyver, in particular, who has been involved in almost every aspect of the conference; Gayle Mahoney, who supported the publications committee and whose design and layout speaks for itself in the Call for Participation, Advance Program and other publications; and last, but not least, Paul Henning and his crew from CLC, who worked closely with us to make sure your experience at CHI '92 is a most memorable and enjoyable one.

Corporate Sponsors

CHI '92 offers its thanks to the following
corporate sponsors. Their generosity
has enabled us to expand the breadth of
the conference and take advantage of
opportunities that we otherwise might
have missed. Their participation as
sponsors also indicates their interest in
and commitment to the field of
Human-Computer Interaction.

APPLE COMPUTER, INC.

HEWLETT-PACKARD

MICROSOFT

NCR

SUNSOFT, INC.

XEROX

AMERITECH SERVICES, INC.

IBM

NYNEX SCIENCE & TECHNOLOGY, INC.

CORPORATE SPONSORS

Technical Program

A Guide to the CHI'92 Proceedings: A Record of the Technical Program

The annual CHI Conference attracts participants who have a variety of backgrounds and interests — from production of technology to basic research. People participating in the program all share the common goal of advancing the design and development of useful and usable systems. Throughout our planning for CHI '92 we were conscious of this variety of backgrounds and we have sought to "strike a balance" when making choices that shaped the technical program.

The CHI Conferences have become dynamic multi-faceted international events offering many activities for conveying information about the design, development, testing, and use of systems that involve human-computer interaction.

Presentations at the Conference are grouped in sessions featuring plenary events, papers, panels, laboratory overviews, demonstrations, and formal videos. In this proceedings volume we can only capture the parts of the Conference that can be preserved on paper.

Submissions received before November of 1991 went through an extensive peer review process, and descriptions are archived here. The descriptions appear in the order of presentation at the Conference.

Plenaries

The opening Plenary for CHI '92 gathers leading figures from the CHI community to discuss the accomplishments and the future directions for Human Computer Interactions (HCI). The panelists are Austin Henderson, Bill Buxton, Stuart Card, Bill Curtis, Marilyn Mantei, and Donald Norman. In the closing plenary, "Designing for Leveraging the Social Mind: Tapping into the Invisible Resources of the Periphery", John Seely Brown challenges us to extend HCI beyond its traditional center focus to include the context of the periphery. Descriptions of the plenary sessions are not included in these proceedings.

Papers

Papers are the traditional format for documenting completed work. Sixty-seven papers from three hundred five submitted were accepted by the Papers Committee.

Panels

Panels are a popular forum for controversial or innovative topics discussed by knowledgeable people. The sessions are designed as extensive opportunities for panelist and audience questions. Nine regular panels were accepted by the Panels committee along with a special panel, "Sci-Fi at CHI: Cyberpunk Novelists Predict Future User Interfaces".

Laboratory Overviews

Laboratory Overviews highlight the scope of work going on at selected industrial and academic sites. Institutions apply and are chosen so that over a period of years we have a record of research and development work going on around the world. The Laboratory Overviews Committee selected nine sites to present this year.

Demonstrations

Demonstrations provide an opportunity for guided tours and discussion of new concepts and systems. The Demonstrations Committee accepted seventeen demonstrations this year. The descriptions are included here.

Formal Video Program

Formal Videos were reviewed and compiled into a two-hour tape available for purchase at the Conference. Abstracts for the videos accepted by the Videos Committee are included.

Additional formats were established for late-breaking results, and submissions for these categories were reviewed early in 1992. Brief representations of these elements are included here as memory aids for attendees and to record the breadth of the CHI Conference experience.

Posters and Short Talks

Sixty-two posters offer an opportunity for one-on-one discussions with the presenters. A total of twenty-six short talks are presented in four sessions. These submissions were refereed by the Posters and Short Talks Committee in a peer review process similar to that for papers but completed on an accelerated schedule. A Posters and Short Talks booklet is available at the conference.

Special Interest Groups

Applications were accepted to reserve meeting space for ad hoc Special Interest Groups (SIGs), an additional venue for specialized interaction opportunities.

Other Conference Events:

Tutorials offer an in-depth view of special topics in classroom-like presentations.

Workshops allow small groups with particular interests and experience to meet for one to two days in intensive sessions.

The Doctoral Consortium provides dissertation-level graduate students with an opportunity to meet each other and to exchange ideas with experienced HCI researchers.

The Interactive Experience offers hands-on exploration of innovative systems.

The Interactive Performance provides live entertainment featuring artistic use of HCI technology.

Special Videos featuring videos on Graphic Design and suggesting Future Scenarios were accepted in a separate submission, and these videos can also be purchased.

The technical program remains the central focus of the Conference. CHI conferences have become the premier venue for professionals representing all aspects of human factors in computing. We thank all the Chairs who, along with their committees, guided the gathering, reviewing, and successful presentation of these works. We invite you to join the active CHI community as together we help to shape the evolution of the discipline and the Conference.

Gene Lynch and John Bennett
CHI '92 Technical Program Co-Chairs

TECHNICAL PROGRAM

EDIT WEAR AND READ WEAR

William C. Hill and James D. Hollan
Computer Graphics and Interactive Media Research Group
Bellcore, 445 South Street, Morristown, NJ 07962-1910

Dave Wroblewski and Tim McCandless
US West Advanced Technologies
4001 Discovery Lane, Boulder, CO 80303

Email: willhill@bellcore.com, hollan@bellcore.com, davew@uswest.com, mccand@uswest.com

ABSTRACT

We describe two applications that illustrate the idea of *computational wear* in the domain of document processing. By graphically depicting the history of author and reader interactions with documents, these applications offer otherwise unavailable information to guide work. We discuss how their design accords with a theory of professional work and an informational physics perspective on interface design.

Keywords: Graphical user interfaces, informational physics, interface mechanisms, professional work, reflective practitioner.

INTRODUCTION

The research described here grew out of a question implicit in Schoen's [11,12] analysis of professional work: how might we employ computation to improve, what Schoen refers to as, the *reflective conversation with work materials*? Previously we have addressed this question in the realm of computer systems administration [14]. That effort focused on the application of an object-oriented system, DETENTE, to embed agendas in complex application interfaces, to track and handle scheduled and unscheduled computer maintenance.

In this paper we address the same underlying question in the more general realm of document creation. The basic idea is to maintain and exploit object-centered interaction histories:

Record on computational objects (e.g. documents, menus, spreadsheets, images, email) the events that comprise their use, and then, on future occasions, when the objects are used again, display useful graphical abstractions of the accrued histories as parts of the objects themselves.

Two document processing applications resulted from considerations of this basic idea: *Edit Wear* and *Read Wear*. The choice of the term *wear* comes from an analogy to physical wear. Specifically, use leaves wear. By modifying an existing editor, these applications arrange for every edit of a document and every episode of reading to leave wear on the document. In the case of *Edit Wear*, this means to graphically portray the document's authorship history by modifying the document's screen representation. In the case of *Read Wear*, it means to graphically portray the document's readership history.

Using a technique called *attribute-mapped scroll bars* [15], wear appears to users as marks mapped onto document scroll bars in positions relative to line positions (see Figure 1). The length of the mark depicts the magnitude of the wear or other wear quantities. Attribute-mapped scroll bars can be used in a variety of ways. For example, we have used them to map word search hits in a document onto their respective scroll bar positions [15]. The placement of the edit wear and read wear information inside the scroll bar serves to frame the wear marks. Since the length of the scroll bar represents the length of the document and relative position in the scroll bar represents relative position in the document, the scroll bar provides a geometry within which to interpret the wear marks in relation to the structure of the document. As a display technique it has the nice property of reusing precious screen space. More importantly it co-locates information display with navigation control points, a topic we analyze later in the theory section.

Figure 1 shows five examples of what users see. Scroll bar (a) is a normal scroll bar unadorned with wear. Bar (b) shows a snapshot of edit wear on a document. The width of individual wear marks is proportional to the the largest magnitude of edits per line. The fact that some sections have been edited more than others is visible and it easy to get to those sections by clicking on them. Bar (c) is the same document at a later stage, with two categories of wear in right and left vertical scroll bar bands. Edit wear displayed in (b) has been compressed into the left band. A second category of edit wear is displayed in the right band. Groups of edits in the second category of edit wear are visible along with a smattering of small edits. Bar (d) shows total read wear on a source code file. Bar (e) shows the same read wear as in (d) but now partitioned in three bands according to its three constitutive categories.

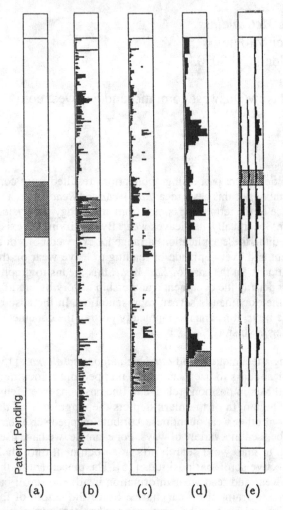

Figure 1. Five Sample Scroll Bars

By displaying an edit-by-edit history of a document in progress, *Edit Wear* graphically answers questions such as: Which sections of the document are most stable (i.e., changing the slowest)? Which sections are most unstable (i.e., current editing hot-spots)? What are the relative ages of document sections? How often have sections of the document been edited? What edits were made during the last editing session? In the case of co-authorship, edit wear distinguishes contributions by author, and answers questions graphically and immediately: Who wrote what? Who edited what and when did they edit it? What have co-authors written and edited since I last saw the document?

Similarly, by use of a line-by-line readership history, *Read Wear* addresses questions concerning how documents have been read: How often and how much have sections of the document been read? Which sections of this document been read by various categories of readers? Who were the last people to read this section, and when?

Answers to these questions should be useful in a number of areas, e.g. co-authored reports, large source-code libraries, and on-line reference document sets. But there is a cost to pay. Without compression techniques, saving all the extra history information on a per line basis results in storage costs being one to two orders of magnitude greater than without *Edit Wear* or *Read Wear*. We have not worked at all on optimizing storage but as storage costs fall, this becomes less of an issue.

From among the myriad ways one might implement the basic idea of *Edit Wear* and *Read Wear*, we chose to base it on a theory of professional work since reading and authoring are ubiquitous professional activities. We follow others [2,3,4,5,9] in applying Schoen's theory of professional work to the design of interfaces. The ways in which *Edit Wear* and *Read Wear* display their information were influenced by Schoen's theory, and much of their utility and usability can be described by Schoen's phrase, *the reflective conversation* that their design engenders.

The rest of this paper divides into two main sections. In the first, we describe the implementation: the role of *categories of wear* as a concept and data structure, selected aspects of how *Edit Wear* and *Read Wear* work internally, the state of our implementation, and undesirable properties of the current implementation. In the second section, we describe the theoretical underpinnings of *Edit Wear* and *Read Wear* and how they illustrate a number of interface design theses. In particular, we examine them from three perspectives: how they embody an interpretation of Schoen's theory of professional work, how they exemplify an informational physics view of interface design and might be generalized, and how they illustrate a computer-supported cooperative work thesis, namely that small group cooperation is better organized by shared artifact than by group process control.

IMPLEMENTATION

Edit Wear and *Read Wear* were implemented by modifying Zmacs, the editor for Symbolics lisp machines. Zmacs is similar to Emacs. It supports both major and minor editing modes on a per buffer basis. Major modes are mutually exclusive specializations for editing specific types of documents. Lisp mode, C mode, and Tex mode are examples. Minor modes are editor specializations that work within all major modes and co-exist with other minor modes. Auto Fill mode, Abbreviation mode, and Electric Font Lock mode are examples. *Edit Wear* and *Read Wear* are implemented as minor modes.

One turns on *Edit Wear* mode and *Read Wear* mode on a per buffer basis. Normally *Edit Wear* is turned on in an editable buffer and *Read Wear* is turned on in a read-only buffer. Usually one doesn't have both modes on in a single buffer, though nothing prevents this. *Edit Wear* and *Read Wear* history data persist across editor sessions. When document files are saved, a shadow file is automatically generated and saved to permanently record the editing or reading activity. Similarly, Zmacs was modified to restore the existing *Edit Wear* or *Read Wear* history when a file is loaded. From the user's point of view, nothing is different about the way one loads, edits, reads, navigates, or saves document files and no extra work is involved in getting the information that *Edit Wear* and *Read Wear* provide. What changes for the user is how the document looks and the addition of a few additional editor commands.

Categories are unique identifiers that serve to label categories of wear. Their purpose is to serve later as indices into wear history records according to category. A set of such categories is associated with each author and reader. Thus author *A* might have the list: (John Q. Public, project 0891, marketing, manager level A3), while reader *B* might have the list (Mary Doe, research, unix expert). An individual can have both author and reader category lists. When *Edit Wear* mode or *Read Wear* mode is entered for a buffer, the editor begins to record editing or reading events for that buffer for each of the active record categories. Editing or reading activity can then be indexed, filtered, and played according to these categories.

How *Edit Wear* and *Read Wear* Work

The main modification to Zmacs required to implement *Edit Wear* and *Read Wear* was to provide a hook that allowed an arbitrary function to be run whenever a document line was edited. Care had to be taken not to degrade editor performance. We experimented with two versions of edit activity recording. The first and most expensive indexes a timestamp for each edit and line for all active edit record categories. The second keeps a list of edit timestamps per line and increments sums of edits per category.

Read Wear attempts to record for each active category associated with the reader and for each document line how many seconds of reading per category the document line participates in. The resulting measures are approximate but precise enough to be useful. In our implementation, reading a line has three requirements: the line is visible in the editor window, a user is logged in, and no lack-of-interaction timeouts (e.g., screen-dimming) have occurred to indicate that the user is not attending to the screen. *Read Wear* keeps its own lack-of-interaction time-out, set currently to 3 minutes. So for each visible line *Read Wear* figures out how many seconds of viewing time it has received and counts that as read time. *Read Wear* suspends and resumes the count properly as users swap around to different buffers.

A few details are needed to explain how this works. Two buffer variables are kept updated: *last-displayed-lines* and *current-displayed-lines*. When text-movement commands are issued by keystroke or mouse, just before the window is scrolled, *last-displayed-lines* takes the value of *current-displayed-lines*. Just after the text-movement command has taken effect, *current-displayed-lines* is updated to whatever lines are now visible. After these two variable assignments are complete, an equality test is performed. If the two variable values are equal (meaning that the lines that are displayed haven't changed) no action is performed. If on the other hand, new lines are visible and some old lines are not visible anymore, processing proceeds. Newly visible lines are given a timestamp for when they became visible. Lines that went out of the viewer get read seconds computed by subtracting their *became visible* timestamps from the time of the text movement command. Nothing happens to the lines that remain visible across the text movement command. This is enough to produce the desired accumulation of read wear. Initial, save-time, swap-buffer, and end-session special situations proceed according to variants of this method.

Experimentation with the current implementation has pointed out a number of possible improvements. First, wear attaches to lines in the document. We would prefer wear attach to individual characters but the storage requirements jump by another two orders of magnitude. Per-character edit wear offers a precision that would be useful in the case of source code documents where single character differences matter. Per-word or per-token read wear is a compromise. Second, the legends that describe different type of wear show up in the editor mini-buffer window which is a half inch below the bottom of the document scroll bar. It is not as easy to apply the legend to the wear as one would like. Third, we have as yet done nothing about making wear show up on the text itself rather than just in the scroll bar. It would be interesting to explore uses of color and texture mapping for this. Fourth, wear doesn't show up in hardcopy. Since its common to use hardcopy to support co-authoring, a program that generates wear-displays on hardcopy would be useful.

THEORETICAL PERSPECTIVES

We now turn to examining *Edit Wear* and *Read Wear* from three perspectives: how they embody an interpretation of Schoen's theory of professional work, how they can be generalized as examples of an informational physics view of interface design, and how they illustrate a CSCW thesis, namely that small group cooperation is better organized by shared artifact rather than by group process control.

Schoen's Theory of Professional Activity

Schoen's theory implies a scheme of interface evaluation in terms of *reflective conversation*. We describe two theoretical constructs concerning reflective conversations and their application to interface design. We then note how physical wear in the world considered as an *interface* often succeeds in the implied interface evaluation scheme. From this we derive the notion of computational wear and show how *Edit Wear* and *Read Wear* fair in the same evaluation scheme.

Opposing the analytical view that "professional activity consists in instrumental problem-solving made rigorous by the application of scientific theory and technique" [11, p.

21], Schoen proposes a reflection-in-action analysis of professional work:

> When the practitioner tries to solve the problem he has set, he seeks both to understand the situation and to change it. ... Through the unintended effects of action, the situation talks back. The practitioner, reflecting on this back-talk, may find new meaning in the situation which leads him to a new reframing. **Thus he judges a problem-setting by the quality and direction of the reflective conversation to which it leads.** [11, pp.134-135, emphasis ours]

Here, Schoen emphasizes problem-setting over problem-solving. What does Schoen mean by problem-setting? For Schoen, *problem setting is a process in which, interactively, we name the things to which we will attend and frame the context in which we will attend to them.* [11, p. 40] Problem-setting precedes problem-solving. Considering interfaces for professional work in the light of Schoen's analytical point of view, we might add and paraphrase:

> Interfaces permit and encourage certain problem-settings and should be judged by the quality and direction of the reflective conversations that result from the problem-settings they engender.

Often interfaces presume an implicit immutable problem-setting and concentrate on supporting problem-solving within the resulting constrained framework. Interfaces don't often support the fuzzy work of problem-setting which according to Schoen is the hallmark of professional work. What Schoen terms the *perceptual emergence of the unnamed and unframed* is a critical aspect of supporting professional problem-setting in computation. For, unless an interface displays perceptual groupings that have yet to be named and framed in Schoen's sense, all phenomena are already labeled and classified and creative problem-setting is constrained.

Edit Wear and *Read Wear* were designed with this in mind. We wanted patterns of editing activity and reading activity to emerge on the documents. We meant the displays of wear to foster sense-making out of otherwise unavailable data. As documents are edited or read, wear builds up in various categories on a per line basis. Eventually, these new wear spots attract attention relative to other wear spots, occasioning the opportunity for authors or readers to name the pattern of wear (actually patterns of author or reader activity) with such phrases as "The July work", "Dave's section", "The network guys' release 2.0". Authors and readers can then use these now named patterns of wear to adjust what they are doing. *

Another notion from Schoen of importance to the design of *Edit Wear* and *Read Wear* is his concept of the *action present*:

> A practitioner's reflection-in-action may not be very rapid. It is bounded by **the action present**, the zone of time in which action can still make a difference to the situation. The action-present may stretch over minutes, hours, days or even weeks or months depending on the pace of activity and the situational boundaries that are characteristic of the practice. [11, p. 62)]

As a result of the desire to embed prior activity information in the action present, *Edit Wear* and *Read Wear* were designed to make patterns of past use apparent during all phases of editing and reading rather than as an after-the-fact summary to be consulted in some other context.

Edit Wear and *Read Wear* were designed to display themselves in the action present of document navigation, a document's scroll bar. One of the most beautiful aspects of this design is that document wear appears in the exact screen position on which a user clicks to scroll to the document section that has that self-same wear. SuperBook [1], a document-oriented information retrieval system, provides another example of this by graphically displays retrieval hits in the context of a document's table of contents. This embedded display method renders the distribution of retrieval hits interpretable and useful to readers.

Physical and Computational Wear

Another way of thinking about this is to employ the notion of physical wear as an organizing metaphor for what we wanted computationally. Physical wear is emergent and generally remains unnamed and unframed until it causes a problem. It is also embedded, unavoidably tattooed directly on the worn objects. It appears exactly where it can make an informative difference.

Consider some serendipitous uses of wear that everyday life presents. The bindings of cheap paperbacks bend and crack in a manner that allows one to find the last page read. In an auto parts store, the most often consulted pages among many linear feet of catalog are identifiable by smudges, familiar tears, and loose pages. The smudges, tears, and loose pages index to information users are likely to consult. Switching from auto parts catalogs to door handles, the polished part of an otherwise patinaed brass door handle shows where others succeeded in grasping it. The best recipes cards in a stack are often dogged-eared and stained. Weaver [12, pp.270-271] describes a rediscovery of the law of first significant digit distribution due to odd smudge patterns on logarithm tables. These examples remind us that wear sometimes encodes useful information.

Wear is gradual and unavoidable change due to use. As a source of useful information, wear is particular appealing

---

* We [6,10] previously demonstrated advantages of displaying unnamed/unframed perceptual configurations. It was observed that unplanned configurations of process control displays, computed from deviations from states of normal operation, have potential for assisting users in coming to consider alternative hypotheses and helping with what Norman [8] has termed *cognitive hysteresis*.

since it is a by-product of normal activity and thus essentially free. No extra effort, nor scheduling of additional tasks are required to get its effects. In the realm of computation we have rudimentary analogs of wear. For example, command histories and system activity logs accrete automatically. File descriptors usually identify the date and time the file was last touched. These examples bear a kind of superficial resemblance to physical wear. We are interested in extending the notion of wear to *computational wear* that might engender reflective conversations with useful task-specific properties. The notion of computational wear exemplifies a new conceptual framework for theorizing about and implementing interfaces. It is related to our work on informational physics [7]. We think of *Edit Wear* and *Read Wear* as examples of an informational physics for documents.

Taking a physics perspective provides another way of looking at the design of interfaces. Computation enables the creation of virtual worlds that resemble the real world and allow us to exploit our extensive knowledge of the world in interacting with them. This is certainly the primary benefit of taking a metaphor-based view of interface design. Of greater importance from an informational physics perspective is the fact that these same techniques also allow us to create virtual worlds that give concrete existence to abstract entities operating according to a physics of our choice. The entities and their physics can be designed to highlight aspects of phenomena not normally available to us but that are important for supporting understanding and task performance. For our point of view it is crucial to emphasize that the physics can be motivated by understandings of the

characteristics of cognition and tasks. The lawful relations that make up the informational physics should be such that the interface operates in ways that are specifically designed to facilitate our apprehension of important relationships.

Generalization of Edit and Read Wear

Edit and *Read Wear* are useful document processing facilities. But suppose we generalize their basic idea of recording user activity and displaying it later in useful ways to other areas of the interface. For example, consider menus. The idea of *Menu Wear* is that statistics of previous menu-selections by category of user and by category of context get painted onto the menu items themselves (see Figure 2)

Edit wear also makes sense for use with spreadsheets employed in *what-if* scenarios. Cells are colored according to the number of times they have been edited. Horizontal and vertical scrollbars are colored to show total edits by row and column. This kind of edit wear makes it apparent where users have been reworking budget lines the most.

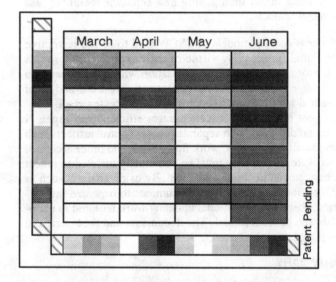

Figure 3. Mockup of Spread Sheet Wear

It is in keeping with the generalization of *Edit Wear* and *Read Wear* that *all* interaction histories should be recorded permanently, event by event, and be made accessible for later redisplay by interface objects such as menu-items, individual text characters in editor buffers, color swatches in paint programs, individual cells in spreadsheet programs, etc. Taking the generalization of *Menu Wear* and *Spread sheet Wear* to the limit, we arrive at an intriguing and problematic interface design issue associated with permanently registering the interaction events of interface objects. We mention it here primarily as a topic worth further discussion.

Suppose *all* interaction history is recorded, structured and indexed for later use. In such a world, *every* menu choice, *every* document edit would be available. But to whom and for what purposes? To make the discussion more concrete, consider the records of editing and reading activity that

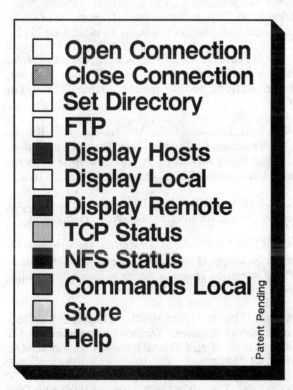

Figure 2. Mockup of Menu Wear exhibits embeddedness and emergence of the unnamed/unframed

we've already collected with *Edit Wear* and *Read Wear*. To whom do they belong? Who should use them for what purposes?

We believe this raises significant ethical issues. One position is that the use of interaction event records should be untransferrably subject to the will of the participating users. *Edit Wear* would belong to the editor and *Read Wear* belongs to the reader. This topic is complex and we expect there to be vigorous discussion and debate about it.

Edit Wear and *Read Wear*: A CSCW Thesis

Edit Wear and *Read Wear* serve as kinds of computer-supported cooperative work applications in the sense that they mediate coordination and cooperation. Co-authors get more precise information about what each other is doing. Co-readers find out who else is reading a particular topic or which sections are read by specific individuals or groups. The CSCW thesis that *Edit Wear* and *Read Wear* illustrate is that there may be advantages to enhancing already-existing interaction-organizing artifacts, such as reports, diagrams, and code rather than posing new separate social process control artifacts.

Process control models of CSCW tend to be too restrictive for small groups. By virtue of their explicitness, process control models curtail improvisation which is frequently a resource for small groups. In contrast, *Edit Wear* and *Read Wear* do not attempt to control social processes at all. They present information that encourages efficient exchanges. A second difficulty with separate process control artifacts such as meeting schedules, work flow charts, and process control software, is that they must be continually updated to reflect changes that occur despite them. By using artifacts such as *Edit Wear* and *Read Wear* documents to organize interaction, there is no additional updating work required to maintain the process model. The documents and their wear are self-updating.

SUMMARY

In summary, *Read Wear* and *Edit Wear* modify document processing as we know it in three significant ways. They move some reading and editing from the realm of private to semi-public activity. In specific settings, the cost of this subtle cultural upheaval may be offset by advantages in coordination that the techniques offer. Second, they exemplify the trend of intentionally designing the forensic qualities of new computation-based media, a trend we may expect to see continue. Third, the wear patterns they display occasion useful conversations, increasing the probability of efficient and effective exchanges among collaborating professionals. The categorical indices into *Read Wear*, for instance, allows readers to find other readers with similar interests.

The entwined concepts of authorship and readership are changing in these ways to accommodate their emerging computational forms. *Read Wear* and *Edit Wear* are examples that provide novel utility in the realm of document processing, without imposing new demands on authors and readers. We have viewed these applications from the perspective of Schoen's theory of professional work, showed how they are examples of a more general informational physics perspective on interface design, and argued that their generalizations have wide applicability and raise important issues for interface design.

ACKNOWLEDGEMENTS

We thank Gerhard Fisher, Ray McCall, Andreas Lemke, Anders Morch, Mark Rosenstein, Larry Stead, and Loren Terveen for discussions about this paper and about the applicability of Schoen's theory to interface design.

REFERENCES

1. Egan, D.E., Remde, J.R., Gomez, L.M., Landauer, T.K., Eberhardt, J. and Lochbaum, C.C. Formative Design-Evaluation of SuperBook., ACM Transactions on Information Systems, 1989, 7:1, pp.30-57.

2. Fischer, G. and Lemke, A.C. Construction Kits and Design Environments: Steps Toward Human Problem-Domain Communication, Human-Computer Interaction, 1988, 3:3, pp. 179-222.

3. Fischer, G., McCall, R., and Morch, A. JANUS: Integrating Hypertext with a Knowledge-based Design Environment, Proceedings of Hypertext'89 (Pittsburgh, PA), ACM, New York, November, 1989, pp. 105-117.

4. Fischer, G., McCall, R., and Morch, A. Making Argumentation Serve Design, Tech. report, Department of Computer Science, University of Colorado, Boulder, CO, 1991.

5. Fischer, G., Lemke, A. C., Mastaglio, T., and Morch, A., The Role of Critiquing in Cooperative Problem Solving, ACM Transactions on Information Systems, 1991, (in press).

6. Hollan, J. D., Hutchins, E. L., McCandless, T. P., Rosenstein, M., Weitzman, L. Graphical Interfaces for Simulation. In B. Rouse (Ed.) *Advances in Man-Machine Systems Research*, Greenwich, CT: JAI Press, Inc, 1987, 129-163.

7. Hollan, J.D. and Hill, W. C. Towards an Informational Physics Perspective for Interface Design, In preparation.

8. Lewis, C. and Norman, D. Designing for Error. In D. Norman & S. Draper (Eds.) *User Centered System Design: New Perspectives on Human-Computer Interaction,* Hillsdale, NJ: Lawrence Erlbaum Associates, 1986, 411-432.

9. McCall, R., Fischer, G. and Morch, A. Supporting Reflection-in-Action in the Janus Design Environment in M. McCullough et al., (Eds.), The MIT Press, Cambridge, MA, 1990, pp. 247-259.

10. McCandless, T. P., PDP Mechanisms of Intelligent Display Control, Society for Computer Simulation Conference

on Intelligent Simulation Environments, San Diego, pp. 87-91, 1986.

11. Schoen, D. *The Reflective Practitioner: How Professionals Think in Action* Basic Books, New York, 1982.

12. Schoen, D., *Educating The Reflective Practitioner.* Jossey-Bass Publishers, San Francisco, 1987.

13. Weaver, W. *Lady Luck.* Double Day, Garden City, NY, 1963.

14. Wroblewski, D., McCandless, T., and Hill, W.C., DETENTE: Practical Support for Practical Action, Human Factors in Computing Systems, CHI'91 Conference Proceedings (New Orleans, LA), ACM, New York, 1991, pp.195-202.

15. Wroblewski, D., Hill, W.C., Mccandless, T. Attribute-mapped Scroll Bars, U.S. Patent Applications: Serial No. 07/523,117 filed May 14, 1990, Serial No. 07/626,130 filed Dec 11, 1990.

THE COMPUTER SCIENCES ELECTRONIC MAGAZINE: TRANSLATING FROM PAPER TO MULTIMEDIA

W. Randall Koons, Anne M. O'Dell, Nancy J. Frishberg, and
Mark R. Laff
Interactive Media Project

Computer Science Department
IBM T. J. Watson Research Center, Hawthorne
P.O. Box 704
Yorktown Heights, New York   10598

Contact telephone number: (914) 784-7971
email: anneg@watson.ibm.com

ABSTRACT
In this paper, we discuss issues in design and usability of
the IBM Computer Sciences Electronic Magazine (CSEM).
The CSEM is an interactive multimedia translation of a
paper magazine. It contains articles describing Computer
Sciences projects at the four IBM Research Labs. Combining aspects from print, television, and computers, it is
a useful vehicle for studying what we see as a completely
new communication medium. We report both our design
rationale in creating the magazine and the results of several
user studies which helped us understand our successes and
failures. These studies are a part of an iterative process
through which we have redesigned and improved the
CSEM.

KEYWORDS: Electronic Magazine, Interactive Design,
Multimedia Design, Navigation, Indexing, Usability,
Hypermedia, Metaphor

INTRODUCTION
The current generation of input/output hardware and software enables system designers to choose many new ways
of representing information on computers. High-resolution
displays enable multi-font proportional-spaced text. Audio
and video adapters provide the capability for presenting
motion, sound, and realistic images. While opening up
new possibilities for rich and effective interaction, this new
flexibility confounds the interface designer. At one level,

the **multimedia computer** is simply a collection of new
adapter boards; at another level it represents a combination
of the capabilities of print, television, and the computer,
yielding a completely new communication medium. As
with all media, there are inherent rules for design based
on sociology, psychology, and physiology, which will be
an adaptation of the design disciplines from the three
components: print, television, and computers.

Our research team, the Interactive Media Project (IMP), is
conducting a series of exploratory studies in designing for
this new medium. In particular, we are building examples
of interactive multimedia applications and studying their
use and effectiveness. From these individual examples,
we hope to derive a general set of design principles. This
paper presents our experience with one such application,
the Computer Sciences Electronic Magazine (CSEM).

Integrating Three Metaphors
The multimedia computer enables the fusion of what have
been three distinct media: print, television, and computing.
However, few applications have been widely disseminated
that take advantage of this integration. Contemporaneous
with our work on the CSEM, Verbum Inc. issued their first
interactive CD-ROM Multimedia Magazine (on the
Macintosh platform) with innovative incorporation of motion video, music, speech and animation[4]. We believe
that electronic magazines share design characteristics with
public-information walk-up-and-use kiosks such as found
in museums, libraries, train stations, airports, but an electronic magazine is likely to be targeted to a more focused
audience, incorporate more text, and involve longer interactions. Hypermedia educational applications such as
Intermedia, at Brown University [12], and "A Field Guide
to Insects and Culture", at Cornell University [7], are re-

lated to electronic magazines in that they link text with video, graphics, animation, or other media, and research in this area tackles many of the same design challenges. Nonetheless, we are early in the evolution of interface standards and conventions for interactive multimedia[3, 5]. Re-examining design issues for interactive media, Richmond reminds us: "Designing for an interactive videodisc project presents a very different set of design problems than a noninteractive project, such as a book. A reader always knows where he or she is in a book-beginning, middle, or end. A book is meant to be read linearly. Interactive media is meant to be viewed in any order the viewer wants. Viewers need visual clues to know where they are, and how to get where they want to go."[11]

By calling our application a *Magazine* we made the analogy with familiar print magazines obvious to readers. The content is intended for the scientific community, who might read publications such as "Scientific American" or "Discover". Some of the terminology we used also promotes the metaphor of a magazine: **cover, article, departments, sidebar**. However, the reader must now decide how the metaphor of **magazine** gets translated into a multimedia format.

By incorporating motion video into the CSEM, we draw on viewers' familiarity with narrative (linear) video and with VCRs. Unlike most print magazines, which are composed of text supplemented by graphics and photos, the bulk of each CSEM article is motion video. Like a broadcast television show or a movie newsreel, CSEM allows for a passive viewer who simply selects a channel (here an article) and watches. However we did not include the familiar VCR controls: pause, play, fast forward, etc.

The CSEM runs on an IBM PS/2 computer with a laserdisc player attached.[1] A touch screen is provided for the user interface. Even though the usual input devices (keyboard and mouse) are not present, users are aware of the computer's random access capabilities. Users are likely to be familiar with ATMs and arcade games, computer applications where limited input devices permit only specific interaction.

Framing the Problem
We set out to translate a paper magazine/technical journal using the best aspects of print, video/television, and computer. We assumed that the users' expectations and familiarity with each of these three metaphors (print magazine,

linear video, and computer game) would contribute to their understanding of the interface for the CSEM. We also found that the expectations and familiarity introduce barriers toward the construction of principled design guidelines for interactive multimedia productions[1, 2]. The purpose of this study is to examine our choice of elements from each of the three metaphors in our design of the CSEM, and to provide direction for the iterative re-design of future CSEM issues. The translation of a magazine from the paper medium to multimedia would allow us to identify interface design issues and attempt to solve them.[2]

Previous Multimedia Applications
This work builds on our previous experience designing two interactive multimedia kiosks. Following a history of work in walk-up-and-use kiosks at T. J. Watson [8, 9], we created two kiosk applications prior to the CSEM. The "Research Information Kiosk" (RIK), for two years provided information to visitors to the IBM T. J. Watson Research Center, Hawthorne, NY. Phone lookup linked to floor plans, current events, local driving directions, and other helpful information was available in a touch screen presentation. It also contained a laserdisc-based **magazine** section which was the predecessor of the current CSEM. Another application, "John Cocke: A Retrospective by Friends," commemorated the career of IBM Fellow John Cocke, recipient of the ACM Turing Award, IBM Bertram Award, and National Medal of Technology[6]. Commissioned for a symposium honoring Cocke's 35th anniversary with IBM, this kiosk featured a scrapbook-style presentation with informative, warm, and often very humorous video interviews of 14 of his colleagues as well as Dr. Cocke, himself.

BUILDING THE MAGAZINE
The CSEM presents articles about research projects in the Computer Sciences Department of IBM's Research Division. The magazine was intended to be a communication vehicle for the IBM Research Computer Sciences community, which is spread over four laboratories worldwide.

The IMP team included members with backgrounds in computer science, communications, video graphic design, video production, human factors, and linguistics. This varied group was particularly well suited for the problem at hand: evolving design and implementation from the old to the new media. Based on our earlier experience with the RIK/Magazine, we began building the CSEM in late April, 1991, and installed it in the lobby of our facility in Hawthorne, New York, in August, 1991. It was also fea-

---

1   The CSEM hardware configuration consists of an IBM PS/2 Model 95 with 16mb memory, an IBM 8514 Display with Microtouch overlay, an IBM M-Motion Adapter/A, an IBM M-Audio Capture & Playback Adapter/A and a Pioneer LD-V8000 laser disc player using CLV format. No keyboard or mouse is available to the end user.

2   A complex application such as the CSEM also drives the development of our multimedia tool set. Our ultimate goal for the tools is to create an environment usable by non-programmers to build a variety of multimedia applications.

tured in the "Tomorrow's Realities" Gallery at SIGGRAPH '91, Las Vegas, in late July. Future issues are scheduled for release at four month intervals.

Design Assumptions

Many design assumptions from our work with previous applications were incorporated into the design of the CSEM. These assumptions had an effect on the graphic design and navigation structure of the CSEM. The results of testing determined how well our design worked, and which areas could be improved.

We used video material that was originally produced and edited to be viewed linearly.[3] Each video piece was quite different in editorial style. These factors placed restrictions on how much interaction could be introduced. Some video pieces were easily divided into discrete topics, while others were difficult to divide due to transitions (of narration or music) between topics. When we wanted to provide additional information on a topic, we used text and still images when there was no more video to choose from.[4]

Our previous human factors testing [6] identified two types of users: "passive users," who want to view the application with minimal effort, and "active users," who want to take control of navigating through the material. We assumed we needed to design for both user groups.

Earlier applications included an "attract sequence" similar to a video game, that automatically triggered a prepared sequence of material if no one was actively using the kiosk. The attract sequence was a highly successful feature of "John Cocke" in three areas. First, it satisfied passive users who wanted to watch the material. Next, the moving images caught the attention of potential users. Finally, it modelled users' behavior (i.e. taught them how the application works). We assumed we should include an attract sequence in the CSEM.

Earlier applications also used "default time-out destinations" If no navigational button is touched after an interval, the application automatically returns to an author-specified destination (for example, the cover). We assumed that since the Magazine would be a walk-up-and-use kiosk, it should use the same type of design.

Structure of Content

Our work with previous applications proved that users prefer the structural tree as "flat" as possible to enable quick and easy access to information. To parallel the paper magazine metaphor, the CSEM had to have a **cover** (see Koons, Plate 1). The cover became the base of the structural tree. Next, we divided the content into **articles** (see Koons, Plate 2), about the IBM CS research projects, and **departments** (see Koons, Plate 3), regular features to appear in every issue of the CSEM. Further division would have made the hierarchy too complex and difficult to navigate.

Each article was designed to have a path of primary information which gave the user an overall description of the research project. The article was divided into **topics** (see Koons, Plate 4), short segments that could stand on their own. Interactive branching allowed the user to "dig deeper" into the content to find more detailed information that was not presented in the primary path. This detailed information, called a **sidebar**, might have been video or text (see Koons, Plate 5). Thus, the structure became article title → topic → sidebar.

As we began laying out the structure of each individual article, we found one article had too much material to easily fit into our structural model. To solve this problem, the material was divided further into **chapters** (see Koons, Plate 6), so the structure of one article was article title → chapter → topic → sidebar. This added undesirable structural complexity, but it was necessary to deviate from our original design in order to accommodate the size of the article.

We tried to simplify the use of the CSEM to truly be walk-up-and-use, but we knew there would be some users who did not understand the various functions. We provided context-based digital audio help, available in every part of the magazine.

Terminology

We examined over 50 paper magazines to determine how their content was organized. Though the terminology and the content structure varies somewhat from magazine to magazine, the basic structure is simple. Most magazines contain articles directed at a particular group of readers, and departments (usually called departments or regular features), parts of the magazine which appear in each issue. We wanted the articles to be the main focus, not the regular items, so we settled on "Departments" as the heading for these regular features.[5] We felt "features" implied the main emphasis of the magazine, similar to "feature film" in the world of moving pictures.

---

3 Video for future magazine articles will be scripted and shot specifically for interactive viewing [10].
4 The video storage medium, laservision video disc, can store a maximum of one hour of video and audio material on a single side.
5 We anticipated the potential ambiguity in using "Departments" to refer to features of the magazine about the activities of the Computer Sciences Department at each of the four research laboratories.

Navigation

Navigation, or wayfinding,[6] in a paper magazine is primarily accomplished by using the cover or table of contents to find each article's starting page. The end of a page or column indicates a continuation of content (and where to resume - "continued on page xx"), or the reader assumes it continues on the next content (non-advertising or non-illustration) page or column. A header (short title or "continued from page xx") indicates resuming of previous content.

Navigation in television is not an issue; the material is simply viewed from beginning to end.[7] Non-broadcast video provides some navigation; the viewer can rewind, fast forward, pause, or stop at any point. Users' navigation through information stored on computers varies with the application. It is widely understood that vast amounts of data may be stored and randomly accessed.

A paper magazine is designed so that the pictures, captions, and banners draw readers to an article. To emulate flipping through a magazine, we developed the concept **Cruise** (see Koons, Plate 7), which made the entire contents of the magazine available from one screen. Selecting Cruise sampled the CSEM as a sequence of topics in five-second intervals. This automated function also served as an "attract sequence".

The **"Last Topic"** and **"Next Topic"** buttons allow the user to flip forward or backward through the material. However, since users focused on the moving video of the article, we offered another means of navigation. At the end of a video segment a set of three buttons appears offering the choices **"Repeat this Topic"** , **"Choose from List of Topics"** , and **"Explore the Next Topic"** (see Koons, Plate 4).

As we neared completion of the CSEM, we added **"Super Jump"**, a popup menu used for navigation (see Koons, Plate 8). Users would not have to return to the cover to select a new article or department.

Graphic Design

The graphic design for the CSEM had to accommodate the constraints imposed by the hardware configuration, structure, content, and navigation. These constraints defined the primary screen for viewing video in both the "explore" and "watch" modes and for all "departments" screens. Other screens had different layouts based on function.

The touch screen interface imposed physical limitations on how the available space on the display was used. A touch sensitive area (**touchpad**) had to be a reasonable minimum size. Also, if the touchpads were too close together, the user would be prone to making undesired selections inadvertently. An area touchable by a finger is *larger* than can be targeted by a mouse, lightpen, or other popular pointing devices. The use of text labels on the touchpads also determined to the minimum size of some buttons.

We decided that the video image should be unencumbered by text or buttons. The maximum size of the video window was established by carefully allocating space for the size and number of touchable buttons that would be on screen at any given time.

The graphic design for the other major screens was as follows: The CSEM's **cover** was a full-screen still frame of video with the title and buttons overlaid (see Koons, Plate 1). The **departments list** was a graphics screen listing all the magazine department names on buttons (see Koons, Plate 3). **Topics** screens were graphics-only and contained buttons for topics in a given **article** or **chapter**. Bi-colored buttons were used for topics containing **sidebars** (see Koons, Plate 4). The **chapter list** screen contained a picture from each chapter with a text label below it (see Koons, Plate 6). A different background color was used to differentiate between parts of the magazine.

Feedback to Users

The use of visual and audio feedback was an important feature of this application. We provided the user with visual and audio cues for touch location, disk operation and an incorrect touch. The normal selection cursor was a hand with the index finger pointing.[8] If there was any disk operation, an hourglass cursor appeared to indicate the user should wait a moment. The negative feedback for touching an inactive area of the screen was the normal pointing finger with the familiar red-circle-with-diagonal-slash for negation over it and a digital audio message, "Whoops, try again." (See Figure 1 for these three icons).

USABILITY TESTING

We performed two series of controlled usability tests. The objective of one round of usability testing ("Paper Study") was to observe and categorize how subjects interact with paper magazines, and to determine if familiarity with a particular magazine influences time on task. The other round of usability testing was done on the CSEM ("CSEM Study") to determine how our translation of the paper magazine metaphor, as described above, fulfilled the test

---

6   **Wayfinding** involves getting to a place you can't see." [11]
7   With the option of changing the channel, of course.
8   Our choice of pointing finger for touch confirmation was natural for the IBM OS/2 PM environment, but Macintosh users who have tried the CSEM
    at conferences mistook our icon for the neutral mouse pointer.

Figure 1. Icons for visual feedback on screen-touches.: These icons represent (left to right) the visual feedback for touching a sensitive object on the screen, touching an inactive area of the screen, and "Please Wait" during disk activity.

subjects' expectations, and to determine to what extent familiarity with the CSEM influences time on task.

In addition, we observed visitors using the CSEM at the SIGGRAPH '91 conference. The results of the testing and observation determined the areas of our design that were successful and what areas of the CSEM needed redesign.

Procedure

In both experimental studies, subjects were seated in a quiet office. One experimenter remained in the room to provide guidance and to control the video recording equipment; a second experimenter observed the users' actions using two video monitors (one for each of two camera angles) and audio headphones. The second experimenter logged data in the following categories:

- user's actions
- comments by user
- requests for help
- usability problems
- comments by experimenter
- task completion and timing

Subjects were asked to perform tasks specifically designed to investigate each design area (for both the paper and electronic magazines). Finally, subjects were asked debriefing questions.

Paper Magazine Usability Study

Nine subjects, all IBM Research Division employees, were tested individually in single sessions lasting less than an hour. The tasks focused on structure, terminology, navigation, and graphic design issues.[9] Subjects were asked to find articles, topics, sidebars and pictures. Some of the tasks were phrased to give clues (such as the name of an article that a sidebar appears in) and some were deliberately vague. Subjects were asked to think aloud as they performed the tasks.

We tested subjects in either of two conditions, to determine whether familiarity with a particular publication would affect performance. In condition 1 (Unfamiliar), we gave five subjects the choice of fifteen different magazines to look through for ten minutes while we observed their behavior. Fifteen magazines would ensure a wide variety of design styles and content for the subject to select from. They were then asked to complete six tasks on each of two magazines that were not included in their original selection. In condition 2 (Familiar), we gave four subjects only four magazines to look through for ten minutes. Four magazines would guarantee that the subject would explore at least two publications. They were then asked to perform the same six tasks on each of two magazines that they had browsed. Subjects in both conditions were asked debriefing questions concerning their performance of the tasks.

CSEM Usability Study

Thirteen subjects, all Research Division employees, were tested individually in single sessions of an hour each. The tasks were designed to be as similar as possible to those used in the Paper Magazine Usability Study and included the additional issue of feedback. Subjects were asked to think aloud as they performed the tasks.

To determine if familiarity with the application was a factor, we tested subjects in two conditions. In condition 1 (Unfamiliar), eight subjects were asked to complete six tasks without having seen the CSEM beforehand. In condition 2 (Familiar), five subjects were given ten minutes of free time to explore the CSEM before being asked to complete the six tasks.

Observations - Uncontrolled Environment

Exhibiting the CSEM at the SIGGRAPH '91 "Tomorrow's Realities" Gallery provided us the opportunity to sample usage by a large and varied population. Attendees to the show typically include people from computer disciplines, the arts, and the business world. We captured and analyzed six hours of screen interactions selected at random from the five day exhibition. Analysis of navigation choices and time delays (pauses) indicated what was interesting to users, what was perplexing, and how usable our design was.

RESULTS OF TESTING

Users of the CSEM expected that they would be able to use it as easily as a paper magazine, yet both CSEM conditions identified a large gap between this expectation and what they experienced. All subjects in the paper magazine study completed the experimental tasks. In the CSEM study, however, 20% (1 of 5) of the condition 2 subjects (Familiar) and 63% (5 of 8) of the condition 1 subjects (Unfamiliar) failed to complete one or more of the tasks.

---

9   rather than on content

The usability problems we identified influenced our iterative re-design as described in "Redesign" below.

We observed no training effects between the two conditions (Familiar and Unfamiliar) in the paper study. The time to complete the tasks was identical for either condition. In the CSEM study, however, the condition 2 subjects (Familiar) completed the tasks an average of 1.75 times faster than the condition 1 subjects (Unfamiliar), a significant difference. The positive effect of the training time on performance for the "Familiar" group means that our interface is not yet "walk-up-and-use".

Paper Magazine Usability Study Results

These results were based on observations of subjects browsing through magazines and performing tasks, and their responses to debriefing questions. As previously stated, we found that experience with a particular paper magazine made no difference in how easily subjects completed the tasks.

Our observations identified three clear styles of paper magazine use:

1. Page flippers - two of the nine subjects used the magazine by flipping through the pages, whether backward or forward in order, and skimming the articles to find something of interest;

2. Cover scanners - two of the nine subjects looked at the cover and went directly to the cover story or other article mentioned on the cover; and

3. Contents page scanners - five of the nine subjects who flipped pages until they found the contents page, scanned the contents page for an article that interested them, and went to the article from the contents page.

These categories, derived from observation, were found to be very similar to those listed by J. V. White [13].

CSEM Usability Study Results

Our general finding is that the CSEM failed where it did not remain true to the magazine (and/or VCR) metaphor. It did not meet viewers' expectations based previous experience with the traditional paper and video media. In Figure 2 we identify the CSEM's major usability problems, and indicate which design aspect (as described in *"Building the Magazine"*, above) contributed to the problem. This figure reports usability problems noted in the logged data: observations by the experimenter, overt comments from the subjects, as well as actions of the subjects. Only problems occurring at least once in each condition are included in the figure. (Additional difficulties may have been observed for subjects in only one condition.) It is clear that decisions

in each of the five design areas[10] have interacting consequences for the usability of the CSEM. Most of the usability problems we identified require redesign in several areas. In addition, we discovered an additional focus area, **User Control**, representing the user interaction with isochronous material such as video and fixed-paced screen transitions.

Valid Design Assumptions

The CSEM studies identified areas in which the CSEM's design was clearly understood, and the specific areas that needed improvement to make it as easy to use as a paper magazine. They also underscored the importance of designing the interface to be as familiar and intuitive as paper, while improving it through the use of interactive multimedia technology.

Users like the overall concept of an electronic magazine, a magazine enriched by presentation on a multimedia computer. They recognize the power that the combination of video, text, audio, and graphics on a computer can have to convey information. We consider the following aspects of our design valid, receiving positive comments during the usability sessions.

- Many users commented positively about the content. They liked the "look" of the magazine and, in debriefing, urged us to make the CSEM available in the library or at their desks.

- The RETURN TO THE COVER button provided the ability to return to a "home state", an important feature to users.

- The RESET FOR NEW USER button was used when each user in the uncontrolled environment finished with the magazine, akin to a reader closing a paper magazine for the next reader.

- Users liked the layout of the SUPER JUMP and DEPARTMENTS screens because these two screens visually resembled the Table of Contents of a paper magazine.

- A still frame of video on screen with text surrounding it, similar to a page of a paper magazine, was considered easy to read and interesting.

ITERATIVE DESIGN

The August 1991 issue of the CSEM was an important milestone in the IMP's iterative design process. The usability testing clearly defined the problem areas that need to be addressed to achieve the goal of an electronic magazine that is as easy to use as a paper magazine. The solutions which address these problem areas were

---

[10] **Structure, Terminology, Graphic Design, Navigation,** and **Feedback** originally identified in *"Building the Magazine"*

Usability Problem	UnF N=8	F N=5	Structure	Terms	Graphic Design	Navi- gation	Feedback	User Control
Lack of Table of Contents	7	2	x	x	x	x		
"Last Topic" Ambiguous	5	4	x	x		x		
Busy-Looking Screens	5	3			x		x	
Color Coding Not Perceived	4	4	x		x	x		x
Path & Pacing Not Understood in Attract Sequence ("Cruise")	3	5		x	x	x		x
Headings for Topics Not Salient Enough	6	1	x		x	x	x	
Inconsistent Visual Cues for Touch-Sensitive Areas	5	2			x	x	x	
Wayfinding Difficulties	4	3	x			x		x
"Department" Misinterpreted	5	2	x	x				
"Chapter", "Topic", "Article" Confusing	4	2	x	x				
Too Much or Too Small Text	4	1			x			
No VCR-like Controls	3	2			x	x		x
"Explore", "Watch" Modes Not Differentiated	3	2	x	x	x	x		x
"Intro", "Abstract", "Overview" Confusing	3	1	x	x				
Help Insufficient or Unexpected Behavior	3	1	x	x		x		x
Negative Audio Feedback Annoying; No Positive Audio Feedback	2	2			x	x	x	
Positive Feedback Icons (Hand and Hourglass) Not Noticed or Not Understood	1	1			x	x	x	x

Figure 2. CSEM Study - Usability Problem Summary: This table shows usability problems identified in the CSEM Study reported or observed for at least one subject in each condition (UnF<amiliar> vs. F<amiliar>) in decreasing order of frequency of occurrence.

implemented in the design of the December 1991 issue of the CSEM.

- **Make it look like a magazine**: We added a table of contents, an index, and a glossary. To further strengthen the magazine metaphor, we introduced pages for navigation (see Koons, Plates 9, 10, 11).

- **Make it act like a VCR**: We added VCR-like control over the video segments for pause, play, reverse, fast forward, fast reverse, and single-step (see Koons, Plate 12).

- **Simplify the graphic design**: Fewer choices on each page have made the layout less confusing, and bigger, simpler, easier-to-touch buttons are labeled in a bigger, easier-to-read font (see Koons, Plate 12).

- **Give Positive Visual Feedback**: Touchable areas were given a visual emphasis that highlights when the user is touching them. Select-on-liftoff was used instead of select-on-touchdown (see Koons, Plate 12).

In summary, we changed the design of the CSEM to more closely match existing paradigms with which the user has experience. In many cases one design change effected several categories (structure, navigation, content, graphic design, terminology, feedback, and user control).

CONCLUSION

The CSEM is a study in a new communication medium, interactive multimedia. As designers, we selected elements and styles from each of the areas from which multimedia is evolving: print, television, and computers. As part of the iterative design process, our usability studies helped us understand which of these choices were successful, and which were not.

We learned that users themselves bring scenarios from their experiences in using the three original media. The closer the user interface matches familiar scenarios, the more usable the CSEM becomes. Finally, in general, we learned that when designing an electronic x (in our case a magazine), begin with the existing x and use the capabilities of the multimedia computer to enhance and extend it.

ACKNOWLEDGEMENTS

This work would not have been possible without Mary S. Van Deusen, who initiated the CSEM, has been a major part of the design team, and who has created most of the video content. The authors also appreciate the design, programming, and video contributions of the other members of the Interactive Media Project: Moe R. Desrosiers, Paul R. Kosinski, and Neil I. Sarnak. Special thanks to Clare-Marie Karat for her assistance with our usability testing and task analysis.

We also appreciate the ongoing support of our department Vice President, Dr. Abraham Peled, who continues to take a special interest in this work.

References

1. J. M. Carroll, R. L. Mack, and W. A. Kellogg. Interface Metaphors and User Interface Design. In M. Helander, editors, *Handbook of Human-Computer Interaction*, 67-85, Elsevier Science Publishers, North Holland, 1988.

2. J. M. Carroll and J. C. Thomas. Metaphor and the Cognitive Representation of Computing Systems. *IEEE Transactions on Systems, Man, and Cybernetics*, SMC-12(2):107-116, March/April 1982.

3. B. Laurel, ed. *The Art of Human-Computer Interface Design*. Addison Wesley, New York, NY, 1990.

4. M. Gosney, ed. *Verbum Interactive, Issue 1.0*. Verbum Inc., San Diego, CA, 1990.

5. S. Ambron, K. Hooper, ed. *Interactive Multimedia*. Microsoft Press, Redmond, WA, 1988.

6. N. Frishberg, M. R. Laff, M. R. Derosiers, W. R. Koons, and J. F. Kelley. John Cocke: A Retrospective by Friends (An Interactive Multimedia Scrapbook). In Scott P. Robertson, Gary M. Olson, and Judith S. Olson, editors, *Human Factors in Computing Systems (CHI'91 Conference Proceedings)*, 423-424, Addison Wesley, New Orleans, LA, 1991.

7. G. Gay and E. Raffensperger. Considerations and Strategies in the Design of Interactive Multimedia Programs. *Academic Computing*, 24ff., September 1989.

8. Kelley, J.F. RIK+GEDD Case Study: Rapid Prototyping and the 1987 CHI+GI Conf Poster Demonstration at CHI '88 in Washington D.C., 1988.

9. Kelley, J.F., Gursky, M.C., and Kannan, K. RIK+GEDD - Research Information Kiosk + Graphic Editing and Database Delivery system: Rapid prototyping and iterative design of public access information applications. Internal publication., 1989.

10. M. Naimark. Shooting for Interactivity Paper delivered at the 191st SMPTE Technical Conference, L.A., October,, 1989.

11. W. Richmond. *Design & Technology*, pages 181-186. Van Nostrand Reinhold, New York, NY, 1990.

12. K. Utting and N. Yankelovich. Context and Orientation in Hypermedia Networks. *ACM Transactions on Information Systems*, 7(1):58-84, 1989.

13. J. V. White. *Designing Covers, Contents, Flash Forms, Departments, Editorials, Openers, and Products for Magazines*, pages 33-36. R. R. Bowker, New York, NY, 1976.

Hypertext or Book: Which is Better for Answering Questions?

Barbee T. Mynatt, Laura Marie Leventhal, Keith Instone,
John Farhat and Diane S. Rohlman

Computer Science Department
Bowling Green State University
Bowling Green, Ohio 43403
(419) 372-2337   FAX (419) 372-8061
e-mail: mynatt@opie.bgsu.edu

ABSTRACT

An important issue in the evolution of hypertext is the design of such systems to optimally support user tasks such as asking questions. Few studies have systematically compared the use of hypertext to books in seeking information, and those that have been done have not found a consistent superiority for hypertext. In addition, designers developing hypertext books have few guidelines. In the present study, users performed information-seeking tasks and answered a variety of types of questions about Sherlock Holmes stories using either a conventional paper encyclopedia or a hypertext encyclopedia. The questions varied on the amount of information needed to derive an answer (fact or inference), the location of the question's key phrase in the hypertext (entry title or entry content), and the format of the information (text or map). Accuracy and time were recorded. The hypertext group excelled in answering fact questions where the information was embedded in a text entry. The book group excelled only in answering fact questions based on maps. In spite of having far more experience using books, the book group was not significantly faster overall and did not perform as well on an incidental learning task. Our results suggest that a hypertext book with a nonlinear structure and including a variety of navigational tools can equal or surpass conventional books as an information-seeking medium, even with minimal training.

KEYWORDS: experimental research, question answering, usability of hypertext, hypertext

INTRODUCTION

An important issue in evaluating the usability of any system is how well the system supports the user in attaining task goals. One task integral to many hypertext systems is answering questions. While many adults are highly skilled in using books to answer questions, hypertext systems can offer additional functions and alternative modes of interaction. These new approaches need to be systematically assessed in order to provide designers with empirically-based design guidelines. In general, little research has been done on the strengths and weaknesses of hypertext *vis a vis* more traditional media. McKnight, Dillon and Robertson (1989), for example, have suggested that there is a great need for experimental work to compare hypertext and paper media in a variety of situations.

The studies that have been done to date on the issue of books versus hypertext have not always painted a rosy picture for hypertext. An initial problem with hypertext is that users read textual material more slowly from screens than from paper media (e.g., Wright & Lickorish, 1983; Gould, Alfaro, Fin, Haupt & Minuto, 1987). Prior studies that compared hypertext books to conventional paper books have reported mixed results, with neither media emerging as uncontestably better. A variety of factors, including the form of computer implementation and the type of task, appear to influence usage patterns and user satisfaction. Marchionini and Shneiderman (1988) described studies that compared utilizing information in hypertext systems to conventional paper materials. In one study comparing a paper versus hypertext version of a maintenance manual, the paper version resulted in significantly faster times for 12 different tasks. A second study (also reported in Shneiderman, 1987) compared a paper versus a hypertext version of a database on the holocaust, developed in Hyperties. For simple fact retrieval questions, the paper version was faster. But as query complexity increased, the Hyperties system became equally fast. There was no difference between the groups in accuracy. In addition, users greatly preferred the Hyperties system.

Egan, Remde, Gomez, Landauer, Eberhardt, and Lochbaum (1989) compared performance on a variety of tasks using a printed statistics book and three different versions of a hypertext facsimile of the same book, developed in SuperBook. The SuperBook version presented the text in multi-window format and supported word look-up and entry into the book from a table of contents. Subjects took part in a one-hour training session and five evaluation sessions. In a structured search task, the subjects attempted to answer questions that could be found by searching for key phrases in either headings only, text only, text or headings, or neither. With the improved hypertext versions, Egan, et al.

found that the SuperBook users were significantly more accurate. The paper book users were marginally more accurate only for searches where the key phrase was in neither the heading nor the text (e.g., key phrases using synonyms). Egan, et al. also found that search times were not statistically different for the two media overall in one version. However, SuperBook users had faster search times for questions whose keywords could be found in the text only. Users of the paper version were faster for searches where the key phrase was in neither the heading nor the text. The MiteyBook version, which included a number of refinements, resulted in 25 percent faster search times overall, compared to the paper version. In an open-book essay task, subjects from the SuperBook group obtained significantly better overall scores and factual content scores than subjects from the paper group. SuperBook users rated the documentation, the system, and affect for statistics as subjectively higher than the paper group. Finally, in an incidental learning task, SuperBook users recalled significantly more chapter headings than the paper group.

In this paper we report an experiment comparing the success users have answering different sorts of questions using either a hypertext encyclopedia, HyperHolmes™, or a paper version of the same encyclopedia. The goal was to determine the relative strengths and weaknesses of paper versus hypertext for this user task, and to determine, from a designers' perspective, what hypertext features make hypertext most effective for this type of application. More specifically, the current study addresses the following issues:

- *The effectiveness of hypertext interface features in answering assorted types of questions.* In prior research using a different sort of hypertext system, Egan, et al. varied the types of questions that subjects were to address. They found that SuperBook was faster for answering questions where the answer was in the text only, and book users were marginally more accurate for finding questions requiring synonyms. In our study, we explore a wider variety of question types, and utilize a different sort of hypertext system.

- *The use of materials which are non-linear.* In the Egan, et al. study, the statistics book represented in the SuperBook version was a standard format text book, organized into sequential chapters with subheadings. Thus, the naive reader would typically be required to go through the book sequentially in order to acquire a coherent understanding of the material. While it is clear that hypertext must be able to successfully present sequential material, it is perhaps a more natural medium for non-linear information with many interconnections. By non-linear information, we mean information that can be understood in isolation, and that does not assume that previous (non-general) information has been acquired. Reference materials, such as dictionaries, encyclopedias and cookbooks are common examples

of non-linear information. Marchionini and Shneiderman (1988) did use non-linear information, but found no superiority for hypertext.

- *The incorporation of more "hyper" features than previous hypertext versus book studies.* In addition to using non-linear materials, the HyperHolmes system includes a number of features that were not used in the earlier studies. These include the use of graphics, backtracking, and searching based on links. More specific descriptions are provided below.

- *The amount of training necessary to be an effective user.* Tombaugh, Lickorish and Wright (1987) have shown that skill level and training can influence hypertext use. However, there are wide variations in the amount of training given to users in previous studies. Egan, et al. used a one-hour training session, and then examined performance across 5 additional hours of interaction with the system. In contrast, Marchionini and Shneiderman used a 7 to 8 minute training period. In the present study, a modest amount (approximately 30 minutes) of training was used.

A DESCRIPTION OF HYPERHOLMES

HyperHolmes: The Electronic Encyclopædia Sherlockiana™ incorporates information from Jack Tracy's *Encyclopædia Sherlockiana* (1977). The *Encyclopædia Sherlockiana* is an alphabetically arranged list of keywords and key phrases related to the Sherlock Holmes stories. Each keyword or key phrase has an accompanying description, and possibly references to other entries in the encyclopaedia. The book is not indexed and entries are found strictly alphabetically. Tracy's book is considered by Sherlockians to be the definitive encyclopedia of information on Sherlock Holmes as depicted in Sir Arthur Conan Doyle's stories.

The HyperHolmes system was implemented in HyperCard 1.2.5, using the Dialoger and aGHASt tools (Instone, 1990). The system contains over 3200 cards. A single card consists of an entry (as copied from the encyclopedia) of text, graphics or a combination of the two. Any entry may contain one or more direct references to other entries. Direct references to other entries are completely capitalized. Each entry is a window on a card. In addition to the entry, other icons and information are present on the card.

HyperHolmes provides a number of navigation tools and methods. The simplest way to move among the cards is to click on any word or phrase in the current entry that is displayed in all capital letters. (See sample screen in Figure 1.) Every capitalized string is a button that takes the user to the indicated card.

A backtrack tool (represented by the bent arrow icon) takes the user back to the most recently visited card. Repeated use of the backtrack tool steps the user back through prior cards in reverse historical order. An alphabet slide bar (seen on the right side of Figure 1) approximates the use of a thumb index followed by page turning in a book. A sliding box

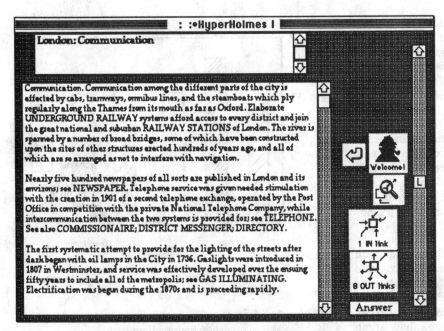

Figure 1: A typical HyperHolmes card

inside the bar can be moved towards the top to select from cards at the beginning of the alphabet, and towards the bottom to select cards later in the alphabet. When the slide box is released, the box contains the letter of the alphabet which matches the title of the card displayed in the main window. Once in the approximate area, clicking on an up or down arrow moves a single card at a time up or down alphabetically.

The search tool (represented by a magnifying glass icon) provides text-searching capabilities. The user types in a target word or phrase and selects the desired search space. The search space can be either the entry titles or the entire textual contents plus titles. (In the current version, the text on maps and drawings is not part of the search space.) Once activated, the search tool displays a list of the titles of cards containing a match, and the contents of one matching card are displayed in the main window. The user may then select any of the displayed titles, select the displayed card and/or dismiss the search tool.

Finally, HyperHolmes includes the Incoming Links and Outgoing Links tools. Clicking on the Incoming Links tool produces a list of all cards in HyperHolmes which reference the current card. The Outgoing Links tool lists all cards referenced by the current card (this is equivalent to the set of buttons associated with the current card). To our knowledge, HyperHolmes is the first hypertext system to incorporate such tools.

In HyperHolmes, several specialized types of cards are used to provide organization, way-finding information and help. These include the Holme card, overview cards and help cards. The Holme card is the first card displayed when the system is initially activated. It contains the title, a large logo (silhouette of Sherlock Holmes) and several buttons, including Getting Help and Overviews. The Holme card can

be directly reached from any other card in the system by clicking on a button that is always present and consists of a miniature version of the logo. Thus the Holme card serves as both the entry point and home base. The Getting Help cards describe how to use the system and include visual "snapshots" of examples. The Overview button produces a table of the various overviews (seven total) that are available. Each overview is similar to a table of contents, but focused on one topic. For example, there are overviews of all the stories in publication order, Sherlock Holmes, London, maps and so on. Cards cited in the overviews are directly accessible from the overviews.

METHOD AND PROCEDURES
Experimental Design

The experiment used a combination of between- and within-subjects experimental design and consisted of three independent variables: question type (described below), medium (book vs. hypertext) and trials. Dependent measures included the accuracy of users' responses and their speed in answering the questions. In addition, the extent of incidental learning was assessed.

Materials

Five types of questions were used: Fact/Text/Title, Fact/Text/Contents, Fact/Nontext, Inferential/Text, and Inferential/Nontext. (There were no Fact/Nontext/Contents questions because the system did not provide the ability to search on textual material in nontext cards.) The questions varied in the amount of information needed to answer them (a single fact or an inference drawn from combining two or more facts), the location of a matching keyword (entry title or entry content) and physical format of the target entry (text or nontext). To answer a Fact question, information from only one entry was needed. Title questions were questions whose answers could be found if the user searched the entry titles using a keyword from the question. An example of a Fact/Text/Title question is "What is a spud?" If the user did a search through entry titles using the keyword "spud," the search would find and display the text entry entitled "Spud," which contained a definition of the term. Contents questions were questions whose answers could only be found by searching for a keyword embedded in the text of an entry (a search on title would not yield any hits). To answer an inferential question, information from more than one entry was needed. An example of an inferential question is: "Name two countries Holmes visited in 'The Final Problem.'" To answer this question, the user must find at least two entries related to "The Final Problem" which mention Holmes traveling through a particular country. The incoming links tool is potentially quite useful in answering inferential questions. In the "Final Problem" question, a user might go to the node about "The Final Problem." Clicking on the incoming links button brings up a list of the nodes which reference this story.

Included in this are several countries (like Luxembourg and Italy), which the user can learn more about by selecting the name from the list. A total of fifteen questions, three of each type, were used in this study. Each user received one of four different random orders of the questions. The orders were restricted in such a way that blocks of five questions, one question of each type, were created within each order.

Following the questions, users also completed an incidental learning task. The incidental learning task consisted of a list of titles of entries. Half of the titles were ones the user must have seen if she or he answered the questions correctly. Half were titles that were probably not seen. The users were asked to circle the titles they remembered seeing.

Users

Novice users were studied because we felt that an important aspect of many hypertext systems is that they be accessible even to novices with a minimum of training. Twenty-nine college students enrolled in Introductory Psychology who were in their first to third year of college were recruited. As a prerequisite for participation, all users had some experience using computers. Fifteen used HyperHolmes and 14 used the paper version of *Encyclopædia Sherlockiana*.

Training

Because users in both groups answered the task questions on a Macintosh II computer, all were given an introduction to the Macintosh II. A guided tour was used to review mouse skills such as pointing, clicking and dragging. The users in the HyperHolmes group also received instruction on working with more than one window, scrolling a window and closing windows. Following the Macintosh training, the experimenter read a tutorial to the users that explained the basic features of either the paper version of *Encyclopædia Sherlockiana* or HyperHolmes. The paper tutorial explained the organization of the book and gave examples demonstrating how the entries were related. The training for the paper book lasted approximately 15 minutes. The HyperHolmes tutorial explained the organization of the software, the Holme card, the Overviews, and how to work the buttons. Each tool was demonstrated and explained. The users practised using each tool while it was explained. Next, they were asked to complete eight exercises using the tools. These exercises reviewed how each tool worked and gave them an opportunity to practice using the tools. The exercise did not give any practice in answering questions. The combined training and exercises with HyperHolmes took approximately 30 minutes.

Procedure

The users assigned to the HyperHolmes condition first received the Macintosh and HyperHolmes tutorials. They were then given a booklet containing the three blocks of questions and asked to search for the answers. They were told to use the remaining time of the two-hour session. When an answer was found, the user clicked on an "Answer" icon on the screen. This caused a text window to appear where the answer was to be entered. If the user was unable to find the answer after searching for 15 minutes, (s)he

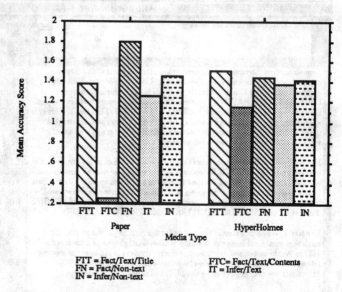

FTT = Fact/Text/Title   FTC= Fact/Text/Contents
FN = Fact/Non-text   IT = Infer/Text
IN = Infer/Non-text

Figure 2: Mean accuracy scores as a function of type of question and medium type

entered "I don't know" in the answer space and went on to the next question. The users using the paper version of *Encyclopædia Sherlockiana* first received the Macintosh and *Encyclopædia* tutorials. They were then given the three blocks of questions to answer. The answers were entered into the computer using the same answer icon/text window as the video users. These users were also told to type "I don't know" in the answer space if they could not find the answer after 15 minutes of searching. After completing the questions all of the users completed the incidental learning task.

RESULTS
Accuracy

Every answer was scored using a 0 to 2 rating scale. A score of 0 indicated the answer was incorrect or missing. A score of 1 indicated partially correct. Only the answers to questions requiring a two part answer (i.e., Inferential/Text and Inferential/Nontext) could potentially receive a score of 1. A score of 2 indicated a completely correct answer.

The mean accuracy scores for the five different types of questions as a function of medium type are shown in Figure 2. Question type had a significant effect on accuracy of responses, $F(4,104) = 20.62$, $p < .0001$. Scores were highest overall for the Fact/Nontext questions (mean = 1.61) and lowest for the Fact/Text/Content questions (mean = 0.74). The interaction between question type and medium was also significant, $F(4,104) = 8.81$, $p < .0001$. Figure 2 illustrates this interaction and shows that Fact/Text/Content questions were harder for both media groups, but were extremely hard for the Paper group. The Fact/Nontext questions were particularly easy for the Paper group, but only of average difficulty for the HyperHolmes group. Overall, the scores were higher for the group using HyperHolmes than for the Paper group (means = 1.38 vs. 1.23). This difference was marginally significant, $F(1, 26) = 3.41$, $p < .08$.

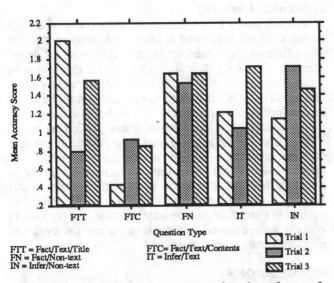

FTT = Fact/Text/Title   FTC= Fact/Text/Contents
FN = Fact/Non-text   IT = Infer/Text
IN = Infer/Non-text

Trial 1
Trial 2
Trial 3

Figure 3: Mean accuracy scores as a function of type of question and trial collapsed across medium type

The difficulty the Paper users had in answering Fact/Text/Content questions is understandable. These questions required finding material embedded in the content (body) of an entry whose title was not keyed to the question. We believe that the reason the Paper group did as well as they did do on the Fact/Text/Content questions was somewhat accidental. One question asked "What are the names of two sea monsters?" There was no entry titled "sea monsters"; however, the entry containing the answer, "Scylla and Charybdis", happened to be on the same page where the entry for "sea monsters" would have been. One-third of the Paper group found the answer to this question, but only one user found the answer to either of the other two Fact/Text/Content questions. This serendipitous finding points to a possibly overlooked advantage of books. Incidental information is much more a "fact of life" with books, and is typically not a feature of hypertext. (However, note our findings in regard to incidental learning discussed below.) The HyperHolmes search tool made finding Fact/Text/Content answers easy, *if* the user understood and used the content-searching mode. The fact that the HyperHolmes group performed worst on this type of question suggests that using the content-searching mode was not always intuitive. This is not surprising, because it is perhaps the content-search feature that potentially makes an electronic version of a book most different from a paper version. Searching line-by-line through text is simply not feasible in a paper book, and so is not a frequently-used problem-solving approach.

The finding that paper book users performed best on Fact/Nontext questions while the HyperHolmes users performed only at an average level on such questions was unexpected. Fact/Nontext questions involved answering a single, factual question based on a map. One explanation for this outcome is that in the paper book the maps were inserted alphabetically in with the rest of the materials. Thus, if the user looked up "India", (s)he would find not

only a text entry, but one or more maps in the same physical location. In HyperHolmes, the search facility listed "Map of India" as one of possibly several matches. The user had to specifically select "Map of India" in order to view the map; this is an additional step that is not required with the book. Although there was an overview of all maps available in HyperHolmes and there was no such listing in the paper book, this added information did not overcome the apparent handicap of the extra steps necessary to access a map. A second possible explanation for the somewhat poorer performance of the HyperHolmes group on the map questions is related to screen size and acuity. The maps represented on the screen were physically smaller than those on paper. Furthermore, a number of the maps from the book had to be divided into two or more screens. If this occurred, arrow buttons were added to the map to quickly take the user to the adjacent map. Nonetheless, division reduced the amount of information simultaneously available.

Interestingly, the HyperHolmes users did not have improved accuracy for the inferential questions, in spite of having the incoming links tool. We speculate that this is due to a lack of familiarity with this function, because books do not have this function available.

The use of three repeated sets of questions allowed us to look at learning effects. Although there was a significant effect of trials, F (2,52) = 4.19, p < .03, there was no interaction with medium type. Performance on the last trial (mean = 1.45) was the best, while performance on the first trial (mean = 1.29) and second trials (mean = 1.20) was poorer. There was also a significant interaction of question type and trials collapsed across medium type, F(8, 208) = 5.78, p < .0001. These data are shown in Figure 3. Perhaps the most noticeable effect contributing to the interaction is the great difference in accuracy on Trial 1 between the Fact/Text/Title questions and the Fact/Text/Content questions. All subjects in both conditions on Trial 1

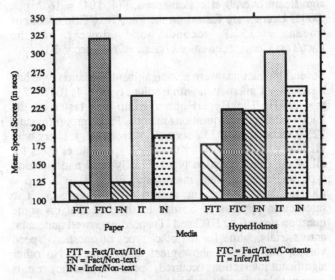

FTT = Fact/Text/Title   FTC= Fact/Text/Contents
FN = Fact/Non-text   IT = Infer/Text
IN = Infer/Non-text

Figure 4: Mean speed in answering questions as a function of medium and type of question

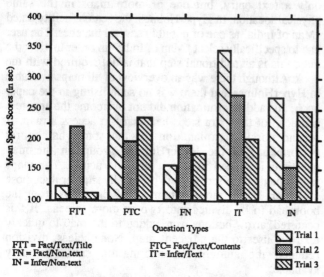

Figure 5: Mean speed in answering questions as a function of type of question and trial

FTT = Fact/Text/Title
FN = Fact/Non-text
IN = Infer/Non-text
FTC= Fact/Text/Contents
IT = Infer/Text

Trial 1
Trial 2
Trial 3

answered their Fact/Text/Title question correctly, but did the most poorly of all on the Fact/Text/Content question. Perhaps this large difference on the first trial reflects the initial intuitiveness of the operations required to find the answers.

Speed

Time to complete each question, in seconds, was recorded for each medium. The results are shown in Figure 4. There was a marginally significant main effect due to medium, $F(1,26) = 3.31$, $p < .08$. The Paper book users were slightly faster overall (mean = 200.9 seconds) than the HyperHolmes users (mean = 235.5 seconds). There was also a significant training effect overall, $F(2, 52) = 9.90$, $p < .0002$. Users got progressively faster on each trial (means = 254.8 seconds on Trial 1, 208.1 seconds on Trial 2 and 195.4 seconds on Trial 3). Finally, question type also had a significant overall effect on speed, $F(4, 104) = 16.7$, $p < .0001$. Users were fastest on the Fact/Text/Title questions (mean = 152.2 seconds) and slowest on the Fact/Text/Contents questions (mean = 269.5 seconds).

Several interactions were also significant. Question type had a significant interaction with medium type, $F(4, 104) = 7.9$, $p < .0001$. The HyperHolmes group was faster on the Fact/Text/Contents questions than the Paper group (means, 223.0 seconds and 323.2 seconds, respectively). Users with the Paper book were faster than the HyperHolmes users for all of the other question types. Finally, trial and question type had a significant interaction, $F(8,208) = 5.9$, $p < .0001$. This interaction is shown in Figure 5. The interaction appears to be due to the fact that on some question types (i.e., FTC and IT) speed improved quite a bit across trials, while for the other types of questions speed varied, but did not show great improvement. No other significant interactions occurred. Speed and accuracy results were not significantly correlated.

Incidental Learning

A Mann-Whitney U test comparing the number of correct answers on the incidental learning task showed that the HyperHolmes group exhibited significantly more incidental learning, $U = 46.5$, $p < .02$. That is, the HyperHolmes group correctly identified more previously-seen entry titles, and correctly rejected unseen titles compared to the Paper group. Incidental learning is of interest because it indicates that unmotivated, nonintentional learning is taking place. That is, if incidental learning does occur, the user is getting "bonus" knowledge with no intentional expenditure of effort. Heller (1990) points out that incidental learning in hypertext-assisted instruction is a desirable feature. Our finding of greater incidental learning from the hypertext version is also of interest because although the book users actually were exposed to more information, the hypertext users apparently learned more.

CONCLUSIONS

The results of this experiment highlight how the functionality offered by a system, the task to be performed and characteristics of the user all interact (Eason, 1984). For some types of tasks, such as Fact/Text/Content questions, HyperHolmes users clearly had advantages over the paper group, because this type of search is more difficult or impossible in a paper book. However, on the Fact/Text/Content questions the performance of HyperHolmes users was still worse than their performance on other question types. In this case, the problem was that the users did not effectively use an available tool that would have made the task easy. An issue for further exploration is how to draw the user's attention to appropriate tools at appropriate times. A tutorial system or knowledge-based system would probably be necessary. The performance on the inferential questions was much the same across the two medium. These result suggest that even when the system supports a type of access, if it is an unfamiliar strategy, the users probably will not use the strategy as effectively as more familiar ones. Our results further suggest that question types that deal with visual and non-textual information are challenging for hypertext book users. In HyperHolmes, maps apparently need improvement to become at least equally accessible as the same information in the paper book.

It is perhaps not amiss to point out again that the book users were highly practiced in using books, while the hypertext users had only one-half hour of training. Considering this large discrepancy in training, our results suggest that well-designed hypertext has great potential for giving users enhanced functionality at little cost to the user.

REFERENCES

1. Duchastel, P.C. Examining cognitive processing in hypermedia usage, *Hypermedia.* 2 (3), 1990, 221-233.

2. Eason, K. D. Towards the experimental study of usability. *Behaviour & Information Technology*, 3(2), 1984, 133-143.

3. Egan, D. E., Remde, J. R., Gomez, L. M., Landauer, T. K., Eberhardt, J. & Lochbaum, C. C. Formative design-evaluation of SuperBook, *ACM Transactions on Information Systems*, 7(1), 1989, 30-57.

4. Gould, J.D., Alfaro, L., Finn, R., Haupt, B., Minuto, A. Reading from CRT displays can be as fast as reading from paper, *Human Factors, 29* (5), 1987, 497-517.

5. Heller, R. S. The role of hypermedia in education: A look at the research issues. *Journal of Research on Computing in Education*, 22(4), 1990, 431-441.

6. Instone, K. A General Hypertext Authoring Stack for Macintosh. Department of Computer Science Technical Report (90-AUG-01). Bowling Green State University, 1990.

7. Marchionini, G. and Shneiderman, B. Finding facts vs. browsing knowledge in hypertext systems, *IEEE Computer*, 21 (1), 1988, 70-80.

8. McKnight, C., A. Dillon and Richardson, J. Problems in HyperLand? A human factors perspective. *Hypermedia. 1*(2), 1989, 167- 178.

9. Nielsen, J. *Hypertext and Hypermedia*. Academic Press, New York, 1990.

10. Shneiderman, B. User interface design and evaluation for an electronic encyclopedia. In G. Salvendy (Ed.), *Cognitive Engineering in the Design of Human-Computer Interaction and Expert Systems.*, (New York: Elsevier Science Publishers), 1987, 207-223.

11. Tombaugh, J., Lickorish, A. and Wright, P. Multi-window displays for readers of lengthy texts, *International Journal of Man-Machine Studies*, 26(5), 1987, 597-615.

12. Tracy, Jack. *The Encyclopædia Sherlockiana*. Avenel Books, New York, 1987.

13. Wright, P & Lickorish, A. Proof-reading texts on screen and paper, *Behaviour and Information Technology*, 2 (3), 1983, 227-235.

REALIZING A VIDEO ENVIRONMENT: EUROPARC'S RAVE SYSTEM

William Gaver, Thomas Moran, Allan MacLean, Lennart Lövstrand,
Paul Dourish, Kathleen Carter, William Buxton

Rank Xerox Cambridge EuroPARC
61 Regent Street, Cambridge CB2 1AB, U.K.
gaver@europarc.xerox.com

ABSTRACT

At EuroPARC, we have been exploring ways to allow physically separated colleagues to work together effectively and naturally. In this paper, we briefly discuss several examples of our work in the context of three themes that have emerged: the need to support the full range of shared work; the desire to ensure privacy without giving up unobtrusive awareness; and the possibility of creating systems which blur the boundaries between people, technologies and the everyday world.

KEYWORDS: Group Work, Collaboration, Media Spaces, Multi-Media, Video

INTRODUCTION

Work at EuroPARC involves collaboration among people separated by the architecture of our building and the distance to overseas colleagues at PARC. We have turned this difficulty into an opportunity to research technologies that support collaboration. Many of the most important facets of this work involve the Ravenscroft Audio Video Environment (RAVE). RAVE is an example of a "media space" – a computer-controlled network of audio-video equipment used to support collaboration – which shares features with systems being developed elsewhere (e.g., 9, 19, 23, 25).

In this paper, we focus on three aspects of our research in order to provide an introduction to our media space:

- We want to support shared work over its entire range – from the sort of casual awareness that keeps us informed about the whereabouts and activities of our neighbors to the more focussed and planned work that is involved in joint problem-solving. The current controls of our media space reflect this concern, having evolved with our use of a user-tailorable interface to the system.

- We are concerned about privacy, but are hesitant about achieving it at the expense of media spaces' ability to provide unobtrusive awareness. We consider the attributes of privacy as many-dimensional. Currently, we combine control and feedback in RAVE to maintain privacy without a loss of functionality.

- We are developing the RAVE system to allow a seamless transition between support for synchronous collaboration and systems which support semi-synchronous awareness over long distances and of planned and electronic events. In this way, we hope to blur the traditional boundaries between people, technologies, and the everyday world, relying both on new technologies and an understanding of people's interactions in the everyday world (cf. 20).

We have been developing a number of systems which use the RAVE infrastructure to enhance our working environment and promote collaboration. In this paper, we discuss examples of systems which have been in relatively wide-spread use at EuroPARC in order to give a taste of the environment we have been developing and to sketch out the philosophy behind this research.

Figure 1: *The RAVE system lets us work together in a "media space" as well as the physical workspace.*

THE RAVENSCROFT AUDIO VIDEO ENVIRONMENT (RAVE)

EuroPARC was founded in 1987 and there are currently about 30 staff members. Our building, called Ravenscroft House, has 27 rooms and 5 open areas on 4 floors. Despite the small size of the lab, the layout separates us to a surprising degree, so that the building is effectively a collection of relatively isolated sites. One of the motivations for the work described here was to turn this problem into a research opportunity: Because EuroPARC is a small research lab, we were able to install complete data, audio, and video networks throughout the lab. Each room in the building has several audio and video cables running to and from a central switch as well as access to digital networks (see 3 for details). The resulting system, called *RAVE*, provides all rooms with some form of an audio-video "node," consisting of a camera, monitor, microphone and speakers, which users can move and turn on or off at will. Connections among nodes are completely computer controlled, so that people can display the views from various cameras on their desktop monitors, set up two-way audio-video connections, etc. (see Figure 1). Using this system, we live in a *media space* (25) as well as the physical workspace.

The RAVE system provides us with a great deal of potential functionality. An important design issue concerns how best to constrain it, both to support and encourage its use in ways that enhance existing work practices and to discourage possible misuse (e.g., spying, monitoring, etc.). In considering this question, it is helpful to consider our first design theme, that of supporting the range of collaboration from casual awareness to focussed engagement.

From Awareness to Collaboration

What is collaboration? One perspective – assumed implicitly by much of the current work on CSCW – is of two or more people focussed intensely on a single task. We prefer a broader approach, one we feel better reflects the range of activities involved in shared work. Figure 2 provides a simple representation of our view of what it means to work together.

Two dimensions characterize this framework. The first, *degree of engagement*, refers to the extent to which a shared focus is involved. The second, *amount of planning*, refers to the extent that shared activities occur spontaneously or are planned in advance. Although the space of shared work is probably characterized by many more than two dimensions, this framework allows us to consider four relevant landmarks of the space.

Underlying all is *general awareness*. This simply refers to the pervasive experience of knowing who is around, what sorts of things they are doing, whether they are relatively busy or can be engaged, and so on. Neither planned nor involving a great degree of interaction, this sort of awareness acts as a foundation for closer collaboration – one of the reasons that physical proximity is a highly

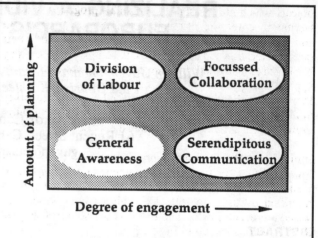

Figure 2: Shared work involves fluid transitions among general awareness, focussed collaboration, serendipitous communication, and division of labour.

accurate predictor of collaboration (15). At the other extreme is *focussed collaboration*. This refers to occasions when people plan to work closely on a shared task. Most CSCW applications seem designed to support this kind of shared, focussed activity.

There are two way-stations between these extremes. The first, *division of labour*, refers to the common practice of splitting a task into its component parts and allowing different people to address them separately. Division of labour does not require the intensely shared focus of attention implied by focussed collaboration, but does require planning and coordination. On the other hand, general awareness often leads to *serendipitous communication*, in which an unplanned interaction may lead to the exchange of important information or the recognition of shared interests.

The description of collaboration illustrated by this framework suggests the need to provide support for a range of activities, from spontaneous to highly planned and from disengaged to highly focussed. Moreover, we want to support the *movement* between these forms of shared work. In the workaday world, people move fluidly between degrees of engagement: maintaining awareness of their colleagues, engaging in serendipitous communication, collaborating intensely for a time, and dividing labour. It is important that we support not only different sorts of shared activities, but fluid movement among activities.

The RAVE Buttons

In providing access to the audio-video network, then, we have emphasized its use in supporting the entire range of shared activities. Because we had few *a priori* notions of how audio-video connectivity would extend current work practices, we have supported access to its functionality in a flexible way, using tailorable onscreen buttons such as those shown in Figure 3.

Buttons are the product of research both at Xerox PARC (14) and at EuroPARC (17). They are simple graphical objects which allow users to run small programs without having to enter the relevant commands explicitly. In addition, they are tailorable in a number of ways: Their onscreen location and appearance can be modified, they may be copied and emailed, they are often parameterized so that application-specific variables can be changed easily, and their encapsulated code can be edited. Their flexibility allowed us to explore our media space, developing more useful control structures as we gained experience.

Initially, the RAVE buttons provided access to relatively low level functionality, allowing single connections to be made or broken. Over time, the buttons have been modified by users to reflect the higher-level tasks they wished to accomplish. The result is the series of generic RAVE buttons shown in Figure 3.

These buttons reflect the range of engagement in collaboration discussed above – indeed, the buttons and our account of collaboration evolved together. The *background* button, for instance, allows people to select a view from one of the public areas to display on their monitor. This is typically the default connection. Many of us, for example, maintain a view of our largest public space on screen when not actively using the audio-video system. This allows us to notice people come and go to check their mail or get coffee, to see meetings form, or to watch for somebody with whom we want to talk. The effect is similar to having the common area outside one's door (without the noise). We can maintain a general awareness, not of our immediate surroundings, but of important areas that are more remote.

The *sweep* button provides another way to maintain awareness of remote locations of the building. This button makes short (~1 second) one-way connections to various nodes in the building. It is customizable, so one can sweep all nodes or a subset of relevant ones. Typically this is used to find out who is around and what they are doing (cf. 23). The *glance* button, which makes a single 3-second one-way connection to a selected node, allows more focussed attention to particular colleagues. Glances are often used to find out if a particular person is in and whether or not he or she is busy. Because both the sweep and glance buttons allow one way connections for only a

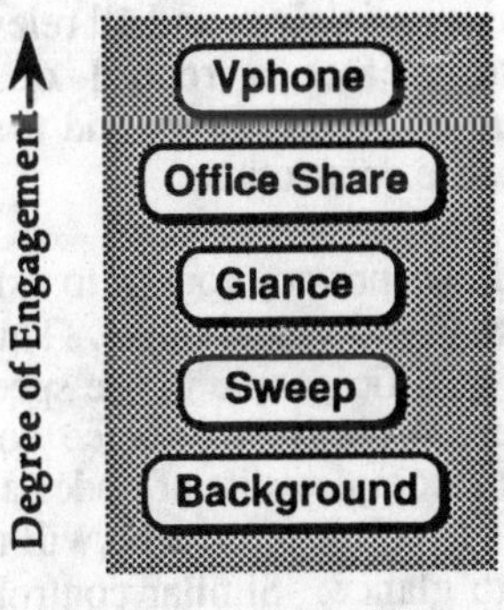

short time, the effect is similar to walking by somebody's door and glancing in: general information about somebody's presence and activities can be obtained without jeopardizing privacy (an issue to which we return below).

More focussed interactions are supported by the *vphone* and *office share* buttons. The first is a two-way audio and video connection which allows colleagues to engage in the video equivalent of a face-to-face conversation. When a vphone call is initiated, the recipient must explicitly accept the connection. Thus this sort of connection is closest to traditional telephone calls. Office share connections are identical to vphone connections, but are meant to last longer – for hours, days, or even months. The effect is one of sharing an office, but because audio volume can be controlled and the video image is relatively small, the other person's "presence" allows but does not demand social engagement.

It is interesting to note here that the vphone and office share buttons offer exactly the same functionality, that of setting up a two-way audio and video connection. The buttons are differentiated solely in terms of the intentions with which the connections are made. Vphone calls are typically used to support relatively short and focussed conversations, while office share connections typically support longer lasting shared work in which the degree of engagement varies fluidly. This is a good example of interface tools which emerged to control our system in terms of users' tasks, rather than technological functionality.

In sum, the five generic RAVE buttons emerged through a process of interconnected use and design supported by an interface system that affords flexible tailoring. The resulting functionality supported by these buttons reflects the range of shared work from general awareness to focussed collaboration to a remarkable degree. The system is even more useful in conjunction with other tools, as we will describe below. But first, it is worth addressing a common set of concerns about the RAVE system.

WHAT ABOUT BIG BROTHER?

Accounts of cameras in every office, one-way glance connections, long-term monitoring of public spaces and so forth can often have Orwellian overtones. Clearly there is a need to protect privacy in audio-video systems such as ours. But there is a trade-off between protection of privacy and provision of functionality that makes the development of such safeguards a non-trivial task.

For instance, one way to assure that our work on media spaces will not add new threats to privacy would be simply to remove all audio and video equipment from EuroPARC – but this would clearly do away with any and all services these technologies offer. More subtly, privacy might be ensured by enforcing symmetrical connections, so that seeing or hearing somebody implies being seen or heard oneself (indeed, this strategy has been taken at BellCore; 23). But one-way connections have advantages we are unwilling to give up. Glances allow us to maintain our

Figure 3: *RAVE buttons reflect different degrees of engagement.*

awareness of colleagues without actually engaging in interaction with them. Thus they are a valuable prelude to communication; just as we might look in someone's door to see if they are busy before entering, so we can look at their video image before vphoning them. Video provides an excellent means to gain general awareness unobtrusively; enforcing symmetry for the sake of privacy would undermine this functionality.

It has become clear to us that privacy is a complex issue that must be disentangled in order to understand the tradeoffs involved in its protection. In particular, four important facets of privacy which may be considered separately are:

- The desire for *control* over who can see or hear us at a given time;

- The desire for *knowledge* of when somebody is in fact seeing or hearing us;

- The desire to know the *intention* behind the connection; but

- The desire to avoid connections being *intrusions* on our work.

The trade-off between privacy and functionality involves a conflict between the desirability of control and knowledge and the intrusion implied by activities needed to maintain them [cf. 9]. Having to allow explicitly every connection made to our cameras would give us control, but the requests themselves would be intrusive. Having somebody's face appear on our monitors every time they connect to us would similarly demand some sort of social response and might well disrupt previous connections. Having to specify and be informed of the intention of various connections would likewise transform an simple process into a relatively effortful and attention-demanding one. The challenge of safeguarding privacy, then, is not just one of providing control and notification, but doing so in a lightweight and unobtrusive way.

At EuroPARC, our privacy protection depends to a great degree on social convention – indeed, our culture initially provided our only protection. It is assumed that people will use the system with "good" intentions; that is, that they will not seek information with the intent of using it to harm anybody. Simply speaking, we trust one another. At the same time, social convention encourages people to control their own equipment: They are free to turn their camera to face a wall or out a window; they may keep their microphones switched off, and so forth.

We took this initial strategy for several reasons. First, being "willingly naive" about privacy meant that we did not assume the degree to which software support for privacy would be necessary, but instead could treat the question as a research issue. Second, explicitly relying on trust established clear social norms about the use of the media space – instead of building software on the assumption that privacy would otherwise be invaded, we assumed it would not be and expected people to behave accordingly. Finally, this strategy allowed us to concentrate on developing the functionality of the system rather than security measures. Nonetheless, as the equipment has become ubiquitous in our own lab and we begin to export it to other settings, we have started to explore other ways to tackle privacy issues. Our current system now provides services which make intentionality an implicit feature of connections and which allow us to provide both control and notifications.

Offering Control: Godard

A certain amount of control over connections is offered by the basic software used to control the audio-video switch. This software, called *iiif* (for integrated, interactive, intermedia facility; see 3), instantiates a simple patchbay metaphor in which device "plugs" are linked to form single point-to-point connections. Each plug and device is "owned" by an associated user and its access is accordingly controlled. Thus people could restrict access to their video-out plugs, for instance, to some subset of users.

In practice this strategy is awkward to use effectively. Control is offered at the level of individual connections rather than relevant tasks, while the generic RAVE services described above – glances, vphone calls, etc. – usually involve a number of individual connections. Although buttons can make this transparent to the initiator by combining a number of connection requests into one button, the system has no way of knowing the intention of individual connections. Thus it is difficult, using simple plug control, to design the system so that a glance can be allowed but a vphone call denied.

For these reasons, a new layer of software called *Godard* (7) has been added to the basic iiif software. Godard uses iiif's underlying protection mechanism to control device plugs so that no connections can be made without its permission. Because Godard mediates all connection requests, explicit services can be defined and control can be handled at the service level. When an initiator requests a service, Godard uses information previously obtained from potential recipients to determine whether to perform the service (and occasionally relies on interactive input to request permission for individual connections or to resolve conflicts). If permission is given and all relevant plugs are available, Godard creates a record of pre-existing connections so they can be restored, and then makes and protects the appropriate connections.

This architecture allows privacy control to exist at the level of services rather than individual plugs. Thus people can set permission for specific people to use specific services. For instance, Figure 4 shows a "glance control panel." The panel presents a complete list of nodes at EuroPARC, and allows the user to select those who will or will not be given permission to glance. Similar control panels exist for vphones, office share connections, and the like.

With the addition of Godard, our system now affords a degree of *control* adequate to preserve privacy: We can now explicitly allow or deny connections to our equipment. In addition, because these connections are represented as higher-level services, the system also provides a useful (if implicit) representation of the initiator's *intentions*. Finally, it serves as a foundation for the provision of the third aspect of privacy suggested above, that of *knowledge* of actual events – notifications about the system state.

Providing Notifications: Auditory Cues

Feelings of privacy are not only supported by control over who can connect to one's equipment using various services, but by feedback about when such connections are actually made. Because Godard knows about connections to recipients' audio-video nodes at the service level, it facilitates the provision of such feedback. Several kinds of feedback can be requested by users in current instantiations of interface software, including text messages displayed on their workstations and spoken messages played over the audio network. Less obvious than these, and in our experience quite valuable, are *auditory cues* used to provide information about system state (11).

For example, when a glance connection is made to a camera, Godard triggers a sound to be played at the relevant location (the default is that of a door opening). The sound typically comes several seconds before the connection is actually made, so it provides forewarning rather than concurrent information. When the connection is broken, another sound (typically that of a door closing) is triggered. In addition, different sounds indicate different sorts of

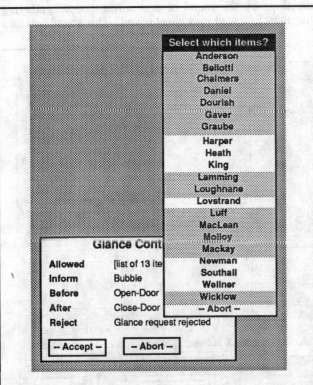

Figure 4: Control panels allow users to give permission to specific individuals for specific services.

connections (and thus the intentions behind them). A knock or telephone bell indicates a vphone request; door sounds indicate glances; footsteps might indicate sweeps; and a camera whir indicates that a framegrabber has accessed one's node. Thus auditory cues provide information about what kind of connection is being made, over and above information about the existence of a connection alone.

Playing sounds such as opening and closing doors may seem frivolous, but nonspeech audio as a medium has several advantages over graphics, text or speech:

- Sound indicates the connection state without requiring symmetry – that is, it provides information without being intrusive.

- Sounds such as these can be heard without requiring the kind of spatial attention that a written notification would.

- Non-speech audio cues often seem less distracting and more efficient than speech or music (although speech can provide different sorts of information, e.g., *who* is connecting).

- Sounds can be acoustically shaped to reduce annoyance (22). Most of the sounds we use, for instance, involve a very gradual increase in loudness to avoid startling listeners.

- Finally, caricatures of naturally-occurring sounds are a very intuitive way to present information. The sound of an opening and closing door reflects and reinforces the metaphor of a glance, and is thus easily learned and remembered (cf. 12).

These sorts of auditory cues have provided an flexible and effective way to unobtrusively inform people that somebody is connecting to their node, and thus serve as another means of safeguarding privacy. More generally, with Godard and auditory cues, we have provided control, feedback, and intentionality – three prerequisites for privacy – at very little cost in terms of intrusiveness. Big Brother would have a difficult time at EuroPARC, both because we can restrict his access and because we can hear him coming.

AWARENESS OVER TIME: THE KHRONIKA SYSTEM

Our audio-video system has helped us maintain awareness of ongoing events in distant locations Khronika (16) is a software "event notification service" that supports selective awareness of *planned* and *electronic* events. Khronika is related to online calendar systems, but supports a more general notion of events than most. It tells us when a video connection has been made, reminds us about upcoming meetings, provides information about visitors, and can even be used to gather people to go to the pub.

Khronika is based on three fundamental entities: *events*, *daemons*, and *notifications* (see Figure 5). Events are defined in terms of their class, their start time, and their

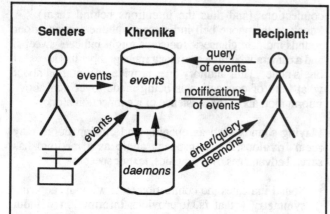

Figure 5: *Khronika maintains a database of events entered both by people and other systems. Daemons watch for specified events and post notifications when they are detected.*

duration. Examples of events include conferences, visitors, local movies, and arriving email. Because they are represented as objects in a hierarchical classification structure, they can also be manipulated in terms of more abstract classes such as "professional," "electronic," and "entertainment."

Event daemons watch for specified event types and produce notification events when they are detected. Daemons are created by users as a set of constraints, so recipients choose the information about which they wish to be informed. For example, a user may create a daemon which watches for all seminar events occurring in the conference room with the string "RAVE" as a part of their description. They can then instruct the daemon to generate notifications

five minutes before relevant seminars are due to begin.

A number of interfaces to the Khronika system have been explored, including buttons which allow users to browse the event database and to create new events and daemons. One of the more interesting and useful interfaces is the *xkhbrowser*, shown in Figure 6. The browser serves as an online calendar, with events shown as fields extending over their relevant times. But the event database may be displayed at varying levels of specificity, from the most encompassing ("event") level to more specific ones such as "meetings," "glances" or "sound." In this way, the xkhbrowser provides a general and powerful mechanism for exploring the database of events.

Notifying Users About Events

Khronika is the mechanism with which Godard generates feedback about audio-video connections. When a request for a connection is made, Godard enters an event into Khronika; an appropriate daemon (created using the various privacy controls already described) then triggers the requested notification.

Notifications can be generated by daemons in several different forms – for instance, a daemon watching for meetings might send out an email message the day before, display a message on a workstation window, or generate a synthesized speech message. Nonspeech audio cues are commonly used to inform us about the state of the audio-video system; there are also a number of cues which inform us about other events (see 11).

For example, we are often reminded about upcoming meetings by the sound of murmuring people gathering together, followed by a gavel sound. This sound acts as a

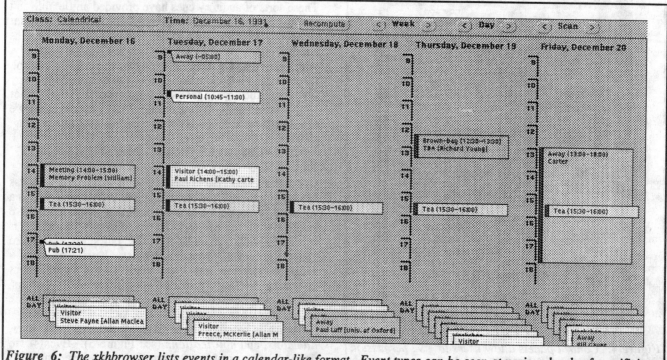

Figure 6: *The xkhbrowser lists events in a calendar-like format. Event types can be seen at various levels of specificity.*

memorable stereotype of naturally-occurring meeting sounds and is thus quickly learned and immediately recognizable. In addition, the sound is designed so that it grows in amplitude quite slowly, so that is not interruptive. Finally, the sharper gavel sound at the end lends a sense of urgency to the sound. Sounds like these are effective yet unobtrusive reminders about remote events – as evidenced by the fact that approximately 50 sounds a day are requested from the Khronika system.

In general, then, the Khronika system in conjunction with audio reminders has a number of the system features we are exploring at EuroPARC. It enhances our general awareness of ongoing events and thus promotes collaboration. It does so in a way that blurs the boundaries between the electronic and everyday worlds, allowing information to be entered from and disseminated by both. Finally, it allows for a great degree of user customization and, like all our systems, is in a continual state of evolution guided by use.

AWARENESS OVER SPACE: POLYSCOPE AND PORTHOLES

RAVE is useful in providing awareness of local nodes. But for technical and financial reasons, we cannot make connections to our overseas colleagues, nor can we connect to more than one node at a time. In order to extend our awareness over a greater distance and to a number of people simultaneously, we have been experimenting with distributing low-resolution video images via our digital networks.

An initial prototype, *Polyscope* (2) is a system which we used to distribute digitized images within our building every 5 minutes or so. The resolution of the images is not very high – only 200 by 150 bits, with no grey scale. Nonetheless, people and objects in their environments are usually visible. In addition, a simple animation facility is available, in which a few images are digitized successively and looped on display. Although such animations are often jerky (and sometimes deliberately frivolous, as when one researcher arranged to periodically transmogrify into Elvis Presley), they make movement obvious and are an effective way to disambiguate scenes. Moreover, Polyscope acts as an interface to the audio-video network. Buttoning an image produces a pop-up menu which allows glance or vphone connections to be initiated.

We are currently using a more recent version of this kind of system called *Portholes* (8). The major advantage of Portholes over Polyscope is that it runs between EuroPARC and PARC – this means that we can see images of colleagues in a building about 6,000 miles away with those of people in our own building. Not only does this support awareness, but it has helped to create and develop a new research community within EuroPARC and PARC – for instance, researchers who have never been co-present nonetheless speak of "knowing" one another through their experience with Portholes.

Both Polyscope and Portholes allow several remote locations to be presented simultaneously, affording passive awareness of distributed workgroups without the necessity of explicitly setting up video links and so on. This facilitates smooth transitions between general awareness and more focussed engagements. In addition, the spatially-distributed but asynchronous functionality offered by systems like Portholes and Polyscope complements our synchronous but single-channeled video services quite well. Perhaps most importantly, Portholes allows us to extend this awareness out of our building to colleagues at geographically distant locations.

EXPERIENCE, EXPERIMENTS, AND EXPORT

We have said little about our experiences using these systems. In general, our development efforts rely on what might be considered a form of participative design, in which designers work closely with users in shaping useful systems (4). At EuroPARC, as with most research labs, the division between designers and users is often blurred. Nonetheless, the group can be divided into technical and non-technical staff, and much of our development is guided by the experiences and input of non-technical users (see 17 for an example of this process). In addition, a number of users have been keeping diaries of their experiences with various systems. These accounts are a valuable source of insight about audio-video mediated collaboration.

More formal techniques have also been useful in better understanding the nature of our media space. Ethnomethodological and participative design techniques have been employed to study the everyday use of the RAVE system and to assist in its development. For example, observations of video-mediated communication have indicated that the medium can undermine the effectiveness of subtle communicative gestures (13), leading us to explore ways to enhance our system. In addition, a series of open-ended interviews have been used to identify problems with the system as well as new possibilities for its design (5).

We have also used more traditional experimental studies to examine a range of issues. For instance, a recent study assessed the utility of a collaborative text editor called ShrEdit and the effects of shared video on its use (21). Another study examined patterns of gaze associated with task and meta-level conversations among co-located or remote partners working in a shared software environment (24). In a third study, we found that nonspeech audio feedback changed participants' perception of a complex collaborative system and their tendency to collaborate while using it (10).

Finally, we have begun exporting these technologies to new sites to better understand how they interact with and support existing work practices. For example, recent research on participative design has involved the installation of a limited audio-video link in a London architecture firm (6). Building on this, a new project is using audio-video technologies to support designers working together but based in different countries – England and the Netherlands (18).

REALIZING A VIDEO ENVIRONMENT

In this account we have been concerned with describing RAVE and several of the related systems we use to support shared work at EuroPARC. We have suggested ways these systems work together to form an integrated environment, and have sketched some of their philosophical foundations.

We hope to have given a feeling for the kinds of systems we are developing. Moreover, we hope to have shown that the three themes of our research – supporting the range of collaboration, maintaining privacy, and extending media spaces to include awareness of planned, electronic, and semi-synchronous events – provide a valuable foundation for research on collaborative systems which are integrated across the working environment. Above all, we have tried to convey a sense of why we find the research at EuroPARC fun, exciting, and important.

ACKNOWLEDGEMENTS

Our work at EuroPARC has depended on the collaborative efforts of many people. In particular, Bob Anderson, Ian Daniel, Christian Heath, Paul Luff, Tom Milligan, Wendy Mackay, Mike Molloy, Toby Morrill, Gary Olson, Judy Olson and Randall Smith have all contributed to the development of the research described here, as have our colleagues at PARC Sara Bly, Steve Harrison, Austin Henderson, Scott Minneman, and John Tang. More generally, the entire EuroPARC research community has provided invaluable support for this work simply by using these systems as part of their everyday environment. Finally, the surrounding philosophy has been emerging from our research community at PARC and EuroPARC for years; it is impossible to assign credit for most of these ideas.

Tom Moran's current address: Xerox PARC, 3333 Coyote Hill Drive, Palo Alto, CA. 94304.

Bill Buxton's current address: CSRI, University of Toronto, Toronto Ontario, Canada M52 1A4

REFERENCES

1. Bellotti, V., Dourish, P., & MacLean, A. (1991). From users themes to designers DReams: Developing a design space for shared interactive technologies. EuroPARC/ AMODEUS Working Paper RP6-WP7.

2. Borning, A., and Travers, M. (1991). Two approaches to casual interaction over computer and video networks. *Proceedings of CHI'91* (New Orleans, Louisiana, 28 April - 2 May, 1991). ACM, New York, pp. 13-19.

3. Buxton, W., and Moran, T. (1990). EuroPARC's integrated interactive intermedia facility (iiif): Early experiences. In *Proceedings of the IFIP WG8.4 Conference on Multi-User Interfaces and Applications* (Herakleion, Crete, September 1990).

4. Carter, K. (forthcoming). Interacting with users: A practitioner's experience. To appear in *Sociology of Software,* Woolgar, S., and Murray, F. (eds).

5. Carter, K. (July, 1991). Usage of the AV network. Presentation at EuroPARC RAVE Review, Cambridge U.K.

6. Carter, K. and Harper, R. (1991). Searching for problems and answers: An empirical report on CSCW. Technical Report No. EPC-91-101, Rank Xerox EuroPARC, Cambridge U.K.

7. Dourish, P. (1991). Godard: A flexible architecture for AV services in a media space. Technical Report No. EPC-91-134, Rank Xerox EuroPARC, Cambridge U.K.

8. Dourish, P., and Bly, S. (1991). Portholes: Supporting awareness in a distributed work group. *Proceedings of CHI'92* (Monterey, California, 3 - 7 May, 1992). ACM, New York.

9. Fish, R., Kraut, R., Root, R., and Rice, R. (1991). Evaluating video as a technology for informal communication. *Proceedings of CHI'92* (Monterey, California, 3 - 7 May, 1992). ACM, New York.

10. Gaver, W. W., Smith, R. B., and O'Shea, T. (1991). Effective sounds in complex systems: The ARKola simulation. *Proceedings of CHI'91* (New Orleans, Louisiana, 28 April - 2 May, 1991), ACM, New York.

11. Gaver, W. W. (1991). Sound support for collaboration. In *Proceedings of ECSCW'91* (Amsterdam, The Netherlands, 25-27 September 1991).

12. Gaver, W. W. (1986). Auditory icons: Using sound in computer interfaces. *Human-Computer Interaction,* 2, pp. 167-177.

13. Heath, C., and Luff, P. (1991). Disembodied conduct: Communication through video in a multi-media office environment. *Proceedings of CHI'91* (New Orleans, Louisiana, 28 April - 2 May, 1991), ACM, New York.

14. Henderson, D. A., and Card, S. (1986). Rooms: The use of multiple virtual workspaces to reduce space contention in a window-based graphical user interface. *ACM Transactions on Graphics,* 5, 3, 211-243.

15. Kraut, R. and Egido, C. (1988). Patterns of contact and communication in scientific research collaboration. In *Proceedings of the CSCW'88* (Portland, Oregon, September 1988) ACM, New York. pp. 25-38.

16. Lövstrand, L. (1991). Being selectively aware with the Khronika system. In *Proceedings of ECSCW'91* (Amsterdam, The Netherlands, 25-27 September 1991).

17. MacLean, A., Carter, K., Moran, T., and Lövstrand, L. (1990). User-tailorable systems: Pressing the issues with Buttons. In proceedings of CHI'90 (Seattle, Washington, 1-5 April, 1990) ACM, New York, pp. 175-182.

18. Mackay, W., and Harper, R. (1991). WAVE: The Welwyn and Venray Experiment. Technical Report No. EPC-91-135, Rank Xerox EuroPARC, Cambridge U.K.

19. Mantei, M., Baecker, R., Sellen, A., Buxton, W., Milligan, T., and Wellman, B. (1991). Experiences in the use of a media space. *Proceedings of CHI'91* (New Orleans, Louisiana, April 28 - May 2, 1991) ACM, New York, pp. 203 - 208.

20. Moran, T. P. and Anderson, R. J. (1990). The workaday world as a paradigm for CSCW design. In *Proceedings of CSCW'90* (Los Angeles, California, October 1990). ACM, New York.

21. Olson, G., and Olson, J. (1991). User-centered design of collaboration technology. *Journal of Organizational Computing, 1,* 61-83.

22. Patterson, R. D. (1989). Guidelines for the design of auditory warning sounds. *Proceedings of the Institute of Acoustics 1989 Spring Conference. 11*, 5, 17-24.

23. Root, R. W. (1988). Design of a multi-media vehicle for social browsing. In *Proceedings of the CSCW'88* (Portland, Oregon, September 1988) ACM, New York, pp. 25-38.

24. Smith, R. B., O'Shea, T., O'Malley, C., Scanlon, E., and Taylor, J. (1989). Preliminary experiments with a distributed, multi-media, problem-solving environment. *Proceedings of the First European Conference on Computer-Supported Cooperative Work* (Gatwick, England).

25. Stults, R. (1986). Media space. Xerox PARC technical report.

Evaluating Video as a Technology for Informal Communication

Robert S. Fish, Robert E. Kraut, Robert W. Root
Bellcore
445 South Street, Morristown, N.J. 07962-1910
robf @ bellcore.com
&
Ronald E. Rice
SCILS, Rutgers University
4 Huntington Street, New Brunswick, N.J. 08903

ABSTRACT

Collaborations in organizations thrive on communication that is informal because informal communication is frequent, interactive, and expressive. Informal communication is crucial for the coordination of work, learning an organization's culture, the perpetuation of the social relations that underlie collaboration, and, in general, any situation that requires communication to resolve ambiguity. Informal communication is traditionally mediated by physical proximity, but physical proximity cannot mediate in geographically distributed organizations. The research described here evaluates the adequacy of a version of a desktop video/audio conferencing system for supporting informal communication in a research and development laboratory. The evaluation took place during a trial in which the system was used by summer employees and their supervisor-mentors. While the system was used frequently, the most common uses and users' assessments suggest that it was used more like a telephone or electronic mail than like physically mediated face-to-face communication. However, some features of its use transcended traditional media and allowed users to gain awareness of their work environment. The paper concludes with a discussion of requirements for successful technology to support informal communication.

KEYWORDS: Informal meetings, evaluation, video, desktop videoconferencing, group work, collaboration.

INTRODUCTION: INFORMAL COMMUNICATION

Communication in organizations can be more or less formal [2]. Formal communication goes through organizational channels following the hierarchy of an organization's structure. In contrast, informal communication cuts across these organizational boundaries. Operationally, informal communication differs from formal communication in its greater frequency, expressiveness and interactivity [6, 16, 29]. These attributes give organizational members the flexibility to deal with highly uncertain and ambiguous topics, tasks, and decisions. Informal communication is especially important for the less directly task-oriented aspects of organizational membership, for example, learning the organizational culture, becoming loyal to an organization, making judgments of others, and forming relationships.

Typically, informal communication is mediated by physical proximity. The chance encounters and ease of access among people who are physically close to each other in an organization provide many opportunities for organizational members to come into contact and communicate [21]. When people are physically close to each other, communication typically occurs through face-to-face conversations or meetings. Compared to other communication channels, face-to-face communication is socially oriented and rich. According to social presence theorists [14, 28] visually-oriented, face-to-face communication supports informal communication because it highlights the other people in an interaction and consequently interpersonal relationships in general. From a media richness perspective [7], visually-oriented face-to-face communication is a rich medium that is interactive (providing opportunity for timely feedback and the tailoring of messages to personal circumstances) and expressive (having the ability to convey multiple cues and to use language variety). Hence, it should be useful to increase understanding and reduce the amount of equivocality in a given communication situation.

Potential of Video/Audio Technology for Informal Communication

Both analyses of the ways the visual channel is used to support informal interaction in face-to-face settings and analyses of early experiments using video to support distributed work groups suggest that video communication systems might provide a basis for informal communication at a distance. Below we review the reasoning based on the prior literature that suggests that a visual channel in general and video in particular 1) is helpful in increasing the spontaneity and frequency of communication, 2) helpful in supporting social relationships, 3) helpful in coping with the most complex and equivocal communication problems encountered in work groups, and as a result 4) helpful in integrating members into and supporting the work in research and development groups.

Frequency and spontaneity of interaction. Close observation of spontaneous, face-to-face communication episodes led Kraut, Fish, Root and Chalfonte [16] to conclude that the visual channel is important in initiating informal communication. The visual channel increases the probability of informal interaction by helping organizational members simultaneously identify a partner, topic, and moment for conversation and by helping them manage the transition from lack of engagement to engagement in interaction. Recent studies of the use of video conferencing systems in R&D laboratories show that they can lead to spontaneous interaction, although less than in face-to-face settings [9]. A recent demonstration project at Xerox PARC provided a continuous video and audio connection between two of its research facilities located hundreds of miles apart [1, 10]. Usage data indicated that over seventy per cent of the interpersonal communication between the two sites consisted of short, casual, "drop-in" interactions and that most of these interactions would not have occurred in the absence of a continuous video link.

Richness and social-orientation of interaction. Both media richness theorists [7] and social presence theorists [14, 28] array communication channels along a continuum anchored by face-to-face interaction at the richer, social end and written documents at the other. To the extent that audio/video communication mimics the features of face-to-face communication in being expressive, interactive, and focusing attention on personal attributes, it should function like face-to-face communication. Thus, the media richness and social presence perspectives suggest that video teleconferencing should be well suited for informal communication, and especially good for aiding the more social, the more uncertain, and the more equivocal aspects of communication. For example, the evidence from early studies of video conferencing suggest that video conferences, face-to-face meetings or written exchanges are roughly equivalent for information transfer tasks, but are differentiated when consensus formation and conflict are at issue [28].

Support for research and development environments. Early trials of telemedicine [24] attempted to use video for medical information transfer, diagnosis, consultation, and patient contact. While the technology had only mixed success in supporting information transfer and diagnosis tasks, Rockoff

[25] offers a "clinical impression ... that this technology improves the cohesiveness and sense of organizational unity experienced by health care providers in a geographically dispersed system, i.e., it facilitates their functional integration (Pp 1087)." This observation is consistent with the hypothesis that at least some of the effects of the technology were in aiding the formation of social relationships and other outcomes associated with informal communication.

More recent studies of video networks in R&D organizations [1, 4, 9, 10] have illustrated the value of video communication networks, as well as showing some of their limitations. In the Xerox PARC experiment described earlier, participants' experiences suggest that having this video link was adequate to promote a shared context and culture that supported joint work across the two R&D locations, but just barely. In discussing this experience, Olson and Bly [22], among others, note the crucial importance of having a shared work space in which participants in a discussion could jointly view and manipulate the objects in their world.

Purpose of current study

The present research examines in a less anecdotal manner than previous studies the usefulness of audio/video conferencing for the support of informal communication in a realistic setting. We were interested in the degree to which visual communication could attain the characteristics of frequency, expressiveness, and interactivity that are the hallmarks of informal communication.

We addressed this question in the context of a four week field trial in which temporary employees and their supervisor/mentors at Bellcore used a new audio/video conferencing technology called the CRUISER™[1] system [9, 26]. Since it supports standard videoconferencing, the CRUISER system should have the attributes discussed above that make it appropriate for rich communication with social presence. In addition, this system included features designed to use video to increase the opportunities for communication and thus increase the frequency of spontaneous conversation. These features included system-initated calls, brief, self-terminating calls, and call sequences, all designed to simulate the experience of walking down a hallway, viewing others as they work in their offices, and taking advantage of a random contact to have a conversation. These features are described in more detail below.

METHODS

The experiment was conducted as part of the summer internship program for college and graduate students at Bellcore. Students in telecommunications engineering, computer science, mathematics, psychology, statistics, and other disciplines worked for 10 weeks with senior researchers in their field. From a pool of about 50 volunteers, we randomly selected 23

---

[1] *Cruiser* is a trademark and service mark of Bellcore.

volunteers --11 students and their 12 mentors -- to use the CRUISER system.

The CRUISER environment in the summer of 1990 consisted of a software controlled audio and video telecommunications network of 30 nodes. The nodes were distributed over four wings and two floors of a large R & D facility. Each user was equipped with a multi-windowed computer terminal that controlled the CRUISER application and provided conventional computing including c electronic mail. In addition to the computer terminal, the CRUISER station consisted of a 12-inch color video monitor, a small speaker, and a microphone. Audio connections were full duplex. This allowed both parties to a conversation to talk at the same time with no audio echo or feedback.

This version of the CRUISER application used three novel calling methods to encourage spontaneous conversation. These methods were:

• *Cruises*, in which users initiated one or a series of audio/video calls. They differed from conventional telephone-like calls in three ways. First, when the caller issued the command, the system opened an immediate audio and video connection to the called party, which timed out after about three seconds unless one party explicitly continued it by issuing a "Visit" command. During the connection, both parties could see and hear each other. Second, if users supplied a list of names (e.g., 'Cruise john, alice, mark'), the system stepped through each in turn, stopping only if one party issued the visit command. Finally, if the user supplied no name (i.e., 'Cruise'), the system selected a called party at random from among the users currently logged into the system.

• *Autocruises*, in which the the system itself initiated calls between selected users at random times. Except for initiation, the protocol was the same as a Cruise. A connection was made and timed out if neither party issued a Visit command. The intended analogy for the Autocruise was wandering in a corridor and seeing other people, with whom one could speak or not.

• *Glances*., which were very brief video-only connections to one or a series of other people. When users issued a Glance they received an approximately one second glance into the called party's office; this Glance could not be converted into a sustained connection without subsequently issuing a Cruise command. If users issued the Glance command without an argument, the system initiated a series of five brief glances of randomly selected logged-in users on the system.

The system included two features to deal with privacy concerns. First, users could issue a "private" command. This caused all others who tried to call them to see a notification that they were busy. Second, the system imposed a reciprocity rule on all calls. Users were assured that if someone else could see and hear them, they could see and hear that person as well.

Finally, to increase awareness of the other CRUISER users, the system included one feature that showed users an active directory listing the availability status of all other users and a second feature that maintained a list showing users a history of who called them.

RESULTS
System usage

There were a maximum of 23 users, both interns and mentors, on any day. During the 21 business days of the trial, users made 1295 call attempts to 1556 recipients[2] or about 2.7 call attempts per potential user per day. As with most new communication facilities introduced into organizations, users showed an early burst of activity as they tried out the system. Figure 1 shows the distribution of call attempts per potential user per day[3], both over all users and separately for the 5 dropouts, users who attempted two or fewer calls during the second week of the trial, and for the 18 sustained users, who attempted more than two calls during the second week of the trial. Throughout the trial, the sustained users were placing 4 to 5 calls per business day, with call frequency understandably dropping on the weekends (days 6 & 7, 13 & 14, 20 & 21). These numbers are comparable to the frequency distribution for telephone usage whose mode is 2 outgoing calls and mean is 4 outgoing calls per user per day [20].

As described previously, calls can be either cruises or glances initiated by callers or autocruises initiated by the system, calls can be placed to one or more people simultaneously, and the name of the called party can be supplied by the caller or supplied by the system. Table 1 shows the distribution of call attempts across these call types and the percentage of each call type that were accepted. As can be seen, the modal use of the system (1015 attempts) was one in which a user intentionally placed a call to one other named party.

Call type	# of called parties		% calls accepted
	1	> 1	
Cruise - caller supplied name	1015	8	54%
Cruise - system supplied name	67	NA	18%
Glance- caller supplied name	174	9	NA
Glance - system supplied name	NA	51	NA
Autocruise - system supplied name	236	NA	3%

---

2 Some call attempts were to a series of recipients.

3 Because of uncertainty about who was present on a given day, the total number of calls per day was uniformly divided by 23, the maximum number of users. Thus, Figure 1 underestimates per person usage on a typical day.

Use over time

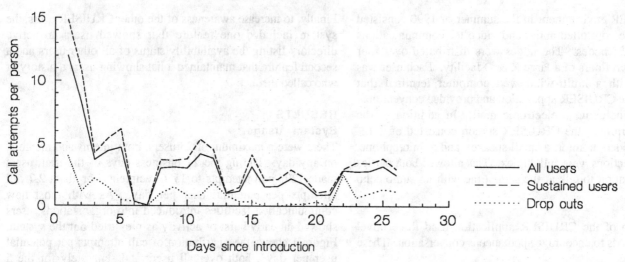

Figure 1. Number of calls over days.

Table 1 . Frequency and outcomes of call attempts

However, about a quarter of user-initiated calls seem to be cases in which people are monitoring their environment rather than communicating with particular individuals. In about half of these calls, callers made a quick glance to a party they named, often to see if that person was available before placing a cruise call or visiting in person. Other calls served a more generalized awareness function. In these cases, users allowed the system to connect them to each other with the possibility for conversation (cruise) or to give them a quick, purely informational peek into the offices of people (glance).

Hence, while the most frequent use of the system was in a mode that was something like a telephone call, there was also significant use that was quite different. While telephone users may call a business to see whether they are open, individuals rarely call each other just to stay aware of who could be contacted, if and when they wanted to. We believe that the Glance mode was often chosen because users perceived that it was quicker and less intrusive than a Cruise call, and therefore provided a better balance between convenience to themselves and the degree to which the call recipients were disturbed.

Figure 2 shows the distribution of Cruise calls and Glances over time. These data substantiate the hypothesis that the two types of calls were used for different functions, since they have distinctive distributions over time (Pearson χ^2 = 21.08, df = 11, $p < .05$). Glances were especially likely to be performed

early in the morning, right after lunch, and on weekends, when uncertainty about who was around was highest and perhaps before the callers themselves had become fully absorbed in their work.

CRUISER calls were typically short. The modal CRUISER call was under 5 seconds, and the median call lasted 62 seconds. Approximately 25% lasted less than 30 seconds, 25% lasted 3 minutes or longer, and 5% lasted more than 30 minutes. The longest calls were over 4 hours. This distribution of call duration is comparable to that observed in telephone calls [20], where the modal call is less than 30 seconds, the mean is about 4 minutes, and the distribution has a similar long tail. Long CRUISER calls include both sustained work sessions similar to those conducted by telephone and two interesting behavioral innovations that we believe were specifically enabled by this technology.

The first of these innovations might be called the *virtual shared office*. On occasion some intern-mentor pairs connected their offices for an extended period, without engaging in sustained conversation. Rather, the pair would work relatively independently, occasionally having conversation to ask a question or to get help on a problem. The open connection reduced the behavioral cost of communication during periods when the participants anticipated they would need multiple episodes of unscheduled conversation. Other researchers studying the use of other desktop conferencing systems have reported similar phenomena [3,11,19].

The second innovative use of long calls might be called the *ambush*. Here one member of a work team with a pressing communication need makes a connection to the other's office. If they are not there, instead of disconnecting and trying again later, they simply maintain the connection and wait for them to come to their office. The "waiter" can monitor the other's office through peripheral awareness, but is still able to focus on his or her own work. This is a nice example of where the technology effectively permitted people to be in two places at the same time.

Comparisons to other media

We have seen, based on system logs, that the typical CRUISER call was short and this finding was confirmed in our self-report data. In the debriefing interviews, subjects estimated the length of their last CRUISER call and the length of their last face-to-face conversation with the same partner. They reported having about 4 minute CRUISER calls versus having about 30 minute face-to-face conversations.

Not only did the conversations differ in length, but they also differed in content and outcome. During our interview, users compared a recent CRUISER conversation with a face-to-face conversation with the same partner. In Table 2 we summarize the length, content, and outcomes in their reports of the conversations.

Conversations using the CRUISER system involved more greeting and scheduling, but involved less problem solving and decision making. Of the 23 student-mentor pairs, most reported using CRUISER conversations to inquire about or to inform each other about the status of work activities, to get quick answers to short questions, or to schedule work. In essence, they reported that during CRUISER conversations they mostly prepared for work, while during face-to-face conversations they actually performed the work.

Why was this? Time and again users said that they used face-to-face communication rather than the CRUISER system because it wasn't able to support all the communication demands of conventional work activities. From a media richness perspective [7], this version of desktop teleconferencing was still insufficiently rich compared to face to face communication. For instance, a major problem that 90 per cent of respondents mentioned was that they could not share work objects when conversing with someone by using the system. One mentor, for example, called a student just as she was in the midst of trying to understand and solve a problem in a computer program she was writing. Taking advantage of this opportunity, the student asked questions and sought advice. However, after some brief discussion, the mentor walked to the student's office so that they could jointly work at the computer terminal and examine printouts. Similarly, one student reported that he often called his mentor whenever he was stuck on a problem. By using CRUISER, he could quickly tell if his mentor was available for assistance. They would briefly discuss the problem and then schedule an immediate or deferred time to meet, mainly so that they could jointly use a blackboard. In a third case, a student had a virtual office connection to his mentor while working on an outline. The student noticed the mentor at his desk and opportunistically asked him a question about the outline. This brief question led to an extended discussion. The conversation progressed to the point where the mentor asked the student to come to his office so that they could jointly use the blackboard.

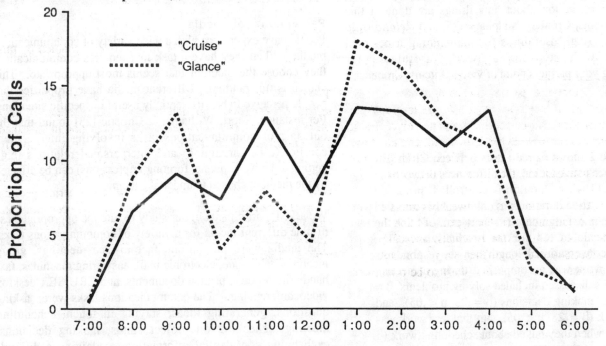

Figure 2. Call attempts by time of day.

Sometimes the resource needed to continue a conversation was another person. Several respondents complained that while CRUISER communication was appropriate for pairs, it was unsatisfactory for communication in a larger group because there were no satisfactory multiperson conferencing facilities available in it.

Other needs for communication richness occurred when people were dealing with social relationships and ambiguities, rather than work objects. Thus, many of the mentors reported that they used the CRUISER system to inquire about status, but met face-to-face when giving students feedback about their personal performance, for example, after a student presentation. One mentor said he scheduled a face-to-face feedback session because he anticipated a long meeting in which the parties would need a "richer" (his term) communication environment, including the ability to move around and to see and respond to subtle reactions.

These differences in topics of conversation led to differences in the perceived usefulness of CRUISER conversations versus face to face conversations. Respondents reported that CRUISER conversations were less useful, both for getting work done and for learning about their conversational partner as shown at the bottom of Table 2.[4] These data were derived by measuring respondents' assessments of a series of 7-point Likert items. These items were then combined into three scales, with item assignment based on a principal components factor analysis with varimax rotation. The scales were: *Productivity* (e.g., usefulness for getting your work done; relevance to your on-going work; 4 items, Cronbach's alpha = .73), *Organizational culture* (e.g., usefulness for keeping up with company people, politics, policies, and other news; usefulness for providing background information about how things are done at this company; 2 items, Cronbach's alpha = .75) and *Relationship maintenance* (e.g., usefulness for maintaining a personal relationship with someone at work; usefulness for understanding your partners point of view; 3 items, Cronbach's alpha = .53)

---

[4] While Table 2 shows paired t-tests between CRUISER and face-to-face conversation, the differences between the modalities hold when duration is controlled, primarily because conversation duration was only weakly correlated with the outcome judgments (r's between -.14 for the relationship scale to .14 for the productivity scale). Rather than conversational length per se, respondents reported that work was accomplished during a meeting when the topics discussed included solving problems (β = .34, p < .005), making decisions (β = .23, p < .05), and assigning work (β = .28, p < .05), but that less work was accomplished when they talked about scheduling work (β = .–.20, p < .10; R^2 for the model = .34).

Measure	Modality		
	CRUISER	Face to face	Paired t-test
Conversation length (in minutes, self-report)	3.9	35.7	-3.96***
% meeting work related	90	89	.00
Meeting topic (% of number of meetings)			
Schedule meetings & tasks	48	19	2.03
Assign tasks to people	14	19	-.57
Report work status	71	81	-1.00
Solve problems	48	86	-2.61**
Make decisions	33	57	-1.75
Discuss workplace information	0	10	-1.45
Discuss nonworkplace topics	5	5	.00
Greet another	33	19	1.83
Outcomes of meetings			
Productive work done	4.77	5.94	-3.92***
Learn organizational culture	1.88	2.10	-0.81
Relationship maintenance	4.29	5.19	-4.26***

Table 2. Duration, topics discussed, and outcomes of conversations

Perceptions of media

People have experience with a wide variety of communications media. When they have a task that requires communication, they choose the medium that seems most appropriate. This choice is not random. Different media have properties that people perceive to be differentially useful in specific situations. For instance, Short, Williams, & Christie [28] found that the outcome of communications tasks involving interpersonal conflict (e.g., bargaining) and interpersonal relations (e.g., getting to know someone, forming impressions) can be affected by the medium chosen to undertake them.

We asked participants in our study to rate the appropriateness of nine different media for a variety of communications tasks. The media were one-on-one face-to-face meetings, group meetings, telephone, electronic mail, answering machines, fax, handwritten notes, printed documents, and CRUISER desktop videoconferencing. The communications tasks were: asking questions, generating ideas, staying in touch, scheduling meetings, checking on project status, making decisions, exchanging confidential information, explaining a difficult

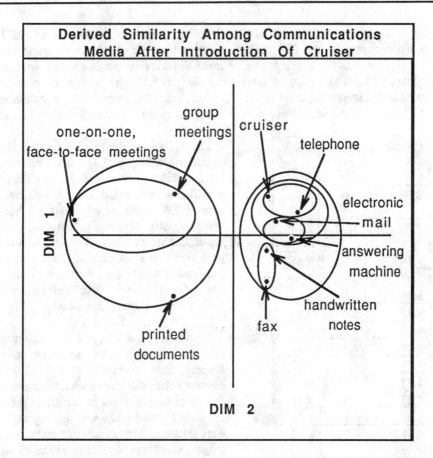

**Derived Similarity Among Communications
Media After Introduction Of Cruiser**

Figure 3. Similarity of communication media.

concept, making commitments, resolving disagreements, exchanging time-sensitive information, negotiating and bargaining, exchanging information, and getting to know someone. This list includes many of the same communication activities that Short et. al. used in their study of the utility of teleconferencing systems [28]. Participants were asked to do this set of ratings twice, once at the start of the study, before they had used the CRUISER system, and once after using the CRUISER system for a month. Because users were not yet familiar with the CRUISER software, the first set of ratings did not include the CRUISER system among the media.

To derive a similarity measure between each of the media we first calculated the mean appropriateness of each medium for each task. We then computed Pearson correlation coefficients between the ratings for each of the media on the 14 communication activities. This resulted in a matrix of 36 pairwise correlations for the ratings collected after the CRUISER system was introduced. This matrix of correlations was treated as similarities and used as input to the KYST [18] nonmetric multidimensional scaling program. This technique [17, 27] attempts to create from the similarities a dimensional representation in which distances between points are related to their similarity. In addition, a hierarchical clustering solution was derived for the same sets of data using the methods of Johnson [12].

Figure 3 shows the two dimensional solution (stress = .008, Formula 1) from these multidimensional scaling and hierarchical clustering procedures. The vertical dimension can be interpreted as the degree of interactivity that a particular medium provides. For instance, group meetings, electronic mail and the telephone are seen as being highly interactive while fax, handwritten notes and printed documents are perceived as less so. The horizontal dimension can be interpreted as the amount of information exchanged through a medium in a typical communication. Thus, users perceived that in one-on-one face-to-face meetings a great deal of information is transmitted while much less is transmitted in the typical telephone call or answering machine message.

The media on the right side of the plot differ from each other primarily in terms of their interactivity. CRUISER and the telephone are clustered with electronic mail and answering machines, but are more interactive, presumably because they offer real-time communication. CRUISER, in turn, is perceived to be a slightly more interactive and information bearing version of the telephone with which it is clustered. This makes sense, since the CRUISER system adds visual information to the audio information transmitted by the telephone.

Table 3 shows the mean rating of appropriateness for the same set of communication tasks listed above for the CRUISER system, face-to-face communication, and the telephone. Ratings were judged on a 1 (Inappropriate) to 5 (Appropriate) scale and the tasks are shown below in increasing order of the appropriateness of the CRUISER system for doing them.

Task	CRUISER	Face to Face	Phone
Exchanging confidential information	2.66	5.00	3.50
Explaining a difficult concept	3.00	5.00	2.61
Getting to know someone	3.14	5.00	2.68
Resolving disagreements	3.59	5.00	3.50
Negotiating, bargaining	3.68	5.00	3.64
Generating ideas	3.82	5.00	3.39
Making decisions	4.00	4.95	3.73
Making commitments	4.14	4.86	4.14
Scheduling meetings	4.18	4.41	4.50
Exchanging information	4.27	4.77	4.14
Asking questions	4.27	5.00	4.41
Staying in touch	4.32	4.73	4.64
Exchanging time-sensitive information	4.41	4.23	4.68
Checking project status	4.50	4.86	4.14

Table 3 Appropriateness of three media for different tasks

Note that both the CRUISER medium and the telephone medium were judged inferior to one-on-one, face-to-face communication for most tasks. The CRUISER system was judged especially useful for checking on project status, keeping in touch, and exchanging information of various types. As the tasks become more socially sensitive or intellectually difficult, both CRUISER and telephone media are judged less adequate, while face-to-face communication is judged more adequate.

Taken together, these data support the conclusion that in this study, the CRUISER service was judged to be useful for similar tasks as the telephone and was perceived as being quite different from face-to-face conversation.

Privacy
The debriefing interviews asked users about their privacy concerns after four weeks of system use. In contrast to concerns expressed while the system was being designed, most users did not think privacy violations were a problem, especially within a small, collaborative community. Only 4 of the 23 users did not want strangers to have the ability to look into their offices. As we said earlier, mentors and interns

described a recent face-to-face and CRUISER conversation with their partner. For each conversation they were asked, "How much did this conversation violate your privacy?" Since people are likely to feel more intruded upon when they are the recipient rather than the initiator of a conversational attempt, the interview ascertained who had started the conversation.

An analysis of variance of these data shows a main effect of initiation (F=2.85, p<.01) i.e., the recipient of a conversational attempt felts more intruded upon than the initiator, but no significant main effect of communication modality, i.e., on average, CRUISER conversations and face-to-face conversations were equally privacy invasive. However, there was a significant interaction between initiation and modality (F=2.39, p < .05) that showed that the recipients of conversational attempts felt substantially more privacy violation when the attempt was made via CRUISER than when it was made face-to-face. This interaction is shown in Figure 4.

Surprisingly, the privacy of outgoing messages was as large a concern as the fear of others snooping into one's office. Because cameras have only a fixed field of view, typically narrower than the human visual system, users were concerned that other people might be present at the called party's location but invisible when they were having a conversation. They also were aware that the hands-free audio in the CRUISER system meant that others physically in the vicinity of a conversation could overhear it. As a result, employees sometimes held face-to-face meetings when they wanted to insure that they were not disturbing others or that others could not overhear them.

Autocruises
CRUISER was designed to support informal communication and increase opportunities for contact in a manner analogous to physical proximity. As we have seen, the glance was a mechanism with a reasonable degree of use and success. The *autocruise* was another mechanism, designed to mimic the opportunities for conversation that people have when they pass by another in the hallway. The autocruise was a system-initiated call attempt, in which two randomly selected users who were currently logged in were connected using the standard *cruise* protocol (i.e., a several second connection that timed-out if neither party accepted the call).

The probability of accepting an autocruise was substantially less than accepting a human-initiated CRUISER call. Of the 236 autocruises conducted during business hours, from 8AM to 5PM, about 3% were accepted compared to 54% of user-initiated calls. This 3% includes only those calls that were converted to a more substantial conversation and does not include the many acknowledgements, greetings and other brief exchanges that occurred during the several second interval before the autocruise timed-out.

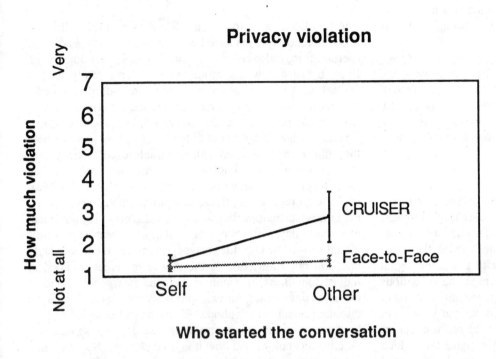

Figure 4. Perceptions of privacy violation.

There are multiple reasons for the low conversation rate for autocruises. For an autocruise to be accepted two parties need to be in their offices, they need to notice that a call attempt occurred, and they need to want to talk to the potential partner at just the moment that the conversational opportunity presents itself. The combination of these probabilities is probably the reason that few autocruises were converted into conversations. In addition, our results suggest that users found autocruises highly disconcerting. When asked to describe features of the CRUISER system they disliked most, 40% of users mentioned autocruises.

DISCUSSION
Did we succeed?
Were we able to show the value of desktop videoconferencing for informal communication? If we use the criteria of frequency, expressiveness, and interactivity as the hallmarks of informal communication that we would like see in the use of a new medium, how did we do with respect to these criteria? The CRUISER system was certainly used a lot, with a frequency equal to or exceeding that of a long established and much more ubiquitous medium like the telephone. This indicates that the system was convenient to use. It also provides evidence for the prediction that desktop videoconferencing will be used more frequently than special-purpose videoteleconferencing facilities because desktop placement reduces the behavioral cost of gaining access to the technology [9].

Expressivity, however, was not as well served. The short call length, its use for scheduling and status reporting rather than problem solving or decision making, and its perceived similarity to other media where the amount of information typically transmitted is limited all indicate that there were many expressive functions for which users did not find the CRUISER system sufficiently suitable. This result is probably related to the lack of support for access to other tools and artifacts (e.g. shared blackboards and editors, etc.) within the context of the conversation and the lack of support within the version of the CRUISER system tested here for multiparty conversations.

In terms of interactivity, we had thought that because we supported both a high quality full-duplex audio channel and a high quality, full-motion video channel that this would be sufficient. It wasn't. Although conversations, once started, seemed quite normal and interactive and the use of the glance mechanism showed that the system was used for some of the exploratory behaviors that are necessary to maintain awareness of possible conversational partners, other features designed to promote the interactivity of informal communication were not successful. The infrequent completion of autocruise calls, the perception of the autocruise mechanism as intrusive, and users' judgments that receiving CRUISER calls was more privacy invading than face to face interactions, all indicate that the implementation of the visual channel mechanism that allowed users to assess, negotiate, start, and end a conversation was not good enough. The specific conversational protocol that people use for informal face to face communication was not able to operate and it was not replaced by something that was sufficiently functional.

Hence, while the version of the CRUISER system we tested here had some successes, it by no means achieved the degree of support for informal communication that we would have liked. For the most part people perceived it and used it like a telephone or an electronic mail system; they adopted the new technology to old uses.

What happened and why?

Perhaps the most important failure of the system was that it inadequately provided users the resources they needed to ease into communication. In the workaday world, when people pass each other in the corridor or pass by another's office, they have subtle, but well practiced mechanisms to assess or signal readiness for communication and to manage the transitions between lack of engagement to engagement and from engagement to disengagement [13,15]. If one party does not wish to communicate with another, he or she can use lack of eye contact and other nonverbal displays to signal this, which in turn often aborts the conversational attempt. The potential initiator can assess another's engagement in a task without the other being aware that an assessment took place. In these cases, the failure to hold a conversation is a cooperative act, in which neither party is explicitly rejected by the other.

In contrast, the conversation opportunity mechanism we used was abrupt, intrusive, and lacking in subtlety. A conversational opportunity was announced when a potential conversational partner instantaneously showed up on one's screen already at speaking distance. Because the screen filled with an image with sudden onset (and the call was frequently announced with a ring as well), the presence of the other was often highly intrusive. Converting an opportunity into a conversation required explicit and one-sided action, when one party to a call issued the "visit" command. These conditions placed too much pressure on the parties to acknowledge each other before they had conducted any negotiation about whether to have a conversation. Users complained that being suddenly confronted with another compelled conversation, even when they didn't want one. In these circumstances, a failure to have the conversation became a explicit rejection, as well. As one user described it, "There is no half way with CRUISER."

To support the expressivity dimension of informal communication, communication tools for casual conversation must also support sustained task-focused work and must allow graceful transition to it. Users repeatedly described attempting to use the occasion of running into an appropriate partner as an opportunity to seek help for a current problem. They were stymied because they couldn't illustrate their dilemma with diagrams or share the object that was vexing them and this contributed to the brevity of their conversations.

The traditional uses to which CRUISER and other desktop teleconference systems have been put and perceptions of their usefulness may also reflect their novelty in several other ways. First, because new communication systems rarely have a critical mass of users at the start, they are indeed less useful than more entrenched systems. During the experiment period, users could only contact 22 other people using CRUISER, several of whom dropped out of the trial and over half of whom they didn't know well enough to initiate even a single call. Second, when new technologies are introduced, people often judge them by the standards of the current world, being critical of the ways they violate the current order without appreciating the new opportunities they allow. Thus, Perry [23] notes that in its early days, telephony, particularly in Great Britain, was thought of as an impolite, privacy invasive medium. Only later did other attributes -- the ability to screen visitors, to reduce loneliness, to summon help in emergencies, and to increase convenience, for example -- become part of the public discourse about the telephone. Third, as technologies mature, both new uses and new norms about use develop, so that over time the technology and how it is used change. New uses that extend beyond standard telephony -- for example, the virtual shared office and orientation glances -- were starting to develop over the course of the experiment.. In summary, while the data presented here suggest that during the trial, the dominant use of the CRUISER system was as a visual telephone used for checking status, asking questions, and passing brief messages it is hard to predict what later use will be from these early experiences.

What will we try next?

Our experience with the CRUISER system leads us to believe that supporting informal communication will require managing some of the tensions and transitions in human behavior. We must balance the costs of providing opportunities for communication with the benefit of any particular opportunity. To provide these opportunities we must balance the tensions between accessibility, privacy and solitude. Moreover, from the point of view of technology design, we must develop better mechanisms to support the transitions between conversational states that people easily manage in their workaday world -- the transitions between non-engagement and engagement, between engagement and disengagement, and between casual conversation and work.

Communication technology to support informal interaction must provide *light weight opportunities* for interaction. In social interaction, a light weight opportunity would be one in which getting into a preconversational attitude is a side effect of other activity and thus allows conversation with little incremental effort. From the preconversational state, potential interactants, by small adjustments and subtle cues, can cooperatively determine whether an acknowledgement, greeting, conversation, or nothing will take place. The failure of the relatively gross techniques that we tried suggests some of the subtlety of everyday conversational coordination and suggests that substantial ingenuity will be required to provide analogous mechanisms in a synthetic world.

Balancing the three factors of accessibility, privacy, and solitude is a must. Accessibility is the ability of one individual to have easy access to another. This is one of essential properties of informal communication. Privacy is the ability of an individual to control the information about him or herself available to others. And solitude is the ability of an individual to control others' intrusion into his or her space or consumption of his or her time. Individuals would like to have all three, but at the level of the group, they are incompatible. Having access to other people at a convenient time often violates their solitude. The use and abuse of telephones, open offices, and private secretaries has shown that even in conventional environments achieving this balance is neither automatic nor static.

Finally, managing the transition between pure conversation and doing work will require the integration of *conversational props* [5]. Conversational props are the artifacts and resources needed to sustain group work. For these props to be used spontaneously in the support of ongoing conversation, they must be easily and quickly accessible during the course of the conversation and they must be easily shared. All members of the conversation must be able to view, point at, and if appropriate, modify objects outside the conversation itself - data, diagrams, and files, for example.

CONCLUSIONS

Based on our own intuitions and the literature on informal communication we have speculated that some form of desktop videoteleconferencing could prove useful in preserving informal communication channels for geographically distributed organizations. We've presented in this paper some results from our initial attempt to prototype such a system. While our results indicated that we were able to produce a system whose frequency of use conformed to our expectations, there was substantial room for improvement in the system along the dimensions of expressivity and interactivity. Some of the necessary improvement will come as users develop experience with these sort of systems and some will come through the sort of iterative technology improvements we've outlined above. We remain relatively confident, however, that technologies of this sort remain the best hope for providing an informal communications mechanism that will lead to successful and productive distributed organizations.

ACKNOWLEDGMENTS

Robert Fish, Robert Kraut and Robert Root designed the CRUISER application, and Richard Clayton and Robert Root programmed it. Bill Campbell, Chris Colasante, Jennifer Murray, and Mark Shifflet provided critical assistance in setting up the network, assisting users, and gathering and analyzing data. Tom Judd and David Braun provided help in hardware and software design, respectively.

REFERENCES

1. Abel, M.J. (1990). Experiences in an exploratory distributed organization. In J. Galegher & R. Kraut (Eds.), *Intellectual teamwork: Social and technological foundations of group work*. Hillsdale, NJ: Lawrence Erlbaum Associates.

2. Altman, S., Valenzi, E. & Hodgetts, R. (1985) *Organizational behavior: Theory and practice*. Orlando, Florida: Academic Press.

3. Borning, A. & Travers, M. (1991) Two approaches to casual interaction over computer and video networks. In *Proceedings of CHI '91, Conference on Human Factors in Computing Systems*. (New Orleans, Louisiana) Association for Computing Machinery, New York.

4. Bulick, S., Abel, M., Corey, D., Schmidt, J. & Coffin, S. (1989) The U.S.West Advanced Technologies prototype multi-media communications system. *Globecom'89: Proceedings of the IEEE Global Telecommunications Conference*. Dallas, Texas.

5. Cruz, G.C., Gomez, L.M., & Wilner, W.T. (1991) Tools to support conversational multimedia. In *Globecom '91, Proceedings of the IEEE Global Telecommunications Conference*, Phoenix, Arizona.

6. Daft, R. L., & Lengel, R. H. (1984). Information richness: A new approach to managerial behavior and organization design. In B. Staw & L. L. Cummings (Eds.), *Research in organizational behavior* (Vol. 6). Greenwich, CT: JAI Press.

7. Daft , R. L. & Lengel, R. H. (1986) Organizational information requirements, media richness, and structural design. *Management Science, 32*, 554-571.

8. Fish, R. S. (1989) CRUISER: A multimedia system for social browsing. *Siggraph Video Review*, Vol 45, No. 6 New York: Association for Computing Machinery

9. Fish, R.S., Kraut, R.E., & Chalfonte, B.L. The VideoWindow system in informal communications. In *Proceedings of the Conference on Computer Supported Cooperative Work (CSCW '90)*, pp. 1-11, Los Angeles, California, ACM Press.

10. Goodman, G. O. & Abel, M. J. (1987) Communication and collaboration: Facilitating cooperative work through communication. *Office: Technology and People, 3,* 129-146.

11. Heath, C. & Luff, P. (1991) Disembodied conduct: Communication through video in a multi-media office environment. In *Proceedings of CHI '91, Conference on Human Factors in Computing Systems.* (New Orleans, Louisiana) Association for Computing Machinery, New York.

12. Johnson, S.C. Hierarchical clustering schemes. *Psychometrika, 32,* 241-254.

13. Kendon, A. & Ferber, A. (1973). A description of some human greetings. In R. Michael & J. Crook (Eds.), *Comparative ecology and behavior of primates.* London: Academic Press.

14. Kiesler, S., Siegel, J. & McGuire, T. (1984). Social psychological aspects of computer-mediated communication. *American Psychologist, 39,* 1123-1134.

15. Knapp, Mark L.(1978). *Social intercourse: From greeting to goodbye.* Boston: Allyn & Bacon.

16. Kraut, R.E., Fish, R.S., Root, R.W., & Chalfonte, B.L. (1990). Informal communication in organizations: Form, function, and technology. In S. Oskamp & S. Spacapan (Eds)., *Human Reactions to Technology: The Claremont Symposium on Applied Social Psychology.* Beverly Hills, CA: Sage Publications. Pp 145-199.

17. Kruskal, J. (1964) Multidimensional scaling by optimizing goodness of fit to a nonmetric hypothesis. *Psychometrika, 29,* 1-27.

18. Kruskal, J., Young, F. & Seery, J. (1977) How to use KYST- 2A, a very flexible program to do multidimensional scaling and unfolding. Unpublished paper, Bell Laboratories

19. Louie, G., Mantei, M., & Buxton, W.A.S. (1991) Making contact in a multi-media environment. HCI Consortium on CSCW, Ann Arbor, MI., February, 1991.

20. Mayer, M. (1977). The telephone and the uses of time. In I. de Sola Pool (Ed.) *The social impact of the telephone.* Cambridge, Massachusetts: MIT Press. Pp 225-245.

21. Monge, P. R., Rothman, L. W., Eisenberg, E. M. , Miller, K. L. & Kirste, K. K. (1985). The dynamics of organizational proximity. *Management Science 31,* 1129-1141.

22. Olson, M. & Bly, S. (1991). The Portland experience: A report on a distributed research group. *International Journal of Man-Machine Studies, 34,* 211-228.

23. Perry, C. R. (1977) The British experience 1876-1912: The impact of the telephone during the years of delay. In I. de Sola Pool (Ed.) *The social impact of the telephone.* Cambridge, Massachusetts: MIT Press.

24. Rockoff, Maxine (1975a). An overview of some technological/heath-care system implications of seven exploratory broad-band communication experiments. *IEEE Transactions on Communications,* COM-23 , 20-30.

25. Rockoff, Maxine (1975b). The social implications of health care communication systems. *IEEE Transactions on Communications,* COM-23 (10), 1085-1088.

26. Root, R.W. (1988). Design of a multi-media system for social browsing. *Proceedings of the Conference on Computer-Supported Cooperative Work.* Portland, OR, 25-38.

27. Shepard, R. N. (1962) The analysis of proximities: Multidimensional scaling with an unknown distance function. *Psychometrika, 27,*127-140, 219-246.

28. Short, J., Williams, E., & Christie, B. (1976) *The social psychology of telecommunications.* London: John Wiley & Sons.

29. Stohl, C. & Redding, W. C. (1987). Messages and message exchange processes. In J. Jablin, L. Putnam, K. Roberts, & L. Porter (Eds.), *Handbook of Organizational Communication.* Newbury Park, CA: Sage Publications. Pp. 451-502.

SPEECH PATTERNS
IN VIDEO-MEDIATED CONVERSATIONS

Abigail J. Sellen*

Computer Systems Research Institute
University of Toronto
6 King's College Rd.
Toronto, Ontario
M5S 1A1 Canada

ABSTRACT
This paper reports on the first of a series of analyses aimed at comparing same room and video-mediated conversations for multiparty meetings. This study compared patterns of spontaneous speech for same room versus two video-mediated conversations. One video system used a single camera, monitor and speaker, and a picture-in-a-picture device to display multiple people on one screen. The other system used multiple cameras, monitors, and speakers in order to support directional gaze cues and selective listening. Differences were found between same room and video-mediated conversations in terms of floor control and amount of simultaneous speech. While no differences were found between the video systems in terms of objective speech measures, other important differences are suggested and discussed.

KEYWORDS: CSCW, videoconferencing, conversation patterns.

INTRODUCTION
People meet for a variety of reasons: to discuss and share ideas, to argue and make decisions, to plan, and to socialize. Video and audio technology has obvious potential for bringing people together at remote locations. Cameras and microphones provide electronic eyes and ears; monitors and speakers deliver visual and auditory information. Combined with computer supported groupware such as electronic whiteboards, all the right ingredients for a simulated face-to-face meeting seem to be in place.

There are nonetheless important differences between video and face-to-face (or same room) meetings. Some of these are rather obvious. Unlike eyes, cameras have a fixed field of view and usually cannot be controlled by the viewer. Failure to make eye contact tends also to be a problem because of separation of camera and monitor. In video-mediated meetings, the principle of reciprocity does not

always hold (i.e., if I can see you, you can see me). There is no concept of a negotiated mutual distance between speakers, and speakers have no sense of how their voices are perceived by listeners. Other differences are more subtle and harder to define, such as the relative impotence of gestures and gaze in securing another's attention through video [13], and the feeling of being "distanced" from others.

Many of these problems are compounded when one is restricted to a single camera and monitor in order to converse with multiple parties. One way of supporting multiparty conversations is to use a "picture-in-a-picture" device which divides the screen into quadrants with one participant occupying each quadrant. However, when multiple participants occupy a single screen, participants are limited in their ability to: 1) direct their gaze to various participants; 2) establish eye contact with other participants; 2) be aware of who, if anyone, is visually attending to them; 3) selectively listen to different, parallel conversations; 4) make aside comments to other participants; and 5) hold parallel conversations.

This experiment was conducted in order to compare same room conversations with video-mediated conversations, and also to compare conversational behavior in two video systems. One video system uses the picture-in-a-picture (PIP) approach and thus suffers from the limitations listed above. The other, called *Hydra*, was designed specifically to support these abilities.

A series of analyses are planned for the data collected in this study. This paper reports on the first analysis — an examination of the gross structure of conversation for each of the three conditions. The general question of interest is how video-mediation affects conversational structure in terms of the on-off patterns of speech. A more specific question is whether the properties of the Hydra video system are sufficiently different from the PIP approach to affect speech patterns. For example, head turning and gaze cues are thought to be important in regulating the flow of conversation. Since Hydra is intended to support these kinds of cues, this may be reflected in objective measures of speech. These issues are addressed in the context of discussions involving four people.

While there are many interesting theoretical issues that arise, there are also practical issues motivating this work. This study is being carried out within the larger context of

*Author is now at Rank Xerox Cambridge EuroPARC, and the MRC Applied Psychology Unit, Cambridge, UK. E-mail: sellen@europarc.xerox.com

the CAVECAT project [16], a project which is exploring a variety of issues in technology supported cooperative work. In particular, this study is part of a more comprehensive design effort examining different ways of supporting multiparty videoconferencing.

The "Hydra" System

Hydra is a system which uses multiple cameras, monitors and speakers to support multiparty videoconferencing [19]. Hydra simulates a 4-way round-table meeting by placing a camera, monitor and speaker in the place that would otherwise be held by each remote participant. Using this technique, each person is presented with a unique view of each remote participant, and that view, and its accompanying voice, emanates from a distinct location in space. Figure 1 shows Hydra in use in a four-way conversation.

The fact that each participant is represented by a separate camera/monitor pair means that gazing toward someone is effectively conveyed. In other words, when person A turns to look at person B, B is able to see A turn to look towards B's camera. Looking away and gazing at someone else is also conveyed, and the direction of head turning indicates who is being looked at. Furthermore, because the voices come from distinct locations, one is able to selectively attend to different speakers who may be speaking simultaneously.

Audio and video connections for Hydra are configured by software which ensures that a consistent "around the table" mapping is made for each person. In other words, the switching network ensures that if person A appears in the center unit for person B, then B appears in the center unit for person A. Similarly, if person C appears to person A's

right, then person C appears to person B's left, and so on. In this way, head turning and gaze cues deliver consistent and meaningful information.

Gaze and the Regulation of Conversation

In this experiment, whether directional gaze cues were present in the conversation was one factor of interest. It is estimated that 60 percent of conversation involves gaze and 30 percent involves mutual gaze [1]. Gaze serves at least five functions [2,15]: to regulate the flow of conversation; to provide feedback on how the communication is being perceived by the listener; to communicate emotions; to communicate the nature of the interpersonal relationship; and to avoid excess information input. Video systems which fail to support gaze and mutual gaze may affect any of these five functions.

One effect which may reveal itself in patterns of conversation is in the regulation of conversation, or how floor control is passed from speaker to speaker. There are a variety of different cues which are used to coordinate turn-taking such as intonation, paralanguage, body motion, and syntax [10]. Among these, gaze and head turning have been well established as being used to keep the floor, to take the floor, to avoid taking the floor, and to suggest who should speak next [2,10,11,12,15]. Kendon [15] found that gaze by a speaker at a listener increases just before ending a long utterance, and that when there is no such terminal gaze, there was more likely to be a pause before switching speakers. In general, a speaker will tend to look away at the beginning of a turn and then terminate the turn with a sustained gaze, usually at presumptive next speaker. A speaker wishing to hold the floor at a pause point will look away from the listener.

Figure 1. A user is seated in front of three Hydra units. Each Hydra unit contains a video monitor, camera, and loudspeaker.

As Short, Williams and Christie [21] have noted, reintroducing the visual channel via conventional video systems may exacerbate problems in regulating conversation. Not only do head turning and directional gaze cues tend to be eliminated, asymmetry may also be an important aspect of the problem. For example, one participant may believe that they are making eye contact, but this is not perceived by the other participant. Similarly, participants from time to time will look at the camera, and this may be interpreted as a signal by the receiver of the look. There is some empirical evidence to support the fact that asymmetry can be problematic. Argyle, Lalljee, and Cook [4] found that asymmetry in the amount of visibility between conversants led to greater effects in terms of pauselength and interruptions than symmetrical lessening of visual cues.

The Experiment

In this study four-person groups were used. Number of participants is an important consideration. Dyads are typically the basis of research on conversational structure, in part because they are simpler to study. However, as soon as a third party is introduced, "next turn" is no longer guaranteed to the non-current speaker. Further, three party conversations are notably different from four-party conversations in that four people provides for the possibility of two different ongoing conversations. Four people in a discussion also means that it is potentially more difficult to gain the floor. Thus it was hoped that using a larger group would accentuate differences between conditions in terms of regulation of conversation.

There are few studies which have objectively measured patterns of spontaneous speech across media. Studies of dyadic conversations in audio-only conditions (e.g., telephone) have found that when one takes away visual cues, there tend to be fewer interruptions [7,18], shorter periods of simultaneous speech [14,18], and longer utterances [18]. However, there is some conflicting evidence. Argyle, Lalljee and Cook [4] found *more* interruptions during dyadic conversations when visual cues were reduced. The findings with regard to pauses are also inconsistent. Argyle, Lalljee and Cook [4] found longer pauses when visual cues are reduced. Cook and Lalljee [7] found no difference between media for length of pauses. Jaffe and Feldstein [14] found slightly shorter pauses within utterances and between switching speakers in a no-vision condition, for mixed sex pairs only.

Only Cohen [6] has objectively measured conversational parameters for groups of more than two people in the context of face-to-face versus video conditions. Cohen compared a face-to-face condition with a meeting using Bell's Picturephone Meeting Service (a voice switched system consisting of 3 cameras in each of two rooms, with three to four people per room). Objective measures of conversational structure showed that the face-to-face condition resulted in more speaker turns and more simultaneous speech than the Picturephone Meeting Service. It seems then, that these results are consistent with most of the studies of dyads, and that video conditions

may have similar effects on conversation patterns as audio-only conditions.

Some have taken these findings to mean that technology-mediated conversations are *better* synchronized than face-to-face meetings. Technology mediated conversants experience fewer interruptions, and turn-taking appears to be more orderly. Regulation of turns is obviously not wholly dependent on face-to-face visual cues. The audio channel also carries synchronization cues and perhaps compensates for the loss or attenuation of visual cues. However, what has been called more "orderly" conversation may in fact reflect a reluctance on the part of listeners to interject and try to seize the floor when visual cues are attenuated. Rutter [17] showed that no-vision discussions are perceived to be less spontaneous, more formal and more socially distant than face-to-face discussions.

Experimental Hypotheses

Because Hydra is designed to simulate a four-way meeting using video surrogates, the overriding expectation was that Hydra would tend to produce conversational patterns more similar to same room conversations than a PIP approach. The PIP approach not only fails to support selective gaze and listening, but it is designed so that a viewer sees themselves in addition to the other three people. This design feature also is unlike a face-to-face situation, and thus was thought to contribute to its "unnaturalness", perhaps to the extent that it affects the structure of conversation. With this in mind, and by extrapolating from the existing literature, the following hypotheses were put forth:

H1. Same room conversations will result in the highest number of turns per session. The fewest will occur in the PIP condition.

H2. The average duration of turns will be shortest in the same room condition, and longest in the PIP condition.

Hypotheses 1 and 2 are based on Cohen's [6] finding that there were almost twice as many speaker switches in a face-to-face meeting than in a Picturephone meeting. If this finding holds for other kinds of video systems, we would expect more frequent and shorter turns in a conversation, all else being equal.

H3. There will be the most unequal distribution of turns among speakers in the PIP condition, and the most equal distribution in the same room condition.

This hypothesis is based on the assumption that if it is more difficult to switch speakers (i.e. in the video conditions), it will be done less often. Thus in the video conditions, and especially in the PIP condition, dominant speakers will dominate more, and non-dominant speakers will attempt to take the floor less often.

H4. There will be more simultaneous speech in same room condition than in the two video conditions.

The Hydra system will produce more simultaneous speech than the PIP condition.

This hypothesis is based on Cohen's [6] results which found more simultaneous speech in face-to-face meetings than in Picturephone meetings. Cohen concluded that face-to-face meetings were thus less polite, less orderly, and more interactive. If Hydra is more like a same room meeting than the PIP system, Hydra conversations should be more interactive, and less orderly than PIP conversations.

No specific hypothesis regarding time between speaker switches was put forth. As discussed previously, the data regarding the effect of visual cues on switch pauses are inconsistent. However, if perfect coordination between speakers means minimizing interruptions and minimizing pauses, then a zero switching time is ideal. The average switch pause is typically in the range of .62 to .77 seconds [14]. As coordination gets worse, we would expect longer switch times to occur. However, we might also expect more overlapping speech during speaker switches. These overlaps are typically not examined separately but are classified as simultaneous speech. One alternative is to conceptualize switching time as a single metric which is sometimes negative (an overlap) and which is sometimes positive (a switch pause). The effect of video-mediation on this measure remains to be explored.

METHOD

Subjects
Twelve groups of four adults participated: 15 women and 33 men. With only a couple of exceptions, none of the subjects knew each other previously.

Task and Experimental Design
Each group was asked to participate in a set of three informal debates lasting approximately sixteen minutes each. Subjects were randomly divided into teams of two, and each team was randomly assigned either to the "Pro" or "Con" side of the issue. Three different topics were introduced with the help of one or two short newspaper clippings. The topics were: the right to smoke in public, mandatory drug testing, and censorship in the news. Each group discussed all three topics, one in each condition. Teams remained the same for all three topics and topics were counterbalanced across conditions.

This was a simple one-factor repeated measures design, comparing performance in three conditions: Same Room, Picture-in-a-Picture video system, and the Hydra video system. Order of condition was counterbalanced using a Latin square design.

Experimental Conditions and Apparatus
The three conditions are described below. Both audio and video records of each conversation were made using a video camera and a VCR located in a separate control room. In addition, specialized speech tracking equipment (also described below) was used in order to record on-off patterns of speech in the conversation.

Same Room Condition. In this condition, all four subjects met in the same room around a table. A video camera was set up in one corner of the room and the video output was channeled through coaxial cable to a VHS videorecorder in the experimental control room. In addition, each subject wore a headset microphone. This audio output was also fed through coaxial cable to the experimental control room. There, it went both to a mixer where all four voices were laid down on the audio track of the video cassette, and to the speech tracking equipment, also located in the control room.

Picture-in-a-Picture (PIP) Condition. Each subject was seated in separate room outfitted with a color video monitor, video camera, a speaker, and a headset microphone. The camera was mounted on top of each monitor and the speaker was located immediately adjacent to each monitor. A video board allowed the display of four composite images as illustrated in Figure 2. This configuration allowed each participant to see the other three participants as well as an image of themselves. Each subject saw exactly the same configuration of images as the other subjects.

As in the Same Room condition, video and audio recordings were made of each conversation. Also as before, the audio output from each microphone was mixed and laid down on the videotape, in addition to being sent to the speech tracking equipment.

Hydra Condition. The Hydra system was set up in each of the same rooms used in the PIP condition. Each of the three Hydra units was constructed from a Sony Watchman color monitor (8 cm diagonal), a black and white camera from a Radio Shack surveillance unit mounted 4.5 cm below the screen, and a speaker mounted just below the camera, also from a Sony Watchman. Each unit tilts back and forth for best viewing position. In the other three rooms, simulated Hydra units had to be used due to budget constraints. In these rooms, three Radio Shack black and white monitors were used (12 cm in diameter), along with two black and white Radio Shack surveillance cameras, and the color camera used in the PIP condition. The color camera was used to feed the prototype Hydra units in order to take advantage of the color monitors in those units. Each camera was mounted directly on top of each monitor. In addition, each camera/monitor pair was mounted directly on top of a speaker. In all cases, the Hydra or simulated Hydra units were located 15 cm apart on the desk top, and set back 38 cm from the edge of the desk.

Figure 2. A meeting using the picture-in-a-picture (PIP) device. Each person sees the other three people in addition to themselves, on one screen. All participants see the same image.

Speech Tracking System

The conversion of speech into digital on/off patterns was accomplished by obtaining audio output from each of the four subjects using unidirectional dynamic, headset microphones. Each microphone output controlled its own externally keyed audio noise gate. When a subject spoke louder then a preset threshold, the corresponding audio noise gate would open, allowing a fixed pitch generated by a Yamaha TX802 synthesizer to pass through. When a subject fell silent the gate would close and cutting off the pitch. Each of the output signals from the four noise gates were fed into four input channels of an IVL Pitchrider 7000 Mark II pitch tracking device. The pitch tracker converted the pitch on/off signals into digital on/off signals and send them, via a MIDI connection, to a Macintosh II computer. These on/off events were stored in the computer and each event was time stamped with SMPTE time code. This time code was simultaneously laid down on the videotape so speaker events could be later synchronized when playing back the videotape.

Procedure

On arrival, subjects on the same team were introduced to each other and given approximately 15 minutes to get acquainted while completing the experimental consent forms. Following this, they were introduced to the members of the other team and were instructed to read the first topic for debate. They were then placed in separate rooms (in the case of the PIP or Hydra conditions) or in the same room, and were instructed on wearing the headset microphones. All three conditions used a similar procedure. Subjects discussed the prescribed topic for 16 minutes, and then were asked to complete a questionnaire about the conversation they had just experienced, independently of each other.

RESULTS

Analysis of Speech Data

Each 16 minute conversation was checked for accuracy against the videotape data, edited where necessary, and coded using specialized software designed for this purpose. Despite the impressive accuracy of the speech tracking system, some sporadic crosstalk did occur from time to time which had to be deleted. In addition, 200 msec pauses were filled in, in order to account for stop consonants (a procedure also used by Brady, [5]). Laughter and also backchannel responses were coded so as to differentiate these data from speaker turns or attempts to take turns. Backchannel responses are vocalizations such as "mmm-hmm", often used to show attentiveness, which do not constitute turns or attempts to take turns [10].

Definitions

The data were analyzed using definitions taken both from Jaffe and Feldstein [14] and Dabbs and Ruback [8,9], and then modified slightly. Dabbs and Ruback's scheme is an extension of that of Jaffe and Feldstein to better account for groups larger than dyads.

The following definitions were used:

Turn. A turn consists of the sequence of talkspurts and pauses by a speaker who "has the floor". A speaker gains the floor when they begin speaking to the exclusion of everyone else and when they are not interrupted by anyone else for at least 1.5 seconds.[1] The duration of a turn begins with the first unilateral sound, and ends when another

---

[1]Without this criterion, even the shortest unilateral sound would be designated as a turn. 1.5 seconds was chosen because this is estimated to be the mean duration of a phonemic clause and there is evidence for the phonemic clause as a basic unit in the encoding and decoding of speech [14].

individual turn or a "group turn" begins (see below). Note that turns therefore include periods of mutual silence at the end of utterances, when no one else has yet taken the floor.

Group Turn. Using Dabbs and Ruback's [8] definition: "A group turn begins the moment an individual turn taker has fallen silent and two or more others are speaking together; the group turn ends the moment any individual is again speaking alone" (p. 519). Dabbs and Ruback proposed the group turn to cover instances where individual turn takers are effectively "drowned out" by the group.

Speaker Switch. A speaker switch occurs whenever one person or group loses the floor, and another person or group gains it.

Switch Time. Switch time consists of *switching pauses* and *overlaps*. A switching pause is a period of mutual silence bounded by different turn takers (individuals or groups). Unlike existing definitions, I also include as a related measure the concept of overlap. An overlap is a period of simultaneous speech immediately before and leading to the person who utters it taking a turn. The two measures can be conceptualized as a single continuous parameter which measures the relationship between one person ending a turn and another starting. A negative switch time is thus an overlap, while a positive switch time is a switch pause.

Simultaneous Speech. Simultaneous speech is speech by one or more speakers who do not have the floor. I further distinguish between overlaps and simultaneous speech which does not lead to a speaker switch. Simultaneous speech which does not precede a speaker switch is called *non-interruptive simultaneous speech* . Overlaps are synonymous with *interruptive simultaneous speech*.

Turn Analysis

The number, duration and distribution of speaker turns is shown in Table 1. Statistical tests using one-tailed analyses of variance at the .05 level showed:

1. No difference across conditions in the number of individual turns per session.

2. No difference across conditions in the mean duration of individual turns.

3. No difference across conditions in the number of group turns per session.

4. No difference across conditions in the distribution of turns among speakers.

Turn distribution among speakers was calculated after Dabbs and Ruback [8] who used Shannon and Weaver's [20] equation for calculating information (in information theory terms). This equation defining H, or amount of information, is essentially a way of calculating the average amount of uncertainty about who has the floor at any given time. H is defined by:

$$H = -\sum p_i \, log \, (p_i)$$

If one person talks all the time, H is equal to its minimum value of zero (no uncertainty). If all four people hold the floor for an equal number of turns, H is equal to 2, its maximum value.

Table 1. Average number and duration of individual turns, average number of group turns per session, and distribution of speaker turns. Standard deviations are shown in brackets.

	Overall F Tests	Same Room	PIP	Hydra
1. Number of Turns per Session	not sig.	62.6 (17.4)	64.1 (19.5)	68.7 (24.25)
2. Turn Duration (sec)	not sig.	15.92 (3.66)	16.46 (6.66)	16.62 (10.31)
3. Number of Group Turns per Session	not sig.	3.8 (3.8)	4.6 (5.0)	3.8 (6.9)
4. Distribution of Turns (H value)	not sig.	1.83 (.10)	1.82 (.17)	1.83 (.17)

Simultaneous Speech Analysis

Table 2 presents the data summary for simultaneous speech and switching measures. Analyses of variance (two-tailed tests at the .05 level) showed:

5. *Percentage of time one person spoke* did not differ significantly across conditions. However, this measure almost reached significance ($F(2,22) = 2.87$, $p < .078$). Percent time of one person talking was based on the summation of all time intervals during which one person only spoke, expressed as a percentage of total session time (960 secs).

6. *Percentage of simultaneous speech* was significantly different across conditions. Means comparisons showed Same Room conversations to contain more simultaneous speech than the video conditions ($F(1,22) = 6.78$, $p < .016$), but showed no difference between the two kinds of video conditions. Percent of simultaneous speech refers to the proportion of time during which two, three or four people were speaking simultaneously.

7. No difference was found in the total amount of *non-interruptive simultaneous speech* across conditions, although the differences were close to significant ($F(2,22) = 2.56$, $p < .10$). Amount of non-interruptive simultaneous speech is the sum of all simultaneous speech events not leading to a speaker switch.

8. *Amount of interruptive simultaneous speech* was found to differ across conditions. Means comparisons showed that Same Room conversations gave rise to more interruptive simultaneous speech than the video conditions ($F(1,22) = 7.04$, $p < .015$), with no difference between video conditions. Amount of interruptive simultaneous speech is the sum of all simultaneous speech events which result in the interrupting speaker taking the floor.

9. *Percent of simultaneous speech taking control* did not differ across conditions. Percent of simultaneous speech taking control is the percentage of simultaneous speech which is interruptive (as opposed to that which does not eventually take the floor).

10. *Percent of speaker switches consisting of overlaps* (as opposed to pauses) did differ across conditions. More speaker switches consisted of overlaps in the Same Room conditions than the video conditions ($F(1,22) = 7.85$, $p < .01$), with no difference between video conditions. Percent of overlaps in speaker switches calculates what percentage of speaker switches takes place with a negative switching time (an overlap), rather than a switch pause.

11. *Switching time* was significantly different across conditions. The Same Room condition gave rise to a mean switch overlap, while the video conditions gave rise to a positive switch time value, or switch pause. The difference between Same Room and video conditions was significant ($F(1,22) = 27.67$, $p < .0001$), but no difference between video conditions was found. Switching time is an average of switch pauses (positive values), and overlaps (negative values).

Table 2. *Summary statistics for simultaneous speech, percent of simultaneous speech taking control of the conversation, and switching time. Standard deviations shown in brackets.*

	Overall F Tests	Same Room	PIP	Hydra
5. % Time One Person Talking	(*) $p < .078$	71.3 (3.7)	72.9 (4.1)	74.7 (5.5)
6. % Simultaneous Speech	* $p < .033$	9.7 (7.4)	7.1 (6.9)	5.4 (7.1)
7. Am't of Non-Interruptive Simultaneous Speech (sec)	(*) $p < .10$	98.1 (86.9)	72.1 (67.7)	57.8 (80.0)
8. Am't of Interruptive Simultaneous Speech (sec)	* $p < .038$	56.6 (39.2)	40.1 (39.5)	33.6 (39.7)
9. % Simultaneous Speech Taking Control	not sig.	38.5 (6.6)	34.4 (5.9)	41.6 (15.6)
10. % Overlaps in Speaker Switches	* $p < .029$	54.1 (18.9)	46.3 (24.1)	43.5 (21.1)
11. Switching Time (sec)	** $p < .0001$	-.46 (.66)	.04 (.79)	.25 (.67)

Questionnaire Data
The mean scores from the questionnaires averaged across 48 subjects are shown in Table 3. Analysis of variance tests found four statistically significant results:

12. Subjects rated the Same Room meeting as allowing them to better take control of the conversation than both video conditions (F(1,47) = 10.59, p < .002). There was no difference between video conditions.

13. Subjects rated the Same Room conversation as being more interactive than either video condition (F(1,47) = 5.65, p < .022). There was no difference between video conditions.

14. Subjects rated the Same Room conversation as allowing them to selectively attend to one person at a time most easily (F(1,47) = 8.73, p < .005). While the Hydra video system gave rise to a higher overall mean than the PIP system, this difference did not reach significance.

15. Subjects rated the Same Room condition the best for knowing when others were listening or attending to them. This was rated significantly better than the Hydra system (F(1,47) = 22.18, p < .0001), which was rated significantly better than the PIP system (F(1,47) = 12.13, p < .001).

DISCUSSION

Turn Frequency, Duration, and Distribution
Mediating conversations with video technology appeared to have no discernable effects on the number of turns taken per session, the average length of those turns, or on the distribution of turns among speakers. These results were unexpected, especially considering previous research which generally finds that audio-only conditions, and in one case, a video-mediated condition [6], tend to increase turn length relative to face-to-face conversations. In light of the lack of differences between same room conversations and video-mediated conversations, it is perhaps not surprising that no difference was found between the two video conditions on these measures.

Table 3. The mean scores for each of the nine questions administered in the questionnaires averaged over 48 subjects. A score of 7 represents "Strongly Agree", while a score of 1 represents "Strongly Disagree".

Question	Same Room	PIP	Hydra
I was able to talk and express myself freely.	6.1 (0.9)	5.8 (1.4)	5.7 (1.4)
I was able to take control of the conversation when I wanted to. (p < .002)	6.0 (1.0)	5.4 (1.5)	5.5 (1.4)
There were too many inappropriate interruptions.	2.4 (1.5)	2.4 (1.4)	2.2 (1.4)
This was an unnatural conversation.	2.7 (1.7)	3.1 (1.7)	3.0 (1.6)
The conversation seemed highly interactive. (p < .006)	5.9 (1.3)	5.4 (1.3)	5.3 (1.2)
There were many unnatural and uncomfortable pauses.	2.5 (1.7)	2.3 (1.1)	2.6 (1.4)
I could selectively attend to one person at a time. (p < .0001)	6.1 (1.1)	4.8 (1.8)	5.3 (1.8)
I knew when people were listening or paying attention to me. (p < .0001)	6.3 (0.9)	4.3 (1.9)	5.3 (1.5)
I found it difficult to keep track of the conversation. (p < .09)	2.0 (1.5)	2.6 (1.7)	2.2 (1.2)

The discrepancy between Cohen's [6] results and these results may be due to the design of the Picturephone Meeting Service she used. Picturephone is a voice activated system which, in her study, switched between six different cameras depending on who in the group was talking. This meant that the whole group could never be viewed simultaneously. She also introduced a 705 msec audio and video transmission delay in order to simulate round-trip satellite conditions. These two factors could well account for differences in turn length and frequency, since this design would presumably more radically reduce the effectiveness of both verbal and visual cues to regulate turn-taking behavior.

Perhaps the results of this study with respect to turn frequency, duration, and distribution speak to the success of both the PIP and Hydra approach in preserving the structure of the conversation, at least at this level. The results of the questionnaire confirm that subjects did not feel that any of the three different situations was especially unnatural or uncomfortable. In both systems, and unlike the Picturephone system, participants are visually available all the time. Thus each person can monitor all other members of the group whether they are speaking or not and non-verbal signals for turn-taking can be perceived. Showing that this factor alone accounts for differences between Cohen's results and these results would require running a voice switched video condition with no audio or video transmission delay.

A final point to note is that the groups were highly variable in overall amount of talking, amount of simultaneous speech, and distribution of turns among speakers. Pronounced between group differences can be contrasted with relatively stable group characteristics across conditions. This emphasizes the importance of using within-group designs for this kind of study.

Simultaneous Speech and Floor Control

Subjects did feel it was more difficult to take control of the conversation in the video conditions than in the Same Room condition (as evidenced by the questionnaire data). Nonetheless, this difficulty was not reflected in the distribution of turns among speakers, as might be expected. Where differences do emerge, however, is in the amount of simultaneous speech that occurred and in the time between switching speakers.

A lower percentage of time was occupied by one speaker talking, and a higher percentage of time was occupied by simultaneous speech in the Same Room condition relative to the two video conditions. This result is in line with previous findings for audio-only and video-mediated conversation, although some researchers have found more interruptions when visual cues are reduced [4].

A more informative analysis may come from asking what function simultaneous speech serves, or what it may indicate. On the one hand, simultaneous speech may be taken to indicate a problem in floor control. Participants may mistime their bids for floor control, or may bid for the

floor and fail. Studies which label simultaneous speech as "interruptions" make this tacit assumption. On the other hand, simultaneity may also be taken to be an indication of the degree of interactivity and spontaneity of the conversation. Conversations which have more simultaneous speech may be due to participants who feel more engaged in the conversation, and are more willing to attempt to take the floor.

Rather than attaching a value judgement to simultaneous speech, it may be more useful to distinguish between simultaneous speech which gains control of the floor versus that which does not. One can then discover how often attempts at floor control occur, and how often they are successful. Most existing studies do not make this distinction.

Video conversations gave rise to less non-interruptive simultaneous speech (although not significantly less), and less interruptive simultaneous speech overall. In addition, the Hydra system gave rise to less simultaneous speech of both types than the PIP system, although this difference was not significant. What this may indicate is a reluctance on the part of conversants to attempt to take the floor in video-mediated conversations. This is in line with many subjects' spontaneous comments. Many reported feeling "distanced" by the video systems, and less a part of the conversation. Perhaps they felt that bids for floor control would be less effective in video-mediated conversations.

The actual effectiveness of bidding for the floor while someone else is talking can be estimated by calculating the percentage of simultaneous speech that gains the floor. As is shown in Table 2, simultaneous speech was successful in gaining the floor about 34 to 42 percent of the time, and the differences across conditions was not significant. Thus, there was no *real* difference in the probability of bids for the floor being effective in Same Room versus video conditions.

If subjects were more reluctant to bid for the floor in the video conditions, and bidding was equally effective, why would this not result in fewer speaker switches in the video conditions? The answer may lie in the fact that speaker switching in the Same Room condition was more likely to occur with an overlap between speaker turns than a pause. Speaker switching in the video conditions, on the other hand, was more likely to occur with a brief pause. The analysis of switching time confirms this finding. Switching time in the Same Room condition was -.46 seconds on average, while mean switching time in the video conditions was a positive value (.04 sec for the PIP condition, and .25 sec for Hydra). It is as if conversants in video-mediated conversations were more opportunistic or polite, waiting for a pause or for a speaker to finish before attempting to take the floor. This theory is speculation at this point, however. A clearer picture will likely emerge after a more thorough analysis of the videotape data.

PIP versus Hydra Systems

Contrary to expectation, there were no differences between the two video systems in terms of objective measures of on-off patterns of speech. However, both the questionnaire data and informal discussions with subjects after each experimental session confirmed that subjects did notice differences between the systems, and most had strong opinions on which system they preferred.

The majority of subjects preferred the Hydra system. Reasons given included the fact that they could selectively attend to people, and could tell when people were attending to them. Another frequent comment was that they liked the multiple sources of audio in the Hydra system, and that this helped them keep track of one thread of the conversation when people talked simultaneously. The questionnaire data confirm that keeping track of the conversation in the PIP condition was the most difficult. Thus, it is reasonable to conclude that Hydra was successful in facilitating selective listening and selective gaze, in line with the original intent behind its design.

A preliminary analysis of the videotape data also confirms that Hydra was successful in affording aside and parallel conversations. Separate conversational threads occurred concurrently a total of four times in the Hydra condition, and three times in the Same Room condition, but never in the PIP condition. Therefore, even though no differences appeared in the structural analysis of speech, it seems likely that an in-depth analysis of the videotapes will reveal differences that do exist between these two systems.

Why the selective gaze and headturning cues did not affect the structure of the conversation is an interesting issue. Head turning and directional gaze could be readily observed in the Hydra conversations. However video-mediation may render these kinds of cues ineffective for their recipients. As Heath and Luff [13] have pointed out, movements in the periphery which appear on a screen lose their power to attract attention. Presumably this is even more of a problem for small screens. Speakers may also face difficulties in knowing how their gestures are received. Indeed, many subjects commented that they wanted a mirror to see how they were framed from the point of view of others. Thus even though Hydra is designed to support directional gaze cues, video mediation may nonetheless detract from the ability of such cues to affect behavior.

Finally, about one third of the subjects preferred the PIP system to the Hydra system. It was interesting to find that most of these subjects commented that they enjoyed having all of the participants on one screen because it meant that head turning was *not* necessary. Some subjects said they liked to see themselves to know how they were seen by others, even though this could sometimes be distracting. One subject commented that seeing herself on the same screen as the others made her feel more part of the group, and said that otherwise she would have felt quite distanced from them. Thus, simulating aspects of face-to-face situations need not always provide the correct design solutions. The PIP system seems to overcome some of the problems inherent in video mediation, such as the feeling of being distanced and its inherent lack of reciprocity.

CONCLUSIONS

This paper provides some statistics on differences between same room and video-mediated conversations for multiparty conversations. However, some unexpected similarities were also discovered. Videoconferencing did not seem to have much effect on how often people spoke, or for how long, or on the patterns of distribution of turns among group members. Both video systems used in this experiment have the characteristic that participants are visually present all the time and no one person "owns" the audio channel. This may account for the lack of drastic differences between conditions. Other kinds of systems such as voice-activated video switching systems have the characteristic that only the current speaker is displayed to the other participants. This aspect of design may result in much larger effects on conversational structure. We currently have such a system in place and are running a second study to test this assumption.

Very few, if any, studies exist which compare objective measures of conversation for different kinds of video systems. This paper provides some of those statistics, and has also shown that such measures may be relatively insensitive to more subtle but nonetheless important aspects of videoconferencing system design. One factor which may have downplayed any differences was the small monitors used in the Hydra design. Because image size was so small, this may have decreased the effectiveness of directional gaze cues in peripheral vision.

Despite this finding, there is every indication that significant differences between the two systems examined here do exist. Both the ability to selectively attend to different audio streams, and to different video images appeared to be successful in making aside conversations possible. In addition, subjects commented that multiple speakers made it easier to follow the conversation. These are clearly important aspects of design, and a more in-depth, qualitative analysis of the videotapes is planned to explore them further.

ACKNOWLEDGEMENTS

I owe a great deal of thanks to four people who became entangled in a complicated technical undertaking in order to realize this experiment. Bill Buxton is responsible for much of the conceptualization behind the design of the various systems. He also contributed to the content of this paper. Gordon Kurtenbach configured the hardware for the speech tracking equipment, and invested a great deal of time writing the software for recording, editing, and analyzing the speech time lines. Tom Milligan and Gary Hardock helped to set up and run the experiment, and helped troubleshoot when necessary. The patience of all the people in the CAVECAT project and the Dynamic Graphics Project at the University of Toronto is also much appreciated.

I also gratefully acknowledge the contribution of the Arnott Design Group of Toronto for the design and fabrication of the *Hydra* models. The work described in this paper has been supported by the Ontario Information Technology Research Centre, the Natural Sciences and Engineering Research Council of Canada, Xerox Palo Alto Research Center, Rank Xerox Cambridge EuroPARC, The Arnott Design Group (Toronto), Object Technology International (Ottawa), Digital Equipment Corp. (Maynard, MA.), and IBM Canada Laboratory Centre for Advanced Studies (Toronto).

REFERENCES

1. Argyle, M. (1975). *Bodily communication*. London: Methuen & Co. Ltd.

2. Argyle, M. and Cook, M. (1976). *Gaze and mutual gaze*. London: Cambridge University Press.

3. Argyle, M., Ingham, R., Alkena, F. and McCallin, M. (1973). The different functions of gaze. *Semiotica, 7,* 10-32.

4. Argyle, M., Lalljee, M., and Cook, M. (1968). The effects of visibility on interaction in a dyad. *Human Relations, 21,* 3-17.

5. Brady, P.T. (1968). A statistical analysis of on-off patterns in 16 conversations. *The Bell System Technical Journal, Jan.,* 73-91.

6. Cohen, K. M. (1982). Speaker interaction: Video teleconferences versus face-to-face meetings. *Proceedings of Teleconferencing and Electronic Communications,* University of Wisconsin, 189-199.

7. Cook, M. & Lalljee, M.G. (1972). Verbal substitutes for visual signals in interaction. *Semiotica, 3,* 212-221.

8. Dabbs, J.M. Jr., & Ruback, R.B. (1984). Vocal patterns in male and female groups. *Personality and Social Psychology Bulletin, 10(4),* 518-525.

9. Dabbs, J.M. Jr., & Ruback, R.B. (1987). Dimensions of group process: Amount and structure of vocal interaction. In *Advances in Experimental Social Psychology, 20,* 123-169.

10. Duncan, S. (1972). Some signals and rules for taking speaking turns in conversations. *Journal of Personality and Social Psychology, 23(2),* 283-292.

11. Duncan, S. & Fiske, D. W. (1977). *Face-to-face interaction: Research methods and theory*. Hillsdale, NJ: Erlbaum.

12. Duncan, S. & Niederehe, G. (1974). On signalling that it's your turn to speak. *Journal of Experimental Social Psychology, 23,* 234-247.

13. Heath, C. & Luff, P. (1991). Disembodied conduct: Communication through video in a multi-media office environment. *Proceedings of CHI '91,* ACM Conference on Human Factors in Software, New Orleans, LA., 99-103.

14. Jaffe, J., & Feldstein, S. (1970). *Rhythms of dialogue*. New York: Academic Press.

15. Kendon, A. (1967). Some functions of gaze direction in social interaction. *Acta Psychologica, 32,* 1-25.

16. Mantei, M., Baecker, R., Sellen, A., Buxton, W., Milligan, T. & Wellman, B. (1991). Experiences in the use of a media space. *Proceedings of CHI '91,* ACM Conference on Human Factors in Software, New Orleans, LA., 203-208.

17. Rutter (1987). *Communicating by telephone*. New York: Pergamon Press.

18. Rutter, D.R. & and Stephenson, G.M (1977). The role of visual communication in synchronizing conversation. *European Journal of Social Psychology, 2,* 29-37.

19. Sellen, A., Buxton, W. & Arnott, J. (1991). *Using spatial cues to improve desktop video conferencing*. 8 minute videotape. Toronto: Dynamic Graphics Project, Computer Systems Research Institute, University of Toronto.

20. Shannon, C.E., and Weaver, W. (1949). *The mathematical theory of communication*. Urbana, IL: University of Illinois Press.

21. Short, J., Williams, E., and Christie, B. (1976). *The social psychology of telecommunications*. London: Wiley & Sons.

HUMAN-COMPUTER INTERACTION RESEARCH AT GEORGIA INSTITUTE OF TECHNOLOGY

James D. Foley
GVU Center, College of Computing, Georgia Institute of Technology
Atlanta, GA 30332-0280, email: foley@cc.gatech.edu

Christine M. Mitchell
School of Industrial and Systems Engineering, Georgia Institue of Technology
Atlanta, GA 30332-0280, email: cm@chmsr.gatech.edu

Neff Walker
School of Psychology, Georgia Institute of Technology
Atlanta, GA 30332-0280, email: nw7@prism.gatech.edu

HCI research at Georgia Tech is found in three cooperating groups: the Engineering Psychology and Experimental Psychology Programs in the School of Psychology, the Center for Human-Machine Systems Research in the School of Industrial and Systems Engineering, and the interdisciplinary Graphics, Visualization and Usability (GVU) Center. We cooperate via cross-listed courses, having students in one area take a minor in another area, collaborative research projects, serving on Ph. D. committees, joint colloquia and brown bag lunches, and joint appointments. The GVU Center (housed in the College of Computing) and Cognitive Science Program (sponsored by Psychology, Industrial and Systems Engineering, and the College of Computing) involves a number of the same faculty, further enhancing our collaborations.

CENTER FOR HUMAN-MACHINE SYSTEMS RESEARCH

The Center for Human-Machine Systems Research was founded in 1981 to study how humans interact with complex systems. An interdisciplinary group of faculty and students in engineering, computer science, and psychology pursue research in analysis, modeling, and design of human-machine systems. Center research explores human decision making and problem solving in such diverse areas as aircraft, aerospace systems, process plants, information systems, ships, communication networks, and manufacturing systems. Typical research projects include:

Intelligent Tutoring Systems: This program involves the design and evaluation of intelligent tutoring systems for operators of complex dynamic systems, e.g., marine power plants or process control plants. We use qualitative models and other knowledge-based techniques to develop a dynamic model of the student and present instructional material adapted to individual student needs. (T. Govindaraj)

Decision Support Systems: This program addresses the real-time decision-making needs of supervisors in highly automated control systems, e.g., near-earth satellite ground control systems. Normative models of decision making, human information sampling, and integration are begin developed in order to create a human- computer interface that dynamically and adaptively supports real-time decision making. (C. M. Mitchell)

Operator's Associate: A dynamic model of operator decision making is used to derive an on-line representation of operator intentions decomposed from functions into subfunctions, tasks, and actions. Using this model, the operator's associate can offer timely advice, assume portions of the control task dynamically at the operator's request, and generally amplify the capabilities of a single human decision maker responsible for the supervisory control of a complex dynamic system. (C. M. Mitchell)

Faculty: T. Govindaraj, A. Kirlik, C. M. Mitchell, and K. Vicente.

SCHOOL OF PSYCHOLOGY

The school of psychology consists of three programs, two of which conduct research in the area of human-computer interaction. Faculty in the engineering psychology program conduct research that emphasizes perceptual and motor skills involved in computer usage and aviation displays. One line of research has focused on understanding movement control as it relates to computer input devices and the design of menu systems. Research on visual processing has focused primarily on instrument displays, with some recent research extending into the area of interpretation of graphical displays.

The research of the faculty in the experimental psychology program focuses on two broad areas of human-computer interaction. One area concerns building models of the computer users. This work has explored the acquisition of procedural knowledge and how acquisition and retention are affected by the prior knowledge of the individual. The second area of research concerns developing instructional techniques to speed acquisition and aid retention of procedural knowledge required for skilled performance.

Faculty: S. Bovair. R. Catrambone, G. Corso, E. Davis, T. Simon, N. Walker

GRAPHICS, VISUALIZATION, AND USABILITY CENTER

The key focus of our center is effectively conveying information between the computer and user. We build software tools to facilitate user interface design, evaluate the quality of photo-realistic and abstracted representations of information, develop tools for animating algorithms and other real-time or simulated processes, develop and evaluate multi-media and non-visual interfaces and help systems, develop CSCW systems, use models of human performance to aid in evaluating interface designs, and use a knowledge of psychophysics to enhance visual displays. Typical research projects include:

User Interface Designer's Aide (UIDE): This system uses a single unified representation of the user interface for multiple purposes: to check the interface design for consistency and completeness, transform the design into a different but functionally equivalent interface, evaluate the interface design with respect to speed of use, create and execute the interface, and generate context-sensitive run-time animated help for the end-user. (J. Foley, P. Sukaviriya)

Algorithm Animation: We are exploring ways to use algorithm animation techniques as aids for program development and debugging. For display of data structures, we seek to supplement traditional debuggers with operations that will allow users to quickly and easily create application-specific animated views using simple commands, buttons, menu selections, and direct manipulation graphics editing. (J. Stasko)

Non-Visual Network Computing Interface: We are adapting graphical user interfaces for use by visually impaired persons, by mapping the interface to a synthetic 3-D audio space in which the user can manipulate objects using a combination of voice input, speech recognition and synthesis, keyboard input, and pointer devices. Built on top of X, the system will provide users with access to the same applications, resources, and networking capabilities that are available to sighted users. (W. Putnam)

Knowledge-based Monitor for Human Computer Interaction: We are developing a user interface monitoring capability for semantic-level interactions. The system will work either with or without being embedded in a UIMS; supports specification of the relevant part of the semantics of the application; allows remote monitoring of interface usage; provides for an open and user-selectable set of metrics; and supports adaptive user interfaces. (Albert Badre)

Faculty (only those involed in HCI are listed): A. Badre (CoC), N. Ezquerra (CoC), J. Foley (CoC), B. Guenter (CoC), Larry Hodges (CoC), Laurie Hodges (GTRI), S. Hudson (CoC), D. Lawton (CoC), B. Mynatt (CoC), W. Putnam (CoC), W. Ribarsky (Computing Services), J. Stasko (CoC), P. Sukaviriya (CoC).

SELECTED PUBLICATIONS (Georgia Tech Authors in **Bold**)

1. Adelson, S., **A. Badre, L. Hodges**, A. Lunde Comparison of different techniques for determination of shape and relative position of objects, *Society for Information Display Digest*, 21, 1990, 351-354.
2. **Bovair, S.**, D. Kieras, P. Polson The acquisition and performance of text editing skill: A cognitive complexity analysis, *Human-Computer Interaction*, 5, 1988, 1-48.
3. **Catrambone, R.** Specific versus general procedures in instructions, *Human-Computer Interaction*, 5(1), 1990, 49-93.
4. **Davis, B.** Modeling shifts in perceived spatial frequency between the fovea & the periphery, *Journal Optical Society of America*, A, 7, 1991, 286–296.
5. **Foley, J.**, and **Sukaviriya, P.** Coupling a UI framework with automatic generation of context-sensitive animated help, *Proceedings SIGGRAPH 1990 Symposium on User Interface Software and Technology*, 152–166.
6. **Govindaraj, T.** Qualitative approximation methodology for modeling and simulation of large dynamic systems: Applications to a marine steam power plant, *IEEE Trans. Systems, Man, and Cyberentics*, SMC-17 (6).
7. **Hudson, S.** Adaptive semantic snaping – a technique for semantic feedback at the lexical level, *Proceedings CHI '90*, 65–70.
8. **Kirlik, A.** What kinds of models are needed to support cognitive engineering? J. Flach (Ed,) *The Ecology of Human-Machine Systems*, Lawrence Erlbaum Associates, Hillsdale, NJ, to appear.
9. Lohse, G., **N. Walker**, K. Biolsi, H. Rueter Classifying graphical information, *Behavior and Information Technology*, (in press).
10. **Mitchell, C.**, et al. OFMspert: Inference of operator intentions in supervisory control using a blackboard architecture. *IEEE Trans. Systems, Man, Cyberentics*, 18 (4), 1988.
11. Payne, M. and **Corso, G.** Effects of range on category scaling of loudness judgements, *Perceptual and Motor Skills*, 60 (2), 1985, 619-624.
12. **Simon, T.** and Young, R. GOMS meets STRIPS: The integration of planning with skilled procedure execution in human-computer interaction. Jones and Winder (Eds.), *People and Computers IV*. Cambridge: Cambridge University Press, in press.
13. **Stasko, J.** Using direct manipulation to build algorithm animations by demonstration, *Proceedings ACM SIGCHI 1991 Conference on Human Factors in Computing Systems*, New Orleans, LA, 1991, 307-314.
14. **Vicente, K.** Coherence- and correspondence-driven work domains: implications for systems design, *Behavior and Information Technology*, 9 (6), 1990.

The Virginia User Interface Laboratory

Primary Contact: Randy Pausch

University of Virginia, Thornton Hall
Charlottesville, VA 22903
(804) 982-2211
Pausch@Virginia.edu

OVERVIEW

The User Interface Laboratory at the University of Virginia is based in the computer science department and includes researchers from the psychology and electrical engineering departments, and from the medical and education schools at UVa. Our overall mission is to produce real solutions to real problems, especially involving new interaction media. This area is sometimes referred to as non-WIMP (windows, icons, menus, and a pointing device) user interface design.

The laboratory formally began in 1988, although some projects were already in existence before the laboratory was founded. The laboratory currently includes fifteen faculty and students, and active projects involve virtual reality, gesture input for the disabled, software architectures for creating real-time, multi-modal interfaces, and SUIT, a platform-independent interface builders. Interesting hardware includes several SGI VGX graphics engines, a high-resolution VPL Eyephone (HRX model) and a variety of spatial tracking and voice I/O devices. In many respects, we are similar to the MIT Media Lab: we are highly interdisciplinary, we do innovative long-term research, and our real strength is the high quality of our students, both graduate and undergraduate. The culture of the lab is best expressed as *tenacious* - for example, before we received enough funding for high-quality virtual reality equipment, we built a system with $5,000 in components and began producing research results with it. We are young, we are determined, and we have a great deal of fun.

We produce both concrete research results and engineering artifacts. Although we are willing to do both, we believe that it is important to be able to distinguish when we are doing basic science, such as when we measure how the human perceptual system interacts with head-mounted displays, or when we are doing engineering, such as developing and/or applying a new tracking technology. At all times, we try to use the "Fred Brooks" model for computer science research: find somebody else's problem and try to help them solve it. Our major projects all have this flavor, and we believe that it helps us readily identify the real problems that arise when using non-traditional human-computer interfaces. The lab has a number of active projects:

CANDY & Tailor

The CANDY Project (Communication Assistance to Negate Disabilities in Youth) seeks to provide a real-time speech synthesizer for disabled individuals, particularly non-vocal children with cerebral palsy. Existing speech synthesizers convert user input into discrete linguistic or phonetic symbols which are converted into sound. Complicated sentences must be created by concatenating lower level symbols, precluding real-time conversational speech. We have developed an articulator-based speech synthesizer which simulates the motion of the human tongue and produces the corresponding speech sounds in real time. The synthesizer is driven by two continuous input signals and non-disabled users can produce real-time speech with a joystick. Disabled users will drive the synthesizer via passive tracking of their body movements. The Tailor project is responsible for generating the custom mappings for each user. Magnetic trackers attached to the user report their location and tailoring software allows each user to move the tracker in an optimal orientation and range. The user motion is then converted into the two continuous signals that drive the speech synthesizer. In this way, we hope to allow each child to compensate for their inoperative vocal tract by using their "best" set of muscles to operate a simulated vocal tract. The motion mapping software may also have future potential as a physical therapy aid. (to appear in the May 1992 issue of *Communications of the ACM*).

VIRTUAL REALITY ON FIVE DOLLARS A DAY

Virtual reality systems using head-mounted displays and glove input are gaining popularity but their cost prohibits widespread use. We have developed a system using an 80386 IBM-PC, a Polhemus 3Space Isotrak, two Reflection Technology Private Eye displays, and a Mattel Power Glove. For less than $5,000, we have created an effective vehicle for developing interaction techniques in virtual reality. Our system displays monochrome wire frames of objects with a spatial resolution of 720 by 280, the highest resolution head-mounted system published to date. We have confirmed findings by other researchers that low-latency interaction is significantly more important than high-quality graphics or stereoscopy. We have also found it useful to display reference objects to our user, specifically a ground plane for reference and a vehicle containing the user. (appeared in SIGCHI '91).

PERCEPTUAL PSYCHOLOGY FOR VR

Current virtual reality environments are based on the presumption that inclusive simulation is an effective means for humans-computer communication. While this seems obvious for entertainment purposes where the experience itself is all that matters, major questions persist when one examines doing useful work inside a virtual reality. We are beginning a long term project to examine the perceptual phenomena surrounding head-mounted displays and spatial input devices. Another aspect of this work uses head-mounted displays as a research apparatus for basic perceptual psychology experiments that cannot be produced with real world objects or traditional computer displays.

SUIT: THE SIMPLE USER INTERFACE TOOLKIT

User interface support software, such as UI toolkits, UIMSs, and interface builders, are currently too complex for undergraduates. Tools usually require a learning period of several weeks, which is impractical in a semester course. Most tools are also limited to a specific platform, usually either Macintosh, DOS, or UNIX/X. This is problematic for students who switch from DOS or Macintosh machines to UNIX machines as they move through the curriculum. The situation is similar to programming languages before the introduction of Pascal, which provided an easily ported, easily learned language for undergraduate instruction.

SUIT (the Simple User Interface Toolkit), is a C subroutine library which provides an external control UIMS, an interactive layout editor, and a set of standard screen objects. SUIT applications run transparently across Macintosh, DOS, and UNIX/X platforms. Through careful design and extensive user testing of the system and its documentation, we have been able to reduce learning time. We have formally measured that new users are productive with SUIT in less than two hours. SUIT currently has over one hundred students using it for undergraduate and graduate course work and for research projects. We pursue SUIT as an engineering project in how to produce the software, but as a basic science project to study what users find difficult when learning a new widget/object-oriented programming environment (presented at UIST '91).

MEMBERS

The founder of the laboratory is Assistant Professor *Randy Pausch*, who came to Virginia from Carnegie Mellon. Dr. Pausch has recently been named a National Science Foundation Presidential Young Investigator. Randy directs the virtual reality, Tailor, and SUIT projects.

Ron Williams, Associate Professor of electrical engineering, is the leader of the CANDY project, and is responsible for guiding the implementation of a novel, articulator-based model of speech synthesis.

Janet Allaire, Assistant Professor of Pediatrics, provides the CANDY project with the speech pathology and pediatrics expertise for developing articulator-based models of speech synthesis.

Dennis Proffitt, Associate Professor of Psychology, leads our efforts in measuring perceptual phenomena, particularly as they relate to the use of head-mounted displays and spatial input devices. Dr. Proffitt has experience working with NASA researchers on VIEW and other related head-mounted display projects.

Laura Vogtle, Occupational Therapy Supervisor, provides expertise in assessing and implementing user studies for the Tailor project, and on providing general guidance for motion-mapping strategies for the disabled.

RECENT PUBLICATIONS

Randy Pausch, *Virtual Reality on Five Dollars a Day*, ACM SIGCHI: Human Factors in Computing Systems, April, 1991.

Randy Pausch and Ronald D. Williams, *Giving CANDY to Children: User-Tailored Gesture Input Driving an Articulator-Based Speech Synthesizer,* Communications of the ACM. (to appear).

Randy Pausch, Robert DeLine and Nathaniel Young, *SUIT: The Pascal of User Interface Toolkits*, ACM UIST '91: Fourth Annual Symposium on User Interface Software and Technology, November, 1991.

Randy Pausch and James H. Leatherby, *An Empirical Study: Adding Voice Input to a Graphical Editor,* Journal of the American Voice Input/Output Society, 9:2, July, 1991.

Randy Pausch and Ronald D. Williams, *Tailor: Creating Custom User Interfaces Based on Gesture,* ACM UIST '90: Third Annual Symposium on User Interface Software and Technology, September, 1990, pp. 123-134.

Randy Pausch and John Detmer, *Node Popularity as a Hypertext Browsing Aid*, Electronic Publishing: Original Dissemination and Design, 3:4, December 1990, pp. 3-10.

Randy Pausch and Rich Gossweiler, *UserVerse: Application-Independent Object Selection From Inaccurate Multi-Modal Input,* Multimedia and Multimodal User Interface Design, edited by Meera Blattner and Roger Dannenberg. Addison-Wesley, 1991. (to appear.)

Randy Pausch, Pramod Dwivedi, and Allan Christian Long, Jr., *A Low Cost Stereographic Head-mounted Display*, SPIE/SPSE Symposium of Electronic Imaging Science and Technology, February 26, 1991.

System Ergonomics and Human-Computer Interaction at SIEMENS Corporate Research and Development

H. Raffler, M. Schneider-Hufschmidt, T.Kühme

Siemens Corporate Research and Development
ZFE ST SN 7, Otto-Hahn-Ring 6
D-W8000 München 83
{raffler | msch | kuehme}@ztivax.siemens.com
{raffler | msch | kuehme}@ztivax.uucp

OVERVIEW

SIEMENS ZFE ST SN 7 was founded in 1987 as part of the Siemens Corporate Research and Development to concentrate research on communication techniques that was previously performed in diverse sectors. Within the department a group of approximately 35 people dedicate their work to topics of human-computer interaction. Additionally a varying number of PhD-students, undergraduates and visiting scientiest are employed in our department.

The research areas include User Interface Management Systems, Computer Graphics, Animation, Multi- and Hypermedia as well as Speech Processing. The goal of the department is both to develop new methods and tools for human computer interaction and to be a center of competence for problems regarding human factors and user interface design. We serve as consultants for all branches of our company.

There is an approximately even split between effort spent for research topics and development projects. Several of our research projects are performed in cooperation with various European and American universities and research institutes. In our projects we try to integrate research and evaluation of ergonomic properties into the development of methods and tools for HCI. While our focus is on computer science aspects of human-computer interaction (and so is the main educational background of our staff members) human factors research and evaluation is done within another central department of our company with which we have close links. This department is responsible for the evaluation of the social and ergonomic impact of our products and research results.

PROJECT SUMMARIES

Computer Animation

Traditionally computer animation is created by different production steps: modelling of complex 3D objects, describing an animation scene, defining the motion of objects and making the animation scenes look realistic by rendering. Together with cooperation partners we develop a system to support these steps. It runs in a UNIX environment on X-Windows. The system will integrate the functionalities mentioned above and supply a homogenous user interface based on OSF/Motif. During the design special consideration has been given to ergonomic aspects. New input devices will enhance the user interface for defining 3D-coordinates or for navigation in virtual worlds.

The current version of our animation system offers traditional key-framing. Creation of animation sequences with support of this kind of animation tools requires much work effort and good feeling for natural motion. Future enhancement of the functionality of this system will both enlarge the area of different applications and ease the process of creating animation sequences. Our team works on simulation of motion dynamics as well as on real-time and interactive animation. Resulting animation sequences can be stored either as scripts or as pixmaps for later imbedding within multimedia documents.

Multimedia

In the field of multimedia interaction the team has worked on the integration of a speech command recognizer as a new input device for an interactive animation system. We center our activities in multimedia around a powerful text- and graphics editor, which will be extended by tools for voice annotation, animation, video and other media. The different multimedia tools will be connected by a flexible link protocol and will run in a distributed UNIX environment. The authoring system will also contain a time-line editor allowing the author of a multimedia application to define the presentation of media in time.

Evaluation of our authoring system is planned for applications like "maintenance of complex technical equipment" and "computer based teaching" in the framework of EC-funded cooperation projects.

Hypermedia

The research project "Hypermedia Dialog" intends to find out how Hypermedia and CSCW (Computer Supported Cooperative Work) methods and techniques can support social interaction. Hypermedia as a semi-formal representation of the structure and CSCW as a technique to model the process of such interaction will be evaluated.

One application will be "design rationale", a tool which will support large groups working together in such fields as software engineering. The project aims to use existing knowledge and to develop new methods in capturing the argumentation that underlies the cooperative design of large systems. We intend to build a generic prototype which will be used to evaluate different argumentation and cooperation models.

Speech Processing

Our research work in speech processing covers a wide range of topics from basic articulatory and phonetic research to on-line translation of spoken dialogs via telephone. Questions of recognition of single words, fluently spoken sentences, syntactic, semantic, discourse and pragmatic analysis are tackled in different projects. In the application area of train table information systems we build up a complete continuous speech understanding system.

One important sector of our research deals with the online translation of continuous speech. We are involved in a large research effort called VERBMOBIL, a joint program by a number of industrial and university partners funded by the German Ministry of Research and Technology (BMFT). The final goal of VERBMOBIL is the development of a portable translation unit for continuous speech. The "Interpreting Telephony" project works on translation of spoken dialogs (English, Japanese, German) over telephone lines.

Several of our projects are joint efforts with diverse universities and industrial research institutions and funded by national and European research agencies. Among the university partners are Carnegie Mellon-University, USA and the University of Karlsruhe, Germany.

User Interface Management Systems

We are developing the User Interface Development System (UIDS) SX/Tools that follows the principle of Direct Composition. The UIDS has been designed with specific consideration for requirements coming from industrial automation and control applications.

The most important feature of SX/Tools is its ability to handle interactive graphics (e.g. polylines, circles, etc.) and widely used control elements (e.g. buttons, menus, etc.) in a uniform way. Other important characteristics of this UIMS are extensibility, end user modifiability and openness towards the integration of existing and new interaction techniques.

SX supports the reuse of existing widget sets (e.g., OSF/Motif, Sun OLIT). Currently we are enhancing the system to support multi-media user interfaces. SX/Tools serves as the research environment for our project "Adaptive User Interfaces".

Adaptive User Interfaces

Our research project "Adaptive User Interfaces" deals with methods and tools for the design of user interfaces which can be adapted to individual users or user groups and to specific tasks. We call a user interface adaptive if it can easily be adapted by its user as well as if it is truly self-adaptive based on a model of the user and the relevant tasks.

The project has two main goals. We want to use existing techniques and tools for adaptive user interface behaviour and we will develop own methods for adaptivity. We intend to integrate the project results into existing user interface tools and to build up a prototypical implementation of an adaptive user interface which will be subject to extensive user acceptance tests. Finally we will analyse to which degree the results of the prototypical realisation can be used in different application domains. Part of the work will be done in cooperation with Georgia Institute of Technology, Atlanta.

SELECTED PUBLICATIONS

J. Grollmann and C. Rumpf: *Some Comments on the Future of User Interface Tools*, In: D. A. Duce et al. (Eds.): *User Interface Management and Design.* Proceedings of the Workshop on User Interface Management Systems and Environments, Lisbon, Portugal, 1990, Springer Verlag, pp 71 - 87.

U. Harke, M. Niemöller and K. Zünkler: *Towards a Multi-Media System: Integrating Computer Animation and Speech-Dialog Interface*, Proceedings of the MULTIMEDIA '90, 3rd IEE ComSoc International Workshop in Multimedia, Bordeaux, 1990.

H. Höge: *SPICOS II - A Speech Understanding Dialogue System*, Proceedings of the ICSLP '90, Kobe, Japan, 1990

Th. Kühme, G. Hornung and P. Witschital: *Conceptual models in the design process of direct manipulation user interfaces.* In: Proceedings of HCI International '91, Stuttgart, FRG, Sep. 1991, Elsevier, Amsterdam, 1991.

G. Niedermair, M. Streit and H. Tropf: *Linguistic Processing related to Speech Understanding in Spicos II*, Speech Communication 9 (1990), pp 565-585.

M. Niemöller and U. Leiner: *Simulation of Motion Dynamics: An Approximative Approach to Motion Specification in Computer Animation*, Proceedings of Computer Graphics 90, London, 1990, pp 229-240.

M. Schneider-Hufschmidt: *Designing User Interfaces by Direct Composition - Prototyping Appearance and Behavior of User Interfaces,* to appear in the proceedings of the NATO-Workshop on User-centered Requirements for Software Engineering Environments, Chateau Bonas, France, September 1991.

P. Witschital: *Why we need "composable" user interfaces.* In: D.G. Bouwhuis (Ed.): *Cognitive Modeling & Interactive Environments*, NATO ASI, Series F, Springer Verlag, Berlin, 1991.

ANTHROPOMORPHISM:
FROM ELIZA TO TERMINATOR 2

Moderator: Abbe Don
IN CONTEXT
3435 Clay Street #4
San Francisco, CA   94118
415-567-8130
abbe@well.sf.ca.us

Panelists: Susan Brennan, State University of New York at Stony Brook
Brenda Laurel, Telepresence Research
Ben Shneiderman, University of Maryland

INTRODUCTION

"I feel depressed."
"WHY DO YOU FEEL DEPRESSED?"
Eliza, 1966

"Open the pod bay door, Hal."
"I CAN'T DO THAT DAVE"
2001 A Space Odyssey, 1968

"MAN OF THE YEAR"
Time Magazine, 1982

"YOUR DOOR IS AJAR"
Chrysler Le Baron, 1983

"I WILL ERASE YOUR MESSAGES"
Phonemate Answering Machine, circa 1988

"YOUR FRIEND JILL GILBERT HAS PUBLISHED AN ARTICLE ABOUT DEFORESTATION IN THE AMAZON AND ITS EFFECTS ON RAINFALL IN THE SUBSAHARA"
Knowledge Navigator, Apple Computer, 1988

"HI, MY NAME IS BRENDA, AND I'LL BE YOUR COMPANION AS YOU USE THE AMERICANA SAMPLER."
Guides 3.0, Apple Computer, 1990

"HASTA LA VISTA, BABY"
Terminator 2, 1991

Within the human-computer interface design community, there is a longstanding tradition against the use of anthropomorphism in the interface. Like any taboo, simply sweeping away the issue   (assigning human characteristics to the computer) does not make it go away. The examples above highlight some of the contexts in which scientists, designers and filmmakers have explored the implications of anthropomorphizing the human-machine interface. Some techniques, such as talking cars, have dissipated in response to users' distaste. Others, such as the Guides approach, need further refinement; and still others, like the images floating through popular culture, warrant examination as they help us define both our fantasies and fears about our relationship to machines.

With command line interfaces and text only systems, the effect of the anthropomorphism taboo translated as, "don't use the first person in error messages." As Ben Shneiderman notes, a message that avoids pronouns altogether such as "To begin the lesson, press return" is preferable to "I will begin the lesson when you press return" [7]. However, as the field has matured, we are working with more sophisticated systems that involve graphics, full-motion video, sound and speech, virtual environments, and telepresence, as we collaborate with designers who come from traditions where anthropomorphism is not only accepted, but encouraged.

There are a variety of task domains in which representing the system in the interface runs up against this wall of resistance. The design of multimedia authoring tools and content may be the fastest growing domain as these systems move off of our desktops and into our living rooms now that CD-I, CDTV, and other consumer devices are actually on the shelves of department stores. With video on the computer screen, the human figure often plays a prominent role in the interface. Recently, there has been a discernible increase in the gratuitous use of the human figure with poorly lipsynched talking heads or systems that fool the user into thinking that the system is intelligent. However, there are also examples of effective uses of human characteristics that take advantage of the semiotic shortcuts provided by costume, gesture, facial expression or voice intonation to help explain why the system is behaving in a certain way.

Another task domain involves representing autonomous behavior in an information retrieval system or more general operating system. While the human figure is not always necessary for representing agency as defined by Alan Kay [2] or Brenda Laurel [3], anthropomorphism can be a useful tool for designers if its strengths and weaknesses are understood. In addition, a distinction between delegation and agency is emerging. While the act of delegating may make the user feel more in control than a system that implicitly forms a model of the user, the issues of representation and communication remain. When delegating the task of filtering email, for example, to whom or to what are we delegating the task? What is the nature of this entity and how do we communicate with it? What is the nature of the distinction between delegation and agency and how does it affect representations in the interface?

The limits of direct manipulation and desktop metaphors are most evident when we leave our desktops altogether and enter the immersive world of virtual reality systems or the portable world of "personal digital assistants" [4] a highly anthropomorphic term now in vogue among Apple Computer's marketeers used to describe portable electronic calendars, organizers and cellular communicators. Agency on the part of the system will need to be adequately represented while the conversational component of direct manipulation is enhanced.

Finally, it is difficult to discuss anthropomorphism without also re-examining the moral and philosophical issues associated with the debate. At the philosophical level, we are constantly redefining what it means to be human. As Sherry Turkle observes, "people have a stake in seeing themselves as different" [9] from machines. The inability to distinguish between human and machine, the real and the constructed, or to be unable to "pull the plug" plagues many characters in science fiction. According to Donna Haraway, "Late twentieth-century machines have made thoroughly ambiguous the difference between natural and artificial, mind and body, self-developing and externally designed, and many other distinctions that used to apply to organisms and machines. Our machines are disturbingly lively, and we ourselves frighteningly inert" [1].

PANELISTS' POSITION STATEMENTS

Susan Brennan
Susan Brennan a psycholinguist, received her Ph.D. in Cognitive Psychology from Stanford University. She also holds an M.S.V.S. from the MIT Media Lab, where she worked on computer-generated caricature and teleconferencing interfaces. She has done research in human-computer interaction at Atari, Apple Computer, and Hewlett-Packard Labs, including five years on HP's

Natural Language Project. She is currently Assistant Professor of Psychology at the State University of New York at Stony Brook. Her current research interests include the role of mutual knowledge in human communication, lexical choice, mental models of conversational partners, and conversational repair.

Those who debate the value or evils of anthropomorphizing the interface are missing the point. Certainly it's irritating to interact with a system that's superficially anthropomorphized or cute. And in an electronic medium, where communication takes place over a channel much narrower than face-to-face, imitating a human being can be misleading. But that is not a good reason to throw away all of speech and language as a communication modality.

There are classes of things that are done better with speech and natural language than with direct manipulation. These things include delegating complex or redundant actions and doing anything that's not in the here and now. When Sutherland [8] presented the first direct manipulation system, the idea was to enable people and computers "to converse rapidly through the medium of line drawings". What makes direct manipulation work is NOT the fact that it's visually conducted, but it is conversational. A conversational interface, whether it is visually or verbally conducted, results in a coherent sequence of behavior. And when speech and language interfaces become more conversational, they will take their place along with direct manipulation in the interface.

We should stop worrying about anthropormorphism and work on making systems capable of behaving as coherent interactive partners. Whether these partners are anthropomorphized or not, they should present their limitations frankly. People are used to dealing with many categories of partners: friends, strangers, the hard of hearing, disembodied voices on the telephone, readers who will come along after they are gone, foreigners, children, and dogs. This flexibility has been documented even among the very young; 5 year olds use more simple language when talking to 3 year olds than they do talking to adults (6). It is this fundamental adaptability of human beings to their partners that makes the whole human/computer enterprise possible in the first place.

Brenda Laurel
Brenda Laurel has worked in the personal computer industry since 1976 as a programmer, software designer, marketeer, producer, and researcher. Her academic background is in theatre, and she holds an M.F.A. and a Ph.D. in theatre from Ohio State University. In 1990, she joined Scott Fisher in founding Telepresence Research, a company to conduct research and development in virtual environments and remote presence technology and applications. Brenda has published extensively on such subjects as virtual reality design, computer-based agents, and interactive fiction. She is editor of the book, The Art

of Human-Computer Interface Design *[Addison-Wesley, 1990]* and *author of* Computers as Theatre *[Addison-Wesley, 1991]*.

"Virtual reality" is a medium that brings the whole issue of what an interface is into high relief. With more conventional systems, interfaces are conceived as ways of representing preexisting computational functionality to human participants. In virtual reality, on the other hand, the interface - that is, a multisensory medium that aims to establish a sense of presence in a representational context - is often a solution in search of a problem. The questions that most VR designers wrestle with are: What kinds of actions might one perform in this medium, and to what end? How can activity be paced? Without the familiar accoutrements of desktops, windows, or command lines, how can participants be constrained - that is, how does the world reveal its potential to a person, and how can a person be prevented from falling off the edge of the world? In the same way that people and other animate beings provide such constraints in "real life" situations through observation, interaction, and dialogue, agents are an obvious and powerful source of such constraints in virtual worlds.

In virtual environments, as in scientific visualization systems with conventional graphical interfaces, the whole point is to represent information, theories, processes, and ideas in ways that are directly accessible to the senses. The same theory applies to the representation of sources of agency. The central premise of virtual environments is to replace sensory input from the physical world with technologically mediated sensory information, without disrupting the connections between sensation, perception, cognition, and emotion. The aim is to enable people to respond holistically to such environments. There is no place in the theory of virtual environments for a disembodied "system" as a source of agency, communication, or collaboration; indeed, such disembodiment forces its mirror image on the participant and precludes the possibility of holistic response.

In the sense that the dogma of direct manipulation prohibits the use of anthropomorphic or animistic representations for complex agencies that exhibit organicity and/or emergent intelligence, it also precludes our use of such agencies as tools for thought, creativity, or productive work. It is not the notion of anthropomorphic agents that is the real obstacle to human empowerment through computers, but rather the straitjacket of interface orthodoxy and the persistent devaluation of any phenomenon which cannot be neatly measured in controlled experiments.

Ben Shneiderman

Ben Shneiderman is a Professor in the Department of Computer Science, Head of the Human-Computer Interaction Laboratory, and Member of the Systems Research Center, all at the University of Maryland at College Park. His technical interests include user interface design, human factors research in programming, hypertext, and computers in education. His 1987 book Designing the User Interface: Strategies for Effective Human-Computer Interaction *(1987), Addison-Wesley Publishers, Reading, MA (464 pages), has recently been published in Japanese, translation by Nikkei-McGraw-Hill, in its second edition.*

Every technology passes through an immature phase in which human and animal models are used as metaphors for design. Lewis Mumford describes the process in his chapter on "The obstacle of animism" in Technics and Civilization (1934): "the most ineffective kind of machine is the realistic mechanical imitation of a man or another animal...for thousands of years animism has stood in the way of...development."

The artificial intelligentsia have made the same mistake in their misdirected pursuit of human-like robots, natural language speech recognition to support interaction, and now human-like agents that magically maintain a user model and cleverly anticipate user needs like a perfect butler or secretary. I believe that these scenarios are obstacles in the development of truly powerful and simple tools that will empower users through direct manipulation of objects and actions.

My sentiments are based on my reading of historical precedents and on empirical studies. The talking automobiles and cash registers are gone, the human-like bank teller machines seem like anachronisms, and natural language interaction seems archaic and slow. By contrast, the dynamic visual world of direct manipulation brings us powerful spreadsheets, effective simulations, lively videogames, intuitive data visualizations, convenient page layout packages, and engaging graphical user interfaces. Users are empowered by having a clear predictive model of system performance and a sense of mastery, control, and accomplishment. Empirical studies consistently find support for direct manipulation styles of interaction. I call on those who believe in the anthropomorphic scenarios to build something useful and conduct usability studies and controlled experiments to compare their designs with direct manipulation. Direct manipulation designs can often be improved, but they are a more appealing direction, as far as I am concerned. I am sympathetic to human faces appearing onscreen if they are to represent human beings. My objection is when the computer is portrayed as a human; such misrepresentations are deceptive, counterproductive, and morally offensive to me.

REFERENCES

1. Haraway, Donna. *Simians, Cyborgs, and Women.* Routledge, New York, New York, 1991.

2. Kay, Alan. Computer Software. In *Scientific American.* 251,3 (September, 1984), pp. 52-59.

3. Laurel, Brenda. Interface Agents: Metaphors with Character. In *The Art of Human-Computer Interface Design*. Addison-Wesley, Reading, MA, 1990.

4. *MacWeek*, January 13, 1991, pp. 1.

5. Mumford, Lewis. *Technics and Civilization*. Harcourt Brace and World, Inc., New York, NY, 1934.

6. Shatz, M., & Gelman, R. The development of communication skills: Modifications in the speech of young children as a function of listener. *Monographs of the Society for Research in Child Development*. 38,5 (1973), 1-37.

7. Shneiderman, Ben. *Designing the User Interface: Strategies for Effective Human-Computer Interaction* Addison-Wesley, Reading, MA, 1987.

8. Sutherland, I.E. Sketchpad: A man-machine graphical communication system. M.I.T. Lincoln Laboratory Technical Report no. 296, Lexington, MA. 1963.

9. Turkle, Sherry. *The Second Self: Computers and the Human Spirit*. Simon & Schuster, New York, NY, 1984.

Action Assignable Graphics
A Flexible Human-Computer Interface Design Process

Matthew D. Russell, Howard Xu, Lingtao Wang

TAO Research Corporation

39812 Mission Blvd., Suite 205, Fremont, Ca. 94539

(510) 770-1344

ABSTRACT

As the state of graphical user interface design theory continues to mature from its beginnings in the mid-eighties, emphasis on reducing the burden of interface programming has become more prevalent. Across the many popular computer platforms used professionally today, a myriad of interface building packages have been designed with this concern in mind. Currently, however, no standard design methodology exists and more importantly, no construction package has emerged that significantly reduces programming effort while still providing the application interface programmer with full control over the design process.

Most interface construction tools are implemented so that the software developer retains full control over the elements of the design process that dictate interface object placement and interface control, but has no ability to completely specify how these components will look and how they function in unison. Interface look and functionality in most cases is rigidly controlled by the design software based on "standards" that exist on the hardware platform in use. While these pseudo standards, demonstrated by such systems as Microsoft Windows and Apple Macintosh, may have many commonalities, defining a design methodology that is applicable to all systems, providing the designer with the ability to make full use of the system capabilities, while still allowing some artistic creativity, has been difficult to achieve.

The importance of combining the issues of interface consistency and streamlining the interface for the needs of each individual application's needs has often been overlooked with emphasis always placed on consistency alone. The argument, as justified by certain research projects [1], is based on the idea that if every application a

user encounters has the same, or at least similar, interface design then the process of learning to use that application becomes much easier. However, this perspective is based on the concept of a generalized target audience in situations where the application design engineer will have trouble gaining a meaningful understanding of the end user's specific task requirements. In these cases consistency for the sake of easy learning makes sense.

Where this approach seems most likely to become a hindrance,however, is when an application is targeted specifically at a knowledgeable and highly skilled audience. In these situations, a "standard" interface appearance is either undesirable or impractical: "If a consistent interface supports learning but impedes skilled performance, and if its major use is by skilled users, then consistency is working against good design" [2]. Indeed, forcing standard appearances can often lead to decreased performance.

A good example of this is the current state of interface design found on the IBM-PC platform. Most interface building packages are either low level interface toolkits, like XVT Software's XVT system, that do little to help the non-programmer design a thoughtful interactive interface or higher level User Interface Management Systems (UIMS), like Microsoft Windows' Visual Basic, that provide a template approach to interface construction that inhibits the creation of an individualized look and feel (refer to Hix and Schulman [3] for a good definition of the differences between an interface toolkit and a UIMS),

As a first step in addressing these problems of interface design, a methodology is proposed (currently implemented on the PC platform) as part of an overall UIMS, in which the interface control program is constructed by allowing designer control over the look and feel as well as the content of a graphical interface. This paradigm is achieved by separating the graphical appearance of interface controls and other objects from the available choice of actions those objects may take. The methodology is labeled Action Assignable Graphics (AAG) to emphasize this separability. The only restriction placed upon the designer using the Action Assignable Graphics approach is that the implementation of the interface be created using one of seven basic control types common to the IBM and Macintosh environments, namely push buttons, radio buttons, check boxes, movable object icons, resize object icons, editable text entry fields (text input/output objects), or client area objects (graphics input/output objects).

By allowing an application designer control over the look and feel of the user interface, the trend towards user-centered design, which allows for considerations of the user's "cognitive abilities and cultural, professional, or personal preferences" [4], can be more easily achieved. The AAG process assumes that whenever construction of an interface begins, the designer has some specific goals in mind that may or may not be realized using previously built user interface appearances. Thus, building interface control programs proceeds from the ground up where the color, shape, and pattern of each individual interface component is defined by using geometric primitives controlled by a drawing package toolkit. Once created, the components may be assigned one of the fundamental action types to define their behavior and purpose during run-time. To produce more sophisticated behavior, the methodology allows for the specification of the group definitions that form sets of interface components. Grouped objects function as a combined whole and exhibit specialized run-time behavior depending on the fundamental action types assigned to the individual components. This type of component creation combined with a group formation and subsequent specialized behavior provides an interface designer with the ability to emulate the functionality of any type of interface behavior desired, as implemented on any system, while still retaining complete artistic control over the interface.

The AAG design method allows the application interface programmer to iterate a prototypical interface control program as part of the editing process to achieve a final product. The prototyping loop incorporates the process of physical design (the graphic appearance) and logic design (the action responses) and is terminated by a code generation step where the graphic and action information

is converted to a computer language equivalent written in the code used by the programmer's system, preferably C. Once this is accomplished the programmer may link the specific application modules to each desired interface component created in the interface control program skeleton. This means that the programmer's burden is reduced from complete interface creation down to simply filling in the details of an object-oriented interface specification structure.

Current work on the AAG methodology is by no means complete. The current direction of our research follows several parallel paths. The current implementation achieves its object-oriented design by residing on top of an underlying event driven run-time control structure that must still to some degree by considered by the interface programmer before a final application package can be completed. Therefore, one future development path is to completely remove all consideration of the event driven structure from the design process. Another line of possible evolution is to port the methodology onto other platforms such as UNIX. Should these endeavors prove successful, the next logical step will be to develop AAG interface compiler technology which would work to improve many areas of systems interface design research, such as techniques for generating high-quality code from basic conceptual models, assistance in semi-automated design decisions, and creating computerized verification of conceptual interface models compared against their global constraints.

REFERENCES

1. Polson, P. The consequences of consistent and inconsistent user interfaces. In Cognitive science and its applications for human-computer interaction. Lawrence Erlbaum. Hillsdale, N.J., 1988.
2. Grudin, J. The case against user interface consistency. Communications of the ACM. 32, 10 (Oct. 1989). 1166.
3. Hix, D. and Schulman, R.S. Human-Computer interface development tools: a methodology for their evaluation. Communications of the ACM. 34, 3 (Mar. 1991). 76.
4. Marcus, A. and van Dam, A. User-Interface developments for the nineties. Computer. 24, 9 (Sept. 1991). 52.

The AT&T Display Construction Set User Interface Management System (UIMS)

Joseph P. Rotella, Amy L. Bowman, Catherine A. Wittman
AT&T Bell Laboratories

The AT&T Display Construction Set UIMS is a software tool that can be used to build and provide interactive graphics displays. The user interface is separated from the application, typically a large software system that performs data collection, data manipulation, or communicates with other external applications.

Although the Display Construction Set uses the X Window System™ and OPEN LOOK™*, the application developer and the display builder do not need programming knowledge of either in order to build a system using graphical displays[1]. Before building displays, the format and types of data the application will present to the user interface are defined in the domain definition file, an ASCII representation of the data model of the application. For example, the domain definition file can model a network hierarchy of switches and cities. Integer values for traffic at each switch can be aggregated together to determine the total traffic for each city. Although many applications already describe a data model in a database schema and this appears to be

---

*The X Window System is a trademark of the Massachusetts Institute of Technology. OPEN LOOK Graphical User Interface is a trademark of UNIX Systems Laboratories, Inc.

a duplication of information[1], these models serve different purposes and may be structured differently. The application database schema may contain much more data than would be appropriate to present in the user interface and may be structured for optimal storage, retrieval, data collection or data manipulation. The user interface data model represents the data according to the conceptual model users have of the application and contains only data relevant to the user interface.

Communication between the application and the Display Construction Set is with ASCII messages sent through named pipes. An application sends data messages to populate the data model and does not need to contain any information about the user interface, achieving a desired separation between the application and the user interface [2]. For those times when this separation must be bridged, a vocabulary of messages have been defined that allow the application to duplicate most user interactions, including popping up, iconifying, resizing and quitting a window, and manipulating user controls like sliders and menus.

This architecture facilitates rapid prototyping by using a simple simulator to send application data messages over the named pipe. The prototype becomes the final user interface with no re-work when the simulator is replaced by an application on any hardware platform writing real data to the named pipe [3]. This architecture also facilitates multiple applications, often written at different times on different hardware to be integrated at the user interface level by sending data messages to a single Display Construction Set process using a data model that incorporates all of the available information.

User interactions can also generate messages that are sent out of the Display Construction Set process over named pipes, allowing a dialog between the application and the user interface and facilitating communication among the modules that make up the overall system [2].

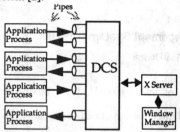

Figure 1. Display Construction Set Architecture

After the data model is defined, displays are built by placing graphical objects in windows and describing their behavior through the object's attributes. For example, the attributes of a polygon include its position, number of sides, color, and mouse button behaviors. An expression describes the value of each attribute.

This functionality has some similarity to a spreadsheet. In a spreadsheet model, the contents of a cell may be defined by writing an expression based on other cells. Attributes are bound to incoming data described in the data model, the value of graphical controls (such as a slider or exclusive choice), or environment variables by expressions. In a spreadsheet, if a number that a cell depends on changes, the cell changes too. Similarly, in the Display Construction Set, when the data that an object depends on changes, the object changes accordingly. The changes can be graphical or behavioral and are dynamic.

There are not two modes (construction and run-time), but one environment where changes are immediately reflected in the display. This "What You See Is What You Get" (WYSIWYG) environment advances the concept of suspended time editing by allowing changes to be made to the user interface while the interface is running and responding to dynamic data [3]

Every attribute contains a default expression. These defaults

were determined by looking at 4 large applications using the Display Construction Set to find the most frequently used expression for every attribute of every object. An expression editor guides the display designer through the syntax of the expression, so no programming skills are required to write expressions, only a knowledge of simple algebra. Over 65 operators and operands are available ranging from addition and subtraction to bit-wise manipulation of data to pattern matching [2] on text..

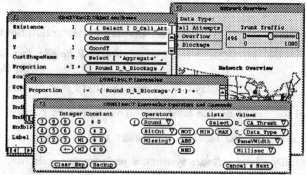

Figure 2. WYSIWYG Editing of *Proportion* Attribute

The Display Construction Set provides a construction interface to build and modify displays, as well as support tools to build display components. These tools are used to define the palette of colors used in displays, vector based background images and custom foreground shapes, pixel backgrounds, icons, and coordinate information.

The Display Construction set is suitable for many applications including network management, fleet management, forms, factory automation, process control, etc. The simplicity of its construction interface makes the Display Construction Set suitable for an application desiring to rapidly build, modify, and integrate a dynamic user interface.

[1] Green, M. Directions for User Interface Management Systems Research. *Computer Graphics 21*, 2 (April 1987), 113-116.

[2] Hill, R. Some Important Features and Issues in User Interface Management Systems, *Computer Graphics 21*, 2 (April 1987), 116-120.

[3] Rhyne, J., Ehrich, R., Bennett, J., Hewett, T, Sibert, J., and Bleser, T. Tools and Methodology for User Interface Development, *Computer Graphics 21*, 2(April 1987), 78-87.

AN INTERFACE FOR INTERACTIVE SPATIAL REASONING AND VISUALIZATION

James R. Osborn and Alice M. Agogino

Mechanical Engineering Department
University of California at Berkeley
Berkeley, California 94720
(510) 548-8464 • (510) 642-6450
osborn@me1.lbl.gov • aagogino@euler.berkeley.edu

ABSTRACT
An interface for software that creates a natural environment for engineering graphics students to improve their spatial reasoning and 3D visualization skills is described. The skills of interest involve spatial transformations and rotations, specifically those skills that engineers use to reason about 3D objects based on 2D representations. The software uses an intuitive and interactive interface allowing direct manipulation of objects. Animation capability is provided to demonstrate the relationship between arbitrary positions of an object and standard orthographic views. A second skill of interest requires visualization of a cutting-plane intersection of an object. An interface is developed which allows intuitive positioning of the cutting-plane utilizing the metaphor of a "pool of water" in which the object is partially submerged. The surface of the water represents the cutting plane. Adjustment of the pool depth combined with direct manipulation of the object provides for arbitrary positioning of the cutting-plane. Subjective evaluation of the software thus far indicates that students enjoy using it and find it helpful. A formal testing plan to objectively evaluate the software and interface design is underway.

KEYWORDS: spatial reasoning, three dimensional visualization, direct manipulation, engineering graphics

INTRODUCTION
Spatial reasoning is a mental process that involves thinking about relationships between three-dimensional (3D) objects. In the context of mechanical engineering, spatial reasoning frequently involves the skill of internally representing 3D objects described by two-dimensional (2D) representations displayed on paper or on a computer screen. However, many individuals drop out of engineering programs because of a lack of confidence in their abilities when confronted with the traditional presentation of introductory engineering graphics material such as descriptive geometry. The purpose of this development effort is to create interactive software that incorporates a user interface allowing these

students to improve their spatial reasoning abilities in a natural, intuitive, and self-motivating way.

SPATIAL REASONING TASKS AND SKILLS
Why is spatial reasoning necessary within many fields of engineering including mechanical and civil? The obvious answer is that these fields involve the design of 3D structures which are often interrelated in complicated ways. A more relevant answer from the perspective of a student in an introductory course in engineering graphics is that engineers often must abstract 3D information and relationships from 2D representations of objects.

Until recently, perhaps, almost all engineering design information was conveyed in the form of descriptions and 2D drawings on paper. The chosen 2D views are usually a standard set of orthographic views, which taken together, should unambiguously specify the 3D objects being represented. With the growing use of computers to store engineering design information, it is now common for engineers to work directly with 3D representations of objects. Nevertheless, these representations are still typically displayed on a 2D medium, the computer screen. Therefore, even if engineers use computers exclusively for representing design information, they must still be able to form a mental connection between the 2D representations that they are working with and the true 3D nature and relationships of the objects being represented.

Cognitive Science Literature
Some basic strategies have been identified that individuals typically use when solving spatial problems [3]. Consider a problem in which an individual must determine if several orthographic views are consistent with an isometric view. This type of problem is a task which involves the mapping between a 3D representation and several 2D representations of an object (Figure 1).

One possible strategy to solve this type of problem is to form a mental image of the object based on the given 3D representation of the object, then mentally rotate that internal representation into the corresponding orthographic positions, and finally test to see if it matches the given 2D views [8]. Another strategy could be to mentally compare

© 1992 ACM 0-89791-513-5/92/0005-0075   1.50

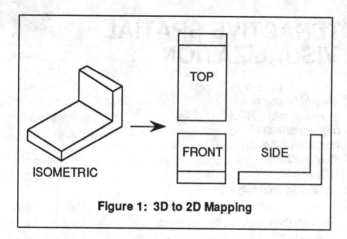

Figure 1: 3D to 2D Mapping

edges and edge intersections to procedurally test if the given isometric view is consistent with the given 2D views. As one might guess, the mental rotation strategy produces faster responses for individuals who are capable of using it. The procedural technique tends to be more accurate but is less efficient particularly for complicated objects. Evidence suggests that high aptitude spatial reasoners switch between both strategies flexibly to adapt to changes in processing demands and structural characteristics of individual problems [3].

Problems involving the opposite mapping are also important. In this case, the task involves the interpretation of a set of 2D orthographic representations of an object to determine if they are consistent with a 3D representation of the object. This skill is important to engineers who must understand 3D information represented with 2D drawings. In any case, visualization skills help individuals solve spatial reasoning problems by allowing them to create accurate internal spatial representations of objects.

Improving Spatial Abilities
The renovation of the engineering graphics curriculum is the focus of many current research efforts. Much of the motivation for this focus is based on the assumption that 3D solid modelling tools or other computer-aided tools will dominate engineering design in the future [1, 7]. Recent studies have shown a broad diversity in spatial abilities and learning styles [5]. Thus, regardless of the mode of instruction of engineering graphics, there is a need to improve general spatial reasoning and visualization skills. The premise of this software development effort is that spatial reasoning and visualization abilities can be improved by means of interactive courseware to build intuition and successful reasoning strategies.

Interactive Spatial Reasoning Software
The foregoing discussion indicates that it is desirable to enhance spatial reasoning abilities by increasing an individual's ability to form internal 3D representations of objects given 2D representations. Why use computers to accomplish this? Computers offer capabilities that are difficult to implement with paper exercises or static physical models. These capabilities include the possibility of a structured or guided interactive nature with dynamic

feedback. Computers are able to display moving images that capture the user's imagination and thereby create a "fun" environment for self-motivated improvement in spatial reasoning skills. The modern personal computer offers an effective platform for the creation of interactive graphics software that can be used to tap into a user's curiosity. Usage of this type of software could naturally enhance the connection between 2D representations of an object and its true 3D nature.

Several computer based approaches have been suggested to improve spatial reasoning abilities. One of these approaches utilizes solid modelling software as an environment to teach engineering graphics in a context which simultaneously enhances spatial reasoning and visualization skills. However, this approach provides less immediate feedback since considerable training is required before a student can begin to work with objects.

This development effort is primarily concerned with creating an interactive environment that students of all ability levels can use immediately, without training, to improve spatial reasoning and visualization skills. Usage of this software does not preclude any other approaches to engineering graphics instruction and should be used in parallel with whatever methods are taught including the more traditional approaches. In order to make the software immediately interactive, students should work with pre-constructed relatively simple objects. By keeping the chosen objects simple and using a simple internal software scheme, such as polygonal facets, to render the objects, this type of interactive nature with direct manipulation can be achieved.

DEVELOPMENT GOALS AND SPECIFICATIONS
The goal of the software is to improve the user's 3D to 2D mapping and 3D visualization skills. These skills are important in many aspects of engineering, but the primary focus of this software should be to improve the student's abilities at interpreting 2D representations such as engineering drawings. The standard orthographic top, front, and side views are fundamental to engineering drawing representations. Therefore, the software should give the user experience with these views and their relationship to the object being represented.

The view of an object from any arbitrary position is essentially a process of projection. The second fundamental goal of the software is to improve the user's understanding and experience with the concept of cutting-plane intersections. This type of experience can be very difficult to demonstrate dynamically with physical models. Since there are few everyday experiences which directly correspond to cutting-plane intersections, special attention must be made to ensure that the cutting-plane interface is not confusing.

One final goal that should be stated explicitly is that the software should be as intuitive and interactive as possible. This will ensure a positive and self-motivating result.

Ideally, the software should satisfy all of these goals and require no training, no manuals, and no keyboard input.

Based on these goals, the following software specifications emerged:

1. Provide an environment which allows the user to interactively explore any arbitrary position of a given object using direct manipulation.

2. Provide the capability to demonstrate standard orthographic and isometric views with animation.

3. Provide a cutting-plane mode which allows interactive arbitrary positioning of the cutting-plane relative to the object and displays the resulting cutting-plane intersection.

4. Provide all functionality of the software with a single-button mouse as the only required input device.

SOFTWARE DEVELOPMENT AND RESULTS

Direct Object Manipulation

The design of a user interface control strategy for direct manipulation of 3D images was of primary importance early in the software development. Fortunately, research which explores various methods for manipulating 3D images with 2D controls was available. In Chen et al. [2], several controllers are presented for manipulation of 3D images with a mouse. A software demonstration of five different types of controllers described in this paper was used to subjectively evaluate the "intuitiveness" of each.

Ten subjects who participated in this evaluation favored the two controllers called the "Continuous XY with Additional Z" controller and the "Virtual Sphere" controller. Both of these controllers define two regions within which mouse clicks are interpreted differently. The two regions are delimited by a circle which is circumscribed about the displayed object (Figure 2). The type of manipulation that occurs is defined by which region that the user clicks in. The other three controllers use more abstract metaphors for manipulation and were not considered further.

For both of these two controllers, the user can manipulate the object about any axis in the plane of the screen (XY control or rolling) by clicking inside of the circle and holding the mouse button down. The axis about which the object is rotated lies in the plane of the screen and is perpendicular to the path that the mouse is dragged. The user can manipulate the object about an axis perpendicular to the plane of the screen (Z control or spinning) by clicking outside of the circle and holding the mouse button down. The difference between the two controllers is that the "Virtual Sphere" allows some spin control within the circle as well as outside of it.

Though the subjects thought these two controllers were the most intuitive of the five controllers they tried, they felt the action was still somewhat non-intuitive since it required the artificial boundary created by the circle to discriminate the two dominate modes of operation for each controller. Brainstorming yielded the suggestion that the boundary of the object itself could be used instead of the artificial circle (Figure 3). The final control strategy is essentially equivalent to the "Continuous XY with Additional Z" controller but uses the object boundary to discriminate the two modes of operation instead of an added circle. The resulting action is very intuitive and a user requires very little practice to understand how to directly manipulate an object.

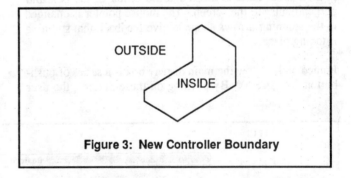

Figure 3: New Controller Boundary

Mouse Pointer Feedback

The capability of changing mouse pointer shape can be used to give added visual cues about the active regions of the interface and the behavior of the software (Figure 4). The normal "arrow" pointer (used for selecting menus, dragging windows, and clicking in buttons) is changed to a "hand" shape to indicate when direct manipulation is possible. When direct manipulation is initiated, the pointer changes to a "crossing-arrows" shape for rolling manipulation and to a "spinning-arrows" shape for spin manipulation. When the cutting-plane depth is being adjusted (described below), the pointer changes to a "grabbing-hand" shape.

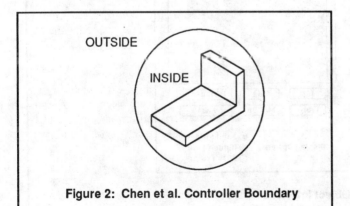

Figure 2: Chen et al. Controller Boundary

Figure 4: Arrow, Hand, Crossing-Arrows, Spinning-Arrows, and Grabbing-Hand Pointers

Display Options

Color was used as one display option to create a more realistic "solid-model" representation of objects. The usage of color is optional and secondary, however, and thus should not present any comprehension problems to color-blind users [6]. Hidden-line and wire-frame display modes in black and white are also provided. The availability of these three display modes allows the user to choose the particular representation most helpful and revealing for the particular object being viewed.

Display Object Interface

The primary element in the Display Object interface is the large square box in the upper-right portion of the interface window (Figure 5). In this box, the currently open object is displayed. As the mouse pointer enters the box, it is changed to the hand shape to indicate that direct manipulation of the object is possible. To perform rolling of the object, the user clicks on the object, and while holding the mouse button down, drags in the desired direction. The object is rotated about an axis in the plane of the screen which is perpendicular to the dragged path. To give the user feedback that rolling is taking place, the mouse pointer is changed to the crossing-arrows shape. To perform spinning of the object, the user clicks within the box, but not on the object, and while holding the mouse button down, drags in the desired direction. The object is rotated about an axis located at the center of the box and perpendicular to the screen. The mouse pointer is changed to the spinning-arrows shape to give feedback that spinning is taking place.

Immediately below the main display box is a series of push-buttons (Figure 5). By clicking on these buttons, the user

can choose to see the object animated into positions which correspond to the standard orthographic top, front, and side views. The object can also be returned to the isometric reference position or back into the last position that the object was in prior to directly manipulating or animating it. Finally, the object can be placed in an arbitrary position (mix up) without animation. This is provided so that the user can test his or her skills at manipulating the object into the standard orthographic positions.

The process of rolling the object is depicted in Figures 6 and 7. In Figure 6, the user has moved the mouse pointer into the main display box to prepare to manipulate the object. In Figure 7, the mouse has been clicked, held down, and dragged to roll the object in a new position.

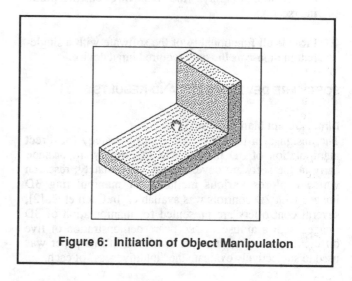

Figure 6: Initiation of Object Manipulation

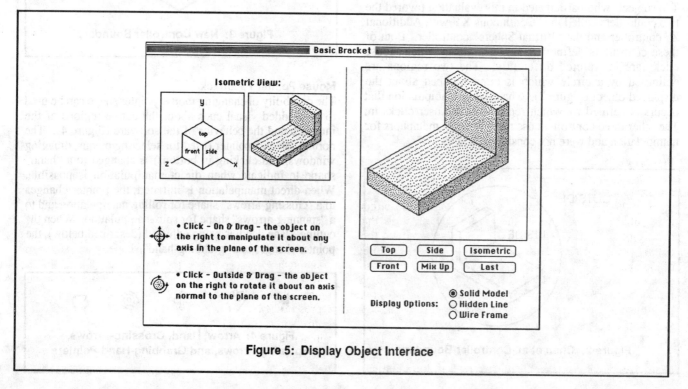

Figure 5: Display Object Interface

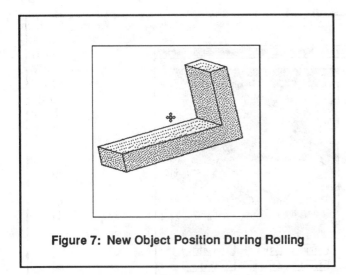

Figure 7: New Object Position During Rolling

To the left of the main display box are two small static images (Figure 5). One of these images is the current object displayed at one half its size and in an isometric position. This image is always in the isometric position. Next to this object image is an isometric cube which shows the position of the x, y, and z axes for the standard isometric position. The three visible faces of the cube are shown with the corresponding top, front, and side labels. These two images, taken together, are intended to provide a reference to the user which defines the standard views for the current object.

Immediately below the two reference images is a brief description of two direct manipulation techniques described above (Figure 5). The shapes into which the mouse pointer changes during object manipulation are visually reinforced by a pair of icons next to the descriptions.

In the lower-right portion of the window, three radio-style buttons are provided to select the object display option (Figure 5). This style of button indicates a set of mutually exclusive choices. Solid Model displays the object in color, Hidden Line displays the object in black and white with hidden edges removed, and Wire Frame displays all edges of the object in black and white.

Cutting-Plane Manipulation

The original idea for manipulation of a cutting-plane, and perhaps the most intuitive, involved always displaying the object in an isometric position and then providing a rectangular "plate" that would slice this image. By direct manipulation of the plate, the user could position the cutting-plane. However, to give complete control of the cutting-plane position, a lateral or front to back positioning of the plate would also be necessary. Thus, a cutting-plane control strategy based on this concept would need much more than the object manipulation control discussed previously since that control provides only for rolling and spinning.

A second problem with the above concept for cutting-plane control has to do with the display of the resulting cutting-plane intersection. If the user can directly manipulate the cutting-plane while the object remains stationary, then that plane could be flipped or rotated relative to its original position and will rarely be in a position parallel to the screen. When the corresponding cutting-plane intersection is displayed in a second area on the screen, the user might become confused by the relationship between the intersection and the cutting-plane itself.

An inversion of roles in the above concept solves the associated problems. Instead of leaving the object stationary, the cutting-plane is held stationary while the object is directly manipulated. With this type of control strategy, there is a one-to-one correspondence between the cutting-plane (now always parallel to the screen) and the separately displayed cutting-plane intersection. All that is needed to give the user complete control of the cutting-plane position is a front to back depth adjustment. This control strategy is a direct extension of the direct manipulation controller introduced with the Display Object interface. Therefore, it should be easier for the user to become accustomed to its action.

A "pool of water" metaphor can be associated with this control strategy. The surface of the water represents the cutting-plane. The depth of the water pool corresponds to the depth of the cutting-plane. The pool is represented by the color gray. The parts of the object behind the cutting-plane are dimmed to indicate that they are submerged.

A difficulty associated with this cutting-plane control method is that when the object is displayed in color, some users misinterpret the dimmed colors as shadows. Once the user understands the water pool metaphor, this confusion usually ceases. However, in an effort to provide a more intuitive cutting-plane user interface, the choice of a surface representation picture was added. The picture is drawn between the portion of the object behind the cutting-plane and the portion in front. A user can select one of several pictures or none at all.

Cut Object Interface

The main element of the Cut Object user interface for cutting-plane manipulation is the large square box in the upper-right portion of the interface window (Figure 8). The main display box is placed in the same position as it is in the Display Object interface, because once again, this box is used for direct manipulation of the object. As before, the mouse pointer is changed to the hand shape when it passes into this box, and is changed to the crossing-arrows or spinning-arrows shape when the object is manipulated. The display box itself now represents a portion of the cutting-plane. The background color within the box is gray to represent the pool of water. The parts of the current object behind the cutting-plane are dimmed to simulate submersion into the pool. Below the main display box, the same animation buttons and display option radio-style buttons are provided as in the Display Object interface.

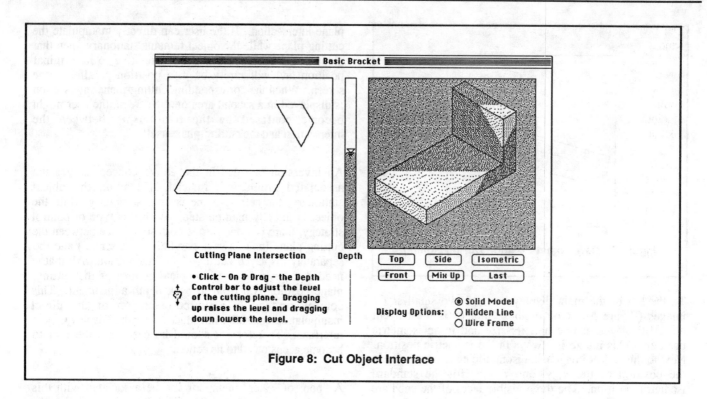

Figure 8: Cut Object Interface

Immediately to the left of the main display box is the water pool depth control (Figure 8). The mouse pointer is changed to the hand shape when it passes into the depth control region. By clicking in the depth control, holding the mouse button down, and dragging up and down, the user can adjust the pool depth and hence the cutting-plane position relative to the object. The mouse pointer is changed to the grabbing-hand shape to give the user feedback that depth adjustment is taking place. The partially submerged object is redrawn as necessary while the user continues to adjust the depth (Figure 9).

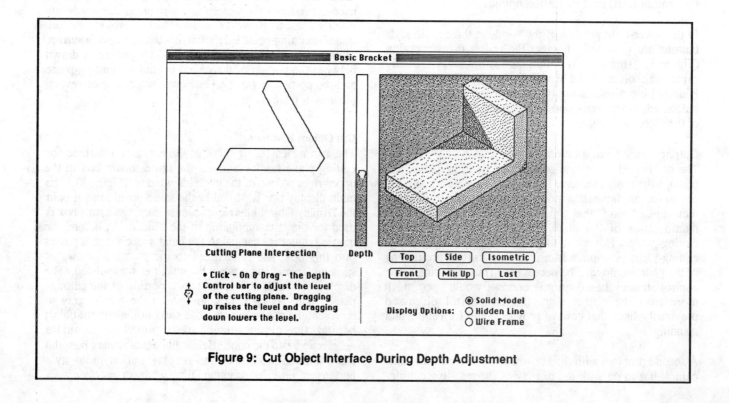

Figure 9: Cut Object Interface During Depth Adjustment

The large square box in the upper-left portion of the window displays the cutting-plane intersection (Figure 8 or 9). The intersection is drawn with the same scale as the object itself so that the one-to-one correspondence between the two images is emphasized. The intersection image is updated as necessary while the object is directly manipulated in the main display box and while the water pool depth is adjusted.

Below the cutting-plane intersection, a brief description is provided for water pool depth adjustment (Figure 8 or 9). This description is accompanied by a grabbing-hand icon to visually reinforce the mouse pointer feedback which occurs during depth adjustment.

A surface menu is added to the standard menu bar (at the top of the screen) to provide the user with a selection of pictures to serve as surface representations. The selected surface picture, if any, is displayed between the submerged and unsubmerged portions of the object. Several different types of pictures are possible including grids, wavy lines (to represent the water surface), or even lily pads! Figure 10 shows the Cut Object main display box with a surface picture reminiscent of a cartoon representation of glass using several groups of diagonal lines.

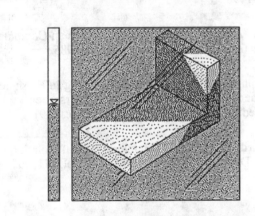

Figure 10: Cut Object Main Display Box With "Glass" Surface Picture

Implementation

The Apple Macintosh personal computer was selected as the development platform because of its graphics capabilities, its pre-existing intuitive interface, and its availability to a large number of users. The necessary Macintosh hardware configuration requires a minimum of 8 bit color to enhance the realistic representation of objects and a floating-point coprocessor to maintain the interactive nature of the software.

The selection of the Macintosh as the development platform allowed development efforts to focus primarily on the object manipulation aspect of the software. The usage of menus and windows in the software is consistent with the

rest of the Macintosh interface and hence did not require special attention.

The software was written in C using the THINK C development environment and makes full use of the Macintosh operating system graphics routines. The code which performs all transformations and other internal object representation algorithms were written from scratch in an effort to make the software as fast, and therefore as interactive, as possible. The objects are represented using polygonal facets. Back-face determination is used to sort the facets for simple convex objects. Optionally, a depth sort or a binary space partitioning tree can be used to sort the facets on more complicated objects [4]. The drawing of the objects is double-buffered to enhance the smoothness of the display.

Software Evaluation

Evaluation is currently in the formative stages. During the course of development, over 60 subjects have had the opportunity to use the software. Subjects ranged from junior-high school students to mechanical engineering undergraduate and graduate students. Over half of the subjects were given paper exercises before and after using the software. The exercises involved sketching orthographic views given an isometric view and vice versa. For the cutting-plane mode, subjects were given isometric views of objects and asked to predict if certain intersection depictions were consistent with those views. In another exercise, subjects were given the cutting-plane intersection (such as that shown in the left box in Figure 9) and asked to draw the cutting-plane onto a given isometric picture. Subjects universally had the subjective opinion that using the software was intuitive, helpful, and fun. Some subjects also reported improved self-confidence and increased motivation on spatial reasoning tasks.

An interesting observation drawn from some subject's descriptions is that the dynamic nature of the software makes the orthographic views more understandable. For these subjects, the capability to move the object slightly off of an orthographic position was enough of a hint to clarify their intuitive understanding of the object. Other subjects reported that color was extremely helpful in understanding the objects.

To obtain an objective evaluation of the software in terms of its usefulness in improving spatial abilities and visualization, a similar series of exercises will be administered to a larger group of subjects who are all students in the introductory engineering graphics course at U. C. Berkeley. The course typically has an enrollment of over 100 individuals. A strategy utilizing tests before and after software use with a control group that does not use the software is planned for the spring semester of 1992.

CONCLUSIONS

Based on subjective evaluation, the goal of producing an intuitive interactive software environment for manipulation of objects has been satisfied. Students do find the resulting environment intuitive, fun, and motivating. The design of an intuitive cutting-plane user interface was successful as a result of creating a novel "pool of water" metaphor which simplified the required user interaction and built on user interaction skills learned from direct object manipulation. However, the success of the software in improving spatial reasoning and visualization abilities has yet to be objectively verified. Plans are underway to accomplish this in the Spring of 1992.

Future development efforts include addressing the reverse spatial reasoning process involving mapping from 2D to 3D representations. Current concepts include a user interface which allows users to directly manipulate multiple orthographic representations of an object to see the relationship to the resulting 3D representation. Efforts will also be directed at the creation of a variety of exercises for use with the software and software integration with a hyper-scripting program to allow the development of intelligent tutoring interactive courseware.

ACKNOWLEDGEMENTS

The project discussed here was supported by the National Science Foundation as part of "Synthesis: A National Engineering Education Coalition," which is focused on the renovation of engineering education. The Spatial Reasoning Group at U. C. Berkeley (in alphabetical order) consists of: Alice M. Agogino, John E. Bell, Fred Beshears, Tom Knudsen, Howie Lan, Debbie Lee, Dennis K. Lieu, Marcia C. Linn, James R. Osborn, Alice Wong, and William Wood. The authors would also like to gratefully acknowledge the contributions of the collaborators at the Synthesis Coalition institutions: Rollie Jenison at Iowa State University and Adebisi O. Oladipupo at Hampton University. The authors would also like to thank Michael Chen for making controller demonstration software available. The software described here was developed using equipment donated to the University of California at Berkeley by Apple Computer, Inc.

REFERENCES

1. Barr, Ronald E., and Davor Juricic. The Engineering Design Graphics (EDG) Curriculum Modernization Project: A White Paper Summary. In Proceedings of the NSF Symposium on Modernization of the Engineering Design Graphics Curriculum (Austin, Texas, August 5 - 7). University of Texas Printing Department, Austin, Texas, 1990

2. Chen, Michael, S. Joy Mountford, and Abigail Sellen. A Study in Interactive 3-D Rotation Using 2-D Control Devices. In Proceedings of ACM SIGGRAPH (August). Vol. 22, no. 4, ACM, New York, 1988

3. Cooper, Lynn A. Strategic Factors in Complex Spatial Problem Solving. Invited paper presented at the 56th annual meeting of the Midwestern Psychological Association (May 4). Chicago, Illinois, 1984.

4. Foley, James D., et al. Computer Graphics Principles and Practice. 2nd Ed., Addison-Wesley, 1990

5. Linn, Marcia C. and Anne C. Peterson. Emergence and Characterization of Sex Differences in Spatial Ability: A Meta-Analysis. Child Development, 56 (1985), 1479-1498.

6. Monk, Andrew. Fundamentals of Human-Computer Interaction. Academic Press, London, 1985

7. Oladipupo, Adebisi O. Solids Modeling in Freshmen Engineering Graphics Using Silverscreen. In Proceedings of ASEE Annual Conference, 1991

8. Shepard, R. N., and J. Metzler. Mental Rotation of Three-Dimensional Objects. Science, Vol. 171, 1971

GRAPHICAL FISHEYE VIEWS OF GRAPHS

*Manojit Sarkar**

Department of Computer Science
Brown University
Providence, RI 02912
ms@cs.brown.edu

Marc H. Brown

Systems Research Center
Digital Equipment Corporation
Palo Alto, CA 94301
mhb@src.dec.com

ABSTRACT

A *fisheye* lens is a very wide angle lens that shows places nearby in detail while also showing remote regions in successively less detail. This paper describes a system for viewing and browsing planar graphs using a software analog of a fisheye lens. We first show how to implement such a view using solely geometric transformations. We then describe a more general transformation that allows hierarchical, structured information about the graph to modify the views. Our general transformation is a fundamental extension to the previous research in fisheye views.

KEYWORDS: Fisheye views, information visualization

INTRODUCTION

Graphs with hundreds of vertices and edges are common in many areas of computer science, such as network topology, VLSI circuits, and graph theory. There are literally hundreds of algorithms for positioning nodes to produce an aesthetic and informative display [1]. However, once a layout is chosen, what is an effective way to view and browse the graph on a workstation?

Displaying all the information associated with the vertices and edges (assuming it can even fit on a screen) shows the global structure of the graph, but has the drawback that details are typically too small to be seen. Alternatively, zooming into a part of the graph and panning to other parts does show local details but loses the overall structure of the graph. Researchers have found that browsing a large layout by scrolling and arc traversing tends to obscure the global structure of the graph [6]. Two (or more) views — one view

---

*Supported by summer research internship from Digital Equipment Corporation's Systems Research Center.

of the entire graph and the other of a zoomed portion — has the advantage of seeing both the local detail and overall structure, but has the drawbacks of requiring extra screen space and of forcing the viewer to mentally integrate the views. The multiple view approach also has the drawback that parts of the graph adjacent to the enlarged area are not visible at all in the enlarged view.

This paper explores a *fisheye* lens approach to viewing and browsing graphs. A fisheye view of a graph shows an area of interest quite large and with detail, and shows the remainder of the graph successively smaller and in less detail. Thus, a fisheye lens seems to have all the advantages of the other approaches and without suffering from any of the drawbacks.

A typical graph is displayed in Figure 1, and a fisheye version of it appears in Figure 2. In the fisheye view, the vertex with thick border is the current point of interest to the viewer. We call this point the *focus*. In our prototype system, a viewer selects the focus by clicking with a mouse. As the mouse is dragged, the focus changes and the display updates in real time. The size and detail of a vertex in the fisheye view depend on the distance of the vertex from the focus, a preassigned importance associated with the vertex, and the values of some user-controlled parameters.

Our work extends Furnas's pioneering work on fisheye views [4, 5] by providing a graphical interpretation to fisheye views. We introduce layout considerations into the fisheye formalism, so that the position, size, and level of detail of objects displayed are computed based on client-specified functions of an object's distance from the focus and the object's preassigned importance in the global structure. In Furnas's original formulation of the fisheye view, a component is either present in full detail or is completely absent from the view, and there is no explicit control over the graphical layout.

TERMINOLOGY

A graph consists of *vertices* and *edges*. The initial layout of the graph is called the *normal view* of the graph, and its coordinates are called *normal coordinates*. Vertices are graphically represented by shapes whose bounding boxes are square (chosen arbitrarily). Each vertex has a *position*, specified by its normal coordinates, and a *size* which is the

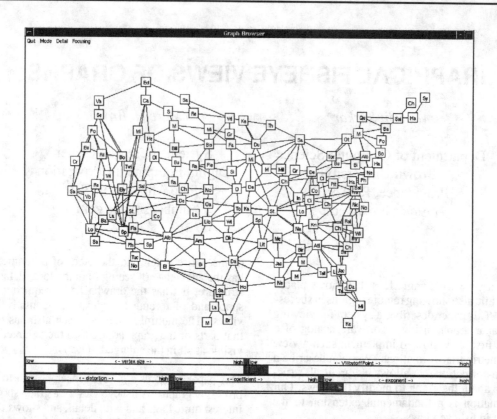

Figure 1: The initial layout of a graph with 134 vertices and 338 edges.

length of a side of the bounding box of the vertex. Each vertex is also assigned a number to represent its relative importance in the global structure. This number is called the *a priori importance*, or the *API*, of the vertex.

An edge is represented by either a straight line from one vertex to another, or by a set of straight line segments to simulate curved edges. Edges consisting of multiple straight line segments are specified by a set of intermediate *bend points*, the extreme points being the coordinates of its corresponding vertices.

The coordinates of the graph in the fisheye view are called the *fisheye coordinates*. The viewer's point of interest is called the *focus*; it is a point in the normal coordinates. Each vertex is the fisheye view is defined by its position, size, and the *amount of detail* to display. Finally, each vertex in fisheye view is assigned a *visual worth*, or *VW*, computed based on its distance to the focus (in normal coordinates) and its *a priori* importance.

GENERATING FISHEYE VIEWS

Generating a fisheye view involves magnifying the vertices of greater interest and correspondingly demagnifying the vertices of lower interest. In addition, the positions of all vertices and bend points must also be recomputed in order to allocate more space for the magnified portion so that the entire view still occupies the same amount of screen space.

Intuitively, the position of a vertex in the fisheye view depends on its position in the normal view and its distance

from the focus. The size of a vertex in the fisheye view depends on its distance from the focus, its size in the normal view, and its API. The amount of detail displayed in a vertex in turn depends on its size in the fisheye view. We now formalize these concepts.

The position of vertex v in the fisheye view is a function of its position in normal coordinates and the position of the focus:

$$P_{feye}(v, f) = \mathcal{F}_1(P_{norm}(v), P_{norm}(f)) \qquad (1)$$

The size of vertex v in the fisheye view is a function of its size and position in normal coordinates, the position of the focus, and its API:

$$S_{feye}(v, f) = \mathcal{F}_2(S_{norm}(v), P_{norm}(v), P_{norm}(f), API(v)) \qquad (2)$$

The amount of detail to be shown for vertex v depends on the size of v in the fisheye view and the maximum detail that can be displayed:

$$DTL_{feye}(v, f) = \mathcal{F}_3(S_{feye}(v, f), DTL_{maximum}(v)) \qquad (3)$$

Finally, the visual worth of vertex v depends on the distance between v and the focus in normal coordinates and on v's API:

$$VW(v, f) = \mathcal{F}_4(D_{norm}(v, f), API(v)) \qquad (4)$$

One has to choose the functions $\mathcal{F}_1, \mathcal{F}_2, \mathcal{F}_3, \mathcal{F}_4$ appropriately to generate useful fisheye views. Readers familiar with Furnas's work will note that our fundamental contributions are the existence of arbitrary functions $\mathcal{F}_1, \mathcal{F}_2$, and $\mathcal{F}_3$. In

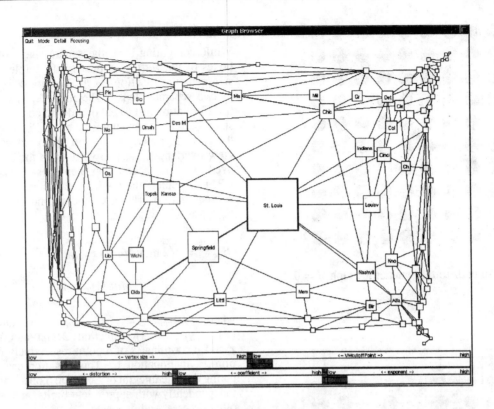

Figure 2: A fisheye view of the graph in Figure 1, $d = 5.71, c = 0, e = 0, VWcutoff = 0$

the next section, we present the set of functions we used in our prototype system.

FISHEYE TRANSFORMATIONS

Generating fisheye views is a two step process. First we apply a geometric transformation to the normal view in order to reposition vertices and magnify and demagnify areas close to and far away from the focus, respectively. Second, we use the API of vertices to obtain their final size, detail, and visual worth. In some applications, the API of all the vertices are equal, so the final size of all the vertices are equal and the second step is therefore unnecessary.

Mapping Position

Transforming from normal coordinates to fisheye coordinates, using focus position P_{focus} requires us to implement the function $\mathcal{F}_1$ in Equation 1. The function we used was

$$P_{feye} = \mathcal{G}(P_{norm})D_{max} + P_{focus}$$

where

$$\mathcal{G}(P_{norm}) = \frac{(d+1)\frac{D_{norm}}{D_{max}}}{d\frac{D_{norm}}{D_{max}} + 1} = \frac{d+1}{d + \frac{D_{max}}{D_{norm}}} \quad (5)$$

Note that the x and y dimensions are treated completely independently in the above mapping. This mapping is called the *cartesian* transformation. Later, we show a slightly different transformation called the *polar* transformation which is based on the polar coordinate system.

D_{max} is the distance of the boundary of the screen from the focus. The constant d in Equation 5 is called the *distortion factor*. The function $\mathcal{G}(x)$ is monotonically increasing and continuous for $0 \leq x \leq 1$ with $\mathcal{G}(0) = 0$, and $\mathcal{G}(1) = 1$. The derivative of $\mathcal{G}(x)$ is

$$\mathcal{G}'(x) = \frac{d+1}{(dx+1)^2} \quad (6)$$

This indicates that for large values of d the slope of the plot x versus $\mathcal{G}(x)$ near $x = 0$ is very high. This results in high magnification. The plot has a very low slope near $x = 1$ which causes high demagnification. The behavior of the function for $d = 0$ and $d = 5$ is as follows:

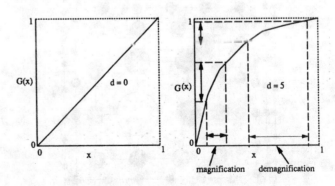

When $d = 0$, the normal and the fisheye coordinates of every point are the same.

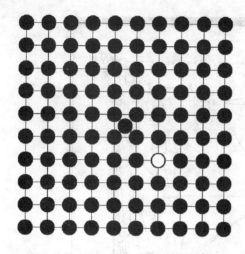

Figure 3: An undistorted symmetric graph, $d = 0$

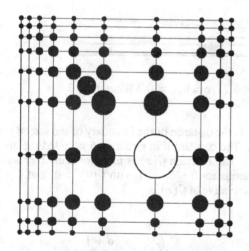

Figure 4: Cartesian transformation of symmetric graph, $d = 4$

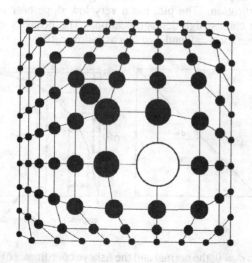

Figure 5: Polar transformation of symmetric graph, $d = 4$

Mapping Size

While computing size, the square shape of the bounding boxes of the vertices is preserved. Implementation of the size mapping function $\mathcal{F}_2$ in Equation 2 is described here in two separate steps. The first step uses the geometric transformation just found in order to compute the geometric size $S_{geom}(v, f)$ by ignoring v's API. This mapping has the special property that if no two vertices in the normal view overlapped, no two vertices in the transformed view overlap. The second step then uses $S_{geom}(v, f)$ and v's API to complete the implementation of $\mathcal{F}_2$. However, the vertices may overlap after the second step. We compute S_{geom} as follows:

$$S_{geom} = \sqrt{2} \min(MapX(x_{norm} + \frac{S_{norm}}{2}) - x_{feye},$$
$$MapY(y_{norm} + \frac{S_{norm}}{2}) - y_{feye})$$

where $P_{norm} = (x_{norm}, y_{norm})$ and $P_{feye} = (x_{feye}, y_{feye})$. The functions $MapX$ and $MapY$ map the x and y coordinates of a point respectively using the function $\mathcal{F}_1$ in Equation 1. This equation can be derived by taking definite integral of Equation 6 on x and y dimensions independently with appropriate limits, and then by making other necessary adjustments.

Finally, the function $\mathcal{F}_2$ in Equation 2 is implemented by

$$S_{feye} = S_{geom}(c \cdot API)^e s \qquad (7)$$

where the coefficient c, exponent e, and scale factor s are constants.

Computing Detail and Visual Worth

The functions $\mathcal{F}_3$ and $\mathcal{F}_4$ are implemented by Equation 8 and Equation 9 below. Both equations utilize S_{feye} computed by Equation 7.

$$DTL_{feye}(v, f) = \min(DTL_{maximum}(v), \alpha S_{feye}(v, f)) \qquad (8)$$

where α is a constant.

$$VW(v, f) = \beta S_{feye}(v, f) + \gamma \qquad (9)$$

where β and γ are constants. The *detail* and the *visual worth*, as calculated here, are essentially linear functions of size.

Mapping Edges

Straight line edges of the normal view get mapped to straight line edges in the fisheye view automatically when vertices at their end points get mapped. The edges with intermediate bend points can be mapped by mapping each bend point separately. Figure 4 demonstrates the effect of straightforward cartesian transformations on a symmetric graph.

Unfortunately, this straightforward approach does not preserve parallelism between edges. This problem can be circumvented by mapping a very large number of intermediate points on each straight line segment individually. However, mapping a very large a number of points may not be computationally feasible for real time response.

The mapping, however, has the property that all the vertical and horizontal lines remain vertical and horizontal after the transformation. Because of this property, our transformation is ideally suited for graphs with edges consisting of mostly horizontal and vertical line segments, for example VLSI circuits.

DISTORTION

Early users of our prototype system commented that transformations seemed somewhat unnatural, especially when applied to familiar objects, such as maps. Our framework allows us to address this complaint by using domain-specific transformations.

Consider for instance, the non-fisheye view of a map of the United States shown in Figure 6 and a corresponding fisheye view in Figure 7. A more natural fisheye view of such a map might be to distort the map onto a hemisphere. To do so, we developed a transformation based on the polar coordinate system with the origin at the focus (see Figure 5). In this transformation, a point with normal coordinates (r_{norm}, θ) is mapped to the fisheye coordinates (r_{feye}, θ) where

$$r_{feye} = r_{max} \frac{(d+1)\frac{r_{norm}}{r_{max}}}{d\frac{r_{norm}}{r_{max}} + 1} \qquad (10)$$

Here, r_{max} is the maximum possible value of r in the same direction as θ. Note that θ remains unchanged by this mapping. Figure 8 shows a resulting fisheye view of the map of the United States. This can be contrasted to Figure 7 which shows a fisheye view of the same outline using the cartesian transformation of Equation 5.

Another factor contributing to the perceived unnaturalness of the fisheye view is that the shapes of vertices remain undistorted and edges remain straight lines (ignoring bend points). We could remedy this by mapping many points on the outline of the vertex, and mapping a large number of intermediate points for the edges, thus allowing the vertices and edges to become curved. However, in our prototype browser, we chose not to do so, in order to achieve real time performance.

THE PROTOTYPE SYSTEM

Our system displays a fisheye view of a user-specified graph, and updates the display in real time as the user moves the focus by dragging with the mouse. Sliders allow the user to control of the value of the distortion factor d in Equation 5, the coefficient c and the exponent e in Equation 7, the vertex scaling factor s also in Equation 7, and a cutoff point at which vertices and their incident edges should no

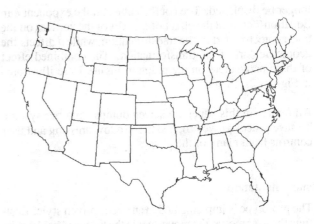

Figure 6: Outline of the United States

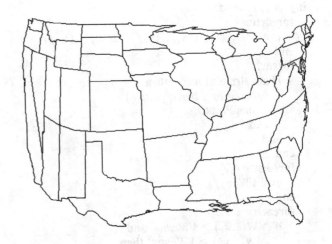

Figure 7: A cartesian transformation of Figure 6. The focus is at the point where Missouri, Kentucky, and Tennessee meet.

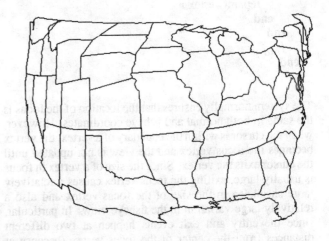

Figure 8: A polar transformation of Figure 6. The focus is at the point where Missouri, Kentucky, and Tennessee meet.

longer be displayed. The coefficient c and the exponent e in Equation 7 control the effect of the API of the vertices on the non-geometric part of the transformation, while d affects the geometric part of the transformation. The combined effect of these parameters on the graph in Figure 1 are illustrated in Figures 2, 12, and 13.

All figures in this paper are screen dumps from our system. To save space, we've cropped the window dressing and user controls from many of the images.

Implementation

The prototype is implemented in an event-driven style. Each time the user moves the mouse while the button is held down, the function $GetFocus$ returns the position of the mouse:

```
loop
    f := GetFocus()
    if f ≠ f_old then
        foreach v ∈ V
            eval P_feye(v, f), S_feye(v, f), DTL_feye(v, f)
        end
        foreach e ∈ E
            if not straightLine(e) then
                foreach bp ∈ bendPoints(e)
                    mapPoint(bp, f)
                end
            end
        end
        foreach v ∈ V
            eval VW(v, f)
        end
        foreach e ∈ E
            if VW(e.v_1) ≥ VWcutoff and
               VW(e.v_2) ≥ VWcutoff then
                repaint edge between v_1 and v_2
            end
        end
        sort V in order of VW
        foreach v ∈ V in nondecreasing order of VW
            if VW(v) ≥ VWcutoff then
                repaint vertex v
            end
        end
        f_old := f
end
```

The system normally ensures that the location of the focus is the same in both normal and fisheye coordinates. However, when the cursor is within the boundary of a vertex, the vertex becomes the focus vertex and the view is not updated until the cursor exits the vertex. Since the size of a vertex in focus is usually large, exiting the focus vertex causes a relatively large shrinkage in the size of the focus vertex and also a relatively large variation in the fisheye view. In particular, since the entry and exit events happen at two different distances from the center of the focus vertex (because at exit-time the size of the vertex is larger than its size at entry-time), without careful coding an exit event causes the most

recent focus vertex to shift away by a large distance from the cursor in a jerky motion. One approach to solving this problem is to force the cursor to be positioned just outside the boundary of the most recent focus vertex on each exit event.

Sorting the vertices in order of their visual worth produces a very useful order. First, if the position of two vertices are in conflict, their VW can be used to resolve the conflict in favor of displaying the vertex with higher VW. Second, the order can be used to maintain the real time response of the system, as we shall discuss below.

Response Time

Our prototype system is able to maintain real time response on a DECstation 5000 for graphs of up to about 100 vertices and about 100 horizontal or vertical edges. Computing fisheye views takes an insignificant amount of time compared to the time required for painting. Real time response cannot be maintained for graphs with significantly larger number of vertices and edges. Performance also suffers when the the percentage of edges that are neither horizontal nor vertical is increased.

An alternative "inner loop" is to display "approximate" fisheye views by painting only a fixed number of vertices and edges, irrespective of the size of the graph. Each time there is a new focus, quickly compute the new fisheye view for all vertices, but repaint only those nodes and edges which will give the best approximation to the perfect fisheye view. Nodes with highest change in their VW and nodes with highest current VW are good candidates. One can take a suitable mix of these two types of nodes, as well as all the associated edges. Each update operation will then involve erasing and painting a fixed number of nodes and edges.

System Notes

The prototype is implemented using Modula-3 and Trestle, a portable X-toolkit [8]. This project was the first Trestle application to be written,[1] beyond the handful of small examples in the distribution package. A number of features that we needed for real time animation (e.g., fast double buffering), and aesthetic drawings (e.g., curves and lines of arbitrary thickness) were not functional when the initial prototype was developed during the summer of 1991. We are currently upgrading to the latest release of Trestle.

GENERALIZED FISHEYE VIEWS AND RELATED WORK

Our work follows from the *generalized* fisheye views by Furnas [4, 5]. Furnas gave many compelling arguments describing the advantages of fisheye views, and performed a number of experiments to validate his claims. The essence of Furnas's formalism is the "degree of interest" function for an "object" relative to the "focal point" in some "structure". Our notion of "visual worth" (see Equation 4) is nearly identical to Furnas's degree of interest. The difference is that we

---

[1] A Modula-2 version of Trestle that doesn't use the X-toolkit has been operational for a number of years at DEC SRC.

have (thus far) described distance as the Euclidean distance separating two vertices in a graph, whereas Furnas defined the distance function as an arbitrary function between two objects in a structure. Our system supports generalized fisheye views by recoding the distance function used explicitly in Equation 4 and implicitly by Equations 1–3.

For instance, consider the graph in Figure 9 (all edges point downwards). The graphical fisheye view of the graph is shown in Figure 10. The API of each vertex is related to its display level (e.g., the root has the highest API of 8, node 33 has an API of 4, and node 86 has an API of 2). The distance between vertices is their Euclidean distance. A vertex is displayed only if its visual worth is above some threshold, and its position, size, and level detail are computed using Equations 1, 2, and 3, respectively. A "generalized" fisheye view of that same graph, with the same focus, is shown in Figure 11. Here, the API is as before, but the distance function not geometrical; it is the length of the shortest path between a vertex and the vertex defining the focus, as proposed by Furnas [5]. Notice that in the generalized fisheye view, each node is either displayed or omitted; there is no explicit way to vary size and and level of detail.

Furnas raised the question of multiple foci [5], but left it unanswered. Our framework can be extended to multiple foci. A simple approach is to divide the screen-space among all the foci (using some criteria), and then apply the transformation independently on each portion of the screen.

Furnas cites a delightful 1973 doctoral thesis by William Farrand [3] as one of the earliest uses of fisheye views of information on a computer screen. The thesis suggests transformations similar to our cartesian and polar transformations, but provides few details.

Last year at CHI '91, Card, Mackinlay, and Robertson presented two views of structured information that have fisheye properties. The *perspective wall* [7] maps a wide 2-dimensional layout into a 3-dimensional visualization. The center panel shows detail, while the two side panels, receding in the distance, show the context. The *cone tree* [9] displays a tree with each node the apex of a cone, and the children of the node positioned around the rim of the cone. The fact that the tree is beautifully rendered in 3D, including shadows and transparency, provides the basic fisheye property of showing local information in detail (because when it is close to the viewer it is large), while also showing the entire context. It would be interesting to experimentally compare cone trees and generalized graphical fisheye views as techniques for visualizing hierarchical information.

It may be fruitful to combine fisheye views with other techniques for viewing extremely large data. For example, related nodes can be combined to form cluster nodes, and the member nodes of a cluster node can be thought of as the detail of the cluster node [2]. The amount of detail to be shown can then be computed using the framework we have presented in this paper. In situations where the information associated with the nodes is very large, one can use fisheye views as navigation tool while the actual information in nodes can be displayed in separate windows.

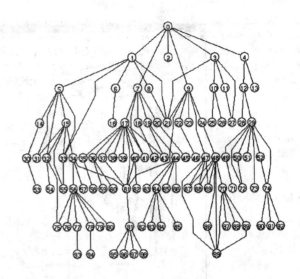

Figure 9: A graph with 100 vertices and 124 edges.

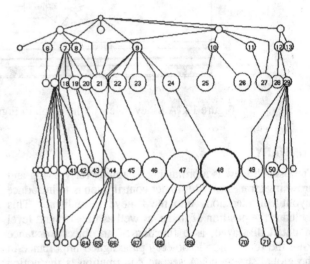

Figure 10: A graphical fisheye view of 9. The focus is on the vertex labeled 48

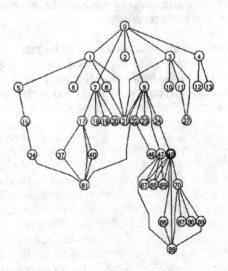

Figure 11: A generalized (non-graphical) fisheye view of 9. The focus is on the vertex labeled 48.

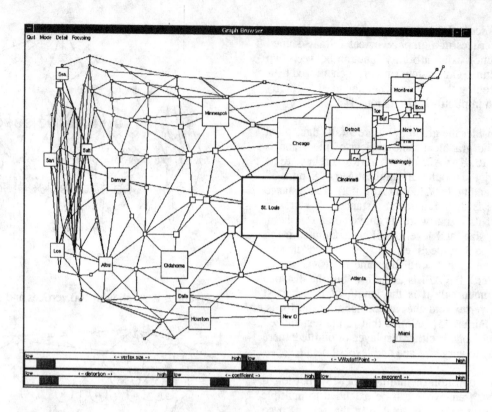

Figure 12: A fisheye view of the graph in Figure 1, $d = 2.38$, $c = 1.0$, $e = 1.14$, $VWcutoff = 0$

SUMMARY

The fisheye view is a promising technique for viewing and browsing structures. Our major contribution is to introduce layout considerations into the fisheye formalism. This includes the position of items, as well as the size and level of detail displayed, as a function of an object's distance from the focus and the object's preassigned importance in the global structure. A second contribution is the notion of a normal coordinate system, thereby allowing layout to be viewed as distortions of some normal structure. As we pointed out, our contributions apply to generalized fisheye views of arbitrary structures (by changing the interpretation of "distance"), in addition to graphs.

It is important to realize that we do not claim that a fisheye view is *the* correct way to display and explore a graph. Rather, it is one of the many ways that are possible. Discovering and quantifying the strengths and weaknesses of fisheye view are challenges for the future.

ACKNOWLEDGMENTS

Jorge Stolfi helped with various ideas concerning geometric transformations. Steve Glassman, Bill Kalsow, Mark Manasse, Eric Muller, and Greg Nelson extricated us from numerous Modula-3 and Trestle entanglements. George Furnas helped to improve the clarity of this presentation considerably.

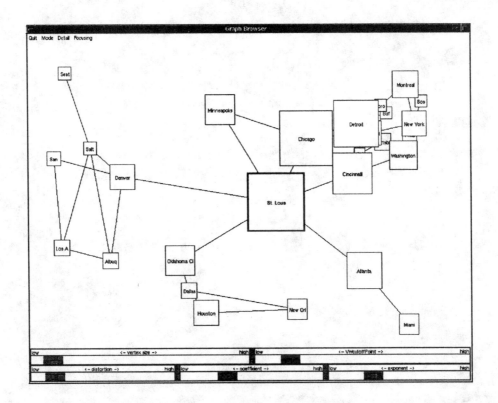

Figure 13: A fisheye view of the graph in Figure 1, $d = 2.38, c = 1.0, e = 1.14, VWcutoff = 0.27$

REFERENCES

[1] Peter Eades and Roberto Tamassia. Algorithms for drawing graphs: An annotated bibliography. Technical Report CS–89–90, Department of Computer Science, Brown University, Providence, RI, 1989.

[2] Kim M. Fairchild, Steven E. Poltrok, and George W. Furnas. SemNet: Three-dimensional graphic representations of large knowledge bases. In *Cognitive Science and Its Applications for Human Computer Interaction*, pages 201–233, 1988.

[3] William Augustus Farrand. Information display in interactive design. Ph.D. Thesis, Department of Engineering, UCLA, Los Angeles, CA, 1973.

[4] George W. Furnas. The fisheye view: A new look at structured files. Technical Memorandum 82–11221–22, Bell Laboratories, 1982.

[5] George W. Furnas. Generalized fisheye views. In *Proc, ACM SIGCHI '86 Conf. on Human Factors in Computing Systems*, pages 16–23, 1986.

[6] Tyson R. Henry and Scott E. Hudson. Interactive graph layout. In *Proc. ACM SIGGRAPH, SIGCHI Symposium on User Interface Software and Technology*, pages 55–65, 1991.

[7] Jock D. Mackinlay, George G. Robertson, and Stuart K. Card. The perspective wall: Detail and context smoothly integrated. In *Proc. ACM SIGCHI '91 Conf. on Human Factors in Computing Systems*, pages 173–179, April 1991.

[8] Greg Nelson, Editor. *Systems Programming with Modula-3*. Prentice Hall, Englewood Cliffs, NJ, 1991.

[9] George G. Robertson, Jock D. Mackinlay, and Stuart K. Card. Cone Trees: Animated 3D visualizations of hierarchical information. In *Proc. ACM SIGCHI '91 Conf. on Human Factors in Computing Systems*, pages 189–194, April 1991.

A Magnifier Tool for Video Data

Michael Mills, Jonathan Cohen and Yin Yin Wong

Human Interface Group/Advanced Technology
Apple Computer, Inc.
20525 Mariani Ave., MS 76-3H
Cupertino, California 95014
Mills@apple.com

ABSTRACT
We describe an interface prototype, the Hierarchical Video Magnifier, which allows users to work with a video source at fine-levels of detail while maintaining an awareness of temporal context. The technique allows the user to recursively magnify the temporal resolution of a video source while preserving the levels of magnification in a spatial hierarchy. We discuss how the ability to inspect and manipulate hierarchical views of temporal magnification affords a powerful tool for navigating, analyzing and editing video streams.

KEYWORDS: Interface Metaphors, Time-Varying Data, Hierarchical Representation, Multimedia Authoring, Information-Retrieval, Video Editing, Granularity of Information

INTRODUCTION
Compared to a real desktop, today's electronic desktop is a cramped work area. There is not enough space on a typical computer screen to spread out the actual-size pages of a document nor to show a normal size photograph in its entirety. Hence, one of the classic challenges of human interface design is to overcome the spatial bounds of small, limited resolution screens—to design electronic workspaces which allow users to work with partial, detailed views of objects, while maintaining a sense of context.

In the last few years, there have been a number of innovative interface techniques designed to provide users a sense of simultaneous awareness of detail and context when working with large information spaces. For example, Spence and Apperley [6] built a "Bifocal Display" to help people work with office documents at different levels of granularity — journals, volumes, issues, etc.. In a similar vein, Furnas [2] has experimented with a Fisheye Lens in order to facilitate smooth navigation between detailed and global views of large amounts of information. More recently, Mackinlay and his colleagues [4] have begun to apply techniques of 3D modeling and animation (a manipulable 3D "Perspective Wall")

in order to make the integration of detail and context even more natural: closer to the way the human visual system provides fine foveal detail, yet maintains awareness of peripheral context.

WORKSPACES FOR TIME-VARYING DATA
Just as users need tools for working with static images and text at different levels of detail, so they need *temporal* magnification tools when working with dynamic data types--movies, animations and sounds. In editing a movie, for example, someone might want to "zoom-in" on a small temporal chunk--say a second's worth of video -- in order to analyze subtle effects of a scene transition. At the next moment, they may want to switch to a high level overview of the movie in order to navigate to a neighboring scene.

Being able to vary the "grain" of detail in viewing an object, whether spatial or temporal, may not in itself provide an effective workspace. The problem is how to give users a sense of orientation--to help them understand how the part they are looking at (a small region of an image, a small chunk of video) relates to the whole. In working with spatial objects, for example, not having a context view can make navigation difficult. It can be a perceptual challenge to locate specific sections of a large image if one is limited to seeing, at any one time, blow-ups of smaller regions: i.e., where the image as a whole must be constructed in the "mind's eye" out of successive partial views [3]. Similarly, it can be hard to navigate, with any precision, to different segments of a long video source if one is restricted to viewing small temporal fragments.

To provide users a sense of spatial orientation when working with large images, many paint programs let them edit magnified, partial views, while providing a "proxy" of the entire image in a separate window or inset. A proxy is a kind of low-resolution surrogate for the real data. (See Moore, *et al* [5] for a discussion of proxies and their interface implications.] In this paper, we describe an interface prototype, the Hierarchical Video Magnifier, whose goal is to address the problem of providing users a sense of *temporal orientation*. How can we enable the user to work with large amounts of time-varying data at fine levels of detail, while at the same time maintaining a sense of temporal context?

Many present-day computer-based video editing systems attempt to provide the user a limited sense of temporal context by using a spatial timeline. This often takes the form of a slider or scrollbar whose horizontal axis represents the total duration of the event. An example is shown in **Figure 1**. Playing the video at normal speed will update the horizontal position of the indicator (the rectangular "thumb") along the timeline at the appropriate rate. If the video is a controllable source such as a laserdisk or digital movie, the user can quickly "scan" the video by dragging the indicator along the scrollbar. If there are fewer pixels constituting the horizontal length of slider than there are frames in the video, the player will "skip" frames during dragging—a form of temporal compression.

Figure 1. A real-time scrollbar for video data

The scrollbar *qua* timeline serves as a frame-of-reference for the currently displayed video frame (a detailed view). For example, the indicator's position on the timeline helps the user visualize the location of the currently visible frame relative to the total duration of the video. By observing this relationship the user can answer such questions as: "Given that I'm looking at the skyline scene, about how much of the video remains?" Or, "Show me the frame that is half-way into the movie." Hence, the timeline provides a temporal overview which can be used to navigate the video.

While the scrollbar does provide a temporal context, it is an extremely impoverished representation of the video source. Consider such questions as, "Does the carousel scene come

before or after the roller-coaster scene?" "Does the stabbing scene occur in more than one place throughout the movie?" "Is the cigarette-lighting scene part of the bedroom scene or part of the eating-dinner sequence?" There is no explicit information on the scrollbar which provides answers to such questions. Nor does the scrollbar give any clues as to where one should click on the scrollbar to find the answers. In sum, the impoverished contextual information on the scrollbar limits its usefulness as a navigational aid. It contains no clues about the content and structure of the video source.

The Hierarchical Video Magnifier attempts to overcome some of the limits of the basic timeline representation described above. It combines a navigable timeline with a richer representation of the video source in order to provide the user a more powerful tool for working with the structure and content of video data. The basic idea is as follows. We begin with a timeline to represent the total duration of the video source. But instead of just using it to navigate a video source at a single level of granularity, we supply the user with: (1) a series of low-resolution video frame samples arrayed along the timeline to give some sense of the video content, (2) a "temporal magnifier"—a tool which can be used to "expand" or "reduce" the effective temporal resolution of any portion of the timeline; and (3) perhaps most uniquely, we maintain a context view — an explicit spatial hierarchical structure of the video source— which results from successive applications of the temporal magnifier.

HOW THE VIDEO MAGNIFIER WORKS

Let us examine how the Hierarchical Video Magnifier might be used to explore the contents of a fairly large video source—30 minutes worth of full-motion video stored on a controllable laserdisc. (While our example concerns examining the contents of an analog source, the interface technique is general: i.e., could apply to a digital movie or even a waveform representation of a sound). The Magnifier application is currently implemented on a Macintosh-II equipped with a video digitizing card. **Figure 2** shows the initial state of the application when it is opened. There are three main windows. First, is a "video source" window for monitoring the real-time play back of the laserdisc contents. Second, is a software controller for navigating the analog video. Third, is the window containing the hierarchical magnifier.

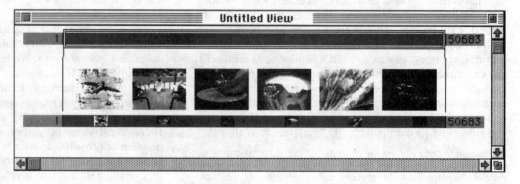

Figure 2. The three main elements of the video magnifier application.

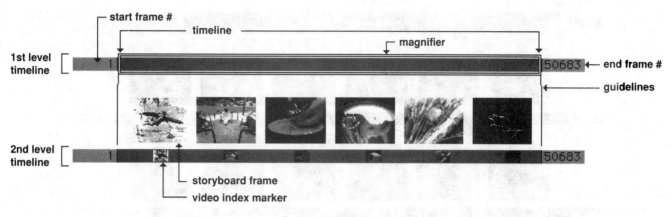

Figure 3. The hiearchical magnifier.

Let's look more closely at the elements of the Magnifier window. See **Figure 3**. At the very top is a timeline — the gray bar — which represents the total duration of the video source; in this case, a laserdisk containing 50,683 frames. The numbers corresponding to the first and last frames are shown at the boundaries of the timeline. A rectangular magnifier surrounds the entire length of this top-level timeline. Note that there are "guide wires" descending from both ends of the magnifier to a second timeline below. This second timeline represents the range of the magnifier. In this case, the magnifier covers the entire length of video. Below the gray magnifier are six low-resolution frames (60 x 80 pixels) equally spaced along the timeline. These six frames represent an extremely compressed view of the entire video source. They have been generated by digitizing still-frame samples at regular intervals from the video stream--in this example a sample for approximately every 8000 frames. This view is not meant to convey the precise temporal relationships among the frames. Rather, it serves as a kind of "storyboard" giving the user some information about the *order* of events across the entire video source. (In future implementations, we plan to use scene change detection algorithms to generate the storyboard frames. By adjusting the threshhold for scene-change detection, we can vary the number of frame samples per row.)

This second level timeline contains miniatures of the larger frames appearing the storyboard view. These miniature frames serve as "video markers"—position indicators which can be dragged along the timeline to "scan" the video source. Dragging a frame marker to the right, for example, will update: (1) the contents of the video source window, (2) the video marker's own contents (display the frame corresponding to its new position along the timeline) and (3) the larger storyboard frame to which it corresponds. By manipulating the video markers, the user can quickly customize the contents of the second-level timeline.

The Temporal Magnifier

In its initial state, the range of the temporal magnifier (the rectangular outline surrounding the top most timeline) extends across the entire length of the timeline. This gives the greatest degree of temporal compression — the coarsest view— of the video source. The six frames have been sampled from roughly 50,000 frames ($\approx$ 8000:1 ratio). By changing the width of the magnifier, the user applies the magnifier to a smaller region of the timeline, as shown in **Figure 4**. This effectively lowers degree of temporal compression ($\approx$4000:1 ratio) and hence, gives a more fine-grained view of a smaller chunk video ($\approx$ 25,000 frames). Note that the contents of the frames, the video index markers and the frame numbers of the second level timeline have been updated to reflect the smaller range of the magnifier. In addition to adjusting its width, the user can position the magnifier over any segment of the timeline. Hence, the magnifier is a tool which can be used to sample the entire stream of video at different effective levels of temporal resolution.

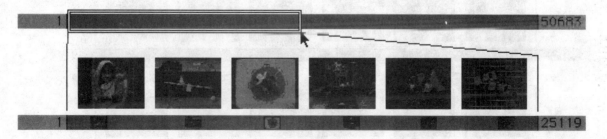

Figure 4. Adjusting the range of the magnifier.

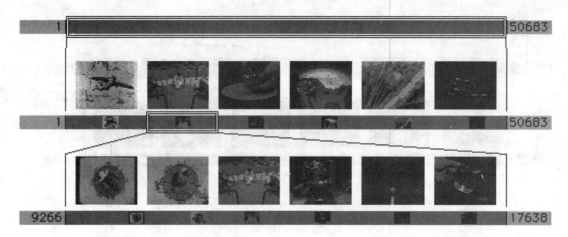

Figure 5. An expanded view of the region surrounded by the magnifier.

Generating Hierarchical Views of Temporal Data

We have seen how the user can vary the temporal resolution of the top-level storyboard. But now s/he may want to "zoom-in" on one part of the timeline—to expand the level of detail surrounding one of the video proxies. Suppose that the user wants to see, in greater detail, what kinds of events surround the carousel scene (the second frame from the left). By clicking on the second-level timeline in the region of the carousel video marker, the user can bring up a new magnifier positioned over this smaller region. See **Figure 5**. A new

storyboard and timeline, corresponding to the region surrounded by the new magnifier, appears below. The "guide wires" descending from the ends of the magnifier help the user visually parse the display—see the second level storyboard as an "expansion of detail" of the magnified region.

What is unique about the current approach is that the first storyboard — the coarsest view— is not simply replaced by the second, more finely-detailed storyboard. The first storyboard remains visible and *can be inspected* -- serves as a

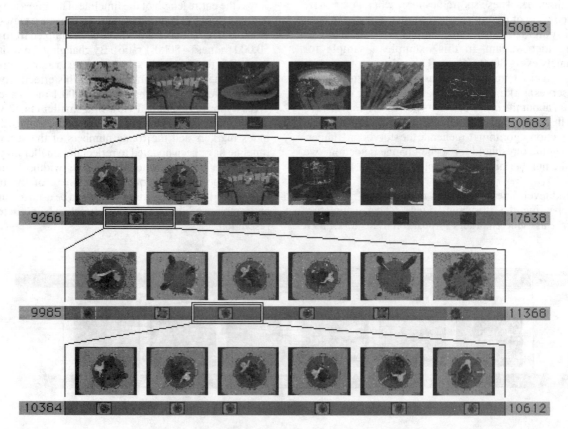

Figure 6. Applying the magnifier two more times.

Figure 7. Switching views via the pull-down menu.

frame of reference for the expanded sub-part. Of course, the user does not have to stop after a single level of magnification. In this example, the user could continue to expand the magnification of the carousel event by recursively applying a new magnifier to successive levels. **Figure 6** shows the effects of applying the magnifier two more times. Note that the six frames of the bottom-most storyboard represent a very small chunk of video (about 8 seconds worth), but at a high sampling rate.

HOW WOULD THE VIDEO MAGNIFIER BE USED?
At the very least, the current approach provides a powerful tool for navigating a video source. The primary cognitive benefit is that the user does not have to depend solely on the "mind's eye" to recall what other scenes surround the segment which s/he is currently examining. In **Figure 6**, for example, I can examine the low-level structure of the bottom storyboard (showing a top-view of the carousel event). Yet I can see, two rows up, a that there is a frame showing this carousel scene from a different camera angle--a side view. I could easily expand this side-view scene by repositioning the magnifier on top of its corresponding video marker.

An Iconic Outliner
Beyond navigation, the hierarchal magnifier could be used to construct a customized iconic "outline" of the video source. The top row of frames, maximally compressed, provides a set of iconic "chapter headings"—a high level overview. Successive rows, providing increasingly greater amounts of temporal resolution, serve as pictorial "sub-headings". The last row might be an uncompressed layer, a "continuous" set of frames constituting a short video chunk — the equivalent of a video "word" or "phoneme". To build an iconic outline of a large video source will require more than a single hierarchical view. Hence, the application allows the user to label each view and store it in a list. The user can switch among views on the list by selecting its label under a pull-down menu. **See Figure 7.**

A powerful feature of the application is that the hierarchical views do not just provide information about the video source; they can also be used to *control* it. See **Figure 8**. For example, suppose the user wanted to play a real-time segment in the video window which corresponds to a given video frame on a storyboard. To do this, the user does not have to punch in a frame number nor enter time code to reset the laserdisc. The user simply drags a copy of the particular frame from the

storyboard and drops it into the video source window. (8a) Because the digital frame has stored information about where it came from (its location in the original video source), it can reset the laserdisk to begin playing at this location. (8b) In this way, someone could customize a set of views — build an iconic log or outline — of a source which could be used as a front-end to navigate the video without having to deal with frame numbers. Finally, the ability to use the hierarchical views to control a video source would make the magnifier a useful component of a video editing system. For example, frames from any row could be selected to define "begin" and "end" points of a segment which could then be digitized from the original video source.

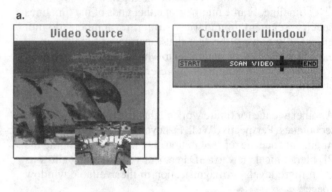

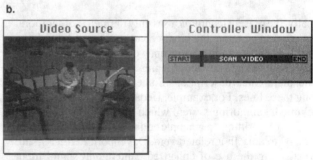

Figure 8. Dropping a frame from the storyboard onto the video source window (a) resets the laserdisk to begin playing at this location (b).

CONCLUSION
We have described a magnifier tool for video data—one which allows users to vary the temporal resolution of a video source, while maintaining an awareness of the hierarchical structure of the levels of magnification.

Preliminary user testing of the technique indicates that while people grasp the basic concept—the recursive magnification of portions of a timeline to generate hierarchical structure—other parts of the interface need to be improved. For example, in the current implementation, people have some difficulty parsing the display—especially understanding how the miniature video markers on the timelines map to their corresponding frames in the storyboard view. This difficulty arises because a video marker, which can be dragged along the timeline, can become spatially displaced vis-a-vis its matching frame on the storyboard. For example, instead of appearing directly beneath its matching frame, a video marker might be dragged to a position almost directly beneath an adjacent, but non-matching, storyboard frame. In this case, the user's eye is presented with a perceptual dilemma--a contest between matching content vs. spatial proximity. Does it perceive the miniature marker as being paired with the spatially displaced frame on the basis of identical video content? Or does it pair the marker with the spatially proximal, but non-identical frame, under which it appears. We need to investigate better methods of helping users perceive the links between video markers and their matching frames.

We also need to explore methods for strengthening the graphical depiction of hierarchical nesting. At present, the only graphical devices used to convey "belongingness" are the "guide wires" which emanate from the edges of the magnifier to the next-level timeline. Frame numbers at either ends of the timelines specify segment boundaries. But the numbers do not graphically convey the fact that a particular timeline is an expanded view of the magnifier to which it belongs. We need to find stronger graphical representations of hierarchical structure.

Another avenue for future work might be to look at how recent techniques (Perspective Wall, Fisheye Lens) mentioned earlier might enhance the representation. For example, mapping the 2D hierarchical view to a 3D Perspective Wall might allow us to fit more levels of magnification in the available window space.

Finally, the present technique uses only the metric of temporal resolution to generate the hierarchical structures. It might be worthwhile examining how recent work in image processing, scene analysis and knowledge representation could help build richer hierarchical descriptions. Some work has already started along these lines. For example, Ueda, et al [7], have built a multimedia authoring system which uses motion and object detection algorithms to generate editable storyboard views of a video stream. In a related vein, Davenport, et al [1], are investigating the use of enhanced camera and sound input techniques to annotate video streams: to enable the user to attach, at the time of recording, information about semantic and structural variables (camera position, lighting, causal actions, narrative structures). The goal is is to represent these annotations in "strata" -- hierarchical layers -- which can be used to enhance video editing and multimedia browsing applications.

Bringing together richer semantic representations of a video source with the ability to manipulate hierarchical temporal views, should lead to even more powerful workspaces for video material.

REFERENCES

1. Davenport, G., Aguierre-Smith, T., and Pincever, N. Cinematic primitives for multimedia. 67-75. *IEEE Computer Graphics and Applications.*, *11(4,)*, July 1991.

2. Furnas, G.W. Generalized fisheye views. *Proceedings of CHI '86 Human Factors in Computing Systems*, 16-23. New York: ACM, 1986.

3. Hochberg, J. In the mind's eye. In R.N. Haber (Ed.) *Contemporary Theory and Research in visual perception.* New York: Appleton-Century-Crofts.

4. Mackinlay, J.D., Robertson, G. G., and Card, S. K. Perspective wall: detail and context smoothly integrated. *Proceedings of CHI '91 Human Factors in Computing Systems,* 173-179. New York: ACM, 1991.

5. Moore, R., Morrison, J. and Oren, T. Proxies and their applications. *Apple Viewpoints*. July 10, 1989. Apple Computer, Inc.

6. Spence, R. & Apperley, M. Data base navigation: An office environment for the professional. Behaviour and Information Technology 1 (1), 43-54, 1982.

7. Ueda, H., Takafumi, M. and Yoshizawa, S. Impact: An interactive natural-motion-picture dedicated multimedia authoring system. *Proceedings of CHI '91 Human Factors in Computing Systems*, 343-350. New York: ACM, 1991.

A RESEARCH PROGRAM TO ASSESS USER PERCEPTIONS OF GROUP WORK SUPPORT

John Satzinger

Department of Management
The University of Georgia
Athens, GA 30602
(404) 542-3746
jsatzing@ugabus

Lorne Olfman

Programs in Information Science
The Claremont Graduate School
Claremont, CA 91711
(714) 621-8209
olfmanl@clargrad

ABSTRACT

Computer support for group work is a technological innovation receiving considerable attention from developmental researchers. This paper reports the preliminary results from two surveys which assessed user perceived needs for various types of group work support. The instruments, distributed to managers and professionals in a variety of organizations, described group support scenarios and associated functions/tools and asked for an assessment of their usefulness to one of the respondent's organizational work groups. Support for between meetings group work was perceived to be more useful than support for either face to face or electronic meetings. Common single user tools were generally perceived to be more useful than multi-user group tools. Individual differences and implications are addressed.

KEYWORDS: Computer supported cooperative work, CSCW, groupware, technology acceptance model.

INTRODUCTION

Despite the variety of research projects and development efforts concerned with computer support for group work, not much is known about user attitudes toward or perceived needs for this support. Support for group work has been referred to as computer supported cooperative work (CSCW), "groupware", group support systems (GSS), group decision support systems (GDSS), and electronic meeting systems (EMS). Researchers from a variety of disciplines and with a variety of research paradigms are working in the area [11]. A number of empirical studies conducted in the laboratory have been reported which assess the impact of this technology on groups, primarily for group meetings [2, 5, 14, 15, 23, 24]. A few field studies have also been conducted [6, 18]. Other researchers are developing and evaluating innovative group support applications and interfaces thought to be of use to groups, either for meetings or for between meeting group activities (c.f., [10, 21, 13]).

A recent report on the state of research in group support concluded that the number one research priority is to describe the nature of group work in organizations so applications which better support group work can be designed [9]. Members of a panel at CHI'90 (Computer Human Interaction Conference) similarly concluded that we need to better understand the nature of group tasks and needs if computer support for groups is to be made more practical [8]. Group support applications must directly benefit end users in their working relationships to be successful [12], and although the use of field surveys has been discussed as a promising research methodology for investigating user needs for group work support [22], no such studies have been found. The only survey found reported current use of group support [1, 20]. Additional information about group work, and about the perceived need for various types of group work support technology, should help software designers and researchers to better understand the potential users for these products.

This paper reports the preliminary findings from a series of field surveys which directly asked potential users about their needs for various group work support technologies. Two surveys have thus far been conducted with the goal of answering three broad questions: (1) what are user's perceived needs for group work support?, (2) how important is technological support for various group work contexts and tasks? (e.g., face to face meetings vs. other contexts and decision making vs. other group tasks), and (3) are developmental researchers working on tools that are perceived to be appropriate and actually useful to the context and task? An additional question underlying this research is whether survey research can provide useful information about user needs for technological support. This research program is the first known attempt to ask for user input about group work support through a survey.

RESEARCH MODEL

Because most group work support technology is in the developmental stages, potential end users of group work support have little if any direct experience with the technology. User satisfaction instruments and surveys assume direct experience with a specific system [7]. This study sought to assess user beliefs about the usefulness of general types of support which might be provided.

COMPUTER SUPPORT FOR FACE TO FACE MEETINGS

Face to face meetings occur when the members of the work group physically meet to discuss issues, report progress, or finalize agreements. A special room can be built to provide extensive technological support for face to face meetings. It can be equipped with unobtrusive computer workstations mounted in the conference table and connected to a computer network. Each participant can use a workstation during the meeting if desired. The contents of each computer display screen can be projected onto large screens visible to everyone in the room for presentation and discussion. During a meeting, participants can have access to information in data bases, display information prepared with presentation graphics software, analyze information using tools such as electronic spreadsheets, selectively share information or send messages to each other, and produce information using special software tools developed for meetings (such as group brainstorming, group authoring, alternative rating and ranking, and consensus building).

COMPUTER SUPPORT FOR ELECTRONIC MEETINGS

Electronic meetings occur when work group members need to work with each other in real time when they are not physically at the same location. Participants have computer workstations in their offices which are connected to a computer network. They might also have portable workstations which can be connected to the network when they are out of the office. During the electronic meeting, participants can have access to information in data bases, distribute information prepared with presentation graphics software, analyze information using tools such as spreadsheets, selectively share information or send messages through the computer network, and produce information using special software tools developed for electronic meetings (such as group brainstorming, group authoring, alternative rating and ranking, and consensus building). The participants could also speak to each other as with conference calls and perhaps see each other as with video conferencing.

COMPUTER SUPPORT BETWEEN MEETINGS

Electronic support for work groups between meetings includes communication and work coordination activities that are necessary for planning future meetings and following through with tasks after the conclusion of meetings. These activities do not require communication or information exchanges in real time. Participants have computer workstations in their offices which are connected to a computer network. They might also have portable workstations which can be connected to the network when they are out of the office. Between meetings, participants can have access to information in data bases, analyze information using tools such as spreadsheets, selectively send information and memos through electronic mail systems, and produce information using special software tools developed for work group use (such as group brainstorming, group authoring, alternative rating and ranking, and consensus building). Other tools available through the computer network would include project management, meeting scheduling, and FAX.

Figure 1: Descriptions of Three Group Work Support Scenarios

The Technology Acceptance Model (TAM) described by Davis [3, 4] was therefore chosen as the basis for survey instrument development for this study. TAM predicts that user intention to use a software package can be determined by assessing user's beliefs about the usefulness of the software. Perceived usefulness is defined as "the degree to which a person believes that using a particular system would enhance his or her job performance" ([3], p.320). TAM was developed to assess behavioral intention to use a software package after a brief exposure to the package. Thus far, TAM has shown reliable results when users are shown a short video tape demonstrating an application, when users are shown a live demonstration of the application, and when users have worked with the application over time [4]. Perceived usefulness is measured with a seven point semantic differential scale which asks for degree of likelihood that a statement about the usefulness of an application is true.

The research model for this study predicts that the context of computer support (support scenario), the type of exposure to the support technology, and individual differences will influence perceived usefulness. Perceived usefulness is assumed to be a surrogate for measuring intention to use the technology, although intention to use the technology was not measured in this study. The three support scenarios used are based on Johansen [16]: computer support for face to face meetings, computer support for electronic meetings (real time, distributed in space), and computer support for group work between meetings. Individual differences include attitudes of the end user toward computers and group work, the nature of the end-user's position in an organization (level, functional area, work experience, etc.) and the characteristics of a specific work group the end-user is involved in (task type, membership, size, meeting frequency, etc).

The type of exposure the end user has to the technology might include actual use, demonstration, or simple verbal description. For a survey of a cross section of end users, actual use of technology or demonstration of technology were not feasible. Instead, it was hoped that a simple description of the conceptual models and architecture underlying each support scenario would allow end users to form an opinion about the usefulness of the technology to one of their specific organizational work groups. Although Davis [3] did not test TAM using written descriptions of applications, Satzinger [19] measured user comprehension of cooperative work applications following either a demonstration of the applications or reading a description of the applications and found no difference in conceptual knowledge or usage knowledge. Only procedural knowledge was greater in the demonstration group. This provided evidence that potential users could understand enough about the concepts and uses of group support applications to form an opinion about their usefulness by reading a simple description. An additional test was conducted by having graduate students complete the survey during a pilot test of the instrument. One group of students completed the survey after listening to a lecture about group work support and the other group completed the survey after participating in a training session with an electronic meeting system. There were no significant differences in perceived usefulness for the students exposed only via the lecture.

Short descriptions of the three support scenarios developed for this study are shown in Figure 1. In addition, a glossary was provided which described specific tools mentioned in the scenarios. The survey instrument included a description of a scenario and then asked questions about perceived usefulness. A sample statement about a scenario would be "overall, this type of computer support would be useful to my work group." The respondent was asked to place a check mark on the seven point semantic differential scale which ranged from extremely likely to extremely unlikely. Specific tools were evaluated for each scenario with a statement such as "retrieving information from databases during a face to face meeting would be useful to my work group."

SURVEY APPROACH

Two surveys have been developed and distributed. The first survey instrument was pilot tested by graduate students in a systems planning course at The Claremont Graduate School, who offered suggestions for clarity in the descriptions and questions. The second instrument was developed following analysis of the results from the first survey. The survey respondents to date have come from a convenience sample. The graduate students in the systems planning course distributed surveys to colleagues at their place of employment. The students were employed in professional positions and attended courses in the evenings. They were asked to distribute the instruments to managers

and professionals in a variety of functional areas. The procedure involved distributing a cover letter, background questionnaire, and the survey instrument to colleagues who agreed to participate. The student surveyor then collected the completed instruments and submitted a short questionnaire on their organization.

	Survey 1	Survey 2
Number of Organizations	34	38
Number of Responses	153	142
Responses by Org Type		
Services	82	81
Manufacturing	62	31
Finance, Insurance, Real Estate	7	19
Other	2	10
Level/Position of Respondent		
Director, VP, CIO	11	6
Group Leader, Manager, Dept Head, Supervisor	45	61
Engineer, Scientist, Analyst, Consultant, Programmer, Technician	75	45
Sales, Service, Educator, Clerical	16	27
Education Level of Respondent		
No Degree	16	28
Bachelor's	60	39
Beyond Bachelor's	77	67

Table 1: Respondent Data: Frequencies by Organization Type, Position & Education

	Survey 1	Survey 2
Age	38.0 (10)	36.0 (10)
Years at present job	5.9 (5.2)	4.9 (5.0)
Total Years Experience	15.0 (9.6)	13.5 (9.6)
Computer Use (max 7)	5.7 (1.8)	5.2 (2.0)
Computer Knowledge (max 7)	5.8 (1.2)	5.8 (1.2)
Number of Work Groups	2.8 (2.0)	3.3 (2.4)
Hours in Meetings per Week	7.0 (7.0)	5.6 (4.7)

Table 2: Respondent Data: Means & (std dev)

SURVEY RESPONDENTS

The respondents in both surveys were on average mature, well-educated and experienced. In the first survey, 153 responses were received from 34 different organizations. The average age was 34, average work experience was 15 years, and 50% were educated beyond the bachelor's degree. Thirty-seven percent were managers and 49% were technical professionals such as engineers, scientists, analysts, consultants and programmers. The balance were in sales, services and education. In the second survey, 142 responses were received from 38 organizations. The average age was 36, work experience averaged 13.5 years, and 47% were educated beyond the bachelor's degree. A slightly higher percent were managers (46%).

Computer use was measured by intensity rather than hours

per week.. The intensity of use was 5.7 on a seven point scale for the first survey and 5.2 for the second survey. Attitude toward computers and attitude toward group work were generally favorable (averaging over 5.5 on a seven point scale). The number of work groups reported per respondent averaged 2.8 in the first survey and 3.3 in the second survey. Hours spent in formal meetings per week averaged 7.0 and 5.6 respectively. These statistics are shown in Table 1 and Table 2.

departments, and in the second survey this was 73%. About half of the groups in both surveys included members from multiple locations. Group size averaged 10.7 and 8.7 on the two surveys. These groups met on average about once a month. Communication intensity was measured by the number of phone calls made per month and the number of memos (or E-mail messages) sent per month regarding the group. Calls averaged 13.2 and 9.1. Fewer memos or messages were sent.

	Survey 1	Survey 2
Has Formal Leader	87%	88%
Meetings Have Written Agenda	46%	62%
Multi-Department Membership	31%	73%
Members in Multiple Locations	46%	58%
Number of Members	10.7 (12.4)	8.7 (6.0)
Number of Meetings/Month	4.6 (4.3)	4.0 (3.7)
Number of Calls/Month	13.2 (19.6)	9.1 (14.7)
Number of Memos/Month	6.9 (12.9)	5.1 (9.8)

Table 3: Descriptive Data on Specific Work Groups

Committee to Coordinate Computer Courses
Corporate MIS Disaster Recovery Team
Data Center Operations Personnel
Database Advisory Group
Department Managers Support Group
Division Strategic Planning
Environment Information Systems
Faculty Rank and Tenure Committee
Fixed Assets Support Group
Flight Project Sequencing Team
Launch Approval Planning Group
Mature Worker Task Force
Mental Health Awareness Team
Product Engineering Group
Project Management Improvement Committee
School District Management Council
Social Events Committee
Task Force to Reduce Invoicing Problems
Task Force to Reduce Specimen Problems
Theoretical Model Verification Group

Figure 2
Representative Work Groups Reported by Respondents

SPECIFIC WORK GROUPS

The respondents were asked to describe one of their work groups that was particularly important to them in more detail. They were then asked to answer questions about the usefulness of group support scenarios and tools in terms of the one work group. Table 3 provides descriptive data on the chosen work groups from both the first and second surveys. Figure 2 lists a sample of the work group names. Most of the chosen groups had a formal leader, but fewer used a written agenda for meetings. In the first survey, 31% of the work groups had members from multiple

	Avail And Used	Avail Not Used	Not Avail
White Board/Chalk Board	105	15	22
Overhead Projector	78	23	41
Video Tape Player/Monitor	56	35	51
Computer Workstation	40	41	61
Flip Chart Pad	63	13	65
Speaker Phone	50	19	72
Electronic White Board	17	10	115
Video Conferencing	11	8	123

Table 4: Availability and Use of Meeting Room Technology from Survey 2

	Mean	St Dev	Range
Action-Oriented Planning	23.0%	13.3	0-80%
Creativity/Idea Generation	24.5%	14.3	0-70%
Decision Making /Agreement Making	23.7%	13.1	0-80%
Briefing/Information Exchange	28.2%	16.4	5-90%

Table 5: Percent of Meeting Time Spent on Task Types from Survey 2

In the second survey, additional questions were asked about the technology available in meeting rooms used by the work group and about the percent of meeting time spent on various group tasks. The availability and use of meeting room technology is shown in Table 4. A computer workstation was available in a meeting room to 57% of respondents, and half of these reported that the computer was used during meetings by their work group. Four group meeting tasks were described based on McGrath [17] -- action oriented planning tasks, creativity/idea generation tasks, decision making/agreement making tasks and briefing/information exchange tasks. Table 5 shows the means, standard deviations and ranges of percent of time spent on each type of task for the work groups. A variety of meeting task profiles are represented in the sample.

SURVEY 1: SUPPORT SCENARIOS AND TOOLS

The first instrument, referred to as Survey 1, described the three support scenarios and asked for an assessment of the overall usefulness of each to a particular work group selected and described by the respondent. For each scenario, specific functions/tools potentially used within the scenario were assessed separately. These included common tools such as database retrieval, presentation support, spreadsheets/DSS, and message sending. Group support tools described included brainstorming, group authoring, rating/ranking, consensus building, and project management.

Four questions were asked about each scenario overall -- the overall usefulness to the work group, the likelihood of efficiency benefits, the likelihood of effectiveness benefits, and the likelihood of acceptance by the work group members. The means and standard deviations of the four questions across scenarios are shown in Table 6. Paired t-tests across scenarios indicated no difference between the face to face and electronic meeting scenarios. The between meeting scenario was rated higher on all four questions (p<.01). These scores indicate that on average respondents were either neutral or thought support for face to face and electronic meetings was slightly likely to be useful. In comparison, scores for between meeting support were either slightly likely or quite likely to be useful.

	SUPPORT SCENARIO		
	Face to Face Meeting	Electronic Meeting	Between Meeting
Overall Usefulness	4.66	4.54	**5.72***
	(1.71)	(1.97)	(1.38)
Efficiency Benefits	4.56	4.49	**5.61***
	(1.74)	(1.95)	(1.41)
Effectiveness Benefits	4.66	4.48	**5.58***
	(1.66)	(1.89)	(1.40)
Acceptance By Group	4.18	4.24	**5.36***
	(1.74)	(1.88)	(1.57)

Table 6: Mean Scores and Std Dev of Overall Scenario Questions (* indicates p<.01)

Table 7 shows the means and standard deviations of the usefulness of specific functions/tools across scenarios. The same pattern emerged as the overall evaluation for database retrieval, presentation support, spreadsheets/DSS, group authoring and project management, with function/tool usefulness higher in the between meetings scenario (p<.01). Message sending differed on all three scenarios, seen as the least useful in face to face meetings and the most useful between meetings. That message sending was seen as one of the most useful tools during an electronic meeting provides evidence that the respondents

understood the difference between face to face and electronic meeting scenarios. Presentation support and database retrieval were ranked in the top three of all scenarios, while consensus building and rating/ranking were ranked in the bottom three.

	Face to Face Meeting	Electronic Meeting	Between Meeting
Database Retrieval	4.74	4.68	**5.54***
	(1.70)	(1.69)	(1.48)
Presentation Support	4.93	4.80	**5.37***
	(1.69)	(1.74)	(1.54)
Spreadsheets/DSS	4.28	4.23	**5.14***
	(1.75)	(1.80)	(1.59)
Message Sending	3.67	**4.69***	**5.71***
	(1.93)	(1.81)	(1.56)
Brainstorming	4.35	4.44	4.63
	(1.67)	(1.72)	(1.66)
Group Authoring	4.26	4.21	**4.66***
	(1.68)	(1.73)	(1.70)
Rating/Ranking	4.06	4.07	4.22
	(1.67)	(1.70)	(1.63)
Consensus Building	4.02	4.09	4.24
	(1.73)	(1.78)	(1.65)
Project Management	4.45	4.32	**4.90***
	(1.72)	(1.75)	(1.77)

Table 7: Mean Scores and Std Dev of Specific Functions/Tools (* indicates p<.01)

Additional analyses were run to study the effect of individual differences on perceived usefulness. Individual differences included variables not related to group work (level in organization, computer knowledge, and attitude toward computers), variables related to group work overall (use support now, attitude toward group work, number of work groups, and hours spent in meetings), and variables related to a specific work group described by the respondent. These were recoded as binary variables. A factor analysis was run for the set of questions about each scenario, and in all three cases the four overall questions clustered into one factor and the specific functions/tools questions clustered into two additional factors (one corresponding to the common tools and the other corresponding to the group support tools). For the individual differences by scenario analyses, the four overall questions for each scenario were therefore summed. Then a 2 by 3 analysis of variance was run for each individual difference (a binary classification of an individual difference variable by the three support scenarios as a blocking factor).

The scenario main effects were all significant at p < .01, as expected from the paired t-tests, with support between meetings rated higher than the other scenarios. Significant differences (p < .05) were detected for six individual differences main effects. Computer support for group work was perceived to be more useful by those (1) who have higher attitudes toward computers, (2) who use computers now for group work, (3) who have higher attitudes toward group work, (4) who spend more time in meetings, (5) who work in a group that spanned multiple departments, or (6) who work in a larger group. There was one significant interaction for the number of memos and messages sent per month. In this case the overall usefulness was rated higher for electronic meetings and for between meetings scenarios for those sending more memos or messages regarding the specific group, but there was no difference in the face to face meeting scenario.

The functions/tools were grouped into two types within each scenario -- the common tools and the group support tools. Individual differences were tested with a 2 by 3 by 2 analysis of variance with scenario and tool type as blocking factors (individual difference by scenario by tool type). The function/tool type main effects were highly significant, with common tools rated higher than group support tools (p<.01 in all cases). The scenario main effects were again highly significant, with tools used between meetings rated higher than with either face to face or electronic meetings. Seven of the individual difference main effects were significant following a similar pattern to the individual difference by scenario analysis. A number of significant interactions were also present, which showed greater differences between common tools and group support tools in the between meeting scenario.

The results from the first survey indicated that group support between meetings was perceived as more useful than support for face to face meetings or electronic meetings. In addition, the more common functions/tools were perceived as more useful than the group support functions/tools, particularly in the between meetings scenario. One interpretation is the respondents spent more of their time working on between meeting tasks than in meetings. Support between meetings might be expected to be proportionally more important. This interpretation would argue for the validity of simply describing support technology and asking for an assessment. The high reliability of the instrument (.961), the factor analyses, the highly significant differences for between meeting support, the individual difference main effects, and the face validity of a number of tool/scenario interactions analyzed indicated the respondents understood the scenarios and tools and made reasonable assessments.

There are several alternative interpretations. First, those who use computer support now for group work would most likely be using such support for between meetings tasks. This use, particularly the use of successful applications such as electronic mail, might have biased the responses. Second, the between meeting scenario implied single user tools rather than multi-user group tools (at least in terms of

simultaneous use), and the respondents would be more likely to understand or be confident about this type of support. The function/tool main effects might argue for this interpretation as well. This might indicate the respondents had difficulty understanding the face to face and electronic meeting scenarios or how the group support tools might be used with their work group. An additional survey was conducted to gather additional information on end user needs and to further validate this survey approach.

SURVEY 2: FACE TO FACE MEETINGS & TOOLS
The second survey focused only on face to face meetings to reduce the number of concepts presented and to allow more questions about the functions/tools used within the scenario. The survey described the face to face meeting scenario and asked the same overall questions as the first survey to see if the results were similar. As described above, additional questions were asked about the availability of support in meeting rooms and the percent of time spent in meetings on four group tasks. For each function/tool, five questions were asked: one overall usefulness question and one question about the usefulness of the function/tool for each of the tasks. This instrument also proved to be highly reliable (.977).

The means on the overall questions about the face to face meeting scenario were almost identical to the first survey, showing a neutral to luke-warm response. An analysis of the frequencies of responses, though, revealed a bimodal distribution not present in the first survey. Only 8.9% of responses were actually neutral. A large group of responses (34%) were fairly positive about the usefulness of support for face to face meetings. A smaller group (23%) tended to be fairly negative. This addressed two issues: (1) the respondents were able to form an opinion based only on the description, which provides support for the validity of the survey instrument, and (2) even if end users readily change their opinion following demonstration or actual use, implementation of this technology might be hampered by significant initial resistance. Individual difference variables which correlated positively with the overall questions included the number of meetings per week, communication intensity (calls and memos) and the current use of a computer workstation in a meeting room (p<.05). Age and years of experience correlated negatively (p<.05). No differences were found for group size, attitude toward computers or attitude toward group work.

Five questions were asked about the usefulness of each of nine functions/tools. A factor analysis of all function/tool questions revealed eight factors. Seven factors corresponded to seven separate functions/tools -- database retrieval, presentation support, spreadsheets/DSS, message sending, brainstorming, group authoring and project management. These were therefore seen as distinct functions. Rating/ranking and consensus building grouped together. The scores on the five questions were then summed for each function/tool. The absolute ranking of the nine tools was identical to the functions/tools for face to face meetings on the first survey. Paired contrasts showed presentation graphics, database retrieval, project management and group brainstorming more useful than the other tools. Message sending in a face to face meeting again had the lowest score, and it was significantly different from the other eight.

An analysis of variance and paired contrasts were run for each of the nine functions/tools with usefulness for the four types of tasks as a blocking factor. This was done to check hypotheses about the usefulness of meeting tools for specific group tasks. The results are shown in Table 8, which lists the nine functions/tools in order of the summed score discussed above, grouped by most useful, less useful and least useful categories. The hypothesized task types where the function/tool would be more useful have the mean usefulness scores underlined. All but message sending were thought to be more useful for two task types. An asterisk appears by the scores where the anova was significant (those indicated were $p < .01$) and where the score was significantly different in the contrasts.

Meeting Task:	Plan	Create	Decide	Brief
Most Useful:				
Presentation Support	4.72	4.89	4.87	5.23*
Database Retrieval	4.75	4.72	4.97*	5.04*
Project Management	5.17*	4.45	4.90	4.77
Brainstorming	4.47	5.14*	4.59	4.49
Less Useful:				
Spreadsheets/DSS	4.37	4.31	4.51	4.54
Group Authoring	4.39	4.27	4.37	4.43
Rating/Ranking	4.38*	4.14	4.53*	3.99
Consensus Building	4.17	4.08	4.37*	3.84
Least Useful:				
Message Sending	3.71	3.72	3.78	3.79

Table 8: Perceived Usefulness of Function/Tool for Four Types of Tasks (* indicates $p < .01$)

The use of presentation graphics was most useful for briefing/information exchange tasks. Database retrieval was most useful for both decision making/agreement making tasks and briefing/information exchange tasks, etc. Spreadsheets/DSS, group authoring and message sending were not significantly different across task type. Again, these results provide evidence that the respondents understood the scenario and the potential use of the functions/tools within a face to face meeting and made reasonable responses. Two common functions and two group support functions were included in the most useful function/tool group.

IMPLICATIONS AND FUTURE RESEARCH

The preliminary results presented here demonstrate a clear pattern. Support for between meetings group work was perceived to be more useful than support for either face to face or electronic meetings. This might be because more time is spent on group tasks between meetings than in meetings. A closer look at the face to face meeting scenario in survey 2 revealed a bimodal distribution. A sizable number of respondents thought support for face to face meetings very useful. Another sizable group was fairly negative. The implication for developmental researchers is that support for between meetings group work activities is important. The implication for those implementing group support, especially for meetings, is the possibility of significant resistance that must be overcome by either training or marketing.

The function/tool analyses in the first survey showed common functions, which are single user in terms of simultaneous use, were perceived more useful than group support functions, which are usually multi-user tools (brainstorming, group authoring, rating/ranking, consensus building and project management). For those designing and implementing group support, careful attention to the user interface and user support might make a difference. For face to face meetings, two common tools (presentation support and database retrieval) and two group support tools (project management and brainstorming) were perceived to be the most useful. For developmental researchers, this implies the meeting room environment should provide access to information and allow presentation of information as well as support group tasks such as brainstorming. Additionally, perceived needs for support in a meeting vary with the type of meeting task, so a variety of tools should be made available.

Finally, those involved in developing or implementing work group support will find more receptive users when they are involved in larger groups, groups with multi-department membership, or groups that spend more time in meetings. Additionally, users with positive attitudes toward computers and group work or those who now use some form of support for group work are likely adopters.

These initial analyses provide encouragement that this survey approach to assessing perceived needs for group work support is promising. Additional surveys and interviews are planned to follow up on these findings in other populations and cultures.

REFERENCES

[1] Beauclair, R. & Straub, D. Utilizing GDSS technology: Final report on a recent empirical study. *Information & Management, 18*, 5 (May 1990), 213-220.

[2] Connolly, T., Jessup, L. & Valacich, J. Effects of anonymity and evaluative tone on idea generation in computer-mediated groups. *Management Science, 36*, 6 (June 1990), 689-703.

[3] Davis, F. Perceived usefulness, ease of use, and user acceptance of information technology. *MIS Quarterly, 13*, 3 (Sept. 1989), 319-340.

[4] Davis, F., Bagozzi, R. , & Warshaw, P. User acceptance of computer technology: A comparison of two theoretical models. *Management Science, 35,* 8 (Aug. 1989), 982-1003.

[5] Dennis, A., George, J., Jessup, L., Nunamaker, J. & Vogel, D. Information technology to support electronic meetings. *MIS Quarterly, 12,* 4 (December 1988), 591-624.

[6] DeSanctis, G., Poole, M., Lewis, H. & Desharnais, G. Using computing to improve the quality team process: Some initial observations from the IRS-Minnesota project. In J. F. Nunamaker, Jr. (Ed.), *Proceedings of the 24th Annual Hawaii International Conference on System Sciences,* IEEE Computer Society Press, Los Alamitos, CA, 1991, Vol 3 750-757.

[7] Doll, W. & Torkzadeh, G. The measurement of end-user computing satisfaction. *MIS Quarterly, 12,* 4 (March 1988), 258-274.

[8] Ensor, B., Crowley, T., Kraut, B., Rein, G. & Sproull, L. How can we make groupware practical? (panel). In *Proceedings of CHI, 1990* (Seattle Washington, April 1-5, 1990) ACM, New York, 1990, 87-89. .

[9] Gray, P., Alter, S., Dickson, G., DeSanctis, G., Harris, S., Johansen, R., Kraemer, K., Olfman, L., & Vogel, D. Report to the ISDP project on research issues in GDSS. In Stohr, E. & Konsynski, B. (Eds.) *The Information Systems and Decision Processes Project,* Los Alamitos, CA, IEEE Computer Society Press, in press.

[10] Greif, I. (Ed). *Proceedings of the Conference on Computer-Supported Cooperative Work (CSCW 86).* Austin, Texas (1986), ACM, New York.

[11] Grudin, J. CSCW: The convergence of two development contexts. In *Proceedings of CHI, 1991* (New Orleans, Louisiana, April 28-May 2, 1991) ACM, New York, 1991. 91-98.

[12] Grudin, J. Why CSCW applications fail: Problems in the design and evaluation of organizational interfaces. *Proceedings of the Conference on Computer Supported Cooperative Work (CSCW 88),* Portland, Oregon, ACM, New York, 1988, 85-93.

[13] Halasz, F. & Tatar, D. (Eds.). *Proceedings of the Conference on Computer-Supported Cooperative Work (CSCW 90).* Los Angeles, Calif., ACM, New York, 1990.

[14] Jarvenpaa, S., Rao, V. & Huber, G. Computer support for meetings of groups working on unstructured problems: A field experiment. *MIS Quarterly, 12,* 4 (December 1988), 645-666.

[15] Jessup, L., Connolly, T. & Galegher, J. The effects of anonymity on GDSS group process with an idea generating task. *MIS Quarterly, 14,* 3 (September 1990), 313-321.

[16] Johansen, R. *Groupware: Computer Support for Business Teams.* The Free Press, New York, NY, 1988.

[17] McGrath, J. *Groups: Interaction and Performance.* Prentice Hall, Inc., Englewood Cliffs, NJ, 1984.

[18] Nunamaker, J., Dennis, A., Valacich, J., Vogel, D. & George, J. Electronic meeting systems to support group work. *Communications of the ACM, 34,* 7(July 1991), 40-61.

[19] Satzinger, J. User interface consistency across end-user applications programs: Effect on learning and satisfaction. Unpublished Ph.D. Dissertation, The Claremont Graduate School, 1991.

[20] Straub, D. & Beauclair, R. Uses of GDSS technology. *Journal of Management Information Systems, 5,* (Summer 1988), 101-116.

[21] Suchman, L. & Tatar, D. (Eds.). *Proceedings of the Conference on Computer-Supported Cooperative Work (CSCW 88).* Portland, Oregon, ACM, New York, 1988.

[22] Vogel, D. & Nunamaker, J. Group decision support system impact: Multi-methodological exploration. *Information & Management, 18,* No. 1 (Jan 1990), 15-28.

[23] Watson, R., DeSanctis, G. & Poole, M. Using GDSS to facilitate group consensus: Some intended and unintended consequences. *MIS Quarterly, 12,* 3 (September 1988), 463-480.

[24] Zigurs, I., Poole, M. & DeSanctis, G. A study of influence in computer mediated group decision making. *MIS Quarterly, 12,* 4 (December 1988), 625-644.

GARDENERS AND GURUS: PATTERNS OF COOPERATION AMONG CAD USERS

Michelle Gantt
Bonnie A. Nardi

Hewlett-Packard Laboratories
Human-Computer Interaction Department
1501 Page Mill Road
Palo Alto, CA 94304
Internet: nardi@hplabs.hp.com
(415) 857-5121

ABSTRACT

We studied CAD system users to find out how they use the sophisticated customization and extension facilities offered by many CAD products. We found that users of varying levels of expertise collaborate to customize their CAD environments and to create programmatic extensions to their applications. Within a group of users, there is at least one local expert who provides support for other users. We call this person a *local developer*. The local developer is a fellow domain expert, not a professional programmer, outside technical consultant or MIS staff member. We found that in some CAD environments the support role has been formalized so that local developers are given official recognition, and time and resources to pursue local developer activities. In general, this formalization of the local developer role appears successful. We discuss the implications of our findings for work practices and for software design.

KEYWORDS: Cooperative work, CAD, end user programming.

INTRODUCTION

Recent empirical studies of end user computing have found a strong pattern of cooperative work among users of a variety of software systems, including spreadsheets, word processing programs, and Unix. Users with different levels of computer expertise and interest work together to customize their environments [5,15,16] and to program applications [23]. Nardi and Miller [23] identified a continuum of three kinds of users: end users, local developers, and professional programmers. End users have little or no programming education and tend to lack an intrinsic interest in computers; they are focused on their own domain interests. Local developers are domain experts who have acquired more advanced knowledge of computing, and in particular, knowledge of one or more specific software systems such as spreadsheets or CAD products. They serve as a resource for end users, training them and developing code for them. Programmers have a much broader, deeper knowledge

of computing than local developers (e.g. knowledge of compilers, operating systems, languages, architectures, programming methodologies) acquired through professional training. Programmers contribute code to the programs of end users and local developers, and help them learn new things.[1] Mackay [15] and MacLean, Carter, Lovstrand and Moran [16] described a similar continuum of expertise among the users they studied.[2]

In this paper we describe patterns of cooperation among users of CAD systems. We chose an ethnographic approach so that we could discover what CAD users are actually doing, and what they think about what they are doing. Ethnography is well suited to studies of collaborative work as patterns of collaboration extend over many users, and are richly nuanced in a way that cannot be replicated in the artificial environment of the laboratory. In the everyday world, people work out ways to solve problems that accommodate and take advantage of the varying expertise and interests of group members. Such methods of work will not emerge under the short time frame and controlled conditions of laboratory experiments, but can be studied naturalistically.

The objectives of this paper are: (1) to document the nature of cooperative work among CAD users, as further empirical evidence of the pattern of collaborative end user computing practices reported in other studies; (2) to highlight the importance of the formalization of the local developer role that we discovered in some of the groups we studied; and (3) to discuss the implications of the cooperative nature of end user application development for work practices and software design.

Many recent studies have suggested that the introduction of computers into offices and factories does not correlate with increased productivity [3,10,12,30,35]. One key reason is that computers are not being used to their best advantage because we are still trying to discover just how to do that [3,10,12]. We believe that human-computer interaction researchers have a contribution to make to this discovery process as our con-

---

[1] There are end users who do not become local developers but who do become quite sophisticated computer users. They are in a minority. The local developer role would not have evolved if they were the common case.

[2] For *local developer* Mackay used the term *translator* and MacLean et al. the term *tinkerer*.

cerns encompass both work practices and technology, which must be considered together as we learn to utilize technology more effectively. Here we focus specifically on the cooperative nature of end user computing. We believe that a description of how users actually get applications written will inform our understanding of how to better organize and manage work practices, and how to better design computer products and research prototypes.

Our study of CAD use partly confirms what other studies have found, i.e. that end users collaborate with more experienced users to create applications. As described in detail in [5,15,16,23], the range of applications end users can create is much greater than it would be in the absence of collaboration for two reasons: end users are learning from more sophisticated users, and they are getting code from them. This sharing of knowledge and code among a community of cooperating users is a mainstay of end user computing.

However, our study found a significant difference in the pattern of collaboration among CAD users compared with users in the previously mentioned studies: the role of local developer has changed from an informal, ad hoc, unsupported position to a formal or semi-formal role in some organizations using CAD. Managers recognizing the benefits of having a local developer in place have begun to support the role. In the CAD world, local developers are taking on many of the functions usually assigned to a customer support organization or MIS department. Because of the tremendous backlog in such organizations, they may not deal with users' problems in a timely manner (or may not deal with them at all). In contrast, local developers serve smaller, more localized constituencies, and they already know the domain and associated problems. Formal support of local developers is exactly what Mackay [15], based on her study of Unix users, recommended: local developers should be given the time and resources to provide computer support to their fellow domain experts. In this paper we will describe the formalized and semi-formalized local developer roles in some of the organizations we studied, and evaluate the advantages and problems of acquiring local developers from the ranks of domain experts.

The "gardeners and gurus" of our paper are terms from the argot of one large corporation we studied where local developer roles have become formal or semi-formal (depending on the needs of the division or department within the corporation). Local developers supporting mechanical engineers in the corporation are called *gardeners,* and those in electrical engineering are *gurus.* The term gardener comes from the corporation's attempt to "grow productivity" by making a gardener responsible for nurturing fellow employees and providing support so that they can perform as effectively as possible. Gardeners and gurus are a special case of local developer. They are distinct from other local developers in that they are given recognition, time, and resources for pursuing local developer activities. In this paper, we will use "gardeners" as a convenient cover term for gardeners and gurus and whatever else they may be called in other organizations.[3] Where our comments apply to either

local developers or gardeners, we use "local developer" as the more general term.

There are a number of studies of CAD use, including studies of CAD tasks from a cognitive perspective, the management of CAD users, and ways to use CAD systems more productively. Ullman et al. [33,34], Dillon and Sweeney [7], Cuomo and Sharit [6], and Pikaar [27] studied aspects of the cognitive processes of individual CAD users; for example, Dillon and Sweeney [7] compared the mechanical engineering design process with that of designers using traditional drawing board techniques. Petre and Green [26] compared the cognitive efficiency of graphical vs. textual notation in electrical engineering design. Sinclair, Siemieniuch and John [31] and Badham [1] described the work process, and design and drafting roles in CAD environments. Maver [20] and Krouse, Mills, Beckert and Dvorak [14] made recommendations for managing CAD environments to maximize user acceptance and productivity. Perzanowski [25] provided a primer of CAD specialization, describing how to write macros, and other aspects of CAD use. Sebborn described the use of customization for automating the work process [29]. Majchrzak, Chang, Barfield, Eberts and Salvendy [17] discussed the technical and user interface aspects of CAD, and the management of CAD users. Brooks and Wells [4] and Manske and Wolf [18] also studied management of CAD users, noting that formalizing the role of local developer can be a valuable support for end users, though they did not elaborate further. Graham [13] advocated developing a network of experts, each specializing in a different CAD tool, to increase productivity. We did not find any in-depth studies of interactions among different kinds of CAD users, or of how users cooperate in building applications.

CAD SYSTEMS

What exactly do we mean by CAD? Computer-aided design (CAD) began in the mid-1960s. Sutherland's SKETCHPAD [32], created at MIT in 1963, is credited with being the first (prototypical) CAD system, and with providing the impetus for future development [17]. Researchers at large automotive and aircraft companies such as General Motors, Lockheed, and Boeing began developing proprietary mainframe-based systems. Because these early systems were very expensive, their use was limited to those industries that could afford the necessary capital investment. The development of minicomputer technology made CAD commercially viable. In the late 1960s, electrical engineers began to use CAD as design and drafting aids for printed circuit board production. During the 1970s, CAD moved into architecture and mechanical and civil engineering. Today CAD has become a standard tool in all of these industries, and a wide variety of products are in use. (See [9,11,17] for the history of CAD development.) CAD systems

---

[3] A recent InfoWorld article entitled "Nurturing the Flock" describing various support arrangements for PC users featured a cartoon showing the PC Manager as a mother hen surrounded by chicks representing different kinds of

users (novices hatching out of shells, demanding users fighting over worms, etc.) [28]. While we doubt that "Mother Hen" will emerge as the next term for local developer, the metaphor does highlight the problem of supporting users. Another use of the term gardening comes from the Soviet Union. In an article in the July 1, 1991 *San Jose Mercury News* it is reported that two Soviet management consultants advocate that managers must be persuaded to stop thinking like "mechanics" and start thinking like "gardeners" who want to cultivate new and improved organizations. It is interesting to see metaphors of the natural world (gardeners, chickens) pressed into service in technical environments.

run on workstations, PCs, and Macintoshes. CAD users have a relatively sophisticated computing environment (at least compared with many end users who are still in the world of standalone PCs and floppy disks). A typical CAD workstation includes a large color monitor, a drawing tablet with stylus and/or mouse, and often network access to other CAD users, printers and plotters, library file servers, and backup systems.

CAD packages are, at their most basic level, drawing and drafting aids. What makes them different from simple drawing packages is that behind each graphical representation is a dataset that enables the program to perform a variety of functions such as autodimensioning,[4] creating wireframes and solid models,[5] and generating parts lists.

Many CAD programs[6] are specialized by the manufacturer specifically for a particular industry such as architecture, electrical engineering, mechanical engineering, or site planning. Other programs, such as AutoCAD, have open environments that can be specialized by users to meet the needs of a wide variety of task domains.

Some CAD programs perform specific tasks within a particular domain. For example, within electrical engineering, there are several tasks: schematic capture, simulation, and physical layout/design. A few systems such as Chipbuster manage all of these processes, but usually each is handled by a separate software package.[7] There are also CAD systems that provide frameworks that integrate such task-specific applications; for example, ASG runs with AutoCAD to automate the entire architectural design process. Traditionally, many of the nondrawing processes (e.g. simulation) came under the rubric of computer-aided engineering, but the line between computer-aided design, engineering and manufacture (CAD, CAE and CAM) is becoming increasingly fuzzy as software companies integrate their tools to support the entire process, from design to manufacture.

METHODOLOGY

To study CAD use, we conducted in-depth interviews with 24 informants (21 users and 3 managers), collected and analyzed informants' CAD artifacts (printouts of macro programs, designs, etc.) and studied and used a CAD system (HP ME30). Informants were found through an informal process of referral. Interviews were tape-recorded in informants' offices or work settings.[8] A set of open-ended questions was asked of each informant in the course of the interview (see Appendix). We discussed the users' tasks and how they used CAD to accomplish them, and how CAD fit into the overall workflow. The order of the questions varied depending on the course of the conversation. Additional conversational leads were followed as they arose. Informants showed us examples of their work on-screen and in paper form. Approximately 325 pages of transcription were obtained from the interviews.

Our informants included architects, mechanical engineers, electrical engineers, and industrial designers. They came from seven companies ranging from a three-person architecture design office to Fortune 100 companies. Most informants had college degrees and all had at least two years of college. Most had been using CAD for at least five years. Informants' computer experience ranged from those who were completely self-taught to one engineer with a degree in computer science (and a degree in electrical engineering). Most informants had taken some formal programming or product classes. Many had also put in long hours studying on their own.

CAD software varies extensively by industry. In our study informants discussed many different CAD systems (all of which are named in footnote 6). The numerous software products discussed reflect the fact that often an individual uses several different products, and that users sometimes referred to products they had used on previous projects.

We introduce seven informants in some detail to give a more concrete flavor of CAD use and CAD users. Informant names used here are fictitious. Verbatim segments from the interviews of these informants will be given to illustrate aspects of CAD use.

- **Ben** is an electrical engineer/designer who works in the R & D laboratory of a large corporation. He has a BS in physics and an MS in electrical engineering. Ben is a self-taught programmer, with no formal programming education. He is a local developer and provides support to twelve people.

- **Steve** is an electrical engineer at a small computer company. He is working on the design of the company's product, which is not on the market yet. He has degrees in electrical engineering and computer science. Steve is a local developer.

---

[4] Autodimensioning is placing dimension lines and corresponding numerical measurements after two points are specified.

[5] A wireframe is a view of each surface of an object incorporated into one 3D view. A wireframe model contains no information on the content of an object that would be needed to compute, for example, volume, mass or stress. In solid modelling, such information is available because the inside or outside of an object can be determined [see 17].

[6] Product credit and trademark notification for the CAD products we refer to in this paper are given here: Abacus is a product of Hibbitt, Karlsson, Sorensen. Adobe Illustrator and PhotoShop are registered trademarks of Adobe Systems Inc. ADS, AutoCAD, AutoLISP and AutoShade are registered trademarks of Autodesk, Inc. ASG is a trademark of Archsoft Group. Cadence, SPICE and Verilog are trademarks of Cadence Design Systems. Calay is a product of Calay Systems Inc. Chipbuster is an internal Hewlett-Packard product. DCS and PCDS are trademarks of Hewlett-Packard. Design Architect is a trademark of Mentor Graphics Corporation. Dynaperspective is a trademark of Dynaware Corp. FlexiCAD is a trademark of Amiable Technologies, Inc. HILO is a trademark of Genrad. HP ME10 and HP ME30 are products of Hewlett-Packard. 20/20 is a registered trademark of Home Depot. KST, ArchT2 and ArchT2/3D are trademarks of Kativ Technologies Inc. Macintosh is a registered trademark of Apple Computer Inc. Mentor Graphics is a registered trademark of Mentor Graphics Corporation. ModelShop is a trademark of Paracomp. OrCAD is a registered trademark of OrCAD. Patran is a registered trademark of PDA Engineering. Pro/Engineer is a registered trademark of Parametric Technology Corp. Synopsys is a registered trademark of Synopsys Inc. Unigraphics is a trademark of McDonnell Douglas. Vellum is a trademark of Ashlar Inc. VersaCad is a registered trademark of VersaCad. Vivid is shareware. Unix is a trademark of AT&T.

[7] For example, Mentor's Design Architect is used for schematic capture, PCDS for printed circuit board layout, and Verilog for digital logic simulation of integrated circuits.

[8] The interviews were conducted by the first author.

- **Rick** is the CAD administrator (or "gardener") for a medium-sized architecture firm. His formal education includes BS and MS degrees in architecture. He has taken many programming classes. He and another system administrator support forty users, including ten CAD users.

- **James** and **Carol** are mechanical engineering production drafters for a large corporation. They support the production engineers in their division. Both have drafting degrees. James has taken many programming classes and is very interested in computers. He has taken on a semi-formal gardener position that includes overseeing the specializations done for a group of 100. In addition, James provides one-on-one support to five people in his group. Carol is an end user. She has no programming experience and does no specialization.

- **Mark** is the gardener for a medium-sized mechanical and industrial design firm. He began working as a mechanical engineering drafter fourteen years ago and was the first person to begin specializing the CAD system when his group began using computers. He has taken a few Unix classes but is primarily self-taught. He also maintains the office's other computers (used for databases and word processing) for forty-five engineers.

- **Warren** is an electrical engineer in a research and development group. He has taken many programming classes and studied extensively on his own. He is a full-time "guru" supporting seven engineers.

PATTERNS OF COOPERATION AMONG CAD USERS

In our study, we found that CAD system users follow the general pattern of collaborative customization and application development found in other studies [5,15,16,23]. CAD users cooperate both to customize their environments (as Mackay [15] found among Unix users) and to program applications (as Nardi and Miller [23] found among spreadsheet users). Two interesting differences from previous studies emerged: (1) the general level of computer sophistication is higher among CAD users such that professional programmers are rarely involved in the collaboration process; and (2) the role of the local developer has been formalized in some cases, with institutional recognition and support accorded the activities of local developers. We will describe general patterns of cooperation among CAD system users, and then discuss the implications of these patterns for supporting end user application development.

Customizing and Programming in CAD Systems

To better explain how CAD users cooperate, we briefly describe the kinds of specializations CAD users make to customize and extend their systems.

Simple customizations include changing the color of a menu, the location of a menu item, line widths and colors, drawing size, and so on. Such customizations are made by editing parameters in macros.[9] A more elaborate customization might involve writing a new macro. For example, the user

might want to create a circle with the center lines automatically drawn in, and add the new circle to a menu. The user would write a macro, assembling the appropriate circle-creating commands and line-creating commands, specifying certain parameters, and then linking them to a menu slot.

The most complex form of specialization requires writing programs in languages such as C or AutoLISP,[10] writing Unix shell scripts, or writing programs in the complex macro languages of some products. Such programming is required, for example, to perform calculations needed for CAD applications (e.g. calculating part placement) or to link a CAD application to other programs (for example, users might need enhanced plotting utilities or links to simulation or database programs).

CAD macros may be called from within a programming language such as AutoLISP. For example, in an architectural application, when a symbol (such as a door or window) is selected from a menu, an AutoLISP function may call a macro that queries the user for values for height and width, which are then used to size the symbol before the user places it in the drawing.

End Users

Of the seven end users in our study, four had done no customization or programming. One was not allowed to do any, as his manager insisted on maintaining established conventions. The other three preferred not to specialize, and because they had local developers or gardeners supporting them, they did not have to. Three end users made simple specializations, as described below.

An end user's first efforts at specialization usually involve customizing the CAD environment by creating keyboard macros and/or changing parameter values within existing macros. These macros may come from many sources: from the software package itself, from macro sets already created for a particular division, department, or site within a corporation, from macros created by fellow users (other end users as well as local developers), and from macros published in magazines and electronic bulletin boards.

Like spreadsheet end users [23], CAD end users generally avoid manuals. They work by: (1) editing existing macros; (2) using existing macros as templates; (3) learning new program features by asking other end users and local developers how to do new things; and (4) asking others, especially local developers, for help in debugging macros.

As was found with spreadsheet users [23], end users of CAD systems tend to be focused on the domain and the task at hand, rather than showing an intrinsic interest in computers. Carol, one of the users who did not do any specializing, explains her focus on drafting skills:

---

such as loops and conditionals. The complexity of the macro languages varies by product; some are quite simple, and others approach the functionality of conventional programming languages. Macros are organized into text files as with conventional programming languages.

[10]AutoLISP is a subset of XLISP and Common LISP, with some additional functions to support design tasks.

---

[9]Many CAD "macro" languages are programming languages with features

Carol: And it does seem like probably just because of different personalities, we all sort of have our area of expertise that when a certain job comes in, [we can say], "Oh, Harry would be good for this" because technical illustration is really his high point . . .

Interviewer: What's yours?

Carol: Ummm, I think I'm very good at drafting skills; I know what those views should be, where they should be placed, and I think I'm very good at being a checker on all the specs on the drawing – that when this goes into production, we won't have to scrap parts, we won't have to bring it back for revision after we've gone through with the final tooth and comb. And that's what I enjoy about it . . . I tackle it like a puzzle, I want to comb everything out and cover every aspect of it and then know that . . . everything's perfect. I like that part. And like I said, James really likes the computer side of it and, "What can I get this thing to do?"

Interviewer: Yeah, "What can I make it do next!" Well, and by not having to worry about the integrity of your lines, you can spend more time checking the integrity of the specs. . . . So . . .

Carol: So the content . . . is the main focus.

Rick, a gardener, summarized his role in terms of end users' focus on "content": "That's why I'm here, because I know that when these guys are designing, they just want to design. They don't want to have to look at a manual, they don't want to have to . . . get into any of that."

Local Developers

In the CAD world, local developers write the macros, programs, and shell scripts that are needed for many applications, but that are beyond the scope of end users' interests and abilities. End users rely on the output of local developers and incorporate their macro, program, and shell script files into their own environments.

Local developers also help end users write, complete, and debug macros. For example, two engineers at a mechanical engineering consulting firm wanted a macro that could create a parabola, a function that the firm's CAD system did not include. They did not know how to write macros, and the local developer did not know the math behind parabola creation. They worked together, each adding their particular expertise, to create the macro for drawing parabolas:

Mark: Two women were dealing with a lens for a lamp and they wanted to . . . be able to define a parabola easily, and they were doing it somewhat laboriously. As it turned out, the ellipse command that is the standard ME10 command is a very complex macro that has you defining the major axis, the minor axis, and then it uses the spline command and repeats with all of the points. It's sort of a left-brain, right-brain thing. I can't explain it. I understand [it] when I'm writing it. So I was

able to take that and simplify it greatly and make a parabola macro out of it . . . So, by just looking in a standard engineering book, we were able to take the math and I knew the [macro] language, they knew the math, and they just told me how we were supposed to manipulate the numbers that we got out of it.

In our study, the eight local developers (informal local developers, not gardeners) among our informants evolved from end users; they were not hired from the outside. They grew into the position because they started specializing on their own initiative, usually out of frustration with the existing software, and because they got interested in seeing how far they could push the software.

Ben explains how he got to be a local developer:

Interviewer: You mentioned there were two reasons why you customize so much: one is because it's so easy [using Chipbuster], and I don't think we actually got to the other one . . .

Ben: The other was aptitude, interest, frustration. I know it can be done, therefore I must.

Interviewer: So how did you learn to write [macros] – the manuals?

Ben: There's a tutorial manual, but mostly it's by learning from examples of how do people do similar things. . . . Very often what I want to do is tweak one of these existing commands so it does something a little differently . . .

Local developers evince a higher level of interest than end users in acquiring computer expertise. They are willing to wrestle with software and with manuals to achieve their aim:

Rick: . . . [Local developers] tend to be hackers: "I don't read manuals, I just start a program and say, 'Ah, let's see what it does! Oh, I have this other package that does the same thing.'" Then you look and see how it does it, and then you get stumped, and then you go look in the manual for reference. And you know in an afternoon you can figure out everything about a package. That's usually what I do.

For macro writing, local developers generally use manuals as a reference when they got stuck, or if they are the first one at a site creating specializations. Many informants spoke ill of manuals, as though they were necessary evils (we return to manuals in the Discussion section). Local developers doing complex programming in C, AutoLISP, or other languages use manuals for learning those languages – indeed there seems little alternative, as it is not possible in conventional programming to rely on editing existing code and/or pure experimentation, as one can for simpler specializations.

These findings about the activities and interests of local developers in CAD are consistent with reports of local developers in other domains [15,16,23]. The main difference we found in CAD is that local developers show considerably more computer sophistication than their spreadsheet counterparts (and, we believe, the users in [15,16]). While local developers of spreadsheets generally work within the macro language (and other specialized aspects of spreadsheets such as facilities to create fancy charts and graphs, or new formats for presenting cell values), local developers in CAD go beyond that level by writing in general programming languages or the complex macro languages of some CAD products, creating shell scripts, and becoming knowledgeable about operating systems. When spreadsheet users need to link to other programs, write complex macros, or do similarly advanced things, they typically call in professional programmers (e.g. from a customer support organization). In the CAD world, a class of users who are not professional programmers, but who come from the ranks of domain experts, have taken on such tasks themselves. It is as though the level of computer sophistication distributed across the different kinds of users has shifted up a level, popping programmers off the end.[11] In the Discussion section we explore the implications of this situation.

Gardeners and Gurus: A Special Case of Local Developer

One of the main findings of our study is that the informal position of local developer has evolved into a formal or semi-formal position in some organizations. In three of the seven companies we studied, gardeners were present. We interviewed six gardeners. As managers begin to notice the time and effort being expended by local developers – and to notice the benefits of local developer activities – they realize that formalizing the position can increase user productivity. In the semi-formal situation, local developers continue with their local developer tasks (as well as their regular duties), but they are at least now given recognition, appreciation, and possibly resources for the functions being performed. When the local developer position becomes fully formalized, the local developer is given a new job title, and time and resources to pursue local developer activities, usually full-time. Managers benefit from recognizing the local developer role in that there is now someone who can officially be relied upon to help end users, and to maintain standardization of the macros and programs they use.

What exactly do gardeners do that is different from informal local developers? In addition to performing traditional local developer duties, gardeners are responsible for writing and disseminating standard macros and programs at the corporate, division, or department level, and for researching and providing new tools to end users. The macros and programs they write may originate from their own observations of what is needed, or they may be created in response to user requests for certain capabilities, or requests from management. Sometimes a gardener sees a macro or program a user has written that looks useful for the whole group. The gardener takes the user's file, tests the code, modifies it if necessary, and then disseminates it to the rest of the group. Gardeners are always on the lookout for tools to enhance the group's productivity.

James, a drafter who has become a gardener, describes a gardener's activities:

> **James:** The gardener has to have a good working knowledge of Unix . . . Because your IT [Information Technology] group is only going to know how to do the administration-type part. They're not going to know the ME30 part. Your end users are only going to know the ME30 part and they're not going to know the systems part. So a gardener is like a cross between both worlds. And he's got to be able to communicate what IT is trying to do with the standardized configurations and hardware ordering, and he's also got to be able to speak the language of the end user who's sitting there saying, "I'm unproductive and I need to be productive real fast." . . . So, it's a juggling act . . .

As James's comments show, a gardener has both domain and computer knowledge. James has educated himself through programming classes and self-study to the point where he can handle the Unix and HP ME30 problems effectively. He has the drafting background to understand domain experts' problems and frustrations. James is effective with two constituencies – the systems administrators and the domain experts. Given appropriate tools such as CAD products, it seems that being a good gardener is generally easier if one starts on the domain side and acquires the necessary computer expertise, rather than starting on the computer side and trying to acquire a working knowledge of a domain. A gardener who is a domain expert need learn only a subset of computer science – that which applies to the specific jobs to be done within a domain. It would be more difficult for a computer specialist to acquire the understandings that accrue over time to a domain expert. Such understandings involving workflow, group work practices, and the problem areas and frustrations of the job are important to the gardener role, and are acquired over time, through the experience of actually doing the job.

In our study we found that informal local developers may coexist with gardeners in large organizations. In this situation gardeners take on the standardization and system maintenance tasks, and local developers tend to provide the one-on-one support to end users. There is potential here for a natural progression for some local developers to eventually become gardeners when gardeners leave or move within the organization.

DISCUSSION

Forester [10] notes that there is a "new wave of skepticism" regarding the productivity benefits of automation. Many studies suggest that the introduction of computers into offices and factories has not generally correlated with increased productivity ([3,10,12,30,35]). Forester calls this the "productivity puzzle." There are many complex reasons why automation has not produced the expected productivity gains,[12] but a key piece of the puzzle is that our work practices and technology have not yet

---

[11]Professional programmers are used to write proprietary CAD systems. We did not study any such systems.

[12]The puzzle has many pieces, including some that have nothing whatsoever to do with technology. Productivity is difficult to measure. A net decline in productivity can occur when countervailing forces (e.g. the need for increased legal and personnel staff to monitor government regulations and employee entitlements) depress productivity more than automation, which is contributing

evolved to the point where we can take full advantage of the potential benefits of automation [3,12]. Given the short history of computing this is not surprising, but it is time for us to take a careful look at the insufficiently evolved social and technical bases of our present computing practices, and try to see where we can do better. Our findings on the cooperative nature of CAD use have practical implications in terms of both work practices and software design. We will argue that: (1) despite a few problems, managers will be well served by growing local developers into gardeners; and (2) software companies designing new products or enhancing existing products should consider how software is actually used – by groups of cooperating users with different levels of computer expertise and interest.

Cultivating Gardeners

Our study supports Mackay's contention [15] that the activities of local developers should be recognized and promoted. In the organizations that we studied in which gardeners have become formal or semi-formal positions, our assessment is that the benefits far outweigh the costs. End users are comfortable with CAD software because they are assured assistance in all aspects of CAD use – whether they are writing macros, learning new tools, or keeping abreast of the latest developments in CAD. Gardeners – who enjoy tinkering with computers – are given official leave to do so. Their communication talents are engaged as they provide an important bridge between system administrators on the one side and domain experts on the other, as well as communicating with users as they help them in debugging, learning new capabilities, and so forth. A gardener can save time and money by making it unnecessary for users to spend their time re-inventing the wheel (creating redundant macros and programs); instead, the gardener offers standard versions of these resources to the entire group. Employees can be more productive because they are concentrating on their domain-related tasks. Establishing a gardener creates a finer-grained division of labor among software users that increases efficiency and motivation because it is firmly grounded in users' interests and abilities.

An important benefit of gardening is that managers can feel confident that the standardization and integrity of the macros, programs, and data used by their staffs will be maintained. Many managers and MIS personnel are made somewhat nervous by the whole notion of end user computing because the potential for chaos is real: data can disappear, users may waste time managing their systems instead of doing their work, and esoteric, personalistic specialization can reduce the utility of the programs developed by end users (see [24]). With a gardener in place these concerns can be dealt with. It is the gardener's job to maintain standards, and to offer users standard programs that they can use to get their work done. A gardener is someone between management and users, and is trusted by both. Because gardeners are fellow domain experts and not outsiders who lack understanding of the everyday patterns of work and group interaction, gardeners are more likely to be effective in dealing with the group's concerns. They can in fact anticipate these concerns and handle them proactively in a way that is impossible for outsiders such as systems analysts

---

to productivity, can increase it. But even taking these factors in account, we do seem to be underutilizing our technology [3].

or MIS personnel.

A problem with formalizing the local developer role that we found is that not all managers recognize the benefits of having a "productivity" person on board. They may feel that this is a waste of a person who could be working to "contribute to the product." Where a higher level of management mandates a gardener, the lower-level manager may feel that he or she is less effective and cannot utilize available resources in the best possible way (see [4]). When this happens, at a minimum it would seem useful for managers to evaluate whether a project really does have enough resources. It may be that a manager has not thought through the benefits of including a productivity person in the group, or that the manager is truly in a situation of insufficient resources. Adding a gardener to a group will involve some kind of economic analysis to determine just when the shifting of resources really makes sense. An indication of the need for a gardener is the situation in which a local developer is devoting considerable time to group support activities, without official recognition and support. Experimentation with the gardener role will undoubtedly be necessary to make it fit the needs of the individual group. Some groups may feel the need for a full-time, fully formal gardener, while others can get along with a semi-formal, part-time person.

Another problem with gardening is that there is not always a person with the right combination of technical and social skills available to assume the job. A person who is technically skilled but uninterested in intensive interpersonal interaction may not have much of a green thumb when it comes to helping other users. By the same token, a person without sufficient technical skill would not be an effective gardener. In our study we found a somewhat reluctant local developer, Steve, who typifies at least part of the problem of finding the right mix of skills. Steve is a highly technically skilled electrical engineer. He and another engineer work on a project where they are creating complex simulations. Some of the other teams within the company are doing similar simulations, and, instead of learning how to program the simulation themselves, they ask Steve and his partner to help them. Steve's ambivalence about acting in a support role comes through in the following only half-humorous exchange:

> **Interviewer:** So you guys are sort of the experts?
>
> **Steve:** We're supposed to be, but . . .
>
> **Interviewer:** (laughing) But you're not really? Well, do people come and ask you for help?
>
> **Steve:** (laughing) Well, the thing is, I'm no smarter than any of those guys and . . . we try not to answer their questions.
>
> **Interviewer:** So you don't like to share what you've done?
>
> **Steve:** No, no, we will help. It depends on the time . . .

How do organizations cultivate gardeners? The right mix of skills is important, as the above example illustrates. A gardener cannot be randomly chosen out of a group of users; there must be genuine interest and enjoyment in assisting less knowledgeable users on the one hand, and the desire to learn one's way around the operating system and a programming language, on the other hand. Brooks and Wells [4] noted that when users are learning a new system in a training class, often one person stands out in interest and ability, and can be identified fairly early as a potential local expert. More generally speaking, their point is well taken: rather than selecting someone to be a gardener at the introduction of a new system, it is better to wait until users have had some exposure to the system, looking for those who gravitate naturally toward its use.

The results of our study indicate that another factor that contributes to gardeners' effectiveness is that they come from the rank and file: they know the domain, the users, the frustrations and problems. The need to expend great effort translating domain knowledge to computer experts is avoided. Gardeners who are domain experts have "been there before" – and, as we saw with James, they show concern and empathy for their users. They know how it feels to be frustrated and unproductive because of software or hardware limitations. This is a considerable advantage: CAD users work within a very challenging environment – design and manufacturing processes are changing, deadlines are getting shorter as managers scramble to reduce time to market [2], and the software itself is quite sophisticated, and constantly changing.

All the gardeners in our study had started out as domain expert/end users. Manske and Wolf [18] reported that in the organizations in Germany that they studied, the CAD administrator was a mechanical drafter with computer expertise, but not design expertise, hired from the outside. They did not provide an evaluation of how well this arrangement works, but it would be interesting to know more about the exact functions of such CAD administrators, and to compare them with their gardener counterparts.

A problem that Mackay reported in her study of Unix customization [15] was that the local developers (or translators as she called them) often were not as knowledgeable about computers as would have been desirable, and as a result, they sometimes distributed buggy code throughout the organization. We did not find this to be a problem among the CAD local developers/gardeners we studied because their level of computer expertise was high, and they were able to meet the technical challenges. While CAD users may typically start out with an advantage in having a good "technical" background, users in other fields can strive to attain a high level of computer competence through training and studying on their own. (Indeed, many of our CAD users had taken programming and product classes, and had devoted a great deal of time to self-study.) Cultivating gardeners should involve making the time and money available for such training and study. More generally, solving the problem of distributing quality code means supporting the local developer role in a formal way, to ensure that adequate time is devoted to testing and debugging code to be given out to the group.

If an organization can manage to train gardeners to a high enough standard, the need for professional programmers largely disappears, at least with respect to the well-designed commercially available products that support end user comput-

ing, such as CAD systems. In our study we found no instance of users resorting to programmers for assistance in specializing their CAD software. When macros and programs are written by gardeners, it is with group use in mind (so idiosyncratic code is not produced), and with a good command of the domain and the end users' concerns. In Mackay's study, the Unix customizations were written by professional programmers for their own use, and the "translating" needed before end users could make use of the customizations was considerable. Of course that was a different setting, and the comparison cannot be stretched too far,[13] but the point is that gardeners can produce code from the outset that is intended for group use, and, most importantly, with a very clear picture in mind of the group's needs and preferences.

While we believe that a major strength of gardeners is their origin as domain experts, we can also see a potential problem in this arrangement. Over time, full-time gardeners may lose touch with the domain side of gardening as their activities come to be defined purely in terms of support. The most effective gardeners will make a special effort to keep up with advances in their field, and to be cognizant of the changing work practices in which they themselves are not directly participating. Some gardeners may want to rotate out of gardening periodically to renew and update their domain knowledge.

Another of Mackay's recommendations was that local developers and programmers should supply end users with extensive examples so that they do not have to start from scratch [15]. As we have described, the users in our study typically had a rich body of macros from which to choose to begin their customizations and programs. This worked well, and we think that an important aspect of gardening is providing such examples. However, two qualifications to an enthusiasm for examples are in order. First, examples seem to work best when they are in a language that end users can understand well, e.g. for CAD end users, the macro language. It will not do to overload people with elaborate examples in complex languages – the presence of examples alone is not enough (see [8]). Second, we noticed that what the less experienced CAD users were doing with examples was simply changing parameter values. This suggests that examples should be set up so that much can be accomplished by making such changes. The use of examples – at least for beginning users – becomes a simple form-filling exercise, not an attempt to replicate functionality involving complicated datatypes, control structures, and so on. MacLean et al. [16] followed this rule to good effect in their "Buttons" prototype.

Cooperative Work and Software Design

There are lessons to be learned from the study of collaboration among CAD users that can be applied to software design as well as to work practices. In doing this study, we were surprised at the level of computer sophistication attained by the local developers and gardeners we talked to – which was generally higher than that of the spreadsheet local developers we studied [23], as we have described. It is important for software designers to think about two things: (1) the continuum of

---

[13]No criticism of the programmers in Mackay's study is intended in any way; they had no charter to create end user customizations.

expertise of a group of users who will cooperate in creating applications; and (2) the endpoints of the continuum.[14] We hear many exhortations to "Know the user!" but there is not a *single* user to know – there is a *community of cooperating users lying within a particular range of computer expertise*. Of all the things software designers might want to know about users, understanding their tasks, and their levels of interest and expertise with computers should be among the highest priorities.

Software designers need to find out, for a given product, where the continuum of computer expertise starts and ends, and then incorporate into the product a range of capabilities that takes advantage of the range of users arrayed along the continuum – just as today's most advanced CAD systems provide the basic drawing and drafting capabilities, a macro language, and a programming language such as AutoLISP.[15] Software products should have a carefully designed set of capabilities targeted specifically for end users, such as the drawing and simple macro editing/writing capabilities in CAD systems, or formula writing capability in spreadsheets. Then, moving along the continuum, more advanced users – local developers, gardeners and sometimes programmers – need to be supported with more sophisticated functionality for their own use, and because they will be the conduit to end users for the product's advanced capabilities.

Organizing functionality around different kinds of cooperating users makes the range of things end users can do with software products much greater. It also acknowledges that some end users will eventually attain more expertise with a program as they become more familiar with it (whether they come to act in the supporting role of local developer or not) and will want to be able to learn more sophisticated capabilities. Some approaches to end user computing, such as programming-by-example [19,21] and user modeling [36], assume that not only do end users remain rather deficient, but that they work in isolation, without a community of cooperating users. This is a limited view of end users, and will ultimately mean inhibiting their growth and the kinds of applications they can create. Three of our users brought this point up in their interviews spontaneously. (We did not ask about it; it was a topic they introduced because they thought we would be interested.) Rick described three levels of users who should be supported – in his terms: "the idiot level, the full-fledged program level, and the power user level." Warren, whose CAD system (for electrical engineering) offers few facilities for specialization, expressed dismay at the limitations of his system compared with another more sophisticated system:

> **Warren:** I'm very jealous because they have this incredible flexible ability to change and do anything. One of the problems with people who write tools is that they assume . . . they try to protect the users too much. And they don't recognize that

there's different levels of users. You can have beginners, general users and experts, and for the expert user, a lot of places will hire somebody to be an expert user just to [do] the customization, to do all the neat productivity things that make such a difference. But you have to have that flexibility to start with. . . . I find myself with most of the PC [printed circuit] tools, there's not much I can do with them.

The upper end of the continuum of expertise is perhaps trickiest to assess – just how far can users who have a strong interest in computers but who are are not professional programmers go? It seems reasonable for at least some CAD programs to support a programming language such as AutoLISP, while such a language might not be suitable for other domains where users are less familiar with computer technology. Of course to some extent what we have here is a moving target, but we believe it is worth the effort to do a detailed assessment of potential users' computer abilities and interests before launching a product.

Another way that software companies can provide better products is to take advantage of local developers in planning manuals. Everyone complains about manuals; end users avoid them, and local developers use them when they "get stuck." We believe that manuals need to be radically re-thought, and that local developers ought to be part of that process – they should be hired by software companies as consultants in the planning and reviewing of manuals. A set of manuals geared specifically toward local developers, who are the ones apparently making the most use of them, would be useful. The standard reference manual format does not fit the bill – at least the complaints suggest that it does not. Our users mentioned the importance of well worked examples as being critical; such examples are often in short supply in reference manuals. Because local developers report that they use manuals when they "get stuck," much more extensive indexing of manuals would seem to be a promising solution. Given the complexity of today's software products, there is a huge number of highly specific places one can get stuck, and they often fall between the cracks of the relatively gross categories that comprise the average index.

SUMMARY

We described cooperative work among CAD system users, focusing on the different activities of end users, local developers and gardeners. We found that in some organizations the local developer role has evolved into the formal or semi-formal role of "gardener," obviating the need for professional programmers. The advantages and problems of the gardener role were discussed. Suggestions for improving cooperative work with software systems were given with respect to managing and supporting users, and for product design. We conclude that more effective use of software systems will be made when managers cultivate gardeners, and when software design efforts take into account the patterns of cooperation among different kinds of users working together to create applications.

---

[14]The notion of a continuum of cooperating users may not apply to every kind of software product, but it does apply to a large class of products. Cooperation among users is increasing, not decreasing. Even home users join user groups, make use of telephone support, read bulletin boards, ask friends for help, etc.

[15]Not every CAD system need provide the more advanced capabilities of course, but there clearly is a demand for them as people attempt applications of ever-increasing complexity.

APPENDIX: LIST OF INTERVIEW QUESTIONS

1. What is your job/position?
2. What is your educational and job-related background?
3. What is the work process/flow and where does CAD fit in?
4. Do you share your work with others in your group? If so, how ? (Do you share CAD files, paper drawings, etc.?)
5. What CAD system is used? For what function?
6. Has your system been customized? If so, who does it and what specific customizations have been done?
7. How did you learn to customize (if applicable)?
8. Is there a CAD expert in your group? If so, how did that person get to be the expert?
9. What do you like/dislike about the system you use?
10. What would make it easier to use (manuals, better organized program, etc.)? What other features would you like to see?

ACKNOWLEDGEMENTS

Many thanks to Janice Bradford, John Drabik, Chuck Habib, Dan Hirano, Russell Sanchez, Debbie Schultz, Celeste Welch, Julie Wilker, Jonathan Yen, and Pete Zivkov for their help in providing valuable information and names of possible informants. Jeff Johnson, Nancy Kendzierski, Jim Miller, Andreas Paepcke, and Craig Zarmer gave helpful comments on earlier drafts of this paper. We are very grateful to our informants who willingly donated their time to this study and shared their work and thoughts with us.

REFERENCES

1. Badham, R. Computer-aided design, work organization and the integrated factory. *IEEE Transactions on Engineering Management* 36, 3 (1989), 216-226.

2. Berardinis, L., Dibble, M., Dvorak, P., and Rouse, N. CAD/CAM industry report. *Machine Design* (May 23, 1991), 47-58.

3. Bowen, W. The puny payoff from office computers. In *Computers in the Human Context*. T. Forester, Ed. Basil Blackwell, New York, 1989, 267-271.

4. Brooks, L., and Wells, C. Role conflict in design supervision. *IEEE Transactions on Engineering Management* 36, 4 (1989), 271-281.

5. Clement, A. Cooperative support for computer work: A social perspective on the empowering of end users. *Proceedings CSCW'90*. (Los Angeles, 5-7 October, 1990), 223-236.

6. Cuomo, D., and Sharit, J. A study of human performance of computer-aided architectural design. *International Journal of Human-Computer Interaction* 1, 1 (1989), 69-107.

7. Dillon, A., and Sweeney, M. The application of cognitive psychology to CAD. *People and Computers IV: Proceedings of the Fourth Conference of the British Computer Society Human-Computer Interaction Specialist Group*. (University of Manchester, 5-9 September, 1988), 477-488.

8. DiSessa, A. A principled design for an integrated computational environment. *Human-Computer Interaction* 1, (1985), 1-47.

9. Encarnacao, J., and Schlechtendahl, E. *Computer Aided Design: Fundamentals and System Architectures*. Springer-Verlag, Berlin, 1983.

10. Forester, T. *Computers in the Human Context*. Basil Blackwell, New York, 1989.

11. Foundyller, C. *CAD/CAM, CAE: The Contemporary Technology*. Daratech Associates, Cambridge, Mass., 1984.

12. Franke, R. Technological revolution and productivity decline: The case of US banks. In *Computers in the Human Context*. T. Forester, Ed. Basil Blackwell, New York, 1989, 281-290.

13. Graham, B. Applying software tools to enhance engineering group productivity. *Proceedings of the Fifth Annual Applied Power Electronics Conference and Exposition*. (Los Angeles, 11-16 March, 1990), 612-618.

14. Krouse, J., Mills, R., Beckert, B., and Dvorak, P. CAD/CAM planning: 1990 - Managing people and the technology. *Industry Week* 239, 13 (1990), CC4-CC10.

15. Mackay, W. (1990). Patterns of sharing customizable software. *Proceedings CSCW'90*. (Los Angeles, 7-10 October, 1990), 209-221.

16. MacLean, A., Carter, K., Lovstrand, L., and Moran, T. User-tailorable systems: Pressing the issues with buttons. *Proceedings, CHI'90*. (Seattle, 1-5 April, 1990), 175-182.

17. Majchrzak, A., Chang, T., Barfield, W., Eberts, R., and Salvendy, G. *Human Aspects of Computer-Aided Design*. Taylor and Francis, Philadelphia, 1987.

18. Manske, F., and Wolf, H. Design work in change: Social conditions and results of CAD use in mechanical engineering. *IEEE Transactions on Engineering Management* 36, 4 (1989), 282-292.

19. Maulsby, D., Witten, I., and Kittlitz, K. Metamouse: Specifying graphical procedures by example. *Computer Graphics* 23 (1989), 127-136.

20. Maver, T. Social impacts of computer-aided architectural design. *Design Studies* 7, 4 (1986), 178-184.

21. Myers, B. Text formatting by demonstration. *Proceedings CHI'91*. (New Orleans, 27 April - 2 May, 1991), 251-256.

22. Nardi, B., and Miller, J. The spreadsheet interface: A basis for end user programming. *Proceedings Interact'90*. (Cambridge, England, 27-31 August, 1990), 977-983.

23. Nardi, B., and Miller, J. Twinkling lights and nested loops: Distributed problem solving and spreadsheet development. *International Journal of Man-Machine Studies* 34, (1991), 161-184. (Reprinted in *Computer Supported Cooperative Work and Groupware*, S. Greenberg, ed. Academic Press, London, 1991.)

24. Panko, R. *End User Computing: Management, Applications, and Technology*. John Wiley and Sons, New York, 1988.

25. Perzanowski, P. Scheduling CAD productivity. *AACE Transactions* (1991), I.1.1-I.1.5.

26. Petre, M., and Green, T.R.G. Requirements of graphical notations for professional users: Electronics CAD systems as a case study. In press. *Le Travail Humain* (1991).

27. Pikaar, R. Situation analysis of design tasks for CAD systems. *Behaviour and Information Technology* 8, 3 (1989), 191-206.

28. Raths, D. Nurturing the flock: As the PC population grows, so does the burden on support staff. *InfoWorld*, 19 August, 1991, 38-40.

29. Sebborn, M. Customising of a two-dimensional CAD system to service the needs of a small high technology company. *Computer-Aided Engineering Journal* (February, 1989), 13-15.

30. Shaiken, H. The automated factory: Vision and reality. In *Computers in the Human Context*. T. Forester, Ed. Basil Blackwell, New York, 1989, 291-300.

31. Sinclair, M., Siemieniuch, C., and John, P. A user-centered approach to define high-level requirements for next-generation CAD systems for mechanical engineering. *IEEE Transactions on Engineering Management* 36, 4 (1989), 262-270.

32. Sutherland, I. SKETCHPAD: A Man-Machine Graphical Communication System. *Proceedings of AFIPS 23*, 329-346 (Detroit, May, 1963).

33. Ullman, D., and Dietterich, T. Mechanical design methodology: Implications on future developments of computer-aided design and knowledge-based systems. *Engineering with Computers* 2, 1 (1987), 21-29.

34. Ullman, D., Wood, S., and Craig, D. The importance of drawing in the mechanical design process. *Computers and Graphics* 14, 2 (1990), 263-274.

35. Warner, T. Information technology as a competitive burden. In *Computers in the Human Context*. T. Forester, Ed. Basil Blackwell, New York, 1989, 273-280.

36. Wolz, U. The impact of user modeling on text generation in task-centered settings. *Proceedings Second International Conference on User Modeling* (Honolulu, 29 March - 1 April, 1990).

BEYOND BEING THERE

Jim Hollan and Scott Stornetta

Computer Graphics and Cognitive Science Research Groups
Bellcore, 445 South Street, Morristown, NJ 07962-1910

Email: hollan@bellcore.com, stornetta@bellcore.com

ABSTRACT

A belief in the efficacy of imitating face-to-face communication is an unquestioned presupposition of most current
work on supporting communications in electronic media. In
this paper we highlight problems with this presupposition
and present an alternative proposal for grounding and motivating research and development that frames the issue in
terms of needs, media, and mechanisms. To help elaborate
the proposal we sketch a series of example projects and
respond to potential criticisms.

Keywords: Telecommunications, CSCW.

INTRODUCTION

Face-to-face conversation provides a richness of interaction
seemingly unmatched by any other means of communication. It is also apparent that living and working near others,
whether that be in the same house, adjacent offices, or the
same city, affords certain opportunities for interaction that
are unavailable to those not co-located.

Research has clarified and substantiated both of these com-
monsense intuitions. It has been shown, for example, that
there is a predictable fall-off in likelihood of collaboration
between two researchers as a function of separation distance, even after correcting for factors such as organizational distance and similarity of research interest [5, see also
8]. This is understood to occur because of the large number
of informal interactions necessary to create and maintain
working relationships. There are also well-developed theories of interaction that predict why some interactions seem

© 1992 ACM 0-89791-513-5/92/0005-0119   1.50

to only work when face-to-face, while others can work over
the phone, and still others through written correspondence
[12,3,14].

This research supports the idea that we as humans have
developed a broad range of mechanisms for social interaction, which seem to meet well our needs for initiating and
maintaining friendships and working relationships, for discussing, negotiating, planning, and all other types of social
interactions. These are known to be complex processes, and
ones which physical proximity facilitates.

Many of us in the telecommunications field would like to
create systems that allows the same richness and variety of
interaction, but with distance no longer an issue. Ideally,
these systems should work so well that those at a distance
should be at no disadvantage to those who are physical
present. This in large measure is the telecommunication
problem. But how best to accomplish it?

BEING THERE

*If, as it is said to be not unlikely in the near future, the
principle of sight is applied to the telephone as well as
that of sound, earth will be in truth a paradise, and distance will lose its enchantment by being abolished altogether.* Arthur Strand, 1898 [7].

Roughly speaking, the response of telecommunication
researchers has been to follow the path that Strand implicitly outlined nearly 100 years ago: solve the telecommunication problem by creating a sense of *being there*, by
establishing some form of audio and video connections
between two distant locations (A notable exception to this is
email, about which we will have more to say later). Hence
the introduction of the telephone itself, and its enhancement
through the addition of video, for teleconferencing, shared
informal spaces [1,5], and one-on-one conversation. It is not
too far from the mark to characterize the goal of the
research by quoting from one of the stated goals of a recent
informal telecommunication experiment: *"the total effect is*

to produce an environment at each end... which is as close as possible to being there [10]."

How successful have the many efforts directed at this goal been? To measure progress towards the direct face-to-face part of this goal, social psychologists have evolved measures of *social presence* [12] and *information richness* [3] to estimate how closely telecommunication tools capture the essence of face-to-face communication. To simplify matters slightly, it is generally agreed that various communication options can be ranked on an axis, in order of decreasing social presence, as face-to-face, audio/video communication, audio only, and written correspondence/email. While it is encouraging that the addition of the video channel seems to increase the social presence, it is often (though not always) the conclusion of studies that the audio/video medium is much closer to the audio only medium than it is to the face-to-face condition.

It is tempting to think that with perhaps a little more screen resolution, a little more fidelity in the audio channel, a little more tweaking to bring the machinery in conformance with subtle and long-established social mechanisms such as eye contact, telecommunications systems will achieve a level of information richness so close to face-to-face that for most needs it will be indistinguishable.

But will they ever be close enough? It is clear they can, for example provide a cost-effective and efficient alternative to business travel to a distant location, and may be superior to audio only telephone for some communicative needs. We have no argument with that. But is this general approach going to be adequate for the long term? Is it powerful enough to see us through to achieving the goal that those at a distance will be at no real disadvantage to those co-located?

A recent study of the Cruiser video system suggests that in one important respect, systems designed using this approach may *never* be "close enough." In a recent trial aimed at seeing whether a video/audio system provided enough information richness, it was found that subjects used the mechanism to set up face-to-face conversation with friends down the hall, but not in lieu of them[6]. The result is not surprising. Perhaps we are demanding too much. After all, its purpose is to enable communication between two distant locations, where going into the next office to talk to the person is not an option. When you have the choice between face-to-face and an imitation, no matter how good, it is natural to choose the real thing. This is a problem inherent with imitation, but we think it is particularly telling for communication. When we make a choice between two channels to use for informal interaction, discrepancies between the two channels are decisive. Thus, if one channel is half as good as another, we don't use it half as often, we probably don't use it at all, so long as the other is readily available. And that fundamental edge of real face-to-face and physical proximity over its imitation, accumulated over the hundreds of interactions it takes to form friendships or successful collaborations means, we believe, that organizations will continue to decouple into geographical groups (See, for example, the discussion of group cohesion in chapter 8 of [12]).

It seems to us that there is no real solution to this situation so long as people use one medium to communicate with those at a distance and another for those for whom distance is not an issue. Those distant will always remain at a disadvantage to those present. It is not really even a question of the quality of the device. It is what it is trying to achieve. It could be 3-D holographic with surround-sound, but if people use an imitation to talk to some people but the "real thing" to those physically proximate, a fundamental difference will always remain.

A logical extension to this line of thinking is that the people at a distance will never stop being at a disadvantage until we use the same mechanisms to interact with each other when we are physically close as when we are physically distant. And that means that to make real progress on the telecommunication problem, we must develop tools that people prefer to use even when they have the option of interacting as they have heretofore in physical proximity. We must develop tools that go beyond being there. But what would it mean for something to be better than being there? And how could we design such a device?

Perhaps a brief analogy could get us moving in the right direction. It is customary for a person with a broken leg to use crutches, but how odd it would be if they continued to use the crutches after their leg was restored to its natural condition. In contrast, one wears shoes because they provide certain advantages over our natural barefoot condition. Special purpose shoes, such as running shoes, are designed to enhance our best performance. Now crutches and shoes are both tools of a sort, but there is a difference. The crutch is designed specifically to make the best of a bad situation -- to let someone hobble around until they are back in shape. On the other hand, shoes are to correct some of the problems of our natural condition, and, in the case of athletic shoes, to enhance our performance.

In telecommunications research perhaps we have been building crutches rather shoes. What we are getting at is this: telecommunications research seems to work under the implicit assumption that there is a natural and perfect state -- *being there* -- and that our state is in some sense *broken* when we are not physically proximate. The goal then is to attempt to restore us, as best as possible, to the state of *being there*. In our view there are a number of problems with this approach. Not only does it orient us towards the construction of crutch-like telecommunication tools but it also implicitly commits us to a general research direction of attempting to imitate one medium of communication with another. A research direction which, as we indicated above and will discuss more fully below, has serious limitations.

BEYOND BEING THERE

No man putteth a piece of new cloth unto an old garment, for that which is put in to fill it up taketh from the garment, and the rent is made worse. Neither do men put new wine into old bottles: else the bottles break, and the wine run-

neth out, and the bottles perish: but they put new wine into new bottles, and both are preserved. Matthew 9:16-17.

To start to elaborate an alternative approach to the telecommunication problem, let's take a step back. For the purpose of discussion, let's frame human communication in terms of needs, media, and mechanisms.

We'll say that communication needs are those human requirements which, when met, encourage and facilitate interaction. They span the whole range of human needs and are the underlying human requirements that get served by communication. They are independent of the medium with which we communicate. For example, we would characterize Daft and Lengel's [4] suggestions of characteristics of information rich channels, *cue variety, feedback, and message personalization*, as candidate needs. Other researchers [6] suggest *simultaneously being reminded of a need to talk to someone* and *having a communication channel* as key aspects of informal communication. Schegloff [15] and others have discussed t*urn taking, repair,* and *stylized openings* as seemingly essential to conversation. It is such underlying needs that we are referring to in the framework we are proposing.

Media are simply what mediates communication. For face-to-face interactions the medium is physically proximate reality. Viewing physical proximity as a medium might at first seem odd but it is of central importance to our argument since the way it has come to mediate face-to-face interactions serves as *the model* for communication. This in turn we will argue has led to a focus on and imitation of the basic characteristics of face-to-face interactions such as their 3-dimensional high-resolution visual and auditory character.

Finally, mechanisms are ways to meet informal communication needs that are enabled by a medium. While needs are media independent, mechanisms are closely, perhaps inextricably, connected to specific media. Examples of mechanisms that seem to work well for physically-proximate interactions might include eye contact, body posture, stereotypical openings and closings in spoken language, or even the strategy of going down to the lounge to see who's taking a break from work.

In an important sense, computationally-mediated communication is a new medium, potentially as good or better than the physically proximate medium we are used to. Here we mean to include not just email, as if sometimes intended by the term, but all communication that is mediated by any type of electronic or computational device, whether it be an audio amplifier, television camera, or email system. As the quote beginning this section suggests, new mechanisms are required for new media. It is thus crucial to consider what mechanisms of communication the new computational medium enables and to realize that mechanisms that may be effective in face-to-face interactions might be awkward or ineffective if we try to replicate them in an electronic medium. This is one of the inherent limitations in imitating one medium with another. As we discussed above, the imitation will never be as good as the real thing. This is true by definition if one is strict in using the old medium as the stan-

dard of measurement. However, even with a more relaxed standard, the new medium will seldom measure up because of discrepancies in the strengths and weaknesses of the two media. Requiring one medium to imitate the other inevitably pits strengths of the old medium against weaknesses of the new. At the same time, to the extent that the goal is imitation, one will not be led to exploit the distinctive strengths of the new medium.

The assumption that the *media* and *mechanisms* of face-to-face interaction are actually the *requirements* for ideal communication is so pervasive that it is implied in the very name of the industry currently most concerned with supporting informal communication in the new medium -- *tele-*communication. The implication is that we are trying to find ways to communicate at a distance as if we weren't at a distance. But it is our contention that such an approach will always limit our thinking to replicating or imitating the mechanisms of one medium with another.*

In contrast, we argue that a better way to solve the telecommunication is to not focus on the *tele-* part, but the *communication* part. That is, to make the new medium satisfy the needs of communication so well that people, whether physically proximate or not, prefer to use it.

The framework of needs, media, and mechanisms also suggests a way to achieve a level of performance for communication tools that goes beyond being there. First, it frees us to ask "what's right with the new medium?" For example, three significant features of the new medium are its ability to support asynchronous communication, anonymous communication, and to automatically archive communication. Yet all of these potentially important features are ignored when the medium is used just to recreate synchronous face-to-face interactions between distant sites.

It also creates a framework in which it becomes meaningful to ask the question: what's wrong with (physically proximate) reality? That is, when we view physically proximate reality as simply *a* medium, we can ask what requirements it meets well, and also what ones it meets poorly, inefficiently, or not at all. We can then explore new mechanisms to meet those needs, mechanisms which leverage the strengths of the new medium.

EXAMPLES

To further illustrate the approach we are proposing, we offer a sampling of projects which are in various stages of devel-

---

* We are reminded of a colleague's description of his reaction to a demonstration of the clarity of a fiber communications link. He responded that often when one was calling a friend or relative far away what one wanted to communicate was the message that "I am far away and thinking of you." He suggested that the new fiber medium made that harder to say. With the old medium one could *hear the distance* and thus the medium itself helped to convey the message.}

opment in our group. We conclude each example with a set of hypotheses that we expect the project will help us evaluate.

Email communication is surely the paramount success of computationally-mediated informal communication. It's design fits well with the framework we propose since it satisfies a number of communicative requirements primarily by exploiting the asynchronous nature of the electronic medium rather than by attempting to imitate synchronous physical interactions. It meets our critical litmus test of being used by groups even when in close physical proximity. In fact, in our own experience, it is not uncommon to send email to someone in the next adjacent office, or even someone sharing an office. In this light, it is not surprising that email was viewed as one of the most (if not the most) successful communication tools in an extensive study that explored the ability of a research group to function when located at two sites, separated by several hundred miles [1].

Yet the sense that we must imitate face-to-face is strong. In a recent popular article on email communication it was noted almost apologetically: "Electronic mail that includes graphics, pictures, sound and video will eventually become widely available. These advances will make it possible to reintroduce some of the social context cues absent in current electronic communications. Even so, electronic interactions will never duplicate those conducted face-to-face [9]."

One direction that our approach leads one to consider is other elaborations of email that are not at all imitative, but move in complementary or even opposite directions. Four of our examples can roughly be considered as such. The fifth example looks directly at those tasks for which the very rich, synchronous interaction and immediate feedback that face-to-face communication provides seems essential.

Ephemeral Interest Groups

Successful informal discussions often take place when there is both an opportunity to communicate and a natural topic of discussion. For example, suppose you have a colleague you would like to know better. It is easier to start up a conversation when both are sitting in a lounge reading a newspaper, or both are waiting for a meeting to start, than interrupting his work by knocking on his office door. In both of these desirable situations, ones' presence in the lounge or in the meeting room indicates that one is available for conversation, and the approaching meeting or newspaper provides an natural topic of conversation.

A problem with these mechanisms, however, is that both parties need to be free at the same time. Thus, without being too precise, the likelihood of these opportunities goes roughly as the *product* of the fraction of the time that each person is available in these circumstances.

The potentially asynchronous nature of computationally-mediated interactions increases the potentially available time for informal interaction to approximate something proportional to the fraction of time available to each person considered separately. This is a much larger value, and implies the makings of a more effective way of having informal interactions, either to get to know a colleague better, or to maintain contact with a close associate. But how to create natural topics of conversation?

The idea of an ephemeral interest group is to create a mechanism that allows a (typically) short-lived discussion to be attached to any object in a community's electronic "space." Thus, items on an electronic calendar listing research talks, apnews stories in electronic form, and even postings to a company-wide bulletin board can provide a seed for an ephemeral interest group.

The word ephemeral helps to emphasize that these discussions differ from those handled by specialized bulletin boards, netnews groups, or special interest mailing lists. In those cases, interests of a more long-standing nature are well served. The intent is to provide a mechanism that allows a group to be created at virtually zero cost to a potential user, and that these groups can be thought of as disposable, intended only to last a few hours or at most a few days.

We have been operating a first version of such a service for over four months at Bellcore. It has been reasonably successful. Users report that it creates a greater sense of informality than postings to the general bulletin board, while allowing them to potentially reach all the readers of the bulletin board, without bothering those that are not interested in that discussion. And, true to its email heritage, allows those not located at the site to keep up on what's going on with a system that puts them at no apparent to disadvantage to those co-located.

As a result of formal interviews and more general user feedback, we have recently begun limited use of a redesigned system, emphasizing increased visibility, and lower user cost of access and interaction. With these changes, there are preliminary indications of increased participation, and the ability to handle topics that are more ephemeral. We plan to report on this work in more detail elsewhere [2]. These ephemeral interest groups provide a means of initiating friendships electronically which we discuss in the next section.

Hypotheses: People using this system that aren't present rate themselves as more a part of the community than those who don't use it and are present.

Meeting Others

While there is currently much discussion of electronic access to information resources and new kinds of information services that may soon be offered, one might conjecture that many people are more concerned with meeting interesting people and having richer fuller relationships than with access to most forms of electronic information. Let's briefly consider what kinds of systems we might be led to propose based on our framework.

First, we are exploring providing users in our lab with a sort of electronic persona that provides people with access to information about others. This includes their publications, picture, state information that is automatically recorded about activity on their workstation, as well as the opportunity to include the kinds of information that many people now attach to the doors of their offices (cartoons, quotes, etc.). The goal is not to replicate in the electronic media what is available in other media but to provide low-cost access to the information so that when reading about a topic, such as an ephemeral interest group posting, one has ready access to other information about them and an opportunity to initiate a conversation. More importantly we think that these pieces of information can provide opportunities for initiation of informal communication.

A second project is a more ambitious variant of the first. It's goal is to provide a form of what one might call *computing personals* in which people would have the opportunity to compose structured profiles describing themselves and allow those profiles to enter into negotiation with other profiles on the net to attempt to locate other people that they might be interested in meeting. The issues of how to construct initial profiles and tailor them as well as the design of the process of negotiation is challenging. Yet one can project that such a form of interaction might provide an interesting alternative way of meeting others.

Hypotheses: Allowing low cost electronic access to information about others will provide an effective way of learning about people for the first time, decrease the cost of initiating contact, and support the maintenance of interactions over time.

Anonymity

One characteristic of an electronic medium that is not shared with face-to-face interactions is an ability to be anonymous. Sproull and Kiesler [9] note that people are in some cases more truthful in email than in face to face, in part because the interaction is more anonymous. Could one not exploit this property to create a new type of email in which exchanges could happen anonymously? This has the potential of satisfying a set of requirements that are not readily satisfied in face-to-face communications. Anonymity could permit exchanges without some of the costs associated with nonanonymous encounters.

Our point is not primarily that such anonymous exchanges will necessarily be valuable (there are certainly many problems that they might generate) but rather that looking at mechanisms enabled by characteristics of a medium and how they might satisfy needs of individuals and groups leads one to posit systems and services that differ from those that follow from an imitative approach.

Hypotheses: Anonymous exchanges will encourage people to discuss issues that they are reluctant to discuss in face to face encounters and lead to discussion of those issues much earlier in a relationship. There is some evidence already available on this issue. One sees anonymous posting services arising on the internet to allow people to interact about very personal topics that it is clear they would be reluctant to discuss in initial fact-to-face encounters.

Semisynchronous Discussions

The perspective we are proposing also encourages one to explore needs, media, and mechanisms independently as well as the linkages between them. As mentioned earlier the asynchronous nature of email is quite effective in supporting certain communicative requirements but focusing on the medium also leads one to ask how the mechanism might be varied. It is clear that the plasticity of the electronic medium allows us quite a bit of flexibility. One does not need to view things as either synchronous or asynchronous. One can imagine semisynchronous mechanisms that might be useful in meeting certain requirements.

Consider for example the following problem of communicating via an electronic bulletin board system. The problem is that the tone and direction of a discussion can be set from the first few responses to a message and people who might well have responded to the original message are reluctant now to enter the discussion. A variant of this problem is not uncommon in meetings or in the classroom in which the first response to a topic can lead the discussion away from what many people might have thought would have been a more productive direction.

The synchronous nature of face-to-face communication does not afford one many options here but in the electronic medium we can explore a variety of semisynchronous mechanisms. Suppose for example that people sending messages intended for discussion could avail themselves of such a mechanism. One variant would permit people to respond to a message at any time but all responses would get batched up and come out at fixed times.

Hypotheses: Use of semisynchronous mechanisms will encourage a greater range of responses than the normal asynchronous or synchronous mechanisms.

Beyond Face-To-Face

The previous examples have emphasized the idea that many things which currently occur in face-to-face, synchronous interactions might actually benefit from being handled in a way that is not, at least superficially, very imitative of face-to-face encounters. However, we certainly feel that some interactions require very rapid, synchronous feedback, and as much information richness or social presence as can be brought to bear.

There is a great deal of enthusiasm, both among telecommunications researchers and the general public, for the possibilities that widespread use of cellular/PCS phone systems, and pen-based wireless computers will allow. How will they change our world? Certainly we can imagine simple extrapolations of current phone and computer use, making computers easier to work with, and phones more readily available. Does the beyond being there approach suggest more imaginative possibilities for these new technologies?

We'll start by asking a question that's easy to ask in our framework. Much telecommunication research has aimed at achieving the level of information richness that we currently have in face-to-face interactions. But no one seems to be asking the question, "what would happen if we were to develop communication tools with a higher information richness than face-to-face?" In the framework proposed in this paper, such tools are actually not all that hard to imagine. We begin by thinking of needs that are not well met in unassisted face-to-face interaction. While we are just beginning to investigate this area, the following examples illustrate the style of approach we are advocating.

Clarity: Could things be clearer in spoken natural language than they are today? American Sign Language provides an intriguing possibility. In ASL, pronoun reference is handled by indicating spatial locations for objects of discussion, and then referring to the various objects by pointing. Thus, while there may be a reference ambiguity in an English sentence using the word "he," there need be no such confusion in ASL.

Feedback: Facial expressions, head nodding, and verbal cues all are used to indicate back to the speaker that one understands and is following the conversation. We would argue that all these mechanisms are rather imprecise. The speaker may wonder: what aspects of what I am saying does the listener understanding? What does the listener think my key point is? But with the spatial location of key pieces of the discussion in a shared visual space, the listener may be able to use tablet gestures to provide a rich range of feedback that simultaneously indicates what aspect of the speaker's comments he is responding to.

Archive: One problem with spoken words in unenhanced physical proximity is that they leave no easily-searchable archive or trace. Recording and making transcriptions, or annotating records after the fact seems a cumbersome process at best. We are pursuing a way to make a system tightly integrated into the spoken interaction, in such a way that the combination of audio and visual record is created without additional effort beyond that needed to converse, and is easily searchable.

What we are suggesting here is a kind of auditory paper, a real-time visual extension to natural language itself.

Hypotheses: Face-to-face conversations using auditory paper will be rated as having higher social presence than unassisted face-to-face interactions. We conjecture that auditory paper will some day, even without the face-to-face component, be viewed as having greater social presence than unassisted face-to-face conversations.

RESPONSES TO POTENTIAL CRITIQUES

We admittedly are trying to present an extreme position as our use of the phrase *beyond being there* might suggest. Our purpose in taking such a position is to highlight our argument and make crisp an alternative approach to support of informal communication in the electronic medium that we feel isn't currently being adequately pursued. Here we respond to a collection of potential critiques.

Advantages of Imitation

There surely are advantages that arise from the imitation of physically proximate reality. An obvious one is that people are used to it and so they will know how to act in the new situation. We would like to suggest though that there can be subtle problems, even when the imitation is successful, because of slight differences in what the media can support. An example is the eye contact problem associated with

video conferencing systems. More importantly though our concern is that in trying to build things that are easy to get use to because they are familiar we will never get beyond the level that the familiar solutions have taken us. In addition, all of the novel representational and communicative uses of the electronic medium almost by definition fall outside of what people are used to now.

Culture

A more difficult criticism is that in advocating our beyond being there position we do not adequately address the issues of culture that surround the use of any media. This criticism would take us to task for failing to give adequate due to culture. That culture provides an important backdrop for our informal communication with others can not be minimized. Our position is that as we explore the new characteristics of media and how they might better meet our requirements we may well see culture change to incorporate and support mechanisms enabled by the new medium because they provide better ways of meeting underlying requirements.

Intersubjectivity

One of the factors that makes face-to-face communication so compelling is how it supports intersubjectivity. Intersubjectivity is a topic that a number of modern philosophers of communication have discussed. Simply put it refers to the creation of a context in which I know that you know that I know what we are talking about. In face-to-face interactions it is constructed via mechanisms of facial expressions, tone of voice, and body language. Much of the richness of face-to-face conversation has to do with exploiting mechanisms of intersubjectivity. Careful examination of almost any encounter will demonstrate their pervasiveness. One will see how a glance can be used to convey a question or to elaborate or even change the underlying context of a discussion.

No matter how powerful and important such mechanisms are there is no reason in principle that the underlying requirements might not be better serviced via mechanisms of other media or via a combination of mechanisms of multiple media. While current techniques, such as embedding little pictures of smiles in email text, to afford the electronic media some of the mechanisms of face-to-face pale in comparison to the richness of direct interactions, one must remember that the electronic medium is still very young. More importantly, looking at nonimitative approaches that focus on underlying requirements and the distinctive characteristics of the electronic media rather than on imitation of the mechanisms of face-to-face might lead to even better solutions.

For example, the ability to remove or selectively enable intersubjectivity might itself have distinct advantages. This is something that is certainly easier to accomplish in electronic forms of communication. A number of people have commented that they can operate more efficiently when viewing a lecture via video or using multiple authoring software precisely because others are not provided with information about them that would be communicated in face-to-face interactions. They can, for example, timeshare their attention with other activities without making the kinds of statements that doing that would do if they were attending the lecture. Thus, they are able to meet other requirements that might have higher value to them precisely because they don't have the kinds of intersubjectivity afforded so readily in face-to-face interactions.

Thus, it is instructive to realize that since there are certainly costs associated with the maintenance of intersubjectivity there may well be occasions when being able to decide not to bear those costs is advantageous.

SUMMARY AND CONCLUSION

Let us summarize our argument:

1. The general telecommunication problem seems to be to create a system that affords us the same richness and variety of interaction that we have when we are physically proximate, even when we are physically distant.

2. Many current efforts to accomplish this attempt to create a sense of "being there," chiefly by establishing audio and video channels between distant locations.

3. Any system which attempts to bring those that are physically distant into a physically proximate community by imitating physical proximity will always keep the former at a disadvantage. This is not because of the quality of the systems, but because of what they attempt to achieve.

4. If we ever hope to solve the telecommunication problem, we must develop tools that people prefer to use even when they have the option of interacting in physical proximity as they have heretofore. To do that requires tools that go *beyond being there*.

5. To create such tools, we suggest framing the problem in terms of needs, media, and mechanisms. The goal then becomes identifying needs which are not ideally met in the medium of physical proximity, and evolving mechanisms which leverage the strengths of the new medium to meet those needs.

In conclusion, we return to the quote at the beginning of this paper. At least since 1898, people have had a vision of a future where new technologies would allow us to interact with others that are far away just as we do with those that are near. We share that vision, but differ from Strand's quote in how best to accomplish it. In our view of the future, it is not so much distance that will be abolished, but rather our current concept of *being there*.

ACKNOWLEDGMENTS

We want to acknowledge the efforts of Steve Abney and Laurence Brothers as well as the other members of the *Beyond Being There* working group. We also thank Will Hill, Jakob Nielsen, Ed Hutchins and Jonathan Grudin for comments on earlier versions of this paper.

REFERENCES

1. Abel, M. J. Experiences in an Exploratory Distributed Organization. In Galegher, Kraut, & Egido (Eds.), *Intellectual Teamwork: Social and Technological Foundations of Cooperative Work*, Lawrence Erlbaum Associates, 489-51., 1990.

2. Abney, S., Hollan, J., & Stornetta, S. The j-key and Ephemeral Interest Groups, in preparation.

3. Daft, R.L. and Lengel, R.H. Organizational Information requirements, media richness, and structural design. Management Science, 32, 554-571, 1991.

4. Emmory, Karen et al., The Activation of Spatial Antecedents from Overt Pronouns in American Sign Language, *Language and Cognitive Processes*, p. 207, vol. 6, no. 3 1991.

5. Fish, R. S., Kraut, R. E. Chalfonte, B. The VideoWindow System In Informal Communications. Proceedings of the Conference on Computer Supported Cooperative Work (CSCW '90), 1-11, 199, 1990.

6. Fish, R. S., Kraut, R. E., Root, R. W., & Rice, R Evaluating Video as a Technology for Informal Communication. Bellcore Technical Memorandum, TM-ARH017505, 1991.

7. Mee, Arthur, The Pleasure Telephone, the *Strand Magazine*, pp. 339-369, 1898.

8. Monge, P.R. et al. . The dynamics of organizational proximity. *Management Science* 31, 1129-1141., 1985.

9. Sproul, Lee, and Kiesler, Sara, Computers, Networks and Work, *Scientific American*, p. 116, September, 1991.

10. Posting at one location of Videowindow informal communication experiment, Morristown, NJ.

11. Root, R. W. Design Of A Multi-Media Vehicle For Social Browsing. Proceedings ACM CSCW'88 Computer-Supported Cooperative Work, 25-38, 1988.

12. Short, J., Williams, E., and Christie, B., *The Social Psychology of Telecommunications*, London: John WIley and Sons, 1976.

13. Williams, E. . Experimental comparisons of face-to-face and mediated communication: A review. *Psychological Bulletin*, 84, 963-976, 1977.

14. Zmud, R.W., Lind, M.R., and Young, F.W. An attribute space for organizational communication channels. *Information System Research*, 1, 440-457, 1990.

15. Schegloff, E. A. Identification and Recognition In INteractional Openings, In The Social Impact of the Telephone, (Ed.) I. de Sola Pool, MIT Press, 1977.

Evaluating Two Aspects of Direct Manipulation in Advanced Cockpits

James A. Ballas, Constance L. Heitmeyer and Manuel A. Pérez

Human-Computer Interaction Lab
Naval Research Laboratory
Washington, D. C. 20375-5000
(202) 767-2774, ballas@itd.nrl.navy.mil

ABSTRACT

Increasing use of automation in computer systems, such as advanced cockpits, presents special challenges in the design of user interfaces. The challenge is particularly difficult when automation is intermittent because the interface must support smooth transitions from automated to manual mode. A theory of direct manipulation predicts that this interface style will smooth the transition. Interfaces were designed to test the prediction and to evaluate two aspects of direct manipulation, semantic distance and engagement. Empirical results supported the theoretical prediction and also showed that direct engagement can have some adverse effects on another concurrent manual task. Generalizations of our results to other complex systems are presented.

KEYWORDS: Direct manipulation, interface styles, interface design, adaptive automation, intermittent automation, aircraft interfaces, intelligent cockpit.

INTRODUCTION

The rapid evolution of user interfaces is occurring not only in office systems but also in modern cockpits, which are computer-based and include advanced graphical displays [14]. However, modern cockpits differ from traditional office systems in several fundamental ways. First, unlike office systems, they often include sophisticated automation, such as the ability to fly on automatic pilot. Moreover, unlike office applications, the cockpit application is dynamic and complex. The pilot must not only handle large quantities of real-time, often continuous, input data; he must also perform several demanding tasks concurrently, usually under severe timing constraints. Finally, unlike users of office systems who typically communicate via electronic mail, the pilot of a modern cockpit communicates in real-time via networked voice and data links. Given these differences, the cockpit interface presents many design challenges that the developers of office systems seldom encounter.

An important question in designing the user interface of modern cockpits is how to handle automation. Our research is part of a larger research program in adaptive automation whose role is to allocate tasks between the pilot and the computer system in an optimal manner [10]. In adaptive (i.e., intermittent) automation, the pilot performs a task only intermittently. Given a dual task situation, a rise in the level of difficulty of one task causes automation of the second task. Having the computer system take over the second task allows the pilot to focus his efforts on the increased difficulty task. Once the difficulty level of the first task returns to normal, the pilot resumes control of both tasks. Such an approach to automation is expected to result in better overall pilot/system performance [10]. Because the pilot only performs the first task intermittently, a challenging problem, and the problem that this paper addresses, is how to design an interface that supports a smooth transition from automated to manual mode.

This paper presents the results of our empirical research on interface styles for adaptive automation. Our research is designed to test predictions from a theory of direct manipulation. A fundamental goal of the research is to determine whether a direct manipulation interface has performance benefits in adaptive automation; i.e., does direct manipulation lead to improved performance when a pilot must quickly resume a task that has been previously automated? A related goal is to separate and evaluate two aspects of direct manipulation identified by the theory, namely, distance and engagement. In this paper, we introduce the direct manipulation theory, present our hypothesis about the effect of interface style in adaptive automation, describe the interfaces developed to test our hypothesis, and summarize the empirical results. We conclude with a discussion of the implications of our results.

BACKGROUND

Designing an interface for an adaptive system involves many issues and decisions, but little theoretical guidance or empirical information is available. There is general agreement on what the interface should accomplish. As a first priority, the interface should enable the pilot to maintain both situational awareness and system control

[10]. We define *situational awareness* as the extent to which the pilot has the knowledge needed to perform a specified task or tasks. Clearly, this knowledge depends upon the specific state of the aircraft and selected aspects of the aircraft environment. In adaptive (i.e., intermittent) automation, the pilot shifts from manually performing a task to monitoring its automated performance and then back to manual operation. In this situation, the key to assessing situational awareness is how well the pilot can resume a task that has been previously automated. We claim that a critical factor in achieving a smooth transition from automated to manual performance of a task is interface style.

Hutchins, Hollan, and Norman (HHN) have developed a theory of direct manipulation [6]. They characterize direct manipulation interfaces according to a model world metaphor; the user interacts with an interface that represents the task domain itself, the domain objects and the effect of user operations on those objects. Command language interfaces behave according to a conversational metaphor; the user and the interface have a conversation about the application domain. The interface acts as an intermediary between the user and the domain. Although typically associated with office computer systems, direct manipulation is also being considered for large safety-critical systems, such as nuclear power plants [2]. HHN concluded that two aspects of direct manipulation account for its performance advantages, low distance and direct engagement. The first aspect is the "information processing distance between the user's intentions and the facilities provided by the machine". Performance advantages come with less distance, because there is less cognitive effort needed to understand and manipulate the domain objects. HHN call such an interface *semantically direct* and claim that it can be achieved by "matching the level of description required by the interface language to the level at which the person thinks of the task".

Distance is of two types, semantic and articulatory. *Semantic* distance is the difference between the user's intentions and the meaning of the expressions available in the interface, both expressions that communicate the user's intentions to the computer and expressions whereby the computer system provides user feedback. For example, if the user wishes to delete all files whose names end in *text* and the computer system (e.g., the Macintosh) has no single expression for this purpose, then significant semantic distance exists between the user's intentions and the expressions available in the interface. *Articulatory* distance is the difference between the physical form of the expressions in the interface and the user's intentions. For example, when a Unix user wants to display a file and to do so he must invoke a command named "cat", significant articulatory distance exists between the name of the Unix command and the intended user operation. Our studies have focused on semantic distance. We have proposed followup studies to investigate issues concerned with articulatory distance.

The second aspect of direct manipulation is *engagement*, i.e., the involvement that comes when the user is able to interact directly with the application domain and the objects within it rather than interacting through an intermediary. The key to direct engagement is interreferential I/O, which permits "an input expression to incorporate or make use of a previous output expression". For example, if a listing of file names are displayed on the screen, one of these names can be selected and operated on without entering the name again. In Draper's view [5], the important aspect of interreferential I/O is that the user and the computer system share a common communications medium. This takes the notion of interreferential I/O beyond the Unix concepts of channels and pipes. In direct manipulation, the shared medium is usually a visual display which presents an explicit, often graphical, view of the task domain.

Related Research on Direct Manipulation
An early study comparing several interfaces concluded that usability depends more on specific interface design than interface style [12]. Contrary to expectations, iconic interfaces were inferior to menu systems and command language interfaces for new and transfer users. More recent studies have generally shown advantages for direct manipulation over command language interfaces [15]. For example, Karat [7] found consistently faster times for several file management tasks in a direct manipulation interface that used pointing and dragging operations on iconic representations of files. However, Karat did find an advantage for the command language interface on one particular type of file management task. Thus, evaluations of interface styles need to be sensitive to task-specific effects. Along this line, Elkerton and Palmiter (cited in Kieras [8]) suggest that the basic principle of direct manipulation lies in the replacement of complex cognitive operations with perceptual and motor activities. Thus the advantage of direct manipulation may lie in tasks with complex cognitive operations that can be transformed into motor and perceptual operations.

Research on direct manipulation has been mostly on conventional applications, such as word processing and file management. A notable exception is a study by Benson and her colleagues [3] which compared a conventional interface to a direct manipulation interface for a parts manufacturing system. The conventional interface used menus, function keys, typed commands, displayed textual information, and paged displays. The direct manipulation interface used a mouse as the only input device and provided a continuous display of important information. The evaluation of these interfaces used performance measures relevant to manufacturing, such as cost, inventory levels and status, and late deliveries. Performance with direct manipulation was superior on three of five dependent measures.

All previous research on direct manipulation has not attempted to tease apart semantic distance and direct engagement, and determine which is important in user performance. Furthermore, previous research has evaluated applications designed for purposes other than evaluation of an interface style. The interfaces in our study were designed specifically to study direct manipulation by separating and evaluating the two aspects identified in the HHN theory.

Direct Manipulation in the Cockpit

The effectiveness in the cockpit of a direct manipulation interface and its two aspects remains an open question. Some studies suggest that navigation displays should present a model world to the pilot. For example, in 1987, Marshak, Kuperman, Ramsey, and Wilson [9] found that moving-map displays in which the viewpoint is similar to what would actually be seen by looking outside the plane led to improved performance. However, in other kinds of displays, a graphical representation of the model world does not provide an advantage. For example, Reising and Hartsock [11] found that in warning/caution/advisory displays, a schematic of the cockpit showing the controls that were needed to handle an emergency did not improve performance. The important factor in improved performance was a checklist of the required procedures (which is closer to what a command language interface would offer).

Ironically, in modern flight control systems, some trends have been away from direct manipulation. For example, fly-by-wire systems remove the pilot from direct control of wing surfaces. Bernotat [4] argues against this trend, suggesting that, in such systems, the pilot needs direct sensory feedback about the aircraft's performance. Such feedback is consistent with the notion of direct manipulation. Other trends in cockpit controls suggest a move toward direct manipulation, e.g., the incorporation of touchscreen displays. However, the incorporation of pointing devices into the flight deck needs to be carefully evaluated; e.g., what is the effect of the pilot's use of two pointing devices concurrently (a touchscreen and a joystick)?

Direct Manipulation in Intermittent Automation

An issue in interface design for intermittent automation is *automation deficit*, the initial decrease in pilot performance that occurs when a task that has been previously automated is resumed. This deficit may reveal itself in several ways: slower human response, less accurate human response, subjective feelings of not being in control, subjective feelings of stress, etc. Some previous studies have shown an automation deficit for manual control tasks, while others have not [10]. In our research we are interested in automation deficits in response time and the effect of interface style on automation deficit.

Our hypothesis is that direct manipulation interfaces lead to a reduction in automation deficit that is reflected in decreased response times right after automation ceases. The rationale underlying this hypothesis is that decreased semantic distance and improved direct engagement enhance a pilot's ability to monitor a task that is automated and then to quickly resume the task. Besides testing the general hypothesis, we evaluated the importance of each

aspect of direct manipulation in minimizing automation deficit.

To test our hypothesis we evaluated the effect of interface styles on a person's ability to resume a task quickly after a period of automation. More specifically, we compared performance in the first few seconds of the manual mode to performance a minute later on, using different types of interfaces.

EXPERIMENTAL DESIGN

Subjects

Twenty subjects were recruited from NRL personnel, with five randomly assigned to each of the four types of interfaces used in the tactical assessment task. All were screened for normal color vision. Two of the subjects were licensed pilots.

General Procedure

The experiment required subjects to perform two tasks, a pursuit tracking task and a tactical assessment task. To establish a setting for adaptive automation, the difficulty of the tracking task alternated between moderate and high throughout the experiment. During the moderate difficulty phases of the tracking task, the subject performed both the tracking task and the tactical assessment task. Each time the difficulty of the tracking task rose to high, the tactical assessment task was automated, and the subject performed the tracking task only. The display screen used in the experiment was partitioned into two nonoverlapping windows, one for the tracking task, the other for the tactical assessment task.

Tracking Task

The tracking task simulated air-to-air targeting of an enemy aircraft using a gunsight similar to the pipper and reticle on a typical head-up display. The target on the display was a graphical representation of an enemy aircraft. The tracking control was a self-centering, displacement joystick. The two levels of tracking difficulty, high and moderate, were produced by changing the movement rate of the target. Performance measures included RMS amplitude calculated for each axis. In addition, the target's and the subject's movements were recorded for later analysis.

Tactical Assessment Task

The second task, tactical assessment, is a critical task in a tactical aircraft and one that has become more challenging with the increased capabilities of modern aircraft. Our hypothesis was tested on interfaces for the tactical assessment task. The simulated tactical situation included three classes of targets - fighters, aircraft, and ground-based missiles - and contacts on the targets by sensor systems. The targets first were designated as possible threats using black color coding, but as they got closer to the *ownship* (the symbol for the aircraft the pilot was in), they were designated as neutral, hostile, or unknown, using blue, red and amber color coding, respectively. The subjects were told that simulated sensor systems were assigning these designations.

The subjects were required to perform two operations, confirm and classify. If the system designated a target as neutral or hostile (i.e., the target was colored blue or red), the subject had to *confirm* the designation by picking the target and then indicating the proper designation, i.e., neutral for blue targets and hostile for red targets. Thus, confirm decisions only required the subject to discriminate colors. If the system designated the target as unknown (i.e., the target was colored amber), the subject had to *classify* the target as hostile or neutral based on its behavior. Table 1 provides the rules for designating a target as hostile or neutral. The target class determines what target attribute the subject uses to determine the target's designation.

Target Class	Hostile	Neutral
Fighter	Constant bearing	Bearing away
Airplane	Air speed ~ 800	Air speed ~ 300
Missile site	Within threat range	Outside threat range

Table 1. Rules for tactical assessment of targets

To classify the amber targets, the subject needed to monitor heading for fighters, speed for aircraft, and projected lateral distance for ground missile threats. The responses were timed and analyzed to produce measures of accuracy and response time.

Training was provided on each task alone and on the dual task without automation. A total of twenty subjects were tested on the intermittent automation, five on each of the four interfaces. Twelve subjects were retested four months later. They received a 3 minute retraining session on both tasks. Further details of the experiment are presented elsewhere [1].

Interfaces for the Tactical Assesment Task

To test our hypothesis, we designed and built four interfaces, using prototyping and iterative development. These four interfaces, which include a direct manipulation interface, a command language interface, and two hybrid interfaces, represent the four combinations of semantic distance and engagement shown in Figure 1. Below, we briefly describe each interface and discuss how each implements some combination of semantic distance and engagement.

The *direct manipulation interface* (Figure 2a) has direct engagement and low semantic distance. It uses a shared communications medium: both the subject and the computer use the entire tactical assessment window to communicate. This interface simulates a radar display with continuously moving symbols representing the targets. The symbol used to represent a target is an intuitive graphical representation of the target class. Each target symbol is initially colored black but changes to red, blue, or amber once the system assigns the target a designation. A touchscreen overlays the display. The subject confirms or classifies a target by picking a target symbol on the display and selecting one of two strips, labeled HOSTILE and NEUTRAL, located on either side of the display. The

subject accomplishes both the pick and the select by touching the appropriate part of the display screen. The words 'HOSTILE' and 'NEUTRAL' in the two side strips are colored red and blue, respectively. For classify decisions, the subject needs to observe the behavior of the graphical symbol that represents the target to determine the proper target designation. For confirm decisions, the subject needs to interpret the color of the target symbol.

		Semantic Distance	
		Low	High
Engagement	Direct	Graphical Display with Touchscreen (Direct Manipulation)	Tabular Display with Touchscreen
	Indirect	Graphical Display with Keypad Input	Tabular Display with Keypad Input (Command Language)

Figure 1. Levels of engagement and semantic distance in the four interfaces for the tactical assessment task.

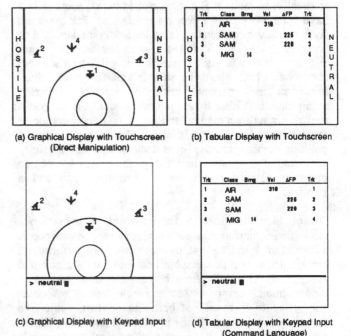

(a) Graphical Display with Touchscreen (Direct Manipulation)

(b) Tabular Display with Touchscreen

(c) Graphical Display with Keypad Input

(d) Tabular Display with Keypad Input (Command Language)

Figure 2. Four interfaces for the tactical assessment task, combining levels of semantic distance and engagement.

The *command language interface* (Figure 2d) has indirect engagement and high semantic distance. This interface uses a split visual medium: the tactical assessment window is partitioned into a top portion, which displays a table of target names and attributes, and a bottom portion, which is for subject input and error feedback. Each entry in the table describes a single target, providing the target's name (an integer), the target's class, and continuously updated data about the target. The name of the target class carries the system designation; initially black, it changes to red, blue, or amber once the system has assigned a designation. The table is decluttered: i.e., it only presents the critical attribute for the given target class. After the subject has completed a classify or a confirm operation on a target, the system removes the target entry from the table by scrolling the table. The subject uses a keypad to invoke a confirm or classify operation. For each operation, two sequential keypresses are required, one designating hostile or neutral, a second indicating the target number. For classify decisions, the subject needs to interpret the data in the table to determine the appropriate target designation. For confirm decisions, the subject needs to interpret the color of the word identifying the target class.

One important difference between the command language interface described above and the command language interfaces associated with more traditional office systems is that the table of target data is updated continuously. Such an approach is dictated in an aircraft context by the impact of external factors on the domain objects (i.e., the targets) and the real-time demands of the tactical domain. The approach makes less sense in an office system where, in most cases, changes to domain objects are made solely by the user and rapid response times are not as crucial.

The third interface (Figure 2c), the *graphical/keypad interface*, combines the low semantic distance of the first interface with the less direct engagement of the second interface. Like the command language interface, this interface splits the tactical assessment window into two portions. The top portion contains the simulated radar display; the bottom portion is for subject input and error feedback. The subject uses the keypad to enter his classify and confirm decisions.

Finally, the fourth interface (Figure 2b), the *tabular/pointer interface*, combines high semantic distance with direct selection of the tactical targets on the display using a touchscreen. The subject picks a target by touching the appropriate table entry. He designates the target by touching either the HOSTILE or NEUTRAL strip at the sides of the display. This last interface is similar to a menu interface, except that the table items are updated dynamically. Scrolling in this interface occurs just after the subject completes entry of the confirm or classify decision and is thus associated with the completion of a user action.

Distance and Engagement In the Interfaces

Although the four interfaces intuitively represent different combinations of semantic distance and engagement, it is important to understand the theoretical rationale for the level of distance and engagement in each interface. Metaphorically, the direct manipulation interface represents a model world of the task domain, the command language interface a verbal description. A graphical representation more closely matches the way that a pilot thinks about the tactical situation. More importantly, these two interfaces support the user's goals differently. We distinguish two user goals: to remain aware of the current tactical

configuration, and to perform the assigned task. The low distance display was designed to support both goals. To support the first goal, the display continuously provided a graphical representation of the target's location and how the target was moving. To support the second goal, all relevant information about each target was encapsulated by this graphical representation.

The high distance display was designed to support only the second goal, user performance of the assigned task. In developing the high distance display, considerable effort was required to design a table that effectively supports the assigned task. For example, the target's spatial coordinates (x, y positions) were not provided because they are not relevant to the task and would have made the table harder to interpret. Moreover, the color code indicating the type of decision required was shown in the class column only, thus separating the system-assigned designation from the target attribute information. Finally, the columns were arranged to support efficient eye movements.

The levels of engagement can also be considered from several perspectives. We provide a pointing device (i.e., a touchscreen) for high engagement and a keypad for low engagement. The keypad uses a mode shift for two keys in order to preserve a common aspect of command language interfaces and to avoid introducing direct engagement with labelled keys for each action and object, a feature that Shneiderman associates with direct manipulation [15].

The theoretical difference between the levels of engagement in the interfaces is based upon the notion of a shared medium. In the direct engagement interfaces (the direct manipulation interface and the tabular/pointer interface), both the user and the computer system use a shared communications medium; that is, they both operate on the same objects. In the direct manipulation interface, the shared medium is the spatial display. The objects to be operated on are the target symbols and the strips labeled 'HOSTILE' and 'NEUTRAL'. In the tabular/pointer interface, the shared medium is the table, and the objects to be operated on are the table entries. In both direct engagement displays, the objects to be operated on and the strips share the same color code. Thus, for example, red in either the spatial display or the table of target attributes indicates that the subject should select the strip with the red wording.

In the indirect engagement interfaces (the command language interface and the graphical/keypad interface), the computer communicates to the user through one medium (i.e., section of the tactical display) and set of objects, while the user communicates to the computer through another medium (a keypad and another section of the tactical display) using a different set of objects. Thus there is a separation of the user input and computer output.

RESULTS

We found considerable support for our hypothesis: automation deficit was least with the direct manipulation interface and greatest in the interfaces that lacked one component of direct manipulation. We assessed automation deficit by comparing subject performance on the first decision after the tactical assessment task was resumed to performance on the seventh decision. This effect was significant in the 12 subjects tested twice, F(3,8) = 11.9, p < .002. Similar results were found in the initial testing with the larger set of 20 subjects. As shown in Figure 3, with the direct manipulation interface, initial performance was as good as later performance. In other words, virtually no automation deficit was found with the direct manipulation interface. In contrast, automation deficit was clearly present in the two hybrid interfaces. Later performance was improved if either component of direct manipulation was present. This is shown by the reduction in response time for the later response in the two hybrid interfaces. If neither component of direct manipulation was present, as in the command language interface, both initial and later performance were poor. Further analysis has suggested that there may still be a deficit after a minute or so in handling events at a high rate with the command language interface when the tactical task is completely automated [1].

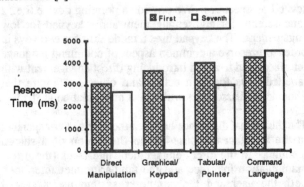

Figure 3. Interface effect on automation deficit in response time.

We also analyzed the effect of the type of decision and the type of display on automation deficit. We found that automation deficit was related significantly to the interaction between the type of decision and the type of display, F(1,16) = 7.89, p < .02. On classification decisions, automation deficit was greater with the tabular displays. On confirmation decisions, the deficit was greater with the graphical displays. The interaction is best illustrated by calculating the difference between the first response and the seventh response (see Figure 4). This pattern was also seen in the retesting four months later, although it was not as strong.

Looking at all the responses, not just the first and a later comparison response, we found no significant differences either in response time or in accuracy between the four interfaces. The reason is that responses with the non-direct manipulation interfaces improved during periods when the event rate was lower (i.e, fourth through sixth targets). Thus the four interfaces supported comparable performance in "normal" operation. In addition, although response times were slower in the retesting four months later, the effect was not significant and was not related to interface

style. Accuracy was related to the type of decision and the type of information that had to be interpreted. Accuracy for the confirmation decisions was 95% and for the classification decisions was 78%. Accuracy was lowest for classification decisions which depended upon monitoring whether a number was changing. This occurs when the subject monitors the bearing of a fighter.

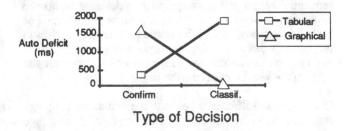

Figure 4. Automation deficit for different decisions with two types of tactical displays

Intra-Task Effects of Interface

In a multiple task domain, the interface for one task might have effects on other tasks. An interesting intra-task effect of engagement (keypad versus touchscreen) was found when the performance on the tracking task was examined. Those using the keypad for the tactical assessment task had better tracking in the initial phase of resuming the tactical assessment task than those using the touchscreen. To understand this result, it is useful to consider touchscreen usage as a form of tracking, and initial performance of this additional tracking task may interfere with making required adjustments to the other (joystick) tracking task. This result suggests that the touchscreen in the tactical assessment task induces an automation deficit in the tracking task. This occurs even though the subjects have been continually doing the tracking task.

Questionnaire Results

Twenty-four rating scales were used to obtain subjective judgments about feelings of control, feelings of awareness, preferences for the interface, judgments of the difficulty in learning and performing the tasks and specific aspects of the tasks, and ability to anticipate the changes in automation. Significant results were found on five scales. The most interesting results were the ratings of ability to anticipate changes in automation and awareness of the tactical situation at the end of automation. Ability to anticipate the changes in automation was dependent upon the type of tactical display. Those with the graphical display felt that they were able to anticipate the changes more often than those with the tabular interface. Furthermore, those with the graphical display felt that they were significantly more aware of the tactical situation at the end of automation. Debriefing confirmed that subjects with the graphical interface noticed the ebb and flow in activity during automation (i.e., activity picks up just before the task switches from automatic to manual), but those in the two tabular interfaces did not. This effect occurred despite the fact that tactical events were appearing in both types of display at the exact same time, that the number of items in both is always the same at any particular moment, and that the ebb and flow of activity is exactly the same in each type of display.

These results show that subjects using the graphical display were able to monitor events during automation. Their ability to anticipate the changes could have produced improved performance, at least for those who had the graphical display and the touchscreen. Several other questions were asked about activity during automation, and subjects accurately described some global characteristics of what had occurred during automation (i.e, how many targets had been present), but not details.

DISCUSSION

Our research has implications for the theory of direct manipulation as well as for the design of interfaces for dynamic, multitask systems. The theoretical implications are based upon both empirical results as well as observations we made during the course of developing the interfaces and conducting the experiment.

On the positive side, we found that the theoretical predictions that we made were generally supported. This result is noteworthy for several reasons. First, this research is a rare example of designing interfaces to test a theory explicitly. Previous studies of direct manipulation and command language interfaces have used interfaces for established applications which may not fairly represent the theoretical concepts. Second, our predictions concern a specific aspect of performance (automation deficit) in a complex, multitask situation. Either challenge---specificity of prediction or complexity of context---would put demands on a theory. Both were present in this research, which makes the successful predictions of the theory especially impressive.

However, we also found that the theory has limitations. First, the theory does not address interfaces which include a mixture of interface styles and which are probably the rule more than the exception in complex applications. The reason is that complex applications involve different types of tasks. A single interface style may not support all tasks in an optimal manner. In the HHN theory, a general interface for the application is assumed. This requires choosing a representation that is suitable for most tasks. But it may not be optimal for certain tasks. Thus choosing a single interface style for a complex application may produce suboptimal performance on some aspects of the application.

This point is important because it is based not only on observation but on empirical results. In our data we found evidence that the optimal display for reducing automation deficit depends upon the type of decision. Simple decisions were served better by the tabular display, complex decisions by the graphical display. In terms of theoretical predictions, the shortcoming of the HHN theory is that it (and we) did not make predictions about the simple decisions. In retrospect, it is evident that the theory would

have to be modified to address decision complexity. It is likely that the confirmation decisions were best supported by the tabular display because the user did not need complete information about the object but simply needed to know the value of a single parameter. If the model world metaphor is implemented faithfully, then different representations for different decisions are not directly possible. Thus an extension of the theory should be considered to support different levels of representation for different requirements.

Second, we found that the theory does not always help with detailed aspects of interface design. Our goal was to evaluate interfaces that had different levels of distance and engagement. The iterative design process we used forced many decisions about details of each of the four interfaces. Many of these decisions were based upon performance considerations and could not be based upon logical derivations from the tenets of the theory. Furthermore, the performance constraints were related to the specific application. For example, the relative placement of the two windows (horizontal or vertical) had an impact on how easy it was to use hands dedicated to the two tasks. This is a stimulus-response compatibility issue that the theory does not address. In essence, the theory is not performance based as are other formal models such as GOMS. It is most relevant in dealing with aspects of the interface that relate to its cognitive complexity.

Finally, we found that distance and engagement are difficult terms to define operationally and to evaluate. Our experiment required interfaces that combined different levels of distance and engagement. In other words, these were design requirements for the interfaces. One of the problems is how to distinguish between distance and engagement. Our empirical results suggest that they are not independent, in that the degree of automation deficit in the command line interface was not a combination of the deficits in the two hybrid interfaces, which each lacked an aspect of direct manipulation. HHN themselves point out that engagement is only present when both semantic and articulatory directness is present.

The interfaces that we produced represented combinations of different levels of distance and engagement. What is not clear is how much distance and engagement were actually present. It is apparent that any interface that allows the person to perform a task successfully has bridged the distance of the gulfs of execution and evaluation as HHN discuss them. The command language interface we produced supported the user's goal of performing the task and therefore reduced semantic distance to a greater degree than an interface which would not support this goal. And yet, it did not provide a view of the model world as a pilot would normally think of it, so considerable distance still remained. Better precision about the degree of distance and engagement in an interface would be helpful.

CONCLUSION

Based upon our findings, we expect that intermittent operation of complex tasks will be more effective with direct manipulation interfaces in a variety of dynamic, real-time systems. Although our results were found in a cockpit application, extension to other systems is appropriate, particularly systems in which the operator is intermittently moving from one task to another. To envision potential generalizations, it is helpful to characterize our application in abstract terms. The dual task application we tested included 1) a continuous task with simple perceptual demands, rigorous manual demands and minor cognitive complexity; and 2) an intermittent task with varying cognitive and perceptual complexity and minimal manual demands. The cognitive complexity of the intermittent task was manipulated by changing the interfaces and by changing the decisions. The results can be interpreted at an abstract level: increases in the cognitive complexity of an interface adversely affect the resumption of its use after a period of automation. This principle certainly holds for systems that include the two types of tasks. The principle would probably hold for systems which have greater complexity on the continuous task. In fact, the effects of interface would probably be greater. The key to appropriate generalization is that there was relatively little cognitive interaction between the two tasks. There was some manual interaction as noted below.

Generalization may not be warranted if the system includes multiple tasks which use similar cognitive processes. In a multitask application, there may be different forms of expressions to the various tasks; the interaction of these expressions is an important issue. Direct engagement in particular may introduce incompatibilities. We found that tracking performance was adversely affected in the initial seconds of resuming pointing with the touchscreen. The cause was an incompatibility between the two forms of manual manipulation. The important issue is whether direct manipulation interfaces to different tasks could compete. According to Wickens [13], the answer is yes. In his resource theory, competition for attentional resources occurs whenever information to the user is in similar modalities or is in a similar code (e.g., spatial or verbal). Competition also occurs whenever responses are similar. Thus two direct manipulation interfaces which both have spatial graphical displays, and which both require pointing devices could produce competition for attentional resources. Thus the generalization of our results to other multiple task systems should be made with consideration given to possible competition between aspects of the direct manipulation interface.

ACKNOWLEDGMENTS

We acknowledge Rob Jacob for contributing to the initial idea for the hypothesis and Rob Carter and Diane Damos for contributions to the design. Many individuals reviewed the interfaces and contributed to their development. We thank the subjects for their participation. This research was supported by the Office of Naval Technology.

REFERENCES

1. Ballas, J. A., Heitmeyer, C. L., and Pérez, M. A. *Direct Manipulation and Intermittent Automation in Advanced Cockpits*. Technical Rep. 9375. Naval Research Laboratory, Washington, D. C. (in press).

2. Beltracchi, L. A direct manipulation interface for heat engines based upon the Rankine cycle. *IEEE Transactions on Systems, Man and Cybernetics*. **17**(3), pp. 478-487 (1987).

3. Benson, C. R., Govindaraj, T., Mitchell, C. M. and Krosner, S. P. Effectiveness of direct manipulation interaction in the supervisory control of FMS parts movement. *Proc. IEEE International Conference on Systems, Man, and Cybernetics*. Cambridge, MA, pp. 947-952 (Nov. 14-17, 1989).

4. Bernotat, R. K. Man and computer in future on-board guidance and control systems of aircraft. In B. Shackel (Ed.) *Man-computer interaction: Human factors aspects of computers and people*. Sijthoff & Noordhoff, Rockville, MD (1981).

5. Draper, S. W. Display managers as the basis for user-machine communication. In D. A. Norman & S. W. Draper (Eds.) *User-centered system design*. Erlbaum Associates, Hillsdale, NJ, pp. 339-352 (1986).

6. Hutchins, E., Hollan, J. D. and Norman, D. A. Direct manipulation interfaces. in D. A. Norman & S. W. Draper (Eds.) *User-centered system design*. Erlbaum Associates, Hillsdale, NJ, pp. 87-124 (1986).

7. Karat, J. Evaluating user interface complexity. *Proceedings of the Human Factors Society 31st Annual Meeting*. Human Factors Society, Santa Monica, CA, pp. 566-570 (1987).

8. Kieras, D. E. An overview of human-computer interaction. *Journal of the Washington Academy of Sciences*. **80**(2), pp. 39-70 (1990).

9. Marshak, W. P., Kuperman, G., Ramsey, E. G., and Wilson, D. Situation awareness in map displays. *Proceedings of the Human Factors Society 31st Annual Meeting*. Human Factors Society, Santa Monica, CA pp. 533-535 (1987).

10. Parasuraman, R., Bahri, T., Deaton, J. E., Morrison, J. G. and Barnes, M. *Theory and design of adaptive automation in aviation systems*. Cognitive Science Laboratory, The Catholic University of America, Washington, D. C. (1990).

11. Reising, J. M. and Hartsock, D. C. Advanced warning/caution/advisory displays for fighter aircraft. *Proceedings of the Human Factors Society 33rd Annual Meeting*. Human Factors Society, Santa Monica, CA. pp. 66-70 (1989).

12. Whiteside, J., Jones, S., Levy, P. S. and Wixon, D. User performance with command, menu, and iconic interfaces. *Proc. ACM CHI'85 Human Factors in Computing Systems*. ACM, New York. pp. 185-191 (1985).

13. Wickens, C. D. and Liu, Y. Codes and modalities in multiple resources: A success and a qualification. *Human Factors*. **30**(5), pp. 599-616 (1988).

14. Wiener, E. L.. Beyond the sterile cockpit. *Human Factors*. **27**(1), pp. 75-90 (1985).

15. Ziegler, J. E. & Fahnrich, K. P. Direct manipulation. In M. Helender (Ed.) *Handbook of human-computer interaction*. Elsevier Science Publishers, North-Holland, pp. 123-133 (1988).

Iterative Design of an Interface
for Easy 3-D Direct Manipulation

Stephanie Houde

Human Interface Group, Advanced Technology
Apple Computer, Inc.
20525 Mariani Ave., MS 76-3H
Cupertino, California 95014

ABSTRACT

Although computer tools for 3-D design applications are now widely available for use on personal computers, they are unnecessarily difficult to use. Conventions for establishing and manipulating views of 3-D objects require engineering-oriented dialogues that are foreign to most users. This paper describes the iterative design and testing of a new mechanism for moving 3-D objects with a mouse-controlled cursor in a space planning application prototype. Emphasis was placed on developing a design which would make 3-D interaction more intuitive by preserving users' experiences with moving objects in the real, physical world. Results of an informal user test of the current interface prototype are presented and implications for the development of a more general direct manipulation mechanism are discussed.

KEYWORDS

3-D manipulation, direct manipulation, iterative design, space planning, hand gestures, narrative handles, bounding box, handle box

INTRODUCTION

Interface strategies that make computer tools for graphic design easy to use have not been equally well developed for 3-D design applications. Page layout and illustration programs provide users with an interface that meets their expectations based on previous experiences. Designers use *rulers,* size type in *points,* cut *masks,* and draw with *pencils* in many available programs. In contrast, 3-D design tools require architects and industrial designers to comprehend engineering-oriented dialogues in order to input, modify and view 3-D data. An understanding of *X, Y, Z* coordinates, *local and absolute frames of reference,* and *yaw, pitch and roll* is required when working with most 3-D design software.

Techniques for directly manipulating 2-D and 3-D objects also differ greatly in their ease of use. For example, moving a mouse cursor to position 2-D pictures and blocks of type on a computer screen is comfortably similar to sliding paper cutouts on a drafting table. In contrast, directly manipulating 3-D objects on a computer display is usually a much less

familiar experience. Movement is often constrained in a manner that does not replicate the experience of moving real, physical objects. Results of manipulations are also hard to understand, because it is difficult to correctly perceive 3-D object positions and orientations in a flat screen view.

This paper describes the iterative design and testing of a new mechanism for moving 3-D objects. The aim of the project presented here was to develop a direct manipulation interface that would make it easy to move 3-D objects on the computer. Emphasis was placed on making 3-D accessible to a broad audience of users. Concepts developed were designed to be usable on personal computers with video display monitors and a conventional one button mouse.

This work was completed within the context of a larger 3-D interface investigation by a team in the Advanced Technology Group of Apple Computer. In order to pursue general interface improvements in a focused manner, the project team chose to prototype a direct manipulation interface for a specific 3-D task. The task chosen was space planning – the application to be built would allow users to arrange furniture within a simulated room. The direct manipulation interface technique presented here was designed specifically to be useful in this context. However, by concentrating on improving users' experience with a familiar 3-D task, we aimed to form some general concepts which might be used to simplify any 3-D direct manipulation interaction.

In this paper, issues addressed by this project and relevant previous work are first identified. Next, the series of design iterations which led to the current interface implementation are described. Finally, the results of a user test used to evaluate the interface are presented and implications for the design of a more general solution are discussed.

IDENTIFYING THE ISSUES

The project began with a user observation aimed at identifying the types of controls users would want for directly manipulating objects in a space planning application. In this informal study, six participants of varying skills were asked to interact with a small foam-core model of a furnished office. Subjects were encouraged to *think out loud* [6] while re-arranging furniture. The model contained a desk, a table, two chairs and two pictures hanging from the 'walls.' Users completed a series of tasks which encouraged them to move various pieces of furniture in different ways.

The basic findings of this observation were: 1) each person manipulated each piece of the foam-core furniture in a different manner, indicating that any 3-D interaction method must allow individuality or flexibility in the functions it provides; 2) most manipulations could be categorized as sliding an object along a plane, lifting an object, or re-orienting (rotating) an object; and, 3) users had expectations about the way objects should move, based on the identity of the piece of furniture each object represented.

In response to these observations, three goals which guided the development of the interface described by this paper were identified. First, the interface should allow a smooth change of modes between sliding, lifting, and turning activities. Second, objects should respond to manipulation in ways that reflect their simulated identities as real furniture objects, and third, emphasis should be placed on providing a means of interaction that can be easily understood by many different users.

Based on these goals, a set of rules were defined for simplifying access to the elemental sliding, lifting and turning manipulations. All furniture objects were defined to have natural *resting planes* to which they would stick by default when not being lifted. Pictures, for example, would stick to walls while chairs and tables would sit on floor planes. Resting objects would continue to stick to their planes when they were slid or turned. To facilitate simple re-orientation, objects were constrained to turn only about their central axis, perpendicular to the resting plane. These constraints were designed to limit full freedom of movement, in favor of giving users easy access to the most important space planning manipulations.

Mapping 2-D input onto 3-D tasks

Since a conventional mouse with a single button was chosen as the sole input device, the problem of how to map two degrees of spatial input onto a 3-D task needed to be addressed. Several issues related to users needs in the context of space planning were identified. These included: how should mouse movement be mapped onto the three distinct activities of sliding, lifting, and turning; and how should fluid switching between these activities be accomplished.

Several strategies for mapping 2-D mouse input onto 3-D manipulations exist. A method developed by Nielson and Olsen [11] constrains object translation along a single axis, defined by a selected object's local coordinate system. A more general solution by Bier [3] allows a user to attach a different coordinate system to an object to allow translation along axes of any orientation. The Virtual Sphere developed by Chen et al [4] allows fluid rotation about an arbitrary 3-D axis by simulating cursor interaction with a 3-D trackball. A mechanism commonly found in 3-D applications on the Apple Macintosh® computer is a palette of individual tools for rotation about three world coordinate axes and translation in two dimensions [12][13]. Users select a specific tool by using the cursor to point and click, then typically click and drag on an object to apply that tool's manipulation capability.

None of these existing 2-D input solutions offered a sufficiently easy transition between rotation and translation to

allow smooth switching between sliding, lifting and turning activities desired for the space planning interface. While Nielson's and Bier's methods provide rotation and translation control, they do not discuss any way of switching between these manipulations. Similarly, the Virtual Sphere addresses only rotation, without providing for translation. While the tool palette interface provides both rotation and translation capabilities, switching between manipulations requires repetitive, non-fluid mode changes to select tools from the palette apply them to objects.

DESIGN ITERATION

The current state of the prototype was achieved by using the project goals to initiate a series of design iterations. Each iterative cycle consisted of rough prototyping, followed by group discussion and casual user observation. Prototypes were created in MacroMind's Director™ [9], an animating and scripting environment, which enabled rapid production of 2-D simulations of 3-D interface ideas. As the design progressed, C++ code allowed us to test more fully formulated solutions in a 3-D environment with proper perspective and manipulation constraints.

We move things with our hands

Development of the prototype began with a consideration of real world object manipulations – people move objects around with their hands. When sliding, lifting, and turning furniture, hands are placed in positions which are physically optimal for each task. People even gesture with their hands when describing such actions. It therefore seemed promising to investigate the use of hands, and meaningful hand gestures, as potential interface mechanisms.

Hands have been used as interface elements in several previously developed 2-D and 3-D manipulation interfaces. A cartoon style hand cursor can be used to slide a page around within several 2-D paint programs, such as MacPaint [5]. A hand with a finger pointing upward functions as a 'browse mode' cursor in the HyperCard program [2]. Hand gestures function as narrative symbols for *File*, *Delete*, *Shear*, *Rotate*, *Move* and *Copy* operations in tool palettes designed by Peter Tierney of Cybermation, Inc. [7]. Using the data glove from VPL Research, Inc. [15], Sturman et al [14] provide 3-D manipulation control by mimicking a user's gloved hand gestures with a simple hand representation on the screen.

Hands as cursors

In the first design, pictures of hands, rendered in different positions, were defined and used as cursors for each of the

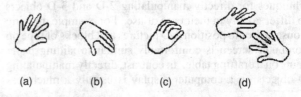

(a)   (b)   (c)   (d)

Figure 1: Different hand positions were used as cursors to indicate interaction possibilities. In (a), and open hand position indicates a ready state, (b) shows a hand pressing down parallel to the plane on which an object rests to indicate sliding, while (c) shows a grab position to indicate lifting. In (d) two hands pushing toward each other in opposite directions indicate rotation.

Figure 2: One of the first prototypes used a living room setting created in MacroMind Director. Even though this prototype was based on 2-D, painted objects, it helped to identify 3-D interface issues.

desired sliding, lifting and turning actions. Initial assumptions were made about which hand positions were appropriate for each type of interaction (Figure 1). These representations might give users an intuitive notion of what kind of action could be undertaken with a given cursor, as well as feedback on actions performed.

In order to test the feel of this proposed interaction, a Director prototype was created. This prototype included a perspective view of a living room with movable pictures of a chair, a floor lamp, a rug and a framed painting, as shown in Figure 2. The open or *ready* hand (Figure 1a) was defined as the default pointing cursor. When the mouse button was pressed, a picture of the *lifting* hand (Figure 1b) would replace it.

Use of this prototype identified two problems immediately. First, while it looked and felt good to use the mouse button for changing the ready hand to the lifting hand, it was not clear how a smooth transition to the sliding or rotating hand cursors could be accomplished. Second, most people who used the prototype felt bothered by the fact that the 2-D hand cursor in the 3-D environment didn't behave like a real hand (Figure 3). Most thought the lifting hand cursor should grab objects in the way they would, using their own hands. For instance, several people agreed that they would pick a real lamp by grasping its

long neck pole. Therefore, they wanted the hand cursor to wrap around the neck of the graphical lamp in the same manner.

Active areas

Initially, it seemed feasible to correct these problems while continuing to use hands as cursors. The 2-D hand cursors could act more like real hands in a 3-D environment if each object *knows* how it can grabbed. Therefore, hidden *active areas* where manipulation could take place were defined for each object in the living room prototype. When these areas were clicked on by the open hand cursor, lifting, sliding, or rotating cursors that were designed to fit each object's contour were activated. Thus the hand cursors appeared to behave more like real hands as shown in Figure 4.

This method enabled the desired smooth switching between sliding, lifting and turning actions. Rather than indicating a cursor action change with a tool palette click, users could simply touch the appropriate area of an object to obtain the hand cursor needed for a given action. Manipulation controls were located directly on each object. This allowed for greater concentration on positioning the piece of furniture being moved, as there was no need to change focus from object to tool palette.

Although the use of active areas effectively solved the earlier cursor problems, a new problem was created. The locations of the active areas defined on furniture objects were not well perceived by users. When initial assumptions about their locations were not reinforced, users tended to click blindly all over objects in search of them. This typically led to frustrations, such as a user wanting to lift a chair, but not being able to make the cursor change to the lifting hand because the correct area of activation could not be found.

Narrative handles

It seemed appropriate to visually expose the active areas for sliding, lifting and turning on each object. The same hand symbols previously used as cursors were therefore implemented as handles. In this new interface prototype, users operated an arrow cursor with their mouse and selection was indicated by pointing to an object and clicking the mouse button once. Upon selection, sliding, lifting and turning hands appeared on the object (Figure 5). Pointing to a specific hand

Figure 3: A "ready" hand cursor is moved toward a lamp. When the mouse button is clicked, a "lifting" hand cursor appears and allows a user to pick the lamp up from the floor of the living room. Users were disturbed by watching a hand grab objects in the "wrong" way. In this case, for instance, the grabbing hand should wrap around the neck of the lamp.

Figure 4: An active area is defined on the neck of the lamp. When the open hand cursor is placed in this area and the mouse is clicked, the cursor becomes a lifting hand which appears to grab around the neck of the lamp.

Figure 5: When hands were implemented as handles, a user could first click anywhere on the lamp with their cursor to select it. Then, the sliding, lifting, and rotating hands would appear as handles. Clicking and dragging on any of these handles would allow manipulation of the lamp in the manner suggested by the position of the hand.

Figure 6: The bounding box, which appeared around an object upon selection, was designed to look like a wire frame, or clear glass box, so that the enclosed furniture object could always be seen clearly.

and holding the button down while dragging the mouse, allowed the selected object to be manipulated in the manner indicated by the hand's particular gesture. Thus, the user could operate these *narrative handles* via the same click and drag actions often applied to rectangular handles in 2-D graphics programs [1].

This design preserved the smooth change of modes between rotation and translation, because all manipulation areas were still directly located on each object. However, determining intuitive locations for controls continued to be a problem. A unique set of handles would have to be defined for each object if the handles were to narrate their afforded actions effectively. While it seemed straightforward to design intuitive locations for some objects, it was hard to define them for others. A natural lifting handle for the lamp appeared to be a hand grasping the neck of the lamp. But, where would a lifting handle be attached to an oddly shaped object like the winged back chair? On the back? Underneath? On the arms? Every user introduced to the handles prototype had a different expectation.

This problem might have been anticipated based on the initial user study, in which subjects moved furniture objects in the foam-core model of an office. It was noted that each user handled any given piece of furniture in a completely different manner. Thus, it became apparent that it would be impossible to design narrative handles that could work for every object, let alone for every person interacting with those objects.

Direct manipulation of a bounding box

A strategy for simplifying the contours of all objects was subsequently introduced. A bounding box that surrounds the 3-D extent of a furniture object, as shown in Figure 6, was included in the interface prototype. The box appeared whenever an object was selected. By directly manipulating this box, the user could manipulate the object inside simultaneously. Therefore, a user only needed to learn how to manipulate one simple 3-D shape, that of the bounding box, to control any object.

Narrative handles were used as controls for manipulating the bounding box. They were positioned on the surface of the box to form a *handle box* (Figure 7). Pictures of hands which

appear to grasp physical handles attached to the box were used as narrative handle forms. Clicking and dragging with the arrow cursor anywhere on the hand or the handle it grasped would allow the manipulation depicted to take place.

Handles for lifting and rotating were designed to suggest the way that users might use their hands to lift and turn a real box. A hand grasping a handle on top of the bounding box – as if ready to pull away from an object's resting plane – was implemented as the *lifting handle*. A selected object could be lifted by clicking on the lifting handle and dragging upward. The hands grasping the handles on the box's four corners – as if to pull the box around – were implemented as *turning handles*. Clicking and dragging on any of the four turning handles allowed an object to be rotated about its central axis, perpendicular to the resting plane.

Hands which appeared to push the flat sides of the box were initially designed to be *sliding handles*. Their implementation was eventually rejected because users tended to ignore their presence, preferring to click and drag directly on the central mass of each object. This tendency may derive from users' previous experiences with manipulating 2-D objects in this manner. Therefore, no handles were provided for sliding objects. Instead, clicking and dragging anywhere on the surface of the bounding box allowed users to slide a selected object.

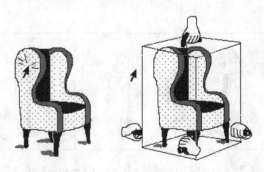

Figure 7: The handle box had a lifting handle, and four rotation handles attached to it. No handle was provided for sliding, on the assumption that the most direct way to slide an object would be to click and drag on the object inside the box itself.

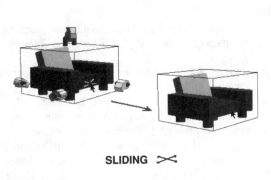

SLIDING ✕

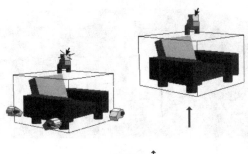

LIFTING ✛

Figure 8: Sliding on the chair's resting plane is executed by clicking and dragging anywhere on the surface of the bounding box. Unused handles disappear while the mouse button is held down to remove unnecessary visual clutter while positioning takes place.

Figure 9: The chair can be lifted off its resting plane when the lifting handle is clicked and dragged upward. In this view, note that the chair literally moves vertically on the screen as it does when sliding. However, the explicit use of a lifting handle distinguishes this action from sliding.

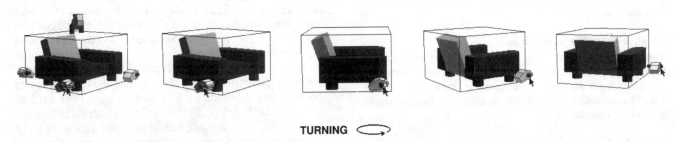

TURNING ⟲

Figure 10: Any of the four rotation handles can be clicked and dragged on to turn the chair about its central, vertical axis. Note that the interface is simplified so that rotation handles only appear for orientations that are appropriate in the space planning context. For instance, the chair cannot be tipped on it's back.

Placing handles in consistent locations on the box seemed to define a simple visual vocabulary for manipulation that was easy to recognize when an object was selected. The presence of handles on the bounding box indicate the range of manipulation possibilities. Missing handles indicate that an object cannot be acted on in a particular way. For example, in the given task domain, a picture on the wall would not offer rotation handles because it has only one appropriate orientation.

Integration of the handle box interface in the larger space planning application prototype was explored through the development of a usage scenario. The rearrangement of furniture in a living room to accommodate a new television set was chosen as a sample task. The handle box interface was animated in a Director sequence, showing the furniture moving into a new configuration. Several concerns were clarified by this exercise. For small objects, the bounding box and handles become too small for the handles to be recognized as hands. In addition, a selected object's handles might easily be obscured by other objects in a crowded room. Handles might also intersect with walls and other pieces of furniture because they protrude from the box.

A more general prototype of the handle box interface was also implemented in a coded prototype on an Apple Macintosh IIfx. This prototype allowed further exploration of the integration concerns introduced by the animated scenario study. Users could manipulate three furniture objects in a room

where real constraints were simulated, and the scale of objects changed to reflect their depth in the scene. This was important for testing the *feel* of the interface, as it was not possible to create this level of simulation in the Director prototypes.

THE USER TEST
The next step was to conduct a user test to evaluate the handle box as an interface for space planning and to identify features which should be preserved in a more general 3-D interface The method of testing was informal, resembling the kind of user observation described by Nielsen [10] and Gomoll [8], in order to provide quick results that could be used in further design iterations.

Method
Ten Apple Computer employees, five men and five women, were selected as subjects for the user test. Three subjects were intermediate level users who primarily use word processing applications, four were advanced users who use word processing as well as 2-D graphics programs, and three were expert computer users with some experience using 3-D programs. The test consisted of three parts: a legibility test, a single object manipulation task, and a multiple object manipulation task.

Legibility test
Four static images of different chair representations (see Figure 12) were shown to users. Possible ordering effects were avoided by varying the sequence in which these images

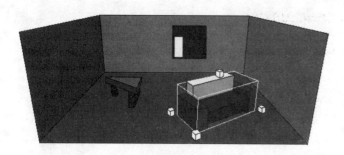

Figure 11: A C++ prototype used in a multiple object manipulation test. Note that the handles were cube-shaped, rather than hand-shaped, to simplify rendering.

were presented. Users were asked to describe what they saw in each picture and to describe how they might use an arrow pointer controlled by a single button mouse to slide, lift and turn the chair.

Single object manipulation task
The chair with the working handle box interface, shown in Figures 8, 9 and 10, was introduced to subjects. They were presented with an interactive Director prototype and were asked to use the mouse to move the chair to various places in a 3-D room model.

Multiple object manipulation task
Participants were asked to use the mouse to manipulate three furniture objects with handle box interfaces in a 3-D room. The C++ space planning prototype shown in Figure 11 was used.

Findings
Our previously undocumented observations of intuitive use of the handle box as an interface for space planning were reinforced by the user test. Every participant was able to use the handle box to manipulate 3-D furniture objects easily and without instruction. The success of the interface appears to derive from the intuitive attributes of the handle box, the context in which it was used, and the identities of the specific objects which were manipulated. Specific findings are described below.

Legibility test
Users' reactions to how they would manipulate each of the four representations show in Figure 12 were as follows:

The chair alone. To turn the chair in Figure 12a, most users said they would click on a "corner" or "exposed edge" and drag it around with a horizontal motion. To slide the chair on the floor, most said they would click in the middle of the chair, and to drag to a new position. When describing how to lift the chair, most users said they would again click in the middle of the chair, and drag upward. Users said the chair should behave like a real chair. Typical comments included: "There is a sense of gravity and the chair is going to obey the laws of gravity," and "this is a chair, we know how to deal with chairs."

A bounding box. When shown the picture of the chair inside the bounding box (Figure 12b), most users said that the chair was now enclosed by "a glass box." Most thought the box was as a selection cue, and many assumed it was there to be used to manipulate the chair. Most users indicated that they would click on and drag the bounding box by an edge or corner to turn the chair. To lift or slide the chair, half of the users indicated that they would first click any face of the box. The other half said they would click on the "center," which appeared to be the center of the 2-D image of the chair and box on the screen. All but one user would then drag the box and chair to their new location – above the floor if lifting, or somewhere on the floor if sliding.

Cube shaped handles. The cubes in the image of the chair shown in Figure 12c were usually identified as handles. Several users said that available functionality was indicated by them. However, users were confused about whether the cube handles were for moving, stretching, or both. All of the users indicated that they would lift the chair by clicking down on the topmost cube and dragging upward. Although most users would grab one of the bottom corner cubes to turn the chair, their impressions of how the chair would turn were inconsistent. Some said the chair would turn around its center, while others thought it should pivot around the opposite corner cube. The question of how to slide the chair yielded the most varied responses. Some users indicated that they would

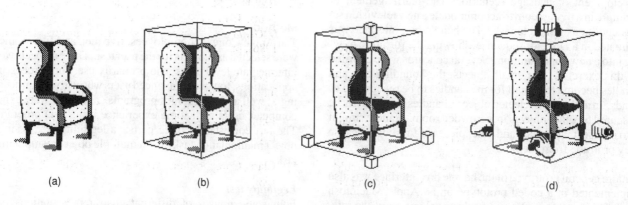

(a)	(b)	(c)	(d)

Figure 12: Images of the chair alone (a), in a bounding box (b), in a handle box with cube-shaped handles (c), and in a handle box with hand-shaped handles (d), were shown to users in the legibility test.

click on the center of the 2-D image of the chair and box on the screen and drag them to a new position on the floor. Some would click on a face of the box to "push" the box, while others would grab one of the bottom corner cubes to "drag" the box around.

Hand shaped handles. Several users indicated that they would click and drag on the handles which the hands appear to grasp, rather than the hands themselves, to manipulate the chair shown in Figure 12d. Some thought that if they clicked on the hands themselves, that the hands would perform the anticipated action. For example, clicking once on the lifting hand would cause the box to move upward automatically. Others said the hands were there simply to indicate what actions could be accomplished with each handle. "I guess the hands give it away right away," said one user as he pointed to one handle grasped by a hand, " it [means] grab here."

Users referred to the handles by their action names. When asked how they would turn the chair, all users said they would click and drag one of the "rotation hands," or "turning hands" – indicating the lower hands grabbing the handles at the bottom corners of the box. All but one of the users said they would grab the "lifting handle," – indicating the handle at the top of the box – to pick up the chair. Some users said they would click and drag the middle of the chair in the box – indicating the 2-D projection of the image – to slide the chair on the floor. Others said they would "grab any side of the box" to "push" it.

Single object manipulation task

When users were asked to try manipulating the chair, most clicked directly on it and dragged to slide it around. Upon selecting the chair, the handle box appeared, and most recognized it from the legibility test. Everyone was able to slide, lift, and turn the chair without apparent difficulty.

Some users wondered if they could use the rotation hands to turn the chair around axes other than the local axis of the chair perpendicular to the floor. Most assumed they could not. Most users appeared to accept this constraint because of the chair's identity as an object that would normally stand upright. As one user said "if it were a generalized 3-D program, I would find [rotation about only one axis] to be a limitation - but if it were a house planner - why would you want to turn the chair on its side?"

Multiple object manipulation task

Users switched between moving the different objects easily, and seemed generally satisfied with their ability to put objects where they wanted them. When sliding, people noticed and liked the fact that an object's scale changed as a distance cue.

Some users said that while they would like to turn the chair over on its side "for kicks" – as one user put it, they didn't mind not being able to because "it *is* a chair." Users thought of examples of other furniture object types which they would want to rotate more freely due to the object's specific properties.

CONCLUSIONS

A number of things were learned during the development and testing of the handle box interface that may be applicable to other, more general 3-D interaction interfaces. They are summarized as follows:

- Controlling object positions by manipulating a bounding box provides a consistent and local direct manipulation mode for many different object shapes.

- Placing controls directly on the box in positions which reflect those one would use to move a similar shape in the real world makes the interaction more intuitive.

- Creating a composite mode for allowing easy access to rotation and translation allows users to make repetitive position adjustments in a smooth manner.

- Using narrative handles – whose shape indicates their manipulation capability – informs users about what they can do with any object.

- Reducing the number of possible degrees of 3-D manipulation freedom via context specific constraints, contributes to ease of use and a user's feeling of control in a 3-D environment.

ACKNOWLEDGMENTS

The hands investigation was part of a larger 3-D interface project led by Lewis Knapp. Thanks are extended to the team for their support and assistance, and in particular to Penny Bauersfeld who conducted the office model user study, Laurie Vertelney who designed the user scenario, and Michael Chen who wrote the C++ space planning prototype. Special thanks to S. Joy Mountford who supported this research, Richard Mander who helped design the user test, and Gitta Salomon and Tom Erickson for helpful comments on this paper.

REFERENCES

[1] Apple Computer, Inc. Human Interface Guidelines: The Apple Desktop Interface, Addison Wesley Publishing Co. Inc., USA, 1987, p. 115.

[2] Apple Computer, Inc. *HyperCard* 2.0 © 1987-1990.

[3] Bier, E. A. Skitters and Jacks: Interactive 3-D Positioning Tools. In *Proceedings 1986 Workshop on Interactive 3-D Graphics* (Chapel Hill, North Carolina, October 1986), pp. 183-196.

[4] Chen, M., Mountford S. J., Sellen, A. A Study in Interactive 3-D Rotation Using 2-D Control Devices. Proceedings of SIGGRAPH'88 (Atlanta, GA, August 1988). In *Computer Graphics* 22,4 (August 1988), pp. 121-129.

[5] Claris Coroporation, *MacPaint*®. Version 2.0. 1985-1987.

[6] Erisson, K.A., and Simon, H. A. Protocol Analysis. Cambridge, Massachusetts: MIT Press. 1984.

[7] Foley, J. D., van Dam, A., Feiner, S. K., Hughes, J. F. Computer Graphics: Principles and Practice , Addison Wesley Publishing Co. Inc., USA, 1990, plates 1.19 - 1.21. pp 376-381.

[8] Gomoll, K. Some Techniques for Observing Users The Art of Human Interface Design (ed. Brenda Laurel) Addison-Wesley. 1990. pp.85-90.

[9] MacroMind, Inc., *MacroMind Director* 2.0. ©1989.

[10] Nielsen, J. Usability Engineering at a Discount. In G. Salvendy and M.J. Smith (Eds.), Designing and Using Human-Computer Interfaces and Knowledge Based Systems. Amsterdam: Elsevier. 1989, pp.394-401.

[11] Nielson, G. M., Olsen, D. R. Jr. Direct Manipulation Techniques of 3D Objects Using 2D Locator Devices. In *Proceedings 1986 Workshop on Interactive 3-D Graphics* (Chapel Hill, North Carolina, October 1986), pp. 175-182.

[12] Paracomp Inc., *Swivel 3D™*. Version 1.1. 1987-1990.

[13] Specular International., *Infini-D™* 1.0.1. 1989-1991.

[14] Sturman, D., Zeltzer, D., Pieper, S. Hands-On Interaction with Virtual Environments, In *Proceedings of UIST '89: ACM SIGGRAPH/SIGCHI Symposium on User Interface Software and Technology*, Williamsburg, VA, Nov. 13-15, 1989, pp. 19-24.

[15] Zimmerman, T. G., Lanier, J., Blanchard, C., Bryson, S., Harvill, Y., A Hand Gesture Interface Device. In *Proceedings of CHI + GI* (Toronto, Canada, April 1987), pp. 189-192.

Computing for Users with Special Needs and Models of Computer-Human Interaction

William W. McMillan

Department of Computer Science
Eastern Michigan University
Ypsilanti, MI 48197
(313) 487-1063
bill@emunix.emich.edu

ABSTRACT

Models of human-computer interaction (HCI) can provide a degree of theoretical unity for diverse work in computing for users with special needs. Example adaptations for special users are described in the context of both implementation-oriented and linguistic models of HCI. It is suggested that the language of HCI be used to define standards for special adaptations. This would enhance reusability, modifiability, and compatibility of adaptations, inspire new innovations, and make it easier for developers of standard interfaces to incorporate adaptations. The creation of user models for subgroups of users with special needs would support semantic and conceptual adaptations.

KEYWORDS: Human-computer interaction, models, handicapped, special education, rehabilitation, accessibility.

INTRODUCTION

Computing for users with special needs (CUSN) is an active field with many successes, but is not well-unified theoretically. Models of human-computer interaction (HCI) can serve as a basis for better understanding CUSN, relating the diverse research in that field, accurately specifying the structure and function of special computing adaptations, developing industry-wide standards for adaptations, and promoting compatibility between different adaptations. Viewing CUSN within the framework of HCI can advance the latter discipline as well by providing in a familiar language clever ideas about the modification of interfaces, and by encouraging the incorporation of special adaptations into standard interfaces.

The target population for CUSN includes those whose needs are not currently met by off-the-shelf computing systems,

most importantly people diagnosed as having impairments that are physical (sensory or motor), cognitive (in learning, attention, perception, or language), or emotional. (See the Appendix for some entry points to the field.) Developments in CUSN include alternate keyboards for users with motor problems, text-to-speech systems for blind users, cognitive therapy programs, augmentative communication systems, programs that teach social skills, and many other varied products. Most work on CUSN is carried out by professionals in education, rehabilitation, and communication disorders, usually in isolation from more theoretical research in the field of HCI. (A notable exception is the activity of ACM's Special Interest Group on Computers and the Physically Handicapped, which is one of the cooperating societies for CHI'92.)

Over the past several years my computer science students and I have collaborated with professionals in special education and rehabilitation to develop applications for physically, cognitively, and emotionally impaired users. In addition, I have interviewed dozens of professionals actively involved in CUSN, including teachers, therapists, administrators, and academicians. During the 1990-1991 school year, I spent a half-day per week at a school for the physically handicapped as an observer, computing consultant, and teaching assistant. This experience has shown the need for better theory in CUSN. Because most existing CUSN products are developed *ad hoc* and their documentation provides little or no specification about how they work, it is often next to impossible to tailor them for a particular user, to combine them in a single system, or to reuse them in a new application. A striking comment made by some who work in CUSN is that there is no such thing as computing for special education or for the handicapped. This does not mean that great work is not being done, but rather that the field has few unifying principles.

By planting our feet firmly within the science of HCI, it is hoped that we can see CUSN as a whole, and encourage HCI researchers to keep CUSN at least within their peripheral vision. Some comments will be made about what it means to be handicapped and about current movement of standard interfaces toward inclusion of features for users with special needs. Then two standard models of HCI will be used as a framework for describing some example adaptations for special users. These demonstrations of the value of specification will support an argument for the development of standards for CUSN. Finally, some directions for research in both HCI and CUSN will be suggested.

WHO IS A SPECIAL USER?

From the point of view of a computer, all human users are handicapped. No one can receive text as fast as a computer can send it, or draw a shape as quickly and precisely as a computer would gladly receive it. The study of human-computer interfaces and dialogues is the study of how to overcome, and capitalize on, the weaknesses and strengths of very different kinds of participants in an interaction. "Standard" interfaces are those that have been designed for the capabilities of the great majority of users. "Special" or "adaptive" interfaces are those that have features not included in off-the-shelf computing products, and so must be crafted for a subset of the user population (possibly consisting of a single individual). Before the advent of graphical user interfaces, people who could not abide cryptic textual commands were too handicapped to use a computer efficiently; they required some "special adaptation", possibly a kindly human intermediary. Today the needs of the "point-and-click user" are met by the computing industry in almost every new operating system and application program that appears.

As society becomes more committed to principles of accessibility and inclusion (shown, for example, by the Americans with Disabilities Act of 1990) and as computing systems become more powerful, the definition of special needs can be expected to shift. An example probably unknown to many Macintosh users is "Easy Access", a utility included with their computer that eliminates the need to press multiple keys simultaneously or to use the mouse to point. What was yesterday a special adaptation is today a standard feature. One of the goals of this paper is to promote an industry-wide understanding of special adaptations, making it more likely that developers of standard interfaces will incorporate them, or at least provide well-documented "hooks" to which others may connect adaptations.

(An important aside before proceeding: The use of company and product names in this paper should not be considered as endorsements or recommendations for their use. I have chosen examples with which I happen to be familiar, or for which I could find adequate information. I have no affiliation with, or support from, any company.)

IMPLEMENTATION-ORIENTED MODEL OF HCI

Figure 1 presents a generic model of a user interacting with a computing system without special adaptations. It has similarities to Marcus and van Dam's *implementation-oriented*

model [3], but includes a more general software structure and is more explicit about some of the information flows. The user's sensory, speech, and motor systems are depicted to make the model detailed enough to handle common adaptations. Output devices include video displays, speakers, speech synthesizers, printers, etc. Input devices include the keyboard, mouse, graphics tablet, microphone, etc. The software that controls the interaction resides in the operating system and in the application program. (The operating system is broadly defined here, and includes any system software that manges the computer or the I/O devices.) Different computer systems partition management of the interface in different ways. In an MS-DOS system, for example, the application must manage any windows that are used, but with MicroSoft Windows, X-Windows in a Unix environment, or the Macintosh, the operating system (or other system routines external to the application) can take that responsibility. The CPU and memory are shown as a single unit simply because there is usually no need to represent them separately when considering HCI. Several aspects of typical computing systems are glossed over in this model. For example, the following are not shown: direct memory access (between I/O devices and memory); support hardware for I/O such as a character generator, special screen memory, and device interfaces; non-I/O interactions between the application and operating system; direct control of devices by applications; and so on. The model can obviously be made more detailed, and this is necessary to model some I/O adaptations for special users.

Some readers may have a degree of understandable discomfort with this model of HCI because it is so hardware and systems software oriented. It seems to pull us toward the *interface*, the

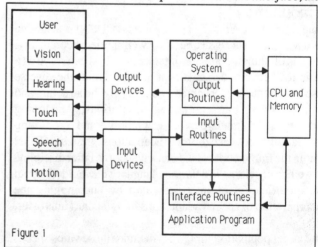

Figure 1

details of how information is transmitted, and away from the meaningful *dialogue*, the exchange of symbols between human and application [2]. The linguistic model, presented in a later section, will return some of the focus to the dialogue. The implementation-oriented model is probably easier to understand, and will be better suited for depicting adaptations for users whose main difficulty is in pure information transmission.

ADAPTATIONS & THE IMPLEMENTATION MODEL

This section will place some fairly common adaptations in the context of the implementation-oriented model of HCI. Rather than redraw the entire model for each modification, "threads" of information through the system will be extracted. Figure 2a shows the standard thread related to keyboard use. The user's hand motion operates the keyboard, which is read and interpreted to some extent by the keyboard driver, one of the operating system's input routines. (The keyboard driver can be considered here to also include any hardware dedicated to reading the keyboard.) Figure 2b shows the same thread, modified in the most logically simple way. The user, who has precise head motion but inadequate hand control, wears a headset with a forward-pointing stick and depresses keys on the regular keyboard by moving the stick. Assuming that simultaneous key presses are unnecessary, the modification is completely external to the computing system. In Figure 2c the regular keyboard is used, but the keyboard driver has been replaced by an alternate routine, possibly obviating the need

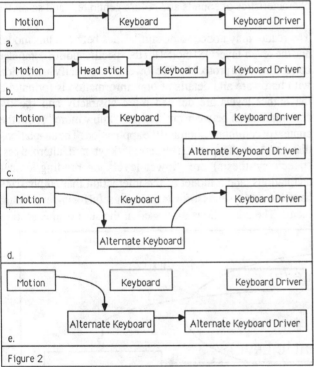

Figure 2

for simultaneous keypresses or modifying key repeat rate. Apple's Easy Access (specifically Sticky Keys) works this way. Diagraming the adaptation in this manner makes it clear that the operating system has been adapted, not the application, and it implies that the modification will work with multiple applications. The specifier, designer, and buyer of such an adaptation can understand and agree on exactly what it does. The thread for an alternate keyboard using the standard driver is shown in Figure 2d. Some users require enlarged keyboards because of imprecision in hand and finger movements. To make special keyboards as general as possible, some manufacturers, e.g., Prentke-Romich, make them fully

compatible with regular keyboards. The operating system doesn't know the difference. Finally, Figure 2e shows an alternate keyboard that requires an alternate driver. If the alternate keyboard is a single switch for a user with very limited motion, some modification to the operating system is necessary. Another example is the Unicorn Keyboard for the Apple II family, which, because the Apple II keyboard is not easily replaceable, requires a special card and software. In this case, a description including the hardware modification requires a more detailed model.

The thread in Figure 3a is for output to the screen. The screen manager includes software and dedicated hardware to support the display. Figure 3b depicts the situation of a blind user who gets textual output through a speech synthesizer. A modification to the operating system channels selected text through a text-to-speech program that drives a speech synthesizer. Another operating system modification (not diagramed) allows the user to interrupt the application and request that various sections of the screen be read aloud. An example for IBM PC-compatible computers is the program Arctic Vision, used in conjunction with the SynPhonix 200 speech synthesizer. In theory, any application that respects the operating system's domain should work with such a configuration. The application in Figure 3c does its own text-to-speech translation and drives the synthesizer. This is not very flexible, but it allows the application to tailor the speech to its own operation, possibly saving the user work in searching the screen for text relevant to current functions.

These examples show how a standard model of HCI can be used to show explicitly what a special adaptation does. This is not only helpful for the maker and buyer of the product, but also for other developers who would like to build a new application using the adaptation, or combine several different adaptations in a single computing system. The current practice of not specifying exactly how an adaptive device or program changes the system sometimes makes it impossible to use

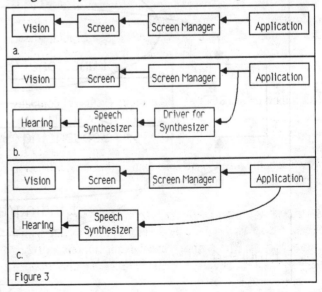

Figure 3

such products in even moderately novel ways — not a situation conducive to the incorporation of adaptations into standard interfaces.

LINGUISTIC MODEL OF HCI

What about adaptations more closely linked to the functions of the application? One example might be an alphabet-tutoring program that keeps its displays uncluttered (unlike most educational programs) so that students with perceptual problems are not overwhelmed. Another might be a primary-level arithmetic program that uses pictures appropriate for a 20-year-old student, rather than forever displaying teddy bears and pink bunnies. It is helpful to look at a model of the HCI that emphasizes the levels of human-computer dialogue when considering such adaptations.

Figure 4 is Marcus and van Dam's linguistic model [3], drawn slightly differently. (A related discussion is by Marsh [4].) Communication between the person and the computer can be thought to occur at the level of meaning (the ideas communicated) and form (the actions taken, the symbols transferred, and their arrangement). The conceptual level of meaning is the level of the user's "world model", or "task model". It is at this level that the concepts of the domain reside, including the objects that exist, their features, relationships, and operations. For example, for a mathematics tutoring program, the conceptual level includes the objects and operations of mathematics (numbers, addition, greater than, etc.) and concepts related to tutoring (questions, answers, determination of correctness, etc.) The communication at the conceptual level is not so much between user and computer as between user and system designer. At the functional/semantic level, the ideas from the conceptual level are placed in the context of the computing system. The abstract operations

from the conceptual level are fully defined in terms of objects and functions represented in the system, including, for the mathematics tutor, limits on computations, error results, complexity of possible questions and answers, exact effects of arithmetic operations, etc.

At the sequencing/syntactic level, the "grammar" of the interaction is defined, including the arrangements of actions that are legal for the user to take and possible for the computer to generate. For the math tutor, this would encompass possible orderings of events after a question has been asked of the user (just give an answer, or ask for a hint then give an answer) the syntax of commands and requests, and the language of the computer's questions, explanations, hints, feedback, etc. At the binding/lexical level, the primitive elements of the language "spoken" in the interaction are bound to manipulation of input devices by the user and to various output devices of the computer. This level determines whether the user points with a mouse, joy stick or touch screen, whether the computer displays text or uses a speech synthesizer, the exact characteristics of sounds and colors generated, and so on.

The reader may notice some similarities between this model and the seven-layer OSI model for the specification of computer communication protocols. The lower levels specify interaction with hardware and details of how information is formatted; the higher levels are defined more abstractly and specify communication between entities that "know more" about the context of communication and the application. The adaptations discussed in the previous section (keyboard alternatives, speech synthesis) are "lower-level" or binding/lexical adaptations, and a model of the interaction that emphasizes hardware and systems software is most useful for understanding them. The adaptations discussed at the start of this section

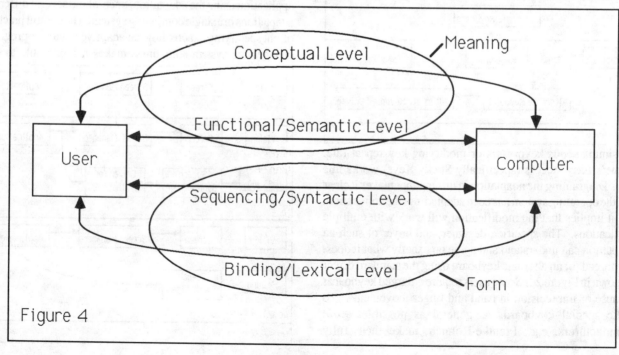

Figure 4

(age-appropriate graphics, uncluttered screen) are at the sequencing/syntactic level (or higher, depending on their exact nature). A program that uses a teaching strategy appropriate for a student with a learning disability has been tailored at the functional/semantic level, and possibly at the conceptual level. A specification of the objects and operations of the domain at these levels would make the program readily understandable to a wide community. Instructional or interaction theories stated in terms of conceptual models would lead directly to designs for software.

WHAT AND WHERE: IDEAS FROM MODELS

It may appear that the implementation-oriented model is only good for describing binding/lexical adaptations, because the higher-level adaptations are all hidden inside the box labeled "Application". But why couldn't some syntactic or semantic adaptations occur in the operating system (or some other system software outside the application)? Consider the user whose perceptual difficulties make the typical window-oriented, menu-driven display too busy for easy use. It is conceivable that the operating system could provide simpler (but possibly less powerful) alternatives for showing information and getting commands. The application's calls to standard system routines that drive the interface could be reinterpreted in the operating system to invoke alternate interface routines. Such an option would have to be set in the operating system, but, once it was activated, *the application wouldn't know the difference*. In principle, any application could be adapted. Programs that magnify screen displays for visually-impaired users are simple examples of this idea (but are best modeled at the lexical/binding level). The two models discussed describe two aspects of an adaptation: its linguistic level and where in the computing system it is implemented.

As part of a research project on computing for the visually impaired, researchers at the Environmental Institute of Michigan (ERIM) have developed a prototype of a tutoring program called On-Line Trainer (OLT) (R. Emaus and D. Winfree, personal communication). It resides in the "background", coexisting with any application program. OLT observes the user's keystrokes and offers the possibility that a blind user could be coached about use of the keyboard or other aspects of the interface when OLT recognizes the need for help. OLT could be tailored to help many kinds of users with many kinds of applications. It is an example of an operating system modification that intervenes at all of the linguistic levels.

Another example is WordWriter, a program ("desk accessory") for the Macintosh that provides an alternate method of typing text. In almost any application, the user can "type" by clicking keys on an image of a keyboard. This is for the user who can move the screen pointer and click either with the mouse or with simple switches, but cannot type. In addition, the utility predicts different ways the word being typed will conclude

and the user can often save typing by selecting the word desired from a list on the screen. This adaptation to the operating system is at the binding/lexical level (different way to type) and, for word prediction, is at all of the higher levels (new concepts, semantics, and syntax).

By thinking in terms of the models presented here (or some other good models of HCI), many such ideas may come to mind. Rather than developing adaptations in whatever way seems intuitively satisfactory, a developer who starts from theory will, in the long run, push frontiers farther and provide a better map for other developers to follow.

STANDARDS

As technology matures, it requires standards. Just as automobiles, televisions, and computer interfaces have benefited from industry agreements about structure, function, and methods of specification, CUSN will become less "special" and better integrated into everyday computing systems as adaptive products become more standardized. As pointed out in the context of the examples presented earlier, many existing adaptations are inadequately specified, erecting barriers to reuse and modification. The most critical need is for ways to specify, and guidelines for, adaptations within the context of a detailed implementation model. The group to develop standards would most logically include the ACM, IEEE, and organizations representing education and rehabilitation professionals. The following need to be defined:

1. Generic implementation models, layered by level of detail.
2. Specialized implementation models for some common classes of computers, also layered by level of detail.
3. A classification scheme for adaptations according to where in the system they intervene.
4. Guidelines for how to intervene at different points.
5. Guidelines for formally specifying interventions in the language of generic and specialized models.

Standards based on linguistic or other semantic models are also desirable, but will probably be more difficult. They would depend on detailed behavioral and learning models of various classes of users, making the standards much more dependent on knowledge in special education and rehabilitation than on theory in computer science. The obvious crossroad is again research in HCI, especially that on user modeling. One approach might be to develop from clinical and educational literature a set of user "stereotypes" [1, 5], that could be used in many different adaptations to customize interactions. Robust, portable user models could possibly be included in standard interfaces.

CONCLUSION

In this paper, two models of HCI have served as the basis for descriptions of some example computing adaptations for users with special needs. If the models are made more detailed, such descriptions can serve as specifications that would support the reuse and modification of both hardware and software adaptations. Good models might also inspire innovative adaptations that would not be obvious otherwise. Viewing CUSN within the framework of HCI leads to greater theoretical unity for the former, and encourages continued developments for accessibility in the latter.

It would be helpful for future work to address the development of standards for adaptations, the elaboration of semantic and conceptual models related to CUSN, the development of more detailed implementation models, the enhancement of standards for off-the-shelf computing interfaces to include adaptations for special needs (or "hooks" for adaptations), and the development of user models for different subsets of users with special needs.

REFERENCES

1. Brajnik, G., Guida, G., and Tasso, C. User Modeling in Expert Man-Machine Interfaces: A Case Study in Intelligent Information Retrieval. *IEEE Trans. on Sys., Man, and Cyber., 20*, 1 (Jan./Feb., 1990), 166-185.

2. Hartson, H.R. and Hix, D. Human-Computer Interface Development: Concepts and Systems. *ACM Computing Surveys, 21*, 1 (March, 1989), 5-92.

3. Marcus, A. and van Dam, A. User-Interface Developments for the Nineties. *Computer, 24*, 9 (Sep., 1991), 49-57.

4. Marsh, S. Human-Computer Interaction: An Operational Definition. *SIGCHI Bulletin, 22*, 1 (July, 1990), 16-22.

5. Rich, E. Users Are Individuals: Individualizing User Models. *Int. J. of Man-Machine Studies, 18*, 3 (March, 1983), 199-214.

APPENDIX
Some sources of information on CUSN:

Publications
Closing the Gap Newsletter
Green, P. and Brightman, A. J. *Independence Day: Designing Computer Solutions for Individuals with Disability.* Apple Computer, Cupertino, CA, 1990.
Journal of Special Education Technology
Lindsey, J. D. (Ed.) *Computers and Exceptional Individuals.* Merrill, Columbus, OH, 1987.
SIGCAPH Bulletin
Technology Review

Organizations
Apple Computer Worldwide Disability Solutions Group
　　20525 Mariani Ave.
　　Cupertino, CA 95014
　　408-974-7910
Closing the Gap Solutions
　　P.O. 68
　　Henderson, MN 56044
　　612-248-3294
IBM National Support Center for Persons with Disabilities
　　P.O. Box 2150
　　Atlanta, GA 30301-2150
　　800-426-2133
RESNA
　　Suite 700
　　1101 Connecticut Ave., N.W.
　　Washington, DC 20036
　　202-857-1199
SIGCAPH, ACM
　　1515 Broadway†
　　New York, NY 10036
　　212-869-7440
Trace R&D Center
　　University of Wisconsin, Madison
　　S-151 Waisman Center
　　1500 Highland Ave.
　　Madison, WI 53705

DESIGNING USABLE SYSTEMS UNDER REAL-WORLD CONSTRAINTS: A PRACTITIONERS FORUM

Moderator: Robert M. Mulligan, AT&T Bell Laboratories
101 Crawfords Corner Rd, Rm. 2D-608A, PO Box 3030, Holmdel, NJ 07733-3030
908-949-7777; rmm1@hound.att.com

Panelists: Mary Dieli, Microsoft
Jakob Nielsen, Bellcore
Steven Poltrock, Boeing Computer Services (Discussant)
Daniel Rosenberg, Borland International
Susan Ehrlich Rudman, U S West Advanced Technologies, Inc.

KEYWORDS: Design process, organizational issues, usability, user interface.

INTRODUCTION

Designing the user interface for an interactive computer application is a difficult task and by no means an exact science. Experience has taught many designers that interfaces based exclusively upon intuition, artifacts, or even existing design principles often have poor usability. Fortunately, several empirical methods exist that, when applied, nearly always improve usability. Collecting input from users throughout the design process, rapid prototyping and other iterative design techniques, formal usability testing, and integrated design are now proven methods for assuring good user interfaces. In the years since Gould & Lewis's "Designing for Usability" paper [2], evidence for the value of these methods has been steadily accumulating. Refinements and extensions of their "key principles" continue to appear at this conference and elsewhere in the CHI literature. They have made their way into handbooks and textbooks, and are taught in the human factors curriculum.

In the real world, however, we often work on projects where it is difficult to put these methods into practice. User interface designers (aka, usability engineers) often get involved in projects too late, have little political clout, are under-funded, have limited or no access to users, etc. Even when organizational politics, budget, and other factors are favorable, pressure to reduce development cycle time often makes it difficult to apply these methods which, because they are empirical and iterative, tend to be time consuming. To contend with these problems, UI designers must call upon other skills and techniques that allow us to design usable applications under a variety of constraints.

Knowledge about these techniques is, thus far, not taught in the mainstream CHI curriculum, but does exist among the practitioners in our community. In this panel, we want to tap into that knowledge, explore it, and share it in a more formal way.

Our discussion will be organized around two hypothetical projects, each with its own set of UI design problems, organizational obstacles, and resource constraints. Panelists will describe their approach to each project and offer their opinions about the compromises and tradeoffs that should and should not be made, which methods apply best in different situations, and how to allocate scarce resources to optimize usability.

Project 1: A Space Station Workstation

This project involves the design of a workstation for NASA's space station project. Your job is to design the user interface for a hypermedia database application, including tools to build and modify as well as access the database. The system will contain information that will be used by ground-based scientists working with astronauts to control in-flight experiments. The data collected in these experiments will be entered into the database. Users will also access data manipulation and data analysis tools through the workstation. The user interface work includes design of both ground-based and in-flight versions of the workstation. You will also evaluate some alternative UI technologies including large vocabulary, quasi-speaker-independent connected speech recognition and handwriting recognition for input, and full-motion video and synthesized speech output.

Constraints.

1. *Schedule:* Development timeframe is 12-18 months.
2. *Resources:* You are budgeted for a full-time user interface designer for one year, and half-time technical position that could be used to support a programmer or someone to help in running usability studies. You have access to a fairly sophisticated prototyping tool. It is good for standard, character-based and graphical UIs,

but has no speech production/recognition or handwriting recognition capabilities.

3. *Relationship with Development Organization:* The sponsoring organization (NASA), recognizing the importance of good user interface design, has mandated the presence of a human factors engineer on all development projects. However, the development organization contracted to do the work normally has software engineers design and build the user interface. They are somewhat skeptical of human factors types and are not sold on their added value. In addition, this group is half way across the country in California. You are in Houston, near the user population.

4. *Availability of Users:* The population of potential users is a small (15 to 20), highly trained group of scientists whose time is scarce and very valuable. You don't need to pay for their time, but they are very busy people. You may get a total of about ten person-hours of their time (across all users) over the course of the project.

Questions.

1. What would you do first?
2. What is the most important thing you could do for this project?
3. What percentage of your time would you expect to devote to the following types of activities:
   - focus groups, task analysis, user needs analysis and other up-front activities
   - designing and prototyping
   - doing "formal" usability testing
   - writing user interface requirements
   - addressing UI standards and consistency issues
   - attending meetings, design reviews, demos, etc.
4. Should you take time to learn as much as possible about the application domain or rely on other project team members and subject matter experts to answer your questions?
5. Should you fight to get responsibility for writing system help messages and user documentation or should you let this work work be done by others? If the former, what would you spend less time on?
6. Would you spend time incorporating the new UI technologies into your prototyping system, or prototype on the real system in close cooperation with the development effort? How would you deal with the geographic separation from the developers?
7. How would you deal with the problem of limited access to your users?

Project 2: A General-Purpose Project Planner

The goal of this project is to develop a new project planning/management software product. The application uses powerful heuristics that will make it trivially easy to plan and manage small to mid-sized projects (involving 5 to 50 people). A small team of developers has been working on the guts of the program for over a year. The current prototype version exists on a high-powered graphics workstation. Users will input information about project goals, schedule parameters, resource requirements, deliverables, etc. using a PC-based graphical user interface. The system will provide typical capabilities like the display and manipulation of Gantt and PERT charts. It will also include some hypertext-based functionality (e.g., linking PERT chart objects to detailed task information). Your marketing organization is convinced that, when "productized," this software will change the the course of human history – if only it can be ported to a PC and made more "user friendly." Feedback from one focus group has indicated that the existing user interface is horrible. Also, it does not comply with your company's GUI standards. Your job is to design a Windows-based UI for the program and prove its usability with typical users.

Constraints.

1. *Schedule:* The product must be developed in three months, ready to ship in four. Don't ask why.
2. *Resources:* You are budgeted for one full-time technical headcount for four months and a reasonable sum for lab support, including funds for about 20 hours of participation by external subjects in focus groups, usability testing, or whatever seems most useful to you. You have access to an off-the-shelf prototyping tool with which you can simulate much of the look and feel of the user interface in your lab.
3. *Relationship with Development Organization:* You have a reasonably good working relationship with these developers. They are fairly receptive to user interface design input. They have assigned two people to begin coding the user interface in a few weeks, and are willing to consider doing some iterative prototyping. The developers are at another location, about 30 minutes from yours. They will make a desk available to you at their location.
4. *Availability of Users:* The population of potential users is fairly large. Availability shouldn't be a problem, but the marketing organization wants to keep the product under wraps as much as possible.

Questions.

1-5. Same as those for Project 1.
6. Would you prototype using your familiar, if somewhat limited tool, or on the real system in close cooperation with the development effort?
7. How would you distribute your twenty hours of subject money over (1) focus groups; (2) usability testing of an early, partially-functional prototype; (3) usability testing of a later, fully-functional prototype; (4) other?

PANELISTS' POSITION STATEMENTS

Mary Dieli founded and manages the Usability Group at Microsoft Corporation. Her major tasks there are to continue to develop and refine a flexible approach to usability in industry (i.e., holistic testing) and to ensure that the group is positioned for maximum effectiveness within the organization.

Position Statement: A question fundamental to usability studies of user interfaces is: Can users map the tasks they want to accomplish onto the interface the system presents? A goal for a usability group is to supply that information to product teams during the design process, along with analyses and recommendations. My approach to adding the usability voice to the others designing user interfaces is guided by several assumptions:

- Different types of data from users can contribute to the usability of a UI. The usability testing group is not the only source of usability data.
- Usability specialists' contribution is unique: they typically supply a particular type of data not supplied by the other sources.
- A user interface consists of not just what users see on the screen, but also of any supporting online and print documentation and training.
- Usability specialists' success in affecting the usability of a product is determined partly by correct positioning in the organization or in relationship to the clients.
- A usability group can function effectively in an organization when it is a catalyst to the design process.
- Usability testing is a process of tradeoffs.

My design of usability plans for the two projects would proceed from these assumptions. They dictate a holistic approach: usability testing that considers the interface, its supporting documentation and training, and its use context. To succeed, this approach needs product team involvement and realistic consideration of constraints.

Bob Mulligan has been a Member of Technical Staff in the User Interface Planning and Design Department at Bell Labs for the past five years. He has designed user interfaces for a variety of telecommunications and computer products and services.

Position Statement: User interface designers must be flexible and eclectic in their approach to different projects. We must develop a battery of techniques, from the "quick and dirty" to the "formal and complete," that will allow us to follow design principles to the greatest extent possible. Although we rarely get to do everything we might like to do to ensure usability, nearly all projects offer some opportunities to use usability engineering methods. We must look for these opportunities, which differ from project to project, and focus our resources where they can provide the greatest return.

In the first scenario, although there are many obstacles, there are also two bright spots – support of human factors by the sponsor and proximity to the user group. I would find ways to leverage these advantages in favor of usability. To take advantage of NASA's support, for example, I would quickly write up a work plan describing my responsibilities and usability goals for the project, and get buy-in from the project team.

In the second scenario, the first thing I would do is move in with the developers. Being "around" for the daily, low-level decision making, especially given the tight schedule, can make all the difference. I would also take advantage of the good working relationship with the development organization and of their willingness to do iterative design. I would quickly prototype some key screens to jump-start the development effort; then shift work to the development system, iterating the real code.

Jakob Nielsen is a Member of Technical Staff at Bellcore's Applied Research Area in Morristown, NJ. His interests include usability engineering with special emphasis on low-cost, practical methods for the improvement of user interfaces – the so-called discount usability engineering approach. He is the author of a forthcoming book entitled "Usability Engineering."

Position Statement: My basic approach to practical usability is called discount usability engineering and can be summarized by the following slogans:

- Anything is better than nothing!
- You can do it!
- Any data is data!
- Do not put all your eggs in one basket!

People faced with the prospects of starting usability engineering activities can be put off by seemingly complex requirements of full-blown research methodologies. For example, reading about the wonderful anthropological studies conducted by leading researchers might lead you to contemplate doing a field study of your own. Some people will immediately abandon the thought because they are not anthropologists and do not have such people on their staff. Others will realize that field studies come in many flavors. Sure, you might learn more if you know all the right tricks, but even hard-core computer scientists can get their fundamental view of users adjusted to the real world by simply visiting a few customer sites and observing what goes on.

Thinking about usability will not improve your products. Doing something will. Often, user interfaces contain such horrendous flaws that any reasonable usability study will reveal them and considerably improve the product. There is no justification anymore for releasing products with usability catastrophes that could have been found just by looking at the smallest amount of real-life data. Any actual usability data is better than pure speculation. Finally, I warn against spending your entire usability budget on a single activity. Nothing can guarantee complete success in user interface design, and I certainly do not provide such guarantees to users of my methods. The various methods supplement each other.

Daniel Rosenberg is currently the user interface architect for Borland International. He (and his design staff) provide UI and graphic design support for Borland language, applications and database products. He is also responsible for coordinating cross- product UI consistency and usability testing within Borland.

Position Statement: It is not possible to take many short cuts when building GUI software if product usability will affect sales or performance. Task analysis, prototyping, and user testing are required as discussed in the HCI literature to assure that the user interface meets both customers needs and market requirements. Unfortunately adequate development resources are not always available. User interface design, like all engineering endeavors, is a calculated risk. As a design professional, you must anticipate where the high risk areas are and allocate your time and resources accordingly.

These two projects provide contrasting situations, each with its own set of risks. Faced with limited resources, I would direct the HCI effort to maximize DEPTH of coverage for a single design concept in the first scenario and BREATH of coverage (for multiple concepts) in the second scenario. In the first scenario, performance is more important than sales. When the target population is small, highly trained and motivated, it's best to apply UI design and testing resources at the back end of the process, shaking out the really bad parts of the design with formal usability testing. In Project 1, it does not matter if you have the best conceptual model for the interface, as long as the design can meet the project's performance and reliability goals.

The second scenario typifies UI design in the commercial "shrink wrap" software business. In this case, most of the resources should be applied at the front end of the process, developing prototypes which explore different conceptual models. All user testing should be devoted to determining which model is most appropriate for a wide audience, using focus groups as opposed to real user testing. If the product is revolutionary, the finer details of the design can be fixed in later versions but you are stuck forever with the basic program structure.

Susan Ehrlich Rudman is currently a Member of Technical Staff at U S West Advanced Technologies. She has most recently been responsible for the design of the user interface for a large database application used for service negotiation. She was formerly manager of the Human Factors Department at Wang Labs.

Position Statement: Human factors engineers must take a long range perspective in selecting methods for design and evaluation. A goal for a first project is to establish credibility and effectiveness at meeting project goals. A second goal is to get substantial sign-off responsibility for the design. With an established track record, we can gain control over budget allocation for key ingredients to good design (field evaluations, participatory design, rapid prototyping and usability testing). If we can demonstrate

these techniques work and do not have any negative impact on other team members, they will be used.

In the space station workstation project, first demonstrate your domain knowledge to the development team and project management. Set up informal interviews with future users even before a formal plan for your work is put in place ("just to get a feel for the project"). Bring all of your knowledge engineering skills to the task. Your users will be flattered at your level of interest. Invite the lead UI developer to an overview of the domain information and then to a prototyping session, stressing the iterative nature of the process. Capture the developers' ideas in the prototype and acknowledge their merit as appropriate.

For the second project, the first step is to spend a lot of time with the existing prototype and its developers. Bring with you an extensive knowledge of spreadsheet and project planning applications (having reviewed all the competitive products). Locate the prototype's strong points. Feel out the developers about who has tried to use it and their reactions. Show them an informal usability test. Pick up on any good suggestions the developers make. Make them partners in designing a usability testing plan.

Steve Poltrock is a Senior Computer Scientist in Boeing's Computer Science organization. He has designed interfaces for research and advanced development applications, including AI, three-dimensional graphic, and groupware applications. He and Jonathan Grudin recently completed a study of interface design and development practices in large product development organizations.

Position Statement: Principles and methods are known for designing and developing effective interfaces. Four principles proposed by Gould, Boies, and Lewis [1] are early focus on users, early and continual user testing, iterative design, and integrated design. Real-world constraints and organizational dynamics frequently prevent implementation of these principles. For example, limited access to users in the first project may prevent valuable analyses of users' tasks or limit user testing. Involvement in the second project is too late for an early focus on users or early testing. As panel discussant, Steve Poltrock will describe ways that these principles frequently break down in development organizations and analyze the plans proposed by other participants in terms of these principles.

REFERENCES

1. Gould, J.D, Boies, S.J. & Lewis, C. Making usable, useful, productivity-enhancing computer applications. *Communications of the ACM,* 34, 1 (Jan. 1991), 75-85.

2. Gould, J.D. & Lewis, C. Designing for usability: Key principles and what designers think. *Communications of the ACM,* 28, 3 (Mar. 1985), 300-311.

PROTOTYPING AN INSTRUCTIBLE INTERFACE: MOCTEC

David L. Maulsby

Department of Computer Science
University of Calgary
Canada T2N 1N4

email: maulsby@cpsc.ucalgary.ca

ABSTRACT

Moctec is a set of interactive mockups of an interface for programming search and replace tasks by example. The user guides inference by pointing at relevant features of data.

Keywords: demonstrational interface, prototyping

1. INTRODUCTION

The mockups described here are being tested to find out whether users could control an interface that infers search patterns, and whether particular instruction devices are helpful. Critical questions are: 1. Can the system guide the user to insights needed in order to give it appropriate operational instructions? 2. Are demonstration and focussing useful alternatives to formal description? 3. Do users find the system beneficial despite its errors? 4. Through which instructions do they attain sufficient control over it?

1.1 Instructible interface

An instructible interface acquires procedures and concepts (criteria for selecting objects) from example demonstrations, deictic or verbal hints to focus attention, and exact formal specifications. A complete interface gives the user access to every computable description of objects in the system, which means the user can form boolean combinations of all system-defined predicates for object attributes and relations. Although inferring such combinations is intractable, the use of focus hints, and an ordering of candidate predicates on expected frequency of applicability in a given context, vastly reduce the search for generalizations. Previous demonstrational interfaces have relied on strict rules to limit search [2, 4, 5, 6]; as a result they learn far too little. Some systems [3, 6, 7] escape this trap by letting the user edit a formal description. The research described here is concerned with filling the gap between these extremes. The goal is an interface that tends to match the effort of instruction to the complexity or "oddity" of target concepts, so that users teach simple or common patterns without interrupting the flow of work.

1.2 Find & Do

Moctec simulates a utility that can: search for patterns of attributes or relations over one or more objects; seek several alternative patterns (cases); do "replacements" comprising multiple actions; and map cases to different replacements.

The Find & Do dialog is shown in Figure 1. To train the computer, the user selects objects in the search pattern and then edits them. Every object selected during the edit becomes part of the pattern. The user can also make examples in the application window. After each edit the user presses "Find" or "Do" to advance to the next instance. If it cannot predict, the system asks the user to demonstrate again.

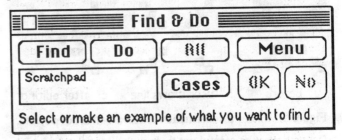

Figure 1. Control panel for "Find & Do"

The system marks all the objects (called *focus items*) with special icons; the user can cancel a focus by clicking it. The user creates a focus item by selecting an object. To edit its description, the user pops up a *focus window* which offers a menu of "obvious" alternatives as well as access to full-blown query dialogs. To express negation, the user can pick "reject items like this". The system hilites relationships it finds amongst objects. The user can indicate that focus items are related by multiple-selecting their icons, and specify the relation by popping up a menu.

2. MOCTEC

Moctec is a cross between a "live" program and a hypermedia slideshow. Interaction devices operate live, but the system's "knowledge state" transitions are pre-defined and it processes only a limited variety of inputs. The user cannot reach the vast majority of (mostly erroneous) states that would be reachable in a real system. By this means we reduce the influence of program bugs on test results, and prevent users becoming hopelessly lost, while giving them enough rope that we can spot simple errors or initial steps towards novel ways of instructing.

3. SCENARIOS

Moctec test users do several tasks with and without Find & Do. After teaching a task once, they are encouraged to teach again by more efficient means. The expected difficulty of teaching varies from trivial (demonstration suffices) to impossible (required predicates are not in the system). Most tasks can be taught provided the user gives focus hints.

3.1 "Swap bold and italics"

The first task is to change all occurrences of **bold** text in a file to *italics*, and vice versa. This can be taught using three examples. First, the user selects, say **"widget"**; the initial search pattern inferred is text(S, "widget"). The user reformats the word, which puts feature *format* into the system's focus. Thus, when the user selects **"gadget"**, the generalization proposed is format(bold), rather than text-ends("dget"). When the user selects *"wicket"* and makes it bold, the system forms a new case rather than generalize the old one, because the action differs; it proposes format(S, italic).

3.2 "Recolor a row of squares"

In this task the user edits the X logo shown in Figure 2. All squares on one arm are to be colored black. Though the system will eventually propose collinear(all-instances(B)), the user can teach the task with one example and a construction line, as shown in Figure 2b. Here, the system tries to form a predicate referring to the line, producing touch(B, Line).

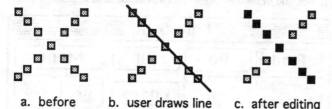

a. before   b. user draws line   c. after editing

Figure 2. Use of a construction to identify a set of objects.

The user must be careful not to draw the line as part of a Do sequence. To avoid this, the user can choose "Do not record" from the Menu. Otherwise, the user must reject the action when Do predicts it, so that it is forgotten.

3.3 "Find games won by Boston"

Boston 2, New Jersey 0

Boston 3, Quebec 1

Calgary 4, Boston 2

Toronto 2, Boston 5

Figure 3. Portion of hockey scores table.

In the third task, the user is asked to find games won by the Boston Bruins in a list of hockey scores. Part of the data is shown in Figure 3. Note that the winning team may appear on the left or the right. An operational search pattern is:

B = text("Boston") & L = line-containing(B) &
P = number-word-following(B) &
R = number-word-in-line(L) & P > R.

A well-designed text pattern analyzer might induce two cases (for winner at the left or right) from very few examples, but the viability of the interface should not depend on such power. In the Moctec scenario the user should focus on the two numbers by clicking them; the system hilites objects in its focus by boxing them as shown in Figure 4.

Figure 4. Hiliting focus items.

When the user clicks 3 and 1, the system adds the features *number* and *number-pair* to its focus. The first two scores (2,0) and (3,1) are consistent with several "preferred" predicates, shown on the popup menu in Figure 5. The user can specify P > R by selecting from the menu, or else by typing "3 > 1" in the Scratchpad.

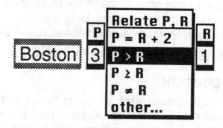

Figure 5. Specifying a relation between focus items.

4. CONCLUSION

A number of Moctec scenarios will be user tested over the coming months. A learning algorithm based on PRISM [1] will process users' action traces off-line to "validate" these scenarios. If the study indicates that an instructible Find & Do is feasible and desirable, a live prototype will follow.

ACKNOWLEDGEMENTS

Apple Computer Inc. and the Natural Sciences and Engineering Research Council of Canada fund this research.

REFERENCES

1. Cendrowska, J. PRISM: an algorithm for inducing modular rules. IJMMS 27,4, pp. 349-370. 1988.

2. Cypher, A. EAGER: programming repetitive tasks by example. *Proc. CHI '91*, pp. 33–40. May 1991.

3. Halbert, D.C. Programming by example. Research report OSD-T8402. Xerox PARC. Palo Alto. 1984.

4. Lieberman, H. Mondrian: a teachable graphical editor. Technical report, MIT Media Lab. 1991.

5. Maulsby, D.L., I.H. Witten, K.A. Kittlitz, V.G. Franceschin. Inferring graphical procedures: the compleat Metamouse. *Human Computer Interaction* 7,1. 1992.

6. Myers, B.A. *Creating User Interfaces by Demonstration.* Academic Press. San Diego. 1988.

7. Stearns, G. R. Agents and the HP NewWave application interface. Hewlett-Packard Journal, August 1989, pp. 32-37.

Interface Support for Comet:
A Knowledge-Based Software Reuse Environment

Sherman Tyler and Jon Schlossberg
Lockheed AI Center, 96-20, B/254F
3251 Hanover Street
Palo Alto, CA 94304
tyler@titan.rdd.lmsc.lockheed.com
schlossberg@casablanca.rdd.lmsc.lockheed.com

Previous approaches to software reuse have been largely ineffective because designers have difficulty locating a software module to reuse and then understanding the ramifications of this new software module on the other parts of a software system. We take the view that software modules need to be represented in a reuse library using a high-level behavioral description language that can support Artificial Intelligence reasoning techniques such as classification and constraint propogation. Given this information, we then provide software designers with a knowledge-based interface for interacting with this software reuse library. Specifically, we employ a Design Memory approach for presenting relevant views of the reuse library to the designer. Our research prototype, **Comet**, uses this approach to locate candidates for software reuse and to compute their ramifications. The goal of this work is a software design environment supporting all stages of design, from the initial exploratory phases through to final implementation.

We take the view that all design is redesign. In any design effort, designers reuse ideas, methods, engineering drawings, specifications, and partial solutions from previous design efforts. This design reuse usually involves individual designers reusing information from their own past design experience. This is precisely what makes an experienced designer a good designer—this experience, readily available, to apply to new design situations. This reuse of experience is the basis of the Design Memory approach (Mark and Schlossberg, Banff Knowledge Acquisition Workshop, 1990), which seeks to encode this information explicitly.

Despite the large body of existing code, software is rarely reused when creating new systems. There are two significant obstacles to reuse: 1) determining which modules from a library of software components are appropriate reuse candidates and 2) understanding the ramifications on the rest of a software system of choosing one of the reuse candidates. We address both these issues by extending our Design Memory approach to the software realm.

As a simplistic example of determining a pre-existing software module's utility in the context of an evolving design, consider an attempt to replace a system's existing search algorithm with a binary search software module. This replacement is only appropriate if the input to the binary search module is already sorted. Therefore, one ramification of using the binary search module is the need to have the input data sorted. We call this kind of ramification a *commitment*.

Knowledge in **Comet** is represented in the LOOM language (MacGregor, AAAI-91). LOOM provides powerful classification and constraint propogation engines along with rigorous methods of structuring the knowledge bases. To support commitments, three knowledge bases are needed: a behavior taxonomy, a module taxonomy, and a taxonomy of domain concepts. **Comet's** underlying knowledge structures are rigorously explored in Mark, et al. (Mark, et al., Lockheed Technical Report, 1992).

We will now present a **Comet** scenario from the domain of sensor-based target tracking which has served as our initial test case for this approach.

Given that **Comet** already contains architectural information about software modules and their associated behaviors organized into a reuse library and has reasoning capabilities to determine commitments, software developers need seamless, efficient access to this data. A detailed interaction scenario is explored in Mark, et al. (Mark, et al., Lockheed Technical Report, 1992); this abstract presents an abbreviated form of that interaction. The developer's goal is, within the domain of sensor-based tracking, to produce a multiple hypothesis tracker (one that keeps several alternatives in working memory). The key interface concepts addressed by **Comet** include: 1) showing users the current commitment structure and 2) giving casual users access to behavior descriptions.

Initially, the designer is presented with a high-level taxonomy of tracker architectures, culled from the module taxonomy. Developers browse this hierarchy looking for an architecture close to their current problem.

Let's assume the developer chooses a single-hypothesis air-to-air tracker as the starting architecture. While browsing this architecture, the developer notices that the behavior of **Coarse Contact Screening** will have to be altered (this module does rough assignment of a contact to a pre-existing radar track). After further inspection of each of this module's submodules, the developer realizes that the module **Assign Contact to Track** will have to be modified; the current module assigns the contact to only one track.

To present this behavior, **Comet** does template-driven natural language generation based on the behavior primitives that comprise the module description. We then allow restricted editing of the result, so that only transformations that map back to known behavior primitives are allowed.

Given this new information, LOOM is asked to classify the user-specified behavior in the module taxonomy. A list of modules that implement the specified behavior are retrieved and the commitments of each module relative to the current architecture are determined; **Comet** presents this information in the Design Memory window (see Figure 1).

In this figure, the top portion of the screen is devoted to a traditional architecture view of the evolving design. The lower window is the Design Memory view into the reuse library. Continuing the example, **Comet** has found exactly one pre-existing module that fits the new user-specified behavior, **Multi Assign Contact to Track**. To the right of this node in the Design Memory window is a presentation of this module's commitments, relative to the current architecture. To make the architecture compatible with the **Assign Contact to Track** modification involves at least resolving all the commitments listed in the Design Memory window. [1]

When presenting commitments, there are several issues that arise. We want to notify the designer as commitments are resolved. In fact, it might often be the case that commitments are resolved right away (for instance, a binary search module is incorporated into the design and there already exists a sorting procedure on its input). To reflect resolved commitments we use a dashed line; unresolved commitments are shown with a solid

---

[1] Clearly, we can never guarantee knowing all of a module's commitments.

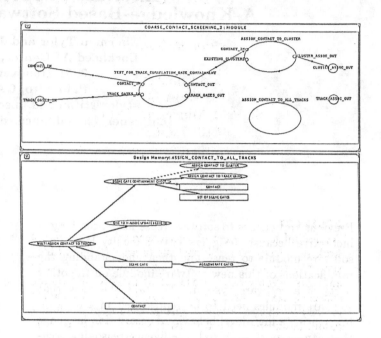

Figure 1: A **Comet** snapshot showing a Design Memory view of a reuse candidate, Multi Assign Contact to Track, along with its commitments.

line.

Some commitments will be to data structures, others to procedures. Commitments to data structures are shown as boxes in the Design Memory window; commitments to procedures are shown as ovals. In Figure 1, we notice four commitments for Multi Assign Contact to Track: two data structure commitments and two procedure commitments.

It will often happen that more than one possible replacement module will be found. In this case, each module, along with its commitments, will be presented in the Design Memory window. The designer would then browse each replacement candidate, and its commitments, to understand which choice would be most appropriate.

The designer now begins to navigate the commitments. For data structure commitments, "selecting" a node produces a list of modules that would resolve the commitment. For procedure commitments, the sub-commitments of introducing the presented new module into the design is shown.

The designer would then continue working with the commitments until they have all been resolved. At this point, the user would select Multi Assign Contact to Track to replace Assign Contact to All Tracks. The result would be a multiple hypothesis tracker, partially implemented.

The Art of Search: A Study of Art Directors

Sharon R. Garber

3M Company
260-4A-08
St. Paul, Minnesota 55144
(612) 736-6854
srgarber@3m.com

Mitch B. Grunes

3M Company
260-6A-08
St. Paul, Minnesota 55144
(612) 733-8064
mbgrunes@3m.com

ABSTRACT

We formulated a model of visual search by conducting a work flow study and task analysis of art directors as they searched for images to use in an advertisement. The analysis revealed the presence of artistic and image concepts, flexible structures which guide the search and are molded by them. Analysis results were used to build a model-based interface for visual search. Results from presenting the interface to users indicate that the interface has the potential to make significant contributions to the visual search task, both in time savings and as an aid to the creative process.

KEYWORDS: User models, cognitive models, user interface design, task analysis, navigation, searching, visual problem solving.

INTRODUCTION

Searching through large volumes of information can be a formidable task particularly when the information is complex or poorly organized [2]. The problems are compounded when the information includes images because aspects of visual search add an additional level of complexity. The task of the art director illustrates this problem well. In an advertising agency, the art director works on a team with a copywriter to develop a creative concept. The director handles the general layout of the concept and selection of the images and graphics for the project. At various stages of the process, the director searches for images which meet the constraints of the layout. The search may take from a few hours to several days and is complicated by the fact that "the perfect image" may not be available. Furthermore, the director may have only a fuzzy idea about what is needed and the idea may change as new images are found.

Good interfaces and visual search techniques may ease the problem but they are most likely to be effective when they match the user's model of the task. Techniques such as iterative search [11,12] and the use of rough approximations [10] have been proposed to guide interface construction but they have not been tested in visual domains. The mental model for images may be quite different from models for other symbols [7]. Work that has been done in visual domains has resulted in intriguing interfaces [5,8,9] but much of the work has been based on intuitions of the developer rather than a model of the user.

In the present study, we formulated a model of visual search by conducting a work flow study and task analysis of art directors as they searched for images to use in an advertisement. We then used the model to create an interface for search through image sets. The interface was presented to 6 groups of users in a set of focus sessions. Focus session results indicate that this model-based interface has the potential to make significant contributions to the visual search task, both in time savings and as an aid to the creative process.

DEFINITION OF TERMS

art director - The director, one of the creative people at the agency, handles the general layout of the concept and selection of images and graphics for the project.

art buyer - The art buyer talks to the art director to determine the image needs for a job, helps decide whether to use a photo shoot or a stock photo and handles all aspects of organizing the shoot or ordering the stock photo. In some agencies the art directors do this step themselves.

comprehensive (comp) - The comp is a layout with images, copy and/or sketches which provides a realistic idea about the look of the final ad. The comp is shown to the client to secure approval of the concept.

photo shoot - The photo shoot is one option to acquire an image for an advertisement. A photographer is hired to shoot a photograph according to the director's specifications.

stock photo house - A stock photo house is a company which collects photos from a variety of sources and rents them to art directors to use in an advertisement. At any one time, a stock photo house may have from several hundred thousand to more than a million photos on hand.

stock photo researcher - The researcher communicates with a client (typically an art buyer or art director) to determine image needs and searches through image files to find appropriate images. On occasion, the client comes to the stock photo house and does the search, with minimal help from the researcher.

STUDY PROCESS
We studied three ad agencies, 1 marketing-design agency, and 1 stock photo house.

Although our major emphasis was the art director, we studied 4 art buyers and 2 stock photo researchers in addition to 9 art directors. We felt that it was important to study the people who work with and help the art director in order to gain a full understanding of the work flow.

We used the following techniques to conduct the studies:

Interview: Interviews were used to gather general information about work flow. We were given tours of the facilities, and collected information about the people who work at the facility, the tasks they do and the resources they use to accomplish their jobs.

Analysis of previous work: Each person selected a previous job and described in detail each step taken from the start to finish of the job, including as much detail as possible about the selection and use of images. This type of post-hoc analysis, in conjunction with interviews, provides guidance in the interpretation of concurrent analyses [6].

Description of current project: Each person described in detail the tasks being completed in a current job.

Observation of creation of ad: We observed two art directors as they took a job from initial job description to creation of comp. The directors were asked to "think aloud" as they worked [1]. The verbal component of the think-aloud protocol was augmented by visual cues by collecting photocopies of layouts, making sketches, and annotating images.

Observation of discussion between art director and art buyer: We observed an art director describe image needs to an art buyer.

Observation of discussion between ad agency and stock photo researcher: We observed a stock photo researcher as she talked to an art buyer to assess needs and then completed a search for photos for the buyer.

Observation of search at stock house by customer: We observed 2 art buyers/directors as they searched for images at a stock photo house. They were asked to "think aloud" as they searched [1]. As in the ad creation task, the protocols were augmented with visual cues.

RESULTS OF WORK FLOW AND TASK ANALYSIS
The work flow study revealed that there are 20 high-level tasks from initial definition of a job to securing of final approval for creation of a printed advertisement. A condensed version of the work flow is presented in Fig. 1. The job begins when a client provides an initial job definition which may be fairly specific such as "we want an updated version of our ad for milk," or it might be broad such as "we need a way of increasing our visibility in the 20-45 year age group."

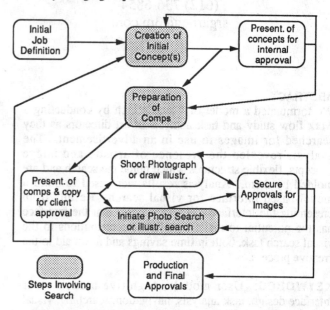

Figure 1: Ad Agency Work Flow for Print Media

After the job is defined, the art director and copywriter work as a team to generate one or more artistic concepts. The process can be very free form and continue for several days. During this stage, the art director might page through magazines or previous ads to look for ideas for the concept.

During preparation of comps, one or possibly two concepts are refined for presentation to the client. The input to the process is a set of initial concepts. The output of this stage is a comp. A variety of resources, varying from sketches to newspapers or encyclopedias might be used at this stage.

When the client has approved the concept and comp, the director decides whether to send the image out for a photo shoot or to search for a stock photo. If a stock photo is requested, the director tells the art buyer what he/she wants and the buyer tries to find it. The buyer calls one or more stock photo houses and describes the needs. The stock photo house sends a set of images back to the buyer within 1 to 2 days. Occasionally, directors or buyers may visit a stock house and search for images themselves.

After the images have been acquired and approved, the job is sent to production.

The work flow analysis reveals that images are used at three main stages, creation of initial concept, preparation of comps and initiation of photo search. These three stages were examined in more detail in the remainder of the study.

MODEL OF THE SEARCHING PROCESS

As we begin to describe the mental model used for searching we will be making use of sections from two protocols to illustrate the main points. Fig. 2 provides sections of a protocol of an image search conducted in a stock photo house by an art buyer. Fig. 3 provides sections of a protocol from a session in which two art directors worked together to create a brochure of items.

Both protocols have been altered to maintain the confidentiality of the work since the jobs being completed were real.

An important part of the mental model for our users is a set of concepts which both guide the search and become molded by it. The first concept is the *artistic concept*, which is a general idea about the layout and goals of the advertisement. It may be difficult to articulate the nature of the artistic concept, particularly at early stages, but it influences the search and decisions.

The second concept is the *image concept*. This is a component of the artistic concept. The image concept is a collection of ideas about the desired image which can take

several different forms. Both the artistic and image concepts will be described more fully below.

The flow of the searching process can vary from job to job. In many cases, the art director starts with the artistic concept. The artistic concept determines the image concept which, in turn, guides the search. This process was used in the job illustrated in Fig. 3.

Action		Interpretation
Instruction to Directors: Create a brochure of items		
Discussion:	*"Can we group the items?"* *"Maybe we could put them in 3 groups, 1 per page of the brochure."* *"We want people in the shots."* *"Action shots would be good."* *"Homey shots"* *"Animal shots"*	*Discuss artistic concept*
Create Formats:	Format A Format B	*Create alternative artistic concepts*
Discussion:	*"Animal shots are overrated."* *"Better with Homey than Animal."*	*Discuss image concept*
Revise Format:	Format C	*Revise artistic concept*
Discussion:	*"What can we show for widgets?"* *"Homey and animal are easy, but how do we find images for widgets?"* *"Maybe we could put animal and widget together."* *"Or just homey."*	*Revise Image Concept*
Image Search:	browse through catalogue using sequential search mark an image which might fit the cover select images at random from favorite books select an oblique animal shot	*Image Search using flexible criteria* *Select target image*
Discussion:	*"We could give it the intended look with an oblique shot."*	*Revise image concept*
Revise Format:	Format D (including oblique animal shot)	*Revise artistic concept*
Image Search:	Seach for oblique shots of homey and widgets Select image of homey	*Search by similarity using target image*
Revise Format:	Format E (including 2 oblique shots)	*Revise artistic concept*
Discussion:	*"That's it. It solves the problem of the intermediate stuff that doesn't fit with a category."*	
Image Search:	Search for oblique shot of people for the cover Select image	*Search by similarity using target image*

Figure 3: Sections of Protocol from Session in Which Advertisement was Created

Action	Interpretation
"I need a picture of a flower from Puerto Rico."	Initial Criteria objects
"There will be text across the middle of the image in the brochure."	format
"I want it to 'say Puerto Rico'."	fuzzy criterion
"I'll look for textures and patterns like waves breaking, flower images."	
"I've had sunsets and beaches before so I want flowers."	restriction
Begin Search	
Reject image: *"This isn't as colorful."*	Add criterion
Reject image: *"This won't fit with my text."*	
Close-up and reject: *"Not enough color."*	
Reject image: *"Distinctive shoreline but has hotels."*	Add restriction
Select image: *"it's got sunflowers, distinctive shoreline."*	
Close-up and reject: *"too much water in the foreground."*	Add restriction
Select Image: *"not flowers but it is colorful"*	Alter criteria
Reject Image: *"it's got people and buildings"*	Add restriction
Select Image: *"not flowers but it 'says Puerto Rico'"*	Alter criteria
Reject Image: *"not interesting enough"*	Add criterion
Select Image: *"not Puerto Rico but looks like it is"*	Alter criteria
Select Image: *"This is horizontal, but I could crop it"*	

Figure 2: Sections of Protocol from Image Search

Occasionally, the process begins with an image search. In this case, the director searches for concept ideas by browsing through images. The concept isn't formed until the search begins.

In all cases, as the search proceeds, images are set aside and kept as a set of current contenders. This image set can affect both the image and artistic concepts. This is illustrated in Fig. 3. The directors began the process by discussing the artistic concept for the brochure. Each director then created a slightly different artistic concept as a starting point. Further discussion induced a change in the artistic concept. When the image search began, the selection of a particular image caused them to change both the image concept and artistic concept. The final version of the artistic concept was determined to large extent by the images which were retrieved during subsequent searches.

The searching process is illustrated in Fig. 4.

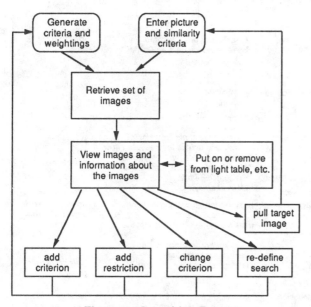

Figure 4: Searching Process

The image concept may start as a loose structure containing a number of flexible components. Usually, there are a number of descriptive terms or criteria. The terms may be fuzzy such as "interesting" (Fig. 2) or more constrained such as "a picture of a flower from Puerto Rico" (Fig. 2). The terms may describe objects in the image such as "a picture of a flower" (Fig. 2), objects which should NOT be in the image such as "no sunsets or beaches" (Fig. 2), or general characteristics of the image such as "oblique shot" (Fig. 3). The number of terms used may be large, 14 and 24 terms in two cases studied.

The criteria may be accompanied by explicit or implicit weightings of importance. At one point (Fig. 2), the searcher indicates that although he prefers a colorful picture of a flower, the color is more important than the presence of a flower.

The image concept is not limited to descriptive terms. In many cases, the concept is formed by viewing images and comparing the concept to the actual images. This is illustrated in Fig. 3. Toward the beginning of the search, an oblique animal shot is selected and then used as a target for further searching as the directors look for other images with the same camera angle but different subject matter.

The director uses the image concept to retrieve a set of images and then uses a variety of devices to compare and contrast the images. During this process, the director may alter or re-define the nature of the search by adding or changing criteria, adding restrictions, or finding an image and using it as a template to search for other similar images. Several of these processes are illustrated in Fig. 2.

Weighting of criteria also may shift as the search proceeds. This process is illustrated in Fig. 2. At the start of the search the user wants a picture of a flower from Puerto Rico. As the search proceeds, he decides that it is more important for the image to be from Puerto Rico than it is for the image to include a flower. It is typical for many shifts in criteria to occur during a search. In one search we observed, 18 shifts in criteria were made. In a second search, 11 shifts were made.

As the search continues and shifts occur, the image concept becomes more well-defined. In Fig. 3, the directors begin by looking for animal, widget or homey shots without knowing quite what they want. Toward the end of the search, they have a more constrained view of the desired image, an oblique view of a group of people. But, even in more constrained searches, it is unusual for the user to find a single, ideal image. In one of the searches we observed, 11 images were set aside for further consideration. In another search, 38 images were set aside. Eventually, of course, a single image must be selected but the process is an iterative one which goes through many steps before coming to a conclusion. In one extreme case, an art director examined images from 26 stock photo houses over a period of many days before making a final selection.

The model described above generates a set of criteria for tools and interfaces to aid in searching. Some of the more important criteria are described below.

The Image Concept: It should be possible to describe an image concept by providing a set of criteria, restrictions and weightings and/or one or more target images which help to define the concept. The system should help the art director define and modify the image concept by providing a way of setting aside and organizing images of interest.

Similarity Searching: Since the concept is a flexible and fluid structure, searching should also be flexible. During a search, a system should provide a range of items which overlap the concept to varying extents. Exact matches to the criteria may be important, but close matches might also be useful.

Idea Generation: At the beginning of the process, image search may be used to help define or refine the artistic or image concepts. The system should help in this creative idea generation stage by providing images which extend beyond the initial bounds of the concepts.

DEVELOPING THE USER INTERFACE

Our methodology to develop the user interface was to:

1. brainstorm design concepts,

2. develop an initial prototype that could be demonstrated to focus groups of art directors,

3. refine the prototype based on focus group comments,

4. conduct user testing to establish usability, productivity measurements and determine user attitudes about the program, and

5. iteratively refine and test the user interface.

We have completed the first two steps of this process with a team of user interface designers, programmers, art directors and marketing personnel. We discuss our plans for the remaining steps later in this paper.

Description of the Initial Prototype

Garber, Plate 1 shows two snapshots of the user interface. In the upper portion, the user has requested a **Search for Similar Images** to find images that are similar to the Boy-with-Dog image. To accomplish this, the user first placed an image of interest onto the "Target." The criterion settings, displayed in the uppermost window, were automatically updated to reflect the characteristics of the target image. The user then modified the full set of criteria by removing unwanted search restrictions while leaving the basic characteristics of the image intact. Importance weightings were set and the search was initiated.

The results of the search are presented in the "Search Space" window. In this space, images are sorted by how closely they match the specified criteria taking into account the relative importance weightings. The first few images (starting at the top-left) completely match the criteria. They are followed by images that are close, but not exact matches. Scanning through the search space we see that "Boy" is replaced by "Girl" in a Girl-with-Dog image, and later we see images with two animals when no more human-animal images are available. When the search space is scrolled, images that are semantically further from the target are displayed.

In the lower part of Garber, Plate 1, the user has decided to explore alternatives to a given target image. The user moved an image to the target and modified the criteria to establish the characteristics of interest for this search. This time, instead of requesting a search for similar images, the user asked to **Explore Alternatives**. The images resulting from this search are organized into columns, where each column "explores" alternate directions from a given criterion setting. In this example, alternatives to "Man" are, in order of closeness, "Woman", "Boy", "Girl",

"Baby", etc. The list scrolls until all alternate directions are exhausted.

For each alternative, an image is displayed showing an example of an image that varies from the established criteria by only one characteristic. When no image exists, the next closest image is displayed. For example, under the "Man" column, the image in the "Woman" direction is the image closest to the characteristics of "Woman - Woman - Florida - 2 Item."

These snapshots of the user interface represent two different ways the user interface supports searching through image spaces. More traditional searching strategies like browsing, index or keyword searching are also useful strategies at different times of the work flow. We did not prototype these more traditional techniques because they are readily available in existing programs.

How the User Interface Supports the User Model

The user interface design supports the model of the user as described earlier. The image concept is supported by allowing the user to describe an image by entering explicit descriptions of an image (criterion settings). Alternatively the user may target an identified image and use that as a source for finding similar images. A scale is provided below each criterion to allow the user to indicate relative importance weightings (+: somewhat important to ++: very important). A weighting of "NEED" is also provided when the user only wants to consider images possessing a given criterion. Images may be set aside and organized using a "Pasteboard" window. The pasteboard functions similar to the way a light table might be used to set aside and organize images of interest.

The user can enter criteria by selecting from a number of system-defined characteristics or by entering desired features of an image. Criteria may be added or restricted (i.e., "Not").

The aspect of similarity searching is also supported by this user interface design. Instead of rigidly requiring that all images exactly match all established criteria, images are included in the search space that overlap the specified concept to varying extents. Flexibility in the searching process is facilitated by tiling the search space, target image and criterion settings on the display so that they may all be viewed and updated at any time. The tiling of information also supports the highly visually oriented art director by minimizing the information that is invisible.

Idea generation is supported in our implementation of exploring alternatives. In this function, we present images that extend beyond the initial bounds of the criterion settings. This is one way of trying to support the creative needs of our user. In our discussion of future work, we discuss other ways in which this might be addressed.

The next step in the development process was to present this prototype to art directors in a focus group setting.

FOCUS SESSION RESULTS

The interface was demonstrated to 6 groups of 3-4 people each. The members of the focus groups were primarily art directors. A few art buyers were included. The group saw two systems in the focus panels. First, they saw a prototype searching system which uses a metaphor of a stock photo catalogue. Users could browse through the catalogue by turning pages or search by image name, category, page number, or keyword. After seeing and using the first system, the present interface was demonstrated. A facilitator then solicited general comments about the interface and asked a set of specific questions about the utility of various features such as similarity searching and presentation of alternatives.

Selected comments may be found in Fig. 5. Comments which were repetitious or which could not be understood without additional context were removed. The remainder of the comments are reproduced without modification.

The comments in all categories were very positive. The general comments indicate that users think that the system is fun, is a significant improvement over their traditional way of working, and that it would be a valuable addition in their job.

There were several comments indicating that there would be a time savings with a system of this nature. Part of the reason that there might be a time savings is because of the increased effectiveness of the search. Participants commented that it is "more of a visual search," and it helps assure that an image will be found. A typical comment is that "the first system is like going to the library, you might not find the image. Here you would find it."

Many people felt that the system would be an aid to creativity, particularly because of the option to ask for alternatives. An example is, "this would bring greater creativity and help me think in a far reaching way." This

---

General Comments:
More fun.   This is wild.

This would now add value.   This is a work horse.

It's more like a computer than just a catalogue.

The only thing I notice, it doesn't follow Mac interface guidelines but that isn't important - It's great.

It's like when I call up and someone else does it for me.

I'm questioning the second one because it's making decisions for me, I think my options are limited here.

This is what it should be ... to make it usable.

Its like the computer has a brain.

Comments on Time Savings:
You start with an image and say what you want exactly, it would take 4 hours otherwise.

That would be a true time saver.

There is no question that this would be a much bigger time saver than the initial system alone.

I could see how some interesting accidents might happen — would save time.

Comments on the Aid to Creativity:
More inspiring if are at dead end.

It facilitates finding new ideas.

It opens up a new creative avenue that I didn't think of.

It is doing exotic thinking for you. It's great.

It suddenly expands to a tool I can use for initial concepts.

Very helpful for brainstorming.

This would bring greater creativity and help me think in a far reaching way.

It's a tool for creative problem solving.

The other makes it more convenient, but this makes you feel that in your hour of desperation ...

Comments on the Effectiveness of Search
Better job of weeding things out.

It did more of the searching.

It's much better to let the machine do the search for you.

It's good ... if you exhaust the options it finds it for you.

I like the feeling of comfort that I have found all (pictures).

It's narrowing it down for us.

It allows you to utilize more because you don't have to be so specific.

You can sift through more.

The first system is like going to the library, you might not find the image. Here you would find it.

Its much easier to find what you want.

More of a visual search.

The other one was just scanning images into a catalogue ... this one really helps you find things.

Comments on the Fit to the User Model:
I like the fuzzy logic, the fact that a category is not defined exactly, because you aren't ever really sure what you want.

This is more similar to the way we use books now. We page through until something catches your eye. Then we go back to the beginning and look for more of those.

I've looked through catalogues and looked for things and not found them, then I change my idea and have to look all over again.

This is more visual. It's better for art directors because they're visual. I know what I like because I see it.

Greater acceptability by directors cause they feel in more control of creative process.

The first version is just a catalogue, this is a tool.

The first is linear, this way you have things on the right and left; That's how art goes, it isn't linear.

Figure 5: Comments About the Searching Interface

reinforces the idea that the image concept is a flexible structure and that users sometimes want help expanding or modifying the structure and other times want help focusing it.

Several comments indicated that we had captured the user's mental model. For example, the following comment suggests that the search by similarity feature fit the mental model well, "this is more similar to the way we use books now. We page through until something catches your eye. Then we go back to the beginning and look for more of those." Other comments indicate that the alternatives feature fits the mental model well, for example, "the first is linear, this way you have things on the right and left; That's how art goes, it isn't linear."

FUTURE WORK AND DIRECTION
User Interface Development
The next step is to begin user testing. Specific goals for the testing process to measure user productivity and attitudes about the program will be established. We plan to measure productivity in terms of time to find an image and enhancing the creative process. Measurements will be compared to existing methods of accomplishing similar tasks, with and without the use of a computer.

We plan to develop more ways to support *idea generation*, since this is the most creative aspect of the user model. Although the exploring alternatives function seems helpful in many situations, we plan to investigate some interfaces that take a more random approach, similar to the way many art directors work during initial concept development.

Image Cataloging
The success of this type of system depends on the way that images are cataloged and how the relationships among terms and concepts are established. We have already conducted some general research in this area [3,4] but need further study to apply that research to this domain and to this user interface. At the same time, we plan to further study user interface alternatives that allow art directors to specify criteria when they are not aware of the terms that have been set up for the images.

Implementation Strategies
The type of searching embodied in this user interface requires data structures and algorithms beyond what is found in traditional hierarchical or relational data bases. We have already developed some of these techniques [3,4] and it is our goal to further refine and test our approaches with very large image spaces (20,000 - 500,000 images).

Generalization to other Domains
Aspects of the user interface and the implementation strategies developed for this application may be transferable to other domains that require searching through large information spaces (even when they do not include images). We plan to identify some other applications in which searching is an inherent need and explore the application of this work to those other areas.

ACKNOWLEDGEMENTS
We would like to thank Martin Kenner for help in preparing this paper. We would also like to thank Comstock, Inc. for the use of their images. All images appearing in Garber, Plate 1 are copyright COMSTOCK, INC.

REFERENCES
1. Ericsson, K.A. and Simon, H.A. Protocol Analysis: Verbal Reports as Data. MIT Press, Cambridge, Mass, 1984.

2. Fischer, G. and Stevens, C. Information Access in Complex, Poorly Structured Information Spaces. In CHI' 91 Human Factors in Computing Systems (New Orleans, Apr. 27-May 2, 1991), ACM Press, pp. 63-70.

3. Garber, S.R. Managing Multimedia Information: A Description of Research. Paper presented at the 1991 Nebraska Interactive Media Symposium (Lincoln, May 6-May 9, 1991).

4. Garber, S.R., Kozak, D.J., Kruse, J.M., and Clare, M.K. Intelligent optical navigator dynamic information presentation and navigation system. U.S. Patent 4,905,163 (Feb., 1990).

5. Hodges, M.E., Sasnett, R.M., and Ackerman, M.S. A construction set for multimedia applications. IEEE Software (Jan. 1989), 37-43.

6. Johnson, P.E. Cognitive Models of Expertise. Paper presented at the Symposium on Expert Systems and Auditor Judgement (University of Southern California, Feb. 1986).

7. Johnson-Laird, P. Mental Models. Harvard University Press, Cambridge, Mass., 1983.

8. Kato, T., Kurita, T., and Shimogaki, H. Multimedia interaction with image database systems. SIGCHI Bulletin 22,1 (July, 1990), 52-54.

9. Laurel, B., Oren, T., and Don, A. Issues in Multimedia Interface Design: Media Integration and Interface Agents. In CHI '90 Human Factors in Computing Systems (Seattle, Apr. 1-5, 1990), ACM Press, pp. 133-139.

10. Srinivason, P. The importance of rough approximations for information retrieval. International Journal of Man-Machine Studies 34,5 (May 1991), 657-671.

11. Williams, M.D. What makes RABBIT run? International Journal of Man-Machine Studies 21 (1984), 333-352.

12. Yen, J., Neches, R., and DeBellis, M. Specification by Reformulation: A Paradigm for Building Integrated User Support Environments. In AAAI '88 Conference on Artificial Intelligence (St. Paul, Aug. 21-26, 1988), Morgan Kaufman Publishers, pp. 814-818.

BROWSER-SOAR: A COMPUTATIONAL MODEL OF A HIGHLY INTERACTIVE TASK

Virginia A.Peck
School of Computer Science

Bonnie E.John
School of Computer Science
& Department of Psychology

Carnegie Mellon University
Pittsburgh, PA 15213
(412) 268-3620
virginia.peck@cs.cmu.edu

ABSTRACT
Browser-Soar models the perceptual, cognitive, and motor operators of a user searching for information in an on-line help browser. The model accounts for 90% of the browsing behavior observed in ten episodes. This result suggests that much of browsing behavior is a routine cognitive task, describable by GOMS, and extends the boundary of tasks to which GOMS applies to include highly interactive tasks. Further, it also suggests that GOMS analyses can be used to evaluate browser interfaces, as they have been used to evaluate text-editors and other computer applications, and to help focus design effort.

KEYWORDS: Browsing, cognitive models, GOMS, Soar

THE IMMEDIATE INTERACTION CYCLE IN HCI
Cognitive modeling of user behavior in HCI research has historically centered on user-paced, routine cognitive skills with character-oriented computer systems (text-editing for example, see [8] for a review), but much of what we use computers for today does not fit this category. We write papers with WYSIWYG editors, interactively manipulate data in spreadsheets, draw diagrams, and browse through extensive information spaces. Progress in computer technology has changed the nature of computer use to where it imposes a much tighter loop between the user's actions and the computer's reactions than in the days of line editors. We have studied the interaction of a user with an information browser to begin to understand the nature of this *immediate interaction cycle*.

There is little detailed understanding in cognitive psychology about the immediate interaction cycle, in contrast to our understanding of reaction-time tasks or problem solving. For instance, most good chronometric experimentation concerns the single arc from stimulus to a single pulse of cognition to an indicative response -- actions that take about a second overall but are not integrated into a cycle of coordinated intentional behavior. This single arc of behavior has been described successfully

in GOMS models [1] as the sequential execution of a perceptual operator, a series of cognitive operators necessary to map the stimuli into the appropriate response, and a motor operator that produces the result [5]. These models can be considered degenerate GOMS models where there is a single goal defined by the experimental task and a single method for accomplishing the task, hence no selection rules.[1] On the other hand, problem-solving concerns situations where the subject deliberates for long periods of time. This behavior has been successfully described as search through a problem space [7], a very different situation where there are no well-known methods of applying operators to transform the present state into the goal state, even if the goal is well defined and operators are easy to apply. From yet a third perspective, most investigations of situated action are focused on how being embedded in an environment defines and shapes the formulation of task, without concern for the dynamics of the interaction. In fact, radical positions on situated action claim that plans (roughly comparable to methods in GOMS terms) play only an orienting role in a situated task and will not be found in the actual performance of that task [9].

Therefore, lacking clear evidence from previous research, we approached the study of the immediate interaction cycle with an open mind about what form the mechanisms that produce such behavior would take. It was possible that browsing tasks would display mechanisms reflecting the heavy dependence on complex visual comprehension. It was also possible that the rapid pace of the interaction would impose a structure unlike subject-paced problem-solving or previous GOMS research. With the alternatives in mind, we began to explore the possibilities.

OUR STUDY OF AN INFORMATION BROWSER
Information browsers are a class of interface systems through which users can both access large amounts of data and change their access to the data. The prototypical computer browser displays a map of an access structure to a

---

[1]There may be more than one method for accomplishing each S-R task. However, research suggests that each subject tends to use a single method and does not select between methods on each trial of the experimental session.

database and provides direct manipulation of the display of data and of the access structure. This definition also applies to the browsing that happens in a library: the books in the library are the information space, the map of the access structure is what the user can see at the current physical location in the stacks, and the acts of visually scanning the shelves or walking through the stacks directly manipulates the access structure. Browsers typically involve recognition of access paths, as opposed to description of access paths used in query languages, which makes perception an important component of browsing. Unlike many query-based databases, browsers typically respond to user actions very quickly, thus provide an example of the immediate interaction cycle in a real-world task.

We chose to study the help browser in the cT programming environment, implemented on the Macintosh[2]. The cT environment provides two main windows, a code window where the programmer edits source code and an execution window where results of the last run are displayed. The help browser can be brought up in a third window and provides access to the on-line reference manual, which is an exact duplicate of the hard-copy reference manual.

Figure 1. cT Help Browser, Macintosh interface

The help browser contains three scrollable windows, as shown in Figure 1. The largest one, at the bottom of the browser, is the text window. Text in this window gives information about cT features, the syntax and semantics of cT commands, and executable examples of command use. The hierarchical menu in the upper left corner is basically a table of contents for the information space. The keyword menu in the upper right corner lists all available cT command words in alphabetical order. Each window scrolls as in a typical Macintosh interface, and clicking on items in either menu window brings up the relevant help

---

[2] cT is a trademark of Carnegie Mellon University. Macintosh is a registered trademark of Apple Corporation.

text in the text window. Clicking on a item in the keyword menu also changes the hierarchical menu to show the relevant section in the table of contents.

We videotaped a non-professional but experienced computer programmer, who had never used cT before, as she wrote a graphing application for her own use. To answer questions about the language, she used the cT on-line help system exclusively, rather than the reference manual. She also thought-aloud as she worked. In the three and one-half hours videotaped, the user referred to the help browser approximately 85 times, in several characteristic ways. She used the hierarchical menu to provide an initial introduction to cT, primarily reading for general information about the capabilities and structure of the language. She used both the hierarchical menu and the keyword menu when she did not know the specific command to implement a desired function. She used the keyword menu to get the syntax of a known command. Some of her searches were immediately successful, some were circuitous but eventually successful, and some were long and eventually unsuccessful.

THE BROWSER-SOAR MODEL

We constructed a computational model of this user's browsing behavior, using the Soar unified theory of cognition. Soar is a detailed theory of cognition embodied in a production system architecture. It provides an integrated architecture for exploring a variety of behavior from routine execution of simple tasks to problem-solving, learning, and long-term development of concepts and skills [6]. Soar has been used by researchers to model users in several HCI environments, including using automatic teller machines [10], playing a video game [4], and learning task-action mappings for an interface [3]. We chose to use Soar because this architecture does not impose a structure onto the task *a priori*. The Soar architecture is flexible enough that the task structure could emerge from the model itself, be it problem-solving-like search, opportunistic behavior afforded by the browsing environment, or methodical operator executions typical of routine cognitive skill.

To construct the model, called Browser-Soar, we examined a single browsing episode, selected because the browse succeeded and contained several changes in search strategy based on the information displayed by the browser. This single episode delineated the basic structure for Browser-Soar (26 operators in 14 problem spaces). Three more episodes were needed to refine that structure, adding 4 new operators and modifying the proposal conditions for 2 previously defined operators. Six additional episodes were subsequently modeled, only requiring the modification of the conditions of 3 previously defined operators. The basic structure of Browser-Soar consists of problem-spaces and operators that produce generic browsing behavior.

Along with the problem-spaces, operators, and other knowledge that comprise Browser-Soar, our modeling of the browsing episodes includes a simulation of the cT help browser itself, with which Browser-Soar interacts. That is, there is a LISP simulation of what is displayed on the cT screen, which Browser-Soar must inspect to determine what to do next. Then, for example, when Browser-Soar determines that a window should be paged up, it moves the mouse and clicks the mouse button by sending output commands to this Lisp simulation. The Lisp simulation then changes the representation of the cT screen to reflect what would be on the real cT screen if such mouse actions actually occurred. Thus, Browser-Soar works with its "eyes open" and its "hands moving"; it simulates motor and perceptual interaction with an external environment.

To illustrate the basic structure of Browser-Soar, we will compare a transcript of a typical browsing episode (Figure 2) to the problem-spaces and operators in Browser-Soar (Figure 3). In the transcript, each mouse action (movement, button press, button release, or button click) and verbal utterance in the protocol appears on a separate line, labeled sequentially. In the Browser-Soar diagram, the triangles represent problem-spaces that contain knowledge and operators for browsing. When lines connect a higher problem-space to a lower one, the lower one is used to implement an operator of the same name in the higher space. Unconnected problem-spaces, Macintosh and Natural Language in this model, are *skill spaces*, containing operators and spaces that can be used by several other spaces throughout the Browser-Soar model.

This browsing episode begins when the user does not know the command to display the content of variables on the screen and goes into the help browser to find an appropriate command. She says "write...write...write" (v2-v4), indicating her generation of a keyword to search for; Browser-Soar models this with the Generate-search-criterion operator. She then says "can I write out the value of something?" (v5), generating an evaluation criterion to decide if "write" is the most appropriate command, given what she reads in the "write" help-text; Browser-Soar models this with the Generate-evaluation-criterion operator.

The user then searches for "write" by scrolling through the keyword menu; Browser-Soar models this with the Search-for-help operator. Search-for-help chooses an appropriate menu window for the search (in this case, the keyword window) and applies an operator to find the search criterion in that chosen window. This operator, Find-criterion, evaluates the current window and changes its contents if the search criterion does not appear in the current window display. Evaluate-current-window uses the knowledge and operators in the Natural-Language skill space to evaluate the words currently visible in the menu with respect to the search criterion. Change-current-window uses the knowledge and operators in the Macintosh skill space to perform the correct mouse actions (m7-m8, m10, m13-m15) to manipulate the window. When "write" scrolls

into the keyword window, the user moves the cursor to it and clicks (m20-m21). Browser-Soar models these actions with the Access-menu-item operator, which uses the Macintosh skill space to perform the mouse actions of clicking to "open" an item.

When the help text for "write" appears in the text window, the user reads it (v22) and discovers that the "show" command can be used to display the contents of variables (v26-v29, v31). Browser-Soar models this with the Evaluate-help-text operator, that in turn applies an Evaluate-current-window operator, which uses the Natural-Language skill space to comprehend the text and compare it to the evaluation criterion. The user goes back to the menu and searches for "show" (the episode continues beyond the excerpted transcript in Figure 2) and eventually succeeds in finding the appropriate command for her program. In Browser-Soar, the Evaluate-help-text operator applied to the help text for "write" changes the search-criterion to "show", which sends the model back to the Search-for-help operator, which eventually finds the help text for "show". Evaluate-help-text then determines that the help text indexed by "show" does indeed satisfy the evaluation criterion and Browser-Soar successfully terminates its search.

ANALYSIS OF THE BROWSER-SOAR MODEL

Ten episodes of browsing behavior, each approximately one-half to two minutes long, were modeled with Browser-Soar. The first four episodes were chosen to cover a wide range of browsing behavior; the remaining six were chosen at random from all browsing episodes in the videotaped behavior. As stated earlier, the structure of Browser-Soar problem-spaces and operators did not change to model the last six episodes (only the conditions on 3 operators were revised slightly) We compared the trace of the operators Browser-Soar executes for each episode to the observed user behavior. Three types of behavior were observed in the protocols: verbal utterances, movements of the mouse, and mouse button actions (clicks, presses, and releases). Browser-Soar does not directly model verbal utterances; that is, it has no Say operator. However, the utterances of the user can be used as indirect evidence of what are considered internal, cognitive, unobservable operators, because the user is "thinking aloud". For example, when the user reads the prose in the help text (v22), we take it as evidence for the Evaluate-current-window operator. On the other hand, Browser-Soar does have directly observable mouse-action operators. For example, the model predicts when the mouse will be moved to an item in the keyword menu and clicked, in service of an Access-menu-item operator. These predictions can be compared directly to the user's mouse actions (m20-m21). However, another type of mouse movement is also observed in the protocol, movements that trace along as the user reads text and menu items.

Time code	Verbal utterances	Mouse movements, button actions	On-screen events
v1	I believe		
v2	write		
v3	write		
v4	write		
v5	can I write out the value of something?		
m6		M to just left of keyword menu down arrow	
m7		M to keyword menu down arrow	
m8		D	keyword menu scrolls
v9	write		
m10		U	
m11		M to right of keyword, 'wrong'	
v12	wrong?		
m13		M to keyword menu up arrow	keyword menu scrolls
m14		D	
m15		U	
v16	no		
m17		M to 2nd keyword from bottom, 'xin'	
v18	ha ha haaa		
v19	write		
m20		M to 3 items up,'write'	
m21		C	'write' help text appears
v22	convenient way to write out short pieces of text that looks tidier in your program than the text command, okay		
m23		M to help text scroll bar, below elevator	
v24	umm...		
m25		M to bottom right of help text window	
v26	show command		
v27	are used		
v28	to display the contents of variables		
v29	so that's what I really want		
m30		M to middle of keyword menu scroll bar	
v31	is show command		

Figure 2. Transcription of browsing behavior in which the user attempts to find the command for writing out the value of a variable. The actual browsing episode continues, beyond this excerpt of the transcript, until the help text for the "show" command is displayed and judged to be appropriate to solve the coding problem.

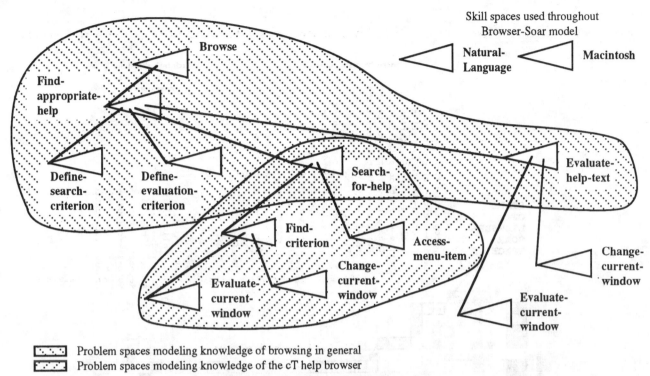

Problem spaces modeling knowledge of browsing in general
Problem spaces modeling knowledge of the cT help browser

Figure 3. The structure of Browser-Soar

Browser-Soar does not predict these movements, but, like the verbal utterances, these movements can provide evidence for unobservable operators in Browser-Soar. For example, when the user moves the mouse to an item in the keyword menu (m11), we predict that she is tracing the word as she reads it and we take this as evidence for the Evaluate-current-window operator that the model has predicted at this point.

Figure 4 illustrates the beginning of a trace of Browser-Soar performing the browse in the transcription in Figure 3. The horizontal axis lists the operators in the Browser-Soar model. The vertical axis orders all user behaviors, verbal (v#) and mouse (m#) as in the transcription. To follow the trace of Browser-Soar's predicted behavior, start at the upper left-hand corner and follow the boxes and arrows lined up underneath the operator names. A solid black box indicates that the model has predicted a directly observable mouse action and the user has performed the corresponding action. A dark gray box indicates that the user's action can be seen as evidence for an unobservable operator predicted by Browser-Soar. A light gray box indicates that the model has predicted an unobservable operator at this point in the trace but no evidence appears for this operator in the user's behavior. Thus, the more black or dark gray boxes in the trace, the more behavioral evidence for the existence of Browser-Soar operators.

Conversely, a similar color-coding scheme is used on the extreme left of Figure 4 to indicate how much of the observed behavior is modeled by Browser-Soar. A black box indicates that this behavior is modeled by a directly

observable operator in Browser-Soar. A gray box indicates that an unobservable operator in Browser-Soar is consistent with this behavior. Thus, the more black or gray boxes in the diagram, the more behavior is being accounted for by the model.

We can now calculate the correspondence between the behavior predicted by the model and the user's observed behavior (Table 1). An average of 90% of user behaviors were accounted for by Browser-Soar operators across the 10 episodes. The 10% of behaviors not accounted for by the model include verbal utterances that were too brief for drawing meaningful correspondences (for example, "um"), meta-verbal utterances that reflected on the process of browsing (e.g., reflection on the decision to scroll in a window rather than drag the elevator), mouse movements that occurred outside the current window under consideration, mouse movements that overshoot target areas, and mouse movements that land outside the browser altogether.

Conversely, we can also calculate how many operators predicted by Browser-Soar are supported by behavioral evidence Browser-Soar has a total of 30 distinct operators that are used repeatedly, sometimes with different arguments, to produce the browsing activities. For each episode, Table 2 lists the number of operators in several categories used by Browser-Soar to model that episode, and the number of occurrences of those operators for which behavioral evidence exists. We used strict criteria for judging whether an observed verbal utterance or mouse movement provided evidence for an unobservable operator.

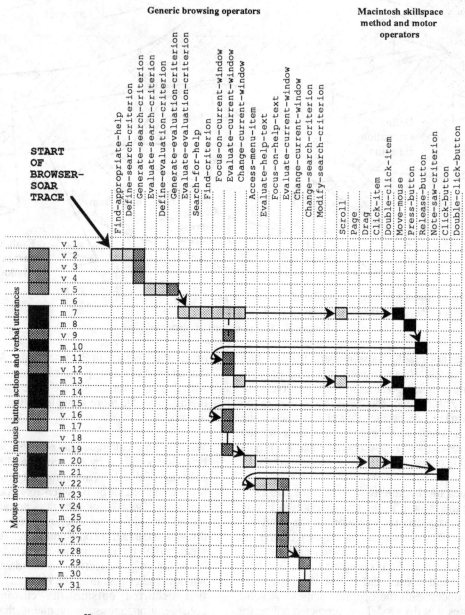

Figure 4. Representation of fit between observed behavior during the "write" browsing behavior excerpt (see transcription in Figure 2) and behavior predicted by the Browser-Soar model

For instance, if the user said "now I want to scroll the window" this utterance would provide evidence for the unobservable operator that chooses to the method to scroll a window, Scroll. However, if the user just moved the mouse to the scroll-down arrow and clicked, without declaring the intention to scroll, this behavior would provide evidence only for the Move-mouse and Click-button operators. Across all the episodes, all the directly observable predicted operators describing mouse activities are observed and 15% of all unobservable operator occurrences have behavioral evidence (94 of 626 operator occurrences). Since different episodes use a different subset of all the operators, all episodes provide evidence for 57% of the 30 distinct operators used by Browser-Soar.

In constructing the computational model, we separated the knowledge about browsing in general from knowledge about the particular browser, from knowledge about the Macintosh, and from knowledge of natural language. (See Figure 3.) This allows us to profile how much of the Browser-Soar's behavior falls out of routine application of the operators constructed without reference to the specific episode and how much required knowledge has to be separately hand-coded to allow Browser-Soar to reproduce the observed behavior. This profile reveals several characteristics of the browsing task. The generation and selection of the search and evaluation criteria for each browsing episode comprises about 10% of the model's behavior and requires specific natural-language knowledge to be provided. This generate-and-test procedure is common in problem-solving behavior and sets the goal for the subsequent browsing episode. Another 10% of the model's behavior involves the understanding of prose, for example, comprehension of the help text, for which we do not currently have a detailed model; we hand-coded the necessary natural-language knowledge. This leaves approximately 80% of the model's behavior that follows smoothly from the structure of the browsing task.[3] Less than 2% of the operators chosen by the model are in violation of the general selection rules defined in our analysis, requiring hand-coded information to make the model track the user's performance.

DISCUSSION

The model and analysis is significant to the study of human-computer interaction for several reasons. The most important is that much of this rapid, display-based, information browsing behavior turned out to be routine cognitive skill. Browser-Soar turned out to be primarily a GOMS model, describing the goal of the search, the perceptual, cognitive and motor operators necessary to accomplish the search, common methods for sequencing those operators, and selection rules for deciding between

Episode Name	Verbal Utterances		Mouse Movements		Mouse Button Acts		Total Behaviors		
Circle	29	(26)	14	(12)	14	(14)	57	(52)	(91%)
Write	25	(21)	20	(14)	24	(24)	69	(59)	(86%)
Unit	16	(13)	9	(5)	21	(21)	46	(39)	(85%)
Array	27	(26)	41	(38)	33	(33)	101	(97)	(96%)
Labelx	18	(16)	9	(6)	1	(1)	28	(23)	(82%)
Precision	7	(6)	8	(6)	9	(9)	24	(21)	(88%)
Axes	33	(31)	7	(6)	8	(8)	48	(45)	(94%)
Markers	22	(18)	15	(9)	5	(5)	42	(32)	(76%)
Vars	11	(10)	11	(8)	47	(47)	69	(65)	(94%)
Zcommand	32	(28)	14	(8)	94	(94)	140	(130)	(93%)
Total	220	(195)	148	(112)	256	(256)	624	(563)	(90%)

Table 1. User behaviors observed.
Numbers in parentheses indicate behaviors predicted (directly or indirectly) by Browser-Soar

Episode Name	Directly Observable Operators				Unobservable Operators		Total Operators		
	Mouse Movements		Mouse Button Acts						
Circle	7	(7)	14	(14)	70	(14)	91	(35)	(38%)
Write	6	(6)	24	(24)	60	(12)	90	(42)	(47%)
Unit	3	(3)	21	(21)	47	(6)	71	(30)	(42%)
Array	8	(8)	33	(33)	81	(15)	122	(56)	(46%)
Labelx	1	(1)	1	(1)	17	(4)	19	(6)	(32%)
Precision	2	(2)	9	(9)	29	(6)	40	(17)	(43%)
Axes	3	(3)	8	(8)	36	(7)	47	(18)	(38%)
Markers	3	(3)	5	(5)	27	(5)	35	(13)	(37%)
Vars	6	(6)	47	(47)	89	(8)	142	(61)	(43%)
Zcommand	5	(5)	94	(94)	170	(17)	269	(116)	(43%)
TOTAL	44	(44)	256	(256)	626	(94)	926	(394)	(43%)
DISTINCT	1	(1)	4	(4)	25	(12)	30	(17)	(57%)

Table 2. Operators predicted by Browser-Soar.
Numbers in parentheses indicate operators for which there is behavioral evidence

---

[3]Six percent of the model's behavior includes information about the alphabet, the spelling of words, and synonyms, which is easily included in the model but has not yet been implemented. At the present time, such knowledge is hand-coded, but we do not count reference to such knowledge as not GOMS-like.

methods. Defining the search and evaluation criteria appears to be typical problem-solving behavior, (implemented by a generate-and-test procedure, in an attempt to match a likely cT command with the desired programming function). However, once these are defined, the bulk of the rest of the behavior is clearly routine. The fact that so much of the observed behavior was accounted for by the model, with so little forcing of the simulation, is evidence that the observed browsing is an instance of GOMS-like behavior situated in a dynamic environment. The changing browser display can introduce subgoals or changes in goals, but even then, the observed behavior can be described as the execution of a routine cognitive skill. As we described at the outset, GOMS-like behavior in the immediate interaction cycle was not anticipated; this discovery advances the understanding of the mechanisms behind the immediate interaction cycle.

This work is the first step towards understanding browsing and the immediate interaction cycle - the discovery that GOMS can describe this behavior takes the form of a hypothesis. We are continuing to pursue this hypothesis by examining other users in this and other browsing situations. If browsing behavior shows itself to be primarily routine cognitive skill in more situations, then an implication of this discovery is that the comparison of browsers can be done from a profile of their GOMS methods, just like the comparison of text-editors [1] or telephone operator workstations [2]. In addition, our analysis provides a mechanism for focusing design effort through the profiling allowed by the separation of knowledge into problem-spaces. For instance, in Browser-Soar's modeling of use of the cT browser, about 80% of the operators employed by the model are in service of manipulating the browser, as opposed to 10% for setting up the criteria and 10% for reading text. Thus, it may be worth expending design effort to redesign the browser to be easier to manipulate and therefore more efficient to use. If, on the other hand, profiling showed that only 20% of the behavior was in the actual browsing, and 70% was in reading the text, it may be more advantageous to re-write the text so that relevant information can be found more quickly.

ACKNOWLEDGEMENTS

The authors would like to acknowledge Allen Newell and Stu Card for helpful collaborations and comments, Sandy Esch and Diane Randolph for transcribing the browsing episodes, the Soar research community, and the anonymous reviewers.

This research was supported by the Office of Naval Research, Cognitive Science Program, Contract Number N00014-89-J-1975N158 and by a grant from Xerox Corporation. The views and conclusions contained in this document are those of the authors and should not be not interpreted as representing the official policies, either expressed or implied, of the Office of Naval Research, the U.S. Government, or Xerox Corporation. The first author is also supported by an NSF Graduate Fellowship.

REFERENCES

[1] Card, S.K., Moran, T.P., and Newell, A. *The Psychology of Human-Computer Interaction.* Lawrence Erlbaum Associates, Hillsdale, NJ, 1983.

[2] Gray, W.D., John, B.E., and Atwood, M.E. Project Ernestine: Validating GOMS for predicting and explaining real-world task performance. *Human-Computer Interaction.* In preparation.

[3] Howes, A. and Young, R.M. Predicting the learnability of Task-action mappings. In *Proceedings of Human Factors in Computing Systems,* SIGCHI '91, New Orleans, LA, 1991, pp. 113-118.

[4] John, B.E., Vera, A.H., and Newell, A. *Towards Real-Time Goms.* Carnegie Mellon University, School of Computer Science Technical Report. CMU-CS-90-195, 1990.

[5] John, B.E. and Newell, A. Toward an engineering model of stimulus-response compatibility. In *Stimulus-Response Compatibility: An Integrated Perspective*, R. W. Proctor and T. G. Reeve, eds. North-Holland, New York, NY, 1989.

[6] Newell, A. *Unified Theories of Cognition.* Harvard University Press, Cambridge, MA, 1990.

[7] Newell, A. and Simon. H. *Human Problem Solving.* Prentice-Hall, Englewood Cliffs, NJ, 1972.

[8] Olson, J.R. and Olson, G.M. The growth of cognitive modeling in human computer interaction since GOMS. *Human Computer Interaction*, 5, pp. 221-266, 1990.

[9] Suchman, L.A. *Plans and Situated Actions.* Cambridge University Press, Cambridge, UK, 1987

[10] Wharton, C. *Implications of the Differences Between Cognitive Architectures for Human-Computer Interaction.* Ph.D. Dissertation, University of Colorado. In preparation.

TOWARDS TASK MODELS
FOR EMBEDDED INFORMATION RETRIEVAL

H. Ulrich Hoppe and Franz Schiele

GMD-IPSI,
Dolivostr. 15, 6100 Darmstadt (FRG)
schiele/hoppe@darmstadt.gmd.de

ABSTRACT

This paper investigates to what extent task-oriented user support based on plan recognition is feasible in a highly situation-driven domain like information retrieval (IR) and discusses requirements for appropriate task models. It argues that information seeking tasks which are embedded in some higher-level external task context (e.g. travel planning) often exhibit procedural dependences; that these dependences are mainly due to the external task; and that they can be exploited for inferring the users' goals and plans. While there is a clear need for task models in IR to account for situational determinants of user behaviour, what is required are hybrid models that take account of both its "planned" and "situated" aspects. Empirical evidence for the points made is reported from a probabilistic analysis of retrieval sessions with a fact database and from experience with plan-based and state-based methods for user support in an experimental travel planning system.

Keywords: task models, information retrieval, plan recognition, planned vs. situated action

INTRODUCTION

For an intelligent interface to be able to infer the users' goals or plans, and to give adequate support, it must have some representation or model of their tasks. It is characteristic of most task models in HCI – whether they are used as a knowledge-base for intelligent interactive systems or are construed as cognitive models of the user   that they describe user behaviour as goal-directed procedural patterns of action. In contrast to this view, information retrieval is to a considerable extent driven by situational triggers (e.g. intermediate search results), making it difficult to capture user behaviour in predefined procedures. In fact, information retrieval appears to be so paradigmatic of what has been termed "situated action" [25] that attempts to infer user *plans* may seem futile. To us, such conclusions are premature, and indeed unjustified. Instead of discarding the possibility of formally modelling and supporting information seeking tasks based on preconceived notions of them being "situated action", we rather consider such tasks as a challenge to test and possibly extend the scope of task models.

Cognitive task models in HCI

Over the last years, a number of formal or semi-formal models of users' task knowledge and performance have been proposed and with some success applied as analytic methods for assessing various aspects of system usability, examples being the GOMS model [2], Cognitive Complexity Theory or CCT [15], and Task-Action-Grammar or TAG [21]. While these models differ in some important aspects (cf. [9]), they also have much in common.

Of main interest here is that all of them include a representation of how users map goals or tasks onto overt actions (*task-action mapping*): they reflect the user's decomposition of tasks as determined by his goals, the means provided by the system for achieving them, and possibly some parameters of the current work environment. This kind of procedural knowledge corresponds to plans in the AI view. If viewed in the "problem space" framework which construes cognitive behaviour as search through a space of problem states [20], plans or task schemata can be seen as problem solving macros with some degree of generality. The search control knowledge for choosing operators may refer to the state of the environment, as for instance in the "selection rules" of GOMS models; but as it is routine skills that are modelled, control knowledge is assumed to be sufficiently complete to effectively eliminate search in the choice of operators.

In these models, control is mainly determined by the goal structure. More recently, growing awareness of the role of the external environment for human problem solving and task performance has led to attempts to more adequately represent the use of external information in cognitive models. Larkin's production system model of "display-based problem solving" [17] accounts for problem solving behaviour in situations where the external environment is used as the main representation of the current problem state. More specifically with regard to HCI, Howes & Payne [14] suggest an extension of Task-Action-Grammar (D-TAG) to model the "display-based competence" of users relying on visual cues for structuring their actions – as exemplified e.g. by the "label-following heuristic" in menu systems [22]. In these models, the visually perceived environment essentially forms an external extension of the user's memory.

Display-based models of task performance or problem solving capture some aspects of "situated action" [25]. Elaborating on this relationship is beyond the scope of this paper. In the following, we will use the term *situated action* to characterize the dominance of external triggers (vs. internal goals and associated plans) for controlling the execution of a task.

Task models for knowledge-based user support

Not only the scientist interested in modelling user knowledge and performance – task-oriented user support mechanisms in intelligent interfaces too require some representation of tasks. These representations need not necessarily lend themselves to a cognitive interpretation. However, to serve as a basis for reliably assessing the user's tasks and goals and for providing relevant assistance, they too must adequately reflect the user's decomposition of tasks.

In the field of AI, most work on goal and plan recognition in interactive systems is geared towards making NL dialogues with advisory or consulting systems more robust (cf. [16]). This not only adds the full range of problems associated with NL processing to the problem of recognizing user plans. It also implies a focus on phenomena peculiar to conversational settings where a speaker explicitly intends to convey his goals to the listener (i.e. the system) as opposed to non-conversational settings where a user pursues his goals directly in using the system as a tool. This distinction has also been referred to as "intended" vs. "keyhole" recognition (cf. [14]). In the latter case, which is the one assumed in this paper, plan recognition is based on the observation and interpretation of sequences of direct (non-linguistic) user *actions* as task-related procedures in the system's application domain.

Text editors and operating systems are the most prominent application domains for which "keyhole" monitoring and plan-recognition has been used to implement intelligent help systems [3, 6, 10]. Similar methods have been employed for diagnosing user behaviour in a variety of tutoring environments (cf. [8]). Task-adaptive advisory systems are not necessarily based on plan recognition, though. The HICCUPS advisor [19] for configuring statistical analyses is based on a planning mechanism which is essentially triggered by the state of the working environment. The state-based approach is also dominant in a variety of critic systems [7]. It is typically based on global quality criteria for evaluating the outcome of the user's actions irrespective of the dynamics of action (as e.g. the evaluation of chess positions as opposed to combinatorial analyses).

The problem of recognizing plans and goals underlying the users' actions is equivalent to inverting task-action mapping. For grammar-based task models, this means using the grammar for parsing purposes, which is formally and technically well-understood. The parsing approach is one of two dominant AI approaches to plan recognition (cf. [26]) – together with logical representations [14] which are computationally less tractable. In an HCI context, Hoppe [11] suggests the use of TAG-like attribute grammars for *task-oriented parsing*. A comparative review of different techniques for the parsing of user actions is given in [4].

The utility of task models for run-time support depends on how much of the user's actions can be subsumed under one of the plans or task schemata. This is a question of both the generality and flexibility of the representation and of the coverage of task libraries as a function of the knowledge acquisition process. The problem of acquiring a sufficiently covering set of task schemata has recently been addressed using machine learning techniques (e.g. [23]).

TASK MODELS FOR INFORMATION RETRIEVAL

While information search in databases and document retrieval systems has some relation to display-based task performance or problem-solving, the situation is different in several respects: The sought information is *hidden* and has to be retrieved using certain clues. Finding these clues requires semantic knowledge. Another difference is due to the fact that in information retrieval the sought information is the ultimate *end* of the task, whereas in display-based problem solving the external information is used to find operators which have the function of *means*. Also, there is *uncertainty* as to the impact of information found on the future course of action.

Due to such characteristics, information retrieval tasks are very much like situated action: In the incremental retrieval process it is mostly impossible to plan or anticipate longer sequences of actions, because the semantic evaluation of intermediate results (co-)determines the selection of the next action. Nevertheless, several lower level "moves" or tactics as well as more global strategies have been identified in the behaviour of professional searchers [1, 5]. These strategies such as "citation pearl growing" or "block building" are highly iterative, flexible and underdetermined. They impose only weak constraints on the relation between the actions in a sequence and can thus hardly be used as a knowledge base for the generation of help and advice. Therefore, most approaches to constructing intelligent interfaces for information retrieval focus on query formulation from natural language input and on terminological support for query reformulation, e.g. based on semantic or associative networks and an automatic analysis of results.

Intelligent support for information retrieval is typically based on the assumption that the user has a specific information need. The problem is that the user's specification of the requested information does not usually provide the adequate clues to extract the information as represented and stored inside the system. Information retrieval is concerned with overcoming this mismatch problem using techniques like partial matching between documents and queries, ranked output of documents, and relevance feedback based on the user's evaluation of the retrieved document set. This leads to an iterative approximation of the user's information need in terms of the system. This approach is rather robust in that it does not break down if the user's information need undergoes gradual revisions and changes during the retrieval process, i.e. it will still approximate a continuously moving target. But the model breaks down if there are discontinuities in the information request, e.g. if a user who is content with the response to a previously formulated need, now looks for something that is essentially different. Then, the "semantic weights" of the previous queries will be superimposed to the new query and thus misdirect the search.

Embedded Information Retrieval

In practice, information seeking activities are embedded as sub-tasks in a higher-level task context where information of different types and potentially from different sources is assembled and integrated to solve a given problem. In document retrieval, this context may be very difficult to assess and to respond to in an adequate way (e.g. the problem of writing a PhD thesis). In contrast, the use of structured factual databases is much more directly guided by external task structures. Travel planning with a database containing such heterogeneous information as flight tables, descriptions of regions and locations, hotel facilities and prices, etc. may be considered as an example. In such an environment, discontinuities in the information request are natural and the assumption that the user's global goal is finally expressed by one query is not reasonable. Indeed, there is no single information source against which the client's goals could be matched in a query and which could return a completely specified travel plan. The overall task comprises information search as well as other subtasks such as calculation of costs, checking for compatibility of partial results, deciding on priorities in cases of goal conflicts, etc..

Composing a travel plan which satisfies the preferences and requirements of a client shows many features of an open-ended design task. There is a global goal which is usually specified on a different and more general conceptual level than the level on which solutions must be described. Depending on the generality of the goal specification and the available repertoire of solution components, there is often a multitude of solutions. As with other design tasks, finding a satisficing solution may be more important than finding the optimal one [24]. The process is iterative in that (partial) candidate solutions are repeatedly revised and incrementally completed until a fully specified travel plan is finally accepted.

Travel planning is an example domain for what we call *embedded information retrieval*. Embedded IR is characterized by the existence of an external task context which imposes a hierarchical structure and partial sequential ordering on the information-seeking goals and actions. Rather than trying to satisfy a single information need through searching in one given database, the task requires that different kinds of information be acquired through access to different information sources (databases or tables) - with the information needs and the choice of information sources partially arising from the implications of intermediate results.

Our central conjecture is that embedded information retrieval can be interpreted as goal-driven behaviour and can thus be supported by plan-based mechanisms like "task-oriented parsing". Before we report on an attempt to do this in an experimental travel planning system, we present empirical evidence for the basic assumption concerning the existence of task-related procedural regularities in information seeking behaviour. It stems from a probabilistic state-transition model for query evolution which is applied to a data collection of query sessions with a structured factual database.

A STATE-TRANSITION ANALYSIS OF QUERIES

Information retrieval operations do not change the state of the underlying system, i.e. of the given database. Therefore, the user's goals cannot be adequately described in terms of system states in this sense. To capture the effects of retrieval operations, it is necessary to refer to an *information environment* in which the information extracted from the database is an explicit parameter. The incremental nature of information retrieval is reflected by regarding changes between successive queries (and not the queries themselves) as operators. Accordingly, the specification of the current query becomes part of the state description.

In order to be able to operationalize this notion of a dynamically changing information environment expressed in terms of query states, certain properties of the underlying database

management system must be taken into account. Here, we assume the information source to be a database in relational format, i.e. it may contain several basic relations or tables as well as virtual relations or views with their respective attributes. The query mechanism is restricted to what can be done with separate forms where certain attributes may be constrained to certain values and other attributes may be requested to be instantiated in the query result. This allows for an homogeneous presentation of input and output in similar forms. Different forms may correspond to physical tables or views, but the user is not concerned with view definition. This type of a form-based query interface implements a simplified version of "Query by Example" (cf. [18, 27]) which is easy to use and sufficient for many purposes.

Let us now define a *query state* (QS) as a tuple with the following components:

$$QS = (V, A_r, A_s, N, R), \text{ where}$$

V stands for the *table or view*,
$A_r = \{\text{Attr*}\}$ is the set of *requested attributes*,
$A_s = \{ [\text{Attr, Val}]* \}$ is the set of *search attributes*
N is the *number* of tuples found, and
R is the current *set of tuples*.

In order to abstract from the concrete instantiation of a query state, we introduce the notion of a *query pattern* (QP), which is a triple made up of the table or view (V), the set of requested attributes (A_r), and the set of search attributes without values ($A_s' = \{\text{Attr} \mid [\text{Attr,Val}] \in A_s\}$).

Transitions between successive query states are effected by certain "moves" as described by Fidel [5] for document retrieval. A move is characterized by its type and parameters. It is useful to distinguish between *structural moves* which change the query pattern, and *content-oriented moves* (essentially term replacements). In retrieval from a relational database, structural moves may e.g. be of type "add-requested-attribute", "add-search-attribute", "drop-requested-attribute", "drop-search-attribute", or "change-view". "Broaden", "narrow", or "change-attribute-value" are the typical content-oriented moves. Broadening and narrowing are specific term replacements in search attributes that can be classified according to a given thesaurus. Characteristic parameters of moves are the affected attributes and tables or views, and, in case of search attributes, the concrete instances of search terms. Again, we will abstract from the concrete attribute values and define a *generalized transition* δ in the following way:

$$\delta = (QP, M), \text{ where}$$

QP stands for the initial query pattern, and
M is the move defined by its type and its general parameters (attributes and views).

Given QP and M, the resulting query pattern is implicitly determined, but there may be different types of moves leading from one query pattern to another (e.g. narrow/broaden). The probability of a transition δ is defined as the conditional probability of applying M if the current query state is an instance of QP:

$$P(\delta) = P(M|QP).$$

$P(\delta)$ can be estimated as the relative frequency of move M for all instances of QP in a collection of recorded query histories.

A probabilistic interpretation of information retrieval being "situated action" leads to a first order Markov model of query evolution where the probability of a transition is assumed to be independent of previous states or moves. Deviations from this assumption can be detected by looking at the probability of sequences of transitions. The simplest case is a pair of transitions $\delta = (QP,M)$ and $\delta' = (QP',M')$ with move M transforming QP into QP'. Let $P(\delta\delta')$ denote the probability that δ' follows directly after an instance of δ, given the current query state is an instance of QP. If moves are purely situated actions we have to assume that both transitions are independent events, so that

$$P(\delta\delta') = P(M,M'|QP) = P(M|QP) \cdot P(M'|QP')$$
$$= P(\delta) \cdot P(\delta').$$

But in general, we have

$$P(\delta\delta') = P(M|QP) \cdot P(M'|QP,M,QP')$$
$$= P(\delta) \cdot P(\delta'|\delta),$$

where $P(\delta'|\delta) = P(M'|QP,M,QP')$ is the probability of applying M' to an instance of QP' if the preceding transition was δ. Estimates of $P(\delta'|\delta)$ can again be computed from query histories. The comparison between $P(\delta'|\delta)$ and $P(\delta')$ can be based on the ratio

$$r(\delta,\delta') = P(\delta'|\delta) / P(\delta').$$

Ideally, in the sense of situated action, r should be 1. If for a given pair (δ, δ') we have $r(\delta,\delta') > 1$, this indicates a positive dependence of δ' on the previous transition δ, and accordingly $r(\delta,\delta') < 1$ indicates an inhibitory effect of δ on δ'.

Applying plan-based task models to information seeking activities is only reasonable if there is evidence that information seeking behavior is not purely situated action but also to a considerable extent goal-directed. According to our hypothesis that "embedded information retrieval" with structured factual databases is more likely to comply with this criterion than document retrieval, the QP-transition model is well suited for complexly structured databases and less expressive for classical document retrieval, since the selectivity of transitions depends on the variety of views and attributes. The model is consistent with the situated action paradigm in that it does not assume plan-like control structures. On the other hand, higher order transition probabilities can be used as indicators for deviations from the assumption of information retrieval being purely situated action.

We have studied search behavior with the EXPRESS system [12], an experimental retrieval interface to a relational database which contains information on wood protection products and their potential applications and risks. EXPRESS offers a form-based "Query by Example" interface with uniform query entry and result forms which are associated with database views. Previous queries with their respective hit rates are displayed in a history window from which they can be selected for reuse. The reformulation of queries is supported by a mechanism that analyzes the given query and suggests new search terms from a semantic network which serves as a thesaurus. Reformulations are only suggested upon request by the user and are not applied automatically. This kind of support is limited to content-oriented moves (*broaden* or *narrow*).

As yet, we have analyzed data which had been collected for other purposes with the EXPRESS environment. In this experiment, a series of complex tasks was performed by 14 subjects. The tasks showed characteristics of embedded information retrieval in that most of them could not be accomplished by using only one specific query pattern. Instead, they required focus shifting between views and switching be-

tween attributes. The suggestion mechanism, which is not of interest here, was disabled in one of the two experimental conditions; when enabled, it was not very often used. The total number of queries collected from 14 individual transcripts amounts to 722, from which 72 query patterns, 219 generalized first order transitions, and 352 generalized transition pairs were derived.

Figure 1 shows the distribution of logarithmic r-values (lr = $\log_{10}(r)$) in 0.2 intervals between -1.0 and 2.0. The line at $\log_{10}(r)=0$, i.e. r=1, marks those second order transitions where the first component transition has no impact on the probability of the second (as compared to its first order probability).

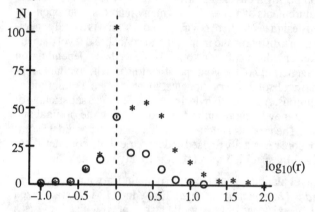

Figure 1. Distribution of lr-values

The upper plot (marked with "*") shows the unfiltered data. A problem with these data is that they include generalized transition pairs (δ,δ') for which there is only one instance of δ, so that the successor δ' too is uniquely determined and thus $P(\delta'|\delta) = 1$. This typically leads to a high r-value. To reduce this effect, only generalized transition pairs with a minimum frequency of 5 for the first transition are further considered (circle plot). Then, the number of remaining second order transitions is 131. But there is still a bias which favours high r-values. Therefore, the fact that the mean (non-logarithmic) r-value for the reduced data set is 1.82, i.e. the second order probability is on an average 82% higher than the first-order probability, should not be overestimated. However, if the minimum criterion is strengthened to a frequency of 10, we still get r = 1.53 (based on 86 pairs).

Table 1. Distribution of lr-values for categories

	C_0	C_1	C_2	Σ
$lr < -0.2$	12	9	1	22
$-0.2 \leq lr < 0.2$	19	28	13	60
$0.2 \leq lr < 0.6$	10	23	5	38
$0.6 \leq lr$	10	1	0	11
Σ	51	61	19	131

An interesting observation can be made if the second order transitions are categorized and their distributions are compared. Table 1 distinguishes three categories: C_2 - both moves are content-oriented, C_1 - one of the moves is content-oriented, and C_0 - none is content-oriented (i.e. both moves are structure-oriented). The distributions of lr-values for C_0

and $C_1 \cup C_2$ (i.e. the category of transition pairs with at least one content-oriented move) are significantly different ($\chi^2 = 18.63$, $p < 0.001$). Evidently, the frequency of extreme lr-values (positive or negative!) is higher in C_0 than it is in $C_1 \cup C_2$. In other words: A high degree of determination of a transition by its predecessor appears to be more probable for purely structural moves. A value of lr ≥ 0.6 means that the second order transition probability is at least four times higher than the first order probability. A typical example pattern in C_0 is a change of view followed by a change of the requested attributes. The observed effect cannot be induced by the suggestion mechanism of EXPRESS, because this could only explain a higher predictability of content-oriented moves.

Structural moves indicate discontinuous search behavior ("the target is shifted"), whereas content-oriented moves are typical in phases of iterative query reformulation driven by a constant or only gradually changing information need. Thus, it seems that *discontinuous structural changes of queries are less "situated" than continuous reformulation processes.* Embedded information retrieval is characterized by the importance of discontinuous actions. The empirical findings provide plausible evidence for procedural dependences in embedded information seeking activities. In the following, we will study how such procedural aspects of user behavior can be modeled and supported by knowledge-based interfaces.

TASK MODELS FOR TRAVEL PLANNING

To explore the feasibility of and requirements for task-models for user support in embedded IR, we implemented an experimental system for composing travel plans. While the scenario of travel planning underlying this system is one of limited complexity, it includes some of the basic features of the domain as described above. A travel plan in this environment consists of a destination, an accommodation, a travel means and travel route, and the costs. The system's functionality comprises an information retrieval component for accessing a relational database which contains data on destinations, accommodations, and travel connections and additional functions for generating travel routes and for calculating costs. Queries are formulated and modified incrementally by adding or removing search attributes and requested attributes.

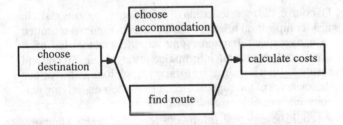

Figure 2. Global structure of the travel planning task

The top-level task "compose a travel plan" includes the following subtasks whose outcomes partially constrain subsequent subtasks (see Figure 2):
(1) Choose a destination,   (2) Choose an accommodation,
(3) Find a travel route,   (4) Calculate total costs.
Apart from subtasks (2) and (3), which are order-independent, the tasks must be performed in the given order. If an impasse occurs at some stage due to a mismatch between options available and the user's requirements, or because con-

straints of the overall task, e.g. cost limits, are violated, the user may need to backtrack and redo preceding subtasks.

Database search is required for the tasks of choosing a destination and an accommodation, respectively. Both tasks typically involve a cycle of specifying relevant search attributes and requested attributes, and evaluating and modifying queries, until a (preliminary) decision is made concerning the desired destination or accommodation. While this pattern of behaviour is common to most information retrieval tasks, there are some important differences which have implications for the system's capability to provide task-oriented user support: Due to the structure of the external task, the number and kinds of users' information needs are constrained. Although the user's precise goals are unknown and cannot be directly mapped to a specific query, it can be safely assumed that at some stage he will have the goals of searching for destinations or accommodations. This eliminates some of the uncertainty about users' intentions that renders user behaviour in IR so elusive. In addition, these goals can be related to particular types of information being searched for or being specified as search criteria by the user.

In our case, particular attributes of database relations can a priori be considered as being especially relevant or even mandatory for achieving a certain goal, while others can be discarded as irrelevant. For instance, the goal of choosing a destination necessarily implies that "DestName" is a requested attribute in the user's current query and implies with high probability that vacation activities are specified as search attributes. Thus, knowledge about the external task in combination with knowledge about the structure of the database and the retrieval functionality provides a basis for forming plausible hypotheses about the user's plans.

Modeling task performance as plans of actions

Based on an extended version of the "Task-Oriented Parser/ Generator", TOP/G [11], we formulated a number of task-composition rules which capture typical procedures performed in composing a travel plan with our experimental system. TOP/G is a bi-directional parser for plan recognition and plan extrapolation which operates with a representation of plans as attributed grammar rules. These rules represent the hierarchical decomposition of a higher-level task into elementary or composite subtasks. Elementary tasks are represented by a task-name and a list of features. Composite tasks cannot introduce new features but may "inherit" and constrain features of component tasks. The control structures for executing a task's components includes *sequence-of*, *set-of* (order-independent composition), and *optional* components. Repetitive tasks are modeled by recursive rules.

The task-composition rules are used as a plan library for parsing the user's actions, forming hypotheses as to the most likely current user plan, and making suggestions to the user for continuation of incomplete candidate plans. Upon the user's request, the system would not only propose an action according to the extrapolation of an hypothesized incomplete plan, but make explicit its assumptions about the user's goals and subgoals by referring to the goal structure as reflected in the parse tree. Thus, rather than confronting the user point-blank with a suggested action, the system helps the user to establish its relevance by offering an interpretation of the user's present task context (see below).

In the following presentation of this approach as applied to the travel planning domain we concentrate on the information-seeking tasks involved. The subtasks of choosing a destination or an accommodation share the following structure:

(a) specify requirements relevant to the choice of a target object (destination or accommodation),

(b) search database for objects satisfying these requirements,

(c) revise requirements and search again if answer set is unsatisfactory,

(d) get more selective information about candidate objects,

(e) make (preliminary) decision.

The rules in Figure 3 illustrate how such procedures are captured in TOP/G's representation scheme. Rule 1 describes one of several procedures for the task of choosing a destination. It comprises four subtasks, including an optional one (rules 1.1 to 1.4), which in turn correspond to procedures for steps (a) to (d) in the task description given above. The optional subtask *mult_revise_requirements* of rule 1 is represented by a recursive rule which accounts for multiple revisions of search attributes. Rule 1.3 captures just one type of possible revisions. The elementary tasks which occur in these rules include: adding search attributes or requested attributes (*add_search_attr*, *add_req_attr*) to the current query; omitting a search attribute (*drop_search_attr*); evaluating a query in terms of the number of hits (*count_hits*); and displaying the query results (*display_result*). The rules express (partial) order constraints on the sequencing and semantic constraints on the instantiation of component tasks. The latter are strongly determined by the semantic structure of the database and its relation to the respective task.

Task-composition rules could also be formulated for domain-independent procedures such as e.g. "broaden" or "narrow". However, since these lack constraints imposed by the external task, and since establishing an action sequence as a broadening procedure requires particular situational conditions to hold that are presently not processed by TOP/G, they are not selective enough to be usefully employed for task support.

```
1    find_destination ::=
        sequence-of (
            spec_dest_requirements_act_reg
            search_dest,
            set-of (optional (mult_revise_requirements),
                    get_info_act_desc ) ).

1.1  spec_dest_requirements_act_reg ::=
        set-of (   mult_add_search_attr [attr_name = 'Activities'],
                   add_search_attr [attr_name = 'Region'] ).

1.2  search_dest ::=
        sequence-of ( add_req_attr [attr_name = 'DestName'],
                      optional (count_hits) ).

1.3  revise_requirements ::=
        sequence-of ( drop_search_attr [attr_name],
                      count_hits ).

1.4  get_info_act_desc ::=
        sequence-of (
            set-of ( add_req_attr [attr_name = 'Activities'],
                     add_req_attr [attr_name = 'Description']),
            display_result ).
```

Figure 3. Information-seeking procedures in travel planning

When parsing user input, any sequence of actions up to the last one which forms a partial instantiation of the top-level

rule (1) is considered as a currently pursued but yet uncompleted plan for the task of choosing a destination. For instance, assuming that the user had just specified values for a 'Region' and some 'Activities', and now asked for a suggestion on how to continue, the support mechanism would come up with the following message:

If you are searching for destinations ...

... and have finished specifying search criteria,
you should mark the destination name ('DestName') as a requested attribute.

More suggestions? (y/n)

This message paraphrases information that is represented in the candidate parse tree resulting from parsing the input with the rules in Figure 3, i.e. that the input actions can be interpreted as an uncompleted plan to search for destinations, where the subtask of specifying search attributes has been completed and the appropriate next step would be to specify "DestName" as a requested attribute. To the extent that TOP/G can produce alternative parse trees using additional rules, the user may get further suggestions.

What we found in informal tests of the plan-based support mechanism was that the task-composition rules we defined covered a broad range of possible procedures in using the travel planning system, and in many situations enabled the system to give relevant suggestions.

It is evident that in information-seeking tasks the support most valuable to users is not so much advice on the ordering of actions, since the process of query formulation and evaluation does not pose complex planning problems. (This does not necessarily hold for the external task, in which they are embedded.) Rather, it is advice on what information to specify or request in queries, that helps the user achieve his goals. In our experimental system, this takes the form of suggestions concerning the choice of attributes which are considered relevant for the hypothesized goals of the user. This kind of help addresses a major problem for inexperienced users querying factual databases. Apart from a check for allowed terms, terminological support concerning appropriate values of search attributes (search terms) is presently not supported in the travel planning system, but could be achieved exploiting thesaurus information and techniques as used in the EXPRESS system [12].

Of course, the representation of information-seeking tasks in task-composition rules such as the ones in Figure 3 is limited in many respects. It ignores some important factors that influence user behaviour in information retrieval (e.g. hit rate and results). But it is instructive to take a closer look at the various deficiencies of the support mechanism, their underlying reasons, and possible amendments.

As could be expected, information encoded in task-composition rules about action ordering turned out to be more fragile than information about the various patterns of search attributes (indicating different priorities) and requested attributes that may be specified by different users. The breakdown of higher-level plans due to some unaccounted-for user action is a problem faced by any plan-recognition mechanism that works with a finite set of predefined plans. There is a tradeoff here between making plans more general and flexible to account for variation in procedures at the risk of sometimes providing extraneous suggestions and making plans more specific to always warrant precise interpretations at the risk of not being able to interpret some individual action sequences at all. TOP/G's hierarchical representation of plans makes for some robustness in that when the system fails to track a user's higher-level plan, it may later resume a correct interpretation of the user's goals on a lower level, based on subtask rules.

An effective means to prevent inappropriate suggestions based on incomplete or incorrect hypotheses on the user's current plan would be to consider additional information about the state of his work environment which is currently not expressed in the task-composition rules. For instance, consideration of the current "query state" as defined earlier could prevent suggestions to specify search or requested attributes that are already specified (which may occur if the system loses track of the user's higher-level plan). Representing and processing this kind of state information could not only provide additional evidence for or against plan-based inferences about user goals. (For example, information about the hit rate of an initial query could provide clues as to whether to suggest to examine the query results or to revise the specified search attributes.) It would also allow to make suggestions more specific with respect to the particular task context. If coupled with a thesaurus, it could provide the basis for suggesting appropriate search terms for reformulating queries. Finally, it could lend semantics to domain-independent task-composition rules which lack semantic constraints imposed by the external task but instead derive their meaning from the state of the current task environment.

Modeling task performance as state-based condition-action rules

Our experience with the plan-based approach indicates what kinds of information would be required for making task support more responsive to the user's current task context. While TOP/G's representation scheme does not presently allow for processing these kinds of information, much of it is available in the travel planning system's protocol of the dialogue history. To see how far exploitation of state-based information would get us in providing task-oriented support, we implemented a support mechanism based on condition-action rules which rely exclusively on such information, namely the search attributes and requested attributes specified in the current query and its hit rate.

1	IF	requested ('DestName')
		hit_rate (not_evaluated)
	THEN	count_hits
2	IF	requested ('DestName')
		hit_rate = 0
	THEN	drop_search_attribute
3	IF	requested ('DestName')
		not requested ('Activity')
	THEN	add_requested_attribute ('Activity')
4	IF	requested('DestName')
		not requested('Description')
	THEN	add_requested_attribute('Description')

Figure 4. Examples of state-based rules

Figure 4 gives a few examples of such rules. The condition-part of rules may test for the presence of particular search attributes and/or requested attributes in the current query and for the query's hit rate (not evaluated/number of hits). The action-part specifies the action that should be suggested to the user if the condition holds. If the conditions of several rules

match the current situation, they are applied in descending order.

The rules in Figure 4 apply to states which may evolve if e.g. the top-level plan shown in Figure 3 is executed and the user has specified "DestName" as a requested attribute. Rule 2 shows how information about a query's hit rate can provide clues as to what are likely or appropriate further actions. At first glance, it might seem that such rules are capable of anticipating user goals and actions as well as plans – without the processing overhead incurred by the plan recognition mechanism. However, strictly speaking, information about hit rate in these rules is not purely state-based information. It also implies some information about action ordering, namely that the *last* action either was or was not "count_hits". If this implicit information were missing, the lack of focus in these rules on the intentions and plans of a particular user would be even more apparent.

State- or situation-based rules and, consequently, the suggestions based on them are, by definition, insensitive to the dynamics of the user's actions. To the extent that the dynamics of actions carry information about goals and subgoals pursued, this information is ignored. For example, if a user searching for destinations has specified only "Activities" as search criteria (which accords with a possible plan for choosing a destination), and has already proceeded to the subgoal of requesting information on the resulting set of destinations, the state-based support mechanism would still keep suggesting to specify a "Region" as an additional search criterion. It has no means for distinguishing between variants in task performance that are caused by variation in the users (sub-)goals and therefore is not responsive to them.

Purely state-based task support appears to work best in domains with a single and persistent goal which can be achieved incrementally with minimal interaction between subgoals. The assumption is that all user actions contribute to and their effects can be matched against this goal [7]. Despite the situated aspects of information-seeking tasks, state-based task support cannot completely replace a plan-based approach.

CONCLUSIONS

Information retrieval tasks are generally considered as difficult or impossible to represent (and therefore to support) by means of goal-directed procedures or plans because of their highly situation-driven nature. The limited set of general retrieval strategies and tactics identified in the literature seems to corroborate this view.

The picture changes though, if we not only acknowledge that information seeking nearly always serves some purpose in an external task or problem to be solved, but that the external task context often imposes considerable structure on the information-seeking processes involved. It is our conjecture that this is the case in many domains which can be characterized as "embedded information retrieval". Both the analysis of transitions between query patterns in searching factual databases and of plan-based task support in a travel planning system provide evidence to that.

Its present limitations notwithstanding, the performance of the plan-based support mechanism suggests that procedural task support becomes feasible, if the system can draw on procedural and conceptual *domain knowledge* about the external task for inferring user goals and plans. It also showed what kinds of information about the state of the task environment could and should be used to account for the "situatedness" of user behaviour and thereby to make procedural task support more reliable and more specific to the particular situation. Work on integrating such state-based information into the plan-recognition mechanism is under way.

While we agree with the "situated action" paradigm's emphasis on the impacts of the situation on the course of action, we contend that user behaviour is (if not exclusively) controlled by goals and that this shows to a considerable extent in the dynamics of his actions. To neglect this would mean to ignore valuable information that a responsive system could capitalize on in giving task-oriented support.

ACKNOWLEDGEMENTS

We wish to thank Johannes Bellert for developing an initial version of the travel planning system, Regina Schilder for implementing the SQP-mechanism in EXPRESS, and Karin Ammersbach for providing us with the data collection.

REFERENCES

1. Bates, M.J. (1979). Information search tactics. Journal of the American Society for Information Science, Vol. 30, pp. 205-214.

2. Card, S.K., Moran, T.P., & Newell, A. (1983). The Psychology of Human-Computer Interaction. Hillsdale (NJ): Lawrence Erlbaum.

3. Desmarais, M.C., Larochelle, S., & Giroux, L. (1987). The diagnosis of user strategies. Proceedings of the 2nd IFIP Conference on Human-Computer Interaction, Stuttgart (FRG), August 1987, pp. 185-189.

4. Desmarais, M.C., Giroux, L., & Larochelle, S. (1991). Plan recognition in HCI: the parsing of user actions. In: Tauber, M.J. & Ackermann, D. (Eds.). Mental Models and Human-Computer Interaction 2. Amsterdam: Elsevier. pp. 291-311.

5. Fidel, R. (1985). Moves in online searching. Online Review, Vol. 9, pp. 61–74.

6. Fischer, G., Lemke, A., & Schwab, T. (1985). Knowledge-based help systems. Proceedings of the ACM SIGCHI Conference on Human Factors in Computing Systems, San Francisco (CA), April 1985, pp. 161-167.

7. Fischer, G., Lemke, A., & Mastaglio, T. (1990). Using critics to empower users. Proceedings of the ACM SIGCHI Conference on Human Factors in Computing Systems, Seattle (Washington), April 1990, pp. 337-347.

8. Frederiksen, N., Glaser, R., Lesgold, A., & Shafto, M.G. (Eds.) (1990). Diagnostic Monitoring of Skill and Knowledge Acquisition. Hillsdale: Lawrence Erlbaum.

9. Green, T.R.G., Schiele, F., & Payne, S.J. (1988). Formalisable models of user knowledge in Human-Computer Interaction. In: van der Veer, G., Green, T.R.G., Hoc, J.-M., & Murray, D. (Eds.). Working with Computers: Theory versus Outcome. London: Academic Press.

10. Hecking, M. (1987). How to use plan recognition in order to improve the abilities of the intelligent help system SINIX Consultant. Proceedings of the 2nd IFIP Conference on Human-Computer Interaction, Stuttgart (FRG), August 1987, pp. 657-662.

11. Hoppe, H.U. (1988). Task-oriented parsing – a diagnostic method to be used by adaptive systems. In Proceedings of the ACM SIGCHI Conference on Human Factors in Computing Systems, Washington D.C., May 1988, pp. 241-247.

12. Hoppe, H.U., Ammersbach, K., Lutes-Schaab, B., & Zinßmeister, G. (1990). EXPRESS: an experimental interface for factual Information Retrieval. Proceedings of the 13th ACM SIGIR Conference on Research and Development in Information Retrieval, Brussels (Belgium), September 1990, pp. 63-81.

13. Howes, A. & Payne, S.J. (1990). Display-based competence: towards user models for menu-driven interfaces. Int. J. Man-Machine Studies, Vol. 33, pp. 637-655.

14. Kautz, H.A. (1991). A Formal Theory of Plan Recognition and its Implementation. In: J.A. Allen, H.A. Kautz, R.N. Pelavin & J.D. Tenenberg. Reasoning About Plans. San Mateo: Morgan Kaufmann.

15. Kieras, D.E. & Polson, P.G. (1985). An approach to the formal analysis of user complexity. Int. J. Man-Machine Studies, Vol. 22, pp. 365-394.

16. Kobsa, A. & Wahlster, W. (Eds.) (1989). User Models in Dialog Systems. Berlin: Springer.

17. Larkin, J.H. (1989). Display-based problem solving. In: Klahr, D. & Kotovsky, K. (Eds.). Complex Information Processing. Hillsdale: Lawrence Erlbaum. pp. 319-341.

18. McAlpine, G. & Ingwersen, P. (1989). Integrated Information Retrieval in a knowledge worker support system. Proceedings of the 12th ACM SIGIR International Conference on Research and Development in Information Retrieval. Cambridge (MA), June 1989, pp. 48-57.

19. McKendree, J. & Zaback, J. (1988). Planning for advising. In Proceedings of the ACM SIGCHI Conference on Human Factors in Computing Systems, Washington D.C., May 1988, pp. 179-183.

20. Newell, A. (1980). Reasoning, problem solving, and decision processes: The problem space as a fundamental category. In: R. Nickerson (Ed.). Attention and Performance VIII. Hillsdale, NJ.: Lawrence Erlbaum Associates.

21. Payne, S.J. & Green, T.R.G. (1986). Task-action grammars: a model of the mental representation of task languages. Human-Computer Interaction, Vol. 2, pp. 93–133.

22. Polson, P.G. & Lewis, C. (1990). Theory-based design for easily learned interfaces. Human-Computer Interaction, Vol. 5, pp. 191-220.

23. Schiele, F. & Hoppe, H.U. (1990). Inferring task structures from interaction protocols. Proceedings of the 3rd IFIP Conference on Human-Computer Interaction, Cambridge (UK), August 1990, pp. 567-572.

24. Simon, H. (1969). The Sciences of the Artificial. Cambridge (MA): MIT Press.

25. Suchman, L. (1987): Plans and Situated Actions. Cambridge (MA): Cambridge University Press.

26. Vilain, M (1990). Getting serious about parsing plans: a grammatical analysis of plan recognition. Proceedings of the 8th National Conference on Artificial Intelligence, July 1990, Cambridge (MA), pp. 190-197.

27. Zloof, M.M. (1983). The Query-by-Example concept for user-oriented business systems. In: Sime, M.E. & Coombs, M.J. (Eds.). Designing for Human-Computer Communication. London: Academic Press.

KNOWLEDGE-BASED EVALUATION AS DESIGN SUPPORT FOR GRAPHICAL USER INTERFACES

Jonas Löwgren

Dept. of Computer and Info. Science
Linköping University
S-581 83 Linköping, Sweden
jlo@ida.liu.se

Tommy Nordqvist

Nat. Defense Research Est. (FOA 531)
P.O. Box 1165
S-581 11 Linköping, Sweden

ABSTRACT

The motivation for our work is that even though user interface guidelines and style guides contain much useful knowledge, they are hard for user interface designers to use. We want to investigate ways of bringing the human factors knowledge closer to the design process, thus making it more accessible to designers. To this end, we present a knowledge-based tool, containing design knowledge drawn from general guideline documents and toolkit-specific style guides, capable of evaluating a user interface design produced in a UIMS. Our assessment shows that part of what the designers consider relevant design knowledge is related to the user's tasks and thus cannot be applied to the static design representation of the UIMS. The final section of the paper discusses ways of using this task-related knowledge.

Keywords: user interface evaluation, design support, guidelines, style guides.

INTRODUCTION

The need for human factors knowledge in the design of information systems has been increasingly acknowledged over the last decade. It is by now unanimously agreed that issues such as usability, consistency and overall appreciation can all be facilitated by the application of human factors expertise to the design process.

A popular medium for the propagation of human factors knowledge has been documents containing general or environment-specific design rules. The former kind

---

[a]Both authors contributed equally to the contents and the presentation of this work.

is called *guidelines*; the latter *style guides*. The knowledge in these documents is characterized by being supported by general consensus, often validated through experience or controlled experiments and by being exhaustive. Style guides in particular often represent *de facto* industrial standards and the knowledge is often prescriptive rather than suggestive (i.e., "must" rather than "should"). However, several objections have been put forward to this type of knowledge dissemination. Hammond *et al* [9] point to the problem that guidelines have to be general in order to be applicable in most situations, which in turn makes them too general for any specific situation. The context dependencies present in real design problems are also hard to capture in general guidelines. Hence, human factors knowledge in the form of guidelines can be hard for designers to use in their daily work. There is also some empirical evidence to support this conclusion; de Souza and Bevan [4] showed by means of an experiment that designers had difficulty in interpreting over 90 percent of the general guidelines given for a design task. Tetzlaff and Schwartz [19] reported similar findings.

The Need For Support

It would appear that guidelines and style guide documents are inefficient ways of communicating human factors knowledge to the designer. Not only are the documents difficult to use, but it is also hard for the designers to remember to apply all relevant rules to a particular design problem. Our answer to this dilemma is to investigate ways of bringing human factors support closer to the design process, thus making the human factors knowledge more accessible and operative. The approach we have chosen is to augment the design and implementation environment of a User Interface Management System (UIMS) with a knowledge base containing human factors knowledge. This knowledge is used to evaluate the design built in the UIMS on the designer's request, yielding what is known as a *critiquing* system. The aim is to provide *formative* evaluation, which is defined as evaluation during system design, intended to

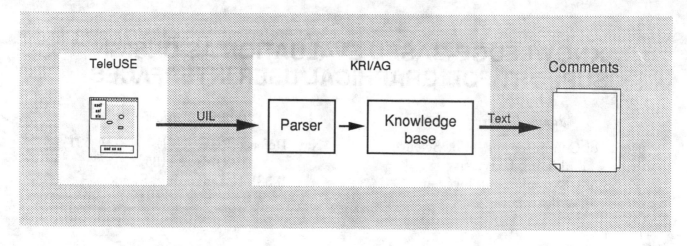

Figure 1: The overall architecture of the current implementation.

provide feedback for subsequent design iterations [10]. We have chosen to address user interfaces built with the Motif^{TM} toolkit since it is one of the emerging *de facto* standards in the software industry, and since the Motif Style Guide [15] contains much design knowledge on a detailed level.

Related Work

Automatic evaluation of user interface design representations has been investigated for at least ten years; some early examples include Reisner's work [16] on assessing simplicity and consistency of commands represented in a BNF grammar and the work by Bleser and Foley [1] on evaluation of a grammar representation with respect to high-level design issues. A more recent approach, using knowledge-based techniques, is illustrated by the Framer system by Lemke and Fischer [11] which is a user interface design environment containing a critiquing system based on general design knowledge. The major differences between Framer and our work are our emphasis on improving upon available knowledge sources, particularly guidelines and style guides, and our notion of runtime evaluation as described below.

ARCHITECTURE

The overall architecture of the KRI/AG prototype system is illustrated in figure 1. The current design environment is the widget editor of the TeleUSE UIMS from Telesoft, which runs under the X Window System^{TM}. This editor, called the VIP, is a graphical widget builder where the various Motif widgets are used as building blocks in constructing a user interface. The design representation can be stored in UIL [5], a *de facto* standard representation for widget instances, which is the language understood by the evaluation system. It is important to point out that the UIL representation covers only the "static" user interface, i.e., the components which can be designed in the UIMS prior to execution of

the system. This includes buttons, menus, forms, etc. but typically excludes the appearance and behaviour of the domain objects. In the current prototype, the VIP runs on a Sun SPARCstation.

KRI/AG is implemented in Epitool, a hybrid expert system shell from Epitec featuring an object-oriented concept representation with inheritance as well as a rule language for writing forward or backward chaining rules. The UIL representation of the user interface to be evaluated is transferred to the DECstation on which KRI/AG runs and parsed into the internal object representation of Epitool. The knowledge base is then applied to the user interface representation, possibly yielding a number of comments on the design.

The Knowledge Base

As stated above, the knowledge base of KRI/AG is built mainly from publicly available sources such as guidelines collections (e.g., Smith and Mosier [18] and Brown [3]) and the Motif Style Guide [15]. The reason for this is that in an earlier project [13], we performed knowledge acquisition almost exclusively along more conventional lines (i.e., eliciting knowledge from a user interface evaluation expert). In this project, we wanted to represent the human factors knowledge of the public sources in a more accessible form.

It can be noted that there is still a fair amount of human expertise represented in the process. One of us, who did most of the interpretation of the guideline documents, is an expert in user interface evaluation. We also used a scenario technique, where an independent expert was given 20 examples of user interface design flaws together with our tentative comments upon them. This material formed the basis for the knowledge acquisition session with the expert, and the results served to validate our analyses of the guidelines. To summarize, the task of building a knowledge base from guidelines and style guides is by no means trivial or mechanical.

```
Rule PopupMenuTitle in OSF_Motif Is
ForAll ?inst WhichIs Motif$XmPopupMenu;
  If
    Not (Class(MenuItem(?inst, 1) = "XmLabel"))
  Then
    MakeComment("The popup menu ", ?inst.Name,
    "does not have a title. Every menu should
    have a unique title placed at the top.
    (Motif Style Guide 4.2.3)");
End;
```

Figure 2: A rule from the KRI/AG knowledge base. Note the typical structure where the user interface representation is examined with respect to design flaws (in this case a missing title in a popup menu).

	General	Motif
Graphical layout	10	4
Menu layout	16	28
Menu dialogue	15	7
Other dialogue	20	0

Table 1: A breakdown of the topics covered by the current KRI/AG knowledge base and the distribution over general guidelines and Motif Style Guide rules. Numbers are percent of the total knowledge base.

In its current state, the knowledge base of KRI/AG comprises about 70 rules and 30 functions[1]. The technique used for producing the comments is what is known as *analytical* critiquing [6], which means that the proposed solution (in this case, the user interface design) is analyzed with respect to possible flaws. The alternative is the *differential* approach, where the critiquing system generates its own solution to the problem and compares it with the one proposed by the user, pointing out the differences and deviations. We have argued elsewhere [12] that the domain of user interface design in general is not eligible to a differential treatment; the reasons are mainly that the problem is not well-defined and that there are many examples of multiple solutions with equal validity.

Figure 2 shows an actual rule from the KRI/AG knowledge base, illustrating the type of knowledge used in analytical critiquing systems. The level of the knowledge is obviously limited to what can be represented in UIL, viz. the layout and composition of widgets. This means that the level of evaluation is accordingly limited to the levels of presentation and syntax.

Table 1 shows a more detailed view of the current contents of the knowledge base in KRI/AG. We can see that roughly 60% of the knowledge base consist of general rules, constructed from the guideline documents. The reason for this is mainly that we spent more time on analysing those documents and validating the results. The remaining 40% consist of Motif-specific knowledge. Almost all of it is concerned with menu layout, organization and interaction. This is an important part of

the Motif Style Guide, but not as dominant as it might appear in our knowledge base. We expect to be able to extend the Motif-specific part of the knowledge base as the analysis of the Style Guide proceeds.

EXAMPLE

This section illustrates the use of KRI/AG to evaluate the user interface of an actual application, built using the TeleUSE UIMS.

The Tactical Map Editor...

Figure 3 illustrates the appearance of the application we chose for evaluation. It is an editor for tactical maps in a military setting, developed at FOA 531. The main window shows a detailed view of an area, with a static map overlayed with symbols representing military units and borders between the areas of responsibility for the different units. The small window to the left is an overview of the whole area covered by the geographic data available. The square indicates the area currently presented in the main window.

Six tools (shown beneath the overview window) are available for the manipulation of the overlay symbols on the map: **Create Unit, Create Border, Create Position, Clear, Move** and **Edit** ("Förband", "Gräns", "Position", "Radera", "Flytta" and "Redigera", respectively). The form in the lower left corner is used to inspect or edit attribute values for the selected unit and to provide new values when a new unit is created. Seven of the nine fields are actually option menus which pop up on a mouse click, giving the user a choice of all permissible values for the field in question.

There are two pulldown menus containing global commands. The left one ("Arkiv") is the typical **File** menu, containing commands such as **Load, Save** and **Exit**. The right one contains commands to set various presentation properties. Finally, the text field at the bottom right is used to present various kinds of textual information.

---

[1]The Epitool environment uses the concept of *functions* to denote procedural domain knowledge units which return values. For purposes of knowledge base size assessments, they may be considered equal to rules.

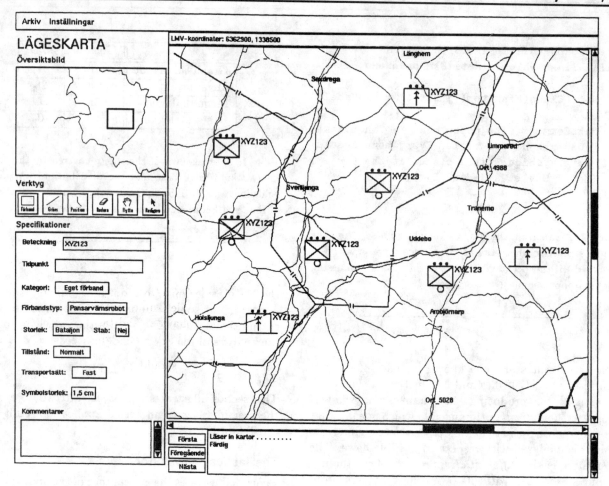

Figure 3: The user interface of the tactical map editor.

...Evaluated

We used VIP to generate a UIL description of the user interface shown in figure 3 and passed the description to KRI/AG. The system generated a number of comments in Swedish, which we present below (translated to English and aggregated since the system, for example, generated the same comment for each of the seven option menus).

- The [text field at the bottom] does not have a label. There should be a label or header above or to the left of it. (Smith and Mosier 1.4:5 and 1.4:17)

- The text fields in [the dialog boxes which appear when the user selects **Save As** or **Open**] do not have default values. (Smith and Mosier 3.1.2:3 and 1.8:1)

- The items in the option menus are in alphabetical order. If there is a logical order, it should be used. Otherwise, if the frequency of use is known, it should be used in ordering the items. (Smith and Mosier 2.5:16–17)

- There is no **Help** menu in the menu bar. Every application should have a **Help** menu. The recom-

mended standard menus in the menu bar are **File**, **Edit**, **View**, **Options** and **Help**, in that order. (Motif Style Guide p. 7-42)

- The menus in the menu bar do not have mnemonics. Specifically, the **File** menu should have the mnemonic **F**. (Motif Style Guide 3.3.3, pp. 7-42, 7-46)

- The items in the **File** menu are not standard. The following items should be in the menu: **New**, **Open**..., **Save**, **Save As**..., **Print** or **Print**..., **Close** and **Exit**. (Motif Style Guide p. 7-23)

- None of the items in the menus of the menubar have accelerators. It is a good idea to use accelerators for the most frequently used items. (Motif Style Guide 3.3.2, 4.2.3, pp. 7-3, 7-4)

By empirical assessment of our previous project [13], we found that references to the guidelines documents were central to acceptance of the evaluation tool. In that system, there was an option which displayed the relevant guideline for each comment generated during evaluation. In KRI/AG, we provide only a reference to the source documents. It would, however, be straightforward to provide an option to present the actual guideline texts and pictures online.

DISCUSSION

Recall that the motivation for our work was the observation that guidelines and style guides seem to be hard to use in practice. The KRI/AG prototype described above represents a first step towards facilitating the use of these knowledge sources in design. This section discusses two of the most important issues raised by our approach: *how to support designers*, and *the appropriate level of evaluation for a design support tool*.

How To Support Designers

In their study of the use of guidelines for user interface design, Tetzlaff and Schwartz [19] concluded that since guidelines were found hard to use, the dependence upon them should be minimized. Instead, toolkits and interactive examples of good designs should be used and the role of the guidelines should be mainly to provide information which is intrinsically unavailable through those vehicles. The similar idea can be found in implemented form in the Framer design environment [11] where a library of initial design skeletons is available to provide starting points for the designer.

Widget builders such as the VIP actually represent a move towards the idea of reusable examples, since some of the widget templates in the modern toolkits are fairly complex and come with a good deal of encapsulated appearance and behaviour. Prominent examples are the FileSelectionDialog and other ready-to-use popup dialogues in Motif. However, as many examples from practice show, it is still not impossible to construct user interfaces which violate general design rules and toolkit-specific style rules. These violations, of course, impair usability as well as the overall impression of the produced system. A particular issue when toolkit-specific style rules are concerned is inter-application consistency (recall the missing mnemonics and **Help** menu in the map editor example above). We believe that a good way of reducing these violations is to augment the design environment with knowledge of general design and specific style, as demonstrated by the KRI/AG system.

When And How? The current system prototype reviews the design only when the designer explicitly requests comments. This is contrary to other work in the area of knowledge-based design environments. In particular, Lemke and Fischer [11] report that their initial Framer system worked in the same way as KRI/AG. They found that it was sometimes hard for the system to give meaningful comments on a design, since the designer had chosen a suboptimal path in the design space early on and pursued it too far before submitting the design for comments. When they reworked

the critiquing module to continuously monitor the designer's work and react as soon as it found anything worth commenting, the resulting system was "more effective." Unfortunately, they do not report any controlled experiments. We regard the issue of critiquing strategy to be a question in need of empirical studies, and we hope to be able to carry out such studies in the near future. This can be done either by implementing an active design evaluation module or by Wizard-of-Oz techniques.

Level Of Evaluation

During the evaluation of our previous user interface evaluation tool [13], we found that evaluation on the level of user tasks was highly desirable. This can also easily be established by examining the knowledge sources used for KRI/AG; both the general guidelines and the Motif Style Guide contain many rules concerning the user's behaviour and tasks. One example from Motif [15, p. 4-21] is the following.

> Applications should provide accelerators for frequently used menu items. In general, accelerators should not be assigned for every menu item in an application.

The crucial word here is "frequently", since there is no way of determining by analysis of a Motif design representation whether a menu item is going to be used frequently. This means that rules such as the one above cannot be properly implemented in an evaluation tool of the KRI/AG type. What we had to do there (compare the seventh comment to the map editor example above) was to leave the judgment to the designer.

There are in general two ways of achieving evaluation on the task level. One is to use a rich design representation where user tasks and domain semantics are specified in the design tool. An example of a design environment based on this idea is UIDE by Foley *et al* [7] where the designer specifies the semantics of the user actions and the domain objects. The other way is to collect and analyze logs from actual tests of the user interface under construction. We believe that the second method, which we call *runtime evaluation* or RTE, is preferable since it is more compatible with existing design tools, does not introduce additional complexity for the designer and relies less on *a priori* assumptions. The rest of this section is devoted to a discussion of how to combine runtime evaluation with the design-time evaluation techniques described so far.

Runtime Evaluation. Other researchers have touched upon the subject of logging interaction and automatically evaluating the resulting data. Siochi and Hix [17] started from the hypothesis that repetitions indicate interesting user behaviour. In a small study, they let subjects use a test interface, collected logs of all the

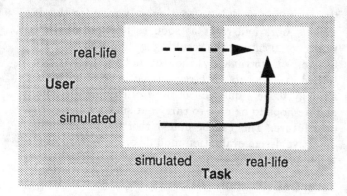

Figure 4: The space of RTE. The solid line shows the approximate time order of different evaluation forms in a traditional waterfall approach to software development, whereas the dashed line illustrates an extremely user-oriented prototyping approach.

interactions and also determined two major usability problems by observation. When their system analyzed the logs with respect to maximal repeating patterns, the same problems were indicated. Olsen and Halversen [14] had earlier shown how logging could be integrated in a UIMS architecture to give metrics concerning the use of different commands. Before we discuss the technical feasibility in our setting, let us introduce a conceptual framework which is intended to relate the idea of RTE to different philosophies of software development.

We propose a two-by-two matrix of RTE where the dimensions are the *task* and the *user* involved in the test situation. The task can be either *simulated* or *real-life*. Simulated tasks can be defined based on the requirement specification or the activity analysis, depending on whether they have been formulated, or they can consist of general handling of the user interface without consideration of the particular tasks in the target environment. Simulated tasks can be tested in the development environment. Real-life tasks, on the other hand, have to be the real tasks that the system is intended to support. Moreover, the tests have to take place in the delivery environment.

On the user dimension, we have *simulated* and *real-life* users. The simulated user can be the original developer, a customer representative, a subject person chosen at random or anyone else who is willing to pretend being the intended user of the system. If a user analysis has been produced earlier in the project, it may be used to aid the "impersonator." A real-life user, as the term implies, is one of the users for whom the system is intended.

This matrix can be used to relate the different forms of RTE to different software development philosophies,

as shown in figure 4. Two examples of different philosophies are illustrated, with the traditional waterfall approach (denoted by a solid line) progressing from simulated tasks through real-life tasks with simulated users and then, in the test phase of the project, to real-life tasks and users. The other example (the dashed line) is an extremely situated design approach where prototyping and development with real-life users are paramount (see, for example, Bødker [2]).

A general property of the matrix is that the cost associated with different forms of evaluation increases with the degree of realism. For example, it is more expensive (in terms of money, time or effort) to carry out a test with real-life tasks than with simulated. It also seems to be the case that the degree of realism is transitive, i.e., a user interface property which can be tested with simulated users or with simulated tasks can also be tested with real-life users or tasks. The reverse relation does not obviously hold.

Properties To Evaluate. The TeleUSE architecture is based on the Seeheim model [8] and uses its own event mechanism and language, called D, for synchronizing the user interface with the functionality of the application. We can expect to be able to collect logs consisting of D events as well as the X events which give low-level information such as keyboard input and mouse position. The idea is then to evaluate these logs using a combination of knowledge-based and algorithmic techniques and to generate comments on the user interface design in analogy with KRI/AG.

While we performed knowledge acquisition for KRI/AG, we formulated many user interface properties of the kind that could not be assessed in design-time evaluation. We will now present some of those properties and indicate how they could be measured using the logs collected during user interface testing.

1. *Long sequences for common operations.* In the way demonstrated by Siochi and Hix, the system can detect repeating sequences and comment upon them if they occur often enough. A case which requires particular attention is when the user has to traverse submenus to reach the desired (frequent) operation.

2. *Switching of interaction techniques during the same task.* If the user is found to be switching from, say, keyboard to mouse and then back again for the same input focus and within a small amount of time, it is worth commenting.

3. *Syntactical inconsistency.* In a graphical user interface, it is desirable that the manipulation syntax is the same throughout the system. This means to consistently use either Object-Command syntax (first select an object or several objects and then

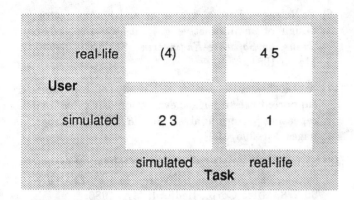

Figure 5: Our sample properties inserted in the evaluation space. An entry in parentheses means that the property can be evaluated to some extent.

apply an operation on it or them) or Command-Object (operation first, then objects). To analyze this, the system can assume that the operations are invoked via the static part of the user interface (buttons, menus, etc.) which is constructed at design-time, whereas the objects of the operations are application-driven.

4. *Detecting errors and help requests.* If the design adheres to Motif standards, errors and help requests can be detected by looking for WarningDialogs and use of the **Help** menus, respectively. Otherwise, the D events corresponding to help request and application errors would have to be tagged in a special way. In both cases, comments showing the dialogue states where more than an average of errors or help requests occurred would be valuable for the designer.

5. *Accelerators for the most frequent operations.* It would be easy to count the number of times different menu items are used and then check for accelerators for the most frequent ones, pointing out possible deficiencies to the designer. Similarly, the system could suggest that a frequently used button in a form containing text input components should be made the default. This would in effect assign the carriage return key as an accelerator for the frequently used button.

To put these properties into the context of user interface development, let us insert them in their cheapest possible places in the RTE matrix, as shown in figure 5. A number in parentheses means that the property can be addressed to some extent. For example, the detection of errors and help requests (property 4) can be done with respect to syntactical errors for a simulated task,

but in order to detect domain errors, a real-life task is needed. If we would now draw a time order arrow reflecting the software development approach used, the resulting picture would show us when we can expect to evaluate the different properties.

SUMMARY

We have shown by means of the KRI/AG prototype how some design knowledge, general guidelines as well as toolkit-specific style guides, can be applied to evaluate a user interface design produced in a UIMS. We believe this to be a valuable step towards bringing human factors knowledge closer to the design process, thus making it more accessible and operative. Our analyses, however, indicate that much of the design knowledge can be applied only by taking into account the actual use situation. We have outlined how data collected during tests of the produced prototype can be used to bring also this use-related design knowledge to bear and presented a framework for relating these tests to the software development approach in use.

ACKNOWLEDGMENTS

The authors want to thank Peter Ericsson from FOA 531 and Lennart Olsson from Enator for implementing the current KRI/AG prototype, and Staffan Löf from FOA 531 for many excellent design ideas and creative discussions. Prof. Sture Hägglund read an earlier version of this paper and gave many useful comments, for which we are grateful. We would also like to thank Nils-Erik Gustafsson from Ellemtel, our expert, for giving us the time we needed with him.

This work has been funded by the National Defense Research Establishment (FOA) and the Swedish Board for Industrial Development of Information Technology (IT4).

Motif is a trademark of The Open Software Foundation, Inc. X Window System is a trademark of the Massachusetts Institute of Technology.

REFERENCES

[1] T. Bleser and J. Foley. Towards specifying and evaluating the human factors of user-computer interfaces. In *CHI'82 Proceedings*, pages 309–314, 1982.

[2] S. Bødker. Through the interface—a human activity approach to user interface design. Lic. thesis DAIMI PB-224, Aarhus University, 1987.

[3] C. Brown. *Human-Computer Interface Design Guidelines.* Ablex Publishing Corp., NJ, 1988.

[4] F. de Souza and N. Bevan. The use of guidelines in menu interface design: Evaluation of a draft standard. In D. Diaper, D. Gilmore, G. Cockton,

and B. Shackel, editors, *Human-Computer Interaction — Interact'90*, pages 435–440. North-Holland, 1990. Participants Edition.

[5] Digital Equipment Corp. *Guide to the XUI User Interface Language Compiler*, 2.0 edition, 1988.

[6] G. Fischer, A. Lemke, T. Mastaglio, and A. Morch. Using critics to empower users. In *CHI'90 Proceedings*, pages 337–347, 1990.

[7] J. Foley, W. Kim, S. Kovačević, and K. Murray. Defining interfaces at a high level of abstraction. *IEEE Software*, pages 25–32, January 1989.

[8] M. Green. Report on dialogue specification tools. In G. Pfaff, editor, *User Interface Management Systems*, pages 9–20. Springer Verlag, Berlin, 1985.

[9] N. Hammond, M. Gardiner, B. Christie, and C. Marshall. The role of cognitive psychology in user-interface design. In M. Gardiner and B. Christie, editors, *Applying Cognitive Psychology to User-interface Design*, chapter 2, pages 13–53. John Wiley & Sons, Chichester, 1987.

[10] S. Howard and M. D. Murray. A taxonomy of evaluation techniques for HCI. In H.-J. Bullinger and B. Shackel, editors, *Human-Computer Interaction — Interact'87*, pages 453–459, 1987.

[11] A. Lemke and G. Fischer. A cooperative problem solving system for user interface design. In *Proceedings Eight National Conference on Artificial Intelligence (AAAI-90)*, pages 479–484, 1990.

[12] Jonas Löwgren. *Knowledge-Based Design Support and Discourse Management in User Interface Management Systems*. Ph. D. dissertation, Linköping University, March 1991. Linköping Studies in Science and Technology # 239.

[13] Jonas Löwgren and Tommy Nordqvist. A knowledge-based tool for user interface evaluation and its integration in a UIMS. In D. Diaper, D. Gilmore, G. Cockton, and B. Shackel, editors, *Human-Computer Interaction — Interact'90*, pages 395–400. North-Holland, August 1990. Also as research report LiTH-IDA-R-90-15.

[14] D. Olsen and B. Halversen. Interface usage measurements in a user interface management system. In *Proc. ACM SIGGRAPH Symposium on User Interface Software (UIST'88)*, pages 102–108. ACM Press, 1988.

[15] Open Software Foundation, Cambridge, MA. *OSF/Motif Style Guide*, 1988. Revision 1.1.

[16] P. Reisner. Formal grammar and human factors design of an interactive graphics system. *IEEE Trans. on Software Engineering*, SE-7(2):229–240, March 1981.

[17] A. Siochi and D. Hix. A study of computer-supported user interface evaluation using maximal repeating pattern analysis. In *CHI'91 Proceedings*, pages 301–305, 1991.

[18] S. L. Smith and J. N. Mosier. Guidelines for designing user interface software. Report ESD-TR-86-278, Mitre Corp., Bedford, MA, 1986.

[19] L. Tetzlaff and D. Schwartz. The use of guidelines in interface design. In *CHI'91 Proceedings*, pages 329–333, 1991.

CONTROLLING USER INTERFACE OBJECTS
THROUGH PRE- AND POSTCONDITIONS

Daniel F. Gieskens

Faculty of Technical Mathematics and Informatics, Delft University of Technology,
Julianalaan 132, 2628 BL Delft, The Netherlands, *e-mail*: daniel@duticai.tudelft.nl

James D. Foley

College of Computing, Georgia Institute of Technology,
Atlanta, GA 30332-0280, *e-mail*: foley@cc.gatech.edu

ABSTRACT

We have augmented user interface objects (i.e. windows, menus, buttons, sliders, etc.) with preconditions that determine their visibility and their enabled/disabled status and postconditions that are asserted when certain actions are performed on the object. Postconditions are associated with each functionally different action on the object. Attaching pre- and postconditions to interface objects provides several useful features, such as selective enabling of controls, rapid prototyping, and automatic generation of explanations and help text.

KEYWORDS: User Interface Tools, Prototyping, Predicates.

INTRODUCTION

Several techniques can be used to describe the dialogue of an application. Some of the best known techniques are transition diagrams, grammars and event languages. As discussed by Green [6], the event model has a greater descriptive power than the former two. A particularly useful form of the event model is to associate pre- and postconditions with dialogue components (actions and/or interface objects). The preconditions of a dialogue component determine when the component would be enabled or activated, while the postconditions are used to describe changes in the state of the interface.

Pre- and postconditions were first used for user interface design by Green [5] as part of a formal specification but were not used at run-time to control the dialogue. In the User Interface Design Environment (UIDE) [2], pre- and postconditions are associated with application actions and are used to describe partial semantics of application actions. These partial semantics are used for many purposes, including selective enabling of menu items, partial explanations of what an action does, providing context sensitive animated help [12], applying correctness-preserving transformations to the interface [1], checking the completeness and consistency of the interface, and dialogue sequencing.

By extending the UIDE mechanism to include all interface objects, we provide finer-grained control than in the original UIDE, which used pre- and postconditions to control only the enabling of individual menu items. While the original UIDE used a set of predefined expressions in its conditions, we now allow arbitrary boolean predicates. The predicates can also be set by the application program, thereby affecting the state of the interface. Predicates can also have special variables which serve to communicate information between interface objects and the application.

Because pre- and postconditions contain semantic information about the dialogue components with which they are associated, they can be used to generate explanations about these dialogue components. For example, if a menu item has a precondition saying that there should be a selected object, a help tool can use this information to tell the user he has to select an object first. If a certain command is not available or if an interface object is disabled, pre- and postconditions of other commands and interface objects can be used to determine the sequence of actions needed to enable the command or the interface object [11].

Pre- and postconditions not only describe semantics, but also encode dynamic behavior. A set of interface objects with pre- and postconditions can implement a complete dialogue without any additional program code.

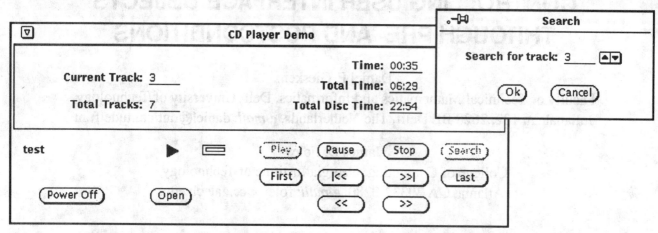

Figure 1   CD player interface implemented with our system. Buttons are selectively enabled and disabled by the preconditions.

Pre- and postconditions also form an interface between a dialogue component and its application. Dialogue components become independent objects which communicate by means of pre- and postconditions. This is somewhat similar to the idea used in VUIMS [10], where the interface consists of objects that communicate by sending tokens to each other. The main difference is that with the pre- and postconditions the messages are predicates that are posted on a 'blackboard', which makes the objects even more independent since they do not need to know who is interested in their information.

In this paper we explain how pre- and postconditions work, then we show how the system supporting this mechanism works. Finally we discuss how a user interface design tool, such as Sun Microsystems' Developers Guide [13], can be experimentally enhanced with this mechanism to support a richer prototyping environment.

In the rest of this article we will use the term widget when we are talking about interface objects. Several examples in this paper use a CD player application. This interface looks similar to the front panel of a real CD player (Figure 1).

PREDICATE MECHANISM

In this system boolean predicates are posted on the "Current State Blackboard" (CSB), which is a list of predicates that are currently true. The CSB is similar to a real-life blackboard: When a predicate becomes true it is written on the blackboard and when it becomes false it is simply erased. Predicates can be written to and removed from the CSB by means of postconditions as well as by the application itself. The application can also determine if a specific predicate is on the CSB. Hence the CSB can be used to exchange semantic information between the application and the interface (UIMS) and thus facilitates separating the application and its interface.

Each predicate consists of a name and two arguments (we can capture any fact or relation in this form). Preconditions are boolean expressions and postconditions are lists of changes to be made in the CSB[1]. Each widget has two sets of preconditions and several postconditions, depending on the type of widget. One set of preconditions determines whether the widget is visible and the other determines whether it is enabled. A button, for instance, may be visible while not being enabled. On the other hand, a widget can never be enabled when it is not visible. Postconditions are associated with each functionally different action on the widget. Some widgets have only one possible functional action (like the select action on a button), while others have several possible actions.

Below are two examples, both taken from the CD player application. Example 1 shows how buttons can be greyed out automatically and example 2 shows how simple program dynamics can be encoded using pre- and postconditions. In the following examples we will describe widgets by stating their type and name (i.e. *menu item save_current_file*), followed by a list of label-value pairs that describe the widget's pre- and postconditions. The labels *pre visible* and *pre enable* stand for the visibility preconditions and the enable preconditions, respectively. The label *post <action>* (i.e. *post select*) describes the postconditions for that specific action on the widget.

Button *stop*
  pre enable: not status(CD,STOPPED)
  post select: status(CD,STOPPED)

Example 1   Selectively enabling of controls - stopping the CD is only available when the CD is not already stopped.

1. Postconditions consist of a list of predicates to be added to the CSB and a list of predicates to be removed from the CSB, an "add" list and a "delete" list, respectively.

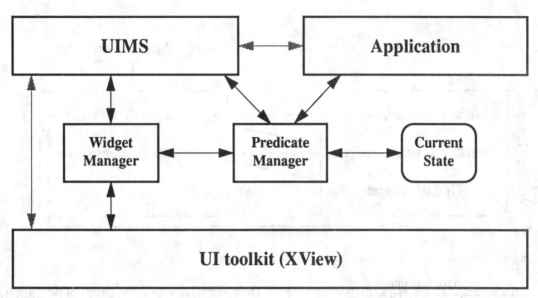

Figure 2   Architecture of the system.

Button *search*
    post select: *popup(SEARCH)*

Popup window *search_track_dialogue*
    pre visible: *popup(SEARCH)*

Example 2   Simple program dynamics - when the search button
             is selected the search-track dialogue window auto-
             matically pops up.

In the previous examples the predicates had literal (constant) arguments, which means the predicate and its arguments must be on the CSB in exactly the same form. Literal
arguments are written in uppercase. Predicates can also have
variable arguments, written in lowercase, in which case the
argument matches with any text (i.e. *current_track(track)*
matches with *current_track(1)*, *current_track(2)*, etc.).
When a predicate containing one or more variables is
matched against predicates in the CSB, both its truth-value
and the literal(s) substituted for its variable(s) are returned.
The literal values are retained, because the same variables
can be used in the postconditions (as in Example 3).

In postconditions functions can be used to modify predicate
arguments. Functions are used to perform simple computations, like increment and decrement (see Example 3), and to
get information from the application.

Button *next_track*
    pre enable: *current_track(curr) and*
                     total_tracks(total) and
                     less_than(curr, total)
    post select: *current_track(inc(curr, 1))*

Example 3   Variables and functions - the variables *curr* and *total*
             get their values, based on what predicates are on the
             CSB. The value of *curr* is used in combination with
             the function *inc* to increment the current track.

Pre- and postconditions form an interface between a widget
and its environment. Its preconditions determine when it is
visible and enabled and the postconditions describe the
changes that result from interactions with the widget. We
define special variables to increase the power of this form of
communication between a widget and its environment. Special variables are variables in predicate arguments with a
special meaning. The currently recognized special variables
are:
  • set_value: sets the value of the widget,
  • get_value: gets the value from the widget,
  • set_image: indicates the name of the bitmap that should
    be used by widgets that display images (icons, messages,
    etc.),
  • upperbound: sets the upper limit of widgets with range
    capabilities (sliders, numeric text items, etc.), and
  • lowerbound: sets the lower limit of widgets with range
    capabilities.

The special variables set_value, set_image, upperbound and
lowerbound can only be used in preconditions, while
get_value can only be used in postconditions. Especially
useful are set_value and get_value, because these allow widgets to communicate their values (as in Example 4) with the
rest of the interface and the application.

Numeric text item *search_track_item*
    pre visible: *visible(SEARCH_WINDOW)*
    pre enable: *current_track(set_value)*
    post changed: *current_track(get_value)*

Example 4   Special variables - the variable *set_value* initializes
             the widget with the current track number. After the
             user has changed the value of the text item, the new
             value is used in the postconditions by means of
             get_value.

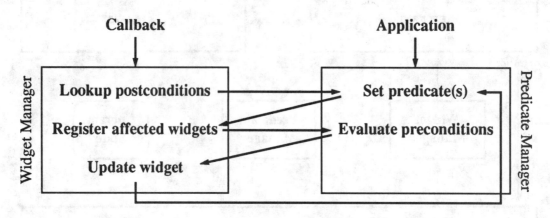

Figure 3   Interaction between the widget manager and the predicate manager.

Normally, when a postcondition is asserted, its effects are propagated immediately. However, sometimes this is not desired. In the search dialogue shown in Figure 1, for instance, the value set by means of the text item should take effect only if and when the 'ok' button is pressed. To make this possible widgets can propose predicates in their postconditions. When the postcondition is asserted, the proposed predicates do not take effect immediately; they are merely recorded as being proposed. Another widget, usually an 'ok' button, can then accept the proposed predicates, as in Example 5.

Numeric text item search_track_item
    pre visible: visible(SEARCH_WINDOW)
    pre enable: current_track(set_value)
    post changed: propose current_track(get_value)

Button search_ok
    pre visible: visible(SEARCH_WINDOW)
    post select: accept search_track_item:proposed

Example 5   Proposed predicates - when the value of the text item is changed a new current track is proposed, but not yet set. When the ok button is selected the proposed change is asserted and the current track is changed.

ARCHITECTURE

The pre- and postconditions are handled by two main components: the predicate manager and the widget manager (Figure 2). These two components form a transparent layer between the application[1] and the toolkit. It is transparent because the application does not need to know about the pre- and postconditions if it does not make use of them.

---

1. The system was originally developed as part of UIDE, where the UIMS part takes care of all the user interface related tasks. However, this system can also be used independently of UIDE. When we talk about the application we mean the application and/or UIMS.

The predicate manager is in charge of the CSB; it is the only part of the system that can write to and read from the CSB. The application is allowed to make changes on the CSB only by calling functions in the predicate manager. This way the predicate manager can always make sure all widgets are updated when there is a change on the CSB. This also allows for changes (in future versions) in the organization of the CSB and the algorithm that evaluates predicate expressions (preconditions). The predicate manager also takes care of parsing and evaluating pre- and postconditions.

The widget manager registers widgets that have pre- and postconditions associated with them. Whenever a widget with pre- and postconditions is to be created, the widget manager asks the UI toolkit to create a normal widget and registers its id, name, pre- and postconditions and predicate variables and stores this information in a 'shadow widget'. The pre- and postconditions supplied by the programmer as text strings are parsed by the widget manager before they are added to the 'shadow widget'. The widget's id is added to a hash table used to find widgets that might need to be updated as a result of changes in the CSB (described later in this section). The widget manager also handles communication with the UI toolkit. When the application wants to retrieve or change widget attribute values, the widget manager first checks if the attributes are of interest to the pre- and postcondition mechanism: In addition to pre- and postconditions, which can be changed and retrieved as normal attributes, the widget manager also needs to know about callback routines, because it has to intercept all callbacks.

When a user interacts with a widget, the underlying UI toolkit generates a callback which invokes a function in the widget manager (Figure 3). The widget manager looks up the postconditions of the corresponding widget and asks the predicate manager to make changes to the CSB. After the predicate manager has done so, it asks the widget manager to supply a list of widgets that might be affected by the changes. The predicate manager reevaluates the precondition for each widget in this list and informs the widget manager about changes in the state of that widget, after which the widget manager asks the UI toolkit to update the widget. After the state of a widget has changed, its children might need to be reevaluated, as a widget cannot be visible if its parent is not visible. Therefore these children are added to the list of potentially affected widgets. The process continues recursively until this list is empty.

EXTENDING DEVELOPERS GUIDE WITH PRE- AND POSTCONDITIONS

Sun Microsystems' Developers Guide (DevGuide) [13] is a user interface layout tool with which the designer can easily lay out a user interface of an application by simply placing and dragging interface objects, such as windows, buttons, sliders, etc. However, it does not incorporate run-time dynamics, such as controlling the (dis)appearing of popup windows. Interface Architect [8] has a built-in C interpreter, which allows the designer to write C callback functions. However, when the designer is laying out a user interface, he usually does not want to write code. In Interface Builder [9] and in version 3.0 of DevGuide it is possible to create 'connections' between interface objects. The designer can drag a connection, displayed as a rubber band line, between two widgets and specify the behavior of the connection. However, this does not address the important need to associate context-specific conditions with the connection, so that it will occur only when the conditions are true: For some dynamic behaviors, semantic information about the state of the application is needed to make the behavior depend on the current run-time context.

We have extended DevGuide to allow the specification of pre- and postconditions. The attributes of widgets created with DevGuide are defined by property sheets, in which the designer can specify properties, such as label text, size, position, color, etc. These property sheets were extended to include fields for pre- and postconditions, so the designer can specify and test run-time dynamics using DevGuide.

Another useful extension would be the mapping of the connections onto pre- and postconditions: the designer specifies connections, while the system generates pre- and postconditions from these connections. This includes the connections in the pre- and postcondition mechanism and allows for better fine tuning; pre- and postconditions generated from connections can be edited, so extra conditions could be added to the connections.

To take full advantage of the pre- and postconditions, we should allow the designer to make changes to the CSB in test mode to simulate changes which would normally be made by the application itself.

CONCLUSIONS & FUTURE WORK

The pre- and postcondition mechanism is useful for prototyping user interfaces, especially in conjunction with other user interface design tools. It allows a designer to change one part of a user interface without affecting other parts. It also allows testing of program dynamics in early design phases. The pre- and postconditions can also be used at run-time to automatically generate help and explanations.

With the architecture presented in this paper, the mechanism can easily be integrated in different environments and can be made to work with a variety of tools and toolkits.

Efficiency does not appear to be a critical issue. However, if better efficiency is needed, several improvements can be made:

- The preconditions are currently evaluated by a rather inefficient backtracking algorithm, which can be replaced by a more efficient algorithm.
- When changes are made to the CSB, the system generates a list of possibly affected widgets. A linear hash table is used to search for these widgets. Using a search tree would improve the time to find these widgets.
- The CSB itself is currently organized as a sorted linear list and determining the truth value of a predicate requires a linear search. The use of a tree structure for the CSB will improve the time to determine the truth value of a predicate.
- Widgets in an interface are organized in a tree structure; most widgets have a parent widget. The system currently uses this information to make sure a child of a non-visible widget is not made visible. This information can also be used to limit the number of widgets of which the preconditions should be reevaluated.

Currently, only one CSB is used for each application. Although this has some advantages, it means all predicates are global. For the same reasons why scoping is used in programming languages, we would like to have some form of scoping for predicates used in pre- and postconditions.

We would like to improve the user interface for specifying pre- and postconditions. This can be as simple as supplying lists of commonly-used predicates from which the designer can select the desired predicates, or as complex as a graphical dialogue editor in which a dialogue is represented by augmented transition networks or petri nets, which can be converted to pre- and postconditions.

Finally we plan to develop a graphical debugging tool, where the dialogue, described by pre- and postconditions, is presented in a graphical form and where the run-time behavior can be traced and possibly modified.

ACKNOWLEDGEMENTS

Daniel Gieskens would like to thank Jim Foley for creating an excellent research environment. We both thank the many George Washington University and Georgia Tech students who provided feedback and help in numerous ways: Dennis de Baar, Won Chul Kim, Piyawadee (Noi) Sukaviriya, Srdjan Kovacevic, Lucy Moran and Jens Kilian. Thanks also to Prof. Hikmet Senay of The George Washington University for his help with predicate logic.

Partial funding for this work was provided by Sun Microsystems' collaborative research program, and by National Science Foundation Grant # IRI-8813179. We thank Bob Ellis of Sun for his skillful management of our research proposal, and Bob Watson, development manager of Sun's DevGuide, for his support and interest.

REFERENCES

[1] Foley, J., C. Gibbs, and W. Kim, "Algorithms to Transform the Formal Specification of a User-Computer Interface" in Proceedings INTERACT '87, 2nd IFIP Conference on Human-Computer Interaction, Elsevier Science Publishers, Amsterdam, 1987, pp. 1001-1006.

[2] Foley, J., W. Kim, S. Kovacevic, and K. Murray, "Defining Interfaces at a High Level of Abstraction", IEEE Software, 6(1), January 1989, pp. 25-32.

[3] Foley, J., D. Gieskens, W Kim, S. Kovacevic, L. Moran, P. Sukaviriya, "A Second-Generation Knowledge Base for the User Interface Design Environment", Report GWU-IIST-91-13, Dept. of Electrical Engineering and Computer Science, George Washington University, Washington D.C., May 1991.

[4] Foley, J., W.C. Kim, S. Kovacevic, and K.Murray, "UIDE - An Intelligent User Interface Design Environment", in Sullivan, J. and Tyler, S. (eds.), *Architectures for Intelligent Interfaces: Elements and Prototypes*, Addison-Wesley, 1991.

[5] Green, M., "The Design of Graphical User Interfaces", Technical Report CSRI-170, Computer Systems Research Institute, University of Toronto, 1985.

[6] Green M., "A Survey of Three Dialogue Models" in ACM Transactions on Graphics 5(3), July 1986, pp. 244-275.

[7] Heller D., "XView Programming Manual", O'Reilly & Associates, Inc., October 1990, ISBN 0-937175-52-8.

[8] Hewlett-Packard Company, "HP Interface Architect Developer's Guide", Hewlett-Packard Company, Corvallis, Oregon, October 1990.

[9] NeXT Computer, Inc., "NeXTstep Concepts", NeXT Computer, Inc., Redwood City, CA, 1990.

[10] Pittman J., and C. Kitrick, "VUIMS: A Visual User Interface Management System" in Proceedings of the ACM SIGGRAPH Symposium on User Interface Software and Technology, Snowbird, Utah, October 1990, pp. 36-46.

[11] Senay H., P. Sukaviriya, L. Moran, "Planning for Automatic Help Generation", Report GWU-IIST-89-10, Dept. of Electrical Engineering and Computer Science, George Washington University, Washington D.C., 1989.

[12] Sukaviriya P., and J. Foley, "Coupling a UI Framework with Automatic Generation of Context-Sensitive Animated Help" in Proceedings of the ACM SIGGRAPH Symposium on User Interface Software and Technology, Snowbird, Utah, October 1990, pp. 152-166.

[13] Sun Microsystems, Inc., "Open Windows Developer's Guide 1.1, Reference Manual", Part No. 800-5380-10, Revision A, of June 1990.

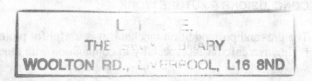

SURVEY ON USER INTERFACE PROGRAMMING

Brad A. Myers

School of Computer Science
Carnegie Mellon University
5000 Forbes Avenue
Pittsburgh, PA 15213
brad.myers@cs.cmu.edu

Mary Beth Rosson

User Interface Institute
IBM T.J.Watson Research Center
P.O.Box 704
Yorktown Heights, NY 10598
rosson@watson.ibm.com

ABSTRACT

This paper reports on the results of a survey of user interface programming. The survey was widely distributed, and we received 74 responses. The results show that in today's applications, an average of 48% of the code is devoted to the user interface portion. The average time spent on the user interface portion is 45% during the design phase, 50% during the implementation phase, and 37% during the maintenance phase. 34% of the systems were implemented using a toolkit, 27% used a UIMS, 14% used an interface builder, and 26% used no tools. The projects using only toolkits spent the largest percentage of the time and code on the user interface (around 60%) compared to around 45% for those with no tools. This appears to be because the toolkit systems had more sophisticated user interfaces. The projects using UIMSs or interface builders spent the least percent of time and code on the user interface (around 41%) suggesting that these tools are effective. In general, people were happy with the tools they used, especially the graphical interface builders. The most common problems people reported when developing a user interface included getting users' requirements, writing help text, achieving consistency, learning how to use the tools, getting acceptable performance, and communicating among various parts of the program.

CR CATEGORIES AND SUBJECT DESCRIPTORS: H.5.2 [**Information Interfaces and Presentation**]: User Interfaces-*Evaluation/methodology, User Interface Management Systems, Windowing Systems*; D.2.2 [**Software Engineering**]: Tools and Techniques-*User Interfaces*;

GENERAL TERMS: Design, Human Factors

ADDITIONAL KEYWORDS AND PHRASES: User Interface Software, Surveys, User Interface Tools.

INTRODUCTION

We were tired of seeing references to papers from 1978 for data about how much of the time and code in applications is devoted to the user interface. Surely with modern window managers, toolkits, interface builders and UIMSs, the data have changed! Therefore, we decided to conduct a new survey to determine what user interface programming is like today. This paper reports on the results of that survey.

These results will be useful for a number of purposes. First, they will help user interface developers demonstrate to their managers that, in fact, most projects spend significant time and resources on designing and programming the user interface portion. Indeed, the numbers reported here might be used by managers to predict the type and amount of resources to be directed toward user interface development. Second, the data clearly show that most projects are using user interface development tools, and that these tools are generally effective and of significant help to the projects. Third, the results can be used to support proposals to research and develop new user interface tools and techniques, and the survey reports on some specific problems and recommendations for new tools. Some of the questions on the survey investigated how the various projects were organized, the process used to develop the user interface, and what tools were used. Therefore, the survey provides a snapshot of how user interface design and implementation is performed today.

Clearly, user interfaces for programs have increased in sophistication, with the use of direct manipulation and WYSIWYG styles, mice, window managers, etc. This, in turn, has made the programming task more difficult. However, tools to help with user interface software have also become more sophisticated and helpful. The data collected tends to suggest that interface builders and UIMSs are helping to decrease the programming task.

RELATED WORK

There have been very few surveys of user interface software. The ones that people usually reference are quite outdated and inconclusive. For example, an IBM study found that the user interface portion of the code was between 29% and 88% [14]. In artificial intelligence applications, an informal poll found it was about 50% of the code [2], which is similar to the results of one AI project which reported 40% [6].

A recent paper discusses a number of reasons why user interface software is *inherently* more difficult to create than other kinds of software, and argues that we should not expect this problem to be "solved" [11]. These reasons include: that iterative design is necessary which makes using software engineering techniques more difficult, that multiprocessing is required to deal with asynchronous events from the user and window system, that the performance of the resulting interface must be fast enough to keep up with users, that there is an absolute requirement for robustness so the interface never crashes, and that the tools for developing user interface software can be very difficult to use.

USER INTERFACE TOOLS

To make user interfaces easier to program, many different kinds of tools have been created. These include window systems, toolkits, interface builders, and user interface management systems (UIMSs). Comprehensive definitions and surveys of these tools can be found in many places [4, 11].

A *window system* is a software package that divides the computer screen into different areas for different contexts. Although a more common term is *window manager*, some systems use that term only for the user interface, and use "window system" for the programming interface.

A *toolkit* is a collection of widgets such as menus, buttons, and scroll bars. When developing a user interface using a toolkit, the designer must be a programmer, since toolkits themselves only have a programmatic interface.

An *interface builder* is a graphical tool that helps the programmer create dialog boxes, menus and other controls for applications. It provides a palette showing the widgets available in some toolkit, and allows the designer to select and position the desired widgets with the mouse. Other properties can then be set. Interface builders are limited to only laying out the static parts of the interface that can be created out of widgets, however. They cannot handle the parts of the user interface that involve graphical objects moving around.

By our definition, a *User Interface Management System* (UIMS) is a more comprehensive tool than an interface builder. A UIMS covers more of the application's user interface than just dialog boxes and menus. Typically, it will provide help with creating and managing the insides of application windows.

Some tool makers have reported significant gains in productivity by users of their tools. For example, the MacApp tool from Apple has been reported to reduce development time by a factor of four or five [13]. As another example, designers were able to create new, cus-

tom widgets about 15 times faster with the experimental Peridot system than by coding the widget using conventional techniques [7].

SURVEY METHODOLOGY

A draft of the survey was circulated on the SIGCHI electronic mailing list, and a number of useful comments were incorporated. The final survey was published in the *SIGCHI Bulletin* [9] and *SIGPLAN Notices* [10]. Also, it was distributed on several electronic bulletin boards and sent explicitly to a number of people. The responses were all received between April, 1991 and November, 1991.

We should emphasize that although some of the respondents were recruited directly, the majority were self-selected. However, given the breadth of the response (as shown in Figure 1), we feel the results will be useful in a variety of personal computer and workstation contexts.

An important goal of the survey was to differentiate the time and code spent on the "user interface portion" of the application from the rest. Unfortunately, previous surveys have shown that many people have difficulty separately identifying these two parts [12]. Therefore, at the beginning of the survey, we included the following paragraphs:

> The term "user interface" is notoriously difficult to define. In this survey, we intend it to mean the software component of an application that *translates a user action into one or more requests for application functionality*, and that provides to the user *feedback about the consequences of his or her action*. This software component (or components) would be distinguished from the underlying computation that goes on in support of the application functionality. Also, we are *not* including the part of the application that generates hardcopy output (e.g., for printing) in the user interface component.

> If you are not happy with our definition, please describe why. However, in answering the remaining questions, please try to apply this definition as best as you can.

No one reported any difficulty with our definition, or entered a different one.

SURVEY RESULTS

We received responses from 74 individuals representing a variety of countries and types of organizations (see Figure 1). 70% came from the US, 15% were from Europe, 8% were from Canada, and 7% were from other places. Most respondents are part of the software industry, either in software development companies (44%) or software research labs (29%), with the remainder from universities (27%). Thus it is not surprising that most of the applications described were developed as commercial, internal or military products (75%). Although the data include a reasonable number of research systems (25%), most of the respondents indicated that they intended these systems to be used by others; virtually none of the systems are "throw-aways."

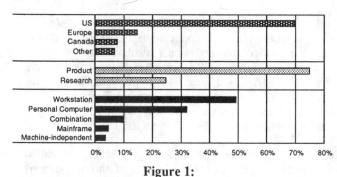

Figure 1:
Distribution of survey responses across countries, type of project, and host computer. The "Combination" systems used multiple types of computers at the same time. The "Machine-independent" systems were designed to run on different kinds of computers.

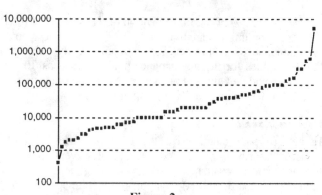

Figure 2:
Total number of lines of code on a log scale (for the 68 systems that reported a value).

Systems

We asked that the answers to the survey questions be based on a single recently-developed application. Application domain was quite varied, including programs intended for sophisticated users (e.g., operating system services and diagnostics, window managers), programming aids (e.g., structured editors and browsers, visual languages), process control and military systems, office applications of many sorts (e.g., database and accounting systems, word processing, data analysis), simulation and CAD systems, educational software, and even a few games. These includes a number of major, well-known commercial products.

As can be seen in Figure 1, the most common hosts for these applications were either workstations (49%) or personal computer systems (32%). The workstations include 8 systems for Sun, 4 for DECStations, 4 for HP, 2 for Silicon Graphics, and one each for RS6000, Intel, Apollo, and Tandem. 14 workstation systems did not specify which platform was used. The personal computer category includes 12 programs for IBM PCs or compatibles, 9 for Macintosh, 2 for PS/2, and one for an Amiga. There were also 4 systems for mainframes, and 3 systems designed to be portable across multiple machines. One of the interesting results is that a significant number of the systems (7, which is 10%) involved a user interface on a smaller computer which was in communication with a bigger computer. These are labeled "Combination" in Figure 1.

A majority of systems (51, which is 69%) used the C programming language. Other languages used included Assembly language (9 systems), Fortran (7), C++ (8), UIL (the OSF Motif description language: 5), Hypertalk (3), Pascal (2), Objective-C (3), Ada (3), Yacc and Lex (2), Lisp (2), and one system each for Basic, Visual Basic, Cobol, Visual Cobol, PL/1, Enfintalk, Smalltalk, Modula-2, Object Pascal, Bliss, Forth, and Self. All the Ada applications were military. A very interesting result is that 58% of the systems were written using *multiple* languages, which is reflected in the counts above. Often, this was a higher-level language and assembly language, or C++ and C, but other times, a special-purpose user interface language was used along with a "regular" programming language.

We asked whether the applications required the end users to have any special training to use the system (assuming they already had knowledge of the application area), and 48% said "none." 24% reported that the system could be learned with just a few minutes of demonstration or exploration, 17% indicated it would take a few hours, and 12% reported that more substantial training (over a period of days) would be needed. Hopefully, this reflects a growing ease of use of the applications being written, rather than an unrealistically optimistic view of the user interfaces. 15 respondents did not supply any data on this question.

Developers

Most of the people who filled out the survey were experienced programmers. The median years of experience was 7, and the median number of applications developed was 5. Most of the projects (72%) involved multiple persons, although only 7% of the development groups had greater than 10 individuals. The largest project reported 200 developers, but some large projects did not report the number. For the multi-person projects, the respondent was usually the manager or the person in charge of the user interface. In some cases, domain experts or future users were part of the development team, and a few projects used consultants to help in designing the user interface.

Size of Applications

There was an enormous range in the size of applications: from 400 lines of code up to 5,000,000 (see Figure 2); the average was 132,000 lines and the median was 19,000. In terms of number of man-years for the entire project, the range was 0.01 man years (about 1 week), up to "several hundred" man years.[1] The median was 2 man years.

Breakdown of Development Time

We asked what percent of the time was spent on each of the phases of the development. 40 projects provided full answers to this question. For these, the results were an

---

[1] To put the upper bound into perspective, it was reported that by the time the WordPerfect word processor program for Microsoft Windows is shipped, an estimated 120 man-years will have been poured into the project by programmers and in-house testers [16].

average of 20.3% of the time spent on design, 49.5% of the time spent on implementation, and 30.3% of the time spent on maintenance. 20 projects were not sufficiently finished to have values for the maintenance phase (or at least they did not provide a value). For these, the average times were 34.8% for design and 65.2% for implementation.

User Interface of Applications

In an effort to characterize the user interfaces of the projects described, we offered respondents several checklists of interface characteristics, covering input (e.g., mouse, keyboard, tablet), output (e.g., bitmap, alphanumeric, audio), interaction techniques (e.g., menus, commands, buttons, dialog boxes), and presentation techniques (e.g., charts, drawings, images).

Most (82%) of the systems used a mouse. Only one system reported using an exotic input device, and it was a scanner to read text. None reported using a DataGlove, touch tablet, video camera, etc. Similarly, few used unusual output devices: 70% supported only bitmap screens, 16% supported only character terminals, and 13% supported both. 72% of the systems supported color. Only 6 systems reported using audio output for anything other than beeping. These included digitized audio in multi-media presentations, audible ticks as feedback during tracing, synthetic speech for blind users, and simple voice messages.

78% of the applications ran under a window system. The most popular were X/11 (40%), Macintosh (16%) and Microsoft Windows (5%); others mentioned were Amiga, Gem, DECWindows, HP-VUE, Next, Presentation Manager, Silicon Graphics, SunView, Symbolics, Vermant Views and Zinc. Six systems used internally developed window packages, and one system supported multiple windowing systems. Of those using X/11, 52% used OSF Motif, 13% used OpenLook, and 35% used a different X/11 window manager, such as uwm or twm. These results are consistent with the distribution of machine types shown in Figure 1.

Independent of whether a window system was used, the survey asked whether multiple windows were used as part of the system's user interface. This is relevant, since a program not on a window system might implement windows internally, and a program on top of a window system may only use a single window. 73% of the applications used multiple windows in their interface. Of these, 57% used only overlapping windows, 20% used only tiled windows, and 22% used both kinds. It is interesting to note that 14% of the applications that were implemented on top of a window system did *not* use windows in their user interface, and 33% of the systems that were not implemented on top of a window system still *did* use windows (presumably, implemented internally in their application). Of the last group, about half were tiled and half were overlapping. Most of these were on a PC; one was on a mainframe. We speculate that they might have built their own window systems because the projects were started before appropriate window systems were available on those platforms.

84% of the applications used some kind of menu. Menus were popular even with applications not using a mouse, with over half of the non-mouse systems having menus. Property sheets (also called forms or dialog boxes), were also very popular, and were used by 89% of the systems. Direct manipulation graphical objects (where graphical objects or icons can be selected and manipulated using a mouse) were used by 55% of the applications.

Most user interfaces incorporated graphical presentation techniques to some extent, with 70% of the applications using 2-D graphics, and 14% using 3-D graphics. Over half of the applications (55%) indicated that they had developed specialized graphical representations of application data (maps, charts, gauges, plots); 23% employed wireframe or rendered drawings.

UI Development Process

We asked respondents to describe the process they followed in developing the user interface. Many (42%) indicated that the work had been very evolutionary in nature, with design and implementation of the user interface proceeding in parallel (intertwined). Almost all (89%) described some effort aimed at gathering and responding to user input, consistent with the iterative development methodology promoted by user interface specialists [1, 3]. 43% reported some level of formal testing with end users prior to release, with only two respondents indicating that the testing had little or no effect. Of the seven respondents not describing any interactions with users, two indicated that the user interface had been based on some other already tested system.

The most common user interface development process (46%) was to build one or more prototypes, which were often offered to users for comments or testing. In a few cases, these prototypes became the released product, but more frequently they were part of earlier design activities. One project complained that the actual implementation team ignored the user interface team's carefully constructed prototype, but most reported that the prototype guided the final design. Other projects (17%) carried out evaluations of paper designs.

Other techniques for considering the needs of end users were also described. In some cases (11%), this involved participatory design in which end users contributed directly to the design of the user interface; in others, the design team interviewed users or observed them at work. 12% of the respondents claimed to have developed user scenarios as part of their design process.

Two projects reported developing a style guide as part of the systems' development. Most of the Motif projects reported using the OSF Motif Style Guide, and most of the Macintosh projects relied on the Apple Human Interface Guidelines. One project reported following the IBM CUA style guide, and one received guidance from several user interface textbooks.

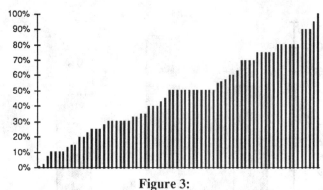

Figure 3:
The percent of the code devoted to the user interface
(for the 71 systems that reported a value).

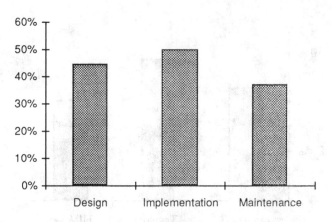

Figure 4:
The average percent of the time devoted to the user
interface during the various phases of the system
development (N = 63 for design, N = 63 for implementation and N = 42 for maintenance) .

Tools Used

Most of the projects (74%) used tools of some sort in
developing the code for their user interfaces. For many
projects (34%) this consisted of a toolkit providing a library
of user interface components (e.g., menus, buttons). As for
the case with window managers, the most common toolkits
were those for X11 systems (e.g., Motif, OpenLook) and
for the Macintosh. Other toolkits mentioned included the
Amiga, Athena Widget Set, DecWindows, Interviews, Objective C library, Silicon Graphics, SunView, and Vermont
Views.

Other projects used more sophisticated tools, often in con-
cert with a supporting toolkit. So, for example, 20 projects
(27%) reported the use of a UIMS. Five of these used
Hypercard; other UIMSs included Designer Forms,
Domain Dialog, Easel, Enfin, Garnet, Lex/Yacc, Menlo
Vista Forms, MetaWindows/Plus, Visual Basic and Visual
Cobol. Two projects used internally-developed UIMSs.
Ten projects (14%) used interface builders; these included
DevGuide, HP-UIMX, MacFlow, Next Interface Builder,
TAE+, VUIT, and WindowsMaker.

User Interface Programming

A major goal of the survey was to assess the code and
effort spent on developing the user interfaces of applications. Thus we asked respondents to estimate the percent
of code devoted to the user interface, as well as the percent
of time spent designing, implementing and maintaining the
interface. The code percentage estimates ranged from 1%
to 100%, with an average of 47.6% (see Figure 3).
Respondents spent an average of 44.8% of design time on
the user interface, 50.1% of implementation time, and
37.0% of maintenance time (Figure 4). These estimates did
not differ significantly as a function of the type of application described, the country in which the work was done, or
the host computer system.

These estimates do seem to be related to the kinds of tools
the projects used in building their user interfaces. We
grouped projects according to the tool use they reported: in
Figures 5 and 6, 'No Tools' refers to respondents who
reported the project used no special user interface programming tools; 'Toolkit' refers to those reporting use of a

toolkit only; and 'UIMS or Builder' refers to those reporting use of a UIMS or of an interface builder (whether or
not they also reported using a toolkit). The code percent
for the 'No Tools' group was 45.2%, for the 'Toolkit'
group it was 57.0%, and for the 'UIMS or Builder' group,
40.6%. Comparable figures for the implementation time
estimates were 44.0%, 64.9%, and 41.2%. These data suggest that the projects reporting use of toolkits devoted more
code and spent more time implementing their user interfaces (the trend is marginally significant for the code percent measure, Kruskal-Wallis Chi-Square (2) = 5.54, p <
.07; Kruskal-Wallis Chi-Square (2) = 10.34, p < .01, for
implementation time).

The differences in these estimates between the 'UIMS or
Builder' group and the 'Toolkit' group are what one would
expect: UIMSs and interface builders are intended to
provide high-level programming support and management
of the kinds of user interface components provided by
toolkits, and thus should reduce the time and code devoted
to user interface development. However, we were
surprised to see that the estimates for projects using no
tools at all were also less than those for the groups using
toolkits. One possibility is that the developers in the 'No
Tools' group were attempting less in terms of user interface, either because they knew they did not have the appropriate tools, or because their applications had simpler
user interface needs.

In an effort to examine this issue, we used respondents'
reports of interface techniques as a rough measure of the
complexity of the user interface, summing together the
number of interface features they had checked from our
lists of input, output, interaction, and presentation characteristics. Although the actual numbers have little meaning,
the comparison across the three levels of tool use was as
expected, with the fewest techniques reported by projects
using no tool support (Kruskal Wallis Chi-Square (2) =
9.88, p < .01). The greatest number of techniques were
reported by the projects using toolkits only. Toolkits are

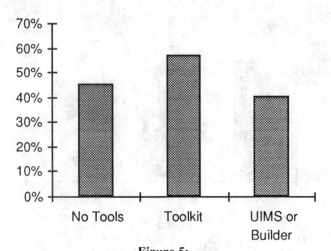

Figure 5:
Comparison of the average percent of the *code* devoted to the user interface for projects with different levels of tool use (N = 18 for No Tools, N = 25 for Toolkit and N = 27 for UIMS or Builder.

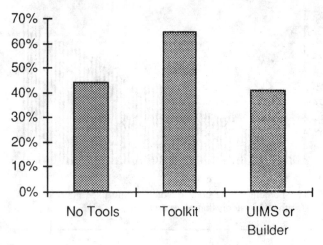

Figure 6:
Comparison of the average percent of the *implementation time* devoted to the user interface for projects with different levels of tool use. (N = 15 for No Tools, N= 22 for Toolkit and N = 26 for UIMS or Builder).

sometimes promoted over UIMSs or builders because they offer greater flexibility to the application programmer [5]. These survey results are consistent with this claim, in that projects relying on toolkits incorporated a larger number of features into their user interfaces, but at greater cost with respect to implementation time and code.

We were also curious about the relative impact of different user interface characteristics, so we did a series of analyses contrasting projects who did or did not incorporate a given feature. Given the post hoc nature of these analyses, the findings must be interpreted with caution. This caveat aside, we found that the strongest predictor of design time was the use of menus (systems using menus devoted 49.1% of design time to user interface vs. 24.6% for those not using menus; Kruskal-Wallis Chi-Square (1) = 6.78, p < .01). This could be due simply to the fact that applications with more complex functionality are more likely to need menus; it could also be that menu organization, terminology and interaction are seen as an important usability concern and thus are likely to increase the relative time spent on user interface design. The factor most likely to increase both implementation time and percent of code was the use of a bitmap display (bitmap applications devoted 55.6% of implementation time to user interface vs. 32.6% for non-bitmap, Kruskal-Wallis Chi-Square (1) = 8.58, p < .01; and 51.9% vs. 32.0% of the code, Kruskal-Wallis Chi-Square (1) = 7.18, p < .01). This seems likely to be due to the enablement of more sophisticated graphical interfaces with bitmap displays, but again at greater implementation cost.

Modifications

51% of the respondents reported that they had been able to re-use part of older code when creating this system. We asked if the system was modularized well enough so that the user interface could be modified without changing the application code. Not surprisingly, most (76%) said yes. However, it is interesting to note that some of the users of

modern toolkits, like Motif, said that their code was tightly coupled to the particular toolkit, and therefore was not well modularized.

18% of the systems claimed to support different natural languages (such as English and French). For those that did not, 28 respondents estimated how long would take to convert to another language, with an average of 1.8 months. The most common technique suggested for separating the user interface from the rest of the application was to put all the text strings into a separate file.

Evaluation of the Tools

In general, the respondents were quite pleased with the tools they used. When available, interface builders were especially appreciated, and were mostly thought to be easy to use. Another important feature mentioned more than once was the ability to execute the interface (including application functions) while still inside the interactive tools. When interactive tools were not available, people wished they had them. Recently, a large number of interface builders have appeared for almost every toolkit, so finding a builder will probably not be a problem for future projects.

Some quotes:

> [The toolkit has a] well-designed look-and-feel and api. [The interface builder] generated good samples of the (then) evolving api.

> [The toolkit] is very easy to learn, even with limited windows experience.

> [The toolkit] gives [us] a lot of low-level control.

> I could get a prototype up to show people relatively quickly.

> [I liked best] the ease of development and fast development and enhancement times involved. After all, we were (and are) able to achieve our objectives the simple way.

The ... interface builder was powerful (very little coding) and easy to use.

[I liked] drawing dialog boxes interactively; [it was] like using a straight-forward drawing program. [I also liked] the code generation ... [and] source code "maintenance" of [the interface builder]. It lets you define source code modules you require and it generates the makefile for you automatically.

Using the [UIMS] enhanced our productivity significantly.

Many of the complaints dealt with performance problems and bugs in the tools. Other common problems were that the tools were difficult to learn to use, and too slow. For example, some comments were:

[The toolkit has a] poorly designed look-and-feel [and an] unusually poor application-programming interface....

Both [the graphics package and the toolkit] are absurdly complex and inefficient. They're slow, poorly documented, plagued by bugs, and eat *incredible* amounts of memory to perform the simplest tasks, which they then neglect to de-allocate. It also requires ridiculous amounts of code to perform those tasks. True, it is quite flexible....

[The toolkit had a] high learning curve. [With it, we are] prone to make mistakes (such as wrong type or number of arguments).

[I like least the] annoying licensing restrictions. We rejected more than one tool simply because we didn't want to sign up for eternal bookkeeping of license fees.

[The tool] doesn't let you create the standard ... look and feel—this is true in many ways, large and small. This was enormously costly in time and salaries as we tried over and over again to compensate for simple flaws....

To be fair, many of these projects used early versions of the tools, and one might expect that some of the problems have been fixed in more recent versions.

Some users called for extended capabilities such as the ability to draw the dynamic parts of windows. Since a few research tools, such as Lapidary [8] and DEMO [15], now support this, we can hope that commercial products will provide this capability in the near future.

Most difficult aspects of the development of the UI

There were many interesting responses to the question about the most difficult aspects of the development of the user interface. Many of these related to the *design* of the user interface, rather than its implementation. The most commonly raised issues about the design were:

- Getting information from users about what they want, and trying to predict their requirements.
- Designing for the naive user while accommodating the experts.
- Writing the help and documentation text so untrained users could understand it.
- Achieving consistency, especially when there are multiple developers.
- Selecting colors and fonts.
- Understanding and conforming to Motif guidelines.
- Finding appropriate user testing subjects.

Some of these problems can be seen as challenges for future tool developers. For example, future tools can probably help achieve consistency, select colors and fonts, and enforce conformance with guidelines.

The issues raised about the *implementation* included:

- Learning how to use the X library. (But one respondent highly recommended the book by Young [17] to help with this.)
- Achieving acceptable performance.
- Communicating between the user interface part and the application part. This includes problems with the use of call-back procedures.
- Communication between different computer languages.
- Getting enough physical memory. (Almost all DOS users and some Macintosh users complained about memory management.)
- Portability across different windowing systems (e.g., PC and X).
- Finding bugs in the user interface software. One large-scale project noted that the automatic testing mechanisms used by the company did not find a number of serious mouse-driven bugs.

Again, these are clearly issues that future tools, and even future versions of today's tools, would be expected to handle.

CONCLUSIONS

From this survey, we can tell that user interface development is a significant part of the design and development task, and that user interface tools are being extensively used to help. Users are being involved in the design of most systems, and the design and implementation are often intertwined. Today's tools seem to be helping designers create more sophisticated user interfaces, and the UIMSs and interface builders are helping to decrease the percent of effort devoted to the user interface. However, the amount of time devoted to the user interface has not yet been substantially reduced by the tools. The challenges for future tool creators seem to be to provide tools which are easier to learn and which significantly increase the efficiency of the user interface designers.

ACKNOWLEDGEMENTS

First, we would like to thank all the respondents for filling out the surveys, as well as their managers for allowing them to. Also, a few people were instrumental in getting us surveys from their organizations. For help with this paper, we would like to thank Brad Vander Zanden and Bernita Myers.

This research was partially sponsored by the Avionics Lab, Wright Research and Development Center, Aeronautical Systems Division (AFSC), U. S. Air Force, Wright-Patterson AFB, OH 45433-6543 under Contract F33615-90-C-1465, Arpa Order No. 7597. The views and conclusions contained in this document are those of the authors and should not be interpreted as representing the official policies, either expressed or implied, of the U.S. Government.

REFERENCES

1. John M. Carroll and Mary Beth Rosson. Usability Specifications as a Tool in Iterative Development. In H. Rex Hartson, Ed., *Advances in Human-Computer Interaction, Volume 1*, Ablex Publishing, New York, 1985, pp. 1-28.

2. Mark Fox. Private communication. Carnegie Group, Inc., Pittsburgh, PA. 1986.

3. J.D. Gould and C.H. Lewis. "Designing for Usability - Key Principles and What Designers Think". *Comm. ACM 28*, 3 (March 1985), 300-311.

4. H. Rex Hartson and Deborah Hix. "Human-Computer Interface Development: Concepts and Systems for Its Management". *Computing Surveys 21*, 1 (March 1989), 5-92.

5. Ed Lee, Mark Linton, John Ousterhout, Len Bass, and Frank Hall. Interface development tools: Feast or Famine (panel). ACM SIGGRAPH Symposium on User Interface Software and Technology, Proceedings UIST'91, Hilton Head, SC, Nov., 1991.

6. Sanjay Mittal, Clive L. Dym, and Mahesh Morjaria. "Pride: An Expert System for the Design of Paper Handling Systems". *IEEE Computer 19*, 7 (July 1986), 102-114.

7. Brad A. Myers. *Creating User Interfaces by Demonstration*. Academic Press, Boston, 1988.

8. Brad A. Myers, Brad Vander Zanden, and Roger B. Dannenberg. Creating Graphical Interactive Application Objects by Demonstration. ACM SIGGRAPH Symposium on User Interface Software and Technology, Proceedings UIST'89, Williamsburg, VA, Nov., 1989, pp. 95-104.

9. Brad A. Myers and Mary Beth Rosson. "User Interface Programming Survey". *SIGCHI Bulletin 23*, 2 (April 1991), 27-30.

10. Brad A. Myers and Mary Beth Rosson. "User Interface Programming Survey". *SIGPLAN Notices 26*, 8 (Aug. 1991), 19-22.

11. Brad A. Myers. State of the Art in User Interface Software Tools. In H. Rex Hartson and Deborah Hix, Ed., *Advances in Human-Computer Interaction, Volume 4*, Ablex Publishing, 1992, pp. (in press).

12. Mary Beth Rosson, Suzanne Maass, and Wendy A. Kellogg. Designing for Designers: An Analysis of Design Practices in the Real World. Human Factors in Computing Systems, CHI+GI'87, Toronto, Ont., Canada, April, 1987, pp. 137-142.

13. Kurt J. Schmucker. "MacApp: An Application Framework". *Byte 11*, 8 (Aug. 1986), 189-193.

14. Jimmy A. Sutton and Ralph H. Sprague, Jr. A Study of Display Generation and Management in Interactive Business Applications. Tech. Rept. RJ2392, IBM Research Report, Nov., 1978.

15. David Wolber and Gene Fisher. A Demonstrational Technique for Developing Interfaces with Dynamically Created Objects. ACM SIGGRAPH Symposium on User Interface Software and Technology, Proceedings UIST'91, Hilton Head, SC, Nov., 1991, pp. 221-230.

16. . "WordPerfect for Windows in The Final Stretch". *WORDPERFECT REPORT 5*, 3 (Fall 1991), 1-3.

17. Douglas A. Young. *The X Window System: Programming and Applications with Xt*. Prentice-Hall, Englewood Cliffs, N.J., 1989.

ORDERABLE DIMENSIONS OF VISUAL TEXTURE
FOR DATA DISPLAY: ORIENTATION, SIZE AND CONTRAST

Colin Ware and William Knight
Faculty of Computer Science
University of New Brunswick
P.O. Box 4400
Fredericton, NB. E3B 5A3
Canada
cware@UNB.ca

ABSTRACT

Vision research relating to the human perception of texture is briefly reviewed with a view to arriving at the principal dimensions of visual texture useful for data display. The conclusion is that orientation, size (1/spatial frequency), and contrast (amplitude) are the primary orderable dimensions of texture. Data displayed using these texture parameters will be subject to similar distortions to those found when color is used. Textures synthesized using Gabor function primitives can be modulated along the three primary dimensions. Some preliminary results from a study using Gabor functions to modulate luminance are presented which suggest that: perceived texture size difference are approximately logarithmic, a 5% change in texton size is detectable 50% of the time, and large perceived size differences are do not predict small (just noticeable) size differences.

KEYWORDS: Scientific visualization, visual texture, Cartography

INTRODUCTION

A single pixel on a colour monitor can display three dimensions of information. This fact derives from the three cone receptor types in the human eye (which requires that three differently coloured phosphors are required to display coloured images on a monitor). From the standpoint of information display this means that it is theoretically possible to represent a trivariate map, a map with three kinds of information continuously represented on a plane (although even bivariate colour coded maps can be confusing [22]). If more than three dimensions of map information are to be represented then two choices exist: either a time varying image can be constructed, or some

spatial resolution can be sacrificed so that information can be stored in the patterning or texturing of the image. The purpose of this paper is to present a model for visual texture optimized for information display. This model is derived from some of the fundamental results of visual psychophysics which suggest that the primary ordered dimensions of visual texture are orientation, size and contrast.

The analysis of the human visual response to sinusoidal grating patterns and Gabor function stimuli has yielded a great wealth of information concerning the human visual response to texture.[1] The first essential concept concerns spatial units. Vision researchers commonly describe repetitive patterns by the angle subtended at the eye of each component. The spatial frequency of a repetitive pattern of stripes is the the number of pattern cycles per unit angle (typically degrees) subtended at the eye. Over the last two decades, beginning with the now classic papers by Campbell and Robson [9] and Blakemore and Campbell [6], hundreds of researchers have probed the human vision system in its responses to simple patterns consisting of sinusoidally modulated gratings. Based on this research it has been proposed that the visual system contains "channels" which are selectively sensitive to spatial frequency and to orientation. A short lived, early view that the visual system might be doing a global fourier analysis of the visual field has given way to the view that the visual system does a coarse local frequency and orientation sampling[11].

CONTRAST SENSITIVITY

Human threshold sensitivity to grating patterns is illustrated in Figure 1. This shows that observers are most sensitive to patterns with a periodicity of approximately three cycles/degree with declining sensitivity to both higher and lower spatial frequencies. This curve gives a measure of how much contrast will be needed for a texture to be

---

[1] There is another approach based on order statistics [3,16] for the statistical combinations of features. However, the primitive features are not well understood and many of the phenomena explained by the order statistics approach can also be accounted for by the spatial frequency properties of the visual system [18].

perceived [9]. As an example, one hundred times as much contrast will be needed for a thirty c/deg pattern to be perceived as for a three c/deg pattern. The practical meaning of this curve is that it restricts the range of useful textures to [1:10] c/deg. At normal viewing distances this translates to a wavelength range of 4 to 40 pixels on a high resolution monitor.

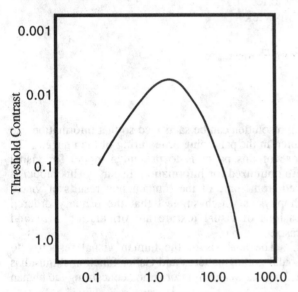

Figure 1. Spatial contrast sensitivity function for the human visual system.

ORIENTATION AND SIZE

The evidence from a number of experiments which are both electrophysiological and phsycho-physical is that the visual cortex contains large numbers of detectors which are sensitive to elongated oriented stimuli [15]. These detectors vary from one another in both their preferred orientation sensitivity and their preferred spatial sensitivity (they are said to have spatial and orientation tuning) and they are held to be responsible to most of the psychophysical results discussed here.

The neural detectors are quite broadly tuned with respect to orientation and size (see Blake and Holopigan, [5] for orientation). The issue of the number of resolvable textures has been addressed in a study by Caelly and Bevan [7] in which they found that textures sampling textures to 18 orientations (in the polar frequency domain of a 2D fourier transform) was sufficient to preserve the pattern on short exposures. The number of frequency channels has been variously estimated as between four and ten [8,21] . Some caveats should be made to the deduction that 18*7 numbers are all that is required to preserve a visual image. This is clearly not the case. Acuity for the orientation of extended lines, for example, is at the level of small fractions of a degree. Also, phase information is not taken into account. However, the results do give an estimate of the number of parameters required to synthesize statistical textures which lack regularity, symmetry and extended pronounced features. These kinds of textures are exactly those most likely to be used in information display.

ORIENTATION AND SIZE ILLUSIONS

It is instructive to compare texture illusions to brightness and colour contrast effects. Brightness contrast illusions are known to cause distortions in data display [10]. A grey patch with a bright surround is darker than the same grey with a dark surround and the distortion may be as much as 20% of the range between black and white[27]

Similar distortions will occur in texture fields [13]; the perceived size of a pattern is distorted by the size of surrounding patterns, as can be seen in Figure 2. The orientation of a pattern is distorted by the orientation of surrounding patterns.

Adaptation effects also occur, prolonged viewing of a high contrast pattern with a particular size will reduce sensitivity to patterns with the similar sizes and orientation [9]. These effects are attributed to interactions within and between "channels" which are tuned in size and orientation and for which the physiological mechanism is presumed to be the neural detectors describe above.

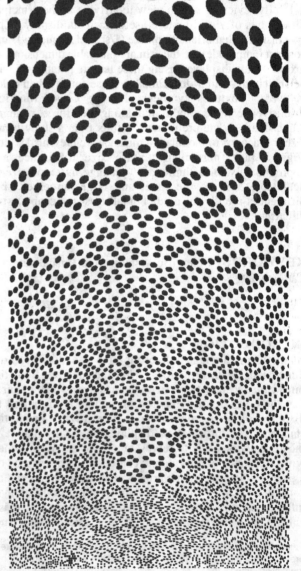

Figure 2. Texture Size Illusion. The background dots vary from small at the bottom to large at the top. Two patches of identically sized dots appear to be larger at the bottom than at the top.

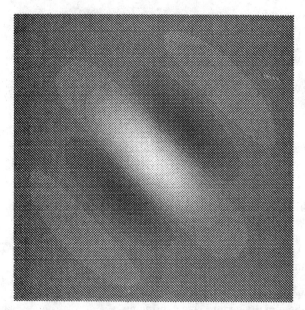

Figure 3. Gabor function. The function is smooth. The distinct boundaries are an artifact of halftoning.

GABOR DETECTORS

According to the second dogma of Barlow [2]
The visual system is organized to achieve as complete a representation of the visual stimulus as possible, in both spatial and 2D spectral terms, with a minimum number of detectors.

A currently favored mathematical model of the neural detectors found at intermediate stages of visual processing is the Gabor function. This function has the form of a one dimensional sinusoidal grating multiplied by a circularly symmetric gaussian [11]. See figure 3. This kind of detector is local because of the gaussian window and has spatial and orientation tuning because of the sine function. It detects a local packet of orientation, size information and contrast information in a way that optimizes joint information in the spatial and frequency domains as has been shown by Daugman[11] in a 2D generalization of Gabor's theory of communications. There is a fundamental uncertainty principle at work here, in order to be highly tuned to spatial frequency or orientation, a detector must be relatively large, but this causes a corresponding loss in position sensing accuracy.

A sine wave grating Grat(x,y) can be represented as a luminance pattern on the (x,y) plane

$Grat(x,y) = C + A.\sin(2\pi((x-x_0)u + (y-y_0)v) + \phi)$
such that the orientation
  $q = \arctan(v/u)$
the spatial frequency
  $w = \sqrt{u^2 + v^2}$
the wavelength
  $\lambda = 1/w$
the amplitude $= A$
the mean Luminance $= C$

and the phase $= \phi$ offset from the starting point x_0, y_0. If the phase is set to $\pi/2$ this gives a cosine function.

A form of the Gabor function is obtained by multiplying the grating by a circularly symmetric gaussian damped window centered at (x_0, y_0). and mapping the result to Luminance. This is simplified by only allowing circularly symmetric Gaussian and a ratio of Gaussian width to wavelength determined by a/w.

$$Lum(x,y) = Grat(x,y).e^{[-((x-x_0)^2+(y-y_0)^2)/(a\lambda)^2]}$$

The Gaussian decays to amplitude 1/e by $a\lambda$. For our studies we link the Gaussian width to the wavelength by making a = 1.5.

THE ORDERABLE DIMENSIONS OF TEXTURE

The Gabor packet encodes three ordered dimensions of texture perception, namely frequency, orientation, and amplitude. It has other dimensions such as the phase of the sine component and the ratio of the size of the gaussian window to the spatial frequency of the sine component. However, perception of phase information is not well understood [1], sensitivity to phase is low and it seems unlikely that ratio of components is critical, so we are left with three dimensions to display data.

The spot noise method elaborated by van Wijk [20] provides a straightforward method for synthesizing texture fields from Gabor primitives. In Figure 4 a texture is reproduced which varies in the two dimensions of size and orientation. Figure 5 shows some spatially distributed variance data mapped to the contrast of a texture field [24].

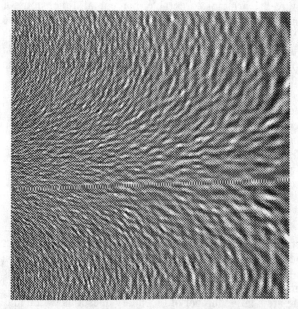

Figure 4. Synthesized texture field made using Gabor primitives. Size is varied from left to right and orientation varies from top to bottom.

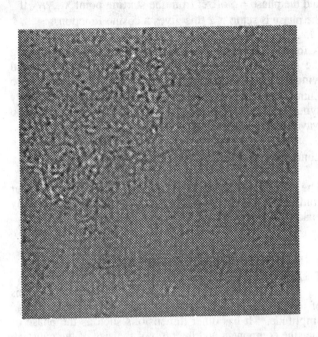

Figure 5. Synthesized texture field made using Gabor primitives. Data standard deviation is presented as texture contrast. High contrast regions represent highly variable data. Orientations are random. Since halftoning has introduced a fine, high contrast texture, this is best viewed from a distance at which the halftoning vanishes.

THE OSC TEXTURE SPACE

Based on the above analysis of psychophysical results the OSC texture space is constructed for the purposes of information display. The intention is to capture the principle orderable, perceptual dimensions of visual texture in a way that is easy to use, much as the HSV or RGYB colour spaces make colour easily accessible to computer graphics for the purposes of information display. We define texture at the point (x,y) on the plane by three variables.

texture(x,y) = (o,s,c)
where
o: orientation (linear between $0 .. \pi$)
s: size (1/frequency, approximately exponentially scaled to anticipate the results)
c: contrast (amplitude exponentially scaled between 0.1 and 1.0)

It is worth noting that texture density is the inverse of size according to this model. This is different from some other models, such as Bertin's for which texton size and texton density are independent variables [4]. Aside from the primary question of the validity of the OSC texture space there are a large number of secondary questions which may be asked concerning how the texture dimensions may best be used to display data. Such as:

Which texture dimension are most effective for perceptual image segmentation?

Which texture dimensions are perceptually orthogonal?
How accurately can information be read from a texture scale (contrast illusions are relevant here)?
What kind of information density can be presented using texture.
What are the interactions between texture dimensions and colour dimensions?
Can a uniform texture space be developed (by analogy with the uniform colour spaces)?

Some of these questions can already be answered by reference to the large body of published psychophysical studies. Others will require further work.

In this paper we present some of the first results of a major study we are undertaking into the properties of the three texture dimensions described above. The results we present here relate only to the size (1/frequency) dimension of texture and to the following two issues:

1) Resolution. How many just noticeable differences (jnds) are there in the texture size continuum.

2) Linearity. What is the mapping between perceived texture differences and physically defined texture differences.

In designing these experiments it was necessary to choose whether to study texture fields or responses to individual texture elements. Both methods have advantages: If we use the texture field we are directly studying the relevant phenomena. Unfortunately we are also introducing noise into the experiment because the stimuli must be generated by stochastic methods. Because of this problem we have initially chosen to do scaling experiments with individual Gabor functions as textons.

There are a number of hypotheses which can be applied to the perception of size differences.

1) Subjects may perceive size proportional to the linear size of the texton.
2) Subjects may perceive size proportional to the logarithmic size of the texton.
3) Subjects may perceive size proportional to the area of the texton.
4) Some other function may best fit the data; for example, brightness is perceived proportional to the cube root of Luminance (for no good theoretical reason)[25].

STIMULI

The stimuli we use are luminance patterns modulated by Gabor functions. The extremes of the wavelength continuum are 1/8 deg .. 1 deg which corresponds to a spatial frequency range of 1 cy/deg ... 8 cy/deg, or three octaves.

We measure the size dimension at each of three logarithmically spaced contrast values.

      0.1   0.285   8.0

and at each of two orientations

      0 deg.   45 deg.

yielding 6 subdivision sequences for each subject.

PROCEDURE

The methodology we adopted has been adapted from studies of uniform colour spaces. [25]. According to this method the user is first given two samples representing the end points of the continuum to be measured. For example a small pattern on the left and a large pattern on the right. The subject then adjusts the texture element in the middle until it appears to lie midway in size between the two flanking patterns. By this method the subject divides the continuum into two perceptually equal intervals. On subsequent trials this midpoint becomes the end point for each of two subsequent settings, dividing the texture continuum into four perceptually equal distances. In the early brightness studies this subdivision process was only carried to 4 or 8 intervals. In our procedure we subdivide until the textures are indistinguishable, to obtain a single *uniform sequence measurement*. The subdivision process is halted (for a part of the continuum) when the selected midpoint is outside the interval which the subject is supposed to bisect. The final level of subdivision (the leaves on the subdivision tree) yields an estimate of the number of just noticeable differences in the entire sequence. In addition, by determining how many leaf subdivisions there are for each high level subdivision, we can determine whether the uniform sequence function is the same for small difference as for large differences.

We apply the subdivision technique to each of the three variables. But here we only present results on the size (1/frequency) dimension. For practical reasons we divided the three doublings (octaves) size sequence into 144 equal ratio steps, 48 intervals per doubling. Each subdivision sequence took about 20 min.

RESULTS

There was no apparent difference between the results for the two orientations therefore these were have been merged together in the following analysis.

It is well known that large perceived differences and small perceived differences need not be related in lightness scaling experiments. This turned out also to be the case for our experiments. Thus, the first subdivision made by subjects was not significantly different from the linear midpoint between the largest and the smallest pattern

mean wavelength = 4.53, true wavelength = 4.5 sd = 0.9

However, the scaling at the jnd level was quite different. Figure 6 shows a histogram of the mean number of subdivisions in each quarter of the sequence scaled according to area, linear size, log size, and the cube root of size. Clearly area and linear size are not the appropriate functions to create a uniform scale of just noticeable differences. Log size and cube root size create a more uniform histogram, and of these cube root size gives probably the best result. The other effect which is apparent in these graphs is the expected fall-off in the number of jnds as contrast is reduced.

To answer the question about the discriminability of size differences we performed a probit analysis[12]. A single experimental run for one subject comprises about 100 trials in each of which the subject has tried to bisect an interval. A trial is scored as a success if the putative midpoint at least lies between the two endpoints, as a failure otherwise.

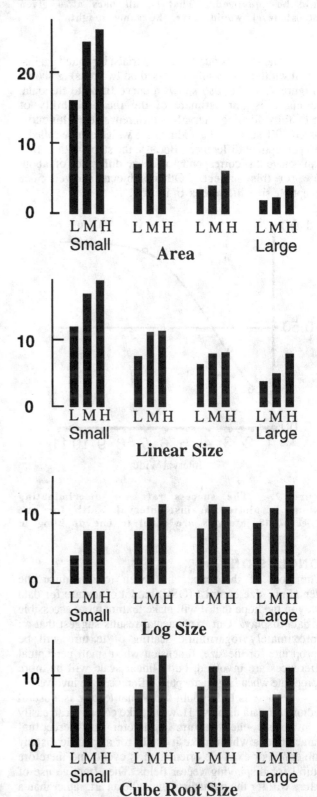

Figure 6. data histograms. Each plot shows L= low contrast, M=medium contrast and H= high contrast, subdivision data partitioned into four equally sized bins. Each plot illustrates the effects of a different transformation. If a

transformation were to result in a perfectly perceptually uniform scale in terms of just noticeable differences, (jnds) then the histogram would be equalized. That is, all bars at a given contrast level would have the same height.

The success rate, successes/trials, is plotted against interval width for one subject (based on two runs) as shown in Figure 7, which also shows a curve fitted to the data. The curve is our estimate of the the probability of successfully dividing intervals of different sizes. This curve crossed 50% success at a width of 3.8 which can be called a 50% perceptible difference. Because the step width is 1/48 of an octave this correspondes to a size difference of about 5.6% for this subject. Other subjects showed 50% perceptible size differences of up to 11%.

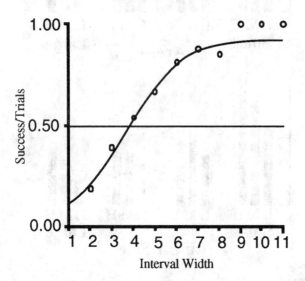

Figure 7. The success rate for discriminating textons is plotted against interval width for one subject. 48 intervals are equal to one doubling in size.

CONCLUSION

The goal of this paper has been to introduce the orientation, size contrast (OSC) model of texture for data dislay in the hope that it will make texture more accessible for data display. Our expeimental results suggest that an approximately logarithmic scaling of texture will be appropriate for the size dimension when small perceptual differences are involved, but a linear scale will be more appropriate when large perceptual differences are involved.

There is little doubt that visual texture is a useful medium for data display. However, like colour it can easily be misused; each texture parameter has perceptual characteristics which make it useful for a specific display problem. For example orientation is cyclic and therefore natural for displaying vector fields. The effective use of texture will for the immediate future be an art, rather than a science, but it is to be hoped that guidelines can be based on the OSC model, much as they are based on the HSV model of colour.

In addition to the work reported here we have a major series of experiments in progress which include:

scaling size, amplitude and orientation, and using texture fields in addition to individual textons as stimuli. We are also developing a package to allow flexible interaction with texture parameters.

Acknowledgements
Thanks are due to Donald Bouck for considerable work on a set of preliminary studies which paved the way for the present work, and to Tim Goss who coded the experiment, calibrated the system and ran the subjects. Kevin Marinelli provided invaluable system support.

REFERENCES
[1] Badcock, D.R., (1984) Spatial phase or Luminance Profile discrimination, Vision Research, 24(4), 613-623.

[2] Barlow, H.B., (1972) Single units and sensation: A neuron doctrine for perceptual psychology? Perception 1, 371-394.

[3] Beck, J. (1983) Textural segmentation, second order statistics, and textural elements. biological Cybernetics, 48, 125-130.

[4] Bertin, J (1983) The semiology of graphics, University of Wisconsin Press.

[5] Blake, R., and Holopigan, K. (1985) Orientation selectivity in cats and humans assesses by masking, Vision Research, 25(10) 1459-1467.

[6] Blakemore, C. and Campbell, F.W. (1969) On the existence of neurones in the human visual system selectively sensitive to the orientation and size of retinal images. Journal of Physiol, 203,237-260.

[7] Caelli, T and Bevan, P. (1983) Probing the spatial frequency spectrum for orientation sensitivity in stochastic textures. Vision Research, 23(1), 39-45.

[8] Caelli, T and Moraglia G, (1985) On the detection of Gabor Signals and Discrimination of Gabor Textures, Vision Res. 25(5) 671-684.

[9] Campbell, F.W. and Robson, J.G. (1968) Application of fourier analysis to the visibility of gratings. Journal of Physiol. 197, 551-566.

[10] Cleavland, W.S. and McGill, (1983) A color-cause optical illusion on a statistical graph. American Statistician, 37(2) 101-105.

[11] Daugman, J.G. (1984) Spatial Channels in the Fourier Plane, Vision Research 24(9), 891-910.

[12] Finney, D.J., (1971) Probit Analysis, Cambridge University Press.

[13] Georgeson, M.A., (1985) Apparent Spatial frequency and contrast of gratings: separate effects of contrast and duration. Vision Research, 25(11), 1721-1727.

[14] Hess, R.F. (1987) Evidence for spatially local computations underlying discrimination of periodic patterns in fovea and periphery. Vision Research. 27(8), 1343-1360.

[15] Hubel, DH. and Wiesel, T. (1968) Receptive Fields and functional architecture of monkey striate cortex. Journal of Physiology, 195,215-243.

[16] Julesz, B. (1975) Textons, the elements of texture perception and their interactions, Nature, 290, 91-97.

[17] Mitchell, D.E, Freeman, R., and Westheimer, G. (1967) Effect of orientation on the modulation

sensitivity for interference fringes on the retina. Journal of the Optical Society of Amer. 57, 245-249.

[18] Northdurft, H.C. (1991) Different effects from spatial frequency masking in texture segregation and texton detection tasks, Vision Research, 31(2), 299-320.

[19] Triesman, A. (1985) Preattentive processing in vision. Computer Vision, Graphics and Image Processing, 31, 156-177.

[20] van Wijk, J.J. (1991) Spot Noise: texture synthesis for data visualization. Computer Graphics, 25, 4, 309-318.

[21] Wilson, H.R., and Bergen, J.R., (1979) A four mechanism model for threshold spatial vision, Vision Research, 19, 19-32.

[22] Wainer, H. and Francolini, C.M. (1980) An empirical enquiry concerning human understanding of two variable color maps, American Statistician, 34, 81-93 .

[23] Ware, C. (1988) Color Sequences for univariate maps: theory, experiments and principles. IEEE Computer Graphics and Applications, 8(5) 41-49.

[24] Ware, C. Knight W. and Wells, W. (in press) memory intensive statistical algorithms for multibeam bathymetric data, Computers and Geosciences.

[25] Wyszecki, G and Stiles, W.S. (1982)Color Science: Concepts and Methods, qualitative data and formulae. New York: Wiley.

THE PERCEPTUAL STRUCTURE
OF MULTIDIMENSIONAL INPUT DEVICE SELECTION

Robert J.K. Jacob
Linda E. Sibert

Human-Computer Interaction Lab
Naval Research Laboratory
Washington, D.C.

jacob@itd.nrl.navy.mil
sibert@itd.nrl.navy.mil

ABSTRACT

Concepts such as the logical device, taxonomies, and other descriptive frameworks have improved understanding of input devices but ignored or else treated informally their pragmatic qualities, which are fundamental to selection of input devices for tasks. We seek the greater leverage of a predictive theoretical framework by basing our investigation of three-dimensional vs. two-dimensional input devices on Garner's theory of processing of perceptual structure in multidimensional space. We hypothesize that perceptual structure provides a key to understanding performance of multidimensional input devices on multidimensional tasks. Two three-dimensional tasks may seem equivalent, but if they involve different types of perceptual spaces, they should be assigned correspondingly different input devices. Our experiment supports this hypothesis and thus both indicates when to use three-dimensional input devices and gives credence to our theoretical basis for this indication.

KEYWORDS: Input devices, interaction techniques, gesture input, Polhemus tracker, perceptual space, integrality, separability.

INTRODUCTION

In studying interaction techniques, each new piece of hardware that appears raises the question *What tasks is this device good for, and how should it be incorporated into interface designs?* Such questions

1992 ACM 0-89791-513-5/92/0005-0211

are typically answered specifically for each new device, based on the intuition and judgment of designers and, perhaps, on empirical studies of that device. Greater leverage would be achieved if such questions could be answered by reasoning from a more general predictive theoretical framework, rather than in an *ad hoc* way. We provide one example of how the answer to this question can be derived from a theoretical framework (as, for example, Card, Moran, and Newell [5] have done for pointing devices).

We begin by posing the question for the three-dimensional position tracker, such as the Polhemus 3SPACE or Ascension Bird trackers. While directly answering the question *What is a three-dimensional tracker good for?* we will also try to shed light on the next level question, i.e., *How should you answer questions like* What is a three-dimensional tracker good for?

Concepts such as the logical input device (discussed further below) provide descriptive models for understanding input devices, but they tend to ignore the crucial pragmatic aspects of haptic input by treating devices that output the same information as equivalent, despite the different subjective qualities they present to the user. Taxonomies and other frameworks for understanding input devices have tended to hide these pragmatic qualities or else relegate them to a "miscellaneous" category, without further structure.

Instead, we draw on the theory of processing of perceptual structure in multidimensional space [8,9]. The attributes of objects in multidimensional spaces can have different dominant perceptual structures. The nature of that structure, that is, the way in which the dimensions of the space combine perceptually, affects how an observer perceives an object. We posit that this distinction between perceptual structures provides a key to understanding performance of multidimensional input devices on multidimensional tasks. Hence two three-dimensional tasks may seem equivalent, but if they involve different types of perceptual spaces, they should be assigned to correspondingly different input devices.

The three-dimensional position tracker can be viewed as a three-dimensional absolute-position mouse or data tablet; it provides continuous reports of its position in three-space relative to a user-defined origin. (In fact, the Polhemus and Ascension devices also report their orientation, but we have focused on position only in the present study.) The device thus allows a user to input three coordinates or data values simultaneously and to input changes that cut across all three coordinate axes in a single operation. (A mouse or trackball allows this in only two dimensions.) Such a device is obviously useful for pointing in three-space, but it is also applicable in many other situations that involve changing three values simultaneously. We concentrated on task spaces that do not directly map to three-dimensional physical space, and on manipulation rather than pointing tasks, in order to frame a balanced comparison. Specifically, we considered two tasks that both involve three degrees of freedom, i.e., that require adjusting three variables. For comparison with the three-dimensional tracker, we used a conventional mouse (for two of the three variables in the tasks) and then provided a mode change button to turn the mouse temporarily into a one-dimensional slider for the third variable.

A naive view of these two alternatives suggests that the three-dimensional tracker is a superset of the two-dimensional mouse, since it provides the same two outputs plus a third. Thus the three-dimensional tracker should always be used in place of a mouse (assuming ideal devices with equal cost and equal accuracy), since it is always at least as good and sometimes better. Our intuition tells us that this is unlikely—but why? The goal of this research is to develop a firmer foundation from which to draw such judgments.

APPROACH

To do this, we extend Garner's theory of processing of perceptual structure [9], first developed with fixed images, to interactive graphical manipulation tasks and thereby use it to shed light on the selection of multidimensional input devices. Our objectives are thus twofold:

- To answer the original question, *What is a three-dimensional tracker good for?* In so doing, we hope to provide by example a step toward putting the study of multidimensional input devices on a firmer theoretical footing.

- To extend Garner's theory of perceptual space from perception of fixed stimuli to interaction techniques.

Our hypothesis is that the structure of the perceptual space of the interaction task should mirror that of the control space of the input device.

BACKGROUND

The present work builds on two separate threads of research. One is the understanding of input devices in human-computer interaction, from the logical device concept through more recent taxonomies and tools. The other is the theory of perception of relationships between dimensions of a multidimensional space.

Study of Input Devices

A number of frameworks have been proposed to organize knowledge about input devices. An early abstraction is that of the logical device found in device-independent graphics packages based on standards such as ACM's Core Graphics System [10]. Fundamental user actions form the basis for the logical device equivalences. The idea is to separate the interaction device from the code needed to handle it in order to gain flexibility and facilitate rapid prototyping. However, experience shows that a system configured with a joystick is quite different from the same system with a trackball, although the logical device approach considers both equivalently as locators.

Foley, Wallace, and Chan's taxonomy of interaction techniques improves upon the logical device concept [7]. It maps elementary interaction tasks to the devices that can perform those functions but adds a middle layer that makes explicit the fact that there are many interaction techniques with which to perform a given elementary task. However, because the taxonomy is organized by task, a device can appear at more than one leaf in the techniques trees, hiding the structure of the device space as well as the qualitative differences that differentiate devices.

Buxton [4] calls these qualitative differences pragmatic attributes. He developed a taxonomy that organizes continuous input devices into a two-dimensional space whose dimensions are property and the number of dimensions sensed. In this way, the similarities and differences in the structure of the devices are highlighted. A tablet, light pen, and two-dimensional joystick are two-dimensional and sense position, but they differ from a two-dimensional trackball because it senses motion. This approach can thus point out that substituting a trackball for a joystick is incorrect; but it does not explain why it results in an awkward interface.

Mackinlay, Card, and Robertson [6,13] expand Buxton's taxonomy into a methodology consisting of three parts: a three-dimensional design space of most input devices; a functional mapping of information from the raw transducers of an input device into the semantics of the application; and evaluation techniques for comparing alternative designs in terms of expressiveness and effectiveness. This scheme, along with a defined set of connectors, allows continuous and discrete devices to be described and simple input devices to be combined into complex controls. Their approach both furthers our understanding of the structure of input device space and recognizes that human performance issues are important to understanding how a device actually works in a given situation. Although some relatively straightforward human factors issues are handled formally, such as matching the size of the domain and range of a value, the more subtle pragmatics of input device usage and task characteristics are still handled by a set of specific rules.

Bleser [3] developed a device taxonomy and input model that explicitly incorporates the physical attributes of input devices, including the notion of the physical separability of input degrees of freedom, and knowledge about task requirements. The taxonomy and model are used in an interactive design tool to suggest one or more natural interaction techniques based on a description of an interaction task [2]. The model depends on a set of heuristic rules and a pattern matching procedure rather than a more general, theoretical framework, but it highlights the need for such information in the design process.

Processing of Perceptual Structure

A multidimensional object is characterized by its attributes. A red circle has size, color, shape, and location, and these attributes define a perceptual space. Garner [9] observed that relationships between the attributes of an object can be perceived in two ways that differ in how well the component attributes remain identifiable. Some attributes are *integrally* related to one another—the values of these attributes combine to form a single composite perception in the observer's mind, and each object is seen as a unitary whole; while other attributes are *separably* related—the attributes remain distinct, and the observer does not integrate them, but sees an object as a collection of attributes. For example, value and chroma are perceived integrally, while size and lightness are perceived separably [11]. The horizontal and vertical positions of a single dot in the middle of an outline square are integral [9], while color and shape are separable [12]. This leads to two classes of perceptual space, one whose coordinate axes are perceived integrally, and one, separably, although there is really a continuum rather than a sharp dichotomy. There are two operational methods to measure integrality or separability. First, subjective judgments of similarity between

stimuli in an integral space (as measured in a direct scaling experiment) obey a Euclidean distance metric, as if the observer is responding to the overall composite distance between the points in the space; while similarity judgments in a separable space obey a city-block metric, as if the observer perceives the similarity along each axis separately. Second, in a classification task, where an observer groups objects into classes to maximize perceived difference between classes and perceived similarity within classes, integral objects are grouped by their overall similarity, while separable objects are grouped by their individual attributes.

We can extend the notion of integral and separable attributes to interactive tasks. In an interactive graphical computer system, the user varies attributes of a fixed visual object over time. Interaction is thus simply movement through the perceptual space to vary the attributes of an object. Integral movement is Euclidean and cuts across the dimensions defined by the attributes; separable movement is city-block and moves parallel to the axes of the space.

We can view the control spaces of input devices in a similar way. Input devices with more than one degree of freedom can be characterized as integral or separable based on whether it is natural (or possible) to move "diagonally" across the dimensions. With an integral device, movement is in Euclidean space and cuts across all the dimensions of control. A separable device constrains movement to a stair-step pattern; movement occurs along one dimension at a time.

METHOD

Our hypothesis is that the structure of the perceptual space of an interaction task should mirror that of the control space of its input device. To examine it, we considered two interactive tasks, one set within an integral space and one in a separable one, and two input devices, one with integral dimensions and one, separable. This yields a two by two experiment, with four conditions. We expect performance on each task to be superior in the condition where the device matches that task in integrality/separability. That is, the interaction effect between choice of task and choice of device should far exceed the main effects of task or device alone.

For the integral three-attribute task in the experiment, the user manipulates the x-y location and the size of an object to match a target, since location and size tend to be perceived as integral attributes, as observed in studies of sets of fixed stimuli [9]. For the separable task, the user manipulates the x-y location and color (lightness or darkness of greyscale) of an object to match a target, since location and color are perceived separably [9]. The difference in perceptual structure between these two tasks is in the relationship of the third dimension (size or greyscale) to the first two (*x* and *y* location); in all cases, the *x* and *y* attributes are integral.

For the integral device condition, we use a Polhemus tracker, which permits input of three integral values. For the separable condition, we use a conventional mouse, which permits two integral values, to which we added a mode change to enable input of a third—separable—value. Our hypothesis predicts that the three degree of freedom input device will be superior to the two degree of freedom (plus mode change) device only when the task involves three integral values, rather than in all cases, as with the naive hypothesis mentioned above.

Design

We used a repeated measures design, with each subject performing all four experimental conditions. Forty subjects (26 men and 14 women) were assigned randomly to four groups for different presentation orders. Order was counterbalanced for practice and fatigue. Within each group, one task is performed with both devices before the second task is presented, to emphasize device differences within task and control for variability caused by practice with a device. Subjects were clerical, administrative, and technical personnel from the Information Technology Division of the Naval Research Laboratory who volunteered to participate without compensation.

Stimuli and Apparatus

A stimulus is a pair consisting of a user-controllable object and a target object. The user is asked to adjust the moveable object to match the target on each trial. For the size task, the moveable object is a solid square whose intensity is 50% of the greyscale range and whose location and size are adjustable (see Figure 1). The target object is a black outline square showing the desired size and position. The range of possible sizes varied from 0.7 to 6.2 inches on a side.

For the greyscale task, the moveable object is a square of size 2.8 inches (the midpoint of the size range), containing an embedded circle 1.5 inches in diameter whose color is adjustable and an outer region displaying the target color (see Figure 2). Color varies between 10% and 90% of the greyscale range. The target object is a black outline square the same size as the moveable object, which presents the position to be matched; the outer area of the moveable object gives the color to be matched. In both tasks, the moveable object is translucent so it never obscures the target.

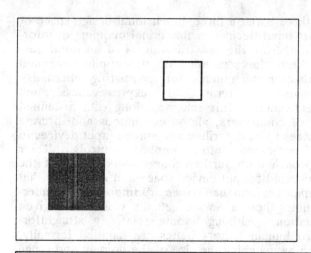

Figure 1. Stimulus for the integral (size) task. The outline square is the target. The user adjusts the location and size of the solid grey square to match the target.

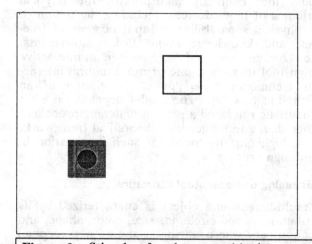

Figure 2. Stimulus for the separable (greyscale) task. The outline square gives the target location, and the outer area of the solid square gives the target color. The user adjusts the location of the solid grey square to match the target outline and the color of the inner circle on the grey square to match that of the outer area.

The maximum possible space of stimuli is a cube 13.75 inches on a side. However, not all of these targets can be used, because we require that the entire target square fit within the 13.75 inch by 11 inch screen and because we reserve colors near black and white for the target outline and screen background. Since these restrictions reduce the stimulus space differently for each task, we further adjusted the two spaces by matching their centroids, aligning the ranges of size and greyscale, equating the extent of hand motion needed to traverse them, and adjusting the monitor gamma correction to enhance greyscale range.

The stimulus set for each of the four conditions was randomly generated, but constrained by a script so that the distances in three-space from one trial to another were the same across conditions. Corresponding trials thus have equal distances, facilitating comparison across conditions. In addition, we required that each stimulus differ from the preceding one by at least 0.5 inches in each dimension, to avoid degenerate trials, which the user could complete without exercising all three dimensions of motion. Each stimulus trial is a three-dimensional point (x,y,z), and the software is identical except for how the z dimension is displayed on the screen. The x and y dimensions of both tasks are mapped as position, but z is mapped as either size or greyscale color.

The three-dimensional tracker used in the experiment was the Polhemus 3SPACE magnetic tracker. It consists of a transmitter that generates electromagnetic fields and a wand housing three orthogonal coils that sense the fields. The position and orientation of the wand is transmitted to a host computer. Only the three position values were used in this experiment. The Polhemus is an absolute device with the origin located at what would be the forward end of an armrest of the chair. The source was permanently fixed under the subject's chair. The control-display ratio for the Polhemus was one inch of device movement to one inch of screen movement. The data from the Polhemus was filtered with a small moving average filter to help smooth out device response. To improve the performance of the Polhemus, we eliminated as much metal as possible from the surrounding area. We used wooden furniture, and the metal mouse pad and its table were removed when not in use. The Polhemus was calibrated in one of two standard ways (one for left handed use, one for right) so that the operating area was consistent across subjects and its axes were orthogonal. Movement in the plane parallel to the screen moved the cursor in x and y. Moving the Polhemus toward screen made the object either bigger or darker, away made it smaller or lighter.

The mouse used was the standard optical mouse supplied with the Silicon Graphics workstation. It is a relative device, and the mouse pad was located under the preferred hand of the subject. The x and y mouse coordinates, combined with a mode change into a one-dimensional slider, provided the three dimensions of control for the experiment. We chose this control strategy because it is similar to those currently used in applications with multiple variables. Movement over the optical pad corresponded to movement in x and y. Holding any button down and moving the mouse toward the screen made the object either bigger or darker, away made it smaller or lighter.

The computer was a two-processor (16 MHz) Silicon Graphics Iris workstation, model 4D/120G. The program was divided into two processes, which ran concurrently on the two processors. One continuously monitored the Polhemus over a serial port and fed data into an event queue in shared memory, while the other drew the images and supervised the experiment. Most other system processes and all network daemons were eliminated. This architecture was effective in greatly reducing the often-observed lag in response to movements of the Polhemus. Position data from the mouse or Polhemus were recorded continuously throughout the experiment, approximately every 20 milliseconds. The monitor was a 19-inch Hitachi running under a gamma correction of 2.7.

Procedure

The subject was seated in a chair without arms, in front of a monitor on a desk 29.5 inches high, with either the mouse (placed on a small, moveable table) or the Polhemus in the subject's preferred hand and a 5.5 inch square flat button located on another small table under the non-preferred hand. The chair was located 36.25 inches away from the desk and the subject's eyes were approximately 56 inches from the monitor. This distance allowed enough room for the subject to manipulate the Polhemus and reduced the interference between the electromagnetic fields of the monitor and the Polhemus. The experimenter sat at a terminal in the rear of the room. The experiment was conducted in a special purpose laboratory designed for such work [1].

Each trial consisted of changing the position and either size or greyscale color of a moveable object using one of the two devices until it matched the position and size or color of the target. The subject pushed the button located under the non-preferred hand when the match was considered good enough. For each condition, the subject was presented first with 33 practice trials, followed by 88 experiment trials. The trials were subdivided into sets of 11, with the first in each set not scored because it measured the time to home the moveable object from an uncontrolled starting position. The home position for the first trial in each set was located in the middle of the screen and was either mid-sized or mid-colored. Within a set, as soon as the subject pushed the button indicating a target had been matched, the trial was ended and another target presented. An instruction screen separated the sets of trials and a subject determined when to start a set. The subjects were instructed to rest as long as they needed between sets of trials.

The subjects were encouraged to ask questions during practice but not during the experimental trials. They were instructed that accuracy and speed were of equal importance. Subjects completed a short questionnaire at the conclusion of the experiment. Each subject took approximately 1.5 hours to complete the experiment, which was run during March and April, 1991.

RESULTS

The data were analyzed in two ways: the first and simpler one measures overall time per trial; the second combines speed and accuracy into a single measure. The mean time per trial (time from appearance of the target until the subject pressed the button) for each of the four experimental conditions is shown in Figure 3 and graphed with dotted lines in Figure 4. The data suggest that neither task nor device alone produces as large an effect as the interaction of the two: that is, matching the integrality/separability of the device to that of the task gives superior performance. To evaluate this observation, we performed a repeated-measures analysis of variance on these data. First, we checked the effect of order of presentation of the four conditions, found no significant effect for experimental group ($F(3,36) = 1.09$, $p > .30$), and thus aggregated the groups in further analyses. There were significant effects for both task ($F(1,39) = 7.40$, $p < .01$) and device ($F(1,39) = 7.80$, $p < .01$) and a highly significant effect for interaction between task and device ($F(1,39) = 69.34$, $p < .0001$), as predicted.

| | Device: | |
Task:	Integral (Polhemus)	Separable (Mouse)
Integral (Size)	4981 *(2065)*	6274 *(2518)*
Separable (Grey)	5357 *(1613)*	4838 *(1269)*

Figure 3. Mean time per trial in msec. *(and standard deviation)*.

The second analysis measures the time required to reach a fixed accuracy criterion on each trial (where accuracy is overall Euclidean distance to target in three-dimensional space). This combines speed and accuracy into a single measure and removes the effect of individual subjects' "personal" accuracy criteria for terminating trials. To facilitate this analysis, we had recorded the position of the mouse or Polhemus approximately every 20 ms. during each trial. This enabled us to simulate retroactively an experiment in which the subject would have been required to reach a certain accuracy criterion, which would then automatically terminate the trial. Since a subject may briefly, inadvertently pass through a point that corresponds to good accuracy, retroactive analysis allows us to correct this by measuring the time until the subject reached our criterion for the *last* time during a trial. Figure 5 and the solid lines in Figure 4 show the results of this analysis, where the criterion was set at the 75th percentile of the final accuracies actually achieved over all trials, conditions, and subjects (which was 0.11 inches in three-dimensional Euclidean distance to the target). The results are similar to those in Figure 3. (The choice of 75th percentile accuracy is not criti-

cal; analysis with other criteria gave similar results.) An analysis of variance, with repeated measures, shows a significant effect for task ($F(1,39) = 5.78$, $p < .05$) but not device ($F(1,39) = 1.91$, $p > .2$), and, again, a highly significant effect for interaction between task and device ($F(1,39) = 52.07$, $p < .0001$).

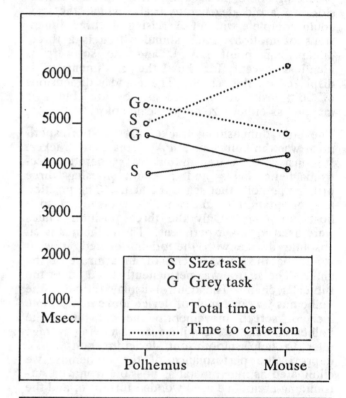

Figure 4. Graph of mean times in msec., illustrating interaction effect. This figure contains two graphs superimposed on the same axes; the two dotted lines show the results for total time per trial (as in Figure 3); the two solid lines, time to criterion (as in Figure 5). Lines marked **S** show performance on the integral (size) task; **G**, the separable (grey) task.

Our questionnaire asked how subjects felt about the experiment and for their prior experience with various input devices. Subjects preferred the mouse to the Polhemus and thought they performed faster and more accurately with it, but significantly more so on the greyscale task than on the size task (*t* test at $p < .05$), as expected. Overall, however, they preferred the mouse on both tasks, despite the fact that they performed worse with it on the size task. They considered the Polhemus more tiring for both tasks and the mouse a little easier to learn for both tasks. The input device familiarity question suggests why the mouse was easier to learn: 37 of the 40 subjects used one daily, while only two had ever used a Polhemus or other three-dimensional tracker. What was surprising is that the Polhemus did not seem to be hard to learn even though the device was new to most subjects, and some subjects were very enthusiastic about the Polhemus. Data from the practice trials show that subjects developed good performance with the Polhemus relatively quickly. While it is an inherently less stable device and might initially cause strain, some highly practiced users in pilot runs reported that the more they used the Polhemus, the less tiring and more natural it became.

Task:	Device: Integral (Polhemus)	Separable (Mouse)
Integral (Size)	3892 *(1430)*	4320 *(1323)*
Separable (Grey)	4739 *(1298)*	4000 *(893)*

Figure 5. Mean time in msec. to reach criterion accuracy *(and standard deviation),* where criterion was the 75th percentile accuracy attained over all the trials.

DISCUSSION

The results converge toward the conclusion that neither device is uniformly superior to the other in performance. Instead, we find significantly better performance in the experimental conditions where the task and device are both integral or both separable and inferior performance in the other two conditions. These results support our extension of the theory of perceptual space to interaction techniques, which predicts that the integral task (size) will be performed better with the integral device (Polhemus) and that the separable task (greyscale) will be performed better with the separable device (mouse).

Design rules for input device selection thus cannot be written from an examination of the input device space alone but must match the perceptual structure of the task space with that of the control space of the device used to perform the task.

APPLICATION

How might these results be used in designing controls for zooming and panning of a geographic display? Zooming and panning, taken together, involve three degrees of freedom. The most common design uses a mouse or trackball for two-dimensional panning and a separate control for zooming. We claim that a user typically does not really think of zooming or panning operations separably, but thinks rather of integral operations like "focus in on *that* area over there." The space is thus Euclidean, like that of the size task in the experiment, and, therefore, making the user do the two separately violates perceptual compatibility. It would be more natural to permit a user to make a gesture that performs the overall operation he or she had in mind, using an integral three-dimensional input device. The user moves the puck around in a volume directly in front of the display screen. Moving it in the *x* or *y* direction parallel to the display surface causes panning; moving it perpendicular to the display (directly toward or away from it) causes zooming. The user typically moves the puck in all three dimensions simultaneously, resulting in some combination of zooming and panning and directly reaches the view of interest. We have successfully demonstrated a mockup of this application.

CONCLUSIONS

This work shows how understanding of multidimensional input devices can be placed on a firmer theoretical footing. It introduces in a more formal way two important considerations in input device selection, which heretofore have not been so treated:

- the nature of task space—more specifically, the way its dimensions compose perceptually;

- the pragmatics of the input device—again, specifically, the way its dimensions compose.

Early research on input devices ignored these considerations; more recent work has begun to address them, but still lacks a theoretical framework that can support formal reasoning about multidimensional input device selection.

We therefore contribute:

- An answer to the original question *What is a three-dimensional tracker good for?* That is, when you want to vary three integrally-perceived attributes simultaneously. We found that the Polhemus is neither uniformly better nor worse than the mouse-based approach, but that it depends on the perceptual space of the task.

- An extension to the theory of perception of structure from fixed stimuli to interactive manipulation.

- The demonstration of an approach to answering questions like *What is a three-dimensional tracker good for?* based on extending a perceptual theory rather than on *ad hoc* testing or expert judgment. We derived our answer to the original question from the theory and then verified it experimentally.

ACKNOWLEDGMENTS

We thank Jim Ballas and Astrid Schmidt-Nielsen for help and advice, particularly in experimental design and data analysis; Jeff Brown, Robert Carter, Connie Heitmeyer, Dan McFarlane, Preston Mullen, and Stan Wilson, for all kinds of help with this research; and our NRL colleagues who took time from their own work to serve as experimental subjects. This work was sponsored by the Office of Naval Research.

REFERENCES

1. L.B. Achille, "Considerations in the Design and Development of a Human Computer Interaction Laboratory," NRL Report 9279, Naval Research Laboratory, Washington, D.C. (1990).

2. T.W. Bleser and J.L. Sibert, "Toto: A Tool for Selecting Interaction Techniques," *Proc. ACM UIST'90 Symposium on User Interface Software and Technology* pp. 135-142, Addison-Wesley/ACM Press, Snowbird, Utah (1990).

3. T.W. Bleser, "An Input Device Model of Interactive Systems Design," Doctoral Dissertation, The George Washington University (May 1991).

4. W. Buxton, "Lexical and Pragmatic Considerations of Input Structures," *Computer Graphics* **17**(1) pp. 31-37 (1983).

5. S.K. Card, T.P. Moran, and A. Newell, *The Psychology of Human-Computer Interaction*, Lawrence Erlbaum, Hillsdale, N.J. (1983).

6. S.K. Card, J.D. Mackinlay, and G.G. Robertson, "The Design Space of Input Devices," *Proc. ACM CHI'90 Human Factors in Computing Systems Conference* pp. 117-124, Addison-Wesley/ACM Press (1990).

7. J.D. Foley, V.L. Wallace, and P. Chan, "The Human Factors of Computer Graphics Interaction Techniques," *IEEE Computer Graphics and Applications* **4**(11) pp. 13-48 (1984).

8. W.R. Garner and G.L. Felfoldy, "Integrality of Stimulus Dimensions in Various Types of Information Processing," *Cognitive Psychology* **1** pp. 225-241 (1970).

9. W.R. Garner, *The Processing of Information and Structure*, Lawrence Erlbaum, Potomac, Md. (1974).

10. GSPC, "Status Report of the Graphics Standards Planning Committee," *Computer Graphics* **11** (1977).

11. S. Handel and S. Imai, "The Free Classification of Analyzable and Unanalyzable Stimuli," *Perception and Psychophysics* **12** pp. 108-116 (1972).

12. S. Imai and W.R. Garner, "Structure in Perceptual Classification," *Psychonomic Monograph Supplements* **2**(9) (1968). Whole No. 25.

13. J.D. Mackinlay, S.K. Card, and G.G. Robertson, "A Semantic Analysis of the Design Space of Input Devices," *Human-Computer Interaction* **5** pp. 145-190 (1990).

EXTENDING FITTS' LAW TO TWO-DIMENSIONAL TASKS

I. Scott MacKenzie[†] and William Buxton[¶]

[†]Department of Computing and Information Science
University of Guelph
Guelph, Ontario, Canada N1G 2W1
519-824-4120, mac@snowhite.cis.uoguelph.ca

[¶]Dynamic Graphics Project, Computer Systems Research Institute
University of Toronto
Toronto, Ontario, Canada M5S 1A4
416-978-1961, willy@dgp.toronto.edu

ABSTRACT

Fitts' law, a one-dimensional model of human movement, is commonly applied to two-dimensional target acquisition tasks on interactive computing systems. For rectangular targets, such as words, it is demonstrated that the model can break down and yield unrealistically low (even negative!) ratings for a task's index of difficulty (ID). The Shannon formulation is shown to partially correct this problem, since ID is always ≥ 0 bits. As well, two alternative interpretations of "target width" are introduced that accommodate the two-dimensional nature of tasks. Results of an experiment are presented that show a significant improvement in the model's performance using the suggested changes.

KEYWORDS: human performance modeling, Fitts' law, input devices, input tasks.

INTRODUCTION

Since the advent of direct manipulation human-computer interfaces (using, for example, the mouse), research in human performance on computing systems has enlisted many traditional techniques and models from human factors. An example is Fitts' law, a speed-accuracy model of human movement developed from research in man-machine systems for air traffic control [4, 5].

In early applications of the law, an operator manipulated a control (e.g., a lever, slider, or rotary knob) over a specified amplitude to a terminal position of a specified accuracy [e.g., 13]. Since the 1970s, many researchers have adopted a different paradigm. Objects of interest are often "iconic" — represented on a two dimensional CRT display and selected by a mouse, joystick, or trackball [e.g., 2, 3, 12]. Unfortunately, and as we shall demonstrate, the law is inherently one-dimensional; so, many such experiments include confounding variables such as approach angle and target shape.

The contribution of the present paper is in extending Fitts' law to 2D target acquisition tasks and in alleviating common weaknesses in applying the model. Following a brief introduction, we demonstrate — with examples from published research — that inaccurate, even erroneous, measures often emerge in typical applications of the model. Modifications are introduced and an experiment is presented to compare alternative models.

FITTS' LAW

According to Fitts' law, the time (MT) to move to and select a target of width W which lies at distance (or amplitude) A is

$$MT = a + b \log_2(2A / W) \qquad (1)$$

where a and b are constants determined through linear regression. W corresponds to "accuracy" — the required region where an action terminates. The log term is the index of difficulty (ID) and carries the unit "bits" (because the base is 2). If MT is measured in "seconds", then the unit for a is "seconds" and for b, "seconds/bit". The reciprocal of b is the index of performance (IP) in "bits/second". This is the human rate of information processing for the movement task under investigation.

Variations of the law have been proposed by Welford [15],

$$MT = a + b \log_2(A / W + 0.5), \qquad (2)$$

and MacKenzie [10, 11],

$$MT = a + b \log_2(A / W + 1). \qquad (3)$$

These equations differ only in the formulations for ID. On the whole, Equation 3, known as the Shannon formulation, is preferred because it
- provides a slightly better fit with observations,
- exactly mimics the information theorem underlying Fitts' law, and
- always gives a positive rating for the index of task difficulty.

The Geometry of Input Tasks

The experiments conducted by Fitts tested human performance in making horizontal moves toward a target. As seen in Figure 1, both the amplitude of the move and the width of the terminating region are measured along the same axis. It follows that the model is inherently one-dimensional. This implies that the minimum A is $W/2$, otherwise the starting position is inside the target.

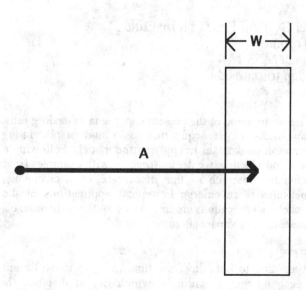

Figure 1. Fitts' law paradigm. The law is inherently one-dimensional since target amplitude (A) and width (W) are measured along the same axis.

Most Fitts' law research employs a task paradigm consistent with Figure 1 [e.g., 9, 14, 12]. However, many investigations vary the angle of approach to "smooth over" or to investigate directional effects [e.g., 1, 3, 8]. If the targets are circles (or perhaps squares), then the 1D constraint in the model remains largely intact (because the "width" of a circle is the same, regardless of the angle of measurement). However, if targets are rectangles, such as words, the situation is confounded. The amplitude is still the distance to the centre of the target; but the role of target width is unclear. This is illustrated in Figure 2.

If the approach angle is 0° (Figure 2a), then the 1D scenario applies. If the approach angle is 90° (Figure 2b), then the roles of width and height reverse (from the perspective of the model). Unfortunately, this has not been accommodated in past research. Card et al. [2], for example, tested several devices in a text selection task and varied the angle of approach. The horizontal measurement was always considered the target "width", regardless of approach angle; so, some unusual interpretations of task difficulty (ID) emerged. For example, when selecting a 10-character (2.46 cm) target from a distance of 1 cm, ID was calculated using Welford's formulation as $\log_2(A/W + 0.5) = \log_2(1/2.46 + 0.5) = -0.14$ bits. This unreasonable value, although not explicitly cited, appeared in the scatter

plot of MT vs. ID (Fig. 6, p. 609). In another Fitts' law experiment using similar conditions, Gillan, Holden, Adam, Rudisill, and Magee [6] required subjects to select a target 26 characters (6 cm) wide from a distance of 2 cm. Again, Welford's formulation was used, so ID was $\log_2(2/6 + 0.5) = -0.26$ bits.

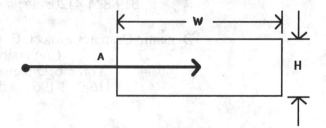

(a)

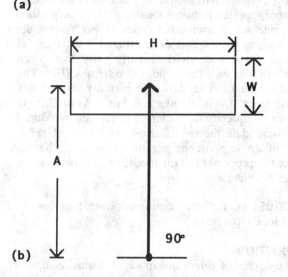

(b)

Figure 2. Fitts' law in 2D. The roles of width and height reverse as the approach angle changes from 0° to 90°

Obviously, a negative rating for task difficulty poses a serious theoretical problem. (What does "negative difficulty" mean?). We suggest two complementary ways to correct this. The first is to use the Shannon formulation in calculating ID (see Equation 3). For example, under the condition cited above ($A = 2$ cm, $W = 6$ cm), ID becomes $\log_2(2/6 + 1) = +0.42$ bits. It is easily shown that the Shannon formulation always yields a positive (or zero) ID. Using the Fitts or Welford formulation, however, the rating is negative when the $A:W$ ratio drops below 1:2.

A second and additional strategy is to substitute for W a measure more consistent with the 2D nature of the task. Consider Figure 3. The inherent 1D constraint in the model is maintained by measuring W along the approach axis. This is shown as W^1 (read "W prime") in the figure. Notwithstanding the assertion that subjects may "cut corners" to minimize distances, the W' model is appealing because it allows a 1D interpretation of a 2D task.

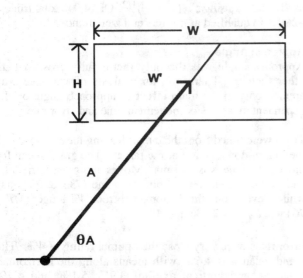

Figure 3. What is target width? Possibilities include $W^{\dagger}$ (the width of the target along an approach vector) or the smaller of W or H.

Another possible substitution for target width is "the smaller of W or H". This pragmatic approach has intuitive appeal in that the smaller of the two dimensions seems more indicative of the accuracy demands of the task. We call this the "SMALLER-OF" model. This model is computationally simple since it can be applied only knowing A, W, and H. The $W^{\dagger}$ model, on the other hand, requires A, W, H, θ_A, and a geometric calculation to determine the correct substitution for W (see Figure 3).

The objective of the present research was to test the viability of the $W^{\dagger}$ and SMALLER-OF models as alternatives to a "STATUS QUO" model, whereby W is always the horizontal extent of a target. As well, two other models were considered. Gillan et al. [6] although addressing different issues, tested $W+H$ and $W \times H$ as possible substitutions for target width. The area model ($W \times H$) has some appeal, since it is not limited to rectangular targets, and since area also seems to reflect the accuracy demand of the task. Substituting $W+H$ seems implausible, however. Gillan et al. [6] justified $W+H$ because it represents "the border of the text object closest to the start button" (p. 231).

In the following paragraphs, we describe an experiment that was conducted to test the models described above. A target selection task was used with rectangular targets approached from various angles.

METHOD

Subjects
Twelve computer literate subjects (9 male, 3 female) from the authors' university served as paid volunteers. Subjects used their preferred hand.

Apparatus
An Apple *Macintosh II* was used with the standard mouse for input. The C-D gain was set to 0.53 using the "fast"

setting on the control panel. The output display was a 33 cm colour CRT monitor (used in monochrome) with a resolution of 640 by 480 pixels.

Procedure
Subjects performed multiple trials on a simple target selection task. For each trial, a small circle appeared near the centre of the display, and a rectangular target appeared elsewhere (see Figure 4). Subjects were instructed to manipulate the mouse and move the cursor inside the circle, then wait for a visual cue before beginning. The cue was a small, solid rectangular bar which appeared on the left of the screen and expanded in size for about 1 second. After the bar stabilized, a move could begin. Subjects prepared their moves as long as necessary, but were told to move as quickly and accurately as possible once the cursor left the circle. Timing began when the cursor left the circle. The goal was to move to the target and select it by pressing and releasing the mouse button. A beep was sounded for trials in error.

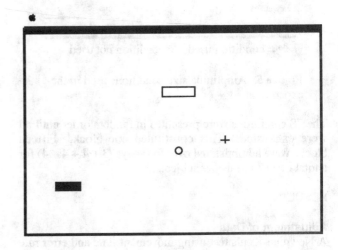

Figure 4. Sample experimental condition.

If a move started before the solid bar stabilized, a beep was heard and the subject restarted the move. Subjects were instructed to balance speed and accuracy for an error rate around 4%. An examiner was present for all trials.

Design
A fully within-subjects repeated measures design was used. Controlled variables were approach angle ($\theta_A = 0°$, $45°$, & $90°$), target amplitude ($A = 2, 4, 8, 16$, & 32 units), target width ($W = 1, 2, 4$, & 8 units), and target height ($H = 1, 2, 4$, & 8 units). Each unit mapped into 10 pixels for a maximum amplitude of 320 pixels (15.3 cm). Dependent variables were movement time (MT) and error rate (calculated from the x and y selection coordinates).

Only 78 of 240 possible cells were used. This kept the experiment manageable and exhausted a wide and important range of conditions. Twenty-six amplitude/size conditions (see Figure 5) were crossed with the three approach angles. Conditions with $W = H$ (viz., squares) were excluded since they yield only small differences in IDs among the models tested. Amplitudes were selected in power-of-four increments starting at the larger of W or H. The latter requirement ensured that the starting position was outside the target for all approach angles.

		Amplitude[a]					
Width	Height	2	4	8	16	32	No.
2	1	•	.	•	.	•	3
4	1	.	•	.	•	.	2
8	1	.	.	•	.	•	2
1	2	•	.	•	.	•	3
4	2	.	•	.	•	.	2
8	2	.	.	•	.	•	2
1	4	.	•	.	•	.	2
2	4	.	•	.	•	.	2
8	4	.	.	•	.	•	2
1	8	.	.	•	.	•	2
2	8	.	.	•	.	•	2
4	8	.	.	•	.	•	2
						Total	26

[a] • = condition used; . = condition not used

Figure 5. Amplitude/size conditions used in the experiment

The 78 conditions were presented in random order until all were exhausted. This constituted one block. Fifteen blocks were administered over four days (3 + 4 + 4 + 4) for a total of 1170 trials per subject.

RESULTS

Adjustment of Data

A Newman-Keuls test using movement time and error rate as criterion variables showed no significant differences in the 15 block means. The data were then entered in a test for outliers, whereby trials with selection coordinates more than three standard deviations from the mean were eliminated. The deviations from the mean were expressed

as 2D vectors using $z = (x^2 + y^2)^{1/2}$. Of 14,040 total trials, 42 (0.3%) qualified as outliers and were removed.

Approach Angle

Approach angle was the only factor fully crossed with other factors. Therefore, an analysis of variance was applied only to the main effect of approach angle on the dependent measures of movement time and error rate.

Trials were timed from the cursor leaving the start circle to the button-down action at the target. The grand mean for movement time was 743 ms. Moves along the horizontal and vertical axes were about the same (733 & 732 ms) while moves along the diagonal axis took 4% longer ($MT = 764$ ms, $F_{2,22} = 23.86$, $p < .001$).

Error rates were very close the optimal rating of 4%. The grand mean was 4.6%, with means along the horizontal, diagonal, and vertical axes of 3.9%, 5.1%, and 4.7% respectively. Statistical significance was achieved ($F_{2,22} = 4.33$, $p < .05$).

The above results were expected based on previous findings [e.g., 2]. Although the differences should be noted, they do not give one model an advantage since a range of short-and-wide and tall-and-narrow targets were used.

Fit of the Models

Our main objective was to compare several interpretations of target width when the approach angle varies. Five models were tested:

Model	Target Width
STATUS QUO	horizontal extent (W)
$W+H$	sum of width and height
$W \times H$	area
SMALLER-OF	smaller of width or height
W'	width along line of approach

Each model was entered in a test of correlation and linear regression using the Shannon formulation for index of difficulty. The results are given in Figure 6.

	ID Range (bits)				Regression Coefficients		
Model for Target Width	Low	High	r^a	SE^b (ms)	Intercept, a (ms)	Slope, b (ms/bit)	IP (bits/s)
SMALLER-OF	1.58	5.04	.9501	64	230	166	6.0
W'	1.00	5.04	.9333	74	337	160	6.3
$W+H$	0.74	3.54	.8755	99	402	218	4.6
$W \times H$	0.32	4.09	.8446	110	481	173	5.8
STATUS QUO	1.00	5.04	.8097	121	409	135	7.4

[a] $n = 78$, $p < .001$
[b] standard error of estimate

Figure 6. Correlations and regression coefficients for five models for target width.

Comparison of Models for Target Width		Correlations of *ID* with Movement Time			Hotelling's *t* test[a]	
1st Model	2nd Model	1st Model	2nd Model	Inter-Model	*t*	*p*
SMALLER-OF	W'	.9501	.9333	.8502	1.32	-
SMALLER-OF	STATUS QUO	.9501	.8097	.7881	6.31	.001
W'	STATUS QUO	.9333	.8097	.6992	4.86	.001

[a]two-tailed test, $n = 78$, $df = 75$

Figure 7. Test for significant differences between models.

The correlations were above .8000 ($p < .001$) in all cases. The SMALLER-OF model had the highest correlation and the lowest standard error, while the STATUS QUO model (W) had the lowest *r* and the highest *SE*. Correlations and *SE*s for the W' model were comparable to those for the SMALLER-OF model. Performance indices (*IP*) were in the range of 4.6 to 7.4 bits/s. The intercepts were all positive with the SMALLER-OF model yielding the intercept closest to the origin.

The highest correlation in Figure 6 was for the SMALLER-OF model. Using this model we conclude that the predicted time (ms) to point to and select a rectangular target, regardless of approach angle, is

$$MT = 230 + 166 \log_2(A / W + 1), \qquad (4)$$

where W is the smaller of the target's width or height. Furthermore, the standard error of estimate can provide a 95% confidence window on the prediction. For example, a task rated at 5 bits of difficulty should take $230 + 166(5) \pm 2(64)$ ms; that is, between 932 ms and 1188 ms.

Model Comparisons
Due to the ranking of correlations in Figure 6, further comparisons between the models were undertaken using Hotelling's *t* test for the difference between correlation coefficients [e.g., 7, p. 164]. The correlations were not significantly different between the STATUS QUO and $W+H$ models ($t = 2.00$, $df = 75$, n.s.), or between the STATUS QUO and $W \times H$ models ($t = 0.91$, $df = 75$, n.s.). Therefore, the $W+H$ and $W \times H$ models were excluded from further pair-wise comparisons.

The correlations for the STATUS QUO, SMALLER-OF, and W' models are compared in Figure 7. As evident, the correlation was significantly higher for the SMALLER-OF and W' models than for the STATUS QUO model ($p < .001$). Furthermore, the SMALLER-OF and W' models did not differ significantly from each other ($p > .05$). An initial conclusion, therefore, is that the SMALLER-OF and W' models are empirically superior to the STATUS QUO model. As noted earlier, the W' model is theoretically attractive since it retains the one-dimensionality of the model. In a practical sense, the SMALLER-OF model is appealing because it can be applied without consideration of approach angle. This is also true of the STATUS QUO model, but not of the W' model.

DISCUSSION
Since these results are potentially important to researchers interested in applying Fitts' law to two-dimensional target acquisition tasks, discussions should continue in more detail. The role of target height and approach angle varies in each model and therefore the comparisons may not be equitable. For example, the STATUS QUO model does not use H and θ_A. Is this a strength or a weakness in the model? In one sense, it is a strength, because fewer parameters brings generality and ease in application. On the other hand, if an additional and commonly varied parameter is shown to effect the dependent variable of interest, and the effect is to degrade a model's performance in comparison to another, then the absence of the extra parameter is a weakness.[1] Of course, the conditions tested must be representative of the application. The present experiment measured the time to acquire rectangular targets in two-dimensional tasks. The levels of factors were not unlike those in interactive computer graphics systems, with the possible exception of text selection, where the majority of targets are short-and-wide (see below).

On generality, the same argument applies in comparing the SMALLER-OF and the W' models. Although applying the W' model requires A, W, H, and θ_A, the SMALLER-OF model only considers A, W, and H. This is both a strength and a potential weakness in the SMALLER-OF model. Perhaps angles between 0° and 45°, for example, would yield variations in movement time more consistent with the W' model than the SMALLER-OF model. This remains to be tested. Nevertheless, the simplicity in applying the SMALLER-OF model with one less parameter is noteworthy.

Text Selection Tasks
In the limited case of text selection, targets are letters, words, or word sequences. The ubiquity of such tasks necessitates a model comparison under the relevant conditions; that is, with target height held constant.

---

[1]It should be noted that the so called "extra variable" is not participating in a multiple regression model, where each new variable *always* improves the fit. The extra variable contributes to the calculation of target width in the index of difficulty. Including target width (or approach angle) does not necessarily improve the fit.

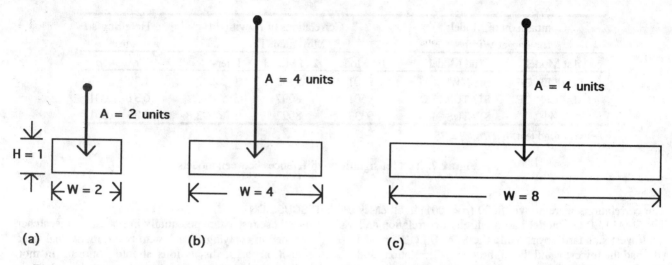

Figure 8. Three sample tasks. Is task (a) harder than task (b)? Is task (b) harder than task (c)? See text.

By a STATUS QUO model, *ID* is a function only of *A* and *W*, where *W* is the width of the text object. So, as the number of characters increases, *ID* decreases (see Equations 1, 2, & 3) and, therefore, the predicted *MT* decreases. Is this a reasonable expectation? Intuitively, yes. After all, the larger a word, the easier it is to select! Upon closer examination however, it is evident that expectations disagree with predictions.

Considering only the STATUS QUO model initially, it is easy to demonstrate that erroneous predictions follow under extreme, yet reasonable, conditions. As noted earlier, a negative *ID* emerges using the Fitts or Welford formulation when *A:W* is less than 1:2. Although improbable for 1D tasks, this situation is perfectly common for 2D tasks. Using the Shannon formulation the limit in *ID* as *W* —> ∞ is 0 bits. This seems reasonable, but as we now demonstrate, the rating for *ID*, although not negative, can become unrealistically low in 2D tasks using a STATUS QUO interpretation of target width.

Figure 8 is a clear refutation of applying the status quo definition — that width = horizontal extent. Intuitively, target selection time for task (a) will be somewhat less than for task (b). But this is not predicted by a STATUS QUO model. Intuitively, target selection time for task (b) should be about the same as for task (c). Again, this is not predicted by a STATUS QUO model. Predictions do match expectations if the task difficulties are computed using the SMALLER-OF or *W'* model.

For further evidence, we need only examine the observations of Gillan et al. [6], who used conditions of *W* = 0.25, 1.0, 3.5, and 6.0 cm with *H* held constant at 0.5 cm (the height of a character). The targets were words or phrases of length 1, 5, 14, or 26 characters. The contour lines in Figure 9 support the SMALLER-OF model over the STATUS QUO model. The observed selection time decreased from the 1-character to the 5-character

conditions for each amplitude condition (as expected for both models); however, *MT* remained the same across the 5-, 14-, and 26-character conditions. The latter effect, although not accounted for by the STATUS QUO model, is fully expected with the SMALLER-OF model because the target height was unchanging and consistently smaller than the target width. Gillan et al.'s [6] data clearly show that *MT* depends on *A* but not on *W* over the latter three conditions.

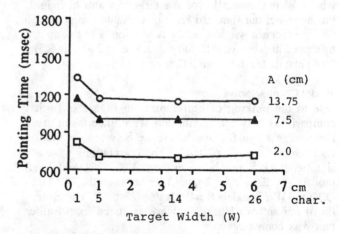

Figure 9. Results from Gillan et al. [6]. Movement time for the larger three targets (where *H < W*) depends only on pointing distance, as consistent with the SMALLER-OF model.

The *W'* Model

The *W'* model, although slightly more difficult to apply, performed as well as the SMALLER-OF model in Figure 7. The model assumes that subjects move toward the centre of the target. No doubt, behavioural optimization would follow under extreme conditions, such as selecting a "very wide" target at close range. If the starting point is below at 45°, for example, movement distances could be reduced by advancing along a more direct path. Such extremes were not tested. To prevent biasing the comparisons for any one model, the experiment fully crossed the three approach angles with all A-W-H conditions; thus, the minimum amplitude for each condition could be applied at each approach angle. Conditions such as $A = 2.0$ cm and $W = 6$ cm (as used by Gillan et al., [6]) preclude the possibility of $\theta_A = 0°$ since the starting position would be inside the target (see Figure 1). In fact, the designs employed by Card et al. [2] and Gillan et al. [6] would have provided even stronger evidence for the W^l and SMALLER-OF models had their data been analyzed as in Figure 6 and Figure 7. The present design, whereby both short-and-wide and tall-and-narrow targets were fully crossed with 0°, 45°, and 90° approach angles, is unbiased with respect to the models tested.

Optimization trends were investigated by calculating the *actual* amplitudes and approach angles for all 78 conditions. As expected, optimization was most evident for the extreme short-and-wide and tall-and-narrow targets. The largest deviation occurred under the condition $W = 1$, $H = 8$, $A = 8$, and $\theta_A = 45°$, where means for the actual amplitude and approach angle were 7.1 units and 36.9°. For the vast majority of conditions, however, actual amplitudes and angles were remarkably close to the specified conditions. Analyses using actual measures for A and θ_A were not pursued further.

When non-rectangular targets are used, applying the SMALLER-OF model is problematic; whereas, the W^l model is applied in the usual way. Nevertheless, one can imagine odd-shaped targets without an obvious "centre". The W^l model may yield unreasonably large or small estimates for target width in some instances. The area model ($W \times H$) has some intuitive appeal in this case. Perhaps an odd-shaped target should be reduced to a minimum-circumference shape — a circle — having the same area. The $W \times H$ model would substitute the area for W, while the W^l model would substitute the diameter.

CONCLUSIONS

The results in Figure 6 and Figure 7 illustrate a problem with traditional applications of Fitts' law to two-dimensional target acquisition tasks. We have shown that the interpretation of target width and the formulation used in the calculation of a task's index of difficulty play a critical role in the accuracy of the model.

The Fitts and Welford formulations suffer by yielding a negative rating for a task's index of difficulty, particularly in 2D tasks since the A:W ratio can be very small. The Shannon formulation alleviates this by always providing a positive (or zero) rating for ID.

Consistently using the horizontal extent of a target as its "width" (the STATUS QUO view) also weakens the model and leads to inaccurate and sometimes erroneous predictions. Two models performed significantly better than the STATUS QUO model. The first — the W^l model — substitutes for W the extent of the target along an

approach vector through the centre. This model is theoretically attractive since it retains the one-dimensionality of Fitts' law; however, the approach angle (as well as the width, height, and amplitude) must be known a priori. The second — the SMALLER-OF model — substitutes for W either the width or height of the target, whichever is smaller. This model is easy to apply, but is limited to rectangular targets, unlike the W^l model. Both models, in tests of correlation, performed significantly better than the STATUS QUO model; however, no difference was detected between them. These findings should prove useful in subsequent applications of Fitts' law to target acquisitions tasks on computing systems with graphical user interfaces.

ACKNOWLEDGEMENT
This research was supported by the Natural Sciences and Engineering Research Council of Canada, Xerox Palo Alto Research Center, Digital Equipment Corp., and Apple Computer Inc. We gratefully acknowledge this contribution, without which, this work would not have been possible.

REFERENCES
1. Boritz, J., Booth, K. S., & Cowan, W. B. (1991). Fitts's law studies of directional mouse movement. *Proceedings of Graphics Interface '91*, 216-223. Toronto: CIPS.
2. Card, S. K., English, W. K., & Burr, B. J. (1978). Evaluation of mouse, rate-controlled isometric joystick, step keys, and text keys for text selection on a CRT. *Ergonomics*, *21*, 601-613.
3. Epps, B. W. (1986). Comparison of six cursor control devices based on Fitts' law models. *Proceedings of the 30th Annual Meeting of the Human Factors Society*, 327-331.
4. Fitts, P. M. (1954). The information capacity of the human motor system in controlling the amplitude of movement. *Journal of Experimental Psychology*, *47*, 381-391.
5. Fitts, P. M., & Peterson, J. R. (1964). Information capacity of discrete motor responses. *Journal of Experimental Psychology*, *67*, 103-112.
6. Gillan, D. J., Holden, K., Adam, S., Rudisill, M., & Magee, L. (1990). How does Fitts' law fit pointing and dragging? *Proceedings of the CHI '90 Conference on Human Factors in Computing Systems*, 227-234. New York: ACM.
7. Guilford, J. P., & Fruchter, B. (1978). *Fundamental statistics in psychology and education* (6th ed.). New York: McGraw-Hill.
8. Jagacinski, R. J., & Monk, D. L. (1985). Fitts' law in two dimensions with hand and head movements. *Journal of Motor Behavior*, *17*, 77-95.
9. Jellinek, H. D., & Card, S. K. (1990). Powermice and user performance. *Proceedings of the CHI '90 Conference on Human Factors in Computing Systems*, 213-220. New York: ACM.
10. MacKenzie, I. S. (in press). Fitts' law as a research and design tool in human-computer interaction. *Human-Computer Interaction*.

11. MacKenzie, I. S. (1989). A note on the information-theoretic basis for Fitts' law. *Journal of Motor Behavior, 21*, 323-330.

12. MacKenzie, I. S., Sellen, A., & Buxton, W. (1991). A comparison of input devices in elemental pointing and dragging tasks. *Proceedings of the CHI '91 Conference on Human Factors in Computing Systems*, 161-166. New York: ACM.

13. Sheridan, T. B., & Ferrell, W. R. (1963). Remote manipulative control with transmission delay. *IEEE Transactions on Human Factors in Electronics, 4*, 25-29.

14. Ware, C., & Mikaelian, H. H. (1989). A evaluation of an eye tracker as a device for computer input. *Proceedings of the CHI+GI '87 Conference on Human Factors in Computing Systems and Graphics Interface*, 183-188. New York: ACM.

15. Welford, A. T. (1968). *Fundamentals of skill*. London: Methuen.

When TVs are Computers are TVs (Panel)

Moderator: **S. Joy Mountford**
Manager, Human Interface Group/ATG, Apple Computer, Inc.,
20525 Mariani Ave., Cupertino, CA 95014. Tel # 408 974-4801

Panelists:

Peter Mitchell: President, Big Animated Digital Productions, Melbourne, Australia

Pat O'Hara: Professor, Tisch School of Arts, New York University, New York, NY

Joe Sparks: President, Pop Rocket, Inc., San Francisco, CA

Max Whitby: Director, MultiMedia Corporation, London, England

KEYWORDS: Interface Design, Multimedia Design.

ABSTRACT:
This panel brings together experts from TV production with those in the computer multimedia business. They will discuss what is likely to happen when the two media coexist. An exciting opportunity exists in merging the strengths of both media together synergistically to create pervasive and powerful Interactive Television.

INTRODUCTION:
Many personal computer companies are asking themselves how to move successfully into the home market. If we examine consumer electronics statistics we find the household penetration of personal computers is only about 30%. However, about 97% of households have television sets, and of the households with children between ages of 7-14 years, 98% have Nintendo game devices [1]. So it is important for computer companies to consider how to take advantage of what is already resident in peoples' homes. It is likely that a merging of the two medium, television and computing, will gradually occur. The interface community needs to better understand the opportunities afforded by each medium, and help create a successful bridge between them.

Currently the computer industry is seeing a trend towards multimedia which has arguable emerged from the collision of the TV and computer cultures. The issue is how to best balance users' expectations from watching highly produced TV with the ability of the computer to present in a non-linear format. However, most multimedia computer systems are used as stand alone systems. Without the power of networks the computer does not qualify in any sense as television, since no signals are being transported. It is likely that Nintendo will

tap the unused phone port that they had the foresight to build into their boxes, which is already attached to a TV. Simultaneously higher speed computer networks are being installed to support full motion video. In turn connecting these computers to networks will enable them to qualify as interactive televisions.

The so-called passive viewing model of watching television has a powerful allure, capable of creating many complex emotions. The computer culture would be wise to study the development of successful TV conventions. The nature of interactive media is to allow divergent, personalised paths without necessarily providing the reassuring consensus view of broadcast television. The shift from broadcast television culture to computer culture is likely to be slow. Ultimately interactive media could serve the same function as passive television by providing a collective mythology or world view.

Many interactive services are sneaking on to your TV. Providing the user with additional channels and trivial interaction through remote controls, has already had an effect on cinematic convention. The FCC has recently allocated bandwidth to companies willing to provide interactive programming. They will need to use new user input devices and ultimately support broadcast of full motion video. Other companies are utilising the existing input of the telephone to allow up to 10,000 callers at once to control programming.

Public Access Television will probably be the birth place of Interactive Television, where computers are already being used as production tools for such shows as "Wayne's World" [1]. Members of New York University using Manhattan Cable, are enabling users to engage in such activities as surrogate travel through "Dan's Apartment", play musical instruments and reallocate the city's budget using touchtone phones. These trends indicate that Cable networks are putting computer people and television people in close proximity in a free-form counterculture. It is likely that something interesting will happen where they meet, and the computer industry should be aware of this opportunity and learn from the TV community. Interface designers need to further benefit from observing other communities to design compelling and usable interfaces [2].

PANELISTS:

S. Joy Mountford manages the Human Interface Group in Apple's Advanced Technology Group. Her group is responsible for designing prototypes that show new interface directions. Within this charter she has begun to see the emerging contribution of traditional media to the design of new media. Users have high expectations based on their exposure to TV, film and books whose conventions are hard to 'recreate' with computers. Each media has its own unique contribution and as interface designers she believes that we need to design to maximise the strengths of each. There is a need for computer interface designers to better understand the basic premises of traditional and entertaining communication media such as TV.

Peter Mitchell is President of Australian-based Big Animated Digital Productions Inc. Peter creates tools, content and interfaces for interactive multimedia projects, interactive speaker support material, touch screen kiosks, as well as interface and product simulations. He will show examples of tools and interfaces that he uses in the design, production and display of interactive multimedia systems.

I believe that the future involves integrated Data/Audio/Video broadcasts running across different networks using a range of playback devices. In the future a broadcast station would be able to run a channel dedicated to interactive programs. At the broadcast station the host computer would auto edit the program on an hourly basis; adding and deleting segments of data, from audio and video sources to be ready for the next transmission .

On the receiving end, the client computer would be instructed to wait for the next broadcast window to receive the production parameters as computer code. This code would determine the interactive branching elements to be incorporated into the program, then the instructions for digitising audio and video sequences would immediately follow. On completion of the broadcast the client machine would have created locally stored multimedia database. Problems such as hardware load times and true nonlinear interaction are essential to solve for this to be viable in real time.

Users could directly connect via modems to interact with each others identical multimedia databases, without having to transfer data, only commands that control the locally stored data. There are several enabling technologies essential to creating such environments:

1. Local area video networking. One or more video channels being transmitted using low powered transmitters and receivers. This type of system would be most usefully implemented in; video conference systems, point of sale systems and information kiosks.

2. Multimedia playback devices. Pop in a disc, plug in the stereo and TV, and the user will be able to navigate with a simple remote control pointing device, through their favourite multimedia databases.

3. ISDN communication networks. Interactive multimedia data should be able soon to be piped through the telephone lines at high speeds into homes, offices and schools.

The press imply that users will all be swimming in a sea of interactive multimedia data. This data will be used to learn from, be entertained by, shop through, communicate and present with. However, to enable this to successfully happen companies must realise the need to first design, create, direct, edit, test, and manage all this data coming from various distributed and disparate sources, before it can be released on unsuspecting users.

Production tools, user interface creating templates and good production design are essential to the success of multimedia titles and services. Small efficient production companies armed with custom tool sets and templates will have the advantage with low operating overheads, multi disciplinary production skills and productivity enhancing systems.

Computer human interface design will be the catalyst to the wide acceptance of this emerging technology. The market place may be as volatile as the music industry. Products could appear and disappear over a short period of time. Only those that are easy to use and actually meet users' expectations will survive. When will we see the "Dark side of the moon", "Ninja Turtles" or "Star Wars Trilogy" of the Interactive Multimedia age?

Pat O'Hara, is a Professor at the Interactive Telecommunications Department within the Tisch School of Arts, at New York University. Pat was Program Director of the Reading Project and is Associate Director of the Alternate Media Center in New York. She is currently a Professor at NYU teaching about the theoretical implications, as well as the production elements involved with Interactive TV.

At the Interactive Telecommunications Program at NYU, we've been experimenting with television and computing since 1980. Our early work with broadcast teletext (at WETA, under an NSF grant) made it clear that the integration would not be a simple addition of one medium to the other. Those early, crude attempts to "insert" computer graphics/text/volatility/interactivity into the broadcast environment demonstrated the importance of studying the attributes and contextual frame of both computers and television.

In 1982 we developed Apple Bytes, the first cable television program to use an automated computer interface for the display of a text and graphic bulletin board. Renamed WINDOW, the project has changed technologies and styles many times as we continue investigating new relationships of computers and TV.

As multimedia technology developed, animation and sound were added, video disc and tape were added, and finally, telephone interaction was added, using a simple telephone keypad interface to allow home viewers to select segments of video or animation for the entire cable audience to view. Subject matter includes issues of concern for the community: homelessness, art in the community, racism, freedom of expression, AIDS, life in the city, ecological concerns, and poverty.

What questions do we ask ourselves at each iteration of WINDOW? How can we exploit the best attributes of each medium and its contextual frame?

1. What does computing add to television?

- Democracy - Anyone in Manhattan with a touchtone phone has an equal chance of having a brief stint as a program director of WINDOW. Over time the show can reflect a true consensus of our viewers as opposed to that of a media elite.
- Flexibility - Using modems and sound recording we can allow viewers to send in the actual programming on a daily basis. For instance an asynchronous political debate could be conducted where a politician's comments are not just presented unchallenged, but instead their views must stand up to nightly rebuttals sent in by viewers using digital video over modems.
- Simulation - Slick computer animation has been standard fare for network logos and sports statistics for some time. Increasingly we will see the computer's unique ability to represent things that exist only in simulation used on television.
- Personalization - The computer can be used as an off-line production tool to enable individuals or small interest groups to create persuasive and compelling programming.

2. What does television add to computing?

- Shared Viewing - Television allows billions of people across thousands of miles and hundreds of cultures to share a frame of reference.
- Moral Issues - Even the most inane sitcom episodes are centered around some moral conflict, however superficial. Currently, the computer is typically applied to issues that are easily put into digital form, without having much emotional impact.
- Accessibility - All family members are comfortable operating a television.

3. The inevitable blurring.

As affordable production tools fall into the hands of non-professional producers, there is increasing amounts of low production quality programming being provided by previously unheard voices. In addition we are seeing what is primarily reordered linear programming being called interactive. The two forms are merging technically, but the appropriate language and form of Interactive Television is likely to be a long time before it develops fully.

Joe Sparks is President of the newly formed Pop Rocket Inc., which produces interactive multimedia titles to appeal to broad audiences. Last year he was Director of Research and Development at Reactor Inc., who produced the fastest selling Macintosh CD-ROM title regardless of category in 1991, Spaceship Warlock. This interactive CD is a very highly produced space adventure game which takes people days to complete.

I believe that the race is on amongst computer manufacturers to give the public a computer disguised as a TV. This is understandable, as consumer products hold potentially the largest market for selling both computer hardware **and** software. The day is drawing near when the public at large will communicate directly with your company and purchase products via software interfaces, the same interfaces that will also allow them to screen television broadcasts, play the games of the future and rent movies.

As the computer and television merge into a smart, networked Interactive TV medium, we will be seeing a different kind of interactive software emerge. This new software must be usable by people who have never touched a computer before. For the first time, software will be competing directly with sitcoms and movies, as well as established phone services.

This approaching Interactive TV will open up vast new marketing possibilities and business opportunities. The demand for good software will be great. The challenge is this: How do you design software that allows the non-computer user to operate the software, without boring, frustrating, or otherwise debilitating them?

Perhaps a good place to look for clues is in the latest video games and computer entertainment pieces. Many computer games require the user to do many complex tasks, but if the experience fails to be entertaining or engrossing, the product will fail regardless of how powerful or capable the interface may be.

User interface elements such as; 3D, graphic design, audio feedback, and animation are now available to be used effectively to allow the user to understand the options available. The consumer market demands to be entertained and amused, but this must not occur at the expense of the user being confused or frustrated by screen glitch. As a designer on two interactive CD-ROM entertainment products I will share some of my experiences in their development. I will also demonstrate these products, and point out solutions and problems to avoid when designing usable consumer product interfaces.

Max Whitby, is a Director at the MultiMedia Corporation, London, England. MMC is an associated company of the BBC formed after the spin-out of the BBC ITU (Interactive Television Unit) in early 1990. Max is an experienced so-called 'old fashioned' TV producer and continues to make films for the BBC. He is well known for a broadcast show called "HyperLand", a history of Virtual Reality which went out last year called "Colonizing Cyberspace," and is working on a new documentary about sex.

I would like to examine the question of linear vs non-linear consumption of information. Conventional linear television is often dismissed by new media evangelists as a contemptible form of passive narcotic. Chewing gum for the eyes. Couch potato mode.

I said this sort of thing myself a few years ago when I left TV production for the wonderful new world of multimedia. Computers, I argued, can make TV smart. Films can start responding to the viewer. People can be liberated, follow their interests and inclinations, free from the tyranny of the producer, creating their own TV.

This vision is persuasive and widely shared. It ignites passionate enthusiasm for the new media. It motivates many of those attracted to the emerging computer-based information and entertainment industry.

There is only one problem. The analysis is wrong. Conventional linear television, for all its faults, is actually an incredibly powerful, sophisticated and mature medium of communication. I will argue that the best TV (of which there is actually a great deal) is far superior to anything we have yet seen on a computer. Those of us attempting to design the first titles intended for the coming information appliances would, I believe, do well to learn from the success of TV rather than to dismiss it.

One interesting fallacy is that watching TV is a passive activity. I believe computer people are fooled into this perception primarily because there is no evident mouse pushing or key tapping going on. In fact there is usually plenty going on in the average "passive" viewer's head. Elaborate realities are constructed, emotions and motivations ascribed to the characters on screen, complex issues and questions addressed. Film grammar and filmic narrative conventions have evolved over many decades to become incredibly sophisticated. The directness and transparency of the medium can lead us to forget the elaborate construction process involved in making even a simple TV program.

I believe we are years away from achieving anything comparable in the non-linear realm. Most interactive multimedia to date is interrupted multimedia. It consists of short bits of (sub-standard) linear media stuck together with icons and buttons. We need, I believe, to look in entirely different directions. One such direction demands a return to the linear as a way of giving our information purpose and structure. We must seek to design interfaces that work within a linear framework to add the value and liberating power that computers promise.

REFERENCES:

[1] Thanks to Dan O'Sullivan for assistance in providing source material for this panel

[2] Mountford S. J. et al, A Day in the Life Of... *Proceedings of CHI '91 Conference on Human Factors in Computing Systems. (New Orleans, LA)*

Transportable Applications Environment (TAE) Plus User Interface Designer WorkBench

Martha R. Szczur

Code 522
NASA/Goddard Space Flight Center
Greenbelt, MD 20771
Phone: (301) 286-8609   FAX: (301) 286-4627
email: mszczur@postman.gsfc.nasa.gov

ABSTRACT

TAE Plus was built at NASA's Goddard Space Flight
Center to support the building of GUI user interfaces for
highly interactive applications, such as realtime processing
systems and scientific analysis systems. TAE Plus is
designed as a productivity tool for the user interface
designer. Human factor experts and user interface designers frequently do not want to have to learn the programming details of the windowing environment before they
use a GUI development tool to prototype and/or develop
an application's user interface. TAE Plus has been developed with this user in mind. TAE Plus is a user interface
management system that supports (1) interactively
constructing the visual layout of an application screen, (2)
rehearsing the UI, (3) generating the application source
code to manage the UI, and (4) providing run-time
services to manage the UI during application execution.

KEYWORDS: design tools, user interface, development
tools, productivity, user interface management system

INTRODUCTION

Development of TAE Plus began in the mid 1980s when
the emergence of low-cost graphic workstations enabled
graphical user interfaces (GUIs) to become a viable and
popular computer-human interaction technique. However,
developing a GUI with color, windows, icons, etc. is much
more complex than building a user interface for an ASCII
terminal. As a method of improving our developer's
productivity we created TAE Plus as a tool for developing
an application's GUI and managing the GUI in the runtime
environment.

The design philosophy was to build a tool that would not
require the GUI developer to understand the underlying
toolkits or windowing system (which were, and still are,
evolving); to provide an easy migration from the tool's

prototyping capabilities to its support of the GUI in the
operational system; and to provide higher level runtime
services that support separation of the user interface code
from the application code.

By not assuming that the WorkBench user is well versed in
the details of the underlying windowing system
technology, TAE Plus strives to make the process of
developing the GUI as easy as possible, while still
providing rich functionality. The approach has been to
abstract out the design and development process from the
details of the underlying support software (e.g., Motif and
X Windows) and allow the designer to immediately begin
designing the user interface without having to study the
details of the supporting software's widget's structure.

After several years of prototyping TAE Plus, an operational
version became available to the public in 1990. Based on
the TAE Plus user community's feedback, new features and
capabilities have been added, and the latest version (TAE
Plus V5.1) is built with the X11R4 windowing system and
the OSF/Motif™ toolkit.

DEVELOPMENT ENVIRONMENT

To support the GUI developer, TAE Plus provides the
WorkBench tool, which allows the application developer to
interactively construct the layout of an application display
and manipulate a set of interaction objects. [Note: The
term, interaction objects, is used in the generic sense to
include those components of the display screen with which
the user interacts.] This set includes user-entry objects
(e.g., radio buttons, check boxes, text entry fields, pulldown
menus) and data-driven objects, which dynamically change
based on values of realtime data (e.g., dials, thermometers,
a set of discrete pictures and stripcharts.)

A WorkBench user specifies the windows and interaction
objects that will make up the GUI and dynamically
specifies the sequence of the user interface dialog (e.g.,
which window to display if a specific radio button is
selected.) A drawing editor (Linton, 1989) is provided to
enable the designer to create the dynamic and static
portions of the data-driven objects. For instance, to create a

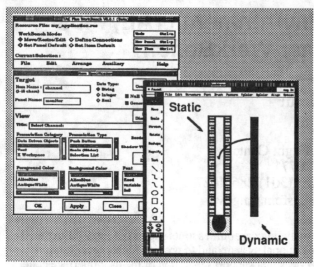

Figure 1.
Using the WorkBench to create a Data-Driven Object

data-driven thermometer object, the drawing editor would be used to create, edit and arrange a static background of a thermometer layout and a dynamic foreground of the *mercury*. Figure 1 shows the WorkBench user in the drawing editor creating the thermometer object. Color thresholds are defined from within the WorkBench. During runtime, the foreground portion, representing the mercury, stretches and changes color based on the associated data's realtime value. A rehearse capability allows the developer to review the user interface during the earlier stages of the development process.

At the end of the WorkBench session, the designed user interface is saved into application resource files. As an aid to the developer going from the user interface design process into the application implementation phase, the WorkBench provides the option to generate fully annotated and operational code which will display and manage the entire WorkBench-designed GUI. Currently, code generation is available for C, Ada and the TAE Command Language (TCL). This code provides the skeleton program into which the application programmer can insert or branch to application-specific functions. The WorkBench tool is not needed in the run-time environment.

RUNTIME ENVIRONMENT

Within the runtime environment the management of the WorkBench-designed GUI is handled by a higher level application program interface, called the Window Programming Tools (WPTs). The WPTs are layered above the Motif and X toolkit routines. They provide a compact set of routines (70 routines versus over 400 Motif toolkit services), which act as a buffer between the complexities of the underlying windowing system and the application code. Guided by the information in the application resource file, the WPTs display and manage the user interface defined in the WorkBench. This approach offers significant advantages whenever it is important to minimize the effects

of changing technologies (e.g., evolving toolkits) on applications. Because it is the WPT services that communicate directly with the Motif and X windowing services, and not the application program, when changes/upgrades are made to the underlying window software, only the WPTs require changes. The application is then relinked to the updated WPT libraries, and the application code itself does not require any changes. The WPTs also provide a buffer from any changes made to the structure or contents of the resource file. Since the applications only access information from the resource files via WPT services, upgrades or enhancements can be made to the resource file without the applications being affected. Figure 2 shows the relationship between the development and runtime environments of TAE Plus.

TAE Plus is an evolving system. Feedback from TAE Plus users (which are an assortment of end scientist users, programmers, and user interface design experts) is guiding the development of future releases of TAE Plus. New directions for TAE Plus include extensions to the interaction objects; introduction of hypermedia technology; integration of expert system technology to aid in making user interface design decisions; and implementation of additional user interface designer tools.

ACKNOWLEDGEMENTS

TAE Plus is a NASA software product being developed by the Goddard Space Flight Center with prime contract support by Century Computing, Inc. It is distributed through NASA's software distribution center, COSMIC™, (404) 542-3265. For more information, contact the TAE Support Office at GSFC, (301) 286-6034.

REFERENCES
Linton, M., Vlissides, J., Calder, P., "Composing User Interfaces with Interviews, "*IEEE Computer*, Feb., 1989.

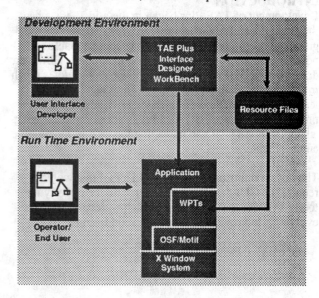

Figure 2. TAE Plus Environment

CHIRP: The Computer-Human Interface Rapid Prototyping Toolkit

Bob Remington

Lockheed Missiles & Space Company
1111 Lockheed Way, O/78-20, B/564
Sunnyvale, California 94089
(408) 743-7007
E-Mail: remington@lmsc.lockheed.com

INTRODUCTION

The dramatic increase in the complexity and quantity of software associated with the computer-human interface (CHI) component for modern computer systems has prompted tremendous interest in the development of new methods and tools that will expedite the production of usable software. Our review of the major CHI prototyping tools being developed at universities, software companies, and corporations shows that they vary greatly in their capabilities with respect to the degree of programming skills required to use them, their ability to allow rapid modifications, their support for user-interface evaluation, their ability to deal with interactive graphics, and their ability to generate directly usable code. Several CHI prototyping projects, such as Lapidary [3] and Views [1] show great promise for the future. However, none of the commercially available prototyping products have the right balance of capabilities to support rapid prototyping of the more demanding command and control applications using advanced interactive graphics.

At CHI '89 Manheimer [2] described the rapid prototyping tool called the Lockheed User Interface System (LUIS). The experience gained from a variety of LUIS-based prototyping activities involving CHI development for modern command and control systems. has led to the identification of additional c apabilities and tools required to support the development of the ground segment of new space systems. Building on LUIS, the Lockheed Space Systems Division Rapid Prototyping Lab in Sunnyvale California is developing and demonstrating a working version of the CHIRP Toolkit. The main objective of this project is to develop advanced CHI rapid prototyping tools that (1) support the requirements of key Lockheed programs to develop and demonstrate modern forms of effective computer-human interaction, and (2)

minimize the labor-intensive, time-consuming, and error-prone aspects of X Window System-based interactive graphical software development.

CURRENT TOOLKIT

As seen in Figure 1, the CHIRP Toolkit contains many of the GUI objects and application-related graphics that you would expect to see in a user interface for a typical command and control application. The CHIRP Toolkit allows the CHI designer to access, via simple menu selections, either primitive GUI objects (e.g., popups, buttons, textfield, etc.), or higher-level prefabricated reusable interface modules such as a panel of buttons, a complete menu structure, a digital or analog clock, and a scrollable help box. GUI objects, graphical objects (e.g.,maps, globes, images, graphs, etc.) stored in application libraries, and graphic application creation utilities (e.g., 2D mercator mapping and 3D orbital mechanics routines) selected from the menus displayed on the left side of the screen immediately appear in the "work area" (i.e., the whole screen area to the right of the menus). A form of visual programming is supported by providing the designer with a direct manipulation interface to position and size objects to create the "look" of the user interface. The CHIRP Toolkit also supports the definition of the functional behavior, or "feel" of the user interface by allowing the designer to interactively specify basic display-control relationships and make calls to external applications via simple menu selections. During 1991 the CHIRP Toolkit was extended to accommodate the first in a series of powerful commercial-off-the-shelf (COTS) X Window System GUI builders called UIM/X.

A number of external application packages containing callable subroutines to perform specific functions have been integrated into the CHIRP Toolkit. Examples of external applications are mapping and tracking, orbital mechanics displays, and signal processing. Integrating the application design support utilities into the Toolkit allows the designer to use these prototyping tools within the context of a single interactive scenario building session. In many cases, the CHI designer can now create and test-drive an interactive graphical interface without writing any actual code.

THE FUTURE

We are developing new capabilities in accordance with a strategy which calls for (1) expanding our custom space systems application software base, (2) adopting COTS application modules whenever possible, (3) implementation of emerging industry standards related to CHI development (e.g., X/ Motif, PEX, VEX etc.), and (4) incorporation of new CHI enabling technologies including 3D visualization and interactive video The evolving CHIRP Toolkit will provide seamless integration of all the existing and planned prototyping capabilities into a single designer's toolkit.   Figure 2 presents the model for our CHIRP Toolkit approach toward integration of future and current prototyping capabilities.

REFERENCES

1. Barfield, L. Boeve, E., and Pemberton, S. The Views User-interface System. *CHI '91 Conference Proceedings*, New Orleans, LA, April, 1991, pp. 415-416.

2. Manheimer, J.M., Burnett, R.C., and Wallers, J.A.   User Interface Management System Development and Application. *CHI '91 Conference Proceedings*, Austin, TX, May ,1989, pp. 127-132.

3.   Vander Zander, B., and Myers, B.A. The Lapidary Graphical Interface Design Tool. *CHI '91 Conference Proceedings*, New Orleans, LA, April 1991, pp. 465-466.

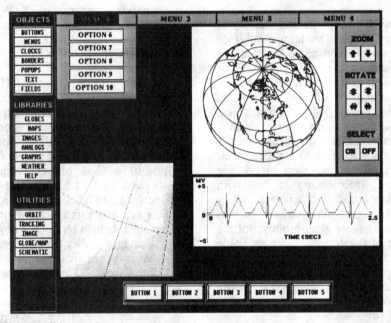

Figure 1. The CHIRP Toolkit user interface and sample graphic objects.

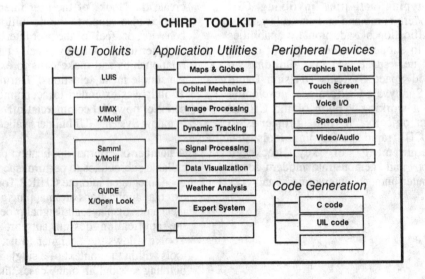

Figure 2. Overview of the CHIRP Toolkit integration approach.

THE ART OF THE OBVIOUS

Automatically processed components of the task of reading frequently used documents.
Implications for task analysis and interface design.

Nygren E, Lind M, Johnson M and Sandblad B

Center for Human-Computer Studies
Uppsala university, Uppsala, Sweden
Phone: int + 46 - 18 18 33 21
E-mail: Else.Nygren@CMD.UU.se

ABSTRACT

In addition to normal reading, knowledge can be gained from a paper document by pattern recognition and encoding of characteristics of the information media. There are reasons to believe that this can be done automatically with very little attentional demand. The knowledge gained is accessible to consciousness and can be used for task components like orientation, navigation, detection of changes and as a complement to normal reading. When information is computerized, and is read from a screen instead of from a paper, the conditions for automaticity are often radically changed. In most cases the reader has to gain the corresponding knowledge by effortful cognitive processes. This means adding to the cognitive load leaving less attentional capacity for the main task at hand. This problem can be avoided by a careful analysis of a reading task into its automatic and non-automatic components, followed by a dedicated user interface design where information relevant for orientation, navigation etc is presented in a way that the reader can perceive rather than read.

KEYWORDS: User interface design, task analysis, user models, reading, tacit knowledge.

THE OBVIOUS

This paper will outline how interface design can benefit from dealing with "the obvious". And especially so in interfaces for advanced users in daily work situations.

One of the characteristics of a good interface is that it appears obvious to the user. Ideally the entire attentional capacity of the user can be concentrated on the main task at hand. Manipulation and orientation in the information on the screen is then performed automatically like driving a car. To design this kind of interface, we argue, it is necessary to identify and deal with information processes within the user which are so obvious that he or she is not aware of their importance.

THEORIES THAT HELP US UNDERSTAND THE OBVIOUS

Some models of human cognitive information processes distinguish between two levels of information processing, [15], [16]. The highest level is closely identified with consciousness and working memory. It has powerful analytical, feedback driven, information processing capabilities. But it is also severely resource limited, slow and sequential. On this level we read, and understand information.

The lower level on the other hand is more senso-motoric in nature, and its capacity has no known limits. It can process familiar information rapidly, in parallel, and without conscious involvement or effort. On this level we look rather than see. We perceive rather than read.

Given certain conditions, the successful repetition of an activity results in the gradual devolution of control from the higher to the lower level. The activity becomes automatic.

Schneider & Schiffrin show that under certain conditions, visual search tasks can be trained to automaticity, [14]. In these experiments subjects were trained to perform automatic detection of alphanumeric characters called targets, which were presented together with other alphanumeric characters called distractors on a computer screen. The task of detecting a target could be performed simultaneously with a second task without any need for more conscious capacity than if the second task was carried out by itself. Thus a task which has become automatic can be added to a persons current set of tasks without any additional need for conscious capacity. Automaticity can be tested by comparing performance of a set of tasks including the task to be tested with performance of the same set of tasks exclusive of the task to be tested. If performance in both conditions are equal, the task is performed automatically, [6], [15]. Other experiments have shown automatic detection when targets and distractors differ in features like colour, size, category or spatial position, [1], [13], [14]. Also detection of a conjunction of features like colour and category, or category and spatial position, can be automatized, at least weakly, [12], [15].

Almost all tasks in working life situations will involve multiple processes with some automatic components, and some controlled, [5]. So will the task of visually encoding a document or a screen-display. It is possible to break down the task into subcomponents that can be shown to be either automatic or controlled. Encoding of digits was investigated by Francolini and Egeth 1980. They concluded that this is never an automatic process which means that it always requires conscious capacity, [2], [5]. Encoding of spatial position however, is almost always an automatic process. When a person attends to an input, for instance a written number on a document, some of its attributes are automatically encoded into memory. One of these attributes is spatial location, [4], [7]. This means that if we for instance read a number on a document we will also, without any extra effort, register the position on the page where the number is located. The knowledge gained by automatic processes is accessible to consciousness and can be used in a number of ways, [4].

So it seems that at the lower level we cannot read, but we can automatically scan a familiar document for patterns in features like colour and spatial position of values.

The concept of "tacit knowledge", as used by Polanyi, is also of interest in understanding the obvious, [11]. Polanyi refers to tacit knowledge as the knowledge which we use but are not aware of in a conceptual sense. He uses the term "focal awareness" and "subsidiary awareness". Focal awareness is directed to what we are aware of consciously. Simultaneously we have our subsidiary awareness directed to, and processing, information without conscious involvement. Polanyi argues that tacit knowledge can be made conscious if it can be brought to focal awareness. If Polanyi is right this means, in our terms, that we can be conscious of, at least some of, the information used on the lower levels, given that it can be brought into focal awareness. This also means that, given the right circumstances, it can be communicated to other people like interface designers.

HOW TO CAPTURE THE OBVIOUS.

Methods for task analysis as well as most experiments trying to shed light on problems related to interface design, deal with consciously processed information only. An example is experimental reading research which deals mainly with two types of reading, proofreading and reading for comprehension, [3]. In both types of reading, the reader is doing first-time reading of an unfamiliar text. As automaticity develops only under certain preconditions and after a large number of trials (typically more than 200), [13], it will not expose in a laboratory setting with unfamiliar material.

In many work situations, however, there is a set of documents which are used very frequently. The structure and the contents of these documents becomes very familiar to the reader. In order to study reading as an integrated part of daily work there is a need for methods which allow us to capture and study information use at the lower level as well as information which is used on the higher conscious level.

Polanyis theory of tacit knowledge indicates that if we can change the normal focus of attention, we can capture at least parts of these information processes. There are many ways to achieve this shift of awareness by manipulating the form of presentation of familiar information, for instance:

1) Withdrawal of high level information. If the high level information content is withdrawn, the users attention will focus on the low level information.

2) Causing artificial interrupts. Artificial interrupts can be caused by introducing errors, or a change in the physical presentation. These interrupts will focus the users attention on the lower level information process that caused the interrupt.

3) Withdrawal of low level information. The low level information can be withdrawn, as a whole or in parts. The lower level processes will cause an interrupt when information is missing. This will focus the users attention on the information which is not there when it is needed.

Method 1 was used in a study of reading in an intensive care unit, [8], [10]. We asked a doctor what information he read from a lab data list which presented results of blood tests for a patient. He answered that he read the numerical values relevant for the situation, of course. We then deprived the list of all numerical information by replacing all letters and numerals by x´s and showed it for just a glimpse to the doctor, (figure 1). The list still gave him information. A row of x´s showed that regular tests were being made. The spatial position of the row showed to which group the tests belonged. Some marks down to the right showed that liver tests had been taken. It also showed that they were taken once and that they therefore probably were normal. He was able to recognize a column as typical for the battery of tests taken when a patient enters a ward and so on. In fact the list deprived of its high level information content, still gave the doctor a fairly good picture of the patient. This is low level information which is not exact, but cheap and fast and which the doctors get practically automatic with no effort at all.

As a contrast we see a corresponding screen display of blood test results treated the same way, (figure 2). The data is tightly packed and there is no mapping of type of test or of time onto position. As a consequence the document is "pattern dead". To coordinate values in time the reader has to encode several numerical data of the form 1991.09.22 23.40. This is an activity which we have seen is never automatic, but a controlled high level process requiring conscious capacity. We believe that this is one of the reasons why there were severe problems to use this screen document in a computerized ward.

Method 2 can be illustrated by writing an extra erroneous ordination in a position of a document where the doctor had stated that he never read, because it was the nurses data field. The fact that the document was more filled than usual in that position caused an interrupt making the doctor attend to the error. Thus it seems that low level processes scan the form even if the content is not consciously processed.

An example of method 3 is to replace an original document with a Xerox copy. This caused an interrupt which made nurses on the same ward realize that they needed to see which values were written with a pencil and which were written with a pen, as the former were approximate but the later were more reliable.

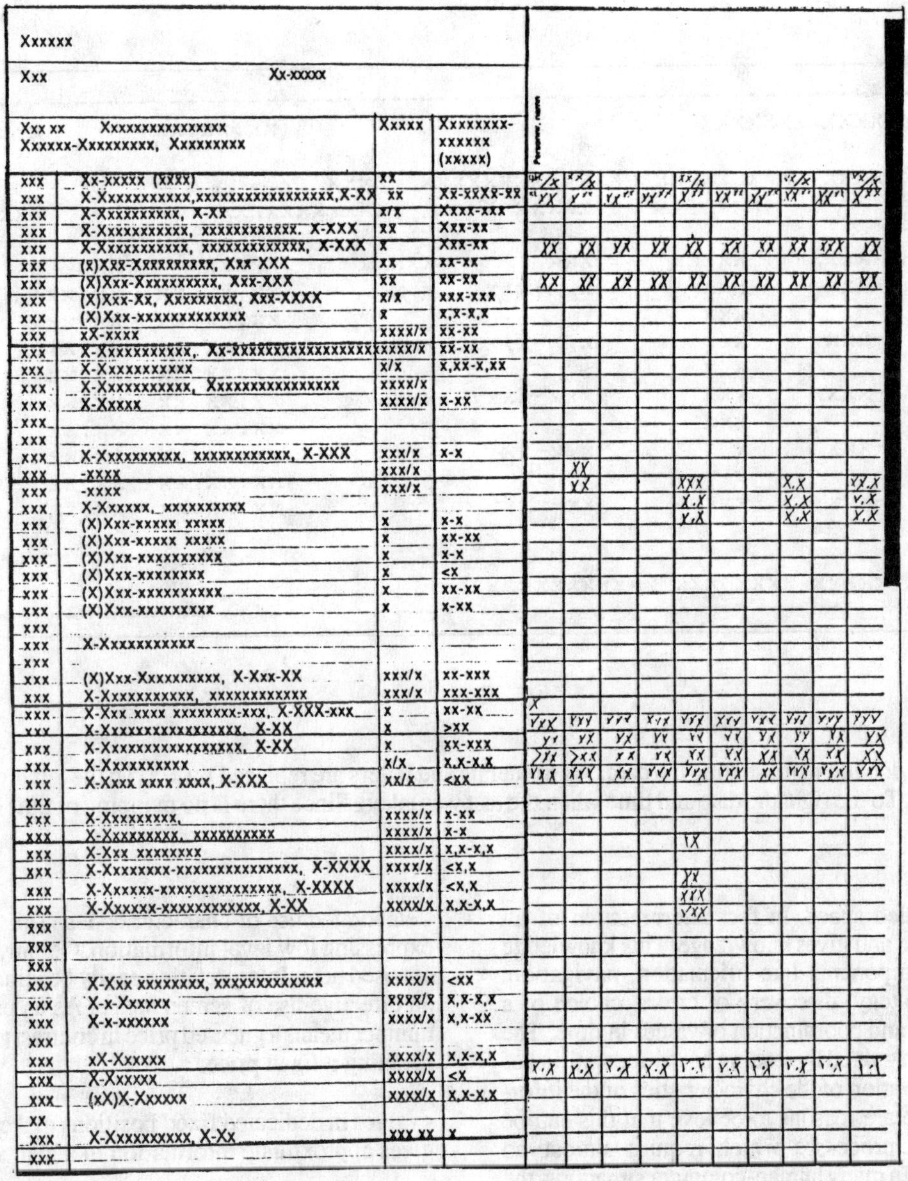

Figure 1. A list of laboratory test results for a patient where all letters and numerals have been replaced by x´s. The pattern was sufficient for giving the doctor a fairly good picture of the patient.

In a study of doctors reading the medical record we have seen that skilled physicians are very familiar with the structure of the medical record, [9]. The mere thickness of the bundle of papers, gave an immediate indication of the case, "this patient must have a chronic disease". Yellowing of the paper and the kind of typewriter font used was effectively used to assess document age. Remembrance of position on page was used as an effective cue for searching information which had been seen before.

It seems that the task of reading, where orientation and navigation is seen as an integrated part, involves a number of components or micro tasks. These are so obvious to an experienced reader that they are taken for granted.

Some features of paper documents are thickness of a bundle, the length of a list, the appearance of a document, spatial relations between documents, appearance of letters and numerals, the pattern made of filled values against a

```
-------------------------------------------------------------------------
   XXXXXXXXXXXXXXXX                                  xx:xx:xx         x:xx:xx

   Xxxxxxx   Xxxxxxxxx   Xxxxxxxxxxxxx   Xxxx
             <xx>        <xxxxxx>        <Xxxxxxxxxxx        >    Xxxxx

   Xxxxxxx   Xxxxx       Xxx             Xxxxx      Xxxxx        Xxx
   X-Xx      xxx         xxx-xxx         x/x        xx.xx.xx     xx:xx
             xxx                                    xx.xx.xx     xx:xx
   X-xxx     x           x,x-x,x         xxxx/x     xx.xx.xx     xx:xx
             x.x                                    xx.xx.xx     xx.xx
   X-xxxx    xxx         xxx-xxx         xxxx/x     xx.xx.xx     xx:xx
             xxx                                    xx.xx.xx     xx:xx
   X-xxx     x           x.x-xx          xxxx/x     xx.xx.xx     xx:xx
             x                                      xx.xx.xx     xx:xx
   X-xxx     xxx         xx-xxx          xx         xx.xx.xx     xx:xx


   Xxxxx xxxxx xxxx xxx xxxxxxxxxxxx
-------------------------------------------------------------------------
```

Figure 2. The screen document presenting lab data. All numerals and letters are replaced by x´s. To the left are the names of tests that have been taken. To the right the date and time when the test was taken. Since there is no mapping of time onto position there is no pattern.

background of unfilled space. In fact interpretation of all these features is made and gives knowledge. This knowledge is used for task components like orientation, navigation, choice of search strategy, discovery of errors, choice of a proper reading level and coordination of values in time. The knowledge is thus not gained by reading but by recognition of patterns and interpretation of the characteristics of the information media. There are reasons to believe that this can be done by automatic processes which require almost no attentional capacity. In many human-computer situations, the corresponding information is no longer obvious but has to be read. For instance, the number of documents can be presented as "number of pages = 45". Physical and graphical features may no longer reflect meaningful relationships, but rather be decorative. The corresponding micro tasks generally have to be performed on a controlled level thus requiring much more attentional capacity leaving less attention available for the main task at hand. We believe that this is the reason for many of the problems with document reading that are referred to as high cognitive overhead but also in some extent to overview problems and orientation problems.

AN OBVIOUS INTERFACE

By paying attention to the obvious information processing we can design better user-interfaces for a frequent reader. We can be aware of the low level information and we can control it. This interface designed for buyers at Volvo car corporation gives some examples, (see Nygren, Lind, Johnson, Sandblad, plate 1 and 2):

- elaborated use of character codes. This is a rich source of expressing low level information. Colour, typeface and style are used here. Interpretation easily becomes automatic and is an effective use of screen space. As an example, a slanting number means a guessed price in contrast to a straight number meaning a fixed price.

- values in dedicated fixed positions make up patterns which gives approximate information in a glance.

- pseudo-physical properties are added. The edge of these bundles gives an approximation of the total number of items as well as their distribution on different colour coded projects.

Automaticity can be tested by the procedure mentioned earlier. This requires a controlled laboratory setting. For design purposes some much more simpler tests will do. The essence of the test procedure is "you know it even if you didn't look for it". This suggests for instance "the one glance test". Find out what will be seen by an experienced user by one glance at the screen. The memory picture which stays in mind, (colours, positions and patterns) should be possible to be consulted. In the Volvo example a buyer can consult such a memory-picture to find out for example if the leftmost column in the middle of the document was filled or not. This means that a certain factory will have a delivery of a certain item or not.

A similar test is the "seen from a distance test" or if you are short-sighted, "take off your glasses test".

Another simple test is "the x-test". What can an experienced user find out if all letters and numerals are replaced by x´s? By this test we see the effect of character coding, colour coding and positional coding.

THE OBVIOUS CONCLUSION.
We have shown that it is plausible that the information conveyed by the physical form of the presentation is used at a low cognitive level without conscious involvement and also that this cognitive activity constitutes a fundamental basis for the information processing on the higher cognitive level.

Thus a user interface should be designed in a way that permits the user to do a substantial part of the information-processing on the automatic high capacity level. The low capacity sequential processor should be saved for reasoning and problem solving.

We propose that prior to interface design, an information analysis shall be made which identifies use of both high- and low level information.

In design of an interface for a specific task, one should ask which information shall the user read, and which shall the user perceive.

In conclusion, we are convinced that this is a fruitful way of attacking problems with high cognitive overhead, but also to some extent orientation and overview problems.

REFERENCES
1. Eberts, R., and Schneider, W. The automatic and controlled processing of temporal and spatial patterns. Human Attention Research Laboratory, University of Illinois (Report 8003), 1980.

2. Francolini, C.M., and Egeth, H. On the non-automaticity of "automatic" activation: evidence of selective seeing. Perception and Psychophysics 27, (1980), 331-342.

3. Frenckner, K. Legibility of Continuous Text on Computer Screens - A Guide to the Literature. Report from Royal Institute of Technology, Stockholm, KTH-IPLab 25:1990.

4. Hasher, L., and Zacks, R.T. Automatic and Effortful Processes in Memory. Journal of Experimental Psychology: General 108, (1979), 356-388.

5. Jonides, J., Naveh-Benjamin, M. and Palmer, J. Assessing automaticity. Acta Psychologica 60, (1985), 157-171.

6. Logan, G.D. On the Use of a Concurrent Memory Load to Measure Attention and Automaticity. Journal of Experimental Psychology: Human Perception and Performance, 5, (1979), 189-207.

7. Lovelace, E.A. and Southall, S.D. Memory for words in prose and their locations on the page. Memory & Cognition 11, (1983), 429-434.

8. Nygren, E. Reading documents in intensive care. I. Pattern recognition and encoding of characteristics of the information media. Report 21/91 from Center of Human Computer Studies, Uppsala university, Uppsala, 1991.

9. Nygren, E., and Henriksson, P. Reading the medical record I. Analysis of physicians ways of reading the medical record. Accepted for publication in Computer Methods and Programs in Biomedicine, 1992.

10. Pettersson, E. Automatic information processes in document reading. A study of information handling in two intensive care units. Proceedings of the First European Conference on Computer Supported Cooperative Work, London, 1989.

11. Polanyi, M., Personal knowledge. University of Chicago Press, Chicago, 1958.

12. Schneider, W., and Eberts, R. Automatic processing and the unitization of two features. Human Attention Research Laboratory, University of Illinois (Report 8008), 1980.

13. Schneider, W., and Fisk, A.D. Automatic category search and its transfer, Journal of Experimental Psychology: Learning, Memory, and Cognition, 10, (1984), 1-15.

14. Schneider, W., and Shiffrin, R.M. Controlled and automatic human information processing: I. detection, search, and attention. Psychological Review 84, (1977), 1-66.

15. Shiffrin, R.M., and Dumais, S.T. The Development of Automatism. in: Cognitive Skills and their Acquisition. Anderson JR Ed., Hillsdale, NJ, Erlbaum 1981.

16. Shiffrin, R.M., and Schneider, W. Controlled and Automatic Human Information Processing: II. Perceptual Learning, Automatic Attending, and a General Theory. Psychological Review 84, (1977), 127-190.

A COMPUTATIONAL MODEL OF SKILLED USE OF A GRAPHICAL USER INTERFACE

Muneo Kitajima

Industrial Products Research Institute
1-1-4 Higashi
Tsukuba Ibaraki 305, Japan
+81 298 54 6731
i8001@ipri.go.jp

Peter G. Polson

University of Colorado
Institute of Cognitive Science
Boulder, Colorado 80309-0345
+1 (303)492-5622
ppolson@clipr.colorado.edu

ABSTRACT

This paper describes a computational model of skilled use of a graphical user interface based on Kintsch's construction-integration theory [4, 8]. The model uses knowledge of a detailed representation of information on the display, a user's goals and expectations, knowledge about the interface, and knowledge about the application domain to compute actions necessary to accomplish the user's current goal. The model provides a well-motivated account of one kind of errors, action slips [14], made by skilled users. We show how information about the intermediate state of a task on the display plays a critical role in skilled performance, i.e., display-based problem solving [10].

KEYWORDS: user models, graphical user interfaces, display-based problem solving, action slips

INTRODUCTION

The goal of this paper is to present a computationally-based performance model of the skilled use of applications with graphical user interfaces like that of the Apple Macintosh. The model provides a theoretical analysis of some basic attributes of skilled human-computer interaction showing in detail how information about the intermediate state of a task on the display plays a critical role in skilled performance, that is, display-based problem solving [10]. Skilled users make a surprising number of errors [3, 14], and the model provides a well-motivated account of this behavior as well as other phenomena consistent with the assumption that skilled performance is not based on detailed, prestored plans [13, 15]. We summarize results from four sets of simulation experiments exploring the parameter space, demonstrating how skilled users can make errors, and validating the sufficiency of the model.

Display-based Human-Computer Interaction

Recent empirical studies of display-based human-computer interaction have provided evidence against standard plan-based theories (*e.g.* [3, 7]) of expertise in HCI. Mayes,

Draper, McGregor and Oatley [13] report that experienced MacWrite users have poor recall memory for the names of menu-items. In addition, Payne [15] has shown that experienced users do not have complete knowledge about effects of commands.

These results provide support for theoretical frameworks that assume that a sequence of user actions is not pre-planned. Each action is selected making use of display feedback during the course of generating a sequence of actions necessary to complete a task [10, 15]. The display plays a crucial role in successful and smooth interaction; the interaction is *truly* mediated by the display.

Other researchers have developed theories of skilled performance in which successful interactions are mediated by the representations of intermediate states of a task presented in a display. Howes and Payne [5] extended the task action grammar framework to display-based, menu systems, which is a competence model of users' knowledge

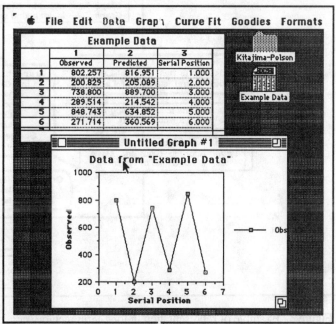

Figure 1. Example of the display in the task to plot the data from document "Example Data" using Cricket Graph, a Macintosh application.

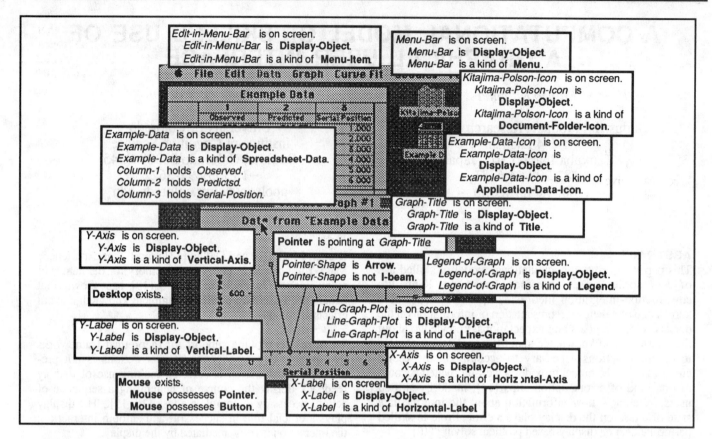

Figure 2. The propositional representation of the display shown in Figure 1 that is input into the model. See text for a description of the propositional notation.

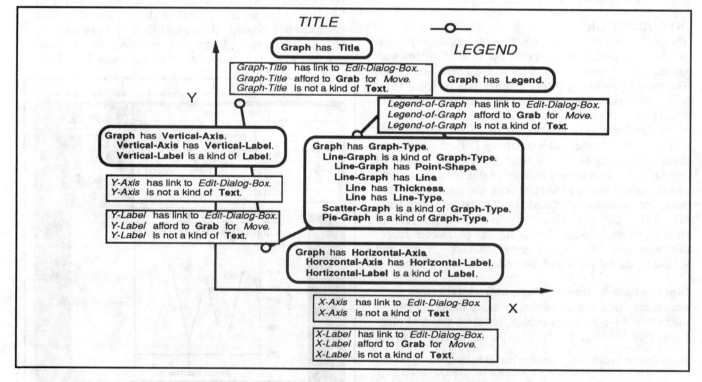

Figure 3. Example of representation in long-term memory concerning graphical domain knowledge.

of display-based systems for evaluating the consistency of an interface. Larkin [10] calls her framework display-based problem solving.

An Example Task

We want to account for the performance of a skilled user in tasks like the one shown in Figure 1. A user is plotting the data in the document "Example Data" using the Macintosh application Cricket Graph. On the screen are numerous objects that represent the current state of this task: the active window displaying the default version of the graph, a spreadsheet containing the data, the document icon for the data file, and an open folder.

An intermediate state of the task is shown in the display presented in Figure 1. The user has just completed plotting the column of numbers labeled "Observed" as a function of "Serial Position" and is starting to perform the subtask of editing the default version of the graph title. The user positions the arrow pointer on the title. The next correct action is to double-click on the title.

A Comprehension-Based Theory of Human-Computer Interaction

Our model is based on Kintsch's construction-integration theory of text comprehension [8]. It is related to similar models proposed by Mannes and Kintsch [12], Doane, Kintsch, and Polson [4], and Wharton and Lewis [18]. These models generate in real-time an action sequence necessary to perform a task in a manner analogous to a skilled reader constructing a contextually appropriate interpretation of a text during reading. In these models, the action selected in a specific situation is generated by a comprehension process which takes as input a representation of the user's current situation. This situation is defined by the user's current goal and expectation, information on the display, and facts about objects on the display and the task retrieved from long-term memory.

A MODEL OF SKILLED USE OF A GRAPHICAL USER INTERFACE

In this section, we begin with an overview of our theory of skilled performance of tasks using a graphical user interface. Next, we describe the construction-integration process. More details about the theory are provided in [8]. The following sections describe the different kinds of knowledge used by the model to generate correct action sequences, how parts of this knowledge are retrieved from long-term memory, how all of this knowledge is interconnected in a network, and the parameters of the model that control the retrieval and the integration processes.

An Overview

The model selects an eligible action given the current state of the display, user's current goal, and user's expectation concerning a desirable display state. Actions in the model are defined at a very small grain size. They include using the mouse to move the arrow pointer to an object, single-clicking an object, double-clicking an object, pressing and holding the mouse button, releasing the mouse button, typing, and the like. However, there is no direct

representation in the model of sequences of actions that perform common subtasks like selecting a command from a menu. The model generates a sequence of actions when a sequence of display states and an associated goal and expectation are provided to it.

The Action-Selection (Comprehension) Processes

The construction-integration theory [8, 12] assumes that selection of the correct action (comprehension) is a two-phase process with construction and integration phases. In the construction phase, propositions representing a user's current goal and expectation, the state of the display, and knowledge retrieved from long-term memory are incorporated into a network using argument overlap to define links between individual propositions. The construction processes are driven bottom-up; they are not constrained by context. As a result, the network contains inconsistent information retrieved from long-term memory and representations of the correct action as well as many wrong actions.

In the integration phase, the correct action is selected using a spreading activation process. The action that is selected for execution is the one whose representation has the highest activation value and whose condition for execution is satisfied. The condition is considered to be satisfied when all propositions in it are found in the network. Some propositions in the condition describe the display state; these are incorporated in the network as display representations. The others extracted from knowledge stored in long-term memory; these are incorporated in the network by a probabilistic sampling process in the construction phase. The action changes the state of the display, defining a new display state. If necessary, a new goal or new expectation is retrieved. The cycle starts again with a new display and, if changed, a new goal or expectation as input to the construction phase.

The Knowledge

There are five kinds of knowledge used by the action selection process: goals, expectations, the representation of the display, general knowledge, and action plan knowledge. All are represented as propositions. A proposition is a tuple of the form (predicate, $argument_1$, $argument_2$, $argument_3$, ..., $argument_n$). In this paper, we will paraphrase the propositional representation paraphrased as simple sentences enclosed in square brackets. The predicate is represented in plain type. Arguments referring to specific objects on the screen are represented in italics, and bold arguments refer to abstract concepts.

Goals

Goals are representations of a user's intentions to perform actions on objects [6]. The same goal can be associated with a long sequence of display states. The goal proposition for the example task shown in Figure 1 is shown in (1).

[Goal is to perform **Edit Graph-Title**
on the object *Graph-Title*] .   (1)

Expectations
An expectation is the representation of the consequences of
an action or sequence of actions in terms of the appearance
of one or more objects on the display. It is associated with
one or a sequence of display states. The model assumes
that expert users can generate detailed representations of
consequences of the next action. Expectations are closely
related to Selz's anticipation schema [17]. The expectation
proposition for the example task shown in Figure 1 is
shown in (2).

[Expectation is to see entry into **Edit Graph-Title**
environment associated with *Graph-Title*] .   (2)

Goals and expectations are stored in long-term memory and
are retrieved at the appearance of an associated display state.
However, the retrieval process is not simulated in the
current model.

Representation of the Display
The model assumes that the visual image of a screen is
parsed into a collection of objects, each represented by
propositions. Display-objects represent the state of a
screen. They include objects that define the style of a
particular interface, such as windows, menus, dialog boxes,
file icons, the mouse, the pointer, and the keyboard. Other
display objects are defined by an application or task, such
as editing or drawing a graph, and are usually the contents
of windows.

Figure 2 shows the representation for Figure 1. Each
object is represented by at least three propositions. The
first asserts that the object is on the screen. The second
identifies the object as a display object.   The third
establishes a token-type relationship.   Additional
propositions for an object describe additional information
about that object.   For example, [*Column-1* holds
Observed] represents a component of *Example-Data*.

The representation of displays contains limited information
about appearance. Only information reflecting underlying
system states that are relevant to the user are included in the
representation. The representation of an object reflects the
current internal state of the system and is used to let the
user know legal actions on the object. For example, the
mouse pointer in the Macintosh interface changes its
appearance depending on the internal system state. In
Figure 2, such representations as [*Pointer-Shape* is **Arrow**]
and [*Pointer-Shape* is not **I-beam**] are indicating system's
internal state. The mouse pointer takes on the arrow shape
on the desktop and the I-beam shape when over an object
that is editable. This distinction is crucial in defining the
result of an operation such as horizontal dragging. With
the I-beam pointer, it results in selection of that portion of
the text; with the arrow pointer, it results in dragging the
pointed-at object.

General Knowledge

General knowledge is knowledge about the components of
the display objects, the attributes of an object or
component, and the functions of or operations that can be
performed on an object or component. It is represented as a
collection of propositions. For descriptive purposes, we
have partitioned this collection into different domains
corresponding to the interface, tasks, and applications. This
knowledge is stored in long-term memory and is
incorporated in the network during the construction phase
by a probabilistic memory retrieval process described in a
later section.

For the task described in Figure 1, nine domains of
knowledge are assumed. The Macintosh graphical user
interface environment is represented in the domains of
dialog box, icon, interface objects, menu, and mouse. The
remaining domains are general facts about application,
application objects like graphs and spreadsheets, and
application functions like editing. The number of
propositions totals to 271.

Figure 3 is an example of the general knowledge about the
components of the graph domain, the properties of these
components and the functions that can be performed on a
component.   Propositions stating [**X** has **Y**] define
properties or components. Examples are [**Graph** has
Title], and [**Graph** has **Horizontal-Axis**].
Propositions of the form [**X** afford to **Y**] assert that **Y** can
be performed on **X**. An example is [*Graph-Title* afford to
Grab for *Move*] .

Action Plan Knowledge
The users modeled in this paper are assumed to have highly
generic low-level action plan knowledge required to use the
interface. The action plan knowledge is a set of plan
elements that represent knowledge about relations between a
user's action and the interface's visible response. An action,
such as pointing or single-click, is associated with multiple
plan elements which describe different responses of the
system depending on the current states of display objects.
The types of actions and the number of variation of each
action used for the simulation experiments described later
are six plan elements for pointing, three for single-click,
four for press-and-hold, two for release, two for double-click
and two for type.

Plan elements are stored in long-term memory in a generic
form and do not refer to specific objects in the current
display. However, when retrieved from long-term memory
and incorporated into the network in the construction phase,
the variables in the generic form are bound to objects in the
display. All plan elements are always incorporated into the
network in the construction phase.

A plan element consists of three fields. An example of a
plan element is shown in Table 1. The name field describes
the action, double-clicking on particular graph title, and its
result, bringing up a particular edit dialog box.   The
condition is a set of one or more propositions that must be
contained in the network in order for the plan to be able to

be executed. The outcome holds a set of one or more propositions that describe the consequences of executing the plan element in terms of changes in the display.

Links Within the Network

The network is defined by links between individual propositions. Different kinds of links have different strengths. The link strengths between propositions are defined by the following six parameters; the argument overlap weight, W_{arg}, free association weight, W_{assoc}, plan relation weight, W_{plan}, plan inhibition weight, W_{inhib}, the goal magnification factor, F_{goal} and the expectation magnification factor, F_{exp}. The free association weight is defined in the discussion of the retrieval process.

Argument Overlap Weight

Argument overlap is the most basic link between propositions. This link type connects propositions defining goal, expectation, the display representation, general knowledge and the name fields of plan elements. In the example used above, the argument *Graph-Title*, which appears in the goal, expectation, representation of the display, and the general knowledge retrieved from long-term memory, serves as an argument for linking among them. For example, the display representation, [*Graph-Title* is a kind of **Title**], has connection to [**Graph** has **Title**], [*Graph-Title* has link to *Edit-Dialog-Box*], [*Graph-Title* affords to **Grab** for *Move*], and [*Graph-Title* is not a kind of **Text**] stored in long-term memory. When two propositions share one argument, they are connected by a link of strength of W_{arg}.

Plan Relation Weight and Plan Inhibition Weight

Plan elements are different from the other kinds of knowledge since they describe procedural knowledge; they have condition and action parts and there are causal relations among them. If a condition of plan A is disabled by the execution of plan B, then plan A inhibits plan B. Or if a condition of plan A is satisfied by the execution of plan B, then plan A supports plan B. The strengths of causal relations are parameterized by W_{plan} and W_{inhib}.

Table 1. One of the two double-click plan elements bringing up an edit dialog box or starting an application.

Name:	Double-Click *Graph-Title* by **Arrow** for starting *Edit-Dialog-Box*
Condition:	If *Graph-Title* is on screen, *Graph-Title* is pointed at, above two *Graph-Title* s are identical *Graph-Title* has link to *Edit-Dialog-Box*, *Pointer-Shape* is **Arrow**, and *Pointer-Shape* is not **I-beam**
Outcome:	Then start *Edit-Dialog-Box*

Goal Magnification Factor and Expectation Magnification Factor

The links from goal and expectation to the rest of the network are treated differently from other links. The strengths of goal and expectation related links are calculated by multiplying the sum of W_{arg} and W_{assoc} by the manification factors F_{goal} and F_{exp}, respectively.

Retrieval of General Knowledge from Long-Term Memory Cued by Display, Goal, and Expectation

Recall that the display representation does not contain any knowledge of the attributes of an object or component, nor of the functions of or operations that can be performed on an object or component. These kinds of knowledge, which are retrieved by the probabilistic sampling process cued by display representations, goal, and expectation in the construction phase, play a crucial role in selecting a correct plan element to be executed. In order for the correct plan to fire, it must have the highest activation value among the executable plans, and all propositions in the correct plan's condition part must be incorporated in the network; part of them are found in the display representation and the rest in long-term memory. Plan elements receive activation from goal, expectation, and display representation propositions directly and/or via paths of links formed by general knowledge propositions, and from other plan elements by causal relations.

For example, the correct plan for the example task shown in Figure 1 is shown in Table 1. In order to make this plan executable, the proposition in the condition part, [*Graph-Title* has link to *Edit-Dialog-Box*], has to be retrieved from long-term memory because it is not a part of the display representation (see Figure 2 and Figure 3). The goal (1), expectation (2), and display representation (Figure 2) serve as retrieval cues for the proposition to be incorporated into the network.

The probabilistic sampling process works as follows. Each proposition in the goal, expectation, and display representation serves as a retrieval cue. The simulation first finds the set of all propositions in the general knowledge stored in long-term memory that are linked via argument overlap to a retrieval cue. Then the propositions in this set are sampled probabilistically based on the strength of the links between the retrieval cue and members of the set in long-term memory. Members of this set are sampled-with-replacement [16]. The number of retrieval attempts using the current proposition as the cue is specified by the sampling parameter, N_{sample}. Because of the nature of the sampling-with-replacement process, dominant associates may be retrieved more than once, but only one example of the proposition is included in the network. Each time a proposition in long-term memory is retrieved, the link strength between the cue and this proposition is increased by W_{assoc}.

RESULTS OF SIMULATION EXPERIMENTS AND DISCUSSION

We carried out four sets of simulation experiments. The first two were designed to evaluate the knowledge representations described in previous sections and to explore the model's parameter space.

The first set of simulations used a simple task of starting an application program by double-clicking its icon. The second set of experiments used a task that involved editing an icon label by inserting text.

The third set of simulations, using the same task as the second simulation, was designed to investigate the process by which the model makes errors by changing the sampling parameter a range of 4 to 14.

The fourth set of experiments simulated execution of part of the task shown in Figure 1. The simulated action sequence started with the spreadsheet containing the raw data on the screen. The model simulated two major subtasks. The first was to plot the observed data points as a function of serial position leading to the graph shown in Figure 1. The second subtask, shown in Figure 1, involved double-clicking the graph title to bring up a dialogue box which enabled the user to change the text of the title and font and point size of the text.

Exploration of the Parameter Space

A detailed report of the first two sets of simulation experiments is contained in Kitajima and Polson (in preparation). We briefly summarize the results here. The first set of simulation experiments showed that W_{assoc} had little or no effect on performance of the model and therefore that parameter was set equal to 1.0 in all of the remaining experiments. In addition, W_{plan} and W_{inhib} should be set to 1.0 and -1.0, respectively, for optimal performance of the model.

In the second set of experiments, N_{sample} was set to a large value, 14, assuring that the all necessary knowledge would be included in the network by the sampling process, F_{goal} and F_{exp} were set equal and manipulated over a range from 1 to 16, W_{arg} from 1 to 4, and the other parameters were set as above. The results showed that the larger W_{arg} becomes, the faster the integration phase converges, and the model consistently activates the correct plan element with the magnification factors (F_{goal} and F_{exp}) set to 16. The model will not activate the correct plan for small values of the magnification factors.

An Attentional Mechanism

The magnification factors had to be set to 16 before the correct plan would reliably get the highest activation and be executed. With the magnification factor equal to 16 and an overlap weight of 4, the link strength equals 64 for propositions in the network whose arguments overlap with the arguments of the goal and expectation propositions.

There are two reasons for this behavior. The magnification factor is a kind of "attention" parameter. During the construction phase, the large value of the magnification factor causes the model to preferentially sample propositions in long-term memory that overlap with the goal and expectation. In the step shown in Figure 1, the model will prefer to retrieve knowledge from long-term memory that elaborates the representation of the graph title. These elaborations are the critical propositions that provide links, a path, from the goal and expectation to the correct plan element.

During the integration phase, the large values of the link strengths between goal and expectation and the rest of the network, 64, cause the goal and expectation to be powerful sources of activation. Thus, paths that overlap arguments that appear in the goal and expectation will be highly activated. However, it is exactly one of these paths that leads to the correct plan element.

Errors

Studies of skilled users in a number of domains have shown that they have fairly high error rates. One of the earliest was Card, Moran, and Newell's [3] study of text editing, in which they observed about a 10% error rate. They hypothesized that experts were willing to trade off speed for accuracy because error correction was a routine skill and in most circumstances was not very costly.

There are numerous failure modes in the construction-integration model that can occur during the comprehension process. In this paper, we focus on the processes that cause errors due to action slips by expert users [14]. The model can make errors even when it is provided with correct goals, expectations, display state representations, all possible actions, and general knowledge. The stochastic memory retrieval process describe earlier can fail to sample critical pieces of general knowledge during the construction phase for small values of the sampling parameter. During action selection, the model uses the goal, expectation, and contents of the display to sample associatively related knowledge from long-term memory. Large values of the sampling parameter make it almost certain that all relevant knowledge will be included in the network. This memory retrieval process is part of Kintsch's [8] original model of text comprehension.

Sampling failures cause the model to build an incorrect representation during the construction phase. A skilled user fails to retrieve relevant information from long-term memory. As a result, critical information is missing from the network. The correct action may not be executable because its prerequisites are missing from the network, or the wrong action receives the highest activation because of the incomplete representation. We have assumed that the size of the sampling parameter is determined by a speed-accuracy trade off process.

Figure 4 shows the results of the third set of experiments that were conducted using the second task. Simulation runs were carried for each of the following set of values of the sampling parameter (4, 6, 8, 12, and 14). Figure 4 plots the probability of successfully completing the label editing task as a function of the sampling parameter. It is particularly interesting to note that the model is capable of performing in a region, 90 to 95% correct, that is characteristic of expert behavior.

There are other error modes. The model may build a correct representation but the parameters describing the activation process are wrong, leading to an incorrect action receiving the highest activation. This occurs when the magnification factors were set to small values.

Many current models [1, 2] of skilled performance do not provide well-motivated explanations of errors. These models use collections of production rules to generate a task's goal structure in working memory and the action sequences to perform the task. However, there are no mechanisms in these models that would cause working memory failures or incorrect rule execution accounting for errors.

The simulation results from the second task shown in Figure 4 demonstrate that the comprehension-based model reported in this paper can make occasional errors and still be able to perform complex tasks. Errors are caused by the failure to use necessary general knowledge stored in long-term memory. The important point to emphasize is that the model does not guess. Errors are due to misunderstandings of the current display state leading to selection of the wrong action.

Display-Based HCI
This section describes how the model is display-based in the sense used by Larkin and Simon [11] and describes the

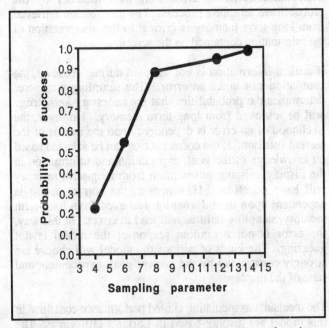

Figure 4. The probability of success plotted as a function of N*sample*.

results of the fourth set of experiments that simulated plotting and editing the graph shown in Figure 1.

Howes and Payne [5], Larkin and Simon [11], Larkin [10], and Kitajima [9] have all proposed models that made extensive use of information about intermediate states of a task contained in the environment or a display. Howes and Payne [5] took a grammatical approach to model roles of display in order to make analyses on the consistency of display-based interfaces. Larkin and Simon [11] were concerned with providing a principled account of why various kinds of visual displays could often dramatically facilitate problem solving processes. Larkin and Simon's [11] argument was that display-based problem solving enables individuals to substitute powerful perceptual operations for difficult and unreliably performed cognitive operations.

Classical information-processing models usually assume that users generate and maintain in working memory a complex goal structure that enables them to execute a sequence of actions necessary to perform a task [1, 2]. Larkin [10] and Kitajima [9] show that the state of the display can partially substitute for a complex goal structure stored in working memory. Both the display and the knowledge necessary to interpret to it substitute for a complex, potentially fragile, and difficult to maintain goal structure in working memory.

The Interactions of Goals, Expectations, and the Display
Table 2 presents the goals and expectations incorporated into the simulation that generated the sequence of actions to perform the task shown in Figure 1. The model has a few

Table 2. Goals, expectations and correct action steps for the third task.

G1 to draw line graph	
E11 to see entering into line graph environment	
step 1:	*Move Pointer to "Graph"*
step 2:	*Hold Down Mouse Button*
step 3:	*Move Pointer to "Line"*
step 4:	*Release Mouse Button*
E12 to see that "Serial Position" is selected as X axis	
step 5:	*Move Pointer to "Serial Position" in "Horizontal (X) Axis" Scroll Window*
step 6:	*Click Mouse Button*
E13 to see that "Observed" is selected as Y axis	
step 7:	*Move Pointer to "Observed" in "Horizontal (Y) Axis" Scroll Window*
step 8:	*Click Mouse Button*
E14 System draw line graph	
step 9:	*Move Pointer to "New Plot"*
step 10:	*Click Mouse Button*
G2 to edit graph title	
E21 edit graph title	
step 11:	*Move Pointer to "Title"*
step 12:	*Double Click "Title"*

general subgoals. Expectations provide most of the knowledge that organizes the sequence of actions that performs the task. As we described earlier, the large value of the magnification factor for links between the expectation and display causes the model to focus its "attention" on the part of the complex display relevant to the current sequence of steps. By attention, we mean that the model preferentially retrieves information from general knowledge stored in long-term memory linked to the arguments of the expectation. The model also strongly activates paths from the expectation to plan elements with overlapping arguments in their name fields.

Each expectation in Table 2 describes the final result of a sequence of steps, which means that there is *not* a new goal-expectation pair for each step. The successive selection of the most eligible plan element at each display state associated with an expectation, that is, the sequencing of steps, is controlled by the condition field of the plan elements, whose truth value is sensitively affected by the step-by-step changes in the display state.

Another critical fact of our model is that it makes extensive use of information about intermediate states of a task contained in the display. The construction-integration cycle

enables the model to bring all relevant knowledge to bear on the problem of selecting the next correct action. The importance of a given knowledge domain in selecting the action is shown by the amount of activation of propositions in that domain.

Figure 5 shows activation values per proposition in each domain. These values are calculated by dividing the activation values collected by each domain by the number of propositions in the domain. The domains shown in Figure 5 changed their values very sensitive to the content of the display and the current expectation. From the figure, it is clearly seen what part of knowledge was doing work in the network. The other domains had relatively constant activation values throughout the task, including mouse, icon, graph, editor, and spread sheet. Their averages were around 0.002 which was remarkably smaller than those values shown in Figure 5.

SUMMARY

This paper has provided a detailed account of a computational model of the skilled use of a graphical user interface. It is highly flexible and is capable of making mistakes, hallmarks of skilled behavior.

Our most important contribution is the explanation of errors made by expert users who have complete, well-learned knowledge of how to perform tasks. The model can make errors because it must compute each correct action. It does not have a verbatim representation of the correct action sequence which is always successfully retrieved from memory. In our current models, the simulation is provided with the correct sequence of goals and expectations required to perform a task. The representation of the current situation is constructed from information in the goal, expectation, and the display. It is then augmented by information retrieved from long-term memory by the probabilistic sampling process. The information retrieved from long-term memory is critical to the interpretation of the information contained on the screen.

If critical information is not sampled during retrieval, the simulation can make an error. The sampling parameter determines the probabilities that the necessary knowledge will be retrieved from long-term memory. However, the likelihood of an error is dependent upon the details of the current situation. If the correct action can be selected based on knowledge of the goal, expectation and information in the display, missing information from long-term memory will have no effect. If, however, the correct action is dependent upon the information retrieved from long-term memory, sampling failures will lead to errors. In this way, the error is not a random response; the model is not guessing. The kinds of actions the model will choose are strongly constrained by the current goal, expectation, and state of the display.

The mechanisms mediating skilled performance contained in this model are display-based in Larkin's [10] sense. The results of the fourth set of simulation experiments show

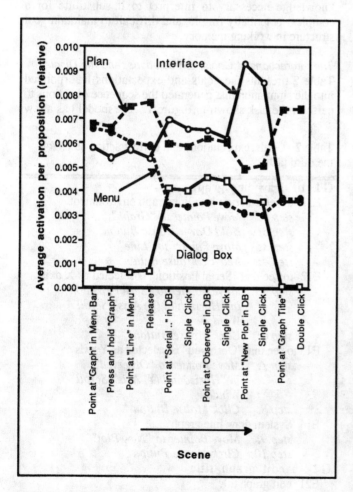

Figure 5. Knowledge use in the integration process.

how a model is able to compute the action sequence necessary to plot and edit the graph shown in Figure 1. Expectations described in terms of expected changes in the display guide execution of the task and focus the model's "attention" on the part of the display relevant to the current task. The model preferentially samples information from long-term memory providing a detailed elaboration of the relevant parts of the display. Utilization of information in the various knowledge domains varies as a function of step in this complex task. These variations are jointly determined by changes in the expectation and the state of the display. The step-by-step changes in display state are used for sequencing the actions to complete a task.

ACKNOWLEDGMENTS

We wish to thank Clayton Lewis, Walter Kintsch, David Kieras, and Stephanie Doane for their contribution to this research program. We thank John Rieman, Adrienne Lee, Peter Foltz, and Dannielle McNamar for their comments on earlier version of this paper. Muneo Kitajima was a visitor at the Institute of Cognitive Science, University of Colorado during our collaboration. Peter Polson's participation in this research was supported in part by NSF Grant IRI 87-22792 and by Army Research Institute Contract MDA903-89-K-0025.

REFERENCES

1. Anderson, J. R. Skill acquisition: Compilation of weak-method solutions. *Psychological Review*, 94 (1987), 192-211.

2. Bovair, A. S., Kieras, D. E., and Polson, P. G. The acquisition and performance of text-editing skill: a cognitive complexity analysis. *Human Computer Interaction*, 5, 1 (1990), 1-48.

3. Card, S. K., Moran, T. P., and Newell, A. *The Psychology of Human-Computer Interaction*. Lawrence Erlbaum Associates, Hillsdale, NJ., 1983.

4. Doane, S. M., Kintsch, W., and Polson, P. G. Modeling UNIX command production: What experts must know. ICS Technical Report #90-1. Institute of Cognitive Science, University of Colorado, Boulder CO., 1990.

5. Howes, A., and Payne, S. J. Display-based competence: towards user models for menu-driven interfaces. *Int. J. of Man-Machine Studies*, 33 (1990), 637-655.

6. Kieras, D. E. Towards a Practical GOMS Model Methodology for User Interface Design. In M. Helander (Ed.) *The Handbook of Human-Computer Interaction*. Amsterdam, NV: North-Holland , 1988.

7. Kieras, D., and Polson, P. G. An approach to the formal analysis of user complexity. *Int. J. of Man-Machine Studies*, 22 (1985), 365-394.

8. Kintsch, W. The role of knowledge in discourse comprehension: A construction-integration model. Psychological Review, 95 (1988), 163-182.

9. Kitajima, M. A formal representation system for the human- computer interaction process. *Int. J. Man-Machine Studies*, 30 (1989), 669-696.

10. Larkin, J. H. Display-based problem solving. In D. Klahr and K. Kotovsky (Eds.). *Complex Information Processing: The Impact of Herbert A. Simon*. Lawrence Erlbaum Assoc, Hillsdale, New Jersey, 1989, 319-342.

11. Larkin, J.H., and Simon, H.A. Why a diagram is (sometimes) worth 10,000 words. *Cognitive Science*, 11 (1987), 65-100.

12. Mannes, S. M., and Kintsch, W. Routine computing tasks: Planning as Understanding. *Cognitive Science*, 15 (1991), 305-342.

13. Mayes, J.T., Draper, S.W., McGregor, M.A., and Oatley, K. Information flow in a user interface: the effect of experience and context on the recall of MacWrite screens. In *People and Computer IV*, D.M. Jones and R. Einder, Eds., Cambridge University Press, Cambridge, UK., 1988.

14. Norman, D.A. Categorization of action slips. *Psychological Review*, 88 (1981), 1-15.

15. Payne, S. J. Display-based action at the user interface, *Int. J. of Man-Machine Studies*, 35 (1991), 275-289.

16. Raaijmaker, J. G., and Shiffrin, R. M. Search of associative memory. *Psychological Review*, 88, 1981, 93-134.

17. Selz, O. The laws of cognitive activity, productive and reproductive: A condensed version. In Frijda, N.H. and De Groot, A. *Otto Selz: His Contribution to Psychology*. Mouton Publishers, The Hague, The Netherlands, 1990, 20-75.

18. Wharton, C., and Lewis, C. Soar and construction-integration model: Pressing a button in two cognitive architectures. Technical Report #CU-CS-466-90. Department of Computer Science, University of Colorado, Boulder CO., 1990.

A GOMS Analysis of a Graphic, Machine-Paced, Highly Interactive Task.

Bonnie E. John
School of Computer Science
& Department of Psychology

Alonso H. Vera
Department of Psychology

Carnegie Mellon University
Pittsburgh, PA 15213
(412) 268-7182
bej@cs.cmu.edu

ABSTRACT

A GOMS analysis was used to predict the behavior of an expert in a graphic, machine-paced, highly interactive task. The analysis was implemented in a computational model using the Soar cognitive architecture. Using only the information available in an instruction booklet and some simple heuristics for selecting between operators, the functional-level behavior of the expert proved to be virtually dictated by the objects visible on the display. At the keystroke-level, the analysis predicted about 60% of the behavior, in keeping with similar results in previous GOMS research. We conclude that GOMS is capable of predicting expert behavior in a broader range of tasks than previously demonstrated.

KEYWORDS: user models, cognitive models, GOMS, Soar, video games.

GOMS AND HIGHLY INTERACTIVE TASKS

GOMS analyses have been used to model many tasks in a diversity of domains [13]. Early analyses were of tasks with a static visual display. Editing tasks used red marks on a paper copy, choice reaction time stimuli were presented at a single position on a CRT screen, spreadsheet formulae and database queries were described on hard-copy, and typing tasks primarily involved transcription from hard-copy or from a single position on a CRT screen. Also, in many of the tasks, the user was free to work at his or her own pace; the user did not have to wait for critical information to appear, and critical information did not disappear. Subtasks were not thrust upon the user by a changing environment. Thus, these early studies did not demonstrate the appropriateness of the GOMS method for interactive tasks.

Recently, we extended the scope of GOMS analyses with an analysis of telephone operator call handling ([6], [3]). This task involved fleeting auditory and visual input, that

could occur before or after the information was needed in the task. It also included speech input and output. Although the input was in real-time and the rate of task completion primarily driven by the task environment rather than the operator's skill, the knowledge of the goals, operators, methods, and selection rules associated with the task was sufficient to predict behavior. Additionally, we have also discovered GOMS-like behavior in an information retrieval task with an interactive computer browser [14].

The goal of the present work is to apply GOMS to even more highly interactive tasks. We believe video games are extreme examples of such tasks. The interaction in many video games seems largely driven by the game rather than by the player. Goals seem to be interrupted, suspended and returned to. Yet, similar to other domains successfully modelled by GOMS, an expert's behavior looks to be highly knowledge intensive and eventually becomes routine.

Some researchers have suggested that GOMS-style analyses cannot model behavior in real-time, dynamic, interactive tasks [1]. They argue that such tasks can only be modeled with completely reactive systems involving no planning at all. The question is therefore whether real-time constraints prevent the application of expert knowledge in such tasks or whether an expert's knowledge of a highly interactive, perceptually-driven motor task can be applied under these time constraints to yield routine plan-like behavior. If the latter is true, then this behavior should be captured by GOMS's goals, operators, methods, and selection rules. In this paper we argue that planning-based methods successfully describe behavior in such highly interactive domains and that this is a significant extension of these tools.

THE TASK

In response to a professional challenge (a panel at the Human Factors Society Meeting 1990), we did a GOMS analysis of Nintendo's Super Mario Bros. 3®.[1] This is a typical adventure game with treasures to collect, enemies to avoid or kill, and super powers to acquire and use. The

---

[1] Super Mario Bros. 3, Nintendo, and the games and characters discussed in this paper are trademarks of Nintendo of America Inc.

player manipulates the character Mario through the world by pressing buttons on a hand held controller. Four buttons on the controller are pressed with the left thumb to move Mario left, right, up or down; two buttons are pressed with the right thumb to make Mario jump, pick up objects, or increase speed.

The task used in this analysis is to traverse part of World 1, Level 1, collecting as many points as possible. A videotape of a nine-year-old expert, KP, performing the task provided observed behavior against which to measure the predictions of the GOMS analyses.

TWO GOMS ANALYSES IMPLEMENTED IN SOAR

GOMS suggests that the goals, operators, and methods can be defined from an objective analysis of the task. We conducted the GOMS analyses with as little reference to the expert's behavior as possible, opting instead, for taking the knowledge explicit in the instruction booklet and reasoning about the task itself.

The analyses were carried out at two levels: the *functional-level*, where operators are at the level of searching a block that or killing an enemy, and the *keystroke-level*, where operators are at the level of individual finger movements on the game's control panel. Each level is considered a separate GOMS analysis, as in Chapter 5 of Card, Moran, & Newell [2]. The two analyses will be described in parallel, beginning with the goals, operators, methods and selection rules for each, then describing the process of applying this information to the task of playing the game.

Goals, Operators, Methods, and Selection Rules

The instruction booklet [12] provides the overall *goals* of the game: to finish each level, to increase your standing (e.g. with points, or coins), and to avoid danger. These goals can be accomplished by performing *functional-level operators*. Functional-level operators appear in the instruction manual as direct commands or warnings. For instance, the command "Hit blocks...A useful item might pop out!" is implemented as a functional-level operator called `search-in-block`, and the warning "BEWARE! THE FOLLOWING ARE DEADLY" is implemented as a functional-level operator called `avoid-danger`.

Functional-level operators are accomplished through *keystroke-level operators* [2], which correspond to pressing the buttons on the controller described above. The instruction booklet also provides *methods*, or sequences of motor operators, for accomplishing some of the functional-

---

2 The terms *goals, functional-level operators* and *keystroke-level operators* are used to distinguish between three different levels in the typical GOMS goal hierarchy. This distinction is drawn to fascilitate exposition, and does not reflect a theoretical distinction between goals and operators. As Kieras [9] observes for GOMS analyses in general, "this distinction is intuitively-based, and it is also relative; it depends on the level of analysis."

level operators. For instance, the booklet shows the keystrokes necessary to pick up a shell, run with it, throw it at a block on the ground, and thereby break the block to find the treasure within.

Occasionally, there is more than one method available for accomplishing a functional-level operator, e.g. an enemy can be attacked either by jumping on its back or hitting it with Mario's tail (a desirable appendage acquired when a series of treasures are collected). Although the instruction booklet describes the alternative methods, it does not provide the selection rules necessary to decide between them. These are presumably acquired by the user as he or she experiments with the different methods in the course of playing the game. We produced selection rules for our analysis by preferring the method that gave the most points. For instance, in one case, the jump-on method described above gives 200 more points than the hit-with-tail method. Where there were no point differences, we produced a selection rule favoring an old technique familiar from previous versions of the game over a new technique peculiar to this version. For this segment of the game, these two considerations were sufficient to explain all of the expert's method selections.

The Soar Implementation of the GOMS Analysis

These goals, functional-level operators, keystroke-level operators, methods, and selection rules, were built into a computational model using the Soar architecture. Soar is a unified theory of cognition embodied in a production system architecture that has been used by researchers to model users performing several HCI tasks, including using automatic teller machines [15], browsing through a help system [14], and learning task-action mappings for an interface [4]. We chose to create a Soar implementation for several reasons. First, a Soar model can be run dynamically, like a computer program, making it easier to assess interactive behavior than typical hand-simulation of GOMS models. Furthermore, as will be discussed later, Soar allows us to back-up from the expert GOMS model and use Soar's inherent learning mechanisms to investigate how methods and selection rules might be acquired through experience.

HI-Soar (for Highly-Interactive-Soar) was constructed as a direct implementation of the GOMS analysis. Functional-level operators are proposed in response to objects appearing on the display, and accomplished through methods comprised of individual keystroke-level operators. HI-Soar interacts with a Lisp system which simulates the content of the display after each keystroke-level operator is applied. This simulation is not real-time, nor is it a full simulation of the game, rather, it gives HI-Soar an encoded representation of the objects on the display that would result from the particular keystroke at that particular point in the game.

Since many relevant objects appear on any one display, more than one functional-level operator is applicable at any one time. An analogous situation occurred in early GOMS analyses of text-editing [2] because the stimulus manuscript had between 3 and 11 editorial marks per page; the user had to select which edit to perform next and comprehend the editing marks to set the goal of the unit task. Card, Moran and Newell incorporated these selection processes into the GET-NEXT-TASK operator. Because text manipulation is highly regular in a left-to-right, top-to-bottom sequence, these selection processes were not discussed at length in early GOMS work. However, in a videogame, the selection of what to do next has much more importance to the outcome of the game and is more subject to individual differences. For our analysis, we developed preferences to select between functional-level operators based on common-sense reasoning about the game. For instance, when many blocks are available, search-in-block is proposed for each of them. We posited a preference for searching in the block closest to Mario. A description of the full set of preferences is beyond the scope of this paper; we refer the reader to John, Vera and Newell [8] for a more detailed account.

As an example of operator proposal and preferences, at the start-up display of the game there are four Question Boxes (QB1 through QB4, where QB1 is closest to Mario and QB4 is the furthest away) and one enemy (a "Goomba") visible on the display. This causes the functional-level operators search-in-block(QB1), search-in-block(QB2), search-in-block(QB3), search-in-block(QB4), and attack-enemy(Goomba) to be proposed. The preferences dictate that search-in-block(QB1) be chosen because it is closest to Mario and the Goomba is not an immediate threat.

Once a particular functional-level operator is selected HI-Soar must determine what method to use to accomplish the functional-level operator. The selection of the method is contingent on many aspects of the situation: powers possessed by Mario, tools available, etc. HI-Soar then selects and applies the appropriate keystroke-level operators to perform the method. When a keystroke-level operator is applied, it sends a message to the external Lisp system which provides information about the contents of the new display back to the perceptual level of HI-Soar.

After each keystroke-level operator is performed, the state of display changes and must be re-evaluated. New functional-level operators have an opportunity to take precedence over the current functional-level operator. Continuing the example, in service of search-in-block(QB1), Mario moves to the right under the control of the press-right-button keystroke-level operator. Simultaneously, the Goomba moves left, closer to Mario. At the point where the Goomba becomes an immediate threat, the preference for attack-enemy(Goomba) overrides that for search-in-block(QB1) and the current functional-level operator changes to attack-enemy(Goomba). This invokes the jump-on method and, in turn, the press-A-button keystroke-level operator. After the Goomba is killed, the preference for search-in-block(QB1) again takes precedence and

Mario is moved right until he is under QB1; press-A-button is again invoked causing him to jump to complete the search-in-block operator.

Thus, given the changes visible on the game screen as input, HI-Soar model predicts the sequence of functional-level operators, methods, and keystroke-level operators that the expert will perform.

RESULTS OF THE GOMS ANALYSES

We compared the operators predicted by HI-Soar to the operators observed in the videotape for the first 30 seconds of the expert's game. Figure 1 shows the comparison at the functional-level and Figure 2 shows the comparison at the keystroke-level. In both figures, the operator names are listed along the vertical axis. The horizontal axis is labelled with a display number that indicates the opportunity for new functional-level operators to be selected. This designation corresponds roughly to time, where each display represents about a second's worth of activity.

In the figures, a black dot marks the inferred function of the expert's observed behavior at each display and a gray dot marks the operator HI-Soar performed at that display. The sense of these figures is that when the black and gray lines track each other, the model is making good predictions of observed behavior. Where the black and gray lines do not track, the model is not predicting the observed behavior.

Occasionally, the expert's behavior cannot be unambiguously inferred. For example, moving to the right could be in service of searching in a block located to the right, attacking an enemy located to the right, or just moving toward the end of the world. In these cases, no black dot appears in the display column and all the HI-Soar operators consistant with that behavior are shown as thin black circles. Where there is a haze of thin black circles above or below the gray dots, the behavior is consistent with many possible functions and it is likely that any prediction will track behavior; where black circles are few, the observed behavior is consistent with only a few functions and the model must be accurate to track behavior.

Figure 2 uses the same graphic conventions as Figure 1 for the keystroke-level operators. For the operators and predictions, each horizontal unit, delineated by dotted lines, corresponds to the functional-level operator implemented by the keystroke-level operators shown in that unit and also to the display that caused the selection of that functional-level operator. Therefore, each horizontal unit is labelled at the top with its corresponding display number and at the bottom with its associated functional-level operator.

Figure 1, the comparison of the observed behavior to the predicted functional-level operators, shows some interesting features of the analysis. Most striking is the excellent agreement between the predicted functional-level operators and the observed behavior. Only once in 31 opportunities is a functional-level operator selected that is inconsistent with observed behavior (Display.21). This instance is at a point

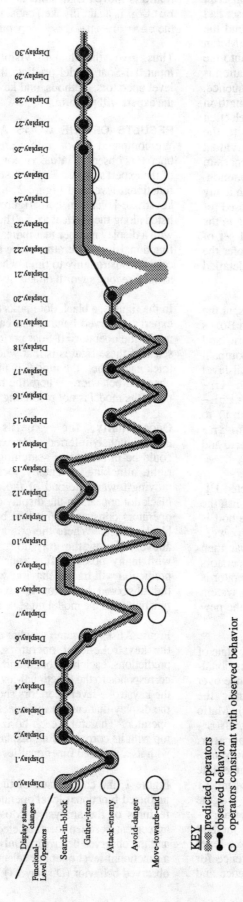

Figure 1. Comparison of the function-level model predictions with the observed behavior.

Black dots indicate functions inferred from the observed behavior. For instance, when Mario hits a block, we inferred that the intended function was to search in that block. Gray dots indicate the predicted functional-level operators. When an functional-level operator is predicted but a corresponding function cannot be unambiguously inferred from the observed behavior, a gray dot appears, but no black dot is drawn in the same Display column. In that case, all the functional-level operators consistent with the observed behavior are indicated with thin black circles. Gray lines connect the predicted functional-level operators and black lines connect the inferred functions. When no function can be unambiguously inferred, the black line passes through the predicted functional-level operator if that operator is consistent with the behavior, and does not pass through the predicted functional-level operator if that operator is contradictory to the observed behavior. Elongated gray circles represent consecutive displays in which the same functional-level operator, with the same argument, is selected. Elongated black circle indicate that the behavior observed throughout those displays is inferred to be in the service of the same function.

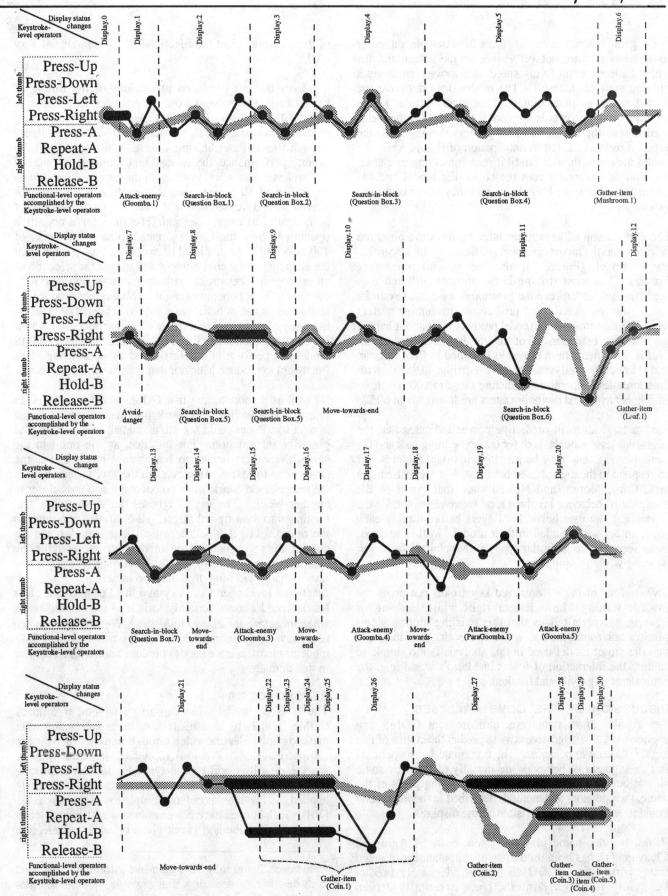

Figure 2. Comparison of keystroke-level predictions to observed behavior
(description same as that of Figure 1.)

in the game where the expert seems to anticipate gathering some coins that are not yet visible on the screen and for which he must attain flying speed. He moves left to get a running start for take-off. The model does not have the prior knowledge that coins will eventually appear to the right, and moves towards the end of the level (to the right) until it sees the coins, and then gathers them. Thus, the expert moves to the left in anticipation of flying, while the model moves to the right until it sees something to gather. As soon as the model sees the coins, the model and the expert have the same knowledge and they come back into synch.

The comparison of keystrokes inferred from the observed behavior and the motor operators predicted by the keystroke-level model, (Figure 2), also has several interesting features. The most striking is the dramatic difference in predictive power between the functional-level and keystroke levels; the functional-level predictions are almost perfect while the keystroke-level model predicts only about half of the observed behavior (46 of the 96 observed keystrokes). This is the same pattern of results obtained in Card, Moran, and Newell's analyses of text editing (1983), with functional-level operators predicting close to 100% of text-editing behavior and motor operators predicting about 60%.

Such a large drop in predictive power indicates that the keystroke-level models, both for the text-editing task and the game-playing task, may be missing important features that correspond to the unexplained behavior. For the text-editing task, Card, Moran, and Newell state that much of the unexplained behavior involved hand movements outside the model, e.g. the user licked her fingers before turning each page, an act not included in their model. In this analysis, there seems to be a similar type of unexplained behavior, twisting while jumping.

Twenty-four of the 37 observed keystrokes not predicted involve turning Mario left or right while jumping or floating. Experts tell us that this twisting motion slows Mario's horizontal motion while in the air. This indicates that the motor model used in this analysis is too simple to capture the interaction of forces in Mario's world (e.g. the equivalents of gravity and friction).

DISCUSSION OF THE GOMS ANALYSES

The results of this analysis indicate that GOMS can capture the knowledge necessary to predict the course of this highly interactive behavior. The functional-level operators in this segment of behavior are literally dictated by some simple heuristics derived from the overriding goals of the game, the operators and methods described in the instruction booklet, and the elements visible on the display.

Pengi, a video-game playing system built by Agre and Chapman [1], has been used to argue that planning-oriented frameworks such as GOMS cannot adequately predict behavior in highly-interactive, externally-driven environments. We believe that the results presented here demonstrate that this is not the case. Clearly, the sequence

of expert behavior at the functional level is predicted very well.

We have not yet produced predictions of the timing of keystroke-level operators from our analyses, as we have in other GOMS analyses (e.g., [7], [3]). However, preliminary analyses indicate that this model will behave reactively enough to simulate the time-course of the game. In the expert's performance, the average time between the onset of keystrokes is about 300 msec, with the range for same-hand keystrokes of 50 msec to over 2 seconds, and the range for alternate-hand keystrokes of 0 msec (simultaneous use of both hands) to over 1 second. The time for a cognitive operator in Soar has been estimated to be on the order of 100 msec [11]. At this level of expertise, Soar predicts that the elements in the environment will trigger the selection of an appropriate keystroke with only one or two cognitive operators. These operators could be buffered to produce the simultaneous use of both hands and the delay between same-hand keystrokes equal to a single cognitive operator (similar to the typing model in [5]). Thus, we believe that a GOMS model can perform in this fast-paced situation using plans (methods) to produce behavior that is sufficiently reactive.

As well as demonstrating that GOMS could produce such interactive behavior, this work provides evidence that a system like Pengi could not mimic human behavior without plan-like information. For instance, at one point in the game, the expert begins to search in a block that is the closest one to Mario. However, on the way to searching in the target block, Mario must go beyond it and pass closer to another block. The expert ignores the closer block and continues to the original target. HI-Soar also continues to the original target block because it has a preference for continuing to implement an incomplete method for the current `search-in-block` functional-level operator rather than switching to a new `search-in-block` functional-level operator. A system like Pengi, on the other hand, would almost certainly switch to the second block when it became the closest to Mario.[3] We would argue that some level of planning, similar to the methods in GOMS models at least, is necessary to produce human-like behavior in this domain.

BEYOND GOMS

The HI-Soar model allows us to go beyond traditional GOMS models to investigate how users can acquire the methods and selection rules through experience with the computer system. Previous studies of the acquisition of routine cognitive skill have typically involved directly providing subjects with a set of methods that, if properly applied, will lead to successful completion of the task (e.g., [10]). Such studies have not examined what happens when the appropriate method is not given or when no selection

---

[3] However, Pengi may have plan-like information encoded in its deictic representation. For example, "the-block-I-am-going-to-search-in", as distinct from "the-block-closest-to me", would allow it to prevent interruption of the goal.

rules are supplied. How do people acquire methods or selection rules through experience? The Soar unified theory of cognition provides an inherent learning mechanism, *chunking*, with which to address these questions. By examining the content of the HI-Soar model, we can identify knowledge that the expert exhibits but is not in the instruction booklet, remove that knowledge from the model, and show how the HI-Soar can learn that knowledge though playing the game.

For example, we described the first display of the game, where four Question Blocks and an enemy could be acted upon. The expert version of HI-Soar has a preference for searching in the closest block, hence, `search-in-block(QB1)` is selected. We eliminated the selection rules from a second version of HI-Soar and, instead, gave it an evaluation function based on how many points would be gotten from each of the proposed functional-level operators. This version of the model successfully chooses the same functional-level operator for the start-up display as the model with the explicit selection rules.

In another case, we looked at how the method of jumping onto a scaffold to search an otherwise unreachable block might be learned. The expert HI-Soar model has hand-coded knowledge that when searching in a block that is out of reach, Mario should jump on the scaffold under it. In a less expert version of HI-Soar, the model can recognize that a block is out of reach and use means-ends analysis to figure out that jumping on a scaffold would allow Mario to reach the block. Chunking integrates the solution as a new method and HI-Soar then transfers that knowledge to all subsequent blocks that are out of reach.

These investigations into how HI-Soar can learn methods and selection rules provide predictions about how people can learn from experience. We are continuing these explorations into learning by manipulating the knowledge in HI-Soar, the situations presented to it, and by comparing its predictions to the behavior of humans as they learn to play the game.

CONCLUSIONS

In summary, this work indicates that a GOMS model can predict functional-level behavior in the highly interactive domain of video games. To a lesser extent, GOMS can predict keystroke-level behavior as well, although a more detailed model of perceptual-motor behavior and the dynamics of the game world would probably lead to more accurate predictions. This work, therefore, represents an extension of the GOMS methodology to much more interactive, machine-paced, and graphic-based applications than has been previously demonstrated. However, given the limited nature of this demonstration, with a single user for less than a minute of behavior, continued investigation is necessary to establish the veracity of these conclusions. In addition, the implementation of these GOMS analyses in a Soar model allows us to investigate how GOMS methods and selection rules might be learned through experience.

ACKNOWLEDGEMENTS

This research was done in preparation for a panel at the Human Factors Society Meeting in Orlando, Oct. 5-12, 1990, organized by Wayne Gray and Mike Atwood of the Intelligent Interfaces Group at the NYNEX Science and Technology Center and we thank them for the professional challenge. This work was supported by the Office of Naval Research, Cognitive Science Program, Contract Number N00014-89-J-1975N158. The views and conclusions contained in this document are those of the authors and should not be interpreted as representing the official policies, either expressed or implied, of the Office of Naval Research or the U. S. Government. We would also like to thank Kyle Gray, Jay Anderson, and Billy Esch for their expert advice about playing Super Mario Bros. 3®.

REFERENCES

1. Agre, P. E. and Chapman, D. Pengi: An implementation of a theory of activity. In *Proceedings of the Sixth National Conference on Artificial Intelligence*, 268-272. Menlo park, Calif: American Association for Artificial Intelligence, 1987.

2. Card, S. K., Moran, T. P., & Newell, A. *The psychology of human-computer interaction.* Lawrence Erlbaum, Associates, Hillsdale, NJ, 1983.

3. Gray, W. D., John, B. E., & Atwood, M. E. (submitted to Human-Computer Interaction) Project Ernestine: Validating GOMS for predicting and explaining real-world task performance.

4. Howes, A. and Young, R.M., Predicting the Learnability of Task-Action Mappings, In proceedings of *CHI 1991* (New Orleans, April 30-May 4, 1989) ACM, New York, 1991.

5. John, B. E. *Contributions to engineering models of human-computer interaction.* Doctoral dissertation, Carnegie Mellon University, 1988.

6. John, B. E. Extensions of GOMS analyses to expert performance requiring perception of dynamic visual and auditory information. In proceedings of *CHI 1990* (Seattle, Washington, April 30 - May 4, 1990) ACM, New York, 1990, 107-115.

7. John, B. E. & Newell, A., Toward an engineering model of stimulus response compatibilty. In *Stimulus Response Compatibillity: an Integrated Perspective.* R. W. Procter & T. G. Reeve (eds.) North-Holland: New York, NY, 1990.

8. John, B. E., Vera, A. H., and Newell, A.. *Towards real-time GOMS.* Carnegie Mellon University, School of Computer Science Technical Report CMU-SCS-90-195, 1990.

9. Kieras, D. E. Towards a practical GOMS model methodology for user interface design in M. Helander

(ed.) *Handbook of Human-Computer Interaction.*. North-Holland: Elsevier Science Publishers B. V., 1988.

10. Kieras, D. E. and Bovair, S. The acquisition of procedures from text: A production system analysis of transfer of training. *Journal of Memory and Learning,* **25**, 507-524, 1986.

11. Newell, A. *Unified theories of cognition.* Cambridge, Mass: Harvard University Press, 1990.

12. Nintendo of America, *Super Mario Bros. 3 Instruction Booklet*.

13. Olson, J. R. & Olson, G. M. The growth of cognitive modeling in human computer interaction since GOMS. *Human Computer Interaction.*, 1989.

14. Peck, V. A., & John, B. E. (Submitted) "Browser-Soar: A computational model of a highly interactive task" School of Computer Science, Carnegie Mellon University.

15. Wharton, C. (In Preparation) Implications of the Differences Between Cognitive Architectures for Human-Computer Interaction. Ph.D. Dissertation Thesis, University of Colorado, Boulder.

COUPLING APPLICATION DESIGN AND USER INTERFACE DESIGN

Dennis J.M.J. de Baar
Faculty of Technical Mathematics and Informatics, Delft University of Technology,
Binnenwatersloot 3, 2611 BJ Delft, The Netherlands, *email*: winfddb@duticai.tudelft.nl

James D. Foley
College of Computing, Georgia Institute of Technology
Atlanta, GA 30332-0280, *email:* foley@cc.gatech.edu

Kevin E. Mullet
Human Interface Technology Group, SunSoft Inc.,
2550 Garcia Ave. MS 1-07, Mountain View, CA 94043-1100, *email:* mullet@sun.com

ABSTRACT

Building an interactive application involves the design of both a data model and a graphical user interface (GUI) to present that model to the user. These two design activities are typically approached as separate tasks and are frequently undertaken by different individuals or groups. Our approach eliminates redundant specification work by generating an interface directly from the data model itself. An inference engine using style rules for selecting and placing GUI controls (i.e., widgets) is integrated with an interface design tool to generate a user interface definition. This approach allows a single data model to be mapped onto multiple GUI's by substituting the appropriate rule set and thus represents a step toward a GUI-independent run-time layout facility.

KEYWORDS: User Interface Software, Automatic User Interface Design, Data Models

INTRODUCTION

An early step in the design of an interactive application is the definition of the application's data model. In an object-oriented design, the data model consists of an object class hierarchy in which each object has an associated set of attributes and methods. Single or multiple inheritance is typically used to avoid repetitive specification of shared methods and attributes. The attributes and methods of an object are either internal or external. Internal attributes and

methods are meant for use within the application and are not exposed in the user interface. External attributes and methods are represented in the user interface as standard interaction objects such as buttons, settings, or sliders (hereafter referred to as "controls") or as data manipulated directly by the user.

The design of the user interface normally takes place only after the application data model has been completed. The external attributes and methods of the data model must be mapped onto a set of controls in the target GUI. These controls must then be divided among one or more application windows and arranged to fit within the available space while maintaining the organizational characteristics required for clear communication and aesthetic quality. Guidelines for control selection and arrangement are provided by GUI-specific style guides such as the OPEN LOOK GUI Application Style Guidelines [13], the OSF/Motif Style Guide [11], the Apple Human Interface Guidelines [1] and the CUA Style Guide [7]. These documents provide high-level rules and principles that help to maximize consistency across applications in the respective GUI's.

A number of commercially-available software tools provide a GUI interface to the GUI design task. *GUI builders* such as Devguide [14], Interface Builder [9], and Interface Architect [6] present the designer with standard user interface components that can be dragged onto the work surface and arranged using direct manipulation. Each of these tools can be used to generate source code or executables for a particular configuration of GUI components, but all rely on the skill and knowledge of the user interface designer to create the desired configuration themselves by manually selecting the appropriate controls and specifying their locations within the parent window. This limitation means that the interface designer is required to repeatedly perform three tasks that are at least potentially unnecessary:

(1) Access details of the data model, either from documentation or from (the designer's) memory.

(2) Access and apply GUI-specific control selection rules that determine how each element of the data model is mapped onto a particular control in the target GUI.

(3) Access and apply GUI-specific layout rules governing the placement of each control in the target GUI.

To create a property window, for example, the designer must know the attributes (properties) of the object represented by that property window, decide on a particular GUI component to use for each attribute, and arrange the components within a window according to the layout conventions established by the target GUI.

Automatic generation of window and menu layouts from information already present in the application data model can relieve the application designer of unnecessary work while providing an opportunity to automatically apply style rules to the interface design. A number of existing systems demonstrate the feasibility of automating one or more of the design tasks identified above. Mickey [10] generates a Macintosh user interface (menus and dialog boxes) from interface descriptions embedded in Pascal. ITS [15] and Jade [16] use a set of style rules created by a style expert and a specification of the dialog content to generate dialog boxes. Jade also includes graphical editing capabilities, which allow the designer to refine the user interface generated automatically by the system. Chisel [12] includes a set of "hints" which assist in placing dialog box elements. DON [8] combines a User Interface Design Environment (UIDE) specification [4] with a set of layout rules to design dialog boxes that reflect visual design goals such as weight and balance.

This paper describes an approach to automating the interface design process that addresses all three of the potentially redundant design tasks identified above. Our system integrates *D2M2edit* [2], an interactive tool for creating data models, *Devguide* [14], an interactive user interface design tool, and a set of *design conventions* embodied in the OPEN LOOK GUI Application Style Guidelines [13]. We will describe the relation between the application data model and the user interface, mechanisms used to select a set of controls to represent a data model and arranging them within a target window, and a design environment that integrates the semantic data modelling and user interface design capabilities. A companion video tape segment is included in the conference video tape.

DATA OBJECTS AND INTERACTION OBJECTS

In the data model of an object-oriented application, every *data object* has associated *attributes* and *actions*. Together, these constitute the semantic layer of the application. In a user interface management system (UIMS) such as UIDE [4], the actions are associated with pre- and post-conditions describing the state of the application before and after the

action is invoked. This information, when available, can be a valuable aid in determining the most appropriate means of presenting the application semantics to a user. *Interaction objects* are controls such as buttons, sliders, or menus that can be manipulated directly by the user. Every interaction

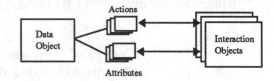

Figure 1 The relation between application data and interaction objects.

object in the user interface is associated with an action or attribute in the application data model (Figure 1). In Figure 2, for example, the attribute 'volume Input' in the application data model is linked to a slider that can be used to change its value.

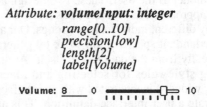

*Attribute: **volumeInput: integer***
    range[0..10]
    precision[low]
    length[2]
    label[Volume]

Volume: 8   0 ▬▬▬▬▯ 10

Figure 2 An attribute and its descriptors from the application data model along with its representation as an interaction object in the user interface.

In this example, the data model includes information that specifies the number of digits (length), the allowable values (range), and the associated label string (label). All of these characteristics are inherent attributes of the data object. The data model may also include supporting information, or *metadata*, that can be used by the modeler to clarify the intended semantics of the data object. In this example, a piece of metadata (precision) provides a rough estimate of the accuracy users will expect in manipulating the data object. Metadata describes the way a data object will be *used* instead of the qualities inherent in the data object itself.

Metadata provides guidance in control selection that is essential if the flexibility of the graphical user interface is to be fully exploited. Sophisticated control selection schemes can be devised if extensive metadata is available, but this approach tends to defeat the goal of isolating the data modelling task from the interface design task. Metadata specified as part of the application data model should therefore address only characteristics that are inherent in the intended usage or structure of the data object; it should not simply provide hooks on which to hang interface design decisions.

Dependencies between the data modelling and interface design environments can be reduced by making interface related metadata an optional part of the data modelling task. If the metadata is omitted during data modelling, an appropriate control can still be selected on the basis of the default for that characteristic. The resulting selections will be satisfactory, but may not be optimal.

MAPPING DATA OBJECTS INTO INTERACTION OBJECTS

In the current system, objects from the application data model are used as input to an automatic control selection and layout facility. An inference engine uses the actions and attributes of the data objects to generate a set of interaction objects in a direct manipulation interface design environment, which instantiates the interaction objects using a GUI toolkit and produces a textual specification describing the GUI components and their locations within one or more windows (see Figure 3).

Following the selection of specific interaction objects, a set of layout rules determines the location of each object. The layout rules implement a set of high-level graphic design conventions addressing the size, spacing, and alignment of individual controls.

The inference engine consists of a control selection component and a layout component. Both components are implemented as linear lists of simple *if-then* rules that can be easily modified and extended to accommodate local design conventions or different GUI standards. The inference engine is designed to be independent of the particular interaction library, or toolkit, that implements the standard GUI components in the target environment. The engine produces general conclusions that can be used to select and lay out appropriate controls for any target GUI toolkit for which an appropriate set of mapping rules has been defined. The following sections provide an overview of the two rule sets needed to generate an interface design.

CONTROL SELECTION RULES

The control selection rules make use of the OPEN LOOK GUI components shown in Figure 4. Additional widget types can be added to the rule base easily enough, though to make iterative design practical, the new widgets must be available in the design environment as well. On the following pages we present the control selection rules in a decision-table format. In Tables 1-4 below, a blank space means that the value is unchanged from the previous row in the same column. The value, *any*, means that the outcome for that row in the decision table is the same regardless of the value taken by the parameter in question.

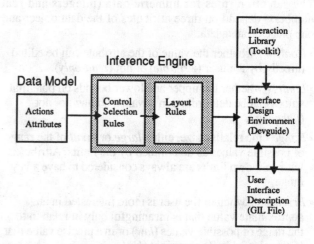

Figure 3   Information flow in the automatic control selection and layout process.

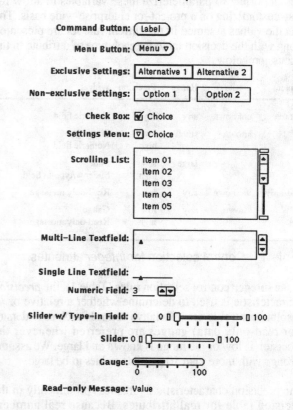

Figure 4   OPEN LOOK GUI components used by the system.

Five different attribute types (boolean, integer, real, enumerated, and string) are covered by the control selection rules. The control selection rule for individual **boolean** attributes is trivial: check boxes are used for all booleans. The OPEN LOOK GUI does provide an alternative control - the nonexclusive setting - but the more intuitive syntax and semantics of the check box make it clearly preferable for isolated boolean attributes.

The selection rules for numeric data (integers and real numbers) depend on three attributes of the data object and one piece of metadata:

- *Content* - whether the value of the attribute can be edited directly by the user (*writable*) or not (*read-only*).

- *Limits* - whether the upper and lower bounds on potential values can be determined in advance (*known*) or not (*unknown*).

- *Range* - the relative size, either *large* or *small* of the range of possible values as determined by the limits. Attributes with unknown limits are always considered to have a large range.

- *Precision* - whether the user is more interested in an approximate value that is meaningful only in relation to the range of possible values (*low*) or in a precise value that is meaningful in its own right (*high*).

It is important to parameterize these variables to allow for easy customizing on a project- or enterprise-wide basis. The specific values assumed in the current rule set are presented along with the decision table for each type of attribute in the discussion below.

Content	Limits	Range	Precision	Widget
editable	unknown	any	any	Numeric field
	known	small	low	Slider
			high	Numeric field
		large	low	Slider
			high	Slider w/type-in field
read-only	unknown	any	any	Read-only message
	known	any	low	Gauge
			high	Read-only message

Table 1   Control selection for *integer* attributes.

In the **integer** control selection rules (Table 1), the *precision* characteristic is used to determine whether a relative or an absolute control is used. Relative controls such as sliders or (for read-only data) gauges are preferred whenever the precision is low or the range is known and large. We assume a *range* with more than 10 possible values to be large.

The precision characteristic figures less prominently in the decision table for real attributes. Because real numbers represent continuous variables, inherently discrete controls such as sliders (whose possible values are limited to the number of pixels spanned by the slidable area) are appropriate only when the range is extremely small. A slider representing the range 0..10 in hundredth-unit increments, for example, would span the entire width of the typical workstation display.

Content	Limits	Range	Precision	Widget
editable	unknown	any	any	Textfield
	known	small	low	Slider
			high	Textfield
		large	any	Textfield
read-only	any	any	any	Read-only Message

Table 2   Control selection for *real* attributes.

The selection rules for **real** data objects (Table 2), specify a slider for real values with high *precision* only when the *range* is within -1 to +1. Otherwise, a standard textfield is used (the OPEN LOOK GUI does not define a numeric field for real numbers).

Items	Set Size	Label	Min	Max	Widget
few	static	short	1	1	Exclusive setting*
			0	1	Variation on exclusive setting
			0	1+	Nonexclusive setting
		med	1	1	Exclusive setting*
			0	1	Variation on exclusive setting
			0	1+	Check boxes
		long	1	1	Exclusive settings menu*
			0	1	Variation on excl settings menu
			0	1+	Nonexclusive settings menu
	dynamic	any	1	1	Exclusive settings menu
			0	1	Variation on excl settings menu
			0	1+	Nonexclusive settings menu
many	any	any	1	1	Abbreviated scrolling list
			0	1	Variation on excl scrolling list
			0	1+	Nonexclusive scrolling list

*Two-item enumerates whose labels contain opposing terms (e.g., On/Off, True/False, etc.) should use *check boxes*.

Table 3 Control selection for *enumerated* attributes.

The control selection rules for **enumerated** attributes (Table 3) are based on several characteristics:

- *Items* - the total number of items in the enumerated set of choices. The current rule set distinguishes only between enumerations with 9 or fewer choices (*few*) and those with 10 or more (*many*).

- *Set Size* - whether the number of choice items is fixed (*static*) or allowed to vary at run-time (*dynamic*).

- *Label* - the length of the label for the longest choice item in the enumeration. Characters are the unit of measure in the current rule set, which distinguishes between three label lengths: *short* (0-10 chars), *medium* (11-50), and *long* (51+). Ideally, the unit of measure should be pixels or points, especially if a proportional font is used for labels.

- *Min/Max* - the minimum and maximum number of simultaneous choices that is possible at any time in the enumeration. If the choices are *exclusive*, than exactly one item is chosen at all times. A *variation on exclusive* enumeration allows zero or one item to be chosen, while a *non-exclusive* enumeration allows any number of choices, including zero.

The amount of space consumed in the parent window is an important criterion for selecting the interaction object for an enumerated attribute. The total space occupied by the widget for an enumeration is a function of the number of items and the length of the character strings serving as the item labels.

Whenever possible, it is desirable to make all of the choices visible at all times. When the number of choices is relatively small and does not vary at run-time, a setting of the appropriate type is preferred. The settings are placed on a menu when the number of choices can vary dynamically. A menu might also be used - even for a small number of choices - when vertical space is at a premium in the parent window. When the number of items is large, a scrolling list is always used.

Check boxes, for example, are normally preferred over non-exclusive settings in the current rule set, both because their semantics are somewhat more intuitive and because they are less confusable with OPEN LOOK exclusive settings. Check boxes, however, do not group well with their labels when arranged with more than one item per row. The rule set thus prefers nonexclusive settings when the item labels are short enough to permit three or more settings in the same row. When the label is too long to fit within the available space, a settings menu displays the complete label on demand.

One problem encountered in the development of the control selection rules is that any set of attributes that can be modeled as a non-exclusive enumerate can also be expressed as a series of apparently unrelated booleans and might be represented as such in the data modelling environment. Communication is improved by presenting the booleans as a set of options in a non-exclusive enumerate. The problem is to identify boolean attributes that are truly independent of all other attributes so that they can be collected in a single group with a generic, "Options," label.

The selection rules for **string** attributes (Table 4) are fairly straightforward. A single or multi-line textfield is chosen based on the size of the string represented by the field. The *length* characteristic is the maximum length, in characters, of the text string. The current rule set distinguishes only between *short* (1-50 chars) and *long* (50+) strings.

Content	Length	Widget
editable	short	Single line text field
	long	Multi-line textfield
read-only	short	Read-only message
	long	Read-only multi-line textfield

Table 4 Control selection for *string* attributes.

Actions from the application data model are realized as commands appearing in menus in an OPEN LOOK base window. The individual menu commands can be of one of three types. If the action is invoked directly by the menu item, a *command item* is used. If the action causes a pop-up window to be displayed, a *window item* is used. If the action causes a submenu to be displayed, a *menu item* is used.

The control selection rules produce a set of standard GUI components that provides an interface to the associated data object, but these controls must still be arranged within the application window before they can be used. The following section describes how this task has been automated.

LAYOUT RULES

The output of the control selection rules is fed directly into the layout portion of the inference engine. The layout rules take a set of interaction objects and a parent window as input and produce a spatial arrangement of the controls within the window as output. In the current implementation, interaction objects whose parent is a base window (actions) are arranged within a control area at the top of the window. Those whose parent is a pop-up window (attributes) are arranged in an OPEN LOOK command or property window.

The current rule set creates layouts that are consistent with the OPEN LOOK Application Style Guidelines [13]. Figure 5 shows a layout generated automatically by the rule set. The example window contains two strings, an integer, two enumerates, and a boolean. (The Apply and Reset buttons appear in every OPEN LOOK property window and are present by default.)

Figure 5 An OPEN LOOK compliant property window generated by the system.

A few simple spacing guidelines help ensure a consistent and aesthetically pleasing result. A virtual layout grid is used to align objects and provide adequate visual separation and grouping within the window. The grid is made up of regular units whose size depends on the scale of the window, which is usually determined by the size of the font used in the window's controls. With the default 12-point font, a 10-point grid unit is used. Five basic constraints are sufficient to satisfy the OPEN LOOK layout requirements:

• 1 grid unit vertical space between controls.

• 1 grid unit between the colon and the left of the control.

• 2 grid unit between groups of controls.

• 2 grid units of space between the edges of the pane and the outermost extents of the labels and controls within it.

• Execution buttons centered at the bottom of the window.

Controls are arranged in a single column with their boldface labels right-aligned to the left of the controls themselves (see Figure 5). The spacing between controls depends on the baseline of the text contained in the control or its label. The system automatically adjusts the size of the window to match the amount of space required by the set of controls.

A similar approach is used to arrange the menu commands in a series of menus at the top of a base window. Commands are assigned to a standard menu location if possible. The OPEN LOOK GUI defines four standard menus whose contents are standardized along the following high-level principles:

• *File* - contains commands that operate on entire filesystem-level objects without directly altering their contents.

• *View* - contains commands that control the presentation of information within the window without affecting the actual data itself in any way.

• *Edit* - contains standard, generic commands that can be used to alter the data itself, regardless of the manner in which the data is displayed.

• *Properties* - contains commands that alter the characteristics, or properties, of the application, the window, the document, or the currently selected data.

The current implementation uses a *glossary*, shown in Table 5, of common command names to place each command into one of the standard menus. Matching is based on textual comparison of the command label. A wild card (*) is used to match any string appearing with the critical word. Commands that cannot be assigned to one of the standard menus are collected in a fifth menu labeled "Other."

After commands are grouped appropriately in the top-level menus, they can be added to the control area of the parent window. The system attempts to optimize the use of the control area by adjusting the size of the window or the

File	View	Edit	Properties
New	* Size	Undo	Selection
Load	* %	Again	Object
Save	Hide *	Cut	Font
Save as	Show *	Copy	Line
Browse		Paste	Character
Revert	Find	Delete	Paragraph
Import		Select All	Number
Export		Clear	Page
Print			Document
Print Optns			Application

Table 5   Menu Glossary.

layout of the menus to take full advantage of the available space. If the window is too small to accommodate all of the menus, its size is increased as necessary. When the window has extra space in the control area, submenus and then individual items are promoted from the shortest remaining menu to the top level until the available space is filled.

INTEGRATING THE DATA MODELLING AND USER INTERFACE DESIGN ENVIRONMENTS

The OPEN LOOK Developer's Guide (Devguide) is an interactive user interface design and specification tool from Sun

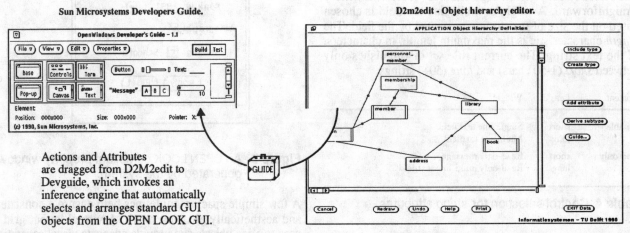

Actions and Attributes are dragged from D2M2edit to Devguide, which invokes an inference engine that automatically selects and arranges standard GUI objects from the OPEN LOOK GUI.

Figure 6   Devguide and D2M2-Edit.

Microsystems [14]. Devguide's base window contains a graphical palette (see Figure 6) from which standard GUI objects can be instantiated and added to a user interface by dragging them onto the screen. The designer uses a combination of direct manipulation and property sheets to specify the attributes of each interaction object. Devguide produces a textual description of the resulting user interface in a format (Guide Interface Language, or GIL) that serves as input to one of several toolkit-specific code generators that create user interface source modules for the application.

D2M2-Edit is the Delft University of Technology's Direct Manipulation Manager Editor [2]. It features an interactive graphics editor that uses semantic data diagrams to visualize the application data model. The data model describes all of the data objects used by the application, the relations between objects (both part-whole relations and class hierarchy relations), the available actions on objects, the pre- and postconditions on the actions, and the attributes, or properties, of the data objects. Every data object has an associated property sheet in which the attributes, actions and pre- and postconditions can be viewed and modified.

To create a user interface directly from the data model, the designer selects one or more actions and attributes from the D2M2-Edit window and drags them onto one of the windows being defined within the Devguide environment or onto the base window of Devguide itself (see Figure 6). Devguide has been experimentally modified to invoke the inference engine directly. It applies the control selection and layout rules to the application data objects and adds an appropriate configuration of OPEN LOOK controls to the destination window. If the data is dropped onto the Devguide base window, a new pop-up window is created to contain the automatically generated controls.

Devguide can then be used in the traditional manner to modify or refine the automatically generated interface. New controls can be added, either from within Devguide or by dragging additional objects from the application data model in D2M2-Edit onto the target window. To support iterative or incremental design, controls can be added to existing interfaces represented as GIL specifications and provided as input to the layout component of the design tool. Together these tools provide an easy way to generate a "quick and dirty" prototype of the application's user interface while eliminating much of the work in the final implementation.

CONCLUSIONS AND FUTURE WORK

Automatic generation of the user interface directly from an application data model is a logical next step in the continuing evolution of user interface design tools. The ability to formally link the semantics of the application data objects to the stylistic conventions and interaction objects of a particular GUI environment brings traditional software engineering and user interface design one step closer together. Automating control selection and layout can increase the quality and consistency of the resulting user interfaces even in the absence of significant design expertise in the target GUI.

Another important application of the automatic layout capability may be seen in object-oriented systems that allow instance-specific or user-specific attributes to be associated with objects. Objects whose set of attributes can be extended or modified by users or by other objects require a run-time window layout facility since the exact set of attributes and values cannot be known until after the design stage. End-user customization can also be simplified greatly if users can rely on the system to provide an adequate layout as soon as a desirable subset of the available features has been identified.

The automatically generated interface designs do not have to be perfect to be valuable in any of the above applications. The current rule set generates usable solutions that are consistent with the OPEN LOOK GUI style guidelines. This research effort demonstrates the feasibility of integrating the modelling and design environments and establishes the foundation for a simple run-time control selection and layout system. There is of course much room for further development and extension of the present work.

The most promising areas for future investigation involve more extensive use of the semantics available in the form of pre- and postconditions in the application data model. This information, perhaps augmented by additional metadata supplied by the application designer, could be used to support a number of additional design capabilities:

- *Prioritizing of controls* - in the current implementation, the order in which controls appear in their parent window depends on both the order in which they are selected in the data modelling environment and the order in which they are introduced into the interface design environment. Future versions should be able to identify critical actions and attributes - based either on the inherent semantics of the data model or on additional metadata provided by the application designer - and prioritize layouts accordingly.

- *Grouping of controls* - a great deal of information about the relatedness of controls could be derived by examining the objects they affect and the state of the application before and/or after they are invoked (as reflected in their pre- and post-conditions). The automatic control selection and layout technology should be able to identify important functional groups and to visually distinguish them within the window using additional space, hierarchical labeling, or appropriate rules and borders.

- *Hierarchical menus* - more sophisticated structuring of the command hierarchy and resulting menu system should be possible based on an analysis of the semantics of the menu items as reflected in their pre- and postconditions.

- *Allocation of controls to windows* - all of the attributes selected in the data modelling environment are currently assigned to a single pop-up window in the interface design environment. In the future the designer will be able to select hundreds of application data elements, all of which have interdependencies. The automatic layout technology should be able to allocate the functionality appropriately among multiple pop-up windows.

• *More sophisticated visual design* - the current rule set implements the simple layout rules defined by the OPEN LOOK Application Style Guidelines. A more sophisticated approach would consider the interior widths of individual controls and enhance the overall visual order by manipulating the sizes of individual controls to increase the consistency and modularity of the interface design.

• *Consideration of available space* - this is currently limited to parameterization of the control selection rules. In the future, the automatic layout technology should augment the default control preferences by considering the actual amount of space available and should simultaneously adjust the size of the window and the arrangement of controls to optimize the use of display space.

• *Integration with a user interface management system* - a complete user interface development environment, such as UIDE [5], in which a single application specification is used both as the basis for an automatically-generated interface design and to provide context-sensitive help to the user at run-time.

ACKNOWLEDGMENTS

Dennis de Baar thanks Jim Foley for his help and support during this project. We all thank Daniel Gieskens, Noi Sukaviriya, Srdjan Kovacevic, Won Chul Kim, Mark Grey, Jens Kilian, other colleagues at Georgia Tech and The George Washington University and Jarrett Rosenberg at Sun Microsystems for their help and feedback. Partial funding for this project was provided by Sun Microsystems' Collaborative Research program, and by the National Science Foundation Grant # IRI -8813179. We thank Bob Ellis of Sun for his skillful management in establishing our collaborative research project and Bob Watson of Sun for arranging pre-release access to the Devguide software. We also thank the Technical University of Delft for providing access to D2M2-Edit, and to Charles van der Mast and Johan Versendaal of Delft for their feedback.

REFERENCES

[1]   Apple Computer, Inc. *Human Interface Guidelines: The Apple Desktop Interface*. Reading, MA: Addison-Wesley, 1987.

[2]   Beekman, W.H.R. *D2m2edit*, Master's Thesis, Delft University of Technology, The Netherlands, July 1990.

[3]   Beshers, C. and S. Feiner, "Scope: Automated Generation of Graphical Interfaces," *Proc. ACM SIGGRAPH Symposium on User Interface Software and Technology*, October 1988, pp. 76-85.

[4]   Foley, J.D., C. Gibbs, W. Kim, S. Kovacevic, L. Moran, P. Sukaviriya, "A Knowledge-Based User Interface Management System," *Human Factors in Computing Systems, CHI'88 Conference Proceedings*, May 1988, pp. 67-72.

[5]   Foley, J.D., W. C. Kim, S. Kovacevic, and K. Murray, "UIDE - An intelligent User Interface Design Environment," in Sullivan, J and S. Tyler (eds.), *Architectures for Intelligent Interfaces: Elements and Prototypes*, Addison-Wesley, Reading, MA, 1991.

[6]   Hewlett-Packard Company, *HP Interface Architect Developer's Guide*, Hewlett-Packard Company, Corvallis, Oregon, October 1990.

[7]   IBM Corporation. *System Application Architecture, Common Access Panel Design and User Interaction*. SC26-4351-0. December 1987.

[8]   Kim, W. and J. Foley, "DON: User Interface Presentation Design Assistant," *Proc. ACM SIGGRAPH Symposium on User Interface Software and Technology*, October 1990, pp. 10-20.

[9]   NeXT Computer Inc., *NeXTstep Concepts*, Redwood City, CA: NeXT Computer, Inc., pp. 8-1 to 8-53.

[10]   Olsen, D. "A programming Language Basis for User Interface Management," *Human Factors in Computing Systems, CHI'89 Conference Proceedings*, May 1989, pp. 171-176.

[11]   Open Software Foundation. *OSF/Motif Style Guide*, Revision 1.0, OSF 11 Cambridge Center, Cambridge, MA 02142, ISBN 0-13-640491-X, 1990.

[12]   Singh, G. and M. Green, "Chisel: A System for Creating Highly Interactive Screen Layouts," *Proc. ACM SIGGRAPH Symposium on Software and Technology*, November 1989, pp. 86-94.

[13]   Sun Microsystems, Inc. and AT&T, *OPEN LOOK GUI Application Style Guidelines*. Addison-Wesley, Reading, MA, 1990.

[14]   Sun Microsystems, Inc., *Open Windows Developer's Guide 1.1, Reference Manual*, Part No. 800-5380-10, Revision A, June 1990.

[15]   Wiecha, C., et. al., "Generating Highly Interactive User Interfaces," *Human Factors in Computing Systems, CHI'89 Conference Proceedings*, May 1989, pp. 277-282.

[16]   Zanden, B. Vander and B.A. Myers, "Automatic, Look-and-Feel Independent Dialog Creation for graphical User Interfaces," *Human Factors in Computing Systems, CHI'90 Conference Proceedings*, April 1990, pp. 27-34.

WORKSPACES: AN ARCHITECTURE FOR EDITING COLLECTIONS OF OBJECTS

Dan R. Olsen, Jr., Thomas G. McNeill and David C. Mitchell

Computer Science Department
Brigham Young University
Provo, UT 84602
(801) 378-2225, olsen@cs.byu.edu

ABSTRACT
Many tools create new user interfaces by compositing them out of smaller pieces. This usually leads to variations on the dialog box to edit a single composite object. Workspaces are a model for compositing together various editors to manipulate sets of objects and their attributes. The workspace components communicate in terms of a *selected set* and the attributes possessed by objects in that set. This model has been implemented as part of the Sushi UIMS.

KEYWORDS: Collection editing, user interface management systems, editors, interactive software.

INTRODUCTION
The history of UIMS research has been dominated by the quest for models which allow designers to easily expression interface designs. A most fruitful approach has been the composition of complex interactions out of simpler ones. Almost all such work has used the model of laying out a series of small interactors in a 2D space, each editing some component of a more complex object. Essentially this is the dialog box in a variety of forms. This yields a single interactor which edits a single composite object. The model is simple, the metaphor is clear and the results are limited. Such a model will not implement MacDraw, the Macintosh finder, HyperCard's card editor, nor the variety of widget layout tools that have been developed for Motif. All of these examples edit collections of objects rather than complex individual objects. To use a programming language metaphor, the dialog box composition model describes record data structures but fails to support arrays and lists.

The Workspace Model, which is discussed in this paper, defines a framework for composing complex collection editors from small individual pieces. There are other systems which can support editing of collections of objects.

Both Garnet [3] and Unidraw [2] address these issues but not with the point of view of composing big interactors out of little interactors. Suite [1] does edit arbitrary collections but is limited to textual interactions.

There are a number of advantages to the composition model. First, it is very easy to explain to designers. Second, it is easy to make the model visually concrete in a design tool. Selecting components from a palette and composing them together like tinker toys has proven its effectiveness as a design metaphor. Third, the orthogonality of the pieces allow for a mixing and matching of pieces in a variety of combinations. This creates a huge design space in which a designer can work.

The workspace model fits within the framework of browse/edit UIMSs [4]. Such UIMSs view their interfaces a composition of editors which edit and perform actions on pieces of semantic information. As such the remainder of the paper will refer to editors rather than interactors.

WORKSPACE MODEL
In discussing the workspace model it is helpful to use a simple drawing application as an example (Figure 1). This application can create drawing with lines, rectangles and text. The lines and rectangles have a line thickness attribute and the rectangles have a fill attribute. The text objects have a typeface and a point size.

The heart of the workspace is a collection editor. The collection editor manages a list of objects to be edited. Each object in the collection is managed by an item editor. In this example the collection editor is a 2D drag oriented editor. There are a variety of other collection editors that can be used in a workspace. The 2D drag editor is the most appropriate for a draw application. Prototypes are sample objects which can be inserted into a collection. Lastly attribute editors are editors which can change some properties of objects in the collection.

Each of these four types of components communicate with each other in terms of a selected set and the classes and attributes of the objects in the collection. The workspace model is very much driven by the classes of the objects in the collection and must know about classes and the methods and fields of a class. This information is automatically provided within the Sushi system [5] where workspaces have been implemented.

COLLECTION EDITORS

There is a symbiotic relationship between collection editors and item editors. The item editors can edit, display and select individual objects in the collection. The collection editor manages the collection as a whole, including insertion, deletion and interacting with the workspace's set of currently selected objects.

In summary a collection editor has the following functionality

1) Manage a collection of data objects
2) Visually organize the item editors
3) Communicate with the workspace's selected set of objects
4) Perform insertions and deletions on the collection

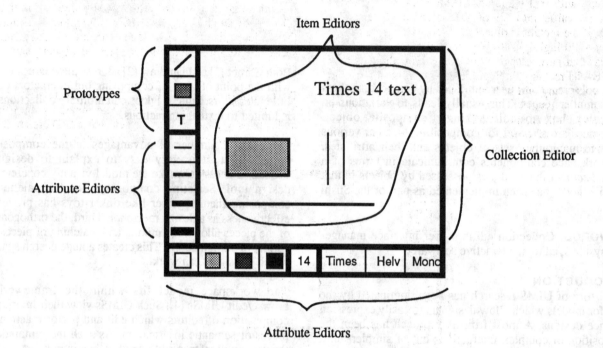

Item Editors

Prototypes

Times 14 text

Collection Editor

Attribute Editors

14 Times Helv Mono

Attribute Editors

Figure 1 — Workspace Components

There is great flexibility in the relationship between a collection editor and its item editors. If, for example, object classes were defined for scrollbars, buttons and type-in fields, and item editors created for each of these classes, then the same collection editor used for the draw example would manage the HyperCard card editor. A similar change to the object classes would produce a Motif widget layout editor such as VUIT. Yet another change of object classes and item editors would produce the window handler in the Macintosh Finder. Each of these are examples which take different object classes and their item editors and composite them within the 2D drag collection editor to create a variety of applications.

A variety of collection editors is possible. The simple scrolling list editor is the first example. If one has an item editor for files which will display a file's name this list collection editor will produce the standard Macintosh dialog for opening files. A change of item editor will produce the Macintosh Finder's View by Name option. Collection editors in 3D are also possible. The spatial arrangement and item editors are, of course, very different but the relationship to the rest of the workspace is not.

An item editor's functionality is:

1) Display an object of a particular class
2) Select oneself in response to user input (such as a mouse click)
3) Communicate selectedness with the collection editor
4) Perform limited editing on the object (such as editing file names in the finder or text strings in the draw application)

ATTRIBUTE EDITORS

The collection editors themselves are only a part of the workspace functionality. With only the collection editor, the draw application could not change the line thicknesses or typefaces of objects in the collection. This type of functionality is the role of the attribute editors. An attribute editor has two purposes: 1) to visually present some attribute of the objects in the selected set, and 2) to edit or change the value of that attribute on all objects in the selected set. Again the selected set and the objects in it form the fundamental communication mechanism among components of the workspace. Figure 2 shows the example application with all attribute editors and objects labeled for reference.

Types of Attribute Editors

There are basically two types of attribute editor: single valued and multivalued. In our example the single valued editors are *d - k* and *m - o*. A single valued attribute editor has an icon, an attribute value, and an attribute name. (In Sushi an attribute name is sufficient for any editor to find and set a field of any object at run time.) A single valued attribute editor indicates whether the selected objects have an attribute with that value and if the editor is selected it will set its value into all of the selected objects. For example, if the rectangle object (2) were selected, attribute editor *e* would highlight itself to indicate that the selected object has that particular line thickness. If attribute editor *f* is selected the rectangle's line thickness will be changed to the new value and *f* will be highlighted and *e* unhighlighted. As will be discussed later, neither *e, f* nor the collection editor know about each other. They each know only about the selected set of objects. The workspace handles the communication and preserves their independence.

3)   Selected - this attribute can be set and it already has this value
4)   Undetermined - this attribute can be set but not all objects in the selected set have the same value for this attribute.

There are a variety of ways in which an attribute editor can present these four states. Figure 3 shows possible examples for the point size editor (a multivalued editor) and one of the line thickness editors (a single valued editor). A multivalued attribute editor does not present the unselected state because it can change its value to reflect the attribute value that is selected. A single valued attribute editor does not present the undetermined state because the unselected state is sufficient to show that not all selected objects have the editor's value

Determination of Attribute Editor State

The state of an attribute editor is determined by the values and classes of the objects in the selected set. There are three major cases which need to be accounted for: 1) a single

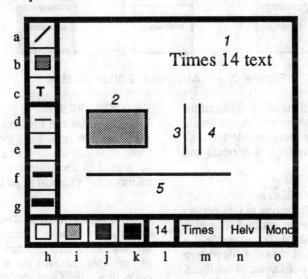

Figure 2 — Labeled Components

Attribute editor *l* , which edits the point size, is an example of a multivalued attribute editor. In our example case it is a simple type-in box for numbers where the user can type in any point size. If object *l* is selected then editor *l* would set itself to 14 since that is the point size for the selected object. If the user types in another value, then the corresponding attribute in the selected object is changed. In Sushi it is possible to generate, or select from a list, an editor for any class of object. Any simple Sushi editor can serve as a multivalued attribute editor for the class of object it edits.

States of an Attribute Editor

An attribute editor must be able to visually present four states.

1)   Disabled - this attribute cannot be set.
2)   Unselected - this attribute can be set but this is not the current value.

object is selected, 2) multiple objects of the same class are selected, and 3) multiple objects of different classes are selected.

Single Selected Object

If a single object is selected, then all attribute editors which edit attributes not possessed by that class of object are disabled. If the text item (*1*) is selected then the line thickness (*d-g*) and fill pattern (*h-k*) attribute editors are disabled because they cannot function on an object of class Text. Among the typeface editors (*m-o*), editor *m* is put in the selected state because its value matches that of the selected object. The point size editor (*l*) is set to 14 to reflect the value of the selected object.

Multiple Selected Objects of the Same Class

If multiple objects of the same class are selected, then the set of disabled attribute editors functions as in the single object case because the attributes which can be manipulated is determined by the class of the object. The selected objects may, however, not have the same values. If objects 3 and 4 are selected attribute editors *h-o* are disabled, attribute editor *d* is selected (because all selected objects have thin lines), and attribute editors *e-g* are unselected.

If, however, objects 3 and 5 had been selected, then the line thickness attribute can be set but there is not a consensus on its current value. Attribute editors *f - g* are set to unselected because no selected object has those attribute values. Attribute editors *d - e* are also set to unselected because even though some objects have their values, not all of them do.

Interchanging Attribute Editors
A key feature in the compositing metaphor is that a variety of alternatives can be selected for a specific function. Take for example the point size editor. Since point size is an integer, any editor which can edit integers can be used. The type-in could be replaced by a scroll bar, for example. The multivalued editor could be replaced by a series of single valued editors which enumerate the available point sizes. All three can be used simultaneously. Because each attribute editor monitors the objects in the selected set, changing the point size of an object using the scroll bar would cause the type-in editor to be notified that it must update its display. Any single valued attribute editors for point size would be similarly notified.

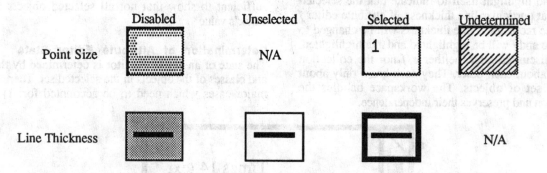

Figure 3 — Attribute Editor States

In this situation if there were a multivalued attribute editor for the line thickness, say a text type-in box, then it would become undetermined. Multivalued editors are selected if all selected objects have the same value for that attribute and are undetermined otherwise.

Multiple Selected Objects of Different Classes
This case only differs from the previous one in that editors are disabled if there is any object in the selected set which does not have a corresponding attribute. For example if a rectangle and a line are both selected then the fill pattern attribute is disabled since lines do not have that attribute. We have arbitrarily decided to disable attributes which are not possessed by *all* selected objects. It would be just as easy to disable attributes only if *no* selected object had the attribute, and indeed this behavior is seen in many Macintosh drawing programs, where fill pattern in our example would remain enabled as long as at least one rectangle were selected.

Selecting or Setting an Attribute Editor
Attribute editors which are in a disabled state cannot be selected or manipulated by the user. If a single valued editor is selected then all objects in the selected set will get that attribute value. Once the value is set, the states of all editors are updated to reflect the new setting. This updating is handled by the workspace rather than the individual editors which do not know about each other. If, for example, objects 2,3 and 4 are selected and then the fattest line width attribute editor is selected each of these objects would have their line width changed to reflect that value.

PROTOTYPES
Prototypes are the mechanism for inserting new objects into the collection. Each prototype is itself an editor and owns an object which is one of the kinds of objects that can be placed in the collection. In most cases our prototype editors simply consist of an icon as in the example (*a-c*).

Relationship to the Collection Editor
When a prototype is selected it notifies the workspace that the selected set should now consist only of the prototype object. This removes the selected set from control of the collection editor and the collection editor is so notified. Selecting objects in the collection editor would give control of the selected set back to the collection editor. When a prototype has the selected set it should highlight itself. Selecting another prototype transfers control of the selected set with a corresponding change in highlighting.
As mentioned earlier, the collection editor is responsible for the insertion of new objects into its collection. The problem was which objects were to be inserted. When a collection editor does an insertion it makes a copy of the currently selected set. Collection editors are written to know when they do not control the selected set and use this to tell the difference between selection, manipulation of objects, and insertion.

Relationship to Attribute Editors
By changing the selected set to itself, a prototype causes the attribute editors to reflect its own values. Changing an attribute will change the prototype object. This allows the modification of the default objects which are inserted into a collection.

Example

In our example one might select the rectangle prototype (*b*) which would cause certain attribute editors to be selected, say *e* and *i*. If the user then selected attribute editor *j* then the prototype would be modified accordingly. If the user then selected in the collection editor (in a place where there is no other object) the collection editor would copy the object in the selected set (the prototype object) and insert it into the collection.

There are times when existing editors are not sufficient, however. In that case the designer must write a custom Sushi editor. The Sushi editing model makes this task relatively easy, however. The Sushi protocol only requires that an editor know how to extract by name the value it is to edit and to monitor the edited object for changes. The job is even easier in the case of single value attribute editors. A single valued attribute editor consists only of a button with an icon, an associated value, an attribute name, a reference

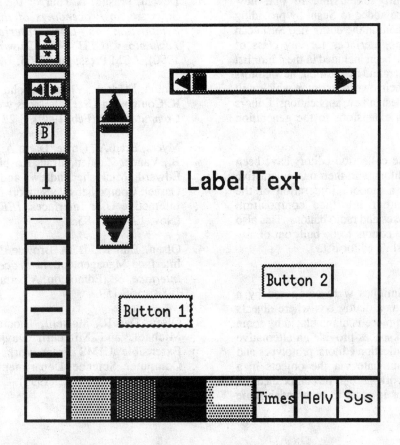

Figure 4 — Interface Layout Workspace

ADAPTING THE WORKSPACE TO A PARTICULAR DOMAIN

User interfaces must often be tailored to the application domain in order to be acceptable. The workspace model offers three avenues for customization of the interface. The designer can choose to customize the attribute editors, write a new collection editor, or change the way the collection editor handles individual objects through the alteration of a declarative specification.

Domain-Specific Attribute Editors

The easiest way to customize an attribute editor is simply to choose a different one. For example, line width is a integer and can be edited by any integer editor. We have implemented a graphical resource editor for the Workspace which allows the designer to select any Sushi editor of the appropriate class to edit an attribute. For example, the designer might choose to use a scroll bar instead of, or in addition to, a type-in box for editing a numeric attribute such as point size.

to an object, and the machinery for applying the associated value to the named attribute of the object when the button is pressed. Setting up a single-valued attribute editor can be handled interactively by Sushi's interface editing facilities with no programming required.

Domain-Specific Collection Editors

Adapting the workspace to an application domain sometimes involves customizing the collection editor. The draw program seen in Figure 1 was changed to an interface layout editor by substituting item editors for text boxes, buttons and scroll bars for the item editors for lines, rectangles and text (Fig. 4).

A workspace implementation of the Macintosh Finder could use a scrolling text editor for the filenames and related information, yielding a View by Name view of the files instead of the Finder's usual View by Icon view. This example illustrates that a collection editor need not use item editors. In fact, the first collection editor we implemented consists only of a scrolling list of selectable strings. The strings cannot even be edited, but this collection editor still conforms to the protocol since it displays a string for every object in the collection, allows the objects to be selected, and communicates the selected set with the rest of the Workspace.

IMPLEMENTATION

The workspace model has been implemented within the Sushi UIMS. Sushi is fully extensible in that new interactive techniques can be added to Sushi by providing new editors and including them in the editor list. Sushi can automatically generate user interfaces for any class of object. New editors that have been included in the editor list are available to Sushi's generator. In addition, new editors can provide an editor for their own descriptor which will allow users to interactively design new applications. Editors can also provide their own extensions to the generation mechanisms.

Workspaces and each of the collection editors have been added to Sushi as special editors with their own interactive design tools. This allows a smooth integration of the workspace model with other interface composition techniques such as dialog boxes and radio buttons. This also allows multivalued attribute editors to be built out of any of the existing editors in Sushi's editor list.

SUMMARY

Previously, interactive techniques were composed by a decomposition model such as a dialog box where objects consisted of pieces and each piece is manipulated by some lower level technique. Workspaces provide an alternative composition model where collection editors, prototypes and attribute editors all communicate via the objects in a selected set. This allows a workspace to be composited out of a variety of smaller pieces in order to accomplish some larger goal. Models which allow simple extension of new widgets or interactive techniques can only define an interface design space that grows linearly with the number of techniques that are added. A composition model defines a design space that grows exponentially as the outer product of the set of interactive techniques.

REFERENCES

1. Dewan, Prasun. A Tour of the Suite User Interface Software. In *Proceedings of the ACM SIGGRAPH Symposium on User Interface Software and Technology (UIST '90)*, (Snowbird, Utah, Oct. 3-5, 1990), ACM Press, pp. 57-65.

2. Linton, Mark A., Vlissides, John M., and Calder, Paul R. Composing User interfaces with InterViews, *IEEE Computer* 22,2 (Feb. 1989), 8-22.

3. Myers, Brad A., Guise, Dario A., Dannenberg, Roger B., Vander Zanden, Brad, Kosbie, David S., Pervin, Edward, Mickish, Andrew, and Marchal, Philippe. Garnet: Comprehensive Support for Graphical, Highly Interactive User Interfaces, *IEEE Computer* 23, 11 (Nov. 1990), 71-85.

4. Olsen, Dan R., Jr. A Browse/Edit Model for User Interface Management. In *Proceedings of Graphics Interface '88* (Edmonton, Alberta, Canada, June 6-10, 1988), 155-159.

5. Olsen, Dan R., McNeill, Thomas G., Burbidge, A. Michael, and Mitchell, David C. SUSHI: An Extensible UIMS Framework, Technical Report, Computer Science Department, Brigham Young University, Provo, UT, (1991).

Selectors:
Going Beyond User-Interface Widgets

Jeff Johnson

Hewlett-Packard Laboratories
Human-Computer Interaction Department
1501 Page Mill Road, 1U
Palo Alto, CA 94304
Internet: jjohnson@hplabs.hp.com
(415) 857-7661

ABSTRACT

Most UI toolkits and UIMSs make use of widgets, e.g., buttons, text fields, sliders, menus. Designers construct user interfaces by choosing and laying out widgets, then connecting them to application semantics. This approach has four problems. First, most widgets are too low-level; constructing interfaces from them takes too much work. Second, working with widgets focuses attention on appearance and layout issues, rather than on more important semantic design issues. Third, designers can easily make poor widget choices, yielding poor interfaces. Fourth, widgets do not mesh well with application semantics; they know nothing about the variables they control. We are developing an application construction environment in which designers and implementers work with semantic-based controls called Selectors rather than with widgets. Selectors are classified according to their interface semantics (e.g., mutually-exclusive choice), rather than their appearance. Each type of Selector can be presented in a variety of ways; this may be chosen semi-automatically. Selectors mesh well with application semantics: their values are application data-types and their views determine how to present valid values automatically.

KEYWORDS: User-interface toolkit, UIMS, widgets.

INTRODUCTION

User interface management systems (UIMSs) and user interface toolkits commonly support application software development by supplying a set of "widgets" that can be used to create user interfaces. The widgets supplied by a UIMS or UI toolkit include such interactive devices as editable text or number fields, sliders, scrollbars, buttons, knobs, dials, meters, and menus.

One problem with UIMSs and toolkits is that they require applications designers to spend a great deal of time fiddling with the appearance and layout of their interfaces. Are the

labels for these two settings aligned properly? Should the designer present this number as a digital number readout or as a position on a dial? How is a menu changed into a set of radio-buttons? Time spent on such matters would be better spent conducting user studies and performing analyses of the task and work-context, i.e., determining the right functionality and matching the interface to it.

Conventional widget sets also allow designers to make poor choices, like using the wrong widget for a setting. The widget may look good, but that's a minor detail if it's the wrong widget. For example, designers using conventional widgets often provide users with no clue whether a button initiates a command (e.g., Cancel) or sets a variable (e.g., Bold), or whether a set of adjacent buttons is mutually-exclusive or not [3]. Though there are user-interface standards that attempt to guide designers away from such mistakes (e.g., Motif and OpenLook), they often go unheeded because the tools make compliance difficult.

Finally, conventional widgets are poorly connected to application semantics. The traditional UIMS/toolkit approach assumes that widgets know nothing about application data-types. To create a widget, information about the possible values of a user-editable setting already represented (implicitly) in the type declaration of the application variable must be provided again in the widget specification (e.g., labels for possible values). For example, an application might have a Font variable that is an enumerated type {helvetica, times, century, courier}. To display a set of radio buttons to allow a user to set the Font, a programmer would have to, when creating the radio button widget, provide labels for the values: "Helvetica", "Times", "Century", "Courier". Also, widgets in most toolkits return generic indices that must be converted or cast into valid application values. If the user selects "Times", the widget indicates only that the second value was chosen; the application must interpret this. This is type-unsafe, because (e.g., as a result of modifications) the application and the widget may order the possible values differently, resulting in erroneous program behavior.

The Application Architectures Project in the Human-Computer Interaction Department of HP Labs is developing an Application Construction Environment (ACE) that attempts to simplify the task of developing task-specific applications [13]. Part of the design philosophy behind ACE is that there is much more to a good user interface than just nice-looking widgets, and that higher-level aspects of the design (e.g., appropriateness of the widgets for what they control, task-specificity of the interface and of the application) are more important than the lower ones. Important goals of ACE are to support:

- higher-level aspects of design,

- developing application semantics as well as interfaces,

- developing interfaces that are well-matched with, and well-connected to, application semantics, and

- a style of application development in which end-users and local developers[1] play a central role.

ACE is part of a growing trend in application development systems to move beyond the limitations of UIMSs and UI toolkits [5]. ACE builds upon work by Foley et al [1] and Szekely [8], who assert that enough is now known about application semantics and interface design-spaces that we can encapsulate and reuse semantic components, high-level interface components, and relationships between components; application development tools no longer need treat these as unpredictable. In particular, ACEKit, the foundation of ACE, is an intellectual descendent and extension, in C++, of Szekely's *Nephew* system [8].

The primary components of ACE applications will not be widgets or anything like them, but rather *Visual Formalisms* (VFs): re-usable components that embody significant pieces of functionality commonly found in interactive applications, and familiar presentations thereof [7]. Tables, graphs, and panels are examples of VFs. End-users, local developers, and programmers build applications by composing VFs and constraining their components to produce the desired behavior, much as spreadsheet-based applications are constructed. Programmers provide specialized components and complex constraints as needed [13].

VFs are, however, not sufficient to build applications. Simple interactive controls -- something akin to widgets -- are needed, for controlling aspects of VFs, task-domain variables, and program parameters. In ACE, we fulfill this need not by supplying a set of widgets, classified and selected according to appearance, but rather by supplying interface components that are classified according to their interface semantics and that provide a much better connection to application semantics.

Rather than choosing and laying out widgets, designers select components based upon the semantics of the various choices and settings that an application will have. If they don't like the default presentations selected by the system,

---

1. "Local developer" is our term for users who, officially or not, are computer experts who often act as consultants for their peers [6].

they choose different ones. The idea is for designers and developers to: 1) pay more attention to application semantics and less to the appearance and layout of applications, and 2) provide the system with much more information about the application and interface semantics than they traditionally have, both to force them to design in those terms and to allow the system to assist if it can.

ANTECEDENTS: VIEWPOINT, JADE, AND ITS

Developing a set of semantic-based controls that covers the space of possible application-controls completely from scratch would be a daunting task. The Xerox *ViewPoint* (formerly called *Star*) property mechanism [3], the *Jade* system of Vander Zanden and Myers [10], and the *ITS* system of Gould et al [2] provide good starting points.

In many UIMSs and UI toolkits, the semantics of the interface and of the available widgets plays little role in their selection by a designer. With such systems, the widgets are very low level visual interaction components: buttons, menus, text fields, etc. User interfaces are built by arranging low-level components spatially and assigning them procedures that affect application data and other components. There is no direct support for compound interactive components, e.g., an array of radio buttons presenting a choice of one value from a set of N values. A compound "widget" for such a case would have to be constructed by juxtaposing N buttons and "wiring them up" so that clicking one of the buttons selects it and deselects all others (in addition to setting a variable to the selected value). The Athena Toolkit for X Windows is an example of this sort of widget set [9]. InterViews 2.6 is another [4]. Systems such as these are flexible in that they allow programmers to construct a wide variety of high-level interface components, but, in doing so, they provide no more support for common arrangements of low-level components than they do for uncommon ones.

The main reason for examining ViewPoint, Jade, and ITS in designing our own approach to interface components is that in these three systems, semantic considerations play a role in the categorization and choice of widgets: designers work at a higher level than arranging buttons, text fields, and relations between them.

If a ViewPoint application designer wants to allow a user to select one of ten possible values, s/he does not place ten buttons near each other and then constrain or program them such that turning one on turns others off; s/he simply uses a Choice parameter and supplies it with labels for the ten possible values. Similarly, On/Off controls in ViewPoint are not implemented by wiring generic buttons so that they flip the value of a boolean variable and remain inverted when ON; rather, there is a Boolean parameter type with a built-in state-variable and an appearance that contrasts with push-buttons. ViewPoint's property sheet toolkit provides widgets of type Command, Boolean, Choice, Choice-with-Menu, Multiple-Choice, Pop-up-Menu, Text, and Text-with-Menu[2]. These high-level widgets make an application programmer's job much easier than do the widgets provided in most UI toolkits. Also, because each setting type has a built-in presentation, user-interface designers have more control over the interface look-and-feel than they do when programmers have more freedom.

However, the ViewPoint property sheet toolkit has several limitations from our perspective. First, it is a true UI toolkit: interfaces are specified in the Xerox application programming language, *Mesa*.

Second, widgets and application semantic variables are poorly connected in the sense described in the previous section. Presentations for the alternative values offered by a widget are limited to either textual labels or bitmaps, which must be provided to the widget independent of the application data-type. The values returned by widgets must be interpreted to yield the corresponding application value.

Third, note that ViewPoint's widget-types are a mixture of semantic types and presentation types. For example, several of the widget-types are just different ways of presenting one-from-many choices. Text fields are, in ViewPoint as in most toolkits, used to present many different semantic setting-types and are thus a presentation type rather than a semantic type. Choosing among these widgets requires a designer to make decisions about presentation as well as decisions about interface semantics. This confounding of setting-type and presentation obscures the intended semantics of the interface and requires programmers to change setting types when they just want to change presentation, and so is problematic.

We believe that there is great value in encapsulating the semantics of the various kinds of settings that applications offer users, independent of how those choices are presented, and then to offer alternative presentations for a given type of choice or setting. Thus, though ViewPoint's approach is "more semantic" than that of many other toolkits, it is not semantic enough for our purposes.

Jade's approach is "more semantic" than that of most UIMSs and toolkits, including ViewPoint's. Jade widgets may have different presentations. Designers specify interfaces in a declarative language, stating, for each desired widget, its category, widget-label, and value-labels. Jade offers widgets of type Command, Single-Choice, Multiple-Choice, Text, Single-Choice-with-Text, Multiple-Choice-with-Text, and Number-in-a-Range. Specifications are compiled to produce interface code. The exact appearance of the various types of widgets is not built into the interface-compiler, but rather is specified in a "look-and-feel" stylesheet. Compiling a given interface specification with different stylesheets produces different-looking widgets. For example, one can define a dialog box and then have it (i.e., all of the widgets on the dialog box) rendered in either the OpenLook look-and-feel or the Macintosh look-and-feel. This is clearly closer to what we want than is ViewPoint.

---

2. Choice-with-Menu is used have a few common choices explicitly displayed, with the rest available via a pop-up menu. Text-with-Menu is used when values are to be entered by typing, with a menu as an accelerator for likely values.

One problem with Jade from our point of view is that, as in ViewPoint, specifications of controls must include labels for their possible values, redundantly (and potentially in conflict) with the application data-type.

Also, Jade's widget-classification is not free of presentational considerations. As in ViewPoint, the Text-widget is present, both by itself and in combination with Single- and Multiple-Choice widgets. We claim that text-fields are not a semantic type, but rather just a way of viewing many different semantic types (e.g., choice of a filename, choice of a user-ID, choice of a dollar amount, specification of a check-memo).

A third problem for our purposes is that look-and-feel stylesheets in Jade determine the appearance of <u>all</u> widgets of a given type. Designers don't have presentation-control over individual widgets. For example, using one stylesheet when compiling an interface would cause all number-setting controls in the interface to be rendered as sliders; using another would cause them all to be rendered as editable number fields. Since we require independent control of presentation for individual widgets within an interface, Jade's approach to providing alternative presentations is not sufficient for ACE.

ITS takes the separation of interface style and content seen in Jade one step further by having presentation style rules classify semantic components by the various attributes that they possess, rather than according to a simple, one-dimensional categorization. This allows different instances of the same semantic component type (e.g., one-from-N choice) to be rendered differently depending upon their attributes. Thus, a one-from-N choice that represents a task-domain variable may be rendered as a set of radio-buttons, while one that represents a control-parameter for the program itself (e.g., number of lines of text to display) may be rendered as a pull-down menu.

ITS' approach to application controls is close to what we want in ACE, but has some drawbacks. The connection to application data-types is not as tight as we would like: as with ViewPoint and Jade, when designers specify Choice or Range blocks, they must provide labels for the choices.

Also, specification is not interactive in ITS: the semantics of user-visible controls is described declaratively and compiled to produce running applications. Changing setting-type requires editing the specification and recompiling; changing presentation requires changing the style rules and recompiling. We are trying to create an environment in which applications across a variety of domains are constructed in a manner similar to the construction of spreadsheet-based applications today [13]. We therefore require the ability to construct applications interactively and to change presentations at runtime.

ACE SELECTORS

We have analyzed the types of interactive controls used in computer applications, and have classified them according to their semantics. Our purpose in doing so is to determine abstractions that can be encapsulated for re-use across a wide variety of applications.

Most widgets display values of application variables and allow users to set them. They set application <u>state</u>. Some widgets indicate available actions and allow users to invoke them. They trigger application <u>operations</u>. Both sorts of widgets show users their options (values or actions) and allow them to <u>select</u> the ones they want. We therefore call semantic controls in ACE *Selectors*, and provide a class Selector. Selectors that display and set application variables are called *Data* Selectors, and those that display and invoke actions are called *Command* Selectors. ACE provides these as subclasses of class Selector.

Data Selectors

One goal of ACE is to facilitate the construction of task-specific applications and interfaces. Task-specific applications are those that offer task-specific objects and actions to users. One obstacle to the development of such applications is that the proliferation of task-domain-specific objects and operations can easily result in a proliferation of interfaces for manipulating and controlling them. Attempting to provide specialized widgets or editors for modifying every type of object would be not only hopeless, but also pointless from a reuse standpoint. Though some application object-types occur often enough that it may make sense to build them into ACE (e.g., time, date, filename, phone-number, dollar-amount, color), most are -- rightly -- specialized for particular applications and therefore not very reusable. The same is true of presentations of these objects.

Fortunately, there are some higher-level aspects of the semantics of making choices and altering settings that can be encapsulated to great advantage:

- Some application controls allow selection of one of a small, discrete, explicitly-populated set of values (e.g., Border: NONE, SOLID, DASHED, DOTTED).   A special case of such controls allows selection of one of two "opposite" values (e.g., Boldface: ON, OFF).

- Other controls allow selection of <u>several</u> values from a discrete set (e.g., Vote for any three of these candidates: John Redneck, Lucille Incumbent, Sally Bleedinghart, Dan Happycamper, Estelle Radical, Leroy Middleroad).

- Still others display and allow selection of a single value from a potentially-large, quasi-continuous range of values (e.g., Loudness: 0 - 1000).

- Finally, some controls allow selection of several values or subranges from a large, ordered range (e.g., Periods when Nurse was with Patient on 6 May: 00:01 - 24:00).

This classification of controls implies a great deal of re-usable semantics, independent of the type of values being selected among. In other words, one choice of a single value from N values is similar to another whether the value being selected is a day of the week, a font size, or a fill-pattern.

Data Selectors encapsulate the semantics of value-choices. Data Selectors are application semantic variables that have (runtime) restrictions on the values they may assume. First, they are restricted to a particular static data-type or class, referred to as the *base-type* of the Data Selector.   Any C++ class that is a subclass of the ACE root class *Object* may serve as a base-type for a Selector. These include Integers, Colors, Dollar Amounts, and even Tables or Object Presenters. Data Selectors are additionally restricted to those values of the base-type that are contained in a specified *Set*, referred to as the *domain* of the Data Selector. Sets can be defined by explicit enumeration (e.g., {red, green, blue}), by a range (e.g., [10..50]), or by a predicate function (e.g., Odd(n)). Finally, the value of a Data Selector is itself a Set, which is restricted in size to a specified minimum and maximum. For example, one Data Selector may offer a choice of from zero to five Dates, while another Data Selector defined over the same Set may allow one and only one Date to be chosen.

Whereas widgets in traditional UIMSs and toolkits are poorly connected to application semantics because they return generic values that must be converted or cast to yield meaningful application values, Data Selectors <u>are</u> application semantic variables. Their values need not be converted or cast, but can be used directly by applications.

Whereas Data Selectors encapsulate the semantics of <u>choice</u>, Data Selector *Presenters* encapsulate that of <u>presenting and editing</u> choices. Though widgets in traditional UIMSs and toolkits know nothing about the variables they represent and control, Data Selector Presenters are based upon the assumption that there is a definable protocol between semantic variables and the interfaces that allow users to set them, and that alternative Presenters can be selected among based upon features (e.g., textual *vs.* graphical, tall *vs.* wide). Data Selector Presenters make use of that protocol to get the information they need about possible values and presentations for them from the Data Selector they present. For example, if a Fill setting can have one of the Color values in {white, light grey, dark grey, black}, the designer creates a semantic variable (i.e., a Data Selector) that accepts only those values, then gets from ACE a suitable Presenter for that Selector, which gets the legal values from the Selector and suitable Presenters for them from ACE (see Fig. 1).

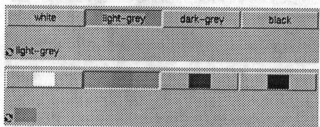

Fig. 1 -- A single 1-from-N Data Selector defined over a Set of Colors {white, light grey, dark grey, black}, viewed using two different Data Selector Presenters (box buttons & cycle button) and two different Color Presenters (name & patch).

This protocol between Data Selectors, Presenters, and base-data-types allows Data Selector Presenters to concern themselves only with the overall appearance and behavior of the setting, leaving the display of individual values wherever the presentation requires them (e.g., the current value, the possible values, or the limits of the range of possible values) to a Presenter for the base-type. For example, let's say a choice of Withdrawal Amount is presented as an array of radio-buttons. The appearance of the individual buttons, the overall layout of the button array (including the positions of the button labels), and the behavior of the button array are provided by the Selector Presenter, but the <u>content</u> of the button labels (i.e., the strings "$20", "$40", etc.) is provided by ACE, which looks for a Presenter for the Selector's base-data-type that matches the Selector Presenter's feature-requirements.

In addition to abstracting out what is common about presenting and making choices across different base-types, Data Selectors also abstract out what is common about presenting and making choices across different presentations. For each Data Selector type, ACE registers several alternative Presenter types; applications can add more if they need them. For example, a Data Selector for a single value from a small number of choices may appear as a set of radio-buttons, a box array (joined row of selectable boxes), a cycle button (shows the current value and switches to the next when pressed), a type-in field that accepts only valid value-names, or a menu (see Fig. 2). Similarly, a slider, a number field, and a dial are all possible presentations of a Data Selector for a single value out of a large ordered range of values.

ACE allows multiple Presenters to present the same Data Selector simultaneously (see Fig. 2). Any change in the value of the Selector, whether instigated programmatically or by the user (through any of the Presenters) causes all Presenters of the Data Selector to be updated automatically.

To summarize the design of Data Selectors, ACE provides:

- a collection of basic semantic objects for representing data-values (e.g., numbers, truth-values, colors, times, dollar-amounts),

- a collection of presentations for basic objects, each of which implements a particular way of presenting its target type of object (e.g., a color can be presented as a color patch, a color name, etc.) and registers its availability along with a list of its relevant features,

- a collection of choice semantic objects, each of which encapsulates the semantics of a particular kind of choice (e.g., a one-from-N choice), independent of any interface for making a choice, defined in terms of a <u>set</u> of basic semantic objects, and

- a collection of possible presentations for choices, each of which implements a particular way of presenting its target type of choice (e.g., a one-from-N choice can be presented as a set of radio-buttons, a pop-up menu, a button that cycles through successive values) and gets its information about what the alternative values are and how to display them from the choice object it presents.

By crossing choice-types with choice-presentation, value-types, and value-presentations, ACE can provide a much greater variety of interactive controls than can most UI toolkits or UIMSs, increasing the likelihood that the right presentation for a particular application setting can be constructed. The requirement that widgets be provided with value-labels independent of the data-type being controlled is eliminated, as is the restriction that value-labels are textual. In unusual cases, when no combination of Data Selector Presenters and base-type Presenters provides a satisfactory presentation of a setting, applications can register special-purpose Presenters for their Data Selectors (e.g., a baseball diamond for a 1-from-4 choice of base-positions).

Command Selectors

Most conventional UIMSs and UI toolkits include the notion of a "button", i.e., a mouse-sensitive region that reacts to a mouse-button press by either executing a specified procedure or emitting a specified event. Some widget sets allow buttons to vary in appearance; some even allow buttons to be invisible or transparent, so they can be laid over other objects to make them mouse-sensitive.

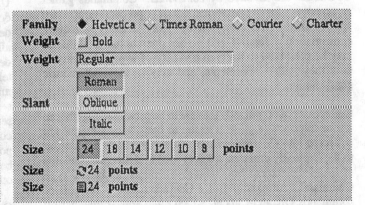

Figure 2. Two interfaces for an application for browsing text fonts, created using Data Selectors. The application contains a 1-from-N Data Selector for each of font Family, Slant, and Size, and a 1-from-2 Data Selector for font Weight. Each interface has two Presenters of Weight, three of Size, and one each of Family and Slant. Changing the value of a Data Selector causes all Presenters of it to be updated. Changing the left interface into the right one required only choosing different Presenters.

As described in the Introduction, many UIMSs and toolkits are primitive in the sense that controls of many different kinds are built by putting a few simple widget types together. In addition to requiring unnecessary, tedious, low-level work by application programmers, such systems rarely distinguish between buttons intended for invoking application operations and those intended as components in property settings. The same generic button used to trigger commands is used to control ON/OFF or multivalue settings. This lack of a distinction -- semantic or visual -- can confuse application programmers and users about the distinction between setting data-values and invoking operations.

More sophisticated user-interface tools (e.g., the ViewPoint property sheet toolkit, Jade, and ITS) enforce a visual distinction between invoking an operation and setting a data-value. In such systems, command buttons are provided as a way to invoke application operations, rather than as a building-block for constructing controls for setting data-values.

ACE Command Selectors differ from the Command widgets of even the more sophisticated UI tools in that they, like Data Selectors, embody a notion of choice. In the case of Command Selectors, the choice is between available operations rather than data-values. Also as with Data Selectors, ACE's approach is to downplay and postpone concerns about appearance, instead focussing concern on specifying: 1) the role of the interactive component in the interface, and 2) the connection between the interface component and the application semantics.

The Command Selectors design builds upon the ACEKit concepts of *operations* and *commands*. In ACE, applications provide *operations*, which allow users to manipulate data at the task-domain level. Operations take arguments, have preconditions for applicability, and produce effects on application data-state and side-effects on the external world (e.g., displaying, printing). How arguments are gathered, how preconditions are satisfied, and how effects and side-effects are manifested are all left unspecified by operations.

Operations are invoked by *commands*. Commands gather arguments for operations, test preconditions for applicability, test arguments for legality, request confirmation if desired, and invoke operations. Commands may be presented to users in a variety of ways, may vary in how they gather arguments, and may or may not require confirmation.

Collections of commands that are to be presented together in a user interface (e.g., as a group of buttons or a menu) are collected into *Command Lists*. Command Lists are similar to the explicitly enumerated Sets used to define the domains of Data Selectors, but require elements to be of type Command. An example of a Command List is the pair of commands OK and Cancel, which often appear together on dialog boxes. Commands placed into a Command List should "go together" in some way; they should be ones that a designer would put into the same menu or into one button row.

Command *Selectors* are semantic objects that provide invocation access to any of a set of related commands. A Command Selector has a domain, specified by a Command List. It also has a value, which serves only to indicate which of the Selector's commands are active. Finally, a Command Selector has a minimum number and a maximum number, which limit the number of commands that may be active at once.

Finally, ACE provides Command Selector *Presenters*, which present -- in a coherent way -- the collection of Commands that define a Command Selector. Several Command Selector Presenters will be available for each type of Command Selector. For example, a Selector for the commands OK and Cancel might be presented as a pair of buttons, a menu with two entries, or a text field that accepts either "ok" or "cancel".

Like Data Selector Views, Command Selector Views handle overall display and behavior of the Selector, relying upon ACE to supply appropriate Presenters for the individual Commands they present.

SUMMARY AND STATUS

In traditional UIMSs and toolkits, different presentations are achieved by using different widget types. This has several adverse affects. First, designers must decide early how they want things to look and behave (at a keystroke level), perhaps before they have fully worked out the semantics of the application, perhaps even diverting their attention permanently away from semantics. Second, changing, say, a slider into a number field is a major design change because it requires replacing one widget with another and "wiring" the new widget into the application. Third, semantic information about widgets' roles in the interface (e.g., that two different widgets are both four-position switches) that could be useful in analyzing the interface if explicitly represented is, in conventional interfaces, only implicit, "hidden" by the choice of different widgets.

Abstracting interface semantics away from presentation, but without the strict, "know-nothing" separation seen in most UI toolkits and UIMSs, eliminates these adverse effects. It decreases the importance of appearance considerations in design and lets designers focus on semantics (perhaps even allowing the system to make preliminary appearance decisions). It makes changing appearance easy. Finally, it tells the system much more about what the designer has in mind. For example, the most appropriate presentation for a setting may depend upon space considerations. The same setting that appears as a horizontal array of radio buttons could, if space were limited, appear as a single value with a pop-up menu to change values. Such determinations might be made by the system as the designer adds Selectors and other components to an application.

Our approach to providing appropriately abstract components for controlling applications is to:

• encapsulate the semantics of interface controls separately from their presentation, such that these semantic controls can serve a dual role as application variable and as state variables for interactive controls,

- encapsulate the presentation of choices between values separately from the presentation of individual values,

- provide a small set of simple semantic-based Selectors that provides the means, when crossed with presentation types and base-types, to easily construct a wide variety of application controls,

- provide a mechanism for registering and finding appropriate presentations for an object, based upon features,

- provide, for each Selector type and each data-object type, a "canned" set of presentations that we expect to be common, and

- allow and encourage designers and implementers to specify applications and user interfaces in terms of their semantics, i.e., in terms of what the application allows users to manipulate and what kinds of choices users must make in using it.

This approach does not eliminate the need for UI toolkits and widgets; there is still a role for them. Selector Presenters are implemented based upon the widgets provided by a UI toolkit. However, Selectors eliminate the need for designers and implementers to think in terms of widgets.

To-date, we have implemented, in C++ on top of InterViews 2.6 [4], a prototype Selectors library (called IVSelectors) that embodies some of the concepts described in this paper, but in which interfaces are specified in C++ rather than interactively. Interfaces built using IVSelectors are specified at a much higher level, requiring far less code, than interfaces built using plain InterViews.

More recently, we have implemented, in C++ on top of InterViews 2.6 and ACEKit [11], a second implementation of Selectors (called ACE Selectors), which allows interactive creation of Data Selectors and interactive choice of presentations. When the implementation is more complete, we will have come significantly closer to our goal of making ACE a tool for developing real applications, rather than a research prototype.

REFERENCES

1. Foley, J., Gibbs, C., Kim, W.C., and Kovacevic, S. "Knowledge-based User Interface Management System." *Proceedings of the ACM Conference on Computer-Human Interaction*, 1988, ACM Press, 67-72.

2. Gould, J.D., Boies, S.J., and Lewis, C. "Making Usable, Useful, Productivity-Enhancing Computer Applications." *Communications of the ACM*, 34(1), January, 1991, 74-85.

3. Johnson, J., Roberts, T., Verplank, W., Smith, D.C., Irby, C., Beard, M., Mackey, K. "The Xerox Star: A Retrospective." *IEEE Computer*, September, 1989, 22(9), 11 - 29.

4. Linton, M.A., Vlissides, J.M., and Calder, P.R. "Composing User Interfaces with InterViews." *IEEE Computer*, February, 1989, 8 - 22.

5. Myers, B.A. "Tools for Creating User Interfaces: An Introduction and Survey." *Technical Report CMU-CS-88-107*, 1988, CMU.

6. Nardi, B. and Miller, J.R. "Twinkling Lights and Nested Loops: Distributed Problem Solving and Spreadsheet Development." *Int. J. Man-Machine Studies*, 34, 1991, 161-184.

7. Nardi, B. and Zarmer, C. "Beyond Models and Metaphors: Visual Formalisms in User Interface Design." *Proceedings of the Hawaii International Conference on System Sciences (HICSS-24)*, 2, 1991, IEEE Computer Society Press, 478 - 493.

8. Szekely, P. "Standardizing the Interface between Applications and User Interface Management Systems." *Proceedings of the ACM SIGGRAPH Symposium on User Interface Software and Technology*, ACM Press, 1989, 34-42.

9. Swick, R. and Weissman, T. *X Toolkit Widgets - C Language X Interface, X Window System*, X Version 11, Release 2, MIT Project Athena, 1988.

10. Vander Zanden, B. and Myers, B.A. "Automatic, Look-and-Feel Independent Dialog Creation for Graphical User Interfaces." *Proceedings of the ACM Conference on Computer-Human Interaction*, 1990, ACM Press, 27-34.

11. Zarmer, C. "ACEKit: An Application Construction Toolkit." *HP Laboratories Technical Report HPL-91-134*, 1991.

12. Zarmer, C. and Johnson, J. "User Interface Tools: Past, Present, and Future Trends." *HP Laboratories Technical Report HPL-90-20*, 1990.

13. Zarmer, C., Nardi, B., Johnson, J., and Miller, J. "ACE: Zen and the Art of Application Building." *Proceedings of the Hawaii International Conference on System Sciences (HICSS-25)*, 2, 1992, IEEE Computer Society Press, 687-698.

HUSAT - 21 YEARS OF HCI

THE HUMAN SCIENCES & ADVANCED TECHNOLOGY RESEARCH INSTITUTE

Brian Shackel

HUSAT Research Institute and Department of Human Sciences
Loughborough University of Technology
Loughborough, LE11 3TU, England

phone +44-509-223010 *fax* +44-509-610724 *email via JANET* B.Shackel@lut.ac.uk

THE INSTITUTE

The Human Sciences and Advanced Technology (HUSAT) Research Institute is the largest centre for the study of human factors and advanced technology in Europe. Established on 1 August 1970, it has grown rapidly in recent years and now has 46 member and 5 associated scientists, supported by 16 secretarial and administrative staff. The 51 researchers have a wide range of skills, experience and training in ergonomics, psychology, computer and information sciences, and engineering. The Institute is led by five Directors (Prof. Brian Shackel, Leela Damodaran, David Davies, Brian Pearce & Prof. Ken Eason). The full-time research staff are employed by the University on fixed term personal contracts not tied to the external contracts.

The multi-disciplinary nature of the group ensures that a broad approach can be taken to research problems and facilitates an integrated 'systems design' view of applications projects and consultancy work. The Institute undertakes research on the human issues associated with emerging forms of advanced technology, for example on the human user aspects of continuous speech recognition and of electronic publishing, but is also particularly concerned with the translation of research into practice. In its balance between research and application HUSAT seeks to influence technological systems as they are developed; it aims to work directly on systems development or to convert research results into forms suitable for use by system designers.

AIMS

The 'Mission and Aims' of HUSAT are:

1. To undertake research studies and consultancy on the human aspects and implications of advanced technology.

2. To use the concepts and methodology of the various human sciences, where appropriate, in the design, implementation and use of advanced technology.

3. To disseminate our knowledge of human factors and ergonomics, and also the information and experience gained from continued involvement in the above activities.

Last year 1990 HUSAT reviewed the position of human factors in the design of IT systems and concluded (as have others) that it is still a situation of 'too little too late'. We consider this problem of technology transfer to be a crucial issue for this decade; therefore, we have set a general HUSAT 'Mission' for the 90s to be the Institutionalising of Human Factors into the Design Process.

WORK AREAS

Following from the three aims stated above, the work of the Institute can be divided into three broad categories: research, consultancy and information dissemination. In these three categories the Institute aims for about 40% of effort to be on research, 40% on consultancy or application projects and 20% on dissemination. This balance is intended to ensure that research concentrates on real issues, that application projects can benefit from the most recent research findings, and that dissemination builds upon results of both research and application projects (ie. basically as in the original aims of 1970).

HUSAT's areas of research and application cover the complete range of ergonomic and human factors issues involved in the design, installation and use of computer systems and advanced technology. Typical examples include the design and evaluation of hardware/software interfaces; workstation design and evaluation; environmental factors including vision and lighting; usability assessment; job design and work organisation; facilitating and evaluating the process of introducing new technology; and assisting the integration of the human factors contribution into IT design processes.

SOME THEMES

Some of the main themes of HUSAT'S past and present work are now briefly outlined below. Because of our particular concern with the translation of research into practice, these themes are discussed under headings relevant to the areas of technological application.

Mobile Information Systems

The work includes accident analysis, the effects of introducing in-vehicle technology into the driving environment, and the design of the in-vehicle interface across a range of applications, from carphones to screen-based technology such as route navigation and guidance systems. Particular emphasis is placed on rapid prototyping techniques for interface development and evaluation. A multi-disciplinary approach is taken to the analysis of physiological, subjective, behavioural, and vehicle control data. HUSAT is also playing a leading rôle in the advance of European ergonomic standards (Parkes & Ross 1991) for the safe implementation of in-vehicle systems.

Organisational Requirements Definition for Information Technology Systems - ORDIT

There is a wide body of research evidence, supported by much of the applied work undertaken within HUSAT, which indicates that many IT systems fail not because they do not meet the users' functional requirements, but because they do not meet their organisational requirements. Future generations of information systems will be integrated, multi-media, multi-user systems rather than stand-alone products. These will have to be carefully matched to the organisational requirements if they are to be successful. The primary aim of the ORDIT project is to find a method of eliciting and formalising organisational requirements, to enable those involved in the design process to take account of these requirements in the design of an IT system. The project is also committed to developing software-based tools to be used as part of a user-centred, iterative design methodology (Eason & Harker 1991).

Electronic Documentation

For over a decade HUSAT has studied the human issues involved in the design and use of electronic documentation. The BLEND project established the feasibility of an online electronic journal (Shackel 1991), while in Project QUARTET the hypertext electronic journal was developed as a desktop resource for individual scholars. Recent work has investigated hypertext not only as an information interface but also as an environment for collaborative authoring. The design of electronic documentation involves much more than the moving of words from paper to screen, and hypermedia techniques offer a potential which needs to be seen in the wider context of the human use of information resources (McKnight et al 1991).

OTHER THEME AREAS

Some of our other theme areas which cannot be summarised here through lack of space include:

Integrated Speech Technology

Advanced Manufacturing Technology

H F Aspects of the Computer Integrated Enterprise

Usability Factors in Video-Communication Systems

The Usability Evaluation Service

The HILITES Information Service

SOME PUBLICATIONS

Over the years several books have been oriented specifically towards designers. Examples are the Applied Ergonomics Handbook (Shackel 1974); two texts on system and workplace design by Damodaran (et al 1980) & by Stewart (Cakir et al 1980); the possibility of health hazards, addressed in the early days by Pearce (1984); a general text on organisational issues in IT (Eason 1988); and an overview on human factors for IT (Shackel and Richardson, 1991). In 1990 HUSAT produced 1 book, 20 journal papers, 55 reports and 65 contributions to books and conference proceedings.

Cakir A, Hart D J & Stewart T F M (1980) *Visual Display Terminals*. Chichester, Wiley. ISBN 0-471-27793-2.

Damodaran L, Simpson A and Wilson P (1980) *Designing Systems for People*. Manchester, NCC Publications. ISBN 0-85012-242-2.

Eason K D (1988) *Information Technology and Organisational Change*. London, Taylor & Francis.

Eason K D & Harker S D P (1991) Human Factors Contributions to the Design Process. In Shackel and Richardson (eds) (1991), pp. 73-96.

McKnight C, Dillon A & Richardson J (1991) *Hypertext in Context*. Cambridge: Cambridge University Press.

Parkes A M & Ross T (1991) The Need For Performance Based Standards in Future Vehicle Man Machine Interfaces. *Advanced Telematics in Road Transport*. Vol II pp 1312-1321. Amsterdam, Elsevier.

Pearce B (1984) *Health Hazards of VDTs?* Chichester, Wiley. ISBN 0-471-90065-6.

Shackel B (1974) *Applied Ergonomics Handbook*. Guildford, Butterworth. ISBN 0-902-85238-8.

Shackel B (1991) *BLEND-9: Overview and Appraisal*. British Library Research Paper 82; ISBN 0-7123-3231-6.

Shackel B & Richardson S R (eds) (1991) *Human Factors for Informatics Usability*. Cambridge: Cambridge University Press. ISBN 0-521-36570-8.

Acknowledgements

Grateful thanks to all my past and present colleagues in HUSAT and to all our research grant sources & contract sponsors for their excellent support over the 21 years.

The Human-Computer Technology Group
at Bellcore

Rita M. Bush

Bellcore
Room RRC 1N267
444 Hoes Lane
Piscataway NJ 08854 US
+1 908 699 8563
rita2@ctt.bellcore.com

KEYWORDS: Technology Transfer, User-Centered Design, Graphical User Interfaces, User Modeling

INTRODUCTION

The Human Computer Technology group is part of the Computer Technology Transfer (CTT) Division at Bellcore. The division's overall goals include the assessment of emerging technologies in computing, and the transfer of selected promising technologies to other software development projects within Bellcore and to the Bellcore Client Companies directly. The Human Computer Technology group is specifically concerned with technologies and concepts relating to human/computer interaction. The group's work has two major thrusts: 1) investigation of human factors concerns in user interface technology, and 2) application of emerging technologies to the assistance of human/computer interaction. The group is composed of behavioral and computer scientists.

Much of the work involves prototyping to assess the feasibility of new software and design concepts, assessment of new technologies, creation of new methods and technologies, and consultations and collaborations with other Bellcore software applications to promote their use of new technologies. The problems that motivate our efforts relate to the often ineffective human/computer interaction that is caused by the underlying complexity of systems and data that users need to accomplish their business goals. Our aim is to hide that complexity so that users can focus directly on accomplishing their tasks, acquiring information, and solving problems.

THE TECHNOLOGY TRANSFER CHALLENGE

Any organization that purports to do technology transfer is faced with the challenge of turning this noble goal into a reality. We deal with clients who are concerned about real issues of cost, quality, and tight product schedules. They are interested in emerging technologies to the extent that these technologies can help ease the pressure of one of these driving forces. The technology transfer organization, to be successful, must help these clients in a very direct fashion.

We accomplish this through "technology teaming". We typically send one of our subject matter experts to be part of the client software development project team for some period of time and thus act as an agent of change. This expert is charged with demonstrating the use of the relevant technology within the context of the project, and instructing, by example, his or her coworkers on the team. Examples of this process will be mentioned in some of the projects discussed below.

MAJOR PROJECTS

A sampling of the group's current work includes:

Demonstrate and transfer user-centered design methods.
The software development process must increase the involvement of the real users of the system, early and often, to ensure useful and usable systems [1]. We have worked with several major software products in Bellcore to incorporate user-centered design (UCD) methods into their development lifecycle. Our efforts to promote the use of UCD methods have had much success. We were instrumental in putting in place a software development policy (endorsed and enforced by a Bellcore Vice President) that all software development projects will incorporate UCD methods to increase the usability of their products. Prior to the adoption of this policy, UCD activities in Bellcore were hit-or-miss. Each of these products is currently at a different point in the software development lifecycle (i.e., development planning, detailed design & implementation, and live field support), yet we have found that it is possible to positively influence the user interface and system usability at each of these points. The introduction of the UCD policy has led to increased requests for consultations from our group and the formation of separate human factors

groups on several of the software development projects.

We are also exploring innovative participatory design techniques [5] that emphasize the user's role as a member of the design team. The PICTIVE technique [3] has been used by a number of software projects in Bellcore as a means of doing task analysis and initial user interface design [4]. The technique has enjoyed great success because of its simplicity and economy of use. PICTIVE is now being extended into TelePICTIVE, an experimental groupware prototype [9].

Finally, the group maintains a usability testing laboratory, which supports usability testing and videotape analysis, both at Bellcore and in the field. As part of our support of this lab, we have introduced the use of logging software to note user behaviors, and we are instructing the local human factors community in its use. The laboratory may be used by any project in Bellcore.

Promote the appropriate use of workstation front-end devices and graphical user interfaces to our software products. Our goal is to assist the appropriate introduction of workstation technology and graphical user interfaces (GUIs) into Bellcore products, and to identify and assess tools that support user interface development in this environment. To that end, we collaborated with several software development projects in creating software prototypes on several different workstation platforms in order to assess the ease with which those platforms supported software development, and the power, flexibility, and portability provided by those platforms. These collaborations resulted in the recommendation that Bellcore use the X Window System™ with the Motif™ style guide for its workstation-based applications.

We have followed up on this work by performing assessments of emerging Interactive Design Tools (IDTs) being made available by several vendors. We are also providing consultations and education to Bellcore software projects that are beginning to use windowing environments and to develop GUIs. The design of GUIs requires a paradigm shift that we are trying to help Bellcore designers and developers make [2, 6]. Our group is also writing Bellcore GUI design guidelines to augment the Motif style guide. The challenge with this work is to actively influence the design process in many Bellcore software products so that the user interfaces have a similar appearance and behavior.

Assess user modeling techniques to act as intelligent assistants to the user interface. Knowledge of the goals and characteristics of the user can guide system behavior toward the user by having a "user model" resident within the software itself. As part of an exploration of intelligent interface frameworks [7], we are exploring the application of these techniques to a Bellcore software product for work force administration. This work involved prototyping a graphical user interface for a particular task in the work force adminis-

---

X Window System is a trademark of the Massachusetts Institute of Technology. Motif is a trademark of The Open Software Foundation, Inc.

tration system, that of time card approval by supervisors. We built two versions of the GUI prototype, one that incorporated a simple user model and one that did not. We wanted to demonstrate that even a simple, easy to construct model would have measurable benefits to the user in the completion of their task on the system. We tested the two versions of the prototype with 18 users from three regional telephone companies. The results of this study showed that users were able to complete the time card approval task faster and were more satisfied with the prototype incorporating the user model [8].

STAFF

The current members of the Human Computer Technology group are: Rita Bush, Tom Dayton, Alan Gebele, Dave Miller, Nancy Mond, Michael Muller, Robert Root, and John Smith. Recent members of the group were Kathy Cebulka, Jane Daniel, and Peter Clitherow (part of our technology transfer is transfer of group members to other projects in Bellcore!) Members are actively involved in professional societies. Michael is the co-chair of PDC '92, the Demos chair for CSCW '92, and is a member of several CHI '92 committees. Bob served as the Communications Technical Subgroup 1991 Program Chair for the Human Factors Society.

RECENT PUBLICATIONS

[1] Bush, R.M. (1990). Putting the Human in Human/Computer Interaction. In *Proceedings of National Communications Forum*, **44.** Chicago: Professional Education International.

[2] Dayton, J. T. (1991). Cultivated eclecticism as the Normative Approach to design. In J. Karat (Ed.), *Taking Software Design Seriously: Practical Techniques for Human-Computer Interaction Design.* Boston: Academic Press.

[3] Muller, M. J. (1991). PICTIVE - Democratizing the Dynamics of the Design Session. In *Proceedings of CHI '91*, New Orleans, April 1991.

[4] Muller, M. J. (1992). Retrospective on a Year of Participatory Design using the PICTIVE Technique. To appear in *Proceedings of CHI '92*, Monterey CA, May 1992.

[5] Muller, M.J., Wildman, D.M., and White, E.A. (1992). Taxonomy of Participatory Design Practices: A Participatory Poster. Poster submitted to CHI'92, Monterey CA, May 1992.

[6] Nielsen, J., Bush, R.M., Dayton, J.T., Mond, N.E., Muller, M.J., & Root, R.W. (1992). Teaching Experienced Developers to Design Graphical User Interfaces. To appear in *Proceedings of CHI'92, Monterey CA, May 1992*.

[7] Smith, J.G., and Cebulka, K.D. (1991). A Framework for Intelligent Interfaces. Poster at CHI'91, New Orleans, April 1991.

[8] Smith, J. G. & Dayton, J. T. (1992). Empirical Support for the Utility of User Models. Submitted to *User Modeling and User-Adapted Interaction*.

[9] Smith, J.G., Miller, D.S., and Muller, M.J. (1992). TelePICTIVE Groupware for Collaborative GUI Design. Poster submitted to CHI'92, Monterey CA, May 1992.

The Human Factors Group at Compaq Computer Corporation

Human Factors Group

Compaq Computer Corporation
P.O.Box 692000   Mail Code 100801
Houston, Texas   77269-2000

INTRODUCTION

The Human Factors group at Compaq Computer Corporation is devoted to providing information and recommendations that will improve the usability of COMPAQ products, allowing end users to accomplish their tasks more effectively, efficiently, and comfortably. The domain of the group ranges from hardware and software issues, to installation, packaging and documentation issues. Established in March, 1989, the department has grown to a staff of seven full-time professionals, with degrees ranging from B.A. to Ph.D. in such areas as Human Factors, Applied Experimental Psychology, I/O Psychology, Cognitive Psychology, and Industrial Engineering. The department's testing activities have increased from 3 studies in late 1989 to over 60 studies in 1991.

COMPAQ CULTURE

A key factor to the successful growth and impact of the Compaq Human Factors (HF) group is the unique corporate culture at Compaq. The core of this culture is "consensus management". This team approach to decision making provided a channel for HF's voice to be heard. Rod Canion, former president and CEO, made the following comments about "consensus management":

"The real benefit of the process is not that you get the answer but all the things you go through to get the answer. You get a lot of facts, you get a lot of people thinking, and the result is that everybody owns the decision when you get through ... Consensus isn't getting everybody to agree to vote for the same thing. Consensus is getting people to believe that you've got the right facts and the right reasons to make the right decision." (Webber, 1991).

Because of this culture, HF was readily incorporated into the team process by providing objective HCI research to help teams make more educated decisions. The group behaves as a "service organization" to the entire corporation, although it is technically located within the Systems Engineering Division. Any individual or team within the corporation that has a product-related CHI issue can request Human Factors' services.

HF IN THE DESIGN PROCESS

From its inception, the group strove to stay problem-oriented, working on specific issues raised by product design teams. With its formalized approach, based on scientific methods, HF research provided objective data on user interface alternatives. This approach was particularly appreciated by team members who in the past had relied on less empirical methods.

Because of its problem-oriented approach, the group selectively attends project design team meetings or attends when meeting leaders have asked HF to address a particular issue. However, HF is in contact with the appropriate developers and designers on a day-to-day basis. Because of the number of projects going on at one time, and because of the relatively small size of the group, this problem-oriented approach allows the group to remained focused on HF issues.

The testing done by the Human Factors group occurs during all stages of the product design cycle, including:
1) *Feasibility testing*--HF provides information for future product planning, testing out the feasibility of new designs or technology.
2) *Iterative testing*--HF is involved during the entire design phase of a product. The group frequently aids in developing and prototyping alternative user interface designs. The group's iterative testing of these designs provides Engineering and Marketing professionals with an understanding of how well the design meets pre-defined usability goals. Specific user interface issues and

recommendations are identified and help the team focus its development efforts. The iterative testing verifies whether previously observed issues have been successfully resolved.

3) *State of the Union testing*--HF gathers information to help answer: Where does our product stand? Where does the competition stand? Where does our product stand with respect to the competition?

4)*Sustaining testing*--HF tests are used to help Engineering quantify challenges that are raised in the field by one or more customers, providing information concerning to what degree the problem exists, and the potential percentage of users who appear to exhibit the problem. Follow-up studies are used to determine whether proposed solutions are effective and/or to compare solutions with varying implementation costs.

RESOURCES, FACILITIES, AND TOOLS

Lab Facilities: The Human Factors group has three laboratories which have been equipped with both video and audio recording equipment, as well as sophisticated editing equipment. As many as 12 individual workstations can be run simultaneously. An observation room looking into two of the labs allows HF, Marketing and Engineering personnel to view the studies first-hand. Camcorders allow the study of end users in the field.

Lab Tools: The group has developed automated tools for data collection and analysis. Among these tools is an experimenter comment/event recorder.

Research Assistants: Two full-time research assistants have become critical in coordinating lab activities from running test users to editing video tapes and charting study results.

Usability Goal Tables: In order to help synthesize expectations of a product's usability, the Human Factors group frequently encourages design teams to build a "Usability Goals Table", adapted from Whiteside, Bennett, and Holtzblatt (1988). The table is comprised of a list of usability attributes (e.g., learning rate), methods by which these attributes can be measured (e.g., task completion time), and "usability goals" for each of these attributes. The intent is that a product is not ready for release unless the minimal usability goals have been met, as verified through iterative design and testing.

User Interface Consistency: A User Interface Team (UIT) meets weekly to discuss software user interface design issues currently under development. Using a brainstorming approach, the team provides user interface suggestions and recommendations. The team and the internal development of a user interface tool have helped to promote consistency for COMPAQ software utilities.

Standards Committee Work: To stay in touch with both domestic and international ergonomic standards,

Compaq has representatives on both the Human Factors Society Committee on Human-Computer Interaction and the TC159 SC4 Work Group 5 of the ISO 9241 Human-Computer Interface Standards Organization.

HF Lunches: The group meets monthly to discuss particular projects, new user interface design ideas, usability engineering methods, or key talks attended at recent conferences. The group also meets quarterly to discuss ways in which it can do its job more effectively.

EXAMPLES OF HF RESEARCH

"Out of the Box" Study: An initial "Out of the Box" study examined the unpacking and set up process of a COMPAQ DESKPRO in contrast to comparable models made by two competitors. In the study, novice PC users were instructed to unpack, set up, configure, and install an operating system on the COMPAQ DESKPRO. They were asked to do the same on a competitor's system. Not only did the study identify HF issues with the COMPAQ product's unpacking and set up process, it also ascertained how the COMPAQ product compared with the competition. Moreover, an edited video tape of the study proved to be very popular and was requested numerous times by different organizations throughout the company. This helped spread awareness of the HF group and the information HF studies can provide. The study was a catalyst for improvements to hardware, software, packaging, and documentation.

COMPAQ System Manager: Human Factors assisted in the user interface design and testing of the COMPAQ System Manager, which enables network administrators to monitor and manage systems remotely. HF addressed several aspects of this product's UI, including the voice, iconic, and software interfaces. The group reviewed HF research and offered guidance for the technical characteristics, content, selection and presentation of the digitized voice interface. A series of surveys were conducted with users to compare and rate potential voices and icon designs. HF conducted iterative usability studies and worked with developers to improve the interface based on the findings of these studies.

REFERENCES

1. Webber, A. M.. "Consensus, Continuity, and Common Sense: An interview with Compaq's Rod Canion", Harvard Business Review, July-August, 1990.

2. Whiteside, J., Bennett, J., & Holtzbaltt, K. Usability Enginering: Our Experience Evolution. In *The Handbook of Human-Computer Interaction,* M. Helander (Ed.), Elsevier Science Publishers B.V. (North-Holland, 1988).

Interfaces for consumer products:
"How to camouflage the computer?"

Moderator: Maddy D. Brouwer-Janse
                Philips Research Laboratories - Institute for Perception Research
                P. O. Box 513
                5600 MB EINDHOVEN, The Netherlands
                Phone: * 31-40-773831 (secr. 773873)
                Email: brouwer@heiipo5.bitnet

Panelists: Raymond W. Bennett, AT&T Bell Laboratories, US
                Takaya Endo, NTT, Human & Multimedia Lab., Japan
                Floris L. van Nes, Philips Research - Institute for Perception Research, Neth.
                Hugo J. Strubbe, Philips Research Laboratories, Briarcliff Manor, US
                Donald R. Gentner, Apple Computer, Inc., US

INTRODUCTION

User interfaces for consumer products are notoriously bad. The increase of computing power in consumer products, from personal computers and diaries, televisions, video and audio products to kitchen machines provides increasingly more functionality that is theoretically available but not practically accessible to users. Most HCI research is devoted to applications for which the computing systems are clearly present and usable to the trained. In contrast, the users of consumer electronics products do not expect to need computer skills to interact with their TV sets or car stereo's. In consumer products, the computing systems are embedded and hidden from the users by the user interface. Their user interfaces have at least a dual function: platform for the quality of the human-computer interaction and carrier of the system's attractiveness and purchasing appeal.

The design of practical user interfaces for consumer products presents formidable problems which have gone nearly unrecognized by the HCI community. This panel will address these problems using the following issues as a starting point for discussion:

- Many problems with today's consumer products originate from user interface designs that are modelled after the user interface of computer systems.

- Consumer products are characterized by very rigid system constraints, such as, display size, memory, cpu power, input devices, conditions of use, component price, mechanical compatibility, manufacturability and serviceability.

- Usability testing is complicated by the need for informal, natural settings, such as, the living room, a car speeding through rush hour traffic, or simulating the multiple tasks that users accomplish under natural conditions while operating their equipment.

- The user population for consumer products is multivaried. Defining specific and unequivocal populations for consumer products is extremely difficult.

- Users of consumer products are, in general, not at all motivated to spend time on learning to deal with their products or reading their system manuals.

- Consumers confront the product usability carrying expectations built in during the pre-purchase phases, i.e., at retailers, on the shelf, or from advertising. The user interfaces have to deal with these expectations. In addition, the introduction of product concepts that provide entirely new functionalities into the mass market creates extra burdens for the design of user interfaces.

PANELISTS

Raymond W. Bennett is a distinguished Member of the Technical Staff in the Advanced Services Technology Department at AT&T Bell Laboraotories in Naperville, IL. In recent years he has worked on low-bit rate coders, text-to-speech systems, automatic speech recognition, enhanced telephony interfaces, and hypertext and hypermedia information systems.

Takaya Endo is Executive Manager of Human and Multimedia Laboratory in NTT Human Interface Laboratories. Since joining NTT in 1968, he has been active in work on the facsimile communication system, the multimedia database system, and human interface technologies. He is now interested in researches on socially distributed cognition and individual differences in human interfaces.

Floris L. van Nes is coordinator of the Information Ergonomics Group at the Institute of Perception Research - IPO, Eindhoven, a joint venture of Philips Research Laboratories and the Eindhoven University of Technology. He has been active in work on speech user interfaces, car audio products, visual displays, design of characters for videotex and information retrieval from public data bases.

Hugo J. Strubbe, who has a physics and computer science background, became interested in user interfaces 10 years ago. After spending a few years on professional interfaces (like office automation) at PRIME Computer, Inc. he joined Philips Research Labs to work on consumer interfaces (like TVs and VCRs).

Don R. Gentner is a human interface designer at Apple Computer. He is currently trying to make friendlier interfaces to UNIX systems, and has previously worked on interfaces for consumer oriented devices, such as news retrievers and VCRs. Recently, he has been exploring the relations between the engineering model of a system, the system image presented to the user, and the user's model of the task.

Maddy D. Brouwer-Janse is a Senior Scientist at the Philips Research laboratories - Institute for Perception Research, Eindhoven, Netherlands. She is working on MMI concepts and methods for consumer and professional products. Particular areas of interest are human problem solving, cognition and perception pertaining to multimodal human-machine communication.

PANELIST STATEMENTS

Raymond W. Bennett
AT&T Bell Laboratories

In living memory, making a telephone call involved nothing more complicated than banging on the switch hook a few times and announcing the number being called when the operator came on line. With the advent of dial offices, area codes, and even international access numbers, placing a call required a bit more ingenuity, but was in reach of most 7-year olds. While the global telecommunications network has made enormous strides in recent decades, one wonders, how many people reading this, know how to transfer a call on their office telephone? How

many of us could explain in detail what happens if, when trying to make a 3-way call from a residential telephone, you get a busy signal, and then flash the switch hook again?

With some qualifications, if we add functionality to a human-machine system, we must pay with more complex interfaces. Since there can be no doubt we will be adding more functionality to the global network, it seems to follow that telephony is doomed to become more complicated. If call transfer is a significant intellectual challenge for many of us, what are the prospects for multimedia teleconferencing? If we are not sure how 3-way calling works, can we be expected to make good use of hypermedia information systems, or information appliances that integrate residential communications services with home-control and security systems?

While we may be looking at a future with more complex telecommunications interfaces, these interfaces need not be more difficult to use. A rich, expansive interface that allows users to communicate naturally and to focus on the task at hand without concern for the underlying machinery can easily score high on "usability" while still supporting considerable functionality. The interface in a human-machine system must present the user with a coherent view of the system, and must foster a conceptual model of the system that makes functionality apparent and comprehensible. The desktop metaphor for personal computers, as pioneered by Xerox and made commercially successful by Apple in their Macintosh line, has become highly popular because it expresses system functionality by way of an analogy with something more familiar. For telecommunications services, the underlying machinery is complicated and poorly understood and service designers are further constrained by having to use existing capabilities rather than freely creating new ones. We will discuss some approaches we have taken in developing new interfaces for enhanced telecommunication services.

Takaya Endo
NTT Human Interface Laboratories

Telecommunications has great potential to help people share ideas and understand each other. Telecommunication services should be easy to use and enable people to communicate and collaborate with the feeling that they are in the same room. Common communication tools must be freely accepted by all users. The following ideas will help develop such tools.

1. Continuity with household life. Consumers have their household life. The Japanese home is full of electric appliances. Among electric appliances with microprocessors, electric rice cooking pots, automatic washing machines, microwave ranges, etc. are widely accepted and are easily used by everyone, even when they have sophisticated functionalities. Nowadays, some appliances are sold that use fuzzy or neuro technologies to adapt to various kinds of conditions and menus. We, in some sense, have to learn from the acceptance of household consumer electronics.

2. *Adapting to traditional cultures.* Historically, various kinds of telecommunication terminals and systems have been introduced with the aim of connecting people to each other, or to remote databases. Telephones are now widely accepted by everybody. About 15 years ago, we started seriously discussing the post-telephone media, and chose the facsimile. Facsimiles at that time were very expensive, large and extremely complicated to use. Certainly they were not suitable for the home use that was our goal. Product enhancement, simplification and usability activities were intense and proceeded in parallel with standardization. Nowadays, as you know, facsimiles are widely accepted in the world because of their low cost, easy-to-use nature and adaptation to traditional cultures. We also have to learn from the acceptance of home facsimiles.

3. *Enjoying and evolving the way of everyday life.* People are enjoying multimedia worlds in everyday life. The two big ones are the game world and the entertainment world. In some sense, new interactive interfaces or new functionalities will be developed through the game world or entertainment world, such as "TV game", "karaoke", etc. These worlds might change consumers into participants by using advanced recognition and interactive technologies. We also have to learn from such enjoyable interactive interfaces that will evolve.

These ideas give us the design principles accepted by consumers, as follows: a) Adding advanced agent functions with environmental sensory abilities. b) Making interfaces that fuse the system with everyday life. c) Adding the feeling of wanting to participate by using advanced perception or recognition technologies. As a result, we must interface with all aspects of the consumer as a sentient being. We must learn to adapt to individual preferences. These principles will be discussed with a variety of examples, and new telecommunication tools will be presented.

Floris L. van Nes
Philips Research Laboratories - IPO
Even the experimentally proven most usable interfaces for consumer products have to be 'sold' to technical people from development departments and artistic people from design departments. Both have their own ideas of what the interface should look, feel etc. like. To convince them to adopt other ideas requires stamina, ingenuity, diplomatic and psychological skill as well as solid evidence, i.e., preferably quantitative, data from evaluative tests.

One of the biggest problems facing the designer of user interfaces for consumer products is that, compared to professional products, very little is known about the actual users. Their variability is large on many different dimensions; from anthropometry to motion stereotypes. They also come from different cultural and social backgrounds. In addition, application domains have specific requirements and constraints for the user-system interaction. For example, the automotive domain is especially characterized by its potential danger for participants and bystanders. Using consumer products in this domain is a secondary task for the driver of the vehicle. The following examples illustrate some of the issues.

1. *Car audio as a vehicle for usability methods.* The usage of automotive products in general is difficult to observe. Automatically recording the patterns of use in the relevant context partially solves that problem. This technique was applied to an advanced car radio/cassette player, by modifying its control software. Registration of objective, realistic usage data in this way turned out to be unobtrusive, reliable and revealing. The corresponding subjective user reports, that are widely used in the industry for quality control purposes were found to be very unreliable: they highly underestimate the real frequencies of control use.

2. *Car navigation systems.* A tool to plan a route and help in navigating it to save time and money is welcomed by many drivers. Presenting the navigation instructions at a decision point on the route in a non-hazardous way, however, is a precarious task. Several ways have to be investigated, such as, using synthetic speech or visual displays on the front window or dash board to safely pilot the driver.

3. *Mobile telephony in cars.* Mobile telecommunication compounds human factors telecommunication problems. Making a phone call while driving a car through rush hour traffic is a very complex and risky task. Making this safe is a real challenge to the user interface designer. Speeding cars present an environment in which the inherent advantages of speech input and outpu can be taken advantage of; i.e., hands-free and eyes-free communication.

Hugo J. Strubbe
Philips Research Labs - Briarcliff Manor
I have been working for 5 years towards one goal: "Simplify TV watching." TV watching is complicated for consumers who want to watch shows that interest them: they often do not find any good shows being broadcast at the time they want to watch TV. So the consumer buys a VCR to "timeshift" good shows or to watch rented movies. Then a cable descrambler comes into the house to receive premium channels. Then a password is needed to prevent the children from seeing some of these premium channels.

And the list goes on. Each of these additions brings more complexity for the non-technical consumer.

Consumer electronics companies, like most companies, try to build products which their "customers" want. However, the consumer is not a direct customer. The retail salesmen and the management of large stores are the important customers. Their wishes about the products are taken into account. There are two main classes of users: "couch potatoes" (non-technical users who are task oriented) and "wizards" (very technical users who are interested in the inner details of the product). Each of these classes needs a different interface.

Collecting usage data of TV watching is very difficult as each realistic observation session takes several months. Focus groups and lab-experiments give little insight into the way the consumer will use the product in the casual home setting after its "newness" has worn off.

1. Why are the interfaces of consumer electronics products so bad? Because of constraints in product development, most products are built with only one interface. Influential wizards, like salesmen, product planners, development engineers, etc. request an interface which accesses all features in a variety of ways. The task oriented "couch potato" interface disappears, and the general public is unhappy as they are forced to use the "wizard" interface.

2. What should be done to improve consumer interfaces? Product developers should be periodically shown usability test data of their creations. They should be required to observe how the general public struggles with their design.

3. Will the transfer of human factors competence improve consumer products? Human factors techniques have been tried successfully on TV interface prototypes. However, such work typically has little effect on products. Designs made by human factors people are often more expensive than those made by engineers. Cost is an important purchase criterion for consumers. They rarely evaluate ease-of-use in the shop. Therefore, one cannot charge extra for it. Consumers who are unable to use the product at home accept this as their fault and do not return the product. The consumer has to be taught to insist on ease-of-use, and our human factors work does not directly contribute to this.

Don L. Gentner
Apple Computer, Inc.
Radios Meet Microprocessors after 70 Years
Microprocessors are now embedded in many consumer products, from toys to sewing machines to automobiles.

This technological development brings with it both bad news and good news. The bad news is that the incremental cost of adding features is negligible; the good news is that people wanted a computer inside their machines all along.

The cost of mass produced consumer products, such as automobiles or VCRs, is determined primarily by the cost of their physical materials. Design and software development costs are amortized over very large production volumes and become negligible. With mechanical controls, additional features typically required more materials and their consequent higher costs. Now, with microprocessor controllers, additional features may only require software enhancements. The only incremental costs are for additional buttons or displays in the interface, so these are minimized. The bad news is that these economic forces and microprocessors have given us products that are bursting with features but hobbled by minimal interfaces.

An informal survey of how people think about controls for their radios and automobile heaters indicated that most people think that moving a mechanical control is like giving verbal commands. They don't realize that there is a direct connection from the control (via shafts, levers or cables) to the internal mechanism. The good news is that people want to use language to control their products, and microprocessors are better than levers at understanding simple languages.

Early crystal radios were controlled by direct manipulation of the electrical mechanism. Although the mechanism was hidden in later radios, the user interface remained directly connected to it. The first significant improvement in the user interface of radios was the change from multiple tuning dials to a single tuning dial, which required a conceptual divorce of the user interface from the engineering model of the radio. The introduction of radio buttons finally brought natural user concepts into the interface. Economic constraints still dominate radio interfaces, and the direct control of capacitors and resistors persists in radio interfaces sold today. Only high-end radios base the user interface on station push buttons or signal scanners.

Microprocessors in consumer products offer us an opportunity to liberate the interface from the underlying mechanism, but liberation requires two steps. First, we must realize that past user interfaces were economically and logically enslaved to the engineering mechanism and that those shackles are now unlocked. Second, we must use this new freedom to rethink the interface in terms of the fundamental user concepts and tasks, and not just as an opportunity to complicate the interface with new features.

A WINDOW SYSTEM WITH LEAFING THROUGH MODE: BOOKWINDOW

Kyoichi Arai, Teruo Yokoyama, Yutaka Matsushita

KEIO University
3-14-1 Hiyoshi, Kohoku-ku, Yokohama 223 JAPAN
Phone: +81-45-563-1141 Fax: +81-45-562-7625
E-mail: kyoichi@myo.inst.keio.ac.jp

ABSTRACT

This paper describes "BookWindow" that we implemented, a window system based on the "book" metaphor, that displays information not by scrolling but by using the animation of paging through. The BookWindow system equips some bookmarks, tabs, etc, by which we can access to an expected page through our requirements. BookWindow can support our work environment which navigates us through information space flexibly, because human beings are quite familiar with "books".

INTRODUCTION

Recently, computers for office-automation are getting lower in price and higher in performance so that they are much closer and very popular to people. It is now practical to build friendly interfaces consisting of many kinds of technical elements. But it is usually assumed to be still not easy for those users to operate them. For example, it is difficult for users to comprehend which part of the entire document(very big document) being displayed on the screen at that time, since the capacity of a screen is so far insufficient to display the whole part simultaneously.

Human beings are very good at managing and memorizing objects spatially[2]. For example, in the case you go shopping to a grocery store which you use frequently, it does not take so long time to find out bottles of milk. What we mean by this is that you have a spatial map of the grocery store in your mind. At present, it is difficult for us to use such a facility to retrieve the data by computer, although most computers can show them on the screen by scrolling or popping up. The reason of this is that such schemes cannot manage information spatially.

BOOK MEDIA

Imagine that we are in a book store and finding pleasant books out from a bookstack. It must be rare that we choose one among many books for the title only. Usually we take it in our hand and run our eyes through it. Then we decide whether that book is worth while to read or not.

Thus, practical points for deciding are not minute full sentences but a table of contents, pictures or figures in most cases.

Secondly in the case we want to re-refer to one part of a book which we read before, it is unusual that we remember the page numbers or any other information precisely. Ordinarily we find out an object with the help of spatial memories such as "A photograph is located in the upper-right corner in a page."

Two cases described above shows us a doubtless fact that memory of human beings is pretty spatial and so ambiguous. It will be very important and indispensable to provide practical interfaces which will be able to comply with these human-oriented, warm-hearted, requests even in electronic media.

PROBLEMS OF SCROLLING SCHEME

Visual display terminals usually offer scrolling scheme in order to display a large amount of information within computers efficiently. This scheme lets pieces of information move continuously(pan scroll) or line by line(roll scroll) in the direction up, down, right or left on the screen. It is usually assumed that scrolling is suited for pieces of information lying relatively close together, but we can point out some typical drawbacks as follows[2][3]:

1. It is difficult for users to comprehend which part of information is displayed on a screen.

2. It is not easy to refer to the point over again to which a user has paid attention before.

3. It is difficult to refer to the specific points of a large amount of information non-linearly.

The scrolling scheme which is the most popular information providing approach does not fit in the feelings of human beings who are familiar with leafing through pages.

FEATURES OF BOOKWINDOW

BookWindow provides information in the style of a book and displays information by using animation of leafing through pages. Therefore, each piece of information is paginated rather than showed continuously. BookWindow has the following features:

1. Users can easily realize the direction of page flipping(forward or backward) by animation and the amount leafed through by the thickness of pages.

2. It can help even unexperienced users access, because it shows a great resemblance to a book, both in appearance and characteristics.

3. It also takes advantages of electronic media. Users can duplicate any page in an instant, and this helps users refer to the information on multiple pages simultaneously.

To realize those features mentioned above in BookWindow, we fixed a goal as "effectiveness rather than efficiency." Even in such a case that you paid attention to a figure located in the upper-right corner in a certain page and after a while you must refer to the figure again, you can easily access that page by activating spatial memory in your mind. It can be said that BookWindow is the new style of information providing system which can comply with ambiguous humane requests sufficiently.

OUR BOOKWINDOW SYSTEM
Prototype System
We built an electronic catalog of some Japanese cars as one prototype system of BookWindow. It has 25 pages in total and includes some minute descriptions and the price table of those cars. Users can do not only browse sequentially by leafing through pages but also access non-linearly to the expected page, since this system borrowed some ideas from hypertext.

Approaches For Accessing
There are two main approaches to access the information in a book provided in the BookWindow system. They are sequential(linear) and random(non-linear) accesses.

Sequential Access
You may feel that these animations consume capacity of memory wastefully. Actually they occupy more capacity than contents of the real text. But this redundancy scheme can be pretty effective to construct environments which are able to navigate users through information space freely.

This system has four modes(buttons) of leafing through. Two of them are used to turn over the next or the previous page respectively, and others are to leaf through pages forward or backward continuously.

Random Access
On a real book, we use some specific tools in order to refer to a certain page again later. Bookmark is one of these tools. Our system equips some electronic bookmarks that can help users' quick reference to the marked page. Another tool is tabs. They look like small flaps or strips, and each of them is used as an identification of the section itself. Users can start reading from any section as well if they want to by picking it up and turning it over.

In hypertext systems, it is a matter of course that we can access to related information by tracing hypertext links. Also in the BookWindow system, users can trace links to refer to and come back freely beyond pages. They can also add another link if necessary. Next subsection describes other functions supported in our system for more practical use .

Other Functions
"Page Copy"
The BookWindow system also takes advantages of electronic media. By clicking "Page Copy" button, the very current page image will be copied to an other window so that users can refer to more than one page simultaneously.

"Underline" And "Memo"
We usually underline or write a few words down directly onto a book to comprehend better. In the BookWindow system, those can be done by dragging mouse cursor. This system also has a "Memo" function to put longer comments. Users can paste the typed memo on a page for immediate re-reference.

CONCLUSION
In this paper, we discussed a newly developed information providing system based on the book metaphor, named BookWindow which represent each information by means of page flipping, not by scrolling. Human beings are good at managing and memorizing information spatially. So BookWindow's approach is thought of indispensable to establish friendly systems.

Since we are living in the Information Age society where people cannot think or believe in isolated way, there must be better approaches to access large amounts of data effectively. We believe that BookWindow can provide a fair measure of flexible work environments even for unskilled users. In order to build human-oriented interfaces, it is quite necessary to get various ideas and knowledge from our daily lives.

REFERENCES
1. ELMAR SCHWARZ, ION P. BELDIE, and SIEGMUND PASTOOR : A Comparison of Paging and Scrolling for Changing Screen Contents by Inexperienced Users, HUMAN FACTORS, 1983.

2. Mitsumasa Miyazawa, Minoru Kobayashi, Kaoru Kinoshita, Teruo Yokoyama, Yutaka Matsushita :An Electronic Book:APTBook, The 3rd IFIP Conference on Human-Computer Interaction (INTERACT '90), August 1990.

3. Ken-ichi Okada, Kaoru Kinoshita, Yutaka Matsushita: Scrolling or Leafing Through: BookWindow, Proc.of 1st Moscow International HCI'91 Workshop, August 1991.

Value Bars: An Information Visualization and Navigation Tool for Multi-attribute Listings

Richard Chimera

Human-Computer Interaction Laboratory
A.V. Williams Building
University of Maryland
College Park, MD 20742-3255
(301) 405-2757
carm@cs.umd.edu

INTRODUCTION

The need for better information visualization and navigation tools is widely recognized [1], [5]. It is difficult to sort and continuously resort tables or listings by more than one attribute and still maintain an understanding of the origin and natural position of items. The concept of "value bars" was created to help users visualize and navigate large information spaces that have characteristics of a line-oriented listing with multiple, quantifiable attributes. In general, value bars are useful for analyzing multi-attribute listings and tables where a particular sort order should be maintained and analysis of the top percentage of items within each attribute is beneficial. The main features are:

- the ability to see in one view an attribute distribution overview for the "important" items (as defined by attribute values) in a fisheye view [3] variant,
- very small screenspace footprint,
- the ability to see at once many attribute overviews,
- the ability to locate outliers and exceptions, and
- extremely low cognitive load navigation.

This work was spawned from the study of a novel way to visualize large tree data structures, called Tree-maps [4]. A more detailed description, discussion, future value bars research, and results of a usability study can be found in [2].

DESCRIPTION

Value bars are thin, vertical strips added to a text window (figure 1), placed next to the scrollbar if one exists; any number of value bars may be added as screen space allows. Each value bar maps one specific quantifiable attribute shared by items. A partitioning algorithm equates the sum of the items' values, or *weights*, to the value bar height. Each item's weight is converted to a height in the value bar proportional to its part of the total weight of all items. If the height exceeds the minimum threshold height, the

region is stacked vertically in the value bar, placed from top to bottom in the same order as appearing in the listing sequence. The end result is a graphic image that looks like a ladder with varyingly spaced rungs. Once partitioned the value bar regions are not changed, moved, or scrolled, all regions are always in view. Items represented in the value bar provide a global view of the distribution of an attribute's values in the listings, providing another variant of the fisheye view [3]. An item is represented by differing height regions in different value bars; an item may not be represented in every value bar.

Item selection, either by a mouse click in the text window or in any value bar, highlights all representations of that item. Clicks in value bars scroll the text window to center the selected item's text representation. This immediate navigation allows users to jump around and examine individual items as the need arises. There is no guess work as to how much to scroll, users continually concentrate on the task with minimal effort spent at the interface level.

Another value bar component is its "visibility marker." Many scrollbars provide an indicator of how much of the entire listing is currently in view; this concept is a requirement of a good value bar implementation. When the text window is scrolled, the visibility marker in each value bar is moved appropriately up or down within the value bar. Visibility markers change size and move independently of each other (though synchronized with the scroll), further showing attributes' differing distribution characteristics.

APPLICATION TO UNIX DIRECTORY LISTINGS

Consider a Unix directory listing with value bars for file size and file age (figure 1). Along the right side of the window are two value bars. The S value bar maps file size largeness (Size) and the Y value bar maps file modification recency (Youth); both value bars use a linear weighting assignment. The rest of the window is a normal scrolling textpane of the directory listing. In the Youth value bar, more recently modified files have a larger weight. The Size value bar has bigger variances in region heights because its values vary more widely than values in the Youth value bar.

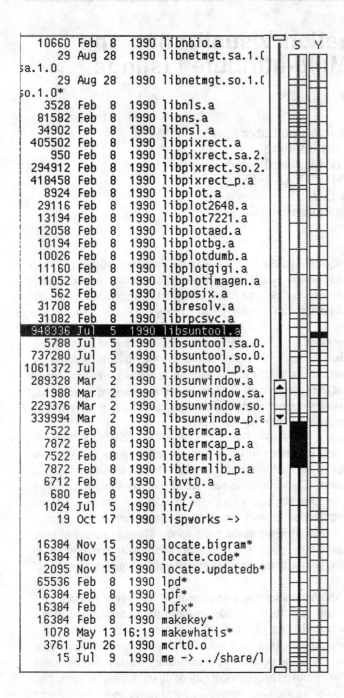

```
 10660 Feb  8  1990 libnbio.a
    29 Aug 28  1990 libnetmgt.sa.1.0
sa.1.0
    29 Aug 28  1990 libnetmgt.so.1.0
so.1.0*
  3528 Feb  8  1990 libnls.a
 81582 Feb  8  1990 libns.a
 34902 Feb  8  1990 libnsl.a
405502 Feb  8  1990 libpixrect.a
   950 Feb  8  1990 libpixrect.sa.2.
294912 Feb  8  1990 libpixrect.so.2.
418458 Feb  8  1990 libpixrect_p.a
  8924 Feb  8  1990 libplot.a
 29116 Feb  8  1990 libplot2648.a
 13194 Feb  8  1990 libplot7221.a
 12058 Feb  8  1990 libplotaed.a
 10194 Feb  8  1990 libplotbg.a
 10026 Feb  8  1990 libplotdumb.a
 11160 Feb  8  1990 libplotgigi.a
 11052 Feb  8  1990 libplotimagen.a
   562 Feb  8  1990 libposix.a
 31708 Feb  8  1990 libresolv.a
 31082 Feb  8  1990 librpcsvc.a
948336 Jul  5  1990 libsuntool.a
  5788 Jul  5  1990 libsuntool.sa.0.
737280 Jul  5  1990 libsuntool.so.0.
1061372 Jul 5  1990 libsuntool_p.a
289328 Mar  2  1990 libsunwindow.a
  1988 Mar  2  1990 libsunwindow.sa.
229376 Mar  2  1990 libsunwindow.so.
339994 Mar  2  1990 libsunwindow_p.a
  7522 Feb  8  1990 libtermcap.a
  7872 Feb  8  1990 libtermcap_p.a
  7522 Feb  8  1990 libtermlib.a
  7872 Feb  8  1990 libtermlib_p.a
  6712 Feb  8  1990 libvt0.a
   680 Feb  8  1990 liby.a
  1024 Jul  5  1990 lint/
    19 Oct 17  1990 lispworks ->

 16384 Nov 15  1990 locate.bigram*
 16384 Nov 15  1990 locate.code*
  2095 Nov 15  1990 locate.updatedb*
 65536 Feb  8  1990 lpd*
 16384 Feb  8  1990 lpf*
 16384 Feb  8  1990 lpfx*
 16384 Feb  8  1990 makekey*
  1078 May 13 16:19 makewhatis*
  3761 Jun 26  1990 mcrt0.o
    15 Jul  9  1990 me -> ../share/1
```

Figure 1. The (familiar parts of a) Unix directory listing using the command "ls -l /usr/lib". The two value bars to the right of the scrollbar represent file size (S) and file modification recency, or youth (Y). The taller the region in a value bar the greater is that listing item's attribute value weight. The currently selected item is the same among the listing and the value bars and is highlighted in inverse video for all representations. Notice the use of value bar specific visibility shading, equivalent in function to the scrollbar's visibility shading, to show which items of the whole are currently visible in the text window. Only the topmost weighted items, different for each attribute, are represented in a value bar.

DISCUSSION

One of the most important value bar advantages is its ability to provide a global distribution overview of attribute values in a single view. Users are able to compare an item's attribute value to other items in the same value bar without the need to scroll or rearrange the sort order many times. Noticing clusters of large regions together may be an important insight to users. The fact that an attribute has values that are relatively equal throughout the items (e.g. all files are similar in size) can be recognized easily. Noticing that one item has large regions in many value bars may be enlightening. There are many ways the single view of multiple attribute distributions can help users distill trends or notice interesting clusters. This also may allow new discoveries that couldn't have been made due to the high cognitive load of resorting a list many times while retaining acquired knowledge about items.

CONCLUSION

The value bar represents a unique combination of information visualization and navigation for multi-attribute listings. The powerful information visualization provides items' local detail in a global context of attribute values and their distributions. Navigation and interaction are simple, clean, and build on generic GUI concepts. Value bars can be applied in many diverse domains whose data have characteristics similar to multi-attribute listings or tables. Value bars are a useful tool which can be integrated unobtrusively into existing application environments.

REFERENCES

1. Beard, D., and Walker, J. Navigational Techniques to Improve the Display of Large Two-dimensional Spaces. Behaviour & Information Technology 9, 6, 451-466.

2. Chimera, R. Value Bars: An Information Visualization and Navigation Tool for Multi-attribute Listings and Tables. University of Maryland Department of Computer Science technical report CS-TR-2773.

3. Furnas, G. Generalized Fisheye Views. In Proceedings ACM CHI'86 Human Factors in Computing Systems Conference (Boston, MA, April 13 - 17). ACM, New York, 1986, 16-23.

4. Johnson, B., and Shneiderman, B. Tree-Maps: A Space-filling Approach to the Visualization of Hierarchical Information Structures. In Proceedings of ACM Visualization '91 Conference (San Diego, CA, October 22 - 25). ACM, New York, 1991, 284-291.

5. Mackinlay, J., Robertson, G., and Card, S. The Perspective Wall: Detail and Context Smoothly Integrated. Proceedings ACM CHI'91 Human Factors in Computing Systems Conference (New Orleans, LA, April 27 - May 2). ACM, New York, 1991, 173-179.

A PERFORMANCE MODEL OF SYSTEM DELAY
AND USER STRATEGY SELECTION

Steven L. Teal

Graduate School of Industrial Administration
Carnegie Mellon University
Pittsburgh, PA 15213
st0i@andrew.cmu.edu

Alexander I. Rudnicky

School of Computer Science
Carnegie Mellon University
Pittsburgh, PA 15213
air@cs.cmu.edu

ABSTRACT

This study lays the ground work for a predictive, zero-parameter engineering model that characterizes the relationship between system delay and user performance. This study specifically investigates how system delays affects a user's selection of task strategy. Strategy selection is hypothesized to be based on a cost function combining two factors: (1) the effort required to synchronize input with system availability and (2) the accuracy level afforded. Results indicate that users, seeking to minimize effort and maximize accuracy, choose among three strategies – automatic performance, pacing, and monitoring. These findings provide a systematic account of the influence of system delay on user performance, based on adaptive strategy choice drive by cost.

KEYWORDS: System response time, strategy selection, interface design, human factors

INTRODUCTION

The effect of system delay on user performance has been of interest to practitioners and researchers since the emergence of timesharing systems in the 1960s [e.g., 11, 15, 19, 22, 24]. While many feel that this problem became a non-issue with the introduction of faster and cheaper computing technologies, many others find that this interaction still remains problematic [18, 23]. In fact, Shneiderman [23] still lists this issue as one of the seven "golden opportunities" for conducting pioneering and productive research in human-computer interaction.

The failure of researchers to adequately address this issue has resulted in a lack of clear, concise guidelines that system engineers can use to support crucial design decisions. Engineers are therefore often forced to either guesstimate "acceptable" delays on a case-by-case basis or test "user satisfaction" with prototype systems under various system response time and/or hardware/software configurations.[1] However, these methods can prove to be ineffective, time consuming and expensive, and provide no long-term solutions to the problem.

A more promising method for addressing this issue would be to work toward the development of a predictive, zero-parameter engineering model that would characterize the relationship between system delay and user performance. The present study lays the ground work for this process by systematically investigating the relationship between system delay and a user's choice of task strategy. We address two questions. First, does system delay in fact have a significant effect on user performance? Second, if delay does affect user performance, can we define a model that adequately describes this relationship?

PRIOR RESEARCH

Most previous research has assumed that system delay has an effect on user performance and that this effect can be evidenced through increased user productivity at decreased system response times. As an example, Martin & Corl [14] investigated the behavior of subjects performing both data entry and problem solving tasks. Results indicated significant effects across conditions, with productivity increasing with decreased system delays; however, further analysis revealed strong productivity increases for the data entry tasks but not for the problem solving tasks. These results support the hypothesis that an inverse relationship exists between system delay and user productivity, and are consistent with the findings of several other studies [e.g., 1, 13, 25].

[1.] Though a technical difference exists between the terms "system response time" and "system delay", for the purposes of this paper these terms should be considered interchangeable.

In contrast, Dannenbring [6] presented results of a data entry task which indicated a marginally significant effect for user productivity with task completion times increasing with decreasing delays. These results run counter to the hypothesis that an inverse relationship exists between delay and user productivity but are consistent with the findings of other studies that either found a similar effect [2] or failed to find any effect at all [e.g., 4, 5, 7].

A survey of the system response time literature reveals additional instances of contradictory findings. The source of these contradictions can be attributed to differences in experimental designs that include:

1. The type of task being studied. Tasks ranged from simple data entry tasks [6] to complex problem solving tasks [14] to open-ended programming tasks [13]. The use of different tasks can account for some of the inconsistencies in results since task effects are generally acknowledged to be a potential intervening variable in studies of system delay and user performance [e.g., 14, 15, 22].

2. The amount of control exerted over the task. Several of the studies were observational in nature and the researchers were not able to systematically control what task (or tasks) the subjects were performing [e.g., 1, 13, 25]. This makes it difficult to make comparisons across studies even for those studies which supposedly used similar tasks.

3. The amount of control exerted over the delay conditions. In a number of studies, researchers were not able to tightly control the delay conditions presented to the subjects [e.g., 1, 13, 25]. This situation normally occurred when data was collected from an active work site with the subjects connected to a host system. While subject transactions were given a high priority, the delays presented were still dependent on the processing load of the host computer and may therefore have varied widely, in mean and variance, from those intended by the researchers.

4. The match between the task and delay conditions. Most studies did not use delay conditions specifically chosen to complement the experimental task [e.g., 3, 6, 14]. For instance, data entry tasks which may call for subsecond response times were tested with multisecond delays [6] while complex problem solving tasks which may require a great deal of external user preparation between interactions were

implemented with subsecond delays [13]. The success or failure of finding an effect may therefore be blurred by the mismatch of task structure and delay condition.

5. The choice of dependent variables. Many studies did not use dependent variables specifically designed to isolate any hypothesized effects [e.g., 6, 14, 25]. More specifically, the use of aggregate variables such as 'total task completion time' and 'total number of errors' may have disguised effects which would have identified through the use of variables which measured performance at a finer grain of analysis.

The present study was designed to avoid these difficulties. First, task effects were minimized by the use of a simple data entry task. Further, a performance model, detailing the interaction of system delay and user performance, was developed to facilitate an understanding of these effects. Second, the study was performed in a laboratory setting, thus providing a means to control the task being performed by the subjects. Third, the study was conducted on a sole-use computer to provide maximum control over the delay conditions experienced by the subjects, and constant delays were instituted to exclude the issues of predictability and variability.[2] Fourth, the delays were matched to the task through performance model predictions and pilot study refinements. Finally, the dependent variables chosen specifically supported testing of the effects hypothesized by the performance model.

DEFINITIONS

Figure 1 presents a detailed analysis of an interaction cycle in terms of system and user events.

System Model

The system model is composed of three components: system response time, display time and lockout time. *System response time* is the time that elapses between when the user initiates an activity and when the computer initiates its response. This measure is composed of three subcomponents: computation, overhead and delay. *Computation* is the time required by the system to perform all operations necessary to support the user's requested activity. *Overhead* is the time required by the system to complete any activity logging after

---

[2.] Constant delays were used to ensure that this initial investigation would not be complicated by potentially intervening variables. Once a basic understanding of the effect of system delay on user performance has been developed several extensions can be added including (1) delay variability and/or predictability, (2) task effects, and (3) user modalities.

all computations have been completed. Finally, *delay* is the sum of all time lags which extend the system response time beyond that required for all computational and overhead requirements.

Along the same lines, *display time* is the time required by the system to display the results of the user's request on the proper output device, and *lockout time* is the time that elapses between when the system displays the results for the current activity and when the system becomes available for entry of the next activity.

User Model

The user model is composed of two events: user planning and acquisition time, and execution time. *User planning and acquisition time* is the time that elapses between when the user initiates the current system activity and when the user begins entering the next task into the computer. This measure is composed of four sub-components: system response time, display time, lockout time, and user delay. The first three of these sub-components are detailed above. *User delay* is defined as the time that elapses between when the sys-

tem is ready for the next system input and when the user actually begins to enter the next activity into the system. The last component of the user model, *execution time*, is the time required by the user to enter the task into the system.

Research Variables

It is our belief that observable changes in user behavior under different system delays can be attributed to shifts between different task strategies. Focusing on these strategy shifts is therefore central to understanding the relationship between system delay and user performance, since users will select task strategies which optimize their performance within the constraints imposed by the system. We can adduce the form of these strategies and track users as they shift between them by measuring the following variables:

1. Initial keystroke latency: Initial keystroke latency is the time that elapses between when the computer signals that it is ready for the next input and when the user actually strikes the first key to begin the activity (i.e., the user delay).

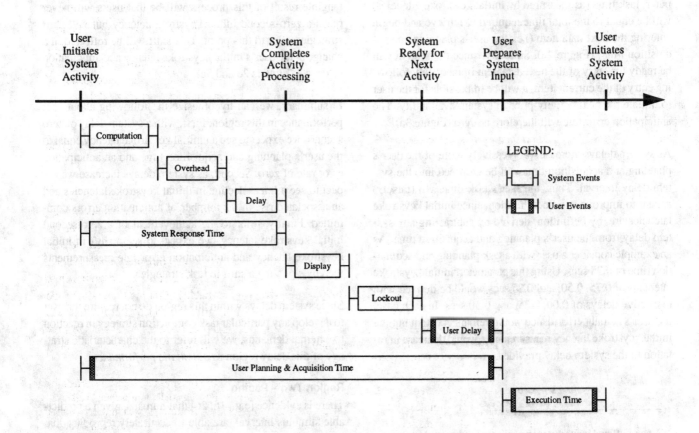

Figure 1. *Model of user and system events occurring during a normal human-computer interaction.*

2.   Subsequent keystroke latency: Subsequent keystroke latencies are the inter-keystroke times for all user inputs other than the initial keystrokes (i.e., the subcomponents of the user's execution time).

3.   Anticipation errors. Anticipation errors occur when the user attempts to enter a keystroke prior to the system becoming available for the next user input.[3]

4.   Keying errors. Keying errors are all performance errors other than anticipation errors (e.g., transcription errors).

PERFORMANCE MODEL

Initial observations indicated that system delays induce three different task strategies, each characteristic of a particular delay region. The choice of strategy was a rational one based on the relative cost of available strategies, where cost reflects the strategy's demand for cognitive resources and the accuracy rate it affords [e.g., 9, 10, 21].

Region One – Automatic Performance

In the simplest case, system delay is equal to zero. Since under this scenario the user will never have to wait on the computer, task time (as measured by initial keystroke latencies) will be equal to the total time required to retrieve and begin entering the next data item (i.e., the user's planning and acquisition time) (Figure 2a). Similarly, since the system will be ready for entry of the next data item immediately following entry of the current item, it will be impossible for the user to initiate the next activity prior to system availability. The anticipation error rate will therefore be zero (Figure 3a).

As system delays increase, progressively more of the user's planning and acquisition time will be absorbed into the system delay interval. Thus, the user's task time will (falsely) appear to improve in a linear fashion, since initial keystroke latencies are, by definition, derived by subtracting any system delay from the user's planning and acquisition time. As an example consider a user with a task planning and acquisition time of 0.75 secs. Using this parameter, initial keystroke latencies of 0.75, 0.50, and 0.25 secs would be derived with respective delays of 0.00, 0.25, and 0.50 secs. In each case, the user's actual performance would remain constant but the initial keystroke latency measurements would decrease in relation to the system delay provided.

This linear decrease in initial keystroke latency will continue until a boundary point is reached where the system delay is equal to the user's planning and acquisition time and an initial keystroke latency of zero is achieved (Figure 2b). At this point the user, theoretically, never waits for the system and the system never waits for the user. However, this boundary point will rarely, if ever, be reached due to the commission and cost of anticipation errors.

Due to the variability inherent in user performance, actual task times will be distributed about some mean value with anticipation errors occurring at a rate corresponding to the shaded region in Figure 4. If a user does not change task strategies and maintains a consistent task time distribution then anticipation error rates in this region will increase with increases in system response times (Figure 3b). The cost of completing the task will therefore increase with increased system response times and, if no corrective action is taken by the user, can become (virtually) unbounded as a 100% error rate is approached. We therefore hypothesize that at some system response level the cost of completing the task will exceed some "acceptable level of effort for the task" and the user will attempt to select a strategy that will successfully accomplish the task but with a lower associated total cost. The tangible result of this process will be that users will never reach a zero-second initial keystroke latency but will shift strategies prior to this point. This shift will be reflected in a change in the user's initial keystroke latency and anticipation error rate (Figures 2c and 3c).

In summary, we can hypothesize the following about user performance in this region. First, with a system delay of zero seconds we expect to see an initial keystroke latency equal to the user's planning and acquisition time and an anticipation error rate of zero. Second, as system delays increase we expect to see a linear decline in initial keystroke latencies and an associated rise in the number of anticipation errors committed. Finally, prior to the achievement of a zero-second initial keystroke latency, we expect to see a shift in initial keystroke latency and anticipation error rate measurements thereby signaling a shift in task strategies.

Since system delays within this region do not require the user to develop any particular task completion strategy in reaction to external demands, we will refer to the characteristic strategy of this delay region as *automatic performance*.

Region Two – Pacing

There is evidence [e.g., 16, 26] that humans, given a predictable stimulus interval, are able to accurately reproduce that interval (as long as the interval remains relatively short).

[3.] A non-buffered input system was chosen to force subjects to contend with the implemented delay conditions (see footnote 2).

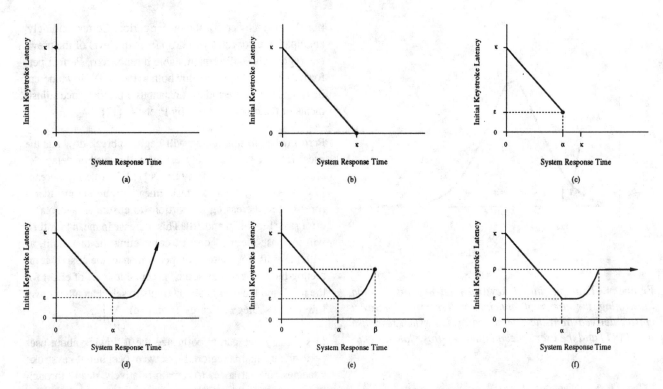

Figure 2. *Hypothesized effect of increased system delay on the user's initial keystroke latency with strategy shift points occurring at α (automatic performance to pacing) and β (pacing to monitoring).*

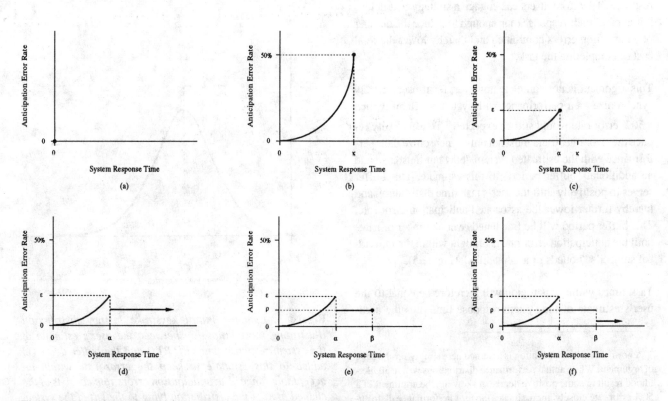

Figure 3. *Hypothesized effect of increased system delay on the user's anticipation error rate with strategy shift points occurring at α (automatic performance to pacing) and β (pacing to monitoring).*

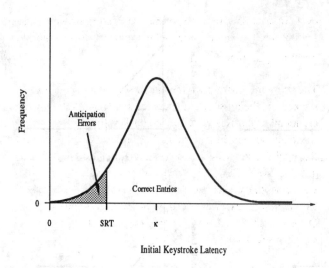

Figure 4. *Example initial keystroke latency distribution illustrating the areas of anticipation errors and correct entries derived from the interaction of the system response time (SRT) and the user's mean initial keystroke latency (κ).*

Such a skill can be brought to bear in the current situation and incorporated into a strategy that takes into account expected system delays. This would allow the user to reduce the anticipation error rate while maintaining a timely rate of response. Therefore, users can engage a strategy that delays initiation of their response long enough to reduce the number of anticipation errors committed and thereby lower the total cost of completing the task.

This argument is not complete however, for if users merely synchronize their performance with system availability then a 50% error rate would still be expected.[4] To effectively reduce the error rate, users must not only synchronize their performance with the estimated system delay but must also add an additional "buffer period" to this estimate. This buffer serves to positively shift the user's task time distribution and thereby further lower the associated anticipation error rate. This buffer period will be fine tuned over a number of trials until the anticipation error rate is brought within the individual subject's "bounds of acceptability" (Figure 5).

Task times within this region will therefore be equal to the user's estimate of the system response time plus the addi-

---

[4.] A normal N(0,1) distribution is assumed here simply for the sake of argument. While actual performance distributions will in all likelihood result in some positive degree of skewing, the argument of a 50% error rate closely approximates the user performance distributions most likely to occur.

tional time included for the buffer period. Correspondingly, anticipation error rates will drop from the level of the previous region and will remain stable but nonzero. Perfect performance is not expected, due both to the variability inherent in user performance and to constant user performance adjustments of the type described by Pachella [17].

Performance in this region will begin to break down as the user's ability to accurately estimate the system delay decreases with increased delay times [16]. With each increase in system delay, the user's task time distribution must therefore shift in increasing proportions to ensure an acceptable error rate (Figure 2d and 3d). This increase in mean task time will increase the total cost of completing the task until, as with the shift from automatic performance, the cost of completing the task exceeds some "acceptable level of effort for the task" and the user again attempts to select an alternative, lower-cost strategy (Figures 2e and 3e).

In summary, we can hypothesize the following about user performance in this region. First, we expect initial keystroke latencies and variances to remain relatively steady through the first part of this region but to rise as system delays increase. Second, we expect anticipation error rates to remain relatively stable.

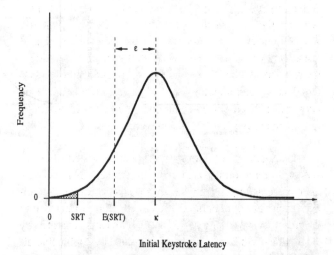

Figure 5. *Example initial keystroke latency distribution illustrating the relationship between the user's estimate of the system response time (E[SRT]) and the buffer delay (ε) added to this estimate to keep the error rate within an acceptable range. The anticipation errors rate consists of the shaded area of the distribution lying to the left of the system response time (SRT).*

Since users attempt to synchronize their performance with the system delay, we will refer to the characteristic strategy of this delay region as *pacing*.

Region Three – Monitoring

At sufficiently long delays, users will no longer be able to synchronize their performance with the system delay and keep the accuracy rate within the "bounds of acceptability". They will then be forced to rely on external stimuli to signal system availability. Initial keystroke latencies will therefore be equal to the user's simple reaction time (Figure 2f) and the error rate will drop to near-zero (Figure 3f).

Since users are forced to rely on an external stimuli to indicate system availability, we will refer to the characteristic strategy of this delay region as *monitoring*.

EXPERIMENT 1 – INITIAL INVESTIGATION

This experiment tested the proposal that system delay affects user performance and that it leads to the selection and use of different task strategies within distinct delay regions.

Method

Subjects. Fourteen subjects were recruited from the general university population. No computer experience was necessary. All subjects were naive regarding the experimental manipulation and were fully debriefed following the experiment. Subjects were paid for their participation.

Apparatus and Materials. The experimental stimuli were presented to the subjects on a Macintosh IIci personal computer. The computer was equipped with a color monitor, and used a standard Macintosh keyboard with the numeric keypad on the right-hand side. To provide maximum control over system delays, the computer was disconnected from all outside networks and all nonessential memory resident programs (e.g., screen savers, RAM disks) were removed.

The materials used for this experiment consisted of seven sets of 90 three-digit pseudorandom numbers. Number sets were presented to the subjects on sheets containing 45 numbers each. The numbers on each sheet were arranged into groups of fives forming a 3x3 matrix with rows separated by single line dividers and columns separated by double line dividers. Each data sheet was encased in a plastic, non-reflective protective cover and placed on an upright typing stand.

The software program which controlled the experiment was written in the cT programming language [20]. A delay module included in the program delayed the computer's response for a predetermined time after the subject entered a complete three-digit number. The timing algorithm had a worst-case cycle time of 35 msecs. Experimental conditions were thus implemented using the target delay minus the worst-case algorithm cycle time.[5]

The software program was designed so that all subject keystrokes and their associated latencies were recorded; however, not all keystrokes were echoed back to the subject on the computer screen. In particular, keystrokes which occurred during the target delay period (i.e., anticipation errors) were not displayed. These keystrokes were recorded to disk but were essentially lost from the subject's perspective. The subject therefore experienced a non-buffered input system. Once the target delay was complete, all subsequent keystrokes were displayed.

Experimental Design. A single-factor, within-subject design was used for this experiment. The conditions were based on a pilot study which provided the following approximations for the strategy shift points: 0.625 sec for shifting to a pacing strategy, and 3.00 sec for shifting to a monitoring strategy. The seven delay conditions used were: 0.00, 0.312, 0.625, 1.25, 2.50, 5.00, and 10.00 secs. An N x 2N Latin square design was used to counterbalance potential ordering effects. Subjects were randomly assigned to the conditions.

Procedure. The experiment was run in a quiet, controlled environment. At the beginning of the session, the task was verbally described to the subject using a sample data sheet. In addition, the following instructions were provided just before initiation of the first task. First, numbers could only be entered into the system using the numeric keypad. Second, any keying errors that occurred could be corrected using the delete key on the main keyboard; however, once a complete number had been entered into the system it could not be corrected. Third, if positional sequencing between the data sheets and the computer screen was lost, the subject was to reorient themselves using the current computer data entry cell as a base and continue with the task ignoring any previously committed errors. Finally, the subject was instructed to perform the task as quickly and accurately as possible. Subjects were also informed during this time that they might experience some delays in the computer's performance due to other processing tasks that the computer was performing. Subjects were not informed of the number of conditions that they would experience.

[5.] Given the sophistication of the equipment used for this experiment, the computer's display time was considered to be virtually instantaneous and was therefore not included as a factor when setting the target delays. Similarly, since a lockout period was not instituted, this response time component did not factor into setting the conditions.

At the beginning of each experimental condition, subjects were given a new set of random numbers which they placed on the typing stand situated next to the computer. Each condition was initiated by the subject striking any key on the keyboard. This action caused the computer screen to be cleared and a replica of the data sheets (minus the random numbers) to be drawn on the screen. At this time, the screen contained only the lines dividing the rows and columns, a box indicating the current data entry position, and an underscore character inside the data entry box indicating where the next digit that the subject keyed in would appear. Subjects then began to enter the current number set into the computer.

Subjects entered numbers into the computer using the numeric keypad on the right hand side of the keyboard. With each key press the appropriate digit was appended to any digits previously keyed into the system and the resulting number centered in the data entry box. Once all of the individual digits had been keyed, the subject entered the resulting number into the computer by pressing either the 'enter' or the 'return' key. If the number in the data entry area consisted of three digits (whether or not it correctly corresponded to the current number of interest), it was accepted for entry and the underscore character and data entry box were erased. If the number contained too few or too many digits then the computer signaled an error with an audible beep and the subject had to correct the error before the transaction would be accepted. Once a valid number had been entered into the system, the target delay for that condition was instituted. After the target delay had lapsed the underscore character and data entry box were redrawn in the next data entry location and the computer was ready to receive the next data entry.

Subjects entered numbers into the computer beginning with the first number in the upper left-hand corner of the first data sheet. They then worked down the sheet until all of the numbers in the first column had been entered. They then moved to the top of the next column to the right and performed the same procedure. This process continued until all of the numbers from the first data sheet had been entered into the system. At this point, the subjects removed the sheet from the typing stand, placed it aside on the desk, and began working on the second sheet.

The computer screen automatically prepared for entry of the second sheet of numbers after a valid number had been entered into the lower right-hand cell of the computer data entry screen. When all of the numbers from the second data sheet had been entered, the subject pressed the 'q' key to end the experimental session. The computer screen then faded black and a message was displayed informing the subject

that the next condition could be started at any time by pressing the 'return' key on the keyboard. Subjects were allowed an optional two-minute rest period after any of the experimental conditions and all subjects were required to take a five minute rest after completion of the fourth condition. This process continued until the subjects completed the task under all seven experimental conditions.

Results

We examined latency variance across the 90 trials in each condition and found it to be elevated over the first 15 trials, but stable thereafter. Presumably the subjects were using these initial trials to adjust their performance for each condition, accordingly we excluded the first 15 trials from subsequent analysis. Figure 6 displays initial keystroke latencies and anticipation errors across the seven conditions used in this experiment. The form of the latency curve agrees quite closely with the curve shown in Figure 2f and the anticipation error curve follows the one shown in Figure 3f. The curves for individual subjects agree with the composite curves, although their location along the time axis varies considerably.

An analysis of variance was performed for the four variables described earlier This analysis revealed significant effects for initial keystroke latency ($F[6,72] = 63.05$, $p < .001$), subsequent keystroke latency ($F[6,72] = 3.53$, $p < .01$), and anticipation errors ($F[5,60] = 6.78$, $p < .001$).[6] Ordering effects were only significant for keying errors ($F[6,72] = 4.77$, $p < .001$). Initial keystroke latency and anticipation error results are presented in Figure 6.

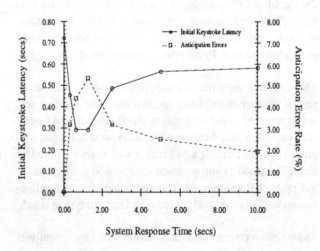

Figure 6. *Double y-axis plot detailing the results of Experiment 1 with initial keystroke latency and anticipation error rate plotted against system response time.*

Analysis using Tukey's HSD revealed significant differences between three system delay regions – 0.00 to 0.625 secs, 1.25 to 2.50 secs, and 5.00 to 10.00 secs – for initial keystroke latencies and anticipation errors. The differences were significant at the $p < .001$ level. There were no significant within-region differences. Neither subsequent keystroke latencies nor keying errors demonstrated significant differences using this more conservative measure.

Discussion

The results of this experiment clearly support an account of system delay effects using the cost-based strategy selection model presented earlier. The results are also consistent with the seemingly contradictory findings reported by others. It is clear from our data, for example, that Dannenbring's [6] failure to find an effect was due to an improper sampling of delays and that delay effects in Martin & Corl's [14] study were masked by an improper choice of dependent variables. In this latter case, if we transform our data into the form used in that study ('total task completion time' and 'total number of errors') and recompute the analysis, we find that our data produce results comparable to those reported earlier.

The results obtained for subsequent keystroke latencies speak to the adaptability of the subjects. Times for this variable decreased with increasing delays as subjects used any "down time" to prepare for the next task by either placing their fingers on the appropriate number keys or practicing the number (without actually pressing the keys) while waiting.

The ordering effects obtained for keying errors can apparently be explained by subject fatigue. Replotting the data by experimental position showed that keying errors increased over the first four trials, dropped off after the mandatory rest period, and then again climbed until the end of the experiment.

Finally, although the data in Figure 6 support our model, it was clear that a high degree of inter-subject variability was present. For example, mean initial keystroke latency for the no-delay condition ranged from 0.583 to 0.979 sec. One consequence of this was to obscure the shape of the (aggregate) curves in Figure 6 as subjects switched task strategies at different system delays. Another consequence was a sub-optimal sampling of delays in the pacing region, hampering analysis of certain other variables of interest, such as latency

---

[6.] By definition, it is impossible to commit an anticipation error with a zero-second system response time. Therefore, data for the 0.00 sec delay condition were excluded from the analysis since its inclusion would have artificially inflated the resulting mean square values. This data correction is evidenced by a decrease in the available degrees of freedom from $F(6,72)$ to $F(5,60)$.

variance. To overcome these shortcomings, we performed a second experiment.

EXPERIMENT 2 – REFINEMENT

This experiment was designed to more closely investigate the region corresponding to the second strategy, pacing. This region is of particular interest since the strategy that the user applies attempts to actively compensate for any delay and requires the user to keep track of the actual delay involved. The delays in the present experiment were restricted to a 3.00 sec range centered on each subject's pacing region, the location of which was determined through a normalization procedure.

Method

Subjects. Twelve subjects were recruited from the general university population. No computer experience was necessary. All subjects were naive regarding the experimental manipulation and were fully debriefed following the experiment. Subjects were paid for their participation.

Apparatus and Materials. This experiment used the same apparatus and materials as experiment 1.

Experimental Design. Delay conditions were set dynamically, based on a pretest using a 0.00 sec delay. The subject's median initial keystroke latency (κ) from the pretest was used as a base point to set the actual experimental conditions. Delays were set at 0.250 sec intervals from ($\kappa - 0.250$) to ($\kappa + 2.50$) secs. Delays beginning at ($\kappa - 0.250$) sec and increasing at 0.50 sec intervals were considered part of condition set one, while the remaining delays were considered part of condition set two. Finally, each data set consisted of 75 rather than 90 three-digit numbers. A Latin square design was used to counterbalance potential ordering effects. Subjects were randomly assigned to orders.

Procedure. This experiment was conducted in the same manner as Experiment 1 with the exception that the experiment was broken into two sessions with each session consisting of six delay conditions. This was done to reduce potential fatigue effects. Subjects participated in sessions on consecutive days at the same relative time of day.

Results

Exploratory data analysis revealed that subjects did pace the system in a relatively stable region. Individual differences were substantially less than those observed in the first experiment. Subject within-condition performance was examined and was again found to stabilize after the first fifteen data points. The first fifteen data points for each condition were therefore removed prior to statistical analysis.

An analysis of variance was performed for the variables of interest. The analysis revealed significant effects for initial keystroke latency (F[11,111] = 27.38, p < .001), anticipation errors (F[11,111] = 8.86, p < .001), and initial keystroke variance (F[11,111] = 33.70, p < .001). Subsequent keystroke latencies and keying errors were not significant. Ordering and session effects were not significant for any of the variables. In addition, a t-test comparing subject performance across pretests was not significant, t < 1. Initial keystroke latency, anticipation error, and initial keystroke variance results are presented in Figure 7.

Tukey's HSD revealed significant differences between five system delay regions (in relation to the subject's median performance) for initial keystroke latency and initial keystroke variance – region 1 [0.25, 0.00], region 2: [0.25, 0.50], region 3: [0.75, 1.75], region 4: [2.00, 2.25], and region 5: [2.50] secs. Similar results were found for anticipation errors with one modification, the third delay region covered a narrow range – 0.75 to 1.50 secs – while the fourth region extended from 1.75 to 2.25 secs. These differences were significant at the p < .001 level. There were no significant within-region differences.

Discussion

The results of this experiment identify a pacing region that lies between 0.75 and 1.75 sec. For delays in this region users appear to have little difficulty pacing the system and are able to maintain apparently optimal levels of response latency and error. The rise in response latency and variance at

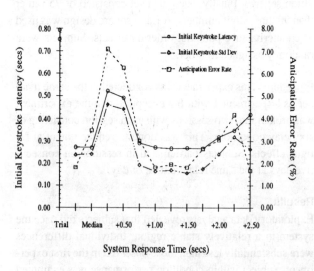

Figure 7. *Double y-axis plot detailing the results for Experiment 2 with initial keystroke latency, the standard deviation of the initial keystroke latency, and anticipation error rate plotted against system response time.*

longer delays (as well as the sudden and significant drop in error rate at the longest delay) are also in accord with the model presented earlier. As users lose control over their ability to pace the system (viz. the increase in variance), errors rise to an unacceptable level and a different strategy (monitoring) becomes preferable.

An unexpected finding was the discovery of significant user difficulty at the crossover between automatic performance and pacing. It is not immediately apparent why this occurs. A possible explanation is that engaging a strategy produces a "blind spot" that interferes with performance. The very high variance at this point suggests that users might be having difficulty consistently using a single strategy, perhaps because the difference in cost is too small to gauge accurately. Alternately, performance difficulties might be due to problems in engaging an internal timer for the short intervals required. Further investigation would be necessary to arrive at an acceptable account.

CONCLUSIONS

User performance is systematically affected by system delays. Results indicate that users choose task strategies suited to a given system delay, with the choice apparently based on the relative cost of a strategy at that given delay. A closer examination of delays inducing a pacing strategy revealed intervals where disproportionate difficulties occurred. The source of this latter effect is unclear at this time, but is consistent with a strategy-based account of performance.

Using this study as a basis, work is currently in progress to extend the performance model into an engineering model which can be used to derive pre-development, zero-parameter response time guidelines for specific tasks. Additional studies should be carried out to (1) evaluate system response time effects across different user modalities, (2) investigate the additional delays dimensions of predictability and variability, and (3) probe the process of strategy engagement.

Development of a model that accounts for the influence of system delay on user performance would support system engineers in the design of new systems and provide additional guidelines for the formulation of system management policies. Our goal is to lower system development and maintenance costs through the inclusion of additional design parameters based on system delay. The inclusion of such parameters will help ensure user acceptance of and satisfaction with new systems, as well as improve productivity.

REFERENCES

1. Barber, R. E., & Lucas, H. C., Jr. (1983). System response time, operator productivity, and job satisfaction. *Communications of the ACM*, 26(11), 972-986.

2. Bergman, H., Brinkman, A., & Koelega, H. S. (1981). System response time and problem solving behavior. *Proceedings of the 25th Annual Meeting of the Human Factors Society*, 749-753.

3. Boies, S. J. (1974). User behavior on an interactive computer system. *IBM Systems Journal*, 13(1), 2-18.

4. Butler, T. W. (1983). Computer response time and user performance. *Proceedings of the Annual Meeting of the ACM SIGCHI (SIGCHI'83)*, 58-62.

5. Dannenbring, G. L. (1983). The effect of computer response time on user performance and satisfaction: A preliminary investigation. *Behavior Research Methods & Instrumentation*, 15(2), 213-216.

6. Dannenbring, G. L. (1984). System response time and user performance. *IEEE Transactions on Systems, Man, and Cybernetics*, SMC-14(3), 473-478.

7. Goodman, T. J., & Spence, R. (1981). The effect of computer system response time variability on interactive graphical problem solving. *IEEE Transactions on Systems, Man, and Cybernetics*, SMC-11(3), 207-216.

8. Grossberg, M., Wiesen, R. A., & Yntema, D. B. (1976). An experiment on problem solving with delayed computer responses. *IEEE Transactions on Systems, Man, and Cybernetics*, SMC-6(3), 219-222.

9. Johnson, E. J., & Payne, J. W. (1985). Effort and accuracy in choice. *Management Science*, 31(4), 395-414.

10. Kleinmuntz, D. N., & Schkade, D. A. (1989). *The cognitive implications of information displays in computer-supported decision making* (Working Paper 88/89-4-11). Austin, TX: University of Texas at Austin, Graduate School of Business.

11. Kosmatka, L. J. (1984). A user challenges the value of subsecond response time. *Computerworld*, 18(24), ID 1-8.

12. Kuhmann, W. (1989). Experimental investigation of stress-inducing properties of system response times. *Ergonomics*, 32(3), 271-280.

13. Lambert, G. N. (1984). A comparative study of system response time on program developer productivity. *IBM Systems Journal*, 23(1), 36-43.

14. Martin, G. L., & Corl, K. G. (1986). System response time effects on user productivity. *Behaviour and Information Technology*, 5(1), 3-13.

15. Miller, R. B. (1968). Response time in man-computer conversational transactions. *Proceedings of the AFIPS Fall Joint Computer Conference*, 33, 267-277.

16. Näätänen, R., Muranen, V., & Merisalo, A. (1974). Timing of expectancy peak in simple reaction time situation. *Acta Psychologica*, 38(6), 461-470.

17. Pachella, R. G. (1974). The interpretation of reaction time in information-processing research. In B. H. Kantowitz (Ed.), *Human information processing: Tutorials in performance and cognition* (pp. 41-82). Hillsdale, NJ: Lawrence Erlbaum Associates.

18. Rudnicky, A. I., & Quirin, J. L. (1990). *Subjective reaction to system response delay: A pilot study*. Unpublished manuscript, Carnegie Mellon University, School of Computer Science, Pittsburgh.

19. Rushinek, A., & Rushinek, S. F. (1986). What makes users happy? *Communications of the ACM*, 29(7), pp. 594-598.

20. Sherwood, B. A., & Sherwood, J. N. (1988). *The cT Language*. Pittsburgh: Carnegie Mellon University.

21. Siegler, R. S., & Jenkins, E. (1989). *How children discover new strategies*. Hillsdale, NJ: Lawrence Erlbaum Associates.

22. Shneiderman, B. (1987). Response time and display rate. *Designing the user interface: Strategies for effective human-computer interaction* (pp. 272-309). Reading, MA: Addison-Wesley.

23. Shneiderman, B. (1991). Human values and the future of technology: A declaration of responsibility. *ACM SIGCHI Bulletin*, 23(1), 6-10.

24. Smith, D. (1983). A business case for subsecond response time: Faster is better. *Computerworld*, 17(16), ID 1-11.

25. Thadhani, A. J. (1981). Interactive user productivity. *IBM Systems Journal*, 20(4), 407-423.

26. Wickens, C. D. (1984). *Engineering psychology and human performance*. Glenview, IL: Scott, Foresman and Company.

THE PRECIS OF PROJECT ERNESTINE
OR
AN OVERVIEW OF A VALIDATION OF GOMS

Wayne D. Gray, [1] *Bonnie E. John,* [2] *& Michael E. Atwood* [1]

1. NYNEX Science & Technology Center

2. Carnegie Mellon University

KEYWORDS: GOMS, analysis methods, empirical studies, user models, cognitive models, methods for analysis/assessment, prototyping, protocol analysis, theory in HCI

INTRODUCTION

Project Ernestine served a pragmatic as well as a scientific goal: to compare the worktimes of telephone company toll and assistance operators on two different workstations, and to test the validity of GOMS[1] models for predicting and explaining real-world performance. Contrary to expectations, GOMS predicted and the data confirmed, that performance with the proposed workstation was slower than with the current one. Pragmaticly, this increase in performance time translates into a cost of $2.4 million dollars a year to NYNEX. Scientificly, the GOMS models predicted performance with exceptional accuracy.

The empirical data provided us with three interesting results: proof that the new workstation was slower than the old, proof that this difference was not constant but varied with type of call, and no evidence of learning in data that spanned four months and 78,240 phone calls. The GOMS models predicted the first two results and explained all three.

It is important to emphasize that the two major parts of Project Ernestine, the field trial and the GOMS analyses, were done separately and during the same time period. It is NOT the case that the GOMS models were built with knowledge of the empirical data. Also, at the time of this writing, we have not observed a single toll & assistance

---

[1] Goals, operators, methods, & selection rules (Card, Moran, & Newell, 1980; 1983).

© 1992 ACM 0-89791-513-5/92/0005-0307   1.50

operator (TAO) using the new workstation.

This paper is the final installment in a series of CHI and other presentations summarizing a major test of the applicability of GOMS to real-world design problems (Gray, et al., 1989, 1990a, 1990b; John 1990). We provide an overview of the methodology of the study, the empirical data, and the GOMS models. This report is a précis only; the complete report on Project Ernestine is provided by Gray, John, & Atwood (submitted). Additional insights into conducting empirical studies and doing analytic modeling in the real-world are provided in Atwood, Gray, & John (submitted).

THE TASK & WORKSTATIONS

The TAO is the operator you get when you dial 0. Their job is to assist the customer in completing calls and to record the correct billing. Among other tasks, TAOs handle person-to-person calls, collect calls, calling-card calls, and calls billed to a third number. The TAO does not handle Directory Assistance calls.

Two TAO workstations were evaluated - the *current* workstation and a *proposed* workstation. The *current* workstation had been in use for several years and employed a 300-baud, character-oriented display and a keyboard on which functionally-related keys were color coded and spatially grouped. This functional grouping often separated common sequence of keys by large distances on the keyboard.

In contrast, the *proposed* workstation was ergonomically designed with sequential as well as functional considerations. The graphic, high-resolution display operated at 1200-baud, used icons and, in general, is a good example of a graphical user interface whose designers paid careful attention to human-computer interaction issues. For example, when the phone being called is ringing, an icon of a telephone with its receiver on-hook appears next to the called number; when the phone is answered, the icon changes to a telephone with its receiver lying next to it. In the *current* workstation, this is indicated by the ASCII characters "CLD 1" (standing for CalLeD line 1) appearing far away from the called number, in the lower part of the screen. Similar care went into the design of the keyboard, where an effort was made to minimize travel distance among the most frequent key sequences and to reduce the number of keystrokes required to complete a call by replacing common two-key sequences with a single function key.

THE FIELD TRIAL

Methodology

Participants
The phone company office used in the study employs over 100 TAOs and handles traffic in the Boston, Massachusetts area. For purposes of the study, 12 *current* workstations were removed and 12 *proposed* workstations installed.

All participants were New England Telephone (NET) employees who had worked as TAOs for a minimum of two years. Twenty-four participants were selected for the *proposed* workstations (the *proposed* condition) from a list of approximately 60 volunteers. Each *proposed* participant was paired with a control participant matching for shift worked (that is, time of day), and average worktime on the *current* workstation (the *current* condition). TAO worktimes were taken from data routinely collected by office managers for the six months prior to the start of the trial (while both groups were using the *current* workstation).

Trial Procedures
Proposed and *current* participants worked their normal shifts during the four month trial. From the perspective of the proposed participants their tasks and duties as a TAO were identical to their pretrial job in all respects but one; namely, a new workstation was used. For the *current* participants nothing had changed. To obtain our data, we extracted the calls handled by our 24 *proposed* and 24 *current* participants from a NYNEX database that routinely samples one out of every ten calls.

Call Categories
To concentrate our effort for both the empirical and analytic comparisons we decided to focus on calls categories that were either high volume or of special interest to NYNEX Operator Services. The final list of 20 call categories accounted for 88.33% of all completed calls. This percentage is based upon one month's frequency data for all calls handled by all NET TAOs.

Results
For the 48 TAOs (24 *proposed* and 24 *current*) over the four months of the study, the 20 call categories sampled a total

of 78,240 calls. Five call categories were eliminated for some analyses due to insufficient occurrence of those call categories[2].

Collapsing over call category to look at the median work time per call for each participant, for each month, the data show that the *proposed* group is slower than the *current* group by 4%; that is, the *proposed* workstation requires 0.8 seconds more time on an average call than does the *current* workstation. This 0.8 seconds is both statistically[3] and financially significant. The 0.8 second deficit translates into a cost of $2.4 million a year in additional operating costs if the *proposed* workstation were to be installed across the NYNEX operating area.

Reflecting seasonal variations in call-mix, the main effect of month is significant, but not the interaction of groups by month. This lack of a significant interaction suggests that TAOs using the *proposed* workstation mastered it very quickly, reaching asymptotic performance within the first month of performance.

For the analysis by call category we looked at the 15 sufficiently represented call categories. This analysis yielded significant effects of group, call category, and their interaction. The effect of call category was expected due to the different nature of the calls. The interaction shows that the advantage of the *current* workstation over the *proposed* is not constant for all call categories. For some call categories this difference is small (0.2 seconds) while for others it is quite large (3.7 seconds). This is an interesting result that cannot be explained by the field data. This is a result on which analytic models may shed much light.

ANALYTIC MODELING

Benchmark Tasks
Rather than model every possible procedure executed by the TAOs, for each call category we modeled one common, or important, variation. With the help of NYNEX Operator Services personnel, we wrote a single script for each of the 20 call categories originally chosen for study and used these as benchmarks. These benchmarks were validated against observed calls and were found to be representative of the average work time for these call categories.

The GOMS Models
To model these benchmarks, two different approaches were

[2]Note: additional statistical analysis, as well as details of those reported here are available in Gray et al., submitted.

[3]The level of significance choosen for this report is $p <$ .05.

used: observation-based models and specification-based models. The models of the *current* workstation were based upon videotapes of experienced TAOs handling calls for each of the benchmark tasks. In contrast, TAOs were never observed using the *proposed* workstation. Rather, these models were specification-based; that is, they were constructed based upon system response time estimates and TAO procedures provided by the manufacturer.

TAO's do several things in parallel when processing a customer's request: they listen or talk to the customer, they perceive information on the CRT screen, they move their hands to appropriate keys and strike them. To display these parallel activities and calculate total task times, we use the *critical path method* (developed for project management). Because this extension distinguishes between Cognition, Perception, and Motor operators and uses the Critical Path Method, we call it **CPM-GOMS** (John, 1988).

In CPM-GOMS the parallelism of the TAO's task is represented in a *schedule chart* (Figures 1 and 2). Each activity in handling a call is represented as a box with an associated duration. Dependencies between activities are represented as lines connecting the boxes. For example, the TAO cannot hit the *collect-billing* key until s/he hears the customer request a collect call. Therefore, there is a dependency line drawn between the box representing the perception of the word "collect" and the boxes representing the cognitive operators that verify the word "collect" and initiate pressing the *collect-billing* key. The boxes and their dependency lines are drawn according to a detailed understanding of the TAO's task, goal decomposition, and operator-placement heuristics (John, 1990).

An important concept in analyzing the total task time for complex parallel tasks is the *critical path*. When activities occur in parallel, one sequence of activities will take more time than parallel sequences of activities; the critical path is the sequence of activities that takes the longest and determines the total time for the entire task. The critical path is displayed in boldface in Figures 1 & 2.

Each schedule chart is the CPM-GOMS model of the call it depicts. We constructed 30 such models, yielding performance predictions for the 15 benchmarks on the *current* workstation and the 15 benchmarks on the *proposed* workstation, corresponding to the 15 call categories analyzed in the empirical data.

Workstation design features and call handling procedures have an impact on the length of a call which are reflected in the critical path. For example, Figures 1 and 2 show the first and last segments of a CPM-GOMS analysis for one 15 second calling-card call for both the *current* and *proposed* workstations. Figure 1 has two striking features. First,

the analysis for the *proposed* workstation has 10 fewer boxes than the analysis for the *current*, representing two fewer keystrokes. Second, none of the deleted boxes were on the critical path, all were performed in slack time. At this point in the task the critical path is determined by the TAO greeting and getting information from the customer. Removing keystrokes that occur during slack time does nothing to affect the TAO's work time; that is, work time is controlled by the conversation, not by the keystrokes and not by the ergonomics of the keyboard.

For the *proposed* workstation one of the keystrokes eliminated at the beginning of the call (Figure 1) now occurs later in the call (Figure 2). In this analysis, the keystroke goes from being performed during slack time, to being performed on the critical path. As a result, the cognitive and motor time required for this keystroke now adds to the time required to process this call and CPM-GOMS predicts that, for this call category, despite requiring one less keystroke than the *current*, the *proposed* will require more time.

CPM-GOMS Predictions versus the Trial Data

After four months of real-world use, during which we sampled 78,240 calls, the trial data showed that the *proposed* workstation was 4% slower that the *current*. Was this result predicted by the CPM-GOMS models? Despite the fact that the trial result was surprising, the answer is *yes*.

When each of the 15 call categories is weighted by its frequency of occurrence in the trial data the CPM-GOMS models predict that the *proposed* will be 3% slower than *current* workstation. Looking at each of the 15 call categories that were analyzed, the correlation between predicted and observed work times was significant for both the *current*, $r^2=0.69$, and the *proposed* workstation, $r^2=0.65$, showing that the models adequately reflected the variation in work time as a function of call type.

Models as Explanation

Including the CPM-GOMS modeling effort in Project Ernestine had one welcome, but unanticipated result. The trial data were so counterintuitive that, in the absence of a compelling explanation as to why the *proposed* workstation was slower than the *current*, there was a tendency to try to find fault with the trial rather than with the workstation.

The manufacturer had predicted that the *proposed* workstation would be, on average, 2 seconds faster than the *current* workstation. Given the general expectation that an ergonomically engineered, modern workstation should be faster than a five year old, ergonomically indifferent one, this estimate seemed reasonable. When the trial data began to accumulate, the immediate and widely-held conclusion was that something (training, procedures, or equipment)

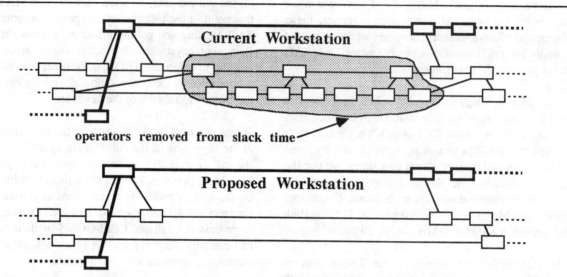

Figure 1. Section of CPM-GOMS analysis from near the beginning of the call. Notice that the proposed workstation (bottom) has removed two keystrokes (which had required 7 motor and 3 cognitive operators) from this part of the call. However, none of the ten operators removed were along the critical path (shown in bold).

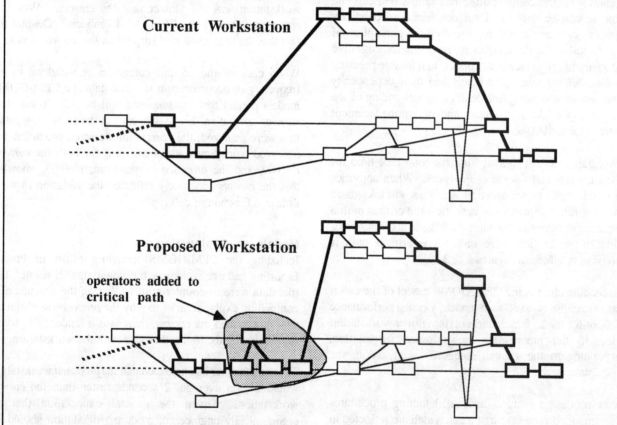

Figure 2. Section of CPM-GOMS analysis from the end of the call. Notice that the proposed workstation (bottom) has added one keystroke to this part of the call which results in four operators (3 motor and 1 cognitive being added to the critical path (shown in bold).

was wrong with the trial.

An initial model of just one call category (Gray et al., 1989) showed us why this *general expectation* was wrong. For example, as discussed above (Figures 1 and 2), although the *proposed* workstation generally had fewer keystrokes than the *current* workstation, the new procedure put more keystrokes on the critical path, rather than in the slack time, increasing the length of the call. In addition, the close spacing of the function keys on the *proposed* keyboard encouraged the use of the right hand for pressing all keys; CPM-GOMS predicted that this would be slower than the old procedure of using the left hand for certain keys that was encouraged by the layout of the old keyboard. Also, while the *proposed* workstation was faster than the *current* workstation in displaying a whole screen of information or in outpulsing large numbers of digits (as in a 14-digit calling card number), the *current* workstation begins displaying information sooner and outpulses a single digit (as for a function key) faster. Since many of these system event are on the critical path, they add to the average worktime of the *proposed* workstation.

Better designed displays provide no advantage to the TAO who knows what information to look for and where it will be displayed. Similarly, a better designed keyboard that reduces the time to move from key to key does not provide a work time advantage when those movements are not on the critical path but provides a deficit when they are.

CONCLUSION
The CPM-GOMS models predicted the empirical field data with remarkable accuracy. In addition, when the empirical data yielded the counter-intuitive result of new technology slower than old technology, GOMS saved the day by explaining why this result occurred. We believe this study validates the usefulness of GOMS models for evaluating real-world systems. Further, this study indicates that GOMS can be used to evaluate design ideas in lieu of empirical studies requiring prototypes or running systems.

The CPM-GOMS models enable us to see the forest rather than the trees. We now understand the TAO's task as a complex interaction involving the TAO, the customer, and various hardware and software. Trying to optimize one component of this interaction, without understanding how it interacts with the others, is unlikely to reduce worktime.

ACKNOWLEDGEMENTS
We thank Sandy Esch, Deborah Lawrence, Jean McKendree, Karen O'Brien, Rory Stuart, Roy Taylor, and Thea Turner for their help and assistance.

Bonnie John's participation was supported, in part, by the Office of Naval Research, Cognitive Science Program, Contract Number N00014-89-J-1975N158. The view and conclusions contained in this document are those of the authors and should not be interpreted as representing the official policies, either expressed or implied, of the Office of Naval Research or the U. S. Government.

NOTE
Request for reprints and additional information should be sent to: Wayne D. Gray, Graduate School of Education, Fordham University at Lincoln Center, New York, NY 10023. gray@mary.fordham.edu. (212) 636-6464

REFERENCES
Atwood, M. E., Gray, W. D., & John, B. E. (submitted). *Project Ernestine: Analytic and Empirical Methods Applied to a Real-World CHI Problem.*

Card, S. K., Moran, T. P., & Newell, A. (1980). Computer text editing: An information processing analysis of a routine cognitive skill. *Cognitive Psychology, 12,* 32-74.

Card, S. K., Moran, T. P., & Newell, A. (1983). *The psychology of human-computer interaction.* Hillsdale, NJ: Erlbaum.

Gray, W. D., John, B. E., & Atwood, M. E. (submitted). *Project Ernestine: Validating GOMS for Predicting and Explaining Real-World Task Performance*

Gray, W. D., John, B. E., Lawrence, D., Stuart, R., & Atwood, M. E. (May 1989). *GOMS meets the phone company, or, Can 8,400,000 unit-tasks be wrong?* Poster presented at: CHI '89, ACM SIGCHI's Conference on Human Factors in Computing Systems. Austin, TX.

Gray, W. D., John, B. E., Stuart, R., Lawrence, D., & Atwood, M. E. (1990a, May). *GOMS meets the phone company: Part 2, or, Data from the world's first, large-scale application of GOMS.* Poster presented at: CHI '90, ACM SIGCHI's Conference on Human Factors in Computing Systems. Seattle, WA.

Gray, W. D., John, B. E., Stuart, R., Lawrence, D., & Atwood, M. E. (1990b). GOMS meets the phone company: Analytic modeling applied to real-world problems. In D. Diaper, D. Gilmore, G. Cockton, and B. Shackel (Eds.), *Human-Computer Interaction -- INTERACT '90.* North-Holland: Elsevier Science Publishers.

John, B. E. (1988) *Contributions to engineering*

models   of   human-computer   interaction.
Doctoral dissertation, Carnegie Mellon University.

John, B. E. (1990). Extensions of GOMS analyses to
expert performance requiring perception of dynamic
visual and auditory information. *Proceedings of
CHI, 1990* (Seattle, WA, April 1-5). New York,
ACM.

Method Engineering:
From Data to Model to Practice

Erik Nilsen,
Lewis and Clark College

HeeSen Jong,
National University of Singapore

Judith S. Olson, and Peter G. Polson
University of Michigan University of Colorado
contact at:
701 Tappan Street
Ann Arbor, MI 48109-1234
jso@csmil.umich.edu

ABSTRACT
This paper explores the behavior of experts choosing among various methods to accomplish tasks. Given the results showing that methods are not chosen solely on the basis of keystroke efficiency, we recommend a technique to help designers assess whether they should offer multiple methods for some tasks, and if they should, how to make them so that they are chosen appropriately.

Keywords: User-interface design issues, design techniques, models of the user.

INTRODUCTION
In attempting to help users achieve high levels of productivity, designers of application software commonly provide users with multiple methods. These are often specialized methods to deal with frequently occurring special cases of important tasks, such as navigation through a document or spreadsheet., or formatting a document bit by bit or through style templates. For example, in Lotus 1-2-3® there are numerous (more than eight) methods for navigating through spreadsheets. Examples include using arrow keys for moving one cell at a time, page keys for moving a screen at a time, and a GOTO command for jumping to a named cell or range. If there were only one navigation method such as arrow keys, there would be significant loss of productivity especially when working with large spreadsheets. The rich collection of navigation methods provided in spreadsheet programs enables users to select a method appropriate to a particular situation and use this method to efficiently move to the location of their next task.

Unfortunately, such multiple specialized methods have surprisingly large cognitive costs.

Improvements in productivity have to be balanced against the cognitive costs of learning the specialized methods and selecting the most efficient method to use in a specific context.

This paper presents data showing how real experts of a piece of popular software (Lotus 1-2-3) select from among a set of methods to accomplish a variety of tasks in a variety of situations. From the results, we show that efficiency in performance is not the only criterion on which people choose methods. We follow the discussion of these results with a technique intended for use by designers to help them determine first whether there is an expected net productivity gain from a special method, and second, how to design the method so users will use it optimally--so they will recognize when to use it and recall it quickly.

EXECUTION COSTS
A specialized method is typically designed to reduce execution time in the particular situation in which it is applicable. The method almost always takes fewer keystrokes, mouse movements, or other user actions. However, there are other time costs: The method has to be recalled successfully. Furthermore, when the method is complicated, the user has to not only recall the command itself but the specialized parameters within it, such as names of ranges or names of locations. And if several methods are retrieved, the appropriate method has to be chosen from the set. The retrieval time and the decision times can be large (approximately one second), nullifying any potential improvements in execution efficiency.

Execution costs can be described by the keystroke level model (Card, Moran, & Newell, 1983; Olson & Olson, 1990). The keystroke model makes the assumption that time to execute a method can be decomposed into a serially executed sequence of operators where the total time to perform the method is the sum of the times for the individual operators. Card et al. (1983) and Olson and

Olson (1990) list a set of perceptual, cognitive, and motor operators that describe performance.

The most common and visible operator is the keystroke, which takes approximately 250 msec. Retrieval of a command or the next step in a method can take from 1000 to 1350 msec. Removing the hand from the home row of the keyboard, acquiring control of the mouse, and selecting a typically sized target can take 1900 msec. In terms of tradeoffs, then, each memory retrieval operations for a well learned command can take from four to six keystroke units of time. The time to select with a mouse is nearly eight keystroke units of time.

Olson and Nilsen (1988) describe in detail how one does the analysis of performance times and how to compare the execution costs of two competing methods.

THE LARGER COGNITIVE CONTEXT
The designers of modern software packages seem to implicitly or explicitly assume that: users can quickly select one of several methods, and that users will select the most efficient method from the set of choices offered. In general, neither of these assumptions is correct.

The time to decide
Specialized methods impose an extra performance burden, possibly reducing total productivity. In order to choose the best method, the user has to recognize the special features of the current situation and recall the appropriate method. Olson and Nilsen (1988) found that users of spreadsheet software who knew two methods for entering formulas were significantly slower than users who knew just one method. This reduction in productivity was due to an increase in planning time, the delay between the completion of the previous task and the start of the new one. The delay was on the order of about 1000 msec or four keystroke units of time. They attributed this increase time to the decision process required to select between the two alternative methods.

Do users always choose the most efficient method?
It is also the case that people faced with several methods do not always choose the method that will maximize productivity. Young and MacLean (1988) presented subjects with a task in which they were to enter values in a matrix of cells. The subjects had a choice of either entering them one by one, moving with a mouse-click and return keys to navigate the cells and rows, or to invest in a significant set-up time to allow a mere "enter" key to move the cursor appropriately from cell to

cell and row to row. Their results showed that in this highly structured, repetitive task situation, people persisted in selecting the method that involved the set-up costs, even when the brute-force, cell by cell method provided a significant (15 second) savings in time.

Since this study is somewhat narrow, in that they tested people in a highly contrived situation where subjects performed a single task over and over again, we decided to investigate people's choices in a more realistic setting. We asked skilled users of Lotus 1-2-3 to enter and change various parts of a number of realistic spreadsheets. We sought both to confirm the results from Young and MacLean that people do not choose efficiently and to reveal, if possible, the bases on which users choose. We expected, from casual observation and personal experience, that factors involving ease of retrieval, avoidance of disasters, and maintenance of context in the global work setting would be significant factors in driving the users' choice of methods.

THE EMPIRICAL STUDY
Subjects
Six expert users of Lotus 1-2-3 were selected from among the MBA and Ph.D. students at the Business School at the University of Michigan. They were selected from their responses to a survey of Lotus use given to all MBA students and Ph.D. students. They indicated that they had used Lotus 1-2-3 continuously for four or more years. In an assessment of their skill level as part of another study on the growth of skill over time, these 6 experts showed that they were far faster, more accurate, and more knowledgeable about the range of possible methods in Lotus than even the best of the students who learned Lotus 1-2-3 at the Business School and used it for two years in class work.

The Tasks they performed
The subjects both entered and then changed a number of realistic spreadsheets. They *navigated* to locations that were either at an edge, to a named location, or within a cluster of cells; *specified a range* of cells within another task (such as a range inside a SUM or a range to which a formatting command was to be applied); entered *sums* of values of various lengths, *edited* the contents of title cells; *centered* titles; set the *width* of a range of columns, and then *altered* those column widths by a certain amount. For each of these tasks, the subjects knew at least two methods. For example, to specify how wide a column should be, all subjects knew that they could either type in a value or move the right hand boundary of the

column with the arrow keys one by one until it is the desired width.

Expecting that one basis for a decision about what method to choose would be the time it normally takes people to perform these tasks, we calculated the time for each method for a variety of task situations. That is, for example, we determined how long it would take to move various distances using the arrow keys, the edge key, the page key plus arrow keys, etc. And, we calculated the time to add a series of numbers using either repeated "+" operators or the @SUM function. The basis for this prediction was the Keystroke Level Model from Card, Moran, and Newell (1983), with the extended set of parameters from Olson and Olson (1991). The predictions were specific to some important physical details of our situation, including the particular layout of the keyboard, where the arrow keys were and the edge and page keys.

We made two modifications to the standard assignment of cognitive parameters, based on extensive study of experts. Experts do not select menu items one at a time (incurring an M before each one), but rather "chunk" them into a unit, as if spelling a word. Thus, for example, to insert a row, the command /WIR incurs an Mk for the "/", and an Mkkk for the "WIR." Furthermore, the Mental operator used was 300 msec., rather than the standard value of 1350 msec. This value was calculated from the experts' own performance of other tasks outside this study. These experts were obviously very skilled and very fast in their performance of these standard tasks. A more detailed discussion of these expert-novice differences in keystroke level parameters are found in Nilsen, Olson, Jong, and Polson (1991) and Nilsen, Olson, Biolsi, Rueter, and Mutter (1991).

We then selected task situations that were clearly favoring one method, some for the alternate method, and some at the very point where the two methods were predicted to take the same amount of time to perform, the point we call the "cusp."

The subjects performed tasks involving 14 different spreadsheets in each of eight sessions over a 6 week period, such that no two sessions were within 3 days of each other, but that there was at least one session per week. These sessions were spaced so that subjects were unlikely to recall the exact form of a spreadsheet they had seen previously, avoiding the situation in which they behave mechanically rather than with their normal thinking and decision making capabilities.

In the first session, they practiced on a small spreadsheet, demonstrating to us that they knew all the methods that we were examining in the study. They also learned the notation we used to indicate what should be done to each cell or column in the experiment. Then they ran through one full set of 14 spreadsheets with the designated tasks noted on them: Twelve small spreadsheets and two large ones, the large ones being necessary to test various aspects of long-distance navigation. In seven successive sessions they edited 14 spreadsheets, just as on day one. We constructed two full sets of these 14 spreadsheets, and alternated them over sessions. These two sets were formally equivalent in the key tasks that had to be performed, but different in actual titles, values, layouts, and the order in which the tasks were to be performed. In four of the later sessions, in addition to these 14 spreadsheets, the experts did a variety of other experimental tasks geared to acquiring baseline data on mental organization and timing, suited for other studies. For each of the datapoints in the results shown in the following sections, there are from 96 to 144 individual data points per cell.

Results

The results are described in two sections. First we discuss the cases having to do with navigation around a spreadsheet. Second, we discuss the behavior in the other tasks, like summing numbers and changing column widths. The navigation tasks tell a story of method choice based on a mixture of time-efficiency and other more situational characteristics; the other tasks elaborate on the features people seem to use in making their choice of methods beyond time-efficiency.

Navigation Tasks For each task situation (e.g., moving 14 cells away), we plotted the percentage that were accomplished using each of the various applicable methods. Figure 1 shows the cross-over in choice for the task of navigating various distances to an ordinary (not named, not at an edge of a block of cells), using either the arrow keys, the page keys, and other methods including the edge key.[1] At short distances, the arrow method is more time efficient, and clearly preferred; at large distances, the page method is more time efficient, and clearly preferred. The dotted line here is the point at which both methods are predicted to take the same amount of time, the cusp.

Two things are of interest in this figure. At long distances, where it is clearly inefficient to use

---

[1]To move to the edge of a block of cells, one hits the "end" key and an arrow key in sequence, indicating which way to move, to which edge.

arrow keys, experts are still using arrow keys 20% of the time. The most time-efficient method, the

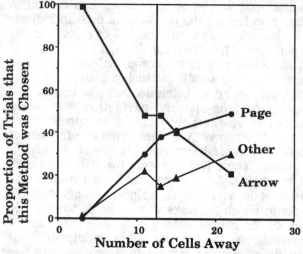

Figure 1. Navigation to a cell that is neither named or on an edge, where appropriate methods are arrow keys, the page key, or other methods, including the edge key.

page key, is used only half the time. The second thing to notice is that the choice of using arrow keys drops below the choice of using the page key very near the cusp, the point that the Keystroke Level Model predicts both methods to be equally fast. At distances below 14 cells, the arrow key should be used exclusively; after 14 cells, the page plus correction arrows is the method that is shortest in execution time. At the longer distances, the edge command is used more often than we predicted, even though it is less time-efficient. We conjecture that the edge method is occasionally preferred to the page command because it moves the view of the spreadsheet to a sensible area (the block or filled spreadsheet area, surrounded by blank columns and rows). The use of these keys preserves the task orientation of the user, rather than merely move a fixed distance.

In summary, the cross-over in choice is at the point at which time-efficiency dictates, but the shape of this function is not optimal. If people were making their choice solely on the basis of time-efficiency, this figure would show 100% choice of arrow before 14 cells away, and 100% choice of page thereafter. The edge key method would be at zero.

Figure 2 shows a second navigation example. Here the people are again navigating around a spreadsheet, but this time to cells that are both named and on an edge. The experts are choosing between using the arrow keys, using the edge key, using the page key plus small arrow corrections, and using the goto-name command. According

to the KLM predictions, the edge key is preferred throughout this range.

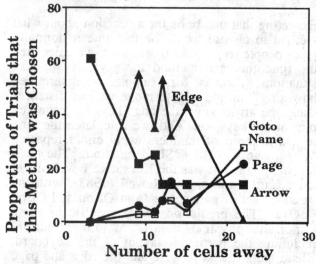

Figure 2. Navigation to a named cell that is also on an edge, where appropriate methods include using the arrow keys, the edge command, and the goto-name command, as well as others.

Two points are striking. At the very short distances, even though the edge key provides the shortest execution time, experts are choosing to use the arrow keys. At the very long distances, the edge key loses to the goto-name command. People recognize that there is something that is needed to move this long distance, and since the cell is named, they choose to use the goto-name command.

It appears in this situation that people are pulled into non optimal methods because of striking situational characteristics. Navigation can always be accomplished by arrow keys and while people work in a local area of a spreadsheet, that is the common method. Because of its high frequency of use, it is retrieved quickly. When the situation calls for *short* navigation to an edge, the arrow key method is chosen, in spite of the actual savings that the edge command can provide. Similarly, looking at a cell that is distant, the experts are choosing a variety of other commands, even though the edge command is once again the most efficient. And, even at the long distances, they are choosing the inefficient arrow method about 15% of the time.

The most interesting phenomenon, however, involves the choices of methods for navigation to an edge when this navigation was *between* tasks or *within* a task, such as specifying a range to format or delete. Although the tasks look different, they are formally equivalent in terms of predicted performance times. For all these conditions, the edge command is the most time-efficient. The results show that experts persist in using the arrow keys *between* tasks, whereas they are more optimally choosing the edge method *within* tasks. In the post-experiment debriefing, the experts reported that they often chose arrows between tasks because it is "mindless." By doing the mindless method, they can think ahead to the next task and prepare for it. If they move more quickly (using the more time-efficient edge key), they would have to take extra time when they get to the target cell to plan the next task. Thus, the choice of method is not confined to efficiency for each subtask separately, but more sensitive to the total cognitive load and global view of performance efficiency.

The other tasks. For the tasks involving summation, altering actual column widths, and formatting, experts chose the method appropriate to execution time-efficiency. But the choice of methods on the other two tasks did not appear to be based solely on time-efficiency. A number of other situational features appeared to drive the choice.

Changing a range of column widths involves a choice between doing it globally or one column at a time. (The early version of Lotus, the one the experts knew, did not allow changing a range of column widths directly). For the task situations we presented them with, it was always more efficient to choose the global command over doing it one at a time. Our experts, however, avoided the global command. As they reported in a post-experiment debriefing session, they did not understand that this command changed only those columns that hadn't been changed explicitly already; they feared it would undo their previous work.

Furthermore, also in the post-experiment debriefing, the experts reported that the only time they used the global command for setting column widths was at the beginning of entering a spreadsheet. Thus, it was a rare choice, and one that was chosen only when the consequences were "safe." This is a good example of "risk control," (Card, et al, 1983), where behavioral choices are determined in part by a combination of the likelihood of making an error and the cost of repairing errors if they occur.

For the task of making editing changes within a cell, the choices facing the subject are to retype the entire title, value, or formula, or after using the edit key (F2) to move to the offending characters, delete them and retype them. There are several specialized ways of moving within a cell: moving with arrow keys, jumping by 5's with the tab or shift-arrow keys, or hitting "home" and moving with arrows from there. Even though the optimal methods often included these specialized jump key-combinations, the experts almost exclusively chose to move with arrows. Although they knew the jump methods, these methods were unfamiliar enough (and therefore infrequent) making them slow to be retrieved or missed altogether.

On what bases do people choose methods?

Our results show that people are looking for efficiency, but that efficiency is not exclusively captured in the calculation of the time to perform the method. Several other situational characteristics often drive the choice:

a) Methods that are commonly used are chosen over rare ones that are more time-efficient (as evidenced in the use of the arrow key over the less familiar page method).

b) Methods that exactly fit the perceived characteristics of the particular situation will be selected more often than pure efficiency would predict (as evidenced in the use of the arrow and named-cell methods over edge).

c) Methods that preserve the context of the task are preferred over ones that change the view without regard to meaningfulness (as evidenced in the choice of the edge navigation method over page command).

d) Methods that steer clear of perceived, potential catastrophic consequences are preferred (as evidenced in the avoidance of the global column width command).

e) And, most importantly, methods are chosen to fit the efficiency of the wider context of work rather than optimizing sub-task by sub-task (as evidenced by the choice of arrow navigation instead of the edge command between tasks, a method that frees cognitive resources for planning ahead).

A MODEL OF THE CHOICE PROCESS

Our model for choice of methods arises as an extension to the simple method selection component of GOMS (Card, Moran, and Newell, 1983). GOMS clearly cannot accommodate the variety of behaviors we have seen here nor their irregularity In this model, we sought to expand the idea of selection of methods to account for the more situational aspects of the choice and its time course.

Our model of method choice substitutes a retrieval and decision process where GOMS had used a simple selection rule. Methods are retrieved in response to cues about the situation and the goal. If multiple methods are retrieved, the user must decide. This decision can involve additional search in the environment for special features, extra memory search for a special "best fitting" method, or a rough calculation of which of several methods will be most efficient. Also, it is unlikely that users will keep accessing memory or searching the environment or calculating precise tradeoffs without limit; we have assumed that if these processes do not converge in a certain amount of time, either the first method retrieved will be enacted or the default will. More precisely:

Stage One. The first stage of method selection involves formulation of the goal and a collection of the significant parameters of the current specific situation. These two sources of information serve as a composite retrieval cue. One or more candidate methods is retrieved. If there is only one, that one is executed. Often the first one retrieved is executed.

Speed of retrieval is heavily dependent on frequency of use *and* the specific fit of the situation to the method. This stage accounts for the emergence of the choice of specialized methods that fit the perceived characteristics, and the frequent methods. We argue also that those methods that preserve the context of the task, those that are easy, and those that avoid risk of error will over time be frequently chosen, and thus quick to be retrieved in this stage. In the long run, frequency of use of methods accounts for much of the quick choice in this stage.

Stage Two. If two or more methods are retrieved quickly, however, the model says that a second stage of processing is initiated. In this stage, the user may attempt to elaborate the situation description by searching for more detail, enough to narrow down the choice to only one appropriate method. For example, having retrieved both the page and goto-name method, as appropriate, one searches memory for the name of that cell. If that name is found, the goto-name method is chosen as more fitting.

The second way in which Stage Two resolves the choice from multiple methods is a quick assessment of the efficiency of each method. One way is to refer to rules of thumb (e.g., choose the method with the lesser mental energy required); the other is to retrieve a past situation for which a method was deemed most appropriate.

Conditions of Time-out. The processes in this second stage are iterative and may not converge rapidly. A user could go through several passes of attempting to formulate better retrieval cues or making more accurate estimates of efficiency. Since we know that users will not persist in analysis indefinitely, the second stage runs under a global time-out. That is, if a sufficient amount of time has been used in the service of retrieval and search, the user will select either the method first retrieved, the one more often used, or the default, the one that *can* be used universally.

DESIGNING FOR MULTIPLE METHODS

The technique outlined below is an attempt to make the results of the above empirical studies accessible to designers. We know that the translation from data and models is not easy for designers to make, and thus they don't do it (Bellotti 1990 a and b). What we present here is a method that incorporates the findings from above and the generalizations from the model into a form that designers can use. It steps designers through questions and activities formulated to help them make the right decisions about adding specialized methods. Designers have to be aware of the fact that a user who acquires a specialized method may or may not experience productivity enhancement. The designer who is contemplating the addition of a specialized method should verify that the new method can lead to significant productivity gains.[2] Since the decision process involved in selecting between alternative methods may impose a penalty of over a second or more, at least *four* keystroke units of time must be saved if the method has any hope of providing an advantage.

The first two stages of this method focus on calculating the potential performance gain from a proposed new method. Since a key piece of the model also focuses on the retrieval of a method, the third stage guides the designer to make salient the situation in which a method is appropriate. One could also train users to recognize situations that favor one method over the other.

The following is a detailed step-by-step procedure for carrying out the above analysis. It is reminiscent of the cognitive walkthrough methods of Lewis, Polson, Wharton and Rieman (1990). In it, the designer "walks through" the

[2]There are many methods that we examined early that *never* produce a productivity gain. For example, editing the contents of a cell in order to change whether it is left, center, or right justified is never faster than changing the alignment through use of menu commands.

actual use of the candidate method from the user's perspective examining performance implications to verify if its use results in actual gains in performance.

Stage I: Considering the set

1. Choose a set of tasks for which alternatives are being considered. Often there are families of tasks that vary on some identifiable dimension (e.g., navigation distance, range of columns that the operation is to effect).

2. List the methods appropriate for each task situation. If appropriate, designate which method is the default method, the one that can cover all possible situations, and which method(s) cover special cases.

3. List the action sequences for each method.

Stage II: Cost-benefit analysis

1. Determine the time to perform each method using cognitive and action parameters from the KLM analysis, as summarized in Olson and Olson (1990). Include in the calculation the time to decide to use a method as well as the time to perform the method.

2. Determine roughly how frequently each method would be appropriate. It is sufficient to merely judge the frequency as common, intermediate, or rare. The important point is to consider the real task situations in which users will be working and looking at the frequency with which the specialized methods might apply.

3. Multiply the time savings of the method by the frequency of use to determine the overall potential savings. If the savings are small, they likely do not warrant the large extra learning time required for reliably remembering the method. A rare method is often forgotten.

Stage III: Making the methods retrievable.

1. For each of the analyzed situations, show how the user will retrieve only the most efficient method by satisfying one or more of the following: a) show that there are appropriate visual (and visibly discriminable) clues that trigger the association (e.g., named cells are highlighted), b) show that there are well known features of this situation that can be remembered easily (e.g., recommend short mnemonic cell names for frequently accessed cells), or c) show that there is a clearcut rule that, if taught, helps users determine when each method is appropriate (e.g.,

for navigating, "use page key if the target cell is more than 8 cells away.")

If the most appropriate method is not likely to be the first one retrieved, then the default will be chosen and the special method will be progressively more rarely used. Effort spent on learning the method will be wasted. If this is the case, then the designer is to either drop the method from the offering, or alter the training, visual clues, or mnemonics to make the special features of the situations more easily noticed and their appropriate methods more easily remembered. A method that is never retrieved never provides a performance enhancement. The effort to develop it is wasted.

CONCLUSIONS.

This paper recommends that part of the interface design process include explicit cost-benefit analysis of the set of methods offered. The user must find significant productivity gains in using a specialized method (far more than 1 second to recoup the time to retrieve it, and even more if the user must choose among several seemingly appropriate ones). And, if there are productivity gains to be had, the designer must insure that the method be retrieved and be the only one retrieved when it is appropriate. Methods must be crafted to be remembered and then more efficient in the global context of work.

ACKNOWLEDGEMENT This research was supported by grant MDA 903-89-K-0025 from the Army Research Institute.

REFERENCES
Bellotti, V. (1990a) *Applicability of HCI Techniques to Systems Interface Design* Ph.D. Dissertation from the Queen Mary and Westfield College, University of London .

Bellotti, V. (1990b) A framework for assessing applicability of HCI techniques" in D. Diaper et al (eds.). *Interact'90 Proceedings*, Elsevier Science Publishers B. V. (North-Holland) IFIP 1990. pp 213 - 218.

Card, S. K., Moran, T. P., and Newell, A. (1983) *The Psychology of Human-Computer Interaction.* Hillsdale, NJ: Lawrence Erlbaum Assoc.

Lewis, C.H., Polson, P.G., Wharton, C. and Rieman, J. (1990) Testing a walkthrough methodology for theory-based design of walk-up-and-use interfaces. *Proceedings of CHI'90 Conference on Human Factors in Computer Systems*. New York: Association for Computing Machinery. pp. 235-243.

Nilsen, E., Jong, H., Olson, J. S., and Polson, P. G. (1991) How experts choose among methods to perform tasks: Keystroke efficiency is not the sole basis of choice. Technical report, Cognitive Science and Machine Intelligence Laboratory, The University of Michigan.

Nilsen, E., Olson, J. S., Biolsi, K., Rueter, H. R., and Mutter, S. (1991) The growth of skill in learning and using software. Technical report, Cognitive Science and Machine Intelligence Laboratory, The University of Michigan.

Olson, J.S. and Nilsen, E. (1988). Analysis of the cognition involved in spreadsheet software interaction. *Human Computer Interaction*, 3, 309-349.

Olson, J.S. and Olson, G.M. (1990) The growth of cognitive modeling in human computer interaction since GOMS. *Human Computer Interaction*, 5, 221-265

Young, R. M., and MacLean, A. (1988) Choosing between methods: Analyzing the user's decision space in terms of schemas and linear models. *Proceedings of CHI'88, Human Factors in Computing Systems*, NY: ACM, 201-206.

The Decoupled Simulation Model for Virtual Reality Systems

Chris Shaw, Jiandong Liang, Mark Green and Yunqi Sun

Department of Computing Science, University of Alberta
Edmonton, Alberta, Canada T6G 2H1
{cdshaw,leung,mark,yunqi}@cs.ualberta.ca

Abstract

The Virtual Reality user interface style allows the user to manipulate virtual objects in a 3D environment using 3D input devices. This style is best suited to application areas where traditional two dimensional styles fall short, but the current programming effort required to produce a VR application is somewhat large. We have built a toolkit called MR, which facilities the development of VR applications. The toolkit provides support for distributed computing, head-mounted displays, room geometry, performance monitoring, hand input devices, and sound feedback. In this paper, the architecture of the toolkit is outlined, the programmer's view is described, and two simple applications are described.

Keywords: User Interface Software, Virtual Reality, Interactive 3D Graphics.

1 Introduction

The Virtual Reality user interface style denotes highly-interactive three dimensional control of a computational model. The user enters a virtual space, and manipulates and explores the application data using natural 3D interaction techniques. This style usually requires the use of non-traditional devices such as head-mounted displays, and hand measurement equipment (gloves). The core requirement of this style is support for real-time three dimensional interactive animation.

This results in the following issues:

1. The real-time generation of synchronized stereoscopic images for a head-mounted display is not supported by most commonly-available 3D graphics workstations. As a result, two workstations must be operated in tandem to provide two video signals. Consistent images must be presented in synchrony to the user.

2. Low-level support for new I/O devices such as position trackers, gloves, and so on must be provided for efficiency and lag minimization, while high-level abstractions are required by the application programmer.

3. Applications must be designed independently of the tracker geometry, room geometry and device configuration, yet correct handling of geometric data is vital to avoid user confusion.

4. The real-time nature of the task demands that a performance monitoring tools be available for performance optimization and for debugging.

The MR toolkit we describe in this paper is developed to address these concerns.

2 Previous Work

Other groups have worked on support for this user interface style. Zeltzer and his colleagues at MIT produced a general purpose package for building interactive simulation systems, especially for task level animation systems [Zeltzer 1989]. The key element in the package is a constraint network to which all the objects are connected. Once the status of an object is updated, all the constraints which involve this object are informed and evaluated. By using constraint propagation, the gestural input from the DataGlove can also be viewed as an object. New DataGlove gestures trigger gesture-dependent constraints which then produce the reaction to the user's activity.

Card, Mackinlay and Robertson at Xerox have produced an architectural model for VR user interfaces called the Cognitive Coprocessor Architecture [Robertson 1989]. The purpose of the Cognitive Coprocessor Architecture is to support "multiple, asynchronous, interactive agents" and smooth animation. It is based on a three agent model of an interactive system. These agents are: the user, the user discourse machine and the task machine. The basic control mechanism is the animation loop, which has a task queue, a display queue, and a governor. The task queue maintains all the incoming computations from different sorts of agents; the display queue contains all the objects to be drawn; while the governor keeps track of the time and helps the application to produce the smooth output. This architectural model is similar to the Decoupled Simulation Model outlined in section 3.

Researchers at IBM have been using multiple workstations to support the real-time requirements of VR user interfaces [Wang 1990, Lewis 1991]. They have assigned a workstation to each of the devices in their user interfaces and an event based UIMS is used to coordinate the input coming from several devices. MR uses a similar device management approach, as described in section 5.2 of this paper.

Holloway at UNC at Chapel Hill has developed a general purpose tracker library called trackerlib for 3D position and orientation trackers.

Our own previous work has addressed the problem of distributing the low level device software over multiple workstations and the production of a skeleton VR user interface that can be used as the basis for user interface development [Green 1990]. The toolkit described in this paper is an extension of this work.

3 Decoupled Simulation Model

A VR application can be broken into four components, represented by boxes in figure 1. Some applications are simple enough to require only the Presentation component and the Interaction component, while others require all four parts. The arrows represent information flows within the system, again with the proviso that some flows are quite minimal in simpler applications. We call this the Decoupled Simulation Model, because the Computation component proceeds independently of the remaining system components.

The Computation component is the item of central interest to the application programmer. This component manages all non-graphical computations in the application, and is usually a continuously running simulation. Typical simulations evaluate a computational model of some process in a series of discrete time steps, periodically updating the application data into a consistent state. When the application data is consistent, the Computation component forwards its data to the Geometric Model component. The simulation can receive two classes of input from the Interaction component. The first input class is user commands. The second input class is the current time, which is used to pace the update rate of the application with the update rate of the graphical presentation. The time updating is needed

to maintain a constant scaling factor between real time and simulation time, since there is no necessary connection between the Presentation component update rate and the Computation component update rate.

The Interaction component is responsible for managing all input from the user, and for coordinating all output to the user. It manages at a high level the various devices available for user input, and dispatches commands to the output devices based upon user actions. The sub-boxes in the Interaction component of figure 1 indicate that multiple devices are used for input. The parenthesized items indicate items that MR does not currently support, but can be supported in the MR framework.

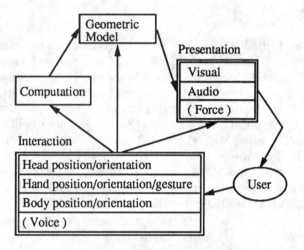

Figure 1: Decoupled Simulation Model.

The Geometric Model component maintains a high-level representation of the data in the computation. The component is responsible for converting the application data in the Computation component into a form amenable to visual, sonic, and force display. For example, the mapping from application data to graphical data could be static, and thus defined at compile time, or it could be dynamic, and under control of the user. The input from the Interaction component can be used to reflect user-proposed changes to the computational model which have not yet been incorporated into the simulation.

The Presentation component produces the views of the application data that the user sees, along with the sonic and force aspects of the application data.

In the visual domain, the Presentation component is the rendering portion of the application, whose input is the graphical data from the Geometric Model, and the viewing parameters (such as eye position) from the Interaction component. The output is one or more images of the current application data from the current viewpoint. These images must be updated each time the application data or the viewing parameters change.

In the sonic domain, the Presentation component presents sonic feedback and application sounds based on the application data and, if 3D sound is used, based on the user's head position. Again, sounds must be updated as the application data and/or the user's position change.

To compare to previous work, Robertson et al's Cognitive Coprocessor Architecture has only one interaction loop that updates a database with small changes. The Cognitive Coprocessor Architecture Task Machine's job is to animate changes from one database view to another, and to animate database updates. There is no direct provision for a continuously-running simulation task in the Cognitive Coprocessor Architecture. The Decoupled Simulation Model has two loops running asynchronously, and therefore has direct support for both discrete event and continuous simulation.

The MR toolkit we describe in this paper was developed to assist in the building of VR applications using the Decoupled Simulation Model. We believe that a clear strategic guideline of this nature can provide a solid basis for building VR applications. These guidelines are bolstered by the toolkit routines, which perform much of the drudgery entailed in managing an interaction of this kind.

4 Application Process Structure

An MR application consists of one or more UNIX-style processes, with one designated as the master process, and others as slave or computational processes. The designation *master*, *slave* or *computation* is called the *role* of the process. An MR application will also establish connection to one or more *server* processes, each of which is uniquely responsible for the management of an I/O device such as a DataGlove, a position tracker, or sound output.

Typically, slave processes perform output tasks. For example, one of the images for a head-mounted display is generated by a slave process. This corresponds to the Presentation component of the Decoupled Simulation Model.

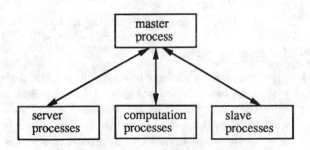

**Figure 2: Process structure
of an MR application.**

A computation process corresponds to the Computation component in the Decoupled Simulation Model, typically performing the simulation part of the application. For example, a computation process could be performing a fluid dynamics calculation, while the user is interacting with the results of the previous time step in the computation.

The master process performs the duties of Interaction component, along with any graphics element of the Presentation component that can reside in the master's local machine. While this tight binding of graphical display with the Interaction component is not required, it is desirable for the purposes of reducing lag. The master process is the first process started and is responsible for initiating the other processes and establishing the communications between these processes. The MR toolkit supports a limited version of distributed computing in which the slave, computation and server processes can communicate with the master process, but they cannot directly communicate with each other. This process structure is illustrated in figure 2. Figure 3 shows the process structure of the example code given in the appendix. Figure 3 shows four processes: The master, the almost-identical slave, and two server processes.

5 Hardware and Software Architecture

The hardware environment that the MR toolkit was developed in consists of a Silicon Graphics 4D/35 workstation, a Silicon Graphics 3130 workstation, a VPL DataGlove (tracked by a Polhemus 3Space Isotrak), a VPL EyePhone (also tracked by an Isotrak) and a third Isotrak digitizer. All the timing figures mentioned in this paper are based on this hardware configuration. We are in the process of porting the MR toolkit to Decstation 5000/200PXG workstations.

The MR toolkit currently supports applications developed in the C programming language, and in the near future at least partial support for applications written in Fortran77 will be provided. The Fortran77 support will allow the addition of VR front ends to existing scientific and engineering computations.

5.1 Internal Structure of MR

The MR toolkit consists of three levels of software. The bottom level of the structure consists of the routines that interact with the hardware devices supported by MR. The structure of this level of the toolkit is described in the next section. The next level of the MR toolkit consists of a collection of packages. Each package handles one aspect of a VR user interface, such as providing a high level interface to an input or output device, or routines for sharing data between two processes. The packages are divided into two groups, which are called standard and optional. The standard packages are always part of the MR toolkit and provide services, such as data sharing and performance monitoring, that are required by all VR applications. The optional packages provide services that may not be required by every VR application. Typically there is one optional package for each device supported by MR and each interaction technique or group of interaction techniques. There can be any number of optional packages, the exact number depends upon the devices that are locally available and the interaction techniques that have been produced. The use of packages facilitates the graceful growth of MR as new devices and interaction techniques are added. In the following sections some of the more important packages are briefly described. The top level of the MR toolkit consists of the standard MR procedures that are used to configure and control the complete application. The routines at this level provide the glue that holds the MR toolkit together.

5.2 Device Level Software

The MR toolkit manages devices such as 3D trackers, gloves, and sound using the client-server model. Depending on the device, one or more server processes are used to drive the device hardware. In our configuration for example, one server manages the head-mounted display's Isotrak, one server manages our DataGlove, and one manages the sound driver.

Each server is solely responsible for all interaction with its device, continually collecting from input devices, and continually updating the values on output devices. When a client wishes to get service from a particular device, it makes a socket connection with the device's server (using TCP/IP over ethernet). The client then sets up how the server should communicate with the device, and instructs the server to commence any special processing that should be performed by the server.

There are several reasons for adopting the client-server model for low level device interactions.

1. Using a separate process to handle each device facilitates distributing the application over several workstations. The server processes can be placed on workstations that have a lighter computational load.

2. Device sharing is facilitated by this approach. The devices used by an application don't need to be attached to the workstation that the application is running on. The application can use them as long as the workstation they are attached to is on the same network.

3. When a new device is added to the system, existing applications are not affected. Applications that don't need the new device simply don't connect to its server.

4. If improvements are made to either the client or server software, these changes usually don't affect programs that use the client code. For example, a new filter was added to our Isotrak server with no change to any existing client code.

5. The rate at which the device is sampled is decoupled from the update rate of the application.

To expand on the fifth point, there are two major benefits to sample rate decoupling. The first benefit is that noise reduction filters and predictive filters can operate at the sampling frequency of the device, not at the application update frequency. Since the server can perform filter calculations at device update rate, filter performance is invariant under application load.

The second benefit is that the client is guaranteed to get the latest filtered data. Moreover, the client-server interaction can be constructed so that the client puts the server into *continuous send* mode, in which the latest data is received by the server, filtered, then sent to the client automatically. Our Isotrak lag experiments [Liang 1991] indicate that continuous mode from Isotrak to server reduced lag by 20-25 milliseconds, and our preliminary measurements show that a similar benefit can be had with continuous data traffic from server to client. Also, network packet traffic between client and server is cut in half, a significant savings.

5.3 Data Sharing Package

The data sharing package allows two processes to share the same data structure. The data sharing package is structured so that one process is a producer of data and another process is a consumer. This fits well with the Decoupled Simulation Model, in which data communication is one way. Two way communications can be achieved by setting up two one-way links in opposite directions. To simplify the implementation, one of the communicating processes must be the master, but this can be easily extended to allow communication between arbitrary pairs of processes.

There are three reasons for providing a shared data package instead of having the programmer directly send data between the processes.

1. The data sharing package provides the programmer with a higher level interface to data communications than is provided by the standard socket software. This reduces the amount of time required to develop the applications and also reduces the possibility of bugs.

2. The data sharing package can optimize the data transfer in ways that the programmer may not have the time or knowledge to perform.

3. The data sharing package increases the portability of the application. If the application is moved to another set of workstations that use different networking software only the data sharing package needs to be rewritten and not all the applications that use it.

To commence data sharing between the master process and a slave or computation process, the programmer declares in both processes the data structure to be shared. The declaration procedure wraps a header around the data structure to be shared, and returns an id that is used by the data sharing calls. This id is common to both processes sharing the data item. Any number of data items may be shared between the master and slave or computation processes. The data sharing action calls automatically update the appropriate data structures. To send data to the other process, the producer process calls send_shared_data, and the consumer process calls one of receive_shared_data or shared_data_sync.

The receive_shared_data call accepts and properly routes all shared items that are sitting in the input queue waiting to be received. If there are no data structures ready to be received, this procedure returns immediately. This allows a process to use the most up-to-date data without blocking for a lack of input. This provides direct support for the Decoupled Simulation Model, in that the Computation component can proceed at its own pace updating the downstream processes asynchronously of the Presentation component.

On the other hand, the shared_data_sync procedure is called when the consumer process must have a particular data item before it can proceed. While shared_data_sync is waiting in the expected item, it will process and update any incoming shared data item that is sent to the consuming process.

Since a shared data model is used, the programmer is usually not concerned with the timing of the data transfers. For most applications this greatly simplifies the programming process, the programmer only needs to state the data that is shared by the two processes, and when the data is to be transmitted. The process that receives the data doesn't need to specify when it is to be received, or take part in any hand-shaking protocol with the sending process.

There are usually two situations where data synchronization is necessary, both of which are associated with the problem of presenting two consistent images simultaneously in the head-mounted display. The first requirement, *consistency*, implies that before image rendering starts, both the master process and the eye slave process must have identical copies and views of the polygonal database to be rendered. The second requirement, *simultaneity*, means that the consistent images must be presented to both eyes at the same time.

The database consistency operation could be performed by having the slave execute a shared_data_sync call to synchronize databases with the master before it starts drawing. However, since the views must also be consistent, MR automatically has the master calculate the view and send it to the slave, which is waiting for the view parameters with a shared_data_sync call. Therefore, if database update is performed before view parameter update, the databases will be consistent after the viewing parameters are synchronized on the slave.

The simultaneous display requirement is usually met by having the master wait for the slave to indicate that it has finished rendering. When the master receives the slave's sync packet, it sends a *return sync* pulse to the slave, and displays its image. When the slave receives the *return sync*, it can display its image. In hardware configurations where the slave workstation is significantly slower than the master workstation, the *return sync* packet is not needed, since the master will always finish first.

There are times when the consuming process needs to know when the shared data is updated. In MR a programmer-defined trigger procedure can be attached to any shared data structure. When a new value for the shared data structure is received, the trigger procedure is called by the data sharing package.

5.4 Workspace Mapping

Because the VR user interface style depends so strongly on the collection of geometric data from the user based upon the user's position in space, this style creates a new demand for geometric accuracy not previously considered by most 3D graphics packages. For example, trackers used in VR applications use their own coordinate systems, which depend upon where they are located in the room. Three-dimensional sound output devices also have their own coordinate systems, and even standard graphics displays have an implicit default view direction. The workspace mapping package removes the application's dependency on the physical location of the devices that it uses.

The workspace mapping package performs two sets of geometric transformations. The first set maps the coordinate system of each device into the coordinate system of the room in which the device is situated. The second transformation set is a single transformation which converts room coordinates into environment or "virtual world" coordinates.

The mapping matrices for every device (including workstation monitors, 3D trackers, joysticks, etc.) are stored in a system-wide **workspace** file. When a device such as 3D tracker is installed in a different location, the workspace file is updated and all applications will automatically use the new position of the device. Because each tracker device is mapped to the common room coordinate system, tracked items drawn in virtual space maintain the same geometric relationship they do in real space. The room-to-environment mapping can be altered by the application's navigation code, but since all devices map to room coordinates, all devices in the room maintain the same relationship as they do in real space.

The workspace mapping package was initially envisioned as a means of solving the problem of each tracker having its own coordinate space. However, workstation monitors and the like were added because some single-screen applications such as our DataGlove calibration program use the same object code on multiple workstations. Having a single fixed viewpoint means that the DataGlove must be held in a particular position to be visible, no matter what screen is used. Instead, such applications now read the workspace file to find the room position and orientation of the monitor, and adjust the viewing parameters so that the DataGlove is visible when it is held in front of the screen that is running the program.

5.5 Timing Package

There are two types of analysis available from the timing package. The first type allows the user to time stamp certain key points in the application program, and thereby monitor the amount of real time that was consumed between each time stamp call. The time stamp call allows the programmer to associate a text string with each section of code for identification purposes. When the program ends, the timing package outputs a summary of the average real time consumed in each section of the code. One summary appears for each process that runs under MR, and so gives the programmer a clear starting point for program optimization. This type of analysis exacts a very small overhead, only 12 microseconds per time stamp call on our SGI 4D/35. On our SGI 3130, each call takes 410 microseconds, so we turn off the time stamping calls on this machine when we are not tuning code for it.

Of course, this timing analysis is only part of the story, since the issue of data communications is ignored. The second type of timing analysis deals with the communications time used by the entire application. In this situation, the data sharing package records each packet that is sent or received. A log file contains the id number of the shared data structure and the real time when it is sent or received. At the end of a run the logs from all the workstations used in the application can be analyzed to determine where the communications delays are in the application.

5.6 DataGlove Package

The DataGlove package provides routines for simple DataGlove interaction. It collects the latest values from the DataGlove server, and transforms the position and location into environment coordinates using the workspace mapping package. The package also supplies a routine that will draw the DataGlove in the current position, in stereo if necessary.

An interactive DataGlove calibration and gesture editing program is part of the package. This program will allow the user to define and name any number of static hand postures, including recognition of hand orientation if necessary.

5.7 Sound Package

The Sound package is an optional package which provides a standard front end to the many possible sound output techniques available. We use the client-server scheme outlined in section 5.2, where in this case, the client is the data producer and the server is the data consumer. MR's current assumption is that sound output will be used mainly as a means of signaling events. When an application needs to signal the user that a command has been received, a single sound package call can be used to dispatch a sound to the server. This is similar to the "Earcon" approach [Blattner 1989, Gaver 1989]. Overlapping events are mixed sonically by the server. The sound package also includes an interactive editing program that allows the user to define and name any number of sounds to be later generated as events in an application.

5.8 Panel Package

Standard two dimensional interaction techniques are provided by the optional Panel package. A panel is a flat rectangle in 3-space that functions as an arbitrarily oriented 2D screen, onto which the application programmer can map menus, graphical potentiometers, buttons and the like. The programmer simply declares a panel and its 3D position and orientation, then allocates screen space, trigger routines, events and so on in the same way the he/she would do with a 2D menu package. The pointer in this case is the DataGlove, whose orientation is used to cast a ray from the hand to any panel in the application. The intersection of the hand ray with the panel is used to determine which interaction technique is active. Hand gestures are then used to perform the operations that would normally be assigned to mouse buttons.

When more than one panel is active, the panel that intersects the hand ray closest to the hand is the one that gets activated. Pop-up panels are also supported, with the default orientation aligned with head tilt, and perpendicular to the line of sight.

6 Examples

In this section, we briefly describe two examples of MR applications. The accompanying videotape has these two examples also.

The first one is the very simple program listed in the appendix. It is the equivalent of the "hello world" program for a programming language. The application consists of a master process, and a slave process. There is no computation process. The flowchart of the application is shown in figure 3, with dashed lines denoting data communications between processes.

The master process first configures the shared data structure, and device set, and starts the slave process. Then both the master and slave processes enter a loop. In the loop, the master process first updates the hand data structure by communicating with the DataGlove server, and performs gesture recognition. Then it updates the EyePhone information by interacting with the EyePhone server, sets up the viewing parameters, and sends them to the slave process. After the shared data is updated to a consistent state, both master and slave processes draw the hand in the environment as an echo of the state of the DataGlove. The update of images are then synchronized before entering next iteration of the loop.

The second example is a simple user interface for fluid dynamics. This user interface forms the front-end to an existing fluid dynamics program written in Fortran [Bulgarelli 1984]. This user interface provides the user with a stereo three dimensional view of the fluid surface using the EyePhone. The user can walk through the flow to view it from different directions. The DataGlove is used to interact with the flow and establish the boundary conditions for the computation, which proceeds while the user is interacting with it.

In terms of software structure, the fluid dynamics example closely follows the Decoupled Simulation Model. The Computation component runs on a CPU server machine at its own update rate. It accepts boundary condition commands from the Interaction component, and sends force vector data to the Geometric component. The Geometric component creates the checkerboard surface that the user sees, and passes it on to the Presentation component. The Presentation update rate is much higher than the Computation update rate, allowing the user to explore slow-moving simulations with limited lag. The fluid dynamics visualization example was produced in three days using this toolkit, with most of the effort being spent on interfacing the Computation component with the Geometric component and the Interaction component.

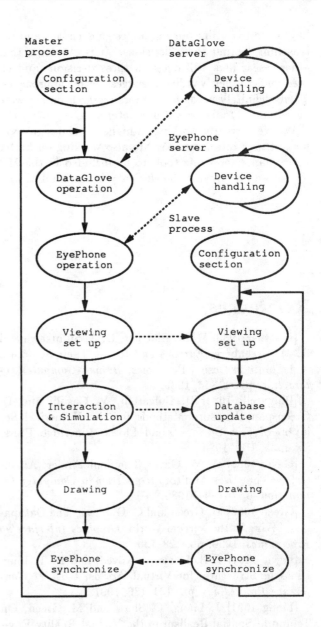

Figure 3: A typical flowchart for an MR application.

7 Conclusions

We have described the Decoupled Simulation Model of real-time 3D animation systems, and a software system to support this model, the MR toolkit. Although it is difficult to demonstrate the flexibility of the toolkit in a paper of this length, it can be seen that it provides the programmer with relatively high level facilities that are most needed in developing a VR application. All the features described in this paper have been implemented. Version 1.0 of MR is available to academic researchers.

We don't make the claim that MR is the best possible toolkit for developing VR applications. Our claim is that it is adequate for our purposes and an excellent start towards developing software development tools for VR user interfaces. In describing the MR toolkit we have tried to outline our major design decisions and the reasoning behind these decisions. It is our hope that other researchers will question these decisions and either confirm their validity or suggest better approaches. There definitely needs to be more research on software development tools for VR user interfaces.

We are currently working on higher level design tools for VR user interfaces. We are also working on better performance modeling tools to be included in the MR toolkit and improving the efficiency of the toolkit.

References

[Blattner 1989] M. M. Blattner, D. A. Sumikawa and R. M. Greenberg, Earcons and Icons: Their Structure and Common Design Principles, *Human-Computer Interaction*, pp. 11–44, 1989.

[Bulgarelli 1984] U. Bulgarelli, V. Casulli and D. Greenspan, Pressure Methods for the Numerical Solution of Free Surface Fluid Flows, Pineridge Press, Swansea, UK, 1984.

[Gaver 1989] W. W. Gaver, The SonicFinder: An Interface That Uses Auditory Icons *Human-Computer Interaction*, pp. 67–94, 1989.

[Green 1990] M. Green and C. D. Shaw, The Datapaper: Living in the Virtual World, *Graphics Interface'90 Proceedings,* 1990, pp. 123–130.

[Lewis 1991] J. B. Lewis, L. Koved, and D. T. Ling, Dialogue Structures for Virtual Worlds, *CHI '91 Conference Proceedings*, pp. 131–136, 1991.

[Liang 1991] J. Liang, C. Shaw and M. Green, On Temporal-Spatial Realism in the Virtual Reality Environment, *UIST'91 Proceedings*, 1991.

[Robertson 1989] G. G. Robertson, S. K. Card, and J. D. Mackinlay, The Cognitive Coprocessor Architecture for Interactive User Interface, *UIST'89 Proceedings*, pp. 10–18, 1989.

[Wang 1990] C. Wang, L. Koved, and S. Dukach, Design for Interactive Performance in a Virtual Laboratory, *Proceedings of 1990 Symposium on Interactive 3D Graphics, Computer Graphics 24, 2 (1990)*, pp. 39–40.

[Zeltzer 1989] D. Zeltzer, S. Pieper and D. Sturman, An Integrated Graphical Simulation Platform, *Proceedings of Graphics Interface'89*, 1989.

Appendix

```
#include <MR/mr.h>
#define machine "tawayik"
#define program "hello_world"
extern  Gtable gtables[];

main(argc, argv)
int      argc;
char     *argv[ ];
{
int            quit_id, count = 0;
Program        slave;
Data           shared_cnt;
Hand           hand;
Gtable         gst_tbl;
Gesture_event  usr_gst;

    /* Configuration section */
    MR_init(argv[0]);
#ifdef MASTER
    MR_set_role(MR_MASTER);
#else
    MR_set_role(MR_SLAVE);
#endif MASTER
    slave = MR_start_slave(machine, program);
    shared_cnt = MR_shared_data(&count,
            sizeof(count), slave, MR_FROM);
    MR_add_device_set(EyePhone);
    MR_add_device_set(DataGlove);
    EyePhone_slave(slave);
    MR_configure();

    /* Computation section */
    read_gesture_file("my.gst");
    assign_gesture_ids();
    gst_tbl = gtables[0];
    quit_id = get_gesture_id("select");
    set_room_reference(1.0, 1.5, 2.0);
    map_reference_to(0.1, 0.0, 0.5);

    while (1) {
        update_hand();
        hand = get_hand();
        usr_gst = recognize_gesture(gst_tbl);
        if (MR_get_role() == MR_MASTER)
            if (usr_gst->id == quit_id)
                MR_terminate(0);
        MR_start_display();
        count++;
        if (MR_get_role() == MR_MASTER)
            send_shared_data(shared_cnt);
        else
            shared_data_sync(shared_cnt);
        draw_hand(hand);
        MR_end_display();
    }
}
```

Interactive Simulation in a Multi-Person Virtual World

Christopher Codella, Reza Jalili, Lawrence Koved, J. Bryan Lewis,
Daniel T. Ling, James S. Lipscomb, David A. Rabenhorst, Chu P. Wang
Veridical User Environments

Alan Norton, Paula Sweeney
Computer Animation Systems

Computer Science Department
IBM T.J. Watson Research Center
Yorktown Heights, New York 10598

Greg Turk
University of North Carolina
Chapel Hill, N.C.

Contact telephone number: (914) 784-7934
email: koved@watson.ibm.com

ABSTRACT

A multi-user Virtual World has been implemented combining a flexible-object simulator with a multisensory user interface, including hand motion and gestures, speech input and output, sound output, and 3-D stereoscopic graphics with head-motion parallax. The implementation is based on a distributed client/server architecture with a centralized Dialogue Manager. The simulator is inserted into the Virtual World as a server. A discipline for writing interaction dialogues provides a clear conceptual hierarchy and the encapsulation of state. This hierarchy facilitates the creation of alternative interaction scenarios and shared multi-user environments.

KEYWORDS: user interface management system, dialog manager, virtual worlds, virtual reality, interactive simulation.

BACKGROUND

A Virtual World is an interactive, multisensory, three-dimensional environment where human-computer interactions are based on the ways we interact with the real world [5, 7]. Virtual World software tends to be complex because it must manage multiple simultaneous devices;

operate as fast as the senses of the human in the loop; incorporate heterogeneous software objects (with a range of operating speeds and hardware bases) seamlessly; and be highly flexible in construction. Our architecture takes into account the need for high performance, coordination of multiple device- and application-generated events, and the need for flexibility in configuring the Virtual World. We have described the architecture in previous papers [1, 12].

We believe that many interesting Virtual Worlds will include one or more simulations [9, 19, 22] – software components with autonomous behavior – as opposed to the simpler spatial-database traversals and preprogrammed animations often seen in today's demonstrations [4, 6, 17]. Such a simulation must be able to update its state (after being perturbed by human input) at interactive speeds. We call this a *real-time simulation*, since its results must be computed within the same elapsed real time as the human's interaction.[1] In particular, this paper will describe a Virtual World called Rubber Rocks, based on the physical modeling of flexible objects [2, 13, 20].

Our Virtual World can be thought of as a set of cooperating servers and clients communicating via asynchronous messages. The flexibility of our architecture stems from an initial design decision to separate the *style* of a Virtual World from its *content* [21]. The content defines the operational characteristics of a Virtual World independent of the user interface. In the case of Rubber Rocks, the content or application is a flexible object simulator. The style, or user interface, is implemented by device servers and a user interface dialogue. Specialized I/O devices needed for the multisensory aspects of the Virtual World are controlled by dedicated server processes, that communicate via asynchronous messages.

The Dialogue Manager, or User Interface Management System [8, 10, 11, 14, 16, 18], provides the methods of interacting with the Virtual World. It is the client process that receives events from input device servers and application programs, and sends data and control information to application programs and output devices. It is the Dialogue Manager that maps device I/O to application parameters and results. Events received from devices and applications are processed by event handlers written in the form of rules. These rules contain embedded C code [18]. In order to achieve high flexibility, device remappability, and reusability, the rule sets should be written as independent modules, each encapsulating its own state. The rule sets are designed according to their purpose in a conceptual hierarchy [12] (see Figure 1). The *specific level* refers to the interface to the servers, such as the I/O devices and application. The *generic level* is a set of rules that merge and filter data from the specific level to derive events that are independent of particular I/O devices. At the top is the *executive level* that defines the scenario or interaction sequences in a Virtual World. These rules form a toolkit for building a variety of Virtual Worlds. We have found that this dialogue structure has successfully scaled up to our latest and most complex Virtual World incorporating real-time simulation, stereoscopic display with head motion parallax, and a shared two person environment. In addition, modifications at the executive level of Rubber Rocks allowed us to easily create different interaction scenarios.

By designing a Virtual World with such a dialogue structure – style cleanly separated from content – it is relatively easy to expand the world to include multiple users [15]. Within the hierarchy of events in the dialogues that make up the interface, a selected group of events at the generic and executive levels can be passed to other Dialogue Managers to create a cooperative multi-user Virtual World. By capturing certain events at the generic and executive levels, the participants of Rubber Rocks are able to interact with each other, as well as have independent views into the Virtual World.

RUBBER ROCKS

Rubber Rocks is a Virtual World simulating a room containing flexible objects. These objects are based on the physical modeling of point masses connected by elastic bonds. They deform and sometimes break as they collide

with each other, the walls and floor, and with the users' hands. Users can create, grab, hit and shoot these simulated objects (see Figure 2). The system provides interactions via hand gestures, speech recognition, speech synthesis, and sound generation. The objects and room are displayed stereoscopically[2] with head-motion parallax[3].

Two users can simultaneously interact with Rubber Rocks. They share a single underlying simulation, the Virtual World content. However, both users have their own style components. That is, both users have their own Dialogue Manager providing independent user interfaces. These do not need to be the same. For example, one user may interact with the system using speech recognition, while the other uses pop-up menus. One user may see the objects rendered with shaded surfaces while the other sees wireframes. Each user's head-motion parallax is managed by the user's own dialogue. In addition, each user's view contains a small amount of state obtained from the other user's Dialogue Manager. For example, each user sees the other's hand.

REAL-TIME SIMULATION

The content of Rubber Rocks is a flexible object simulator [2, 13, 20] that integrates Newton's second law (F=ma) over time. Objects are modelled as a network of point masses and springs (or bonds). The dynamics of the system includes external forces such as gravity, friction and repulsive forces due to collisions. Collision forces occur when an object collides with another object, a room boundary, or one of the hands.

In Rubber Rocks, a number of simple, playful objects are defined. These vary in complexity from octahedra con-

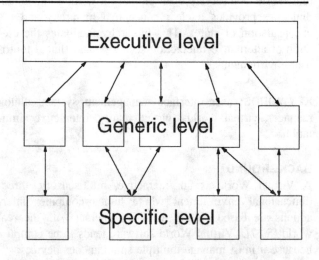

Figure 1. Hierarchical organization of rule sets

---

1   That is, we do not use "real-time" in its stricter technical sense here; we do not limit ourselves to simulations implemented with real-time programming principles.
2   The graphic display is computed and displayed separately for each eye.
3   The observer's viewing location is repeatedly measured, defining a new camera position from which the correct perspective view is calculated.

taining seven points and eighteen bonds, to sheets composed of 36 points and 110 bonds. Cubes, containing 27 points and 86 bonds, are objects of medium complexity. Each object has a set of physical parameters which determines the flexibility and breakability of the object. These objects can break into pieces if a strong external force is applied to the object.

User interactions with these objects result in the direct perturbation of the simulated dynamical equations, through the imposition of either forces or absolute positions. The interactions include slapping, carrying, and shooting objects[4]. Naturally, the execution rate of the simulator depends on both the complexity and the number of objects being simulated. When the simulator runs more slowly, there is a higher ratio of real time to simulated time. But worse than the loss of speed are the effects of changing the

relative velocity between the objects and the user's hand.[5] For example, the user's hand will move faster with respect to the objects when the simulator is slower, and it will appear as if the objects are hit harder. Thus the ungated simulation displays both the unnatural effects of time-varying gravity, and time-varying hand-slapping forces as the contents of the room change. To simulate the flow of time more faithfully, and keep the relative ratio of hand velocity to simulated object velocity constant, we gated the simulator at a constant rate equal to the lowest expected simulation rate.

The ease of integrating the simulator shows the flexibility of our architecture. The simulator is connected into the Virtual World as a server. It communicates its state changes directly with the Dialogue Manager. The amount of state needed to be communicated to the Dialogue Man-

Figure 2.   Rubber Rocks: Two users are interacting with Rubber Rocks. Each is wearing a baseball cap with a position sensor attached for head-motion parallax. Gloves and position sensors are used for gesture input. The two users are looking at a room from opposite sides. Within the room are a number of flexible objects. For this photograph, the simulator is frozen at a time when both users are tugging at a single brick-shaped object. Hands are also displayed in the scene reflecting both the position and the gesture of the users' own hands. Note that one user is viewing the scene on a twenty-three inch display while the second is using a large-screen projection system. Both views are monoscopic for purposes of the photograph.

---

4   Shooting is the application of a force on an object in the direction the user is pointing.
5   Velocity of the hand is computed by the tracker, while the velocity of simulated objects is computed by the simulator. The interface dialog scales the hand velocity to be in units that are proportional to the size of the simulation space.

ager is relatively small, consisting of object collisions, fractures, creations and deletions. The Dialogue Manager passes to the simulator the hand positions, forces and positions to be imposed on objects, and requests for object creation and deletion.

Graphical data is sent directly from the simulator to the renderer. The Dialogue Manager coordinates this connection by directing the simulator to pipe its output to the renderers. The graphical data is sent in the form of surfaces to describe the current shape of the flexible objects. This relatively large amount of data bypasses the Dialogue Manager for performance reasons, but also because it is not needed for computing the state of the interface dialogue.

DISPLAY METAPHOR

The display metaphor of Rubber Rocks mimics a box-shaped room located behind the display surface. In fact, the glass surface of the display forms the near wall of the room. The room is displayed stereoscopically to provide additional depth cueing. However, with traditional stereoscopic displays, the image appears to follow the observer as their head moves. But, by tracking the position of the observer's head and by using an appropriate shear[6], the room is made to appear stationary behind the screen.

The size of the room is scaled to the size of the display. When using a small 19" display, the room is really more like a box. Relatively small amounts of hand motion result in the traversal of the virtual hand across the box. Similarly, small head motions from side to side will change the view from looking down the left edge of the box to looking down the right edge. Correspondingly, with large screen projection, larger motions are needed to be consistent with having a larger virtual box behind the screen.

INTERACTION SCENARIOS: ACTIONS AND GOALS

Interaction scenarios contain two components: the possible sequences of actions the users can perform, and the goals they are trying to achieve. Consider, for example, alternative ways of controlling the camera position in Rubber Rocks. During initial debug and test, the position is controlled by filling in a form. Specific-level rule sets are written for form-widget input and events are passed on to higher-level rule sets for the control of the graphics camera position. When a 3D-tracker device becomes operational, identical events are generated by a new specific-level rule set for the tracker. This general approach allows us to substitute a variety of devices and interaction techniques without having to rewrite any of the higher level rule sets.

In a similar manner, we created scenarios with alternative goals. For general audiences, Rubber Rocks was initially demonstrated as a competitive game for multiple users.

Subsequently a non-competitive version was created. In Rubber Rocks a "game" is a collection of the highest level of dialogue rules. It is generally not concerned with low-level events like hand gestures, head tracking, or graphics rendering frame rates. Sometimes, it may not even be concerned with the number of users playing the game. Rather, it is more concerned with very high-level events such as game-begin and game-end, the creation and deletion of objects, and possibly point scoring. Because the game rule sets are only concerned with this restricted set of events, we are able to quickly devise a variety of games with different goals. We can also select among these different games on the fly by enabling/disabling rules.

Of particular importance, all these alternative interactions were achieved without any changes to the simulator, the world's content.

TWO-PERSON VIRTUAL WORLD

Virtual Worlds are an ideal environment for collaboration [3]. The architecture chosen to implement Rubber Rocks has enabled us to quickly extend it into a multi-user system. The basic notion is that each user has a Dialogue Manager for their interaction with the Virtual World. Each Dialogue Manager sends commands and information to the simulator (see Real-Time Simulation). Connections just between the Dialogue Managers and the simulator would be sufficient if the participants did not need to interact with each other. To accommodate interaction between users, a connection is made between each of the Dialogue Managers. For example, each user would like to see the other's hand within the room. The hand location and posture need to be passed between Dialogue Managers. Since the Dialogue Manager we use is event-based [12], we capture events of interest and broadcast them to the other Dialogue Manager. In the case of the hand data, hand-data events are captured and broadcast to the other Dialogue Manager. Once the remote Dialogue Manager receives the hand data, it is able to update its remote-hand state information and pass the information on to the renderer for display. In addition, this information can be used to determine whether the local and remote hands are colliding. If so, the dialogue can generate events that ultimately result in hand clapping sounds. Also, if one user's dialogue is stopped, the other user's dialogue is unaffected (except that the remote hand stops moving).

Higher-level events in the dialogue structure are of most interest when designing for multi-user Virtual Worlds. In the hand example, the hand information is an aggregate of hand position and hand gesture information. Other interesting information in Rubber Rocks includes the beginning and end of a game sequence. When either user's dialogue begins or ends a game, the game begin/end event is passed

---

6   The view for each eye is created by virtual cameras kept parallel to each other and perpendicular to the screen.

to the other user's dialogue so it can coordinate the interface for such aspects of the interface as game scoring. More importantly, by focusing on the higher-level, and therefore more abstract, events, we need not consider the specifics of I/O devices and views into the Virtual World. For example, the abstract events are the same regardless of whether the input was spoken or chosen from a menu. Another advantage of this high-level approach to sharing of information between dialogues is the reduction of state information that needs to be communicated between Dialogue Managers.

SYSTEM CONFIGURATION

Rubber Rocks is implemented on a distributed UNIX platform. The clients and servers communicate with each other through TCP sockets and therefore Virtual Worlds can easily be implemented across heterogeneous processors [1, 12].

The distributed architecture provides the computational capacity needed for richer Virtual Worlds with complex behavior. Furthermore, the functional partitioning requires relatively low communications bandwidth. Rubber Rocks supporting two users runs on a local area network of seven IBM RISC System/6000 machines. The flexible object simulator runs on a dedicated machine due to its compute-intensive nature. Each user's interface runs on two machines – one for rendering the 3D graphics and one for running the dialogue. Two machines are dedicated to servers driving the I/O devices – gloves, 3D trackers, speech synthesizers and recognizers, and sound generators.

CONCLUSION

We built a multi-user demonstration system coupling a flexible-object simulator with a multisensory user interface, including hand motion and gestures, speech input and output, sound output, and 3-D stereoscopic graphics with head-motion parallax. The experience with the implementation of Rubber Rocks supports the basic architecture for Virtual Worlds we have developed. The flexibility of the system stems from the initial design decision to separate *style* from *content*. In addition, we developed a discipline for writing dialogues based on a conceptual hierarchy. As a result, the alternative interaction scenarios for Rubber Rocks were easily created and could be selected on the fly. This architecture also facilitated the creation of a shared, multi-user Virtual World.

We believe that Virtual Worlds rich in content will contain real-time simulations. Rubber Rocks demonstrated the integration of a simulator into our architectural framework. The simulator is inserted into the Virtual World as a server, requiring relatively little bandwidth to communicate state changes to the Dialogue Manager.

Rubber Rocks is the third in a series of increasingly complex Virtual Worlds that we have implemented on this ar-

chitectural base. In the future, other simulation servers, such as constraint solvers and autonomous agents, will act as building blocks for the construction of even richer Virtual Worlds.

ACKNOWLEDGMENTS

We would like to acknowledge Wayne L. Wooten and Jeremy Stone for developing system components. In addition, we would like to thank Ron Frank for his contributions to making the Rubber Rocks demonstrations at CHI'91 and SIGGRAPH'91 possible.

References

1. Appino, Perry A., Lewis, J. Bryan, Koved, Lawrence, Ling, Daniel T., Rabenhorst, David A., and Codella, Christopher F. An Architecture for Virtual Worlds. *Presence*, 1(1), 1991.

2. Bacon, R., Gerth, J., Norton, A., Sweeney, P., and Turk, G. Tipsy Turvy. *SIGGRAPH Electronic Theater*, 1989.

3. Blanchard, C., Burgess, S., Harvill, Y., Lanier, J., Lasko, A., Oberman, M., and M. Teitel. Reality Built for Two: A Virtual Reality Tool. *Proceedings of the 1990 Symposium on Interactive 3D Graphics (Snowbird, Utah)*, 35-36, ACM, New York, 1990.

4. Brooks, F.P., Jr. Walkthrough - A Dynamic Graphics System for Simulating Virtual Buildings. *Proceedings of the 1986 Workshop on Interactive 3D Graphics (Chapel Hill, North Carolina)*, 9-21, ACM, New York, 1987.

5. Brooks, F.P., Jr. Grasping Reality Through Illusion -- Interactive Graphics Serving Science. *CHI '88 Proceedings*, 1-11, ACM, May 1988.

6. Esposito, Chris, Bricken, Meredith, and Butler, Keith. Building the VSX Demonstration: Operations with Virtual Aircraft in Virtual Space. *CHI '91 Conference*, ACM, April 1991. Short Talk

7. Fisher, S.S., McGreevy, M., Humphries, J., and W. Robinett. Virtual Environment Display System. *Proceedings of the 1986 Workshop on Interactive 3-D Graphics (Chapel Hill, North Carolina)*, 1986.

8. Green, M. A Survey of Three Dialogue Models. *ACM Transactions on Graphics*, 5(3):244-275, July 1986.

9. M. Green. Virtual Reality User Interface: Tools and Techniques. In T.S. Chua and T.L. Kunii, editors, *CG International '90*, 51-68, Springer-Verlag, Tokyo, 1990.

10. Hill, R.D. Supporting Concurrency, Communication, and Synchronization in Human-Computer Interaction: The Sassafras UIMS. *ACM Transactions on Graphics*, 5(3):179-210, July 1986.

11. Jacob, R.J.K. A Specification Language for Direct-Manipulation User Interfaces. *ACM Transactions on Graphics*, 5(4):283-317, October 1986.

12. Lewis, J.B., Koved, L., and Ling, D.T. Dialogue Structures for Virtual Worlds. *CHI '91 Proceedings*, 1991.

13. Norton, A., Turk, G., Bacon, B., Gerth, J., and Sweeney, P. Animation of fracture by physical modeling. *The Visual Computer*, 7:210-219, 1991.

14. Olsen, Jr., D. MIKE: The Menu Interaction Kontrol Environment. *ACM Transactions on Graphics*, 5(4):318-344, October 1986.

15. Patterson, J. F., Hill, R. D., Rohall, S. L., and Meeks, W. S. Rendezvous: An Architecture for Synchronous Multi-User Applications. *CSCW'90 Proceedings*, 317-328, ACM, Los Angeles, CA, October 1990.

16. Pfaff, G. E., Ed. *User Interface Management Systems*. Springer-Verlag, Berlin, 1985.

17. Rheingold, H. *Virtual Reality*, chapter 8. Summit, New York, NY, 1991.

18. Rhyne, J.R. Extensions to C for Interface Programming. *Proceedings of ACM SIGGRAPH, Symposium on User Interface Software (Banff, Alberta, Canada)*, ACM, October 1988.

19. Smith, R. B. The Alternate Reality Kit: An Animated Environment for Creating Interaction Simulations. *Proceedings of the 1986 IEEE Computer Society Workshop on Visual Languages*, 99-106, 1986.

20. Sweeney, P., Norton, A., Bacon, R., Haumann, D., and Turk, G. Modelling Physical Objects for Simulation. *Proceedings Winter Simulation Conference*, Phoenix, Arizona, 1991.

21. Wiecha, C., Bennett. W., Boies, S., and Gould, J. Generating Highly Interactive User Interfaces. *CHI '89 Proceedings*, 277-282, 1989.

22. Zeltzer, D., Pieper, S., and D. Sturman. An Integrated Graphical Simulation Platform. *Proceedings of Graphics Interface '89*, 266-274, 1989.

THE ABSTRACTION-LINK-VIEW PARADIGM: USING CONSTRAINTS TO CONNECT USER INTERFACES TO APPLICATIONS

Ralph D. Hill

Bellcore
445 South Street, 2D-295
Morristown, NJ 07962-1910

(201) 829-4581
rdh@thumper.bellcore.com

ABSTRACT

The goal of the RENDEZVOUS™ project is to build interactive systems that are used by multiple users from multiple workstations, simultaneously. This goal caused us to choose an architecture that requires a clean run-time separation of user interfaces from applications. Such a separation has long been a stated goal of UIMS researchers, but it is difficult to achieve. A key technical reason for the difficulty is that modern direct manipulation interfaces require extensive communication between the user interface and the application to provide semantic feedback. We discuss several communications mechanisms that have been used in the past, and present our approach — the Abstraction-Link-View paradigm. Links are objects whose sole responsibility is to facilitate communication between the abstraction objects (application) and the view objects (user interfaces). The Abstraction-Link-View paradigm relies on concurrency and a fast but powerful constraint system.

CATEGORIES AND SUBJECT DESCRIPTORS: H.5.2 **[Information Interfaces and Presentation]:** User Interfaces--*user interface managements systems*; H.5.3 **[Information Interfaces and Presentation]:** Group and Organization Interfaces--*synchronous interaction*.

ADDITIONAL KEY WORDS AND PHRASES: dialog independence, constraints

INTRODUCTION

Dialog independence, the separation of user interface from application, is a key concept underlying most modern User Interface Management System (UIMS) research and has much to recommend it. There has been a lot of discussion

---

™ RENDEZVOUS is a trademark of Bell Communications Research, Inc.

of the advantages of dialogue independence and problems with the required run-time separation of the user interface from application (e.g., [23], [6], [3], [8], [7]). For us, the key problem is: modern direct-manipulation (DM) interfaces require a lot of information exchange between the user interface and application, in order to provide semantic feedback.

Perhaps it is because of the difficulties with separation that there are many papers in the UIMS literature that discuss the problem, but few reported solutions. We conjecture that while it is easy to make abstract arguments for a clean separation, the need to produce interfaces within financial and temporal budgets often takes precedence over engineering elegance. However, our problem domain *requires* a run-time partitioning into user interface and underlying application, with efficient communication between these two components.

OUR PROBLEM DOMAIN: MULTI-USER USER INTERFACES

Our application domain is based on human-to-human communication augmented by computer-based tools. We are particularly interested in the creation of distributed conversational props. *Conversational props* are artifacts that facilitate conversations. It could either be the object of the conversation, or it could assist the conversation. Examples of common physical conversational props include whiteboards and physical models. In the education domain, photographs, maps and models of atoms and molecules are examples of conversational props. The teacher uses these props to focus the conversation and to illustrate important points.

When conversations become spatially distributed, say, using video tele-conferencing, the usefulness of physical props is severely impaired. The props cannot be shared or manipulated across great distances.

Physical props can be replaced by shared computer applications in the style of [21], [22] and [4]. A shared computer application can present information to multiple users simultaneously, and let remote users point to interesting aspects of the information, or even modify it, allowing all users to immediately see the updated information. One could think of a shared computer application as a simple multi-person virtual meeting space accessed from window-based terminals. Instead of meeting in a physical conference room with physical charts, models and whiteboards, conference participants can meet in a virtual space, communicating via videophone and shared electronic charts, models, and whiteboards.

We are building the RENDEZVOUS language [12] and architecture [19] to assist in the development of shared computer applications which will be used as conversational props. The highest level of our run-time architecture is illustrated in figure 1. We have chosen to have one centralized, shared abstraction (the application semantics) with one view (or user interface) per person.

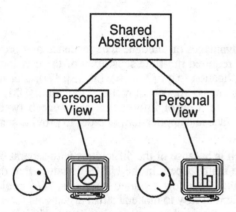

Figure 1. Abstract architecture of
RENDEZVOUS applications.

We made this architectural decision to make many of the hard problems in multi-user systems more tractable. For example, replicated architectures, which have a view and abstraction for each user, make it much harder to provide correct state information to users who join late, and to keep all of the interfaces synchronized [2]. The cost of our architecture is that it forces us to cleanly separate each multi-user application into an abstraction and several, possibly different, views.

The remainder of this paper concentrates on the technical problem of supporting communication between the shared abstraction and the multiple views. "Multiple views" could mean one view (i.e., a traditional single user application) or no views (i.e., a multi-user application is waiting for users to connect to it). The Abstraction-Link-View paradigm is not restricted to interfaces with two or more users and, in particular, is applicable to single user applications.

INTER-MODULE COMMUNICATIONS MECHANISMS FOR INTERACTIVE SOFTWARE

The idea of separating the application from the user interface has been around for a long time, and a variety of approaches to connecting the separated components have been tried. In this section we discuss callbacks and constraints, the two most advanced communications mechanisms currently in use.

Callbacks

Callbacks are a mechanism for communicating among modules that relies on one module, A, registering a procedure p, with another module, B. The registration specifies the conditions under which B will call p.

The Smalltalk Model-View-Controller (MVC) paradigm [13] is based on three objects: the *model* implements or interfaces to the semantics of the application; the *view* presents graphical output to the user; and the *controller* interprets user input. The model object allows view and controller objects to register callbacks with it. Whenever some aspect of the model changes in any way, the callback methods are called. Views and controllers communicate with each other, and back to the model, via conventional method call.

The X Toolkit [17] uses callbacks, but in the opposite direction from MVC. In the X Toolkit, application objects register callback procedures with widgets (user interface objects). When the specified event occurs, the callback procedure in the application is called.

There are three key problems with callbacks. First, they are asymmetric. One module must announce in advance when it wants to be called by the other module. Care must be used in identifying and maintaining the master-slave relationship. Second, the communication is limited by the granularity of the callbacks and the types of conditions (for callback) that can be easily specified. In MVC, and most of its descendants, the module that is called back will often have to query the calling object and compare its current state with its previous state, in order to determine what has changed. Finally, the asymmetry and granularity problems both require that an additional communications mechanism be supported, resulting in complexity and possible confusion.

Constraints and Active Values

Active values can be viewed as variables that allow other objects to register functions with them. Whenever the value of an active value changes, it calls the functions that have been registered with it. Many active value systems are much more elaborate than this, allowing more control over when and how the functions are called. Active value systems are a lot like callback systems, where callback procedures are registered with individual variables rather than objects.[1]

Constraint maintenance systems provide a fast and convenient way to maintain relations among values. In general, constraint maintenance systems allow a set of source variables to be linked to a target variable such that whenever any of the source variables changes, the value of the target variable is set to a specified function of the source variables. Constraints are similar in functionality to active values, but are a higher-level construct, with simpler and more compact specifications, and can result in more efficient execution [9].

---

[1] Active values and callbacks, as discussed above, are both examples of *procedural attachment*. We have defined callbacks to be procedures attached to objects, while active values are slots (within objects) that have attached procedures.

Constraints or active values are used for communication between the user interface and application in several UIMSs including: Garnet [16], which uses constraints in a MVC like architecture, Peridot [15], which used active values, and GRINS [18], which used simple constraints. While there is this experience with constraints as a communication mechanism, the constraints are often used in ad hoc ways, linking values, not objects.

THE ABSTRACTION-LINK-VIEW PARADIGM

While constraints are promising as a powerful communications mechanism, there is little experience using them in a structured manner to link objects. On the other hand, callbacks have been used extensively to link objects, but they are a poor communications mechanism. Our goal in RENDEZVOUS is to gain the advantages of both of these approaches, in the context of multi-user direct manipulation interfaces.

The Abstraction-Link-View paradigm (ALV, pronounced "al-vee") is an architecture and programming method for building multi-user or CSCW applications. ALV is designed to provide rapid feedback (largely) independent of the number of users, while supporting a clear separation of application from user interface at run-time. Redundancy, in the form of caching in the user interface, is used to ensure rapid feedback. Constraints are used to automatically maintain consistency between the caches and the "real" values in the application.

ALV is based on separating an interactive program into three main types of run-time components: abstractions, views and links. A multi-user interactive application implemented using ALV will typically have one abstraction and several views (at least one per user). There will be one link for each view, which connects the view to the abstraction. (See Figure 2).[2]

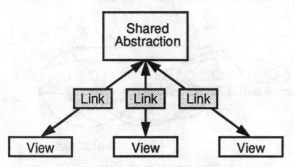

Figure 2. Basic ALV Architecture.

The *abstraction* stores, or provides access to, the abstract information of the application. In the multi-user context, this is all the information that is common to all views (although it is not necessary that all views show all this information).

---

[2] It is possible and useful to have multiple abstractions, and more than one link per view. For example, you might want to take two related abstractions, and make them appear to the user as a single application. This is trivially supported by ALV, but, for simplicity, we only discuss the single abstraction case in this paper.

The *views* present the information to the users, and allow the users to modify the information or the display of the information. All views do not have to be the same, for example, numeric information could be presented in bar chart and pie chart views (see figure 1). One user could have multiple views.

In addition to view-specific information (like pie slice colors in the pie chart view, and bar widths in the bar chart view) each view has all of the information from the abstraction that is required to generate its display. In the case of the pie and bar charts example, the abstraction would store the numbers that are being presented as pie slices and bars. The views would have this information as well, but in the form of bar heights and slice angles, rather than raw numeric values. This redundant, but not replicated, information allows the views to quickly update their displays, even when access to the abstraction is impaired by network delays or high loads on the abstraction.

The *links* are bundles of constraints that maintain consistency between the views and abstraction. In particular, they ensure that the redundant information stored in the views and abstraction is kept consistent. To ensure this consistency, they must, for example, transform bar heights to the raw underlying numbers, and vice versa.

Using ALV, pie chart views can be ignorant of raw numbers, and be only concerned with sizes of wedges. Similarly bar chart views need only be concerned with bar heights. It is the job of the links to map between the underlying data, and the presentation. This keeps the views and the abstractions simple, and encourages re-use of both, which in turn aids rapid prototyping. This gain does not come at the cost of complexity in the links — in practice most links are very simple.

ALV and Hierarchical Toolkits

The run-time architectures of many user interface toolkits are based on a tree of objects at run-time (e.g. Interviews [14], Tube [10]). The RENDEZVOUS architecture is similar, but is based on multiple trees. Each view is a tree of view objects, and each abstraction is a tree of abstraction objects. The links are implemented as a set of objects, where (typically) each link object links one view object to one abstraction object. More complex link structures are possible, but only occasionally needed.

Within a given interface, all the view trees do not have to be isomorphic to the abstraction tree. Typically, the view trees have many more objects (to supply user interface detail). Thus many view objects will not be linked to any abstraction object. (See figure 5 in the next section for an example of this.)

The structures of the trees may change at run-time, either due to re-organization, or the addition or deletion of objects. To ensure that all the views and the abstraction are synchronized, the links must be able to alter the structure of the abstraction or views. This requires links that can move objects within the hierarchy, as well as create and destroy objects.

ALV AND THE RENDEZVOUS LANGUAGE

We have developed the RENDEZVOUS programming language to implement interactive programs that allow multiple users to simultaneously interact with a single instance of an application. The language is an extended object-oriented Lisp. RENDEZVOUS objects are very light-weight processes, and consist of slots, simple multi-way constraints (similar in spirit to the one-way constraints of Garnet [16] and Apogee [9]), and event-handlers for processing input events (derived from Sassafras [11]). The constraints and event-handlers replace the methods of traditional object-oriented programming languages.

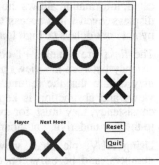

Figure 3. X and O players' views of Tic-Tac-Toe game.

Figure 3 shows the X and O players' views of a Tic-Tac-Toe game we have implemented in the RENDEZVOUS language. In general, multi-player games are good for illustrating the problems associated with multi-user interactive systems. For example, this game illustrates:

Synchronized Views
> Both players get identical views of the board.

Customized Views
> Each player's view is customized with the player indicator. As well, the players can position their board arbitrarily in their window and resize their window.

Enforced Turn Taking
> Players can only leave a mark on the board when it is their turn to move.

Freedom for Simultaneous Action
> Both players can quit or press the reset button at any time.[3]

Bringing Latecomers Up-to-date
> If the X player's view is created first, the X player can place an X before the O player's view is created. The O player's view will automatically be brought up-to-date when it is created.

The run-time structure of this application, at an abstract level, is an abstraction linked to two views (figure 4).

---

[3] It may be more "correct" to make the reset button accessible only to the player who is currently allowed to move. We chose to make it always accessible to illustrate support for simultaneous action.

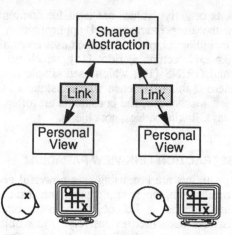

Figure 4. Abstract structure of two-user game.

Each view is really a hierarchy of view objects, for example, the board is a rectangle with nine cells as children. The abstraction is also a hierarchy.

The structure of the links in this program is driven by the structure of the abstraction hierarchy. The abstraction hierarchy consists of a root with nine cell objects as children. The root stores general information on the game such as which player moved first in this game, and which player moves next. The root could also contain code to detect winners, and keep track of the score. The cell objects store the state of the cell (x, o or blank) and their row and column indices.

Two link classes were written for the Tic-Tac-Toe game. One links the root of the view hierarchy to the root of the abstraction. The other links cell objects in the view to cell objects in the abstraction. Figure 5 shows the structure of the abstraction hierarchy and a view hierarchy with the links that connect them. For simplicity, we show only three of the nine cells in each hierarchy.

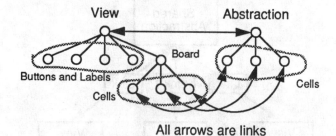

Figure 5. Structure of hierarchies and links in Tic-Tac-Toe (simplified).

The definition of the link class ttt-game-link (which links the root of the view hierarchy to the root of the abstraction) is shown in figure 6. It is a sub-class of Link and defines three dependencies (constraints). The Link class is a RENDEZVOUS library class that defines the slots "view" and "abstraction," and some constraints that will take some clean-up action when the view terminates.

Constraints in RENDEZVOUS look like Common Lisp assignment expressions using the the Common Lisp "setf" assignment operator. Setf takes two parameters, a

```
(defClass ttt-game-link
  :super-class Link
  :dependencies
  ((setf (turn view)
         (turn abstraction))
   (setf (reset-pending view)
         (reset-pending abstraction))
   (setf (reset-pending abstraction)
         (reset-pending view))))
```

Figure 6. Definition of ttt-game-link.

target for the assignment, and a new value.

The first constraint in ttt-game-link has the turn slot of the view, (turn view), as a target, and the turn slot of the abstraction, (turn abstraction), as the new value. The constraint system will ensure that whenever the value of (turn abstraction) changes, the target, (turn view) will be updated. Since the turn in the view does not change on its own, this ensures that the turn in the view and the turn in the abstraction are always the same.

The second constraint copies the value of the reset-pending slot from the abstraction to the reset-pending slot of the view. The third constraint implements the reverse constraint. Thus, the last two constraints implement a cycle that copies the value of the reset-pending slot from the view to the abstraction and vice versa, ensuring that these two values are always the same, no matter where the change originates.

```
(defClass ttt-cell-link
  :super-class Link
  :dependencies
  ((setf (rel-position view)
         (create-position
           :x (* 100  (cell-column abstraction))
           :y (* 100  (cell-row abstraction))))
   (setf (state view) (state abstraction))
   (setf (state abstraction) (state view))))
```

Figure 7. Definition of the ttt-cell-link class.

The definition of the ttt-cell-link class (the link between cells in the view and cells in the abstraction) is shown in figure 7. This class defines three constraints. The first computes the relative position (with respect to the parent object — the board) of the view cell from the column and row indices of the abstraction. In this case the relative position of the view is the target, and the constraint system must update the target when either of the row or column index changes. The last two constraints create a cycle of constraints that keep the abstraction and view versions of the cell state information consistent.

Starting up a Tic-Tac-Toe game requires creating an abstraction hierarchy, two view hierarchies, all of the links, and setting the view and abstraction slots of the links to point at the appropriate objects. This sounds like a lot of objects to create. It practice, it is relatively easy. The abstraction and view hierarchies are created simply by creating their root objects. The substructure is filled in automatically from the class definitions. Once the hierarchies are created the link between the roots can be created, and a simple loop can be used to create the links between cells. As each link object is created, its view and abstrac-

tion slots must be initialized to the appropriate objects in the view and abstraction hierarchies.

ALV and the RENDEZVOUS language have been used to build several other interfaces, including: a card table that supports up to 4 players playing almost any card game by dragging cards on a virtual card table, and into and out of "hands" [20], an elaborate multi-person electronic white board, a collaborative user interface design tool, and many simpler test and demonstration programs.

PROGRAMMING LANGUAGE FEATURES TO SUPPORT ALV

ALV is very demanding in terms of the programming language features it requires. On the surface, links appear to be simply objects with constraints. This would suggest that the object and constraint systems used in Garnet [16] or Apogee [9] may be all that is required. Unfortunately, neither system provides a sufficiently powerful substrate to support ALV. The key requirements of ALV, beyond a basic object-oriented programming language, are:

Multi-way Constraints
> Most user interface construction tools that support constraints support only one-way constraints (e.g., Garnet, Apogee and Tube [10]). A key feature of these systems is only one constraint can be inbound on a value. Links require multiple constraints to be inbound on a value. This implies links require multi-way constraint maintenance systems, since these systems are capable of maintaining consistency in the presence of multiple inbound constraints.

Indirect Sources and Targets for Constraints
> The constraints in links rely on indirect access to slot values in the linked objects. By indirecting off on the slots "view" and "abstraction" the individual constraint specifications are kept simple, and it is easy to create and install links.

Constraints as Inter-Process Communication
> To ensure all users get fair access to processing resources, ALV requires that each view and abstraction hierarchy run as a separate process.[4] This means that the constraints in the links are being used for interprocess communication. Ideally, the constraint system should not just support cross processes constraints, but (like the RENDEZVOUS constraint system) go on to try to protect the programmer from dead-locks and races.

Constraints to Maintain Structure
> User actions will often result in adding and removing objects from the display. Since the links provide the only contact between abstractions and views, the links, and hence, the constraints, must be able to create and destroy objects, as well as restructure the run-time tree. (This can create problems for indirect sources and targets. A discussion of these problems,

---

[4] We go beyond this in RENDEZVOUS, making each object a feather weight process.

and their solutions, is beyond the scope of this paper.)

Some of these features are available from a variety of sources. For example, Garnet supports indirection for source variables in constraints [24], and Delta-Blue [5] supports multi-way constraints. Basic interprocess support can be trivially added by ensuring that no process scheduling occurs during constraint propagation (i.e., constraint propagation must be either done in a monitor or otherwise protected). The use of constraints to maintain structure may be unique to the Rendezvous constraint system. The RENDEZVOUS constraint system is (currently) unique in satisfying all four requirements.[5]

Discussion

The above says that a very powerful constraint system and a multi-process object system are needed to implement ALV. It is tempting to ask "Is it worth the effort?"

We answer this question with three claims that are based on the experience of seven programmers implementing three complex multi-user interfaces, in the RENDEZVOUS language using the ALV paradigm:

1) User interface implementors will want all of this power anyway. Powerful constraint systems and multi-process object systems make advanced interfaces easier to implement.

2) Link objects are far too useful and powerful to ignore. They are an efficient and elegant solution to a difficult problem. The move toward CSCW and shared computing environments emphasizes the need for communications mechanisms like link objects.

3) Using the constraint system for communication is not a performance problem — graphics update consumes far more processor resources.

ALV FEATURES AND ISSUES

In our experience, ALV has many advantages over previous proposals for communicating between user interfaces and applications. Foremost for us is that it makes it easy to build multi-user interfaces where each user can have a different view. There are many other advantages, mostly at the software engineering level — they make it easy to produce reliable, easily maintained code.

Reusability and Independence. All communication is implemented in the link objects. No communications support is coded into the view or abstraction objects. Thus, abstractions and views need very little information about each other (and often have none). Because views and abstractions are independent of each other, they are simpler to design and implement. The simpler designs, which are not heavily influenced by specific uses of the objects, results in greater reusability.

To illustrate the strength of the independence of views and abstractions consider an abstraction object that maintains a set of numbers. Assume we have a bar-graph view object

in our library that we want to use to display these numbers. We simply write a link object that contains constraints that link the values in the abstraction object with the bar-height slots in the bar-graph view object. The implementors of the view and abstraction need not agree on a protocol for inter-object communication or scaling of the values — it is trivial for the link to do this. To use a pie chart view to display the same numbers, or a different abstraction with the bar-graph view requires, at most, a new link. Again, links are in general trivial to write, so this is a trivial requirement.

Redundant Information. When decomposing an interactive system into user interface (view) and application (abstraction) components it is almost certain that there will be information that properly belongs on both sides of the division. Earlier approaches often ignored this enigmatic problem. ALV acknowledges, and exploits the inherent redundancy to improve interactive performance. Abstraction objects contain all the information they require to do their processing. Similarly views contain all the information they require to do their processing and provide feedback. The links keep the redundant information consistent.

Links as Inter-Process Communication. Multi-user interfaces will involve lots of concurrency. This is unavoidable. Concurrent programming is usually considered an advanced topic. This suggest yet another source of difficulty when building multi-user interface. ALV, through the use of constraints, avoids this difficulty. In our experience, constraints and links are easily used interprocess communication mechanisms, even for programmers who have minimal experience with concurrent programming.

Views onto Views. In ALV there is nothing special about abstraction objects, so any object, even a view object, could be an abstraction object (figure 8). With suitable link and view objects, this would make the internal values in the view objects accessible to the user. This is the architecture of a user interface editor and debugger that allows direct observation, and arbitrary manipulation, of any view object, while the interface is running.

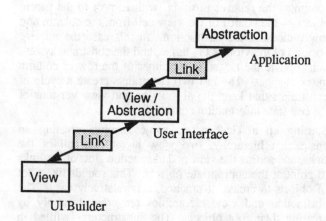

Figure 8. Views onto Views.

---

[5] The full functionality and implementation of the RENDEZVOUS constraint system will be discussed in a forthcoming paper.

ALV VS. MVC

The Model-View-Controller (MVC) [13] architecture is probably the most widely cited and imitated objected-oriented user interface architecture. Therefore, it is appropriate to compare ALV with MVC and some of its descendants.

MVC decomposes an interactive system into three components: model - implements the underlying semantics, view - presents graphical output to the user, and controller - interprets user input. The view and controller register callbacks with the model. Whenever any aspect of the model changes, the callbacks are notified. It is then up to the view and controller to determine what has changed, and what, if anything, to do. All objects run in a single process.

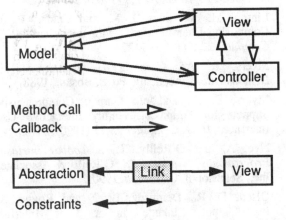

Figure 9. MVC vs. ALV.

Figure 9 compares the basic structure of MVC to ALV. The ALV abstraction object corresponds to the MVC model object. The MVC view and controller objects are combined in the single ALV view object. While MVC mixes method call and callback to provide inter-object communication, ALV uses only constraints. Also, ALV's constraints are installed and maintained by the link objects, so the view can ignore the abstraction and vice versa. This is not true of MVC, where each object must explicitly communicate with the other two.

Many MVC derivatives (e.g., the Andrew Toolkit [1]) combine the view and controller into one object like ALV's view. This reduces some of the communication, but does not provide the advantages of having a third object in charge of communication like ALV's link objects. The following points apply to MVC and most MVC derivatives.

Modularity and Reusability. In MVC the view and controller need to know about the model's internal structure in order to know what has changed and how to react. This makes it difficult to modify any single component without affecting the others.

Callbacks vs. Constraints. MVC callbacks are called when any aspect of the model changes. This is too coarse. But, all callbacks that could possibly be needed must be designed in from the beginning. Calling back on *any* change guarantees that all possible callback conditions are

supported.

Callbacks make it impractical to have a third party manage callbacks like links manage communication in ALV. Thus, the use of callbacks forces the communication to be procedurally coded into all components involved in the communication. This limits the reusability of the components.

Compared to constraints, callbacks are quite static. REN-DEZVOUS constraints automatically retarget themselves as views and view objects are created, restructured or deleted. If callbacks were used, procedural code would have to be written for each interface to ensure that callbacks are registered and de-registered as needed.

Multi-User Interfaces. In theory MVC can support multi-user interfaces with multiple view-controller pairs per model. There are, however, practical problems dealing with concurrency and the bandwidth requirements of the callback protocol. To overcome these problems Shared ARK [21] fully replicates all three components for each user instead of using multiple view/controller pairs per model.[6] This simple replicated approach can only be used when all users have identical interfaces.

SUMMARY

Our goal in the development of ALV and the RENDEZVOUS language has been to support the rapid development of multi-user direct manipulation interfaces. We chose an architecture based on a single shared application, in order to simplify some multi-user problems [19]. Given this decision, ALV was developed to allow multiple user interfaces (views) communicate with the single centralized application (abstraction). ALV is based on the use of links, which are bundles of constraints, to connect views and abstractions. The links are independent objects that install the constraints. Much of the power of ALV comes from the declarative nature of constraints and the fact that neither the views nor abstractions have the communication constraints coded into them. The views and abstractions ignore each other. This makes it easy to reuse views and abstractions in other contexts, and means that it is easy to change one without changing the other.

The independence of views and abstractions, combined with the obvious graphical nature of links, suggests that it is possible to build a graphical direct manipulation user interface builder that allows non-programmers to build interactive systems by selecting views and abstractions from a library, and drawing in the necessary links. The resulting interfaces could support a wide range of graphical direct manipulations with semantic feedback. It is rare for non-programming interface construction tools to support this level of interaction with the application.

Within the RENDEZVOUS project, ALV has been very successful in simplifying the construction of multi-user interfaces. We have found that ALV has properties that are close to ideal for the implementation of multi-user interfaces:

---

[6] Private communication with Randall Smith.

- strict modularity and dialogue independence,
- support for multiple simultaneous user interfaces to a single instance of an application, where the interfaces can be identical or radically different,
- support for rapid semantic feedback,
- conceptual simplicity, and
- a simple programming model, even in the presence of concurrency.

ACKNOWLEDGMENTS

The Abstraction-Link-View paradigm evolved over many months of discussions among a group of people. Major contributors include John Patterson, Steve Rohall, Nathaniel Borenstein, and Wayne Wilner. The presentation in this paper has been improved with help from Tom Brinck, Nathaniel Borenstein, Jacob Nielsen, and Louis Gomez.

REFERENCES

1. Borenstein, N. S., *Multimedia Applications Development with the Andrew Toolkit*, Prentice Hall, Englewood Cliffs, New Jersey, 1990.

2. Crowley, T., Milazzo, P., Baker, E., Forsdick, H. and Tomlinson, R., MMConf: An Infrastructure for Building Shared Multimedia Applications, *Proceedings of CSCW'90*, 1990, 329-342.

3. Dance, J. R., Granor, T. E., Hill, R. D., Hudson, S. E., Meads, J., Myers, B. A. and Schulert, A., The Run-time Structure of UIMS-Supported Applications, *Computer Graphics 21*,2 (1987), 97-101.

4. Forsdick, H., Exploration into Real-time Multimedia Conferencing, *Proceedings of the Second International Symposium on Computer Message Systems*, 1985, 299-315.

5. Freeman-Benson, B. N., Maloney, J. and Borning, A., An Incremental Constraint Solver, *Communications of the ACM 33*,1 (1990), 54-63.

6. Green, M., Report on Dialogue Specification Tools, in *User Interface Management Systems*, G. Pfaff (editor), Springer-Verlag, Berlin, 1985, 9-20.

7. Hartson, H. R. and Hix, D., Human-Computer Interface Development: Concepts and Systems for Its Management, *ACM Computing Surveys 21*,1 (1989), 5-92.

8. Hartson, R., User-Interface Management Control and Communication, *IEEE Software 6*,1 (1989), 62-70.

9. Henry, T. R. and Hudson, S. E., Using Active Data in a UIMS, *Proceedings of the ACM SIGGRAPH Symposium on User Interface Software*, 1988, 167-178.

10. Herrmann, M. and Hill, R., Abstraction and Declarativeness in User Interface Development Systems — The Methodological Basis of the Composite Object Architecture, *Proceedings of the XIᵗʰ World Computer Congress*, 1989.

11. Hill, R. D., Supporting Concurrency, Communication and Synchronization in Human-Computer Interaction — the Sassafras UIMS, *ACM Trans. on Graphics 5*,3 (1986), 179-210.

12. Hill, R. D., A 2-D Graphics System for Multi-User Interactive Graphics Based on Objects and Constraints, in *Advances in Object Oriented Graphics 1*, E. Blake and P. Wisskirchen (editors), Springer-Verlag, Berlin, 1991, 67-91.

13. Krasner, G. E. and Pope, S. T., A Cookbook for Using the Model-View-Controller User Interface Paradigm in Smalltalk-80, *Journal of Object-Oriented Programming 1*,3 (1988), 26-49.

14. Linton, M., Vlissides, J. M. and Calder, P. R., Composing User Interfaces with InterViews, *IEEE Computer 22*,2 (1989), 8-22.

15. Myers, B. A., *Creating User Interfaces by Demonstration*, Academic Press, Boston, 1988.

16. Myers, B. A. and al., Garnet: Comprehensive Support for Graphical, Highly Interactive User Interfaces, *IEEE Computer 23*,11 (1990), 71-85.

17. Nye, A. and O'Reilly, T., *X Toolkit Intrinsics Programming Manual, 2Ed.*, O'Reilly & Associates, Inc., Sebastopol, California, 1990.

18. Olsen, D. R., Dempsey, E. P. and Rogge, R., Input/Output Linkage in a User Interface Management System, *Computer Graphics 19*,3 (1985), 191-197.

19. Patterson, J. F., Hill, R. D., Rohall, S. L. and Meeks, W. S., Rendezvous: An architecture for synchronous multi-user applications, *Proceedings of CSCW'90*, 1990, 317-328.

20. Rohall, S. L., Patterson, J. F. and Hill, R. D., Go Fish! A Multi-User Game in the Rendezvous System, Video tape presented as part of the formal video program at CHI'92, 1992.

21. Smith, R. B., O'Shea, T., O'Malley, C., Scanlon, E. and Taylor, J., Preliminary experiments with a distributed, multi-media, problem solving environment, *Proc. 1989 European Conference on Computer Supported Cooperative Work*, 1989.

22. Stefik, M., Foster, G., Bobrow, D. G., Kahn, K., Lanning, S. and Suchman, L., Beyond the Chalkboard: Computer Support for Collaboration and Problem Solving in Meetings, *Communications of the ACM 30*,1 (1987), 32-47.

23. Thomas, J. J. and Hamlin, G., Graphical Input Interaction Technique Workshop Summary, *Computer Graphics 17*,1 (1983), 5-30.

24. Zanden, B. V., Myers, B. A., Giuse, D. and Szekely, P., The Importance of Pointer Variables in Constraint Models, *Proc. of UIST'91*, 1991, 155-164.

Grace Meets the "Real World":
Tutoring COBOL as a Second Language

Bob Radlinski and Jean McKendree

NYNEX Science & Technology, Inc.
500 Westchester Avenue
White Plains, NY 10604
(914)644-2493
rad@nynexst.com

ABSTRACT

Grace is an intelligent tutoring system for COBOL which has been used to teach both novice and experienced programmers. While the tutor was quite effective in several classes and was designed with cognitive and interface principles in mind, we discuss a number of interesting issues that we have discovered when novice and experienced programmers used the tutor. Most of these problems are related to incompatibilities between the tutor interactions and the students' expectations in two areas: (1) the interactions with the tutor versus the interactions in their usual work environment and (2) the way in which experienced programmers solve problems. We describe these issues along with our solutions in the revised version of the tutor.

KEYWORDS: Intelligent tutoring systems, expert/novice differences, skill acquisition, task analysis, user-centered design, situated learning.

INTRODUCTION

The NYNEX AI Lab has developed Grace, an intelligent tutoring system for COBOL. Grace has been used in several classes, most recently in two courses of *COBOL as a Second Language* at New York Telephone and at Metropolitan Life Insurance Co. The students in these later courses were already programmers with various levels of experience and knowledge. They ranged from knowing 1 to 8 other languages and from having 1 to 20 years of experience in the workplace. Grace was also used in an introductory programming course with students who had no previous programming experience. Both groups will be mentioned throughout the paper.

A comparison of students who used Grace and those who did not showed that Grace is quite effective at teaching COBOL. Overall, the tutored students performed about 10 percentage points better on standardized and customized posttests than their paired counterparts in the group that did not used Grace. They also completed more COBOL programming exercises. Furthermore, the comments collected from the students about their experiences with Grace were generally positive, particularly from the less experienced programmers. Also, less instructor help was required for the tutored students, even on the class programming projects. For a more detailed discussion of these and other trials, see [5].

It is very important to point out here that the first trials of Grace, and the population for which Grace was initially intended, were done with novice programmers taking their very first programming course. Most had never used a computer before. In contrast, our later trials involved programmers experienced in languages other than COBOL. This expert-novice distinction becomes a crucial one for the issues discussed in this paper. This fortuitous circumstance allowed us to become aware of important issues which we would not have realized otherwise. However, it also meant that we were not prepared to gather quantitative measures for comparing the two populations. Therefore, the discussions in this paper will be primarily qualitative.

Grace provides a very sophisticated interface based on menus, type-in windows, and dedicated function keys. Empirical evidence shows that it takes 15 to 30 minutes for a typical student to use the system comfortably. The interface is based on similar practice tutors which have also been shown to be quite effective [2]. We feel that the interface was appropriate and easy to use as was shown by the success of our first trials with the novice students.

However, even though the tutor is undoubtedly effective, we became aware of a number of problems with both the tutor's interface and with its problem solving paradigm. Basically, these problems arose, not because of fundamentally poor design, but because of two underlying mismatches.

The students' frustrations were due, first, to inconsistencies between the interface interactions and their "real world" of programming and, second, to a mismatch between the level of the feedback and problem-solving steps in the tutor versus the level at which the students thought about the problem. In this paper, we will explore some of the sources of these mismatches along with the changes we are implementing in order to bring the tutor more into line with the expectations of the students.

MISMATCHES

The tutorial interaction with Grace is built on a production system model of an "ideal student", much like the LISP Tutor [1] and other "practice" tutors. At each step in the problem, the tutor generates all next possible steps and then compares the next attempt of the student. This technique is quite good at modeling the overt problem solving behavior of a student. However, the level of the problem solving steps are geared to the individual productions which generally corresponded to the single words or numbers in a COBOL statement. It is this granularity of interaction that created the first set of mismatches.

In Grace, the students are given a description of the problem and a portion of code that typically defines data items and other constraints of the solution. They then begin by selecting a COBOL verb from a context-sensitive menu on the right of the screen. (See Figure 1.) That verb appears in the large code window. For example, the first step might be to select "MOVE *identifier/literal*" from the menu. Then, a type-in window would pop up and the student would be prompted to type in the name of an identifier. A new menu would then be generated and they would choose the "TO" phrase. This scenario repeats itself until all the necessary COBOL statements are defined.

While this style of entry does model the overt behavior of students writing code (ie. they enter one "word" at a time), the *step-by-step, one item at a time*, nature of a production system resulted in an interaction style that seemed stilted and unnatural to many of the students, particularly those having years of experience with various tools and languages. These experienced programmers were frustrated by the tutor's word-by-word granularity of input that was imposed upon them. They wanted to input multiple identifiers, full phrases or complete statements as a single action.

In contrast, the students having little or no programming experience were not bothered by the menu structure that often hinted at the correct next step, the unsolicited help and error messages, or the multimodal input requirements and bit by bit input constraints. Since it was their first experience with an interactive system, they had no preconceptions as to the look and feel of programming tools, and appreciated any help that the system offered.

The experienced students soon discovered that the student model underlying the problem selection was very unforgiving. *Typographical slips,* even when they were immediately corrected, often resulted in the student being presented with remedial problems. Also, all errors in Grace are followed by immediate feedback. These error messages were frequently unwanted and annoying. All skill levels of student began to focus more on typing skills than on the solutions and complained that the error messages gave too much away.

The use of *two modes of input* (the mouse for menu selections and the keyboard for specifying identifiers and values) was also frustrating. The students' "rhythm" was disrupted by having to look to the screen to see whether to select or to type and by having to alternate many times per statement between the two. Even the format of some of the menu items was unnatural. For instance, to specify an 'IF' statement and its conditional test, Grace requires the following steps:

(1) Select an IF statement from the menu,
(2) pick the RELATION such as "*item-1 <= item-2*",
(3) specify the first item of the relation such as COUNTER,
(4) specify the second item of the RELATION such as 100.

These steps proved to be unnatural particularly for the experienced students, who wanted to simply type in "IF COUNTER <= 100". The expert programmers also felt that the context sensitive menus gave too much of a hint of what to do next as did some of the novices as they began to feel more confident.

There was a problem caused by Grace allowing *multiple solutions* to a problem. Frequently in a COBOL solution, the students have the option of sequencing statements in any order. One of the strengths of a production system approach is that it can allow this flexibility since it solves the problems dynamically. However, since Grace did not know which of several statements was being started, it interrupted the student for clarification.

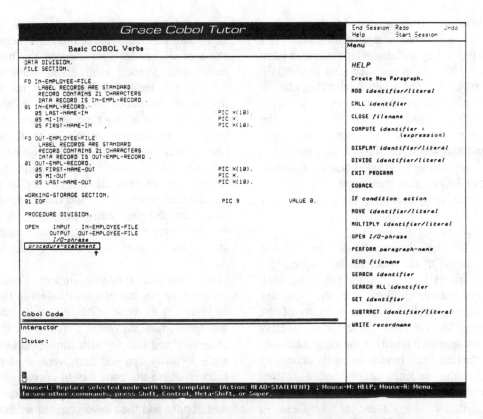

Figure 1: GRACE Interface with Context-Sensitive Menus, subgoal posting and multiple HELP

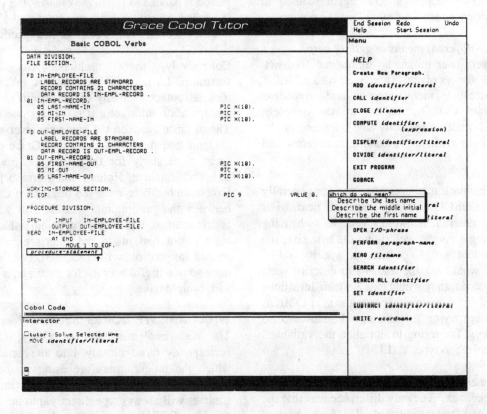

Figure 2: GRACE's "Dopplegangers" for multiple MOVE statements

As an example, in Figure 2, the student has to specify a MOVE statement for a first name, middle initial, and last name. Grace has popped up a dialog window to query the student as to which MOVE was intended after the MOVE menu item was selected. The menu would describe all possible MOVE statements and ask the user to pick one. This extra interaction, which became known as the "doppleganger effect", caused such responses as "Well, why doesn't it wait and *see* what MOVE statement I try, and then tell me if I'm wrong?". It also clued the student as to the number of MOVE statements that were required as well as confusing them by disrupting the goals that they had in mind.

The "dopplegangers" are the result of the tutoring paradigm that we chose at the onset of the project. Our production system solves for all possible solutions, each step of the way, before checking for the students' response. This tutoring style is typical of many of the tutors which use an ideal student model or an overlay paradigm [10]. This approach results in the tutor following many possible paths that could have been easily pruned by simply waiting for the student's action *before* finding possible solutions. In many situations, this order of evaluation is invisible to the student, but in Grace it became frustratingly clear, both because of the "dopplegangers" and because of the sometimes slow response time. The "dopplegangers" again seemed to frustrate the experienced students more than the novices.

Grace offered *five different means of getting help*, four of which were user initiated. Immediate feedback after an error was always given. There were also a 'HELP' key, two mouseable menu items, and hypertext information about COBOL linked to the problem descriptions. All students basically saw only two of the kinds of help: the immediate feedback after an error and the 'HELP' key.

The immediate feedback messages after an error generally indicated which COBOL term was expected next. For example, if they entered the word "VALUE" when the tutor was expecting a number describing the byte size, the error message would say, "You need to specify a PIC size." When we would ask the students to describe what they were trying to do, they would express their intentions in terms of higher-level goals rather than the next COBOL term that they were trying to generate. For instance, a student would say, "I'm trying to initialize the variable." rather than "I'm trying to type 'VALUE'."

The messages attached to the 'HELP' key were the same as the immediate feedback. The only difference was that the request for help was student initiated. This key was used rarely.

Few students used the mouseable help in the menus. None of the students discovered the hypertext COBOL information on their own. Even when we showed them the hypertext facilities, they still did not use it because of the indirect means of accessing the information. Rather than being able at any time to type in or pick a COBOL term and see information about its use and syntax, they had to click on the problem description, locate the term they wanted somewhere in the description, and click on it. A few students used this utility once or twice, but found the response time so slow and the indirection so confusing that they did not continue using it. They instead frequently referred to the text and syntax "cheat sheets" from class.

Grace attempted to cue the students about *subgoals in the problem* by posting nodes in italics in the code window. In Figure 1, the code window has the goals "*I/O phrase*" and "*procedure statement*". However, it was clear from observing and talking with the students that these nodes were virtually ignored and were seen merely as place holders where the code would appear. They did not see any correspondence between the language and position of these nodes and their own goals in writing the code. For example, the "*I/O phrase*" subgoal is used to indicate that another file can be identified for input or output *or* that a period is needed to finish the clause. In this case, a period is needed, so students became confused about whether or not they needed to have another file specified.

Collectively, these problems caused considerable frustration for many of the students. While the interface took advantage of many of the useful qualities of direct manipulation interfaces, it failed for one primary reason. The distance between the goals and everyday work of the students and the interactions that Grace created was too great, particularly for the expert programmers. In the terms of Hutchins, Hollan, and Norman [6], the Gulf of Execution had been enlarged because of Grace's mismatch between the programming tasks with which they were accustomed and the new paradigm which they had to learn. We had made the interface intrude into their immediate goal of writing COBOL code and we had not done so in a useful way as, for example, a good structured editor might have.

WHAT ARE WE DOING INSTEAD?

The new implementation of Grace, on IBM PS/2s, corresponds more closely into the actual environment which the programmers are using in their work. The interaction is reduced to a single window where the students will always type directly into the code window in complete COBOL statements rather then alternating menu selection and typing. Not only did most students say they

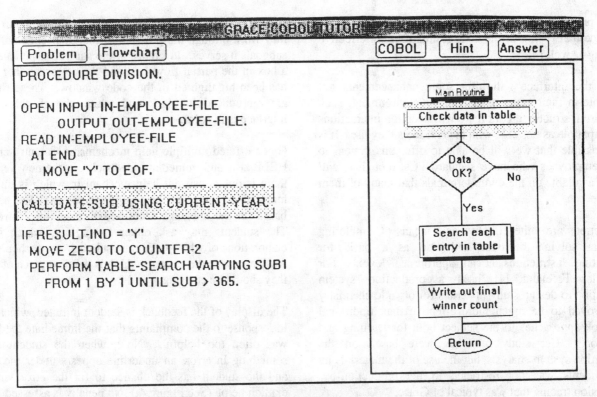

Figure 3: GRACE PS/2 with flowchart used for indicating code for a particular subgoal

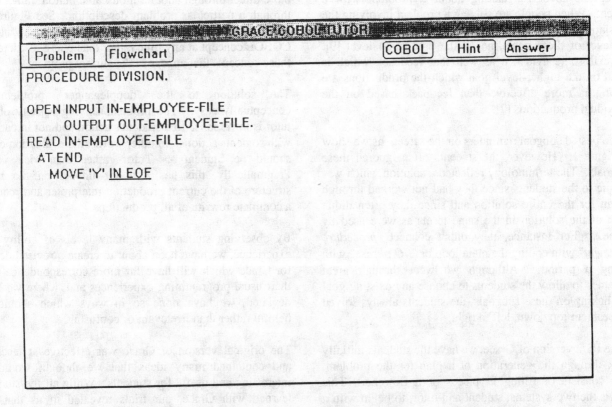

Figure 4: GRACE PS/2 with underlining for errors, button Initiated HELP and hypertext

would prefer being able to just type code, there is some evidence that typing in the code results in more effective learning as well [3].

While the interface will offer some enhancements not available in their actual programming environment, such as a partial structured editor, we will keep the interactions as compatible as possible with the real tools they use. It is also possible that we will be able to offer this system to those employees who have standard PCs, though it will not be available on the dumb terminals that many of them still use.

Productions are quite effective as a means of simulating problem solving behavior and also as a basis for generating instructions at an appropriate level. For example, Freeland [4] used a production system simulation to design study materials for organic chemistry that proved to be much more effective than traditional textbook approaches to the subject both for learning and retention. Her study materials were based on the production system analysis, but the use of the materials by the students was not restricted to the production-by-production tracing that was typical of Grace.

The productions in Grace were also quite useful as a simulation of code generation skills. However, we encountered mounting evidence that it is not the appropriate level for talking about a problem with a student. When people are solving a problem involving the translation of goals into syntactic units, they often talk at the level of these goals, not at the production level [9]. There is some evidence as well that feedback which is based on the higher-level goal which the productions are serving is more effective than feedback based on the individual productions [7].

Grace posted subgoal reminders on the screen, as we show in Figure 1. However, the students often ignored these subgoals. The terminology reflected a solution which was opaque to the students since they had not worked through a plan for the entire solution and since they often didn't think of the solution in the same terms as were used by Grace. For instance, they didn't connect "*procedure statement*" with coding the main loop or "*I/O phrase*" with typing a period. Although we went through great extremes to allow the students to choose any existing goal by clicking on these subgoals, the students always solved the problem top down, left to right.

In the PS/2 version of Grace, we have the students initially work through the generation of a plan for the problem. This consists of filling in pieces of a flowchart. This allows the two systems, student and tutor, to begin with a more consistent vocabulary and understanding of the

subgoals in a problem. The flowchart can also be used as they work through the problem to link their code with the subgoals it serves. In Figure 3, the student has clicked on a box in the partial flowchart and the corresponding code has been highlighted in the code window. These figures are reproduced in black and white, though the actual interface is in color.

Grace offered multiple help mechanisms - menu items, a HELP key, and immediate feedback. In the new version, there is one consistent help mechanism which is through mouseable buttons at the top of the screen. The help is based on the subgoals identified through the flowchart. The students may ask either for a hint, which is an elaboration of the particular subgoal they should be working on, or the answer, which is the next piece of code they should be entering.

The display of the feedback is student initiated, which was in response to the complaints that the immediate feedback was often too helpful. Now, when the student types something in error, an underline appears under the code and the student has the chance to fix the error without explicit help. (See Figure 4.) No penalty is assessed if the correction is made without help on the next try.

We will continue to provide hypertext information about COBOL use and syntax. However, access has been made more direct through another mouseable button, rather than through a particular problem description. (See Figure 4.) In this way, the student can request information about any COBOL concept at any time rather than being restricted to those concepts that appear in the current problem.

The solution to the "doppleganger" problem is conceptually easy. The problem solving activity of the tutor is in *response* to a student's action and not in parallel with students actions. In other words, the evaluation cycle should be Student -> Tutor rather than vice versa. Pragmatically, this has a major impact on the basic structure of the current production interpreter and requires a complete rewrite of all productions.

By observing students with many levels of ability and experience, we have been about to create a revised design for Grace which will have far more correspondence with their usual programming experiences and, where we have deviated, we have done so in ways which should be helpful rather than irrelevant or confusing.

The original version of Grace was effective at teaching and contained many ideas that we thought would be interesting and useful for students. While all the students learned with Grace, our trials revealed to us that, for experienced programmers, many of our design decisions actually got in the way of their learning and enjoyment of the tutor simply because we had not considered the conflict with their previous experience. We believe that the new version of Grace will do much to rectify these mismatches without reducing the effectiveness of Grace as a COBOL tutor.

WHAT ABOUT EXPERT/NOVICE DIFFERENCES?

The redesign of Grace has tried to address many of the problems that were expressed by the experienced programmers. But these practice tutors were originally designed for novice students and we still intend that they be used by this population as well. We believe that our redesign will be able to serve both groups of students well and may actually make the novice students' transition to the workplace easier than the original Grace tutor did.

Even though the inexperienced programmers were very enthusiastic about Grace in the original form, we suspect that the proposed enhancements will have an even more positive impact on novices. Help will always be available through a consistent mechanism over which they will have control. Directly typed input may be more difficult at first, but may enhance learning [3]. The requirement of completing the flowchart prior to specifying the proper syntax will begin to introduce the concepts and vocabulary of good program structure and design. Finally, the higher, goal oriented interaction resembles the feedback generated by human tutors working with novice programmers [8].

CONCLUSIONS

Grace has been shown in several trials to be effective for both novice and experienced programmers. The practice on problems and the immediate, individualized instruction has proven each time to be more effective than doing traditional projects and receiving instructor comments. We believe that many aspects of Grace are useful and should be retained. These include the production system model of problem solving which traces the problem solution along with the student, the immediate feedback when there is an error, and the individualized curriculum based on student history.

However, we learned the importance of keeping in mind the audience for which the tutor is created. If we had been concerned only with novice programmers, we might not have been drawn to look closely at these issues. The experienced programmers pointed out problems that we needed to address and that might have proven to be a source of difficulty for the beginning programmers had we followed them from the class into their first encounter with a traditional system. By redesigning Grace to correspond more closely to the experiences of the "real world" of COBOL programming, we have spanned the Gulf of Execution and allowed Grace to serve as a bridge to new skills for beginning as well as experienced programmers.

ACKNOWLEDGEMENTS: The Grace development team also includes Michael Atwood, Bart Burns, Wayne Gray, Anders Morch, and Haresh Sabnani. We would like to thank New York Telephone Co., Metropolitan Life Insurance Co., and SUNY-Purchase for providing "real" students for these trials. Thanks to John Anderson and his lab for providing some software and much assistance. Special thanks to Barbara Jaslow for her time and effort spent teaching these classes and contributing to the design of the Grace curriculum.

REFERENCES

1. Anderson, J.R. and Reiser, B.J. (1985). The LISP Tutor. *Byte, 10,* (4), 159-175.

2. Anderson, J.R., Boyle, C.F., Corbett, A.T., and Lewis, M.W. (1990). Cognitive modeling and intelligent tutoring, *Artificial Intelligence,* 42, 7-49.

3. Corbett, A.T., Anderson, J.R. and Fincham, J.M. (1991). Menu Selection vs. Typing: Effects on Learning in an Intelligent Programming Tutor, Proceedings of the *International Conference on Learning Sciences,* pp. 107 - 112. Charlottesville, VA: Association for the Advancement of Computing in Education.

4. Freeland, R. (1986). Retention of Problem-Solving Skill in Organic Chemistry: Instructional Design using a Simulation Model. Unpublished doctoral thesis, Carnegie Mellon University, Psychology Department.

5. Gray, W.D. and Atwood, M.E. (in press). Transfer, adaptation, and the use of intelligent tutoring technology: The case of Grace. In M. Farr and J. Psotka (eds.) *Intelligent computer tutors: Real world applications,* New York: Taylor & Francis.

6. Hutchins, Hollan, and Norman (1986). Direct Manipulation Interfaces. In D. Norman and S. Draper, (eds.), *User Centered System Design,* Hillsdale, NJ: Lawrence Erlbaum Associates, pp. 87-124.

7. McKendree, J. (1990). Effective feedback content for tutoring complex skills, *Human-Computer Interaction,* Vol. 5, No. 4, pp. 381-413.

8. McKendree, J., Reiser, B. and Anderson, J.R., (1984). Tutoring goals and strategies in the instruction of programming skills, *Proceedings of the Sixth Annual Cognitive Science Conference*, pp. 252-254.

9. Simon, H.A. and Ericsson, K. A. (1984). *Protocol Analysis*, Cambridge, MA: MIT Press.

10. Wenger, E. (1987). *Artificial Intelligence and Tutoring Systems*, Los Altos, CA: Kaufman.

Evocative Agents and Multi-Media Interface Design

Beth Adelson
Dept. of Psychology
Rutgers University
adelson.chi@xerox.com

Abstract

This paper describes research which focusses on the issue
of possible roles for computerized agents within multimedia educational software.

Keywords: Computerized agents, multi-media software, educational software, foreign language learning.

1 Introduction

In this paper we describe *Love and the Search for a
Cheap Flat*, a french language-learning application using salient cultural agents within a multi-media interface
[14, 16][1]. The application, implemented in *Muse* (Section 4.1), was developed out of our interests in education and cognition; and multi-media interface design. In
terms of educational and cognitive issues we had several
goals. i. We wanted to create an application that would
be highly motivating; therefore, one based on the real-
life concerns of the students using it. ii. We wanted the
application to reflect our belief that language learning,
rather than simply being a matter of learning vocabulary and syntax consisted also of learning to live within a
culture. According to our view, foreign language learning therefore involves understanding individuals within
the foreign culture at both a psychological and sociolog-

ical level. It also involves being able to effectively converse with these individuals based on that understanding. iii. Because active participation leads to longer
lasting and more robust learning, we wanted to create
an application which called for thoughtful and challenging student interaction [8, 7, 17, 6, 5, 4, 2, 3, 1, 13, 15].

In terms of developing a multi-media agent-based application which reflected our ideas about the principles
underlying good interface design our goal was to develop
an interface which would draw the user in without not-
icably doing so. That is, we wanted an interface which
would be, through the use of multi-media and interface
agents, compelling and aesthetically pleasing. However,
we did not want the interface, even given its complexity, to be at all distracting, either in its aesthetics or in
its functionality. To put the functional concerns more
strongly, we believed that the interface could be transparent to the user; simply acting as a vehicle for the
educational experience motivating the application.

In providing a more detailed explanation of our work
on education, cognition and interface design we begin,
in the next section with a description of what it is like
for a student to use the French application. We then
discuss the educational concepts underlying the application. Finally we address issues underlying the design
of the interface.

2 A Walk Through the Application

2.1 Overview

In using this application students encounter and analyze some characters who constitute powerful 'cultural
icons'[2]. The students then construct arguments for the

---

[1] This work was begun while visiting MIT's Muse Consortium
and completed while the author was a Henry Rutgers Research
fellow. Warm thanks go both to the Muse Consortium and Rutgers University for making this work possible. Special thanks go
to Evelyn Schlusselburg for her varied and generous input concerning the development of Muse applications.

---

[2] Thanks to Gilberte Furstenberg of MIT's Athena Language
Learning Project for her thoughtful, continual and creative contributions.

An earlier interface, and the disk used both there and here was
developed by the MIT Athena Language Learning Project. In the

purpose of effecting the actions of these characters.

The scenario in which this occurs runs as follows: The student is presented with a story stored on video disk and presented via the Muse application, on the screen of her workstation. In the story, the student first meets the protagonist, Philippe. Although quite likeable, Philippe has, through his flakiness just lost his job, his sweetheart and his apartment.

As a result, Philippe is faced with a set of challenges: He has to convince an appropriately sceptical realtor, M. Jacot, of the "Paradise Realty Co.", that he would be a responsible tenant. As a fallback position, he feels that he also needs to convince his aunt, a staunch pillar of the bourgeoisie, that he is the perfect choice for house-sitter during her up-coming three month African safari. Additionally, he has to deal with a rather temperamental plumber over the leaky sink in the apartment he has shared with his lost love Elisabeth.

Philippe as a character is too discombobulated to deal effectively with these situations. This creates the opportunity for the student to step in and argue on Philippe's behalf[3]. The intrinsic interest here is that these are challenges which the college-age students using the program are just beginning to face in their own lives. Additionally, stories of lost love tend in their own right to be engaging.

2.2 Two Applications

For reasons explained below we have created two versions of the application.

- Direct Version:

  Here the student directly argues with the realtor, the aunt and the plumber on behalf of Philippe. The exercise presented by the application begins with a scene in which the student sees Elisabeth leave Philippe. Philippe then asks the student to help him with the problems which stem from such a break up.

  The story is presented in the applications's largest window in the center of the screen (Adelson, Plate 1). Here and throughout the application when the student is asked to participate, the request appears above the center window and is accompanied by buttons which allow the student to indicate whether she wishes to. The story continues

only if the student wants to participate. Otherwise the application comes to an end.

Assuming that the student wants to continue she then enters a scene in which she is asked to help convince the realtor that Philippe will be a responsible tenant. The video pauses and she is now confronted with a list of three topic sentences each of which could form the core of an argument for the realtor.

Adelson, Plate 2 illustrates the paused video window in the center of the screen with the three topic sentences in the column to the left. The student chooses the topic which she feels will be most effective given the position and nature of the character Philippe is currently confronting. She does so by pressing the button accompanying a given topic sentence. The English translation of the arguments appear below.

1. "Philippe has always paid his rent on time."

2. "Philippe comes from an old and respected family."

3. "Philippe is a well connected journalist."

Once she has chosen a topic, a window opens in the bottom left corner of the screen and she is asked to construct an argument for Philippe (Adelson, Plate 3). When she has constructed an argument with which she is satisfied, she presses the button at the bottom of the window in which she is working and the argument is sent off to an instructor for later grading[4]; however, the topic she has chosen also has an immediate effect because multiple outcomes are stored on the disk with different choices leading to different outcomes. For example, if the student argues that Philippe is an up-and-coming journalist the realtor becomes quite solicitous, otherwise he remains circumspect.

The student then goes on to participate in a similar way in Philippe's encounter with his aunt for whom he wants to house sit and with the plumber who comes to fix the sink in the apartment he has been sharing with Elisabeth. Philippe's inability to get the plumber to come and fix the

---

earlier project, "A la Rencontre de Philippe", Gilberte Fursten-berg was director of educational design and Janet H. Murray was executive producer. For information on the original interface contact Janet Murray.

[3]The story, the tasks presented to the student, and the responses required from the student are entirely in French.

[4]Interestingly, the argument that will generally convince a Parisian realtor is different from the one which would be most likely to convince her American counterpart. "Well connected journalists" enjoy a privileged position in French society and their presence is welcome even when their credit history is shaky. The student needs to call upon this kind of knowledge of cultural differences when choosing and constructing an argument, but this is not an impossible task since cultural mores are discussed in the French course in which the users of this application are enrolled. Notice also, that during the later interaction with the instructor there is room for the student to successfully disagree with our sense of what constitutes a winning argument.

kitchen sink over the last six months has contributed to the break up of his relationship. Elisabeth has finally made the appointment herself and has asked Philippe simply to let the plumber in to the apartment and to pay him. However, Philippe has not paid attention to where Elisabeth has left the check. If the student can convince the temperamental plumber to, on this one occasion, extend credit to Philippe the story ends with Elisabeth being convinced that Philippe has turned over a new leaf; she therefore gives the relationship another try. If the student is unsuccessful with the plumber but has convinced either the aunt and/or the realtor of Philippe's trustworthiness, Philippe writes Elisabeth a rather cool 'Dear Genevieve'. If none of the characters are convinced, Philippe is left at the conclusion of the story to face another difficult day.

Because the outcome of the story depends very much on the student's understanding the characters well enough to choose a convincing argument we feel that the application provides a striking and therefore effective learning experience. In the next section we present data to this effect.

- Agent Version:
  This version differs from the Direct Version in that at the outset of the story the student chooses an agent to argue on Philippe's behalf [14, 16]. The agent can be either General Charles De Gaulle or Torch Singer Edith Piaf (Adelson, Plate 4). The student chooses the agent after seeing a description both of the agent's role in French society and of the agent's (strong) character. Additionally the student hears and sees a video segment of Piaf singing her haunting theme song "La Vie en Rose" (Adelson, Plate 5) and historical photos of DeGaulle's imposing presence (Adelson, Plate 6).

  For each of the situations that confront Philippe, the agent offers to make one of three arguments. (Again the video freezes and the arguments appear in the left column of the screen). The topics of the arguments are the same as the ones in the Direct Version; here however, the student sees the full argument, rather than just a topic sentence. The English version of the arguments offered by General DeGaulle and Edith Piaf to Plumber Morel appear below. The arguments, written by a French historical novelist, are very much in the distinctive 'voice' of the agent.

  – DeGaulle's arguments for the plumber
    1. "Monsier Morel, looking around, you can surely see that Monsieur [Philippe] Vitaz is perfectly capable of paying you.

He clearly has the means to make good on his debt. A man born as Philippe is will not fail to discharge his debt! It is a question of honor!"
    2. "Monsieur Morel, for the French, each must trust the other. What would happen to our country? Our country without the solidarity which has always been its strength? I tell you, to trust Philippe, it is your obligation."
    3. "Monsieur Morel, your reputation is known. It is said that no plumber is better than you. Monsieur Vitaz, by all evidence, is in need of your good services. May I allow myself to ask you, in this one case, to have the goodness to make this repair?"

  – Piaf's arguments for the plumber
    1. This one doesn't have the air of a guy with money problems. He has what to pay you with. Ones like him, they pay their debts.
    2. Eh Morel, what about trust? Sure it's not the fashion today, but what about other days? Days like yours and mine?
    3. Ah Morel, I know you. There is no other like you. Come on Monsieur.. Come! Come!

The student chooses the argument which she feels would be most effective if presented by the agent[5]. The student then has a chance, as she did in the Direct version, to use her analytic and argument construction skills. She does so by explaining her choice in the lower left window and sending it off for later feedback. Again the choice of argument effects the outcome of the story.

2.3 Why Two Versions?

Both versions have the strength that they provide rich analysis and explanation tasks. However, each has a weakness. In the Direct Version the program knows which topic the student has chosen to argue on and takes a path based on that choice of topic without regard to the *goodness* of the argument. We were uncomfortable with the possibility of the students noticing this limitation. That is, if a student was unable (or unwilling) to

---

[5] Again the winning argument is not obvious. Having seen the video of the plumber the student sees the degree of Plumber Morel's pride. However, from the way in which he takes command of the situation, savors the difficulties of a leaky sink and wields the tools of his trade it can be inferred that his pride in his craft outweighs his pride as a Frenchman. This kind of careful arguing from the evidence is what will allow the student to make a successful choice.

create an explanation which she felt was adequate and the outcome of the situation was still positive the application would suffer in the student's eyes. For this reason we constructed the Agent Version where complete and well formed arguments were provided within the program. However, as mentioned above, in order give the students using the Agent Version an equally rich task we asked them to *explain* their choice rather than construct the argument[6].

We hypothesized that the Agent Version might have two limitations: 1. Since the student effects the outcome of the story in a less direct way she may feel less engaged and therefore she may learn less. 2. Additionally, having the agent intervening for the student might add a confusing layer of complexity. We also considered the alternative possibility that the agents might enliven the application, thereby enhancing the student's learning. In the next section we present data comparing the two versions of the application.

3   Research Motivations

As noted above, we had the goal of fostering students' ability to live and respond effectively within the culture represented by the foreign language. We felt that asking students to deal with individuals who both possessed strong characters and held frequently encountered positions in society was a way of meeting this goal. Having the students analyze these characters in terms of their personalities and their social roles was a first way of having the students learn to deal with them effectively. Having the students then formulate arguments based on these analyses was a second way of aiding them.

Further, active participation fosters learning that is longer lasting and can be used in a larger (more creative) number of ways since the knowledge acquired is more fully integrated into existing knowledge [7, 8, 17, 6, 5, 4, 2, 3, 1, 13, 15]. Towards that end we wanted to have the students participate as fully as possible.

Additionally, we wanted the exercise to be embedded in a context which was relevant and enjoyable to the students. As we noted, the video disk we chose to use in our application had been produced for an earlier non-Muse application created by the Athena Language Learning Project. The disk, with the story about Philippe and Elisabeth clearly gave us relevant and enjoyable material to work with. However, the earlier application created a different learning environment than the one we wished to

---

[6] Of course the problem still remains that the students could construct half-hearted explanations but we felt that this was less serious. That is, it would still make sense to the student that the story was being positively affected by the agent's cogent argument, even if the student's explanation of the argument was less than it should have been.

create. In the earlier application, Philippe asks the student to help him solve some of his problems by exploring the neighborhood in which he lives, by observing conversations and by listening to messages on his answering machine. However, the student interacts with Philippe by answering only factual questions and only via use of a menu system. In using this application the student was not called upon to: understand the cultural aspects which influence the characters' behaviors; identify and structure issues which underlie effective arguments; and generate extended arguments in French.

The Muse authoring language provided us with a vehicle for creating an application which would meet our goals. In terms of maximizing the student's involvement Muse allows the user to experience an engaging multi-media environment [10]. In this environment our students see and hear Philippe's adventures. But more importantly the Muse application allows the student to interact with the Philippe story in a way which would effect its outcome. In our view, this ability to effect the story's outcome is what gives the user the strongest sense of being in Philippe's environment and therefore leads to the kind of powerful learning experience we were seeking.

3.1   Results: The Learning Experience

Ideally we would test our work by comparing the grades obtained by students who did and did not use an integrated set of language learning applications throughout the course of a school year. That is an ultimate goal, but before designing and implementing such a curriculum we need to look at the degree to which the students entered into the learning experience in order to assess at least the software's usability. Towards that end we asked 14 students to use the software. Seven students used the Agent version and seven used the Direct. The students were then asked to rate the software in several ways. A seven point rating scale was used. A rating of 4 indicated a neutral answer and a rating of 7 indicated a most positive answer. Explanations for the ratings were also collected.

Each of the students had studied French for a minimum of four years.

Level of participation: Each of the students spent a good hour using the application and all provided thoughtful arguments or explanations.

Preference to current curriculum: The seven students using the Direct version when asked how they liked using this application as compared to their current language lab in which they heard tapes of spoken French and then answered factual questions on the material gave the application an average preferablity rating of 5.4. The seven students using the Agent version gave the application an average rating of 6.4, so both groups had a more positive than neutral feeling towards the application (Direct Group: $t,6=4.8$; $p<.01$. Agent Group: $t,6=12.02$; $p<.00005$). Additionally, the Agent group preferred the application more than the Direct group ($t,12=2.78$; $p<.01$).

Comparison between the Direct and Agent Versions: The preferability of the Agent over the Direct version was not a foregone conclusion. We had considered the possibilities that the Agent version while more entertaining, might either be less engaging or too busy and therefore confusing. That the Agent group more strongly preferred the application over the current curriculum suggests the Agent version was more engaging.

As a second piece of evidence supporting the goodness of the Agent version, the students in the Agent version felt they were more likely to continue their French studies (an average of 6.6 as compared to 5.6 for the Agent and Direct students respectively: $t,12=2.98$; $p<.01$). This too suggests that the Agent version was the more effective learning experience. These results, if they continue to generalize [14, 16], suggest that interface agents can be valuable educational aids; they can engage students without distracting or distancing them from the learning experience.

A third measure on this issue did not produce a significant result. The application increased the two groups enthusiasm for the class in which they were currently enrolled pretty much to the same extent (an average of 5.0 as compared to 5.1 for the Agent and Direct students respectively: $t,12=0$; $p=.5$). As an aside, when the ratings for the two groups were combined the students did, as a whole, show an increase in enthusiasm for the class ($t,13=3.04$; $p<.01$).

A last question compared the subjective feelings that each group might have had for the version they did *not* experience. When each group was provided with a description of the version they did not see and asked to imagine how they would have liked the other version their feelings were fairly neutral (4.4 and 4.1 for the Direct and Agent versions respectively: $t,12=.27$ $p=.39$). However, the *opinions* expressed on this issue were illuminating. The Direct version students who imagined most liking for the Agent version were the students who found the Direct version difficult and felt that the Agent version might have been a little easier on their French composition skills. The Agent version students who expressed most liking for the Direct version were those who would have preferred the freedom to make up their own version of the arguments, without an agent formulating one for them. This suggests, as we had hoped in our desire to create a highly engaging experience, that the students not only were challenged, but also enjoyed the challenge.

In sum, it seems that while both versions of the software seem usable and enjoyable the Agent version seems to capture the interest of the students to a greater extent.

4 Interface Issues

4.1 Implementation

The motion video information presented to the user was stored on two disks, and the video players for both were controlled by the Muse application. Visual stills were stored in pixmap files whose presentation was also controlled by Muse. Conceptually, Muse moved the user through a state-space[11, 12]. The movement was effected as the user clicked on button objects, causing the story to enfold. The handling of the students' arguments and explanations to the instructor was accomplished by calls to the underlying operating system. Detailed discussion of these issues is presented in the *Technical Issues* section of Hodges[10], but what is important here is that the control of the multiple video players, etc. was transparent to the student.

4.2 Interface Design: Concern for the User

As we discussed in the introduction to this paper we wanted to create an interface which balanced strong aesthetic appeal with easily grasped functionality.

Aesthetics: We chose deep colors (purple and maroon) for the backgrounds to the screens which presented visual information and created borders and buttons for the backgrounds by using muted versions of vividly complementary colors (dusty rose and ochre). These colors, while holding the user's attention, were not distracting because they balanced each others strength. Additionally they were sufficiently dark so as not to be visually fatiguing (Adelson, Plate 4) Although Tufte [19, 18] cogently argues for muted colors in textual media we have found that multi-media educational applications benefit from use of strong color[10].

Functionality: As discussed just above, the user has no need to be aware of the technology which enables her to see visuals from three sources, and Muse handles this interplay seamlessly. A second issue in making sure that an interface is not annoying concerns how easily the functionality of the application can be deduced by the user. In our attempt to avoid annoying the users we were quite intentionally consistent in our placement of information sources. The information leading to the understanding of individuals (both agents and characters such as the plumber or the realtor) was always presented in the center window. Requests for user participation were always placed above this window. The left hand third of the screen was reserved for activity concerning argument construction, with core arguments being presented at the top, and expansions or explanations being entered at the bottom. As a result, despite its complexity, the students needed very little on-line or verbal instruction on the application's use. Additionally, they were able to concentrate on the exercise, rather than on the interface.

5 Closing Remark

In this paper we have described a language learning application which was motivated by our interests in education, cognition and interface design. The multi-media agent-based application provided an engaging but not distracting environment for learning to analyze and argue with individuals from a foreign culture.

References

[1] Adelson, B. Characterizing the nature of analogical reasoning. In Design Theory and Methodology. M. Waldron (Ed.). Springer-Verlag. NY. In press.

[2] Adelson, B. Categorizing Concepts. *Cognitive Science*. December, 1985.

[3] Adelson, B. and Soloway, E. The role of domain experience in software design. *IEEE: Transactions in Software Engineering*. November, 1985.

[4] Adelson, B. When novices surpass experts: How the difficulty of a task may increase with expertise. *Journal of Experimental Psychology: Learning, Memory and Cognition*. July, 1984.

[5] Adelson, B. Problem solving and the development of abstract categories in programming languages. *Memory & Cognition*, 1981 9(4), 422-433.

[6] Anderson, J.R. *The architecture of Cognition*. Harvard University Press: Cambridge, MA. 1983.

[7] Chi, M., Bassok, M., Reimann, P. and Glaser, R. Self-explanations. *Cognitive Science 13*, 1989.

[8] Chi, M., Feltovich, P and Glaser, R. Categorization and representation of physics problems by experts and novices. *Cognitive Science*. 1981

[9] Larkin, J. What kind of knowledge transfrs? In *Knowing, Learning and Instruction* L. Resnick (ed.) Lawrence Erlbaum: Hillsdale, NJ. 1989.

[10] Hodges, M. (ed.) *Applications from the MIT Muse Software Consortium*. NY: Addison-Wesley. In press.

[11] Hodges, M. Sasnett, R. and Ackerman, M. A construction set for multi-media applications. *IEEE: Transactions in Software Engineering*. January, 1989.

[12] Hodges, M. Sasnett, R. and Harward, V. J. *Unix Review*. Vol. 8, 2. 1990.

[13] Larkin, J. What kind of knowledge transfrs? In *Knowing, Learning and Instruction* L. Resnick (ed.) Lawrence Erlbaum: Hillsdale, NJ. 1989.

[14] Laurel,   B.   Interface Agents. In The Art of HCI Design. (B. Laurel, ed.) NY: Addison-Wesley. 1990.

[15] Novick, L. Analogical transfer, problem similarity and expertise. *Journal of Experimental Psychology: L, M and C*. 1988.

[16] Oren,   Salomon, Kreitman and Don, In The Art of HCI Design. (B. Laurel, ed.) NY: Addison-Wesley. 1990.

[17] Schoenfeld, A. *Mathematical Problem-Solving*. Academic Press: NY. 1985.

[18] Tufte, E. *The Visual Display of Quantitativ Information*. Graphics Press: Cheshire, CT. 1990.

[19] Tufte, E. *Envisioning Information*. Graphics Press: Cheshire, CT. 1983.

Graphic StoryWriter: An Interactive Environment for Emergent Storytelling

Karl E. Steiner
Thomas G. Moher

Department of Electrical Engineering and Computer Science
University of Illinois at Chicago
M/C 154, Box 4348
Chicago, IL 60680
steiner@uicbert.eecs.uic.edu
moher@uicbert.eecs.uic.edu

ABSTRACT

The Graphic StoryWriter (GSW) is an interactive system that enables its users to create structurally complete stories through the manipulation of graphic objects in a simulated storybook. A rule-based story engine manages character and prop interaction, guides story development, and generates text. Through the simple interface and story writing engine, the Graphic StoryWriter provides an environment for early readers to learn about story structures, to experience the relationship between pictures and text, and to experiment with causal effects. This paper describes the motivation for and design of the Graphic StoryWriter, and reports on an empirical comparison of childrens' stories generated orally and using the GSW.

KEYWORDS: User interaction, story grammars, educational software.

INTRODUCTION

Storytelling is not an activity restricted to bedsides or campfires. When we tell a friend about a conflict at work, describe to a spouse what happened on the way home from the grocery, or relate an incident from the past to our neighbor, we are actively engaging in storytelling. While the ability to write prizewinning fiction may be a unique gift, the ability to comprehend and create meaningful stories is a basic communication skill.

Still, storytelling is a skill that must be developed. Children grow in their recognition and mastery of story components. Some common story conventions are the inclusion of a formal opening like "Once upon a time," the identification of characters and conflict, the use of a

consistent past tense, and a formal close such as "and they all lived happily ever after." Children as young as two may begin to use these conventions in their stories, and the incidence of inclusion rises as a child ages [1]. Children similarly grow in their ability to recognize story structures [8].

In recent years, the practice of having pre-literate children dictate stories to an adult transcriber has become popular in pre-school and early elementary school classrooms [11]. Children enjoy the activity, and obviously take a great deal of pride in the tangible product of their efforts, which they profusely illustrate and proudly display.

The adult provides two important compensatory services for the young author. First, by acting as a transcriber, the adult helps to bridge the gap between oral and written language. Since the child already knows the content of the story, he or she can approach word recognition and reading as a "matching" activity, in much the same way that illustrations serve to cue expectations in children's story books.

Less explicitly, but equally important, adults typically provide encouragement and guidance in the structure of the story. Questions such as "and then what did the boy do?" or "was he scared?" or "how did they find their way out of the forest?" help children to understand basic elements of character and plot development [2, 5].

Unfortunately, there are many more children than teachers, so this valuable strategy for promoting emergent literacy does not get used as often as it might.

This paper reports on the design of, and user experience with, a practical computer system, the Graphic StoryWriter, which provides some of the services that the adult transcriber offers in the "dictation" technique. We adopted as our target user community children at the developmental stage of "emergent literacy," chronologically four to seven years of age.

The design of the Graphic StoryWriter presented three important challenges. First, economics and technical limitations precluded a system based on oral input, so it was necessary to find an alternative allowing pre-literate children to express their stories. In the GSW, children "write" stories through point-and-click direct manipulation of characters and props in an imaginary setting, and a written story is automatically generated in response to their actions.

The solution to the first challenge introduced the second: how to provide a domain of sufficient richness under the necessary constraints of limited characters, props, and plot options. In designing the GSW, we examined the literature on early writing, and we employed an iterative development technique to try to obtain a reasonable balance between complexity and expressive richness.

The third challenge we faced was how to help the children to create structurally complete stories. At the target developmental stage, children typically tend toward relatively "plot-less" stories consisting of lists of events or characters. In the GSW, an underlying rule-based system is used to gently encourage (but not demand) the development of a story from the introduction of a central conflict through its resolution.

The experiences of young children using the Graphic StoryWriter lead us to believe that it goes a long way toward meeting these challenges for our target population. Unattended six-year old children had little trouble using the GSW after a brief introduction, even those with no prior experience with computers or pointing devices. The children attended strongly to the task for periods of up to ten minutes, and most of them spontaneously expressed a desire to continue to work with the GSW. The stories which they produced were similar (or superior) in expressive richness to spontaneously generated oral stories based on the same stimuli. And finally, the stories produced using the GSW appeared to be much more likely to reflect a complete conflict resolution structure.

USER INTERFACE

A session with the Graphic StoryWriter begins with the child selecting between two alternative story settings: a crater-filled Space World populated by (male and female) astronauts, rockets, and volcanoes, and a Fantasy World of kids, castles, kites, and monsters. The opening screen is shown in Figure 1.

We chose the metaphor of a storybook for the basic screen layout. A graphic of an open book occupies most of the screen. The virtual page is divided into two sections, an illustration area and a text area. The remainder of the screen is reserved for the characters and props which are used in the story. Figure 2 shows a sample screen of a story in progress in the Fantasy World setting.

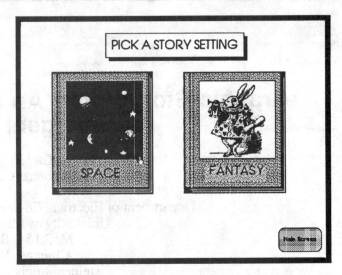

Figure 1. Graphic StoryWriter Opening Screen.

The storybook metaphor was chosen to help children grasp the nature of the software. Picture books are a familiar object in most classrooms. Their format is generally consistent with that of this software; an illustration along with related text. The events on each page are related to what has come before and what will follow [3]. Students can transfer their print awareness and knowledge of picture books to this software.

The characters and props are initially placed in a "staging area" on the far left side of the screen. An object is selected by clicking on it. The object then "follows" the mouse movement until the mouse is clicked again, at which point the character or object is deposited in the illustrated setting. The software will not allow objects to be dragged so that they overlap the text area of the screen. Each movement of a graphical object, either from the staging area or within the illustration, results in the generation of corresponding text at the bottom of the screen. The user terminates a GSW session by selecting the button labelled "THE END."

Figure 2. The Fantasy World screen layout.

Optionally, for children with a simple reading vocabulary, the user is presented with a pop-up menu which allows him or her to specify certain attributes of animate characters, as shown in Figure 3. In the simpler version of GSW, this selection is made randomly for the user without the presentation of the menu.

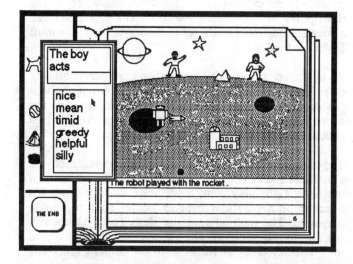

Figure 3. Pop-up Menu for Character Attributes.

Audible and visible feedback is given to make the selection of an object more obvious. The system "chimes" when a valid object has been selected. Also, the cursor changes from a selection pointer (a pointing hand) to a placement pointer (a large "X"). Further movement of the cursor then moves the selected object.

Visual and audio effects reinforce the text, and add a bit of entertainment to the program. When a character plays with the ball, for instance, it appears to bounce in front of that character. When a character eats the pear, the program says "yum yum." Animation effects can help hold user interest and further reinforce the desire to explore the software. [4]

To allow the system to serve additional instructional purposes, a variety of print options are provided. For users wishing a complete record of their story, the system can reproduce each page of their work complete with text and graphics. For users wishing to re-illustrate or re-write their work, the system provides illustrations with no text, or text with a blank illustration area. There is also an option which prints the complete text on a full page without an illustration area. Figure 4 shows the various print options.

With the Authoring Tool, a user, such as a teacher or parent, can create customized scenarios. This tool allows a user to enter an initial text screen, place characters and props, and choose their characteristics. Scenarios could be devised to supplement an instructor's class plan. Not only does this allow for the creation of uniquely relevant materials, but the focused nature and goals of these scenarios can encourage closer attention to the textual responses and clues [4].

Figure 4. Print Options in the Graphic StoryWriter.

DESIGN ITERATION

The design of the Graphic StoryWriter user interface was strongly informed by user reactions to an earlier (but conceptually and functionally similar) version of the software. As part of our design process, we videotaped 16 first-grade students using the original GSW, and reviewed those tapes to identify difficulties students were having with the interface.

The children took several approaches to character and prop manipulation. Some moved an object, then read the results and made further moves based on the feedback. Some moved and read in an exploratory manner without a clear plan. Many simply arranged the characters and props in tableaus that appealed to them. The system accommodated all of these approaches.

The students had no conceptual difficulties with the basic manipulations required. They had no problems relating mouse movements to those of the pointer on the screen, or with the notion of clicking to perform an action. In many cases, the students required no prompting in order to use the buttons.

There were, however, some shortcomings in the user interface to the GSW, and it is instructive to review that design history.

Object manipulation was one problem. Several of the props were small, and the children had difficulty targeting and selecting these particular objects. Also, there was no visible or audible feedback to indicate that an object had been properly selected.

The system required a second or two after each movement/text generation cycle to save the previous work. Input could not be processed during this time, but there was no on-screen indication that the system was busy. This, coupled with the lack of selection feedback, created confusion for several of the students.

Response speed and feedback was also an issue with the print button. The system required several seconds to prepare a print job once the print button had been clicked. Impatient students, unsure whether the machine was printing or not, would click the button several times. When the print command finished, the buffered clicks often triggered a button on the next screen which shared the same location as the print button.

Some students expressed surprise at the system's interpretations of their moves. Most of these complaints concerned issues of character proximity. The system checked first to see if a character had moved next to another character. This allowed for situations where a character moved next to a prop, yet the system chose another nearby character as the subject of the interaction rather than the prop.

Finally, the basic paradigm allowed only for the initial placement of props. Further movement of these inanimate objects could take place only under the influence of one of the animate characters. Several of the students expressed confusion at their inability to move props.

In the end, the study of the children's problems with the original interface resulted in several substantive changes in the user interface for the GWF:

- The smaller props were increased in size to make them easier to select.

- Audible and visible feedback were added to provide feedback on selection and to add entertainment value.

- A busy indicator was added to keep users from mousing and clicking ahead of the current operation.

- Buttons on "adjacent" screens were moved to distinct locations, so that a click-ahead would not trigger a button on the new screen.

- Proximity triggers for character-to-character and character-to-object interactions were replaced with a simple "closest-object" rule.

- The ability to move props within the illustration page was added.

MANAGING STORY STRUCTURES

Each movement of an object in the Graphic StoryWriter results in the generation of descriptive text, which is displayed on the user's screen. The sequence of text passages generated by successive movements in a session with the GSW constitutes the story produced by the user.

The text generation facility in the Graphic StoryWriter is based on a *story grammar* [9, 10] in which each story consists of a *setting* and one or more *episodes*.

Text generated in the setting presents the main character, establishes the central conflict, and sets the physical location of the story. A GSW user can participate in all of these decisions. A place is chosen at the opening screen. The first character selected becomes the main character. The central conflict is a function of the description selected (randomly or explicitly) for the main character. If the description "shy" is chosen, the character's goal is to make a friend. If the main character is "hungry," he or she must find some food.

An episode describes a complete action sequence, consisting of at least three parts: an *initial event*, an *attempt* and a *consequence*. Additionally, an optional *internal response* can occur between the initial event and the attempt, and an optional *reaction* can occur after the consequence.

The initial event describes actions or feelings that motivate a character and induces a goal. For example, a character who was in a fight may want to distance himself from his attacker or a playful character might want to find a playmate. The internal response describes a character's reaction to this stimulus. The attempt describes the action the character takes in response to the initial event. The consequence describes the outcome of this event, and the reaction describes the character's feelings about the result.

An example of a short story conforming to this grammar is shown in Figure 5.

GRAMMAR CATEGORY	EXAMPLE
SETTING	Once upon a time, in a far away land, there was a lonely boy.
EPISODE	
Initial Event	The boy wanted to play a game.
Internal Response	He was sad because he was alone.
Attempt	He got his ball and went to see his friend.
Consequence	They played a game.
Reaction	The boy was happy to be with his friend.

Figure 5. Story Grammar Example

A *structurally complete* story, for our purposes, is one in which the central conflict which was established in the setting is resolved by one of the consequences in an episode. In the GSW, each consequence generated is checked to see if it in fact does resolve the central conflict; if so, the story is brought to an end.

In order to encourage the user to work toward the resolution of the central conflict, the GSW periodically generates "reminders" if the desired consequence is not met. These take the form of such sentences as "The girl still looked for something fun to do."

EXPERIMENTAL SUPPORT

Once the general usability of the Graphic StoryWriter was established, we wanted to look more closely at the kinds of stories which the children produced when using the software.

We approached this problem with two important questions in mind. First, did the GSW present an environment sufficiently rich to allow children to create stories of the type that they would spontaneously produce in oral dictation? If the GSW failed in this respect, if the stories which the children reported spontaneously were consistently richer, more interesting, or more complex than those they produced while using the software, we would feel that the GSW had fallen short of its goals in a fundamental way.

The second question which we faced was whether or not the GSW succeeded in its more ambitious goal of encouraging the students to create structurally complete stories, that is, stories in which the central conflict was resolved before the children pronounced the story completed.

Procedure

We designed a simple experiment intended as a preliminary test of these questions. In our experiment, twenty-three children in their second week of first grade were used as subjects; none of the children had any prior experience with the GSW. The students were randomly assigned to one of three groups.

Children in the first group (ORAL), were presented with a piece of paper showing a picture of the characters, props, and the Fantasy setting used in the GSW, and asked to tell a story, which was recorded on audio tape and later transcribed. (The stimulus material was literally a hand-colored screen dump from the Fantasy illustration.) Children in the second group (AUTO) used the GSW with randomly assigned character attributes. Children in group three (MANUAL) used the GSW as well, but were asked to explicitly select character attributes using menus. In order to eliminate literacy effects, generated text and menus were read aloud to the students. The GSW was instrumented to keep a log of their work.

The collected stories from the three groups were analyzed, and three dependent measures were obtained. The first measure was the total *time* spent on the task. While we expected the GSW subjects to take longer on the task, we were interested to see how long children would comfortably attend to the task, and we wanted to see if there was a difference between subjects who selected their own character attributes as opposed to those who let the system select those attributes.

Second, we counted the number of *events*, defined as the number of times two characters interact, or a character interacts with a prop. This was intended as our basic measure of the complexity of the resultant story.

Finally, we determined for each subject whether their story had reached a *closure*, defined as the resolution of the central conflict in the story. This was our measure of the structural soundness of the generated story.

Results

Subjects in the ORAL group required, on average, just over a minute to tell their stories. Subjects in the MANUAL and AUTO groups required, respectively, 402 seconds and 305 seconds to create stories using the GSW. There was no significant difference between the two groups using the GSW.

ORAL subjects averaged 2.8 events, MANUAL subjects 3.5 events, and AUTO subjects 3.2 events per story. Again, no significant differences were found between groups in an analysis of variance.

Within the ORAL group, only one of the subjects reached a state of closure. In contrast, three of the eight AUTO subjects reached closure, as did all eight of the MANUAL group subjects. Contingency analysis revealed a significant difference among the groups on this measure (p<.01). Chi-squared tests between groups, however, revealed no significant difference between the ORAL and AUTO groups.

Discussion

The results of the experiment offer tentative support for the efficacy of the GSW in providing a sufficiently rich environment for storytelling, and for its ability to encourage the creation of structurally complete stories.

The task times for the GSW subjects reveals that the students were able to attend to the task for five or six minutes at a time without difficulty; in fact, most of the subjects expressed a strong desire to use the GSW to create additional stories. Manual selection of character attributes resulted in marginally shorter task times for our subjects, in spite of the additional time required to read and select from menus, but the difference was not statistically significant.

The stories which were produced by the ORAL group and the two GSW groups were similar in complexity, as reflected by the *events* measure. A larger number of subjects may have resulted in significance on this measure, but at any rate the magnitude of the difference appears to be relatively small, and favor the GSW in direction. We found no evidence to counter the argument that the GSW environment is rich enough to allow students to express the kinds of stories that they would spontaneously generate orally, given the same visual stimuli.

The most interesting results concern the structure of the resultant stories. First graders have an incomplete understanding of story structures and components. Many of the oral "stories" were simply a listing of objects or events, without apparent attention to a plotline:

> *The well is going to be right there. And the cake*
> *is going to be right there. And the fox is going to*
> *be right there. And the people are going to be right*
> *there. And the man is going to be right there.*

Only three of the seven ORAL storytellers began their story with any statement of setting. Of these, two subjects failed to resolve the central conflict, as in the following story, where the boy and girl never find their way out of the forest:

> There was one girl and one boy who were lost in the forest. And they lived in a kingdom and there was a tree and a well. And it was the girl's birthday and they got lost because the girl's father said they could just go in the little forest but they went in the big forest instead. Then they met a fox and the fox asked them why don't you go play baseball? And so he went and played baseball.

In only one case was a structurally complete story created (if one accepts the premise that the "conflict" created by the princess in the following story was her need to find a prince!):

> Once upon a time there was a rich princess. She lived in a pink castle with roses all around it. And the princess had a well by her castle. And she had an apple tree by it. And she had a pet dog. And one day she went for a walk in the woods and she found another castle. And she knocked on the door and so they let her in. And then she saw a prince and they married each other and they went off to their own castle. And they had a dog. And they growed a new apple tree.

The GSW, by its design, demands that the user establish a setting and a central story conflict. However, while it encourages the creation of a structurally complete story, it does not force the central conflict to be resolved, as shown in the following story generated by one of the AUTO group subjects:

> In ages past, in a distant forest, there was a playful girl. She liked toys and games. A dog came along. He was greedy. The girl still looked for something fun to do. A boy was near. He was mean .

Note that although the GSW made an attempt to encourage the subject to pursue resolution of the central conflict (finding the girl something fun to do), the subject never did resolve that goal before calling it quits.

When the software chose the attributes of the characters (AUTO group), we found that while the trend was in the direction of improved closure, we did not obtain a statistically significant difference from the ORAL group.

Very striking, however, is the fact that when the subjects were allowed to select their own character attributes, they all proceeded to structural completeness, as in the following story:

> In ages past, in a strange land, there was a crabby boy. He did not want to do anything. There was a dog. He was brave. He was not afraid of the crabby

boy. They made friends and played a game. The boy had fun. He was not crabby any more.

Our explanation for this differential behavior is that the students who chose their own character attributes had more of a "stake" in the resolution of the associated conflict that those students who let the system select behaviors randomly. While the RANDOM group received the same text output, and became aware of character attributes immediately after selecting a character for the first time, apparently the passive receipt of this knowledge provided considerably less impetus to resolve the conflict than if the subject had actively chosen the attributes themselves.

In addition to the qualitative measures, a more subjective difference was noted. Students who selected character attributes themselves seemed to display more satisfaction and enthusiasm with their efforts. More menu using students commented that their stories felt "right."

It was clear from the empirical study that the addition of menus to select character attributes had a strongly positive effect on the ability of children to produce a good story. However, the menus which we used required at least a small reading vocabulary, or the presence of a human reader to interpret the attribute. At present, we are investigating two alternative means of providing the same capabilities to pre-literate students: graphical depiction of character attributes (smiling face, sad face, etc.) and digitized voice output. Our intuition is to provide all three mutually reinforcing cues in the menu; that is, we will show the printed attribute, its graphic depiction, and the student will hear the attribute pronounced through the computer.

It is important to point out that the oral stories produced by our subjects were not entirely spontaneous, in that we constrained the children to base the story on the setting and characters which we provided. Totally free-form stories may or may not have resulted in more complex or more structurally complete stories than the ones we obtained. Nonetheless, by imposing the constraint, we are able to directly test the impact of the GSW on storytelling.

RELATED SYSTEMS

Storywriting systems developed for research purposes typically investigate the validity or usefulness of certain linguistic or cognitive theories. For example, the MESSY system [6] incorporates a theory of story generation based on the underlying structure of Russian myths. In this system, all actions are explicitly encoded. It operates by "filling in the blanks" with appropriate words. While the MESSY system is capable of producing relatively complex stories at a fast rate (128 words/sec), it does not engage in planning and does not have any "knowledge" of its story domain.

TALESPIN, developed by James Meehan, creates a fictional world, populates it with characters, assigns them goals, then generates text about the activities of the characters.

The characters make appropriate plans to achieve their goals based on their knowledge of the simulated world [7].

These programs offer significant insight into the task of creating text with a computer. The GSW incorporates ideas from TALESPIN and MESSY in its text generation scheme. The use of a grammar as a controlling structure was demonstrated by MESSY and is incorporated by the GSW, along with a fill-in-the-blank approach to text generation. From TALESPIN, GSW gets the ideas of independent characters motivated to action by discreet goals.

Examples from the commercial world of educational and entertainment software also informed the design of the GSW. The "1-2-3 Sequence Me" software by Sunburst Communications allows users to place pictures and text in logical order. "Super Story Tree" by Scholastic allows users to build or navigate branching, interactive stories. The system provides simple menus and stories can include both text and graphics. "Story Maker" by Bolt, Beranek and Newman, works in a similar way. Super Story Tree and Story Maker allow users to explore story structures, but present only limited and predefined options.

"Once Upon a Time" by Compu-Teach and the "Explore A Story" series by William K. Bradford allow students to illustrate, reorganize and add text to original or pre-written stories. The interface of these programs incorporate simple menus and a mouse or cursor key driven pointer. Neither system provides a dynamic story generation capability or feedback on the user's composition.

"The Playroom" from Broderbund allows users to develop early learning skills such as letter recognition, counting and telling time in an exploratory environment. Clicking on objects in a simulated playroom launches appropriate tasks. For example, selecting a book takes users to the letter recognition game. A product with a similar interface is "McGee" by Lawrence Productions. This program allows users to experiment with objects in a simulated house. When a user clicks on a ball, the system shows an animation of McGee playing with the ball, and displays a descriptive sentence. Neither of these products, however, address story structures.

CONCLUSIONS
The Graphic StoryWriter is a work in progress. In this paper, we have reported on the GSW user interface, the design process which led us to that interface, and we have provided tentative empirical evidence concerning the effectiveness of the GSW in facilitating emergent literacy and promoting the generation of structurally complete stories.

While there are no substitutes for reading or writing, the GSW can provide some unique learning opportunities for early readers. The system allows a user with minimal keyboarding skills to generate structurally complete stories. These stories can serve as models of proper story construction and can dynamically reinforce knowledge of story components. The system demonstrates the relationship between illustrations and text, thus supporting emergent literacy. The simple interface and storywriting engine permit users to experiment with interactions in a judgement-free environment.

ACKNOWLEDGMENTS
From Abraham Lincoln Elementary School in Oak Park, Illinois, we wish to thank Jarvia Thomas, Nancy Alaks, Carol Dudzik, Patrice Keleher and especially the children in Mrs. Thomas's First Grade class for helping us with the design and testing of the Graphic StoryWriter.

REFERENCES
1. Applebee, Arthur N. *The Child's Concept of Story*. University of Chicago Press, Chicago, 1978.

2. Cherry, Louise. The Role of Adults' Requests for Clarification in the Language Development of Children. In R. Freedle (Ed.) *New Directions in Discourse Processing: Vol 2, Advances in Discourse Processing*. Ablex, Hillsdale, NJ, 1977.

3. Costanzo, William V. *The Electronic Text*. Educational Technology Publications Inc., Englewood Cliffs, New Jersey, 1989.

4. Geoffrian, Leo and Geoffrian, Olga. *Computers and Reading Instruction*. Addison Wesley Publishing Company, Reading, Massachusetts, 1983.

5. Hough, Ruth, Nurss, Joanne, and Wood, Delores. Tell Me a Story. Young Children 43 (Nov. 1987), 6-12.

6. Klein, Sheldon, *et al.* Automatic Novel Writing: A Status Report. Computer Science Technical Report 186, University of Wisconsin, Madison, 1973.

7. Meehan, James. *The Metanovel: Writing Stories by Computer*. Garland Publishing, New York, 1980.

8. Mason, Jana and Au, Kathryn. *Reading Instruction for Today*. Harper Collins Publishers, 1990.

9. Nauman, April D. Structure and Perspective in Reading and Writing. In T. Shanahan (Ed.) *Reading and Writing Together: New Perspectives for the Classroom*. Christopher-Gordon Publishers, Norwood, MA., 1990.

10. Stein, Nancy and Glenn, Christine. An Analysis of Story Comprehension in Elementary School Children. In R. Freedle (Ed.) *New Directions in Discourse Processing: Vol 2, Advances in Discourse Processing*. Ablex, Hillsdale, NJ, 1977.

11. Sulzby, Elizabeth. Children's Development of Prosodic Distinctions in Telling and Dictation Modes, in Ann Matsuhashi (Ed.), *Writing in Real Time*. Ablex, Hillside, NJ, 1987.

TOWARD A MORE HUMANE KEYBOARD

William Hargreaves, Ph.D.[a]; David Rempel, M.D.[b]; Nachman (Manny) Halpern[c];
Robert Markison, M.D.[d]; Karl Kroemer, Dr.Ing.[e]; and Jack Litewka.[f]

[a]President, Kinesis Corporation, 15245 Pacific Highway South, Seattle, WA 98188, Phone: 206-241-4595, Fax: 241-9252; [b]Director, Ergonomics Laboratory, University of California at San Francisco, 1301 South 46th Street, Bldg 112, Richmond, CA 94804, Phone: 415-237-7400, Fax: 231-9500; [c]Ergonomics Coordinator, Occupational & Industrial Orthopaedic Center, New York, NY 10014, Phone: 212-255-6690, Fax: 255-6754; [d]Associate Clinical Professor of Surgery at UCSF School of Medicine and Hand Surgeon, San Francisco Hand Specialists, 450 Sutter Street, Suite 2215, San Francisco, CA 94108, Phone: 415-956-2525, Fax: 956-6396; [e]Director, Ergonomics Laboratory, ISE Department, Virginia Tech, Blacksburg, VA 24061-0118, Phone: 703-231-5677, Fax: 231-3322; [f]President, Applied Ergonomics, 13734 39th Avenue N.E., Seattle, WA 98125, Phone: 206-361-1890;

INTRODUCTION (W. HARGREAVES)

Occupational injuries related to computer use have become newsworthy.   Most people who work in an office environment know a coworker who has experienced chronic pain or disabling injury to the upper extremities from computer use. Such injuries are commonly termed "repetitive strain injury" (RSI). To date, the focus for remedies has been on providing adjustable furniture and encouraging work breaks. Though the results of such changes have not yet been widely studied, informal inquiries in the workplace suggest that the problem remains and is growing.

The direct interface between most workers and their computers is the keyboard, and the belief that the traditional keyboard may be a major cause of computer-related RSI is gaining acceptance.   Thus alternative keyboard designs are considered by some to be important factors in reversing or preventing RSI. A number of redesigned "ergonomic keyboards" are currently under development.   Of these, three styles predominate: articulated traditional keyboards, chording keyboards, and hand-contoured keyboards.

Articulated traditional keyboards can exactly replicate a traditional computer keyboard, but they have at least one joint or hinge to allow adjustment of the right and left halves to each user's preference. Chording keyboards use key combinations to produce letters. These keyboards typically have only 8-10 keys, though each switch may have several active positions (e.g. ternary chord keyboard). The hand-contoured keyboard has keys arranged in separate right and left sections which are contoured to match the shape and movement of the hands and fingers. Typically the traditional Qwerty layout is retained in hand-contoured keyboards.

Significantly, there has been no forum for the side-by-side comparison of objectives, features, and demonstrated effectiveness for the different styles of ergonomic keyboards. The intent of this panel is to create such a forum. The first two panelists will present objectives and test methods.   The last three will contribute specific attributes of articulated, chording, and hand-contoured ergonomic keyboards.

MEASURING KEYBOARD-RELATED MUSCULOSKELETAL STRAIN (D. REMPEL)

Repetitive strain injuries due to office work more than doubled from 1989 to 1990 [1] and are probably due to the increased time workers spend using a single tool, the computer keyboard.   These injuries range from muscle fatigue to nerve entrapments and tendon-related disorders. Modifications to the current alphanumeric Sholes brothers' keyboard (Qwerty) have been proposed to make the keyboard safer, but few of these modifications have been rigorously tested to determine whether they meet stated claims. Force is considered a significant risk factor for these injuries, and reducing the keyswitch force of activation (light touch keyboard) has been shown to reduce the force that typists apply [5]. Other work-related risk factors are repetition of a specific motion, awkward joint postures (e.g. wrist in extension), and long durations of exertion without adequate recovery time [6]. Engineering modifications to a keyboard can only alter these risk factors to a certain extent. Task modification and appropriate work-rest cycles will probably play a greater role in reducing these risk factors.

To determine the health impact of keyboard designs, tests can be either of short-term (minutes to several days) or long-term (months to years) duration. Although properly conducted long-term testing is more valuable, it as also more expensive. The most important elements in determining the value of either short or long-term tests are (a) study bias, (b) predictive value of the measurement tool, and (c) number of subjects tested.

Study bias is easily introduced, since it is almost impossible to blind subjects or researchers to keyboards of a different design and have them use the keyboards at the same time. Therefore, subjective measures (How does this keyboard feel?, Are your wrists sore after using this keyboard? Is your typing speed better with this keyboard?) are difficult to interpret. Objective measures are available (typing speed, error rate, joint angle, impact force, muscle electrical activity, nerve function, physical examination, intracarpal pressure) but require experience to collect and interpret. Each of these objective parameters measures a different physiologic aspect of typing and each has a different value in predicting repetitive strain injuries. Finally, if a study has too few subjects, the results may be meaningless.

DESIGN CRITERIA — WHAT SHOULD AN ERGONOMIC KEYBOARD DO, AND HOW CAN WE TELL IF IT DOES IT? (N. HALPERN)

The keyboard has become a common human-machine interface due to the widespread use of video display terminals (VDTs). The tasks involved in VDT operations are varied, yet most require a keyboard as the input device. Only a few studies have investigated the effects of keyboard design on the musculoskeletal system of the operators. Most studies looked at the key layout and emphasized the measurements and mechanical parameters of the keyswitches. In order to investigate the ergonomics of keyboard design we need to examine the demands on the human operator.

The demands of keyboard operation relate to *energy consumption* and *information processing*. Design criteria need to address energy consumption from the viewpoint of both localized dynamic muscular work and static postural effort. Information processing demands relate to visual identification and feedback. The design goals of an improved, ergonomic keyboard should be to:

(1) Optimize the work of muscle groups involved in keying.

(2) Optimize tactile feedback.

(3) Reduce static postural effort.

(4) Facilitate visual identification of keys.

The interest in RSI associated with VDT work indicates the need for a special focus on the muscular demands of this work. Static or postural effort in keyboard operation involves the muscles of the upper extremities, mainly to support the fingers; the dynamic component for these muscles may be small. Stress in the upper extremities is caused by a combination of forearm pronation, ulnar deviation of the wrist, extension of the hand to aid the reach of the smaller fingers, arm abduction, and shoulder elevation. An injury mechanism can be inferred from the few relevant studies.

The important design parameters that affect static postural effort are keyboard size and shape, wrist and arm support, and key layout. Dynamic work performed during keyboard use primarily involves the small muscles of the fingers. Design parameters that affect this effort are key travel, key shape, inter-key distance, keying frequency, keyboard shape, and key assignment (layout). The latter probably also affects the dynamic work performed by muscles in the wrists and forearms.

The presentation will outline ways to achieve ergonomic design goals, taking into consideration the influence of workstation design and work organization parameters on the human operator.

DESIGN LESSONS FROM TROUBLED UPPER LIMBS (R. MARKISON)

The human lifespan was 25 years in ancient Greece, and the present human lifespan is three to four times as long. The author's experience in dissecting thousands of troubled limbs over a 17-year period underscores a pressing need to design tools which work with, rather than against, the delicate form and function of the upper limbs.

As a design-minded hand surgeon, I would like to address a handful of issues:

(1) Flat, non-adjustable keyboards violate the golden rule of muscle function by using muscles at inappropriate fiber lengths.

(2) Non-adjustable keyboards abuse the thumb, which after all, is only 40,000 years old in the context of more than two million years of human hand evolution.

(3) Thirty-five percent of hands have congenital linkage of the ring and little finger flexor tendons; this has great design implications for keyboard development.

(4) Pronation of the forearm combined with ulnar deviation of the wrist and abduction of the little finger away from the hand cause significant difficulties with the ulnar and median nerves, as well as with the tendons that traverse nine separate discrete tunnels at the wrist.

(5) Adjustability is absolutely essential, since we have a broad age span of workers and a broad anthropometric variation among workers who may have very tiny hands or very large hands. Examples will be drawn from repetitive strain injuries among musicians [4].

UNCONVENTIONAL KEYBOARDS — FOR EXAMPLE, THE TERNARY CHORD KEYBOARD (K. KROEMER)

RSI, though known for decades to afflict keyboard operators, has now become an area of major concern. This is partly because of the widespread use of keyboards, and possibly because of heightened health awareness. While numerous proposals have been made to change the keyboard layout since the first commercial typewriter was developed about 125 years ago, the current computer keyboard layout is in essence unchanged from the original. Standardized in 1966, the traditional keyboard has features that demand improvements for biomechanical and psychophysical reasons. These include the key *per se*, the large number of keys, their layout on the keyboard, and the arrangement of the keyboard with respect to the operator.

There are several design variables for keys and keyboards currently used, or proposed. These can be categorized by (1) keyswitch parameters (2) position of the keyboard, and (3) data entry mode (see Table 1). Many of the previously proposed alterations were based on theoretical considerations, some of which are still valid (e.g., number of keys, layout, posture) while others are not (e.g. letter-key-digit allocation).

Each of these variables, alone or combined, affect the user's digit posture, wrist posture, arm posture, and movements (and thus energy requirements). These variables, together with the temporary task requirements, determine the person's musculo-skeletal strain (risk of RSI) and performance (number of entries, errors.).

A comparison of existing or proposed designs indicates that, depending on their specific features, they might affect keyboard operators' health and performance in various ways. We performed experiments on specially designed apparatus to measure finger mobility, strength, and speed. We also had subjects perform extensive learning and performance trials on a prototype of a ternary chord keyboard. The comparison of biomechanical digit characteristics and keying performances showed no or little correlation, which is quite in contrast to previous presumptions.

The results of our survey and experiments have implications for the design, arrangement, and use of future keyboards.

HAND-CONTOURED KEYBOARDS (J. LITEWKA)

It was recognized early on that the Sholes/Qwerty keyboard required awkward postures. Over the last 100 years, many concepts and experimental designs have been introduced to remedy this deficiency. Most early improvements were intended to promote faster typing. However, with recent increases in both incidence and awareness of RSI, keyboard safety has become a paramount issue without detracting from the importance of productivity. As a result, there is a new objective for keyboard designers: minimize the stressful postures, force, and repetition which combine to cause keyboard-related injuries.

In the mid-1970s, I participated in initial research and development of the first commercial hand-contoured keyboard [reviewed in 2]. This keyboard, in limited commercial use for ten years, pioneered ergonomic

TABLE 1. KEYBOARD VARIABLES (KROEMER)

Keyswitch Parameters	Keyboard Attitude	Data Entry Mode
Activation mode	Slope	Activation mode
Activation energy	Slant	(displacement, impulse)
Number of states per key	Tilt	Single (traditional)
Number of keys		Multiple (chording)
Key arrangement		

features intended to reduce strain while maintaining or increasing typing speed and accuracy. Its main features are concave wells containing keys for the right and left hands, separated by a central space. Additional sets of keys are operated by the right and left thumbs. The use of these thumb keys redistributes the work load among the digits, reducing the work done by the little fingers and minimizing ulnar deviation which would otherwise occur when reaching for the outermost keys. Overall geometry reduces pronation, ulnar deviation, wrist extension, and little finger abduction, while providing shorter, simpler reaches for all fingers. Long term use by injured users supports the efficacy of this design in reducing or eliminating pain.

In 1991, an enhanced hand-contoured keyboard with additional features and a reduced learning requirement was developed in the U.S. Location and accessibility of function keys and thumb keys were improved, as was keyswitch tactility. By incorporating built-in palm rests, static postural effort was reduced. The standard layout of the 101-type computer keyboard was largely maintained to minimize learning requirements. The product conforms to a broad range of hand sizes and shapes, from those of children to those of large adults, without the need for moving parts. Importantly, neither the British nor the U.S. designs can be misadjusted by a naive user.

A learning-curve study was conducted with healthy subjects in late 1991, using a prototype of the U.S. hand-contoured keyboard [3]. Additional one- to three-day evaluations by RSI-sufferers have been carried out. Most healthy subjects and all injured subjects preferred the hand-contoured design over the traditional one, finding the former more comfortable and requiring less effort. In the learning-curve study, all subjects reported the hand-contoured keyboard easy to learn, with the majority typing faster than on a traditional keyboard (with equivalent accuracy) after less than eight hours. Injured subjects uniformly reported significant relief from symptoms and increased output.

It appears that an optimized hand-contoured ergonomic keyboard can reduce RSI risk factors without sacrificing productivity or imposing a significant learning curve.

REFERENCES

1. BLS Reports on Survey of Occupational Injuries and Illnesses in 1977-1990. Washington, D.C.: Bureau of Labor Statistics, U.S. Dept of Labor, 1991.

2. Hobday, S.W.. A keyboard to increase productivity and reduce postural stress. In Trends in Ergonomics, Human Factors V. F. Aghazadeh, ed., Elsevier Science Publishers B.V., North Holland, 1988, pp. 321-330.

3. Jahns, D.W., Litewka, J., Lunde, S.A., Farrand, W.P., and Hargreaves, W.R. Learning curve and performance analysis for the Kinesis™ ergonomic keyboard — a pilot study. Presented as a poster at the HFS 35th Annual Meeting (San Francisco, Calif., Sep 2-6, 1991). Copies available from Kinesis[a].

4. Markison, R.E. Treatment of musical hands: redesign of the interface. In Hand Injuries in Sports and Performing Arts. Amadio P.C., Hand Clinics 6,3 (Aug 1990), 525-544.

5. Rempel, D., Gerson, J., Armstrong, T., Foulk, J., Martin, B. Fingertip forces while using three different keyboards. In Proceedings of the HFS 35th annual meeting (San Francisco, Calif., Sep 2-6, 1991). Human Factors Society, Santa Monica, Calif., pp. 253-255.

6. Rempel, D., Harrison, R.J., Barnhart, S. Work-related cumulative trauma disorders of the upper extremity. JAMA 267,6 (Feb 12, 1992).

TreeViz: Treemap Visualization of Hierarchically Structured Information

Brian Johnson

Human-Computer Interaction Lab
Department of Computer Science
University of Maryland
College Park, MD 20742
brianj@cs.umd.edu
(301) 405-2725

INTRODUCTION

TreeViz is an Apple Macintosh implementation of the treemap technique for visualizing hierarchical information structures [2,4].

TreeViz enables users to visualize and browse large hierarchically structured information spaces. TreeViz enables the drawing of hierarchies an order of magnitude larger (# nodes) than is possible with typical presentation methods, given the same display space.

BACKGROUND AND GOALS

The primary goal of this project is the development of improved methods for the visualization of large hierarchically structured information spaces.

Scientific visualization has received a great deal of attention in recent years. There are many reasons for this but chief among them is the simple observation that humans have difficulty extracting meaningful information from large volumes of data. Our increasing ability to produce, disseminate, and collect information has quite naturally led to a demand for tools which aid in the analysis of this information and support our intuition.

Visualization tools increase the bandwidth of the human-computer interface. TreeViz harnesses the power of the machine to graphically encode information, and the power of the human visual processing system to analyze and search this graphical information space.

METHODOLOGY

The treemap visualization technique make efficient use of the available display space, mapping hierarchies onto a rectangular region in a space-filling manner. This efficient use of space allows large hierarchies to be displayed and facilitates the presentation of semantic information.

Presentations of hierarchically structured information typically fall into one or more of the following categories:
- **textual** (listings),
- **positional** (outlines), or
- **diagrammatic** (tree drawings [3]).

The treemap **mosaic** approach eliminates white space; each node is a tile in the overall mosaic. The position, size, color and pattern of tiles convey the properties of individual nodes, just as the patterns and colors of the entire mosaic convey properties of the hierarchy as a whole.

Treemaps partition the display space into a collection of rectangular bounding boxes representing the tree structure (Figures 1-3). The drawing of nodes within their bounding boxes is entirely dependent on the content of the nodes.

The display size of a node is based on the magnitude of its weight relative to the weight of the entire tree [1]. A node's weight can be assigned based on any numeric attribute, as long as the weight of each node is greater than or equal to the sum of the weights of its children.

Trees with well over 1000 nodes can be drawn on a 13" display. Interactive control allows users to specify the presentation of both structural (depth bounds, etc.) and content (display properties such as color mappings) information.

PROJECT RESULTS

Results so far are very encouraging and feedback from users has been positive. An initial counter-balanced, within-subject experiment compared TreeViz with the UNIX command line for directory-browsing tasks. TreeViz performance times were faster for "global" tasks such as locating the largest files in the hierarchy, and comparable to UNIX for "local" questions such as determining the size of a particular file. The subjects were given approximately 15 minutes of treemap training; at least one year of previous UNIX experience was required.

CONCLUSION

Space-filling mosaic approaches to the visualization of hierarchies have great potential. The algorithms are general and the possibilities for mapping information about individual nodes to the display are appealing.

Hierarchies are a natural way of organizing information and have become a ubiquitous part of life in the computer age. The treemap approach to visualizing hierarchies enables meaningful drawings of large hierarchies in a limited space. Treemaps can aid decision-making processes by helping users create accurate mental models of the content and structure of hierarchically structured information spaces.

ACKNOWLEDGEMENTS

Information visualization is an ongoing research project at the University of Maryland Human-Computer Interaction Lab. I would like to thank Ben Shneiderman, my advisor and the originator of the treemap concept, David Turo, my treemapping comrade on the Sun workstations, and all of the members of the HCIL.

REFERENCES

[1] George Furnas. Generalized fisheye views. Proceedings ACM CHI'86, pages 16-23. 1986.

[2] Brian Johnson and Ben Shneiderman. Tree-Maps: A Space-Filling Approach to the Visualization of Hierarchical Information Structures. Proceedings IEEE Visualization '91, pages 284-291, October 22-25, San Diego, CA, 1991.

[3] George Robertson, Jock Mackinlay, and Stuart Card. Cone trees: Animated 3d visualizations of hierarchical information. Proceedings ACM CHI'91, pages 189-194. 1991.

[4] Ben Shneiderman. Tree visualization with tree-maps: A 2-d space-filling approach. Technical Report CAR-TR-548, CS-TR-2645, University of Maryland, College Park, September 1990. to appear in ACM Transactions on Graphics.

[5] Edward Tufte. The Visual Display of Quantitative Information. Graphics Press, Cheshire, CT, 1983.

EXAMPLE

A weighted tree with 26 nodes.

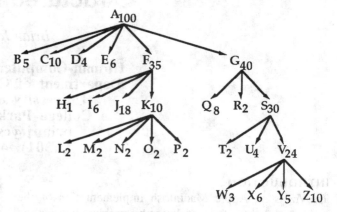

Figure 1: Traditional Tree Diagram Representation.

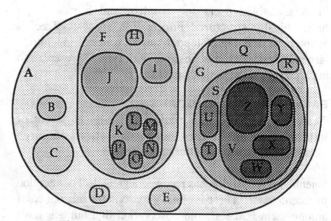

Figure 2: Venn Diagram Representation.
Node size is proportional to weight.

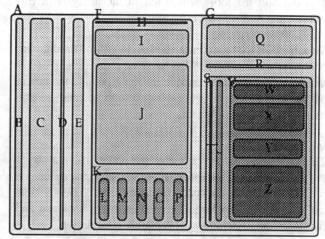

Figure 3: TreeViz Treemap Representation.
Scales transparently to well over 1000 nodes
on a 13" screen. Seeing is believing!

THIS PAGE LEFT BLANK

THIS PAGE LEFT BLANK

FINDING USABILITY PROBLEMS THROUGH HEURISTIC EVALUATION

Jakob Nielsen

Bellcore

445 South Street

Morristown, NJ 07962-1910

nielsen@bellcore.com

ABSTRACT

Usability specialists were better than non-specialists at performing heuristic evaluation, and "double experts" with specific expertise in the kind of interface being evaluated performed even better. Major usability problems have a higher probability than minor problems of being found in a heuristic evaluation, but more minor problems are found in absolute numbers. Usability heuristics relating to exits and user errors were more difficult to apply than the rest, and additional measures should be taken to find problems relating to these heuristics. Usability problems that relate to missing interface elements that ought to be introduced were more difficult to find by heuristic evaluation in interfaces implemented as paper prototypes but were as easy as other problems to find in running systems.

Keywords: Heuristic evaluation, Interface evaluation, Usability problems, Usability expertise, Discount usability engineering, Telephone-operated interfaces.

INTRODUCTION

Heuristic evaluation [17] is a method for finding usability problems in a user interface design by having a small set of evaluators examine the interface and judge its compliance with recognized usability principles (the "heuristics"). Heuristic evaluation thus falls into the general category of usability inspection methods together with methods like pluralistic usability walkthroughs [1], claims analysis [2][3][10], and cognitive walkthroughs [11][19], with the main difference being that it is less formal than the other methods and intended as a "discount usability engineering" [13][16] method. Independent research has found heuristic evaluation to be extremely cost-efficient [8], confirming its value in circumstances where limited time or budgetary resources are available.

The goal of heuristic evaluation is the finding of usability problems in an existing design (such that they can be fixed). One could thus view it as a "debugging" method for user

interfaces. The present article extends previous work on heuristic evaluation [4][12][14][17] by looking more closely at several factors that may influence the probability of finding usability problems. A probabilistic approach is necessary in examining the success of a method that is heuristic and approximate. The factors considered below are the expertise of the evaluators, the severity of the usability problems, the individual heuristics, and the activities needed to identify the problems.

EFFECT OF THE EVALUATORS' USABILITY EXPERTISE

Heuristic evaluation was originally developed as a usability engineering method for evaluators who had some knowledge of usability principles but were not necessarily usability experts as such [17]. Subsequent research has shown the method to be effective also when the evaluators are usability experts [4][8]. Unfortunately, usability experts are sometimes hard and expensive to come by, especially if they also need to have expertise in a particular kind of application.

To investigate the effect of having evaluators with varying levels and kinds of expertise, a study was conducted where the same interface was subjected to heuristic evaluation by three groups of evaluators: "Novice" evaluators with no usability expertise, "regular" usability specialists, and "double" usability specialists who also had experience with the particular kind of interface being evaluated.

A Telephone Operated Interface

A "voice response" system is a computer information system accessed through a touch tone telephone. The user's only input options are the twelve buttons found on a regular telephone (the digits 0–9 and the special characters * and #). The system's only output is through speech and sometimes sound effects. This interaction mechanism provides literally hundreds of millions of terminals to any computer system and allows it to be accessed from almost anywhere in the world [6][7].

Because of the variety of evaluators employed in the present study, a printed dialogue was evaluated instead of a running system. The evaluators were given a dialogue that had been recorded from a voice response system which will be referred to here as the BankingSystem. Evaluating an interface on the basis of a written specification is actually a reasonable task, and is one of the strengths of the heuristic evaluation method. It lends itself to such evaluations as well as to evaluations of implemented systems [14].

The BankingSystem is a telephone operated interface to the user's bank accounts. The user's task in the sample dialogue was to transfer $1,000 from the user's savings account to the user's checking account. The dialogue between the Banking-System (S) and the user (U) in Figure 1 is took place as the user tried to perform this task. This dialogue has actually taken place, the underlying problem being that the user had not authorized the bank to accept transfers over the phone.

The user can be assumed to be provided with printed instructions stating that the system uses the # key to signify the end of the user's input (in the same way as many other systems use an enter key). As long as the user has not hit the # key, it is possible to correct input by pressing ** (the asterisk key used twice). This option is not used in the dialogue in this example, however. The printed instructions were not evaluated as part of the heuristic evaluation.

For the heuristic evaluation, the evaluators were asked to keep in mind those basic technical limitations of the system which were due to the access through a touch tone telephone and not to include criticism of the very use of 12-button input and speech output instead of, say, input though speech recognition or output through graphical dialogues with pull-down menus, etc.

Even the small sample dialogue in Figure 1 contains a rather large number of usability problems as listed below. Readers who are only interested in the general results of the heuristic evaluation and not the individual usability problems can skip ahead to the section titled *Results of the Heuristic Evaluation*. The list of usability problems is ordered according to a rough estimate of the relative seriousness of the problems. Major usability problems are those that have serious potential for confusing users or causing them to use the system erroneously while minor problems may slow down the interaction or inconvenience users unnecessarily. For each problem a brief phrase in italics indicates what well-established usability principle was broken by the dialogue with respect to that problem. These phrases are taken from the list of nine usability heuristics used in earlier papers on heuristic evaluation [12][17] and are discussed in further detail in [16].

Major Problems

Problem 1. The error message in statement 11 appears much too late. It is not reasonable to have the user enter large amounts of information only to learn that it was all in vain. The error message should have appeared immediately after the user's initial choice of the function in statement 2. One evaluator noted that the current form of the dialogue seems to be designed as a front end to a traditional full screen mainframe system where users fill in an entire screen of data before hitting enter and transmitting all of the data to the computer at once. Even if the bank's main computer system with the account database were indeed a traditional transaction-oriented mainframe, one should not let the properties of the backend computer impact the dialogue when a new interaction medium is introduced. In many cases, the best solution would be to prevent the error from occurring in the first place by only listing those functions in the main menu which the user is authorized to use. *(Simple and natural dialogue).*

(First there is a short dialogue in which the user is identified by entering an identification number and a secret access code—this is not part of the evaluation exercise)

(1) S: Enter one for account information, three for transfers between your own accounts, ...

(2) U: **3#**   *{the user interrupts the system}*

(3) S: Enter account to transfer from

(4) U: **1234567890#**   *{savings account number}*

(5) S: Enter account to transfer to

(6) U: **#**   *{an abbreviation for the checking account}*

(7) S: Enter amount in cents

(8) U: **100000#**

(9) S: From account number twelve thirtyfour fiftysix seventyeight ninety to account number primary account, a transfer of one thousand dollars is to be made. Press one to confirm, zero to cancel.

(10) U: **1#**

(11) S: You do not have access to use this function.

Figure 1   *A sample dialogue between a user (U) and the BankingSystem (S). The statement numbers are not part of the dialogue but are used to refer to individual statements in the analysis.*

Problem 2. Users should not be required to convert an amount of money to cents since only a very mathematically inclined person will find it easy to think of $1,000 as 100,000 cents. This problem can be completely avoided by simplifying the system to allow transfer of whole dollar amounts only. Doing so will also speed up the interaction by eliminating two keystrokes. For transfers between the user's own accounts, whole dollars will be completely adequate. For a bill-payment system, it might be still be necessary to have some mechanism for specifying cents. In that case, a solution might be to have users enter first the dollars and then be prompted for the cents. Since the system allows the user to interrupt prompts, a transfer of a whole dollar amount could still be achieved very fast if the user entered **1000##** to signify $1,000. The fact that there were no digits between the two # keystrokes would mean "and no cents." *(Speak the user's language).*

Problem 3. The error message in statement 11 is not precise. It is not clear what "this function" refers to. The problem could be transfers in general, transfers between the two specific accounts, or that the user did not have the $1,000 in the savings account. The system should explicitly state that the user was not allowed to initiate any transfers, thus also avoiding the use of the computer-oriented term "function." The expression "access" is also imprecise as well as being a rather computer-oriented term. An access problem might have been due to system trouble as well as the missing authorization form to allow telephone-initiated transfers. *(Precise and constructive error messages).*

Problem 4. The error message in statement 11 is not constructive. It does not provide any indication of how the user might solve the problem. Users might think that the bank did not want their category of customers to use the transfer facility or that the problem would solve itself if they had more money in their account. *(Precise and constructive error messages)*.

Problem 5. The expression "primary account" in statement 9 is not user-oriented. The system should use user-oriented terms like "checking account." *(Speak the user's language)*.

Problem 6. Instead of having the user enter ten digit account numbers, the system could provide the user with a short menu of that user's accounts. There is a much larger risk that the user will make errors when entering a ten digit account number than when entering a single digit menu selection. A menu-based dialogue would probably speed up the dialogue since users would be required to do much less typing and would not need to look up their account numbers. In statement 6, the current design does provide a shortcut by letting the checking account number be the default but this shortcut again involves some risk of errors. Also note that a menu of account names might be difficult to construct if the customer had several accounts of the same type. Assuming that most customers do limit themselves to one of each account, it would still be best to use the menu approach for those customers and stay with the current interface for the difficult customers only: Just because one cannot solve a problem for 100% of the users, one should not skimp out of solving it for, say, the 80% for which a better solution can be found. *(Prevent errors)*.

Problem 7. It is very likely that the user will forget to press the # key after having entered menu selections or account numbers. Since the number of digits is predetermined for all user input except for the amount of money, the system in fact does not need a general terminator. The system should only require a # in situations where the input has an indeterminate number of digits and it should then explicitly state the need for this terminator in the prompt. In these few cases, the system could furthermore use a timeout function to give the user a precise and constructive reminder after a certain period of time without any user input, since such a period would normally indicate that the user had finished entering input but had forgotten about the #. *(Prevent errors)*.

Problem 8. The feedback in statement 9 with respect to the chosen accounts simply repeats the user's input but ought to restate it instead in simpler and more understandable terms. Instead of listing a ten-digit account number, the feedback message should provide the system's interpretation of the user's input and state something like "from your savings account." By using the name of the account (and by explicitly including the word "your"), the system would increase the user's confidence that the correct account had indeed been specified. *(Provide feedback)*.

Minor Problems

Problem 9. The listing of the main menu in statement 1 should reverse the order of the selection number and the function description for each menu item. The current ordering requires users to remember each number as the corresponding description is being spoken since they do not yet know whether they might want to select the function [5]. *(Minimize the user's memory load)*.

Problem 10. The most natural order of menu options in this type of system would be a simple numeric order, so the main menu in statement 1 should not skip directly from selection 1 to 3. Users who remember that account transfers were the

second option on the list might be inclined to utilize the interrupt facility in the system and simply enter 2 without waiting to hear that the menu choice should have been 3 because there is no option 2 in the system. *(Simple and natural dialogue)*.

Problem 11. Feedback on the user's choice of accounts and amounts appears much too late. Normally a lack of feedback would be a "major" problem, but the present design does provide the ** editing facility as well as some feedback (even though it is delayed). *(Provide feedback)*.

Problem 12. The options in the accept/cancel menu in statement 9 have been reversed compared to the natural order of the numbers zero and one. Actually it would be possible to achieve some consistency with the rest of the dialogue by using the # key to accept and the * key to cancel. Note that some systems (for instance many British systems) have the reverse convention and use * to indicate the answer yes and # to indicate the answer no. The assignment of meaning to these two keys is more or less arbitrary but should obviously be consistent within the system. The choice between the two meanings of # and * should be made to achieve consistency with the majority of other similar systems in the user's environment. *(Simple and natural dialogue)*.

Problem 13. The phrase "account number primary account" in statement 9 is awkward. When referring to an account by name instead of number, the field label "number" should be suppressed. *(Simple and natural dialogue)*.

Problem 14. The term "account" in prompts 3 and 5 should be changed to "account number" as the user is required to enter the number. *(Speak the user's language)*.

Problem 15. It would probably be better to read out the account numbers one digit at a time instead of using the pairwise grouping in statement 9 since users may well think of their account numbers as grouped differently. The change in feedback method should only apply to the account numbers since it is better to report $1,000 as "one thousand dollars" than as "dollars one zero zero zero." *(Simple and natural dialogue)*.

Problem 16. Different words are used for the same concept; "enter" and "press." It is probably better to use the less computer-oriented word "press." *(Consistency)*.

The complete voice response system raises several usability issues in addition to the sixteen problems discussed above. One of the most important issues is the voice quality which of course cannot be evaluated in a printed version of the dialogue. Normally one would caution against using the almost identical prompts "Enter account to transfer from/to" (statements 3 and 5) since users could easily confuse them. But the speaker in a voice dialogue can place sufficient emphasis on the words "from" and "to" to make the difference between the prompts obvious.

Results of the Heuristic Evaluation

The BankingSystem in Figure 1 was subjected to heuristic evaluation by three groups of evaluators with varying levels of usability expertise. The first group consisted of 31 computer science students who had completed their first programming course but had no formal knowledge of user interface design principles. These novice evaluators were

	Novice evaluators	"Regular" specialists	"Double" specialists
Major usability problems:			
1. Error message appears much too late	68%	84%	100%
2. Do not require a dollar amounts to be entered in cents	68%	74%	79%
3. The error message is not precise	55%	63%	64%
4. The error message is not constructive	6%	11%	21%
5. Replace term "primary account" with "checking account"	10%	47%	43%
6. Let users choose accounts from a menu	16%	32%	43%
7. Only require a # where it is necessary	3%	32%	71%
8. Give feedback in form of the name of the chosen account	6%	26%	64%
Average for the major problems	**29%**	**46%**	**61%**
Minor usability problems:			
9. Read menu item description before the action number	3%	11%	71%
10. Avoid the gap in menu numbers between 1 and 3	42%	42%	79%
11. Provide earlier feedback	42%	63%	71%
12. Replace use of 1/0 for accept/reject with #/*	6%	21%	43%
13. Remove the field label "number" when no number is given	10%	32%	36%
14. Change the prompt "account" to "account number"	6%	37%	36%
15. Read numbers one digit at a time	6%	47%	79%
16. Use "press" consistently and avoid "enter"	0%	32%	57%
Average for the minor problems	**15%**	**36%**	**59%**
Average for all the problems	**22%**	**41%**	**60%**

Table 1 *The proportion of evaluators who found each of the sixteen usability problems. "Double" usability specialists had expertise in both usability in general and interfaces to telephone-operated interfaces in particular.*

expected to indicate a worst-case level of performance. Note that they were "novices" with respect to usability but not with respect to computers as such. The second group consisted of 19 "regular" usability specialists, i.e., people with experience in user interface design and evaluation but no special expertise in voice response systems. There is no official certification of usability specialists, but for the purpose of this study, usability specialists were defined as people with graduate degrees and/or several years of job experience in the usability area. The third group consisted of 14 specialists in voice response usability. These "double specialists" had expertise in user interface issues as well as voice response systems and were therefore expected to indicate the best level of heuristic evaluation performance one might hope for.

Table 1 presents the results of the three sets of evaluations and shows that heuristic evaluation was difficult for single evaluators. The above list of usability problems was constructed on the basis of the complete set of evaluations, but no single evaluator found all the problems. Problems 7, 9, 11, 12, 14, and 15 were not included in my own original list of problems but were added after I read the other evaluators' lists. On the other hand, the really catastrophic problems 1, 2, and 3 were found by more than half of the evaluators even in the group without any experience. Just fixing these three problems would improve the interface tremendously.

No group did really well, even though the "double specialists" with both usability expertise and voice response expertise were able to find well over half of the problems on the average. Table 1 indicates that usability specialists are better than people without usability training at finding usability problems and that it helps even more to have usability exper-

tise with respect to the type of user interface being evaluated. The differences between the novices and the regular specialists and between the regular and double specialists are both statistically significant at the $p<.001$ level according to t-tests.

The average performance of individual evaluators may not be acceptable for the use of heuristic evaluation in a usability engineering project, even in the case of the double specialists, but the picture changes when the performance of groups of multiple evaluators is considered. Figure 2 shows the average proportion of the usability problems that would be found by aggregating the sets of problems found by several evaluators. These aggregates were formed in the same way as in previous studies of heuristic evaluation [17]. That is to say, for each group size, a large number of random groups were formed, and for each group, a given usability problem was considered found if at least one member of the group had found it. As can be seen from Figure 2, groups of double and regular usability specialists perform much better than groups of novice evaluators without usability expertise.

For the regular usability specialists, the recommendation from previous work on heuristic evaluation [17] holds in that between three and five evaluators seem necessary to find a reasonably high proportion of the usability problems (here, between 74% and 87%). For the double specialists, however, it is sufficient to use between two and three evaluators to find most problems (here, between 81% and 90%). For the novice evaluators, a group size of fourteen is necessary to find more than 75% of the problems. Using five novice evaluators, which is the upper range of the group size normally recommended for heuristic evaluation, results in the finding of 51% of the usability problems.

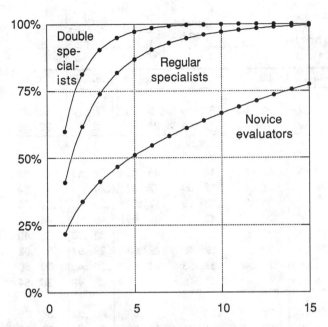

Figure 2 *Average proportion of usability problems found as a function of number of evaluators in a group performing the heuristic evaluation.*

Regular vs. Double Specialists

As mentioned above, the double specialists found significantly more usability problems than did the regular usability specialists. As can be seen from Table 1, the two groups of evaluators actually performed about equally well on many of the usability problems. A large part of the difference in performance is due to the five usability problems for which the probability of being found was thirty percentage points or more higher when the evaluators were voice response usability specialists than when they were regular usability specialists. As outlined below, these five problems were all either specifically related to the use of a telephone as the terminal or were related to the differences between auditory dialogues and screen dialogues.

Problem 9 (read menu item description before the action number) was found by 60% more voice response usability experts than regular usability experts. Even though a similar design issue of whether to list menu selection labels to the left or to the right applies to screen-based menus, the choice would be less crucial for usability. As a matter of fact, screen-based menus are probably better off having the label to the left of the description of the menu item (corresponding to reading the action number before the menu item description) since such a design leads to a uniform, close spacing between the two elements in each line of the menu.

Problem 7 (only require a # where it is necessary) was found by 39% more voice response usability experts than regular usability experts. This problem is much more relevant for telephone-based interfaces than for screen-based interfaces. Actually, the advice to speed up screen-based dialogues by eliminating the need for an enter key wherever possible would probably lead to *less* usable screen interfaces because of the reduced consistency.

Problem 8 (give feedback in form of the name of the chosen account instead of repeating ten digits) was found by 38%

more voice response usability experts than regular usability experts. The underlying issue of providing understandable feedback would also apply to screen-based interfaces but the problem would be less serious in such a system because it would be easier for users to understand the ten-digit numbers in their printed form.

Problem 10 (avoid the gap in menu numbers between 1 and 3) was found by 37% more voice response usability experts than regular usability experts. Even though screen-based menus are also more usable when they are sequentially numbered, the numbering is less crucial in the case where the user can see the complete list of numbers simultaneously. A screen-based menu might have a blank line where menu item 2 would normally have been, thus indicating to the user that the number was reserved for a future extension of the system, if that was the reason for omitting the number from the menu. Often, screen menus for non-mouse systems would actually be based on mnemonic characters rather than numbers.

Problem 15 (read numbers one digit at a time) was found by 32% more voice response usability experts than regular usability experts. This problem could only occur in an auditory dialogue and the regular usability specialists would have no prior experience with this exact problem. A similar problem does occur in traditional screen dialogues with respect to the way one should present numbers such as telephone numbers or social security numbers that are normally grouped in a specific way in the user's mind.

These detailed results indicate that the double specialists found more problems, not because they were necessarily better usability specialists in general, but because they had specific experience with usability issues for the kind of user interface that was being evaluated.

In the discussion below of additional factors influencing the finding of usability problems through heuristic evaluation, the results from the "regular" specialists in the BankingSystem evaluation are used since they are the closest to the evaluators used in the other studies that are analyzed.

USABILITY PROBLEM CHARACTERISTICS

Table 2 summarizes six heuristic evaluations. Teledata, Mantel, and the Savings and Transport systems are documented in [17] and the names from that paper are used as headings. For the BankingSystem, the results are given with the "regular" usability specialists as evaluators. The Integrating System was evaluated by "regular" usability specialists and is discussed in [15]. The table only represents those usability problems that were actually found when evaluating the respective interfaces. It is possible that some additional usability problems remain that were not found by anybody, but it is obviously impossible to produce statistics for such problems.

Table 2 also shows three different ways of classifying the usability problems: by severity (i.e., expected impact on the users), by heuristic, and by location in the dialogue. Table 3 then shows the results of an analysis of variance of the finding of the 211 usability problems by single evaluators, with the independent variables being severity, heuristic, and location as well as the system being evaluated and the implementation of its interface. Two implementation categories were used: Teledata, Mantel, and the Banking System were evalu-

Name of interface:	Tele-data		Mantel		Banking System		All paper prototypes		Savings		Transport		Integrating System		All running systems		All problems	
Number of evaluators:	1	3	1	3	1	3	1	3	1	3	1	3	1	3	1	3	1	3
All problems (211)	.51	.81	.38	.60	.41	.74	.45	.74	.26	.50	.20	.42	.29	.59	.26	.54	.35	.63
Severity of problem:																		
Major usability problems (59)	.49	.79	.44	.64	.46	.77	.47	.74	.32	.63	.32	.65	.46	.79	.38	.70	.42	.71
Minor usability problems (152)	.52	.82	.36	.59	.36	.71	.45	.73	.26	.50	.19	.41	.21	.51	.22	.48	.32	.59
Applicable heuristic:																		
Simple and natural dialogue (51)	.52	.77	.51	.78	.46	.79	.51	.78	.14	.36	.21	.48	.31	.60	.24	.51	.39	.66
Speak the user's language (35)	.60	.90	.47	.70	.53	.88	.55	.83	.33	.62	.14	.32	.25	.62	.24	.51	.41	.68
Minimize user memory load (8)	.44	.81	.94	1.00	.11	.30	.48	.73	.26	.62	.15	.39	.27	.57	.24	.54	.36	.63
Be consistent (33)	.51	.85	.13	.34	.32	.70	.44	.76	.31	.58	.13	.29	.17	.39	.22	.45	.31	.58
Provide feedback (21)	.60	.87	.68	.96	.45	.79	.58	.87	.39	.72	.48	.85	.39	.69	.40	.72	.46	.77
Provide clearly marked exits (9)	.19	.50	.03	.09	•	•	.09	.26	.43	.62	.22	.53	•	•	.32	.58	.20	.40
Provide shortcuts (12)	.39	.78	•	•	•	•	.39	.78	.33	.67	.19	.48	.29	.63	.28	.61	.29	.62
Good error messages (25)	.42	.73	.33	.62	.37	.63	.38	.66	.23	.46	.33	.53	.27	.66	.25	.48	.30	.56
Prevent errors (17)	.50	.86	.17	.39	.32	.70	.29	.59	.19	.45	.21	.48	.37	.79	.22	.49	.25	.54
Where is problem located:																		
A single dialogue element (104)	.58	.85	.42	.66	.40	.75	.49	.77	.26	.53	.22	.45	.30	.59	.26	.53	.38	.66
Comparison of two elements (43)	.52	.85	.13	.35	.32	.70	.48	.80	.27	.53	.14	.34	.24	.56	.24	.51	.31	.60
Overall structure of dialogue (18)	.50	.84	•	•	.53	.84	.51	.84	.33	.67	.24	.50	.21	.53	.25	.54	.35	.66
Something missing (46)	.35	.67	.33	.51	.10	.30	.33	.58	.29	.55	.21	.49	.41	.71	.30	.58	.31	.58

Table 2 *Proportion of various types of usability problems found in each of the six interfaces discussed in this article, as well as in the collected set of 211 usability problems from all of them. The proportion of problems found is given both when the heuristic evaluation is performed by a single evaluator and when it is performed by aggregating the evaluations from three evaluators. Bullets (•) indicate categories of usability problems that were not present in the interface in question. The total number of usability problems is listed in parentheses for each category.*

ated as paper prototypes, whereas the Savings, Transport, and Integrating Systems were evaluated as running programs.

Even though Table 2 would seem to indicate that paper interfaces are easier to evaluate heuristically than running systems, one cannot necessarily draw that conclusion in general on the basis of the data presented in this paper, since different systems were evaluated in the two conditions. Earlier work on heuristic evaluation [14][17] did speculate that heuristic evaluation might be easier for interfaces with a high degree of persistence that can be pondered at leisure, and it is certainly true that paper prototypes are more persistent than running interfaces.

Table 3 shows that the system being evaluated had a fairly small effect in itself. This would seem to indicate a certain robustness of the heuristic evaluation method, but this result could also be due to the limited range of systems analyzed here. More studies of the application of heuristic evaluation to a wider range of interface styles and application domains will be needed to fully understand which systems are easy to evaluate with heuristic evaluation.

Major vs. Minor Usability Problems

Previous research on heuristic evaluation has pointed out that it identifies many more of the minor usability problems in an interface than other methods do [8]. Indeed, heuristic evaluation picks up minor usability problems that are often not even *seen* in actual user testing. One could wonder to what extent such "problems" should really be accepted as constituting usability problems. I argue that such minor

usability problems may very well be real problems even though they are not observable in a user test. For example, inconsistent placement of the same information in different screens or dialog boxes may slow down the user by less than a second [18] and may therefore not be observed in a user test unless an extremely careful analysis is performed on the basis of a large number of videotaped or logged interactions. Such an inconsistency constitutes a usability problem nevertheless, and should be removed if possible. Also note that sub-second slowdowns actually accumulate to causing major costs in the case of highly used systems such as, e.g., those used by telephone company operators.

The top part of Table 2 compares the proportion of the major and the minor usability problems. A usability problem was

	df	Mean Square	p	ω^2
Problem severity	1	.842	.001	6.8%
Heuristic used	8	.118	.01	5.0%
Location of problem	3	.047	.37	0.1%
Implementation of interface	1	.747	.07	1.9%
System (nested in Implementation)	4	.123	.03	3.4%
Implementation × Location	3	.159	.02	6.8%
Residual	190	.044		

Table 3 *Analysis of variance for the probability of finding the 211 usability problems when using single evaluators. Other interactions than the one shown are not significant.*

ω^2 *indicates relative effect sizes in terms of proportion of total variance accounted for.*

defined as "major" if it had serious potential for confusing users or causing them to use the system erroneously. Note that the term "serious" was used to denote this category of usability problems in earlier work [12]. Given that the usability problems were found by heuristic evaluation and not by user testing, this classification can only reflect a considered judgment, since no measurement data exists to prove the true impact of each problem on the users. For the Teledata, Mantel, Savings, and Transport interfaces, the major/minor classification was arrived at by two judges with a small number of disagreements resolved by consensus, and for the Banking System a single judge was used. For the Integrating System, the mean severity classification from eleven judges was used. The simple classification of usability problems into only two severity levels was chosen because of this need to rely on a judgment; it was mostly fairly easy to decide which severity category to use for any given usability problem. See [9] and [15] for further discussions of severity ratings.

It is apparent from Table 2 that heuristic evaluation tends to find a higher proportion of the major usability problems than of the minor, and Table 3 indicates that the difference is statistically significant ($p<.001$) and one of the two largest effects identified in the table. Intuitively, one might even have gone as far as to expect the evaluators performing the heuristic evaluations to focus only on the major usability problems to the exclusion of the minor ones, but the results indicate that this is not the case since they find many more minor than major problems in absolute numbers (8.1 vs. 4.1 per system on the average). So the evaluators pay relatively more attention to the major problems without neglecting the minor ones.

Since the interfaces have many more minor than major problems, the minor problems will obviously dominate any given heuristic evaluation, even though the probability of being found is greater for the major problems. Usability engineers therefore face the task of prioritizing the usability problems to make sure that more time is spent on fixing the major problems than on fixing the minor problems.

Effect of the Individual Heuristics

Since heuristic evaluation is based on judging interfaces according to established usability principles, one might expect that problems violating certain heuristics would be easier to find than others. Table 3 indicates a significant and fairly large effect for heuristic. Even so, Table 2 shows that there are few systematic trends with respect to some heuristics being easier.

Considering all the 211 usability problems as a whole, Table 2 shows that usability problems have about the same probability of being found in a heuristic evaluation with the recommended three evaluators for most of the heuristics. Seven of the nine heuristics score in the interval from 54–68%, with the "good error messages" and "prevent errors" heuristics being slightly more difficult than the others. The only truly difficult heuristic is "provide clearly marked exits" (scoring 40%). The practical consequence from this result is that one might "look harder" for usability problems violating the "provide clearly marked exits" heuristic. For example, one could run a user test with a specific focus on cases where the users got stuck. One could also study user errors more closely in order to compensate for the relative difficulty of applying the two error-related heuristics, especially since

problems related to user errors are likely to prove especially costly if the system were to be released with these problems still in place.

A contrast analysis of significance based on an analysis of variance for three evaluators confirms that usability problems classified under the "good error messages," "prevent errors," and "provide clearly marked exits" heuristics are more difficult to find than usability problems classified under one of the other six heuristics, with $p=.0006$.

Location of Problems in Dialogue

Even though the specific usability heuristic used to classify the usability problems had some impact on the evaluators' ability to find the problems, it might also be the case that other systematic differences between the problems can help explain why some problems are easier to find than others. Since heuristic evaluation is a process in which the evaluators search for usability problems, it seems reasonable to consider whether the circumstances under which the problems could be located have any influence.

The bottom part of Table 2 shows the result of considering four different possible locations of usability problems. The first category of problems are those that are located in a *single* dialogue element. An example of this category of usability problem is Problem 2 (do not require a dollar amount to be entered as cents) in the telephone operated interface analyzed earlier in this article. To find single-location problems by heuristic evaluation, the evaluator only needs to consider each interface element in isolation and judge that particular dialog box, error message, menu, etc.

The second category consists of usability problems that require the evaluator to *compare* two interface elements. This will typically be consistency problems where each interface element is fine when seen in isolation but may lead to problems when used together. An example from the BankingSystem is Problem 16 (both "press" and "enter" are used to denote the same concept).

The third category contains the usability problems that are related to the overall *structure* of the dialogue. An example from the BankingSystem is Problem 7 (only require a # where it is necessary). Another example would be the need to unify the navigation system for a large menu structure. These problems require the evaluator to get a grasp of the overall use of the system.

The final category of usability problems are those that cannot be seen in any current interface element but denote *missing* interface elements that ought to be there. An example from the BankingSystem is Problem 4 (the error message should have a constructive message appended). Note that the issue here is not that the current error message is poorly worded (that is easy to find and belongs in the category of single-location problems) but that the message ought to be supplemented with an additional element.

As can be seen from Table 3, the difference between the four location categories is not statistically significant. However, the interaction effect between location category and interface implementation *is* significant and has one of the two largest effect sizes in the table. As shown in Table 2, problems in the category "something missing" are slightly easier to find than other problems in running systems but much harder to find than other problems in paper prototypes. This finding corresponds to an earlier, qualitative, analysis of the usability problems that were harder to find in a paper implementation than in a running system [14]. Because of this difference, one should look harder for missing dialogue elements when evaluating paper mockups.

A likely explanation of this phenomenon is that evaluators using a running system may tend to get stuck when needing a missing interface element (and thus notice it), whereas evaluators of a paper "implementation" just turn to the next page and focus on the interface elements found there.

CONCLUSIONS

Usability specialists were much better than those without usability expertise at finding usability problems by heuristic evaluation. Furthermore, usability specialists with expertise in the specific kind of interface being evaluated did much better than regular usability specialists without such expertise, especially with regard to certain usability problems that were unique to that kind of interface.

Previous results [17] with respect to the improvement in heuristic evaluation performance as groups of evaluators are aggregated were replicated in the new study reported above, and the general recommendation of using groups of 3–5 evaluators also held for the regular usability specialists in this study. For double specialists, a smaller group size can be recommended, since only two to three such evaluators were needed to find most problems. Of course, the actual number of evaluators to use in any particular project will depend on a trade-off analysis on the basis of curves like Figure 2 and the cost (financial or otherwise) of leaving usability problems unfound.

Major usability problems have a higher probability than minor problems of being found in a heuristic evaluation, but about twice as many minor problems are found in absolute numbers. Problems with the lack of clearly marked exits are harder to find than problems violating the other heuristics, and additional efforts should therefore be taken to identify such usability problems. Also, usability problems that relate to a missing interface element are harder to find when an interface is evaluated in a paper prototype form.

The results in this article provide means for improving the contribution of heuristic evaluation to an overall usability engineering effort. The expertise of the staff performing the evaluation has been seen to matter, and specific shortcomings of the methods have been identified such that other methods or additional efforts can be employed to alleviate them and find more of the usability problems that are hard to find by heuristic evaluation.

ACKNOWLEDGMENTS

The author would like to thank Jan C. Clausen, Heather Desurvire, Dennis Egan, Anker Helms Jørgensen, Clare-Marie Karat, Tom Landauer, Rolf Molich, and Robert W. Root for helpful comments on previous versions of the manuscript. The four studies reported in [17] were conducted by the author and Rolf Molich who also participated in the classification of usability problems as major or minor and in relating the problems to the heuristics. The further analyses and conclusions on the basis of this and other data as reported here reflect the views of the author of the present paper only.

REFERENCES

1. Bias, R. Walkthroughs: Efficient collaborative testing. *IEEE Software* **8**, 5 (September 1991), 94–95.

2. Carroll, J.M. Infinite detail and emulation in an ontologically minimized HCI. *Proc. ACM CHI'90* (Seattle, WA, 1–5 April 1990), 321–327.

3. Carroll, J.M., Kellogg, W.A., and Rosson, M.B. The task-artifact cycle. In Carroll, J.M. (Ed.), *Designing Interaction: Psychology at the Human–Computer Interface.* Cambridge University Press, Cambridge, U.K., 1991. 74–102.

4. Desurvire, H., Lawrence, D., and Atwood, M. Empiricism versus judgement: Comparing user interface evaluation methods on a new telephone-based interface. *ACM SIGCHI Bulletin* **23**, 4 (October 1991), 58–59.

5. Engelbeck, G., and Roberts, T.L. The effect of several voice-menu characteristics on menu selection performance. *Behaviour & Information Technology* **in press**.

6. Gould, J.D., and Boies, S.J. Speech filing—An office system for principals. *IBM Systems Journal* **23**, 1 (1984), 65–81.

7. Halstead-Nussloch, R. The design of phone-based interfaces for consumers. *Proc. ACM CHI'89* (Austin, TX, 30 April–4 May 1989), 347–352.

8. Jeffries, R., Miller, J.R., Wharton, C., and Uyeda, K.M. User interface evaluation in the real world: A comparison of four techniques. *Proc. ACM CHI'91* (New Orleans, LA, 27 April–2 May 1991), 119–124.

9. Karat, C.-M., Campbell, R., Fiegel, T. Comparisons of empirical testing and walkthrough methods in user interface evaluation. *Proc. ACM CHI'92* (Monterey, CA, 3–7 May 1992).

10. Kellogg, W.A. Qualitative artifact analysis. *Proc. INTERACT'90 3rd IFIP Conf. Human–Computer Interaction* (Cambridge, U.K., 27–31 August 1990), 193–198.

11. Lewis, C., Polson, P., Wharton, C., and Rieman, J. Testing a walkthrough methodology for theory-based design of walk-up-and-use interfaces. *Proc. ACM CHI'90* (Seattle, WA, 1–5 April 1990), 235–241.

12. Molich, R., and Nielsen, J. Improving a human-computer dialogue. *Communications of the ACM* **33**, 3 (March 1990), 338–348.

13. Nielsen, J. Usability engineering at a discount. In Salvendy, G., and Smith, M.J. (Eds.), *Designing and Using Human–Computer Interfaces and Knowledge Based Systems*, Elsevier Science Publishers, Amsterdam, 1989. 394–401.

14. Nielsen, J. Paper versus computer implementations as mockup scenarios for heuristic evaluation. *Proc. INTERACT'90 3rd IFIP Conf. Human–Computer Interaction* (Cambridge, U.K., 27–31 August 1990), 315–320.

15. Nielsen, J. Applying heuristic evaluation to a highly domain-specific interface. *Manuscript submitted for publication.*

16. Nielsen, J. *Usability Engineering.* Academic Press, San Diego, CA, 1992.

17. Nielsen, J., and Molich, R. Heuristic evaluation of user interfaces. *Proc. ACM CHI'90* (Seattle, WA, 1–5 April 1990), 249–256.

18. Teitelbaum, R.C., and Granda, R.E. The effects of positional constancy on searching menus for information. *Proc. ACM CHI'83* (Boston, MA, 12–15 December 1983), 150–153.

19. Wharton, C., Bradford, J., Jeffries, R., and Franzke, M. Applying cognitive walkthroughs to more complex interfaces: Experiences, issues, and recommendations. *Proc. ACM CHI'92* (Monterey, CA, 3–7 May 1992).

APPLYING COGNITIVE WALKTHROUGHS TO MORE COMPLEX USER INTERFACES: EXPERIENCES, ISSUES, AND RECOMMENDATIONS

Cathleen Wharton

Hewlett-Packard Laboratories
and
Dept. of Computer Science and
Institute of Cognitive Science
University of Colorado
Boulder, Colorado 80309-0430
cwharton@cs.colorado.edu

Janice Bradford
Robin Jeffries

Hewlett-Packard Laboratories
P. O. Box 10490
Palo Alto, CA 94303-0867
bradford@hplabs.hpl.hp.com
jeffries@hplabs.hpl.hp.com

Marita Franzke

U S WEST Advanced Technologies
and
Dept. of Psychology and
Institute of Cognitive Science
University of Colorado
Boulder, Colorado 80309-0345
mfranzke@clipr.colorado.edu

ABSTRACT

The Cognitive Walkthrough methodology was developed in an effort to bring cognitive theory closer to practice; to enhance the design and evaluation of user interfaces in industrial settings. For the first time, small teams of professional developers have used this method to critique three complex software systems. In this paper we report evidence about how the methodology worked for these evaluations. We focus on five core issues: (1) task selection, coverage, and evaluation, (2) the process of doing a Cognitive Walkthrough, (3) requisite knowledge for the evaluators, (4) group walkthroughs, and (5) the interpretation of results. Our findings show that many variables can affect the success of the technique; we believe that if the Cognitive Walkthrough is ultimately to be successful in industrial settings, the method must be refined and augmented in a variety of ways.

KEYWORDS: Cognitive Walkthrough, group walkthroughs, task-based evaluations, usability inspection method, user interface evaluation.

INTRODUCTION

The need for practical techniques for critiquing and iterating a user interface design early and often in the development process is well recognized. The ideal technique would be usable early in the development cycle and inexpensive in monetary cost, time, and the need for access to scarce expertise. Several evaluation techniques are available that attempt to meet various of those goals, e.g., usability testing, heuristic evaluation, guidelines and style guides, GOMS analyses, and Cognitive Walkthroughs [3, 5, 6, 8, 11]. This paper reports on experiences using the Cognitive Walkthrough method in real development environments.

The Cognitive Walkthrough is a model-specific methodology originally designed for the evaluation of simple *Walk Up and Use* interfaces. Consequently, most applications of the method have been based on interfaces of that type (see [7, 8, 13]). Recently, however, there have been attempts to understand how the method scales up to interfaces that are themselves more complex, but still support infrequent or novice users [2, 5, 7]. Additionally, it has been a goal [of 2 and 5] to conduct these evaluations in more realistic contexts by having them carried out in industrial environments by groups of software developers, rather than by HCI specialists.

In this paper we discuss both issues and recommendations for this methodology in light of our experiences with three complex user interfaces. We describe recurring issues we observed and their implications for the use of the technique by others. The fact that these same issues came up during independent applications of the method by different individuals to different systems lends credence to the robustness of the phenomena we describe; however, one must keep in mind that we are reporting anecdotal evidence, not the results of controlled experiments.

THE COGNITIVE WALKTHROUGH: AN OVERVIEW

The Cognitive Walkthrough is a methodology for performing theory-based usability evaluations of user interfaces. Analogous to the traditional structured walkthroughs used by the software engineering community [17], the Cognitive Walkthrough has the goal of improving software usability by defect detection, amplification, and removal. Like other forms of usability walkthroughs [6, 11], Cognitive Walkthrough evaluations emphasize basic usability principles. In contrast to other types of usability evaluations, the Cognitive Walkthrough focuses on a user's cognitive activities; specifically, the goals and knowledge of a user while performing a specific task.

The Cognitive Walkthrough is designed to be used iteratively, early in the design cycle, by individuals or groups. Either software developers or usability specialists can perform the Walkthrough. It is a task-based methodology that serves to focus an evaluator's attention on the user's goals and actions, and on the system affordances that support or hinder the effective accomplishment of those goals. During the Walkthrough, the steps required to accomplish a task are evaluated by examining the behavior of the interface and its effect on the prototypical user. Both problematic and successful task steps are recorded. Steps are deemed successful if the expected goals and knowledge of the typical user would result in selection of an action that leads the user closer to her ultimate goal; they are problematic otherwise.

The Cognitive Walkthrough is based on a theory of exploratory learning, *CE+*, and some corresponding interface design guidelines, *Design for Successful Guessing*, geared toward *Walk Up and Use* systems [12]. A Walk Up and Use system (e.g., automatic teller machine or airport information kiosk) supports the notion of *learning by doing*[1]. Since the Walkthrough is tightly coupled to the above theory and guidelines, each step in a Walkthrough mirrors the underlying theory by testing whether these principles have been followed in the interface's design.

The Walkthrough is a form and task-based methodology, whereby a task is evaluated by completing a set of forms, each form comprising several evaluation steps. Each step, in turn, is designed to address underlying theoretical concepts through a list of questions to be asked about the interface. See Figure 1 which contains a portion of a Cognitive Walkthrough form to be used when evaluating each interface action [16]. For example, to determine if the user is likely to choose the appropriate action at a given stage of a task, the Walkthrough asks how well an identifier (e.g., a button labelled "time") is linked to the needed action (e.g., pressing the button) and how well the needed action is linked to the user's current goal (e.g., to set the time on an alarm clock).

The Walkthrough method consists of three basic phases: a preparation phase, an evaluation phase, and a result interpretation phase. The forms guide the evaluators through the preparation and evaluation phases with detailed instructions; the interpretation phase, however, is more ad hoc. The preparation phase is used to gather and record basic system information prior to the evaluation phase. For example, the suite of tasks to be evaluated is identified and information about the users is noted. In the evaluation phase questions like those in Figure 1 are asked of each step within a given user task. And finally, in the interpretation phase all information gathered and recorded from the Walkthrough process is interpreted according to the following metrics: positive responses support the inference that the interface is good, whereas negative answers highlight steps that are difficult for the user. The results thus hint at interface problems and the necessary changes.

...

Step [B] Choosing The Next Correct Action:

[B.1] **Correct Action:** Describe the action that the user should take at this step in the sequence.

[B.2] **Knowledge Checkpoint:** If you have assumed user knowledge or experience, update the USER ASSUMPTION FORM.

[B.3] **System State Checkpoint:** If the system state may influence the user, update the SYSTEM STATE FORM.

[B.4] **Action Availability:** Is it obvious to the user that this action is a possible choice here? If not, indicate why.

How many users might miss this action (% 100 75 50 25 10 5 0)?

[B.5] **Action Identifiability:**

[B.5.a] **Identifier Location, Type, Wording, and Meaning:**

_____ No identifier is provided. (Skip to subpart [B.5.d].)

Identifier Type: Label Prompt Description Other (Explain)

Identifier Wording_____

Is the identifier's location obvious? If not, indicate why.

[B.5.b] **Link Between Identifier and Action:** Is the identifier clearly linked with this action? If not, indicate why.

How many users won't make this connection (% 100 75 50 25 10 5 0)?

[B.5.c] **Link Between Identifier and Goal:** Is the identifier easily linked with an active goal? If not, indicate why.

How many users won't make this connection (% 100 75 50 25 10 5 0)?

...

Figure 1: Excerpt From a Walkthrough Form

THE THREE INTERFACES EVALUATED

We have conducted Cognitive Walkthroughs for three different applications that are much more complex than the Walk Up and Use interfaces to which the method has previously been applied. Since the three systems are intended to be productively used by casual or intermittent users (users similar to those the technique is designed to support), the method should still be applicable. Each of the applications was designed for a different domain and class of users, and utilizes a different interface style. The three applications we evaluated are HP-VUE, REPS, and BCA.

The HP-VUE System

HP-VUE is a visual interface to the Unix operating system.[2] It provides graphical tools for manipulating files, starting and stopping applications, requesting and browsing help, controlling the appearance of the screen, etc. A "beta-test" version of HP-VUE was evaluated.

The evaluation of this interface was done by a group of three software engineers similar to the actual designers of HP-VUE. Seven common tasks were evaluated; they were selected by someone who was expert in using the Walkthrough technique, rather than the evaluators

---

1. People use learning by doing in situations where they are knowledge poor, and hence must rely on feedback from the interface to shape or refine their knowledge and behavior.

2. The Hewlett-Packard Visual User Environment (HP-VUE 2.0). HP-VUE is a trademark of the Hewlett-Packard Company. UNIX is a trademark of AT&T. The X Window System is a trademark of Massachusetts Institute of Technology. Motif is a trademark of the Open Software Foundation, Inc.

themselves. The set of paper forms used for this evaluation was developed by Wharton [16].

The REPS System

REPS is an existing system to guide sales representatives through a sales call by providing them with necessary customer and product information. Sales representatives use the system frequently, but new users, who do not receive intensive training on the system, are introduced often. REPS is accessed via ASCII terminals using function keys; it does not support a graphical interface. At the time of the evaluation the system had been taken down because of user complaints. The application of the Cognitive Walkthrough was an attempt to locate and quantify the interface problems.

The evaluation team was made up of a system developer who helped to implement the system, a requirements analyst who served as an advocate for the users and joined the group after the initial design decisions had been made, and a cognitive psychologist who joined the team as a user interface consultant. Four task scenarios were selected by the requirements analyst and the cognitive psychologist. Three simple interactions (i.e., task scenarios) with the system were formally evaluated; paper forms similar to those described in [12] were used. In a fourth task scenario, no forms were used. Instead the group tried to answer the standard questions informally.

The BCA System

BCA is a research prototype CAD tool intended to be used by electrical engineers to design the construction parameters for a bare printed circuit board and to get feedback on the manufacturability of the design. This design task is complex, requiring the specification of many parameters and the weighing of tradeoffs between design choices affecting, among other things, fabrication cost, board production yield, and electrical performance. The targeted BCA user is an infrequent user who needs to do these tasks between one and three times per year. BCA runs on a Unix workstation under X-Windows with a Motif-based interface. The version evaluated had the requisite functionality, but had never been previously tested by a real user.

The Walkthrough was done by the current BCA design team, made up of a project manager, four computer scientists, and one electrical engineer. Only one of these people had been involved in the original design and implementation of the system, and only one other person was familiar with the Walkthrough method. Two tasks were evaluated, one simple and the other complex. The set of paper forms used was developed by Wharton [16].

EXPERIENCES, ISSUES, AND RECOMMENDATIONS

The purpose of this paper is to describe the issues that arose during the Cognitive Walkthrough evaluations of these three applications. Common themes emerged across all the evaluations, which we believe expose the strengths and weaknesses of the current version of the method. Elsewhere we have published more formal analyses of two of these evaluations, including information about the number and types of problems found [2, 5]. Our approach here is more anecdotal. We describe various aspects of our experiences, illustrating the issues with examples from the evaluations, and draw conclusions about improvements to the method.

The three interfaces described above are similar in important ways. First, all are intended to be used by casual users or novices, so the capability to be productive on the system without extensive training is important. Second, all support a broad range of functionality and complex tasks. And third, in all cases the functionality being evaluated has been implemented; we did not evaluate design mock-ups. We now discuss the key issues, experiences, and recommendations relevant to the Cognitive Walkthrough evaluations of these three applications.

Task Selection, Coverage, and Evaluation

The first step in performing a Walkthrough is to select the tasks to be evaluated. Any interface of even moderate complexity supports dozens or hundreds of tasks and task variants, and only a small fraction of them can be evaluated. However, the Walkthrough methodology does not provide guidance on how to select tasks, because task selection is not within the scope of the underlying theory. Nevertheless, to achieve good results during a Walkthrough it is necessary to understand those tasks that are most useful to evaluate, how many tasks are needed for sufficient interface coverage, and issues that arise when evaluating tasks.

How Realistic and Complex Should the Tasks Be? The REPS and BCA evaluation teams selected both simple and complex tasks, evaluating the simple tasks first. This reflected their need to gain experience with the Walkthrough method before doing more complex tasks. The simple tasks tend to correspond to the functional decomposition of the interface by its designers; the more complex tasks correspond to compositions of functionality and relevant transitions among subtasks. Although all evaluators strove for realism in the tasks they selected, the length and complexity of the evaluation process resulted in tasks being selected that were simplifications of what users would do in these rich environments, limiting consideration to only the most direct path through the interface. Consequently, potential problems may have been overlooked.

From our experiences we have found that tasks that mirror a simple, functional decomposition of the interface typically do not expose many problems with the interface. On the other hand, doing a simple task first can provide the experience necessary to perform a more complex Walkthrough. In general, we have found that it is most important to choose realistic tasks which exercise key system functionality; such tasks often comprise multiple core functions of the interface. By doing so, the evaluation covers not just the elements, but their combination and any necessary transitions among the subtasks. An important tradeoff to consider is the degree of realism or complexity of any individual task evaluation versus the number of tasks that can be covered, assuming fixed and limited resources. It is important to select some tasks to be covered as realistically as possible, which will often imply complex action sequences with multiple alternatives, as well as to choose other tasks to cover the full range of functionality.

Where Should Boundaries Be Drawn? Aside from complexity, many other issues need to be considered when determining which tasks to include in the evaluation. For example, evaluators must decide what constitutes the domain of the application. Should the tasks to be evaluated encompass only what the application currently does or what users will expect it to do? This was particularly an issue for HP-VUE, because HP-VUE provides access to functionality provided by both the X-Window system and the Unix operating system; however, the release evaluated did not cover all the functionality of X and Unix. Users have to switch to "native mode" to accomplish some of their tasks. When selecting the tasks to evaluate for HP-VUE, it was difficult to decide what to do about frequent tasks that straddled the boundaries of HP-VUE.

How Many Tasks Are Enough? All evaluations were able to cover only a small fraction of either the set of user tasks or the functionality of the interface. The evaluators were unable to commit the time to fully evaluate an interface of the complexity of the systems considered. To do so would easily take 100 hours or more, a figure inconsistent with the 1-2 sessions the evaluators believed a critique should take. As it was, the actual sessions were often 4-8 hours long. Because all evaluators stopped after 6-15 total hours and 2-7 tasks, we do not have measures of the number or kinds of problems that might have been uncovered had additional tasks been evaluated.

What About Task Variants? Once a candidate set of tasks is chosen, which variants to evaluate must also be considered. Rich interfaces often provide multiple ways to accomplish a task. Should all the paths be evaluated, or only the "most obvious" one for a given context? We have always evaluated only a single path assuming that this is the one the user would choose. Further, by decreasing the number of paths for a particular task, the number of tasks can be increased appropriately. Absolute tradeoffs between the number of tasks and paths, however, are not known.

At What Granularity Should the Evaluation Be Carried Out? Even when a suite of user tasks under evaluation can be refined to address these task selection and coverage concerns, other task-related issues arise when the evaluation is performed. Evaluators often have trouble deciding what the granularity of an individual action should be. For instance, should a user action consist of a meaningful set of keystrokes, e.g., a file name, or should each letter (keystroke) within the file name be counted as an individual user action? An example of this involves the HP-VUE interface, where one may log into the HP-VUE system by using one of two methods: (1) type login name followed by a <CR>, or (2) type login name and then mouse click on the "OK" button. It may seem that these methods would have identical implications, but depending on how the user approaches the task physically and mentally, the termination actions (i.e.,

pressing the <CR> button or the mouse click on "OK"), may lead to significant differences in the evaluation.

We believe the granularity of action evaluations needs to be determined with respect to the interface under evaluation. In most cases it seems that a reasonable collection of keystrokes, such as those used to input a file name, can be counted as a single user action. But if the interface requires different physical actions, such as keystroke and mouse click actions, then these should be treated as two separate actions. (cf. The approach of Card, Moran, and Newell's Model Human Processor [1], where a <CR> is always treated as a separate step.)

What About Identical Subtasks? Another issue is that of identical embedded subtasks within a set of different, larger tasks. When using realistic tasks, several different tasks may contain an identical subtask. Should this be treated as the same subtask each time it comes up, or will there be nuances of the different contexts that may change the evaluation of that subtask? When this situation arises during an evaluation process, the evaluators must decide whether to do a detailed evaluation of those identical aspects. During our evaluations we encountered some pairs of contexts in which the identical subtask would be performed differently. Had the evaluators treated the previously analyzed subtask as a "solved problem" in the second context, important problems would have been overlooked. Thus, for identical embedded actions, all transitions definitely should be evaluated, but it may be safe to short-circuit some of the actual subtask evaluations.

What About a High-Level Treatment of User Tasks? The final issue we raise concerns the Walkthrough's lack of a high-level treatment of the suite of user tasks. Because the tasks are evaluated at the granularity of individual user actions, there is no way to determine if the task as a whole evaluates well. It is only known how the individual user actions evaluate. This is a shortcoming of the method, because the designer also needs to know whether a task itself is sensible, non-circular, too long, or important to the user. The possibility of missing interface problems because the Walkthrough does not encourage evaluators to take a broad view of the task is one for which we have not found a solution. We have relied on informal critiques to ensure that such issues are not missed.

The Process of Doing a Cognitive Walkthrough

As described previously, the Walkthrough methodology consists of a set of forms to be filled out while exploring user actions and system responses during one or more tasks. The central Walkthrough form asks a series of questions about a single atomic action in a task; thus, copies of this form are filled out dozens of times during a complete Walkthrough. Groups who adhered most closely to the Cognitive Walkthrough procedures found the repetitive form filling to be very tedious, enough so that it discouraged some evaluators from using the method in the future.

Similarly, the separation of bookkeeping requirements from the actual evaluation ended up being another procedural impediment — often a wall was thrown up between those people who focused on the interface proper and those who focused on the recordkeeping. In our evaluations, we found that groups who rotated or otherwise shared responsibility for bookkeeping did better in this regard.

While doing a Cognitive Walkthrough, evaluators often noticed problems that were not directly relevant to the current task. For example, while working on a step that involves typing a file name into a text field, the evaluators might notice the absence of wild card options, even though the task being evaluated did not require the use of wild cards. It is always difficult to know what to do with such issues. Taking the time to resolve them greatly lengthens the Walkthrough and causes the group to lose context information about the current task that can be time-consuming to regain. On the other hand, it is easy to lose track of these side issues and never get back to them if they are not captured along the way.

Thus, the methodology needs explicit procedures for keeping track of side issues and changes needed in the interface, together with appropriate context to reconstruct the situation later. The group leader will still need to use judgment about when to allow such digressions and when to refocus the discussion, but the task may be made easier by having a formal way to table important discussion.

A similar situation arose when the evaluators were also the developers. They often wanted to pursue a problem beyond the limits of the Walkthrough — to design a fix, followed immediately with a Walkthrough on the fix. This, too, can be time-consuming, but developers seemed to want closure on understanding what better solutions were available.

We found the looser application of the method, as done by the REPS group on their final task, to be more successful and more satisfying to the evaluators. This group found the process to be less tedious than did any other group. This is consistent with other findings [14]. We believe the REPS group was successful with this "broad brush" approach because they had first explored the interface using the more structured methodology; they had learned when to be precise and when they could be more casual. However, we don't know how to formalize the circumstances under which each of the two different approaches would be most appropriate.

The evaluators suggested many changes to the procedural aspects of the method, several of them having to do with group aspects. One was to capture information that the entire group needed to refer to (e.g., assumptions about the user population) on overheads or flip charts, to make it more publicly available. Another was to share the various recordkeeping tasks, possibly rotating them between user tasks, so that all participants felt involved in both the critique of the interface and the identification of problems. Finally, since evaluators found the main source of tedium to be the task action evaluation form, they would have preferred to have a "review card" to summarize the relevant questions. Using this the evaluators could quickly go over the issues for

a task step, only committing to the paper record those issues for which there was a problem. This would prevent them from overlooking any important aspects, while speeding up the process quite a bit.

Requisite Knowledge for the Evaluators
The Walkthrough methodology presupposes more knowledge of cognitive science terms, concepts, and skills than most software developers have. The forms refer heavily to the specialized vocabulary of cognitive science, containing terms such as *goal structures*, *activation of goals*, and *supergoal kill-off* [3]. The terminology could be changed (or softened as in [7]), but the concepts they represent are equally specialized and will be foreign to the typical software developer. Certain of these concepts are critical to the successful use of the method. For example, one evaluator questioned the whole notion of goals, and whether people actually break their primary goal into smaller subgoals when doing a task. How does one explain the Cognitive Walkthrough notion of supergoal kill-off to someone who does not presuppose the existence of goals?

Because of a lack of familiarity with terminology, misunderstandings can occur. The most common misunderstanding was seen in task decomposition, where goals were often indistinguishable from interface actions. For example, one group came up with the following set of goals for the task of *loading a file*:

> find the file name in the browser
> select file to be loaded
> click to load the file
> wait

These goals are essentially the interface operations that are performed. A more plausible decomposition might be:

> determine the name of the file to use
> select the file
> load the file

Notice that "determine the name" is a purely mental operation that has no analog in the evaluators' list, "select the file" encompasses the first two goals in the earlier list, and "load the file" encompasses the latter two. But, it's not obvious that users would decompose loading a file into "click" and "wait" without either experience or feedback from the interface about the need to wait.

The Walkthrough developers have said that one of the most frequently asked questions they hear is "what is the difference between a goal and an action?" They have pointed out that even if goals have the granularity of interface actions, it shouldn't matter to the results of the Walkthrough, because if there is a mismatch between user goals and system actions, it will just show up in a different place in the evaluation. If goals are described as interface operations, the

---

3. The supergoal kill-off phenomenon occurs when an arbitrary final step, (e.g., typing carriage-return) is forgotten because a prior subgoal (e.g., type in the file name) gets associated with the complete goal; thus the user inadvertently considers the entire goal accomplished when only the distinguished subgoal is done.

evaluator will then have to justify why the user would form those goals from the system state, rather than justify why more realistic goals would lead to the needed actions [Clayton Lewis, personal communication, 1990]. We found that having goals at the granularity of individual actions did lead to problems. The example above demonstrates some of the issues that came up. In particular, for this interface, no salient feedback is given regarding the need to wait while the file is being loaded (which takes a long time). This problem was not noted by the evaluators because they had assumed that the user had the goal of waiting; they expected the user to be unconcerned about the amount of time before the system indicated completion of the load operation. Perhaps the evaluators should have questioned the applicability or obviousness of this goal, but in this instance, they found it to be perfectly natural.

In all but one of the Walkthroughs, at least one evaluator had more than a nodding acquaintance with cognitive science. This seemed to mitigate the effects of the specialized concepts and terminology reasonably well. The group that was least knowledgeable about cognitive science had the most problems at various levels — in task definition, in understanding the forms, and in accepting the results of the Walkthrough. Overall, we believe that it will be difficult to eliminate the need for cognitive science background both to make sense and to take full advantage of the technique. A better approach would be to enlist someone with at least a moderate HCI or Cognitive Science background as a member of the evaluation team.

Group Walkthroughs

All the interfaces were evaluated by groups of two to six evaluators. In general, the method seems to adapt quite naturally to a group evaluation situation. However, in comparing the REPS evaluation, viewed as successful by the REPS team [2], and the BCA evaluation, rated as poor by its participants, we noticed a number of situational parameters that are correlated with the success of the method when applied with a group. These are: division of duties, size of the team, length of the sessions, and the length and format of the particular Walkthrough forms used.

In both of these evaluations, one 'walkthrough advocate' introduced the method to the evaluation team and also emerged as the discussion leader and facilitator. In both cases it appeared to be important to have this person be responsible for bringing the discussion back on focus when it had digressed. The key issue for leading a group walkthrough seems to be the flexible managing of the group process between expansion (giving the team members the chance to discuss related topics to prevent frustration) and turning the focus back on the method. Research by social psychologists on the functions of leaders in small problem solving tasks suggests that an effective leader must function as both a "task leader", who keeps the group focused on the current problem, and as a "social-emotional leader", who motivates members to work hard and coordinates inter-member interaction [9, 15].

The BCA evaluators felt that having six people on the walkthrough team was too many; they suggested a size of three. Having more people can make the discussion less focused; sharing the walkthrough forms and the interface becomes a problem; and the proportion of errors discovered per time investment of each team member is not economical.

The Walkthrough sessions can easily become too lengthy. The BCA session took six hours, whereas the REPS sessions were limited to two hours and spread over several days (as were the VUE sessions). In comparing these two different approaches we found that tiring the team with lengthy meetings seemed more damaging to the process than the possibility of losing momentum between meetings. In the REPS evaluation the previous task evaluation was summarized by two of the group members between meetings, which helped the team stay focused and kept its members aware of already localized problems.

In both the REPS and BCA evaluations we observed two positive side effects not covered by the theory. First, the Walkthrough served as a method of learning about the importance of considering the background knowledge and environment of the intended users, and how to do a careful task analysis. For both the REPS and BCA applications the team members' consciousness about these issues has been raised and they have been taken into account in further steps of those projects.

Second, the Walkthrough served as a method of mediation between the requirements and the development side of the design team. When the design team is divided between requirements analysts and system developers, a communication gap may easily develop between them. Both types of expertise — detailed knowledge of the users' tasks and needs, *and* the options and constraints of the development platform — is needed to optimize the design of a particular interface. In our experience the Walkthrough application gave both parties a neutral ground and shared vocabulary to negotiate these design decisions, and hence to make optimal use of their complementary expertise. Similarly, having a 'Walkthrough advocate' on the team seemed to help to establish this focus on the interface issues and prevent digressions into old conflicts. Research on group decision making has frequently demonstrated that the decomposition of a global decision problem into its components, analysis and decision on each component separately, and then recombination into a group solution is an effective method to reduce or eliminate conflict [e.g., 4, 10]. The Walkthrough may provide similar benefits by imposing an analogous highly-structured, task-driven, component-by-component organization on the group process.

Interpreting Cognitive Walkthrough Results

According to the Cognitive Walkthrough originators [Clayton Lewis, personal communication, 1991], the Walkthrough does not identify problems with an interface; it identifies mismatches between system affordances and user goals. Because of the nature of the underlying theory, the

Walkthrough seems to do a better job of pointing out mismatches that are linguistic in origin (e.g., mislabelled buttons or menu items) than those of a more graphical nature. Whereas the Walkthrough does inform developers of the aspects of the interface that are troublesome, identifying specific problems and generating their solutions are tasks beyond the scope of the Walkthrough proper, although the data generated by doing a Walkthrough would be highly relevant to such a task. In practice, our engineer evaluators went beyond identifying mismatches to identifying problem statements and often immediately to solutions.

The Cognitive Walkthrough technique can sometimes lead evaluators to solutions that are suboptimal. In one task evaluated, the user was required to go back and forth between different windows of the system, know which data entry fields were required and the correct sequence in which they had to be entered, with no cues from the system. The solution suggested by the evaluators was to highlight the data entry field or calculation that was to be done next. This solution is consistent with the Walkthrough forms, which focus on the salience of the appropriate action at the current step, but it is suboptimal to a solution that includes reorganizing the data entry fields and calculation buttons in a task-oriented manner.

We also found that the Walkthrough method can lead evaluators to propose erroneous solutions. For instance, one evaluation team proposed a change that would produce a simpler action sequence in the context of the task they were evaluating without realizing that it would remove functionality required for other user tasks.

As the above examples point out, by deriving solutions for a particular task, the evaluators may not be able to see the larger picture and may come up with an inappropriate problem statement or solution. In spite of this most of the problems identified by the evaluators were appropriate assessments of the interface they were analyzing. Occasionally, the narrow focus on individual task steps introduced what are essentially *set effects*, where the evaluators were so focused on a particular set of solutions that they were unable to recognize when a problem required a solution outside of this set. Consequently, methods that assess an interface more globally are needed as a supplement to mitigate these problems.

CONCLUSIONS

For the first time the Cognitive Walkthrough has been applied to highly complex, high functionality systems by groups of software engineers. If the Walkthrough is to be successful in helping to design better software systems, it must be able to deal with real systems in environments such as those we tested.

Is the Cognitive Walkthrough ready for use by real development teams on high functionality applications? Based on our experiences, we say "not without substantial extensions". There are simply too many caveats for successful use of the method. We believe that these problems

can be overcome by further research and extensions to the technique; however, widespread practical use must await those extensions.

The problems with Cognitive Walkthroughs are at two levels. The first involves process mechanics. Those can be mitigated by straightforward changes to the Walkthrough process; specific recommendations for such changes are summarized in Figure 2. The second class of problems involves limitations in the method as it currently exists. It is those limitations that keep the method from being viable at this time. We hope that the developers of the Cognitive Walkthrough will address these issues in their research.

One limitation of the Walkthrough method is that it doesn't match well with current software development practice, at least in the organizations where these evaluations were done. The developers we work with are interested in usability issues, but don't have the training or the inclination to become expert on the topic. Furthermore, usability is only one of a large number of aspects of the product they must focus on — aspects like reliability and performance demand equal attention, and are more clearly understood by software

---

Task Issues

- Start with a simple task and then work on more complex tasks. Include at least one task whose complexity matches what users will typically encounter. Balance the complexity of individual tasks with the range of functionality to be covered.

- Chose realistic tasks that exercise key system functionality. Look for tasks that cover multiple core functions, so as to evaluate transitions between subtasks.

- When selecting the tasks consider issues of: task granularity, action granularity, identical subtasks, and task variants.

Process and Group Issues

- At least one member of the group should be familiar with the terminology and concepts of cognitive science and with the Cognitive Walkthrough's process and assumptions.

- Provide aids to help organize the task. Possible aids include: a mechanism for keeping track of side issues and solution alternatives for later re-examination, a review card or other mechanism to summarize the questions to be asked at each step, overheads or other group-visible means to capture information frequently referred to, such as assumptions about user knowledge.

- Minimize the impact of bookkeeping tasks. Rotating the tasks is one method; tools to automate the process are another.

- The leader/facilitator needs to pay careful attention to group process issues. Things to consider: size and composition of the group, ensuring appropriate participants' expectations (as to time required, nature of the process, etc.), and the need for effective group management skills, since the walkthrough may expose existing conflicts among group members.

- Break the walkthrough up into sessions of reasonable length (2-3 hours). It is important to break only between tasks, so that context carefully built up will not be lost.

Figure 2: Some Recommendations for an Effective Cognitive Walkthrough

engineers. Developers are under constant time pressure; thus, any technique that takes more than a few person-days would need very strong support, both among management and the technical community to be worth jeopardizing product schedules. They are looking to identify the most critical interface problems; it's hard to relate the detail-oriented procedures of the Walkthrough to the identification of high-impact, pervasive problems. Finally, developers need solutions. The intentional interposing of an intermediate step between problem identification and solution may have benefits, but developers see it as a roadblock to their primary goal in doing the evaluation.

The issues above create problems for other task-oriented, developer implemented usability methods as well. There may need to be significant changes in software development life-cycles before any developer implemented methodology can be successful. On the other hand, requiring major changes to current practice is a serious impediment to the widespread use of Cognitive Walkthroughs.

Another class of limitations concerns task selection. Effective task selection is a critical issue for any methodology based on user tasks. Furthermore, since the Cognitive Walkthrough is intended to be used by developers, the evaluators may not have access to the informed intuitions of a user interface professional to select appropriate tasks. While, in principle, a task selection methodology could be added to the method, the field of HCI simply does not know enough about task selection for a pragmatically viable method to be developed at this time. We believe that, for the foreseeable future, the task suite should be generated by a knowledgeable professional. Finally, the Cognitive Walkthrough is limited by its focus on the lower level interface issues. Evaluators need to be provided with a process for stepping back and looking at the application more globally. This is probably done most directly by combining Walkthroughs with other evaluation methods. However, it could be done as an extension of the Walkthrough method.

The challenges identified above — incongruence with current software development practice, task selection, and the lack of focus on higher level issues — are not unique to Cognitive Walkthroughs. They must be resolved for any user interface evaluation method based on tasks and applied by the developers themselves to be successful. We hope that this paper will spur research into ways to successfully incorporate the Cognitive Walkthrough and other methods of this type into current practice.

ACKNOWLEDGMENTS

We would like to thank the following people for their contributions to this work: Lucy Berlin, Nancy Bruner, Norman Chang, Scott Conradson, Felix Frayman, Bruce Hamilton, Reid Hastie, Stan Jefferson, Clare-Marie Karat, Nancy Kendzierski, Dan Kuokka, Clayton Lewis, Catherine Marshall, Jakob Nielsen, Vicki O'Day, Andreas Paepcke, Peter Polson, John Rieman, Terry Roberts, Craig Zarmer, and the anonymous CHI'92 reviewers.

REFERENCES

1. Card, S.K., Moran, T.P., and Newell, A. *The Psychology of Human-Computer Interaction*. Lawrence Erlbaum Associates, Hillsdale, NJ, 1983.

2. Franzke, M. Evaluation Technique Evaluated: Experience Using the Cognitive Walkthrough. *Proc. of the Bellcore/BCC Symposium on User-Centered Design*. Livingston, NJ, November 1991.

3. Gray, W.D., John, B.E., and Atwood, M.E. The Précis of Project Ernestine, or An Overview of a Validation of GOMS. *Proc. ACM CHI'92*. (Monterey, California, May 3-7, 1992).

4. Hammond, K.R. and Adelman, L. Science, Values, and Human Judgement. *Science*, 1976, Volume 194, pp. 389-396.

5. Jeffries, R., Miller, J.R., Wharton, C., and Uyeda, K.M. User Interface Evaluation in the Real World: A Comparison of Four Techniques. *Proc. ACM CHI'91*. (New Orleans, Louisiana, April 27 – May 2, 1991) pp. 119–124.

6. Karat, C., Campbell, R., and Fiegel, T. Comparison of Empirical Testing and Walkthrough Methods in User Interface Evaluation. *Proc. ACM CHI'92*. (Monterey, California, May 3-7, 1992).

7. Lewis, C., and Polson P.G. Cognitive Walkthroughs: A Method for Theory-Based Evaluation of User Interfaces. Tutorial presented at *ACM CHI'91*. (New Orleans, Louisiana, April 27 – May 2, 1991).

8. Lewis, C., Polson, P., Wharton, C., and Rieman, J. Testing a Walkthrough Methodology for Theory-Based Design of Walk-Up-and-Use Interfaces. *Proc. ACM CHI'90*. (Seattle, Washington, April 1 – 5, 1990) pp. 235–242.

9. McGrath, J.E. *Groups: Interaction and Performance*. Prentice-Hall, Englewood Cliffs, NJ, 1984.

10. Neale, M.A. and Bazerman, M.H. *Cognition and Rationality in Negotiation*. Free Press, New York, NY, 1991.

11. Nielsen, J. Finding Usability Problems Through Heuristic Evaluation. *Proc. ACM CHI'92*. (Monterey, California, May 3-7, 1992).

12. Polson, P.G., and Lewis, C. Theory-Based Design for Easily Learned Interfaces. *Human-Computer Interaction*, 1990, Volume 5, pp. 191–220.

13. Polson, P., Lewis, C., Rieman, J., and Wharton, C. Cognitive Walkthroughs: A Method for Theory-Based Evaluation of User Interfaces. To appear in *International Journal of Man-Machine Studies*, 1992.

14. Rowley, D.E., and Rhoades, D.G. The Cognitive Jogthrough: A Fast-Paced User Interface Evaluation Procedure. *Proc. ACM CHI'92*. (Monterey, California, May 3-7, 1992).

15. Shaw, M.E. *Group Dynamics: The Psychology of Small Group Behavior*. 3rd edition. McGraw-Hill, New York, NY, 1981.

16. Wharton, C. *Cognitive Walkthroughs: Instructions, Forms, and Examples*. Technical Report University of Colorado at Boulder, Institute of Cognitive Science, 1992.

17. Yourdon, E. *Structured Walkthroughs*. 4th edition. Yourdon Press, Englewood Cliffs, NJ, 1989.

The Cognitive Jogthrough:
A Fast-Paced User Interface Evaluation Procedure

David E. Rowley and David G. Rhoades

Varian Associates
2700 Mitchell Drive
Walnut Creek, CA 94598
510-945-2275
rowley@varian.com

ABSTRACT

Walkthrough techniques have been shown to be an effective supplement to empirical testing methods for evaluating the usability of software systems [3, 4]. Unfortunately, structured walkthrough procedures tend to be time-consuming and unpopular with evaluators when used on substantial tasks. To maximize the useful information obtained from walkthroughs while minimizing the overhead of the procedure itself, a fast-paced methodology was developed and used within the constraints of a real-world product development environment. By using video recording equipment and an informal, interactive evaluation session, the "cognitive jogthrough" procedure revealed significant user interface problems that could then be studied using other techniques.

KEYWORDS: User interface evaluation techniques, structured walkthroughs, design methodologies.

INTRODUCTION

This paper describes the in-house development of a user interface evaluation procedure at Varian Chromatography Systems. This procedure was used to evaluate the proposed user interface of a software application package being developed for an existing pc-based chromatography workstation that we manufacture.

Our chromatography workstation is used by industry and regulatory agencies to determine and control the composition of materials such as pharmaceuticals, pesticides, and petrochemicals, and to monitor for the presence of compounds of concern in the environment. It consists of a set of software applications based on Microsoft® Windows 3.0[tm]. These applications control instruments that perform automated experiments to

separate and quantify the individual components of the chemical samples, process the raw data, and generate calculated results in a form which is useful to the chromatographer. Each iteration of this process is termed a *chromatographic run*. In addition to the software that performs these core workstation tasks, application packages may be utilized to perform calculations and generate results that are required by a particular market segment. These application-specific programs may be invoked automatically at the end of each chromatographic run, or interactively by the operator.

One of the primary tasks of the chromatographer is to develop methods that specify and control the actions described above (see figure 1). A *method* is the set of instructions required to perform a single chromatographic run. In a typical methods development scenario, the chromatographer first determines the instrument hardware conditions which result in a satisfactory chromatographic separation of the sample components. Once this has been achieved, the chromatographer specifies the data handling parameters which control processing of the raw data and the basic results calculations. Finally, parameters which control any application-specific calculations and report generation are specified. As shown in the figure, each of these steps consists of specifying the instructions, invoking the actions, and inspecting the textual and graphical results. Chromatographers utilize heuristics derived from knowledge of the application domain to determine whether the results are satisfactory, or whether additional iterations are required.

It has been our experience that users prefer to do methods development in an interactive software environment in which the chromatographer can rapidly perform these separate but related actions in an iterative manner until satisfied with the results. This is facilitated when the individual applications that provide the various chromatography workstation services are easily accessible, interact seamlessly, and are consistent in their look and feel. We have established a user interface evaluation team at our site as a means of working towards these goals. The team is composed of user interface designers, software engineers and in-house "users" who are knowledgeable in the tasks of our target markets. We feel the multi-disciplinary nature of the team is important to provide both a customer perspective and experience in graphical user interface design.

The team's roles are to maintain and to further develop interface consistency in the workstation software, and to ensure that the user interface of the system does not interfere with the work flow of the user. This is especially important when individual applications are developed by

in our organization, no full time Human Factors specialists exist. User interface evaluation is a supplementary activity for all of the participants on the team, and therefore the time that can be devoted to evaluations is limited. This turns out to be a key constraint on the activities of the group and has had a great influence on our evaluation technique.

EVALUATING A PROPOSED USER INTERFACE
We set out to perform user interface evaluations with several goals in mind. Primarily, we wanted to identify problems in the user interface which could either be resolved immediately during the evaluation session, or

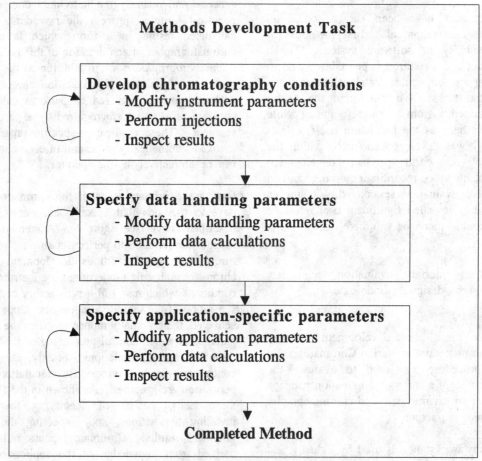

Figure 1

different software engineers, and when new applications are added to an existing product. The team develops project-wide guidelines, templates, and examples, and it evaluates interface proposals for new applications and modifications to existing ones. It also serves as a mechanism for ongoing communication during the development cycle between the software developers and the in-house representatives of the end users.

Since the notion of Human Factors activities as an integral part of the software development process is relatively new

designated as a separate design task. We wanted to develop a procedure that would be suitable both for evaluators with little understanding of the application, and users with little understanding of evaluation techniques. It was important for the procedure to provide a mechanism for a thorough review, with enough structure to avoid tangential diversions, but flexible enough to allow us to skip areas beyond the scope of our influence. The documentation of the procedure was also important as a way to capture significant information brought out by the evaluation, but we didn't want the process of documentation to impede the evaluation.

Due to time and resource constraints placed on the project, empirical usability testing on interface prototypes was not considered to be a feasible evaluation technique for the situation. Co-operative Evaluation had been practiced in-house to gain some insight on what was required to use this procedure successfully [2, 6]. Based on our experiences, we felt that in order to do meaningful evaluation using this procedure, a prototype modeling the system behavior in a rather convincing manner was needed. We also believed that we needed ready access to subjects who were familiar with the application and who adequately represented our customer profile. We had attempted to use in-house customer representatives, but found that the bias they had developed while working intimately with our products influenced the way in which they performed user tasks. Time and resource constraints prevented us from developing a working prototype and doing the field visits that would be necessary to satisfy our criteria.

We reviewed several papers suggesting alternative interface evaluation procedures, including Lewis and Polson's Cognitive Walkthrough procedure [1, 4, 5]. The Cognitive Walkthrough approach appealed to many of the interface evaluators with a background in software engineering who have had good experiences with software design walkthroughs. It provided a satisfactory theory-based mechanism for finding problem areas in the user interface, and because of the familiar nature of the procedure, it seemed to be a good technique to use in an organization that had relatively little prior experience with formal user interface evaluation.

Task Selection

The user interface evaluation team spent time identifying core tasks of our customers, based primarily on experience in the field and knowledge of the market. Two major modes of usage that exist with our product are high-throughput automated analysis and methods development. Automated analysis requires little participation of the user beyond setting up the initial conditions for the sequence of separations to be performed. Methods development is a far more interactive task, requiring constant attention of the user. The burden on the user interface is greater for this task since the "modify-perform-inspect" loop needs to be optimized to the users' work flow. The chromatographer does not wish to be burdened by a system whose user interface gets in the way while performing this task.

The user interface evaluation team selected methods development for the new application as the task to be evaluated. This selection was made because of the interactive nature of the interface, because the methods development task is considered to be a core task of our chromatography workstation, and because it was the portion of the new application interface that had the most unresolved issues. Since the new application was still early in the design stage, the opportunity of "doing it right the first time" was there.

Before the evaluation session began, it was recognized that the entire methods development task was too long to be covered in one sitting. Therefore, only a subset of the task, the specification and verification of the application-specific parameters, was selected for the first evaluation. We hoped (perhaps naively) to cover a substantial portion of this task subset in a single ninety minute session.

The Walkthrough

The ground rules for the walkthrough were derived not only from the Lewis and Polson material, but also from internally developed walkthrough procedures used on software architecture designs [7]. In this procedure, the evaluation participants play one (or two) of four roles: Presenter, Evaluator, Moderator, and Recorder. Moderators and Recorders may act also as Evaluators.

The participants arranged themselves in a meeting room before an overhead projector and a large computer monitor. Drawings of the proposed screens were displayed on the overhead projector while the monitor displayed existing software which could be used to demonstrate the system's proposed behavior. The Presenter described to all participants the task to be evaluated, and the preferred path to the goal state. This was done in a session preceding the actual evaluation session. During the walkthrough, the Presenter traversed the preferred path by executing all the actions required to navigate through it. The Presenter identified alternative paths, and the consequences of pursuing them. Any uncertainties in the proposed design were noted. The Moderator ran the meeting, keeping everyone focused on the walkthrough, and resolving any issues that arose regarding the process. The Recorder wrote down each step taken during the walkthrough on an evaluation sheet. We used a modified version of the evaluation sheet presented in the Lewis/Polson paper (see figure 2). In order to help ease the burden of recording all the evaluators' comments, the Recorder used an electronic template of the evaluation sheet that reduced the amount of repetitive typing required. The Evaluators answered each of the questions on the evaluation sheet for each step taken towards the goal state. Actions and choices were ranked according to the percentage of potential users that were expected to have problems. As likely actions were identified, the Presenter executed the action and the system response was recorded.

After the first immediate goal was presented, the group proceeded to identify the first atomic action that was likely to be taken by most users. The action was executed and the system response recorded. The evaluation proceeded along these lines and several problem areas in the user interface were identified. Suggestions for alternate design approaches were tabled by the Moderator so that the evaluation could continue within the time limits that had been defined. While the Recorder was able

disappointed with the small amount of material covered and the pace with which it proceeded. The thought of repeating the process several more times in order to complete the evaluation for the task subset was discouraging to all of the participants.

The Jogthrough
To address the problems associated with the pace of the walkthrough, we decided to modify the procedure for future evaluation sessions. Instead of transcribing the comments manually into an electronic template, we recorded the evaluation session on videotape. We had

---

Walkthrough Evaluation Sheet

Actions/choices should be ranked according to what percentage of potential users are expected to have problems: 0 = none; 1 = some; 2 = more than half; 3 = most.

1. Description of user's immediate *goal*:

2. (First/next) atomic *action* user should take:
    2a. Obvious that action is *available*? Why/Why not?
    2b. Obvious that action is *appropriate to goal*? Why/Why not?

3. All other available actions *less appropriate*? For each, why/why not?

4. How will the user *execute* the action?
    4a. Problems? Why/Why not?

5. Execute the action. Describe system response:
    5a. Obvious *progress* has been made toward goal? Why/Why not?
    5b. User can access needed *information in system response*? Why/Why not?

6. Describe appropriate *modified goal*. if any:
    6a. Obvious that *goal should change*? Why/Why not?
    6b. If task *completed*, is it obvious? Why/Why not?

Figure 2

to transcribe comments during the evaluation by typing them into a template, the evaluation team spent much of the time waiting for the Recorder to catch up with the action.

At the end of the ninety minute period, only ten atomic actions were covered. This is roughly equivalent to opening a single file and displaying a windowful of application parameters to edit (a minor portion of the task subset that we wanted to evaluate). While the participants were satisfied with the quality of the evaluation, they were

already developed a test logging software package in-house that is used during videotaped usability testing sessions. We were able to make use of this test logging software during the evaluation in a similar manner -- to log significant events in real time. The role of the Recorder, therefore, becomes one of camera operator and event logger. The test logging software allows the Recorder to quickly enter notes about the events of the evaluation and stamp them with a time value that is synchronized with the video camera's timer. The test log is then later used to index into the video tape and review segments of interest.

We noted that during the walkthrough, several good design suggestions were raised, but they were not well accommodated by its structure. The walkthrough, after all, is an interface evaluation procedure and does not lend itself to the design process. For the most part, discussions

ground rules of the evaluation to allow more free discussion and to allow the discussion to stray from the questions on the evaluation sheet when we thought it might provide fruitful suggestions. Questions like "what if it were implemented this way" would spawn discussions about the possibilities of various other approaches to the design problem.

The Jogthrough Setup

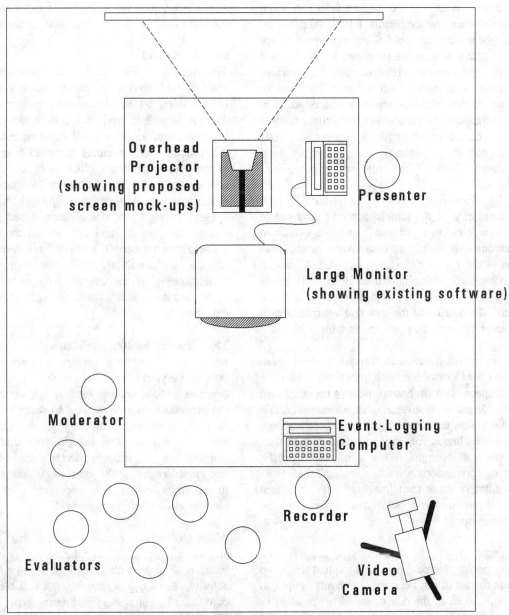

Figure 3

along these lines were suppressed by the Moderator. In the modified procedure, we wanted to encourage these suggestions, as long as they were appropriate, and explore the alternate paths the user might choose as a result of their implementation. To accomplish this, we changed the

The criterion by which the Moderator judged discussions inappropriate for the scope of the evaluation became more subjective with this procedure, since we were no longer bound to adhere strictly to the questions on the evaluation sheet. It was up to both the Moderator and the Presenter to decide when it was appropriate to combine several atomic actions into a single step, and when discussion of a particular design issue was beyond the scope of the evaluation. In some cases it was agreed that certain concerns about the interface could not be resolved in the evaluation session and would require further empirical study.

In the ninety minute jogthrough, roughly thirty user actions were covered. Atomic actions that would have been covered individually in the walkthrough procedure were combined when the evaluators felt that individual examination of the actions would not provide any useful information. Certain areas of the proposed design that had not been fully developed were discussed and various alternative design suggestions were made. The focus of this procedure, as with the Cognitive Walkthrough, is to evaluate how the user might choose from the available options the one considered most likely to result in a state closer to the goal state. When design suggestions were made, they were immediately evaluated with this in mind.

RESULTS

Since the granularity of the atomic actions evaluated in the walkthrough sometimes differed from those evaluated in the jogthrough, it is difficult to make quantitative comparisons of the number of steps evaluated. A rough estimate can be made that approximately three times as much material was covered in the jogthrough than in the walkthrough. The section of the task that we intended to review, however, was not fully covered in either session.

The interaction provided by the jogthrough brought about some modified behavior of the participants, especially the application experts and in-house users who were not familiar with formal review techniques. Since a certain amount of discussion was encouraged, they became more vocal and played a bigger role in the evaluation than they had during the walkthrough. When application-specific terminology or conventions were in question, they were able to immediately share their insights. This increased level of participation was a welcomed benefit of the jogthrough technique.

The documentation of the walkthrough session was definitely the pacing factor during the evaluation. The Recorder was forced to omit certain comments simply to keep up with the flow of the discussion. This resulted in frustration during the session as the participants constantly had to be told to slow down, and frustration later on when the interface designers had to decipher the cryptic abbreviations that the Recorder resorted to under pressure. The video tape generated during the jogthrough, on the other hand, captured all the comments and discussions made by the participants and required little maintenance

during the session. The Recorder was able to log the evaluation of major steps throughout the task without affecting the tempo of the discussion.

The evaluators responded favorably to the modifications made to the walkthrough procedure resulting in the jogthrough. There was a general feeling of accomplishment after the jogthrough that was in marked contrast to the feeling of frustration after the walkthrough. Although we did not cover all that we had anticipated with either technique, there was more willingness to continue the jogthrough than there was with the walkthrough.

CONCLUSIONS

The modified walkthrough, the jogthrough, satisfied our evaluation objectives and provided design inputs that were not afforded by the structured walkthrough procedure. The jogthrough procedure seems particularly well suited to a product development environment where multidisciplinary teams evaluate proposed interfaces, but have primary responsibilities other than user interface design and evaluation. The informal, fast-paced feel of the evaluation encourages participants to make design suggestions, but provides a theory-based framework that can be used to immediately screen them. The active participation of people with different areas of expertise has the additional benefit of increasing each person's understanding of the overall project, and in improving communication and consensus-building across product development teams.

The structure of the walkthrough enforces a rigorous review of all steps necessary to navigate through the proposed system, and therefore makes it difficult to overlook hidden usability errors (although the tedium of the procedure itself may lead to some oversights). This may not be the case with the jogthrough if the evaluation team chooses to skip over a step that is considered insignificant. A greater burden is placed on the Moderator and Presenter during the jogthrough since the criteria used to determine when it is appropriate to discuss design alternatives are left up to them.

Although it was our experience that the jogthrough allowed us to evaluate significantly more of the proposed interface than the walkthrough, it is still a time consuming activity. In fact, it is probably not feasible to evaluate all core tasks in our system in this manner. Therefore, task selection becomes a very important issue, and sometimes decisions have to be made to neglect areas that may present usability problems in the product. These are never easy decisions to make, but the jogthrough procedure provides a mechanism for identifying aspects of the interface that require further attention, and allows evaluators to find these areas of concern faster than with the walkthrough.

By allowing design alternatives to be proposed and discussed during the evaluation session, the jogthrough procedure becomes as much a technique for collaborative design as it is a structured evaluation. By combining these two processes, a more formal approach to the user interface development process was employed than may have been otherwise, given the time constraints on the project. The tight coupling of design and evaluation promotes the rapid development of working breadboards that can be further evaluated using empirical techniques. Problem areas identified in the jogthrough can be focused upon in usability tests when the time and availability of subjects is often limited.

SUMMARY

Under strict schedule constraints, a proposed user interface was evaluated using several techniques. A Cognitive Walkthrough approach was used as an alternative to empirical usability testing due to both schedule and resource constraints. The Cognitive Walkthrough proved laborious and did not make the best use of the evaluators' limited time. A modified walkthrough procedure, a "Cognitive Jogthrough", was developed to gain valuable usability feedback from evaluators in a fast-paced session. The results of the two approaches showed that much the same type of feedback was made available by the jogthrough as with the walkthrough, but far more actions were evaluated and design suggestions were made that were not well accommodated by the rigid structure of the walkthrough procedure.

The Cognitive Jogthrough technique took advantage of the diverse background of our evaluation team members. Application experts and in-house users were given the opportunity to make design suggestions and voice their opinions on the usability of the proposed interface. Design discussions allowed us to resolve some concerns within the structure of the evaluation session, and allowed us to target others as areas for further investigation. We feel that we retained enough structure to provide a thorough review of the interface, but enough flexibility to change the focus of our attention during the session when we felt it appropriate. By using a video camera in conjunction with test logging software, we were able to fully document the session without hampering the pace of the evaluation. The test log provides a convenient way to quickly access information on the tape at a later time.

These aspects of the jogthrough process helped fulfill our goal of employing a user interface evaluation methodology that worked within the framework of our development environment.

ACKNOWLEDGEMENTS
The authors wish to thank Lisa Breslow, Gary Burce, Duncan Carmichael, Jean-Louis Excoffier, Susan Finkelman, Tim Medlin, Bob Palin, Sue Ann Scheppers, and John Sullivan for their participation in the user interface evaluation process. Additional thanks to Susan Finkelman, Marge Levin and Tim Medlin for their valued editing and review inputs.

REFERENCES
1. Bell, B., Rieman, J., and Lewis, C. Usability Testing of a Graphical Programming System: Things We Missed in a Programming Walkthrough. In Proceedings of CHI 1991 Conference (New Orleans, LA, Apr. 27 - May 2). ACM, New York, 1991, pp. 7-12.

2. Haber, J. Proposing Usability Testing to Management - An "It works therefore it's truth" approach. Presented at CHI 1991 Conference (New Orleans, LA, Apr. 27 - May 2) by Lora Davenport.

3. Jeffries, R., Miller, J.R., Wharton, C., and Uyeda, K. User Interface Evaluation in the Real World: A Comparison of Four Techniques.. In Proceedings of CHI 1991 Conference (New Orleans, LA, Apr. 27 - May 2). ACM, New York, 1991, pp. 119-124.

4. Lewis, C., Polson, P., Wharton, C., and Rieman, J. Testing a Walkthrough Methodology for Theory-Based Design of Walk-Up-and-Use Interfaces. In Proceedings of CHI 1990 Conference (Seattle, WA, Apr. 1-5). ACM, New York, 1990, pp. 235-242.

5. Nielsen, J., Molich, R. Heuristic Evaluation of User Interfaces. In Proceedings of CHI 1990 Conference (Seattle, WA, Apr. 1-5). ACM, New York, 1990, pp. 249-256.

6. Wright, P. and Monk, A. Co-Operative Evaluation - The York Manual. University of York, York , UK, 1991.

7. Yourdon, E. Structured Walkthroughs. Yourdon Press, New York, 1978.

COMPARISON OF EMPIRICAL TESTING AND WALKTHROUGH METHODS IN USER INTERFACE EVALUATION

Clare-Marie Karat, Robert Campbell*, and Tarra Fiegel**

IBM T. J. Watson Research Center
PO Box 704, Yorktown Heights, NY 10598
ckarat@watson.ibm.com

* Now at Department of Psychology, Clemson University, Clemson, SC 29634
**Now at Department of Psychology, New Mexico State University, Las Cruces, NM 88003

ABSTRACT

We investigated the relative effectiveness of empirical usability testing and individual and team walkthrough methods in identifying usability problems in two graphical user interface office systems. The findings were replicated across the two systems and show that the empirical testing condition identified the largest number of problems, and identified a significant number of relatively severe problems that were missed by the walkthrough conditions. Team walkthroughs achieved better results than individual walkthroughs in some areas. About a third of the significant usability problems identified were common across all methods. Cost-effectiveness data show that empirical testing required the same or less time to identify each problem when compared to walkthroughs.

KEYWORDS: Empirical testing, walkthroughs, problem severity, cost-effectiveness, scenarios

INTRODUCTION

Software development teams work within cost, schedule, personnel and technological constraints. In recent years, usability engineering methods appropriate to these constraints have evolved and become increasingly incorporated into software development cycles. Human factors practitioners currently rely on two types of techniques to evaluate representations of user interfaces: (1) empirical usability testing in laboratory or field settings; and (2) a variety of usability walkthrough methods. These latter methods have substantive differences and are referred to as pluralistic walkthroughs, heuristic evaluations, cognitive walkthroughs, think-aloud evaluations, and scenario-based and guideline-based reviews [1, 4, 10, 12, 16, 18, 19, 20, 21, 22, 23]. Empirical usability testing and walkthrough methods differ in the experimental controls employed in the former.

Human factors practitioners must make tradeoffs re-

garding time, cost, and human factors issues in selecting a usability engineering method to use in a particular development situation [15]. Use of walkthroughs has been encouraged by development cycle pressures and by the adoption of development goals of efficiency and user-centered design [1, 2, 5, 12, 20, 23]. Many questions remain about how walkthroughs compare to empirical methods of usability assessment, and when and how walkthroughs are most effective.

Questions About Empirical Testing Versus Walkthrough Methods

Usability problems. How do the two methods compare in the number of usability problems identified in a user interface? Is one method better than the other in identifying serious problems? How many of the problems are found by both methods and how many are found solely by one method?

Reliability of differences. If the methods differ in their effectiveness in identifying usability problems in user interfaces, do these differences persist across different systems? Or is the effectiveness of an evaluation method system dependent, based on the type of interface style and metaphor used in the interface?

Cost-effectiveness. What is the relative cost-effectiveness of the two techniques in identifying the usability problems in an interface?

Human factors involvement. What amount of human factors involvement is necessary in the use of the two techniques? What issues arise in analyzing and interpreting data?

Questions About Walkthrough Techniques

Individuals versus teams. Are walkthroughs more effective when conducted individually or in teams? Social psychology has documented that groups seldom perform up to the level of their best member [17]. One exception in this area is that groups do offer the possibility of more accurate judgments than individuals, especially when working on complex tasks [17]. The use of interaction-enhancing procedures may heighten group productivity as well [7].

Evaluator expertise. Are members of development teams and representative end users effective evaluators

1992 ACM 0-89791-513-5/92/0005-0397   1.50

in walkthroughs, or should the evaluators be exclusively human factors or user interface (UI) specialists?

Prescribed tasks versus self-guided exploration. In a usability walkthrough with prescribed tasks, evaluators step through a representation of a user interface (e.g., paper specification, prototype) or the actual system while performing representative end user tasks. Other walkthrough procedures rely on self-guided exploration of the interface by evaluators who may or may not generate scenarios for that purpose. Do evaluators in walkthroughs think that one approach is more useful than the other in identifying usability problems?

Utility of guidelines. What is the role of usability heuristics or guidelines in usability walkthroughs? Are heuristics useful and necessary for experienced members of development teams?

Recent Data
Recent studies provide some data on these issues. Jeffries, Miller, Wharton, and Uyeda [10] compared the effectiveness of usability testing, guideline, heuristic, and cognitive walkthrough [16] methods in identifying user interface problems. The heuristic method diverged from the Nielsen and Molich [20] method as it was completed by UI specialists and did not include the use of written heuristics or guidelines. Prescribed task scenarios were employed in usability testing and cognitive walkthroughs. Results showed that the heuristic method identified the most usability problems and more of the serious problems, and did so at the lowest cost of the four techniques. Usability testing was generally the second-best method of the four in identifying problems. A number of questions arise: Was evaluator expertise the key component in the effectiveness of both the heuristic and usability testing methods? What was the amount of overlap in the problems identified by the four methods? What was the inter-rater reliability of problem identification?

Desurvire, Lawrence, and Atwood [4] compared the effectiveness of empirical usability testing and heuristic evaluations in identifying violations of usability guidelines. The heuristic method differed from others [10, 20] in that evaluators rated guidelines on bipolar scales for each of a set of tasks. Laboratory testing identified violations of six of ten relevant guidelines, while the combined results from the heuristic evaluations identified only one violation of a guideline. The heuristic ratings from UI experts and empirical usability test participants were predictive of laboratory user performance data. Non-UI experts' ratings were not predictive of performance. Heuristic ratings were effective in identifying tasks where problems would occur, but not the specific user interface problems themselves. UI experts' "best guess" predictions of performance were comparable to their heuristic ratings.

Bias [1] describes a systematic group evaluation procedure called the pluralistic usability walkthrough that includes end user, architect, design, developer, publication writer, and human factors representatives who complete scenario-driven walkthroughs of software prototypes. Human factors staff lead the group ses-

sions. The design-test-redesign cycle is reduced to minutes through the use of low-technology prototypes to illustrate alternative designs, and through the presence and cooperation of individuals with the varied skills required to complete the work. This technique highlights the value of multidisciplinary activity in design [6] and group problem solving [7], and the iterative design possible within tight time constraints. A question arises about the group facilitation skills and procedures required for human factors engineers to achieve high group productivity and accurate judgments in the walkthroughs [7, 17].

Nielsen and Molich [20] tested heuristic evaluations completed individually by evaluators who were not human factors experts. In three of the four studies reported, evaluators received a lecture on nine usability heuristics and related reference material. No prescribed task scenarios were employed. Aggregates of data from five computer science students or industry computer professionals generally found about two-thirds of the problems that the authors had previously identified in the interfaces. While the study measured how hard it was to find problems, there was no measure of the severity of the identified usability problems.

There is some evidence that evaluators other than UI specialists can carry out useful and successful think-aloud and heuristic walkthroughs [19, 20]. Also, Jorgensen [12] and Wright and Monk [23] both provide evidence of the success of a think-aloud technique used by developers who had minimal training on the procedure and limited use of human factors resource. Developers observed users who thought aloud while working through tasks on the developers' systems. Walkthroughs were done by individuals in the former study and by teams in the latter. Questions arise about the numbers and types of problems that were not identified in these studies, and how data on problems were interpreted and analyzed.

Goals of the Study
Our study had three goals: The first goal of the study was to better understand the relationship between empirical testing and walkthrough results. This information would improve the understanding of the tradeoffs in selecting one rather than another in a particular situation. This goal included assessment of the number and severity of usability problems identified by the two methods and the resource required to identify them. The second goal was to determine whether the results regarding the relative effectiveness of empirical and walkthrough methods were reliable and would replicate across systems, or whether these results were system dependent. The third goal of the study was to understand how well walkthroughs work in user interface evaluation and how to improve their effectiveness. An effective walkthrough method would be one that identifies most usability problems in an interface, and especially the most severe usability problems. The role of individuals and teams, evaluator characteristics, scenarios, self-guided exploration, and usability heuristics in walkthroughs were explored as part of this third goal.

METHOD
Design
Three user interface evaluation methods were assessed: empirical usability test, individual usability walkthrough, and team usability walkthrough. The usability walkthrough procedure developed and used in this study included components to maximize effectiveness of usability problem identification, based on previous research. The walkthrough included separate segments for 1) self-guided exploration of a graphical user interface (GUI) office system, and 2) use of prescribed scenarios. The procedure utilized a set of 12 usability guidelines. Walkthroughs were conducted individually by six evaluators in one condition and by six pairs of evaluators in another condition. The evaluators in the team condition conversed with each other about issues and problems during the sessions. The evaluators were responsible for documenting the usability problems they identified in the walkthroughs.

The empirical usability test method also had separate segments for 1) self-guided exploration of a GUI system, and 2) use of prescribed scenarios. The six users in the usability tests were asked to describe usability problems they encountered, and problems were recorded by the human factors staff who were observing the sessions.

The usability problems identified through use of the three methods were categorized using common metrics. Thus data could be compared across methods on dimensions including number and severity of usability problems identified in the interface. The three methods were each applied to two competitive software systems in order to assess the reliability of the findings. The usability tests and walkthroughs were completed as if part of a realistic development schedule with resource constraints so that the data could provide practical information on usability engineering in product development.

Participants
Six separate groups of experienced (GUI) users participated in the study of the two systems. For each system, the empirical test and individual walkthrough each utilized six participants, and the team walkthrough utilized six pairs of participants. A total of 48 participants took part in the study. Participants were randomly assigned to methods; team members did not know each other. Participants had not previously used the GUI system they worked with in the study. The six groups were comparable based on background data gathered prior to usability sessions. Participants were predominantly end users and developers of GUI systems, along with a few UI specialists and software support staff. Most of the participants had advanced educational degrees; used computers in home, work, and school settings; and had used a variety of computers, operating systems, and applications. They used computers approximately 20 hours a week, including over 10 hours a week on GUI systems. Except for more formal education, the participants were typical of those who would participate in usability walkthroughs and empirical testing of GUI systems in product development.

Materials
The two systems selected for the study were commercially available GUI office environments with integrated text, spreadsheet, and graphics applications. They will be referred to as Systems 1 and 2. The two systems differed substantially in the type of interface style and office metaphor presented.

Human factors staff consulted with end users and developed a set of nine generic task scenarios to be used with both systems. These scenarios were representative of typical office tasks involving text, spreadsheet, and graphics applications, and use of the system environment. The tasks included a range of one to thirteen subtasks and covered document creation, moving and copying within and between documents, linking and updating documents, drawing, printing, interface customization, finding and backing up documents, and use of system-provided and user-generated macros.

A two-page document of guidelines was developed for the evaluators in the walkthrough conditions. The document told evaluators their assignment was to identify usability problems with the interface initially by exploring the interface on their own and then by walking through typical tasks provided to them. A usability problem was defined as anything that interfered with a user's ability to efficiently and effectively complete tasks. Evaluators were asked to keep in mind the guidelines about what makes a system usable and to refer back to them as necessary. Following the precepts of minimalism [3], the document provided brief definitions and task-oriented examples of twelve guidelines. These guidelines were compiled from heuristics used by Nielsen and Molich [20], the ISO working paper on general dialogue principles [9], and the IBM CUA user interface design principles [8]. The twelve usability guidelines included:

- Use a simple and natural dialog,
- Provide an intuitive visual layout,
- Speak the user's language,
- Minimize the user's memory load,
- Be consistent,
- Provide feedback,
- Provide clearly marked exits,
- Provide shortcuts,
- Provide good help,
- Allow user customization,
- Minimize the use and effects of modes, and
- Support input device continuity.

A usability problem description form was developed for use by the walkthrough evaluators. The form instructed the evaluators to briefly describe each problem and then rate its impact on end user task completion.

Procedure
The authors completed all usability engineering work in the study and became familiar with each GUI system prior to commencement of the usability sessions. All sessions were completed in a usability studio in Hawthorne, NY. The GUI systems were set up on an

IBM PS/2 Model 80 with an 8514 display and a printer. Usability sessions for all methods each took about three hours. The first half of the usability sessions included an introduction by the usability engineer who administered the sessions, and a self-guided exploration of the system by the participants. During the self-guided exploration, participants could go through on-line tutorials, read any of the hard copy documentation shipped with the system, use and modify example documents created using the different applications and system functions, or create new application documents and experiment with system functions. In the second half of the sessions, participants worked through a set of nine typical tasks presented in random order and completed a debriefing questionnaire given by the administrator.

The empirical testing and walkthrough sessions differed in human factors involvement in the session and in how usability problems were documented. In empirical testing, two usability engineers administered each session in its entirety with an individual user. One person in the control studio interacted with users (who were in the usability studio and described usability problems they encountered during sessions), controlled the videotape equipment, and observed usability problems. The second person in the control studio logged user comments, usability problems, time on task, and task success or failure.

Usability staff involvement in the walkthrough sessions was limited to test the resource requirements of the method. One administrator was available on-call during the session in case of unexpected events. A few sample sessions were videotaped and observed by human factors staff; no session logging occurred. One administrator introduced the session and instructed walkthrough evaluators in the use of the guidelines for usability walkthrough document and the usability problem description forms. The administrator emphasized in both individual and two-person team walkthrough conditions that the problem identification sheets were the deliverable for the session. In the team conditions, evaluators were given additional instructions to help each other by providing relevant information [7]. They were told that if either one of the team members thought something was a usability problem, they should record it. Also, team walkthrough evaluators were instructed to take turns with the mouse and with recording usability problems so that each person had direct experience with the interface and with the usability problem description forms. Evaluators read the guidelines document and the administrator then left the studio. After the self-guided exploration phase, the administrator returned briefly to present the task scenarios and emphasize that it was more important to identify usability problems than to complete all the tasks.

RESULTS
Data Analysis
The usability problems recorded during empirical testing and the usability problem descriptions documented during the walkthroughs were classified by the usability engineers using a generic model of usability problems that evolved during the course of the study. The classification completed a content analysis of the problems and prepared the data for subsequent problem severity ratings. The hierarchical model consisted of a total of 47 categories of potential user interface problem areas. Because of the functional differences between the systems, all 47 categories applied to System 1 while only 43 applied to System 2. Subcategories were created when a main category had several problems that were related, yet addressed different aspects of the higher-level category. For example, the fifth main category was Move & Copy and it had two subcategories: 1) Clipboard and 2) Direct Manipulation. We distinguished between problems that were pervasive through the environment and those that were application specific. For example, we classified icon complaints (e.g., cannot understand icon meaning, icons hard to read, no icon status information or it is hard to distinguish) as pervasive office-level problems, while confusion about specific spreadsheet functions (e.g., how does the sum function work?) were regarded as application specific.

Item classification was discussed until consensus was reached about its placement in the model. To assess inter-rater reliability, 50 problem statements were randomly selected from the data for the three conditions and classified by two usability engineers who had not observed the participants or been involved in data analysis. They each classified the data using the generic model of usability problems. The inter-rater reliability scores between the third-party usability staff and the staff involved in the study were 87% for the empirical testing data, 70% for the individual walkthrough data, and 71% for the team walkthrough data. For each empirical testing and walkthrough group, data were analyzed regarding the number of usability problem tokens (all instances), usability problem types (instances minus all duplicates), and problem areas (higher level categories of problem tokens and types, e.g., Move and Copy) in the generic model. These problem areas were assigned Problem Severity Classification (PSC) ratings.

A version of the PSC measure, which is used in IBM, was employed in the study. It provides a ranking of usability problems by severity that can be used to determine allocation of resources for addressing user interface problems (see Table 1). PSC ratings are computed on a two-dimensional scale, where one axis represents the impact of a usability problem on end user ability to complete a task, and the other represents frequency (the percentage of end users who experience the problem). Categories of the impact dimension (high, moderate, low) and frequency dimension (high, moderate) were combined to form an index of PSC ratings that ranged from 1-3 where 1 is most severe. High impact was defined as a problem that prevented the user from completing the task, moderate impact represented significant problems in task completion, and low impact represented minor problems and inefficiencies. Given the small sample sizes in the conditions, moderate frequency was defined as 2 (33%) users, evaluators, or evaluator teams; and high frequency was defined as three (50%) or more of them. For example, if three or more of the six evaluators (high frequency) reported a problem that caused significant difficulty (moderate impact) in completing a task, a PSC rating of "1" would be assigned to the problem area.

Frequency (Percentage of Users)		
	High	Moderate
Impact on Task		
High	1	1
Moderate	1	2
Low	2	3

Table 1. Problem Severity Classification rating matrix.

We generated PSC ratings for each of the categories in the generic model of user interface problems. There were 47 PSC ratings for System 1, and 43 for System 2. To generate PSC ratings in the empirical conditions, the human factors staff calculated the frequency of users experiencing a problem and assigned an impact score. Disagreements about impact scores were discussed until consensus was reached. In the walkthrough conditions, human factors staff calculated the frequency data and averaged the impact scores provided by the evaluators. Problem areas that did not have problem tokens from at least two participants or teams were assigned a PSC rating of 99 (i.e., no action required). Problem areas with PSC ratings of 1-3 were called significant problem areas (SPA), and those with ratings of 99 were called "no action" areas.

For the walkthrough conditions, evaluator questionnaire data on aspects of the walkthrough procedure were collected during the debriefing sessions and analyzed. For the empirical conditions, data on time on task, completion rates, and the debriefing questionnaire were collected but are not reported here.

Empirical Testing and Walkthrough Results

For Systems 1 and 2, empirical usability testing identified the largest number of usability problem tokens (all instances), followed by team walkthrough and then individual walkthrough (see Table 2). For both systems,

	Empirical Test	Team Walk	Individual Walk
System 1			
Problem Tokens	421	115	78
Problem Types	159	68	49
System 2			
Problem Tokens	401	107	64
Problem Types	130	54	39

Table 2. Total identified usability problems.

the total number of usability problem tokens found by empirical testing was about four times the total number of problems identified by team walkthroughs, and about five times the total number found by individual

walkthroughs. The difference in the distribution across the groups of the total number of tokens found was statistically significant for each system at the $p < .01$ level according to χ^2 tests.

Empirical testing also identified the largest number of usability problem types (instances minus duplicates), followed by team and individual walkthroughs. For both systems, the total number of usability problem types found by empirical testing was about twice the total number found by the team walkthroughs, and three times the total number found by individual walkthroughs. Again, the difference in the distribution of the total number of problem types found in the three groups was statistically significant for each system at the $p < .01$ level.

The data on PSC ratings assigned to problem areas for Systems 1 and 2 are presented in Table 3. For both systems, empirical testing identified a larger total number of significant problem areas (Total SPAs) assigned PSC ratings of 1-3 than did either team or individual walkthroughs. However, the variation in total number of SPAs across methods was statistically significant for System 1 ($p < .01$) but not for System 2. For both systems, there was no bias or tendency towards more severe ratings (i.e., more PSC 1s versus 2s) in one group as compared to another.

	Empirical Test	Team Walk	Individual Walk
System 1			
PSC 1	19	9	8
PSC 2	18	13	9
PSC 3	3	1	1
Total SPAs	40	23	18
No Action Areas	7	24	29
Total Problem Areas	47	47	47
System 2			
PSC 1	10	3	6
PSC 2	15	10	10
PSC 3	2	1	1
Total SPAs	27	14	17
No Action Areas	16	29	26
Total Problem Areas	43	43	43

Table 3. PSC ratings of usability problem areas.

Table 4 provides information on the number of unique usability problem areas identified by each of the methods. A problem area that is unique to a method is a SPA that is identified by only one method. For Systems 1 and 2, empirical testing identified the largest number of unique problem areas. For both systems, two-thirds or more of these unique problem areas were assigned a PSC rating of 2, representing relatively important problems in the user interfaces.

A common usability problem area across methods occurred when a SPA was identified by all three methods. For example, a common problem area was the basic model for linking, where empirical testing and team walkthroughs generated a SPA with a PSC rating of 1 and individual walkthrough generated a SPA with a

PSC rating of 2. To analyze the proportion of problem areas that were common, the total number of SPAs for each system was computed. The total number of SPAs identified for System 1 was 41 (40 identified by empirical testing plus 1 unique problem area identified by team walkthrough). The total number of SPAs identified for System 2 was 29 (27 identified by empirical testing plus 2 unique problem areas found by individual walkthrough). Regarding common problem areas for System 1, 13 of the total number of 41 SPAs (32% of total) were common across the three techniques. For System 2, 10 of the 29 SPAs (35% of the total) were common across techniques.

	Empirical Test	Team Walk	Individual Walk
System 1	13	1	0
System 2	8	0	2

Table 4. Unique usability problem areas.

Walkthrough Results

Additional analysis of the effectiveness of team as compared to individual walkthroughs was conducted by studying the total number of problem tokens found by each individual walkthrough evaluator or walkthrough evaluator team. This analysis showed that teams found more problem tokens than did individual walkthrough evaluators for each system ($p < .01$ according to t-tests). For System 1, the average number of problems identified by the walkthrough teams was 19 while the average for individual walkthrough evaluators was 13. For System 2, these values were 18 for team and 11 for individual walkthroughs respectively. However as shown in Tables 2 and 3 above, while more problem tokens and types were identified by team walkthrough conditions, the total number of SPAs identified was similar for both team and individual walkthroughs, and the pattern held across systems.

During the debriefing, evaluators rated the relative usefulness of scenarios as compared to self-guided exploration in identifying usability problems in the systems. The evaluators used a 5-point scale where a score of 1 was the most positive response for use of scenarios. All walkthrough groups favored the use of scenarios over self-guided exploration; the average score across systems was 1.8. Evaluators were also asked about the added value of using the guidelines during the walkthrough. A 5-point scale was again used and a score of 1 was the most positive response for guidelines. For both systems, the walkthrough evaluators thought the guidelines were of limited added value to them in identifying usability problems; the average score across systems was 3.9. The evaluators said they thought the brief document was very effective in explaining and giving examples of the guidelines, and that they would not change the format. They stated that because of their experience with GUI and other systems, they were already familiar with the guideline concepts, but that less experienced users would find it very useful. It was noted that almost all evaluators tried to take the guideline document with them at the end of the session.

When asked about this, they said they were very pleased with it and wanted to keep it for reference.

Cost-Effectiveness Data

Table 5 shows the cost-effectiveness data for the three methods on the two systems. This analysis includes the time required by human factors staff and participants; no laboratory facility costs are included. Human factors time includes preparation of all materials (35-45 hours across methods), administration of sessions (10-55 hours), and data analysis (16-50 hours). Time to analyze the data using the generic model of problem areas and the PSC matrix are included for all groups. As expected, the total hours required (human factors plus participant) for a method was highest for empirical testing for System 1 and System 2.

	Empirical Test	Team Walk	Individual Walk
System 1			
HF staff hours	136	72	70
Participant hours	24	48	24
Total hours	160	118	94
Problem Types	159	68	49
Hours/Type	1.0	1.7	1.9
SPAs	40	23	18
Hours/SPA	4.0	5.1	5.2
System 2			
HF staff hours	116	77	76
Participant hours	24	48	24
Total hours	140	125	100
Problem Types	130	54	39
Hours/Type	1.1	2.3	2.6
SPAs	27	14	17
Hours/SPA	5.2	8.9	5.9

Table 5. Cost-effectiveness data for the three methods.

However, empirical testing needed only about half as much time as the walkthroughs to find each usability problem type. For System 1, the hours required to identify each significant problem area were fairly similar across techniques. For System 2, the resource required for team walkthrough was higher than for both empirical testing and individual walkthrough.

DISCUSSION

The findings regarding the relative effectiveness of empirical testing and walkthrough methods were generally replicated across the two GUI systems. It is not clear whether these patterns would be replicated on non-GUI systems, however, the significant differences in the style and presentation of the two GUI systems in the study support the reliability of the results across these types of systems.

The empirical testing condition identified the largest number of problems, and identified a significant number of relatively severe problems that were missed by the walkthrough conditions. These data are consistent with Desurvire et al. [4] data and at odds with Jeffries et al. [10] data. The difference between our data and those of Jeffries et al. [10] in the number of problems found might be explained by the difference in evaluator expertise, but Desurvire et al. [4] also utilized UI experts, and their data are consistent with ours. All three studies do provide strong support for the value of UI expertise though. We recognize that the basis of our empirical usability testing results was the experimental controls employed, the skills required to conduct the test, experience with the two GUI systems prior to observing test sessions, and the UI expertise required to recognize and interpret the usability problems encountered by the users. Our data suggest that this type of empirical usability testing should be employed for baseline and other key checkpoint tests in the development cycle where coverage of the interface and identification of all significant problems is essential. Walkthroughs of the type in this study are a good alternative when resources are very limited [19] and may be the preferred method early in the development cycle for deciding between alternative designs for particular features. In Jeffries et al. [10] the heuristic method found a larger number of severe problems than usability testing. This might be explained partially by the differences in procedures. Data for the methods in our study were collected across a three-hour time period. In the Jeffries et al. [10] study, the UI experts in the heuristic condition documented the problems they found over a two-week period.

About a third of the significant problem areas identified were common across all methods. The degree of overlap is encouraging, but it should caution human factors practitioners about the tradeoffs they are making in employing one method rather than another. These methods are complementary and yield different results; they act as different types of sieves in identifying usability problems. Jeffries [11] stated that there was less overlap in problems found by any two of the methods in their study [10] than in ours. The higher degree of overlap in our study might be partially due to the fact that all methods used the same scenarios. These scenarios were rich and complex examples of typical work that end users need to perform and may have greatly aided in the evaluation of the systems by all methods. The overlap between the two methods that used their scenarios in Jeffries et al. [10] was no higher than that between the others though, and may reflect differences in the two sets of scenarios.

Team walkthroughs achieved better results than individual walkthroughs in some areas. The fact that any differences emerged between the team and individual walkthroughs is encouraging. The brief period of the usability session, the lack of an established working relationship between team members, and the small size of the teams may have contributed to the small differences found. Many usability walkthroughs in product development are done by moderate-sized teams (e.g., 6-8 people) because of the wide range of skills and backgrounds necessary to identify and then resolve usability problems. Therefore, due to practical and organizational considerations, team walkthroughs may be an area warranting future research. Work by Bias

[1] and Hackman and Morris [7] may help identify ways to facilitate and enhance the performance of team walkthroughs.

All walkthrough groups favored the use of scenarios over self-guided exploration in identifying usability problems. This evidence supports the use of a set of rich scenarios developed in consultation with end users. And as evaluation work attempts to predict what will occur in real world settings, the use of well-founded scenarios can provide some assurance that real world problems will be identified.

The evaluators, who were all experienced GUI users, generally thought that the guidelines for usability were of limited added value to them in conducting the walkthroughs, but would be helpful for less experienced users. These data are consistent with the Desurvire et al. [4] results showing no difference between UI experts' heuristic and "best guess" ratings. Guidelines may serve to promote consensus about usability goals for development teams, and may be more useful for less experienced evaluators during walkthroughs.

The results also demonstrate that evaluators who have relevant computer experience and represent a sample of end users and development team members can complete usability walkthroughs with relative success. Specific UI or human factors expertise may be very helpful but is not required, and there are a multitude of practical, individual, end user, organizational, and product benefits to be achieved by involving more members of development teams in walkthroughs [5, 12, 19, 20].

Cost-effectiveness data show that empirical testing required the same or less time to identify each problem as compared to walkthroughs. The differences between these data and the cost-benefit data for usability test and heuristic methods in Jeffries et al. [10] may be due to the differences in the walkthrough procedures utilized and in the type of data analysis performed in the two studies. If our walkthrough data had been analyzed in other ways or by different individuals (e.g., developers), the resource required might have varied significantly. However, the resource and skills applied to data analysis may be reflected in the quality of the analysis and the resulting changes to systems. Ultimately, the true cost-benefit of these methods will be realized through their ability to facilitate the achievement of usability objectives for systems in iterative development, and to provide measurable benefits that exceed the costs of their use [13, 14, 15]. Analysis of data from one iteration in isolation is of limited utility.

The identification of usability problems is not an end in itself. Rather, it is a means towards eliminating problems and improving the interface. The part of the development process concerned with making recommendations for change based on the usability problems identified is not covered in this study. We did find that the larger the number of problem tokens and types identified regarding a significant problem area of the interface, the richer the source of data was for forming recommendations for changes to improve that portion of the interface. The data from this study show that the empirical and team walkthrough conditions have the advantage over the individual walkthrough conditions in this area. The empirical test data contained four times as many problem tokens describing a significant problem area and providing context about it as compared to team walkthrough data, and teams produced 33-50% more information as compared to individual walkthroughs. The quality of the data analysis completed and the recommendations that arise from them are issues for future research.

How could walkthrough methods be improved? Users in the empirical testing sessions were given opportunities to provide recommendations for changes to the usability problems they encountered, and the walkthrough sessions could be improved to capture evaluator recommendations as well. Another area of walkthrough procedures that needs attention is the difficulty of interpreting problems. Walkthrough evaluators used different language than the staff who analyzed the problem reports, and the data analysts' job of understanding these problem statements was made more difficult by a lack of context and lack of session observation. The difficulty experienced in interpreting walkthrough data was supported by the lower inter-rater reliability data reported for walkthroughs compared to usability tests. Moreover, from walkthrough sessions that human factors staff observed, it became evident that evaluators misattributed the sources of problems. We also observed that evaluators sometimes became so involved in the task scenarios that they forgot to document problems they encountered and identified. We attempted to overcome this demand characteristic of the walkthroughs by emphasizing the importance of problem identification over task completion, but it was not effective in some cases, and further refinement of intervention strategies should be explored [7]. A better debriefing of evaluators that included reviewing identified usability problems, capturing undocumented ones that evaluators mentioned in passing, and collecting evaluator recommendations for changes might improve walkthrough effectiveness.

ACKNOWLEDGEMENTS

The authors thank Amy Aaronson, Catalina Danis, Tom Dayton, John Gould, Robin Jeffries, John Karat, Wendy Kellogg, Jakob Nielsen, John Richards, Kevin Singley, Cathleen Wharton, and the anonymous reviewers for comments on earlier versions of this paper.

REFERENCES

1. Bias, R.G. Walkthroughs: Efficient collaborative testing. *IEEE Software* , 8, 5, 1991, pp. 94-95.

2. Bellotti, V. Implications of current design practice for the use of HCI techniques. In Jones, D.M. and Winder, R., (Eds.), *People and Computers IV*. Cambridge University Press, Cambridge, 1988, pp. 13-34.

3. Carroll, J., Smith-Kerker, P.L., Ford, J.R., and Mazur-Rimetz, S.A. The minimal manual. *Human-Computer Interaction*, 3, 1987-88, pp. 123-153.

4. Desurvire, H., Lawrence, D., and Atwood, M. Empiricism versus judgment: Comparing user interface evaluation methods on a new telephone-based interface. *SIGCHI Bulletin*, 23, 4, pp. 58-59.

5. Gould, J.D., and Lewis, C. Designing for usability: Key principles and what designers think. *Communications of the ACM*, 28, 1985, pp. 300-311.

6. Grudin, J. and Poltrock, S.E. User interface design in large corporations: Coordination and communication across disciplines. In *Proceedings of CHI'89* (Austin, TX, April 30-May 4, 1989), ACM, New York, pp. 197-203.

7. Hackman, J.R., and Morris, C.G. Group tasks, group interaction process, and group performance effectiveness: A review and proposed integration. In Berkowitz, L., (Ed.), *Advances in Experimental Social Psychology*, Vol. 8, Academic Press, New York, 1975.

8. International Business Machines Corporation. *Systems Application Architecture, Common User Access, Guide to User Interface Design*, (SC34-4289), 1991.

9. International Standards Organization. *Working Paper of ISO 9241 Part 10, Dialogue Principles, Version 2* , ISO/TC 159/SC4/WG5 N155, 1990.

10. Jeffries, R.J., Miller, J.R., Wharton, C., and Uyeda, K.M. User interface evaluation in the real world: A comparison of four techniques. In *Proceedings of CHI'91*, (New Orleans, LA, April 28-May 3, 1991), ACM, New York, pp. 119-124.

11. Jeffries, R. J. Personal communication, Sept. 1991.

12. Jorgensen, A.K. Thinking-aloud in user interface design: A method promoting cognitive ergonomics. *Ergonomics*, 33, 4, 1990, pp. 501-507.

13. Karat, C. Cost-justifying human factors support on development projects. *Human Factors Society Bulletin*, 35, 3, 1992, pp. 1-4.

14. Karat, C. Cost-benefit and business case analysis of usability engineering. *ACM SIGCHI Conference on Human Factors in Computing Systems*, New Orleans, LA, April 28-May2, Tutorial Notes.

15. Karat, C. Cost-benefit analysis of usability engineering techniques. In *Proceedings of the HFS Society*, (Orlando, FL, Oct., 1990), pp. 839-843.

16. Lewis, C., Polson, P., Wharton, C., and Rieman, J. Testing a walkthrough methodology for theory-based design of walk-up-and-use interfaces. In *Proceedings of CHI'90* (Seattle, WA, April 1-5, 1990), ACM, New York, pp. 235-242.

17. McGrath, J.E. *Groups: Interaction and Performance* Prentice-Hall, Englewood Cliffs, N.J., 1984.

18. Nielsen, J. Finding usability problems through heuristic evaluation. In *Proceedings of CHI'92* (Monterey, CA, May 3-7, 1992), ACM, New York.

19. Nielsen, J. Usability engineering at a discount. In Salvendy, G., and Smith, M.J., (Eds.), *Designing and Using Human-Computer Interfaces and Knowledge-Based Systems*. Elsevier Science Pulishers, Amsterdam, 1989, pp. 394-401.

20. Nielsen, J. and Molich, R. Heuristic evaluation of user interfaces. In *Proceedings of CHI'90*, (Seattle, WA, April 1-5, 1990), ACM, New York, pp. 249-256.

21. Whitten, N. *Managing Software Development Projects: Formula for Success*. Wiley and Sons, New York, 1990, pp. 203-223.

22. Wharton, C., Bradford, J., Jeffries, R., and Franzke, M. Applying cognitive walkthroughs to more complex user interfaces: Experiences, issues, and recommendations. In *Proceedings of CHI'92* (Monterey, CA, May 3-7, 1992), ACM, New York.

23. Wright, P.C., and Monk, A.F. The use of think-aloud evaluation methods in design. *SIGCHI Bulletin*, 23, 1, 1991, pp. 55-57.

One Dimensional Motion Tailoring for the Disabled:
A User Study

Randy Pausch, Laura Vogtle, and Matthew Conway

University of Virginia, Thornton Hall
Charlottesville, VA 22903
Pausch@Virginia.edu

ABSTRACT

The Tailor project allows physically disabled users to provide real-time analog input to computer applications. We use a Polhemus™ tracking device and create a custom tailored mapping from each user's best range and type of motion into the analog control signal. The application is a simple video game based on *Pong*, where the analog input controls the position of the player's paddle. A group of able-bodied subjects was able to correctly hit the ball with the paddle 77% of the time, and a comparison group of children with Cerebral Palsy performed at the 50% level. More than half the disabled users were able to perform at a higher level than the worst able-bodied user.

KEYWORDS

gesture input, disabled, handicapped, user study

INTRODUCTION

The goal of the Tailor project at the University of Virginia is to allow disabled users to drive computer-based applications through the use of analog control signals. For example, with two analog control signals, one for X and one for Y, a user can smoothly move a screen cursor. Able-bodied users easily perform analog tasks, but many disabled users lack the manual dexterity to control devices such as mice and joysticks. The Tailor project recognizes that many disabled users have *some* repeatable, controllable range of motion, but that it does not correspond to any existing physical input device. Imagine, for example, an individual who could not easily move his elbow away from his waist, but could move his wrist towards or away from his chest. Such an individual is capable of generating a useful control signal, but no existing physical device exists to interpret it.

Tailor's long term goal is to generate an interface for each user which will allow him to produce real-time analog control signals with his best physical motion [8]. Our long term motivation comes from the CANDY (Communication Assistance to Negate Disabilities in Youth) project at the University of Virginia, which is an ongoing research project in augmentative communications. CANDY's overall goal is

to provide a conversational speech prosthesis; a detailed description of which is beyond the scope of this paper [9, 6]. Our initial target population is children with Cerebral Palsy (CP), but individuals with many other disabilities, such as Parkinson's, Muscular Dystrophy (MD), Multiple Sclerosis (MS) and stroke could benefit from our approach.

The class of applications we are examining consists of those that can be driven by two simultaneous analog control signals and possibly an associated on/off switch. All mouse-based interfaces fall into this category. Our approach is called *passive tracking*, a method that detects body motions by means of sensors worn by the user. We then translate the detected motion into the analog signals that drive the application. As an interim goal, we are currently producing a one-dimensional analog control signal from our users. This allows us to gain experience mapping arbitrary user motions in a simpler realm than the two dimensional case.

This paper presents both quantitative and qualitative results from our first user study, which measures how well children with CP use tailored interfaces to play a real-time video game based on the arcade game *Pong*. We use a single player game: by moving a paddle, the user attempts to keep a bouncing ball in the field of play. A player's score is a percentage computed from the number of successful blocks divided by the number of opportunities. In addition to our desire for experience with our approach, we ran this user study to demonstrate that with an appropriate input mechanism, our target population could control a real-time task such as a video game. As a benchmark, we compared how our disabled subjects did with the scores of non-disabled subjects. Non-disabled subjects averaged 77% successful returns, and disabled subjects averaged 50%. More than half of our disabled subjects performed better than our worst able-bodied subject. We begin by explaining our approach to motion mapping for one dimensional analog signals. We then describe the user study, including useful information we gained from early pilot studies. After giving a detailed presentation of the results, we discuss several issues that were raised by the performance of this user study.

RELATED WORK ON PASSIVE TRACKING

When interfaces based on physical devices are problematic, an alternate approach is to passively track the user's body motions. The most obvious advantage of this approach is that we can tailor the interface to each individual's best range of physical motion. Another advantage is that no strength is required to move a physical switch. For the CP community, another advantage is that less coordination is required; with a physical interface, the user much first contact the device, and then move it in some way. The final advantage is that a software interface based on motion tracking can be adapted over time to account for improvement and/or fatigue.

One alternative to tracking body motion is to track eye motion. Eye-tracking is not appropriate for our application for several reasons. First, over 50% of cerebral palsied individuals have eye movement disorders [14]. Second, using eye-tracking for the long term goal of CANDY, a speech synthesizer, makes it impossible to maintain eye contact or receive visual stimulation while speaking. Third, many disabled users are poor candidates for eye-tracking because they tend to move their heads.

Gesture recognition has a long history in many contexts, but most research has focused on converting continuous body motion into discrete tokens. Two-dimensional gesture recognition has been used for printed lettering, cursive handwriting, proofreader's symbols, and shorthand notation. In all cases, the approach is to convert the continuous motion of a stylus into a discrete token as input to a language-driven computation or process. Recognition of three-dimensional gestures has also been attempted, but again the main emphasis has been on converting the body motions into discrete symbols that are interpreted as commands to the system [2, 3]. Systems have attempted to recognize static gestures for the deaf alphabet and motions for a subset of American Sign Language. All of these approaches are based on converting three-dimensional signals into a discrete stream of tokens.

Existing work on mapping gesture into continuous control signals is extremely application dependent. For example, advanced military systems exist which map pilot head motion into weapon trajectories. The pilot's faceshield contains targeting crosshairs, and as the pilot's helmet moves with his head, the system computes the angle of his gaze [5]. More detailed tracking is performed in three dimensional drawing or sculpting applications [12], and virtual reality systems, where sensors attached to gloves [4] provide three-dimensional signals that are mapped into motions in synthetic worlds shown on traditional or head-mounted displays. These systems perform mappings from position and orientation information, but the mappings are significantly less complicated than those we propose.

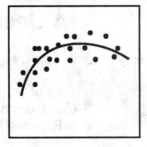 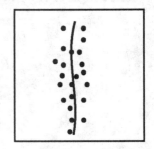

User Moves Wrist   User Moves Wrist
By Pivoting Elbow   Forward and Backward

Figure 1: *Target Curves*

MAPPING TECHNIQUE

Mapping consists of two basic phases, the collection phase and the control phase. The *collection phase* determines the comfortable and preferred motions for the user. The *control phase* performs real-time mapping of user motion based on a mapping function created from the data obtained during the collection phase. Our current mapping approach is based on *target curves*, and allows users to control a device requiring one analog input parameter. In this example, the "device" is a vertical slider on a graphical display which can be moved up and down. During the collection phase, the user is instructed to move the tracker in any manner that is comfortable, while we collect position data from the sensors. During this time, the user receives no visual or auditory feedback from the system.

For example, assume that the user had a tracker attached to a wrist, and was told to keep his hand on a horizontal table during the measurement. This effectively constrains his motion to two dimensions. Based on the on-screen display of this raw data, the therapist creates a piecewise linear curve though the data, corresponding to a dominant path of motion made by the user during the control phase. This is done by invoking a heuristic, manually specifying the curve, or a combination of both. All target curves used in this user study were manually specified. Figure 1 shows typical collection of sampled tracker data and the resultant target curves. The first user pivoted his wrist around his elbow, and the second moved his wrist forward and backward.

During the control phase, the user moves the tracker along the target curve and from his position along that curve, we generate an analog signal. One end of the curve indicates 0 percent of this signal and the other end indicates 100 percent. Intermediate positions along the target curve indicate intermediate signal values and the signal generates visual feedback on a CRT. The user is not expected to move the tracker precisely along the curve; we map tracker data to the nearest point on the target curve, as shown in Figure 2. Although in the previous example we limited the user's motions to a table surface, target curves, in general, are three dimensional.

DESCRIPTION OF THE USER STUDY

Our goal was to measure how well disabled children could control a real-time, one dimensional analog signal. While our long term goal is to drive a speech synthesizer, we chose to use visual rather than aural feedback. We could have played a tone and had our subjects play a second tone, attempting to match the pitch, but this proved unwieldy in early trials. Simple visual feedback, such as moving a slider, as shown in Figure 2, quickly bored the children. We decided to use a video game because it held the children's interest and because it made our scoring mechanism obvious.

The game was a simple variation on original arcade video game, Pong. A ball bounces off the walls of a square playing field, making a pleasant beeping noise as it contacts each wall. The player defends one of the walls, attempting to block the ball with a paddle before the ball reaches the wall. As shown in Figure 3, each child moves the paddle either vertically, defending the right wall, or horizontally, defending the top wall. On a successful defense, the ball bounces off the paddle and play continues. If the player fails to block the ball with the paddle, it reaches the wall behind the paddle and a less pleasant buzz is sounded. The game pauses for two seconds and then puts a new ball into play at the positions marked with an "X" in Figure 3. In order to avoid a lock step pattern of motion, each time the ball contacts the paddle or a wall, its angle of reflection is a slight variation of its angle of incidence.

One major advantage of using this particular video game as our task is that, although control of the paddle is one dimensional, the player needs to quickly perform a two-dimensional perception and planning task in order to anticipate where to move the paddle. Many people have the incorrect impression that children with CP are all mentally retarded. While the incidence of retardation is higher in the CP population (50%-65%) [14] than in

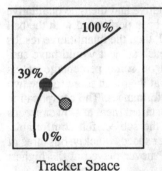
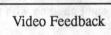

Figure 2:   *Tracker Space to Device Space. The grey dot is a user's position. The black dot is the point on the target curve closest to the current position.*

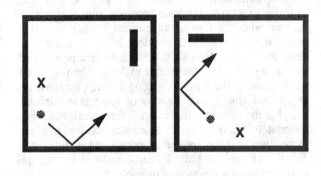

Figure 3:   *Vertical and Horizontal Games. An "X" marks the position where the ball begins.*

the general population, many children with CP are not retarded. By using this two-dimensional game, we make the point that our target population has the planning and cognitive skills necessary for the eventual two-dimensional version of the Tailor system.

The most difficult question was how to evaluate the effectiveness of our mappings. One design might have been to compare subjects with CP using a traditional input device such as a joystick, with a group of subjects using the Tailor system. This would have been pointless, since we know that our target population cannot use traditional input devices. What we were really interested in measuring is how well our mappings could compensate for disability; how well would a child using our system do in comparison to an able-bodied child of the same age? Therefore, we compared a group of able-bodied children to a group of children with CP who had their input mapped by the Tailor system. One problem with this approach is that if we allowed able-bodied children to use physical devices, such as joysticks, we would also be comparing the performance of the input devices involved. The Polhemus tracker is not as accurate a device as a joystick; more importantly, there is a hardware latency of approximately 85ms [7] which makes the game noticeably harder to play.

In order to keep the tracker lag from dominating our results, we had our able-bodied subjects use the Polhemus and Tailor-mapping software. Of course, the tailored mappings are unnecessary for the able-bodied users; they can adapt easily to any reasonable physical motion. By having both groups use the system, we discovered how big a disadvantage it is to have CP — how badly are the users disabled when we compensate by allowing them to use their best range of motion. The only remaining issue was that our able-bodied users, having grown up in Nintendo generation, clearly had practice with video games. We counter-balanced this practice effect by not allowing them to play with their dominant hand. We suspect this decision had little effect; none of our able-bodied subjects expressed a strong desire to use their dominant hand. We had two of the able-bodied subjects attach the tracker to their head in order to gain a direct comparison with the one CP subject who used head attachment. Trials were run between February and September of 1991, using children ranging from age six to seventeen, inclusive. Fourteen able-bodied children and eight children with CP participated in the study. We recognize that we are using an uncomfortably small number of subjects in our analysis, but the difficulty in arranging these trials cannot be overstated. Many of our disabled subjects had to travel more than an hour by car to participate in the study. Table 1 shows the breakdown of body sites used for attaching the tracker to various subjects.

attachment site	able-bodied	CP
head	2	1
Right Wrist	5	2
Left Wrist	5	5
Left Elbow	2	0

Table 1: *Body Attachment Points*

The physical setup includes an IBM-compatible 386 personal computer with a color VGA display and either a 14 or 19 inch monitor. The playing field is a square 420 pixels on a side, and the paddle is 95 pixels wide. Our tracker is a Polhemus Isotrak™ [10]. The ball's speed was always one of three fixed values: slow = 33 pixels per second; medium = 64 pixels per second; fast = 178 pixels per second. With each subject, we began at the slowest speed and moved up to faster speeds as the subject became more comfortable. Three of our eight disabled subjects did not play at the highest speed. This was a trade-off between allowing the subjects to practice, and handling their fatigue; due to the relatively short times span the CP children could support vigorous physical activity.

FEEDBACK ON PILOT STUDIES

We obtained valuable feedback by running several disabled pilot subjects. The physical setup was very important for the disabled users; many have difficulty stabilizing their bodies. The Polhemus tracker cannot be used in an area with large metal objects as it is based on sensing a magnetic field, so we transferred our subjects from their wheelchairs to a specially constructed wooden chair with flexible support for seating. We believe that this may have adversely affected the performance of some of the children, as they are very dependent on the customized seating and support in their individual wheelchairs. For future trials, we will eliminate the need for this by switching to alternative tracking technologies that are less sensitive to metal [1]. CP is often accompanied by poor vision [14]; we acquired a

large monitor and made sure that the subjects were seated close enough that they could easily see the ball and paddle.

We explained to the children that they were helping us experiment with a new device. We had originally not intended to show a running score on the screen, but our pilot subjects demanded it, and began keeping score themselves by counting. This should not have surprised us, as it is a well known phenomenon that children this age require score keeping mechanisms and invent them when they are not present.

The original game design only allowed the game to be played vertically, defending the right wall. This produced cognitive trouble for the children whose target curves were predominantly horizontal, in much the same way that rotating a mouse 90 degrees makes it almost impossible to use. Other researchers have also found that stimulus and response need to be organized in spatially similar ways [13]. What we found interesting was that the two orientations, horizontal and vertical, were sufficient.

The other things we learned during the pilot studies involved our interaction with the subjects. Having limited or no experience with video games, our subjects had trouble understanding whether they were controlling the motion of the paddle or the ball. We overcame this by having the subjects move the paddle briefly in a training session before the ball appeared. A more subtle problem had to do with retracking. The Tailor system works by using a target curve, and during a session it sometimes becomes necessary to stop play in order to establish a new target curve. This can be caused by many things, including fatigue or substantial motion of the child's body in the chair. With some subjects, when we stopped to establish a new curve they often interpreted this as a failure on their part and needed a healthy dose of reassurance before they could continue. During the trails, we took great pains to avoid the need to re-establish target curves.

RESULTS

We address first the quantitative and then the qualitative results. If all the trials had been performed with the ball traveling at the same speed, then the quantitative results would be easy to report: each subject would have successfully blocked the ball on some percentage of his trails. One could then look at the mean score for the two groups and graph their performances. The complication is that for each subject, we started them at slower speeds and then moved up when the subject felt comfortable. Subjects moved up to higher speeds quickly, but three of our eight children with CP never played at the highest speed.

Figure 4 shows the results of all trials run at the medium speed, the only speed for which we have data on all our subjects, and the speed upon which we base our overall quantitative result of mean performance of 77% vs.

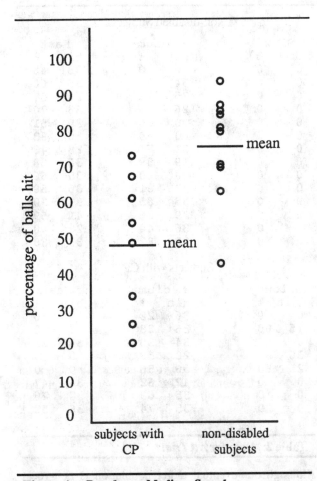

Figure 4: *Results on Medium Speed*

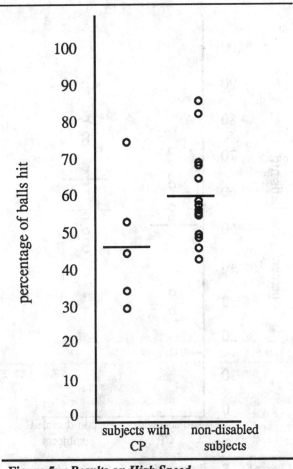

Figure 5: *Results on High Speed*

50%. More important than the mean performance is the large overlap shown between the two groups' performances. Figure 5 shows a similar comparison of all trials run on the high speed; it is less conclusive because three of our eight subjects with CP did not attempt the high speed. Not running at a higher speed seemed to have more to do with fatigue or lack of confidence than performance. The three CP subjects who declined to try the fast speed where not our worst performers at the medium speed; they ranked 4th, 5th, and 7th out of the 8. Therefore, we feel that there is value in ignoring the speed of the trials and lumping them together, the results of which are shown in figure 6. This lumping favors the children with CP, as they include more runs at the slow and medium speed. The full breakdown of trials by speed is given in table 2. In any reasonable interpretation of the data, the children with CP performed much better than we had anticipated at this stage of the project. This is especially true given that most of our subjects had to travel to participate in the study, and several we only obtained because they were traveling to our

area for clinic appointments or to have surgery at a local hospital, hardly an optimal time to participate in a user study.

For most of our subjects with CP, this is the first real-time, continuous task they had ever performed.[1] As such, it provides an interesting opportunity to observe their reactions to the pong game.

Most able-bodied subjects would anticipate where the ball was headed and then move the paddle to the correct position and wait for the ball to approach. The children with CP were much more likely to leave the paddle where it had last hit the ball, or at a particular location (near either side wall was common) and then move to block the ball at the last possible moment. We do not know why this particular motor behavior occurred. One possible explanation is that the children with cerebral palsy have difficulty with response programming. More

---

1. Even though half of our subjects with CP use powered wheelchairs, it is important to realize that for the CP population, wheelchair joysticks are not analog devices but are *multi-way switches*. Push the stick far enough in one of four direction and the wheelchair moves. Anything less and the chair remains where it is.

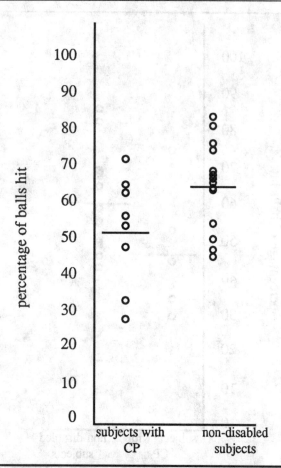

Figure 6: *Results on All Speeds Combined*

Non-disabled Subjects

Slow			Medium			Fast		
#	hit	%	#	hit	%	#	hit	%
	0	0		0	0		33	48
	0	0		34	71		35	60
	0	0		25	96		28	57
	0	0		26	88		33	70
	0	0		0	0		35	51
	0	0		0	0		36	83
	0	0		21	71		28	43
	0	0		19	89		36	58
	0	0		0	0		35	66
	0	0		27	81		36	58
	0	0		35	63		37	70
	0	0		29	86		41	59
	0	0		36	44		28	50
	0	0		33	82		33	88

Subjects with CP

Slow			Medium			Fast		
#	hit	%	#	hit	%	#	hit	%
	0	0		36	22		36	36
	15	100		36	28		0	0
	0	0		34	35		36	31
	36	61		20	50		0	0
	25	80		36	56		0	0
	0	0		42	62		36	47
	0	0		35	69		37	76
	0	0		35	74		36	53

Table 2: *Data for All Trials*

simply, they may be unable to organize and initiate muscular actions to produce a prompt motor response. Alternatively, maintaining the paddle in a "ready" position required more control at an access site [13]. The children with CP typically could not manage this, therefore returned to a consistent resting place.

None of our subjects, either those with CP or able-bodied, had a conscious awareness of the location of the target curve. This is a pleasant observation, because our eventual system will provide open-loop feedback as it is used, constantly determining the shape and location of the target curve as the device is used; the current explicit creation of a target curve is an aberration.

Our most interesting qualitative results focus on the children's reactions to the system. Without exception, they enjoyed the trials. We are encouraged about the approach of passive tracking; although our subjects became fatigued during the trials, we suspect that they continued to perform long after they would have been able to manipulate a physical control, even one built especially for them. In addition, the mapping strategy substantially reduces noise and jitter from the user's motions.

Although our eventual target population is non-vocal children with CP, in this study we included children who could vocalize to some degree so that we could get observations from them. It was from one of the children that we obtained an important insight about passive tracking. Normally, children with CP who attempt a control task "tense up" and hamper their own performance, much like a novice tennis player is often unable to swing properly until he learns to relax. We asked one of our subjects why he was able to control the paddle so well - he replied *"I'm not controlling it; it's watching me."* His perception was that the paddle was doing the work of following his motions, not that he was doing the work of controlling it. This difference seems to be extremely important in helping the children relax.

CONCLUSIONS

The user study we have presented is one step in a series of investigations that will be necessary to realize the long term goals of the Tailor and CANDY projects. We have now established that our mapping strategies make is possible to compensate for physical disabilities such as CP in a task requiring a real-time, one dimensional analog input.

Our results were much better than we had anticipated, especially given the adverse conditions our subjects with CP had to endure. In trials with a simple video game based on Pong, the able-bodied subjects succeeded on 77% of their trials, and the subjects with CP succeeded on 50%. Over half the subjects with CP outperformed the worst able-bodied user.

Our future efforts will be in continued enhancements to the mapping techniques used in one dimension, and in producing mappings from motion into a two-dimensional analog control signal.

ACKNOWLEDGEMENTS

We thank Ron Williams for having the vision to undertake the CANDY project. We are also grateful to Frederick Brooks, Jr. of UNC Chapel Hill, whose suggestion of videotaping the trials led to several insights. The decomposition of the two-dimensional problem into its one-dimensional components is an idea borrowed from Marc Raibert [11]. Finally, we would like to thank our subjects and their families, without whose help this research would not have been possible.

REFERENCES

[1]   Bird input device, Ascension Technology Corporation, PO Box 527, Burlington, VT 05402. Phone:(802)655-7879.

[2]   R. Bolt, *Put-That-There: Voice & Gesture at the Graphics Interface*, Computer Graphics, 14,3 (1980), pp. 262-270.

[3]   W. Buxton, E. Fiume, R. Hill, A. Lee and C. Woo, *Continuous hand-gesture driven input*, Proceedings of Graphics Interface '83, pp. 191-195.

[4]   J. D. Foley, *Interfaces for Advanced Computing*, Scientific American, October, 1987, 127-135.

[5]   T. A. Furness, *Super Cockpit: Virtual Crew Systems*, Armstrong Aerospace Medical Research Laboratory, 1988.

[6]   A. Girson and R. Williams, *Articulator-Based Synthesis For Conversational Speech*, International Conference on Acoustics, Speech, and Signal Processing, April, 1990.

[7]   J. Liang, C. Shaw, and M. Green, *On Temporal-Spatial Realism in the Virtual Reality Environment*, Proceedings of UIST: the Annual ACM SIGGRAPH Symposium on User Interface Software and Technology, November, 1991.

[8]   R. Pausch and R. Williams, *Tailor: Creating Custom User Interfaces Based on Gesture*, Proceedings of UIST: the Annual ACM SIGGRAPH Symposium on User Interface Software and Technology, October, 1990, pp. 123-134.

[9]   R. Pausch and R. Williams, *Giving CANDY to Children: User-Tailored Gesture Input Driving an Articulator-Based Speech Synthesizer*, Communications of the ACM. To appear.

[10] *Apparatus for Generating a Nutating Electromagnetic Field*, Jack Kulpers, Polhemus Navigation Sciences, Inc., 1977. U.S. Patent Number 4,017,858

[11] M. Raibert. *Legged robots*. Communications of the ACM, Volume29, Number 6, June 1986, pages 499-514.

[12] C. Schmandt, Spatial Input/Display Correspondence in a Stereoscopic Computer Graphic Work Station, Computer Graphics, July, 1983, pp. 253-261.

[13] R. Schmidt, *Motor Control and Learning; A Behavioral Emphasis*, Human Kinetics Publishers, Inc. 1988. pp. 86-89.

[14] M. Wolraich, *The Practical Assessment and Management of Children With Disorders of Development and Learning*, Year Book Medical Publishers, 1987. p. 168.

Working with Audio: Integrating Personal Tape Recorders and Desktop Computers

Leo Degen, Richard Mander and Gitta Salomon

Human Interface Group, Advanced Technology
Apple Computer, Inc.
20525 Mariani Ave., MS 76-3H
Cupertino, California 95014
(408)996-1010

ABSTRACT

Audio data is rarely used on desktop computers today, although audio is otherwise widely used for communication tasks. This paper describes early work aimed at creating computer tools that support the ways users may want to work with audio data. User needs for the system were determined by interviewing people already working with audio data, using existing devices such as portable tape recorders. A preliminary prototype system – consisting of a personal tape recorder for recording and simultaneously marking audio and a Macintosh® application for browsing these recordings – was built. Informal field user tests of this prototype system have indicated areas for improvement and directions for future work.

KEYWORDS: audio interfaces, audio browsing, multi–media, user interface, user observation, design process

INTRODUCTION

Today, users primarily create and work with text and graphics on their computers. People rarely use audio, even though it is a communication medium that is well understood and otherwise pervasive in their lives. For example, many people use Dictaphones [9] and small tape recorders to create letters, conduct interviews or capture fleeting ideas. The phone answering machine provides a popular way for people to communicate with others, as well as leave messages for themselves.

Several research projects have addressed computerized audio capabilities within specific task domains. For example, Phone Slave [12] provides users with an enhanced phone answering machine. MediaView [7] allows users to create voice annotations within documents. Voice has been shown to be a desirable medium for this task, because it offers a rich and expressive, yet informal, way to make global comments [2].

Most likely, audio is not widely used on computers today because appropriate tools are not readily available. In this paper, we describe our work on an audio interface that allows users to create and use audio data in a flexible way.

The paper describes our research and prototype development. The first section describes a number of important characteristics of audio use we uncovered by examining how people currently use audio. For example, Dictaphones support portability and the means to capture an idea even when physical constraints make writing impossible. These findings were instrumental in driving our design.

In the following section, we describe the prototype system constructed. It consists of two main elements: a modified personal tape recorder for capturing audio data, and an application that allows users to work with the audio data captured on a Macintosh computer. The interface 'scales' from one machine to the other: industrial design elements on the portable recorder translate to graphical interface elements on the computer.

The third section describes the informal user test conducted and discusses the results and their implications for redesign. In the final section, we offer insight into directions for future research. The system constructed to date constitutes an initial pass at the problem. Our goal was to quickly construct a testable prototype, albeit with known limitations, that would give us insight into the capabilities users would desire in a more sophisticated system.

CURRENT USAGE OF AUDIO

A user study was conducted to determine how people currently use portable tape recorders and where they find limitations in the available technology. We intentionally interviewed people already comfortable with the use of audio data — they could provide insight into interface issues without getting caught up in the question of why one might want to use audio. They were already familiar with the advantages and disadvantages of audio use with existing technology. In a sense, we made several assumptions: people want to use audio; a number of people have found beneficial uses for it supported by current technology; and, these people can provide insight into how a better system could be built utilizing the capabilities of a desktop computer.

From a call for participants throughout Apple Computer, ten people representing a variety of usage patterns were selected. Among them were students who recorded material in class, commuters who recorded while driving, writers and engineers who recorded interviews and meetings, and people who either dictated material for others or worked with dictations others created for them.

Method

The ten participants were interviewed in their offices about their use of personal tape recorders. These informal interviews were videotaped for later analysis. During the interviews, users described the typical use of their recorders, how they had come to use recorders in the first place, what features their recorders offered, and what they did with the material they recorded. We also asked participants about their frustrations with using audio data in general, and in particular what problems they encountered with their own tape recorder.

Results

Microcassette recorders were the most common type of recording device used by our participants. These recorders were valued for their industrial design which supported one-handed recording through a small form factor and convenient placement of controls and the microphone. Users also valued the "cue" and "review" features which allowed them to listen to the audio (though highly distorted) while simultaneously fast-forwarding or rewinding. Other useful features were voice activated recording, a two-speed setting which could be used to playback the audio at slower speeds, and a counter which could be reset and used as a one-time location marker.

Most participants carried a single recorder in their briefcase, although some participants had two recorders – one in the car and the other either at work or at home. Several users left voice mail recordings for themselves or used the 'memo' feature on their telephone answering machines to leave themselves reminders. One participant recorded lectures but listened to the tapes while driving so as to take advantage of a scan feature only available on the car cassette player.

Uses for portable tape recorders. Most participants used the recorders because they wanted a way to record in settings where they could not easily capture information in any other way.

Students described difficulties keeping track of lectures while taking notes. They recorded classes so they could concentrate on the lecturer and used the recording to take notes later.

Commuters mentioned that they often had good ideas about work projects, or remembered things they had to do, while driving in their cars. They found that small tape recorders an effective way to capture information while driving.

Writers used tape recorders to capture material during interviews and meetings in order to later create accurate quotes. In addition, the recordings provided a way for writers to 'attend' meetings again and catch material initially deemed unimportant.

Several users described other situations in which they preferred to use a tape recorder rather than write things down. For example, recorders were used for thoughts, observations, and details while at a conference or trade show. Some participants used a recorder to clear their mind of thoughts about the next day's tasks before they went to sleep.

Working with the recorded material. Most users converted the audio material to text using either a standard word pro-

cessor or, frequently, a specialized outlining application such as MORE™[14]. They often had a routine for dealing with their recordings; for instance, one user sat down every Saturday morning and listened to the tape, transcribing pieces of information into several different MORE files. Another user listened to the tape upon arrival at work to obtain the items he had recorded the night before or on the way to work. One user transcribed the entire tape into a single word processing document, printed the document, and then physically cut and pasted pieces of it into a notebook or onto larger sheets of paper which could be stored in file cabinets. None of the participants archived their tapes, instead they simply recorded over the old material.

Users mentioned that they sometimes needed to access specific material before it had been transcribed, and they used the cue and review features to locate it. One user was able to mark important points in recordings by momentarily stopping the tape. This created small breaks which could be detected and located by the user's car cassette player .

Users who dictated information would hand off their tapes to someone else for transcription and would receive a text version, in return, for review.

Implications for Design

One of the biggest frustrations users reported was the difficulty with finding specific material. Apart from using the cue and review features, the only method for finding a specific section was to create a single 'marker' by zeroing the counter. This allowed them to return to that one place in the recording. Some users attempted to work around this problem by making a note of counter numbers during recordings, but this was not practical in all situations, for instance, while driving.

While recording meetings, users often realized they were capturing items they would want to return to later. For example, the writer often knew that he would want to use a particular statement as soon as he heard it spoken. However, users had no way to mark sections while recording. This clearly points to the need for being able to annotate audio *as* it is being recorded, and later search for those annotations.

Another problem reported concerned the serial nature of the tape medium, which does not allow for random access. Users often knew that interesting material was near the end of a tape, but they had no way of quickly moving there. Several users reported sometimes recording so much material that they never found the time to process any of it. Consequently, potentially valuable information was lost. These frustrations point to the need for a visual display of the audio data, which would allow users to easily access segments based on their relative location.

Users also wanted to be able to quickly review sections, but they felt the pitch shift which occurred with use of the cue and review features on their devices severely reduced intelligibility. They wanted to be able to speed up or slow down the audio playback without experiencing substantial quality degradation.

THE PROTOTYPE DESIGN

Based on our interviews, we designed a system that would support the types of tasks observed and address problems

Figure 1: The personal tape recorder with 'marker' buttons.

with the current technology. The prototype system consists of two components:

- A personal tape recorder that allows users to capture audio data and apply personal 'markers' to that data.
- SoundBrowser, a Macintosh application, that allows the user to browse the data captured by the portable recorder on their desktop computer.

Each component is described below.

Personal Tape Recorder

The personal tape recorder is a standard stereo Walkman (SONY TCS-430). The recorder was modified by adding two buttons which allow users to 'mark' or 'stamp' the audio while they are recording. Figure 1 shows the marker buttons, positioned within easy reach, on the tape recorder.

The user can assign particular significance to each button. For example, one button could be designated as an audio 'bookmark' and it might be depressed at interesting points during a meeting, as it is recorded. The other button might be used as a "To Do" marker – a user could push it just before recording a reminder to look up a reference or call a

certain person. The markers produced by these buttons can be used to find specific pieces of audio at a later time.

Implementation technique. The recorder was modified by attaching a circuit board with two buttons and a tone generator to its outside casing. These buttons create distinct audio tones on one stereo channel. The other channel is available for the user's recordings via the two built-in microphones.

Currently, data is moved from the tape recorder to the Macintosh via a non-automated process. Data is initially transferred via the AudioMedia NuBus board and an application program provided with the board [3]. A custom parser program on the Macintosh then prepares the transferred data for use by locating the embedded markers. It also notes where the tape recorder was turned off and on, and uses this information to create a distinct marker for each audio segment. The resulting file can be viewed by the user in the SoundBrowser application.

SoundBrowser

SoundBrowser allows a user to browse data recorded on the personal tape recorder. It integrates some interaction techniques that have been demonstrated in prototype systems such as [1,4,5,10], along with new functionality. The SoundBrowser window display is shown in Figure 2.

Playback via random access or markers. SoundBrowser provides several ways to browse through audio data. Users can choose to play the entire sound via the play button in the title bar. Alternatively, they can play any piece of sound by placing the mouse at the desired location and clicking the mouse button. If the mouse is moved while the button is depressed, the user can 'jump' backwards or forwards within the sound representation and simultaneously hear portions of the audio in the areas traversed. This facilitates quick replay of specific sections and differs from several existing systems, such as Farallon's SoundEdit[4], in which users are must enact a two step process – first the desired section is selected, then a play command is issued.

Another way of accessing the sound is via the markers created by pressing the buttons on the personal tape recorder. The markers appear in the window, directly below the sound representation (Figure 2). The user can click on any of the markers to start playing the sound at the corresponding location. The color of each marker reflects the color of the hardware button that created it; the interface scales appropriately from the tape recorder to SoundBrowser.

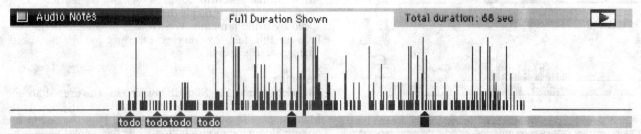

Figure 2: The SoundBrowser window. The majority of the window area is devoted to the audio representation. Time is represented along the horizontal axis, amplitude along the vertical. Duration values for the total audio piece and currently visible portion are shown in the title bar. Markers added by the user appear below the audio representation. In this example, one continuous audio stream was recorded, during which the user depressed the 'to do' marker 4 times, and then highlighted a few points within the last 'to do' item using the other marker button.

These features support two needs indicated by the user study: the ability to randomly access sections of the data, and the ability to relocate and play specific items.

Speed changes without pitch shift. In addition, SoundBrowser incorporates a scheme for speeding up or slowing down the audio while maintaining its pitch and intelligibility. This is made possible by a harmonizing algorithm executed by an external DSP unit. Users can therefore quickly scan the audio without experiencing the 'chipmunk' effect they found undesirable. They can also slow down the audio to comprehend all of its content, which might be useful in musical applications where difficult passages can be 'stretched' in time for analysis.

Macro and micro views. Initially, the full duration of available audio data is shown in the SoundBrowser window. If the audio data is lengthy, this may result in a dense representation. In order to make precise selections or view specific portions in detail, users can 'zoom in' to obtain more information in any area of the sound by depressing the mouse button and moving the mouse upward. Similarly, a vertical downward movement results in a 'zoom out.' Figure 3 depicts three discrete steps from a continuous inward zoom. The zooming movement is visually reinforced by a change in the saturation of the sound wave graphic. The information in the title bar also changes to reflect the duration of the sound shown at the current zoom level. Note that zooming is 'modeless' – the user can play the audio while simultaneously changing the magnification level.

Visual representation of audio. SoundBrowser offers a number of different visual sound representation schemes. These include common dot, line and solid body (Figure 4) amplitude representations that are used in other sound editing environments[3,4,5]. In addition, an amplitude bar graph representation is provided (see Figures 2 and 3). A version of this representation was implemented in "The Intelligent Ear"[10], however the SoundBrowser representa-

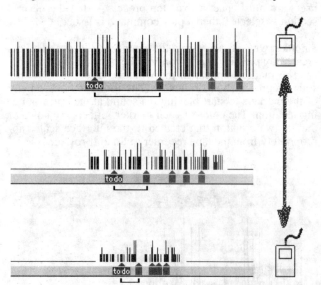

Figure 3: <u>Zooming capability</u>. If the user depresses the mouse button and moves the mouse upwards, the audio data representation expands to show more detail. This figure depicts three discrete stages from a continuous fluid zoom on one portion of the data. Note how the spacing between markers increases as the mouse moves upwards.

Figure 4: <u>Solid body representation</u>. Amplitude is mapped to line offset from the center line. SoundBrowser additionally maps amplitude to line thickness and color saturation.

Figure 5: <u>Color bar representation</u>. Amplitude is quantized and mapped to color saturation only. The places where foreground and background colors are equal will most likely be line or subject breaks.

tion is quantized to exaggerate information about possible line and/or subject breaks[13]. That is, large gaps followed by peaks are most likely to be sentence or subject breaks. Another representation, 'color bar' (Fig. 5), maps quantized amplitude to color saturation only[8]; peaks are highly saturated, silences completely desaturated. This results in a display with little visual noise, and yet provides the same information as the representations mentioned above.

INITIAL USER TESTING OF SOUNDBROWSER

The SoundBrowser interface discussed above is an improved version, which was changed based upon user test results. A usability test, of the kind described in [6] was performed.

Method

Six novice and three expert audio users were asked to complete three tasks with the SoundBrowser. First, the random access features of the SoundBrowser were tested. Participants were asked to locate specific information within three different sound files, varying in length from 1 to 3 minutes. Users were asked to find the start and end of the singing in a musical segment, find the predicted conditions for Oakland city within a weather forecast, and find the second and third items in a voice mail message.

In the second task, we asked users to try the different visual representations and indicate the positive and negative aspects of each.

Lastly, we explored potential boundaries for the variable speed feature. We asked the users to play unknown radio news items and sections of spoken text at both increasing (from normal speed to 200% faster) and decreasing (from 200% faster to normal) playback speeds. Users changed the speed by using a menu. We avoided possible ordering effects in this task by varying the direction of the speed changes across users.

Results

All users found the SoundBrowser easy to use, although some features of the interaction were not readily apparent. Many users did not realize they could play the sound by holding down the mouse button while the pointer was within the sound representation, and they requested standard sound controls such as play, stop and pause. However, once they discovered the ability to initiate play anywhere within the sound, they quickly became adept. The play button itself was frequently mistaken for a zoom control, possibly because it was located within the window title bar where the zoom box usually resides.

Users had problems understanding whether they were seeing a representation of the entire sound or only a part of it. Some remarked that they would like an accompanying overview, or global reference map, that would indicate their current position relative to the rest of the sound. This was particularly desirable during zooming, when many lost track of their relative position. Users also wanted the sound representation to scroll automatically so that the play indicator bar was always visible in the window.

Based on user comments, the solid body and bar graph were the most popular graphic representations. The users had difficulties identifying the exact beginning and ending of the sound. Consequently, the visual representation was changed to include horizon lines that delimit the audio data. This new design feature is shown in Figure 2.

Users were able to understand unfamiliar sounds at a 75% playback speed increase; familiar sounds at a 100% playback speed increase were still intelligible. The expert users all requested that the speed control, rather than zoom control, be mapped to the vertical movement of the mouse.

FIELD TEST OF THE ENTIRE SYSTEM

Our next step was to conduct a field test with the prototype recording device and the SoundBrowser application. Our aim was to find out if the combination of an annotatable tape recorder and SoundBrowser would fulfill the needs identified in our earlier user study. We also hoped to acquire information about using the annotation tape recorder as a device for capturing personal audio data.

Method

The field test group included five participants; a technical writer, an interface designer, a medical practitioner and two engineers. All but the medical practitioner had used a hand held recording device before. The participants were given an annotation tape recorder to use for two days. Although it would have been valuable to study patterns of usage over a longer time period, this was not feasible due to the primitive nature of the prototype and consequent amount of effort involved in transferring the data to the Macintosh.

Participants were encouraged to use the recorder in a variety of settings such as in meetings, while commuting, and as a general note-taking device. We told them to use the annotation buttons in ways they saw fit, and did not assign predetermined meaning to them.

After the two day period, the tape recorders were collected and segments of the audio recordings were processed for use with the SoundBrowser application. In a one-hour test with each of the participants, we gathered information about how they had used the tape recorder and we observed them using the SoundBrowser application. Afterwards we asked the participants about their problems with the prototypes and ideas for improvements.

Results

Applying markers. Generally the users had no problem marking audio data while they recorded it, though one participant wasn't sure whether a marker was applied by a single press of a button or by holding the button down continuously. All users wanted visual feedback on the recorder that their marker had been applied.

The participants attached various meanings to the annotation buttons; some used the two buttons to represent hierarchical subject groupings, some for distinguishing between business and personal matters. All users expressed the need for a flexible number of buttons and control over defining their meaning. All of the users felt that the markers were adequate annotations – none wanted to also include speech annotations, such as "this is the important point."

Finally, users noted that recording and annotating other people in meetings or interviews did not create a social problem; they felt at ease pushing the marker buttons as others were talking. However, the users would prefer the tape recorder to be somewhat smaller and less conspicuous.

Using markers. The graphical representation of the markers in SoundBrowser was well understood. Users intuitively pressed on them to hear the corresponding audio. Most users wanted to be able to edit markers by moving, deleting, and adding new ones. They remarked that while moving a marker the corresponding audio should play so they could hear 'where they were'. In addition, users wanted a way to attach names to markers in order to, for instance, identify people in a meeting. Users also wanted SoundBrowser to provide a filtered display of marker types in order to find specific types quickly.

Organizing and working with audio. The users expressed the need for sound editing facilities, such as drag-selecting and cut, copy and paste. They wanted to be able to place pieces of the audio data in different environments, such as to-do lists. Some users desired a full speech-to-text translation of specific selections.

In order to make precise selections, users acknowledged the need for zooming (as shown in Figure 3). However, the mapping of zoom level to the vertical mouse movement within the audio display was confusing to most users. They said they would prefer a distinct controller, located elsewhere on the window, for adjusting the level of zoom.

Additionally, most users wanted to be able to playback their notes on the personal tape recorder, and they wanted to access them based on the specific annotations applied.

All users were asked to look at their recordings with the different visual representations available in SoundBrowser. Although we did not intend to rigorously test which representations were best, we noted that users seemed to prefer the quantized amplitude representation. One user initially thought that a visual representation was unnecessary, but later found the bar graph representation very useful in combination with quick replay.

All participants expressed interest in using the prototypes in their everyday life. In spite of the rudimentary nature of the prototype, they felt that the prototype was a significant improvement over available technology.

DIRECTIONS FOR FUTURE WORK

The work reported here represents preliminary research into creating general purpose audio tools. It also starts to address a 'scalability' problem – how to create a family of machines that work together and support similar interface features in ways appropriate to each particular machine.

A next step is to create a smaller, digital version of the personal tape recorder that would provide greater functionality. Such a device could pre-process the recorded data for use with SoundBrowser. The digital data could be stored on a cartridge, or on a small removable hard disk, thus providing easy portability of the data from the device to the computer. Using digital data would allow for better-than-actual recording time data transfer rates.

Since users had varying needs for markers, and desired more feedback concerning them on the personal tape recorder, a small, touch sensitive display on the recorder would be advantageous. The display could include data such as the length of recorded pieces and which markers were
applied, and it could provide visual feedback as markers were added. Users could scan through the tape, searching for particular marker types, and return to certain passages to apply markers 'after the fact.' If users could hit a button, speak the marker type, and later use speech recognition to interpret the marker, a single marker button might suffice. Alternatively, the touch screen display could facilitate a flexible number of marker buttons, with unique meanings assigned by the user. Creating these buttons for display on the recorder might best be accomplished on a desktop computer, thereby requiring design of another 'scalable' interface – markers created on the desktop machine would need to be transferred and represented on the personal tape recorder.

The SoundBrowser application can also be improved in several ways. Facilities for editing and creating markers, as well as recording and marking directly on the desktop computer are desirable. Several changes suggested by users, such as moving zooming to a special control panel and mapping speed change onto vertical movement of the mouse will be undertaken. Finally, exploration into appropriate visual representation of audio data will be continued.

Scalability, as discussed in this paper, primarily refers to the fluid transfer of data and interface elements from the tape recorder to the desktop computer. Movement in the other direction poses a number of interesting problems. Users may want to alter the data in SoundBrowser by adding new markers and then transfer it back to their personal tape recorders for use at a remote location. How should the new markers be depicted? Or users may want to share their audio data. How should the interface describe someone else's set of unique markers? Furthermore, how might either the personal tape recorder or desktop computer depict the combined idiosyncratic markers of several people? Issues such as these will be addressed by future work.

ACKNOWLEDGEMENTS

We would like to thank S. Joy Mountford for inspiring us to explore audio and portable devices; Yin Yin Wong for graphic design expertise; Laurie Vertelney for an industrial design consultation; and, Tracy Narine for user testing assistance. Chris Schmandt and several anonymous reviewers supplied useful feedback on the original manuscript.

BIBLIOGRAPHY

[1] S. Ades and D.C. Swinehart. Voice Annotation and Editing in a Workstation Environment. *Proc. American Voice I/O Society 1986 Conference*, September 1986.

[2] B. Chalfonte, R.S. Fish, and R.E. Kraut. Expressive Richness: Comparison of Speech and Text as Media for Revision. In *Proceedings of CHI, 1991* (New Orleans, Louisiana, April 28 - May 2, 1991) ACM, New York, 1991. pp. 21-26.

[3] Digidesign, Inc. *AudioMedia*™. Version 1.2. 1989.

[4] Farrallon Computing, Inc. *SoundEdit*™. Version 2.0.1. 1989.

[5] R. Kamel, K. Amami and R. Eckert. PX: Supporting Voice in Workstations. *IEEE Computer*, August 1990. pp. 73 - 80.

[6] J. Nielsen. (1989). Usability Engineering at a Discount. In G. Salvendy and M.J. Smith (Eds.), *Designing and Using Human-Computer Interfaces and Knowledge Based Systems* (pp. 394-401). Amsterdam: Elsevier.

[7] R.L. Phillips. MediaView: A General Multimedia Digital Publication System. *Comm. of the ACM*, 34, 7, (July 1991), 74 - 83.

[8] J.R. Pierce. *The Science of Musical Sound*. Scientific American Books, Inc. 1983

[9] D.C. Rehr. Dictation Machines: A Long, Colorful History. *The Office*. 112, 6, (December 1990), pp. 37-41.

[10] C. Schmandt. "The Intelligent Ear: A Graphical Interface to Digital Audio," *Proc. IEEE Conference on Cybernetics and Society*, October 1981, pp. 393-397.

[11] C. Schmandt and B. Arons. Getting the Word. *Unix Review* , 7, 10, (October 1989), 54-62.

[12] C. Schmandt and B. Arons. Phone Slave: A Graphical Telecommunications Interface. *Proc. 1984 International Symposium Society for Information Display*, June 1984.

[13] K.R. Sherer, J. Koivumaki and R. Rosenthal. Minimal Cues in the Vocal Communication of Affect. *Journal of Psycholinguistic Research*, 1, 3, 1972.

[14] Symantec Corporation. *More*™. Version 3.0. 1990.

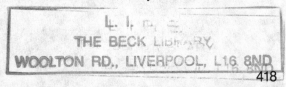

Skip and Scan:
Cleaning Up Telephone Interfaces

Paul Resnick
MIT Center for Coordination Science
Cambridge, MA 02139
presnick@eagle.mit.edu

Robert A.Virzi
GTE Laboratories Incorporated
Waltham, MA 02251
rv01@gte.com

ABSTRACT

The current generation of telephone interfaces is frustrating
to use, in part because callers have to wait through the
recitation of long prompts in order to find the options that
interest them. In a visual medium, users would shift their
gaze in order to skip uninteresting prompts and scan
through large pieces of text. We present *skip and scan*, a
new telephone interface style in which callers issue explicit
commands to accomplish these same skipping and scanning
activities. In a laboratory experiment, subjects made
selections using skip and scan menus more quickly than
using traditional, numbered menus, and preferred the skip
and scan menus in subjective ratings. In a field test of a
skip and scan interface, the general public successfully added
and retrieved information without using any written
instructions.

KEYWORDS: phone-based interface, semi-structure,
audiotex, telephone form, menu, interactive voice response.

INTRODUCTION

Most people in the United States have used telephone
information systems of some sort, many will admit that
such systems are useful, but few people like to use them.
With the current generation of telephone interfaces, callers
are forced to wait through the recitation of long prompts and
information when only selected pieces are of interest. We
describe a new interface style, which we call *skip and scan*,
that gives users more control over the process of listening
and recording. In this style, the implicit structure of recorded
prompts and information is made explicit and available to
users for navigation purposes. Initial evidence indicates that
the new style is preferred by users and lets them access
information significantly faster. This may enable the
creation of more complicated telephone-based information

services, including groupware systems in which callers add
information as well as retrieve it.

Hypermedia graphs are a convenient notation in which to
describe telephone interfaces [2, 11, 12]. A graph determines
what a caller will hear and what commands will be available
during a telephone dialogue. A caller is always located at a
particular node, and the sound associated with that node is
played. Each node has links to other nodes, which are
labelled by the commands a caller can use to traverse the
links. The commands can be either touch-tone button
presses, or verbal utterances entered via speech recognition.
In addition, a default link may be traversed automatically
after playing the sound for the current node, if no other
command is entered. For example, the standard audiotex
interface can be represented as a tree of nodes, with the
sound for each node being prompts as to what buttons to
press to follow links to other nodes (see Figure 1.) As we
shall see later, the graph abstraction can also be used as an
analytic tool, to relate user interface characteristics such as
user control, consistency and simplicity to properties of
graphs. We believe that an understanding of those graph
properties will prove helpful in the design and evaluation of
other new interaction techniques, both for telephones and for
small-screen displays.

RELATED RESEARCH

Much work has gone into optimizing menus like those in
Figure 1. There was some disagreement in the research
community as to whether prompts should be presented in
key-action order ("Press 1 for X") [4] or in action-key order
("For X, press 1") [3, 5], with the more recent research
indicating that action-key is preferable. Most research
indicates that three or four is the optimal number of options
to be presented in a menu [3], though such advice is
frequently not heeded since the categories that seem most
natural often contain more than four items.

Two studies explored more unusual graph structures [13,
14]. Rosson and Mellen created a hierarchical graph in
which each interior node contained a recording of a category
name (e.g. entertainment, restaurants, or hotels.) Subjects
were provided four buttons, two to move back and forth
between categories, one to select the current category, and

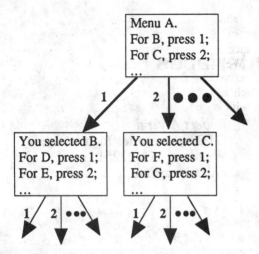

Figure 1: A generic audiotex system viewed as a hypermedia graph. Each node contains the prompts for one menu. Links are labeled by the touch-tone buttons that initiate link traversal.

one to move back up the hierarchy. Unfortunately, the mapping of information to the graph structure was not considered a variable in the study. Its novel features were not discussed, nor was it compared to the more conventional style of providing prompts for all of the categories in one node ("For entertainment, press 1; for restaurants, press 2; for hotels, press 3;...") Roberts and Engelbeck explored a spatial metaphor for navigation, in which information was laid out in a grid of nodes. The commands to navigate between nodes were spatially mapped to the telephone keypad (i.e., **2** up; **8** down; **4** left; **6** right.) They compared the spatial interface to a hierarchical menu interface, but found no significant differences in time required to perform tasks, or in subjective preferences. Our skip and scan information retrieval method builds on and generalizes the ideas in these two studies.

There is also much room for innovation in the way information is entered by telephone. Existing voice mail systems expect callers to leave an entire message as a single recording, thus leaving implicit any structure that the message might have. Most voice mail systems also begin recording when the system is ready rather than when callers

are, which creates many awkward beginnings of messages. Recently, some voice mail systems have begun to give callers the option of reviewing and re-recording their messages.

The PhoneSlave conducted conversations with callers to elicit the several pieces of information it considered essential to good phone messages [15]. The system asked each caller a series of questions ("Who's calling please", "What is this in reference to?", "At what number can he reach you?", etc.) After playing a question, it recorded whatever the caller said, until a long pause was detected, then went on to the next question. While callers fill in the contents of a predefined structure with the PhoneSlave, Hindus [6] is exploring ways for participants in a phone conversation to add structure at their own discretion.

A NEW INTERFACE STYLE

We have developed a new interaction style for both information retrieval and entry. Information retrieval is still based on traversal of a menu hierarchy but the implicit structure of menus is made explicit. That enables users to skip and scan through the prompts within a menu. For information entry, users skip and scan through a series of separate but related entry blanks in a telephone form. Taken together, the retrieval and entry techniques are the basis of a coherent interface style that we call skip and scan. In this section, we first describe the retrieval technique and then the entry technique.

Retrieval: Skip and Scan Menus

The skip and scan style of selecting an option from a menu gives users more control over what prompts they hear. Figure 2 shows the skip and scan version of the top menu node from Figure 1. Each option described in the text of the original node becomes its own node in the new graph. Callers press **9** and **7** to skip forward and back between options and can always select the current option by pressing **1**. While the new menu style may look more cumbersome, it actually allows callers to scan through the options much more quickly, because they can skip ahead without listening to complete prompts. In the next section we present the results of an experiment that confirms this claim.

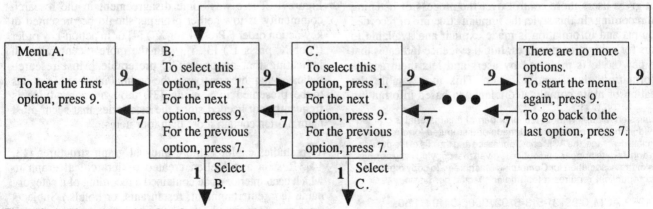

Figure 2: A skip and scan interface for menu selection.

Entry: Skip and Scan Forms

For information entry, we have developed the *telephone form* . We have generalized the PhoneSlave message taking dialogue to capture the structure of information objects other than personal phone messages. We have also turned from a conversational metaphor to a form-based metaphor. We believe that the form metaphor is more helpful, because it suggests an information entry process that is controlled by the user rather than suggesting an equal partnership between the user and a computer.

In a telephone form (Figure 3), there is one *entry blank* (node) for each separate recording that is expected. For example, if the object to be entered were an event announcement, there would be entry blanks for a headline, the date, the time, the location, etc. In addition to buttons **9** and **7** for navigating between entry blanks (note the consistent use of these buttons in Figures 2 and 3), the caller can use buttons **1** and **3** to record and/or erase the contents of the current entry blank. When the caller is satisfied with all of the recordings in the form, the caller presses # to save the entire object, or * to throw it away.

Semi-structured input has two advantages over making one long recording. First, the person recording is reminded of important information to include in the object, such as the admission price for an event. Second, splitting up an object into several separate recordings is a pre-requisite for allowing future callers to skip and scan through the logical segments of the object, a technique we will discuss in the future research section.

Our particular implementation of semi-structured input, the telephone form, provides users with a great deal of control over the entry process. Callers can quickly scan through the entry blanks to find out what information will be requested, so that they can better judge what information to record in each entry blank. They can gather their thoughts before starting each recording. In addition, users can recover from mistakes by re-recording single entry blanks rather than entire objects.

The telephone form concept can also be generalized to allow entry blanks that contain non-voice data. For example, an event announcement could contain a date entered using touch-tones. We have also implemented forms with entry blanks that contain links to other objects and lists of objects, which opens up new horizons for applications. Experience with visual interfaces has shown that lists of semi-structured objects, where the objects can contain links to other objects or lists, form the core of many group communications applications [8, 10].

EXPERIMENT: SELECTING A NAME FROM A LIST

We conducted an experiment that compared skip and scan menus with the more conventional menu style. Users were asked to find a target name from a list of between 3 and 12 names. Two methods of selection were tested in a within subjects design. In the standard method of selection, each name was announced followed by a selection number (Bob Smith, press 1; Paul Jones, press 2; etc.). This was compared to the skip and scan method as outlined in Figure 2, with one node for each name. Although we anticipated that users' overall performance would be faster in the skip and scan method, we expected to find evidence of a learning effect due to the novelty of the new method. We were interested in determining how many trials would be required before users performed as well with the skip and scan method as with the standard interface. We also asked users which style they preferred.

Methods

Subjects Two groups of subjects were run in this experiment. The first group was composed of 12 subjects recruited from a local university (mean age 23). We expected this group to perform well on the tasks and to exhibit relatively fast learning. To test the limits of applicability of this new technique, a second group of 6 subjects was drawn from an older population (mean age 62). We chose this older population because past experience has indicated that older users tend to be resistant to new technology and to have greater difficulty using telephone-based interfaces.

Stimuli A list of 100 names was randomly drawn from the telephone directory of a large corporation. Each name was

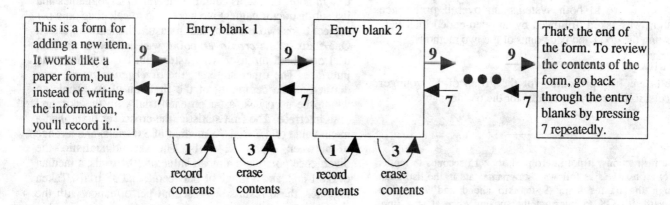

Figure 3: A telephone form containing several entry blanks.

presented as a first name followed by a last name exactly as it had appeared in the directory.

A total of 72 trials were prepared. Each trial consisted of a target name drawn randomly from the list of names and from 2 to 11 distractor names, leading to list lengths of 3 through 12 names. The target name appeared in each of the 12 serial positions 6 times. A random order was drawn for presenting the stimuli, and this same random order was used for both conditions and for all subjects.

A telephone interface was constructed that implemented each of the selection techniques. One female voice was used for all system prompts and a second female voice was used to present each of the names composing the lists. Users interacted with the systems from a telephone by pressing tone generating keys.

Procedures: Subjects were escorted into a testing room and seated before a standard desk set telephone. The general experimental procedures were explained but they were given absolutely no instruction on how they were to interact with the system. Instead they were told that they were to imagine that they had called a company with an automated directory service. They were told to follow the directions given by the system and to select the target name. Half the subjects in each group were presented the standard method first, the other half of the subjects interacted with the skip and scan method first. Between conditions they were warned that the method of selection had changed, and that they should attend to the instructions presented by the system.

Prior to the start of each trial, users listened to a name repeated over the telephone handset. This was the target name for the trial and it also appeared on a printed card next to the telephone as a memory aid. Users were told to press any key on the keypad when they were ready to begin the trial. Timing started when this key was pressed. In the skip and scan method, instructions, which the user had the option of skipping, were then played as part of a header node[1]. No instructions were required for the standard method. After each trial, users were told whether or not they had selected the correct name and then the next target name was announced.

After exposure to both systems, an overall preference question was asked, followed by an open-ended interview regarding the good and bad points of the two methods.

Results

Results are first presented for the group of 12 younger subjects, followed by the results for the 6 older subjects.

---

[1] The instructions, if not interrupted, took 15 seconds to recite. The exact text was as follows: "<n> names are in the list. Scan through the names using 9 to skip ahead and 7 to skip backward. It's OK to interrupt the spoken voice at any time. Select a name by pressing 1. For the first name, press 9."

Younger Group: In Figure 4 the mean correct reaction times for the two conditions are shown as a function of target position. The best-fitting regression lines are superimposed. An Analysis of Variance (ANOVA) was calculated with the factors of Condition (standard menu method vs. skip and scan) and Target Position. The ANOVA confirms what the figure reveals. Overall, subjects were faster with the skip and scan method ($F(1,11) = 83.417$, $p<.001$) and were faster when the target name was earlier in the list ($F(11,121) = 140.572$, $p<.001$). Moreover, the interaction term was significant ($F(11,121) = 14.685$, $p<.001$) showing that the advantage for the skip and scan method is greater as the target name appears later in the list. This is not surprising as in the standard method subjects had to wait for the target item while in the skip and scan method users could jump forward in the list based on a match with the first name.

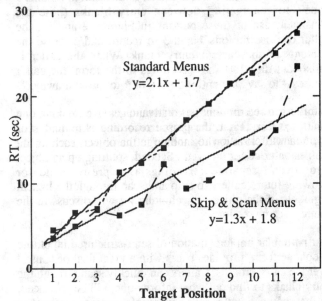

Figure 4. Mean correct reaction time is shown as a function of target position for the younger subject population. The regression equations appear next to each menu style.

We were interested in learning effects as well as overall performance. Because the trials were matched (i.e., the nth trial in both conditions contained identical target names and lists of distractor names) we were able to calculate on a per subject basis two statistics that measure the learning effect. One statistic, the *crossover point*, was defined as the first trial on which the user was faster with the skip and scan interface. The other statistic, the *divergence point*, was defined as the beginning of the first run of five trials on which the user was faster on each trial with the skip and scan interface. The first statistic, the crossover point, had a mean value of 4.7 trials, a median of 3.0 trials, and a range of between 2 and 12 trials. The second statistic, the divergence point, had a mean value of 10.1 trials, a median of 6.0 trials, and a range of between 2 and 38 trials. Taken together, these results suggest that performance with the skip and scan menus surpassed performance with the skip and menus fairly rapidly.

Error rates, although tracked, were too low to warrant analysis. In the skip and scan condition, errors were made on fewer than 1% of all trials. For the standard method, errors occurred on just over 2% of the trials. Most of these errors occurred on trials in which the user had to press two keys to make a selection (e.g., item number 10) when the second key was not pressed before the timeout so that the system interpreted the selection as item number 1.

When asked which system they preferred overall, all 12 subjects expressed a strong preference for the skip and scan method over the standard method (p<.001 by sign test). When probed as to why they preferred it, users stated that they thought it was faster, more efficient, and put them more in control.

Older Group: In Figure 5 the mean correct reaction times for the two conditions are shown as a function of target position with the regression lines superimposed. An ANOVA was performed with the factors of Condition (standard menu method vs. skip and scan) and Target Position. Unlike the younger subjects, the difference between the two methods was not reliable ($F(1,5) = 1.526$, $p>.10$). However, they were faster when the target name was earlier in the list ($F(11,55) = 59.492$, $p<.001$) and the interaction term was significant ($F(11,55) = 4.374$, $p<.001$). For this older population, the skip and scan method was slower when the target name was early in the list, but there was a small advantage when it later in the list.

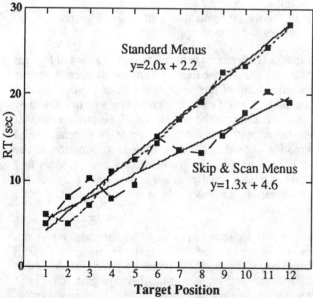

Figure 5. Mean correct reaction time is shown as a function of target position for the older subject population. The regression equations appear next to each menu style.

In general, the learning effect for this population was much more dramatic. As with the younger subjects, two statistics were calculated for each subject. The mean crossover point for the older subjects was 7.5 trials, the median was 12.5 trials, with a range of between 1 and 15 trials. The mean

divergence point was at 21.0 trials, with a median of 13.5 trials, and a range of between 5 and 56 trials. When compared to the younger population, the older group clearly took longer to learn the new technique, primarily because of their resistance to interrupting the prompts.

Older subjects made considerably more errors than the younger subjects, with 9.6% and 10.4% errors for the skip and scan and standard methods, respectively. These high error rates are not surprising since the two interfaces were optimized for younger, faster subjects. Most of the incorrect trials on the skip and scan method occurred when subjects exceeded a threshold for time on the trial[2], often while asking questions of the experimenter. Most of the errors on the standard menus were of two kinds: subjects were too late in typing the second digit of two-digit selectors (e.g., the 2 of 12); or they associated the name with the number that preceded it rather than the one that followed it.

When asked which system they preferred, 5 of the 6 older subjects stated a preference for the skip and scan method (p<.10 by sign test). When asked for the reasons behind their preferences, all indicated that they preferred the one that seemed to be fastest.

Discussion

The results from the younger population strongly favor the skip and scan method. Not only did it lead to overall better performance, this benefit occurred within a few trials. We believe that the learning time might be reduced even further with a better wording of the introductory prompts that were in the header nodes of the skip and scan menus. The skip and scan method was also unanimously preferred to the standard method. Based on these results, it appears to us that the skip and scan menus have wide applicability in the development of voice response systems.

Because we wanted to test the limits of the technique, we ran an older group of subjects, drawn from a population known to be resistant to new technology. The clarity of the results with the younger population led us to believe that six subjects would be a sufficient sample from the older population. This population showed a marginally reliable preference for the skip and scan method, although their performance results were less clearly in favor of it. These subjects took longer to learn the new technique and their performance was better only on the longer menus. We would recommend caution in implementing the new technique to the extent that the user population was older, the system would have a significant number of first-time callers, or the menus tended to be naturally short.

COMPLETE APPLICATIONS

The experiment described above was motivated by two prototype applications, developed independently by the two

---

[2] Trials were counted as errors when the time to complete the trial was more than two standard deviations from that subject's mean, even if the subject selected the correct target.

authors of this paper. One was tested in the laboratory, the other in the field. Both were well received, although neither was compared against alternative telephone interfaces for the same application.

One application (developed by Virzi) was a community bulletin board containing newsclips about the activities of a town. The newsclips were grouped into categories. Category headings were presented as in Figure 2, and users traversed the list of categories using the **4** and **6** keys. Within each category, users traversed a list of up to 25 newsclips. Each newsclip consisted of a headline and contents. Users could traverse this list of headlines until they came upon an article of interest. Pressing the **2** key caused the contents of the article to be played.

Extensive usability testing (to be reported more completely elsewhere) indicated that there was some initial hesitancy and surprise that the system did not conform to users' expectations for a "standard" interface. However, performance was very good, with all users completing the tasks and navigating through the system within minutes.

The second application (developed by Resnick) was an events calendar used by Boston-area peace activists during and after the 1991 war with Iraq. After choosing a category, users could skip and scan through event announcements, sometimes as many as twenty in a category. Unlike the community bulletin board described above, the announcements were not split into separate headline and contents nodes. We hoped to achieve the same effect by having callers interrupt announcements after listening to the headline. Analysis of the keystroke logs for the 1973 calls handled between February 1 and April 5 indicates that they did: of the 1798 callers who pressed at least one touch-tone button, more than 90% interrupted at least one announcement.

The events hotline was very well-received by its users. The phone number was publicized through flyers at public rallies, and by word of mouth. The system sometimes handled more than 90 calls per day, which meant that the phone line was busy virtually all the time. Several individuals who claimed to be technophobes went out of their way to say that they liked it. Still, it is not clear how much of the positive response was due to the utility of the system (it had the most complete, up-to-date information about anti-war activities in Boston) rather than the usability of the interface. A month after the cease-fire, usage was down to 10-15 calls per day, where it has remained since then.

Perhaps most interestingly, the event announcements were added by the general public, using the telephone forms interface described in Figure 3. Each announcement consisted of six separate recordings for a headline, the date and time, the location, and so on. We estimate that at least 40 different people successfully filled out a form at one time or another. A few people had trouble with the concept of a form and added announcements that repeated the entire contents in several entry blanks.

The results from both of these applications are very encouraging. The skip and scan style allowed categories to contain 20 to 25 items. That, in turn, allowed users of the peace events hotline to add new items without necessitating frequent restructuring of the menus. Using conventional menus, with only a few items per menu, frequent restructuring would have been necessary.

The next version of the events hotline, about to be installed, separates the date and time into two entry blanks and prompts callers to type in a date rather than record it. That makes it possible to sort announcements by date and to throw out old announcements automatically. The new version also makes the structure of event announcements usable for information retrieval. Callers can skip back and forth between the segments of an announcement, making it possible, for example, to hear the dates and locations of all the event announcements in a category while skipping the other information.

GRAPH PROPERTIES

What makes it possible for users to skip and scan in a telephone interface? Above we used the hypermedia graph representation as a descriptive tool. Here we use it as an analytic tool: we operationalize the useful but vague principles of increased user control, consistency, and simplicity in terms of graph properties and the mappings of graphs to application concepts. We argue for graphs that have:

1) smaller nodes, each containing a headline;
2) a small number of consistently available links;
3) an easily recognizable mapping of graph nodes and links to application concepts.

Consider the differences between the graph styles of Figures 1 and 2. In Figure 1, the numbered-menu style, each node is larger, consisting of the prompts for all of the options that are available. Even if callers can reject options quickly, they have to wait through the remainder of the prompt for that option in order to hear the next prompt. In general, useful information should not follow useless information in the same node, but what is useful differs among users and contexts of usage. Smaller graph nodes, since they contain less information, are less likely to contain any out of order information.

Note that this argument in favor of smaller nodes does not apply to screen-based hypertext. In a screen-based environment, it is possible to present a large amount of text simultaneously and let users shift their eye gaze in order to skip and scan. The argument for smaller nodes would apply, however, to other "keyhole-sized" interfaces, such as very large print monitors and braille output devices that show only a few words at a time [7], and to the small LCD displays found on advanced-feature telephones, electronic address books, and the like.

Each node should contain a headline that describes the contents of the node. For example, in a telephone form, each entry blank begins with a recitation of the name of the entry blank (e.g., "Date and time" or "Location"). The headline serves three functions. First, it provides an orientation cue as to where the user has arrived after following a link, which is important in visual hypermedia systems as well [9, 16]. Second, the headline summarizes the contents sufficiently to let callers decide whether it is safe to skip the node. Third, callers can get an overview of the contents of a group of nodes, by listening to just the headlines. Notice that the telephone form makes it possible to prompt callers to record a headline as a separate entry blank in new objects. In that way, the graph property of nodes having headlines can be maintained even as the general public adds nodes to a graph.

The ability of callers to control the dialogue depends not only on what actions they *can* take, but also on what actions they *know how* to take. Thus, callers may hear the headline for a node, know that there is something else they would rather be listening to, but not know how to skip to the other node. For example, Arons implemented a speech-only hypermedia graph with speech recognition used to specify which links to follow [2]. He found that his system spent more time prompting users about what links were available than playing the contents of the nodes (which also meant that callers had to listen through the nodes in order to hear the prompts.) He remedied this by making the links predictable, so that users would not always need to hear the prompts. For example, every node has a "more" link that goes to another node providing more details.

To make the links predictable, there should be both syntactic regularities in the graph and an easily understood mapping of the graph structure to the application structure. By syntactic regularities we mean that links with the same labels should be present at all or nearly every node. For example, in Figure 2, every node has a link labeled **9** emanating from it.

Even predicting that **9** is an available command will not be enough unless users can predict what it will do. Users can predict what **9** will do because there is a mapping between the nodes in the graph and the application concept of a set of options arranged in a list. Moreover, this mapping which is reinforced by the wording of the prompts. If callers understand the application concept and the mapping, they can predict that pressing **9** will move them to a node that contains a prompt for the next option in the list.

Contrast jumping between logical units of information, as just described, with jumping a fixed number of seconds, using fast-forward and rewind keys. With fast-forward and rewind, skipping is not coupled to the structure of the information, so users cannot be sure how much information they will be skipping, or what they will hear next. As an analogy, think about how hard it is to find a particular scene on a videotape using a VCR's fast-forward and rewind keys. Contrast this with a hypothetical system that pre-coded scene boundaries and allowed users to skip from scene to scene, always jumping to the beginning of a scene.

FUTURE RESEARCH

We are extending this research in several directions. First, the skip and scan style can be applied to additional tasks, particularly getting help and scanning the contents of a single object. Second, we plan additional experiments. Finally, we plan additional field tests, especially of groupware applications.

Even though our skip and scan menus contain just one "real" prompt per node, there are still "help" prompts for how to skip forward and back and how to select. If we apply the skip and scan style consistently, users should be able to skip through the help prompts to find the actions that interest them, without listening to the entire prompts for the other actions. We are trying different implementations of this idea, since the initial ones that we have tried make it harder for first-time callers to get started.

We are also exploring alternative ways to apply the skip and scan style to navigation through the entry blanks of objects that have been entered previously with telephone forms. One possibility is to use buttons **6** and **4** to skip between entry blanks of a single item, leaving **9** and **7** to skip between items. Another possibility is to play just a headline for each item. If a user selects an item, then **9** and **7** move between entry blanks until the user deselects the item. The latter implementation would maintain the simplicity of the interface but users would have to keep track of whether they were moving through a list of items or through the entry blanks of a single item.

We are designing additional laboratory experiments of different aspects of skip and scan interfaces. One experiment will explore the effects of numbering menu options as callers become more familiar with a graph and can remember the contents of some menus. In addition to the two item selection techniques described in this paper we will test a hybrid version that lets callers manually skip through the prompts in a menu, but still numbers the options, so that users can make a selection with a single keystroke if they do not need the prompts. We also plan an experiment to test our hypothesis that the ability to skip to a meaningful boundary in a long piece of speech is significantly more helpful than simple fast-forward and rewind keys.

The skip and scan interface style may broaden the scope of applications that can be successfully realized by telephone. For example, the telephone form metaphor may be a good vehicle for expressing queries by telephone. As another example, many group communication applications, such as meeting scheduling, organizational memory [1] and sales lead tracking, are just gaining acceptance in organizations in which everyone has access to networked computers. If the skip and scan paradigm makes it easier for callers to find information by telephone, such groupware applications might plausibly be implemented for telephones.

We have developed an application generator, called HyperVoice, to be reported elsewhere, that automatically generates skip and scan interfaces, including the text of the prompts that need to be recorded. We are using HyperVoice to implement and, in some cases, test groupware applications. For example, we recently set up an organizational memory application for a group of teachers that lets them share questions, answers, and success stories related to a new curriculum project that they are participating in.

CONCLUSION

Skip and scan is a promising telephone interface style. Through explicit navigation commands, it gives users some of the control they get from shifting their gaze in visual interfaces. In a field trial, callers with no written instructions successfully used a skip and scan interface to both add and retrieve information. In an experiment, subjects preferred skip and scan menus to the more conventional, numbered menus. After an initial learning period, they also made selections more quickly with the skip and scan menus. The learning period was just a few trials for younger subjects and may be reduced with a more careful wording of prompts, or if skip and scan menus are used widely. Still, the need for a learning period of even one call may limit the utility of skip and scan menus in applications that are to be used predominantly by first-time callers.

ACKNOWLEDGEMENTS

We would like to thank Don Ottens for his able assistance in conducting the experiment reported in this paper. We would also like to thank Sandra Teare and Kate Dobroth for lending their voices, and Tom Lanning for helping to make this collaboration possible. Tom Malone contributed many important ideas throughout the course of this project, including the phrase "skip and scan." Mark Ackerman, Kum-Yew Lai, Jintae Lee, Brian Pentland, Mike Plusch, Troy Jordan, Debby Hindus and Chris Schmandt also contributed to the ideas and presentation of this paper.

REFERENCES

1. Ackerman, M. S. and Malone, T. W. Answer Garden: A Tool for Growing Organizational Memory. In *Conference on Office Information Systems.* (Cambridge, MA, 1990). ACM, pp. 31-39.

2. Arons, B. Hyperspeech: Navigating in Speech-Only Hypermedia. In Proceedings of *Hypertext.* (1991).

3. Engelbeck, G. and Roberts, T. The Effects of Several Voice-Menu Characteristics on Menu Selection Performance. Technical Report ST0401, US West Advanced Technologies, 1990.

4. Gould, J. D. and Boies, S. J. Human Factors Challenges in Creating a Principal Support Office System-- The Speech Filing System Approach. *ACM Transactions on Office Information Systems.* 1, 4 (Oct. 1983), pp. 273-298.

5. Halstead-Nussloch, R. The Design of Phone-Based Interfaces for Consumers. In *CHI '89 Conference on Human Factors in Computing Systems.* (Austin, TX, 1989). ACM, pp. 347-352.

6. Hindus, D. Phone Calls Don't Have to Be Ephemeral: A Semi-Structured Approach to Stored Voice. Technical Report MIT Media Lab, 1991.

7. Ladner, R., Day, R., Gentry, D., Meyer, K. and Rose, S. A User Interface for Deaf-Blind People (Preliminary Report). In *CHI + GI '87.* (Toronto, 1987). ACM, pp. 75-80.

8. Lai, K.-Y., Malone, T. and Yu, K.-C. Object Lens: A "Spreadsheet" for Cooperative Work. *ACM Transactions on Office Information Systems.* 6, 4 (1988), pp. 332-353.

9. Landow, G. P. The Rhetoric of Hypermedia: Some Rules for Authors. *Journal of Computing in Higher Education.* 1, 1 (1989), pp. 39-64.

10. Malone, T. W., Grant, K. R., Lai, K.-Y., Rao, R. and Rosenblitt, D. Semi-structured Messages are Surprisingly Useful for Computer-Supported Coordination. In *Computer-Supported Cooperative Work: A Book of Readings,* Volume I. Greif, Ed. Morgan Kaufmann, San Mateo, CA, 1988, pp. 311-331.

11. Muller, M. J. and Daniel, J. E. Toward a Definition of Voice Documents. In *Proceedings of ACM Conference on Office Information Systems* (Boston, 1990) pp. 174-183.

12. Richards, J. T., Boies, S. J. and Gould, J. D. Rapid Prototyping and System Development: Examination of an Interface Toolkit for Voice and Telephony Applications. In *1986 Conference on Human Factors in Computing Systems.* (New York, 1986). ACM, pp. 216-220.

13. Roberts, T. L. and Engelbeck, G. The Effects of Device Technology on the Usability of Advanced Telephone Functions. In *CHI '89 Conference on Human Factors in Computing Systems.* (Austin, TX, 1989). ACM, pp. 331-337.

14. Rosson, M. B. and Mellen, N. M. Behavioral Issues in Speech-Based Remote Information Retrieval. In *AVIOS.* (San Francisco, CA, 1985).

15. Schmandt, C. and Arons, B. A Conversational Telephone Messaging System. *IEEE Transactions on Consumer Electronics.* CE-30, (1984).

16. Utting, K. and Yankelovich, N. Context and Orientation in Hypermedia Networks. *ACM Transactions on Information Systems.* 7, 1 (1989), pp. 58-84.

DESIGNING COLLABORATIVE, KNOWLEDGE-BUILDING ENVIRONMENTS FOR TOMORROW'S SCHOOLS

Chair: **Anne Nicol Thomas**
Children Using Technology
P. O. Box 2643, Truckee, CA 96160, USA
AppleLink Nicol.A; Compuserve 72330,3565

Panelists:
James Pellegrino, Vanderbilt University
Peter Rowley, Ontario Institute for Studies in Education
Marlene Scardamalia, Ontario Institute for Studies in Education
Elliot Soloway, University of Michigan
Jim Webb, Huron Public School, Toronto, Canada

ABSTRACT
The notion that children learn by constructing their own knowledge is highly popular these days among educational theorists. But what are the particular abilities that enable learners to be successful? And how must computer systems, and in particular their user interfaces, be designed to foster and support those abilities? The panel members represent several nationally-recognized education projects, all designed to give children control over their own learning while, at the same time, providing supports for effective learning strategies. They will discuss the unique design issues -- resolved and unresolved -- that arise as cognitive theories meet classroom realities. CSILE, a collaborative, user-constructed database, JASPER, a video-based mathematics program, and MediaText, a multi-media authoring environment, are available for use and review by CHI92 attendees prior to the panel presentation.

KEYWORDS
Education, Knowledge-Building, Collaborative Learning, Design

INTRODUCTION
In designing our programs, we have been confronting a central issue: How do we design a system for children that encourages and enhances--without mandating--effective, collaborative learning strategies? The aim of our work has been to incorporate into classroom-based computer systems a set of carefully-researched principles of learning and cognition. The basic premise of our systems is that children learn by constructing their own knowledge; but it turns out that there is a fine line between providing appropriate supports for the learning process and regulating or limiting children's styles and strategies. Each project has interface design dilemmas that arise out of its particular mix of educational priorities, technology and classroom testing. The purpose of the panel presentation is to fuel discussion and debate about the learning issues we are confronting, the priorities that we have placed on those issues in designing educational technology, and the interface features we have built for addressing those issues.

WHAT'S NEW IN EDUCATIONAL THEORY AND PRACTICE?
Before discussing technology and interface design, we must take a good look at the ideas and practices that have inspired our work. All of the systems represented here are designed to support a kind of learning and teaching that is different from what many of us knew as children and is different from what is happening in lots of classrooms today. Over the past few years, we have started to see, both in the research literature and in teacher practice, a growing appreciation of the need for learners to determine and control their own learning processes. Scardamalia and Bereiter [3] describe three idealized teacher models that illustrate the progression from a teacher-controlled to a learner-controlled approach to learning: In the first, the teacher prescribes and supervises tasks for which learning is an assumed by-product; the focus is on activities rather than on knowledge. Teachers in the second model focus on knowledge by setting cognitive goals and asking stimulating questions, usually based on children's expressed interests. This approach is child-centered, but the control of learning processes still remains with the teacher. The third type of teacher behaves a lot like the second, but also turns over to the learner control of higher level cognitive processes like goal-setting, directing inquiry, and monitoring comprehension. Most educational software has been designed to fit the first two teaching models, and we are just beginning to learn how to build into technology the supports children need to take control of these higher level thinking skills.

The progression from the the first to the third teaching model can be observed in classroom practices–across teachers and even across activities in one teacher's classroom. In the so-called traditional classroom (an extreme version of the first model), we see teachers in complete control of the learning activities and processes. They often arrange their classrooms so that children are facing towards the "front "of the room where most instruction takes place. They schedule the day's activities according to the texts and guides they are using to plan the curriculum, and they view themselves as the children's primary source of information and expertise, or at least as the critical mediator and interpreter of knowledge.

Teachers who take a more learner-centered approach often have a different classroom arrangement. They set up resource centers for science, math and writing so that the children can move more freely among activities in the classroom and can gain more control over the scheduling and "time" aspects of their learning. There are lists of questions for children to answer and tasks for them to do on their own or collaboratively; the children can often choose when and how. These teachers and types of activities fit most closely with the second model described above.

In classrooms where children are more in control of their own learning processes, we see students themselves making lists of ideas and questions upon encountering a new topic. They identify what they know now and what they want to know; as they go on, they write out their hypotheses and figure out what kinds of learning processes they must undertake to test them. They evaluate their own and their peers' knowledge gains and submit portfolios upon the completion of projects. This last type of teacher is intimately involved in the knowledge-acquisition activities with the students and has an important role as a model for the inquiry process.

Across these three teacher models, we also see an increased appreciation of the social nature of learning. Especially as we get to the third model, learners are encouraged to respond to other learner's questions and share the results of their learning with one another. In these classrooms, we often see children working in collaborative groups: they establish their own rules for productive work and interaction, and they ask for and use peer response to their work.

WHAT MUST TECHNOLOGY PROVIDE TO SUPPORT LEARNING?
If children learn by constructing and controlling their own learning, and if learning is a social process, carried out in collaboration with one's peers and others, then these ideas place special requirements on the design of educational technologies. What works in a "task-oriented" setting is not appropriate for knowledge building, especially for knowledge building among "novices." Many of the elegant design solutions that have been successful in a business environment, and even in a business *learning* context, do

not carry over into the classroom [2]. During our panel presentation, we focus on four of the elements that must be considered if technology is truly to support learning as we understand it now.

New Interface Metaphors to Support and Represent Collaborative Knowledge Building
The desktop metaphor pervades the interface of most "tool" applications we use in schools–word processors, drawing and paint programs, and databases. This metaphor falls short when it comes to representing knowledge-building and collaboration. For example, we need representations and supports for knowledge *synthesis*, not just knowledge accumulation. And, in school settings, collaboration often happens when several students work together at one computer rather than, as CSCW models assume, each at a separate computer.

Supports for Sustained Inquiry and Problem Solving
Rather than presenting discrete activities–no matter how engaging or worthwhile they might be–our technologies are intended to encourage and support extended, in-depth work in exploring, defining, reinterpreting, and coming to understand a body of knowledge.

Effective Means for Democratizing Societal Knowledge Resources
As children take over responsibility for constructing their own knowledge and understanding, they need direct access to authoritative information and ideas. Technology makes it possible, but our designs need to make it feasible and desirable for teachers and students together to have access to important ideas that are not immediately and physically available in the classroom.

Integration of Multimedia Resources and Authoring Tools into the Learning Environment
Our children are growing up with a new set of skills for acquiring and synthesizing information from a wide range of media. But, for the most part, they are using these skills outside the mainstream of their curriculum[4]. As teachers and as designers, we need to be looking at authentic ways to use multimedia in our classroom activities and to integrate multimedia capabilities appropriately into the technology.

THE PROJECTS
We are all working within the "constructivist" framework – the notion that children construct their own knowledge – and we all agree that the list of elements given above represents important considerations for us. But we find that we have developed different priorities in implementation, and that we have come to some very different ways of addressing these elements in the interface design. In the preceding paragraphs, each of the design considerations was described briefly from a general, theoretical standpoint. In the panel discussion, the designers give their own perspectives on these elements and

show how they have dealt with them in the interface design process.

CSILE

CSILE (Computer-Supported Intentional Learning Environments) is a system designed to support collaborative knowledge-building in and beyond the classroom. It is being developed at the Ontario Institute for Studies in Education by a team of cognitive scientists, computer scientists and educators. There are actually several systems being used as part of the larger research project; the version shown at this conference consists of client Macintosh LC's connected to a Macintosh IIci or IIfx which operates as a server. Prior to its use by students, the system is essentially an empty database with tools and capabilities to support children building and elaborating on their own knowledge and understanding of topics being studied in the classroom. All the ideas, questions, hypotheses, and responses that comprise the "data" in the system are generated by the children using CSILE. A typical configuration is eight client computers in a classroom of approximately 25 to 30 students. The computers are networked across classrooms as well, so that students signing on to CSILE in one classroom have access to the notes and comments of everyone else at the school. At this point, CSILE is being field-tested at several sites in the US in addition to the Toronto elementary school where it has been under development for over five years.

JASPER

JASPER is a videodisc-based series of stories and challenges designed to promote problem posing, problem solving, reasoning and effective communication in mathematics[1]. Students see a specially-created adventure story on videodisc and then are challenged to solve a real problem that arises in the story. Optimal solution of the problem requires extensive exploration, review of facts in the story, hypothesis-generation, evaluation of factors against constraints and complex, extended mathematical calculations. The project is guided by a set of design principles based on constuctivist theory, in general, and more specifically on applications of that theory to the learning of mathematics.

MediaText, IByD, and SPIF

These three systems explore different aspects of a "digital workbench" that supports learners (kids and teachers) engaged in project-based learning. They are being developed by the HiCE Project, in collaboration with colleagues in the School of Education at Michigan. MediaText enables learners to compose documents that incorporate video clips, music clips, sound clips, animations, still images, as well as text. SPIF (Software Planning Infrastructure) is a CAD (computer-assisted design) tool that scaffolds the process of learning software design for high-schoolers. And IByD (Instruction By Design) is a CAD tool that scaffolds the learning of unit-lesson design by preservice teachers. All three systems are being used by students and teachers; and they are being

studied and revised in the context of the classroom. From the classroom perspective, we are exploring the types of roles (e.g., information delivery, workspace, communications) that the coming generation of workbenches can play; from a computing technologies perspective, we are exploring the special demands that learning knowledge-intensive practices places on the interface.

THE PANELISTS

James W. Pellegrino is Frank W. Mayborn Professor of Cognitive Studies, Dean of Peabody College of Education and Human Development, and a former Co-Director of the Vanderbilt Learning Technology Center. His research and development activities have focused on children's and adult's thinking and learning and the implications for instructional practice. His work includes studies of spatial, inductive, and mathematical reasoning and problem-solving. Recent work has focused on the role of computers and other technologies in the design of instructional environments that support generative learning.

Peter Rowley heads the Systems Development group at OISE's CSILE Project –the programmers who are actually building and refining CSILE. Over the years, CSILE has been transported across three platforms –from the ICON (the Ontario educational micro-computer) to UNIX (via A/UX on the Macintosh), and finally to the Macintosh LC (running directly on the Macintosh system). He has been involved in the many interdisciplinary discussions that have surrounded the building of CSILE and has been responsible for finding ways to translate cognitive theory into C++ and MacApp code, with all the tradeoffs that entails.

Marlene Scardamalia is head of the Cognitive Science program at the Ontario Institute for Studies in Education. She has been directing the CSILE project, with Carl Bereiter, for the past six years. In that time, they have seen many of their original ideas for computer-supported intentional learning environments implemented, and have been developing and modifying their views of learning based on classroom experiences with CSILE.

Elliot Soloway is an Associate Professor in the Dept. of EECS at the University of Michigan where he directs the Highly-Interactive Computing Environments Project. Our software development efforts are tied directly to real users. e.g., we are involved with the local schools on a range of projects. Needless to say, we are continually learning about schooling.

Jim Webb has been involved with the CSILE project for six years as a teacher at Huron Public School in Toronto. One of the propositions of the program is that the classroom teacher must be involved in the collaborative work of building knowledge -- in fact, the teacher is a model as well as a facilitator of the learning process. Thus teachers like Jim have a critical role in using and in providing feedback to the designers about the effectiveness of the technology.

Anne Nicol Thomas is the panel moderator. Formerly with Apple's Human Interface Group, she is an educational psychologist whose interests focus on the design and evaluation of "interfaces for learning," and is a consultant working on the interface design and classroom field testing of CSILE.

REFERENCES

1. Cognition and Technology Group At Vanderbilt. The Jasper Series: A Generative Approach to Improving Mathematical Thinking, July, 1991 (revised September, 1991). To appear in *This Year in School Science*, American Association for the Advancement of Science.

2. Nicol, Anne. Interfaces for Learning: What Do Good Teachers Know That We Don't ? In *The Art of Human Computer Interface Design*, edited by Brenda Laurel. Addison-Wesley Publishing, Inc., Menlo Park, CA, 1990.

3. Scardamalia, Marlene and Bereiter, Carl. Higher Levels of Agency for Children in Knowledge Building: A Challenge for the Design of new Knowledge Media. *The Journal of the Learning Sciences*, 1(1), 1991. 37 - 68.

4. Soloway, Elliot. How the Nintendo Generation Learns. *Communications of the ACM*, September 1991, Vol 34, No. 9, 23-26, 95.

INTEGRATED DATA CAPTURE AND ANALYSIS TOOLS FOR RESEARCH AND TESTING ON GRAPHICAL USER INTERFACES

Monty L. Hammontree, Jeffrey J. Hendrickson, and Billy W. Hensley

Texas Instruments, Incorporated
P.O. Box 655474, MS 238
Dallas, Texas 75265

ABSTRACT

Our on-line data capture and analysis tools include an event capture program, event data filtering programs, a multimedia data analyzer, and a retrospective verbal protocol recorder for use with the multimedia data analyzer. Off-line observation logging is also supported. Additional plans for development include the integration of an online time-synchronized observation logger, and time-synchronized eyetracking data recording. The tool set provides an integrated multi-source data collection, processing, and analysis system for: 1) comparing and evaluating software applications and prototypes; 2) evaluating software documentation and instructional materials; and 3) evaluating on-line training. The tools currently run on Macintosh^{TM} computers and under Microsoft Windows^{TM}. Plans are to port the tools to run under Presentation Manager^{TM} and Motif^{TM}.

KEYWORDS: Event capture, data filtering, video analysis, verbal protocol, observation logging, eyetracking

INTRODUCTION

The integrated on-line data collection, processing, and analysis tools, described below, were designed to aid in the evaluation of software, prototypes, documentation, instructional materials, and training programs. The tools include: 1) an event capture program, which records events related to objects in the graphical user interface; 2) data filtering programs, which translate and aggregate the user generated events into a meaningful characterization of the user's interaction with the application and system software; 3) a multimedia data analyzer, which directly links event logs and video recordings of interactive sessions (e.g., selecting a logged event of interest will drive the video player to the frame corresponding to the start time of that event); and 4) a retrospective verbal protocol recorder for use with the multimedia data analyzer, which records digitized speech and associates it with the video tape segment and the corresponding logged event of interest. Off-line observation logging (text annotation of video) is also supported.

TOOL DESCRIPTION

Event Capture

The event capture utility records events related to the objects in the Macintosh^{TM} and Microsoft Windows^{TM} graphical user interfaces (e.g., applications, windows/files, dialogue boxes, menus, commands, tools, content area inputs, etc.). The software is transparent to the user and does not degrade performance perceptibly. It gathers information from system level resources and writes it out to event logs along with time stamps and other desired outputs. Capabilities for specifying the types of events (e.g. mouse events, keystrokes, etc.) to be written to the log files have been developed, as well as the ability to define event attributes that are to be collected (e.g. timing and screen coordinate information). The event capture utility will work with any application or any prototyped application, eliminating the need for code instrumentation.

Event Filters

The costs associated with keystroke/event analyses have traditionally been prohibitive. In the past, researchers have typically spent several hours processing each hour of keystroke/event data. This was a hurdle that had to be overcome to make keystroke/event capturing a viable measurement tool.

This hurdle was overcome with the development of filters that quickly translate and aggregate user-generated events into meaningful characterizations of user interaction with application and system software. For example, one filter that has been implemented will extract all instances where commands were selected by the user. The resulting log denotes: the application that was active when the command was selected; the title of the parent menu of the selected command; the name of the selected command; the method by which the command was selected (i.e., by menu or command key selection); the event that preceded the command selection sequence (i.e., a keypress, another command selection, a mouse click, scrolling, etc.); the clock time at which the preceding event occurred; the elapsed time from the preceding event until the target menu was selected; the time from when the target menu was selected until the target command was selected; the combined menu and command selection times; and the number of menus that the user examined before locating the selected command.

The filter described above is a custom filter. A generic filtering tool is under development that will allow events to be filtered by object type (i.e., applications, windows/files, dialogue boxes, menus, commands, tools, content area inputs, etc.), object attributes (i.e., physical appearance, x-y position, etc.), event type (i.e., mouse drags, clicks, key presses, etc.), event attributes (i.e., clock time at which the event occurred, x-y position where event was registered) or combinations of the four.

Multimedia Data Analyzer

A significant amount of behavioral research relies on video tape analysis, which is strong in terms of qualitative information, but weak in terms of quantitative information. Furthermore, it is difficult to locate and access specific events of interest when working with video tape. In contrast, real-time event capturing provides very precise timing and error data, and also allows the experimenter to locate and access specific information very quickly. However, event logs do not convey qualitative information very well. The above mentioned advantages and disadvantages make it clear that real-time event capturing and video recording would complement one another quite well if they were successfully integrated.

The multimedia data analyzer addresses these needs. The event capturing and filtering tools provide a precise, searchable record of subject behavior. Linking the timing information collected via these tools with video tape recordings of user behavior enables the experimenter to directly access video tape segments by selecting timing information contained in event logs. In other words, the experimenter can locate and select the event of interest in the event data log, and the system will automatically find and display the corresponding video tape segment of interest. With integration of observation logging into the system, the experimenter will also be able to drive the video player from observation logs.

The selected video segments can be labeled and annotated with text, providing a retrospective observation logging capability. The resulting segment lists can then be saved for later reference.

Retrospective Verbal Protocol Recorder

The ability to rapidly access video tape segments from event data logs provides a mechanism enabling time cost-effective retrospective verbal protocol. The experimenter can randomly access any segment of video tape by driving the video player from the event log recordings obtained in the experimental session. The comments elicited from the subject are recorded as digitized speech on disk, with an association link to the selected video tape segment and the corresponding logged event of interest.

APPLICATIONS

There are a wide variety of instances where the integrated information available through these tools would be invaluable. The following are some examples.

Prototype Comparison

Timing and efficiency data can be obtained from event logs, providing useful information to weigh when making design decisions. For example, in one experiment, keyboard and mouse-based methods for selecting commands from menus were compared. A command use filter provided hard evidence regarding the efficiency with which subjects were able to locate and select commands with the alternative methods.

Documentation/Instructional Material Evaluation

In many instances, valuable information can be gained by comparing a user or users actions against a target sequence of events. Such is the case when evaluating instructional materials. Judgements regarding the effectiveness of such materials can be made by comparing the event log generated by a participant against the target sequence of events specified in the instructional material.

Augmenting Video Tape Analysis

The event capture and processing tools greatly reduce the time, expense, and inconvenience associated with video tape analysis. This is achieved by using the filtered data log (or observation log) as an index to tape segments of interest.

FUTURE DEVELOPMENT PLANS

Plans for development include the integration of an on-line time synchronized observation logger, and time synchronized recording of eyetracking data. The tools currently run on Macintosh^{TM} computers and under Microsoft Windows^{TM}. Plans are to port the tools to run under Presentation Manager^{TM} and Motif^{TM}.

Multimedia Help: A Prototype and an Experiment

[1]*Piyawadee "Noi" Sukaviriya,* [2]*Ellen Isaacs,* [3]*Krishna Bharat*

[1,3]College of Computing
Georgia Institute of Technology
Atlanta, GA 30332-0280
(404)-894-9105
E-Mail: noi@cc.gatech.edu, kb@cc.gatech.edu

[2]SunSoft Inc.
2550 Garcia Avenue,
Mountain View, CA 94043-1100
(415)-336-1167
E-Mail: ellen.isaacs@eng.sun.com

ABSTRACT

On-line help systems have not paralleled recent advances in user interface technology. In particular, traditional textual help does not support visualization of the interaction processes needed to complete tasks, especially in graphical interfaces. In this demonstration, we present an experimental prototype which is capable of presenting help information in text, audio, static graphics, video, and context-sensitive animation. The prototype is used in a study on how multimedia technology enhances user performance.

KEYWORDS: On-line help, multimedia help, multimedia experiment, animated help, user performance.

INTRODUCTION

On-line help systems have not kept up with advances in user interface technology. As most of us have experienced, describing concepts or explaining what needs to be done to complete tasks in an interface only by words can become cumbersome. Words alone cannot thoroughly describe the actual interaction processes needed to complete a task such that users can visualize them without becoming tedious and distractive. Help suffers in the same fashion. Various graphical media such as static graphics and video potentially can overcome this insufficiency and should be brought into help presentation technology.

In the prototype described in this summary, we introduce *context-sensitive animated help* [5]. Predated work on automatically-generated animated help was done earlier by Neiman [3]. The first author has developed the notion of "context-sensitive" animated help as well as an architecture which can automatically generates this type of help. A part of this architecture has been incorporated in the prototype as another graphical medium. Context-sensitive animated help uses simple 2-dimensional animation to demonstrate how to perform a computer application task within the context in which help is requested. Animated help simply superimposes "moving" animated character of input devices, some of which are shown in Figure 1, on a graphical interface to indicate operations on input devices. Associating operations on input devices with existing objects on the screen and illustrating what actually happens to these objects after each operation directly suggests to users the means by which a task can be completed. Figure 2 shows pulling down a menu to select an item with a mouse-button-down operation, for example.

Figure 1   Animated Characters of a Mouse and
a Keyboard Devices

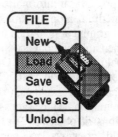

Figure 2   Selecting Load from a FILE menu

We need to understand better the effectiveness of these various media when used in help, singly or in combination, however, before we can properly use them in help presentation. We are studying user understanding of definitions, and user performance in completing tasks and trouble shooting, using the experimental prototype presented in this summary. The capability to use text, audio, static graphics, video, and context-sensitive animated help, in the same prototype allows the study to be designed such that these media can be compared when used in exactly the same situations.

EXPERIMENTAL DESIGN

One of our hypotheses is that a graphical medium is a more direct means to illustrate definitions of objects and task operations in a graphical interface, hence it should enhance user performance when incorporated in help. However, performing tasks through interactions with a graphical interface is rather dynamic and involves moving the cursor, operating various input devices to move around in the screen space, and so forth. A more continuous graphical medium, such as video or animated help, should portray these characteristics of the interface better. Since video and animation provides graphics with continuity, they should enhance user performance further. Context-sensitive animated help not only provides continuous graphical illustrations of actual operations, but it also uses the current context to demonstrate tasks. Therefore, it eliminates the user's mental transfer from help to the current problem context. We hypothesize that animated help will enhance user performance even further. Context-sensitive animated help is expected to be quite useful especially in situations which require trouble shooting.

Booher [1] showed that a combination of written instructions and graphics (pictures) used in combination resulted in faster performance compared to written instructions alone. However, subject's accuracy in the combined media group was not superior to written instructions alone. Palmiter [4] showed that animated help, compared with textual instructions, resulted in subjects performing faster with better accuracy right after training, but slower and less accurate 7 days later. The subjects receiving animated demonstrations also had difficulties applying what they learned to other tasks which were quite similar to the demonstrated examples they saw. Both experiments were on procedural instructions.

These experiments suggest that a graphical medium alone is not sufficient; it has a drawback of insufficient information for inferring actual procedural information. We eliminated using a graphical medium alone in our experiment. It is also foreseeable that graphical help on a more complex task would be incomprehensible without accompanying words to explain semantics behind the graphics. Our experiment has five modes of presentation: (1) text, (2) text and static graphics, (3) audio and static graphics, (4) audio and video, and (5) audio and animation. Three types of information are studied: (1) definitions of objects, (2) procedures, and (3) trouble shooting. This creates a 3x5 experiment in which 5 between-subject groups are studied. Sun Microsystems' Developer's Guide [2] is used as the application domain. We are currently conducting the experiment, in which time spent in help, time used in performing tasks, and errors are dependent variables.

Due to the space limitation, our experimental design cannot be explained here in detail but we discuss some of our design criteria here. For example, we always coupled either text or audio with each graphical medium used: static graphics, video, and animated help. Only audio is used with video and animated help since using text with these two media will visually distract subjects from following help materials. We designed help materials such that verbal explanations, textual or auditory, deliver the concepts being explained while graphics provide more concrete examples of the concepts. This way, verbal explanations will help subjects assimilate concepts so they can apply these concepts to other similar tasks. We also emphasize steps in each instruction to reinforce the concepts of chunking, especially when continuous media are used. We hypothesize that, because of the medium's continuity, learning from animated help is not memorable in [4] since it is perceived as one long piece of information.

EXPERIMENTAL PROTOTYPE

The prototype consists of two components – one is the actual help, the other is a help authoring tool. The help component organizes help materials into topics, each topic has 5 presentation modes to choose from. Each subject will receive help in one presentation mode throughout the experiment for all 3 types of information. All materials are pre-recorded, except the context-sensitive animated help which is generated dynamically at runtime from the prototype's internal supporting representations [5].

The help authoring tool helps organize help materials recorded in different media for different help topics, and for coupling materials to be used in each presentation mode. For instance, we use this tool to associate sound files with various image files recorded for each topic. This tool is also used to associate sound files which narrate video clips with appropriate video files. A help author can play back a scenario being created at any point without actually quitting the authoring mode.

CONCLUSIONS

In this summary, we present a prototype of multimedia help implemented for an experiment to study effectiveness of different media used with different types of help information. In addition to its capability to display help materials in multimedia, the prototype also provides support for organizaing multimedia help materials.

ACKNOWLEDGEMENTS

This research is sponsored by Sun Microsystems, Inc. We would like to thank Jim Foley and Bob Ellis for helping to make this research happen, and John Stasko for improving the clarity of this summary.

REFERENCES

1. Booher, H.R. Relative Comprehensibility of Pictorial and Printed Words in Proceduralized Instructions. *Human Factors*, 17,3 (1975), pp. 266-277.
2. Developer's Guide User's Manual. (1991) Sun Microsystems, Inc.
3. Neiman, D. Graphical Animation from Knowledge, in *Proceedings of AAAI'82* (1982), pp. 373-376.
4. Palmiter, S. and Elkerton, J. An Evaluation of Animated Demonstrations for Learning Computer-based Tasks, in *Proceedings of Human Factors in Computing Systems CHI'91* (May 1991), pp. 257-263.
5. Sukaviriya, P. *Automatic Generation of Context-sensitive Animated Help.* (1991) A Ph.D. Dissertation, George Washington University.

SCI-FI AT CHI:
CYBERPUNK NOVELISTS PREDICT FUTURE USER INTERFACES

Aaron Marcus (Panel Moderator), Principal, Aaron Marcus and Associates
1144 65th Street, Suite F, Emeryville, CA 94608-1109, Tel: 510-601-0994, Fax: 510-547-6125
E-mail: marcus3@violet.berkeley.edu

Prof. Donald A. Norman, Department of Cognitive Science, University of California/San Diego,
La Jolla, CA 92093-0515, Tel: 619-534-6770, Fax: 619-534-1128, Internet E-Mail:
norman@cogsci.ucsd.edu, Bitnet E-Mail: dnorman@ucsd, AppleLink E-Mail: dnorman

Dr. Rudy Rucker, Science Series, Autodesk, Inc,., 2320 Marinship Way, Sausalito, CA, 94965,
Tel: 408-395-7115, E-Mail: rudy@autodesk.com

Mr. Bruce Sterling, Author, 4525 Speedway Avenue, Austin, TX 78751
Tel: 512-323-5176, Fax: 512-479-0912 (Europa Books)

Prof. Vernor Vinge, Department of Mathematical Sciences, San Diego State University, San
Diego, CA 92182, Tel: 619-462-0413, E-Mail: vinge@sdsu.edu

ABSTRACT

This plenary panel will explore ideas about future user
interfaces, their technology support, and their social
context as proposed in the work of leading authors of
science fiction characterized as the Cyberpunk
movement. Respondents will react to and comment
upon the authors' presentations.

KEYWORDS

User/machine systems, computers and society,
history of computing

STATEMENT BY AARON MARCUS: INTRODUCTION

Many of the popular science fiction novels and short
stories in the late 1980s, particularly those of the so-
called Cyberpunk authors (as reported in the *Wall Street
Journal*, among other publications), refocused interest
on the latest scientific technologies: cybernetics,
genetics, neurochemistry, ecology, bio-engineering, and
other leading-edge developments.

Some Cyberpunk authors are programmers, others
have had little direct contact with computers except
through word processors, but all are aware of current
technological/cultural developments and have written
about advanced technologies. Prof. Marvin Minsky of
MIT wrote the introduction for Vinge's *True Names* and
lauded his insights into artificial intelligence.

In many of their writings, Cyberpunk authors
portrayed distinct visions of future advanced user
interface scenarios, for example, the use of direct neural
system implants and the creation of "controlled
hallucinations." In these scenarios, the user interface,

other than the equipment to provide connections,
becomes the fantasy interplay of dramatic personae, real
and imagined, together with signs and symbols in a
three-dimensional, full-media environment.

This panel will provide an opportunity for some of
the leading authors of this science fiction genre to
present excerpts from their work, provide insights into
where they think user interface technology is headed,
and to debate passionately the impact of user interface
technology on future user communities, markets, social
organization, quality of life, and social/cultural values.
In their published works, all of the panel authors have
presented unique, forceful, creative viewpoints about
which technologies will be important, what impact
these technologies will have on society, and how one
should evaluate that impact. These science fiction
authors have something of value to provide the SIGCHI
panel audience: powerful visions of a future technology
and the society in which it is embedded.

Key issues to be discussed in the panel will include
the following:

What are the primary technologies in the scenarios
of future user interfaces?

What new applications and markets do new user
interfaces make possible?

How do user interfaces affect society in these
works?

Do direct neural implants signify the end of
conventional user interface technology and/or the
beginning of a new definition of the user interface?

How do these scenarios affect metaphors, cognitive
models, navigation, appearance, and interaction?

Where do these authors get their information? How
accurate is it?

Has reality caught up with futurist fantasy?

STATEMENT BY DON NORMAN: CYBERNET MEETS INTERNET MEETS CONVENTIONAL ACADEMIC

Weird stuff. These folks present their fantasies, and I am supposed to respond. OK, two ways:

Way 1: To comment on the role of science fiction in general and the strange stuff these three guys have been writing, in specific. I did my homework, carefully reading all their stuff. Hard work, this scientific discussion business.

Way 2: To comment on what was said at this symposium.

What does science fiction offer to us? One is prediction. Second is social sensitivity. And third is scenario generation, the better way to do prototyping. I'll say more about all three of these things when the time comes.

Contrast the three writers. Intelligence is NOT the route to survival, says the Swarm, an ant-like intelligence of distributed automata. A story by Sterling. Intelligence amplification is the way of the future, says Vinge.

Hmm. I have recently been arguing that artifacts don't make us smarter; they change the task we have to do. Vinge says, essentially, that I have a very limited view of an artifact. When the artifact replaces the brain --literally, physically, replaces it, then it really does make us smarter.

As for Rucker, he suggests that this meatware that constitutes the current version of the human is kind of limited, but it has some potential as an erratic, chaotic, generator of interesting interactions.

Would you believe that I will relate all this to CHI? Stay tuned, plugged in, hopped up. Or I'll bobble you.

Why, I just wrote a chapter explaining that technology is the easy thing to predict. The hard thing is the impact on social structure, which you might say is what this science fiction stuff is all about. We better pay more attention. Now, their view of humanity and technology is pretty negative, pretty scary. We have no choice but to be more optimistic, eh?

STATEMENT BY RUDY RUCKER:

There are two points about virtual reality which I would like to discuss:

Firstly I want to note how the eyephones-and-data-glove implementation of VR is displacing the electric-jack-plugged-into-your-brain paradigm of science-fictional cyberspace.

Secondly I would like to suggest that telerobotics represents a "best possible" computer interface in which one sees through a "transparent" machine out into the outer world. Virtual reality is a halfway step towards this goal.

STATEMENT BY BRUCE STERLING: COMPUTER AS FUROSHIKI

"Computer as Furoshiki" is a highly speculative vision of the personal computer as it might evolve if freed of certain current material constraints.

The *furoshiki* is an intimate and ubiquitous accessory to Japanese daily life. It is nothing more than a large square of tough, well-made cloth, usually with a handsome pattern. The furoshiki is used, among other purposes, as a grocery bag, a book-tote, and a decorative wrapper for ceremonial gifts. In its simplicity and multiple uses it is little different from a cowboy's bandanna, except that the skill in wrapping and knotting furoshikis is more arcane and akin to origami.

The computer-as-furoshiki is the computer as a large woven square of lightweight, flexible cloth. It is not, however, "cloth" as that material is currently understood.

The furoshiki's screen is formed by thin bands of color-emitting optical fibers, which are wide enough and bright enough to mimic the scan-lines of a video display terminal. These display-fibers are interwoven with other fiber-optics carrying data.

A second kind of fiber is densely interwoven; it consists of a room-temperature superconductive wire, possibly a novel form of buckminsterfullerene for strength and flexibility. This highly-charged net of superconductors serves as a literal power-grid.

The third fiber is some currently unknown form of piezoelectric filament that can contract, relax, and therefore warp and knot itself in response to precise electrical charges deployed along its length.

A fourth form of fiber serves as a radio antenna and communications grid.

One section of the cloth can be radically stiffened to serve as the diaphragm for an audio speaker.

Computation, memory, and movement are carried out by photonic, photoelectronic, and electronic chips composed of custom-built artificial diamond for low cost and strength. If the tensile fibers are composed of organic proteins (which would seem likely), then the computer-as-furoshiki consists mostly of carbon.

The device is operated with voice-commands, and possibly gesture, through a similarly woven linked glove.

The computer-as-furoshiki is capable of limited movement. Early versions might fold themselves up like a gentleman's handkerchief; later models would resemble aluminum foil or Saran Wrap. Advanced versions can fly.

Although this computer lacks direct video input, it might be capable of optical character recognition if placed on a page, or of image-scanning if placed on a graphic.

When one's head is wrapped completely in the furoshiki, it becomes a virtual reality rig.

When placed on a light-sensitive paper, or film, it generates hard-copies. This computer might displace paper as a medium by usurping not merely the information on paper, but the physical properties of paper as well.

When not in use, the furoshiki is worn, as a scarf, tie, turban, or , of course, the Console-Cowboy's Bandanna. Mainframes can be used as pup-tents, super computers as Big Tops, for a late twenty-first century multimedia circus.

STATEMENT BY VERNOR VINGE

Progress with human/computer interfaces is effectively Intelligence Amplification (IA). Already we are solving problems and managing systems more complex than was possible earlier (though as yet most people do not recognize this as an increase in intelligence). I distinguish two major trends:

1. Interfacing with machines in order to understand and manipulate the physical world. Paradoxically, this is the most important aspect of virtual reality.

2. Interfacing with machines to coordinate with other humans: consensual reality.

Both have the effect of raising intelligence, but with very different flavors. Using one or the other, we may find that superhuman intelligence is first achieved via Intelligence Amplification rather than Artificial Intelligence.

ACKNOWLEDGEMENTS

The idea for this panel stemmed from the panel moderator's awareness of a symposium organized at the Microcomputer Technology Consortium (MCC), Austin, Texas, in 1989, in which a group of science-fiction writers was invited to address and interact with MCC's research and development staff.

SPEAKER BIOGRAPHIES

Mr. Marcus is founder and principal of Aaron Marcus and Associates. He and his staff plan, research, analyze, design, evaluate, and help implement the metaphors, cognitive models, navigation schema, appearance characteristics, and interaction attributes of user interfaces. They also prepare the documents used to manage the development and maintenance of user interfaces. Their work focuses on task and cognitive model analysis; rapic prototyping of screens with effective use of typography, symbolism, color, spatial layout, animation, and sequencing; and design of icons, color sets, and control panels. Their clients include major US and international firms. Mr. Marcus is the co-author with Ronald Baecker of *Human Factors and Typography for More Readable Programs* (1990) and the author of *Graphic Design for Electronic Documents and User Interfaces* (1992).

Donald A. Norman is Professor and Chair of the Department of Cognitive Science at the University of California, San Diego. He is one of the founders of the Cognitive Science Society and has been chair of the society and editor of the journal *Cognitive Science*. He has been an officer of SIGCHI. The basic premise of Norman's research is that the unaided mind is limited in power, but cognition, when distributed across people and objects, can be powerful if the tools are properly designed. Norman believes most are pretty awful. Norman is the author of the book *The Design of Everyday Things*. The book *Turn Signals Are the Facial Expressions of Automobiles* was published in April, 1992.

Rudy Rucker is the author of more than a dozen books on science and science fiction, including *Software* and *Wetware*,(Avon), Mind Tools, (Houghton Mifflin, and Infinity and the Mind (Bantam).He programmed *James Gleek's Chaos: The Software* for Autodesk. He is a professor of mathematics and computer science at San Jose State University.

Bruce Sterling's works include *Islands in the Net* (Arbor House and Ace), *Schismatrix* (Ace and Arbor House), *The Artificial Kid* (Ace and Harper/Row), and *Involution Ocean* (Ace),He is the editor of the cyberpunk anthology *Mirorshades* (Arbor).

Vernor Vinge's works include *True Names* (Baen Books), *Marooned in Real Time* (Blue Jay), *The Peace War* (Blue Jay), *Tatja Grimm's World* (Baen Books), *Threats and Other Promises* (Baen Books), and *The Witling* (Blue Jay). He teaches in the department of mathematical science at San Diego State University.

PARTICIPATORY DESIGN OF A PORTABLE TORQUE-FEEDBACK DEVICE

Michael Good

Digital Equipment Corporation
110 Spit Brook Road (ZKO2-1/N42)
Nashua, NH 03062-2698 USA
1-603-881-2296, good@baviki.enet.dec.com

ABSTRACT

Customer-driven design processes such as participatory design can be used to develop new presence, or virtual reality, technology. Chemists worked together with computer company engineers to develop scenarios for how presence technology could be used to support future molecular modeling work in drug design. These scenarios led to the development of a portable torque-feedback device which can be used with either workstation or virtual reality technology. This paper discusses both the experience with the participatory design process and the novel features of the portable torque-feedback device.

KEYWORDS: Presence, virtual reality, participatory design, force feedback, molecular modeling, chemistry.

INTRODUCTION

Whether it is called virtual reality, artificial reality, cyberspace, or presence, the technology that enables participants to see, hear, feel, and walk around a computer-generated world has captured the public imagination. Accompanying this enthusiasm are serious questions about the usefulness of presence technology. One belief is that "Artificial reality will just be a gadget for rich countries," affecting only military and Nintendo game applications [3].

How might we take presence technology beyond gadgetry and make it useful for diverse people doing different types of work? My approach has been to apply the techniques of participatory design [1, 9] to the development of presence technology. In Digital's Presence project, chemists collaborated with computer engineers to develop new prototypes of presence technology. As Laurel [11] suggests, our starting point is

to design the experience that we want people to have when using computers in their work.

In this paper, I will first set the context by briefly describing the portion of the chemists' drug design work on which we focused, and then describing the technological background in presence that the computer engineers brought to the project. I will then discuss our experience with the participatory design process, and how it led to the development of a new force-feedback device, the portable torque-feedback device (patent pending).

CONTEXT

Participatory design is a collaborative process. Computer users are the experts in their work, while computer designers are the experts in computer technology. Participatory design brings these two backgrounds together to create new systems with the goal of improving the quality of work life, as shown in Figure 1.

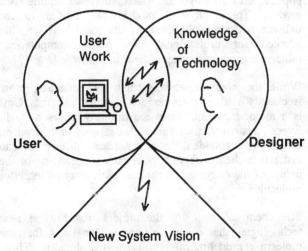

Figure 1: Dynamic Interaction Between Technology and Work

Blomberg and Henderson [1] describe three basic aspects of participatory design: the goal of improving the quality of work life, a collaborative orientation, and an iterative process. An important part of participatory design is what

Ehn [4] calls the balance between tradition and transcendence. In participatory design, new technology explicitly incorporates the history of how work has been done in the past while simultaneously improving how work can be done in the future.

Molecular Modeling

Our customers were members of a molecular modeling group at a pharmaceutical company, working in the drug discovery process. The discovery and development of new drugs is a long, complex process. We focused on one piece of the discovery process for one category of drugs called enzyme inhibitors.

Enzyme inhibitors are small molecules that can dock, or bond, with larger enzyme molecules at an active site. By docking at the active site, the small molecules inhibit or stop an undesired chemical reaction produced by the enzyme. Stopping the chemical reaction can serve to relieve undesired symptoms. The inhibitor might be made up of about sixty atoms while the enzyme itself is made up of thousands of atoms.

One of the many problems in enzyme docking is that neither the enzyme inhibitor nor the enzyme is rigid. Both can twist into many different layouts, called conformations. Exploring these different layouts is called exploring the conformational space of the molecules. One common goal is to look for conformations with low energy for both the enzyme inhibitor and the enzyme, since this tends to make docking easier.

Exploring conformational space is one of many applications of molecular modeling. Chemists have many molecular modeling tools available. Perhaps the most popular tools are physical models, such as Dreiding stick models. These physical models are similar to the ball-and-stick models used in chemistry classes, but adapted for professional use. Many computerized molecular modeling systems are also available [e.g. 13].

While the computerized systems are becoming more frequently used, they are resisted by many chemists. Cost is a major issue, but there are usability issues as well. Even a system that appears well-designed and based on established graphical user interface principles can distance a chemist from a physical understanding of the nature of the enzyme and the candidate enzyme inhibitor molecules.

The chemists' goal for the project was to find new technologies that could be used as the basis for new molecular modeling tools for enzyme docking. These tools would combine the benefits and usability of existing physical and computerized modeling tools.

Presence

The computer engineers brought a particular technical focus to participatory design. This technical focus was to increase the quality of presence for computer users.

Presence has several characteristics. Presence is related to a feeling of computer transparency, where the interface to a computer fades into the background [7]. As presence or transparency increases, so does the experience of working on a task as opposed to working on a computer. This has long been a goal in developing usable systems.

From a design perspective, presence expresses the qualities of a product that can be perceived by one or more of our senses [5]. Research in multisensory human-computer interaction currently focuses on making greater use of the senses of vision, touch, and hearing.

From a perspective in rhetoric and argumentation, presence is the quality which makes certain elements important and pertinent to an audience [15]. One historical method to increase presence is to use concrete rather than abstract objects.

Our use of the term "presence" refers to the quality of human-computer interaction that makes systems more transparent to the user, makes greater use of the senses, and makes the abstract concrete. Presence is not a distinct category of computer technology like menu systems, direct manipulation, or virtual reality [18]. Many different technologies can be used to achieve greater presence through computers, depending on the nature of the work and on individual and group preferences.

Our technological focus started with virtual reality technology [16]. Our participatory design experience expanded that focus to include workstation technology enhanced with multisensory I/O devices. Artificial reality [10] is another technology for achieving presence in some contexts. We did not include it in our technological focus due in part to the lack of tools for developing working prototypes.

The computer engineers' goal for the project was to develop new presence technology that could improve work life for our customers in the future by providing more transparent, sensory, and concrete systems. Molecular modeling has already been a driving problem behind the multisensory research at the University of North Carolina [2]. We expected that working with chemists would be especially useful for developing new ways to support the sense of touch in the use of computers.

PARTICIPATORY DESIGN EXPERIENCE

Participatory design offers rich methodological possibilities for building powerful computer application systems. This project applied participatory design methodology to a somewhat different area: the development of presence technology. The computer engineers worked in the context of product development organizations that have traditionally built general-purpose systems for diverse customers.

My initial conception of the participatory design process was to view it in five steps:

1. Building relationships. We would spend enough time to ensure a good fit between customer-participants and the Presence project. This included familiarizing our customers with presence technology.

2. Contextual inquiry. Contextual inquiry emphasizes interview methods conducted in the context of the participant's work and building an understanding of work in context [19]. The computer engineers needed to build an understanding of the customer's work before we could collaborate as co-designers.

3. Brainstorming. Brainstorming sessions, where all ideas are recorded and criticism of ideas is forbidden, would generate many ideas for how presence technology could improve work life.

4. Storyboarding. Customers and computer engineers would develop some of the most promising brainstorming ideas into illustrated scripts of a "day in the life" of a customer using presence technology in the future [14].

5. Iterative design. Using the storyboards as specifications, the computer engineers would build prototypes that would be tested by the customer-participants on a regular basis. All the previous steps would continue in an iterative fashion.

Our participatory design work with chemists was one of three simultaneous participatory design projects for developing presence technology. In the other projects, where the computer users were toy designers and computer industrial designers, we followed this 5-step process. After spending several months in building relationships, the initial design visits lasted 2 days. The first day was spent in contextual inquiry, and the second day was divided between brainstorming and storyboarding. Subsequent iterative design sessions lasted 1 day.

With the chemists, however, the initial design session was less structured. Contextual inquiry and storyboarding activities flowed together, and brainstorming activity was generally absent. Storyboarding did not produce a full illustrated script, but rather a scenario for use of new technology. We adapted the design techniques on the fly in response to the work context. Participatory design is a collaborative approach to design, not a rigid set of design methods.

In the rest of this section I will describe our experience in working with the chemists in building relationships, contextual inquiry, and storyboarding. The next section will then describe our progress in moving from the scenario to the prototype tested in our first iterative design session.

Building Relationships

Conducting participatory design in a large product development organization presents many challenges. Grudin [6] identifies many of these challenges and their various sources in the nature of product development, in the division of labor within product development organizations, and in the use of standard software development procedures and techniques. Two of these challenges took months for us to overcome: identifying appropriate customer participants, and then obtaining access to the participants.

I tried several approaches in order to find appropriate customer participants for this project. One approach that did not work was simply to call or send electronic mail to the sales representative in charge of a promising account. A much more successful technique was to discuss this project in Digital's VAX Notes conferences, which serve as electronic bulletin boards for a variety of technical and employee interests. Interested sales representatives then contacted me in response to these notes. These contacts could take days or months to develop. Two months elapsed from the time I placed a note in the pharmaceutical industry conference before a sales representative contacted me about the project.

Initial contacts enabled the customers and me to build a working relationship before beginning the actual design sessions. The pharmaceutical customers had already planned a visit to Digital to hear about future technologies in other areas, so my presentation was included in that visit. This meeting took place 2 months after the initial contact with the Digital sales representative. Two months later we arranged the first design meeting.

Overall, 5 months elapsed between the first contact with the sales representative for the pharmaceutical company and the first on-site participatory design visit. It took only half that time to then develop the torque-feedback device and presence software prototypes for molecular modeling and have them ready for the first iterative design session.

Part of the reason that the process took so long is systemic, as Grudin discusses, but part is particular to the nature of this project. We needed to find customer groups who were already familiar with state-of-the-art computer systems for their applications and whose mission included looking for new technology which could help solve their difficult problems. These groups also needed to include intended users of the new technology: chemists who were familiar with computers, not just computer people who were familiar with chemistry. Research and development groups made the best candidates for this work.

Contextual Inquiry

We use contextual inquiry to understand the nature of the user's work, how computers are involved in that work, and how the use of computers supports and disrupts the work process. Interviewing customers as they use a computer system is particularly effective for understanding the ongoing usage of a computer system, rather than the summary experience that customers recollect after the fact. Such interviews are often hit-or-miss regarding job content, though, and are not usually sufficient by themselves to get an overall understanding of the work process.

One technique we use to provide more context is to have customers give us an overview of their entire work process, using artifacts of that process wherever possible. An overview of the entire drug design process would have been too complex for the computer designers to follow. Instead, our customers focused on the portion of drug design that they viewed as most relevant: the creation of drugs from enzyme inhibitors. After reviewing the basic chemistry, the molecular modelers demonstrated some current modeling techniques with both physical models and computer models. All the computer engineers had extensive collegiate math and science backgrounds, which helped in understanding the chemists' work.

One chemist's work was particularly inspiring for future designs. He had found the current computerized representation of the enzyme active site too limiting, even with the use of stereoscopic displays and fast 3-D rendering systems. He constructed an elaborate foam-core physical model of the enzyme active site, with the cavity of the model representing the conformation of the enzyme that was of the greatest interest. After constructing this model he was very excited, so he rushed to get his Dreiding model of the enzyme inhibitor and physically experiment with moving the Dreiding model of the enzyme inhibitor around the foam core model of the enzyme active site. But this did not work either: the problem was simply too complex for either the physical model or the computer model to be fully understandable on their own. The chemist wound up going back and forth between the physical model and the computer model to figure out the proper conformation of the enzyme inhibitor which would lead to a good dock.

This and similar sessions led to the idea of combining the advantages of computer models and physical models. Physical models in many ways provide greater presence for the chemists and are closer to the traditional work practice. Computerized models offer many ways to transcend the current work practice, including the ability to get quantitative results. Why not combine the two into an electronic Dreiding model, where the computer model can be manipulated physically, like existing Dreiding models?

A key element of contextual inquiry involved having the computer engineers tour the work facilities. Most of our participatory design work at the pharmaceutical company took place in conference rooms, but we did tour the molecular modeling laboratory and individual offices, as well as getting a walking tour of the entire complex. Absorbing the physical feeling of the workplace helped

the computer engineers better understand the context of the customers' work.

After doing some storyboarding around the electronic Dreiding model ideas, we returned for further contextual inquiry sessions. Another chemist demonstrated the use of the group's existing molecular modeling software package in more detail. This demonstration then fed into further storyboarding work.

Storyboarding

"Day in the life" scenarios and storyboards both can serve as specifications for prototypes. Both techniques emphasize narrative, rather than theory, as the primary source for design [17]. Scenarios describe situations where customers would use new technology in the future. Storyboarding goes to an additional level of detail by creating an illustrated script for this scenario. Storyboarding thus can provide a more detailed specification for prototype software. In this case, our scenario was simple enough that the lack of an illustrated storyboard did not hamper our later prototyping work.

The molecular modelers developed a scenario based on an electronic version of the mechanical stick models that chemists already use. The electronic model could be physically manipulated like the mechanical models while supporting several new capabilities, such as ease of filing and providing quantitative energy calculations. Physical manipulation keeps the kinesthetic presence that is missing in current molecular modeling software. Quantitative results such as energy calculation and minimization provide important and pertinent information that is not present for chemists when using the mechanical models.

This scenario illustrates the balance between traditional work practice and the new possibilities offered by presence technology. It based on the existing work practice of the Dreiding models, but adds numerous capabilities that are not provided by those models. The visual representation of the electronic Dreiding model would follow the practice of the chemists' existing molecular modeling software.

FROM SCENARIO TO PROTOTYPE

Developing Prototype Hardware

These participatory design sessions confirmed our initial impression that force-feedback devices to support the sense of touch would be particularly useful in molecular modeling.

General-purpose force-feedback devices are not currently commercially available, so we had to design and build our own. Our initial force-feedback prototype, developed prior to our participatory design work, was based on Minsky's 2-D force-feedback joystick [12]. We were also influenced by the 6-D robotic arm used by Brooks et al. for enzyme docking [2], and by the force-feedback steering wheel used in Atari's Hard Drivin' arcade game [16]. Since the work started we have become aware of other related devices, including Iwata's 9-D manipulator [8] and the force-feedback versions of instrumented gloves [16].

Our participatory design sessions suggested a smaller and simpler force-feedback device that would be more useful in molecular modeling applications than the 2-D joystick. This hand-held device would have one torque motor to provide torque feedback: as the participant twisted the shaft, the device could twist back as appropriate. This was directly suggested by the idea for an electronic Dreiding model for molecular modelers, where the modelers could deal with a computer model of a molecule in the same physical ways that they currently deal with physical Dreiding models of molecules.

Our portable torque-feedback device uses the same basic electronics as our version of the 2-D joystick, but much simpler mechanics. The 2-D joystick converts the output of torque motors into position offsets in the X and Y directions, whereas the torque-feedback device has no need for such conversion.

Figure 2, drawn to scale, shows the relative size and shape of our initial 2-D joystick versus the later 1-D device. The 2-D force-feedback joystick was about 28 inches tall and 20 inches square. The portable torque-feedback device was about 7½ inches tall and 2½ inches in diameter.

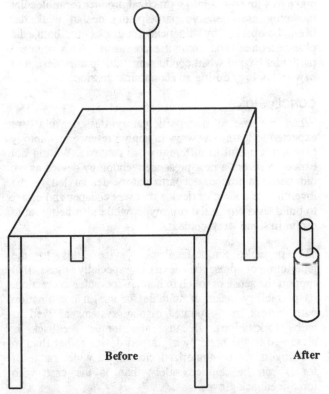

Before

After

Figure 2: Force-Feedback Devices: Before and After Participatory Design with Chemists

Developing Prototype Software

The scenario of electronic Dreiding models led to the development of our initial software prototype which the chemists tested a few months later in a visit to one of our laboratories. In this prototype, the participant selects the molecule to be studied, and data is read in from a text file in standard PDB (Protein Data Bank) format. The chemists provided PDB data for several small 30-60 atom molecules. The molecule was displayed in a window on the screen in a color-coded format similar to that used in the customer's existing molecular modeling software.

After reading in the molecular data, there were several modes available: twisting the entire molecule using a 6-D magnetic sensor, moving the entire molecule using the sensor, and selecting a bond that the participant would like to rotate. All this mode selection, including the specification of the bond, was done via the keyboard. We focused our time developing the presence features within each mode, rather than on improving the usability of the control structures of the prototype.

Selecting a bond to rotate started the mode that used the torque-feedback device. As the participant rotated the molecule around the bond, the device provided feedback based on an estimate of molecular forces. This energy curve was also displayed on the screen along with the graphical display of the molecule. The torque on the device was proportional to the gradient of the energy curve, based on the rotation of the shaft of the torque-feedback device. The graphical display of the energy curve also indicated the current position on the curve. In this first prototype, the energy curves were randomly selected from three precomputed functions, so any relationship to actual molecular forces was coincidental.

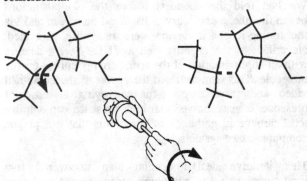

Figure 3: Rotating an Enzyme Inhibitor Around a Selected Bond

Figure 3 shows a black-and-white representation of the color display of a sample enzyme inhibitor. Moving from the conformation on the left-hand side of the figure to the conformation on the right involves two steps. First, the chemist selects the bond (indicated in Figure 3 with the thick dotted line) so that the left-hand side of the molecule would be rotated. The chemist then rotates the shaft of the torque-feedback device about 60 degrees towards him- or herself, and the left-hand side of the molecule also rotates about 60 degrees towards the chemist.

As the shaft is rotated, the chemist feels resistance to the rotation based on the gradient of a molecular energy curve. In this first prototype, this energy curve was based on random data. In a more advanced prototype, the energy gradient would be based on the varying differences in distance between the atoms in the molecule. In the example in Figure 3, this would lead to a decrease of energy at first, as the top-most atoms move further apart. At the local energy minimum, no torque output is produced. The energy would increase again towards the end of the rotation as the bottom-most atoms move closer together, leading to greater resistance or torque output.

Iterative Design Results

Despite the limitation of the arbitrary energy curves, the prototype was compelling for the chemists. The most experienced chemist noted that the prototype was "Very nice... I'm already playing... Feels great to me... This is really neat."

Torque feedback played a different role in exploring the molecular model than the chemists had expected. The senior chemist noted that instead of using torque feedback to find good conformations (how the molecule should be twisted around different bonds), he was using the graphical display for that purpose. The torque feedback aided him in developing a physical understanding of the molecule. The combination of the graphical and force display seemed to provide a "very rapid way to examine the conformational space."

We had told the chemists before the demonstrations began that the energy curves displayed on screen and via the torque-feedback device were randomly generated. Nevertheless, the chemists felt as if they were dealing with an approximation of the actual energy curves for the molecule. This demonstrated the power of the combined video and force display for conveying a sense of presence. It also showed that high presence can amplify the "garbage in garbage out" problems that can plague computer-based systems.

This iterative design session also uncovered two limitations with the prototype torque-feedback device itself. The first limitation was the inability to turn the torque feedback off. In one scenario, the chemist may want to choose a bond, rotate it to the desired position, then keep choosing other bonds and rotating as desired. In this scenario it is important to have a mode where the torque feedback is off, because the chemist may want to leave a bond in a relatively high-energy conformation. That could not be done if the torque feedback is pushing the chemist away from that position towards a local energy minimum. A button on the device is useful for this and other control functions.

The second limitation was the quantization of the device. In this prototype, the torque feedback was quantized in 5-degree increments of the 360 degrees of rotation. The junior chemist believed this reduced the feel of the torque-feedback unit as a high-resolution device, even though this level of quantization was the highest he had seen for computing molecular forces in existing molecular modeling computer software. We speculate that adding some interpolation, or doing unequal sampling where the energy is sampled most at the lowest levels of change (the lowest values of the first derivative) would add more presence. Despite this limitation, the chemist felt the prototype gave "a feel for the degree of fineness of the rotational space around bonds."

Participatory design involves being prepared to discard technological ideas if new paths better meet customer needs. Customer participation includes making decisions, not simply being asked for advice. During our first iterative design session, the molecular modeling customers spent about 1 hour with prototypes involving the force-feedback devices and about 2 minutes with another prototype which used the head-mounted display. Their experience confirmed their initial hunch that force feedback met their needs while the head-mounted display did not. A revised scenario focused on supporting the senses of touch and hearing to complement screen-oriented displays.

Our participatory design sessions have not yet resulted in a finished product. Further work needs to be done to make this invention into a practical product for molecular modeling use. Iterative participatory design work has been hampered by financial cutbacks at both the pharmaceutical and computer companies. This seems a particular hazard when conducting participatory design of new technology during an economic recession.

CONCLUSIONS

When we started our participatory design work, we expected to learn new ways to apply presence technology to make it useful in different work contexts. We did not expect to invent a new presence technology device as we did here. In this case, participatory design led to the invention of a simpler device that was cheaper and easier to build than our initial prototype, while also being more useful in some work contexts.

The portable torque-feedback device adds to the repertoire of presence devices, especially those that support the sense of touch in human-computer interaction. Its portability makes it suitable for use in combination with current head-mounted display systems as well as with workstations. Because the torque feedback is presented to the hand by a grasped device rather than to the fingers via computerized clothing, a wider range of forces can be applied safely than is the case with force-feedback gloves.

Applications of the portable torque-feedback device are not limited to molecular modeling. The device can be used for other applications where torque feedback is useful. These applications could include the industrial design of the feel of knobs and dials as well as general purpose information visualization. Usability for these different applications could be enhanced by a set of "Swiss Army" style attachments to the shaft of the device, such as knobs, dials, and steering wheels.

Participatory design is an approach that responds to its context, rather than a fixed set of procedures used in all situations. Our design sessions with the chemists succeeded, even though they did not take place in the five discrete steps I had initially anticipated. Specific design activities proceeded as needed in the context of a collaborative relationship.

Our difficulties with participatory design came in initiating and sustaining the process, not in applying the process in design sessions at customer and computer company sites. Finding and enrolling appropriate customer participants for the participatory design process remains a challenge for engineers in large product development organizations. Our use of the company's internal electronic network to find participants eventually worked, but it was slow. Sustaining a commitment to participatory design work for new technology also was a problem for us.

Developing useful, enjoyable, and appropriate technology that enhances presence for computer users is an ongoing challenge. Participatory design has steered computer engineers and chemists in some new design directions. This experience indicates that participatory design can be used to develop new computer technology as well as new computer-based application systems.

ACKNOWLEDGMENTS

Tom Stockebrand dubbed our collaboration the Presence project and moved this project from mockups to working prototypes, among many other contributions. James Munson was co-inventor of the portable torque-feedback device. The prototypes were developed by James Munson, RuthAnn Abruzzi, John Gilstrap, Robert Clemens, Pete Pittman, and Pin Fong Ng. Figure 1 was provided by Karen Holtzblatt and Sandy Jones. Eliot Tarlin and Minette Beabes provided the design and rhetoric perspectives on presence, respectively.

DISCLAIMER

The views expressed in this paper are those of the author and do not necessarily reflect the views of Digital Equipment Corporation.

REFERENCES

1. Blomberg, J. L. and Henderson, A. Reflections on participatory design: Lessons from the Trillium experience. In *Proc. CHI '90 Human Factors in Computing Systems* (Seattle, WA, April 1–5, 1990), ACM, New York, 353–359.

2. Brooks, F. P., Jr., Ouh-Young, M., Batter, J. J. and Kilpatrick, P. J. Project GROPE — Haptic displays for scientific visualization. *Computer Graphics*, 24, 4 (August 1990), 177–185. Proc. SIGGRAPH '90 (Dallas, TX, August 6–10, 1990).

3. Ditlea, S. Another world: Inside artificial reality. *PC/Computing*, 2, 11 (November 1989), 90–102.

4. Ehn, P. *Work-Oriented Design of Computer Artifacts*. Arbetslivscentrum, Stockholm, 1988. Available from Lawrence Erlbaum Associates, Hillsdale, NJ.

5. Gilles, W. The presence of products: A question of perspective. *Innovation*, 4, 3 (1985), 5–8.

6. Grudin, J. Systematic sources of suboptimal interface design in large product development organizations. *Human-Computer Interaction*, 6, 2 (1991), 147–196.

7. Holtzblatt, K. A., Jones, S. and Good, M. Articulating the experience of transparency: An example of field research techniques. *SIGCHI Bulletin*, 20, 2 (October 1988), 45–47.

8. Iwata, H. Artificial reality with force-feedback: Development of desktop virtual space with compact master manipulator. *Computer Graphics*, 24, 4 (August 1990), 165–170. Proc. SIGGRAPH '90 (Dallas, TX, August 6–10, 1990).

9. Johnson, J., Ehn, P., Grudin, J., Nardi, B., Thoresen, K. and Suchman, L. Participatory design of computer systems (panel). In *Proc. CHI '90 Human Factors in Computing Systems* (Seattle, WA, April 1–5, 1990), ACM, New York, 141–144.

10. Krueger, M. W. *Artificial Reality II*. Addison-Wesley, Reading, MA, 1991.

11. Laurel, B. *Computers as Theatre*. Addison-Wesley, Reading, MA, 1991.

12. Minsky, M., Ouh-Young, M., Steele, O., Brooks, F. P., Jr. and Behensky, M. Feeling and seeing: Issues in force display. *Computer Graphics*, 24, 2 (March 1990), 235–243. Proc. 1990 Symposium on Interactive 3D Graphics (Snowbird, UT, March 25–28, 1990).

13. Mohamadi, F., Richards, N. G. J., Guida, W. C., Liskamp, R., Lipton, M., Caufield, C., Chang, G., Hendrickson, T. and Still, W. C. MacroModel — An integrated software system for modeling organic and bioorganic molecules using molecular mechanics. *Journal of Computational Chemistry*, 11, 4 (April 1990), 440–467.

14. Mountford, S. J., Buxton, B., Krueger, M., Laurel, B. and Vertelney, L. Drama and personality in user interface design (panel). In *Proc. CHI '89 Human Factors in Computing Systems* (Austin, TX, April 30–May 4, 1989), ACM, New York, 105–108.

15. Perelman, Ch. and Olbrechts-Tyteca, L. *The New Rhetoric: A Treatise on Argumentation*. Trans. J. Wilkinson and P. Weaver. University of Notre Dame Press, Notre Dame, IN, 1969. Original French version published in 1958.

16. Rheingold, H. *Virtual Reality*. Summit Books, New York, 1991.

17. Rorty, R. *Essays on Heidegger and Others: Philosophical Papers Volume 2*. Cambridge University Press, Cambridge, 1991.

18. Wixon, D. and Good, M. Interface style and eclecticism: Moving beyond categorical approaches. In *Proc. Human Factors Society 31st Annual Meeting* (New York, October 19–23, 1987), Human Factors Society, Santa Monica, CA, Vol. 1, 571–575.

19. Wixon, D., Holtzblatt, K. and Knox, S. Contextual design: An emergent view of system design. In *Proc. CHI '90 Human Factors in Computing Systems* (Seattle, WA, April 1–5, 1990), ACM, New York, 329–336.

USER CENTRED DEVELOPMENT OF A GENERAL PRACTICE MEDICAL WORKSTATION: THE PEN&PAD EXPERIENCE

A.L. Rector*, B. Horan*, M. Fitter†,
S. Kay*, P.D. Newton§, W.A. Nowlan*, D. Robinson†, and A. Wilson*

*Medical Informatics Group, Department of Computer Science,
University of Manchester, Manchester M13 9PL.
Tel: +44–61–275–6133, FAX: +44–61–275–6236, EMAIL: rector@cs.man.ac.uk
†MRC Social and Applied Psychology Unit, University of Sheffield
§Centre for Research in Primary Care, Department of General Practice, University of Manchester

ABSTRACT
The goal of the PEN&PAD project is to design and develop a useful and usable medical workstation for day–to–day use in patient care. The project has adopted a user centred approach and direct observations of doctors, participative design and Formative Evaluation have therefore been an integral part of the process of software development. Indeed, doctors have been involved from the earliest stages of the project. The project has focussed on British General Practitioners, but the methods which have been evolved are general. This paper describes the strategy by which doctors can be involved in the successful design and development of a medical workstation.

KEYWORDS: user centred, workstation, medical informatics, methodology, evaluation.

INTRODUCTION
Doctors have often been described as resistant to using computers, and numerous surveys (for example [1]) have purported to show doctors' negative attitudes towards computers. The difficulty of producing information systems which doctors are willing to use has frequently been cited as the major barrier to the wider use of computers in medical care [2]. However, doctors are enthusiastic users of other new technology, and a recent survey in the United Kingdom suggested that although relatively few doctors use computers in the course of the medical practice, more than half of all doctors use computers at home [3].

How can this discrepancy be explained? The most obvious explanation is that doctors do find existing systems neither sufficiently useful or nor easily usable to justify the effort required to use them, whatever their feelings towards 'computers in general'. One possible solution to these inadequacies

is to involve doctors more extensively in the development process. However, mere involvement is not enough, since most projects claim to have involved users, yet the problems persist.

The goal of the PEN&PAD project is to design and develop a useful and usable medical workstation for day–to–day use in patient care [4, 5]. To meet this goal, we set out to make user involvement more effective. We have developed a new methodology for involving doctors in the development process from its earliest stages. The methods are adapted from work by many others including Monk [6], Mumford [7] and Norman & Draper [8]. They have led to an iterative process of rapid prototyping and formative evaluation in which user participation is an integral part.

THE BRITISH GENERAL PRACTICE ENVIRONMENT
Working almost entirely in primary care, the relationship between the British General Practitioner (GP) and the patient is one of 'first contact'. A GP deals with the day–to–day management of patients, tackling conditions ranging from the common cold to acute diabetes. The GP also has the role of referring patients to other hospital–based consultants. A typical British General Practice will consist of 3 full–time doctors, a nurse, a practice manager, and auxiliary administrative staff.

CIRCLES OF USERS AND THE ITERATIVE DEVELOPMENT CYCLE
The user centred strategy employed by the PEN&PAD project relies on the long–term involvement of General Practitioners (GPs). The GPs are described in terms of four categories or 'circles' of doctors; the iterative process embodied in this strategy is described in terms of 'cycles'.

The General Practice Users
There are four categories of GP users:

i) One doctor is employed full time as a member of the development team[1].

ii) An 'inner circle' of five doctors provides the primary input to the design and evaluation process. They are involved in workshops which take place roughly once per month and in individual sessions and preparation equivalent to two or three additional days per month. The doctors

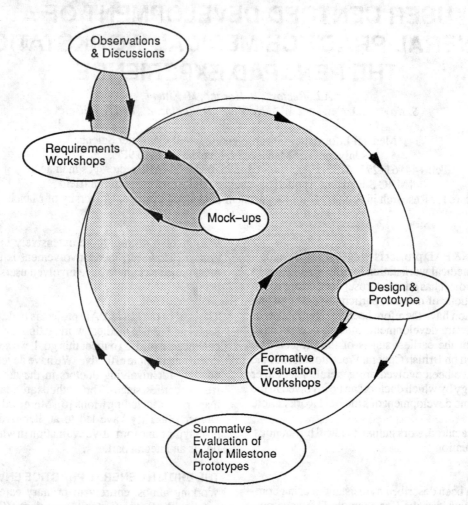

Figure 1: A schematic representation of the User Centred Development Process

were selected to include a range of types of general practice and of attitudes towards computers. All of them have, or have acquired during the course of the study, computers in their practices for at leastadministrative purposes[2]. None of them is involved in academic practice.

iii) An 'outer circle' of twelve doctors participates in major formative evaluation workshops which are held at roughly six–monthly intervals. These doctors were drawn from the British Computer Society Primary Health Care Specialist Group, the primary organisation of general practitioners interested in computing in the UK, augmented by members of the department of General Practice at the University of Manchester.

iv) A group of eight 'naive' users, doctors with no prior connection with the project, who participate in the final 'quasi–summative' phase of the evaluation. These doctors, whose characteristics are similar to the group above, were unpaid. Three had no computer experience whatsoever, the remainder used computers in their consulting room.

The Formative Evaluation Cycle

The project makes a distinction between 'formative' and 'summative' evaluation [9]. 'Formative evaluation' is undertaken for the development team and aims to refine the requirements and thus improve the design. 'Summative evaluation' is carried out either for the development team or for external agencies to determine whether or not the project has reached pre–defined criteria. Formative evaluation is an integral part of the development cycle and is also used to refine the methods employed in the summative evaluation.

The development strategy is shown schematically in figure 1. Each cycle consists of a series of workshops for requirements analysis and preliminary design specification, then a short period in which software is produced, followed by a formative evaluation workshop.

In the first cycle of the development process, a series of workshops was held to determine initial user requirements and to outline proposed designs. The workshops consisted of group discussions supplemented by informal demonstrations and assessments of new ideas. A minority of the demonstrations were computer–based; most relied on paper or overhead transparencies. The design exercises were focussed on doctors' tasks, and their requirements for medical information. In addition, all members of the development team spent time observing doctor–patient consultations.

Based on this information, the development team produced initial computer–based prototypes. The prototypes were largely 'cardboard'—little more than slide shows to demonstrate potential. They were shown first to the inner circle to eliminate the worst flaws in the user interface, and then subjected to a formative evaluation workshop with the outer circle of doctors.

After the formative evaluation workshop, the results were analysed and fed into the next cycle of the development process. A further series of requirements analysis and design workshops was held to explore issues raised by the evaluation workshop and refine the development team's understanding of the requirements. In addition, the workshops were used to propose increasing degrees of functionality for the next prototype. The current prototype was then completely discarded and the new one was implemented from scratch during the next cycle.

At the end of the third cycle, it was felt that the system had reached a plateau in its development. It was also feared that the doctors in both the inner and outer circles were becoming too involved in the project to give unbiased advice. The approach described in this paper stresses the need to involve users in the development process and to thus produce a 'shared culture' between themselves and the developers. One advantage of this is a common language that can enhance the understanding of some aspects of the problem. However, it can also create a set of 'blinkers' which prevent both parties from seeing certain blunders or faults [9]. A series of 'quasi–summative' evaluation workshops were therefore held which involved doctors who had no previous contact with the system and who were chosen to be more representative of the wider GP community. We termed this evaluation 'quasi–summative' because the system was far from complete.

THE WORKSHOP METHODOLOGY
The workshops involve three groups:

i)   The development team who produce the prototypes;

ii) The evaluation team consisting of psychologists and associated observers;

iii) The doctors.

The evaluation team is separate from the development team, but participates in many of the project planning activities. They are, in general, viewed by the development team as colleagues and allies, although they also have a separate responsibility to prepare a final evaluation report for the funding bodies.

The Requirements Analysis and Design Workshops
The pattern of the Requirements Analysis and Design Workshops is highly variable. Each workshop is devoted to a particular design issue. On most occasions, the issue relates to

a prototype which the doctors have seen at a previous workshop. On other occasions, the issue considered has been raised at a previous workshop or during observations and discussions with the doctors outside the formal workshops. Examples of the specific issues discussed are:

• the flow of the consultation;

• what data needs to be entered at each stage of the consultation;

• the degree to which the information presented needs to depend on the context in which it is to be used.

Each doctor is expected to spend at least one paid session before each workshop preparing material and ideas. Frequently, the doctors find it convenient to demonstrate their ideas in the form of screen scenarios created on overhead transparencies. On other occasions, particularly when they are working on the details of the information required in particular areas, they find it more helpful to prepare handouts to be circulated to their colleagues prior to the workshop.

The requirements analysis and design workshops are led by the medical member of the development team and attended by the inner circle doctors, the development team, and the evaluation team. Each workshop consists of a two hour discussion in which the doctors discuss the issue in question with the occasional participation of members of the development and evaluation teams. In many sessions, the development team spend a significant amount of time checking their conclusions with the doctors. The normal outcome of a workshop is a commitment from the development team to prepare additional material or prototypes. Frequently, there is also a commitment from the doctors to prepare more material for a subsequent workshop.

The Formative Evaluation Workshops
The formative evaluation workshops follow a much more standardised format. They are led by the evaluation team and involve doctors from both the inner and outer circles. Some of the workshops also include one or two 'naive' doctors who have not seen the system before. A fundamental principle of the formative evaluation workshops is that the workshops are 'owned' by the evaluators and the users, not the developers. At each workshop, the schedule of events is similar. After a brief introduction, the new prototype is demonstrated by a member of the development team. The doctors are then divided into pairs, and a member of the development team and an observer from the evaluation team are assigned to each pair of doctors. Each pair of doctors is provided with specific 'training tasks' designed to familiarize them with the features of the system. Some doctors choose to perform the tasks quite literally, others use them merely as a starting point for a more general exploration.

The doctors are then given specific 'evaluation tasks' to perform. In almost all cases, these tasks are in the form of role–playing exercises in which one user takes the role of "patient" and the other takes the role of "doctor". The "doctor" is asked to use the system in the course of performing a consultation with the "patient". The development team and evaluation team cooperate to prepare scenarios in advance. Experience shows that most doctors are able to improvise the role of patient from very brief vignettes and that the variation which the doctors' different interpretations introduce into the evaluation task provides valuable extra information on how the system might be used in alternative situations.

Following the evaluation tasks, the doctors complete a short questionnaire and structured interview schedule. There is usually, either spontaneously or formally, a brief discussion between the two doctors and the member of the evaluation team. Throughout the training and evaluation tasks, the members of the development team are restricted to providing only 'on line help' in order to let the doctors complete their tasks. Members of the development team are not allowed to discuss the reasons for different features of the design and are not, above all, to argue about whether or not particular features are sensible, easy to use, consistent, or convenient.

Following the completion of the questionnaires, the doctors, development and evaluation teams meet in a group discussion conducted by the leader of the evaluation team. The first part of this discussion is devoted to high level issues concerning the prototype. After the initial discussion, the development team are officially asked to join in, and much of the subsequent discussion consists of a dialogue between the development team and the users concerning the reasoning behind various features. Finally, time permitting, there is a brief 'brain–storming' session to capture any new ideas which might have been stimulated by the day's activities.

Following the workshop, there is a debriefing session for the development and evaluation teams to gather the immediate responses and impressions. Over the next few days, their observations are written up by all members of the development team, and the evaluation team prepare a formal report for the development team. During the subsequent design and evaluation meetings, these results are used to modify the task analysis, user requirements, and design.

RESULTS OF THE USER CENTRED DEVELOPMENT PROCESS

Education of the Development Team:
Formative Evaluation as Process not Product

The most important result of the user centred development process was that the development team came to understand the doctors' problems. This effect is difficult to quantify, but there is unanimous agreement amongst members of the development team that the workshop process has been instrumental in overcoming their misconceptions concerning medical practice and doctors' needs. The workshops are dramatically more effective in achieving this than mere demonstrations, in which the same team frequently take part. Watching users attempt to achieve realistic tasks with the system is a very powerful motivator to remove problems.

The most dramatic example of the development team learning about the users' needs has been the acceptance of the extent of

user variability. Developers inevitably look for the 'best' way to complete a task and become attached to their pet notions. Invariably we have found that some situations, or some users, require an alternative.

The workshops are also effective in keeping the development team focussed on the doctors' priorities—'keeping their feet on the ground'. All development projects have a natural tendency to create their own agendas. Each workshop provides a valuable corrective.

An important concomitant result is that the inner circle of doctors has come to understand the development team's thinking and to understand the prototypes in much more detail than would ordinary users. They are frequently able to offer valuable suggestions which would be impossible for more naive users.

Specific Results

The evaluation workshop produces three types of output:

- 'Micro level' diagnostic comments on particular ergonomic details which need to be fixed. These comments describe the usability of a particular feature with little regard for its context.

- 'Midi level' comments which tend to be comparative. These relate the current implementation of some large subsystem (such as data entry or chart handling) to its previous implementation.

- 'Macro level' comments which assess the impact of the system on the wider medical environment, the likely response of colleagues, patients, and staff, and the likely impact on the quality of care, organisation of the surgery, and relations with mangers and hospital consultants.

Most workshops uncover a number of micro level problems. Where the development team believe that a micro level defect is so severe that the evaluation of the higher levels is invalid, a subsequent informal assessment is held after the fault is fixed, so that the overall evaluation does not have to await the next major workshop[3].

The workshop tasks are designed primarily to elicit midi level comments: these involve the use of the system both to perform these tasks and to navigate within and between them. The outcome of these comments is a further refinement by the development team of its analysis of the task structure of the consultation. Table 1 gives details of some solutions to the micro and midi level problems raised by previous workshops. The structured interviews and subsequent workshop discussion give rise to macro level comments. Overall, these have produced three major results:

- Most doctors liked the systems and say that we seem to be 'on the right track'.

Micro	Midi
Provide 'clear up' button to remove all but master window	Transform 'scratch pad' into 'comment' area on data entry forms
Automatically position collapsed windows	Indicate normal range on the display of numeric data
Improve switching between graphical and tabular charts	Include the number of available results for each item on the menu of results
Employ users' language, e.g. 'tds' instead of 'three per day'	Adopt model of over–inclusiveness in determining content of data entry forms

Table 1: Some changes at the micro and midi level resulting from the formative evaluation workshops.

- There is no one best way. Medical practice is enormously complicated, and users are highly variable. Consequently, systems must be equally flexible.

- Simple clear presentations are often more effective than sophisticated attempts to provide intelligent summaries. Doctors are remarkably good at recognising patterns if the information is clearly presented.

For the development team the most important outcome of the user centred process is the second of these macro level results: the realisation of the range of variability of users and of medical situations. For example, the user centred process made it obvious that some doctors find the use of a mouse difficult, some are well accustomed to keyboards and good typists, and in some situations, typing a short abbreviation is faster than any conceivable search through menus or forms. Without the user centred process, the project would almost certainly have followed its original remit and produced a system which could only be used with a mouse. A prime requirement now is that all functions be equally accessible from the keyboard.

In addition to the macro level results, the development and evaluation team abstracted a series of overall constraints or 'maxims' for the development of the system from the micro and midi level comments. These maxims reflect our understanding of the basic properties which the system must possess to be usable in medical practice. They include items such as:

- The system must always be interruptable. This means that if the user moves his or her hands completely away from the system, it must be in precisely the same state when he or she returns to it. Therefore, for example, all menus pop up and stay up even when the mouse button is released.

- All, or almost all, options should be immediately visible. The use of multi–state buttons and similar 'hidden' options should be minimized.

- Everything on the screen should convey information about the patient being seen. The doctor should never ask for something—e.g. the result of a test—only to discover that it does not exist in the medical record.

- In organising information and forms, it is better to be inclusive than exclusive. Within limits, doctors will happily ignore superfluous items, provided they do not

have to respond to them in any way. (In this way a pointer–based interface which allows free 'random access' to the screen produces very different results from a keyboard based interface in which, for example, a user must use the cursor keys to skip irrelevant items.)

- There should be no 'modes'. All functions should be possible at every stage of the consultation, since the course of the consultation is highly variable and unpredictable.

Interaction with Project Management

One of the most important effects of the iterative user centred process is that the Formative Evaluation Workshops provide absolute deadlines and milestones for the project. The workshops have to be scheduled several months in advance in order to fit into the participants' diaries. Once scheduled, they are virtually immovable. The goals of the prototype might be scaled down, but a working prototype has to be completed by the given date. The Formative Evaluation Workshops are highly public events and provide much harder deadlines than any internal project management process.

PROBLEMS AND LIMITATIONS
Problem Space vs Solution Space: or
"Users are always right... except when they're wrong"

The most serious problem for anyone attempting to involve users actively in software development is how to treat the multitude of requests and ideas which emerge. Users' groups are notorious for generating endless lists of requests, or 'wish–lists', which suppliers cannot hope to meet.

The PEN&PAD approach to this problem is to divide the conceptual space into

- The problem space which is the province of the user. The problem space is concerned with the needs of the users in terms of their *requirements*, the variability that exists in those requirements, and the usability or acceptability of the system, which can only be discovered by evaluating the *use* of the system in a semi–realistic context.

- The solution or design space which is the province of the development team. The solution space is concerned with the creative design *ideas* generated by the developers and the constraints of practicality and feasibility implicit in the *technology* in which those ideas are implemented.

Users are always right about the problem space. If users say they cannot understand something or that they need to do something—e.g. that they do not understand the meaning of command buttons or if they say that they need a 'scratch pad'—then they must be believed[4].

However, users are usually wrong in their suggestions as to how best to meet their needs or remedy a problem. Users' comments are usually concrete and framed in terms of the problem space, whereas a good design solution is likely to be abstract and must be framed in terms of the design space.

The example of the users' request for a 'scratch pad' is illuminating.

The request for a 'scratch pad' was made early in the project and resulted in the addition of a large free–text window to the second prototype. However, in the formative evaluation exercises, the doctors made almost no use of this facility. Furthermore, it was obvious from the doctors' comments that the literal 'scratch pad' did not serve the need that had provoked the request.

We took the topic of the 'scratch pad' as the subject of one of the Requirements Analysis and Design workshops. It rapidly emerged that there were at least three different functions needed:

- A diary or agenda on which the doctor could record reminders—e.g. to telephone a consultant or make arrangements with social services following the surgery.

- A place for private notes which were not part of the patient's official medical record but of which the doctor wished to be reminded, e.g. 'ask about his cat' or 'Remember to thank her for the Christmas card.' The doctors also wanted to use this space for reminders of things which were worrying them but which they did not want to commit to the medical record because they were too tentative.

- A place for completely private, protected, and confidential items which should not appear even in the most secure part of the patient's medical record.

This example of the scratch pad is typical. Repeatedly, users' requests which were superficially simple, turned out to hide a multiplicity of functional requirements. Conversely, it was often possible to meet a large number of requests with a single design feature. The most dramatic example of a single feature eliminating many individual requests was the provision of a 'clear up' button to remove all the windows except that containing the patient summary. Providing the 'clear up' button eliminated the need for most of the other, more complex, features which had been requested for controlling layout and 'clutter'.

Difficulties with the Prototyping Process
The use of prototypes gives rise to a number of intrinsic difficulties. Users and outside observers have difficulty determining which parts of a prototype are 'real' and which are simply well–crafted mock–ups. This frequently leads the users to have unrealistic expectations as to how rapidly a working system can be produced.

More significantly, users find it difficult to distinguish between those features of a prototype which the development team expects to carry through to later versions and those which are merely accidents of the particular prototyping tools being used. The result can be that the users spend much time discussing things of no relevance to the further design of the system.

The most extreme example of this problem occurred at the first Formative Evaluation Workshop in which the logging–on procedure was particularly unintuitive to users not already familiar with the conventions of the development environment. The development team had been aware that this procedure was awkward, but had not thought it important. However, nearly half the discussion time was taken up with comments relating to logging–on to the system and to subsequent difficulties which followed from it. A similar example is the difficulty which many users experience with an optical mouse[5]. Users who have this difficulty must be quickly moved to a machine with a mechanical mouse or their comments will be almost worthless.

The Role of Medical Content
In a similar way, the medical content of the scenarios and the prototypes may cause controversies which obscure the issues that the evaluation and development teams wish to explore. Doctors are naturally more concerned about medical issues than about computing science and arguments about medicine can easily come to dominate the discussion. For example, a workshop intended to explore various alternative presentations of clinical protocols can easily be side–tracked by discussion of the controversy concerning how aggressively moderate high blood pressure should be treated. Wherever possible we have tried to use example scenarios which minimize this type of medical controversy and focus on the use of the system itself.

Lack of Experienced Users
The biggest defect in the user centred strategy is that none of the users ever becomes really expert in using the system. There is an enormous difference between using the system for a few hours during a formative evaluation workshop and using it routinely, several hours per day, five days per week.

DISCUSSION
To date, the medical informatics community has not been notably successful in producing systems which are widely used in routine medical practice. It is all to easy to blame the doctors for these difficulties, adopting an attitude which might be caricatured as 'Pearls before swine'. The alternative explanation for this lack of success is that our systems have rarely actually met medical requirements or been usable in clinical conditions—an attitude which might be caricatured as 'The emperor's new clothes". The second attitude is far more constructive for members of the informatics community, because it leads to important consequences for the development process.

The User Centred Development and Formative Evaluation methodology reported here has been created in an attempt to take the "emperor's new clothes" attitude seriously. PEN&PAD has not yet been used in real medical settings, so we cannot guarantee that the result is a practical system which doctors will use. However, we can say that the User Centred Development process has helped us to avoid a number of serious blunders which would have rendered the eventual system unusable and that the system has been enthusiastically received in all of our simulations and demonstrations to date. The next step is to put more advanced prototypes into the field and observe how they are used.

The Formative Evaluation Workshops have also been used as part of two European collaborative projects, EURODIABETA and PRECISE. In both cases, they were used in isolation to assess systems which were already well advanced in their construction. These experiences confirmed the effectiveness of the simulations in eliciting convincing responses from doctors, but they revealed significant problems in extending the methodology to other sites where it is not part of the culture. Within the project, the development team and evaluation team have negotiated their relationship over the life of the project, and the evaluation team are familiar with the goals and needs of the development team. No such process had taken place with the other projects evaluated during the European projects, and significant conflict arose concerning the remit of the formative evaluation and the goals of the systems being evaluated. Nonetheless, most participants agreed that the process had been helpful and had resulted in important new insights.

What is the key ingredient in the process? The developers are often asked if they could not elicit the same information from simple demonstrations, and they invariably reply emphatically that they could not. The atmosphere and information gathered in the two situations is entirely different. We believe the key ingredient is the formal structure provided by the workshops and the presence of external evaluators. The demonstrations are 'owned' by the development team but the workshops are 'owned' by the users. The fact that workshops are conducted by the evaluators rather than the developers; the fact that the users must actually attempt to use the system for a practical task; and the rule that the developers can only act as 'on line help' combine to create an atmosphere in which users provide much more frank and honest criticism than in demonstrations or less formal settings.

ACKNOWLEDGEMENTS

This research supported in part by grants in the United Kingdom from the Medical Research Council number SPG8800091, from the Department of Health, and from the European Community initiative on Advanced Informatics in Medicine (AIM) as part of the EURODIABETA and PRECISE projects.

FOOTNOTES

[1] The development team are responsible for the design of the clinical and its implementation.

[2] By 1991 approximately 50% of all British general practitioners had a practice computer system according to UK Department of Health sources.

[3] Note that micro level comments are almost always negative. Good micro–ergonomic design is invisible. The team discovered this to its cost when in the first version of the latest prototype, a number of 'minor' ergonomic features were changed, producing a system which was universally disliked by both our regular and 'naive' users until the original micro–ergonomics features could be restored.

[4] As obvious as it seems to say that there is no point in arguing with somebody about whether or not they understand something or find it easy, we have frequently observed developers doing precisely that when users failed to appreciate one of their pet features. Despite the rules that developers were only to act as 'on line help' during the exercises, there were times when they could hardly restrain themselves. Observations of other groups and demonstrations suggest that our group is far from unique. It was our experience with such discussions early in the development of the Formative Evaluation Workshops which led us to institute the rule that developers could only observe during the formal evaluation sessions.

[5] Without exception, all clinical users expressed a preference for the Macintosh mechanical mouse over the Sun optical mouse. Although most users were able to use both, there was a minority of users who found the optical mouse completely unusable.

REFERENCES

1. Teach, R.L., Shortliffe E.H. An analysis of physician attitudes regarding computer based clinical consultation systems. Comp Biomed Res, 1981;14, 542–58.

2. Shortliffe, E.H. Computer Programs to Support Clinical Decision Making. Journal of the American Medical Association, 1987;258, 63–68.

3. Young, D., Chapman, T., and Poile, C. Physician, reveal thyself. British Journal of Healthcare Computing, 1990,7,9,16–21.

4. Howkins, T.J., Kay, S., Goble, C.A. et al. An Overview of the PEN and PAD Projects. In Moore, R.O., Bengtsson, S., Bryant, J.R., and Bryden, J.S., eds. Lecture Notes in Medical Informatics 40, Medical Informatics Europe 90, Glasgow. Berlin, Springer–Verlag, 1990,73–78.

5. Horan, B., Rector, A.L., Sneath, E.L. et al. Supporting a Humanly Impossible Task: The Clinical Human Computer Environment. In Diaper, D., Gilmore, D., Cockton, G., and Shackel, B., eds. Human Computer Interaction— Proceedings of INTERACT'90. Amsterdam, Elsevier Science, 1990,247–252.

6. Monk, A. Fundamentals of Human Computer Interaction. London, Academic Press, 1984.

7. Mumford, E. Designing Human Systems for New Technology: The ETHICS Method. Manchester, Manchester Business School Press, 1983.

8. Norman, D.A., and Draper, S.W. User Centred System Design: New Perspectives on Human Computer Interaction. Hillsdale, New Jersey, Lawrence Erlbaum Associates, 1986.

9. Hewett, T.T. The Role of Iterative Evaluation in Designing Systems for Usability. In Harrison, M.D. and Monk, A.F., eds. People and Computers II: Designing for Usability. Cambridge, Cambridge University Press, 1986, 196–214.

Retrospective on a Year of Participatory Design using the PICTIVE Technique[1]

Michael J. Muller

Bellcore — Room RRC-1H229
444 Hoes Lane
Piscataway NJ 08854 US
+1 908 699 4892
michael@bellcore.com

ABSTRACT

PICTIVE is a participatory design technique for increasing the direct and effective involvement of users and other stakeholders in the design of software. This paper reviews a year of the use of PICTIVE on products and research prototypes at Bellcore. What we have learned is illustrated through five brief case studies. The paper concludes with a summary of our current PICTIVE practice, expressed as three developing, interrelated models: an object model, a process model, and a participation model.

KEYWORDS: Participatory design, graphical user interface (GUI), text-based interface, design methodology, assessment.

INTRODUCTION

The PICTIVE technique was developed at Bellcore in 1990 (Plastic Interface for Collaborative Technology Initiatives through Video Exploration), within the context of participatory design. It uses low-tech, paper and pencil approaches in order to facilitate the direct participation in software design by users who may not be computer literate. It uses video recording techniques for record-keeping, and to simplify the social dynamics of the design session. PICTIVE has been applied on nine products and projects. Our practice of the technique has grown and evolved through use, and through the insights of the people who have used it. The results have been for the most part positive, although we point out a number of caveats in the project descriptions.

We were fortunate in trying to do this work at a time when user centered design (UCD) was experiencing a renaissance at Bellcore (e.g., [4]); thus, participatory design comes into the development process as an early form of UCD. We have also worked to find an interpretation of participatory design that is appropriate for our North American context (e.g., [19]). This combination of factors has led both to considerable grassroots interest on the part of colleagues, and to relatively firm management support [4].

PICTIVE — AN APPROACH TO PARTICIPATORY DESIGN

Most of our work has involved a technique called PICTIVE (Plastic Interface for Collaborative Technology Initiatives through Video Exploration) [21], which was inspired by mock-up techniques on the UTOPIA project [2,3]. It should be noted that PICTIVE is but one of many approaches to participatory design; for others, see [1, 13, 26]. PICTIVE uses low-tech, paper-and-pencil design objects in conjunction with high(er)-tech video recording. The intent is to provide a non-software-based "rapid prototyping" environment of common office objects, which can be manipulated on an *equal-opportunity basis* by all members of a design team — programmers and non-programmers alike. Typically, these objects include colored pens, scissors, and more specialized representations of user interface objects (windows, menus, icons, etc.). The members of the design team serve as *peer co-designers* and bring their various issues to this common design environment. When the technique works well, the session proceeds as a sort of informal group brainstorming session, through the "mutual validation of diverse perspectives" advocated by Bodker et al [3], without any particular party driving or controlling the session [18].

The PICTIVE object model, process model, and participation model were derived through experiences in applying the technique to specific products and projects. Details of these models will be provided after the case studies on which they are based.

---

1. This paper is based on a position paper at the 1991 ACM Computer-Human Interaction (CHI) conference's workshop, *Participatory Design: Practical Stories and Stories of Practice* [20].

CASE STUDY SYNOPSES
This section of the paper reviews selected projects on which we have used PICTIVE, and what we have learned from them.

Project Management Groupware
The Project Management Groupware (PMG) project was our first experiment with participatory design. The goal was to build an experimental research prototype using an experimental AI software environment [6,32] to support the project planning and project management needs of knowledge workers who were independently writing interrelated and interdependent documents. Our initial design experiences were highly positive: the users were enthusiastic about using paper-and-pencil techniques to express their needs and ideas, and the human factors workers believed that they had found a new means for obtaining requirements information. We reported our design as a success story [25].

Later, we discovered several limitations of what we had done. The most important problem was the poor transfer of the system concept from the design sessions to the developer of the research prototype. This occurred because the developer was not involved in the participatory design sessions. Our initial hope — that the video records would serve as a simple video design document — also turned out to be naive: the design sessions produced over a dozen hours of videotape, and the developer simply didn't have the time to comb through those records to collect information for implementation.[2]

A second weakness — and this was compounded by the absence of the developer — was our initially poor understanding of a process model for this type of participatory design activity. The sessions tended to approve any suggestion that the users made. This turned out to present significant problems to the developer, whose experimental environment did not have the functionality to support certain design options preferred by the users. If the developer had been part of the PICTIVE session, s/he could have initiated a discussion of design alternatives that were more technologically feasible, and perhaps could have led users to new technology-based capabilities that might have enhanced the workplace value of the target system.

Graphical User Interface Re-Design of a Text-Based Interface
In a second project, we made fewer and different errors. This was a graphical re-design of a text-based system. The PICTIVE sessions for this project were actually conducted by the developer, thus obviating some of the most salient mistakes of the PMG project. A more diverse group of participants was

---

2. Reviewers of PICTIVE video records have commented that it is sometimes difficult to understand who is talking about what, because there are sometimes many voices and occasionally two parallel conversations. This is especially difficult if the reviewer was not present during the recording session. We speculate that stereophonic recordings of the audio portion of the video may provide spatial cues to help in this task, but we have not yet tried the experiment.

involved, including the developer, a user, a graphical analyst, a marketer, and a human factors worker.

The design effort was a success: all the participants believed that they had had the opportunity to express themselves, and that they had collaboratively solved their problems. The resulting research prototype in fact worked fairly well. However, the users were somewhat disappointed with certain technological attributes, leading to another design and implementation iteration.

The problem appeared to center on miscommunications regarding the implementation technology. Several members of the design team were accustomed to "dumb" terminal technology, whereas other members' mental models were the X-Windows™ system. The result was undetected miscommunication about certain of the dynamics of the target environment, and consequent mismatch of expectations about a few features of what was to be built. The lesson that we learned from this experience was that the developer's (or technologist's) role in PICTIVE is to provide a detailed understanding of the technology. This level of detail may be difficult to achieve by paper-and-pencil techniques.

Facilities Allocation System
The problem of technology explication appears to have been solved in work on a facilities allocation system product, called FLEXCOM/linc.™ Participatory design of a portion of FLEXCOM/linc was preceded by a design walk-through based on a partially implemented prototype [24]. Thus, by the time that the PICTIVE session began, the users had undergone a 45-minute tutorial on the target technology. These PICTIVE sessions usually involved two users, a developer, a marketer, and one or more human factors workers.

One notable aspect of these sessions was that they contradicted assumptions about users as Luddites. That is, it is often thought that users are conservative, and tend to resist new technologies (e.g., [14]). However, our experience was the opposite: in fact, the users and the marketers urged the developers to take full advantage of the sophisticated capabilities of the target windowing environment, and found novel applications of this environment to meet detailed user-initiated design requests. This suggests that the design walk-through had adequately communicated the developer's technology ideas, supporting a richer interaction to meet the users' needs. However, these provisional conclusions will have to be re-examined in late 1991, when the product is subjected to full usability testing.

Classroom and Workshop Use
PICTIVE has been used in two classroom settings. The *Practicum in Methods for User Centered Design* [36] teaches a number of methods, including PICTIVE as its representative case for participatory design. PICTIVE has also been used in

---

X-Windows is a trademark of MIT.
FLEXCOM is a trademark of Bellcore.

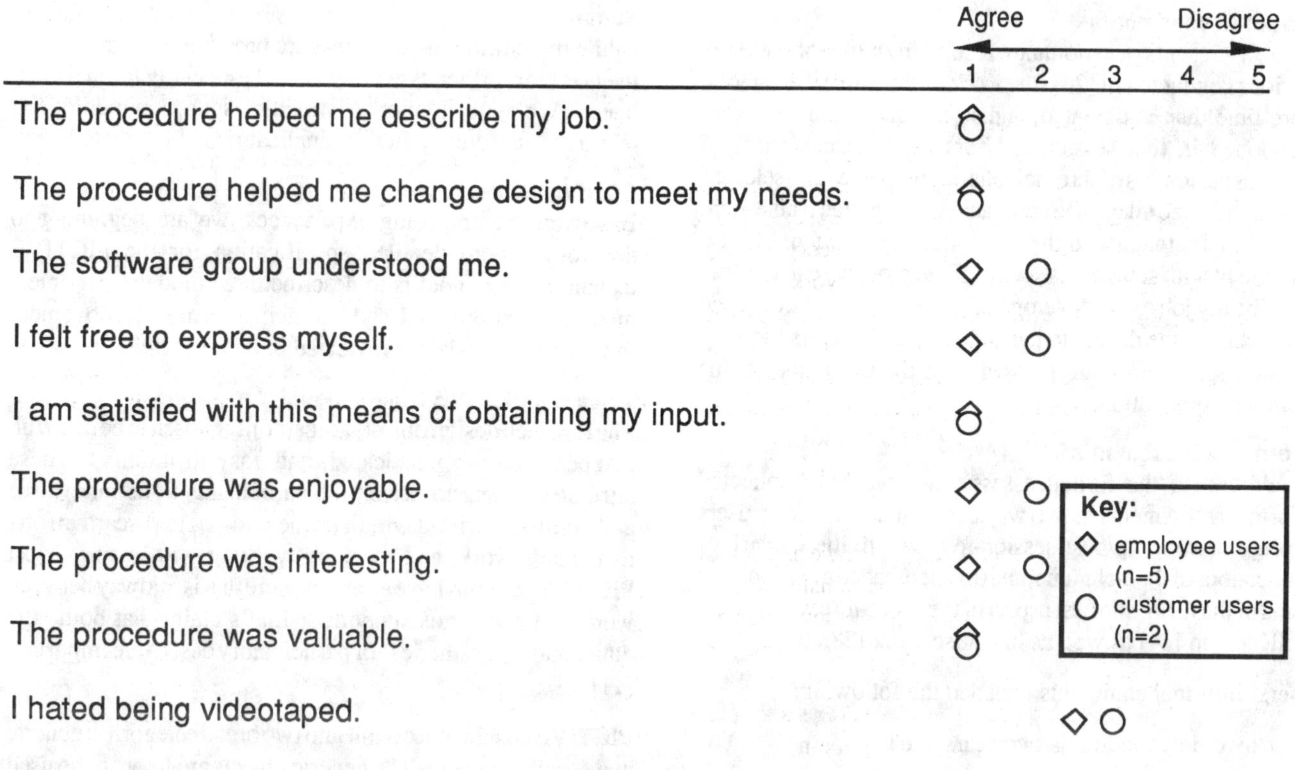

	Agree				Disagree
	1	2	3	4	5

The procedure helped me describe my job.

The procedure helped me change design to meet my needs.

The software group understood me.

I felt free to express myself.

I am satisfied with this means of obtaining my input.

The procedure was enjoyable.

The procedure was interesting.

The procedure was valuable.

I hated being videotaped.

Key:
◇ employee users (n=5)
○ customer users (n=2)

Figure 1. Formal assessments of PICTIVE.

a tutorial workshop on graphical user interface design [28] with the goals of (a) teaching an approach to GUI design, (b) familiarizing the participants with the *OSF/Motif™ Style Guide* [30], and (c) exploring the adequacy of the *Style Guide* to meet certain classes of business needs. Both classroom uses led to the same lesson about PICTIVE practice: There should be a clear decision about how specified the requirements are before the PICTIVE session is begun. With a detailed specification, PICTIVE can be used immediately to begin collaborative design. With a high-level specification, the session often becomes an extended requirements analysis instead. Of course, requirements analysis is also quite valuable. We conclude that the point is not to discourage concretized requirements analysis, but simply know what sort of result or outcome is desired, and to structure the methodology, materials, and process according to the desired outcome.

World of Intelligent Tutoring Systems (WITS)
One other problem surfaced when PICTIVE was applied to a research prototype in the World of Intelligent Tutoring Systems (WITS) project (an earlier report of this project appeared in [31]; see also [23]). PICTIVE was used in this context as a knowledge acquisition tool. Following fairly standard expert system paradigms, the researchers asked their domain expert to use PICTIVE in order to explain how the tutoring software should support the authoring and teaching of curricula. The problem in this case was that the eventual end-users of the

OSF/Motif is a trademark of Open Software Foundation.

system — i.e., the non-expert authors and students — had less of a direct role in the design activities. The system, in fact, failed to meet their needs and expectations in certain respects. This outcome is not surprising in view of the standard user centered design principle of *Know Thy User* [15, 29, 36]. Nonetheless, it may be necessary to point out that PICTIVE is not particularly useful if the actual users of the system are not involved!

Other Projects
It should be noted, in passing, that PICTIVE has proven useful on several other projects. Their breadth may help to indicate the utility of participatory design for different human-computer interface media. As noted above, PICTIVE has been used for graphical and text-based interfaces. It has also worked well to re-design a printed report — i.e., a form of uni-directional, non-interactive user interface for certain repair situations. PICTIVE has also been used on a highly iconic research prototype that provides a form of executable organizational memory.

ASSESSMENTS OF PICTIVE
We have tended to use PICTIVE in applied settings, in order to get a job done for a practical product. This has had an adverse effect upon formal assessments of the technique: The pressures of doing applied work on a limited schedule in the field sometimes worked against the goal of collecting detailed assessment data. Therefore, our assessment is limited at present.

Formal Assessments

Figure 1 presents questionnaire results from two of the three sessions conducted in [24] (the work of the third session took more time than anticipated, and so the questionnaires were abandoned in that session). Users (i.e., selected staff of business customers of three telephone companies and selected staff of the three telephone companies) completed a nine-item questionnaire that asked them to indicate the extent of their agreement with statements such as "The procedure helped me describe my job to the developers," or "The procedure helped me to change the design to meet my needs," etc. As Figure 1 shows, users were quite pleased with the technique in this particular application.

Informal Assessments

In addition to the formal assessments, we have collected informal assessments in two ways: (a) remarks made by users during summing-up/post-session-review activities of various applications of the technique, and (b) open-ended questionnaire items of the form "the best aspect of the procedure was _____" (collected in [24] as well as in course work [28, 36]).

Users' informal comments included the following:

○ Why didn't we do this two years ago?

○ [The best aspect of the procedure was] the freedom to change what was best for my job function.

○ [The best aspect of the procedure was] being asked for input on something that is to be used, rather than being told.

○ I felt that you were really listening to me.

○ I'd like to do this again!

○ Not enough time [in the mixture of design review and PICTIVE].

The informal assessment approach also allowed us to record the views of software professionals (developers, designs, and analysts). The following comments are representative of their responses:

○ We found out things that we never would have discovered otherwise.

○ [PICTIVE] allowed for ideas to be shown more explicitly than conversation alone, with very little expense in terms of preparation time.

○ That certainly opened my eyes!

○ It was difficult to stay on the subject.

○ Participatory design won't help you if you ask the wrong users!

○ [PICTIVE was the most highly rated part of a highly rated course on User Centered Design]

Summary

While these initial assessments are promising, we recognize the need for further assessments, and especially more formal ones. We will attempt to structure such methodological research into future practical applications of the technique.

CONCLUSION

Based on the preceding experiences, we are beginning to develop a more detailed specification for the PICTIVE technique. The goal is to describe three models: an object model, a process model, and a participation model. Movement toward those models is reviewed in this section.

Toward a PICTIVE Object Model

The low-tech design objects are carefully chosen to be colorful, inexpensive, unsophisticated, and easy to modify. These attributes appear to permit the participants to be innovative and confident with them, to try new ideas, to discard efforts that didn't work, and to enjoy working with them. Most PICTIVE sessions have an atmosphere that is midway between work and play, thus supporting Ehn's claim that both "the ethics and the aesthetics" of participatory design are important [11].

PICTIVE design objects fall into two broad categories: generic and specific objects. The generic objects are likely to be used in most exercises. These include colored pens in blues, greens, and earth tones, with relatively little use made of black, and with red and yellow reserved for specific semantics such as warnings and errors (based on Crane's rationale for the use of colors [8]). Colored papers are used for data fields, menus, windows, and the like, as well as for full-screen displays; in general, the papers should use pastels, while the pens should use fully saturated colors, to insure a clean video record of the session.[3] When possible, the colored papers are made of removable labels, or are affixed to the design surface with removable tape. Scissors should be available to customize the generic objects.

Specific objects are usually constructed in advance to meet the needs or constraints of the users' jobs and tasks, or of the implementation environment. These may include icons for particular work-based entities, pop-up events for work-oriented operations, or an interface style based on a particular environment (e.g., in [28], we based our specific objects on the OSF/Motif Style Guide). It is important for the developers or designers to realize that even these specific objects are likely to be changed in the course of the group's work.

Toward a PICTIVE Process Model

In addition to the physical model of PICTIVE (low-tech objects, etc.), there is also an emerging process model. Ideally, each participant carries out a "homework assignment" prior to the session. For the users, this is often to prepare a step-by-step walkthrough of one or more important job tasks or usage scenarios that they want the system to support. For the

---

3. In our experience, colored pencils fail to make high-contrast lines, and are therefore difficult to read on video records.

developers or designers, this usually takes the form of preparing paper-and-pencil versions of certain system functionality — e.g., a starting set of icons, or some templates of windows or dialogue boxes that correspond (a) to the target environment, and (b) to the developers/designers' current understanding of the users' needs. Other participants are asked to prepare materials or concepts that are appropriate to their domains of expertise.

The session begins with a review and introduction to the homework assignments which have been prepared by the various participants. This familiarizes each participant with the others' viewpoints, and it helps to make each participant aware of the personal stake of each of the other participants. This in turn helps people to work to meet each others' needs.

The users' work scenarios are then explored in detail, leading to a discussion of how the developers' technology can be applied to meet the users' human needs. Other participants introduce their needs into the discussion (e.g., designing for testability, designing for marketability, etc.).

The attributes of the emerging process model are as follows:

Reciprocal Education. Each participant has the responsibility to explain her or his perspective, personal stakes, and competence to the other participants.

Reciprocal Preparation. These explanations are most easily done if each participant prepares for the session — e.g., the developer might bring a working, general example of a new technology, the human factors worker might bring paper-and-pencil components of the system, and the user might bring step-by-step scenarios of use.

Reciprocal Validation. The purpose of the session is not for all participants to be convinced of one world view or one vocabulary, but for each participant to understand and give credence to the points of view and vocabularies of the other participants. This permits the participants to collaborate across disciplinary and organizational boundaries through mutual understanding, while nonetheless remaining faithful to their own experiences, personal stakes, and workplace realities, as well as to the other people whom they represent.

Concretized Visual Communication. PICTIVE participants are engaged in the task of making their views and needs clear to one another. Our experience has been that this goal is facilitated by the use of concrete examples, depicted visually. In the case study involving printed reports, we found that an apparent impasse between two groups of users, based on one group's highly abstract analysis, became trivially easy to reconcile once the abstractions were translated into visual terms. For details on the strengths of concrete visual communications, see, e.g., [7, 8, 17, 27, 35].

Checking In. Because the purpose of the session is to hear the views and perspectives of all the people in the group, the participants usually develop a pattern of making sure that no one is being left out or ignored.

Emergent Designs. Often, the design becomes something that none of the participants initially envisioned, through the combination of expertises and perspectives that were, as a set, unavailable to any single participant.

Consensus Decision-Making. The emergence of new design ideas that contain multiple contributions helps to move the group away from entrenched positions. Often, decisions are made by consensus rather than by voting or other approaches that might disenfranchise the minority.

In most PICTIVE sessions, ideas expressed on the design surface are captured on the video recording, for use in interpretation and implementation. This has several benefits. Most obviously, it preserves a record not only of the static layout of design elements, but also of the intended dynamic behaviors of those elements during use. Second, the recording of the discussions surrounding the design provides an informal design rationale that can be of some use in attempting to reconstruct the purpose of certain design decisions. While we initially feared that video recording would have an inhibitory social effect, we discovered exactly the opposite. Because a video record is kept, there is no need for one participant to take the role of a formal record-keeper. This permits the participants to work together, without imposing a social distance between "designers" and "recorder," or between "subjects" and "researcher."

Toward a PICTIVE Participation Model

One of the early challenges that we faced was to find a place for participatory design in a North American corporate context. As noted by Grudin [14], participatory design is more difficult to accomplish outside of the Scandinavian countries because of differences in legislative environment, workplace unionization, and scale and fragmentation of software development organizational models. This section of the paper takes up three convergent motivations and justifications to support of broad participation in the design process.

We believe that participatory design has specific advantages in terms of relatively delimited and (as Floyd [12] has termed them) product-oriented business motivations. Participatory design can help to leverage all the available expertise to improve product quality and market share [22]. Participatory design can also help to increase commitment to the product or project [16], through the involvement of the customers and the "downstream" software development staff.

Expertise. An analysis of the "leveraging expertise" argument leads to the inclusion of a diverse group of professionals. Quality products are based on diverse knowledge and expertise — of technology, of design principles, and of the users' actual jobs and needs. Quality products should also be designed for complete testability, and should be created in a way that makes them easy to explain in documentation or in training courses, and easy to present to potential customers at the point of sale.

Thus, the expertise of developers, users, and human factors workers should potentially be augmented by the expertise of testers, trainers, technical writers, and marketers.

Commitment and Buy-In. Similarly, products tend to be more successful if they receive the commitment of all the people involved in their implementation and use. Certainly the commitment of the customers to the product is desirable. Carter provides evidence that an increase in customer commitment through participation in design activities can lead to increased willingness of customers to try out new technology features [5]. Thus, participatory design can be valuable not only in shaping the technology to the users' needs, but also in persuading the user to be willing to give the technology a try.

In addition, the inclusion of other professionals in the development process — i.e., the testers, technical writers, marketers, and so on, referred to above — can help to increase their commitment. If they participate in the design of the product, they are more likely to view the results as something in which they share ownership. Participation can help to make the product more understandable to all of the production staff as they work on it, and can help them to know how to work together on it, supporting models of shared success [9].

Of course, commitment by the customers and other colleagues must be earned and justified through the commitment of the PICTIVE practitioner to be responsive to those partners. This leads to a third consideration in the participation model:

Stakeholders and Workplace Democracy. The preceding discussions used arguments based on expertise and commitment to justify the inclusion of diverse personnel or roles in the design process. Participation by these same personnel or roles is suggested by the Scandinavian themes of workplace democracy through participatory design [1].[4] One way that we have explicated the workplace democracy theme in terms of our own US history and context is: *no mechanization without representation* [18]. This may be expanded as follows: The people who will be affected by a software system should participate in decisions regarding that system [1, 10, 13, 19, 26].

In one sense, this is simply a restatement of the notion of user centered design. The users receive the most obvious impact of the system, and a commitment to non-exploitative approaches (e.g., [33, 34]) requires their direct participation in the design of that system, rather than an indirect protocol through which requirements analysts attempt to serve as intermediaries. According to this argument, users are among the primary stakeholders of the system, and human factors

workers help them to achieve their goals as stakeholders.

However, there are other workers who may also be understood as stakeholders in the system, because their careers are also affected by the product: developers, technical writers, trainers, marketers, and testers. In this light, human factors workers may be seen as stakeholders, too (rather than simply as agents of the users), because their own careers are affected. Thus, a broad interpretation of participatory design, based in US software engineering practice, provides for the possibility that representatives of some or all of these personnel might also be direct participants in design decisions.

In this way, we support the inclusive nature of participatory design through three different but convergent motivations: product quality (inclusion of expertise), product commitment, and workplace democracy. Maintaining the convergence of these three motivations will be a key requirement for the continued usefulness and success of participatory design in our workplace.

ACKNOWLEDGMENTS
Kathy Cebulka and Tom Dayton have generously given their comments on their use of PICTIVE for the graphical re-design project. Terry Tavener provided the opportunity to work on the printed report project. Rob Farrell and Larry Lefkowitz provided the opportunity to work on WITS. Connie Kaye and John Sauer collaborated on the facilities allocation system work. Todd Moyer and Gary Levin provided the opportunity to work on the executable organizational memory project.

I thank Elizabeth Dykstra for pointing out the importance of a process model as a component of PICTIVE.

I make special and on-going thanks to Danny Wildman and Ellen White, who offered to include PICTIVE in our *Practicum* when it was a largely untried technique. The following people have contributed to an understanding of PICTIVE and participatory design in our context: Jeanette Blomberg, Sara Bly, Rita Bush, Robert Carasik, Kathy Cebulka, Tom Dayton, Elizabeth Dykstra, Shu Hsi, Kari Thoresen, Ellen White, and Danny Wildman.

Finally, I thank Susan Hornstein and Danny Wildman for careful review of this document, and anonymous reviewers for their advice regarding clarity of explication.

REFERENCES
1. Bjerknes, G., Ehn, P., and Kyng, M. (Eds.) (1987). *Computers and Democracy: A Scandinavian Challenge.* Brookfield, VT: Gower.

2. Bodker, S., Ehn, P., Kammersgaard, J., Kyng, M., and Sundblad, Y. (1987). A UTOPIAN Experience: On Design of Powerful Computer-Based Tools for Skilled Graphic Workers. In Bjerknes, G., Ehn, P., and Kyng, M. (Eds.), *Computers and Democracy: A Scandinavian Challenge.* Brookfield, VT: Gower.

---

4. As Winner notes [36], a social motivation that is pursued obliquely or through subtle means may never be articulated. If left unsaid, such a motivation may *become unsayable,* and may thus be forced further into the closet. We have therefore continued to state the democratic nature and motivation of the approach.

3. Bodker, S., Ehn, P., Knudsen, J., Kyng, M., and Madsen, K. (1988). Computer support for cooperative design. In *CSCW88: Proceedings of the Conference on Computer-Supported Cooperative Work*. Portland OR: ACM, 377-393.

4. Bush, R.M. (1992). The Human Computer Technology Group at Bellcore: Laboratory Overview. In *Proceedings of CHI'92*. ACM: Monterey CA.

5. Carter, K. (1991). Participatory Design Work at Rank Xerox Cambridge EuroPARC. Position paper at CHI'91 workshop, *Participatory Design: Practical Stories and Stories of Practice*. CHI'91 meeting, New Orleans LA, 29 April 1991.

6. Cebulka, K.D. (1990b). WISE: An Intelligent Interface for User Modification of Applications. In *Proceedings of 1990 IEEE International Conference on Systems, Man, and Cybernetics*. Los Angeles CA: IEEE Press, 637-639.

7. Crane, D. (1991). Changing the "Demand" for Participatory Design. Position paper at CHI'91 workshop, *Participatory Design: Practical Stories and Stories of Practice*. CHI'91 meeting, New Orleans LA, 29 April 1991.

8. Crane, D. (1990). Workshop on Graphic Recording in Systems Design. In *PDC'90: Conference on Participatory Design*. Seattle WA: Computer Professionals for Social Responsibility, 95-98.

9. Dray, S. (1991). A Sampling of Participatory Strategies at IDS Financial Services. Position paper at CHI'91 workshop, *Participatory Design: Practical Stories and Stories of Practice*. CHI'91 meeting, New Orleans LA, 29 April 1991.

10. Ehn, P. (1988). *Work-Oriented Design of Computer Artifacts*. Stockholm: Arbetslivcentrum.

11. Ehn, P. (1990). Strategies and Tools for Participatory Design. Presentation at PDC'90: Participatory Design Conference, Seattle WA.

12. Floyd, C. (1987). Outline of a paradigm change in software engineering. In Bjerknes, G., Ehn, P., and Kyng, M. (Eds.). *Computers and Democracy: A Scandinavian Challenge*. Brookfield, VT: Gower.

13. Greenbaum, J., and Kyng, M. (1991). *Design at Work.: Cooperative Design of Computer Systems*. Hillsdale NJ: Erlbaum.

14. Grudin, J. (1990). Obstacles to Participatory Design in Large Product Development Organizations. In *PDC'90: Conference on Participatory Design*. Seattle WA: Computer Professionals for Social Responsibility.

15. Helander, M. (Ed.) (1988). *Handbook of Human-Computer Interaction*. Amsterdam: North-Holland.

16. Kvavik, K. (1991). Effecting Buy-In from Participants — Technology Transfer and its Spread. Position paper at CHI'91 workshop, *Participatory Design: Practical Stories and Stories of Practice*. CHI'91 meeting, New Orleans LA, 29 April 1991.

17. McKim, R. (1972). *Experiences in Visual Thinking*. Monterey CA: Brooks/Cole.

18. Muller, M.J. (1991a). No Mechanization without Representation: Who Participates in Participatory Design of Large Software Products? In *Reaching Through Technology: Proceedings of CHI'91*. New Orleans LA: ACM, 391.

19. Muller, M.J. (1991b). Panel: Participatory Design in Britain and North America: Responses to the "Scandinavian Challenge." (chair). In *Reaching Through Technology: Proceedings of CHI'91*. New Orleans LA: ACM, 389-392.

20. Muller, M.J. (1991c). Participatory Design: Practical Stories and Stories of Practice (Workshop). In *Reaching Through Technology: Proceedings of CHI'91*. New Orleans LA: ACM, 501.

21. Muller, M.J. (1991d). PICTIVE — An Exploration in Participatory Design. In *Reaching Through Technology: Proceedings of CHI'91*. New Orleans LA: ACM, 225-231.

22. Muller, M.J., and Cebulka, K.D. (1990). Software Professionals in the Year 2000: Technologies to Support an Enhanced Social Communications Fabric. In *Proceedings of National Communications Forum*, **44**. Chicago: Professional Education International.

23. Muller, M.J., Farrell, R., Cebulka, K.D., and Smith, J.G. (1991). Issues in the Usability of Time-Varying Multimedia. Chapter to appear in Blattner, M. and Danenberg, R. (Eds), *Interactive Multimedia Computing*, in press.

24. Muller, M.J., Kaye, C., and Sauer, J.E. Jr. (1991). Case Study of Transformation of Screen Layout and Dynamics through Participatory Design. Poster at 1991 meeting of the Human Factors Society, San Francisco CA, 4 September 1991.

25. Muller, M.J., Smith, J.G., Shoher, J.Z., and Goldberg, H. (1990). Privacy, Anonymity, and Interpersonal Competition Issues Identified during Participatory Design of Project Management Groupware. *SIGCHI Bulletin*, **23**(1), 82-87 (January 1991).

26. Namioka, A., and Schuler, D. (Eds.) (1990). *PDC'90: Conference on Participatory Design.* Seattle WA: Computer Professionals for Social Responsibility.

27. Nelms, H. (1957). *Thinking with a Pencil.* Berkeley CA: Ten Speed Press.

28. Nielsen, J., Bush, R.M., Dayton, J.T., Mond, N.E., Muller, M.J., and Root, R.W. (1992). In *Proceedings of CHI'92.* ACM: Monterey CA.

29. Norman, D.A. (1988). *The Psychology of Everyday Things.* New York: Basic Books.

30. Open Software Foundation (1991). *OSF/Motif Style Guide, Revision 1.1.* Engelwood Cliffs NJ: Prentice Hall.

31. Silverstein, G., Farrell, R., and Smith, J.G. (1990). Integrating Multiple Instructional Paradigms in Industrial Training Applications. In *Proceedings of AAAI Workshop on Knowledge-based Environments for Learning and Teaching.*

32. Smith, J.G., and Cebulka, K.D. (1990). A Framework for Intelligent Interfaces. Poster at CHI'90.

33. Thoresen, K. (1990a). Prototyping Organizational Changes. In *PDC'90: Conference on Participatory Design.* Seattle WA: Computer Professionals for Social Responsibility, 22-33.

34. Thoresen, K. (1990b). Statement for Participatory Design of Computer Systems (Panel). In *Empowering People: CHI'90 Conference Proceedings.* Seattle WA: ACM, 144.

35. Verplank, W. (1990). *Graphical Invention for User Interfaces.* Tutorial presented at Empowering People: CHI'90, Seattle WA, April 1990.

36. White, E.A., Wildman, D.M., and Muller, M.J. (1989). *Practicum in Methods for User Centered Design.* Tutorial presented at Human Factors Society Annual Meeting, September 1991.

37. Winner, L. (1986). *The Whale and the Reactor: A Search for Limits in an Age of High Technology.* Chicago: University of Chicago Press.

EVOLVING TASK ORIENTED SYSTEMS

Paul Seaton and Tom Stewart

System Concepts
Museum House
Museum Street
London, WC1A 1JT
tel +44 71 636 5912
email Tom_Stewart@Hicom.LUT.AC.UK

ABSTRACT

This paper describes an approach to developing systems which can be summarised as 'analyse top-down, design middle-out, and build bottom-up'. A case study is described in which this approach is used to develop a system to support staff who select new products for a major UK company. The novelty of the approach lies in its use of task analysis to define an appropriate domain for the system and then the use of a working prototype to grow a system from the bottom up. The project involved using simple development tools which allowed the users to start getting business benefit from the system right from the start. Their use could therefore develop as the system evolved.

KEYWORDS: Task Analysis, Prototyping, User Involvement, Design Methods, Evolutionary Design, Bottom-up Methods, Graphical Interfaces

1.0 INTRODUCTION

Our client is a major UK organisation with over 200 retail outlets in the UK and an increasing number worldwide. It is highly centralised with the London-based head office responsible for selecting and buying all merchandise. Within head office the Departments are organised according to groups of products, covering a very diverse range. Mainframe computer systems are a vital part of the buying process, with facilities for monitoring sales, estimating and placing orders with suppliers, but there is a growing recognition, as in so many organisations, that current systems development techniques are failing to deliver the business benefits expected. The systems which are developed are often late, over budget and difficult to use.

Traditional systems analysis techniques have been effective for specifying the functional requirements for new systems, but they have been criticised for placing insufficient emphasis on the usability of the resulting systems.

Other system development approaches have been tried which encourage greater user involvement in system specification and development. However, this has not always been successful. Insufficient analysis early-on in the development process has resulted in system specifications evolving in an ad hoc and sometimes uncontrolled way. Prototypes and demonstration systems have been developed to reflect the preferences of some users without sufficient attention to the technical feasibility or costs associated with full scale implementation.

Putting it another way, analysis-driven designs have tended to be unusable whereas user-driven designs have been unbuildable. To make matters worse, staff in head office User Departments are making increasing use of spreadsheets and other PC tools and are becoming critical of the limitations of the mainframe systems and the outdated style of interface. The scale of development required for mainframe systems prevents them from being sufficiently flexible to reflect the changing commercial priorities of the User Departments. Much of the information used by the User Departments is held on spreadsheets and other PC packages. Up until now these systems have been viewed by the Information Technology Department (IT) as distinctly separate from mainstream systems development.

What is required is a method for developing systems which combines the business benefits of increased usability with the efficiency benefits of more ordered development and better engineered systems.

1.1 The Need for a New Approach

The above problems are wasteful of resource and represent a major lost opportunity. Better usability could allow managers to use the systems directly instead of through intermediaries and assistants, saving staff costs. But experience in other organisations shows that allowing managers to drive systems themselves has significant benefits in helping them to understand the business better and make far more effective use of the information provided. However, this requires much more than just a 'friendly' or 'pretty' interface. It requires that the user interface as well as the functionality of the system is matched to the real business tasks of the users.

Tasks in this sense are defined in business terms not system operation terms. Thus 'estimate sales' is a business task whereas 'update an amend estimate screen' is not. It is simply a means to an end.

Ideally, therefore, a task oriented interface reflects an understanding of the steps, options and requirements for performing the business task. Using well-designed task-oriented software is not only efficient, it is also satisfying. At every stage, the choices available in menus or other navigation match the real decisions. The right options fall easily to hand. The system is intelligent and makes sensible assumptions, based on previous actions. The defaults are sensible guesses and more often right than not. Even when the task is novel, the interface allows the users to reach exactly the information or the choices they require, although perhaps not quite so quickly or so elegantly as in the frequent tasks.

However the task-oriented development approach is in its infancy and there are major risks in rushing into new and untried methods of working. We therefore decided to gain real experience of its use in a limited trial development of an exemplar system before considering scaling up the approach to other areas.

1.2 Creating an Exemplar Task-Oriented System

In choosing the exemplar, we wished to ensure that the task area selected was important for User Departments. However, because we ultimately wanted to change the working practices and the attitudes of designers as well as users, it was important that we did not cut across existing IT activities. There already was a major system design activity adressing the problem of helping buyers (known as merchandisers) to estimate future sales

From early discussions with users in User Departments, the new product development activity emerged as a likely candidate. It is an important task area with little existing IT support. It is currently carried out by staff who are not heavily involved in other IT related activities.

We therefore proposed to develop an exemplar system to support these users in their new product development tasks, to demonstrate the business benefits of a more user centred approach to systems design.

In addition, we believed that:

. A successful system would provide the most powerful illustration of the benefits of a task-oriented interface.

. As a by-product of the development, we would be able to develop usable task analysis techniques and to create the tools necessary to support this approach.

. Since the process required close involvement with the staff in User Departments, our exemplar would demonstrate by example how to involve users in a disciplined way.

. The exemplar would also provide a sound starting point for linking into other areas of buying should the task oriented approach prove beneficial.

. Last, but not least, the exemplar would provide real business benefits to the chosen department, ideally far more than they expected and certainly more than they were promised.

1.3 Assumptions behind the approach

The most important requirement was that we would focus on real tasks. We intended to identify these through task analysis. However, we recognised that one of the dangers of our approach was that the new system would merely mimic the existing working practices. In order to overcome this constraint, we decided to implement a minimal working protoype system. Although this system supported the existing working practises of the users it was also sufficiently flexible to allow these practices to evolve to exploit the full capabilities of the system.

Such 'bottom-up' development helps to ensure that the initial system is useful as well as usable. But it does have the danger that it can be difficult to extend later. To avoid this, we took two important decisions.

First, the task analysis would be performed 'top down' from the departmental level. This would ensure that we could identify tasks which were capable of growth and which were of sufficiently general applicability, ie they are tasks associated with meeting real business requirements rather than operating the existing systems.

Second, the system would be built from a limited set of standard modules to ensure that future growth could be achieved without major redesign. This standardisation included the overall 'look and feel' of the user interface. The modular approach also allowed us to be able to deliver 80% of the users' requirements quickly.

In addition we made it clear that we were not aiming for a 100% solution with the tools we had available. This helped us to manage the user's expectations to a realistic level which proved to be one of the most critical factors in the success of the approach.

We believed that the combination of 'top-down' analysis, middle out design and 'bottom-up' build would give us the best of all worlds.

2.0 ESTABLISHING THE INFRASTRUCTURE

There were two infrastructure components upon which our development depended:

- a user interface standard to serve as a model to guide the growth of the system and which could encompass all the functionality which the system might eventually develop

- a hardware and software platform suitable for immediate applications as well as providing future growth path opportunities

Our inital investigations into this area showed that Microsoft's Windows 3.0 was a suitable vehicle for the provision of a common interface on the IBM PS/2 workstations within User Departments. It is widely accepted across the industry and has an ever increasing portfolio of supporting products, ranging from simple spreadsheet packages to full development environments.

Using a product such as Windows provided us with a Graphical User Interface (GUI) which could potentially encompass all applications within the User Departments. It also provided the basis for a common user interface in that it has its own implied interface standards which are consistent across all its supporting products. Within the Windows framework it is then possible to use further GUIs to front end individual applications and again they adopt the common Windows interface standards. Such a

feature allowed us to remain independent of products and suppliers, allowing new products to be 'plugged in' as and when they become available.

To support the approach a comprehensive in house user interface standard was developed independantly of Windows 3.0 and this ensured the approach could be extened to other technical platforms such as OS/2.

3.0 THE EVOLUTIONARY APPROACH

Some proponents of analysis methods seem to imply that a suitable design emerges almost as a by product of good analysis. We would argue that if this is the case, then it probably means that the analysis was conducted at the wrong level. In other words, the analysis probably focused on potential design solutions rather than on establishing requirements.

No matter how good the analysis method, there is still a vital design activity to create a system which matches these task requirements. If the analysis has been done properly, there will be several design options. The task analysis data may make it obvious that some of these options are more likley to succeed than others but they should still be valid options.

Our priority was to develop a working prototype which provided sufficient functionality and usability to get the users started. One of the key attributes of this approach is that the prototype works from the start ie it delivers value to the users immediately.

Often what are called prototypes are really just demonstrations of 'wouldn't it be nice if' features. These may mislead users about what is realistic and may focus attention on details of presentation or content which are less important than functionality at the early stages.

By providing users with something which works right from the start, we deliberately aimed to focus their attention on task related issues. That is not to say that we ignored their comments on the overall appearance and presentation of the system. First impressions are very important but too many changes can be confusing. Our strategy was to start a process whereby they could evolve a new method of working as the system evolved.

Paradoxically, this places more emphasis on the designers of the prototype understanding the users' real task requirements and anticipating future requirements. Thus the system has to be designed with a degree of 'future proofing' built-in. In practice, this involves adopting a modular approach, paying additonal attention to the maintainability of the design and the code and recognising that some design effort will have to be thrown away as new ideas evolve.

There is no established methodology for developing task-oriented interfaces. Indeed, our own approach evolved during the course of the project. We believe this approach is repeatable and indeed we are currently planning to repeat it for a different application area. We describe it below in its evolved form, which although not final, is sufficiently mature to be useful.

The approach involves the following steps:

. Identify target users and define focus of future system

. Perform Task Analysis

. Agree Scope of working prototype

. Perform Task Modelling

. Perform Task Mapping

. Design working prototype

. Help users to learn through experience

. Manage Change

. Grow system within department

In the following sections, we discuss each of these steps in more detail.

3.1 Identify Target Users and Define Focus

Traditionally it is normal to define a boundary to the system being proposed. With a task oriented approach, this is not appropriate. Until the task analysis has been performed, it is not at all clear where the 'boundary' should be. Indeed, with front end tools such as Easel/Win (a PC based GUI for external databases especially those held on mainframes) it may be unnecessarily restrictive to think in terms of boundaries at all. We therefore identified a focus for our system and left the question of boundary to a much later date.

From our early investigations of User Departments, the New Product Selection Team emerged as a suitable target group for this approach. They play a key role in

new product development and represent a combination of experienced and novice computer users. The staff in the chosen department already used spreadsheets to a limited extent to support their buying activities.

3.2 Perform Task Analysis

Although Task Analysis is an established technique in ergonomics, it has mainly been applied to tasks which have a large physical component eg operating machine tools. Tasks which are primarily mental are much more difficult to analyse not only because almost all the activity is hidden but also because the tasks tend to be ill-structured and involve subtle nuances.

A recent review of task analysis techniques suitable for user interface design carried out by System Concepts had identifed one technique - Hierarchical Task Analysis - as most promising. We therefore used that as our starting point but rapidly found that we had to evolve our own simplified version for it to be effective in a dynamic retail environment.

The main technique used to collect the data involved structured interviews with relevant staff in the User Departments. This enabled us to draw a hierarchy of tasks showing the linkages between the different levels. In this context, a task is an organised sequence of behaviour which is performed by a person or a group of people in order to achieve a business objective.

The first stage in the Task Analysis is to establish the highest level Departmental Tasks. These represent the main mission of the Department as a whole, eg Develop New Product. The next level is the Primary Task. These contribute directly to the business objectives of the Department eg Decide Overall Strategy (for developing a new product).

Below the Primary Task, the secondary task is a task which must be performed in order to perform the primary task eg Establish Lessons Learned (from previous seasons sales figures). Sub-tasks are the lowest level of detail and may be associated with document and screen based information sources and output.

Figure 1 shows the task hierarchy that was adopted throughout the project.

We found that it was important to conduct the analysis from Department Task down to Sub-Task level for the specified area. This helps to ensure that no false assumptions are made during the design phase and that all associated tasks are incorporated in the system.

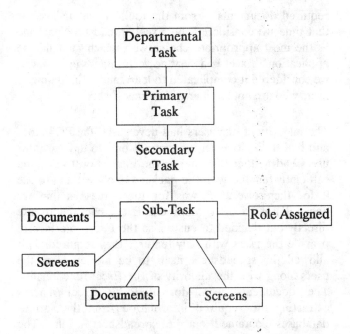

Figure 1 : Task Hierarchy

Figure 2 shows a detailed example of the break down of the Sub-Task : Update Developement Programme.

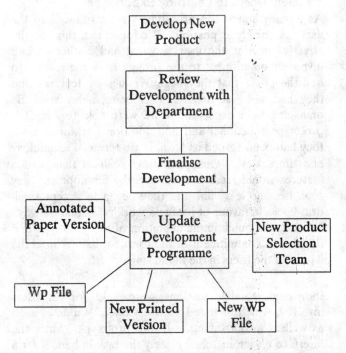

Figure 2 : Task Hierarchy for Sub-Task; Update Development Programme.

These tasks were then further reviewed in order to identify one which would be a suitable target for the working prototype. Ideally this should be a task which is important, which is amenable to computer aid and where improvements in current performance on the task would be important in achieving the departments overall business objectives.

The most suitable candidate was the sub task 'Update Development Programme'. This document formed the basis of the department's information about the characteristics and status of products under development.

3.3 Agree Scope of Working Prototype

The prototype was intended to simplify the maintenance and publishing of the two documents by the provision of a simple 'electronic list' to replace the current manual method. Such a list could form the basis of a different way of working which could help them keep better track of new products and communicate progress within the department.

Each feature of the system was negotiated with the users in terms of timescale to build and the ability of the technology to deliver. This concept was central to our approach in that it allowed us tto quickly provide the users with a working 'prototype/system' that demonstrated its benefit immediately. We therefore had to very carefully manage their expectations of what the system would deliver. By doing this effectively we were able to provide them with the basic system quickly and then use their experiences of using it to 'evolve' the system to better reflect the true user need.

3.4 Perform Task Modelling

Once the Task Analysis had been completed to the Sub-Task level, and the scope of the prototype agreed with the users, then the next stage in the process was to Model the Sub-Task in terms of how it would logically be performed. This process was achieved by the use of a Task Model. This model reflects the Actions and Objects relating to the Sub-Task and should be independent of any pre-conceived view of how the system will function.

Figure 3 shows the Task Model for the Sub-Task Update Development Programme. Subsequent Sub-Tasks can either be incorporated into an existing Task Model or a new Model developed.

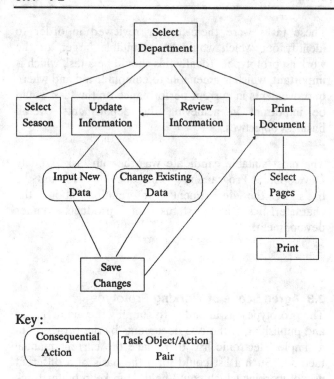

Key :

Figure 3 : Task Model for Sub-Task Update Development Programme. The arrows indicate the sequence in which the Actions are performed. The bottom of each 'column' represents a potential exit point from the dialog.

Both the functionality and the design of the interface are centered around the task model produced. This helps to ensure that the system reflects the tasks performed by the users.

3.5 Perform Task Mapping
The next stage was to map the Task Objects and Actions onto interface objects eg Dialogue Box or Action Bar etc. This required a working knowledge of the In-house User Interface Standards.

Each Task Action/Object pair is taken in turn and the mapping procedure applied to it. The procedure involves establishing the options and rules, (determined from the task analysis and any limitations of the technology being used) and then mapping the Task Action/Objects onto Interface Objects and Controls. Such a process ensures that maximum task orientation is achieved in the specification of the user interface and that the usability factor is maximised.

3.6 Build Working Prototype
Through consultation with the users it was established that the minimum requirement was the provision of a simple 'electronic list' which would allow easy maintainance of the data and automatic generation the

required documents. From the tools at our disposal at that time we considered the Excel spreadsheet package as the most appropriate choice with which to build the application. Excel is a very powerful package however, we considered it complicated to learn and intimidating to users who are not familiar with spreadsheets.

The majority of our users had never used the PC before and had difficulty even switching it on. In any case our users had neither the time or the inclination to become sufficintly familiar with the package to allow them to use it for themselves. It was for these reasons that we decided not to offer them the Excel package to use directly but decided to customise the Excel interface to provide the users with only features they required. This allowed the spreadsheet itself to be hidden from the users along with the majority of the Excel functionality. The documents were formated by Excel macros extracting the required information from the various databases contained on the spreadsheet itself. The update of the database was through an Excel dataform, this had the added advantage of offering the users online reference to the data and it is hoped that with time they will begin to use this facility more often and only produce hard copies when absolutely necessary.

3.7 Help Users to Learn by Experience
As already stated the prototype was introduced to the users as quickly as possible. We found that this had the effect of gaining the users interest and getting a more involved commitment to the project from them. It also had the effect that they began requesting features that they had not at first seen as being necessary. By managing thier expectations we were able to keep the prototype functional and add additional features once they had been agreed as feasible (in terms of technology and timescales). Once the users realised that certain features would mean a more lengthy development they soon became less vital and they began to accept small drawbacks in favour of having a working system quickly. To enable a quick implementation of the prototype and to gain the commitment of the users we had to 'hold the hands' of the users in the initial stages.

Individual training sessions were held for all users involved, which included an overview of Windows itself as well as an introduction to the prototype. Since the interface design matched closely the task in hand after a quick overview of the functions available they soon became comfortable in its use. We then provided support as and when requested and helped the users to actually use the system to produce production documents.

3.8 Manage Change

Although the basis of the approach was to be supportive of the users and to be attentive to their stated requirements, this did not mean that we immediately actioned every request for changes. Indeed, we instituted a degree of change control very early in the process.

Once the prototype was introduced into the department and was being used to manipulate 'real' data, change control was instigated. This was achieved by logging each request to change the system on a change request form.

All such requests were then assessed to determine their full impact on the prototype and estimates made for how long it would take to deliver. A record of each change was kept on a Change Response Form. Once the impact was established, we relayed back to the users what the change would mean to the prototype and how long it would take to deliver. We quickly found that users soon learnt to prioritise requirements in terms of 'nice to have' and necessary features.

3.9 Grow System

The next step is to grow the system within the Department in order to extend its usefulness and value to the New Product Selection Team and to extend its usefulness to other members of the department. Our strategy involves gentle nudging of users and potential users as well as responding positively to ideas and suggestions.

We also expect to be able to suggest extensions ourselves based on further task analyses and also from our continued exposure to real users and their day to day requirements.

4.0 CONCLUSIONS

At the time of writing this paper, the initial stage of the project had been well received by the users. They were using the system as a routine tool to support their work and were beiginning to explore the further potential of the various utilities provided.

From our regular visits and informal discussions, it was clear that there were many possible opportunities for main-frame links and extensions to the functionality which could greatly help the users in their work.

In retrospect, one of the most important parts of the process was to treat the users as partners. However, this did not mean that we 'gave them what they wanted'. Indeed, one aspect of treating them with a degree of respect was to point out that there were constraints and that some of their requirements were easier to achieve than others. Having established a degree of mutual trust, this was not a major problem.

The most significant problem area turned out to be relating what we were doing to conventional system development activities. For example, typical project management reporting required us to answer questions such as 'when will the system be implemented?' and 'when will the project be completed?' which we found difficult to answer. Answers such as 'its already been installed for two months' and 'it depends' are not entirely satisfactory to traditional project managers who like to minimise uncertainty and structure the development process.

Nonetheless, we believe that this approach has considerable potential for identifying worthwhile systems to support the business tasks of real users. That may not be everything but it seems like a worthwhile start.

A VISIT TO A VERY SMALL DATABASE: LESSONS FROM MANAGING THE REVIEW OF PAPERS SUBMITTED FOR CHI'91

John Rieman, Susan Davies, and Jonathan Roberts

Institute of Cognitive Science
University of Colorado
Boulder, CO 80309
(303) 492-4932
rieman@cs.colorado.edu

ABSTRACT

Many of the principles that guide user-interface design for commercial systems do not scale down to simple applications developed on personal computers. These "very small systems" are typically designed within a high-level application such as a database or a spreadsheet. The entire development process may take no more than a few days. In this restricted context, iterative design and usability testing are unaffordable luxuries, while detailed task analysis and early focus on users fail because the task and users will not coalesce until the system is in place. We describe our experiences with developing and using a very small system. We present suggestions for successful design in similar situations.

KEYWORDS: Design methodologies, small systems, databases.

A MISMATCH: SMALL SYSTEM NEEDS . . .

The past decade has seen sweeping changes in the availability of computers. The power that a user would expect from a time-shared slot on a minicomputer ten years ago is now available in a personal computer that costs, with software, less than the minicomputer's terminal once did.

As computers have become more available, the size of application needed to justify computerization has decreased. Ten years ago a computerized mailing list was a luxury for a small business; today it's no surprise to see computer-generated labels on mailings from clubs, charities, or businesses that may have only a few hundred addresses. Similarly, spreadsheets now track budgets that once occupied small-business ledger books, and every organization worthy of its name has a newsletter.

In our experience, many of these "very small systems" are not strictly off-the-shelf packages. Instead, they are developed by customizing high-level database, spreadsheet, word processing, or page-layout systems. Sometimes it is the user who does the customization. Often, however, the user or the small-business owner invests one or two thousand dollars for hardware and software and then realizes that the money will be wasted without some help in customizing the system to fit the intended use. Reluctantly, the system owner budgets several hundred dollars more and buys a few days of expert help from one of the many small-business computer consultants. In larger organizations, computer systems personnel provide similar help to users developing new applications on their desktop machines.

The central focus of these development efforts is the user interface, both in the shallow sense of screens and menus and in the deeper sense of defining an underlying structure that matches the user's task. More traditional programming issues, such as memory management or floating point routines, are typically handled by the application package in which the system is written.

. . . VERSUS BIG SYSTEM METHODS

During the same period that computing has come to the masses, the human-computer interface field has grown from a few people and some general ideas to a large community with various clearly defined methods and principles for interface design. But these methods and principles, we argue, are biased toward the larger systems that have been the focus of commercial software developers. They do not scale down to the development needs of the very small system.

More specifically, we make the following claim: Developing the first iteration of a working system requires a minimum quantum of effort; and at the absolute low end of system size, that quantum is the maximum that the developer's client is willing to fund. Under these conditions, the benefits of iterative design and usability testing, which are powerful approaches for larger projects [6], are moot. The first cut at the system will be the last, and the developer must make it a success.

Worse, even methods intended to define near-miss prototypes for a large project may founder for very small systems. A system that is small by absolute standards may have major effects when brought to bear on an equally small task, significantly changing the task's definition and the work roles of the users. Under these circumstances, detailed

© 1992 ACM 0-89791-513-5/92/0005-0471 1.50

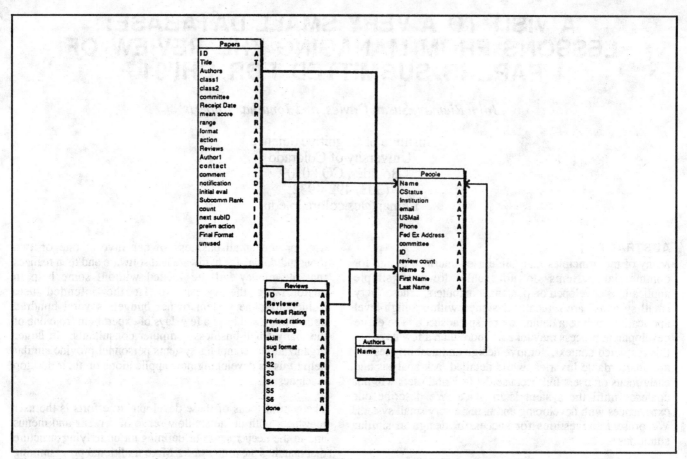

Figure 1. The structure of the database as displayed in 4th-Dimension's graphical programming interface.

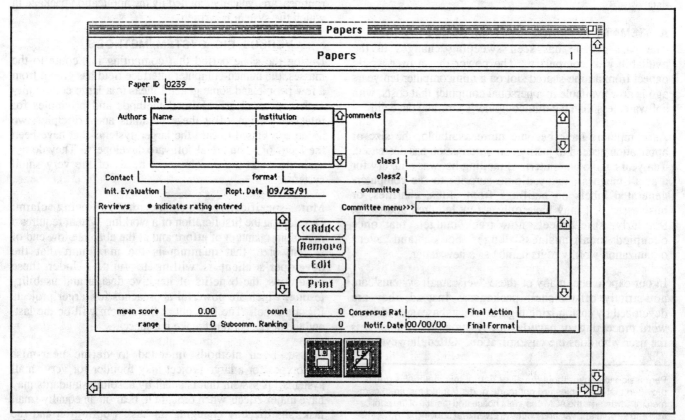

Figure 2. The data entry screen used for each paper. Another custom screen is used to enter author contact data.

task analysis [11] and early focus on users [6], even if resources allow them, are aiming at a target that will move as soon as the lone arrow is fired.

If traditional development methodologies don't apply, how can the developer of a very small system maximize the system's chances of success? What pitfalls can the developer avoid in the mist of changing tasks and unknown users? To provide some insight into these questions, this paper describes our experiences as users (first and second authors) and the developer (third author) of a very small system. We begin by describing the task the system was designed to support; we briefly describe the development phase; and we give details about problems, successes, and changes in our ideas about the system as the task progressed. We conclude with some suggested design principles for other very small systems.

THE TASK AT HAND: TRACKING CHI PAPERS

Near the end of September each year, about 300 papers are submitted in response to the CHI conference call for participation. They arrive, six complete copies of each paper, at the address of the CHI Papers Chair. It is the job of the Papers Chair to send the submissions to about 100 individuals in the CHI community who have agreed to act as reviewers. Most reviewers receive ten papers; each paper is given at least three reviews. The reviews, including a numeric rating, are returned to the Papers Chair, who summarizes the ratings for each paper.

The entire group of reviewers constitutes the Papers Committee, which in turn is broken down into subcommittees covering major areas of the CHI field. At the end of October the committee meets in a single location to discuss their reviews and select which papers will be published and presented at the CHI conference. Within the next two weeks, letters of acceptance or rejection are sent to the first authors of all papers.

The numbers tell the story: 300 papers, more than 500 authors, 100 reviewers, 900 reviews. And about five weeks between the time the bulk of the papers begin to arrive and the time the committee meets to make its final decision. Our task was to use a computer to improve the efficiency and reliability of the process.

DEVELOPING THE PROGRAM

To make the context of this story more concrete, let us briefly identify the players. The CHI'91 Papers Chair was Peter Polson of the University of Colorado's Institute of Cognitive Science. He enlisted the aid of four graduate students, including the first two authors, to help manage the papers review process. The effort was to be centered around a microcomputer-based database that would be created specifically for that purpose. The third author, who is Principal Systems Analyst for the Institute of Cognitive Science and the C.U. Department of Psychology, would act as the system developer. All four of the student workers (two from psychology and two from computer science) had experience with Macintosh and other systems, but they would not be doing any programming for the database.

Work on the database system began late in August, when the Papers Chair described the basic requirements of the system to the developer. The description included an overview of the papers review process, a list of items that should be recorded in the database, and descriptions of the ways data would be entered, manipulated, and viewed. It was decided that the database would be placed on a Macintosh using the ACIUS 4th-Dimension database system. 4th-Dimension provides a hierarchical database substrate and a rich set of traditional and visual programming tools for defining files, relationships, procedures, and interface screens.

Over the next several weeks, the developer spent some 40 hours learning 4th-Dimension and setting up the database. The second author also became involved early in the development effort. Nominally, she was a user. Realistically, she was learning the papers review process as its definition emerged from the needs analysis presented by the Papers Chair and the functionality that the developer was discovering in 4th-Dimension. The development process was incremental rather than iterative – or perhaps decremental would be a better term, as the original ambitious specifications were cut down to a size that reflected the performance demands of interactive work and the limits of the developer's time.

Nevertheless, 4th-Dimension made it surprisingly easy to add fields, redefine data entry screens, and write simple procedures. As a result, the final system included a large number of data fields, on the assumption that it would be good to have all the data in a central location. The system's underlying structure is presented in Figure 1. From the user's point of view, there were fundamentally two related files, one for papers and one for people (reviewers and authors, where some reviewers might also be authors).

UP AND RUNNING

The fully functional version of the system was completed in the middle of September, just as the first submitted papers began to arrive. With the database in place, the other three student assistants became involved in the process.

We started the data entry process by keying in the names and addresses for all of the reviewers. Then for about a week we "coasted," entering the few papers that arrived early, exploring the system's functionality, preparing filing cabinets and office supplies, making procedural decisions. In the last week of September the rate of arrival for papers increased, and we began work in earnest.

Those @!*$#% Shortcuts

For each paper we had to key in the title; the authors' names and affiliations; the first author's mailing address, phone, and e-mail address; and the primary and secondary category that the authors suggested for review of the paper.

In a word processor or a simple spreadsheet, we would have entered every item in a relatively form-free environment. But the database provided us both with structure and shortcuts. The main screen (Figure 2) presented a form with fields for all the information except the first author's contact data. Tabs moved the user from field to field; command-Tab moved out of certain multiple-choice fields; control-Tab moved back. A different screen automatically appeared for entry of the first author's contact information.

There were several shortcuts. If a name was already in the database, the contact-information screen would be skipped, but only if the names were spelled identically. Another shortcut helped with the identical-spelling problem: typing the first part of a name followed by an asterisk would cause the system to find the existing name that matched, if there was one; if not, a "no match" message would show, which had to be clicked away with the mouse.

Still another shortcut allowed affiliations to be selected by clicking on a list; affiliations not on the list could be added at any time, or the affiliation could be typed in without adding it. The list appeared automatically whenever the affiliation field was reached.

These shortcuts were easy to build in 4th-Dimension, and we had high hopes as to their effectiveness. Unfortunately, we had focussed more on their usefulness when appropriate than on their hindrance when inappropriate. Entering each paper turned into a hand-waving mixture of alphanumeric keys, mouse point-and-clicks, and special keys (tabs, returns, enters, commands). The mouse-actions designed to improve efficiency seemed often to do just the opposite, preventing the user from ever establishing a smooth rhythm of typing in data.

Perhaps more noticeable, the decision load was constantly high. Had this name been entered before? Should I add this affiliation to the list? Do I press tab or control-tab to advance to the next field? Can I hit Enter here or do I have to click OK with the mouse? In the end, the four workers had mixed feelings about the shortcuts. The faster typists found them counterproductive, while the slower typists were more forgiving.

The structured data entry produced another problem. If a name had already been entered, the contact information screen didn't appear. But in some cases, the name had been entered as a reviewer, and the contact information supplied with the paper was more up-to-date. Within the flow of data entry there was no way to edit existing contact data.

Will the Real Marilyn Mantei Please Stand?
The data entry had a window-on-a-record nature, which seemed clean and appropriate during design. However, it left us no easy way to view pre-existing data while new data were being entered. So it's not surprising that several names were inadvertently entered more than once, with slightly different spellings: e.g., Marilyn Mantei (first entered as a reviewer) and Marilyn M. Mantei (as an author).

We spent an unreasonable amount of time trying to decide whether this was a problem. At this point in the job, we still didn't have a clear focus on how the data would be used. Did it really matter that an author was in the database

twice, as long as both entries were correct? What if the author had supplied different contact information; which would we use if we went to a single record?

We finally decided that one person, one record was the way to go, the strongest argument being that updating contact information would be easier if there were only a single record. We picked a name for each of the multiples, checked that the contact information was complete, and deleted the extra. This was to have serious repercussions.

The Mysterious Disappearance of George Furnas
We had entered about 100 papers and the submissions were arriving fast when George Furnas's record disappeared from the database. This was not a good sign. Had we deleted him accidentally while trying to resolve a name conflict? Or – as George later suggested – had the agents of darkness invaded the database?

A day later another author disappeared, and then two more. They literally seemed to go away overnight. We increased our backup frequency, stopped deleting people's records for any reason, limited our activities to the core data-entry routines, and crossed our fingers. People stopped disappearing, but we remained uncomfortable. We started to talk about alternative game plans: dump the data into a spreadsheet and live with reduced functionality, or even do everything on paper.

A few days later one of us was entering data when the graphical programming interface to 4th-Dimension suddenly popped up and overlaid the data-entry screen. We hadn't seen the programming interface before, and on a 19-inch screen the effect was considerably more spectacular than Unix's proverbial "Segment Fault: Core Dump." We left a message asking for programming support, shut down the system, and went for a beer.

While battening down the programming interface the next day, we located the reason for the disappearing authors. A stray pointer in a subroutine was causing the wrong record to be deleted under certain editing conditions – editing that we usually performed at the end of the day, just before leaving. The fix was trivial, a single line of code. The disappearing authors and the pop-up programming interface turned out to be our only serious software bugs, but we nervously maintained the frequent backup schedule for the rest of the project.

But Terry Roberts Already Has Ten Papers
The deadline for paper submissions was October 1, and by midnight October 2 we had all the data entered. The next morning we validated our final input and ran another set of backups. Now it was time to decide which reviewers would get each paper.

The process went something like this. On the evening of October 3rd, the Papers Chair and three of the student workers sat down in a very small room with the database. We would pull a paper from its physical file and simultaneously bring it up on the database. We'd look at the review areas suggested by the author, read the abstract, check the references, look over the background interest sheets provided by the reviewers, and come to a decision: The first reviewer on this paper should be, e.g., Terry Roberts. Now we had to find her subcommittee. By default, the committee list displayed with each paper was the subcommittee matching the topic area suggested by the author. But sometimes we selected reviewers from other subcommittees who had appropriate expertise. Eventually the right committee would be found, we would click on the reviewer's name, and the paper would be assigned. One assignment down, only 899 to go.

But it got harder. Eventually many of the reviewers had been assigned their full quota of papers. Some assignments were on the basis of, "Right down her alley, send it to her." Others were more a matter of, "We don't have any real specialists in that area, but so-and-so will do a good job." But what if the reviewer who seemed really right for a paper had already been assigned the maximum ten papers? Obviously, look at those ten, see if any could be given to someone else, and reassign.

Easier said than done. This was a subtask we hadn't anticipated, and there was no way to see which papers were assigned to a reviewer, only how many. Calling for programming support to add this feature at 10 p.m. was definitely not an option. As with many unanticipated tasks, we ended up relying on memory and flipping through our paper files. Actual reassignment, fortunately, was easy. Just click and click. The entire reviewer assignment process spread over a very long evening and part of the next day.

900 into 120 Won't Go
Late Thursday morning, October 4, and we were almost ready to send out the papers for review. The reviewers had all been assigned and the Federal Express packets addressed (on a typewriter; the data were in the database, but we didn't have an impact printer for the carbon forms). Two tasks remained: we had to print the forms that the reviewers would fill in with comments for each paper, and we had to put the papers with the forms and put them in each reviewer's packet.

The forms would have the name of the reviewer, the paper's ID number (the quickest way for us to look it up when we entered the reviewers' ratings), the paper's title and first author, and a set of questions about the paper. It was our first chance to use the database for something other than data entry. We set up a special report that had been defined for this purpose a month earlier, loaded the printer with forms on which everything but the reviewer name, paper ID, title, and author had already been photocopied, and started the job.

That was about 12:30 p.m. By 1 p.m. we had printed 100 forms of the nearly 900 total. The Federal Express office had been notified that we were delivering the packets for all 100 reviewers before they closed at 5 that afternoon, and they had scheduled extra help for the load. To meet the deadline we'd have to finish printing the forms in the next two hours, collate them with the papers, and stuff them into the Federal Express envelopes. It couldn't be done.

After a brief and frantic discussion we cancelled the printout and made up the packets with forms that included only the review questions. A letter asked each reviewer to enter the paper's name and ID. Working from a simple report showing which papers went to which reviewers, five of us spent three hours running up and down a hall and dropping papers onto the packets, laid out alphabetically in two 50-foot lines. We delivered the last of the 100 packets to Federal Express at 5 minutes before 5.

Report Generation: The Big Win
Reviews began to trickle in from reviewers, with a final flood during the week preceding the committee meeting. Entering this information was relatively problem free, a welcome relief after our experiences with the papers. We did need to correct a minor bug in the routine that calculated averages, and we had to make a management decision about how to handle ratings marked as, for example, "2+." This had to be entered as a real number. Should it be 2.2? 2.25? Or perhaps even 1.8, since "+" seems to mean "better," and a 1 rating is better than a 2. We solved the better/worse dilemma by reading the reviewer's comments or, if those weren't decisive, contacting the reviewer, and we went with 0.2 as a standard increment for + or −. Fortunately, the database allowed real numbers in the rating field, so we weren't limited to the integers 1 through 5.

During the week before the committee meeting, we generated a bevy of final reports showing the ratings of each paper, sorted and selected every way we could imagine might be useful. Which were the papers that all reviewers praised? Which were the ones that no one liked? Which had produced conflicting reviews? Which were borderline? How did the data break down by subcommittee? Were there any subcommittees that were overloaded?

It's important to understand that we had only a vague appreciation of these questions during design of the database. Custom reports defined at that time would have missed the mark by a wide margin. During the month of data entry, the subcommittee composition and definitions had shifted, the ratings had raised new questions, and the plan for managing paper selection had become more concrete. But the reports we finally generated were appropriate and, as the committee members later told us, very useful. We credit this success to 4th-Dimension's general-purpose direct-manipulation facility for defining report formats. This was the one point where we were actually able to iterate the design, and the payoff was clear.

If They Like It, Why Don't They Want More?
November 2 through 4 was the committee meeting. It ran without a hitch. Our initial reports were appreciated and used. We had the database set up in the conference center where the subcommittees were working, and we updated it frequently as reviewers reconsidered their reviews and altered ratings to reflect consensus decisions.

But once again our expectations as to how the system would work were less than accurate. We thought we would be printing frequent reports for each subcommittee, with papers sorted to reflect new ratings. For most of the subcommittees, this was a service that was never requested. In retrospect it's clear why not. A subcommittee dealing with 30 papers made short work of eliminating the bottom 20 and accepting the top 3. The rest of the day was spent discussing the few remaining papers, and a printed list would provide no new information to a subcommittee that had the papers themselves stacked on the table.

How Many Mailing Labels Can You Fit on the Head of A Laser Printer?
We left the meeting with each paper's final status, accept or reject, marked in the database. The final job on our end was to print letters and mailing labels to inform the authors of the decisions. This turned out to be another task that sounded trivial but actually required a fair amount of work.

The letters had been typed in Microsoft Word, and the addresses were in the 4th-Dimension database. We sorted by accept/reject, found the 4th-Dimension option to save as a text file, and after a couple of tries saved the information in a workable format. "Workable" here meant that it only took two or three search-and-replace passes in Word to convert the file to a mail-merge format. Another two hours' fiddling with Word's "Table" feature gave us a file that would print the addresses one to a label (we used big labels to reduce fine-tuning).

The letters went out on schedule. We delivered a copy of the database and the mail-merge file to Gary Olson, Technical Program Co-Chair, who used it to generate mailings to authors of the accepted papers. And the database program itself? Ruven Brooks, Papers Chair for CHI'92, picked it up for reuse.

LESSONS FOR DEVELOPERS OF VERY SMALL SYSTEMS
Looking just at the benefits, our efforts were a success. We provided rapid turnaround of papers and reviews, and we supplied accurate reports in a form that the committee found effective. But there were high costs in time spent programming the database, learning to use its features, and entering data. On the balance, we still believe that computer support for the papers management task is appropriate – but our database was too ambitious. The following paragraphs describe some of the lessons we've learned.

Expect the Task to Change
The Scandinavian design approach [4] notes that tasks can't be analyzed independent of the system being developed because the new system will change the task. Carroll's task-artifact cycle describes a similar phenomenon [2,3], as does the contextual design approach described by Wixon and Whiteside [12]. This task mutability may be *a fortiori* the case with very small systems. Often these systems are the first and last cut at a task, not a replacement for an existing method. The task will coalesce around the system.

Further, the small group of workers interacting with the system are not nearly so bound by existing structure as the workers in a large company.

But if the task is going to change, and the developer doesn't have the time or resources to iterate the design, how can an effective system be produced? We believe the answer is to provide a system with robust core functionality and an interface that allows the user high flexibility in working with data. (Wixon and Whiteside present similar guidelines for the initial prototype in a contextual design effort [13].) The rest of our suggestions are more specific pointers in this direction.

Focus on the Core — Just Say 'No' to Frills
In the face of a potentially changing task, we believe the developer must attempt to identify core functionality and direct the development efforts toward those areas. "Core" functions, as we use the term here, have two characteristics: they relate to task activities that appear central to the user's overall operations, so they are less likely to change as the task evolves; and they can provide major savings in time, money, or effort.

For our database, the core functionality was the generation of mailings and reports, supported by the necessary data entry. Not within the core were additional information storage, general look-up facilities, and perhaps the support for assigning reviewers. These functions were either not central to our task or not likely to provide high payback. Of the core functions, report generation was well supported, thanks to our choice of 4th-Dimension as a substrate. Generation of mailings was unreasonably difficult, and what could have been simple data entry was made more difficult by overlaying it with shortcuts and features designed to support look-up and reviewer assignment.

Although it may seem obvious, we want to emphasize the importance of building a robust, "bulletproof" version of the core functionality. The users of very small systems live on the frontier of support. If a system developed by an in-house support person fails, the user may find their problems at the bottom of a very long to-do list, competing with "reboot the VAX" and "fix e-mail." The user who relies on outside consulting may simply be out of funds and out of luck, unless the problem is obviously the consultant's fault.

For the developer with only a few days to build a system, saying "No" to unessential features is the best way to ensure that the core is bulletproof. It's also the best way to build a system that occasional users can learn and use with confidence.

One kind of frill is unnecessary added functionality. In our system, for example, we defined fields for some information that really didn't need to be in the database, even if it was important. The author contact address included a special field for Federal Express address, to be completed in addition to the usual mailing address if the author was also a reviewer. Since we knew from the start that the Federal

Express labels would be typed on a typewriter, we could have avoided the programming and data entry associated with that field and simply kept the addresses on paper or in a text file (most had been supplied to us through e-mail).

A second kind of frill is perhaps even more seductive. This is the "eliminate work for special cases" frill. A line of code can check for a special case and skip a subroutine. In our database, for example, if an author had already been entered, the contact data screen wasn't displayed. In retrospect, this feature saved little time, and we often would have been better off seeing the screen and checking that the data were correct. A general lesson is that truly "special" cases are hard to identify. An additional point is that special-case behavior requires the user to develop multiple expectations for interface behavior in situations that are apparently similar. For the occasional or short-term users of very small systems, who will typically receive no formal training, consistent behavior is especially important. [9,10]

Use the Back of the Envelope
In retrospect it's easy for us to point to unnecessary features and claim they shouldn't have been provided. But how can the designer focus on core functionality if the task is going to change? We think that rough, "back of the envelope" calculations of user time and effort are a powerful method for winnowing the useful features from the frills. The developer can't predict with certainty which features will be used or required; but rough calculations can identify features that would have no significant payback in any conceivable version of the task. This is especially true where, as in our case, a system is known to be a one-time or limited-use effort.

For example, if the user expects to print a list of 300 names and addresses four times, then capturing the keystrokes when the data are first entered will save roughly 3 x 300 x 15 seconds = 3.75 hours. This is meat-and-potatoes functionality. Indeed, this is functionality so powerful that, once the keystrokes are saved, the task may be redefined to include five or six printings of the list. This is functionality that should receive the designer's primary attention.

By comparison, consider our database's feature that allowed affiliations to be selected from a list, instead of being retyped. This might have saved us 100 typings of short strings such as "Digital Equipment Corporation" or "University of Colorado." The back of the envelope shows 100 x 3 seconds = 5 minutes typing time. A mere sprig of parsley. The combined time to program and train on this feature almost certainly exceeded its savings. This is the kind of seductive frill that rough calculations provide justification for avoiding.

Don't Discount Manual Operations
Back-of-the-envelope calculations can be especially valuable in convincing users or clients that a customized computer approach, no matter how seductively modern, is not always the best alternative to doing things by hand [5]. By "doing things by hand" we mean either pulling the job completely

off the computer or leaving it on-line but providing no tailored routines for data entry and manipulation.

The approaches have similar benefits. They require little or no training, they offer unmatched potential for procedural modification as the task evolves, and they reduce the amount of work required of the developer. Paper systems have the additional advantage that they can't be erased by a stray keystroke.

Having the reviewers write the titles on the review sheets turned out to be much more tractable than printing the 900 sheets from the database. The manual approach was also a success for the subcommittees, who managed their deliberations without help from the database after the initial report. And we still wonder whether a manual approach, or some mix of manual and automated, might have been a better approach to assigning and unassigning reviewers. (At least one previous Papers Chair simply built stacks of papers for each reviewer, examining and shuffling papers until the reviewers had a balanced load. [8])

Make Data Visible and Touchable
Our final point recognizes both the changing nature of the task and the value of manual operations. Very small systems are quite different from large commercial databases, where security requires tightly controlled access. Users of very small systems are only one step away from maintaining their own records by hand. They are familiar with the data and they can benefit from direct access to it, just as they expect direct access to word processing or graphics files. Errors will be caught more quickly if stored information is visible, and data that can be modified directly may allow changes in the task to be accommodated without low-level programming. This is the "direct engagement" approach that has been recommended by Hutchins, Hollins, and Norman [7] and other researchers [1].

We saw an important example of the value of direct engagement in our database. The big win of report flexibility came from our ability to do direct-manipulation changes to the report forms. Although we weren't touching the data directly, we felt more in control than during most of our work.

We also saw a number of places where violating the direct-engagement principle caused problems. The name-conflict issue, the destruction of author records behind the scenes by an invisible subroutine, the inability to see which papers were assigned to a reviewer – all might have been avoided or mitigated with visible, touchable data.

Direct engagement is most likely to be enhanced by the choice of substrate. To that end, if we were doing this project again, we would consider a spreadsheet or even a word processor as a competitive alternative to a database. However, even a simple, flat-file, non-hierarchical database would have improved this aspect of our system, by allowing the user to work with all the information about a paper on a single record, instead of splitting the data between a record for the paper and another (hidden) record for each author. We could have built this simpler structure in 4th-Dimension or a less sophisticated package.

SUMMARY

Very small systems, built on top of high-level substrates such as databases or spreadsheets, are becoming increasingly common as the cost of personal computers drops and powerful substrates become widely available. Applications that were once uneconomical to computerize can now be implemented with only a few days of assistance from an experienced developer. The user interface is a critical part of these systems; indeed, the system developer may build little more than the interface, since lower-level routines are provided by the substrate.

But the developer of very small systems often operates under constraints of time and resources that make traditional user-interface design principles difficult to apply. Iterative design guided by usability testing is infeasible when the available resources are barely sufficient to build a single version. And traditional task analysis fails when the task and users will only become defined through interaction with the finished system.

Our experience suggests that successful small systems require simple, robust core functionality, coupled with broad general power to directly view and modify data. Rough calculations can focus the development effort on critical areas, but the final system must be flexible enough that users can adapt it to the rapidly changing nature of their tasks.

ACKNOWLEDGEMENTS

Tamara Sumner provided insightful counterarguments that helped us sharpen our ideas in this paper. Clayton Lewis, a long-time proponent of back-of-the-envelope calculations, critiqued an earlier draft. Cathleen Wharton and Catherine Ann Ashworth were our co-workers in managing the CHI'91 papers review. Their views, while not always in agreement with those presented in this paper, helped us to appreciate the value of a system flexible enough to accommodate alternative approaches. Special thanks to Peter Polson, CHI'91 Papers Chair, for his comments on this paper and for giving us the opportunity to be involved in the CHI'91 review process. Support for research in issues raised by this work has been provided by US West Advanced Technologies and the National Science Foundation, grant IRI 8722792.

REFERENCES

1. Bødker, S. A human activity approach to user interfaces. *Human-Computer Interaction 4* (1989), 171-195.

2. Carroll, J.M. Infinite detail and emulation in an ontologically minimized HCI. In *Proceedings of the Conference on Human Factors in Computing Systems* (Seattle, WA, April 1-5). ACM, New York, 1990, pp. 321-327.

3. Carroll, J.M., Kellogg, W.A., and Rosson, M.B. The Task-Artifact Cycle. In *Designing Interaction: Psychology of the Human-Computer Interface*, Carroll, J.M. (Ed.), Cambridge University Press, Cambridge, 1991, pp. 74–102.

4. Floyd, C., Wolf-Michael, M, Reisin, F.-M., Schmidt, G., and Wolf, G. Out of Scandinavia: Alternative approaches to software design and system development. *Human-Computer Interaction 4* (1989), 253-350.

5. Göransson, B., Lind, M., Pettersson, E., Sandblad, B., and Schwalbe, P. The interface is often not the problem. In *Proceedings of the Conference on Human Factors in Computing Systems and Graphics Interface* (Toronto, April 1-5). ACM, New York, 1987, pp. 133-136.

6. Gould, J.D., Boies, S., and Lewis, C. Making usable, useful, productivity-enhancing computer applications. *Communications of the ACM 34* (1991), 74-89.

7. Hutchins, E.L., Hollan, J.D., and Norman, D.A. Direct Manipulation Interfaces. In *User Centered System Design*, Norman, D.A., and Draper, S.W. (Eds.), Lawrence Erlbaum, Hillsdale, NJ, 1986, pp. 87–124.

8. Lewis, Clayton. Personal communication, August, 1990.

9. Polson, P.G., and Lewis, C.H. Theory-based design for easily learned interfaces. *Human-Computer Interaction 5* (1990), 191-220.

10. Polson, P.G. The consequences of consistent and inconsistent user interfaces. In *Cognitive Science and its Applications for Human-Computer Interaction*, Guindon, R., (Ed.), Lawrence Erlbaum, Hillsdale, NJ (1988), pp. 59–108.

11. Rubenstein, R., and Hersh, H. *The Human Factor: Designing Computer Systems for People*. Digital Press, Burlington, MA, 1984.

12. Wixon, D., Holtzblatt, K., and Knox, S. Contextual design: An emergent view of system design. In *Proceedings of the Conference on Human Factors in Computing Systems* (Seattle, WA, April 1-5). ACM, New York, 1990, pp. 331-336.

13. Wixon, D., and Whiteside, J. Engineering for Usability: Lessons from the user derived interface. In *Proceedings of the Conference on Human Factors in Computing Systems* (San Francisco, CA, April 14-18). ACM, New York, 1985, pp. 144-147.

DESIGNING THEORY-BASED SYSTEMS:
A CASE STUDY

John B. Smith and Marcy Lansman

Department of Computer Science
University of North Carolina
Chapel Hill, NC 27599-3175
919-962-1792 919-962-1979
jbs@cs.unc.edu lansman@cs.unc.edu

ABSTRACT

In this paper, we discuss principles for designing and testing computer systems intended to support users' thinking as they perform open-ended or ill-defined tasks. We argue that such systems inherently and inevitably implement a model of users' cognitive behaviors. Making that model explicit can provide system developers with guidance in making design decisions. However, both model and system must be tested and refined. We discuss these principles in relation to a case study in which our group developed a hypertext-based writing environment and then tested that system in a series of experimental studies of writers' strategies.

KEYWORDS: system design, cognitive modes and strategies, cognitive models, task analysis, user testing

INTRODUCTION

What should be the relationship between human-computer interaction studies and the design and testing of actual systems?

Few would disagree that results of human-computer studies should play a larger role in the design of computer systems. However, we have not seen very many instances where this has actually happened. There are many reasons for this. Most HCI studies have addressed the ways individuals interact with existing systems. Many have been concerned with specific interface issues -- such as representation, layout, use of color, ease of operation for specific commands, etc. -- rather than broad, patterns of behavior that might be more useful for developers. As a result, much of this work remains unknown to system designers or it has been incorporated piecemeal.

One promising development can be seen in recent theoretical discussions that sketch broad approaches to system design, frequently drawing on work from other disciplines including speech act theory [Winograd & Flores, 1986], activity theory [Bodker, 1989], ethnography [Suchman, 1987]. These discussions have provided useful and convincing insights into the situated activities of users; but because of their generality, applying these insights to specific design problems is often difficult. For example, some writers describing the Scandinavian approach suggest that factors as far-afield as the medieval social structure of the nation are relevant for contemporary system designers [Floyd, *et. al.*, 1989].

Thus, much of the work in HCI is either too specific or too general to provide practical guidance for system building. What designers need is *practical* guidance that addresses *overall* system design. Such a method would enable them to reliably and predictably build "whole" systems that have internal consistency and integrity.

During the past seven years, our research group has been engaged in a program of research that relates to these issues. We did not begin with the intention of addressing broad issues of design methodology; rather, we were interested in users' cognitive strategies for a particular task -- technical and scientific writing -- and in building a hypertext-based computer system to support that task. We soon realized, however, that to understand this task would require basic research in cognitive theory and, to be useful, the theory would have to relate in specific ways to the support system we were building.

We have also come to realize that the *method* applies to many tasks other than writing. In our own project, we have extended this approach to the tasks of software development and to collaborative work. But, we believe the method applies to any complex, open-ended, or ill-structured task. Included in this category would be design, planning, extended problem-solving and other tasks that require sustained human thinking that is carried out with the help of a computer system.

Such systems have sometimes been called *intelligence augmenting* or *intelligence amplifying* software [Engelbart, 1973]. An example is hypertext systems in which users represent abstract structures of ideas as networks of nodes and links -- each node corresponding to a concept and each link corresponding to an association or relationship. The computer is said to augment or amplify *intrinsic* human conceptual processes by representing a larger set of ideas than that which can be held in short term memory and by permitting more numerous and more complex traversal operations than would otherwise be possible. IA systems can be contrasted, on the one hand, with systems that enable users to manipulate data structures in accord with *extrinsic*, rather than intrinsic, rules -- for example, accounting systems. They can be contrasted, on the other hand, with *artificial intelligence* systems that, by design, seek to simulate human though, but are intended to operate autonomously rather than cooperatively.

While intelligence amplifying systems were once primarily a curiosity, we believe they will become the predominant form of software for microcomputers and workstations. Indeed, we already see a trend in this direction in multiple window multitasking operating systems, in systems that integrate multiple tools, in the proliferation of hypertext systems, and in the more powerful tools that are appearing for a variety of design tasks.

Building systems that can help users think more efficiently and more effectively requires new methods for their design as well as new methods to test and refine those designs. It seems self-evident to us that a system that seeks to help its users carry out complex, open-ended tasks will be more successful if it implements a *model* of that process than if it does not. Such a model will include a data, or product, component and a set of system operations to affect that product, but it must emphasize the *cognitive* processes and strategies that are used by human beings to build or to understand the complex conceptual structure that is being represented in that product. For example, a good deal is known about the cognitive processes that writers use to produce technical, scientific, and other kinds of expository documents. However, the task is too complex and subject to too many undetermined variables for someone to produce a set of rules that would automatically generate a well-written document. Nevertheless, we could describe at a more abstract level a set of *steps* that can help a human writer select and organize material, plan the document, edit its sentences, etc. And we could build a system that, by design, could help its users carry out those steps. But both the enactment of the steps and the control of the supporting computer system are dependent upon the intellect of the human user, as opposed to an independent algorithm.

This notion of a *set of steps* suggests what we mean by a *model* for open-ended tasks; in the section that follows, we explain this concept more precisely. By a *theory-based system*, we mean a system that is consistent with a particular model for a complex, open-ended task. After the discussion of theory, we describe a general approach for designing such systems, illustrated by one particular system developed by our group. Finally, we discuss issues concerned with testing and refining both system and model.

THEORY

Systems intended to amplify or augment their users' thinking inevitably include in their design a model of those mental activities. This model is inherent in the way conceptual objects are represented, in the operations provided to manipulate them, in options for moving objects from one context to another, etc. But, regardless of whether system designers are aware of it or not, the model is there, embedded in the implementation.

A more effective approach, we believe, is for system designers to be consciously aware of this model. In an ideal world, it would be defined before system design begins; however, in practice, the model is likely to be worked out in parallel with system design and refined after users start working with the system.

Over the past seven years, our group has followed this approach in developing several systems. The models we have developed have been expressed in terms of a set of *cognitive modes* and the *strategies* and *tactics* human beings use to engage the various modes and to move among them. In this section, we first discuss these concepts in general terms; after that, we illustrate them by describing a particular set of modes used for technical and scientific writing. We wish to emphasize, however, that modes and strategies are general concepts that can be used to model a number of intellectual tasks in addition to writing.

We define a cognitive mode to be a particular way of thinking used to accomplish a particular *goal*, that will be realized by producing a particular kind of *product*, drawing on particular cognitive *processes*, in accord with a particular set of *constraints*. The *product* produced in a mode is the symbolization of a concept or relationships among concepts. Different cognitive modes provide different options for representing concepts or structures -- for example, words, diagrams, notes, outlines, and other forms. Thus, different forms prevail in different modes. Cognitive *processes* act on products to define them or to transform one form into another. Thus, certain processes are favored in certain modes, while others are de-emphasized or suppressed. The *goal* of a mode is the individual's intention for engaging that particular way of thinking. While goals are abstract, they are made concrete in the particular product the individual aims to produce in that mode. *Constraints* determine the choices available in a mode. Constraints are relaxed or tightened in accord with the individual's large-scale strategies for engaging different modes of thinking for different purposes.

To illustrate these concepts, consider two modes frequently used by expository writers: exploratory thinking and organizing. During *exploration*, the goal is to externalize ideas, consider different combinations, and to gain a general sense of the information available or missing. Thus, constraints are minimal to encourage creativity and multiple perspectives. The processes that are emphasized are recalling from memory, associating, relating, and building small component structures. The products generated are, thus, notes, jottings, diagrams, perhaps loose networks of ideas. During *organization*, the goal is to plan the actual document to be written; thus, constraints are tightened to produce a logical, coherent organizational plan. That plan is normally expressed as a hierarchy or some other regular form. And the processes are analyzing, synthesizing, sustained conceptual building, and refinement based on noting consistent/inconsistent relations in the structure. *Exploration* and *organization* are, thus, distinctly different ways of thinking. And they differ still from other activities such as actual writing and several forms of editing.

Modes are used *strategically*. With respect to writing, experienced writers use the various modes in accord with a general strategy they know and use to accomplish a particular intellectual activity. But they also switch modes for tactical reasons that arise during the course of work. By strategy, we mean writers' overall understanding of the writing process and the steps they have learned that enable them to get their writing done. By tactics, we refer to the fact that writers shift from one mode to another in response to specific problems that occur. Researchers studying writers' strategies have noted that writers may return to exploration mode after an organizational phase when they realize during writing that the plans they produced earlier are inadequate [Hayes & Flower, 1980]. Thus, modes help writers focus their attention on one set of activities at a time, while strategies provide them with an overall sense of direction as well as the means to resolve problems that arise during the process.

When writers use cognitive modes in accord with a global strategy, they are likely to produce a series of related intermediate products. For example, during exploration some writers represent concepts externally, cluster them, and then link them into a loose network of associations. During organization, they transform that loose network of ideas into a coherent structure for the document. During writing, the individual concepts and relations in the organizational plan are transformed into continuous prose, graphic images, or other developed forms. During editing, they refine the structure and expression of the draft document. Thus, writers produce a *flow* of intermediate products in which the output of one mode becomes the input for another.

However, this flow of products is not one-way and continuous. Rather, as writers shift modes iteratively and recursively to solve problems, the flow of intermediate products goes back and forth, as well. For example, writers may find while organizing that they do not have critical information needed for a particular section. Rather than interrupt their thinking to get that information, they may elect to continue but leave the section undeveloped. Later, when the missing information is available, they may interrupt their writing, revert to organization or perhaps even exploration mode, and build the missing portion of the document's structure. When the missing

piece has been filled in, they resume writing. [Smith & Lansman, 1991]

The concept of cognitive mode can be applied to tasks other than writing. Over a range of intellectual activities, individuals divide tasks into subtasks, set goals and subgoals, produce intermediate objects or subassemblies, and employ different processes during different phases of the work. They do these things whether they are working with physical objects or with information objects. In considering this broader range of tasks, we have found it useful to differentiate between the *general* notion of mode and the *specific* modes used for a given task. The first -- defined as the interdependent configuration of goal, products, processes and constraints -- can be viewed as an *architectural construct*. While different tasks draw on different modes, they can all be described within the general framework of modes and strategies.

A *model*, as we use the term, is a particular set of modes and the rules that account for the relationships among them. Thus, a model of writing identifies a particular set of modes -- those used by particular writers under particular writing conditions -- and the particular strategies and tactics used by those writers, which are learned and/or developed by those writers Consequently, we should not be surprised to see different groups of writers using different sets of modes for a given task. Some sets of modes and strategies, it can be argued, are preferable to others because they are more efficient or suit certain groups better than other sets.

We developed a model of writing that emphasizes separate and abstract planning modes; we call this approach the *strategic method for writing* [Smith & Smith, 1987]. The seven modes included in the strategic method, along with their constituents, are summarized in Figure 1. Since a key step in the methodology we are discussing is mapping model to system design, we describe the different modes of this model in more detail here. In the section that follows, we show how these particular cognitive modes are mapped to various system modes.

Exploration mode is used to gain a general sense of the material available for the document. During exploration the writer retrieves ideas for the text from memory and from source materials, writes them down as short phrases, clusters them and notes specific relations among them. Some people write phrases on "post-its" and cluster the post-its to represent the relationships between ideas. Other writers may express their ideas as rough sentences and link these sentences with arrows. The products of exploration mode are always intermediate, i.e., these products do not show up directly as part of a draft. There are few constraints on the form of the products of exploration. For example, ideas need not be expressed in complete sentences. There is, however, at least one constraint on the process: writers avoid evaluating the ideas that come up during exploration and, instead, simply record them.

Situational Analysis mode is used to identify aspects of the rhetorical situation that affect the text. As was the case for exploration, there are few constraints on the

	Processes	Products	Goals	Constraints
Exploration	•Recalling •Representing •Clustering •Associating •Noting subordinate-superordinate relations	•Individual concepts •Clusters of concepts •Networks of related concepts	•To externalize ideas •To cluster related ideas •To gain general sense of available concepts •To consider various possible relations	•Flexible •Informal •Free expression
Situational Analysis	•Analyzing objectives •Selecting •Prioritizing •Analyzing audiences	•High-level summary statement •Prioritized list of readers (types) •List of (major) actions desired	•To clarify rhetorical intentions •To identify and rank potential readers •To identify major actions •To consolidate realization •To set high-level strategy for document	•Flexible •Extrinsic perspective
Organization	•Analyzing •Synthesizing •Building abstract structure •Refining structure	•Hierarchy of concepts •Crafted labels	•To transform network of concepts into coherent hierarchy	•Rigorous •Consistent •Hierarchical •Not sustained prose
Writing	•Linguistic encoding	•Coherent prose	•To transform abstract representation of concepts and relations into prose	•Sustained expression •Not (necessarily) refined
Editing: Global Organization	•Noting large-scale relations •Noting and correcting inconsistencies •Manipulating large-scale structural components	•Refined text structure •Consistent structural cues	•To verify and revise large-scale organizational components	•Focus on large-scale features and components
Editing: Coherence Relations	•Noting coherence relations between sentences and paragraphs •Restructuring to make relations coherent	•Refined paragraphs and sentences •Coherent logical relations between sentences and paragraphs	•To verify and revise coherence relations within intermediate sized components	•Focus on structural relations among sentences and paragraphs •Rigorous logical and structural thinking
Editing: Expression	•Reading •Linguistic analysis •Linguistic transformation •Linguistic encoding	•Refined prose	•To verify and revise text of document	•Focus on expression •Close attention to linguistic detail

Figure 1: Seven cognitive modes for writing.

products of situational analysis. These products include notes, lists, and diagrams that represent what is known or assumed about potential readers. These products are intermediate and are used to guide decisions made in other modes. During situational analysis, the writer envisions potential readers, establishes priorities among them, imagines what readers know about the subject matter and decides how he would like the text to affect them. Thus, situational analysis allows the writer to make consideration of context a conscious conceptual process.

Organization mode is used to develop a single, coherent structure for the text. The writer uses the ideas and component structures produced in exploration mode as the raw materials for organization mode. He groups sets of ideas under their logical superordinate headings, generating those superordinate concepts when necessary. He breaks other ideas down into their components. He experiments with various organizational schemes to determine which one fits the rhetorical goals he has developed during situational analysis. The processes required by organization involve examining the logical relationships between ideas. The product, for the writer, is a hierarchical structure containing three to four levels of topic headings. The organizational process is constrained by the requirement that the result be a single organizational scheme which includes all the major ideas that are to appear in the text.

Writing mode is used to translate the ideas in the organizational scheme into sentences. The product is a rough draft. Both the organizational scheme and the rules of English grammar constrain that product. While writers vary widely as to the quality of the prose they expect to produce in writing mode, the writer strives for a first draft that is grammatical and rhetorically suitable for the purposes established during situational analysis. But he anticipates making major structural and linguistic changes during the the editing phases.

Editing is done in three different cognitive modes. During *global editing*, the writer addresses the large-scale structure of the document. The purpose is to make sure that the document as a whole makes the right point, that the right parts are present, and that they are in the right order. The primary constraint is that attention is focused on the high-level, structural features of the document and that the details be ignored. During global editing, the writer evaluates large-scale relations, notes logical inconsistencies among the parts of the document, and corrects or manipulates these large, structural components. The product is a refined version of the document - one that has a sharper central focus than the original draft and one in which the large components fit together more comfortably.

Coherence editing requires the writer to shift attention to intermediate-sized units of the text, such as paragraphs and sections. The purpose is to examine the logical, sequential order of, first, the paragraphs within sections and, then, sentences within paragraphs. The primary constraint is again to focus attention on units of a particular size. Cognitive processes include evaluating coherence relations and restructuring paragraphs to make relations clear. Some sentences may have to be transformed or rewritten to make them fit together. The product is a document in which the sentences and paragraphs have clear, logical relations to one another and advance the larger purpose of the section they comprise.

Expression editing represents still a different mode of thinking. Whereas coherence editing is concerned with sentences as discrete objects to be verified and arranged, expression editing is concerned with the insides of sentences - their clarity, directness, and appropriateness for the rhetorical purposes of the document. Thus, expression editing requires close attention to linguistic detail. The processes emphasized are reading, linguistic analysis, linguistic transformation, and linguistic encoding. The product is a more refined document - one with crafted prose.

The seven cognitive modes described here represent one particular model of the writing process. Our subsequent studies suggest to us that it accurately accounts for the behavior of many writers, but not all. Thus, as is the case for any phenomena, alternative models are possible and, indeed, may be required if we are to account for the behavior of most individuals for open-ended tasks, such as writing. In a later section, we return to this issue of alternative models, but, first, we show how this particular model served as the basis for designing a writing support system.

SYSTEM DESIGN

We have suggested above that writing can be viewed as a complex process involving different cognitive modes, such as the particular set of modes just described. A key question for system design, then, is how best to support these different cognitive modes and the flow of intermediate products among them? We will try to answer this question here, both in general but also in more detail for the Writing Environment (WE) developed by our group.

Two basic designs are possible. In a single mode system, all system functions would always be available. For writing, the set of functions would be the union of those required to support all of the cognitive processes for the different cognitive modes discussed above. By contrast, a multimodal approach would divide the environment into separate system modes, each corresponding to one or more of the cognitive modes. If the second approach were followed, each system mode would include only the functions appropriate for its corresponding cognitive mode(s).

We adopted a multimodal system design for WE for several reasons. As we discussed in the previous section, writers manage the overall writing task by dividing that process into phases in which they engage different cognitive modes. Each mode is unique in terms of its particular combination of processes, products, goals, and constraints. Consequently, supporting these large-grained "chunks' of activity, each with its own unique requirements, in separate system modes seemed both natural and efficient: natural, in that system architecture would both mirror and reinforce cognitive strategy; efficient, in that specific system operations could be matched closely with specific cognitive processes and with specific intermediate products developed by writers during the task.

We made this design decision recognizing that it ran counter to widely-held beliefs that systems with multiple user interface modes are less desirable than so-called *seamless* systems that profess to have only a single, all-inclusive interface mode. The case against multimodal interfaces is strongest for systems that are controlled through textual commands. Problems arise when input from the keyboard is interpreted as textual data in one mode or context and as commands to the system in other contexts. The problem is compounded when the system includes multiple control modes, resulting in different command interpretations for the same input. However, the problem with multiple mode systems has always been making the user aware of what mode the system is in at any given moment. A simple remedy is available for graphics-based systems, such as the Macintosh and the other multiple window systems, in the form of visual cues that signal the mode. In fact, one can reasonable argue that today's multiple window multitasking operating systems are inherently multimodal; they are not perceived to be such -- and, indeed, have even been called *seamless* -- because they have solved the multimodal problem so effectively that users are unaware they are switching modes when they switch between applications/windows.

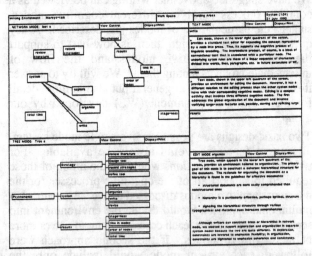

Figure 2: Writing Environment (WE). Overview of the four system modes: Network, Tree, Editor, and Text Modes

Building theory-based systems is relatively straightforward when the task model is expressed in terms of *modes*. For

example, the Writing Environment presents the user with four system modes that correspond with six of the seven cognitive modes included in the *strategic* model, outlined in Figure 1. The default layout of the screen is shown in Figure 2; however, the individual modes can be resized freely. The upper left window, called *network* mode, is intended for *exploration*. The underlying data model in this mode is a directed graph embedded in a two-dimensional space. Thus, the user has maximum flexibility with which to represent concepts as nodes (boxes with a word or phrase to express the idea), move them to form clusters of loosely related ideas, and link them to denote more specific relationships. Small conceptual structures can also be built here and used later in the other modes.

To support the *organization* cognitive mode in which the user builds the actual plan for the document, the system provides a *tree* mode, shown in the lower left corner of Figure 2, in which the user is constrained to create a hierarchical structure. (Reading comprehension research has shown that a hierarchical document is likely to be more easily and more accurately comprehended than documents with other structures [e.g., Kintsch & van Dijk, 1978; Schwartz & Flammer, 1981; Ausubel, 1963; Meyer, Brandt, & Bluth, 1980; Kieras, 1980].) While users could have continued working in network mode to build a tree, they are encouraged to shift to the system mode specifically intended for organization. Thus, system design encourages, but does not demand, users to transform their (loose) network of ideas into a well-formed hierarchical structure.

At any time in the process they can open a node and write or edit a block of text that will be associated with that node. *Editor* mode, shown in the lower right corner, is a conventional text editor. There, writers transform into text the concepts and the relations among them represented in the graph or tree. Eventually, we will provide other editors so that they may express an idea as a drawing. In fact, the general framework of the system is sufficiently general so that it would permit sound, video, or other forms of expression so long as editor and display functions are available.

Finally, the upper right system mode, called *text* mode, is intended for *coherence editing*. While the tree represents the structure of the document and the logical sequence of nodes or blocks of text that comprise it, text mode constructs a linear form of the implied text by stepping through the tree -- top to bottom, left to right. In it, one can see transitions from the text in one node to the text in another node, move sentences from one to another, etc. Eventually, we will replace text mode with a full WYSIWYG editor, but none is currently available that we can use.

In summary, the four system modes correspond with *exploration, organization, writing,* and *coherence editing*. For *structure editing*, writers uses tree mode: by moving branches and nodes around in the tree, users reorganize the text of the associated document. To support *expression editing*, writers may use either editor or text modes. Thus, six of the seven cognitive modes shown i.n Figure 1 are supported by the four system modes in WE. At present, WE does not support *situational analysis* mode. We have developed several heuristics that help writers with this thinking process [Smith & Smith, 1987], but since the products produced in this mode of thinking do not become literal parts of the document, we have not built a system mode to support it.

STUDIES

The third step in theory-based design is to test and refine both system and theory. To refine the model for writing and the WE system that was based upon it, we carried out a series of experimental studies under quasi-naturalistic conditions. Those studies, in addition to serving this purpose, also address a broader set of cognitive and human-computer interaction issues concerned with writers' cognitive strategies and patterns of behavior. Conducted over a 3-4 year period, they produced two different kinds of information that bear on the validity of the *strategic* model and the WE system design. First, we collected comments from participants in the form of responses on written questionnaires completed after several days of system use as well as oral responses made during debriefings. Second, as we explain in more detail below, we collected objective data of users' actions with the system in the form of machine-recorded protocols. By examining these data, we can see quite clearly and concretely which task or system operations caused users problems. Features that cause difficulty -- which we label *turbulence* to indicate interference with the natural flow of information and intent between user and system-- suggest inconsistencies either between the model and users' actual cognitive processes and strategies or between the model and its realization in the system design.

In the remainder of this section, we discuss these data in more detail.

The gist of our approach is this: a user works with an application system we have developed or modified to produce a machine-readable transcript of all *actions* -- rather than *keystrokes* -- performed by that user during the session. That session can take place in the laboratory or in the user's natural working environment. The data can be used to recreate, or *replay*, an approximation of the original session, but in a fraction of the original time. It can also be analyzed automatically by one of the *cognitive grammars* we have developed. These grammars constitute models of users' cognitive strategies for a given task using a particular computer system. The grammars are used to parse the protocols, producing a parse tree that is a concrete representation of a particular user's strategy for a given session. While these parse trees can be examined directly, more often they are further processed by *filter programs* that count various symbols or combinations of symbols in accord with a particular analytic perspective; these derived data are then passed to a statistical utility for

conventional analysis. Finally, these various data are presented to the researcher through a combination of *static* and *animated display tools* to facilitate visualization and interpretation. This methodology has been discussed in more detail in [Smith, Smith, & Kupstas, 1991].

While experiments differed in their particular designs, all took the same basic form. The overall purpose of the experiments was to have different populations of writers use the WE system to plan and write one or more documents approximately two-three pages in length, based upon reading materials supplied to them and addressing particular rhetorical situations that identified purpose, readers, etc. Subjects came to the lab for a series of two to five half-days, normally in the same week. They spent one or two half-days learning the system by completing a structured tutorial and several sample tasks. On the third and subsequent days, subjects planned, wrote, and edited documents using the WE system. Each writing task took two-three hours, during which the system automatically (and unobtrusively) recorded detailed action-level protocols, as discussed above. This design, thus, produced the two kinds of data noted above -- comments and observable patterns in the machine-recorded protocols.

Responses to Questionnaires

At the end of each study, we asked participants to fill out a long questionnaire about their reactions to the Writing Environment. For example, we asked them what they liked and didn't like about the system, how it compared to other word processing systems they had used, and how useful they found each of the system modes. Responses indicated that participants adapted easily to the multimodal nature of the system and to the fact that different system modes appear in different windows on the screen. They particularly liked the fact that they could see the organizational structures of their papers in a separate window as they wrote text. Here are some users' comments:

> The multiple window display is the most useful feature. The ability to see the organization of the document while editing a node is unique.

> I like having the outline section right next to the text section for quick reference.

We studied questionnaire responses for evidence that the system modes of the Writing Environment matched or did not match the cognitive modes of users. Responses suggested that the match was good for Network and Tree Modes, but not good for Edit and Text Modes.

Many users reported that they used Network Mode as we intended - for jotting down ideas and investigating the relationships between them. In response to the question, "Was Network Mode useful?" they wrote:

> Yes because it allowed you to get your ideas down without having to organize them.

> Yes - I liked the 'linking' idea.

Yes - it was useful to get many different ideas down quickly w/o having to worry about order.

Yes. Different ideas could be scattered in the beginning and then connected later.

They also found Tree Mode a useful tool for organizing their articles. In response to the question, "Was Tree Mode useful?" they said:

Yes because one could organize your ideas from the network modes and decide which ideas were useable and which were not.

Yes. It was very easy to move whole connected areas of thought.

An occasional user felt the Network and Tree Mode were redundant, but a greater number reported that they used the two modes for different types of thinking.

Responses to Edit and Text Mode were less enthusiastic. Some users liked the fact that Edit Mode encouraged them to focus on one idea at a time:

Perfect! It kept you focused on one aspect of your paper and helped you move on in writing. I think this is what cut the time consuming task of writing.

But many of the comments on Edit and Text Mode suggested that users had a hard time coordinating the planning modes and the writing modes to produce a text that flowed easily from section to section.

Some users wanted to use the structure they had produced in Tree Mode as a guide rather than as a fixed framework for their papers.

I do not like being constrained in the tree portion to having each topic in the text portion. I would like to be able to write a whole outline and pick and choose which topics will be paragraphs in the text.

I didn't like the fact that every part of the tree diagram acquired it's own title heading. I therefor couldn't include items to a topic which didn't include substantial text also.

Others wanted to see more of the text at one time while editing:

It would maybe be nice to have a screen where differentiation between nodes could be suppressed. - See flow of paper and transitions.

Some of the responses to Edit and Text Mode may reflect the fact that the Writing Environment did not have the polished editing capabilities of modern commercial word processors. But some of them also indicate that there is a mismatch between the way writers edit their texts and the way Edit and Text Modes of the Writing Environment are designed.

Users' comments clearly indicate that they want something like a WYSIWYG editor, in which they can see the text as a single unit. The challenge will be to create a new system mode which, on the one hand, allows users to see and modify the text as a whole and, on the other hand, allows users to rearrange sections of text by moving nodes in a tree.

Machine-Recorded Protocols

While the questionnaires reflect users' subjective reactions to the four system modes of the Writing Environment, the computer-generated protocols give us an objective view of how writers used these system modes. They tell us, for example, how users distributed their time among the various modes. Computer protocols indicated that almost all users spent a significant amount of time in both Network and Tree Modes and did work in both modes. The same is not true of Edit and Text Modes. A number of writers used either Edit or Text Mode exclusively for both writing and revising. Like the questionnaires, the protocol data indicate a good match between the cognitive processes of exploration and organization and the design of Network and Tree Modes but a poorer match between the cognitive processes of writing and revising and Edit and Text Modes.

Several aspects of the protocol data suggest that writers' strategies changed as they became more familiar with the system. During the early stages of practice, they spent a large proportion of their time experimenting with Network and Tree Modes. They often built very large trees, larger than necessary in some cases. As one user commented:

I should have made a simple hierarchy in the tree mode and not made so many nodes. It got to a point where I would have less than a sentence in each node. Better to have much larger chunks in each node.

Later in practice, users spent less time in the planning modes. In the one experiment, in which subjects learned to use the Writing Environment on Days 1 and 2 and wrote separate articles on Day 3 and Day 4, the amount of time spent in Tree Mode decreased significantly from Day 3 to Day 4 as did the number of nodes in the final tree.

Writing strategy also varied with the writers' knowledge of the topics the were writing about. In one study, we asked graduate students in art history and in chemistry to write two articles each, one on a particular type of Japanese Art and one on a type of metal alloy. Users spent more time *planning* their articles when they were writing on an unfamiliar topic than when they were writing on a familiar topic. But they spent more time writing and revising when they were working on the familiar topic.

One of the most interesting characteristics of the data was the pattern of alternations between the structural planning modes and the writing modes of the system. Many teachers advise their students to plan their papers first, by writing an outline, and then to use their outlines to guide their writing. According to these teachers, composing a document should take place in separate stages - first planning, then writing. We used our computer-generated protocols to ask whether our participants used the strategy teachers recommend.

We found that there was huge variability in the extent to which participants finished their planning in Network and Tree Modes before they began to write and revise in Edit and Text Modes. Figure 3 shows two extreme cases. For each subject, two broken horizontal lines represent time spent planning (in Network and Tree Modes) and time spent writing and revising (in Edit and Text Modes). The writer at the top did almost all his planning before he began to write. The writer at the bottom alternated between planning and writing throughout the session. The other 15 writers in this experiment were spread out along a continuum between these two extremes. In general, computer protocols show far more alternation between the planning the writing/revising modes of the system than we had anticipated. This finding emphasizes the need for smooth transitions between system modes.

These observations and data do not conclusively "prove" the theory or its realization in the system design. But

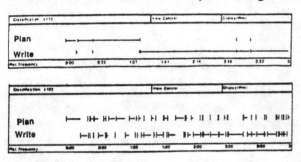

Figure 3: Each panel of this figure shows how an individual subject distributed his time between planning (Network and Tree Modes) and writing/revising (Edit and Text Modes). Time since the beginning of the session is shown on the horizontal axis. Each vertical tick represents the beginning of a planning or a writing/revising episode. The length of the horizontal line attached to the tick represents the duration of the episode. The top panel represents a writer who did almost all of his planning before he began writing and revising. The panel at the bottom represents a writer who alternated often between planning and writing/revising.

they do provide evidence that supports some design decisions while indicating the need to alter others. For example, the system's planning modes seem to closely match writers cognitive planning modes. On the other hand, the evidence suggests that although coherence editing may be a valid cognitive mode, the system mode intended to support that kind of thinking, which we called text mode, was unsatisfactory.

CONCLUSION AND FURTHER RESEARCH

The theory-based method described here is both comprehensive with respect to system design while also providing developers with guidance in making decisions regarding specific functions and their organization within the interface. It also provides ways to test both system

and theory that can produce specific suggestions for changes that could make the system better fit its users' thinking. We have used this method to build and test a hypertext system for expository writing, and we are extending it to two other tasks/systems -- for software development and for collaborative work. While our work to date convinces us of both the efficacy and generality of the approach, much research still needs to be done.

Modes and strategies are really architectural components. Further work is needed to elaborate a more complete cognitive architecture based on them. Similarly, we hope to see other tasks analyzed within this architecture. But to do so, better observational and analytic tools are needed to study patterns of users' behavior under naturalistic conditions and extending over extended periods of time -- months rather than hours -- if we are to take into account longitudinal and adaptive effects. And we need better interface development tools that facilitate building multimodal systems in which user function can easily be edited and reorganized in order to test different modal configurations or to match configuration with particular groups of users.

This program of research will require multidisciplinary teams and will involve basic research in both cognitive science and computer science as well as in HCI. But it promises us computer systems that more closely match the way we think. This is likely to be an increasingly important concern as computing becomes both more universal and more distributed.

ACKNOWLEDGMENTS

This research was supported by the National Science Foundation (Grants # IRI-8519517 and # IRI-8817305), The Army Research Institute (Contract # MDA903-86-C-345), and The Office of Naval Research (Contract # N00014-86-K-0680). A number of individuals have contributed both ideas and effort to the work described here; they include Gordon Ferguson, Steve Weiss, Dick Hayes, Catherine Smith, Matt Barkley, Paulette Bush, Rick Hawkes, John Hilgedick, Hong Li, Mark Rooks, Doug Shackelford, Yen-Ping Shan, Oliver Steele, John Walker, and Irene Weber.

REFERENCES

Ausubel, D. P. (1963). *The psychology of meaningful verbal learning.* New York: Grune & Stratton.

Bodker, Susanne (1989). A human activity approach to user interfaces. *Human-Computer Interaction,* 4,3,171-195.

Engelbart, D. C., Watson, R. W., & Norton, J. C. (1973). The augmented knowledge workshop. *AFIPS conference proceedings,* pp. 9-21.

Floyd, C., Wolf-Michael, M., Reisin, F-M., Schmidt, G., & Wolf, G. (1989). Out of Scandinavia: Alternative approaches to software design and system development. *Human-Computer Interaction,* 4,4, 253-349.

Hayes, J. R. & Flower, L. S. (1980). Identifying the organization of the writing process. In L. W. Gregg & E. R. Steinberg (Eds.), *Cognitive Processes in Writing*. Hillsdale, NJ: Lawrence Erlbaum Associates, pp. 3-30.

Kieras, D. E. (1980). Initial mention as a signal to thematic content in technical passages. *Memory and Cognition*, 8, 345-353.

Kintsch, W., & van Dijk, T. A. (1978). Toward a model of text comprehension and production. *Psychological Review*, 85, 363-394.

Meyer, G. J. F., Brandt, D. M., & Bluth, G. J. (1980). Use of top-level structure in text: key for reading comprehension of ninth grade students. *Reading Research Quarterly*, 1, 72-103.

Schwartz, M. N. K., & Flammer, A. (1981). Text structure and title-effects on comprehension and recall. *Journal of Verbal Learning and Verbal Behavior*, 20, 61-66.

Smith, J. B., & Lansman, M. L (1991). *Cognitive modes and strategies for writing*. Chapel Hill, NC: UNC Department of Computer Science Technical Report # TR91-047.

Smith, J. B., & Smith, C. F. (1987). *A strategic method for writing*. Chapel Hill, NC: UNC Department of Computer Science Technical Report # TR87-024.

Smith, J. B., Smith, D. K, & Kupstas, E. (1991). Tools and techniques for automated protocol analysis. Chapel Hill, NC: UNC Department of Computer Science Technical Report # TR91-034.

Suchman, L. (1987). *Plans and situated actions: The problem of human-machine communication*. Cambridge: Cambridge University Press.

Winograd, T., & Flores, C. F. (1986). *Understanding computers and cognition: A new foundation for design*. Norwood, NJ: Ablex.

Towards a Model of Cognitive Process in Logical Design: Comparing Object-Oriented and Traditional Functional Decomposition Software Methodologies

Jinwoo Kim and F. Javier Lerch

Graduate School of Industrial Administration
Carnegie Mellon University, Pittsburgh, PA 15213
jk2i@andrew.cmu.edu, fl0c@andrew.cmu.edu

ABSTRACT

This study aims at developing and empirically testing hypotheses about professional designers' cognitive activities when using object-oriented methodology (OOD) versus using traditional functional decomposition methodologies (TFD). Our preliminary results indicate that OOD may achieve substantial time savings over TFD in logical design. The verbal protocols from a pilot study show that OOD may achieve these time savings: 1) by simplifying rule induction processes used in functional decomposition; 2) by guiding designers on how to build more effective problem spaces; and 3) by allowing designers to run mental simulation more efficiently and more effectively.

KEYWORDS: Rule induction, mental simulation, object-oriented design, functional decomposition.

INTRODUCTION

In the last two decades several software design methodologies have been developed for guiding and aiding designers in the complex process of software development. Examples of software design methodologies are Data Structure Oriented Design [12], Structured Analysis and Design [18, 27] and more recently, Object-Oriented Design [3, 4, 5, 6, 16, 19]. Most design methodologies that were available before Object-Oriented Design (OOD) utilize a process called functional decomposition for transforming problem requirements into logical design. The proponents of Object-Oriented methodologies claim that OOD is superior to traditional methodologies (e.g. improved productivity) during logical design because Object Oriented methodologies lessens (or eliminates) the complexity of the cognitive processes required by functional

decomposition[1]. Presently there is little empirical evidence that supports these claims [6, 21] but there are several theoretical discussions that speculate why OOD may induce different problem-solving behavior and cognitive processing during logical design [4, 15, 20]. The objective of this research is to develop and empirically test hypotheses about the differences in cognitive problem solving activities between OOD and TFD designers.

In cognitive terms, a software design methodology is a problem solving aid that focuses the designers' attention on certain aspects of the design problem and attempts to facilitate the process of transforming problem requirements into a software solution. This research effort focuses on comparing the cognitive processes that may be induced by OOD and TFD during the logical design processes. Logical design includes understanding of the given problem and the transformation of this understanding into a high-level software design (e.g. pseudo-code). This paper first explains why OOD may facilitate logical design and presents an experiment for testing the differences of cognitive processes between OOD and TFD. The results of our pilot study indicate that when the characteristics of the problem are well suited to OOD, OOD may achieve substantial time savings (4:1) over traditional methodologies in logical design. The verbal protocols from the pilot study show that OOD may achieve these time savings: 1) by simplifying rule induction processes used in functional decomposition; 2) by guiding designers on how to build more effective problem spaces; and 3) by allowing designers to run mental simulations more efficiently and more effectively.

The next section briefly reviews the research on rule induction during problem solving and the role of mental simulation in design activities. Section three elaborates on the potential advantages of OOD during logical design. Section four presents the experimental design and analysis procedures. Section five presents and discusses the results of the pilot experiment. The last section describes plans for future research.

---

[1] Their specific claims are that OOD is more natural [15, 5], OOD is based on the underlying framework of the application domain itself [19], and object-orientation offers a better mapping of problem entities than the procedures and data structures utilized in traditional functional decomposition methodologies [20].

THEORETICAL BACKGROUND

Rule Induction

Rule induction can be classified as a specific problem solving activity that aims at finding a set of rules to solve a group of problems rather than just a single individual problem. Rule induction processes are included in general induction tasks such as concept attainment [23], pattern induction [25], and scientific discovery [24]. The main difference between rule induction and other problem-solving activities is the existence of two problem spaces built for the task: a space of instance and a space of rule [25]. In the rule induction task, the attainment of a solution is determined by applying the proposed rule to instances and by testing whether this application yields a correct result. The test is not applied directly to the rule but rather to another set of expressions, the instance. Therefore, a set of rules are generated in the rule space and those rules are tested in the instance space. It is the existence of this dual space and the use of information drawn from one space to constrain search in the other space that distinguishes rule induction from other forms of problem solving.

Software design requires that designers discover a set of rules for fulfilling user requirements. From this point of view, programs are sets of rules for translating user requirements into computer programming constructs. For example, suppose that a user asks a designer to develop a program that calculates a person's social security tax. The user states that social security tax is 7% of annual income up to $48,000. In this case, the designer should discover a set of rules for calculating a person's social security tax under all possible conditions.

Several studies have shown that software designers utilize two problem spaces during logical design: the task domain problem space and the solution domain problem space [14, 9, 20, 11, 5]. The task domain problem space is the internal representation of the description of the problem used by the designers during problem understanding; this representation is in the language of the problem given to the designer. The solution domain problem space is the internal representation of the full or partial software solution of the problem in the language of the methodology used by the designer. In the social security tax example, the task domain consists of real world entities, such as tax, income, and people, while the solution domain consists of data structure (e.g., a variable for income) and control logic (e.g., if-then statements). The rule induction task during logical design involves generating instances of problem solutions in the task domain problem space and then generating and testing sets of rules. This generation and testing of rules requires moving between solution instances in the task domain problem space and proposed rules in the solution domain problem space.

In the social security tax example, the designer might generate three instances; Tom earned $45,000 until last month, and $2,000 in this month; Jerry earned $47,000 until last month, and $2,000 in this month; Bob earned $49,000 until last month, and $2,000 in this month. By solving these instances, the designer might come up with a set of rules; if a person's cumulative income is less than $48,000, then pay 7% of this month's income; if his cumulative income just exceeds $48,000 in this month, then calculate the difference between the last month's cumulative income and $48,000 and pay 7% of that difference; if his last month cumulative income is already greater than $48,000, then pay nothing. This set of rules can be translated into the solution domain as: IF $(z + y) <$ 48000 THEN $t = z * 0.07$ ELSEIF $y > 48000$ THEN $t = 0$ ELSE $t = (48000-y)*0.07$ where $z=$last month's cumulative income, $y=$ this month's income, $t=$current social security tax.

We expect software methodologies to have a major impact on rule induction processes because they prescribe how designers should approach the problem in the task domain problem space (e.g. focus on objects vs. focus on functions) and they determine the nature of the solution problem space (e.g. OOD elements in the solution problem space are objects, attributes, methods, and messages while TFD manipulates data structures and control logic constructs).

Mental Simulation

Mental simulation is a general problem-solving strategy [13, 26]. In software design, mental simulation is defined as the internal execution of the task or the software solution; several studies have found that mental simulation is pervasive in software design and consumes a large proportion of designers' time [1, 14, 9, 8]. Empirical studies have also shown that mental simulation is error prone in complex design tasks because of the overloading of Working Memory (WM). WM overloading is generated by long sequences of operations and/or by the complexity of the problem states manipulated by the designer during execution. For example, Anderson and Jefferies [2] showed that errors in mental simulation are a major determinant of the amount of time spent in writing Lisp programs because programmers spent a great deal of time identifying and correcting errors generated by faulty mental simulations. In their design studies, Kant and Newell [14] also found that most of the design time was spent making errors during mental simulations and recovering from these errors. We expect that software methodologies should have a differential impact on WM overloading because different software methodologies may induce problem spaces with different states and operators.

Kant and Newell [14] also show that mental simulations have two types of executions: symbolic and test-case. Symbolic simulation is the execution of an internal representation with general symbols as inputs. This type of simulation is only possible if designers are capable of achieving a certain level of abstraction that allows them to generate symbolic representations of the task. In the tax example, a symbolic mental simulation would utilized inputs such as 'calculate tax for a person with current income of $z'. On the other hand, designers are forced to run simulations with specific test cases (test-case execution) when they lack sufficient generalizable knowledge about the problem or its solution. In the tax example, the designer may run a test-case execution such as 'calculate tax for Jim Jones with current income of $2,000.' Although in general a single symbolic execution requires more cognitive resources than a single test-case simulation [14], symbolic simulations are more effective because they are more general: several test-case simulations are required to gain the same knowledge (about the program or the design) generated by one symbolic execution. Therefore designers may prefer to run symbolic simulations if they can actually run the simulation in their heads; otherwise they either generate a large number of errors or switch to test-case simulations.

COGNITIVE PROCESSES IN LOGICAL DESIGN

We expect OOD to radically change the cognitive processes in logical design. The major changes induced by OOD can be identified in terms of: 1) the complexity of the rule induction process, 2) the characteristics of the two problem spaces, and 3) the efficiency and effectiveness of running mental simulations in the two problem spaces. In this section we compare and contrast the cognitive processes we expect designers to execute when following either the traditional functional decomposition methodologies (TFD) or the object oriented methodology (OOD).

We first present the cognitive processes TFD designers are expected to execute in logical design and the performance implications of these processes. We then outline how OOD radically changes these cognitive process. Finally, we summarize the differences between the two methodologies by presenting a set of hypotheses.

Cognitive Processes in Traditional Functional Decomposition Methodologies

TFD methodologies focus the designers' attention on the functional aspects of the software [27, 18, 11]. Because designers are mainly concerned about software functions at the outset of the design process, designers attempt to find a set of rules in the task domain which can be easily translated later on into the functions of the software. TFD therefore makes extensive use of induction processes to specify the rules in the logical design. We speculate that this focus on rule discovery prevents designers from engaging in other processes, such as abstracting problem space elements or mapping elements from the task domain to the solution domain during the early stages of the design effort.

We hypothesize that the rule induction process in logical design is similar to other induction tasks such as pattern induction and rule discovery[25]. We therefore expect TFD designers typically to go through the following steps. First, several test-case problems are solved in the task domain by using mental simulation and then a set of hypothetical rules is generated by finding some common patterns in the problem solutions for the several test cases. Second, these hypothetical rules are tested by executing mental simulations. If the designers find that the hypothetical set of rules cannot solve the problem, they are forced to go back to solve additional test cases. If the hypothetical set of rules turns out to be appropriate for the problem, then the designers will translate this set of rules into the control logic (functions) and the data structures that constitute the software solution. Third, these translated data structures and control logic will be tested by executing evaluative mental simulations [9, 14]. At any time during the rule induction process, designers may decide to decompose the set of rules into several sub-sets of rules or sub-functions if they consider the original set of rules to be too complex.

Problem spaces generated with early focus on the functions of software and on rule induction with less abstraction tend to have some specific characteristics. First, the solution-domain problem space will be different from the task-domain problem space because the solution domain consists of data structures and control logic whereas the task-domain consists of real world entities and constraints [5, 20]. Second, both task-domain and solution-domain problem spaces will include less abstraction because the detailed elements of the task-domain are directly used in the rule-induction process and then translated into data structures and control logic.

We hypothesize that these two characteristics of TFD problem spaces cause Working Memory (WM) to overload during mental simulations. Figure 1 shows a schematic representation of how this process may occur. It also shows how problem space characteristics are expected to be related to cognitive processing predictions.

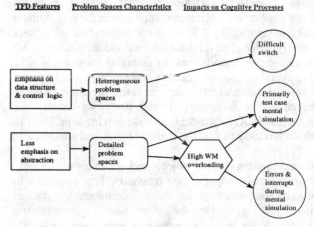

Figure 1: Impact of TFD on the cognitive processes of logical design

The heterogeneity between the elements in the two problem spaces may generate high WM loads because designers have to remember real world elements in the task domain and artificial constructs and constraints in the solution domain. The detailed nature of the two problem spaces causes WM overloading because designers need to remember a large number of symbols while running mental simulations.

If WM overloading is prevalent in TFD design, then we expect a significant number of errors and interrupts during the execution of mental simulations as shown Figure 1. Errors are produced when designers fail to consider some relevant constraints in their mental simulations; interrupts are generated by designers stopping the mental simulation when information needed for execution is unavailable. WM overloading, in conjunction with the detailed nature of the problem spaces, is likely to minimize the number of symbolic mental simulations executed by the designers because symbolic mental simulation requires both an abstracted problem space and considerable cognitive resources. Finally, the heterogeneity of the elements in the two problem spaces increases the difficulty of switching between these spaces and therefore fewer switches are expected than in the case in which the elements in the two problem spaces are more homogeneous.

Cognitive Processes in Object Oriented Methodology

We expect OOD methodology to simplify the rule induction process because of its early focus on objects rather than functions. This focus on objects should also change the nature of the problem spaces and facilitate the execution of mental simulations and the switching between problem spaces.

OOD methodology requires that designers first identify the objects and attributes in the task-domain problem space. Designers are asked to focus on the main objects in the problem rather than on the main functions of the software [4, 11]. All other OOD software components such as attributes, methods, and messages are constructed around objects. OOD also provides detailed templates about how to find objects and attributes in the task-domain problem space [5]. We do not know how designers actually determine relevant objects and attributes. We only have naive guidelines for detecting those entities[3]. However, we do expect that after designers find out correct objects and attributes, the entire process of logical design will be facilitated. In this study, we analyze the impact of OOD when designers are solving a problem in which it is easy to find the correct objects and attributes.

After designers identify objects and attributes in the task-domain problem space, they transform them directly into objects and attributes in the solution-domain problem space [20, 5]. On the other hand, operators and constraints in the task domain require more elaborate transformations into methods and messages of objects.

Operators in the task domain are usually constrained by rules that specify when it is legal to apply these operators. Operator constraints should be reorganized and transformed into methods and messages so that they can be represented in terms of how an object uses a method or message in the solution domain. In other words, OOD prescribes that the designer specifies methods and messages of individual objects rather than a set of rules for the whole program. Therefore the rule induction process in OOD is simplified; rule induction in OOD is the process of identifying and transforming operators and operator constraints into methods and messages of individual objects. This is in sharp contrast to rule induction process in TFD which tries to develop a set of rules for the entire problem. The rule induction process in OOD is modularized based on individual object, and evolves naturally toward general object classes. During this rule induction process, designers are encouraged to abstract all OOD components (objects, attributes, methods, and messages) to emphasize the important points and to suppress details immaterial or diversionary [4].

These characteristics of OOD methodology generates problem spaces that are substantially different from those generated by TFD. First, the objects in the solution domain are regarded as the natural real world objects, not as artificial program constructs. Rosson and Gold [21] empirically found that real world objects are frequently represented in OOD. Second, the objects in the two problem spaces are supposed to be abstracted objects. OOD emphasizes that attributes, methods, and messages should be reconstructed or abstracted around abstract objects. Therefore designers in OOD build problem spaces in which their elements are abstracted and are organized around the main objects. Third, objects have data and procedures within themselves and interact with other objects only through messages [6]. Therefore OOD problem spaces are built around objects which are active and autonomous entities that know what they can do by themselves. This should generate problem spaces that are modularized because they are based on autonomous objects.

We hypothesize that the nature of OOD problem spaces reduces WM overloading during mental simulation as illustrated in Figure 2. The real world solution domain results in low WM load because designers do not have to remember arbitrary constructs and constraints and can rely on their knowledge about the familiar real world [22, 9]. The abstracted problem spaces also decrease WM loads because object-based abstraction decreases the number of unimportant details to be considered in running mental simulations. OOD problem spaces also facilitate partial mental simulation due to the modularity generated by each object having its own data and procedures.

If OOD reduces WM overloading during mental simulation, then designers should be less likely to generate errors or interrupts. Reduced WM loading coupled with abstracted problem spaces should also enable designers to run symbolic mental simulations more extensively. Finally OOD should facilitate switching between the two problem spaces because their elements are similar to each other so designers are required to remember less details about the states in each problem space during problem solving.

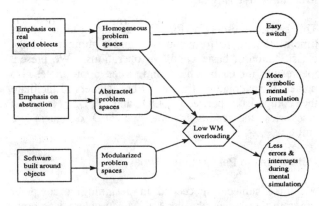

Figure 2: Impact of OOD on the cognitive processes of logical design

Hypotheses

Our hypotheses are that in comparison to TFD designers, OOD designers will

H1. use symbolic mental simulation more extensively,

H2. use test-case mental simulation less extensively,

H3. commit fewer errors during mental simulation,

H4. have fewer interrupts during mental simulation,

H5. switch between two problem spaces more frequently,

H6. use less time executing mental simulations, and
    (because of H1, H2, H3, H4)

H7. spend less time in completing the logical design.
    (because of H1, H2, H3, H4, H5, H6)

PILOT STUDY

Subjects

Three professional software designers participated in the pilot study. Two designers used TFD (Subjects TFD1 and TFD2) and one OOD (subject OOD1). The subjects were recruited through an electronic bulletin board at Carnegie Mellon University and were paid to participate in the experiment. All subjects are professional programmers with programming experience ranging from 8 years for OOD1 to 9 and 17 years for TFD1 and TFD2 respectively. Subjects had at least two years of experience in what they consider to be their predominant methodology.

Materials

All subjects were asked to solve two isomorphs of the Tower-of-Hanoi (TOH) problem; first, the Monster-Change (MC) problem, then the Monster-Transfer (MT) problem. Two problems are isomorphs if any solution of one may be translated step by step into a solution path of the other [10]. Isomorphs have the same basic problem structure which are disguised in different wordings. The descriptions of the two problems (MC and MT) are presented in Figure 3.

We selected the MC problem as the main task for two reasons. First, we hypothesize that OOD designers can identify the correct object (monster) and attribute (the size of the globe) easily for this MC problem because the monster is the only active agent in the problem description. This hypothesis has been supported by empirical studies with subjects solving the MC problem [10]. Second, prior empirical work has shown that the execution of test-case mental simulations for the MC problem is time consuming and error prone [22]. Therefore, since TFD designers are expected to use test-case mental simulations extensively, we can predict TFD designers to require more time during logical design than OOD designers and we expect them to make more errors during mental simulation.

Three five-handed extraterrestrial monsters are holding three crystal globes. Because of the quantum-mechanical peculiarities of their neighborhood, both monsters and globes come in exactly three sizes with no other permitted: small, medium, and large. It is randomly determined which size of monsters are holding which size of globes. For example, it is possible that the medium-sized monster is holding the small globe; the small monster is holding the large globe; and the large monster is holding the medium-sized globe. Since this situation offends their keenly developed sense of symmetry, they proceed *to shrink and expand globes (or, to transfer globes from one monster to another*[a])* so that each monster would have a globe proportionate to its own size starting from any given initial composition.

Monsters etiquette complicated the solution of the problem since it requires that:

1. Only one globe may be *changed (transferred)* at a time.

2. *If two globes have the same size, only the globe held by the larger monster may be changed. (If a monster is holding more than one globe, only the largest of the globes may be transferred.)*

3. A globe may not be *changed to the same size as the globe of a larger monster (transferred to a monster who is holding a larger globe)* .

*a. The two problems differ only in the italic portions. The MT problem is presented in parentheses.

Figure 3: The Monster-Change problem

Our selection of the two monster problem isomorphs was also based on practical considerations: First, we can use the MT problem to measure the depth of understanding about the underlying problem structure since both problems are isomorphs. Problem isomorphs have the same problem structures which are disguised in different wordings. If designers have a deep understanding about the problem after solving the MC problem, they may be more likely to find out that the MT problem can be solved with the same computer program. Second, the problems can be described in a single page allowing designers rapid re-readings during problem understanding and logical design.

Procedure

Subjects were given instructions about the general nature of the experiment and told that verbal protocols would be collected. Subjects were then trained in the thinking-aloud method by using two traditional training tasks (mental multiplication and window visualization[7]).

The experimental sessions were divided into five sections. First, subjects were asked to read the MC problem and to understand it thoroughly. Second, they were asked to build a logical design for solving the problem by writing detailed pseudo-code in their respective methodologies (TFD or OOD). Third, subjects were asked to check their logical design by solving one specific test case of the general MC problem. Then, they were asked to write a computer program based on their logical design. After they finished the MC problem, they were asked to do the same tasks for the MT problem. The subjects were stopped either when they found out that the MT problem is the same problem as the MC problem or when they started to write down new pseudo-code for the MT problem without finding that the two problems are isomorphs.

Analysis Procedure

All experimental sessions were videotaped. The logical design effort encompasses the first two experimental sections (problem reading and writing pseudo-code). The verbal protocols for the logical design were transcribed and segmented into episodes. Episodes are small self-contained phases of highly organized activity as shown in Figure 4 [17]. Each episode was then decomposed into several basic activities (not shown in Figure 4).

Basic activities were classified according to two factors. First, each activity was coded in terms of whether it was in the task domain or in the solution domain. This coding was usually done by using keywords identifying the content of subjects' cognitive activities. For example, task domain activities are characterized by subjects discussing elements of the problem such as rules for applying operators (e.g. changing the size of the globes) while solution domain activities can be identified by references to programming constructs such as pointers and if-then statements. However, in some occasions isolated keywords were not sufficient for classifying activities in a given domain so the actual context of the entire episode was taken into consideration. Second, we identified all mental simulations interspersed in the transcribed protocols. A mental simulation activity was operationally defined as any cognitive process in which subjects

actually traverse the problem space in the task domain or run logical design constructs in the solution domain. Mental simulations were classified either as test-case or symbolic according to the inputs used during the simulation. Furthermore, we also assessed the execution of each mental simulation as completed without error, completed with errors, or not completed (interrupts).

PRELIMINARY RESULTS

This section presents performance results in terms of the time needed to perform the task and a summary of the classification of basic cognitive operations. We present the results for each subject and, when appropriate, also present the average for the two TFD designers to facilitate the comparison between OOD and TFD. In most categories, the results for the two TFD designers are similar.

Differences in Performance Time

All three subjects succeeded in designing a computer program that solves the general MC problem isomorph. However, there was a substantial difference in time between OOD1 and the TFD designers. OOD1 required only one third of the time needed by the TFD designers (69 minutes for OOD1 versus 185 minutes for the average of the two TFD designers). Furthermore, OOD1 finished the logical design four times faster than the TFD designers (the time spent in these activities was 24 minutes for OOD1 vs. 102 minutes for TFD designers). OOD1 took almost the same time to run his logical design with the specific case given for the walk-through (6.3 minutes for OOD1 vs. 4.7 for TFD designers). OOD1 needed approximately half the time spent by the TFD designers for writing and debugging the computer program.

Differences in Logical Design Processes

Figure 4 presents three episodic schemas at an abstract level that represent the entire problem-solving paths of the three subjects during logical design. TFD designers spent most time in rule induction process in which they solved several test cases and generated and tested a set of rules. For example, TFD2 generated and solved several test cases (*56 - *62 in the figure) and then generated two rules based upon the solution (*65, *66). Then he found that these rules had errors and decided to solve several more test cases (*67 -*73). Then he generated and tested three more rules (*74, *76, *78) based on the solution paths of the test cases. Finally he developed control logic (*79 - *83) based on the induced rules. TFD1 performed rule induction processes in a very similar manner to TFD2. In other words, during logical design, the TFD designers spent a large amount of time in rule induction processes, especially in solving individual cases. In fact, TFD1 listed all (twenty seven) possible test cases (*48) and attempted to solve most of them (*25 - *33, *34 - *38, *41 - *46, *50 - *55).

Episodic Schema for OOD1 | Episodic Schema for TFD1 | Episodic Schema for TFD2

Read the problem [a](74)
Build a TD [b]**space (195)**
- *1 Find out objects.
- *2 Find out attributes.
- *3 Define initial & goal states.

Build basic rules (219)
- *4 Generate initial rules.
- *5 Test the initial rules.
- *6 Refine the rules in objects.
- *7 Test the refined rules.

Refine the basic design (257)
- *8 Refine the object.
- *9 Refine the set of rules.
- *10 Solve a symbolic case.
- *11 Refine the set of rules.
- *12 Refine the attributes.

Translate to SD [c] **space (61)**
- *13 Translate the object.
- *14 Translate the attributes.

Transform constraints into a method (494)
- *15 Transform the second constraint into a method.
- *16 Transform the first constraint into a method.
- *17 Transform the third constraint into a method.
- *18 Generate change and change back rules.

Generate & test a main control rule in SD (133)
- *19 Generate a rule.
- *20 Test the generated rule.

Read the problem (130)
Build a TD space (110)

Generate & test several alternative rules (522)
- *21 generate & test a rule.
- *22 generate & test another rule.
- *23 generate & test another rule.
- *24 generate & test another rule.

Generate & solve several test cases (1829)
- *25 Solve a test case
- *26 Solve another test case.
- *27 Solve another test case.
- *28 Solve another test case.
- *29 Solve a test case again.
- *30 Solve a test case again.
- *31 Solve another test case.
- *32 Solve a test case again.
- *33 Solve another test case.

Generate & test several alternative rules (607)
- *34 Solve a test case.
- *35 Solve another test case.
- *36 Solve another test case.
- *37 Solve another test case.
- *38 Solve another test case.
- *39 Generate & test a rule.
- *40 Generate&test another rule.

Generate & solve several test cases (1356)
- *41 Solve a test case
- *42 Solve another test case.
- *43 Solve another test case.
- *44 Solve another test case.
- *45 Solve another test case.
- *46 Solve another test case.

Generate & test several alternative rules (1442)
- *47 Generate&test a rule.
- *48 Generate 27 test cases.
- *49 Generate&test a rule.
- *50 Solve a test case.
- *51 Solve a symbolic case.
- *52 Solve a symbolic case.
- *53 Solve a symbolic case.
- *54 Solve a symbolic case.
- *55 Generate & test a rule.

Translate into pseudo-code (689)

Read the problem(245)
Build a TD space (249)

Generate & solve several test cases (1530)
- *56 Solve a test case.
- *57 Solve another test case.
- *58 Generate a test case.
- *59 Generate another test case.
- *60 Generate another test case.
- *61 Generate another test case.
- *62 Generate another test case.

Build a data structure (302)
- *63 Build a globe array in SD
- *64 Represent the globes in TD

Generate & test several alternative rules (297)
- *65 Generate&test a rule.
- *66 Generate&test another rule.

Generate & solve several test cases (1319)
- *67 Solve a test case
- *68 Solve another test case.
- *69 Solve a test case again.
- *70 Solve another test case.
- *71 Solve another test case.
- *72 Solve a test case again.
- *73 Solve a test case again.

Generate & test several alternative rules (446)
- *74 Generate a rule.
- *75 Solve a test case.
- *76 Generate a rule.
- *77 Solve a test case.
- *78 Generate a rule.

Generate & translate a set of rules (1191)
- *79 Generate an abstract rule.
- *80 Generate a sub-set of rules.
- *81 Generate a sub-set of rules.
- *82 Generate a sub-set of rules.
- *83 Generate a sub-set of rules.

---

a. Number in the () represents time taken for that step in seconds.
b. TD = Task domain
c. SD = Solution domain

Figure 4: Episodic schema for the three subjects.

On the other hand, OOD1 spent very little time in rule induction processes and actually solved only a single test case (*10) during the entire logical design process.

OOD1's design activities closely followed those activities prescribed by the OOD methodology. First, OOD1 identified the objects (*1) and attributes (*2) and defined methods of objects at the abstract level (*6). Next, he elaborated on the definitions of objects and attributes (*8, *12) and then translated the object and attributes in the task domain into the solution domain (*13, *14). He then performed a simplified rule induction process (*15, *16, *17, *18) by simply transforming the three constraints in the problem description into a method. This method specified how an object (a monster) can accomplish its goal states (having its correct size of globe), whereas the constraints in the problem description prescribed the rules for changing the attribute of the object (the size of the globe). OOD1 only needed 8 minutes to perform this transformation.

Although the rule induction process was highly simplified by the OOD methodology, several specific design problem surfaced because OOD1 found it difficult to ignore irrelevant features of the problem. For example, OOD1 was puzzled by the fact that monsters have five hands; this attribute of the monster is completely irrelevant for solving the problem. OOD1 attempted to model the number of hands as an attribute of the main object (the monster) because the OOD methodology clearly prescribes the identification of all attributes after objects have been defined but before we know if these attributes will be needed for building the methods. This type of difficulty was not exhibited by either of the two TFD designers.

Differences in Mental Simulation

OOD1 spent less time in mental simulations than TFD designers in both absolute and relative terms. OOD1 mental simulation time was 5.4 minutes compared to 63.8 minutes for the TFD designers. In relative terms, OOD1 spent 23% of his logical design time in activities classified as mental simulations while this percentage was 62% for the TFD designers.

Table 1 shows the percentage of mental simulation times between symbolic and test-case mental simulation.

ITEM	OOD1	Avg. TFD	TFD1	TFD2
Symbolic MS	90%	44%	54%	31%
Test-case MS	10%	56%	46%	69%

Table 1 : Time distribution of mental simulation categories (% of mental simulation time spent in each category)

OOD1 spent 90% of his total mental simulation time in symbolic mental simulation. On the other hand, TFD designers spent only 44% of their total mental simulation time in symbolic mental simulation and the remaining 56% in test case mental simulations.

Table 2 shows our classification of mental simulations in terms of errors and interruptions.

ITEM	OOD1	Avg. TFD	TFD1	TFD2
# of CN	10	18.5	24	13
# of CE	2	10	12	8
# of Completed	12(80%)	28.5(45%)	36 (46%)	21(42%)
# of INT	3 (20%)	35 (55%)	41 (54%)	29(58%)
Total # of MS	15(100%)	63.5(100%)	77(100%)	50(100%)

CN = Mental simulations completed without errors.
CE = Mental simulations completed with errors.
INT = Mental simulations which were not completed.

Table 2 : Classification of mental simulation (MS)
(# of mental simulation)

This classification indicates that OOD1 completed 80% of his total mental simulation trials while the TFD designers only completed 45% of their mental simulations. Only the completed mental simulations were classified again in terms of errors. Our analysis of completed mental simulations shows that TFD designers made errors in approximately one third of their completed mental simulations whereas less than one fifth of OOD1's completed mental simulations were classified as completions with errors.

Differences in the Activities Between Problem Spaces.

OOD1 spent less percentage of time in the task domain than the TFD designers. Table 3 shows that OOD1 spent 41% of his logical design effort in activities classified as task domain activities.

ITEM	OOD1	TFD Average	TFD1	TFD2
Task Domain	9.9 (41%)	71.6(70%)	75.9(68%)	67.3 (72%)
Solution Domain	13.9 (59%)	30.5(30%)	35.2(32%)	25.9 (28%)
# of Switches	25		1	7

Table 3 : Task domain vs. solution domain (minutes)

On the other hand, TFD designers spent 70% of their logical design time in the task domain mainly because they performed several test case solutions of the problem. More interestingly, the classification of OOD1 activities shows OOD1 switching between the two problem spaces approximately every minute. On the other hand, TFD1 switched between the two spaces in only one occasion during the entire logical design process while TFD2 switched only seven times (every 13 minutes on average).

Differences in the MT Problem

OOD1 discovered that the MC and MT problems are isomorphs in less than 10 minutes by paraphrasing the three constraints in the MT problem into the constraints of the MC problem. On the other hand, both TFD designers attempted to write new pseudo-code without noticing the common underlying structure between the two problems. They spent considerable time in this effort (56.4 minutes for TFD1 & 44.2 minutes for TFD2). Furthermore, both TFD designers were unable to discover this common

structure even after given direct clues repeatedly (e.g., " Don't you think this is the same problem as the first problem?" Subject's answer " No, because now the monsters can have more than one globe").

Discussion

This study shows that OOD1 achieved substantial time savings over the TFD designers in logical design because OOD1: 1) simplified the rule induction processes by focusing on individual objects (monsters) rather than on functions and by transforming the general operators and constraints into the methods of individual objects, 2) built more effective problem spaces (i.e. homogeneous, abstract, and modularized problem spaces) by following OOD methodology, and 3) ran more effective mental simulations (symbolic executions) more efficiently (with fewer errors and interruptions).

The rule induction process is simplified because OOD does not require the designer to solve many specific cases of the problem. Instead, rule induction is only attempted in OOD when methods (linked to specific objects) need to be specified. In our study, the OOD designer simply transformed the constraints in the problem descriptions into the method in the solution domain after the correct objects had been identified. This result indicates that OOD has a distinctive advantage in problems with complex requirements for rule induction and simple object and attribute structures.

TFD designers executed a large number of test-case mental simulations to discover a set of rules to be implemented in the solution domain. These mental simulations, as in other design tasks [14], were time consuming and error prone. Errors in mental simulations compound the difficulty of the rule induction process by generating wrong solutions that produce faulty sets of rules. Consequently TFD designers spent considerable time in the detection and correction of these errors. On the other hand, the OOD designer utilized mental simulation infrequently and mostly with symbolic inputs.

Although the OOD designer spent less time in absolute and relative terms in the task domain, he developed a better understanding of the underlying problem structure. We propose two possible explanations: a) OOD's emphasis on abstraction helps to find the underlying problem structure that is the same in both problems, and b) the mapping needed to find that two problems are isomorphs is similar to the mapping needed to build methods from problem constraints.

FUTURE RESEARCH

The basis of our future research is the manipulation of problem characteristics using problem isomorphs. We expect this strategy to provide two advantages: a) we can compare how problem characteristics influence cognitive processes without changing the underlying structure of the problem, and b) we expect to lessen the difficulty of finding designers with comparable expertise in OOD and TFD methodologies.

In this research, we selected the MC problem as the main task because we expected a substantial superiority of OOD over TFD. It is likely this advantage will be reduced by changing the characteristics of the problem without changing the final logical design. For example, we expect TFD designers need less time for solving the MT problem than the MC problem because the execution of test-case simulations is easier for the MT problem by a factor of 2 [10].

We also expect problem isomorphs will help us to relieve some of the difficulties of empirically comparing between OOD versus TFD. One of the main problems in empirical testing is that it is very difficult to directly control the designers' level of expertise in their predominant methodology. Given this reality, any difference in the cognitive processes between OOD and TFD designers might be attributed to the differences of the designers' expertise in their predominant methodology as well as to the differences induced by the methodologies. Problem isomorphs can be used as a way of isolating the impact of the software design methodology on cognitive strategies and performance because surface characteristics of the problem isomorphs can have a differential impact on OOD and TFD. For example, features that make it difficult to find out the correct objects and attributes may have a detrimental impact on OOD designers but not on TFD designers. Therefore if the performance superiority of OOD and TFD is altered by the type of problem, we can isolate the impact of methodology by randomly assigning designers from each population (OOD and TFD) to each problem isomorph.

ACKNOWLEDGEMENTS

The authors would like to acknowledge the advice and comments of Dr. Herbert Simon.

REFERENCES

1. Adelson, B., and Soloway, E.   A Model for Software Design *(YALEU/CSD/RR #342)*. Shelton, CT: ITT 1984.

2. Anderson, J. and Jefferies, R. Novice LISP Errors: Undetected Losses of Information from Working Memory. *Human-Computer Interaction*, Vol. 1, (1985), 107-131.

3. Booch, G. Object-Oriented Development. *IEEE Transactions on Software Engineering, SE-12*, (1986). 211-221.

4. Booch, G. *Object Oriented Design with applications.* Benjamin/Cummings, Redwood City, C.A., 1991.

5. Coad, P and Yourdon, E. *Object-Oriented Analysis.* Prentice-Hall, Englewood Cliffs, N.J., 1991.

6. Cox, B. J.   *Object oriented programming: An evolutionary approach.* Reading, MA: Addison-Wesley, 1987.

7. Ericsson, A. and Simon, H.   *Protocol Analysis*. MIT Press, London, England, 1984.

8. Guindon, R. Designing the Design Process: Exploiting Opportunistic Thoughts. *Human-Computer Interaction*, 5, (1990), 305-344.

9. Guindon, R., Curtis, B., and Krasner, H. A Model of Cognitive Processes in Software Design: An Analysis of Breakdowns in Early Design Activities by Individuals *(MCC Tech. Rep. No. STP-283-87)*.   Austin, TX: Microelectronics and Computer Technology Corporation, 1987.

10. Hayes, J. R.   and Simon, H.   Psychological Differences among Problem Isomorphs. In H. A. Simon (Ed), *Models of Thought, Vol. I.*   Yale University Press, New Haven, 1977, 498-512

11. Henderson-Sellers, B. and Edwards, J. M.   The Object-Oriented Systems Life Cycle. *Communications of the ACM, 33,* (1990), 143-159.

12. Jackson, M. A.   *System Development.* Prentice-Hall, Englewood Cliffs, N.J. 1983 .

13. Kahneman, D., and Tversky, A.   The simulation heuristic. In D. Kahneman, P. Slovic, and A. Tversky (Eds.), *Judgment under uncertainty: Heuristics and biases.* New York : Cambridge University Press, 1982, 201-208.

14. Kant, E. and Newell, A. Problem solving techniques for the design of algorithms. *Information processing and management, 20,* (1984), 97-118.

15. Korson, T., and McGregor, J. D.   Understanding Object-Oriented: A Unifying Paradigm. *Communications of the ACM, 33,* (1990), 40-60.

16. Meyer, B.   *Object-Oriented Software Construction.* Prentice-Hall, Hemel, Hempstead, 1988.

17. Newell, A., and Simon, H.   *Human Problem Solving.* Prentice-Hall, Englewood Cliffs, N.J., 1972.

18. Page-Jones, M. *The Practical guide for structural design.* Prentice-Hall, Englewood Cliffs, New Jersey, 1987.

19. Rambaugh, J., Blaha, M., Premerlani, W., Eddy, F., and Lorensen, W. *Object-oriented modeling and design.* Prentice-Hall, Englewood Cliffs, N.J., 1991.

20. Rosson, M. B., and Alpert, S. R. The Cognitive Consequences of Object-Oriented Design. *Human-Computer Interaction, 5,* (1990), 345-379.

21. Rosson, M. B., and Gold, E.   Problem-Solution Mapping in Object-Oriented Design *(RC 14496 (#64951))*. User interface institute, IBM T. J. Watson

research center, 1989.

22. Simon, H. A., Kotovsky, K., and Hayes, J. R.   Why Are Some Problems Hard? Evidence from the Tower of Hanoi. *Cognitive Psychology,* 17, 1985, 248-294.

23. Simon, H. and Kotovsky, K. Empirical Tests of a Theory of Human Acquisition of Concepts for Sequential Patters. In H. A. Simon (Ed), *Models of Thought, Vol. I.* Yale University Press, New Haven, 1977, 274-291.

24. Simon, H. and Kulkarni, D.   The processes of Scientific Discovery; The strategy of Experimentation. In H. A. Simon (Ed), *Models of Thought, vol II.* Yale

University Press, New Haven, 1988, 357-382

25. Simon, H, A., Lea, G.   Problem Solving and Rule Induction. In H. A. Simon (Ed.), *Models of Thought, vol. I.* Yale University Press, New Haven, 1977, 329-346.

26. Thorndyke, P., and Hayes-Roth, B. Differences in Spatial Knowledge Acquired from Maps and Navigation. *Cognitive Psychology*, 14, (1982), 560-589.

27. Yourdon, E. *Modern Structured Analysis.* Prentice-Hall, Englewood Cliffs, N.J., 1989.

Requirements And Design of DesignVision, An Object-Oriented Graphical Interface to an Intelligent Software Design Assistant.

Raymonde Guindon

Computer Science Department,
Stanford University
Stanford, CA, 94305
(415) 723-3605
Guindon@cs.Stanford.EDU

ABSTRACT

Key findings from empirical studies—early design is opportunistic; critical role of pictures in design conception; impact of various cognitive limitations—have very effectively determined requirements and design for a set of tools to support early design. Key design features of the tools include respectively: (1) The (simultaneous) display of any software modules at arbitrary levels of abstraction and from any subsystems. The unrestricted, smooth navigation between these software modules. (2) Multiple design notations—pictorial and symbolic—cross-referenced, editable, and maintained consistent across all views. Integrated views of control flow, data flow, and functional decomposition. (3) Automatic layout at arbitrary levels of nesting. Visual display of execution paths in the solution. Automatic completeness and consistency check. Automatic visual indication and listing of modules with constraint violations.

KEYWORDS: Design process, design methodology, design tools, models of user.

REQUIREMENTS AND DESIGN FOR THE GRAPHICAL DESIGN ASSISTANT

The early stage of software design is a most critical phase of software development, yet it is the least well studied, understood, and supported by tools. In fact, there are no tools in use that can qualify as truly supporting the early, creative stages of software design. Most CASE tools in use are nothing more than requirements and de-

sign specification editors [1]. Although they provide invaluable help by eliminating the drudgery of drawing and redrawing diagrams, they leave the bulk of the intellectual work unsupported. Even rapid prototyping systems still focus on programming (e.g., incremental compiling, late variable binding) rather than design.

Recent empirical studies have contributed to our understanding of the early stages of software design [2, 3, 4]. In these studies, verbal protocols of experts in the early stage of designing a realistic system were analyzed to obtain a temporal trace of the shifts between knowledge domains used and levels of abstraction of the partial solutions as they were developed. As the main result, the design plots show that designers do not follow a top-down decomposition. Rather, designers shift drastically between the subsystems developed and the level of abstraction of the partial solutions in these subsystems, and they infer new requirements throughout the entire design process. This observed design process was labeled *opportunistic*. In turn, the key findings from these empirical studies—early design is opportunistic; critical role of pictures in design conception; impact of various cognitive limitations; cognitive reuse of design schemas—have determined the requirements and design for the set of tools to support early design described in this paper.

An alternating sequence of requirements and the corresponding design decisions, derived from these empirical studies, is presented. This paper concentrates on the user interface of the system (See [6] for a description of other parts of the system).

Requirement: Early Design Is Opportunistic

The most influential finding is that the early stages of design are opportunistic and do not follow a top-down dynamics, and moreover, this is *good* design practice. This is very important because in the past, prescriptive models of software design have typically advocated a top-down and waterfall design process. Moreover, CASE tools, which purport to support early design, typically support a top-down design process [7].

Behavioral Characteristics of Opportunistic Design To derive useful design decisions, it is necessary to describe in detail the behavioral characteristics of opportunistic design. These include:
(1) interleaving the development of partial solutions at various levels of abstraction and in different subsystems,
(2) inference of new requirements and design constraints throughout the solution development, often leading to drastic restructuring of the design solution,
(3) extensive mental simulations of scenarios in the task domain triggering the discovery of new requirements and partial solutions in widely different levels of abstraction and subsystems.

A behavioral description is necessary but not sufficient to derive design decisions. It is necessary to also understand *why* opportunistic design occurs. Detailed analyses of the results show that opportunistic problem-solving has multiple causes. It appears to be a natural consequence of any of at least three causes: integration of knowledge domains with different structures; data-driven problem solving in experts; and discovery of new requirements throughout design.

Cause: Integration of Knowledge Domains With Different Structures. These knowledge domains may have very different structures. For example, the software system in Guindon's studies was the control for an elevator system to move N elevators to M floors. Consider the interaction between two knowledge domains: 1) the task domain, why and how people use elevators; 2) the software architecture for systems such as elevators. From a user standpoint, here is a likely scenario of use: first, the user presses an up/down button; second, the user enters the elevator when it arrives at the floor; third, the user presses a floor number button inside the elevator. However, these three contiguous user actions require software control implemented in widely different subsystems and levels of abstraction. First, the pressing of the up/down button may be collected by a central controller which will then allocate one elevator to serve this request. Second, entering the elevator presupposes the detection that the target floor has been reached and the automatic opening of the doors. Third, the pressing of the floor number button is likely handled by an individual controller inside each elevator. So, a designer mentally simulating this user scenario might sequentially design the central controller, the hardware for detection and alignment of floors and lifts and for opening of the doors, and the individual lift controllers. Although a natural consequence of the interaction between sources of knowledge, this sequence of solution development is in violation of the top-down design paradigm.

Cause: Data-Driven Solution Recognition In Experts.

The problem-solving of experts is characterized by the data-driven recognition and application of knowledge. For those requirements that are clear and complete, the designer may immediately recognize the corresponding partial solution. But this might not be possible for the inevitable ambiguous or incomplete requirements. Those requirements that are clear and complete may correspond to partial solutions in different subsystems and at various levels of abstraction. Although a natural consequence of data-driven processing in experts and of the ill-structuredness of design problems, such a solution development violates a top-down design process.

Cause: Inferred Requirements Lead To Solution Restructuring. Design problems have incomplete and ambiguous requirements (goals). New requirements are inferred throughout the design process and may cause designers to restructure their already existing design solution. This intrinsic feature of design problems precludes a top-down process in the early stages of design.

Thus design tools should accommodate and support an opportunistic process because it is a natural consequence of integration of knowledge from multiple domains with different structures, data-driven recognition of solutions in experts, and solution restructuring when new requirements are discovered.

Design Decisions Based On Opportunistic Process

An opportunistic design process is characterized by sudden shifts in levels of abstraction and subsystems. Consequently, the visualization tool supports the following features:
(1) The display of any software modules at arbitrary levels of abstraction—a designer can view any software module at any number of levels of nesting in the calling hierarchy. That is, the software modules called within the calling module will have their definition opened up inline within the definition of the calling module.
(2) The simultaneous display of software modules from different subsystems.
(3) The unrestricted, smooth navigation between these displayed software modules. That is, any picture representing a software component (e.g., module, input, output) is mousable. So designers are able to select any one of these software components. Designers can then request any available viewing, editing, information retrieval operations available. For example, designers can request to visualize the selected software component differently (e.g., with or without I/O, at a different depth of abstraction, see its pseudocode definition). Designers can graphically or textually edit the definition of the module. Designers can retrieve information from the knowledge-base about its status (e.g., whether it is a completely specified module, whether it has associated constraint violations). More importantly, designers are

able to freely shift between selected software modules across different subsystems and across levels of abstraction (nesting). For example, designers can mouse on a module at nesting depth 3 and redefine it, and yet leave undefined any of its ancestors in the calling hierarchy. Designers are also able to freely shift between the different views of a same software module (e.g., action diagrams, data flow diagrams, pseudocode).

Figure 1 shows the display of three software modules at different levels of abstraction. The module to the left, KSINFERENCE, is displayed without I/O at a depth 3 of abstraction. The module KSINFERENCE is again displayed to the lower right, but this time with I/O and at a depth 2 of abstraction. The module at the upper right, EXECUTEKSCLOSURE, is displayed with I/O at depth 2. Note that EXECUTEKSCLOSURE is also displayed within the other two views of the module KSINFERENCE, but differently. Note that all of these software pictures are mousable and any available operations (editing, viewing, retrieving information, etc.) can be performed at any time on these components. For instance, one can mouse the CREATEKSCLOSURE module within the KSINFERENCE module, and request to see it displayed differently or edit its definition. One can mouse any input or output and edit it.

Requirement: Pictorial Representations Are Critical In The Conception Of Designs

The second most influential finding is that pictorial external representations play a critical role in early design, especially in the conception and in the informal testing of design. This was also observed in other studies of early design in mechanical engineering [8]. Again, this is in contrast with most of the current CASE and CAD systems which are computer-based tools for documentation, not conception [7].

For instance, Guindon [3] observed that designers overwhelmingly use pictures and diagrams of two kinds: semi-formal design notations such as action diagrams, structure charts, state transition diagrams, and the likes; informal pictures depicting scenarios of use in the task domain (user scenarios). These pictures and diagrams serve the following purposes related to the conception and informal testing of the design:
(1) to simulate scenarios of system use in the task domain, in order to disambiguate given requirements and validate inferred requirements,
(2) to simulate the behaviors of the software system and test against the behavioral and functional requirements,
(3) to augment short-term memory, especially during the simulations.

Use Of Multiple Semi-Formal Design Notations. Designers use different semi-formal design notations to express different parts of their solution, and they freely shifted amongst these notations. For example, designers could use structure charts to express their architectural design, but use state transition diagrams to capture more detailed algorithms for the functioning of specific parts. Designers could also use non-pictorial notations, such as pseudocode, to express other parts of their solution. Thus, a design visualization tool should support viewing a software component under all these design notations, provide cross-referencing across the different displays for a software component, and keep all these displays consistent after modifications.

Shifting Between Control Flow, Data Flow, And Functional Decomposition Viewpoints. Most diagraming techniques present one viewpoint of a software system, for example the control structure, the data flow, or the functional decomposition, but not in combination. However, designers appear to shift freely between these three types of viewpoints. This suggests that the presentation of a single viewpoint might not be sufficient to fulfill the designers' needs and that a design notation integrating these three viewpoints would be useful.

Design Decisions Based On Pictorial Representations

Multiple Visual Design Notations. It should be obvious from Figure 1 that the main language to represent design is visual. In particular, the interface supports the following visual design notations: action diagrams and data flow diagrams. Designers are free to shift between these design notations to visualize or express different parts of their solution. For example, designers could view or define a module using action diagrams, but view one of its submodules with data flow diagrams. Of course these are not the only design notations intended to be supported, in particular state-transition diagrams and structure charts should be added in the future.

Graphical Editor For Design Solutions. The visual representation of a software component can be edited via the graphical editor. For example, input to, output from, or called submodules can be deleted, replaced, or added from the definition of another module. The editor was designed following these guidelines: (1) keep all views consistent; (2) provide the most specific, informative feedback possible about the state of modification of a software component.

Any changes made to a software component in one window in the desktop is immediately propagated to *all* views of this software component in *all* windows on the desktop. So the designer always receives a consistent view of the state of all the displayed software components.

The designer receives an immediate visual feedback (of

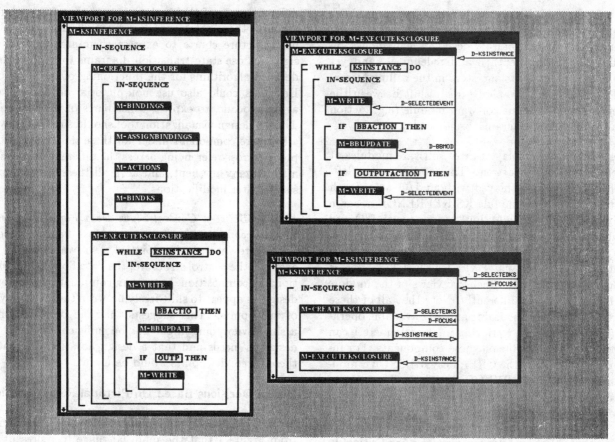

Figure 1: Three different views of software modules. All software component pictures are mousable.

the greatest information content possible) of the state of execution of their planned editing task. For example, if an input has been deleted from a software module, then all views with data flows of this module will indicate visually that this input was deleted (as opposed to replaced or added) and all views without data flows of this module will show that the module was simply edited (since the edited input cannot displayed). As will be discussed later, this kind feedback allows the designer to keep track of which redesign tasks are completed and which are left to do, relieving some of the cognitive burden associated with management of goals and tasks.

Figure 2 shows how all the edited input and output are greyed, to indicate a change in their status, and a different code is given to inform of the type of the modification (add, delete, replace, rename).

The propagation of modifications to all views is not just at the interface level of course. Modifications made via the graphical editor are made in the knowledge-base. As will be discussed later, any modifications that violate consistency or completeness constraints are detected and the software components affected by such violations are immediately signaled visually to the designer. So, the designer receives immediate visual feedback about the legality of the redesign operation.

Integrated Views Of Control Flow, Data Flow, And Functional Decomposition. Another important influence is the perceived need for integrated views of the control flow, data flow, and functional decomposition. So a software diagram was devised to present an integrated view of control structure and data flow at arbitrary levels of nesting. This diagram was synthesized from already existing diagraming techniques to reduce the amount of learning by the designers that would have been otherwise necessary. Designers can select any subset of these three views they want to see together. Note that in Figure 1 some modules are displayed with their input/output flows and others are not, and this can be done at arbitrary levels of nesting in the functional decomposition.

Requirement: Mixed External Representation Modes

Designers also freely mixed pictorial representations with more symbolic or verbal ones, such as, notes, logical or mathematical formulas, and pseudocode. Designers annotated scenario pictures and design diagrams with notes serving many purposes including:
(1) to remind themselves of insights or particular sketches of design solutions which they wanted to handle later in their design session,
(2) to indicate that a particular requirement was inferred and added to the list of given requirements, and conse-

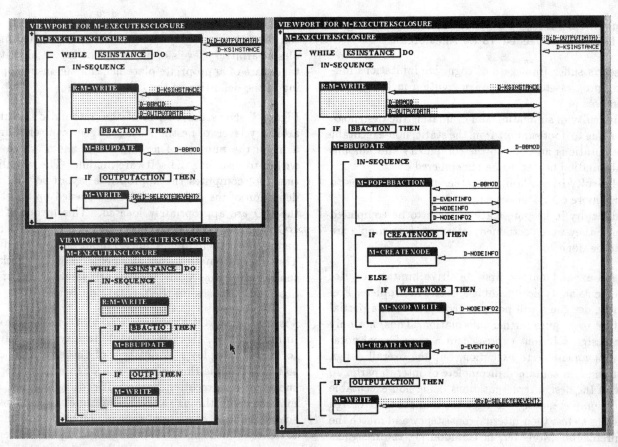

Figure 2: The edited views of a module are all kept consistent. The most specific level of feedback on the state of editing the module is presented.

quently, whose desirability and criticality from the customer's standpoint might be questionable,
(3) to note the importance or criticality of some requirements compared to others, and consequently, order their design activities accordingly,
(4) to detail an agenda of activities they wanted to perform (a to-do list).

Likewise, designers could annotate their pseudocode or formulas with pictures. These pictures most often depicted corresponding scenarios of use of the system in the task domain, which the pseudocode was meant to handle. The observation of mixed representation modes is specially interesting since some of the current (research) visual programming systems, as a matter of principles, will not support any other representations than pictorial, thereby excluding symbolic and verbal representations (e.g., see [5] for a review).

Design Decisions For Mixed External Representations

The visualization tool supports the use of mixed external representations:
(1) the creation, editing, and viewing of pictorial and of symbolic representations of software modules including the use of text and frames with slots and values,

(2) the maintenance of consistent views of the state of a software component across all representation modes (within and between windows).

So, in addition to the pictorial views, designers can also view a symbolic representation of any software module in the library. This symbolic representation is under the form of a frame with slots and values. The slots specify, amongst other information, input, output, what other software modules are called by the module and how they are called. A part of the symbolic representation of the module the designer can also display is its pseudocode definition. An important feature of the visual and symbolic representations is that they are *linked* to each other. The designer can move freely between both representations and request information about the software system from either representations to be presented in either representations. So, a designer can request a symbolic listing of a software submodule from the visual display of its supermodule, and the designer can request a visual display of another module from the symbolic display. Because all the views of an object are linked, any change made to any view of a software module is immediately propagated to all views of the module on the desktop, maintaining matched or consistent views.

Requirement: Designers Suffer From Various Cognitive Limitations Needed To Be Alleviated

Designers suffer from various cognitive limitations hindering progress toward a design solution including (for others, see [4]):
(1) difficulty in simulating and evaluating the design solution due to poor support from the static, non-executable representations and due to the complexity and amount of information needed to be remembered
(2) difficulty in combining together partial solutions to form a more complete design,
(3) difficulty in keeping track of tasks to be completed because they were postponed, interrupted, or simply are yet to be done.

Let me expand on the first cognitive limitation. Requirements are typically ambiguous and incomplete. Frequently, designers will postpone completion of a partial solution to acquire further information. Thus, not only were design solutions expressed in a semi-formal notation not amenable to execution, but the overall design solution often contained incomplete or interim parts. In spite of the design representations being non-executable and incomplete, designers tried to simulate their design solutions to test their internal consistency and match the requirements. Moreover, in Guindon [3], the designers were observed using the external representations of the solution to help them manage the complexity of these mental simulations. Nevertheless, even with the support of the external representations, designers found it difficult to keep track of the execution context when returning from a call to a submodule. As a consequence, the observed mental simulations tended to be shallow in depth, restricted to 2 nesting levels. Moreover, designers also lost track of which possible execution paths had already been taken in the presence of if-then, if-then-else or case control constructs within a module.

The execution of informal, incomplete design specifications is a research topic in itself, but from a user-interface standpoint, design tools should at least help designers keep track of execution context and of selected values at choice points to support the simulation and testing of the design.

Design Decisions To Alleviate Cognitive Limitations

With respect with the first requirement—alleviating difficulty in simulations of design solution— three simple facilities are provided in the system.

Automatic Layout At Arbitrary Levels of Nesting. First, the difficulty in keeping track of execution context during simulations requires that the graphical layout of the called modules helps the designers identify quickly what is the calling module and where should execution continue in the calling module. To this effect, the designers can request the display of a module and its called modules at arbitrary levels of nesting. The layout algorithm takes care of appropriate placement for the in-line opening of the definition of the called module.

Figure 1 shows the output of the automatic layout at arbitrary levels of nesting. The designer can select from a menu the number of nesting levels under which she wishes to visualize the software module. The visualization tool computes the appropriate layout so that the definition of the called modules are opened up and that the I/O are appropriately located. This layout of the I/O supports a quick visual check for I/O consistency, namely, that there are no unused input and output data. Thus this automatic layout also helps designers check visually for internal consistency of their solution, one of the observed purposes for the mental simulations.

Visual Display Of Execution Paths In The Design Solution. Second, there is a simple facility for designers to visually display a simulation of the execution of a software module through all or through a user-selected subset of its execution paths. The designers can also manually step through these visual simulations. The visual simulation consists of showing input flowing in the currently executing module, highlighting the currently executing module, and recursively simulating the execution of its called submodules in the correct order, and finally showing output flowing out of the currently executing module. This is somewhat like a visual display of an exhaustive trace of all the modules pushed on and popped off the call stack. Because the call stack is maintained automatically, this alleviates the short-term memory overloads which occur during mental simulations of a design solution.

Automatic Completeness and Consistency Check. The third facility is an automatic consistency and completeness checker (see [6] for more details). After the creation of or modification of a module, the designer can see a display of all constraints violations the new definition of the module entails. There are three levels of checks for constraint violations made: 1) general software constraints; 2) specific software architecture constraints; 3) task domain constraints. For example, the first level–general software constraints–is the most general and checks that all modules have a definition, that all input to the calling module are used by at least one of the called submodules, that all output from a submodule are either used by subsequent submodules or the calling module. This eliminates the most tedious aspects of simulations of the design solutions to test their completeness and consistency. The details of these different levels are beyond the scope of this paper, but can be found in [6].

Note that this constraint checking facility also helps alleviate the second cognitive limitation, the difficulty in combining together partial solutions (i.e., individual modules), by automatically checking their I/O consistency.

Automatic Visual Indication And Listing Of Modules With Constraint Violations. With respect to the third cognitive limitation—difficulty in keeping track of tasks to be completed—two related facilities are provided. The first one is an automatic visual indication of the presence of constraint violations in any one of the displayed modules on the desktop. Such modules then become displayed with an X-like icon indicating a violation. Thus the designer is immediately reminded that such modules need further work. The designer can then request to see a listing of the violations with suggestions on how to repair them. The second facility is simply the ability to request a listing of all modules (displayed or not on the desktop) that have constraint violations in their definition. The designer can then access a list of violations by selecting one or more modules to inspect. Although these two facilities do not certainly completely alleviate the difficulty in keeping track of all tasks to be completed, they provide designers a simple and unobtrusive way of keeping track of *some* of the tasks that need to be completed.

Requirement: Incomplete, Ambiguous, And Changing Requirements Force Designers To Leave Solutions In Tentative, Interim State

Designers often postpone detailed design commitments until they have acquired additional information or greater understanding of the problem. So, designers can leave a partial solution unfinished and shift to developing another partial solution, contributing to the opportunistic character of the design process. As a consequence the overall solution can be composed of partial solutions at different levels of completeness—some complete, others still in a draft or incomplete state. Modules that the designers consider incompletely specified are typically those modules for which the designers may not yet know some of the input or output, some of the called submodules, or what control constructs should be used in calling the submodules. It has already been mentioned why this creates difficulty during the simulation to test the correctness of the design solution.

Design Decisions To Accommodate Interim Solutions

There are two basic facilities provided (which are related to those previously seen for modules with constraint violations).

Automatic Visual Indication And Listing Of Interim Modules. By default, whenever a new module is created, it is tagged as interim (i.e., incompletely specified) and displayed visually as such (with iconic question marks).

The designers can also manually set or change the status of any module from and to being considered completely specified and being considered incompletely specified. A related facility is simply the ability to request a listing of all modules (displayed or not on the desktop) that have been tagged as incompletely specified. As a consequence, the designer is also helped in remembering which tasks still need to be completed, alleviating a cognitive difficulty already presented.

Different Levels of Consistency Checking For Interim Modules. As much as the writer of a paper desires different kind of feedback on a first draft than on the finished version, software designers need different kind of feedback for modules they tagged as incompletely specified from those modules they considered finished. To this effect, somewhat different levels of consistency and completeness checks are performed for those modules that designers have tagged as incompletely specified than for those modules which are considered finished. The details of these differences are beyond the scope of this paper, but can be found in [6].

PUTTING IT ALL TOGETHER: A SESSION WITH DESIGNVISION

A representative design session will be described to summarize the facilities offered in the system. One of the main purpose of the scenario is to highlight the fact that the designers are provided much more than an editor to document design specifications. The intent behind the design of the tools is to support the *conception* of designs, not just their documentation. This is achieved in particular by the smooth unrestricted navigation between modules at any levels of abstraction, between any subsystems, between any of the views of a module, and between any of the facilities provided (editing, viewing, browsing, simulating, information retrieval, etc). This is also achieved by the intelligent feedback provided on the legality of modifications during redesign, and the ability to visually simulate the behaviors of the design.

Suppose the designer wishes to design a system by reusing already existing modules. She first browses the library of existing modules using the system built-in browser. To help her decides which subset of modules to select, she uses the visualization tools to view a few modules that look particularly promising. At this point, she decides to visualize just the control flow (i.e., without I/O) of the module CONTROL, but at depth 3 in the functional decomposition. She also decides to visualize the module KSINFERENCE with its I/O at depth 2 in the functional decomposition. She also decides to visualize the data flow diagram for the module SCHEDULER, and the pseudocode view for the module EXECUTE-CLOSURE.

At this point, she decides that the module she wants to

create is most like the module CONTROL. So, by mousing on the module CONTROL, she copies it and renames it ACTUATOR. By default, the newly created module ACTUATOR is tagged and displayed as incompletely-specified until the designer indicates otherwise. Using all the viewing tools and their options, and the graphical and symbolic editors, the designer will now redesign the selected software component into a new one. (At this point, only a simple copy-edit redesign paradigm is supported. In the future, others will be offered, such as specialization from classes).

Using the graphical editor, input to, output from, called submodules, and so on, can be deleted, replaced, added, renamed from the definition of a module. The designer can also, instead, elect to use the symbolic editor and modify the symbolic and pseudocode view of the module ACTUATOR. Throughout the redesign process, the designer is informed visually (with X-icons displayed on the modules themselves) and textually (in a diagnostic window) of consistency and completeness violations resulting from modifications. The designer is thus reminded of which modules need to be completed.

Any changes made to a software component in one window in the desktop is immediately propagated to *all* views of this software component in *all* windows on the desktop. So the designer always receives a consistent view on the desktop of the state of all the displayed software components. Moreover, the designer receives an immediate visual feedback (of the greatest information content possible) of the state of execution of the planned redesign task. For example, if an input has been deleted from module ACTUATOR, then all views with data flows of ACTUATOR will show that this particular input was deleted (as opposed to replaced or added) and all views of ACTUATOR without data flows will show that the module was simply edited (since the edited input cannot displayed). This feedback allows the designer to keep track of which redesign tasks are completed and which are left to do, relieving some of the cognitive burden associated with management of goals and tasks.

The designer has the freedom to tag a software component as incompletely-specified through a menu. This is indicated visually by question marks on the left side of the software module and also internally in the symbolic representation. The designer receives different levels of feedback on constraint violations depending on whether the module is tagged as incompletely-specified or not.

Once all consistency and completeness violations have been eliminated from the ACTUATOR module, the designer can check its behaviors against the requirements. To do so, the designer requests to visually simulate the execution of the module ACTUATOR by mousing on the module and selecting the animate option. The designer

can select all or a subset of execution paths by specifying appropriate values at selection points. The designer can also manually step through the simulation.

After a series of requests to view modules under various representations and a number of modifications are performed, the designer is satisfied with the definition of the ACTUATOR module. The designer can redisplay all views to show the resulting software component and save the new module in the library.

To conclude, this paper has presented an effective research and design methodology where requirements are derived from empirical studies of users. It has also presented the software system designed on the basis of this methodology. This is an important practical experience. It shows that in the situation where relevant tools are scarce and our understanding of a process is poor, we can effectively derive useful requirements and design principles from empirical studies of users.

REFERENCES

[1] Fisher, A. S. (1988). *CASE: Using Software Development Tools*. New York: Wiley.

[2] Guindon, R. (1990a). Designing the design process: Exploiting opportunistic thoughts. *Human-Computer Interaction*, 5, 305-344.

[3] Guindon, R. (1990b). Knowledge exploited by experts during software system design. *International Journal of Man-Machine Studies,* 33, 279-304.

[4] Guindon, R., Krasner, H., and Curtis, B. (1987). Breakdowns and processes during the early activities of software design by professionals. In G. Olson, E. Soloway, and S. Sheppard (Eds.), *Empirical Studies of Programmers, Second Workshop*. Ablex Publishing.

[5] Myers, B. A. The state of the art in visual programming and program visualization. In A. Kilgur and R. Earnshaw (Eds.) *Graphic Tools for Software Engineers*, PP. 13-26, University Press, Cambridge, 1989.

[6] Nii, H. P., Aiello, N., Bhansali, S., Guindon, R., and Peyton, L. *Knowledge-assisted software engineering (KASE): An introduction and status-June 1991*. Report KSL 91-28. Knowledge Systems Laboratory, Computer Science Department, Stanford University, 1991.

[7] Schindler, M. *Computer-aided software design*. John Wiley and Sons, New York, 1990.

[8] Ullman, D.G., Stauffer, L.A., and Dietterich, T.G. (1987). Toward Expert CAD. *Computers in Mechanical Engineering*, Nov.-Dec. Issue.

Facilitating the Exploration of Interface Design Alternatives: The HUMANOID Model of Interface Design

Pedro Szekely, Ping Luo and Robert Neches

USC/Information Sciences Institute
4676 Admiralty Way, Suite 1001
Marina del Rey, CA 90292
(213) 822-1511
szekely@isi.edu, ping@isi.edu, neches@isi.edu

ABSTRACT

HUMANOID is a user interface design tool that lets designers express abstract conceptualizations of an interface in an executable form, allowing designers to experiment with scenarios and dialogues even before the application model is completely worked out. Three properties of the HUMANOID approach allow it to do so: a modularization of design issues into independent dimensions, support for multiple levels of specificity in mapping application models to user interface constructs, and mechanisms for constructing executable default user interface implementations from whatever level of specificity has been provided by the designer.

KEYWORDS: Design Processes, Development Tools and Methods, User Interface Management Systems, Rapid Prototyping, Interface Design Representation, Dialogue Specification.

INTRODUCTION

Interface design really begins much earlier than current tools recognize. Long before a designer is ready to experiment with presentation issues like the layout of widgets chosen from a widget library, designers have typically made (often implicitly and unconsciously) strong design commitments about conceptual issues such as the choice of application data structures and capabilities that will be presented, as well as the general nature of interaction techniques which will be used to present them. By and large, the tools that designers use at this point are whiteboards or pad-and-pencil because the conceptualizations are more abstract than interface drawing or mock-up tools support. For example, a designer may decide that a file directory structure needs to be presented in a window, without yet knowing whether to use indented text or a grapher. The fact that those early conceptualizations are not supported on-line inhibits exploration of design alternatives. It is too difficult to walk through scenarios and imagine dialogues when sketching by hand. There is too much work and too much commitment to particular details when using a display layout package.

HUMANOID's contribution to interface design is that it lets designers express abstract conceptualizations in an executable form, allowing designers to experiment with scenarios and dialogues even before the application model is completely concretized. For example, designers can execute an interface after specifying only data types of command inputs, without having said anything about sequencing or presentation. The consequence is that designers can get an executable version of their design quickly, experiment with it in action, and then repeat the process after adding only whatever details are necessary to extend it along the particular dimension currently of interest to them.

Figure 1. illustrates the nature of this refinement process. The figure shows ten snapshots from the evolution of the design for a program to view the slots of an object, starting with an initially empty design and ending with a complete, working application. Each snapshot shows the interface that HUMANOID generates after one or two refinements to the design. The interfaces generated at each step are not just mock-ups of the presentation, but fully working interfaces, to the extent that they have been defined thus far. For example in Version 4 of the evolving design in Figure 1. the designer is able to explore dialogues involving selectable objects, despite not yet having defined how to display those objects. We believe that the design process is substantially enhanced by the opportunity this approach affords to put designs into action faster and earlier, and to test them before all the abstractions are concretized.

HUMANOID belongs to the family of interface design tools and UIMSs centered around the notion of deriving the user interface from a high-level specification of the semantics of an application program [3, 6, 14, 15, 17, 18 and 20]. The application semantics are usually specified as a set of object types and procedure headers. The interface is specified by elaborating the semantic description by annotating it with information used by an interface generating component. We recognize five dimensions along which interface designs can be varied and elaborated. We summarize them below, and expand on each dimension on the following sections.

Application design. The application design specifies the operations and objects that an application program provides. Variations involve changing the parameters of operations,

FIGURE 1. The evolution of the design of a program to browse objects.

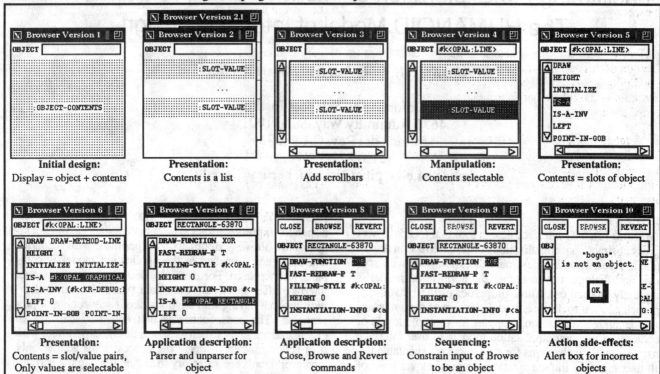

Version 1: **Initial design:** Display = object + contents

Version 2: **Presentation:** Contents is a list

Version 3: **Presentation:** Add scrollbars

Version 4: **Manipulation:** Contents selectable

Version 5: **Presentation:** Contents = slots of object

Version 6: **Presentation:** Contents = slot/value pairs, Only values are selectable

Version 7: **Application description:** Parser and unparser for object

Version 8: **Application description:** Close, Browse and Revert commands

Version 9: **Sequencing:** Constrain input of Browse to be an object

Version 10: **Action side-effects:** Alert box for incorrect objects

Version 1 shows the interface generated for a design that states that the object browser is an application object with a global variable to hold the object being browsed. The presentation shows the global variable, and below it the contents of the object. HUMANOID generates a default interface, choosing a type-in interaction technique for the global variable. The *object-contents* are shown in a schematic way (in a dotted rectangle), since at this point the designer only stated that the display should contain a part to display the contents, but did not represent anything else.

Version 2 refines the presentation of the object contents stating that the contents consist of a list of slot value pairs. Since at this point in the design the designer has not specified how to compute the set of slot value

pairs for the object, HUMANOID shows the list in a schematic way with two *slot-value* parts in dotted rectangles separated with "...".

Version 2.1 illustrates that the design process can involve exploration of alternatives at the same level, not just refinements. Version 2.1 was an alternative presentation of *object-contents* as a graph rather than a list.

Version 3 refines the presentation to include scrollbars.

Version 4 adds a new global variable to the application design: *current-selection*. It adds a manipulation behavior to the design: making the slot value pairs selectable and stored in current-selection. Note that the behavior can be immediately exercised even though the presentation design is unfinished.

Version 5 refines the presentation by specifying an ac-

cess procedure for the slots in the object to be presented. In addition, it refines the presentation method to show the names of the slots. The definition of the selection manipulation was not changed, and it still works.

Version 6 further refines the presentation method to show the values of the slots, and refines the manipulation to only select the value part of the slots value pairs.

Version 7 refines the application description by adding a parser and an unparser for the global variable for the object being browsed. The user can now type the names of new objects. The designer typed in the identifier of a rectangle object and the display is updated automatically. The designer did not have to write any code for keeping the display up to date.

Version 8 adds three commands to the application description. The presentation

was not refined. HUMANOID by default placed the command buttons at the top of the display.

Version 9 refines the application description for the Browse command, constraining its only input to be an object, and linking it to the current-selection global variable in the application. The effect on the interface is to constrain the sequencing of the dialogue. If the current selection is not an object, the Browse button is dimmed, and the user cannot invoke the browse command. In contrast, in version 8, the Browse button was selectable, even though the current selection was not a browseable object.

Version 10 adds what we call an action side-effect. When the object global variable receives an incorrect input, an alert box is displayed and the value is reverted to the previous value.

deleting or adding operations, adding attributes to object types, etc.

Application design is the major direction of refinement in interface design. Our model of design views designers' exploration of design alternatives as a process of incrementally adding information to the application design, generating alternatives along the other four dimensions of variation as needed at each step.

Presentation. The presentation defines the visual appearance of the interface. Variations involve: data to present, major parts of a display, data to be displayed in each part, presentation methods for each part (recursive step), layout of the parts, and conditions for including parts in displays.

Manipulation. The manipulation specification defines the gestures that can be applied to the objects presented, and the effects of those gestures on the state of the application and the interface.

Sequencing. The sequencing defines the order in which manipulations are enabled, or equivalently, the set of manipulations enabled at any given moment. Many sequencing constraints follow from the data flow constraints specified in the application description (*e.g.*, a command cannot be invoked unless all its inputs are correct). Additional constraints can be imposed during dialogue design.

Action side effects. Action side-effects refer to actions that an interface performs automatically as side effects of the action of a manipulation. For example, a newly created object can become automatically selected, closing a dialogue box can reset all the options to their default, typing return in a type-in field can automatically move the cursor to the "next" type-in field. Side-effects can add, set, delete values of command inputs and global variables, and can change the state of commands and inputs, which trigger changes in presentation and sequencing.

The sections following discuss each of these dimensions in detail, together with the benefits for interface design exploration that the variations provide. Then we discuss related work, and close with conclusions.

DESIGN DIMENSION #1: APPLICATION DESIGN

An application design consists of a definition of commands, object types, global variables and the data flow constraints between these entities. The application design specifies the information about an application that is independent of how the objects are displayed, and how the operations are invoked. HUMANOID provides three kinds of objects to specify application designs:

Commands. A command is an object that describes all the information necessary to invoke an operation. The description of a command includes the call-back procedure that implements the command, a set of pre-conditions, and a description of each of the inputs to the command.

Inputs. An input is an object that describes all the information about a parameter of an operation needed to ensure that the interface will invoke the call-back procedure with correct arguments. The description of an input includes the *type* of the input value, a *predicate*, which is a procedure that does semantic validation on input values, the *minimum* and *maximum* number of values that the input can take, *alternatives*, which specify a set of values from which the input values must be chosen, and a *parser* and *unparser* for converting strings to input values and viceversa.

Application Objects. An application object groups together a set of commands and objects. An *application program* consists of one or more application objects. For example, a mail program could consist of an application object to manipulate folders and an application object to edit messages. At run time, a program can make multiple instances of its application objects. For instance, a mail program would have an application object instance to manipulate folders, and perhaps multiple instances of the application object for editing messages, so that the user would be able to compose multiple messages in parallel.

Input objects can also be defined for application objects. In this case they are called *global inputs*, because they are similar to global variables in a program. The value they hold can be accessed from any command in the application.

Application designs can be refined in three ways: by editing the command, input and application objects, by defining data flow constraints, and by defining command and input groups.

Command, input and application modifications. Commands, inputs and applications are organized in an inheritance hierarchy. Designers can define new versions of these objects, inheriting properties from existing ones. Designers can also add, delete and modify any of the properties of the command, input and application objects described above.

Data flow constraints. The data flow constraints specify constraints between the properties of inputs, command and application objects. One can, for instance, constrain the type, value, alternatives or other property of an input to be a function of any property of a command or an input. The constraints are enforced automatically by the underlying representation system [4]. Whenever the value of any of the slots changes, the constrained values are recomputed, and HUMANOID automatically reconstructs the affected portions of the display, enforces the relevant sequencing constraints, and performs the relevant side-effects.

The constraints between command inputs and global inputs can be used to implement selection-based interfaces, and other interface features where commands get their inputs from a global variable. For example, these constraints are used to support the factoring transformations in UIDE [3].

Version 9 of the Object Browser in Figure 1. illustrates the use of data-flow constraints. The *object-to-browse* input of the *browse* command is constrained to get its value from the application global input called *current-selection*. Whenever a value is selected in the *object-contents* part of the display, the value is stored in the *current-selection* global input. HU-MANOID propagates the value to the *object-to-browse* input, and enforces a sequencing constraint by disabling the *browse* button if the selected value is not an object.

Command and input groups. Command and input groups allow designers to add more structure to the definition of an application by grouping command and inputs into named objects. Command and input groups can be installed in application, command and input objects. The groups do not specify any interface feature by themselves, but designers can refine them to specify presentation, sequencing and side-effect interface features.

The application design represents information about an application program's semantics in a central place. This information is shared by the other four dimensions of interface design, and separating it out allows the other dimensions to be varied more independently. Also, since the application design describes the "objects of discourse" for the interface independently of other design dimensions, it represents a start towards explicitly capturing issues that designers are concerned with in the early, conceptual phases of design.

The following sections discuss the presentation, manipulation, sequencing and action side-effect dimensions of interface design refinements, which can be applied to application designs to yield interfaces with particular features.

DESIGN DIMENSION #2: PRESENTATION

The presentation component of HUMANOID is designed to allow designers to specify presentations in stages. The goal is to let designers specify just the amount of information that they can or want at any given time during the design process, and to let them refine the presentation design iteratively as they understand the design better. HUMANOID can prototype the interface given any amount of information.

The presentation component of the user interface for a program is defined via *templates* [21]. A template is an object that specifies a method for constructing the presentation of a data structure. Designers construct presentations by refining the templates in HUMANOID's library.

HUMANOID's template library contains default templates to display application objects, commands and input objects, as well as templates to display lists of objects in columns, rows or tables, to display graphs and trees, and several flavors of scrolling windows.

The default template for application objects can generate menu bars of pull down menus, panels of command buttons, and panels of global inputs using radio buttons, check boxes, and other traditional interaction techniques. This template illustrates the use of command and input groups to specify presentations. For example, to create the application window in Version 8 of the Object Browser example in Figure 1., the designer defined a group called *panel-commands*,

with the *close*, *browse* and *revert* commands. The default template generates the panel of command buttons. Menu bars could have been generated by defining the *menu-bar-commands* command group, and the input panels are generated from the *panel-inputs* input group.

The templates mechanism supports the following kinds of presentation refinements:

Adding parts to existing templates. Designers can start by specifying what data should be displayed in a part, and later on refine the part to specify how the data should be displayed. For example, Version 1 of the Object Browser shown in Figure 1. was created by adding a part called *object-contents* to the default application template. Designers can initially provide some hints about the size and proportions of the presentations of parts so that when HUMANOID prototypes the interface it can generate presentations that approximate the presentations the designers have in mind.

Adding inclusion conditions. Designers can add an inclusion condition to the definition of a part so that it is only included in the display when the conditions are met. The conditionals can be constraint expressions that depend on application data. The constraints are automatically maintained so that when the application information changes, HUMANOID automatically updates the display to exclude or include the part as appropriate.

Adding template applicability conditions. Designers can add applicability conditions to templates to define the situations when the use of a template is appropriate. The applicability conditions can also be constraints. When the data they depend on changes, HUMANOID will automatically re-search the template hierarchy to find a new template to display the corresponding portion of the display.

Refining parameters. Designers can refine the parameters of a template to override default values (*e.g.*, change the font of a class of labels). It is possible to put a constraint in the parameters so that the values will be computed at run-time based on application information. When the application information changes, HUMANOID automatically regenerates the appropriate parts of the display.

Specifying layout. Designers can specify the layout for the parts of a display separately from the specification of the parts. Designers can refine the layout once the design of the presentation of the parts is complete, in order to achieve a pleasing layout.

Specifying a replacement hierarchy. A replacement hierarchy is a decision tree for selecting the most appropriate templates for displaying an object. Each node in the tree is a template. Child templates construct more specific presentations than their parent, and are chosen only if their applicability condition is satisfied in the current context. When HUMANOID is directed to display an object with a template, it will search the replacement hierarchy below that template to find the lowest template in the hierarchy whose applicability condition is satisfied. By calling HUMANOID with a template close to the top of a replacement hierarchy, designers delegate to HUMANOID the selection of presentation method. By specifying a template closer to the bottom of the hierarchy, designers exercise more control.

For example, HUMANOID has a template replacement hierarchy to choose between different presentations of input objects, such as check buttons, radio buttons or type-in buffers. The applicability conditions are based on attributes of the input object such as whether there is a set of alternatives from which the value is to be chosen, the size of the alternatives, the number of values that the input accepts, etc. Designers can build similar replacement hierarchies for the templates for their application data structures.

HUMANOID's template mechanism for constructing presentations has the following benefits:

- Designers can refine the presentation step by step, always seeing the effects of the current design, even when it is only partially specified.

- The part inclusion conditions, and template applicability conditions provide a natural way to create conditionalized displays whose characteristics depend on the run-time values of the data to be presented.

- The template replacement hierarchy provides a convenient way to organize and reuse presentation methods.

- HUMANOID automatically reconstructs displays when the data being presented changes.

DESIGN DIMENSION #3: MANIPULATION

Manipulation specification involves specifying the input gestures that users can perform to manipulate presented information, along with the actions that should be invoked when the appropriate gesture is detected.

Manipulations are specified by adding to templates one or more *behavior* specifications. A behavior specification consists of a specification of the gesture that invokes the behavior (*e.g.*, mouse click, mouse drag), a specification of the parts of the presentation where the gesture applies (*e.g.*, over the widget generated by a template, or over all the parts of a template), a specification of the application data on which the gesture operates, and the actions to be taken at interesting points during the gesture (*e.g.*, for a dragging gesture the interesting points are "mouse press", "mouse move" and "mouse release").

The actions of behaviors can contain arbitrary Lisp code. However, typical actions are very simple. They only set the value of an input object, or change the status of an input, a command, or a group (see the following section on sequencing for an explanation of input, command and group status). Designers do not need to include code to, for instance, activate or deactivate other behaviors, highlight or dim presentations, etc. These are subsidiary actions to setting the value of an input or changing a status, and so are specified in the sequencing and action side-effect dimensions.

Version 4 of the Object Browser shown in Figure 1. defines a mouse-click behavior to select slot-value pairs. The *start-where* slot is the list of all the elements of the *object-contents* part (making all the slot-value pairs selectable), and the action sets the *current-selection* global input to the value presented in the slot-value pair that the user buttons. The action does not contain code to highlight the *current-selection*, or to enable or disable any commands that might use the *current-selection*. These features are specified in the presentation and sequencing aspects of the design. When commands are added later on in Version 8, there is no need to come back to this behavior and edit the actions in order to enable or disable the relevant commands.

The behaviors are implemented on top of the Garnet Interactors package [11]. The library of behaviors includes behaviors for type-in, dragging and moving, button and menu selection, angle specification, two point specification. These behaviors cover most of the gestures used in direct manipulation, mouse-based interfaces [11].

HUMANOID's model of manipulation has several benefits:

- Separates the specification of *what* the behaviors do, *where* they apply, and *when* they are applicable. The separation of what and where derives from the Garnet model of interactors [11]. The separation of when derives from HUMANOID's model of sequencing (see next section).

- When designers refine the presentation of the objects, it is not necessary to modify the definition of the manipulations. The manipulations will continue to work with the refined presentations of the objects.

- Behaviors are easy to specify because their actions are simple: they either set the value of an input, or change the status of an input, a command or a group. Interface designers need not program in order to specify the actions.

DESIGN DIMENSION #4: SEQUENCING

Sequencing design involves specifying the order in which different displays appear on the screen, and the set of behaviors that are enabled at any given moment. In HUMANOID designers do not specify sequencing by directly adding instructions at appropriate places to enable or disable particular behaviors. Instead, HUMANOID computes the set of enabled behaviors at any time based on the data flow constraints in the application design, and by applying a fixed set of policies to a model of the states of individuals or groups of commands and inputs. The sequencing of the displays is computed in a similar way, and is explained in the next section on action side-effects.

We discuss the model of command states below. The model of states for inputs and groups of commands and inputs is similar, and is not discussed in this paper.

The state of a command is defined by the following slots:

Idle/active/running. Commands are *idle* by default. The *idle* state specifies that the command is not being interacted with. The *active* state specifies that the command is being interacted with in order to obtain the inputs needed before it can run. The *running* state specifies that the call-back of the command is executing. HUMANOID automatically returns the command to its default state once the call-back returns.

HUMANOID's policies for determining enabled behaviors from these states are as follows. When a command is *idle*, only the behaviors that set it *active* are enabled. When the command is *active*, the behaviors that set inputs for the command are enabled (subject to one exception, as explained below), and the behaviors that set the command to *idle* are also enabled. The behaviors that set the state to *running* are enabled only if the command is ready to run, as defined by the *ready/not-ready* slot. When the state is *running*, no behaviors are enabled.

Disabled/enabled. When a command is *disabled* it cannot be made *active*, and the behaviors that set the command to *active* or *running* are disabled. The *disabled/enabled* slot can be defined with a constraint so that a command disables or enables itself by testing the state and value of any command or input in the application. By default, commands where one or more inputs are tied to a global input are automatically *disabled* when the value of the global input does not satisfy the *type*, the *minimum* and *maximum* restrictions, and the *predicate* defined for the command input. Commands whose preconditions are not satisfied are *disabled* by default.

Ready/not-ready. Indicates whether a command is ready to run, *i.e.*, whether it is *active*, all its inputs are correct, and no preconditions are violated. Behaviors that change the command to *running* are enabled only if the command is *ready*.

The *disabled/enabled* and the *ready/not-ready* act as guards: they specify the conditions under which the *idle/active/running* slot can change value. Designers control sequencing indirectly by defining additional constraints on the guard slots, and by triggering actions that change the state of other commands and inputs when the value of any of the three slots changes. HUMANOID propagates the effects of the state changes by enabling and disabling behaviors as explained above.

The actions triggered on state changes are specified via methods of commands (similarly, the sequencing constraints of inputs and groups are specified via methods of input and group objects). Whenever a state slot of a command changes from A to B, the method a-to-b is called on the command and all command groups to which the command belongs. For example, when a command changes from *active* to *running*, the method *active-to-running* is called; when a command is no longer ready to run, the method *ready-to-not-ready* is called. The method can then change the status of other commands in the group, or call arbitrary procedures.

The state transition methods provide a general mechanism for designers to control the states of individuals and groups of commands and inputs, and thus a general way to control sequencing. In addition HUMANOID provides a library of objects called *attributes*, which define packages of methods that implement commonly-used sequencing features. For example, HUMANOID provides the following attributes for command sequencing (similar attributes are provided for input sequencing):

- *Only-One-Active.* This attribute specifies that only one command in a group can be *active* at any given time. When a new command in the group is made *active*, the previously *active* command is made *idle*. When no command is *active*, a pre-designated command in the group is made *active*, if one is defined.

- *Only-One-Enabled.* This attribute specifies that when a command in a group is made *active* or *running*, the other commands in the group are *disabled*.

These two command sequencing attributes can be used to implement familiar interface features. *Only-One-Active* can be used to specify the sequencing of the palette of drawing commands in a MacDraw-like drawing program, where the user selects a tool to draw. Only one tool is selected at any given time, and only the behaviors for the selected tool are enabled over the drawing area. *Only-One-Enabled* can be used to disable the menu bar of pull down menus while one of the commands is either executing, or prompting for inputs in a dialogue box. Note that in both examples the attributes are defined for command groups that the designer would define to control the presentation.

To incorporate sequencing constraints into a design, the designer simply lists the relevant attribute in the *attributes* slot of individuals or groups of command and inputs. If an attribute that packages the desired sequencing constraints does not exist, the designer first has to define it, by defining the appropriate methods. This mechanism makes simple, commonly used features easy for designers to use, but provides enough generality so that complex sequencing constraints can also be implemented.

The *browse* command in Version 9 of the Object Browser shown in Figure 1. illustrates the sequencing model. The *object-to-browse* input of the *browse* command is defined to be of type *Object*. The default definition of the *disabled/enabled* slot specifies that if the *object-to-browse* is incorrect, the command is *disabled*, causing the behavior that activates the command to be disabled so that clicking on the Browse button has no effect. So, when the user selects an object in the *object-contents* part of the display, the button is enabled, but if the user selects a non-object such as the constant XOR, the button is disabled.

HUMANOID's sequencing model has the following benefits:

- Provides a much less cumbersome means of specifying sequencing than event-based systems [5], or state transition networks [7]. Rather than specifying sequencing at the level of gestures/behaviors, or a potentially large number of states, HUMANOID derives the sequencing constraints on behaviors by applying a fixed set of policies to simple state model of commands, inputs and groups.

- Provides a framework (states and methods) for designers to express complex sequencing constraints, and provides abstractions (attributes) that make it easy to express commonly used sequencing constraints.

- Provides good support for design exploration because much sequencing behavior falls out from the data flow constraints expressed in the application design, with no extra effort needed from the designer. Additional sequencing constraints are expressed as annotations to individuals and groups of commands and inputs that are often used for presentation purposes too.

DESIGN DIMENSION #5: ACTION SIDE EFFECTS

Action side-effects are actions performed automatically as side effects of the actions triggered by user inputs. For example, a newly created object can become automatically selected, closing a dialogue box can reset all the options to their default, typing return in a type-in field can automatically move the cursor to the "next" type-in field.

Action side-effects are expressed using the command, input and group state transition methods described in the previous section. Whenever a behavior sets the value of an input, or changes the state of a command or an input, methods indicating the change are called.

Designers can specify side-effects by writing methods for the appropriate state transitions, or can define attributes similar to the sequencing attributes. For example, to cause a dialogue box to appear in response to a menu selection, designers can write a method for the *idle-to-active* state transition that calls *present-object* with the command and *dialogue-box-template* as its parameters. Since showing dialogue boxes is a common case, HUMANOID provides a command attribute called *Show-Dialogue-Box*.

HUMANOID provides the following attributes for commonly used side-effects on inputs. A similar library for command and group side-effects is also provided, but it is not discussed in this paper.

Revert-When-Incorrect. When an input is set to an incorrect value, the previously correct value is automatically restored.

Message-When-Incorrect. When an input is set to an incorrect value, an alert box is posted.

Beep-When-Incorrect. When an input is set to an incorrect value, the interface beeps.

Prompt-Ring. This attribute is defined for input groups. When an input in the group is set, the behaviors for the next input in the group are automatically activated.

Version 10 of the Object Browser shown in Figure 1. is an example of side-effect specification. It uses the *Revert-When-Incorrect* and the *Message-When-Incorrect* action side-effect attributes on the *object* global input, where users can enter the object to be viewed. If the user types in an incorrect object, the user will be notified with an alert box, and the value of the object is reverted to the previous (correct) value.

HUMANOID's model of side-effects has several benefits, which derive mostly from linking side-effects to command,

input and group state transitions, rather then specifying them in the actions of behaviors:

- Makes behaviors easier to reuse. Since the side-effects of behaviors are separate from the behaviors, the same behavior can be used in different contexts that require different side-effects.

- Increases modularity. Side-effects are represented centrally in the command, input or group objects, rather than being spread out in the possible multiple behaviors that act on these objects.

- Provides good support for design exploration. The manipulations and side-effect dimensions can be explored independently because the side-effects depend on the effects of the action of a behavior rather than on the behavior itself.

RELATED WORK

The most sophisticated of the UIMSs centered around the notion of deriving the user interface from a high-level specification of the semantics of a program are MIKE [14], UofA* [18] and UIDE [3]. MIKE and UofA* are able to generate a default interface from a minimal application description, and provide a few parameters that a designer can set to control the resulting interface. MIKE allows designers to define the interaction techniques for prompting for inputs, the structure of the menus, and actions to be executed when presentations are selected. However, MIKE has a built-in prefix dialogue structure that cannot be changed. UofA* supports prefix, post-fix and no-fix dialogue structures, supports current selected objects, and open-ended, and close-ended command invocation. Both systems allow designers to refine the layout.

HUMANOID's general model of commands allows designers to exert much finer control over dialogue sequencing. In addition, HUMANOID provides a library of command groups that allows designers to very easily specify the dialogue structures that MIKE and UofA* support. HUMANOID also provides finer control over presentation design, and supports the construction of the "main window" of application programs, which MIKE and UofA* do not support. UIDE's application description is much richer than those used in MIKE and UofA*. Such richer descriptions can be used to support more sophisticated design tools [3] (help generation, consistency and completeness checking, automatic dialogue box and menu design, transformations). Even though we have not constructed such sophisticated design tools, it should be possible to construct them, since our application description provides the necessary knowledge.

HUMANOID's application description is similar to UIDE's. HUMANOID improves on UIDE by providing a richer model of command states, enabling designers to exert finer control over dialogue sequencing. For example, HUMANOID's action side-effect mechanism subsumes UIDE's post-condition one, because it allows commands to assert side-effects on any of the state transitions of a command, not just on the successful execution of a command. In addition, HUMANOID provides more sophisticated facilities for refining the presentation and manipulation dimensions of the interface.

The command and input groups attributes provide a compact mechanism to specify dialogue sequencing similar to Statecharts [23], that avoids the explosion of states that occur in state transition networks. In fact, command and input group sequencing attributes can be used to emulate all the dialogue structures supported in the UofA* UIMS [18], plus provides the framework to define others.

Interface builders such as the Next Interface Builder [13], and OpenInterface [12] are a different class of tools to aid in the design of interfaces. These tools allow designers to draw interfaces consisting of check boxes, radio buttons, labels, type-in areas and other such interface building blocks. These tools make it very easy to construct the particular interfaces they support, but they are poor for design exploration. Designers have to commit to particular presentation, layout and interaction techniques early in the design. Making changes to the dialogue structure is difficult. For example, changing an input prompted in a dialogue box to a global input is difficult because all dialogue boxes that prompt for that input have to be manually edited. Also, making global policy changes such as changing the interaction technique to present choices requires manually editing a large number of displays. Achieving the same results that HUMANOID enables by using an interface builders, if it can be done at all, requires a level of programming sophistication beyond the reach of the designers for whom these tools are intended.

Systems such as ITS [1] and HUMANOID do not have this problem because to change a global policy it is enough to change a rule in ITS, or a template in HUMANOID. HUMANOID and ITS provide similar facilities for constructing presentations, but ITS lacks the facilities to do interface design along the other dimensions that HUMANOID supports.

Interface builders are currently easier to use than application description-centered systems like HUMANOID, MIKE, UofA* and UIDE, for constructing simple displays like dialogue boxes. However, this shortcoming can be overcome. APT [9], SAGE [16] and DON [8] are examples of systems that automatically generate high quality displays from the design knowledge base. APT and SAGE generate high quality charts, and DON, which is based in UIDE, is an initial attempt to generate high quality dialogue boxes.

HUMANOID currently lacks an interactive interface to construct the application description, which MIKE and UIDE have, and an interactive layout editor, which MIKE and UofA* have. We are currently working to remedy this shortcoming. Perhaps the ultimate interactive interface for design should also build on demonstrational systems like Lapidary [10] and Druid [19]. These systems allow the designer to specify the presentation and the behavior of an interface by example. Designers draw the interface as the user will see it, and then demonstrate the actions that users can perform, by graphically manipulating the presentation. These systems generalize the examples, and generate code that implements the general case. The attractiveness of these systems is in

their claims for ease of use. We view these systems as potentially complementary to knowledge-based systems like HUMANOID. For instance, one could imagine a Lapidary-like interface to specify some of the design changes illustrated in our Object Browser example. To specify that the slot-value pairs should be selectable, and highlighted in reverse video, the designer could draw the black, xored, rectangle, and the Lapidary-like tool would make the appropriate generalizations. It is an open research issue, however, whether demonstrational tools can be made sophisticated enough to design complex interfaces.

Our work only partly addresses issues of task analysis and user centered design: HUMANOID facilitates creating designs that act upon realizations obtained through these design approaches, but does not address these methods directly.

CONCLUSIONS

HUMANOID is an interface design system that lets designers express abstract conceptualizations of an interface design in executable form, allowing designers to experiment with scenarios and dialogues before the application model is completely concretized. The novel features of HUMANOID are:

- Supports top-down design. Designers can refine interfaces step by step. At any step designers can ask HUMANOID to generate the interface in order to try it out, or can refine it further.

- Allows designers to delay committing to specific interface features until they want to. Designers do not have to fully specify any aspect of the design in order to prototype it or to refine another aspect of it. For example, designers can specify manipulations for a presentation that has not been fully specified.

- Allows designers to explore the design space in any order. HUMANOID supports both breadth-first and depth-first design strategies, or any combination in between. In the breadth-first strategy, designers can specify the complete interface at a high level before refining any aspect of it. In the depth-first strategy designers can fully specify one aspect of the design (presentation, manipulation, sequencing) before working on a different aspect.

- Supports the specification of all aspects of an interface. HUMANOID supports the iterative specification of the application functionality, its presentation, input behavior and sequencing. HUMANOID supports the construction of the interface for the "main windows" of programs, not just the menus and commands to control the program.

- Provides an extensive library of presentation methods, and defaults for choosing presentation methods based on the types of objects to be displayed. For example, HUMANOID can construct dialogue boxes automatically, choosing check boxes, radio buttons, etc. automatically based on the types of the inputs to be requested. Designers can provide various hints that steer the dialogue box constructions in several directions.

- Defines a novel partitioning of interface design spaces into relatively independent dimensions, allowing designers to refine designs along these dimensions. The example in Figure 1. illustrates how designers can refine the presentation, application description, interactive manipulation and sequencing aspects of the interface in a rather independent manner.

We believe that HUMANOID substantially enhances the iterative design process required for constructing good user interfaces [2, 22] by allowing designs to be put into action faster and earlier than current design tools allow, and by allowing designers to refine designs along multiple, relatively independent dimensions.

ACKNOWLEDGEMENTS

We wish to thank Peter Aberg, David Benjamin, and Brian Harp for helpful comments on earlier drafts of this paper. This work was supported by DLA and DARPA under contracts #MDA972-90-C-0060 and #N00014-91-J-1623. Contents represent the opinions of the authors, and do not reflect official positions of DLA, DARPA, or any other government agency.

REFERENCES

1   W. Bennett, S. Boies, J. Gould, S. Greene and C. Wiecha. Transformations on a Dialog Tree: Rule-Based Mapping of Content to Style. In *Proceedings of the ACM SIGGRAPH Symposium on User Interface Software* and Technology, pp. 67-75, November 1989.

2   W. Buxton and R. Sniderman. Iteration in the Design of the Human-Computer Interface. In *Proceedings of the 13th Annual Meeting of the Human Factors Association of Canada*. 1980, pp. 72-80.

3   J. D. Foley, W. C. Kim, S. Kovacevic and K. Murray. UIDE: An Intelligent User Interface Design Environment. In J. S. Sullivan and S. W. Tyler, editors, *Intelligent User Interfaces*. pp. 339-384. ACM Press, 1991.

4   D. Giuse. Efficient Frame Systems. In J. P. Martins and E. M. Morgado, editors, *Lecture Notes in Artificial Intelligence*, Springer Verlag, Sep, 1989.

5   M. Green. Report on dialogue specification tools. In *User Interface Management Systems*. G. E. Pfaff, editor, Spring-Verlag, 1983, pp. 9-20.

6   P. J. Hayes, P. Szekely and R. Lerner. Design Alternatives for User Interface Management Systems Based on Experience with COUSIN. In *Proceedings SIGCHI'85*, April 1989, pp. 169-175.

7   R. K. Jacob. A specification language for direct manipulation interfaces. *ACM Transactions on Graphics* 5, 4. (October 1986), 283-317.

8   W. C. Kim and J. Foley. DON: User Interface Presentation Design Assistant. In *Proceedings UIST'90*. October 1990, pp. 10-20.

9   J. Mackinlay. Automating the Design of Graphical Presentations of Relational Information. *ACM Transactions on Graphics*, pp. 110-141, April 1986.

10 B. Myers, B. Vander Zanden and R. Dannenberg. Creating Graphical Interactive Application Objects by Demonstration. In *Proceedings of the ACM SIGGRAPH Symposium on User Interface Software* and Technology, pp. 95-104, November 1989.

11 B. A. Myers. A New Model for Handling Input. *ACM Transactions on Information Systems* 8, 3. (July 1990), pp. 289-320.

12 Neuron Data, Inc. 1991. *Open Interface Toolkit*. 156 University Ave. Palo Alto, CA 94301.

13 NeXT, Inc. 1990. *Interface Builder*, Palo Alto, CA.

14 D. Olsen. MIKE: The Menu Interaction Kontrol Environment. *ACM Transactions on Graphics*, vol 17, no 3, pp. 43-50, 1986.

15 D. Olsen. A Programming Language Basis for User Interface Management. In *Proceedings SIGCHI'89*. April 1989, pp. 171-176.

16 S. Roth and J. Mattis. Data Characterization for Intelligent Graphics Presentation. In *Proceedings SIGCHI'90*. April 1990, pp. 193-200.

17 K. J. Schmucker. MacApp: An application framework. In R. M. Baecker, W. A. Buxton, editors, *Readings in Human-Computer Interaction*. pp. 591-594. Morgan Kaufmann Publishers, Inc. 1987.

18 G. Singh and M. Green. A High-level User Interface Management System. In *Proceedings SIGCHI'89*. April 1989, pp. 133-138.

19 G. Singh, C. H. Kok and T. Y. Ngan. Druid: A System for Demonstrational Rapid User Interface Development. In *Proceedings UIST'90*. October 1990, pp. 167-177.

20 P. Szekely. Standardizing the interface between applications and UIMS's. In *Proceedings UIST'89*. November 1989, pp. 34-42.

21 P. Szekely. Template-based mapping of application data to interactive displays. In *Proceedings UIST'90*. October 1990, pp. 1-9.

22 W. Swartout and R. Balzer. On the Inevitable Intertwining of Specification and Implementation. CACM 25, 7 (July 1982), pp. 438-440.

23 P. Wellner. Statemaster: A UIMS Based on Statecharts for Prototyping and Target Implementation. In *Proceedings SIGCHI'89*. April 1989, pp. 177-182.

Collaborating in the World of Interactive Media

Moderator: **Michael Arent**,
               Apple Computer Inc., 20525 Mariani Avenue, Cupertino, CA 95014
               phone: 408.974.3078
               email: arent@apple.com

Panelists: **Donna Cohen**, Interactive Media Producer, Warner New Media, Burbank, CA
               Mike Mills, Human Interface Designer, Apple Computer Inc., Cupertino, CA
               Chris Krueger, Interaction Designer, Arborescence, San Francisco, CA
               Wendy Richmond, Interactive Media Designer, WGBH, Boston, MA

Keywords

design process, graphic design, human interface design, hypermedia, interdisciplinary collaboration

Introduction

Creating, producing, and publishing interactive media is a complex task that most often requires the expertise of different disciplines working collaboratively as a team. This is somewhat similar to the cast of people required to create and produce a feature film or a television commercial. In terms of interactive media, the disciplines could include writers, programmers, producers, human interface designers, design directors, graphic designers, animators, sound engineers, video technicians, and usability testers among others. Teams can be an orchestrated mix of in-house people, design groups, specialized contractors and service bureaus. All in all, these "…different disciplines have different priorities, different thinking styles, different values. When people from different disciplines get together, their values collide. What one person finds valuable others do not even notice. And they do not notice that they do not notice. [1]"

The purpose of this panel is to present how these different professional disciplines have overcome the challenging complexities of professional clashes, resource limitations, technical bottlenecks, budget constraints, demanding consumers and nervous clients in order to create and produce successful computer-based interactive communications and their interfaces [2]. The quest of these presentations from the viewpoints of different professional disciplines is twofold:

1. to provide the CHI'92 audience with an insiders view of the complex issues that professionals face when doing collaborative work.

2. to engage the audience in the discussion of the many issues related to the collaborative process of interactive media design.

What Issues Will Be Addressed?

Some of the issues of interdisciplinary collaboration that will be discussed include:

■ Who has ultimate creative control over the direction of a design? the interaction designer? the producer? the programmer? the content editor? a core group within a team? How is creative control determined?

■ How are collaborative relationships built that are required to develop and produce successful design? What kind of relationships lead to design failure?

■ What are the tradeoffs among design elegance, functionality, communicativeness, and commercial value? [3]

■ When is the right time to engage in testing a design (through focus groups, usability testing, etc.) to determine if end-users or consumers are going to understand the content message(s) and the interface to that content? [4]

■ How do designers and producers work with tool developers to design and build tools that are flexible and provide productivity gains?

The Panel Format

■ The chairperson will introduce the panelists then give a brief statement that sets the tone for the theme of the panel.

■ Each panelist will give a case presentation using video or interactive computer-based examples in which they describe the intention of the design, the target audience, the different disciplines with whom they collaborated, the issues that arose as a result of the collaborative design process, how the issues were resolved or not resolved and what impact these issues had on the outcome of the case project.

■ The chair will present a small, "pop quiz" style problem to the panelists to solve collaboratively. Audience participation will be welcome.

■ Continued discussion in a breakout area

The Panelists

Michael Arent is a human interface designer with the Advanced Technologies Group at Apple Computer. He is currently working with a collaborative team on the design and implementation of the interface to QuickTime, the new multimedia architecture being developed for Macintosh computers. Prior to Apple, Michael has worked with a variety of interdisciplinary teams to design commercial and prototypical interfaces for applications software and interactive media pieces.

The technology for personal computers is evolving to effectively handle a wider variety of data types and allow more sophisticated control of media devices, such as, videotape, laser disc and CD players This technology evolution is in turn expanding the possible uses of interactive media. The interactive media marketplace is predicted to expand with an impact similar to the "desktop publishing" phenomenon. If this explosion occurs, the demand for qualified professionals to collaborate in the creation and production of interactive media products, exhibits, training/educational materials, etc. will increase exponentially. How will the interdisciplinary teams of the future function to produce successful designs? What issues will the people who comprise these teams face?

Donna Cohen is an interactive media producer at Warner New Media and was the driving force behind the design and production of the seminal CD-ROM Audio Notes series, which included "The Magic Flute" and Beethoven's "The String Quartet". In her high energy style, Donna orchestrates musicologists, editors, writers, graphic designers and a cast of other disciplines to produce highly engaging, interactive CD format pieces based on well-known classical music compositions, operas and other content. Donna will give a lively discourse about the rewards and travails of a producer of interactive media. The presentation will be accompanied by examples from the interactive pieces she has produced. The team-related issues she will cover range from content decisions to appropriate "look and feel" for the mass market.

Mike Mills is a cognitive psychologist and human interface designer with the Advanced Technologies Group at Apple Computer. Dr. Mills is also currently working with a collaborative team on the design and implementation of Apple's new QuickTime multimedia architecture as well as leading his team in the research of interfaces for end-user authoring tools. Mike will present some of the salient human interface issues of authoring tools for "the rest of us." He will show interactive demos that provide directions for resolving these issues not only for non-programmers but across members of teams comprised of different disciplines with different programming and authoring skills.

Chris Krueger is a designer at a firm that specializes in interactive software. His firm has recently designed and produced a very successful information kiosk for the California Academy of Sciences Museum in San Francisco that communicates a complex scientific subject in a very user-friendly way for "mere mortals". He is currently involved with a team of people, who are designing an interactive weekly magazine to be distributed on CD format. Chris will talk about the tight collaborative relationship and skills required to create and produce timely interactive media publications. He will address the "look and feel" and the other interface issues that allow efficient interactive media software development as well as consistent service to the consumer.

Wendy Richmond joined WGBH Educational Foundation to form the Design Lab, an interactive multimedia design studio serving both WGBH and outside clients. At the Design Lab she co-directs a variety of interactive multimedia projects. Wendy began designing with and for computers in 1978 as a graduate student at MIT, and was a collaborator in the formation of the design technology companies, Bitstream and Lightspeed Computers. Wendy is also an author

and has written numerous articles on design, computer technology and the collaborative process as well as a book entitled "Design & Technology: Erasing the Boundaries". Wendy will present a collaborative team case situation through the anecdotes of creating a large project in a frighteningly accelerated time frame using developmental software. She will present the Design Lab's largest effort to date, the recently completed (CD-ROM, MPC platform) Multimedia Macmillan Dictionary for Children.

References

[1] Kim, S., *Interdisciplinary Cooperation,* In The Art of Human Computer Interface Design, Addison-Wesley, Reading, 1990, 31-44

[2] Arent, M., Vertelney, L. and Lieberman, H. *Two Disciplines in Search of an Interface*, In The Art of Human Computer Interface Design, Addison-Wesley, Reading, 1990, 45-55

[3] Gentner, Donald R. and Grudin, J., *Why Good Engineers (Sometimes) Create Bad Interfaces*, In Proceedings of CHI'90: Human Factors in Computing Systems (Seattle, April 1990). ACM, New York, 277-282.

[4] Salomon, G.B., *Designing Casual-Use Hypertext: The CHI'89 InfoBooth*, In Proceedings of CHI'90: Human Factors in Computing Systems (Seattle, April 1990). ACM, New York, 451-458.

References

The MidasPlus Molecular Modeling System

Thomas Ferrin, Conrad Huang, Gregory Couch, Eric Pettersen and Robert Langridge
Computer Graphics Laboratory
926 Medical Sciences
University of California
San Francisco, CA 94143-0446

MidasPlus [6, 7] is an interactive molecular modeling system used to depict three dimensional macromolecular structures such as proteins and nucleic acids, to study how these structures spatially and chemically interact, and to study how small molecules such as drugs bind with these macromolecules. Effective interaction with macromolecular structures presents several challenges: the molecules consist of thousands to tens of thousands of atoms and the scientist user is easily overwhelmed by the sheer volume of data if the displayed information is not limitied and presented in a rational manner. The intellectual process of understanding the structure and function of molecules is linked to visualizing the complex spatial relationships within these structures, and since the user is only presented *images* of models, this intellectual process must proceed without being able to physically handle and make experimental "hand driven" modifications of a physical model. Finally, macromolecules are often globular in shape, of course bear no resemblance to macroscopic physical objects in the real world, and hence make it inherently difficult for the human visual system to accurately perceive the complex spatial relationships that are so crucial to chemical activity.

MidasPlus attempts to solve these problems through a variety of methods. Atomic coordinate data is used to create line and surface displays of several interacting molecules while qualitatively monitoring stereochemistry. Three-dimensional rotations and translations are controlled with either the workstation mouse using a "virtual trackball" interaction technique, [4] or by a six-degree-of-freedom "spaceball" device in order to provide concise control of viewing angles and positions. Although a complete model of any molecule is generated, it is possible to view any sub-segment in isolation for clarification. MidasPlus is capable of displaying wire-frame structures with depth cueing, dot cloud solvent accessible [11, 14] and van der Waals surfaces, [1] and shaded color surfaces with multiple light sources and shadows (appropriate for publication purposes) using either an "atomic sphere" form of representation [8] or "ribbon" drawings for depicting secondary protein structure. [3, 12] Several modes of stereo viewing are provided and stereo display coupled with kinetic depth effect is critical to the perception of spatial relationships. Color can be used to denote a variety of quantitative information including atom type, electrostatic potential charge, and hydrophobicity.

The MidasPlus system has been in active use by scientists as a drug design support system for several years [2, 9, 10, 13] and has been licensed to over 200 university, government and industrial research laboratories. The software runs on the Silicon Graphics IRIS family of workstations and NeXT workstations. [5] A port is also underway to the DECstation 5000 series of workstations. The demonstration will illustrate the various ways molecular data can be visualized and interactively manipulated using MidasPlus.

References

[1] P.A. Bash, N. Pattabiraman, C.C. Huang, T.E. Ferrin, and R. Langridge. Van der waals surfaces in molecular modeling: Implementation with real-time computer graphics. *Science*, 222:1325–1327, 1983.

[2] J.M. Blaney, E.C. Jorgensen, M.L. Connolly, T.E. Ferrin, R. Langridge, S.J. Oatley, J.M. Burridge, and C.F. Blake. Computer graphics in drug design: Molecular modeling of thyroid hormone-prealbumin interactions. *J. Med. Chem.*, 25:785–790, 1982.

[3] M. Carson and C.E. Bugg. Algorithm for ribbon models of proteins. *J. Mol. Graphics*, 4(2):121–122, June 1986.

[4] M. Chen, S.J. Mountford, and A. Sellen. A study in interactive 3-d rotation using 2-d control devices. *Computer Graphics*, 22(4):121–129, August 1988.

[5] T.E. Ferrin, G.S. Couch, C.C. Huang, E.F. Pettersen, and R. Langridge. An affordable approach to interactive desktop molecular modeling. *J. Mol. Graphics*, 9(1):27–32, 37–38, 1991.

[6] T.E. Ferrin, C.C. Huang, L.E. Jarvis, and R. Langridge. The midas database system. *J. Mol. Graphics*, 6(1):2–12, 1988.

[7] T.E. Ferrin, C.C. Huang, L.E. Jarvis, and R. Langridge. The midas display system. *J. Mol. Graphics*, 6(1):13–27, 36–37, 1988.

[8] C.C. Huang, E.F. Pettersen, T.E. Klein, T.E. Ferrin, and R. Langridge. Conic – a fast renderer for space-filling molecules with shadows. *J. Mol. Graphics*, 9(4):230–236, 242, 1991.

[9] T.E. Klein, C.C. Huang, T.E. Ferrin, R. Langridge, and C. Hansch. Computer assisted drug receptor mapping analysis. *Artificial Intelligence in Chemistry*, 306:147–158, 1986. ACS Symposium Series, B. Hohne and T. Pierce, ed.

[10] R. Langridge, T.E. Ferrin, I.D. Kuntz, and M.L. Connolly. Real time color graphics in studies of molecular interactions. *Science*, 211:661–666, 1981.

[11] B. Lee and F.M. Richards. *J. Mol. Biol.*, 55:379–400, 1971.

[12] A.M. Lesk and K.D. Hardman. Computer-generated schematic diagrams of protein structure. *Science*, 216:539–540, 1982.

[13] R.A. Lewis, D.C. Roe, C.C. Huang, T.E. Ferrin, R. Langridge, and I.D. Kuntz. Automated site-directed drug design using molecular lattices. *J. Mol. Graphics*, 1992. in press.

[14] F.M. Richards. *Annu. Rev. Biophys Bioeng.*, 6:151–176, 1977.

Simulation-based Learning Systems:
Prototypes and Experiences

Arthur James & James C. Spohrer

Apple Computer
MS: 76-3A
Cupertino, CA 95014
(408) 974-1421
spohrer@applelink.apple.com

KEYWORDS: Simulation, Learning, Authoring

INTRODUCTION

Apple's Business Learning Research group is exploring the development of next generation simulation-based learning environments that integrate artificial intelligence and multimedia technologies [1]. Sample applications include a role playing simulator designed to help engineers learn information gathering skills, and a device simulator designed to help mechanics learn troubleshooting skills. In addition to sample applications, authoring environments that can speed the development of these systems are also being prototyped. The Business Learning Research (BLR) group is part of Apple's Advanced Technology Group (ATG).

RESEARCH PROTOTYPE 1 - ROLE'M

Apple uses a consultative approach to selling computer systems. Sales teams, consisting of a systems engineer and a sales representative employed by Apple or authorized resellers, meet with customers to perform *needs analysis consultations*. During needs analysis consultations, systems engineers work with customers to determine their networking needs, existing organization and information systems, and special constraints. In part, successful consultations require that systems engineers gather the necessary factual information to determine relevant products and propose the best solutions. However, to be truly successful, sales teams must also establish good interpersonal relationships with customers.

The prototype Role'm training system allows a student to perform part of a needs analysis consultation with a simulated executive briefing specialist from Roberts and Company, a fictitious marketing firm [3]. Students use a restricted natural language interface to construct statements that allow them to communicate with a simulated customer. Other role playing simulators have explored different approaches to the problem of natural language input [4]. Customer behavior is modeled by rules, and displayed as video clips in a window. If an SE does not relate his line of questioning to a customer's problems, the customer will become bored and quickly run out of time for the interview. If the SE is successful, then the customer gives the SE an advance to meet with a vice president.

RESEARCH PROTOTYPE 2 - MRFIXIT

Airlines train and employ mechanics to ensure that their aircrafts are maintained in top operating condition. Airline mechanics must learn to maintain and troubleshoot complex systems composed of hundreds of components with various fault modes. Most mechanics learn through on the job experience in an apprenticeship relationship with a master mechanic. Apprenticeship learning is augmented with leader led instruction.

Interactive device simulations can aid instructors efforts to explain complex systems. In addition, instructors find that coached learning environments can help students practice and learn skills by increasing their time on task. However, given the current state of training system authoring tools, advanced computer based training aids with these features are not easily developed by instructors and subject matter experts without the assistance of programmers. The MrFixit system is a vehicle for exploring: (1) how to more easily author detailed interactive simulations of aircraft subsystems, and (2) how to more easily author coached learning environment that teach mechanics troubleshooting.

The prototype MrFixit training system is composed of three main environments: (1) an environment for authoring a device (e.g., aircraft air conditioning system) from a library of graphic components, (2) an environment for interacting with the device to get pictures, digitized sound, and text descriptions of the device components, and (3) an environment for seeding a fault in the device and watching an expert system troubleshoot the problem. The device authoring environment is in the early stages of development, and has been strongly influenced by the IMTS/Rapids system [5]. The prototype expert system uses about twenty rules to illustrate troubleshooting behavior in several dozen fault scenarios. Several hundred rules will be required to troubleshoot the entire system which is made up of a few hundred components. A practice environment will be added to MrFixit. The purpose of the practice environment is to allow students to attempt to troubleshoot the device, and receive remediation when the students' actions differ from the experts.

EXPERIENCES

Building systems like MrFixit and Role'm using existing development tools is difficult, in part because no single tool combines the best features of existing multimedia authoring tools and AI authoring tools [2]. Few AI authoring tools are usable by non-programmers. Few multimedia authoring tools have an extensible object environment or powerful inferencing capabilities. More fully empowering developers of integrated multimedia/AI training systems will require addressing the issues of tool integration and end-user authoring.

Finally, existing multimedia and AI authoring tools do not provide adequate methodology support (e.g., data collection and analysis), computer managed instruction support (e.g., lesson planning, grading), support for customizing paradigmatic training examples for new domains, support for collaborative/group development efforts, or support for integrating training into the workplace as job aids.

CONCLUDING REMARKS

Our goal is to better understand what authoring tools are needed to develop training systems that integrate multimedia and AI (MM&AI) technologies. Our approach is to first develop a few prototype training systems and evaluate existing authoring tools. From our initial explorations it is clear that to meet the needs of today's instructors and subject matter experts, a combined multimedia and AI authoring environment that can be used by non-programmers is required.

ACKNOWLEDGEMENTS

Thanks to Jim Winkles, Mark L. Miller, Tyde Richards, Dave Vronay, Adam Chipkin, Ruben Kleiman, Tom Brinck, Jim Laffey, Kit Abbott, and Greg Czora who have contributed to the development of these systems. We wish to thank all our collaborators at Boeing, especially Frank Ruggiero, Terry Samphire, Terry Swanson, Roger Guay, Pat Henderson, and Brian Didier.

REFERENCES

1. Spohrer, J.C. (1990) Integrating Multimedia and AI for Training: Examples and Issues. Proceeding of the IEEE Systems, Man, and Cybernetics Conference, IEEE Press, pp. 663-664.

2. Spohrer, J.C., Vronay, D., Kleiman, R. (1991) Authoring intelligent multimedia applications: Finding familiar representations for expressing knowledge. Proceeding of the IEEE Systems, Man, and Cybernetics Conference, IEEE Press, pp. 1751-1756.

3. Spohrer, J.C., James, A., Abbott, K.A., Czora, G.J., Laffey, J. Miller, M.L. (1991) A role playing simulator for needs analysis consultations. Proceeding of the World Congress on Expert Systems, Pergamon Press, pp. 2829-2839.

4. Stevens, S.M. (1989). Intelligent interactive video simulation of code inspection. *Communications of the ACM*. 32:7, 832-843.

5. Towne, D.M., and Munro A. (1989). *Rapids: A simulation-based instructional authoring system for technical training*. Technical Report No. 112. Behavioral Technologies Laboratory, USC. Redondo Beach, CA.

ClearBoard: A Seamless Medium for Shared Drawing and Conversation with Eye Contact

Hiroshi Ishii   and   Minoru Kobayashi

NTT Human Interface Laboratories
1-2356 Take, Yokosuka-Shi, Kanagawa, 238-03 Japan
Tel: +81-468-59-3522, Fax: +81-468-59-2332
E-mail: ishii@ntthif.ntt.jp, minoru@ntthcs.ntt.jp

ABSTRACT

This paper introduces a novel shared drawing medium called ClearBoard. It realizes (1) a seamless shared drawing space and (2) eye contact to support realtime and remote collaboration by two users. We devised the key metaphor: "talking *through* and drawing *on* a transparent glass window" to design ClearBoard. A prototype of ClearBoard is implemented based on the "Drafter-Mirror" architecture. This paper first reviews previous work on shared drawing support to clarify the design goals. We then examine three metaphors that fulfill these goals. The design requirements and the two possible system architectures of ClearBoard are described. Finally, some findings gained through the experimental use of the prototype, including the feature of "gaze awareness", are discussed.

INTRODUCTION

A whiteboard (or blackboard) is probably the most typical shared workspace in an ordinary face-to-face meeting. Fig. 1 shows a snapshot of a whiteboard being used in a design session. Participants are concurrently drawing on and pointing to the whiteboard, while speaking and gesturing.

In a design session, the participants' focus can change dynamically. When we discuss concrete system architectures, we intensively use a whiteboard as a shared drawing space by drawing diagrams, marks, and pointing to them. The whiteboard serves as an explicit group memory that each participant can see, point to, and draw on simultaneously [9]. On the other hand, when we discuss abstract concepts or design philosophy, we often concentrate on the partner's face while talking. In face-to-face conversations, mutual gaze (eye-contact), facial expressions and gestures provide a variety of non-verbal cues that are essential in human-human communication [2]. Through the use of TeamWorkStation in design sessions [6], we

Fig. 1 A Whiteboard used in a Design Session

realized that a smooth transition between face-to-face conversations and shared drawing activities is essential in supporting a dynamic collaborative process.

When we design a medium to support these activities, it is not sufficient to simulate the whiteboard function only, the simple video phone function only, or even both functions. It is necessary to integrate a virtual whiteboard with face-to-face communication channels *seamlessly* so that users can switch their focus smoothly from one to another according to the task contents [3].

In a face-to-face meeting, the room is perceived as a *contiguous* space: there are no physical *seams* between the whiteboard and the participants. By simply moving their eyes or heads, participants can look at both other participants and the whiteboard. However, in existing desktop tele-conference systems with shared drawing functions, the participants' images and shared drawing images are usually dealt with separately. These images are displayed in different windows on a screen, or in different screens. Therefore, there are *seams* between the images of participants and the shared drawing images. The virtual meeting space was segregated into several spatially separated windows or displays.

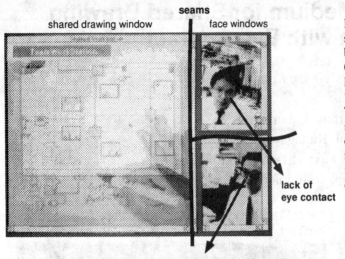

seams
shared drawing window   face windows

lack of
eye contact

Fig. 2   Seam and Eye-Contact Problems in
            TeamWorkStation

Lack of *eye contact* has been another problem of existing desktop video conference systems. People feel it difficult to communicate when they cannot tell if the partner is looking at him or her. Eye contact plays an important role in face-to-face conversations because "eyes are as eloquent as the tongue." Fig. 2 illustrates these two problems: seams between windows and the lack of eye-contact in a shared screen of TeamWorkStation [8].

In order to solve these problems, this paper presents a novel shared drawing medium, ClearBoard. ClearBoard realizes both (1) seamless shared workspace and (2) eye contact. ClearBoard is designed to support realtime and remote collaboration by two users. Therefore, it can be called a "pairware" instead of "groupware" [11].

This paper first reviews previous work on shared drawing support and clarifies the goals of this research. We then examine three metaphors that fulfill these goals. The design requirements and system architecture of ClearBoard prototype are described. Finally, some findings gained through the experimental use of the prototype are discussed.

PREVIOUS WORK

As shown in Fig. 3, there have been several systems proposed to support face-to-face conversations and shared drawing activities. However, there has been no system that fulfills both of the following two requirements: (1) a contiguous space that includes both shared drawings and user image, and (2) eye contact.

Video Tunnel

Video Tunnel [2] is a kind of video phone developed in EuroPARC for a computer-controlled video network. It supports eye-contact between two speakers using the well-known half mirror technique.

	shared drawing	facial expression	eye-contact	seamlessness: contiguity of drawing and user images		
Video Tunnel		O	O		EuroPARC [2]	only for face-to-face conversation
VideoWindow		O			Bellcore [4]	
VideoDraw	O[*1]	O		[*5]	Xerox PARC [13]	for shared drawing and face-to-face conversation
Commune	O[*2]	O			Xerox PARC [1, 10]	
VideoWhiteboard	O[*1]	[*4]	△[*6]		Xerox PARC [14]	
TeamWorkStation	O[*3]	O		[*7]	NTT HI Labs [6, 8]	
ClearFace on TWS	O[*3]	O		[*8]	NTT HI Labs [7]	
ClearBoard-1	O[*1]	O	O	O	NTT HI Labs	

*1 direct drawing with whiteboard marker
*2 direct drawing with digitizer
*3 indirect drawing with pen and computer tools
*4 shadow image of user

*5 different screens
*6 shadow and drawing are contiguous.
*7 different windows
*8 translucent face windows over drawing window

Fig. 3 Previous Work and ClearBoard-1

(a) in front of white board   (b) over a table   (c) through a glass window

Fig. 4 Three Metaphors of Seamless Space for Shared Drawing and Face-to-Face Conversation

VideoWindow
VideoWindow, developed in Bellcore, is a wall-size screen that connects remote rooms to support informal face-to-face communications [4].
Neither Video Tunnel nor VideoWindow support shared drawing activities.

VideoDraw
VideoDraw [13], developed in Xerox PARC, is a pioneering work that supports shared drawing activity using video. It allows a user to draw with a whiteboard marker directly on a transparent sheet attached to the video screen that shows the drawing surface image of the partner. For face-to-face conversations, VideoDraw provides users with another screen.

Commune
Commune [1, 10] is a shared drawing tool based on a digitizer and multi-user paint editor developed in Xerox PARC. It is used with another screen for face-to-face conversation as VideoDraw.

VideoWhiteboard
VideoWhiteboard [14] developed in Xerox PARC, utilizes the shadow of users to convey the gestures of collaborators. Since the marks on the wall-size screen and the shadow of the user are captured by a single camera, it provides remote collaborators with a virtual space in which the marks and the shadow of drawing gestures are contiguous. However, because only shadow images are sent, no facial expression is conveyed.

TeamWorkStation
TeamWorkStation [6, 8] developed by the authors at NTT enables the simultaneous use of heterogeneous tools such as computer tools, printed materials, handwriting and hand gestures in a shared drawing space. Facial images are displayed in different windows on the same display.

ClearFace on TeamWorkStation
ClearFace [7] developed by the authors lays translucent facial images over shared drawing images to utilize the limited screen space more effectively. However, as with TeamWork-Station, the facial images are not contiguous with the drawing space.

THREE METAPHORS FOR SEAMLESS SPACE
In order to design groupware that achieves the two goals of (1) contiguous (seamless) space, and (2) eye contact, we first investigated the following familiar metaphors, and clarified their problems.

(a) talking in front of a whiteboard, and

(b) talking over a table.

(a) is an exact whiteboard metaphor. The advantage of this metaphor is that all the participants can share the common board orientation. However, because two participants share the same space in front of the whiteboard, it is hard to implement a mechanism that can coordinate the use of this shared space. The only way we found of realizing this metaphor is to employ "virtual reality" technology. However, we do not think it is a good idea to force users to wear awkward head-mount displays and special gloves and a suit just to share some drawings. This solution lets users dive into a computer-generated virtual world which definitely increases cognitive loads.

(b) is another quite familiar metaphor, sitting on opposite sides of a table and talking over the table. This metaphor is quite suitable for face-to-face communication because two participants can easily see each other's face. However, the orientation of a drawing becomes upside-down for one of the parties[1]. If we could develop an "L-shaped display", this metaphor could be realized to some extent. However, it is hard to give users a natural sense of sharing the same space over the table.

In order to overcome the problems in metaphors (a) and (b) while utilizing their advantages, we devised the new metaphor (c) as the foundation of our groupware design in September 1990.

(c) talking *through* and drawing *on a transparent glass window*[2].

---

1 VideoDraw [11] and Commune [1, 8] took the human interface close to this metaphor letting users share a common orientation. However, physical seams existed between the separate screens, one for the partner's facial image and the other for shared drawings.

2 VideoWindow [3] and VideoWhiteboard [12] are close to this metaphor. However, as described in Fig. 3, both fail to achieve the two goals of seamless integration and eye contact.

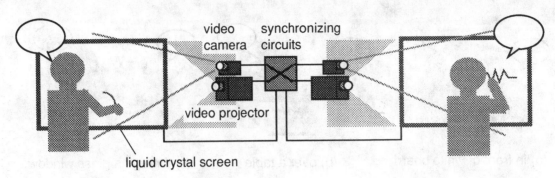

Fig. 5 Liquid Crystal Screen Architecture

Metaphor (c) does not produce any confusion or conflict about shared space use, since each participant's space is isolated from the other partner's space by a transparent glass window. This metaphor has the following advantages. First, as with the table metaphor (b), participants can see the partner's face easily. Second, since the partner's face and drawings are closely located on the board, switching the focus between the drawing and the partner's face requires less eye movements than (a) or (b).

One problem of this metaphor is that participants can not share the common orientation of "right" and "left" of the drawing space. However, this problem can be easily solved in implementing the prototype by mirror-reversing the video image.

We chose this metaphor (c) as the base for pairware design because of its simplicity and the advantages described above.

We coined the name "ClearBoard" for the pairware based on this metaphor (c). There can be several technical approaches to implement this ClearBoard concept. In the following section, we discuss two possible implementations of Clear-Board.

PROTOTYPE IMPLEMENTATION

Design Requirements
In order to implement a ClearBoard prototype which supports remote collaboration, we identified the following three design requirements.
(1) direct drawing on the display screen surface must be supported[3],
(2) the video image of a user must be taken through (behind) the screen surface (to achieve eye contact), and
(3) common orientation of the drawing space, not only "top" and "bottom" but also "right" and "left", must be shared at both sites.

The video tunnel architecture based on half-mirrors satisfies requirement (2). However, the combination of a half-silvered

---

3 Although we had taken the indirect drawing approach in TeamWorkStation [6, 8] to incorporate variety media such as printed materials into shared drawing space, in the design of ClearBoard, we took the direct drawing method to realize the metaphor of glass window illustrated in Fig. 4 (c).

mirror and a CRT display produces the problem of parallax, and does not satisfy requirement (1).

Requirement (3) is important to provide both users with a common orientation of the drawing space. Especially for words, the partner must be able to read the text in its correct orientation. The strict implementation of the transparent glass metaphor does not allow this.

In order to realize a ClearBoard prototype that satisfies all these requirements, we investigated two alternative system architectures based on different techniques.

Liquid Crystal Screen Architecture
In order to take a frontal image of a user who is drawing on a screen, it is necessary to take his or her image through the screen by a video camera placed behind the screen. A liquid crystal screen, which can be rapidly switched between the transparent and light scattering state by the application of a suitable control voltage, can be a key device to fulfill this requirement. Fig. 5 illustrates the system architecture of ClearBoard based on this technique.

Fig. 6 illustrates how this architecture works; the liquid crystal screen is switched between the two states, (1) light scattering

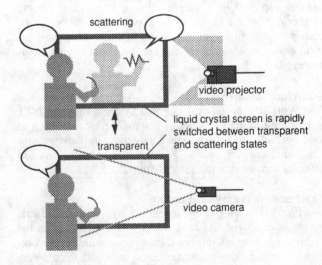

Fig. 6 Light scattering and Transparent States of Liquid Crystal Screen

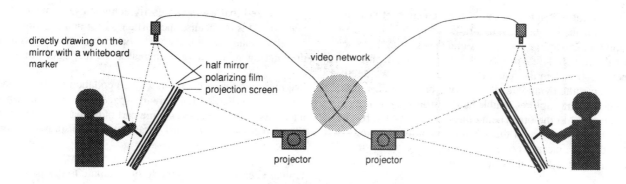

Fig. 7 "Drafter-Mirror" Architecture of ClearBoard Prototype

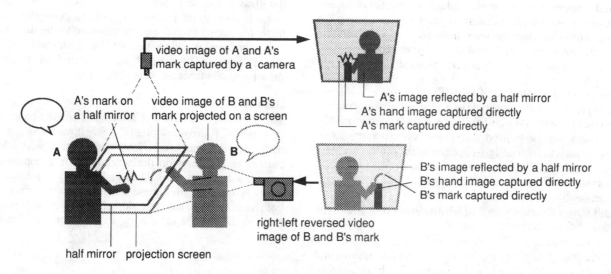

Fig. 8 How Drafter-Mirror Architecture Works

and (2) transparent. In state (1), the screen works as a rear projection screen on which the image of the partner and his or her drawing is displayed. In state (2), the user's image is captured by a video camera located behind the transparent screen. The timing of image capture and image display is synchronized to the switching of liquid crystal display states.

This technique was demonstrated by Shinichi Shiwa [12] at NTT in order to enable eye contact without any shared drawing support consideration. This architecture can be utilized to implement the ClearBoard concept if users are allowed to draw directly on the screen.
The transition frequency of the liquid crystal screen depends on its size. High frequencies, which decrease the physical load on user's eyes, are hard to achieve with large screens. Flickering images can be a serious disadvantage. The high cost of the liquid crystal screen is another drawback. Because of these shortcomings, we devised the next solution, which we refer to as "Drafter-Mirror architecture".

"Drafter-Mirror" Architecture

In order to implement the ClearBoard concept with a *flicker-less* and simpler technology, we devised the new system architecture illustrated in Fig. 7. We call it "Drafter-Mirror" because it looks like a drafter (a desk for architectural drawing) and it uses a half-mirror technique to enable eye-contact.

Each Drafter-Mirror terminal is equipped with a tilted screen, a video projector and a video camera. The screen is angled back at about 45 degrees and is composed of a projection screen, a polarizing film and a half-silvered mirror. Video feedback between the two cameras and screen pairs is prevented by a polarizing filter on each camera lens and a nearly orthogonal polarized filter that covers the surface of each screen. Users can write and draw on the surface of the screen using color paint markers. Water-based fluorescent (luminous) paint markers were used in our experiment because these colors are easy to distinguish from the background images including the user and the user's background. Markers can be erased with a cloth.
Fig. 8 illustrates how this Drafter-Mirror architecture works.

The video camera located above the screen captures the drawings and the image of the user reflected by the half-mirror as a continuous video image. This image is sent to the other terminal through a video network, and projected onto the partner's screen from the rear. The partner can draw directly on this transmitted video image. Because of this architecture, the video camera captures double hand images, one being the direct image, and the other being the image reflected by the half-mirror. The image of the user and his or her drawings is projected on the partner's screen so that both users can shared common orientation of the drawing space.

The drawing image captured by the camera is trapezoidally distorted due to perspective because the screen is at an angle. In order to support shared drawing on the screen, the drawing image must be recreated with the original shape and size on the partner's screen. In the current implementation, the distortion is offset by the opposite distortion caused by projecting the image onto the tilted screen. In order to give a suitable distortion rate, the camera and the projector should be symmetrically arranged with respect to the screen.

EXPERIMENTAL USE OF CLEARBOARD-1

We implemented the prototype of a Drafter-Mirror system in November 1990. (We call this prototype "ClearBoard-1".) Since then we have used this prototype in experimental sessions such as icon design, direction of the routes in a map, and discussions about diagrams for this paper. We informally observed the use of ClearBoard-1 by ourselves and our colleagues.

Fig. 9 shows the appearance of the Drafter-Mirror prototype in one of the experimental sessions.

We realized that users can easily achieve eye-contact when needed. This is because the partner's face and drawings are closely located on the board. Easy eye contact even in drawing-intensive activities increased the feeling of intimacy.

We observed that users often worked collaboratively to coordinate the limited shared drawing space. For example, when a user started drawing over some part of the partner's drawing, the partner often voluntarily erased his or her drawing from the screen.

Unlike ClearFace [7], users do not hesitate to draw over the image of the partner's face. In ClearFace, the partner's image was mixed with the drawing image behind it, and users found it difficult to draw over the facial image. In ClearBoard, we assume that users recognize the partner *behind* the drawing on the glass board, and thus feel no difficulty drawing on the board *in front of* the partner. The transparent glass window metaphor seems to make users sensitive to the distance between the drawing and the partner. Even with this overlapped image, users did not report having trouble distinguishing drawing marks from the video background.

Gaze Awareness

The most novel feature of ClearBoard, and the most important, is that it provides precise "gaze awareness" or "gaze tracking." A ClearBoard user can easily recognize what the partner is gazing at on the screen during a conversation. Precise *gaze awareness* can not be easily achieved in an ordinary meeting environment using a whiteboard because both users stand on the same side of the board. We conducted collaborative problem solving experiment on ClearBoard

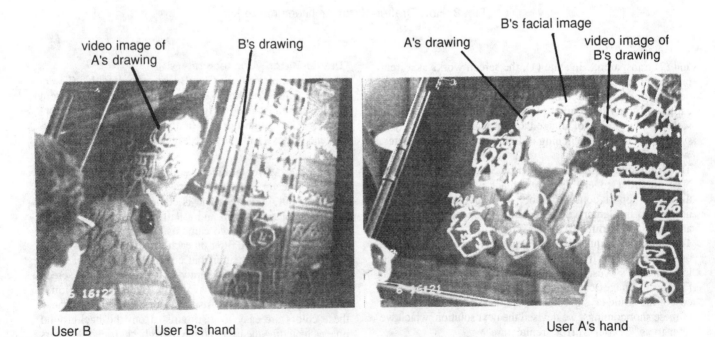

Fig. 9 ClearBoard-1 Prototype in Use
(See also Ishii and Kobayashi, Plate 1 and 2)

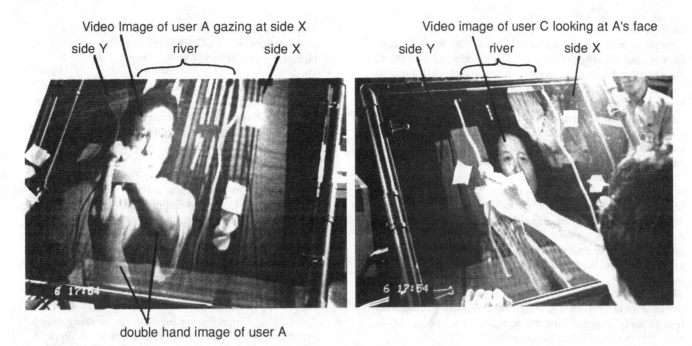

Fig. 10 ClearBoard-1 used for solving the "River crossing" problem
(See also Ishii and Kobayashi, Plate 3 and 4)

using the "river crossing problem[4]."
A separate psychological experiment has determined that the success of this game depends heavily on the *points-of-view* of the players [5]. It is thus advantageous for the collaborative players to know what the partner is gazing at.

Through this experiment we confirmed that it is easy for the players to say which side of the river the partner is gazing at and this information was quite useful in advising each other. Fig. 10 shows a snapshot of one such experiment. User A is gazing at side X of the river, and user C is looking at the face of user A to read his *gaze*.

The importance of *eye-contact* is often discussed in the design of face-to-face communication tools. However, we believe the concept of *gaze awareness* is more generalized and is a more important notion. *Gaze awareness* lets a user know what the partner is looking at, the user's face or anything else on the shared workspace. If the partner is looking at you, you can know it. If the partner is gazing at an object in the shared workspace, you can know what the object is. Eye contact can be seen as just a special case of *gaze awareness*.
We think the notion of *gaze awareness* will be an important goal of the next generation of shared drawing tools. It can not

be easily obtained in conventional meeting environments, and only CSCW technology can provide it. ClearBoard-1 is the first system that provides distributed users with the capability of *gaze awareness*.

Problems of ClearBoard-1
Through the experimental sessions using this prototype, we found the following problems.

(1) clarity of images on the screen
It is hard to achieve sharp focus on all the marks on the screen and on the user's face. Since the screen is tilted, the bottom edge is about 40 cm further from the camera than the top edge. In the current prototype, the camera focuses at the center of the screen, so that the user's face and the edges of the screen are slightly out of focus. The quality of the projected video image is not as sharp nor bright as an ordinary computer screen. Because half-mirrors and polarizing films are used, the screen image of Drafter-Mirror architecture is inevitably darkened.

(2) erasing partner's marks
Since the marks drawn by each user exist on their respective screen surfaces, a user can not erase the partner's drawing.

(3) double hand images
As illustrated in Fig. 8 and Fig. 10, each user "sees" two hands for each actual hand with this arrangement. At first glance, a few users said they were disturbed by this. However, they got used to it soon and had no further complaints.

(4) recording of work results
We mainly used a Polaroid™ camera to make a record of work results. However, if we use the appropriate computer input technologies, it will be easier to record and print the work results.

---

4   The "river crossing problem" is a puzzle to get group A members and group B members across a river using a boat. (In the most traditional case, the groups were missionaries and cannibals.) The boat can hold only two members at a time, and must have at least one member in it to cross the river. The number of group A members must be larger than that of group B members on both banks. We played the puzzle on ClearBoard drawing the river on it and using some pieces of sticky paper (Post-it™) to represent the members of each group.

CONCLUSION

This paper has presented a novel shared drawing medium, ClearBoard. ClearBoard realizes (1) a seamless shared drawing space and (2) *gaze awareness* to support realtime and remote collaboration by two users.

We devised the key metaphor of ClearBoard: "talking *through* and drawing *on* a transparent glass window." We compared this metaphor to the traditional concepts of *whiteboard* and *table*. We implemented a prototype of ClearBoard based on the "Drafter-Mirror" approach and confirmed that the prototype fulfills the two goals.

In addition, through the informal use of ClearBoard-1, we found its most important feature to be *gaze awareness*. By referring to the role of gaze in human communication, ClearBoard is shown to provide a new environment for collaboration. We are planning to conduct empirical studies to understand the effects of gaze awareness in collaborative problem solving.

We are also designing a computer-drawing version "ClearBoard-2" to offer several new functions: recording of working results, easy manipulation of marks (move, shrink, erase, etc.), and the use of data in computer files.

ACKNOWLEDGEMENTS

We thank Naomi Miyake at Chukyo University and Isamu Yoroizawa at NTT for their insightful comments on the ClearBoard concept and experiments. Thanks are also due to William Buxton at the University of Toronto, Jonathan Grudin at the University of California, Irvine, and John Tang at Sun Microsystems for their thoughtful comments on this paper. We thank Kazuho Arita for his technical advice. We express our appreciation to Shinichi Shiwa for introducing his work on eye contact using the liquid crystal technique. We also thank Takaya Endo and Gen Suzuki for their encouragement and support for this research project.

REFERENCES

1. Bly, S. A., and Minneman, S. L. Commune: A shared drawing surface. In Proceedings of Conference on Office Information Systems (COIS'90, Boston, Massachusetts), ACM, New York, 1990, pp. 184-192.

2. Buxton, B., and Moran, T. EuroPARC's Integrated Interactive Intermedia Facility (IIIF): Early Experiences. In Proceedings of IFIP WG8.4 Conference on Multi-User Interfaces and Applications (Heraklion, Crete, Greece, September 24-26), North Holland, Amsterdam, 1990, pp. 11-34.

3. Buxton, B. Telepresence: Integrating Shared Task Space and Personal Spaces. In Proceedings of The Potential of Team and Organizational Computing (Groupware '91, Amsterdam, Netherlands, October 29), Software Engineering Research Center, Utrecht, 1991, pp. 27-36.

4. Fish, R. S., Kraut, R. E., and Chalfonte, B. L. The VideoWindow System in Informal Communications. In Proceedings of Conference on Computer Supported Cooperative Work (CSCW '90, Los Angeles, California, October 7-10), ACM, New York, 1990, pp. 1-11.

5. Hutchins, E. L., and Levin, J. A. Point of view in problem solving, In CHIP Technical Report No. 105, University of California at San Diego, 1981.

6. Ishii, H. TeamWorkStation: Towards a Seamless Shared Workspace. In Proceedings of Conference on Computer Supported Cooperative Work (CSCW '90, Los Angeles, California, October 7-10), ACM, New York, 1990, pp. 13-26.

7. Ishii, H., and Arita, K. ClearFace: Translucent multiuser interface for TeamWorkStation. In Proceedings of European Conference on Computer-Supported Cooperative Work 1991(ECSCW'91, Amsterdam), 1991, pp. 163-174.

8. Ishii, H., and Miyake, N. Toward an Open Shared Workspace: Computer and Video Fusion Approach of TeamWorkStation. Communications of the ACM, December 1991, pp. 37-50.

9. Lakin, F. A performing medium for working group graphics. In Computer-Supported Cooperative Work: A book of readings. Morgan Kaufmann Publishers, San Mateo, California, 1988, pp. 367-396.

10. Minneman, S. L., and Bly, S. A. Managing a trois: A study of a multi-user drawing tool in distributed design work. In Proceedings of ACM SIGCHI Conference on Human Factors in Computing Systems (CHI'91, New Orleans, Louisiana, April 27 - May 2), ACM, New York, 1991, pp. 217-224.

11. Schrage, M. Shared Minds. Random House, New York, 1990.

12. Shiwa, S., and Ishibashi, M. A Large-Screen Visual Telecommunication Device Enabling Eye Contact. In Digest of technical papers of Society for Information Display International Symposium 1991(SID 91), 1991, pp. 327-328.

13. Tang, J. C., and Minneman, S. L. VideoDraw: A video interface for collaborative drawing. In Proceedings of ACM SIGCHI Conference on Human Factors in Computing Systems (CHI'90, Seattle, Washington, April 1-5), ACM, New York, 1990, pp. 313-320.

14. Tang, J. C., and Minneman, S. L. VideoWhiteboard: Video shadows to support remote collaboration. In Proceedings of ACM SIGCHI Conference on Human Factors in Computing Systems (CHI'91, New Orleans, Louisiana, April 27 - May 2), ACM, New York, 1991, pp. 315-322.

SPATIAL WORKSPACE COLLABORATION: A SHAREDVIEW VIDEO SUPPORT SYSTEM FOR REMOTE COLLABORATION CAPABILITY

Hideaki Kuzuoka

Department of Mechano-Informatics, University of Tokyo,
7–3–1 Hongo, Bunkyo-ku
Tokyo 113, Japan
+81-3-3812-2111 (ext 6369), kuzuoka%ihl.t.u-tokyo.ac.jp@relay.cs.net

ABSTRACT

Collaboration in three-dimensional space: "spatial workspace collaboration" is introduced and an approach supporting its use via a video mediated communication system is described. Verbal expression analysis is primarily focused on. Based on experiment results, movability of a focal point, sharing focal points, movability of a shared workspace, and the ability to confirm viewing intentions and movements were determined to be system requirements necessary to support spatial workspace collaboration. A newly developed SharedView system having the capability to support spatial workspace collaboration is also introduced, tested, and some experimental results described.

KEYWORDS: Remote collaboration, CSCW, spatial workspace collaboration, focal point, verbal analysis, video mediated communication.

INTRODUCTION

Most of the current studies on Computer Supported Co-operative Work (CSCW) have considered desk-top or office-work type collaboration methods such as conferencing systems [9, 11] and shared drawings or writing tools [2, 10, 13]. However, as communication networks develop, it is becoming possible to collaborate among geographically distributed laboratories or within an integrated industrial framework (e.g., among design sections, manufacturing sections, etc.). In the present approach, collaboration between a machine designer and a manufacturer could occur, for example, in situations where the manufacturer needs to show the designer how a machine operates in order to explain its manufacturability. In this case, different types of communication problems

Fig. 1: Machining Center (MC).

arise since the workspace consists of a three-dimensional (3-D) space. In such an environment, objects which must be explained may be dispersed in 3-D space, as well as having 3-D motions and directions. Here, collaboration in this kind of environment is classified as **"spatial workspace collaboration"** so as to distinguish it from other types of workspace collaboration.

OBSERVATION OF MACHINERY OPERATION INSTRUCTION

To clarify spatial workspace collaboration activities, face-to-face instruction sessions on the Machining Center (MC) (Fig. 1) were examined. The MC is a numerically controlled machine that performs complex machining functions such as milling, drilling, etc., and can be either manually operated by switches or automatically operated by a computer.

During an instruction session, an instructor taught a subject (operator) to manually operate the machine to cut a work-piece. All subjects in the present study were either graduates or senior undergraduates in the Department of Mechanical Engineering, University of

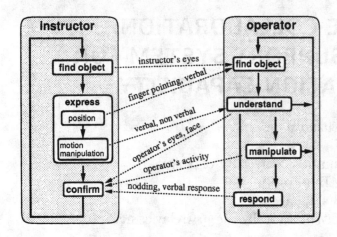

Fig. 2: Communication patterns.

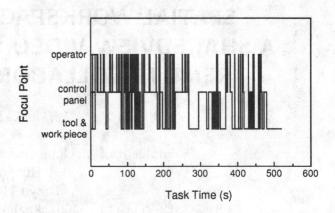

Fig. 3: Changes in the instructor's focal point.

Tokyo. Instruction sessions were video taped for later analysis. It is well-known that both verbal and gestural expressions play an important role in communications [1, 3, 12]; hence the times and locations of these expressions were recorded when used. Since many expressions were also used to direct attention to objects in the spatial workspace, the locations at which the subjects were looking were also recorded. The study's primary objective is to support communication in a 3-D environment, thus analysis of 3-D activities and expressions were subsequently focused on.

Communication Patterns

Following an analysis of the video taped sessions, it was found that structures of communication can be in represented as shown in Fig. 2, with the instructor's actions being categorized as follows:

find object– Directing attention to the object to be explained.

express– Expressing an idea using verbal/gestural means.

confirm– Confirmation that the operator understood the instructor's expressions, i.e. by confirming the viewed object by the operator, or by observation of proper MC operation.

Corresponding to the instructor's actions, the operator acted as follows:

find object– Found the object indicated by the instructor.

understand– Watched and listened to the instructor's expressions so as to understand them.

manipulate– Operated the machine according to the instructor's explanation.

respond– A response by the operator that indicated comprehension; either by affirmatively nodding or saying "OK" for example

In Figure 2, the broken-arrow lines show the direction of the flow of expressions corresponding to each subject's action. It is realized that some actions cannot be included in these categories, however, since only the characteristic activities for a spatial workspace are considered here, other actions are neglected. In addition, it is known that communication patterns cannot be exactly represented as shown in Fig. 2, although this representation was helpful to assist in developing a basic understanding that was useful in designing the presented communication support system.

Changes in Focal Point

The change of focal points in communication patterns is repeated almost every few seconds; and in every "loop" pattern the instructor looks at the objects of attention, the operator's manipulation and facial response, and the MC's motion. Figure 3 shows a typical example of how frequently an instructor changes his focal point, where the y-axis indicates the object at which the instructor is referring to. It was determined that in some instances the instructor changed his focal point almost twice in a second. Hence, to support spatial workspace collaboration, a system must have movable 3-D focal points. Since the system should be able to show locations that the instructor/operator want to see/show, it is also important that the system's focal points accommodate their viewing intention. This is one of the biggest differences of the presented collaboration system as compared to desk-top ones.

Expressions for Spatial Workspace Collaboration

The instructor's expressions that were used in the previously described focal point communication loop were classified as *position*, *motion/manipulation*, and *confirmation*. Many other expressions, e.g., counting numbers and showing the length of an object, were also used, but were neglected since only 3-D expressions were analyzed here.

position: The operator sees the object which the instructor directed attention towards. Verbal expressions

Fig. 4: Typical model task workspace.

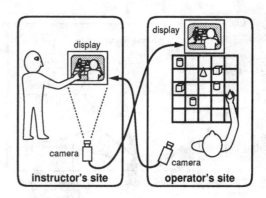

Fig. 5: Case 3 of the model task experiment.

such as "this button" and gestures, such as finger pointing were used. These expressions represent the **express** action which occurs immediately following the instructor's **find object** action.

motion/manipulation: Expressions for describing the motion of a tool, the manner in which to push buttons, the way to turn switches, etc., being verbally expressed as "this direction," "turn like this," etc. These expressions were usually given soon after the *position* expressions during the **express** action.

confirmation: Expressions which confirmed that the operator understood what was being explained, or by motions indicating they were looking at the right location. These expressions were seen during the **confirm** action.

In order for the instructor to give instructions smoothly, a communication system should incorporate features which support the ability to smoothly exchange these expressions.

MODEL TASK EXPERIMENT
Model Task
Use of the MC for experiments requires significant preparation time and not many qualified instructors were available, thus a so-called "model task" was created to enable experiments to be easily and routinely conducted. The task had to include the expressions of *position, motion/manipulation,* and *confirmation,* in addition to having 3-D object movement capability. The task selected used an area divided into 5×5 squares similar to a chess board, with four different 3-D objects being utilized. Initially, several of the objects were placed onto some squares (Fig. 4) and during the task the instructor directed the operator to move objects to another square or to rotate them in some direction. Three types of activities were performed and each one consisted of a specific number of required manipulations (A, 5; B, 6; C, 9).

Experiment
The following four cases of instruction format were evaluated.

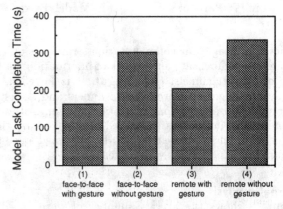

Fig. 6: Model task completion time for each case.

1. **case 1 (face-to-face, with gesture)** Instruction was given face-to-face and the instructor could use any gestures or words, but could not move objects themselves (10 experiments).

2. **case 2 (face-to-face, without gesture)** Instruction was given face-to-face and the instructor could use only words and no gestures (7 experiments).

3. **case 3 (remote, with gesture)** Instruction was given remotely using a VideoDraw-like configuration (Fig. 5) [13, 4]. The instructor's gestures were superimposed on the image received from the operator's site and then sent back to the operator's site (11 experiments).

4. **case 4 (remote, without gesture)** Instruction was given remotely as in case 3, but the instructor was restricted from using gestures (7 experiments).

Expression Analysis Evaluations
Figure 6 shows the completion times of the model task for each case, with gestures clearly increasing the communication efficiency. However, it should be noted that the required time does not necessarily indicate communication variations between different communication cases. When people communicate with each other, more than one sensory channel [8] and expression channel are complementarily used, i.e., if one channel is modified, or re-

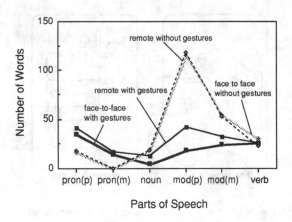

Fig. 7: Parts of speech used in Model Tasks.

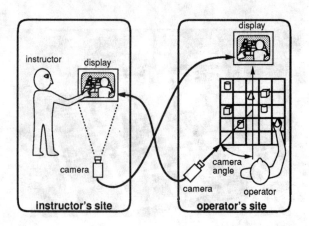

Fig. 8: Experiment using different camera angles.

stricted in usage, our communication strategy is quickly altered to compensate for the lack of information via the use of other channels. As a result, it is beneficial to analyze changes in expressions to understand the effect of modifications in a communication system. Although standard deviation was calculated for the results, their value is not significant enough to be discussed since the number of experiments was limited.

Verbal Analysis

Figure 7 shows the average number of words used in each case for a particular grammatical part of speech. The definitions applicable to the x-axis are respectively "pron" representing pronouns and "mod" representing modifiers, where modifiers include adjectives, adverbs, and spatial words. Spatial words are expressions to describe spatial position and direction, e.g., "up", "down", "right", "left", "inside", "far", and "center" [14]. "Noun" includes nouns which are not considered as modifiers such as "button", "cone", and "cube". Modifiers were classified into two types according to the expressions they were used for, i.e., modifiers to express *position* (p), or modifiers to express *motion/manipulation* (m) expressions (mainly rotation directions). Since nouns were seldom used for expressing motion, "noun" represents words used to express an object's name. Since interest was directed only at words that were used to express *position* and *motion/manipulation*, other words were not counted. Furthermore, since the increase and decrease in the number of words were the primary objective, normalized word counts per part of speech were not utilized.

In Figure 7, the two communication cases that did not use gestures showed almost the same results, pattern, while the other two cases that used gestures are markedly different. The difference in gestures vs. no gestures indicates that the gestural expressions significantly decreased the required number of verbal expressions, especially declarative expressions such as modifiers. For example, when gestures were used, the operator said, "Place this cube here, and turn 90 degrees like this," whereas when gestures were restricted, the operator said,

"Place the cube to the right one step and down one step. Then, horizontally and clockwise, turn it 90 degrees." It is also interesting to note that the use of pronouns decreased considerably without gestures. Although this verbal analysis may require more thorough examination, it is safe to assume that oral channels can be used equally for each case, and that the number of declarative words increase and the number of pronouns decrease when communication is not smooth. Since the number of subjects was limited, the statistical significance cannot be strongly argued here. However, using time results and verbal analysis together, the effectiveness of gestures is clearly evident.

Translation of Directional Expression

Experiment observations indicated that a difference in the directional orientation between the workspace of the instructor and the operator was one of the primary causes in making communication difficult. The effect of different workspace viewing angles was examined by changing the camera angle of the workspace (Fig. 8). Six pairs of subjects were divided into two subclasses, with each subclass subsequently performed activities A, B, and C under certain prescribed circumstances. One subclass performed activities A and C with a camera angle of 45° and activity B at 90°. The other subclass performed A and B at 90° and C at 45°. The data obtained from a 45° angle was classified as category (I), whereas the data using 90° was classified as category (II). This enabled a comparison for the effects of camera angle on performance.

Figures 9 and 10 show that as the camera angle of workspace increases, communication becomes more difficult, i.e., orientational differences vary the visual cognition between two subjects. When the instructor expressed position or rotation instructions to the operator, directional expressions had to be translated so that the operator could understand them. For example, the following conversation was recorded:

Instructor: "180 degrees to the right. This direction."

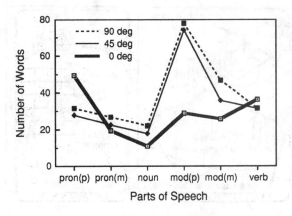

Fig. 9: Relationship between parts of speech and number of words at different camera angles.

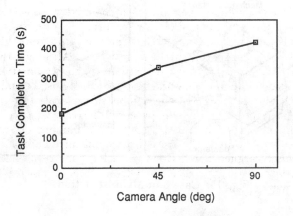

Fig. 10: Relation of task completion time and camera angle.

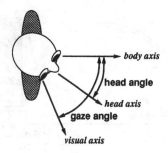

Fig. 11: Diagram showing body, head, and visual axes.

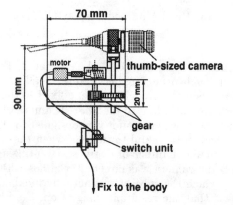

Fig. 12: The SharedCamera's operating mechanism.

Operator:	"That's left, for me."
Instructor:	"180 degrees to the right."
Operator:	"Like this?"
Instructor:	"The other way, the other way."

Another problem which occurred involved the instructor's superimposed gestures becoming more ambiguous for the operator to follow since the screen images were viewed from a different perspective than their own. This caused an increase in the number of total words (Fig. 9) and task completion time (Fig. 10). If the workspace is in 3-D, and the camera location is fixed, directional expression translation frequently occurred; thus the ability to change the focal point is required in this situation.

Communication System Requirements

Based on the results of these experiments, the following communication system requirements are required to effectively support spatial workspace collaboration.

- Variability of focal point to optimally accommodate viewing intentions.
- Ability to share a focal point; thereby minimizing differences in directional expressions.

- Capability to use superimposed gestures.
- Since the focal point should be variable, the operator's display showing applicable instructions (shared workspace [13]) should also be variable.
- Possess the ability to confirm an operator's comprehension and the object's actual manipulation.

SHAREDVIEW: VIDEO COMMUNICATION SUPPORT SYSTEM

A system, named SharedView, was developed to satisfy the requirements to support spatial workspace collaboration, and consists of the following two devices:

SharedCamera

In order for the instructor and the operator to both share the same focal points and to increase the ability to change them, a small camera about the size of a person's thumb was mounted on the head of the operator. However, the head's axis does not always correspond to the eye's visual axis, e.g., when looking sideways a person's head turns although not as much as their eyes (Fig. 11); thus if the camera is rigidly fixed to the head it will not always be directed at the proper location. This necessitates turning the camera so that it faces in the right direction. It was noticed in the experiments that the gaze angle (angle between body axis and visual axis) and head angle (angle between body axis and head axis) were almost proportional, therefore, if the head angle could be

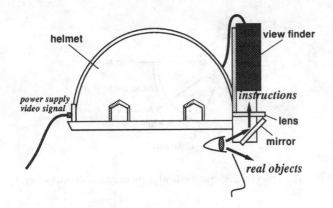

Fig. 13: Head Mounted Display (HMD).

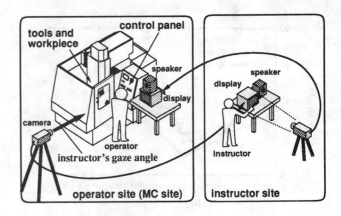

Fig. 14: Case 2 of MC instruction.

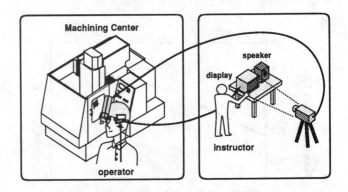

Fig. 15: Case 3 of MC instruction.

detected then the gaze angle could be estimated. For this purpose, the angle occurring between the head and body was detected using a wire with one end fixed to the body and the other end leading to the SharedCamera's switch unit (Fig. 12). The switch unit was designed to turn on when the head turned, and to turn off when the camera turns a particular number of degrees. By utilizing this mechanism the camera was directed at almost the same location in which the subject was actually looking. One concern was that the resultant image from the Shared-Camera might be shaky and difficult to see. However, since a person's head does not move so frequently, head "jiggle" was a negligible effect.

Head Mounted Display (HMD)

The initial experiments showed that superimposing gestures on a shared workspace image was an effective method for instruction. Since the operator's focal point changes frequently, the display is required to be movable. If the operator had to instead look at a stationary display in order to observe the instruction, the Shared-Camera would not be directed towards a specific location in the shared workspace. For this reason, a small display monitor was mounted on the head so that the operator's head need not be turned, i.e., allowing the operator's pupils to move upwards to view the display in order to see the remotely given instruction (Fig. 13). On the other hand, when the operator wanted to see real objects, the pupils moved downwards. The displayed image was approximately equivalent to viewing an 8-inch display.

This head mounted camera was formerly called "Shared-View" [7], although here it is renamed as "SharedCamera" and the integrated SharedCamera and HMD setup called "SharedView."

SYSTEM EXPERIMENTAL USE

The SharedView system was used to perform remote instruction of the MC. To enable comparison the same task was examined using the following three cases:

1. **case 1 (face-to-face, with gesture)** Instruction

was given face-to-face using gestures and words, although no actual control of the MC was allowed (2 experiments).

2. **case 2 (remote, fixed camera and display)** Instruction was remotely given with gestures using a camera and display that were set at a fixed location as shown in Fig. 14 (9 experiments).

3. **case 3 (remote, SharedView)** Instruction was remotely given with gestures using the SharedView as shown in Figs. 15 and 16 (9 experiments).

The MC instructions were given in such a way that the operator only needed to change directions toward the MC by approximately 90°, i.e., to face the control panel, the tools, or a work-piece. For expression analysis, expressions were classified into three types as:

position: Expressions indicating the locations of buttons, switches, etc.

manipulation: Expressions indicating the manner in which switches are turned, buttons are pushed, etc. The operator primarily looked toward the control panel when these expressions were used.

direction: When the instructor was required to spatially describe the MC, expressions indicating 3-D orientation (e.g., direction of the tool's x, y, z axis) and tool movements had to be used (Fig. 17). At this

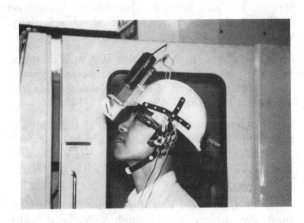

Fig. 16: Wearing SharedView for remote MC instruction.

Fig. 17: Instruction location as displayed on the HMD. Both the instructor's and operator's gestures can be seen.

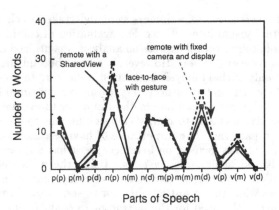

Fig. 18: Effect of SharedView and HMD for remote MC instruction.

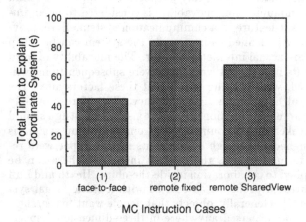

Fig. 19: Elapsed time to explain the MC's coordinate system.

time the operator looked toward the actual direction of the tools or a work-piece.

In the model task expression classifications, a *direction* expression was included in the *motion/manipulation* expressions, although in this experiment it was separated to more clearly show the effect of the SharedView. In Figure 18 the definitions applicable to the x-axis are respectively "p" representing pronouns, "n" representing nouns, "mod" representing modifiers, and "v" representing verbs. Each of them were classified into three types according to the expressions they were used for, i.e., *position* (p), *manipulation* (m), or *direction* (d). Only two instructors (A, B) were available; hence A gave instruction to 5 operators while B gave instructions to 4 operators (case 2 and 3). In case 1, A gave instruction to both subjects. Since the experiment's objective was to compare case 2 with 3, only two case 1 experiments were performed. Results indicated that when using SharedView, modifiers for *direction* decreased (Fig. 18), as did the time required to explain the MC's spatial orientation (Fig. 19). This occurred because in case 2, the direction

of the viewing angles between the instructor and the operator differed by ~ 90° while explaining the MC's internal spatial orientation. A typical example of an actual misunderstanding of a direction expression observed in case 2 is as follows:

Instructor: "Left to right. This direction."

Operator: "Like this? Like this?" (He was showing forward and back directions.)

Instructor: "No, opposite. Right to left."

Operator: "Right to left?"

Instructor: "Yes."

These results showed the effect of SharedView's ability for focal points, although further experiments are required to determine statistical significance.

CONCLUSIONS

In this paper, a new collaboration type, i.e., "spatial workspace collaboration" was introduced. As an example of spatial workspace collaboration using video media, remote instruction experiments were undertaken to clarify actual visual interactions. For evaluation of communicationability, verbal expression analysis was utilized as well as time evaluation. However, it cannot be said that use of only verbal analysis is the best indicator. In fact, it is believed that it is necessary to analyze communication using more than one method in order to evaluate its effectiveness and to clarify complex human communication patterns. The importance of having a movable focal point was focused on here because it has not been investigated in previous systems. Using the presented SharedView system, an instructor can easily show using gestures what they want an operator to see. Also of importance is the need for the instructor to confirm where the operator is looking.

When communication is informal, it occurs at any time, in any place, and for any purpose. To support this kind of communication, movability is considered to be an important feature in a communication system. Here, movability is defined as how easily the system can be setup before actual interactions occur. The movability of focal points in a shared workspace were subsequently investigated, with it being found that these factors affect the overall interaction time efficiency. Therefore, not only the actual interaction stage, but also **setup stage** should be taken into account when a communication system is designed. Although experiments in this paper were remote instructions, the concept introduced here can be applied to collaboration inside-the-office. Heath and Luff addressed problems associated with a static visual system [5]. Generally, objects that people want to see/show may be dispersed anywhere in three-dimensional space. However, people may not always be at a location where a video camera can easily function, nor will they may not always be in a situation where they can conveniently use a video camera. Therefore, it is concluded that for video mediated communication systems to be more widely used, spatial movability of the system must be included.

For good communication system design, movability and an ability to share an image appears to be a common goal. However, these goals should be realized based a qualitative understanding of human activities, i.e., the system should be designed to accommodate the intended tasks of the user. SharedView is an example of such a system.

ACKNOWLEDGMENT

Much gratitude is extended to Dr. Takemochi Ishii, Keio University, and Dr. Michitaka Hirose, University of Tokyo, for all their beneficial advice and suggestions. I am also thankful to Gen Suzuki and Hiroshi Ishii, NTT, for their kind assistance.

REFERENCES

[1] Sara A. Bly, A Use of Drawing Surface in Different Collaboration Settings. In *CSCW88*, Portland, 1988, pp. 250–256.

[2] Sara A. Bly and Scott L. Minneman, Commune: A Shared Drawing Surface. In *SIGOIS Bulletin*, Massachusetts, 1990, pp. 184–192.

[3] Alphonse Chapanis, Interactive Human Communication. In Irene Greif, editor, *Computer-Supported Cooperative Work: A Book of Readings*, Morgan Kaufmann Publishers, 1988, pp. 127–140.

[4] Jack F. Gerrissen and John Daamen, Inclushion of a 'Sharing' Feature in Telecommunication Services. In *13th International Symposium HFT '90 HUMAN FACTORS IN TELECOMMUNICATIONS*, Torino, Italy, 1990.

[5] Christian Heath and Paul Luff, Disembodied Conduct: Communication Through Video in a Multimedia Office Environment. In *Proc. of the Conference on Computer Human Interaction (CHI) '91*, 1991, pp. 99–103.

[6] Hiroshi Ishii and Naomi Miyake, Toward an Open Shared Workspace: Computer and Video Fusion Approach of TeamWorkStation. *Communications of the ACM*, 34(12), 1991, pp. 37–50.

[7] Takemochi Ishii, Michitaka Hirose, Hideaki Kuzuoka, Tsutomu Takahara, and Takeshi Myoi, Collaboration System for Manufacturing System in the 21st Century. In *Proc. of the International Conference on Manufacturing Systems and Environment*, 1990, pp. 295–300.

[8] Robert Kraut, Carmen Egido, and Jolene Galegher, Patterns of Contact and Communication in Scientific Research Collaboration. In *CSCW88*, Portland, 1988, pp. 1–12.

[9] Marilyn Mantei, Capturing the Capture Lab Concepts: A Case Study in the Design of Computer Supported Meeting Environments. In *CSCW88*, Portland, 1988, pp. 257–270.

[10] Susanna Opper, A Groupware Toolbox. *BYTE*, Dec 1988, pp. 275–282.

[11] Mark Stefik et al, Beyond the Chalkboard: Computer Support for Collaboration and Problem Solving in Meetings. In Irene Greif, editor, *Computer-Supported Cooperative Work: A Book of Readings*, Morgan Kaufmann Publishers, 1988, pp. 335–366.

[12] John C. Tang and L. J. Leifer, A Framework for Understanding the Workspace Activity of Design Teams. In *CSCW88*, Portland, 1988, pp. 244–249.

[13] John C. Tang and S. L. Minneman, VideoDraw: A Video Interface for Collaborative Drawing. In *Proc. of the Conference on Computer Human Interaction (CHI) '90*, Seattle, 1990, pp. 313–320.

[14] Atsushi Yamada et al, The Analysis of the Spatial Descriptions in Natural Language and the Reconstruction of the Scene. *Information Processing Society of Japan*, 31(5), 1990, pp. 660–672. (in Japanese).

Portholes: Supporting Awareness in a Distributed Work Group

Paul Dourish

Rank Xerox EuroPARC
61 Regent St
Cambridge CB2 1AB UK
(0223) 341512
dourish@europarc.xerox.com

Sara Bly

Xerox PARC
3333 Coyote Hill Road
Palo Alto, CA 94304
(415) 812 4360
bly@parc.xerox.com

ABSTRACT

We are investigating ways in which media space technologies can support distributed work groups through access to information that supports general awareness. Awareness involves knowing who is "around", what activities are occurring, who is talking with whom; it provides a view of one another in the daily work environments. Awareness may lead to informal interactions, spontaneous connections, and the development of shared cultures—all important aspects of maintaining working relationships which are denied to groups distributed across multiple sites.

The Portholes project, at Rank Xerox EuroPARC in Cambridge, England, and Xerox PARC in Palo Alto, California, demonstrates that awareness can be supported across distance. A data network provides a shared database of image information that is regularly updated and available at all sites. Initial experiences of the system in use at EuroPARC and PARC suggest that Portholes both supports shared awareness and helps to build a "sense of community".

KEYWORDS: group work, collaboration, CSCW, media spaces, distributed workgroups, informal interaction, awareness.

INTRODUCTION AND MOTIVATIONS

Reports on the use of media space technology (e.g. [3], [5], [6], [8], [10], [11]) typically focus on the use of direct audio and video connections as an aid to collaboration among remotely located individuals. The emphasis on real-time connections is not surprising; such uses are highly visible and identifiable mechanisms through which remote

collaboration can be enhanced. However, our experiences of using media space technology at Rank Xerox EuroPARC [4] and at Xerox PARC [9] have also pointed to the importance of a different style of connection. We find that, when their video equipment is otherwise unused, many of our media space users like to observe activities in public areas; they report that they find these connections useful in order to see "what's going on" as members of the group gather for meetings, check their mail, collect coffee, etc. These background connections are used very differently from those of direct connections; in particular, they tend to be long-term and non-engaged. Unlike information which might be gleaned from a direct connection with a colleague, here it is being gathered passively, while other workplace activities progress.

This use of video technology is very similar to the typical awareness activities which occur in a shared physical environment. While sitting at a desk, we are aware of activities going on around us—we hear the sounds of conversations in corridors, see people as they pass by, notice people in offices as we walk down a hallway, and so forth. The *Polyscope* system at EuroPARC [2] and the *Imager* system at PARC were attempts to capture some of this information in the respective media spaces. The basic approach that each took was to present regularly-updated digitised video images from locations around the media space on the workstation screen. These images show activities in public areas and offices. Our media space infrastructures provide the technological base for these applications—users of the awareness services are "inhabitants" of our media spaces.

Following on from positive experiences with Polyscope and Imager, we wished to extend the notion of "awareness" outside a single physical location, and thus support awareness for *distributed* work groups. Such groups, by their nature, are denied the informal information gathered from a physically shared workspace and the proximity which is an important factor in collaboration between colleagues ([1], [7]). We expect that a shared awareness space can be a basis for providing similar information. In addition, awareness services can be achieved with less bandwidth than the usual "live video" connections of existing media spaces. Thus, we

FIGURE 1. A window dump of the "pvc" client to Portholes. The first eight images show EuroPARC nodes; the last seven show PARC nodes. All images were taken at approximately the same time.

could explore the utility of awareness for truly distributed groups without large investment in a technological infrastructure[1].

Our system for distributed awareness is called "Portholes". A multi-site awareness service tackles a number of new issues, including data distribution techniques and the interface problems of dealing with shared information. Portholes consists of a cooperating group of servers which jointly manage a distributed data space. In addition, Portholes includes clients which present the Portholes information in a variety of ways giving users the ability to process and use the information. Figure 1 shows a typical interface to Portholes with images of colleagues who share research interests and projects in both Cambridge and Palo Alto.

This paper focuses on Portholes as an example of the kind of system we think might support our notion of distributed awareness. We will describe Portholes and its existing clients, offer some initial observations of its use, and discuss issues that we consider central to developing an understanding of the role of awareness in everyday work activities and in using technologies to enable that awareness in distributed groups.

---

1. Our infrastructure, of course, is based on an existing media space. In the absence of such a facility, individual Portholes nodes can be set up with separate video cameras and frame-grabbers. Adequate quality can be achieved with relatively inexpensive equipment.

DESIGN CONSTRAINTS AND ARCHITECTURE

Portholes is basically a system for maintaining image information which is both generated and consumed at a number of sites connected via an internet. Essentially, the technical problem is timely distribution of information so that it can be usefully presented to a user, while keeping within the constraints of available network bandwidth. Since we wish to support multiple interfaces and interface styles, we make a strong distinction between the two major system components—a *server* component, which is responsible for maintaining the database, and one or more *client* components, which present the information to users.

Interface Requirements

Interface requirements drive a great deal of the server design, and so it is worth considering what sorts of facilities they might provide, and hence the requirements they impose. An interface client of the Portholes information base will generally be an interactive program running on a user's workstation. It might display not only images, but also information about the image itself (for example, when it was taken). The interface might well provide other information about the source of the image (generally a person), such as office number and e-mail address. In designing the system, we also wanted to allow the image information to be used to access other, externally-provided services (e-mail is an obvious example), and these might well involve some kind of manipulation of the image itself or its associated information. All these needs must be catered for by the server.

Again, the primary problem to be overcome is *latency* in transmitted information. A single interface will typically

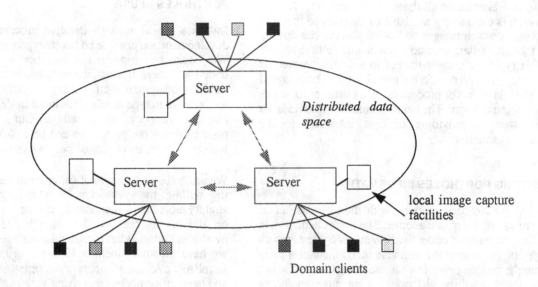

FIGURE 2. The structure of the Portholes system. Portholes consists of a number of cooperating information servers linked by a network. Client programs communicate only with their local servers, although they may display remote information. Servers use local image-processing facilities.

show information from multiple sites, and network access to remote sites will be many orders of magnitude slower than access to local information. We can tolerate a certain amount of latency; image updates may only occur every ten minutes, and so the user will not expect up-to-the-second information. However, latency must not be reflected in the *manipulation* of information in the interface, which must have good interactive response. Thus, all manipulations of image information must result in, at most, an interaction with a *local* information server, rather than with a server at the generating site, possibly thousands of miles away. The image information must be *replicated*, so that a local copy can always be made available when needed.

The Portholes Architecture

Components

The basic architecture of Portholes comprises a set of cooperating information servers, each of which has particular responsibility for a *domain*, typically a media space at one site. A domain contains a number of *sources* of regularly updated awareness information, as well as client programs which *consume* that information. Each server is responsible for distributing information generated by sources in its domain, and for ensuring that information required by client programs within that domain is at-hand. Clients access the shared information base through their closest server. Information flows between the domain servers as required by the various client programs. Client programs access the information space as if it were all located centrally; they need not even be aware that the information is not generated locally. The server, for its part, deals purely with the information distribution, and has no knowledge of the way in which information is presented by

the clients. Thus multiple, very different, client interfaces can present the same information from a single server. The relationship between clients and servers is illustrated in Figure 2.

As well as image information, a source also has a set of *properties*, which hold other information associated with that source. In effect, the image is only a single source property. These other properties then allow clients to perform more useful manipulations based on the awareness data. For instance, most of our clients take advantage of an "e-mail address" property which can be used to provide a user with a mechanism for sending an e-mail message to someone directly from their image in a Portholes window. We can also be more creative, for example by adding audio snippets via the property mechanism.

Data Flow

There are two data sets within Portholes—domain data (e.g. what domains are available, and how they can be reached) and source data (images and property information). The distribution strategy for these two sets is different, because of the way in which they are used.

Although a user will typically only look at a subset of the available source information, browsing all of the domain information is a common activity (e.g. when selecting which of the available sources to display). Therefore, while source information is transmitted only on an as-needed basis, domain data is actively propagated to all sites. This means that domain data is always immediately accessible to the user for browsing and manipulation. Delays in source data, however, can be tolerated, which helps us achieve our goal of keeping network throughput low.

Our clients make use of all these server facilities. Domain information is continually available to the user, so that it is easy to select which images will be displayed. The display space, though, is flat, with no reference made to domains; interfaces typically present images in a single "awareness space". Properties carry information which may be intended for the user directly, for processing by a client, or for inter-server communication. Thus our architecture provides an efficient way of providing multiple interfaces to the awareness information.

PRESENTING PORTHOLES INFORMATION

To date, we have been working with three clients, all of which are variations of one another. The basic client, *pvc*, is an application running under the X Window System, which displays one or more of the available images, automatically updating the images every few minutes. The user can select which images are displayed using an initialisation file or with a menu when the application is running. Another client, *edison*, has the capabilities of pvc and also associates digital audio messages (or "snippets") with images. It allows users to record their audio snippets and listen to those recorded by other Portholes users. Finally, a client *viewmaster* is provided for public use. It is like pvc but with the constraint that the only images available are public spaces; no office nodes are included.

Referring back to Figure 1, note that there are images from both EuroPARC and PARC all taken at approximately the same moment in real-time (all times are presented in the local user's timezone—the times in the figure are British Summer Time). Clicking on an image brings up a dialog box with the properties available for that image (name, phone number, etc.) and a set of action buttons. In pvc, these actions are E-MAIL and GLANCE; edison has an additional action LISTEN for those images with associated audio messages. Clicking on E-MAIL causes a mail system window to open with the *To:* field appropriately completed with the name of the person associated with the selected image. Clicking on GLANCE will invoke a media space glance action[2] at EuroPARC (this feature is not implemented at PARC). Clicking on LISTEN will play the associated audio snippet.

All of the existing clients operate primarily in a broadcast mode. By *broadcast*, we mean that all users of the system have access to all information within the system. Thus, if a user records a voice message in edison, that message may be played by all edison users. Ultimately we believe that Portholes clients will integrate both broadcast and directed information. By *directed*, we mean specifying particular users to be recipients of the information. Note that directed information may come from Portholes (for example, an audio snippet sent only to one recipient) or it may come as an interface to an existing directed system (such as e-mail).

_____

2. Glance provides a one-way video connection of a few seconds' duration to a specific media space node.

PORTHOLES IN USE

Just as we believe in an iterative process of design and development, we practice an iterative process of use as well. We begin by using our prototypes ourselves; as we understand ways in which the system can be used and as we stabilise the system itself, we expand our user base. When we feel a prototype is ready for more in-depth analysis, we employ a variety of study methods. Our goal is to reach a point at which our prototypes can be a part of an everyday working environment outside our own research labs.

We are in the early stages of using Portholes. At the time of this writing, the system has been under development for slightly more than a year, and the clients have been available on and off for the last 8-10 months. When clients are available, Portholes has seen regular use at our two sites, and we have grown to include 10 users at PARC and 12 at EuroPARC. All are members of our respective media spaces, and have office nodes comprising video cameras, monitors, microphones and speakers. In addition to the images of the offices of the users, Portholes also has images available from several public areas: the commons area at EuroPARC, a view out to the green behind EuroPARC (called Parker's Piece), a common area at PARC used by many of the Media Space participants, a view of the construction site for another Xerox facility near PARC, and the PARC media lab.

The Portholes users form a distributed work group. Most have met face-to-face and share research interests, and a few subgroups have on-going collaborations across the two sites. Nevertheless, despite knowing each other and having shared research interests, colleagues typically have relatively few interactions across sites. In addition, a summer student working on Portholes at PARC (who wrote the edison interface) has never met any of the EuroPARC users except through Portholes.

During the earlier development phase, we had a core user group of around 10; since then, others have asked to join, and so our user base has expanded to the 22 people mentioned above. We have noted our own observations regarding the use of Portholes over the past few months, and we have asked our users for feedback. The results indicate that Portholes appears to be playing an active role in providing a basis for distributed awareness.

Initial Observations
Our first informal and anecdotal observations have generally fallen into two categories. The first includes user-suggested modifications or enhancements to the Portholes service; for instance, colour is a frequently-requested feature. The second is user references to people and/or events that have occurred "in Portholes". It is not at all uncommon to hear a user refer to some person that he or she "saw" today, when in fact that person was at the remote site, and only available through Portholes. Such "sightings" are especially common when some unusual activity occurs at the other site. Some examples give a flavour of these:

- Recently a participant at PARC was spending many late nights working in his office; his presence was not only noted by EuroPARC participants but also led them to be quite aware of his dissertation progress!

- Another late night worker at PARC was pleased to tell his local colleagues that he had watched the sun rise in England (over Parker's Piece). Similarly, a EuroPARCer says she likes to "watch the day begin" at PARC.

- Recently a EuroPARCer came in late on a Saturday, prompting a PARC Saturday worker to press E-MAIL in edison and say "I see you". The response back from EuroPARC was "It's nice to know I'm not completely alone!"

- Cross-site visits are a particular source of sightings. For instance, a PARC visitor to EuroPARC was amused to notice a EuroPARC visitor to PARC using her "home" workstation to demonstrate software.

- Our summer student at PARC, not having met his colleagues at the other site, nevertheless feels as though he "knows" some of the Portholes users there, and recognises personal characteristics (snippets of favourite music being one form of the edison audio messages).

User Feedback

In order to get more detailed feedback on the use of, and reactions to, our prototype Portholes system, we asked a group of fifteen users to note their usage of Portholes over a three-day period and to fill out an electronic questionnaire. The questionnaire also asked open-ended questions regarding features they liked and disliked.

We received eleven responses by electronic mail. While we do not believe we're ready to "quantify" the effects of awareness, we can observe some patterns in the typical use of Portholes.

Basic Usage

All but one of our questionnaire respondents reported using pvc and/or edison[3] at least a few times a day through the questionnaire period; e-mail and audio snippets were used only occasionally. As we would expect, there are some problems at this stage with the dependability, accessibility, and amount of information. Particular troubles included:

the erratic performance and unreliable images (eg. when were these really taken?)

[that the pvc window] *takes up too much space on my screen to be up continually so it's overhead to see it*

that not much happens; the turn around for new information is so slow that I'm not too motivated to use it; I'm never guaranteed of seeing much

---

3. Differences in hardware platforms meant that the audio facilities were not available to all users. These users had to use pvc instead of edison.

Despite problems our group was (and is) quite positive about having the system. We've found two main modes of use—using the system as a lightweight information tool and using it as a shared space or community.

Portholes as an Information Tool

As an information tool, Portholes offers a lightweight means of finding out the availability of a colleague and in offering quick reports that are not time-urgent:

I remember seeing [a colleague] *in his office and going down to ask him something—checking for* [that colleague] *over pvc is a common event.*

The sense of general awareness which helps save time on wasted visits or phone calls to empty offices. The information it provides also allows you to predict when people will be free, or certain implications for yourself, such as "[A colleague is] *talking to a visitor this morning so I won't get to see him until after lunch."*

...I notice that [a remote colleague's] *message is an informal bug report.*

Portholes as a Community

In providing a shared space for a community of users, Portholes offers the opportunity to see colleagues who are remote as well as those who are local. Portholes also provides a place for sharing the serious and the whimsical:

I remember seeing people arrive, and leave, people passing through others' offices...

[I remember seeing a few people at the remote site]— *like* [a colleague] *whom I've never met.*

I also liked [a colleague's] *message where he sang happy birthday to himself...*

the sense of whether people were around and seeing my friends; knowing who's around; feeling some connection to folks at [the remote site] *(sharing a "community" with them)*

[I like the fact that pvc/edison] *Brings everybody together, both within* [my local site] *as well as between the labs.*

DISCUSSION: CURRENT RESULTS AND ISSUES

Portholes is meant to provide an awareness of remote colleagues. The image information is intended to be available without necessary actions from the users; other information is intended to be available in a lightweight (without much user involvement) manner. Thus, evaluations are difficult; people are not likely to remember specific experiences, and asking them to think about them too much changes their experiences. In order to understand the system and to plan for future work, we want to consider three different issues:

1. the effect of awareness information in supporting a work group generally;

2. the ability of Portholes to provide meaningful awareness information; and

3. the design of interfaces to present this information usefully.

Although there is considerable attention paid to the value of work group familiarity and proximity in a shared physical space, there has been little research into support of these in a media space environment. Furthermore, there is little research on what role passive awareness itself plays in group work activity and cohesion. We have observed participants in media spaces and in Portholes routinely using these systems for background information. Developing an understanding of how this awareness information is being used in Portholes and what effect it has on the work group interactions will lead to a better understanding of its role in maintaining work group relations generally.

Secondly, the form of the Portholes awareness information should be considered in light of our evolving understanding of awareness itself. As our user observations suggested, the notion of awareness as exemplified in Portholes currently seems to provide a basis for an information tool (community access) and for a shared space (community building). We are exploring the value of other media in providing information in support of both awareness and community building. For instance, audio snippets do not provide *awareness* in the same sense as the automatic images; both sender and receiver must initiate explicit actions to effect the information exchange, making it neither passive nor "background". However, audio snippets do appear to contribute to the sense of community through the awareness they provide of a colleague's personality and nature, and we are interested in exploring this form of information.

Thirdly, the interfaces to systems such as Portholes will have a significant impact on how the information is used. If awareness is a passive and background notion, then the interfaces must be particularly lightweight. At the same time, if the awareness is a basis for more interactive exchanges, then the interface must provide those capabilities. We have already observed with Portholes some of the interface difficulties. Displaying more than a few images takes considerable screen real-estate making it difficult to have Portholes available for peripheral viewing while focusing on other workstation tasks[4]. In addition, many of the actions are still not as flexible for user control as we would like nor as natural for prompting interactions as we would hope.

---

4. A full display of all available images takes almost all of a 17-inch screen, although other windows can be placed on top of it.

The "awareness" often seems inconsequential—late night sightings, a voice message that is part of a song, dinosaurs fighting in a commons area. However, the enthusiasm with which our users take up the system suggests to us that they sense the same potential in "awareness information" as we do, and are eager to access and exploit it. Certainly, we have observed that communications among colleagues across sites has increased, especially informal, unprompted communications of a type which would not have occurred before. Four months after our initial questionnaire, some simple statistics collection in the server tells us that participants continue to be regular users of Portholes. Making information available to colleagues in a way that does not distract from the task at hand but rather adds to the sense of work group community is the use of Portholes we hope to achieve.

CONCLUSIONS

Based on our experiences with the notion of awareness, we have designed, implemented, and brought into a use a prototype system to support lightweight awareness-gathering in distributed work groups. We have extended several of the notions from earlier awareness interfaces (Polyscope and Imager) to support a distributed work group, to expand the underlying system architecture, and to begin studying the use of the system in daily work activities. In looking at the feedback from our users and their patterns of usage of this system, we're pleased by the number of people who frequently use pvc and/or edison and by the ways in which they are using it.

Our user observations suggest that awareness may be a useful basis for community access (an information tool, especially for locating colleagues) and for community building (a shared space for "sightings" and personal snippets). In particular, this second usage helps maintain working relationships in a group which would otherwise have few direct interactions.

Our experiences with Portholes suggest that awareness across distance has meaning, that it can lead positively toward communications and interactions, and perhaps most importantly, that it can contribute to a shared sense of community. Furthermore, systems like Portholes show the potential for media spaces and electronic networks as environments for collaboration in low bandwidth situations. We expect the continued use, development, and evaluation of the Portholes system to contribute to a greater understanding of the nature of awareness and the support of distributed work groups.

ACKNOWLEDGEMENTS

We particularly thank Amin Vahdat for implementing edison and Tom Moran, Alan Borning, and Mike Travers for helping us get started. Scott Elrod, Enrique Godreau, Scott Minneman, and Pierre Wellner contributed to making it run, particularly the frame-grabbing processes. We also very much appreciate the comments from Victoria Bellotti, Francoise Brun-Cottan, Bill Gaver, Steve Harrison, Susan Irwin, Lennart Lövstrand, Allan MacLean, and Wendy Mackay on this paper. Most importantly, we thank the Portholes-Users for their willingness to explore new ideas and new technologies with enthusiasm.

REFERENCES

1. Allen, T. (1977), *Managing the Flow of Technology*, MIT Press, Cambridge, Massachusetts.

2. Borning, A. and Travers, M. (1991), Two Approaches to Casual Interaction over Computer and Video Networks, Proc. CHI '91 Human Factors in Computer Systems, New Orleans, Louisiana.

3. Bulick, S., Abel, M., Corey, D., Schmidt, J. & Coffin, S. (1989). The US WEST Advanced Technologies Prototype Multi-media Communications System, Proc. GLOBECOM '89 Global Telecommunications Conference, Dallas, Texas.

4. Gaver, W., Moran, T., MacLean, A., Dourish, P., Carter, K. and Buxton, W. (1991), Working Together in Media Space: Collaboration Research at EuroPARC, Proc. UNICOM Symposium on CSCW—The Multimedia and Networking Paradigm, London.

5. Heath, C. & Luff, P. (1991), Disembodied conduct: Communication through video in a multi-media environment, Proc. CHI '91 Human Factors in Computing Systems, New Orleans, Louisiana.

6. Irwin, S. (1990), *Technology, Talk and the Social World: A Study of Video-Mediated Interaction*. Dissertation. Michigan State University.

7. Kraut, R., Egido, C., and Galegher, J. (1988) Patterns of Contact and Communication in Scientific Research Collaboration, Proc. CSCW '88 Computer-Supported Cooperative Work, Portland, Oregon.

8. Mantei, M., Baeker, R., Sellen, A., Buxton, W., Milligan, T. and Wellman, B. (1991), Experiences in the Use of a Media Space, Proc. CHI '91 Human Factors in Computer Systems, New Orleans, Louisiana.

9. Olson, M., and Bly, S. (1991) The Portland Experience: A Report On A Distributed Research Group, Intl. Journal of Man-Machine Studies, 34.

10. Root, R. (1988). Design of a Multi-Media Vehicle for Social Browsing, Proc. CSCW '88 Computer Support for Cooperative Work, Portland, Oregon.

11. Stults, R. (1988) Experimental Use of Video to Support Design Activity, Technical Report SSL-89-19, Xerox Palo Alto Research Centre, Palo Alto, California.

A METHOD FOR (RECRUITING) METHODS[1] : FACILITATING HUMAN FACTORS INPUT TO SYSTEM DESIGN

Lim, K. Y. and Long, J. B.

Ergonomics Unit,
University College London,
26 Bedford Way, London WC1H 0AP, UK.
+44 71 3807557 (phone)
+44 71 5801100 (fax)

ABSTRACT

The paper proposes that some current problems in recruiting human factors methods to system design might be alleviated by means of a structured human factors design framework. The explicit stage-wise design scope of such a framework would support the assignment of appropriate human factors methods to specific system design needs. As an illustration, the design framework of an in-house structured human factors methodology is reviewed followed by the assignment of a set of existing human factors methods against its design stages. Subsequent steps to develop the assigned methods into a similar methodology are then described. The potential of such a methodology for facilitating human factors input is discussed.

KEYWORDS: structured design methodology, human factors method recruitment, human factors system design cycle.

CURRENT PROBLEMS OF HUMAN FACTORS INPUT

Recent reports indicate that the uptake of human factors methods may be hindered by inadequate guidance on their recruitment during system design,[2] e.g. selecting a task analysis method, suitable for a particular design context, from a wide range of alternatives [15]; and locating human factors methods explicitly against the system design cycle [8]; etc. Two requirements must be met to alleviate the problem of inadequate guidance, namely:

(a) the design scope supported by existing human factors methods must be well defined;

(b) existing methods must be located explicitly against appropriate stages of the design cycle. The support provided by the methods would then be contextualised to system design needs.

These requirements emerged during discussions at a recent workshop on human factors methods [13]. One solution that was discussed will be assessed briefly to identify what further developments might be desirable.

In response to requirement (a), existing human factors methods might be characterised with respect to their ability to 'illuminate' a set of design issues, e.g. ease of learning, errors, etc. (see Figure 1). To meet requirement (b), existing methods might be categorized according to the resources required for their application (e.g. need for an existing design, time consumption, etc.) and the design support that they provide (e.g. methods for discovering the task, for generating a 'first-cut' design, etc. (see Figure 2)).

While these possible ways of meeting the requirements may provide some guidance for appropriately recruiting existing human factors methods, a number of problems remain. Specifically, the set of design issues used to characterise existing human factors methods need to be more complete and more representative (Figure 1). However, in view of the wide range of human factors system design concerns, it is unclear which design issues could conceivably constitute such a set. Thus, the utility of Figure 1 is limited to the identification of a design issue that is both of interest to any specific design, and is a member of the tabulated set. In addition, since design

---

[1] For the origin of this paper, see acknowledgements.

---

[2]. The term 'system' implies a human-machine system which performs tasks in a particular environment, work being achieved in the process. In the context of the system, Human Factors is primarily concerned with end-user behaviour with respect to devices, while Software Engineering is concerned with device behaviour.

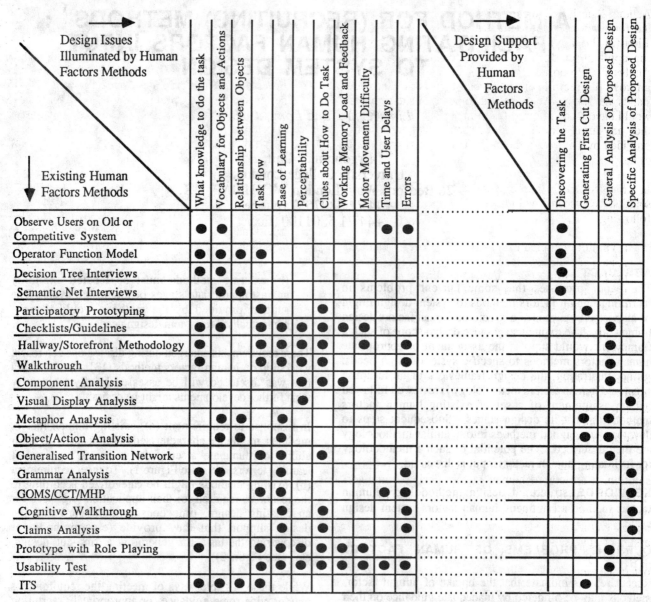

Existing Human Factors Methods	What knowledge to do the task	Vocabulary for Objects and Actions	Relationship between Objects	Task flow	Ease of Learning	Perceptability	Clues about How to Do Task	Working Memory Load and Feedback	Motor Movement Difficulty	Time and User Delays	Errors	Discovering the Task	Generating First Cut Design	General Analysis of Proposed Design	Specific Analysis of Proposed Design
Observe Users on Old or Competitive System	●	●								●	●	●			
Operator Function Model	●	●	●	●								●			
Decision Tree Interviews	●	●										●			
Semantic Net Interviews		●	●									●			
Participatory Prototyping				●			●						●		
Checklists/Guidelines	●	●		●	●	●	●							●	
Hallway/Storefront Methodology	●			●	●	●	●		●		●			●	
Walkthrough	●			●	●	●	●				●			●	
Component Analysis						●	●	●						●	
Visual Display Analysis						●									●
Metaphor Analysis		●	●		●								●	●	
Object/Action Analysis		●	●		●								●	●	
Generalised Transition Network				●	●		●							●	
Grammar Analysis	●	●									●				●
GOMS/CCT/MHP	●			●	●					●	●				●
Cognitive Walkthrough					●		●				●				●
Claims Analysis					●		●				●				●
Prototype with Role Playing	●			●	●	●	●	●						●	
Usability Test				●	●	●	●	●			●			●	
ITS	●	●	●	●								●			

Figure 1 : Design Issues Addressed by Existing Human Factors Methods (following Olson [13])

Figure 2 : Design Support Provided by Existing Human Factors Methods (following Olson [13])

considerations for some issues would pervade the entire system design cycle at some level of description (e.g. 'Task Flow' issues), specific points for recruiting human factors methods could be located using Figure 1 only with difficulty. A result may be a failure to address human factors issues at the earliest possible stage during design specification. Thus, human factors contributions would be incorporated less effectively. An alternative outcome that may result from the categorization of methods against such pervasive issues, is that methods would be poorly distinguished with respect to their suitability for a particular design context, e.g. which one of the ten 'Task Flow' methods is most appropriate for variant design (see Figure 1)?

Consequently, existing methods need also to be matched against stage-wise design context and scope. In other words, to facilitate recruitment, existing methods should be related directly to coherent *groups* of human factors design issues (as opposed to *discrete* issues within a set) that constitute the stage-wise scope of a (structured) design process. A simple example of this is given in Figure 2 for a system design cycle comprising : Discover the user's task --> Generate a 'first-cut' design --> etc. Thus, by using Figures 1 and 2 together human factors methods may be assigned to meet more specific system design needs, e.g. although both 'Object/Action Analysis' and 'Grammar Analysis' are indicated in Figure 1 to be suitable for addressing 'Vocabulary for Objects and

Actions' issues, design context characteristics may indicate the former to be more suited to conceptual design (i.e. 'First-Cut Design'), and the latter to be more appropriate for application during detailed design (i.e. 'Specific Analysis of Proposed Design'). Although Figure 2 might improve the recruitment of human factors methods as it stands, the stage-wise scope and context of its design cycle would have to be inferred (as in the previous example) as they are largely implicit. Thus, better support might be provided by improving the definition of its system design cycle.

In conclusion, further developments of the proposed solution (represented by Figures 1 and 2) should address the following:

(a) a more detailed examination of existing methods. A tabular matrix such as Figure 1 needs to characterise methods more completely to facilitate appropriate recruitment during system design;
(b) a more explicit stage-wise conception of the system design context and scope. In other words, the simple system design cycle adopted in Figure 2 needs to be extended.

Suitable existing human factors methods may then be identified by matching more detailed characteristics of existing methods derived in (a) against the better defined stage-wise design needs in (b). Appropriate recruitment of existing methods might thus be facilitated.

To illustrate the above developments of the proposed solution, a structured human factors design framework derived[3] during the development of an in-house methodology [9, 10] is exploited. The set of existing human factors methods (listed in Figures 1 and 2) is then assigned against system design needs that are explicitly specified by the stage-wise scope of the framework. The outcome is reported as follows :

Section 2 provides an overview of the structured human factors design framework. General categories of human factors methods that are relevant to each of its design stages are listed. The set of existing methods in Figures 1 and 2 is also assigned tentatively against individual design stages of the framework;
Section 3 then suggests what further improvements might be necessary for ensuring effective human factors input during system design;
Section 4 completes the paper with a summary of its conclusions.

A STRUCTURED FRAMEWORK FOR HUMAN FACTORS DESIGN
Figure 3 shows the structured design framework of an in-house human factors methodology for designing human-

computer systems. General characteristics of the framework comprise the following:

(a) the scope of all design stages of the framework is explicitly defined. The identification of human factors methods that are appropriate for each of these design stages is thus facilitated;
(b) design specification is motivated by a user-task oriented approach, i.e. the user model is characterised by particular requirements for task execution and performance;
(c) the design focus is on specification, rather than implementation and evaluation, since the latter design concerns are already well developed. The bias is intended to redress the imbalance arising from the traditionally late recruitment of human factors to system development.
(d) system design is progressed through three phases, each comprising a number of design stages. General design concerns of the phases are as follows : generation of initial design information (Information Elicitation and Analysis Phase); conceptual design (Design Synthesis Phase); and detailed design (Design Specification Phase).

An overview of the design framework follows. For a more detailed account, the reader is referred to Lim et al [8, 9, 10].

(i) The scope of the Extant Systems Analysis Stage comprises the elicitation and analysis of extant system[4] information, e.g. user needs and problems; existing task characteristics, design features and rationale, etc. In addition, extant designs are assessed to determine their potential for recruitment to target system design. The detail to which extant systems are analysed depends on circumstances surrounding the design project, for instance the resources available; the designer's familiarity with the system domain; etc. A wide range of human factors methods are recruited to support design in this stage. Firstly, the elicitation of extant system information is supported by 'off-the-shelf' techniques such as user interviews (including structured, decision tree and semantic net interviews), unobtrusive observations of the end-user, etc. Secondly, the derivation of appropriate task descriptions is guided by task analysis methods, e.g. task decomposition rules pertaining to task frequency, centrality and criticality; and task abstraction and generification techniques [6, 7]). Thirdly, assessments of extant design features are supported by general evaluation methods such as component and artefact analysis techniques, etc.

---

[3] The structured framework was derived by extending a composite of existing human factors design frameworks [8].

[4] It should be noted that *extant* systems includes both the *current* system (i.e. the system (computerised or not) currently in use in the client organization) and *related* systems (i.e. similar systems in use in other organizations).

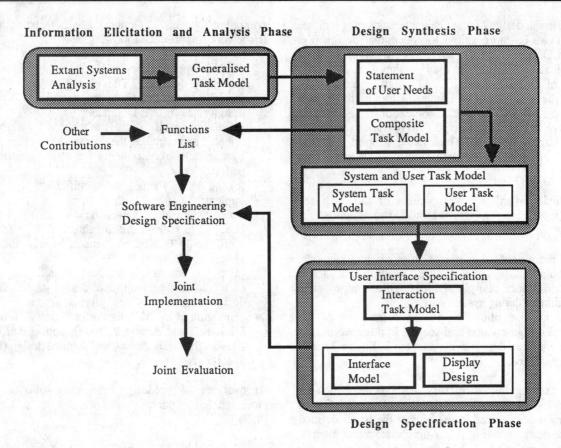

Information Elicitation and Analysis Phase   **Design Synthesis Phase**

Figure 3 : A Structured Human Factors Design Framework

(ii) The concerns of the Generalised Task Model Stage includes the generation of device independent descriptions to facilitate analytic mapping between appropriate extant design features and design requirements for the target system. In other words, a generalised *extant task* model is derived to support the recruitment of extant system features. A generalised *target task* model is also derived at this stage to establish the foundation for design extensions that are required to support novel target system tasks. The derivation of these models is supported by general task analysis methods such as TAKD[5] [5]. The two generalised task models are then carried forward to the Composite Task Model Stage where compatible elements are synthesized based on statements of user needs (see following design stages).

(iii) The Statement of User Needs Stage summarizes the conclusions of extant systems analysis (e.g. the rationale for recruiting particular extant design features to the target system), and defines user requirements for the target system (e.g. performance criteria and domain semantics for the target system). As such, the design stage is supported by general performance specification

methods such as scenario analysis [11] and semantic analysis methods such as metaphor analysis. The statements of user needs are carried forward to constrain subsequent design, e.g. the synthesis of generalised task models at the Composite Task Model Stage.

(iv) The Composite Task Model Stage addresses the generation of a conceptual task for the target system. Thus, the two generalised task models derived previously, are synthesized into a composite task model. On the basis of the latter model, the allocation of function between human and computer may be decided. Function allocation is initiated by designating components of the composite task model as on-line (computer-supported) and off-line (manual) tasks. Sub-tasks of the on-line task are then assigned to the human and computer as appropriate. Existing human factors methods that support this design stage include general task design methods, basic prototyping and simulation methods, and function allocation methods [1, 14].

(v) The scope of the System and User Task Model Stage comprises the detailed design of target system functions. The latter involve a further decomposition of the composite task model. On and off-line tasks

5 TAKD is the acronym for Task Analysis for Knowledge Based Descriptions.

are thus decomposed to yield the system task model and user task model respectively. Functional design is then pursued via the system task model, i.e. human-computer sub-task cycles of the latter model are decomposed further. In addition, job design may also be undertaken on the basis of the system and user task models, e.g. jobs may be specified based on the combined workload. Methods which support the preceding stage are also generally applicable to the present design stage.

(vi) The purpose of the Interaction Task Model Stage is to specify a device level description of the user's task, i.e. to derive an interaction task model. The model may be described in terms of object and action primitives of the chosen user interface environment (if any) and basic keystrokes of the designated hardware. Design iterations with later design stages are particularly important to ensure an appropriate level of description of the interaction task model. Low level actions of the description are then grouped into coherent units of interaction to constrain the specification of error recovery schemes, feedback messages and screen displays. To demonstrate the proposed design to users (and hence incorporate their feedback), more advanced prototyping and simulation methods, and general evaluation methods may be recruited.

(vii) The scope of the Interface Model Stage comprises the detailed specification of screen objects, for instance their behaviour and appearance, changes arising from user inputs, and state changes of representation and real world entities. Object modelling, command syntax and icon design are thus concerns of this design stage. Methods that could potentially support this stage include object/action analysis, visual display analysis, metaphor analysis, usability test, etc. To ensure coherence, interface model descriptions should be specified iteratively with screen composition at the Display Design Stage.

(viii) The Display Design Stage addresses the specification of screen contents (including messages) and layout;[6] the compilation of a glossary of screen objects; and the definition of presentation contexts for error and feedback messages, and for computerised task support functions.

It should be noted that the specifications in (vi) to (viii) are inter-linked explicitly by notation [8, 9, 10]. Taken together, they constitute the human factors specifications of the user interface. This account completes an overview of the structured human factors design framework.

Appropriate locations in the structured design framework for recruiting some members of the set of existing methods

---

[6] Screen displays may be specified on paper or prototyped using a computer-based tool such as Prototyper.™

(Figures 1 and 2) have been indicated in the preceding overview. Figure 4 indicates the locations for the complete set. In summary, these locations for recruitment have been determined intuitively and approximately by intersecting explicit stage-wise system design needs (corresponding to the stage-wise scope of the structured framework) against the support provided by the set of methods. To confirm the appropriateness and so the 'accuracy' of these locations, a more detailed examination of individual methods is required. Specifically, the methods should be examined further to determine whether the information required for application can be met by the design stage, and whether their outputs would address adequately the design concerns of that stage. In addition, the acceptability of resource demands by the method needs to be assessed relative to design priorities at the stage.

In the following section, the assignment of methods as proposed in Figure 4 is extended. The improved solution for facilitating method recruitment and how it may be developed is described.

DEVELOPING A STRUCTURED HUMAN FACTORS METHODOLOGY

Although Figure 4 supports a more specific recruitment of existing methods, it does not help to ensure that project resource allocations are commensurate with the requirements for adequate application of human factors methods. In other words, method application may be thwarted by unrealistic time frames for project deliverables. Such problems have been reported previously [2, 3, 12].

To support better projections of resource demands (and hence alleviate the problems), a solution is to develop and integrate an appropriate set of human factors methods into an overall structured design methodology. Such a methodology would facilitate an explicit accommodation of the *scope* and *process* of human factors design by the system design agenda. The design uptake of human factors methods might thus be facilitated. Another motivation for developing a structured design methodology is that it constitutes the basis for developing computer-based tools for supporting human factors design. Such tools have been developed in Software Engineering on a similar basis, e.g. CASE and IPSE tools [4].

These reasons motivated the development of the in-house structured human factors methodology which was mentioned earlier [8, 9, 10]. A similar methodology may be constructed based on the assigned methods in Figure 4. To this end, general procedures are as follows:

(a) select a sub-set of the assigned methods (whole or part of the methods in Figure 4) that shows promise for supporting in-house design needs;
(b) iterate procedures c1 and c2;
(c1) examine and extend individual methods (as necessary) on the basis of the structured design framework. The objective is to ensure that the design

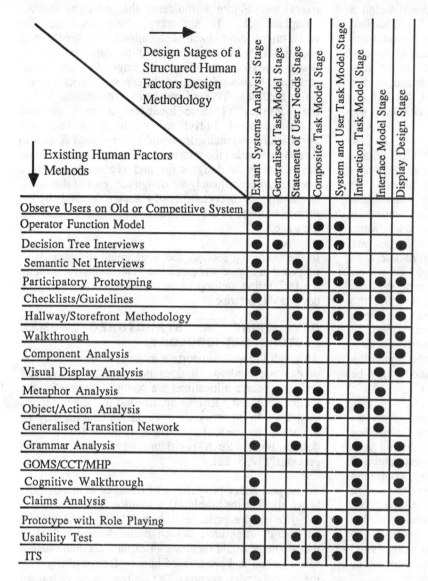

Design stages of the structured framework are supported by the following general categories of human factors methods :

Extant Systems Analysis Stage :
General elicitation, evaluation and task analysis methods.

Generalised Task Model Stage :
General evaluation and task analysis methods.

Statement of User Needs Stage :
General evaluation, task analysis and performance specification methods (e.g. scenario analysis).

Composite Task Model Stage :
General evaluation, task analysis, paper based prototyping, simulation and function allocation methods.

System and User Task Model Stage :
General evaluation, task analysis, paper based prototyping, simulation, function allocation and job design methods (e.g. workload analysis).

Interaction Task Model, Interface Model and Display Design Stages :
General evaluation, task analysis, mock-ups and more advanced prototyping, and simulation methods.

Figure 4 : Existing Human Factors Methods (following Olson [13]) Located against Specific Design Stages of the Structured Framework [8,9]

support provided by the methodology is explicit, comprehensive and complete. For instance, a method may be extended to ensure that the information it generates would meet input requirements of another method that is assigned to a succeeding stage of the methodology;

(c2) on the basis of the structured design framework, examine and concatenate individual methods (as necessary) which have been assigned to successive design stages so that overlaps in their design scope are eliminated;

(d) identify alternative combinations of methods that may be recruited across design stages of the structured methodology, e.g. the methodology might have three design stages {X,Y and Z} which are supported by methods {X1 to X3}, {Y1 to Y3} and {Z1 to Z3}

respectively. Depending on the compatibility of the methods assigned to successive design stages (e.g. see c1 and c2 above), the structured methodology may offer various recruitable combinations of methods to suit different design contexts, e.g. the combination of methods {X1, Y3, Z1}, which emphasizes extant design analysis, may be selected for a variant design scenario; while combination {X3, Y2, Z3}, which include more rigorous design validation methods, may be selected on another occasion to support novel design.

Following the development of a structured methodology, the above procedures could be invoked periodically so that other existing methods may be incorporated incrementally. During incorporation, the characteristics of the methods to be recruited should be assessed to ensure their compatibility with the set of methods currently installed in the methodology. Further research in this direction has been planned. Specifically, the research addresses the incorporation of a range of user requirements specification and domain analysis methods into the existing in-house structured design methodology. Results of the work will be reported in the near future.

CONCLUDING SUMMARY

The paper proposes the explicit location of existing human factors methods against design stages of an appropriately structured design framework. The proposal was motivated by two reasons. Firstly, the well defined stage-wise design scope of the structured framework would support a tighter matching of existing methods with system design needs and contexts. Thus, suitable existing methods may be identified for recruitment at appropriate stages of system design. Secondly, existing methods assigned against a structured framework could be developed further and integrated into an overall methodology. Since the stage-wise design scope and process of such a methodology are well defined, human factors design could be accounted for more explicitly at design outset (e.g. resource allocation at project planning) and during design development. Thus, the uptake of human factors would be facilitated. To illustrate what is entailed by these assertions, a set of existing methods was assigned against a structured human factors design framework. Further steps for deriving a structured methodology were then described. An in-house structured human factors methodology has been developed in this way. Case-study tests have indicated the methodology to be promising for facilitating human factors contribution to system design. Related extensions of the present research have also been undertaken or proposed. Aside from the those projects mentioned in the preceding section, the *inter-disciplinary* integration of structured methodologies was also addressed, i.e. Human Factors and Software Engineering design were integrated via their structured methodologies so that the co-ordination and timing of their design activities with respect to an *overall* design cycle is facilitated. The research has been completed and reported elsewhere [9, 10].

ACKNOWLEDGEMENTS

Although the issue of human factors method recruitment to system development is not novel (and has concerned us for some time), our attention and focus on this issue in this instance was generally stimulated by the Workshop on Human Computer Interface Design : Success Cases, Emerging Methods, and Real-World Context (Boulder, CO, July 23-26, 1991). In particular, the discussant presentation by (and subsequent discussion with) Judy Olson prompted consideration of a possible relation between *structured* human factors methods and human factors methods recruitment. Useful discussions with other workshop attendees (too numerous to mention) are also gratefully acknowledged. The proposal, however, is our own.

REFERENCES

1. Clegg, C., Ravden, S., Corbett, M. and Johnson, G. Allocating functions in computer integrated manufacturing : a review and a new method. *Behaviour and Information Technology*, 8, 3 (1989), 175-190.

2. Eason, K. D. and Cullen, J. Human factors contributions in the context of IT system design and implementation. In : H. J. Bullinger et al (eds.), *Information Technology for Organizational Systems*, 811-816, Elsevier Science Publishers, North-Holland, 1988.

3. Grudin, J. Systematic sources of suboptimal interface design in large product development organisations. *Human Computer Interaction*, 6, 2 (1991), 147-196.

4. Hewett, J. and Durham, T. *Computer-Aided Software Engineering: Commercial Strategies.* Ovum Ltd., 1987.

5. Johnson, P., Diaper, D. and Long, J. B. Tasks, skill and knowledge; task analysis for knowledge based descriptions. In *Proc. First IFIP Conference on Human-Computer Interaction (Interact '84)*, (London, September 4-7, UK, 1984), Elsevier Science Publishers, North-Holland, Vol. 1, 23-28.

6. Johnson, P. and Johnson, H. Generification : a process of identifying generic properties of tasks within a given domain. Queen Mary College Report to ICL, No. 2, 1987.

7. Johnson, P., Johnson, H. and Russell, F. Collecting and generalizing knowledge descriptions from task analysis data. ICL Technical Journal, 1988.

8. Lim, K. Y., Long, J. B. and Silcock, N. Motivation, research management and a conception for structured integration of human factors with system development methods: an illustration using the Jackson System Development method. In *Proc. Fifth European Conference on Cognitive Ergonomics*, (Urbino, September 3-6, Italy, 1990), Golem Press, 359-374.

9. Lim, K. Y., Long, J. B. and Silcock, N. Integrating human factors with structured analysis and design methods: an enhanced conception of the extended Jackson System Development method. In *Proc. Third IFIP Conference on HCI (Interact '90)*, (Cambridge, August 27-31, UK, 1990), Elsevier Science Publishers, North Holland, 225-230.

10. Lim, K. Y., Long, J. B. and Silcock, N. Integrating human factors with the Jackson System

Development method : an illustrated overview. *Ergonomics (Special Issue on Cognitive Ergonomics III)*, 33, 12 (1991), in press.

11. Malin, J. T., Schreckenghost, D. L. and Thronesbery, C. G. Design for interaction between humans and intelligent systems during real-time fault management. In *Proc. Fifth Annual Space Operations, Applications, and Research Symposium*, NASA Johnson Space Center, Houston, Texas, July 9-11, 1991, in press.

12. Meister, D. A Catalogue of Ergonomic Design Methods. In *Proc International Conference on Occupational Ergonomics*, (1984), 17-25.

13. Olson, J. Human-computer interface design : success cases, emerging methods and real world context, (Boulder, Colorado, July 23-26, 1991), Discussion handout on existing human factors methods.

14. Price, H. E. The allocation of functions in systems. *Human Factors*, 27, 1 (1985), 33-45.

15. Whitefield, A., Wight, J., Life, A. and Colbert, M. Assessing the programming language PML as a task analysis method and product. In *Proc. HCI '91 Conference : People and Computers VI*, (Edinburgh, August 20-23, Scotland, 1991), Cambridge University Press, 403-420.

TEACHING EXPERIENCED DEVELOPERS TO DESIGN GRAPHICAL USER INTERFACES

Jakob Nielsen

Bellcore, 445 South Street, Morristown, NJ 07962-1910

Rita M. Bush, Tom Dayton, Nancy E. Mond, Michael J. Muller, and Robert W. Root

Bellcore, 444 Hoes Lane, Piscataway, NJ 08855-1300

Email: nielsen@bellcore.com, rita2@ctt.bellcore.com, tdayton@ctt.bellcore.com, nem2@ctt.bellcore.com, michael@bellcore.com, broot@ctt.bellcore.com

ABSTRACT

Five groups of developers with experience in the design of character-based user interfaces were taught graphical user interface design through a short workshop with a focus on practical design exercises using low-tech tools derived from the PICTIVE method. Several usability problems were found in the designs by applying the heuristic evaluation method, and feedback on these problems constituted a way to make the otherwise abstract usability principles concrete for the designers at the workshop. Based on these usability problems and on observations of the design process, we conclude that object-oriented interactions are especially hard to design and that the developers were influenced by the graphical interfaces of personal computers with which they had interacted as regular users.

Keywords: Graphical user interfaces, GUI, design, transfer of skill, education, standards, object-oriented interfaces, heuristic evaluation, PICTIVE.

INTRODUCTION

By now, graphical user interfaces (GUIs) are fairly old, with a history going back to Ivan Sutherland's Sketchpad system from 1962 [20], Douglas Engelbart's mouse from 1964 [2], several research systems from the 1970s [3], and several commercial systems from the early 1980s [18]. Even so, many (if not most) large-scale computer-using organizations have continued using character-based interfaces for a variety of reasons, including the need to support an existing base of alphanumeric terminals connected to traditional mainframes.

Based on the increasing dominance of graphical user interfaces in most new computer systems since the mid-1980s and with graphical platforms coming down in price, several of

these large organizations are currently contemplating or even implementing a switch from character-based systems to graphical user interfaces. Such a switch necessitates transferring the skills of large numbers of developers who have extensive experience in the design of character-based interfaces but who may never have designed a graphical user interface before.

It can be hard even for experienced programmers to learn the necessary programming techniques and extensive subroutine libraries used when implementing graphical user interfaces (e.g., [16]). The development of new programming systems and user interface management systems holds some promise for alleviating this problem in the future.

This article considers the additional problem of the transfer of user interface design skills in the case of developers with experience designing character-based interfaces. Of course, one possible solution to this problem would be to restrict the developers to handle only the implementation of the interfaces and then bring in a new team of experienced usability specialists and graphics designers for the actual graphical user interface design. In many cases, however, such specialized staff may not be available, and in other cases the usability specialists themselves may need to transfer their designs skills to handle the new interface medium. Furthermore, it is almost always the case that developers without "official status" as usability specialists have to design parts of the interface themselves.

The transfer of developers' design skills from character-based user interfaces to graphical user interfaces is obviously of great practical interest for those development organizations that are currently switching to graphical systems. Furthermore, the study of this phenomenon is particularly interesting in that it provides an opportunity for assessing the difficulties of design for the GUI generation of interaction paradigms; studies of novice designers (like the students used in many studies) would confound the effect of the specific interaction paradigm and the effect of simply learning to design a user interface. Finally, the process of moving from one interaction paradigm to another is of general interest also with respect to ongoing efforts at inventing the next generation of interaction paradigms as evidenced by current research in, e.g., virtual reality interfaces, interaction agents, etc.

A GRAPHICAL INTERFACE DESIGN COURSE

We have developed a short course in graphical user interface design and taught it to five groups of software professionals. In fact, the course is more of a workshop than a traditional training class since it is heavily based on practical exercises where the participants design actual graphical interfaces themselves. Such a reliance on learning-by-doing in a practicum setting seems to be one of the better ways of imparting any kind of usability knowledge [23]. Design skills generally have to be learned through active efforts on the parts of the learners rather than taught through passive attendance at lectures. The practicum method is especially valuable for this learning process [19][24].

Workshop Outline

Due mostly to resource restrictions and the difficulty of having the designers leave their ongoing projects for an extended period of time, the workshops were limited to half a day each. This is obviously a very short time in which to learn a complicated topic like graphical interface design, and several workshop participants expressed a desire for a full-day workshop. On the other hand, the workshop was deliberately intended to sensitize participants to graphical interface design issues without leaving them with a false belief that they had suddenly become graphical interface design experts, and the limited duration was certainly an advantage for achieving that goal. Also, the workshop did succeed in acquainting the designers with a wide spectrum of graphical interface design principles as evidenced by their ability to refer to these principles towards the end of the final design session.

After a short introduction on management goals for moving to graphical interfaces, the workshops started by a lecture on principles for graphical user interface principles, including such issues as

- Definition of "graphical user interface" and the characteristics of graphical interfaces and direct manipulation.
- Design principles and guidelines for usable graphical interfaces. For example, the principle of providing users with a good conceptual mental model leads to the guideline of using real-world metaphors in the graphics whenever possible.

The workshops then proceeded with a guided tour of a live graphical user interface, pointing out the various standard user interface elements and how they were used and combined. As always, the concreteness embodied in the live system generated more participant comments and questions than the abstract principles, but we do believe that the explicit statement of the basic usability principles for graphical dialogues was an important part of the workshops.

After a short description of the PICTIVE-like [8] design method to be used in the practical exercises (described further below), the participants then proceeded to design two graphical interfaces. The first design exercise was the same for all the workshops and was limited to a period of about 30 minutes since it was mainly intended as a warm-up exercise. The second design exercise took about one hour and concerned a design problem from the participants' own project, thus being different for each workshop. The participants were asked to produce a written specification of this second design problem in advance of the workshop, but even so they still needed time during the workshop to limit the scope of the problem to a reasonable size, given the available time. They did so during the break between the first and second design exercise, thus being able to take advantage of their experience from the first exercise.

The first exercise concerned the design of a report generator interface to a database system. Users were to be able to select a number of fields from the database and lay out a report listing those fields with the database records sorted according to one or more of the fields. We provided the designers with a fairly detailed specification of the intended functionality since the goal of this workshop was not usability engineering in general but specifically graphical interface design. For the initial workshops, our specification turned out to be too general and to encompass much too much for a complete design to be generated in the available time. We therefore restricted the problem in subsequent versions, for example by limiting the database to being a single-file system. We learned that it was necessary to provide a very precise definition of a very limited set of functions to avoid having the participants spend most of their time arguing over what features to include in the system rather than on interface design as such. Also, we discovered the need for an active workshop "manager" who could at times interrupt the participants and remind them that the goal of the workshop was to design a graphical interface, and either encourage them to arrive at a more or less arbitrary resolution of the functionality decisions or simply hand down such a decision.

As further described below, each interface design was subjected to heuristic evaluation by a team of usability experts, and the usability problems thus identified were discussed with the participants after each design session. While the specialists performed the heuristic evaluation of the first design, the workshop participants had a break and also discussed the details of the specification of the second design problem. While the evaluation team conducted the heuristic evaluation of the second design, the designers heard a short presentation on the general usability engineering lifecycle [14], emphasizing the need for user centered design, including such methods as participatory design and user testing. This presentation was intended to familiarize the participants with the range of important usability activities related to a software product, and to put our classroom exercises into context as only one of a set of necessary work activities. Since the workshop took place in a closed room in half a day with partially artificial design problems, the participants were required to design without any task analysis or interaction with real users, and they should obviously not do so in a real project.

PICTIVE-like Design Practicum

The design exercises were carried out using a modified form of the PICTIVE method [8][10]. PICTIVE was originally developed for use in participatory design with the goal of allowing users (and other product stakeholders [9]) without programming abilities equal access to the construction of an interface design. Therefore, a PICTIVE design process includes the use of extremely low-tech materials in the form of paper and colored pens, pads of sticky notes, "cursors" on cut-out pieces of transparencies that are moved by hand over the design surface, and the use of overwriting, scissors and tape to "edit" the design. To illustrate the use of these design tools, a few minutes of videotape from a PICTIVE design session were shown, emphasizing the possibility of changing the design elements by cutting them up or writing on them.

Since our developers did not yet know how to program graphical user interfaces, the PICTIVE design tools were well suited for our use. The full PICTIVE methodology also includes additional elements, especially the participation of real users in the design process, which were not used in this workshop, so we would characterize the design practicum as using PICTIVE-like tools rather than being a true PICTIVE process.

In addition to blank paper and sticky notes, we provided pre-printed sheets of paper with graphical design elements taken from the specific interface standard used in the workshop. For example, we had menubars preprinted with the standard *File*, *Edit*, *View*, *Options*, and *Help* menu headers, as well as blank windows with scrollbars, different kinds of dialog boxes (both blank ones, and the standard error dialogs and file selection dialogs), and lists of radio and check buttons with the labels left blank to be filled in by the designers. Having such design element templates readily available corresponds to the way most modern GUI programming toolkits work. The participants initially hesitated to modify (write on and cut up) the preprinted design elements, but after a small amount of prompting by one of the workshop leaders who served as a facilitator of the design process and the use of the PICTIVE tools, they quickly learned to do so.

All of these dialogue elements were blown up by a factor of about two compared to their size on a computer screen to allow the workshop participants to easily add labels and other dialogue elements by hand. The oversized design also made it possible for the entire group of designers to see the design and made it easier for us to videotape it.

Finally, the designers were provided with a large (21×15 inches, 53×38 cm) sheet of paper that served as the design surface. Our initial intention was to have this expanse of paper simulate the full computer screen and have the participants place windows and other dialogue elements on it as their design progressed. It turned out, however, that the designers limited themselves to designs the size of the preprinted windows, so for the later workshops we pre-sketched a main window with the standard menu bar to take up the full sheet of paper to encourage the designers to utilize the entire design surface.

Heuristic Evaluation

In order to provide the workshop participants with immediate feedback on the usability aspects of their designs, the designs were subjected to heuristic evaluation by two usability specialists. Heuristic evaluation [15] is based on having a group of evaluators judge the usability of an interface by going through it and comparing it to a set of heuristics for usable design. The normal recommendation is to use between three and five evaluators for heuristic evaluation since more evaluators find more usability problems [15], but practical considerations prevented the use of more than two evaluators for this workshop. The workshop time schedule required the evaluators to present their list of usability problems immediately after the conclusion of the heuristic evaluation session, leaving them almost no time to coordinate their lists of usability problems. From an instructional perspective, uncoordinated feedback from a larger group of evaluators would have been too confusing to the designers.

The limitation of basing the heuristic evaluation on two evaluators was not too serious in our case since we had the advantage of having two highly skilled usability specialists[*] available as evaluators, and since the instructional goals of the feedback sessions would be served quite well even if not every single usability problem was pointed out. We mainly needed to discuss the most glaring and most conceptually interesting usability problems in order to provide the designers with a better understanding of the usability principles they had violated in their initial designs.

Heuristic evaluation was chosen for several reasons, including the pragmatic consideration that the feedback sessions needed to take place about fifteen minutes after the designers had finalized their designs. This short time frame ruled out the use of user testing and pointed to the use of heuristic evaluation since it is known to be an extremely time-efficient usability method [4]. Also, instructional considerations favored heuristic evaluation's explicit tie-in between specific usability problems and general usability principles since we wanted the participants to learn how these principles applied to GUI design. It was important not just to tear the participants' designs apart on arbitrary and opinionated grounds but instead to relate the usability problems to the recognized usability principles we wanted them to learn. In practice, it turned out to be a challenge for the evaluators to stick to this rule, and evaluations were probably too judgmental in tone at the first workshops.

The entire design sessions were videotaped,[†] and the two evaluators were present in the room while the designs were being developed. Observing the design sessions gave the evaluators a head start on the heuristic evaluation and contributed considerably to the quality of the feedback sessions since the evalua-

---

[*] Also, at least for the report generator exercise, the evaluators had the status of "double specialists" with expertise in both general usability and in the type of interface being evaluated. Heuristic evaluation by such "double specialists" requires fewer evaluators than when "single specialists" are used [12].

tors were able to refer back to the designers' own design discussions. At the end of each design session, the designers were asked to present a simulated walkthrough of a user session with their final design. These walkthroughs had the advantage of freezing the design and making it clear to the evaluators exactly how the various interface elements and sub-dialogues constructed during the design session were intended to interact. The walkthroughs lasted about five minutes each and were also videotaped. The evaluators brought the videotape with the walkthrough to another room equipped with playback facilities allowing them to freeze the tape as well as play it forwards and backwards in slow motion. They had about fifteen minutes to review the videotape and perform the heuristic evaluation.

Workshop Participants

The observations presented below are based on five graphical user interface design workshops with a total of 27 participants. The participants were experienced software professionals who had designed and developed systems with character-based user interfaces but had not previously designed graphical user interfaces.

Group sizes ranged from four to seven participants. The best results seemed to be achieved from groups with about five participants. The larger groups tended to split dynamically into subgroups at each end of the table discussing different aspects of the interface design and it was difficult to get everybody to participate simultaneously in a single design stream on the PICTIVE design surface. Smaller groups sometimes came to a standstill where nobody had good ideas for continuing the design.

For each workshop, the group consisted of people who were already working together on an existing project or in an existing organization. They were therefore able to jump straight into working together on our design exercises without the hesitation one sometimes observes with groups where the participants are not used to working together. Also, the participants were able to draw upon shared knowledge during the second design exercise which used a problem from their respective projects.

Each workshop involved a single group of designers and six usability specialists, so most workshops actually had more teachers than students. This disparity was probably slightly overwhelming for the designers but since each usability specialist had different roles in the workshop, we preferred keeping this large number of "teachers." In fact, not all the usability specialists functioned as teachers in the traditional sense, and the participation of a large number of usability specialists allowed us to play different roles during the design exercises and the interface evaluation sessions. For example,

one of us was the design process facilitator who helped the designers apply the PICTIVE tools and keep the design process going smoothly. Another served the role of keeper of the interface standard and was deferred to with respect to the rules of the particular GUI standard used in the workshop. Others were defenders of the usability principles and used the evaluation sessions to point out problems in the designs. And yet others had roles of workshop managers, including the responsibility for keeping the tight time schedule and making decisions when the designers wondered what to assume about their users. This latter role was important to keep the design flowing during the artificial workshop setting where it was not otherwise possible to investigate conditions in an external reality. For example, in the design of a query interface to a relational database, the participants decided to assume that the users would be familiar with entity-relation diagrams and base the graphical interface on such diagrams. This was an acceptable decision to allow them to proceed with the design process, even though there are obviously many people who are not familiar with these diagrams and who would therefore need another interface.

Even though most of us could probably have played other roles if need be, we believe that the role playing on the part of different usability specialists enhanced the workshop and made the different perspectives clearer to the designers than if a few people had taken on multiple roles. For similar workshops under conditions where fewer usability specialists are available, we would recommend using at least three usability specialists such that different people can serve as design facilitators and evaluators. Normally, at least two design evaluators will be needed due to the demands of the heuristic evaluation method.

Usability Specialists as Technology Defenders

A striking observation from this workshop is that we as usability specialists fell into the role of "owners" or defenders of a technology. A similar phenomenon is often observed when programmers attend user testing of their own software. In such cases, standard usability engineering practice is to encourage the programmers to follow the "shut up" rule and not interfere with the test users even though they will feel a constant urge to correct users as they "misuse" the programmers' designs.

Even though we were well aware of this principle, it was very hard for us not to jump in and "correct" the designers when they misused standard interface elements or were overlooking a good way to utilize graphical interaction principles. Indeed, at the first workshop, we interfered with the designers and suggested that they use a direct manipulation technique to achieve a certain goal. They did so, but when it came time to simulate the entire interface for the walkthrough it turned out that they had not really understood what they had been pressured into including in their design, as evidenced by the following exchange. A is the designer who had been narrating the walkthrough up until the point where the interface element introduced by us had to be used.

   A: *"Help me out with this. Where do we go from here?"*

---

† At the first workshop, we used two videocameras: One filming the group as a whole and one filming the PICTIVE design surface. This camera setup turned out to intimidate the workshop participants, and for the remaining workshops, we relied on a single camera filming the design surface without including the workshop participants themselves in the video frame.

B: *"This is where we use these cursors."*

A: *"OK, This is, eh... If you understand this better at this point, you can describe it, because I don't think I got it. I don't know what to make of it."*

C: *"This is where we sort of changed gears."*

For the remaining workshops, we mostly restrained ourselves and let the designers retain ownership of their designs without interference, but it was often *very* difficult for us to stick to the "shut up" rule.

USABILITY PROBLEMS IN THE DESIGNS

The heuristic evaluation revealed a total of 40 usability problems in the designs. As mentioned above, the heuristic evaluation was performed under resource constraints, so the designs most likely contain additional, undiscovered problems. This number of usability problems is not representative of the eventual quality of these designs if they had been developed into final products. These usability problems were the result of a single, time-limited design session, so it is likely that most of these problems would have been found in subsequent design activities and user testing, just as they were in fact found by us by a simple "discount usability engineering" effort. The discussion of the usability problems below is an indication of the difficulties of learning graphical user interface design and indicative of the issues one will have to look out for when productizing such designs.

It should be stressed that the software professionals in our workshops were not bad user interface designers. The designs discussed in this article were their first graphical interface designs, so to some extent it would only be natural for them to have some problems. In general, one should have the same attitude as when judging results from traditional user testing: When an error is made, it is not because the user (here: designer) is stupid, it is because the system (here: GUI design) is difficult.

Here, we focus on the usability problems in the designs, but there were also several positive aspects, including some creative solutions that were perhaps surprising given that these designs were the designers' first attempt at designing graphical user interfaces.

Classifying the usability problems according to the set of usability heuristics (mostly taken from [7] and [11]) gives the following result (a few problems were classified under more than one heuristic):

Simple and Natural Dialogue: 7 problems. For example, one report generator design had one window where users specified sorting criteria with radio buttons and another window where feedback on the current sorting criterion was listed. A simpler design would have combined the two to a single field with a pop-up option menu. As another example, an application for reviewing and changing information on a mainframe had some protected information that was not user-editable. The distinction between the two kinds of information in the design was a heavy box around the editable data and a thin box around the protected data. An alternative design would have

eliminated the box around the protected data and only had boxes where the user could edit the data. Not only would the graphics have been simpler and less busy for the eyes, but it would also be more natural since any kind of box around a number seems to indicate that users can interact with it.

Speak the User's Language: 3 problems. In the report generator exercise the basic object of the interface was taken to be the database (a system-oriented view of the functionality) rather than the user-generated report (a user-oriented view).

Minimize User Memory Load: 2 problems. One design required users to type in the sorting criteria in the report generator exercise (e.g., < or >). A better design used by the other four groups would explicitly show the available options to the user (for example as radio buttons or in a pop-up option menu).

Consistency: 7 problems. For example, three groups changed the name of the `File` menu to `Database` in the report generator exercise. Even though the term `Database` might at first sight seem an appropriate name for a menu to open and close databases, practically all graphical user interface standards use the common term `File`, so users will normally be used to seeing this term and would know what to expect of a `File` menu.*

Provide Feedback: 4 problems. In one application, users could open objects in separate windows for closer inspection of their detailed contents. Instead of a generic window title, the design should have provided feedback on which object had been chosen by repeating its name in the window title. As another example, an application for assigning certain jobs to service representatives ought to dynamically dim the names of those staff members who did not have the qualifications to handle the current job category.

Provide Clearly Marked Exits: 3 problems. A dialog box where the users could change certain information had an `OK` button but not a `Cancel` button, so users could only escape from the dialog box by manually undoing any changes they might have made.

Provide Shortcuts: 4 problems. For example, a report generator design allowed users several ways to sort the records, and users were required to actively specify one of these methods. A shortcut could have provided the most common sorting method (probably "sort by ascending values") as the default and allowed the users to change it from a pop-up option menu.

Good Error Messages: No problems were found in this category as the workshop participants did not have time to design the error messages.

---

* One can obviously argue whether it is better to use `File` (consistent with other standard-compliant applications) or `Database` (which certainly would seem to have a higher degree of "external consistency" [5] for this particular application). The ultimate decision would have to be made on the basis of an analysis of the degree to which the users' work involved switching between applications

Prevent Errors: 1 problem. In one application where users could shut down certain processes running on a computer system, the default option in the confirmation dialog box should not be *OK* but rather *Cancel* since killing processes is a dangerous and non-reversible operation.

Object-Oriented Design: 7 problems. This category is discussed further below since it seemed to represent the most serious usability problems.

Appropriate Graphics Design: 3 problems. This category only comprised the extent to which the graphics design supported the dialogue and not the broader issue of pleasant or good-looking graphics design. Because of the time constraints of the workshop, the participants did not have time to produce polished graphics for which such a judgment would have been relevant. One example of a graphics design problem was a case where icons represented objects that could be marked for two different activities; execution or deletion. Icons marked for execution were turned green and icons marked for deletion were turned red. Even though these colors provided a good mapping between their common connotations and the functions they were representing, they would cause difficulties for a large number of users with color-deficient vision, so one should provide redundant cues such as, for example, an ✕ or a slash over the icons to be deleted.

User in Control and Modeless Dialogues: 2 problems. A certain application had several subapplications that were linked by buttons in such a way that users were unnecessarily restricted in moving between the subapplications. A user-controlled interface would have provided a global palette or menu of subsystems and allowed users to move to any subsystem at any time.

We observed several cases where the designers were seduced by the graphics capabilities and overlooked textual solutions that might have been more appropriate. For example, in a case where users had to retrieve some information from a file, they were required to find its icon even though it could be buried under other objects. The design did not allow users to simply type in the file name in case they remembered it. Such complete rejection of any character-based interaction technique constitutes an over-reaction against the influence of previous interfaces.

Object-Oriented Design

Most of the usability problems described above are minor in the sense that they can easily be corrected in a subsequent design iteration without having to change the fundamental structure of the interface. Unfortunately, the seven problems relating to the lack of object-orientation in the interface have deeper consequences for the basic structure of the design and are thus harder to correct, meaning that one should pay special attention to them up front before implementing a potentially problematic design.

Practically all the development teams had difficulties in arriving at appropriately object-oriented designs.[*] Of the five groups, four groups designed interfaces with one or more usability problems due to lack of object-orientation, and the

fifth group would probably have done so also. This group was in the process of designing a function-oriented interface when one of the instructors interrupted their design and suggested that they move to an object-oriented design. This interruption was a case of the problem described above with usability specialists as "owners" of a technology which they want to promote. Due to this interference, this fifth group did include the object-oriented features as suggested, but they clearly had not understood the deeper meaning of the suggestion and it mainly served to interrupt the flow of their design. They had a very hard time understanding this design suggestion even though it was actually quite good (as judged by several usability specialists after the workshop) and simplified the interface, thus again indicating the difficulties of getting to grips with object-oriented design.

Object-oriented interfaces are to be seen in contrast to the function-oriented interfaces that were the traditional basis for character-oriented interfaces. In a function-oriented interface, the interaction is structured around a set of commands which the user issues in various combinations to achieve the desired result. The main interface issue is how to provide easy access to these commands and their parameters, and typical solutions include command-line interfaces with various abbreviation options as well as full-screen menus.

Object-oriented interfaces are sometimes described as turning the application inside-out as compared to function-oriented interfaces. The main focus of the interaction changes to the users' data and other information objects which are typically represented graphically on the screen as icons or in windows. Users achieve their goals by gradually massaging these objects (using various modification features that are of course similar to the concept of commands) until their state as shown on the screen matches the desired result. Some examples of problems with arriving at object-oriented designs were:

In one design for the report generator exercise, users generated the report by first selecting the appropriate retrieval parameters and then clicking on a *Report* button. Before seeing the report, they were then forced to select the report style (text, graphics, statistics) from a *View by* menu that would then show a window with the actual report. A more usable object-oriented design would immediately present the report as an object in a window and then allow the users to change its format (several times, if need be) while they could see it and judge what representation would suit their goals best. This object-oriented design would also allow for the use of a default format (say, view as a textual report) that would probably suit users in many cases and make the interface more approachable for novices.

---

[*] Even though it is true that the learning of object-oriented *programming* may sometimes present difficulties [1][17], the focus of the current discussion is the object-oriented nature of the resulting *user interfaces*, independent of what programming language might be used to implement them. For example, it is possible to implement an object-oriented graphical user interface in a traditional procedural programming language by using event-driven programming.

An application for managing certain information was centered around a window for specifying attributes of the information of interest (for example, reports dealing with a specific central office). Several commands were associated with this representation: `Run Query`, `Sort`, `View Data on Screen`, `Print Data`, and `Save`. The design could easily confuse some users as to whether the `Save` command would save the specification of the retrieval or the concrete information retrieved (but not seen) during this specific query. This problem would be avoided by going to an object-oriented design where a new window (with its own menu bar) would appear as the user activated the `Run Query` command. This design would entirely eliminate the `View on Screen` command (which would be implicit in the design), and the `Print` and `Save` commands would then operate either on the object containing the specification or the object containing the retrieved data, making it obvious what they were referring to. The original design was function-oriented and required the user to specify desired functions before the data could be viewed. An object-oriented design allows the user to see the data before it is sorted, thus probably allowing the user a better decision with respect to what would be the appropriate sorting criterion. Also, most users would probably want to check the data before printing it, so making viewing the data a default action would constitute a shortcut.

Interface Contamination

The designers were sometimes influenced by having personal experience as users of graphical interface standards other than the one they were designing for. Indeed, 63% of the designers had regular or extensive experience using a personal computer with a graphical user interface, even though only 19% had regular experience using the workstation graphical interface they were asked to design for in the workshop. Examples of the influence from personal computers with graphical user interfaces include:

- In two groups, designers argued that one should keep the menu title `File` on the basis of their experience as users of a system with such a menu. In one session where almost all the designers had experience with such a system, this argument was successful, but in the other session the name of the menu was changed anyway.

- A designer assumed that highlighting of text in selected fields worked in the same way as on the personal computer he had been using.

- At one workshop, the designers discussed whether a report header could be placed directly on the report without having to create it explicitly as a new object first. Designer **D**: *"I just want to click anywhere on the screen and start typing."* Designer **E**: *"Like in FooBar"* (a personal computer graphics program). Designer **E** later used an example from another personal computer graphics program to explain how the user would interact with a certain part of the interface being designed.

The positive aspect of this influence from other GUIs is that some design principles are communicated by osmosis since most graphical interface standards are fairly similar (see [6]

for a comparison of several such standards). The negative aspect is "interface contamination" in that details native to one interface standard creep over to implementations that are supposed to follow another interface standard. One lesson from this phenomenon is that designers should be immersed in a computational environment for their own computer usage with the same interface standard as the one they are trying to design to. Also, if many designers in a company have previous experience with some other interface standard, it may pay to construct a short guide listing the differences between the new standard (to which they are expected to design) and the standard to which they have been exposed as users. This observation corresponds to previous studies of uses of interface standards [21] which have found that designers are heavily influenced by the actual running systems they know, as well as the observation that widely used applications can have a major impact on shaping designers' ideas of how to design their own applications [22].

FOLLOW-UP STUDY OF A DESIGN TEAM

About seven months after the workshops, one of the design teams had completed a complete prototype graphical user interface for a fairly complex product. This interface was subjected to a heuristic evaluation usability study which is reported in detail elsewhere [13]. As one would expect from a prototype, the interface contained several usability problems, but the consensus of the evaluators was that the overall design was good and employed a variety of graphical user interface features in an appropriate manner. The overall look and feel of the design was definitely that of a cohesive graphical user interface. A first conclusion is thus that the designers had indeed learned graphical interface design.

A second conclusion from the analysis of this interface was that several of the most severe usability problems could be traced to a lack of object-orientation in parts of the interface. Briefly, the interface involved looking at outputs from various queries to external databases, and using parts of that output as inputs to queries to other external databases. The prototype interface treated the database output as plain text event though it was highly formatted and consisted of a predetermined number of fields with specific meaning. Users had access to standard copy–paste mechanisms for use in transferring information from previous queries to new queries, but doing so involved several awkward steps and the possibility for errors. An alternative, more object-oriented interface design would have recognized the individual data elements on the screen as user-oriented objects even though they had been produced as output from external database queries. Instead of the function oriented construction of new queries into which data could be pasted, the object-oriented view would concentrate on the data and allow users to apply further queries to any selected data. For example, one possible redesign would have users select a data field and pop up a list of those external databases for which a query for that datatype would be meaningful, thus at the same time simplifying the interface (by only presenting the relevant databases) and avoiding several steps and usability problems in the construction of the query. Making the interface object-oriented along these lines would fix eight of the ten most severe usability problems in the prototype.

CONCLUSIONS

When teaching user interface design for a new interaction paradigm, practical exercises using a low-tech design method allowed the participants to focus on the design rather than to struggle with implementation details. Following the design sessions by feedback sessions critiquing the participants' designs made the discussions of interface principles engaging and concrete for the designers.

Other lessons from the workshops are:

- Object-oriented interface design is difficult to learn for designers who have been used to the function-oriented interface style, so special care should be taken to teach not just GUI design in general but also object-oriented design in particular. Generalizing this observation, we find that changes in interaction paradigms may often involve deep changes in the way functionality is accessed and not just the more superficial screen changes implied by terms like "graphical" vs. "character-based" user interfaces.

- Designers will often have experienced new interaction paradigms on platforms other than the one they are expected to design for, and this experience can lead to interface contamination unless steps are taken to contain it. We recommend letting designers get extensive experience as users of applications that comply with the same interface standard they are intended to design for, as well as explaining any differences between interface standards they may have been using in the past and the one they are intended to use.

- Concretized demonstrations (like the one we used to illustrate GUIs after the general lecture) and discussions across disciplines and backgrounds help in communicating the diverse and potentially quite abstract issues involved in user interface design.

ACKNOWLEDGMENT

The authors would like to thank Tom Landauer for helpful comments on earlier versions of this manuscript.

REFERENCES

1. Détienne, F. Difficulties in designing with an object-oriented language: An empirical study. *Proc. INTERACT'90 Third IFIP Conf. Human–Computer Interaction* (Cambridge, U.K., 27–31 August 1990), 971–976.

2. Engelbart, D. The augmented knowledge workshop. In Goldberg, A. (Ed.), *A History of Personal Workstations*. Addison-Wesley, Reading, MA, 1988, 185–236.

3. Goldberg, A. (Ed.). *A History of Personal Workstations*. Addison-Wesley, Reading, MA, 1988.

4. Jeffries, R., Miller, J.R., Wharton, C., and Uyeda, K.M. User interface evaluation in the real world: A comparison of four techniques. *Proc. ACM CHI'91* (New Orleans, LA, 27 April–2 May 1991), 119–124.

5. Kellogg, W.A. The dimensions of consistency. In Nielsen, J. (Ed.), *Coordinating User Interfaces for Consistency*, Academic Press, San Diego, CA, 1989. 9–20.

6. Marcus, A. *Graphic Design for Electronic Documents and User Interfaces*. Addison-Wesley, Reading, MA, 1992.

7. Molich, R., and Nielsen, J. Improving a human-computer dialogue. *Communications of the ACM* **33**, 3 (March 1990), 338–348.

8. Muller, M.J. PICTIVE—An exploration in participatory design. *Proc. ACM CHI'91* (New Orleans, LA, 27 April–2 May 1991), 225–231.

9. Muller, M.J. No mechanization without representation: Who participates in the participatory design of large software products? *Proc. ACM CHI'91* (New Orleans, LA, 27 April–2 May 1991), 391.

10. Muller, M.J. Retrospective on a year of participatory design using the PICTIVE technique. *Proc. ACM CHI'92* (Monterey, CA, 3–7 May 1992).

11. Nielsen, J. Traditional dialogue design applied to modern user interfaces. *Communications of the ACM* **33**, 10 (October 1990), 109–118.

12. Nielsen, J. Finding usability problems through heuristic evaluation. *Proc. ACM CHI'92* (Monterey, CA, 3–7 May 1992).

13. Nielsen, J. Applying heuristic evaluation to a highly domain-specific user interface. *Manuscript submitted for publication*.

14. Nielsen, J. *Usability Engineering*. Academic Press, San Diego, CA, 1992.

15. Nielsen, J., and Molich, R. Heuristic evaluation of user interfaces. *Proc. ACM CHI'90* (Seattle, WA, 1–5 April 1990), 249–256.

16. Nielsen, J., and Richards, J.T. The experience of learning and using Smalltalk. *IEEE Software* **6**, 3 (May 1989), 73–77.

17. Nielsen, J., Frehr, I., and Nymand, H.O. The learnability of HyperCard as an object-oriented programming system. *Behaviour & Information Technology* **10**, 2 (March–April 1991), 111–120.

18. Perry, T.S., and Voelcker, J. Of mice and menus: Designing the user-friendly interface. *IEEE Spectrum* **26**, 9 (September 1989), 46–51.

19. Schön, D.A. *Educating the Reflective Practitioner: Toward a New Design for Teaching and Learning in the Professions*. Jossey-Bass Publishers, San Francisco, CA, 1987.

20. Sutherland, I.E. Sketchpad: A man–machine graphical communication system. *Proc. AFIPS Spring Joint Computer Conference 1963*, 329–346.

21. Thovtrup, H., and Nielsen, J. Assessing the usability of a user interface standard. *Proc. ACM CHI'91* (New Orleans, LA, 27 April–2 May 1991), 335–341.

22. Tognazzini, B. Achieving consistency for the Macintosh. In Nielsen, J. (Ed.), *Coordinating User Interfaces for Consistency*, Academic Press, San Diego, CA, 1989. 57–73.

23. White, E.A., Wildman, D.M., and Muller, M.J. *Practicum in Methods for User Centered Design*. Workshop at Human Factors Society 35th Annual Meeting (San Francisco CA, 1–4 September 1991).

24. Winograd, T. What can we teach about human–computer interaction. *Proc. ACM CHI'90* (Seattle, WA, 1–5 April 1990), 443–449.

Integrating Human Factors on a Large Scale: "Product Usability Champions"

Deborah Mrazek
Michael Rafeld

Hewlett-Packard Corporation
8000 Foothills Blvd.
Roseville, California 95678
(916) 785-5615
Internet: rafeld@hpcc01.hp.com

ABSTRACT

This paper describes how a software development division in a large corporate environment found a creative way to integrate human factors techniques into their development processes. It discusses the limitations of a single Human Factors Engineer, the needs of a typical engineer on a software project, and how these limitations and needs produced the *Product Usability Champion Program*.

Product Usability Champions are representatives from each software project in the division who act as usability watchdogs for their respective projects. The Human Factors Engineer's responsibility is to provide support to these Champions. This support includes access to a Usability Lab, technical advice, references, consulting, classroom training, hands-on training, Usability Champion program facilitation and support, and specific project team involvement. This paper describes the program's structure, implementation, and success.

KEYWORDS: Large-scale Human Factors, Consulting, Usability Lab, Usability Toolkit, Championing, Centralized usability resources.

OVERVIEW

In large organizations such as Hewlett-Packard, human factors engineering has traditionally been the domain of a few people, given the title of Human Factors Engineers, who primarily focus on the issues of usability and human-computer interface design [3]. These people may be full-fledged members of product design teams. In many situations, however, these few people are requested to provide input on far more than they can ever reasonably address [1,3].

On the other hand, there are people who are not Human Factors Engineers, yet have interest in the same issues: usability and human-computer interface design [5]. These people are not usually trained in human factors, but have interests in this area that may spring from different sources -- perhaps from previous experiences, or as users themselves. They may be programmers, technical writers, etc.

The inherent problem is having a single Human Factors Engineer who is stretched too far, working apart from others who are interested in usability issues. At the same time, other members of the development teams have the same interests, but are unable to act upon them. In keeping with the CHI '92 theme of "Striking A Balance," we at the HP Roseville site have arrived at a solution that strikes a balance between these two groups of people. In essence, we have attempted to integrate these two groups in such a way that both are strengthened by the joining. The concept we have developed is that of the "Product Usability Champion."

PROGRAM CONCEPTION

Recently, a division at HP in Roseville, California, reorganized and was given a new set of goals. This provided the perfect opportunity to re-think how some of the division's programs worked. One of the programs to be changed was the Human Factors Program.

The first step was to interview each senior division manager to understand their specific business needs and issues. The next step was to develop a list of Human Factors activities or resources that could support the managers' specific needs or help resolve some of their issues. This exercise generated a list of Human Factors activities so large that an army of Human Factors Engineers would have been needed to undertake them all. An army of Human Factors Engineers busily working may be a nice idea, but not very practical from a business perspective.

In reality, the division had only one Human Factors Engineer available to serve 135 people who are responsible for four different sets of products, ranging from PC applications to mainframe operating systems. A possible approach to the Human Factors Program would have been to prioritize all the usability activities and assign to the Human Factors Engineer the first handful. This is the way many divisions within HP provide Human Factors services. Unfortunately, this would have left all the other potential activities postponed or simply undone. This solution would have not begun to support the activities of each manager's specific needs. So, another approach was needed.

The key asset that the Human Factors Engineer contributes is the ability to recognize what usability-related activity is appropriate at a given time and to determine how best to implement that activity [2,7]. To do this in such a large division, however, would consume a great deal of time, requiring that the Human Factors Engineer become a product-expert in all of the products and technologies the division currently supported. Therefore, the new program would have to maximize the contributions while minimizing the effort to become an expert of each product.

The solution, then, would be to find a way to have the Human Factors Engineer strategically combine forces in a more integrated fashion with each specific design team. In other words, the teams would stay current with their own technology and products, and the Human Factors Engineer would stay current in the latest human factors techniques and work on providing usability tools that everyone could use. The Human Factors Engineer would therefore not have to become a product-expert in all the products and technologies.

The concept that arose from this proposition was that of *Product Usability Champions*. That is, at least one "usability-aware" product team member would be actively involved on each product development team. This person would be the designated team Usability Champion. When it was time for a team to use a particular usability technique, the champion would work with the Human Factors Engineer and a few members of the design team to form a multi-disciplinary task force. The representatives would then take leadership, or championing, roles on their respective projects and the Human Factors Engineer would act as their *involved consultant*, rather than a full contributing member of the product development team.

The two keys to the success of such a program would be that management are fully committed to the program and that members of each key project team were willing to become involved.

Selling The Concept

This general concept was presented to the senior division managers and their immediate staff without whose support this concept would not work. The managers needed to understand that each of their design teams would have to be more involved and responsible for their own usability-related activities.

Management was presented with data showing that, based on past divisional history and personal experience, the Human Factors Engineer could be a full contributing member of only two product design teams concurrently [2]. All other teams would have to "fend for themselves" when it came to usability-related activities. One key selling point to this new program was that one Human Factors Engineer could:

1. Support the Product Usability Champion Program.
2. Be actively involved in several product team usability activities.
3. Have representation on **all** the project teams through the team's Product Usability Champion.
4. Develop and deliver usability- related training.
5. Facilitate more sophisticated Human Factors activities as the Product Usability Champion Program matured.

Therefore, more teams could plan and perform usability activities with guidance from the Human Factors Engineer, during the appropriate phase of their lifecycle.

Management agreed to the concept of the program but had certain reservations. They wanted to control the amount of time and effort their teams invested in usability and wanted to make sure that services from the Product Usability Champions Program would satisfy their specific circumstances.

The managers and the Human Factors Engineer agreed that a Champion and his/her manager would determine the level of involvement and could alter it based on their specific needs. Also, the topics addressed through the program would be suggested by the Champions themselves, addressing the concern that each section had specific needs. The program's mission would be:

> To enable the Product Usability Champions
> to act as the usability focus for their teams,
> and for the Human Factors Engineer to
> provide the teams, through their Champions,
> with the appropriate consulting, training and
> tools for them to be successful.

Identifying The Champions

After selling the concept to management, the next step was to find Product Usability Champions on each team. In most cases, Product Managers would approach project team members to see if they had any interest in the issues of usability and human-computer interface design. If so, they were then asked if they were willing to devote some percentage of their time to representing the team in the Product Usability Champion Program, and to act as a champion for the team.

THE PROGRAM IN PRACTICE

An interesting fact, and one that makes for a stronger program, is that the Product Usability Champions are from every area of the organization. This ensures that the program addresses the needs in all areas. There are:

> Software Design Engineers (10)
> Learning Product Engineers (3)
> Quality Engineers (3)
> Support Engineers (1)
> Managers (2)

The Product Usability Champion Program is made up of many pieces. Without any one of the pieces, the program could still exist, but would not be as successful. The components of the program are:

- Management support
- The champion's energy and involvement
- Regular monthly meetings
- Regular channels of communication
- Human factors consulting by the Human Factors Engineer
- A *Usability ToolKit*
- Availability of a *Usability Resource Cube*
- Availability of a *Usability Lab*
- "Just-in-time" training for design teams

Monthly Meetings

During the monthly meetings, many topics can be covered. Some of them are calendar-dependent (e.g., a trip report from SIGCHI), while others are need-dependent (e.g., findings and experience from a usability test). Some of the sample discussion topics that have been covered during monthly meetings are:

- Trip reports from SIGCHI and SIGGRAPH
- Reports on project team usability activities
- Previews of upcoming usability classes
- Discussions of future program direction

Communication Channels

Without the right channels of communication, a program like the Product Usability Champions Program would eventually fall apart. Some of the communications methods this program has found effective are:

- E-mail from the Human Factors Engineer on upcoming activities
- Monthly meetings
- Routing of hardcopy literature
- Networking among Champions on an informal basis

The importance of this network should not be overlooked. With this network, the Champions are able to leverage experiences, review each other's work, and provide moral support.

Human Factors Engineer Consulting

The Human Factors Engineer acts as the consultant to the Champions. This may be as a reviewer, facilitator, trainer or active member of a specific usability-related task-force. The Human Factors Engineer is also responsible for acting as the division's "eyes" for new usability methods and techniques. And, in addition, the Human Factors Engineer is responsible for the care and feeding of the Product Usability Champions Program.

Usability ToolKit

This ToolKit, in the form of a set of hanging files, enables the Champions to be autonomous. It also enforces a common language and methodology when they need to get help from the Human Factors Engineer.

The ToolKit is divided into sections. One section is devoted to each major phase in the product development lifecycle. Within each section are the appropriate "tools" for that development phase. Each "tool" consists of a *Quick Start Sheet* (a high-level overview), simple instructions, examples, recommended forms, and cues as to the right time to get specific Human Factors Engineering input. Very important to the ToolKit is the Usability Map that maps high level team needs into usability activities and results (see Table 1). This map is a guide for design teams at *any* time during the development lifecycle.

Also important is the Activities Chart that compares the various usability activities to the project team's needs, experience level, resources, and stage in the product development lifecycle.

Usability Resource Cube

The Usability Resource Cube is a location (physically, an office cubical) that is the central repository for all the resources available to the Usability Champions. It is also a visible sign that usability is an important function, since it has dedicated floor space. An example of the types of material the Champions can find in this area are:

- A large (4' x 8') Usability Map in bright colors
- The Usability ToolKit
- Training references
- Various conference proceedings

	Understanding The Customer	Needs & Task Analysis	Prototype Evaluation	Iterative Testing	Alpha/Field Testing
Team Need	Design team needs to understand typical user of product	Design team needs details on how users do their work	Need to check prototype of product against user interface design principles and customer data	Need to fill gaps in customer data and optimize proposed product using prototypes	Does final product actually meet customer needs?
Possible Activities	Design team learns through: *Surveys* *Interviews* *Market research*	Design team asks users about: *Expectations from product* *Job responsibilities impacted by using the product* *Step-by-step details of their job*	Design team analyzes user interface against HP User Interface Guidelines and customer data	Design team conducts usability tests or walkthroughs with actual users: *In Usability Lab* *At customer site*	Collect user data at Alpha sites
Results	Design team gains understanding of: *Typical user* *Typical environments* *Likely scenarios*	Design team gets customer data on: *Dependencies* *Expectations* *Desired results* *Step-by-step instructions*	Design team now understands product's deviations from standards and customer data	Product specifications meshed with user expectations and user "hot spots" uncovered	Usability rating and shortcomings of final product to be used in next round of development

Table 1. Usability Map

♦ Archived usability activities from past project teams
♦ Samples of prototyping tools
♦ Reference books, pamphlets and articles
♦ A bulletin board listing upcoming activities, key articles, information about our competitors' usability activities

Usability Lab

When it is appropriate to run formal usability testing, a complete Usability Lab with an equipment operator is available. The lab consists of three hidden video cameras in a product evaluation room, a one-way mirror separating the evaluation room from the control room, and an observation/control room for the product team and equipment operator. Because there is a dedicated operator, a Usability Champion or project team is better able to focus on the product and the test results than the administrative issues involved in running a test.

"Just-in-Time" Training

Just before a team needs to do a specific usability-related activity for which they lack knowledge, the Human Factors Engineer develops and delivers team-specific training in that activity.

COMPARING THE PROGRAM TO OTHERS

It is important to understand how the Product Usability Champions Program compares to other usability programs. As stated before, within this division, the Human Factors Engineer was previously assigned to be a full contributing member to two or three product development teams. Other teams that wanted to do usability activities did so with only minor consulting from the Human Factors Engineer.

Other divisions rely only on the project teams to perform usability activities, without any formal guidance. Yet others contract consultants when they need (usually after the fact) Human Factors consulting. In any of these models there is very little cross-fertilization of usability ideas between teams. This may be because the lone Human Factors Engineer acts as the hub and filter to all usability activities or because there are no formal mechanisms to communicate these efforts.

Fisher [2] addresses the problem of resource limitations, and advocates changing the role of the Human Factors Engineer in to that of an "information provider," rather than a "user interface designer." In his model, the Human Factors Engineer's new role is focused in two areas: using well-defined methodologies to identify and verify user needs in the design process; and providing ongoing feedback throughout the development cycle regarding the appropriateness of proposed design solutions. As in our solution, this allows a lone Human Factors Engineer to be much more accessible and successful. However, the Product Usability Champions Program takes it a step further, and puts into place the mechanisms for the diverse project teams to begin building off of each others' successes, and learning from each others' failures.

CURRENT PROGRESS

Up until the time this paper was written (September, 1991), we have had positive results with this implementation. At least half of the team attends each of the monthly meetings. There is considerably more communication between the different product teams because of the communication between the Usability Champions, and the general level of awareness about usability and human-computer interface issues has been raised because of each team's exposure.

The latter aspect is probably the hardest to quantify, but is the most important achievement that has yet occurred. The more people who are aware of the successes of other applications, and of what role these issues play in product design, the better the products that will eventually be produced.

One example of success was a one day class on survey design and implementation. Twenty-five percent of the division wanted to take it, and everyone that took it found ways to apply what they learned to their job.

Drawbacks/Problems

Since this program has not been in place for that long, we have not had any significant drawbacks. We do, however, anticipate that when the schedule becomes tight many of the Usability Champions -- who are also software developers -- will no longer be able to devote much time to usability. Our approach to this would be to bring the managers back into the decision process, and remind them of their initial commitments.

Another problem is inexperience. Since the Usability Champions are not trained in all areas of the discipline, there will naturally be large areas with which they are unfamiliar. We have addressed this by making the resources described available, as well as advertising how these resources may be of service.

The biggest problem, however, is that of integrating human factors into groups where there is currently no interest. If they are not represented by a Usability Champion, they are, to an extent, outside the activity described in this paper. It has proven true in the past that decrees from above about adopting human factors usually fall on deaf ears [6]. We have tried to address this in a two ways. First, we highlight the successes of other groups in public forums such as

status meetings for the entire section. Second, we attempt to pique interest by including these groups on the distributions of usability-related materials. Only time and patience will tell us if teams with no interest will "see the usability light."

CONCLUSIONS

By understanding who the Human Factors Program's customers are, what their business needs are, and what their key tasks are, we could design a new Human Factors Program that maximizes the human factors input in product development. It's extremely important to understand how usability techniques will contribute to the division's achieving its business goals. We then apply the techniques in a responsive manner. By understanding your customers needs and tasks, you may be able to improve how you can support their usability needs.

VISION

Where will this program go? One way it might evolve is that Usability Champions begin to take on specific roles in which they specialize. For instance, one person might be particularly interested in the design and implementation of surveys which test the usability of products. With access to the resources described above, this person would first learn the basics and, at some point, may become a considered "expert" in the area. At this point, the whole would be quite a bit greater than its constituent parts. In this vision, the Human Factors Engineer now plays the role of adviser and guide, and no longer becomes the central resource for usability questions. The sum total of usability knowledge, and more, would reside with a variety of people. And, as people move on and change positions, this information would gradually be disseminated through the organization.

One final point: it is incumbent upon any attempting this program that they have management buy-in from the top. The only way it will succeed is if they are willing to devote the time of several of their people to this idea. As described above, if they are convinced of the payoffs, they should be convinced to commit the resources. Good luck.

REFERENCES

1. Fisher, W. Increasing Human Factors Effectiveness Within the Organization. In Proceedings of the Human Factors Society - 33rd Annual Meeting (Denver, Colo., October 16-20). Human Factors Society, Santa Monica, Calif., 1989, pp. 460-461.

2. Fisher, W. Increasing Human Factors Effectiveness in Product Design. In Proceedings of the Human Factors Society - 35th Annual Meeting (San Francisco, Calif., September 2-6). Human Factors Society, Santa Monica, Calif., 1991, pp. 471-475.

3. Grudin, J., and Poltrock, S.E. User interface design in large corporations: Coordination and communication across disciplines. In Proceedings CHI '89 Human Factors in Computing Systems. ACM, New York, 1981, pp. 197-203.

4. Hoffman, M. Advanced Product Development Through Market Participation. In Proceedings of the Human Factors Society - 33rd Annual Meeting (Denver, Colo., October 16-20). Human Factors Society, Santa Monica, Calif., 1989, pp. 461.

5. Norback, J. The Complete Computer Career Guide. Tab Books, Blue Ridge Summitt, Penn., 1987.

6. Thomas, J. Human Factors in IBM. In Proceedings of the Human Factors Society - 29th Annual Meeting. Human Factors Society, Santa Monica, Calif., 1985, pp. 611-614.

7. Tynan, P. Human Factors and Time-based Competition. In Proceedings of the Human Factors Society - 33rd Annual Meeting (Denver, Colo., October 16-20). Human Factors Society, Santa Monica, Calif., 1989, pp. 462-463.

OVERVIEW OF
THE INSTITUTE FOR RESEARCH ON LEARNING

William J. Clancey

Institute for Research on Learning
2550 Hanover Street, Palo Alto, CA 94304
USA
Tel. (415) 496-7925
E-mail: Bill_Clancey@irl.com

ABSTRACT
The Institute for Research on Learning (IRL) is a non-profit organization founded in 1986 in Palo Alto, California, committed to understanding what leads to successful learning in the schools, the workplace, and everyday life. A basic premise of IRL research, that people learn best when they are engaged with others, leads IRL's researchers to perceive schools and workplaces as *communities of learners* and to focus on the design of environments, technology, and activities that support learning as a collaborative activity. IRL pursues its research in collaboration with schools, universities, corporations, and government agencies—in the actual settings in which learning takes place.

KEYWORDS: Laboratory overview, learning, design processes, socio-technical systems design, participatory design, communities of practice, ethnographic analysis

MISSION AND THEMES
Understanding design processes and tools in terms of communities of learners is fruitful for inventing new kinds of social-technological interactions that respect and enhance human capabilities. Because of IRL's interdisciplinary character and views about cognition and learning, we have specific concerns about the nature of research, participation of users in design processes, and the appropriate use of computers.

Specifically, IRL engages in "action research," which depends on multidisciplinary research teams forming partnerships with people in target communities (schools and workplaces) to develop technology and organizational processes over a significant period of time. It is through this interaction that new workplace practices can evolve that embody integrated views about the nature of organizations, learning, and knowledge. For example, our design processes aim to avoid deskilling brought about by the computerization of work, to break down organizational and technological barriers to participation and coordination, and to invent new ways of mediating human interactions (e.g., by shared visual workspaces).

IRL research in the workplace attempts to reorient previous attempts to improve productivity that focused too narrowly on individual efforts and modeling only physical and technological processes (as opposed to human communication, creation of ideas, and social construction of values). A key idea is that descriptions of behaviors—in the form of procedures, grammars, or schemas—are always impoverished and potentially demeaning, relative to the dynamic processes by which people create information and construct new representations in the course of everyday, "routine" activity.

In particular, we promote ecological approaches to psychology, which are based on the idea that when people act, they are not executing schemas, rules, or procedures that they retrieve from memory, but are always constructing something new. This perspective helps us understand what is problematic for new users of computer systems. The rejection of memory-as-stored-structures leads us to view perceptual processes not as input to a cognitive processor. Rather, categorizing what we see on a computer screen is intricately tied to our work sequence. What we see and what we do arise together—during interaction—producing new, coordinated compositions of perception and action, which bias future behavior.

BRIEF HISTORY
IRL was founded by David Kearns (now Undersecretary of Education), John Seely Brown (Xerox Vice President of Research), and James G. Greeno (Professor of Education, Stanford University). The initial interests were 1) to combine cognitive and social perspectives of human learning, 2) bring educational research in Artificial Intelligence to industry application, and 3) develop a new kind of multidisciplinary research institute. Funding has been provided by foundation gifts, government agencies, and research partnerships with industry. The Executive Director of IRL is Peter Henschel, a policy specialist with extensive experience relating government, businesses, and schools.

MEMBERS

IRL researchers deliberately frame problems and projects to integrate diverse points of view. For example, we require that every project include computer and social scientists.

IRL's Principal Scientists and Their Areas of Speciality

William J. Clancey	computer science, AI, cognitive science
Penelope Eckert	sociolinguistics, ethnography
Shelley Goldman	education, anthropology
James G. Greeno	psychology, education, mathematics
Rogers Hall	computer science, mathematics
Brigitte Jordan	anthropology, interaction analysis
Charlotte Linde	linguistics, ethnography, discourse analysis
Jeremy Roschelle	computer science, education, physics
Susan Stucky	linguistics
Etienne Wenger	computer science, anthropology

KIND OF WORK

IRL's research and technology development has the following characteristics:

Research-in-Action. Our view of the research process parallels our view of learning. We do not believe that research results can simply be transferred or applied to schools or industry. IRL's projects are examples of research-in-action, of collaborative work between researchers, designers, and educators to produce immediately useful findings throughout the research process.

Real-Life Settings. IRL's researchers study learning as it takes place in real-life situations, rather than relying on conventional survey and laboratory research methods. This allows IRL researchers to analyze actual learning processes, retaining the important aspects of social interaction.

Innovative Research Methods. Studying learning in its natural settings requires new ways of doing research. We are developing methods particularly suited to dealing with the full complexity of actual learning situations. Research methods include ethnography, video-based interaction analysis, discourse analysis, participatory design, and reciprocal evolution.

Socio-Technical Systems. We develop computer programs in order to develop theories about representation creation and use, to gain experience in creating multidisciplinary collaborative teams, and to promote our point of view and methods via prototype demonstrations and tools usable in other communities. Consistent with our views about the relation between computer and human capabilities, we focus on tools that facilitate conversations for constructing information and meaning, rather than trying to automate what people do.

SAMPLES OF WORK

Envisioning Machine — physics simulation program; study of collaborative construction of meaning, role of gestures and computer simulation.

Picasso — communication technology incorporating a fax, file transfer, remote screen sharing and control; study of learnability and usability of alternative designs; study of collaboration at a distance involving multiple representations; study of design evolution in the context of use.

Videonoter — video interaction analysis tool for recording and overlaying multiple streams of data and interpretations.

MultiMediaWorks — multimedia composing tool; Apple Classroom of Tomorrow project; study of collaboration involving "repurposing" of video, pictures, and sound for student compositions.

Workplace Project — study of the ways in which people use technological, spatial, temporal, and social resources in a distributed workplace (focusing on an airlines control room). This collaboration between Xerox PARC and Steelcase (affiliated with IRL through Brigitte Jordan) has developed into a new project that will involve IRL, Steelcase designers, and their customers.

KEY PUBLICATIONS

Clancey, W. J. The frame of reference problem in the design of intelligent machines. In K. vanLehn (ed), *Architectures for Intelligence*, Lawrence Erlbaum Associates, Hillsdale, NJ, 1991.

Clancey, W. J. Situated cognition: Stepping out of representational flatland. *AI Communications*, **4**, 2/3, 107-112, 1991.

Clancey, W. J. Review of Rosenfield's *The Invention of Memory*. *Artificial Intelligence*, **50**, 2, 241-284, 1991.

Jordan, B. Cosmopolitical Obstetrics: Some Insights from the Training of Traditional Midwives. Social Science and Medicine **28**, 9, 925-944, 1989.

Jordan, B. Technology and the Social Distribution of Knowledge. In J. Coreil and D. Mull (eds), *Anthropology and Primary Health Care*. Westview Press, Boulder, 1990, pp. 98-120.

Linde, C. What's next? The social and technological management of meetings. *Pragmatics*, **1**, 297-318, 1991.

Suchman, L. and Jordan, B. Interactional Troubles in Face-to-Face Survey Research (Review paper). *J Amer Stat Assoc* **85**, 409, 232-241, 1990.

Wenger, E. 1990. *Toward a theory of cultural transparency: Elements of a social discourse of the visible and the invisible*. PhD Dissertation in Information and Computer Science, University of California, Irvine.

CHI in Australia

S.Howard[1], I.Kaplan[2] and G.Lindgaard[3]

[1]HCI Group, Centre for Systems Methodologies, Department of Computer Science, Swinburne Institute of Technology, PO Box 218. Victoria 3122. Australia. Phone: (03) 819 8566, e-mail: steve@saturn.cs.swin.oz.au

[2]Australian Centre for Unisys Software, 115 Wicks Road, North Ryde, NSW 2113, Australia. Phone: (02) 390 1382, e-mail: ilana@syacus.acus.oz.au

[3]Human Factors Research Team, Telecom Australia Research Laboratories, Clayton, Victoria, Australia. Phone: (03) 541 6806, e-mail: g.lindgaard@trl.oz.au.

Introduction

CHISIG (Computer Human Interaction Special Interest Group) is the professional organisation for CHI research and practice in Australia. Formed December 1983, it's membership has grown from twelve to over 250 practitioners and researchers from industry, government and academia. CHISIG aims primarily to facilitate high quality basic and applied CHI research in Australia. CHISIG's activities include the publication of a bi-monthly newsletter, and the holding of both regular seminars and an annual conference (see references), usually early in the Australian summer. Although there are many pockets of CHI research activity throughout Australia, some representative centres are discussed below.

Representative Centres *(listed alphabetically)*

Aeronautical Research Laboratory Formed 1980, the Human Factors Group within the Aeronautical Research Laboratory aims to conduct research into aircrew performance and exploit behavioural variables for improving aircrew-avionics capability; to examine the technologies of information display and systems control and devise methods for integrating them into aircrew jobs, and; to develop a comprehensive aircrew human engineering design and evaluation technology. Projects include the analysis of operator workload in tasks involving the control of complex aircraft; prototyping of displays for tactical aircraft; task analysis for helicopter operatives; the development of techniques for the evaluation of aircrew workload, and; an analysis of the problems associated with vision and visual aids in night air operations. Facilities include a vision laboratory; eye and head movement monitoring equipment; auditory and noise monitoring equipment, and; AutoCAD, Design IDEF and Micro-SAINT software. The major participants are Jeremy Manton, Jane Miller and P.Hughes.

Australian Centre for Unisys Software A Human factors consulting service was established at the Australian Centre for Unisys Software (ACUS) in 1989. The Human Factors consultant is responsible for ensuring the quality of the human-computer interfaces developed. ACUS projects range from developing system software to developing application development tools. Human Factors input to the projects include screen design; task and user needs analysis; developing style guides, and; usability testing. Human Factors seminars are also also developed and presented in-house. The major participant is Ilana Kaplan.

Bond University, Bond Research Into User Interface Technologies (BRUIT) Established in 1989, BRUIT carries out research on the design and construction of user interfaces for electronic communications and access to on-line information. Interfaces are being constructed, using Macintosh and X Windows models, in domains as varied as electronic mail; bulletin boards; electronic brochures; other group-ware applications, and; personal and distributed information systems. Major projects to date include a variety of Macintosh interfaces to Unix and X400 mail; electronic mail systems for teaching; post-processing of bulletin board messages; hypertext interfaces to the Smith and Mosier interface guide-lines, and; an on-line information system for the main University library. Major participants include Michael Rees, Renato Iannella and several postgraduate research students.

BHP: Information Technology Research Group The Information Technology Research Group within BHP is concerned with developing AI based solutions to internal customers (in steel, minerals and petroleum areas) as well as servicing external customers. It is focussed mainly in the domains of operator guidance systems; integrated scheduling and flexible manufacturing systems, and; process control systems. Some example systems development projects are a risk management system for BHP Petroleum; continuous caster scheduling at BHP Long Products Division, and; an operator guidance system for blast furnace heat and mass balance process control at BHP Rod and Bar Products Division. HCI issues being tackled include the integration of usability engineering methodologies with knowledge based systems development methodologies; integration of HCI methodologies with conventional systems development methodologies, and; the use and development of graphical user interfaces. The major participants are Laurie Lock Lee, Kee Teh, Steve Garlick and Jukka Rantanen.

Curtin University of Technology, Schools of Psychology and Information Systems Within the Schools of Psychology and Information Systems a number of CHI projects are actively being pursued. The focus of the major research effort is Decision Support Systems. Example projects include the comparison of the relative workload of participants, facilitators and technical support staff in group meetings conducted either with Group Decision Support Systems or with manual support; the comparison of two modes of representing information in strategic problem solving, and; the comparison of linear and matrix representation techniques for decision making. Additional projects are being conducted in the general area of Hypertext technology and its use in student information systems. The major participants are Clare Pollock and Jenny Christmas (Psychology); Peter Marshall, Heinz Dreher, Des Klass, Doug Atkinson and Thomas Sui (Information Systems); and Floyd Lewis (Western Washington University, USA).

Swinburne Institute of Technology, Centre for Systems Methodologies, HCI Group The HCI Group within the Centre for Systems Methodologies at Swinburne Institute of Technology aims to develop and teach undergraduate and graduate level courses in HCI, and perform basic and applied research in the areas of user interface design and modelling the HCI process, particularly with respect to large scale real world systems development. Projects include modelling user interface design in software engineering; user modelling in computer assisted instruction and graphical user interfaces, and; the development of notations and methodologies to support the prototyping of interactive technology. The groups facilities include a suit of UIMS's running on Macintosh, Sun, Hewlett Packard and IBM hardware; various Computer Aided Software Engineering tools, and; a usability laboratory. The major participants are Steve Howard, Ying Leung, Liz Chang, Kon Mouzakis and Ray Anderson, plus a number of post-graduate research students working in the above general project areas. The group has significant links with industry and academia within Australia and overseas.

Telecom Research Laboratories, Human Factors Research Team The Human Factors Research Team of Telecom Australia Research Laboratories comprises three experimental psychologists. Projects include basic research requiring rigorous experimental design and analysis; usability evaluation of existing Telecom systems; human factors support to the design of new products and systems, and; projects involving the design and testing of user documentation. Applications include video-conferencing; screen format design; help systems; auditory prompts for an automatic calling card service; user documentation for various Telecom products, and; interface work on database systems. The team is also involved in writing guide-lines for screen design,

usability testing, user needs analysis, graphical user interfaces and documentation. The major participants are Gitte Lindgaard, Josephine Chessari and Elizabeth Bednall.

University of Canberra, Faculty of Information Sciences and Engineering, HCI Centre Established in 1990, the HCI Centre at the University of Canberra aims to develop courses, teach and perform applied research in the areas of user interface design and usability testing, particularly with reference to computer based systems design for the public sector. Projects include the teaching and evaluation of the design process; usability testing as part of the systems development process, and; the usability engineering of knowledge based systems. The groups facilities include a usability laboratory; a purpose designed meeting/design room; computer laboratory; access to workstations; DEMO prototyping software; portable video cameras, and; UIMS software. The major participants are Penny Collings, Paul Buckley, Renuka Fernandez and Jan Newmarch.

University of New South Wales, School of Computer Science, Visualisation Laboratory Established in 1990, the laboratory provides sophisticated graphics hardware for the CHI research group of the School. The groups interests include the testing of software, in particular of graphics systems. Logging and sophisticated play-back facilities are being developed for use in psychological testing and language assessment. Facilities include Silicon Graphics workstations (of both the IRIS and POWERSERIES range) and ALIAS software packages. The major participants are John Hiller and John Nicholls.

West-Pac, Usability Group Established October 1989, the usability group aim to improve the usability of WestPac's internal product development (hardware, software, documentation, forms, procedures etc), and; provide general human factors consulting and facilities to improve product quality. Activities to date include usability testing; prototyping, and; market research. Facilities include a custom built usability laboratory and supporting facilities (video network, editing suit, one-way mirror); IBM PS/2's; LAN network etc. The major participant is Brendan McManus.

References

HCI Australia '89. Proceedings of the Annual CHISIG Conference, 23-24 November 1989, Monash University/Telecom Australia Research Laboratories, Melbourne, Australia.
Exploring HCI: into the '90s. Proceedings of the Annual CHISIG Conference, 29-30 November 1990, Telecom Australia Research Laboratories, Melbourne, Australia.
People before Technology. Proceedings of the Annual CHISIG Conference, 27-29 November 1991. University of New South Wales, Sydney, Australia.
Your Word Is My Command: towards an Australian capability in human-computer interface design. Australian Science and Technology Council. ISBN 0 644 12571 3.

THE INSTITUTE FOR PERCEPTION RESEARCH IPO, A JOINT VENTURE OF PHILIPS ELECTRONICS AND EINDHOVEN UNIVERSITY OF TECHNOLOGY

F.L. van Nes, H. Bouma and M.D. Brouwer-Janse

Institute for Perception Research/IPO
PO Box 513
5600 MB Eindhoven, The Netherlands
Tel.: 31 (0)40 773873, Fax: 31 (0)40 773876
E-mail: secr@heiipo5.bitnet

ORGANIZATION

The Institute for Perception Research, in Dutch abbreviated to IPO, is the result of a unique partnership between industry and government. Philips Research Laboratories Eindhoven and Eindhoven University of Technology have collaborated closely, on a 50/50 basis, in this joint venture since IPO's foundation in 1957, 35 years ago. The University provides accommodation at its premises, and Philips provides all the necessary equipment and computers for doing research. This has created an excellent technological research environment. IPO is structured in a matrix organization, consisting of three basic research groups or disciplines: Hearing & Speech; Vision; Cognition and Communication, and two applied research or project groups: Information Ergonomics and Communication Resources for handicapped users. IPO recently founded a graduate school, 'Perception and Technology'. It is located in the Institute and conducts a Ph.D. program in English to facilitate international participation, both by students and teachers, who may be visiting research fellows. Collaboration is actively sought for interdisciplinary research in areas outside IPO's basic strengths, thus widening scope and impact beyond the core areas of IPO research. European research projects in which IPO is involved include the ESPRIT project Polyglot, which is concerned with speech recognition and synthesis, the TIDE project 'Visa', which deals with universal access to WIMP software for partially sighted and blind users, and the EUREKA project on high-definition television.

MISSION

IPO's research focuses on human information processing in multimodal interaction with hardware and software. Thus, communication between users and systems constitutes the heart of IPO's research program. The 'systems' may consist of professional or consumer products. The leading requirement for their design should be their aptness for human usage, i.e., how well their design fits in with the relevant user faculties in the domains of perception and cognition. This statement leads to the threefold mission of IPO: First, the study of those user faculties in relation to controlling and using equipment. Secondly, transfer of the insights gained to the product design and development departments of the Philips company; in fact there is a two-way stream of sought and found information in this respect. Thirdly, in relation to the university world IPO's educational mission is to teach both undergraduate and graduate courses related to the research activities. Moreover, many students take part in research projects as part of their Master's or Ph.D. curriculum.

STAFF

The interdisciplinary nature of IPO research calls for a multidisciplinary staff, presently counting about 80 psychologists, linguists, ergonomists, physicists, engineers and industrial designers. The members of the senior research staff include:

Director: Herman Bouma
Speech analysis and synthesis: René Collier, Berry Eggen, Leo Vogten
Psychoacoustics: Adriaan Houtsma, Dik Hermes, Armin Kohlrausch
Vision, image quality, and image coding: Jacques Roufs, Jean-Bernard Martens, Joyce Westerink
Cognition and communication: Don Bouwhuis, Robbert-Jan Beun, Kees van Deemter
Information Ergonomics: Floris van Nes, Maddy Brouwer-Janse, Reinder Haakma
Communication resources: Henny Mélotte, Han Neve.

The Institute has an active program of international research fellowships.

WORK STYLE

In terms of technological facilities there are few limitations now in designing systems that are in principle functional. Making such systems usable, however, and preventing their functionality from remaining hidden often overtaxes our understanding of human information processing, the very basis for this usability. Therefore, long term in-depth research into all relevant areas and phases of human information processing forms the mainstay of IPO. The aim of the research is to develop and broaden theories, often taking the form of a model. This strategic work is primarily done in the three basic research groups. The two project groups do application-oriented research, which is based on the strategic work and contributes in the short term to industrial innovation and needs of the community at large. The majority of the work in the laboratory is done in small multidisciplinary teams, as the nature of the problem tackled requires. Software engineers assist the teams in performing experiments, in analysing the results and in building prototypes. Among the Institute's assets are a well-equipped mechanical and electrical workshop. Publications, patents, and prototypes of products are the major output of IPO. Most of the research is published in professional journals. In addition, the IPO Annual Progress Report publishes about fifteen freely available research papers each year.

RESEARCH THEMES

User Interfaces and Human Factors

Both generic and specific aspects of user interfaces are studied. As a 'generic' example, questions about the strengths and weaknesses of speech as an input or output medium led to the building of a speech interface prototype, both for research and demonstration purposes. A 'specific' example is the design and testing of dot matrix characters for Teletext, displayed on regular TV sets, with legibility therefore of critical importance. The 'IPO Normal' character set is now applied in TVs of most brands as a standard. A human factors-oriented result of IPO research was applied in the design of the Dutch highway emergency phone system. Current innovative projects are concerned with user interfaces for consumer products such as high-end TV sets, remote controls, compact disk-interactive (CD-I), mobile telephones, and for professional products such as medical equipment and analytical instrumentation. In all these projects evaluation, for instance with the co-discovery method, and testing by representative users play an important role. Several special interfaces and products are made and evaluated for people with handicaps such as low visual acuity or impaired speech. Recently our attention has also been directed towards the elderly without special impairments; an increasingly important user group.

Cognitive Functions and Speech

One subtheme within this theme is the study of cognitive functions of hearing and vision. Examples are speech perception, including such prosodic features as timing and intonation; visual search processes; and reading, as such and on various types of display. Speech synthesis is used both as a research tool, to enable the investigation of individual parameters, and for making high-quality text-to-speech systems, hitherto for Dutch, English and German. Another sub-

theme concerns cognitive functions that are not necessarily coupled to the senses, for example, human communicative dialogues, related to applications such as man-machine dialogues in natural language (including speech); and interactive learning, applied in educational computer systems. In addition, human attention is studied (also as a function of age) - the results being applicable to multi-media systems.

Perceptual Functions and Psychophysics

In this theme the information exchange between human and machine at the physical level is studied, be it between visual display and eye, loudspeaker and ear, fingers and keyboard or voice and microphone. The IPO research program starts here, in the psychophysical domain, studying such basic functions as perception of pitch and timbre in the auditory system or spatio-temporal luminance transfer in the visual system. On the basis of these fundamental insights, the assessment of sound quality and image quality is addressed, for instance in the European High Definition TV project and in music coding, as used for the Digital Compact Cassette recorder.

REFERENCES

1. Elsendoorn, B.A.G., and Bouma, H. *Working Models of Human Perception*. Academic Press, London, 1989.
2. Hart, J. 't, Collier, R., and Cohen, A. *A Perceptual Study of Intonation. An Experimental-Phonetic Approach to Speech Melody*. Cambridge University Press, Cambridge, 1990.
3. Taylor, M.M., Néel, F., and Bouwhuis, D.G. *The Structure of Multimodal Dialogue*. North Holland Publishers, Amsterdam, 1989.
4. Nes, F.L. van. Visual Ergonomics of Displays, in *The Man-Machine Interface*. J.R. Cronly-Dillon and J.A.J. Roufs, Eds., MacMillan Press, London, 1991, 15, pp. 70-82.
5. Houtsma, A.J.M. and Fleuren, J.F.M. Analytic and synthetic pitch of two-tone complexes, in J. of the Acoustical Society of America, 90, 3 (1991), 1674-1676.
6. Hemert, J.P. van. Automatic segmentation of speech, in IEEE Transactions on Signal Processing, 39, 4 (1991), 1008-1012.
7. Bouwhuis, D.G. and Collier, R.P.G. SPICOS: A cooperative natural-language dialogue system, in Philips Research Bulletin on Systems & Software, 2 (1990), 13-16.
8. Blommaert, F.J.J. and Martens, J.B.O.S. An object-oriented model for brightness perception, in Spatial Vision, 5, 1 (1990) 15-41.
9. Deemter, C.J. van. Forward references in natural language, in J. of Semantics, 7 (1990) 281-300.
10. Westerink, J.H.D.M., and Roufs, J.A.J. Subjective image quality as a function of viewing distance, resolution, and picture size, in SMPTE Journal (1989), 113-119. (This paper won the Journal Award of the Society of Motion Picture and Television Engineers).

In Search Of The Ideal Prototype

Moderator: Richard Muñoz
                        Oberon Software, Inc.
                        One Memorial Drive
                        Cambridge, MA 02142 USA
                        (617) 494-0990
                        munoz@oberon.com

Panelists: Harold H. Miller-Jacobs, TASC
                        Jared M. Spool, User Interface Engineering
                        Bill Verplank, IDEO

ABSTRACT

Common wisdom states rapid prototyping will result in a better product. Many tools are available to assist the practitioner in producing prototypes. Yet, few indications exist to show rapid prototyping has substantially improved how products are built.

This panel will look at the following issues:

Can rapid prototyping dramatically improve product development?

How do developers integrate rapid prototyping into their existing development process?

Are high fidelity tools helpful or do they actually impede development?

What is the *ideal prototype* and how can we build it?

KEYWORDS

prototyping, design, software development, product development, user interface design, process management, programming tools, participatory design, design process

SPEAKERS

Richard Muñoz has been practicing diplomacy between system developers, UI designers, and advanced development tools for several years. Currently, Rick is senior software engineer for Oberon Software in Cambridge, MA. Oberon is developing an integrated object-oriented visual programming environment, which will allow for seamless software development from prototype to application.

Harold H. Miller-Jacobs has been advocating and using rapid prototyping tools for system definition and development at TASC in Reading, MA. He also teaches at Tufts University, and tries to maintain a listing of the constantly changing and emerging tools for rapid prototyping.

Jared M. Spool is a founding principal at User Interface Engineering, a product design firm in Andover, MA. Jared works closely with developers to help them visualize their products early in the development cycle. He has spent the last few years experimenting with many different techniques for making prototypes more effective.

Since 1986, **Bill Verplank** has been with IDEO in San Francisco (formerly ID TWO) as a product design consultant. He was at Xerox from '78-'86 working on the Star user interface. From 1960-'78, he was at Stanford and MIT in product design and man-machine systems. Bill has taught a tutorial in *Graphical Invention* at CHI conferences for the last several years.

POSITION STATEMENTS

Richard Muñoz

Are prototyping tools really useful? If based on the demand for and the introduction of new prototyping tools, the answer is obviously yes. However, prototyping tools are only useful when used correctly as part of a complete design process. After several years of both using and developing prototyping tools, I have found that many such tools have little impact on the usability of a product, and can even be detrimental to the design process.

My challenge to the panelists and to the audience is to discover why certain prototyping tools fail and what makes other prototyping tools and methodologies succeed.

High Fidelity Tools: With the popularity of "Graphical User Interfaces," many prototyping tools are now available that allow interactive construction of user interface components, such as dialog boxes, buttons, and other interactive objects. Often the products of these tools compares with documents at the onset of the "desktop publishing revolution;" the tools allowed bad designs to be developed more quickly. These tools are mistakenly used as the main interface design tools, often concentrating on details (e.g. "what order should the menu items be in?") before a good understanding of the user's needs is acquired[1]. Also, few (if any) of these tools allow for the prototyping of user data visualization and interaction; most provide for the design of administrative UI features, such as controls and windows.

Low Fidelity Tools: Many CHI researchers have determined the usefulness of "low fidelity" prototyping tools and techniques [2,3]. Unfortunately, these tools are isolated from the rest of the design process. There are no interactive prototyping tools that allow the easy integration of design knowledge acquired using "low fidelity" techniques. Also, low fidelity tools are more susceptible to organization problems, such as management whim. At one company, early UI design involved paper "mock-ups", which got a fair amount of user review. Later, several flaws became apparent with the original mock-up design; nevertheless, management insisted that the mock-ups be followed exactly. Had the developers evolved and used the prototyping technique during the product implementation stage, perhaps this problem would have been avoided.

Functional Core vs. the UI "Component" of an Application: Often prototyping efforts concentrate only on the UI aspects of a software product. In many cases, the UI is designed and implemented separately from the "functional core" of an application. However, usability is determined by the whole functional process, not just the "look and feel" of the UI. Prototyping tools would be more useful if they allowed prototyping of the functional parts along with the UI.

By combining and integrating several prototyping techniques, development tools, and design methodologies, prototype tools could eventually become powerful enough to provide prototyping capabilities for the entire product design and development process, incorporating the best of both low fidelity an high fidelity prototyping tools.

I'd like to conclude my position with a quote from Tufte[4] that strikes some interesting points:

"User interfaces must be designed *on the screen* rather than on paper. The only way to see how elements interact is to see them interact. How else can we make wise decisions about the complexities of color, layout, icons, typography, windowing, interaction dynamics, and design integrity. *It is simply not possible to design a competitive user interface these days without powerful prototyping tools right from the start.* During the development process, screen-capture tools are essential, for design analysis and for communication among various

developers. Specifications should be given by example, by detailed illustration, not by words alone.

"User interface design decisions cannot be made one-at-a-time. Local optimization of design will never yield satisfactory global outcomes; perfecting may little separate pieces and then putting them all together will produce cluttered and fussy screens. For example, when every function on the user interface receives special visual emphasis, then *nothing* at all has gained emphasis - only visual noise has increased, as stronger and stronger elements compete with each other."

One of my questions to the panelist is thus: Is Tufte correct? Is his description of high fidelity prototyping the only way to succeed in producing the ideal prototype?

As an industry, we are still discovering what role prototyping plays in the design of user interfaces and entire products. By expanding our notion of what prototyping tools are, we are more likely to succeed in using them to build usable products.

Hal Miller-Jacobs

So, You Thought Hi-Fi Went Out In The Fifties? Rapid prototyping as a system development tool has just come of age. Few will argue that its just this year's yuppie status symbol, embellished with much techno-hype. The technique continues to impact the system development community, and may even be effecting the authors of governmental specifications. Rumor has it that there may be some concessions to rapid prototyping in future system development specs.

Of the many issues that are being debated these days amongst users and advocates of rapid prototyping, is the "fidelity" of the prototype. I will argue that the closer the prototype looks to the target system, the more beneficial the prototype will be; that is to say, the higher the fidelity the greater the value!

The whole purpose of have a prototype in the first place is to get a glimpse at the ultimate system. The closer the prototype is to the actual system the better the "glimpse." Less pretending and apologizing is needed when explaining the system. The primary purpose of the prototype - namely to identify the functions of the system - is best portrayed when the functions can be clearly symbolized. High fidelity prototypes provide the necessary context and visualization.

One of the major advantages of a high fidelity prototype is that user interactivity can be incorporated. That is, users can implement some of the functions and observe a response, albeit canned. What kind of response can you get from a paper mock-up or a MacDraw screen?

High fidelity prototypes do not necessarily mean more time or effort to generate. Some very high fidelity prototyping tools are as simple as a drawing editor. There is however a direct relationship with cost; the higher the fidelity - the higher the cost of the tool.

As a general rule, I would argue that one should use the highest fidelity tool available for any prototype.

Jared M. Spool

I believe that the problem isn't rooted in the prototyping tools themselves, but in the process in which they are employed. To see this, we first must look at the goals of the product developer.

The ideal goal is to produce a product that meets the user's needs. Reality adds the constraint that you have to ship the product before your money runs out. So the developer is constantly looking for new ways to produce the product faster and cheaper.

I propose that a prototype is effective when it allows the viewer to give pertinent and productive feedback back to the developer. That information is used to update the design of the product.

The sooner information is delivered to the developer, the sooner it gets it into the product. Since changes to the design cost increase by an order of magnitude with every development phase, this argues that you want as much information up front as possible.

This says that for prototyping to have a dramatic impact on the development process, it has to provide information in the earliest stages of development. These are the stages where requirements and basic functional understanding is only just beginning to crystalize.

Also, we can deduce that for prototyping to be effective at this stage, it has to collect massive amounts of pertinent and productive feedback from those who view it.

Unfortunately, most of the tools that are commercially available to developers require that a complete functional description of the program be available. Also, these tools do a very poor job of illustrating the user's perspective of how the product will be used. For example, most tools do not let you put any data in the various dialogs. This is like having a story with all of the nouns removed. You can see the structure of the plot, but you have no idea what is happening.

Low fidelity prototyping techniques can be employed to give quality feedback during these early stages of development. These techniques can demonstrate the flow of information through the product along with how the user will interact with it. It is the case where the 80/20 rule applies: you can get at least 80% of the benefit of prototyping with just 20% of the effort required with high fidelity prototypes. I recommend that developers avoid us-

ing a computer to prototype until they absolutely can't avoid it!

During this panel, I plan to present techniques and tools that developers are using to dramatically reduce the time and money that it takes to ship a product. I will address requirements for future prototyping tools to make them more effective in the development process.

Bill Verplank

Having worked now six years for an industrial designer I will compare and contrast user-interface design with the range of prototypes conventionally used in product design:

idea sketches are 'prototypes'
I suggest that "prototyping" is externalizing and making concrete a design idea for the purpose of evaluation. We could all benefit from being better idea sketchers. This should happen very early in the design process. I will bring examples of sketch scenarios and story-boards that served as early rapid "prototypes".

on the screen vs. on paper
Tufte[4] exaggerates in saying that interfaces should be designed "on the screen rather than on paper." Maybe eventually. Now there are surprises: paint programs are sometimes more effective than any "working" prototypes and traps.

alternatives vs. iteration
User interfaces are too often crafted thru endless iteration instead of designed as competing alternatives. With a computer it is sometimes difficult to see very many alternatives side-by-side.

standard elements vs. graphic representations
I agree that the current interest in window headers, scrollbars, and dialog box standards has distracted from the tough job on designing good graphic representations for direct manipulation.

Bibliography
[1] SPOOL, J.; Five Usability Tests You Can Do Today; *Eye For Design;* July 1991, V2 N4.

[2] MOUNTFORD, S. J.; Designers: Meet Your Users; *CHI '90 Proceedings;* Addison-Wessley, Reading MA

[3] MULLER, M.; PICTIVE - An Exploration In Participatory Design; *CHI '91 Proceedings;* Addison-Wessley, Reading MA

[4] TUFTE, E.; Visual Design Of The User Interface, *IBM Design Program;* IBM, Armonk NY; 1989

THE RAPPORT MULTIMEDIA COMMUNICATION SYSTEM (DEMONSTRATION)

J. R. Ensor   S. R. Ahuja   R. B. Connaghan   M. Pack   D. D. Seligmann

S. R. Ahuja
Room 4F 601
AT&T Bell Laboratories
Holmdel, NJ 07733-3030
(908) 949 5569   sra@vax135.att.com

The Rapport multimedia communication system [Ah 88] allows people to hold long-distance discussions, sharing voice, video, and program displays in real-time. Rapport manages these meetings by coordinating the multiple communication streams among the participants. People can take part in a Rapport meeting using a range of devices, from simple telephones to workstations equipped with specialized peripherals. Conventional telephone calls are managed as voice-only meetings. Meeting participants with appropriate monitors can see each other through video feeds and share displays of other video-based information. Rapport also allows meeting participants to see common program displays on their computer monitors.

Rapport uses the telephone as the primary framework for conducting meetings. The Rapport user controls overall meeting operations with a computer screen-based interface resembling a phone and/or a conventional telephone attached to a computer. Meetings are initiated by dialing a person's telephone number or specifying the name of a person to be called. If used with appropriate ISDN telephones, Rapport allows the user to add and drop members to and from meetings. These phones also permit the user to be a member of several meetings concurrently, entering and leaving meetings by switching among call appearances. Meetings can be started as multimedia calls and voice-only meetings can grow to include information sharing in additional media.

Rapport users with video display devices can see each other via "talking heads" video exchange. This use of video is especially useful for participants who are not well acquainted with each other or for meetings that involve negotiations. Common, shared video streams can also be displayed during Rapport meetings. In this case, video is often used as a medium for display of information that exists apart from any participant, much like the display of program data through drawings and still images.

Existing, user-level computer programs that use a specific window system for their input and output requests may be associated with a Rapport meeting to produce common displays on participants' computer screens. Each meeting participant running the window system is able to provide input to and see output from these programs, which are termed *application programs*. Other systems support shared displays for meeting participants. Some systems, *e.g.* [La 86] and [Wa 90], replicate user input to programs executing on each participant's computer to create shared displays (multi-site mode); while other systems, *e.g.* [Pa 89], send output from a program to each participant's computer to create shared displays (single-site mode). Rapport is apparently unique in its ability to execute application programs in either single- or multi-site mode [Ah 90].

Rapport helps its users participate in meetings without leaving their offices, *i.e.*, meet "virtually." Thus, we say that Rapport is a manager of *virtual meeting rooms*. A meeting (or call) is a period of user interaction within some virtual meeting room. Like Michelitsch [Mi 90], we find that the virtual meeting room serves as the foundation for both synchronous and asynchronous communications. In particular, the meeting room provides a means for delivering active messages. For example, a person might start an application and leave it in a particular state as a message for another person. Thus, the virtual meeting room has served well as a general metaphor for both multi-media communications and environments supporting long-term collaborations.

Because Rapport meeting participants may exchange information through voice, video, and data, we have had the opportunity to observe how different media are used during conferences. Voice is a readily-used medium for information exchange, as participants talk to each other; and it is also used as the primary medium for exchanging the inter-personal signals used to conduct conferences. In fact, we feel that real-time conferences cannot be easily conducted without voice. Video is a useful medium for meetings which involve negotiation, where conferees find value in seeing each other. However, we do not often conduct such meetings in our laboratory. Thus, our use of video in conferences has been biased towards "live" demonstration of procedure or technique. That is, we have used video primarily to show how something is done or how some object looks. Data sharing in Rapport is accomplished by giving conferees the opportunity to interact in real-time with their existing, commonly used computer programs. These programs have been a major source of information for conference participants, and this medium has served as the basis for Rapport's extensions to video teleconferencing.

REFERENCES.

[Ah 88]   Ahuja, S. R., Ensor, J. R., and Horn, D. N. The Rapport Multimedia Conferencing System. Proc. Conf. on Office Information Systems, Palo Alto, March 1988, pp. 1-8.

[Ah 90]   Ahuja, S. R., Ensor, J. R., and Lucco, S. E. A Comparison of Application Sharing Mechanisms in Real-Time Desktop Conferencing Systems. Proc. Conf. on Office Information Systems, Cambridge MA, April 1990, pp. 238-248.

[La 86]   Lantz, K. A. An Experiment in Integrated Multimedia Conferencing. Proc. Conf. on Computer-Supported Cooperative Work, Austin, December 1986, pp. 267-275.

[Mi 90]   Michelitsch, G. A New Metaphor for Multimedia Desktop Conferencing Systems. Proc. IEEE Multimedia '90, Bordeaux, November 1990.

[Pa 89]   Patterson, J. F. The Good, the Bad, and the Ugly of Window Sharing in X. Proc. 4th Annual X Technical Conf, Cambridge MA, January 1990.

[Wa 90]   Watabe, K., Sakata, S., Maeno, K., Fukuoka, H., and Ohmori, T. Distributed Multiparty Desktop Conferencing System: MERMAID. Proc Conf. on Computer-Supported Cooperative Work, Los Angeles, October 1990, pp.27-38.

YAPO: YET ANOTHER PREVIEW ODA

M.A. Apollonio, G. Colasante, P.G. De Luca, A. Diana, A. Gisotti

R & D Division, Multimedia Group, Tecnopolis Csata Novus Ortus, 70010 Valenzano, Bari/Italy

Phone: (39) - 80 - 8770.237
E-Mail:
gisotti@VM.CSATA.IT(BITNET),
apollo@VM.CSATA.IT(BITNET),
apollo@osi1.csata.it(INTERNET)

ABSTRACT

The production of documents aimed at supporting the flow of information in an office enviroment is experiencing an evolution based on the most advanced automation systems which concerns substantially four aspects :

1. the production of manipulable documents showing a high quality of representation;
2. the production of documents that can be integrated (or exported) with other workstation formats on the basis of varying approaches (for istance the ISO standards);
3. the production of processable documents for storage or subsequent post-production;
4. the production of immaterial documents, i.e. documents that do not necessarily need a visual medium (paper, screen) rapresentation for their informative content.

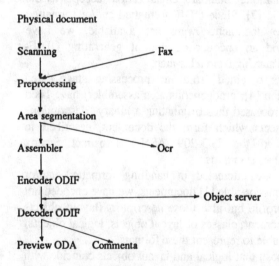

Fig.1 The Document Processing System

In this demo we describe the implementation of a ENCODER/DECODER ODIF , that is a part of a document processing system for the office environment [2]. An automated entry system for printed documents has to trasform documents on paper into a ODIF (Open Document Interchange Format) conforming rapresentation to allow further processing by other tools. In order to achieve this goal the document scanned in pages has to pass through numerous processes (scanning, preprocessing, encoder ODIF, decoder ODIF, preview ODA) [3][5]. For all tools of this work, a common user interface has been developed using the bit-mapped high resolution screen, the mouse and the window system of the SUN 3/80 workstation.

This project(*) is based on the awareness of the crucial role that the office automation market plays today and of the prospect of a rapid growth in the near future. The central idea of the project is an ODA integrated workstation which implies the integration of advanced office automation services associated with the modern concept of dynamic document. The workstation, to be implemented in a UNIX environment, will support the ODA (Open Document Architecture) format ISO 8613/1989 and future extensions.

ENCODER/DECODER ODIF

As to the four requirements mentioned above, difficulties have been encountered in handling and interchanging multi-media documents and it has been necessary to produce the documents using the ODA architecture which ISO (International Standard Organization) accepts as the standard one [7]. Since ODIF formatted and/or formatted processable documents were not available, we have implemented an encoder capable of generating ODIF-documents starting from a bit-map.

The values obtained from the processing stage (area segmentation [4], omogeneous area assembler) have been properly processed thus originating a binary "description" of the objects which form the document, described in according to the ISO-209 ASN-1 (Abstract Synatx Notation One) standards.

Since we are interested in handling formatted and/or formatted processable [1] documents, we have encoded not only the profile but also those descriptors (layout objects and their content, classes of layout objects, logical objects) which are able to represent these formats.

Here we posit that logical and layout objects coincide with a view to integrate them interactively in a subsequent stage. The ODIF document obtained can be analyzed in all its components using the decoder. A "pulverizer" tool operates between the ODIF stream and the decoder; it singles out the individual descriptive components of the ODIF document and transmits each of them separately to the decoder. Data are then processed appropriately, depending on the application (Commenta, Preview).

To implement the encoder/decoder ODIF, the ASN-1 notation of the ODA architecture has been used which is contained in parts 5, 6 and 7 of ISO 8613/1989.

(*) Project granted by C.N.R. (National Council of Research) and AGENSUD (South Development Ministry).

To input this description to the ISODE (ISO Development Environment) tool, which is the compiler of the ASN-1 notation, provides the C procedures which contain the body of the implemented encoder/decoder.

Commenta is useful from a tutorial viewpoint, since it allows to associate the informative content of each single descriptor to its ASN-1 notation.

Preview, which has been implemented in accordance with the directions of the User Interface, permits to collect information on the layout of each ODA object (pages, frames, blocks) to be subsequently processed by the User Interface (display). For each page of the document a set of information will be available for the representation of its layout.

DISPLAYING THE ODIF DOCUMENT

To construct and display in What You See Is What You Get mode (WYSIWYG) an ODIF document requires an environment which allows to integrate and display different medias.

As to Preview, we have used the high graphic quality and high resolution bit-mapped displays of SUN workstations as well as the power of the X Window System. In the first release of prototype, the User Interface of ODA Preview has been implemented using ATK, an object-oriented toolkit which is part of the ANDREW System [6], and the ADEW (Andrew Development Environment Workbench), a System Management User Interface which facilitates considerably the creation of graphic user interfaces. It should be pointed out, however, that the Andrew Toolkit will no longer be used in the following versions of the prototype; in fact, is already working the second release implemented using the OSF/MOTIF user interface system, which is viewed as the most widespread Graphic User Interface for X Window System.

The user interface of the ODA Preview has been implemented following some basic principles:

- display of the document in WYSIWYG;
- a rapid interaction through the use of the mouse;
- simplicity;
- uniformity.

It includes a command desktop able to start the decoding of an ODIF document and its subsequent reconstruction and displaying in WYSIWYG mode. For the time being display is limited to the layout of the document; however, its extension to both the raster content and the character content is under way. The first prototype of the Preview of ODIF formatted documents is therefore limited to a stylized display of the layout. Besides, the display of the document PROFILE, wich is structured as a page including character content objects composed of the information contained in the profile, will be integrated.

REFERENCES

1. Horak, W. et al., Handling of mixed text/image/voice documents based on a standardized office document architecture, ESPRIT '84: Status Report of Ongoing Work, J.Roukens and J.F.Renuart, Elsevier Science Publishers B.V. (North-Holland).

2. Akiyama, T. and Hagita, N., Automated entry system for printed documents, Pattern Recognition pp. 1141-1153.

3. De Luca, P.G. and Gisotti, A., How to take advantages of word structure in printed character recognition, in Proc. RIAO'91 - Intelligent Text and Image Handling (Barcellona, Spain - April 2-5, 1991), pp. 148-159.

4. Roccotelli, M.P. et al., An experimental system for office document handling and text recognition, Proc. ICPR'88, pp. 739-743 (1988).

5. De Luca, P.G. and Gisotti, A., Printed character preclassification based on word structure. Pattern Recognition, Vol.24, No. 7, pp.609-615, 1991. Pergamon Press plc.

6. Palay, A.J. et al., The Andrew Toolkit - An Overview, Proceedings of USENIX Winter Conference, February 1988.

7. ISO 8613 Information processing Text & office systems. Office Document Architecture (ODA) and Interchange Format. 1989.

A Desk Supporting Computer-based Interaction with Paper Documents

William Newman and **Pierre Wellner***

Rank Xerox EuroPARC
61 Regent Street
Cambridge CB2 1AB (United Kingdom)
Newman@EuroPARC.Xerox.Com, Wellner@EuroPARC.Xerox.Com
*also University of Cambridge Computer Laboratory

Abstract

Before the advent of the personal workstation, office work practice revolved around the paper document. Today the electronic medium offers a number of advantages over paper, but it has not eradicated paper from the office. A growing problem for those who work primarily with paper is lack of direct access to the wide variety of interactive functions available on personal workstations. This paper describes a desk with a computer-controlled projector and camera above it. The result is a system that enables people to interact with ordinary paper documents in ways normally possible only with electronic documents on workstation screens. After discussing the motivation for this work, this paper describes the system and two sample applications that can benefit from this style of interaction: a desk calculator and a French to English translation system. We describe the design and implementation of the system, report on some user tests, and conclude with some general reflections on interacting with computers in this way.

Keywords: user interface, interaction technique, display, input device, workstation, desk, desktop, document recognition.

Introduction and Motivation

Today's office, with its dual system of paper and electronic documents, presents users with a range of problems. Electronic and paper documents have very different properties, are not well integrated, and working with one often requires giving up the advantages of the other. Electronic documents lack the portability, tangibility and universal acceptance of paper. Working with paper, on the other hand, denies direct access to the wide variety of interactive functions available on personal workstations—functions that include spelling-correction, electronic mail, keyword searching, numerical calculation and foreign-language translation.

The standard solution to problems of dealing with information on paper is to devise a screen-based alternative. These solutions are often based on a real-world metaphor. Users interact with computer-generated synthetic objects that simulate objects such as paper documents and a desktop. However, the replacement of paper by computer is not always appropriate. For example, reading from a screen is generally slower than from paper [Hans88] and this poses a problem with longer documents. Keeping medical records on-line means that doctors must consult a desktop computer rather than glance through a written record, and this changes the interaction between doctor and patient, not always for the better [Grea92].

An alternative to screen-based designs is offered by the opportunity to *augment* real-world objects with computers instead of simulating them. This is the concept of "embodied virtuality" or "computerized reality." [Weis91, Well91] We apply this idea to the work environment and specifically to the desk. Instead of using the "desktop metaphor" and electronic documents, we use the real desk top and real paper documents. Instead of "direct manipulation" with a mouse, one of our goals is to explore "tactile manipulation" of real artifacts that we augment to have electronic properties. Our ultimate goal is to reduce the incompatibilities between the paper and electronic domains so that interchange is cost-free and users no longer pay a penalty for choosing the "wrong" medium at the outset. The research reported here is a first step towards attaining this goal.

In this paper, we describe a system, Marcel, developed originally for experiments on tracking paperwork (see [Lamm92]), and since extended to allow direct interaction with paper documents in ways that are normally possible

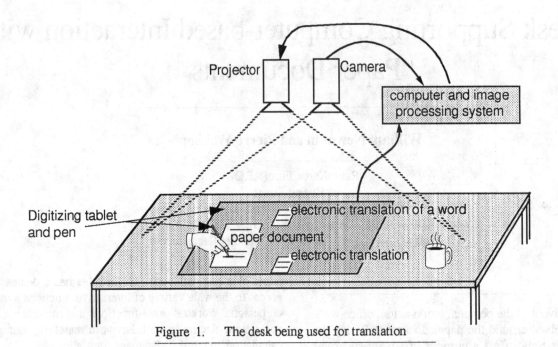

Figure 1.   The desk being used for translation

only with electronic documents. We then explain the way we have gone about designing and implementing Marcel. To explore the characteristics of this technique, we have implemented two simple applications. The first is a desk calculator that allows the user to select numbers printed on paper for input into the calculator. The second is a translation program that allows the user to select French words and display the English translations. We comment on the effectiveness of the approach, which has undergone some user testing, and on the general implications of interacting with computers in this way.

System Description

The system is built around an ordinary physical desk, and can be used as such. It has additional capabilities, however. A video camera is mounted above the desk pointing down at the work surface. Also, a computer-driven projector is mounted above the desk, allowing the system to superimpose electronic objects onto paper documents and the user's work surface (See Figure 1). The camera's output is fed into an image processing system that can see what the user is doing on the surface of the desk. The image processing system is in fact capable of detecting where the user's finger is pointing, but in Marcel a digitizing tablet and cordless pen are used to allow more precise pointing.

Although the system uses unconventional means of input and output, users can still interact with documents in much the same way as on a workstation. Ordinary X Window applications run exactly the same way as on a standard workstation without distinguishing pen or finger-based input from mouse-based input. The system enables new

types of interaction techniques, however, and new applications that exploit the user's direct access to the printed word.

Related work

Electronic and physical objects have been merged together using a half-silvered mirror in an early system for placing virtual labels on physical buttons [Know77]. Like our desk, VIDEODESK [Krue91] uses an over-the-desk camera, but tracks only silhouettes against a light table. The TeamWork-Station [Ishi90] also shares many of our goals in that it attempts to integrate traditional paper media with electronic media. It uses video mixing techniques to merge the images of paper documents on a desk with computer-generated images and the result is viewed on a monitor. In our system the result is viewed on the desk itself instead of a monitor. The main difference, however, is that our system not only provides a merged view of the two media, but also allows the user to perform computer-based interaction on the text of paper documents.

Another example of enhancing paper documents with computer functionality is the technique of barcoding text books [Mill91]. This allows a reader to scan a barcode with a laser wand and automatically play a particular track in a video-disk recording. Our approach presents the computer's response differently, but more importantly, it is much more general in that it does not require specially prepared documents. It can work with any paper document and the interaction is designed to be compatible with users' current work practices: with both electronic and paper media.

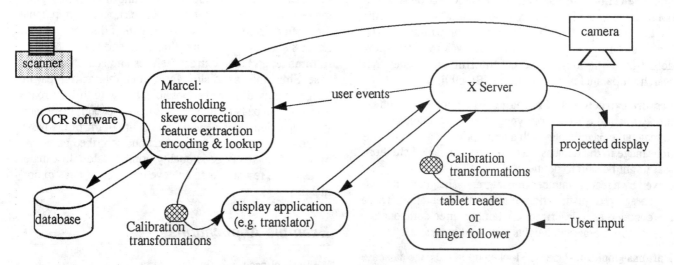

Figure 2.   System Architecture

A currently active area of research and development is pen-based computer interaction (for examples see [Carr91] and [Gold91]). Much of this work is focused on note-pad sized computers instead of desk-sized displays, but the techniques developed for pen-based interfaces, such as handwriting and gesture recognition, will greatly enhance the style of interaction we describe in this paper. Our focus is on the unique aspects of this type of desk system, which allow paper documents to be used on the desk in similar ways as the electronic objects.

The Design of Marcel

The main difficulty in implementing a system to support computer-based interaction with paper documents is to relate a selected location on the paper to the text at that position. The ideal solution would be a high-resolution camera, capable of capturing a selected region of the desk surface and applying optical character recognition (OCR) to it. While there are hand-held scanning devices capable of capturing high-resolution images, they are inconvenient; OCR also poses problems of slow response and sensitivity to skew angle. We are interested in solutions that would allow the user to point with a stylus or even with a finger, at documents lying at various orientations. Devising a means for providing fast response to this form of text input is a major component of the system design. We have tested two solution strategies, both using a video camera mounted over the desk: The DigitalDesk and Marcel.

The DigitalDesk [Well91] uses supplementary cameras zoomed into narrow fields of view to obtain images of paper documents that are suitable for limited OCR, and it uses a finger-following camera for pointing. Although a desk cal-

culator was implemented as an example to illustrate the concept, this means of pointing and OCR is not yet precise enough for real user testing.

Marcel, on the other hand, uses low-resolution video images, corrects them for skew, and correlates them with document images obtained from a printer or a high-resolution scanner. Commercial OCR software is applied to the scanned images ahead of time, and the digitizing tablet enables very precise pointing. The result is a prototype that is reliable enough for user testing.

The system architecture of Marcel is shown in Figure 2. Images are captured from the over-the-desk camera, and are fed through a number of stages: thresholding, skew-detection and correction, feature extraction, encoding and database lookup. Meanwhile, coordinates are read through X Windows from a hand-held stylus or other pointing device. These are used to select contents from the text found in a database, and the contents are passed as arguments to the appropriate computer function. Results are displayed on the desk surface using a projected computer display. The following sections discuss some of the issues this system needed to address; more details can be found in [Newm91].

Image capture and thresholding: Each gray-scale image is converted to binary by means of an adaptive thresholding routine that compensates for variations in lighting across the desk surface. With the camera adjusted to cover a 25 x 18 inch area, the effective scanning resolution is about 30 dots per inch. High Definition TV would of course improve image resolution, and was considered as an alternative but ruled out because it would also increase processing time without producing the quality needed for direct OCR.

Skew detection and correction: Skew correction is essential to compensate for the varying angle at which documents are held while reading them or interacting with them. The low-resolution bitmaps lend themselves to rapid skew detection using morphological filtering techniques that search for parallel picture elements [Bloo90].

Feature extraction and encoding: The purpose of the feature extraction is to exploit typographic layout conventions to match the page image with a description of a high resolution image in the database. The features extracted are those that might be said to define the "shape" of the page as perceived by a reader: number of paragraphs, height of individual paragraphs, justification of text, and indentation. These are encoded as a descriptor containing three components: line lengths, paragraph heights and word breaks.

Database lookup: Pages are looked up in the page database by attempting to match the line-length component of the descriptor. If multiple entries are found with same line-length component, the paragraph-height and word-break components are used to discriminate between them. The word-break component encodes the position of words on the first two full lines of text, and is needed in cases where page shapes are otherwise indistinguishable.

Calibration: The system must be able to map each point of the camera image to a point of the projected display. If the digitizing tablet is used, then each point of the digitizing tablet must be mapped to a point in the camera image and to the display. Vibrations and optical distortions make it difficult to maintain accurate calibration over the entire area of interaction, and errors here make the system inaccurate and difficult to use. We have been experimenting with ways to perform calibration both manually and, with the aid of projected test patterns, automatically.

Display: A projected display provides similar capabilities to using a large flat display screen or a rear-projected display. It has the important advantage, however, that computer-generated images can be superimposed onto paper documents. A problem with overhead projection is shadows; for example, the user cannot lean over to look at a projected image too closely. In practice, however, this has not yet proved to be a problem. Another issue with projection is the brightness of the room. The projector used in these experiments works quite well with the room's normal fluorescent lights, but a bright desk lamp makes the display unreadable. The same would be true of direct sunlight, so this limits the desk's usability in some settings. One last problem is that not all materials make good projection surfaces. The projection area should be white and untextured in order to show the projected images most clearly. An ideal system would have projection both from above and from below.

Performance: A considerable amount of work has gone into ensuring adequate performance to support fast, reliable interaction. In its current implementation the system takes about 8 seconds to capture, threshold and skew-correct a full image, and then extract features and search the database. Since this is too slow for normal interaction, partial images are used whenever possible, and with this approach selection can be performed in less than a second. Error rates vary depending on the layout and quality of the printed text, and in order to support the applications described below we have used relatively good-quality printed material. A major focus of the research is to achieve lower error rates in normal use.

Example Applications

We have chosen two simple applications to illustrate how this system might be used: a calculator and a translation application.

Desk top calculator

People using calculators often enter numbers that are already printed on a piece of paper lying on the desk. They must copy the numbers manually into the calculator in order to perform arithmetic on them. Transcribing these numbers slows down the user of a calculator and contributes to errors.

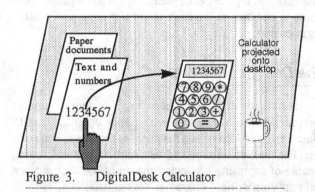

Figure 3.   DigitalDesk Calculator

To address these issues, we project a calculator onto the desktop (see Figure 3), in this instance using DigitalDesk rather than Marcel. This enables finger-tip operation much like a regular electronic calculator. The projected cursor follows the user's finger (or pen) as it moves around on the desktop and the user can tap on the projected buttons to enter numbers. The advantage of this calculator over an ordinary calculator, however, is that it has an additional way to enter numbers. If the number to be entered is already printed on a piece of paper lying on the desk, the user can simply point at it and it appears in the calculator's display as though it had been typed in directly. This calculator can save many keystrokes and errors when making calculations with printed data.

Definition from previous interaction:

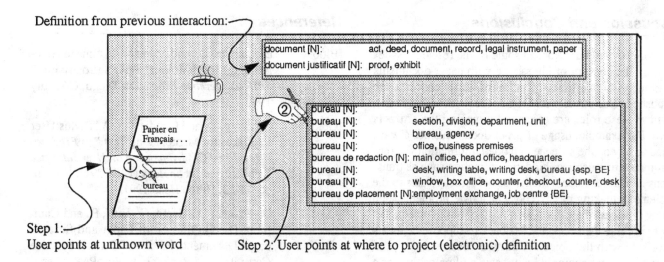

Step 1:
User points at unknown word   Step 2: User points at where to project (electronic) definition

Figure 4.   Using translator on surface of desk

Desk top translation

Another example of an application that can benefit from this desk is foreign language translation. Looking up words in a dictionary can take up a substantial amount of a reader's time when reading documents in a foreign language. The time spent looking up words also makes it more difficult to remember the context of the word or the passage. Some readers find this delay so disruptive to their reading that they prefer to read on despite the presence of many unknown words.

We have implemented a system in which French documents can be read at a desk in their paper form. When the user needs to look up a word, he or she can simply point at the word. The system extracts the root of the word, looks it up in a French-to-English dictionary and displays the definitions in an electronic window projected onto the desk, allowing the user to point to the location where the translation should be placed on the desk (See Figure 4). Any number of words can be looked up, and the user can slide the windows around on the desk or remove them when they are no longer needed.

User Reactions

Although we did not conduct any formal experiments with our system, a small number of people have tested the translation application and we recorded their reactions. These related both to the application and to the digital desk technology, both of which were new to the users.

The on-line dictionary provided much faster lookup of unfamiliar words, partly through automatic determination of the root word (e.g., "aller" from "vais") and partly by avoiding the manual lookup process itself. Although on-line lookup

look several seconds, users were often able to select a word and continue reading uninterrupted, knowing that the translation window would appear. They liked the fact that translations remained visible, sometimes avoiding the need to look up a word twice. We expect these benefits would also be provided by a screen-based system, but only if the document were available on-line.

For the most part, the digital desk was found comfortable and natural by subjects, all of whom had used traditional workstations or PCs before. None was bothered by the projection system or by shadows cast by hands and other objects; indeed after using the system for about fifteen minutes, one user asked if the desk was made of glass and looked under it to see where the projected display was coming from! They were asked at the end of the session how they felt about using the desk as compared to a traditional workstation. Their overall reaction was that it was quite similar, and they commented specifically that they had "more space," that using it was "more manual," "easier on the eyes," and "much more healthy than a screen." Subjects were unsure whether the paper had to stay in a precise location, and one said that it was "irritating that the paper moved around" relative to the projected images. This could have been avoided by providing different feedback and is being investigated. One of our subjects was left-handed and was inconvenienced by the experimental setup, with paper on the left and space for definitions on the right—her arm obscured the paper while she waited to position the translation window. This observation suggests that there may be interesting differences in how handedness affects the layout of applications on a digital desk as opposed to a workstation. More comprehensive tests are still required, but these initial trials have not uncovered any fundamental problems with our approach, and have encouraged us to pursue the research further.

Discussion and Conclusions

Our work to date has exposed some of the research issues posed by the concept of interacting with paper documents and other passive artifacts. One set of issues concerns the established roles of these artifacts in the work environment, and how these roles are affected by making the artifacts active. For example, usage of paper documents has always tended to rely on the absence of hidden information whereas in an interactive context, hidden information such as translations can be revealed. Another set of issues relates to the problems in making passive objects active: problems such as how to access the information content of the object, and how to provide the necessary feedback to support the user's interaction with the object. A printed document is a relatively easy target compared with, say, a filing cabinet or a bookshelf.

Two central issues in supporting interaction with paper documents are the development of effective styles of interaction, and the provision of tools for the design and implementation of paper-based user interfaces. So far, we have made only a little progress in these two areas. In the applications we have built we have tried to adhere to existing workstation interaction styles so as to avoid surprises for our users. We have experimented with paper "command sheets" as a means of offering the user a range of command modes, but recognize that this puts limits on the interactivity of the application.

Our interest in the digital desk stems in part from its ability to support "tactile manipulation" interfaces. These attempt to let the user interact with physical artifacts and electronic objects in much the same way: by touching them. With this style of interaction, manipulation of electronic documents is similar to manipulation of paper documents, and paper can have computer-based properties that make it possible to interact with it like an electronic object.

Ultimately, we hope to integrate paper documents better into the electronic world of personal workstations, making paper-based information usable in the same ways as electronic information, without requiring the user to abandon paper and use an electronic workstation instead. The ideal system that we envision is one in which users are free to choose either medium as the task requires without being constrained to the limitations of either.

Acknowledgments

We wish to thank the many people who have offered advice and help, including Dan Bloomberg, Ian Daniel, Mike Flynn, Ron Kaplan, Martin Kay, Mik Lamming, Linda Malgeri, Ron Mann, Mike Molloy, Atty Mullins, Peter Robinson, Z Smith, Larry Spitz, and our subjects.

References

[Bloo90]   Bloomberg, D., and Maragos, P. "Image Algebra and Morphological Image Processing." *SPIE Conference Proc.*, San Diego, CA, July 1990.

[Gold91]   Goldberg, D. and Goodisman, A. "Stylus User Interfaces for Manipulating Text." in *Proceedings of the ACM Symposium on User Interface Software and Technology* (UIST '91), November 11-13, Hilton Head 1991.

[Grea92]   Greatbatch, D., Heath, C., Luff, P., and Campion, D. "On the use of Paper and Screen-based Documentation in the General Practice Consultation." Rank Xerox EuroPARC Technical Report, Cambridge 1992.

[Hans88]   Hansen, W. J., and Haas, C. "Reading and Writing with Computers: A Framework for Explaining Differences in Performance." in *Communications of the ACM*, vol. 31, no. 9, September 1988.

[Ishi91]   Ishii, Hiroshi and Miyake, Naomi. "Toward an Open Shared Workspace: Computer and Video Fusion approach of TeamWorkStation." In *Communications of the ACM*, vol. 34, no. 12 December 1991.

[Know77]   Knowlton, K. "Computer Displays Optically Superimposed on Input Devices." *Bell System Technical Journal*, vol. 56, no. 3, March 1977.

[Krue91]   Krueger, M. *Artificial Reality II*. Addison-Wesley, 1991.

[Lamm92]   Lamming, M. and Newman, W. "Activity-based Information Retrieval: Technology in support of Personal Memory." Rank Xerox EuroPARC Technical Report 91-03. February 1992.

[Mill91]   Miller, R. "Behold the Humble Barcode." Multimedia and Videodisk Monitor. Arlington VA, Sept. 1991.

[Newm91]   Newman, W. "Interacting with Paper Documents" in *Proceedings of NordDATA '91*, June 16-19; Oslo 1991.

[Well91]   Wellner, P. "The DigitalDesk Calculator: Tangible Manipulation on a Desk Top Display" in *Proceedings of the ACM Symposium on User Interface Software and Technology* (UIST '91), November 11-13, Hilton Head 1991.

[Weis91]   Weiser, M. "The Computer for the 21st Century" *Scientific American*, September 1991.

OBJECT-ORIENTED VIDEO: INTERACTION WITH REAL-WORLD OBJECTS THROUGH LIVE VIDEO

Masayuki Tani, Kimiya Yamaashi, Koichiro Tanikoshi,

Masayasu Futakawa, and Shinya Tanifuji

Hitachi Research Laboratory

4026 Kuji-cho, Hitachi-shi, Ibaraki-ken, 319-12 Japan

email: masa@hrl.hitachi.co.jp

ABSTRACT

Graphics and live video are widely employed in remotely-controlled systems like industrial plants. Interaction with live video is, however, more limited compared with graphics as users cannot interact with objects being observed in the former. Object-Oriented Video techniques are described allowing object-oriented interactions, including the use of real-world objects in live video as reference cues, direct manipulation of them, and graphic overlays based on them, which enable users to work in a real spatial context conveyed by the video. Users thereby understand intuitively what they are operating and see the result of their operation.

KEYWORDS: Object-oriented user interface, direct manipulation, live video, interactive plant control.

INTRODUCTION

People may often click a graphical button on a computer screen, but they do not try to click buttons on a machine being shown in a live video. That is to say, the level of interaction with video differs from that with graphics, although recent advances in hardware allow the simultaneous display of both video and graphics in a single screen. Most interactive graphic systems allow direct manipulation of graphical objects, and its effectiveness is widely acknowledged [10, 14]. But most recent interactive video systems only support frame-by-frame manipulation of recorded video and have not advanced much beyond Movie Maps [7], an early interactive video system, which allowed users to employ an object in a video image as a reference cue. The interactions supported by Movie Maps are more limited compared with direct manipulation of graphical objects. Furthermore, Movie Maps, as well as other interactive video systems, only deal with recorded video and do not address the issue of interacting with objects in live video.

Live video is used in many different applications that require monitoring the status of distant places, especially in user interfaces for remotely-controlled systems, typical examples of which are industrial plants, where various machines are controlled from a remote control center. Operators at remote control centers use live video to grasp the plant status intuitively, in addition to using graphic visualization to understand them analytically. Current user interfaces for plants or other remotely-controlled systems, however, do not support any technique for integrated use of graphics and live video nor do they have the same level of interaction between the two.

This paper describes interactive video techniques that allow interaction with objects in live video on the screen, by having models of the objects monitored by cameras. We call these techniques Object-Oriented Video, analogous to Object-Oriented Graphics (e.g. [6]), which have models of graphical objects. Object-Oriented Video includes the use of real-world objects as reference cues, direct manipulation of real-world objects through live video, and graphic overlays based on objects in live video, which allow the same level of interaction with live video as with graphics and the integrated use of graphics and live video. Furthermore, these techniques enable users to take advantage of real spatial context conveyed by video, such as layouts of objects in the real world. This context helps users to intuitively understand or easily remember the function of an object. These techniques have been implemented in a prototype system called HyperPlant, developed for monitoring and controlling an electric power plant, to demonstrate that they can effectively improve user interfaces for remotely-controlled systems.

USER INTERFACES FOR REMOTELY-CONTROLLED SYSTEMS

Working on a remotely-controlled system consists of two main tasks, that is, (1) monitoring and analyzing the status of the system and (2) operating objects in the system based on the analysis. User interfaces supporting these tasks generally consist of three components (see Figure 1): (1) the data/information visualizer that graphically visualizes data reflecting the status of the system and additional information, such as manuals, operation plans or other

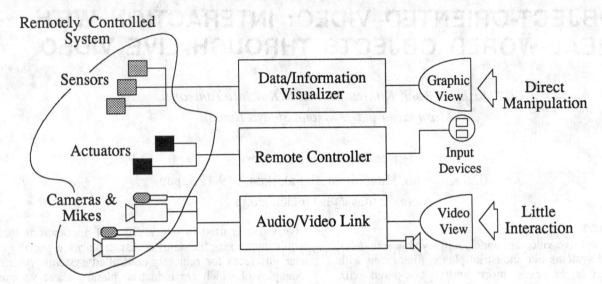

Figure 1. A schematic diagram of user interface systems
for a remotely-controlled system.

documents, to help users to work on the system; (2) the remote controller that provides user interfaces through which users remotely operate objects in the system; and (3) the audio/video link that allows users to see and hear the status of the system. The video link often employs remotely-controlled cameras that users can tilt, pan, zoom, or move to look around the system.

In current remotely-controlled systems, the data/information visualizer and the remote controller provide graphical user interfaces [3,13], but do not support any technique to integrate the audio/video link with them. For example, users have to operate the graphic view and the video view independently and in different ways. There is also no support for relating what is seen in the live video and graphics. The Object-Oriented Video can provide various techniques for integrating those three components. These techniques allow complementary use of graphics and live video.

OBJECT MODELS
Allowing interaction with objects in live video requires determining what is being pointed to by users. The Object-Oriented Video provides object models that teach what is seen at the point specified by the users on a live video.

The object models discussed here deal only with objects whose movement is controlled, which means they limit interactions to objects that stay put or are moved by remote control. In spite of this limitation, the models are useful because most objects in remotely-controlled systems with which users need to interact also stay put or are remotely controlled. The models can be informed about how an object moves because that movement is controlled.

Usual cameras map objects in a three-dimensional scene onto a two-dimensional plane on the screen. This mapping

is modeled as a perspective transformation from the world coordinate system to the display coordinate system (see Figure 2). This transformation is specified by a perspective matrix that is a function of the camera parameters composed of pan, tilt, swing angles, view angle and camera position [11]. There are two basic strategies for modeling objects imaged by cameras: modeling them (1) in the world coordinate system before objects are mapped (called 3D modeling), and (2) in the display coordinate system on the screen after objects are mapped on it (called 2D modeling).

(1) 3D modeling
3D modelling defines 3D shapes and positions of objects in the world coordinate system. Those 3D shapes may be modeled by various levels of approximation according to applications. For example, they can be described by a set of simple 3D graphic primitives, such as cylinders and cubes, for pointing to an object, while more complicated 3D models are needed for naturally overlaying 3D graphics on an object.

Given a point in the display coordinate system, the object seen at that point can be identified from the 3D models and the current camera parameters. The algorithm developed for identifying an object is as follows. This algorithm can take advantage of hardware support for 3D graphics, such as z-buffering and double buffering [5].
1) Assign a different color to each object in the 3D model.
2) Render the 3D model onto the same area as a video image is displayed. This rendering process includes viewing transformation by the perspective matrix specified by the current camera parameters and visible-surface determination, which can be performed in real time by hardware, such as the z-buffer. Using the offscreen plane of the double buffer can prevent the rendered image from appearing on the screen.
3) Read the color of the pixel at the given point on the

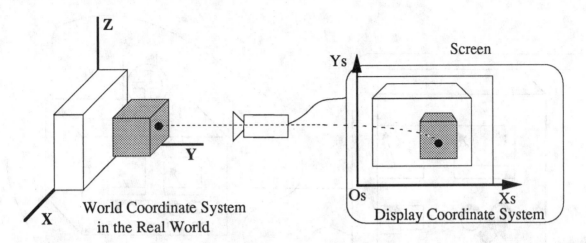

Figure 2. A camera maps objects in the world coordinate system onto the display coordinate system by perspective mapping.

offscreen plane. This color identifies the object.

(2) 2D modeling
2D modeling defines 2D shapes of objects mapped onto the screen by a camera. The 2D shape of an object is described as a set of 2D graphic primitives, such as rectangles, polygons, or circles. Once the 2D model is defined, identifying the object at a specific point in a video image becomes identifying the graphic primitive at that point, which is supported by most graphic systems [5].

Manipulation of the camera, such as zooming, changes its parameters and then changes the 2D shapes and positions of objects on the screen. In simple 2D modeling, the 2D shapes and positions of objects are defined corresponding to each set of camera parameters. This limits video images that allow interactions to only ones mapped by one of the specific sets of camera parameters; that is, users can only interact with objects when the camera is set to one of the predetermined sets of camera parameters.

3D modeling allows users to interact with objects in live video without the limitation discussed above while manipulating the cameras freely, because the 3D models are defined independently of camera parameters, which are taken into consideration when identifying an object. It is however more complex and time-consuming to define 3D models than 2D models. We have used 2D modeling to implement the prototype system HyperPlant for simplicity and because cameras in plants are usually set to one of predetermined sets of camera parameters. HyperPlant provides a tool set to define the simple 2D models of objects. This tool set includes a conventional object-oriented drawing tool used to trace the 2D shapes of objects on a video image (see Tani Plate 1). The tracing results are recorded corresponding to the current camera parameters. The action of an object, executed when users manipulate it, is described by an event-response language.

LINKS TO THE REAL WORLD
The Object-Oriented Video allows objects placed in the real world to be linked with information or an executable code in a computer system through live video used to monitor these objects. By pointing to an object in a live video, users easily retrieve information related to this object or execute codes linked with it.

Tani Plates 2 - 4 show examples of links through live video implemented in HyperPlant. By pointing to the burner of the boiler on a live video (see Tani Plate 2), a document appears which teaches the ignition procedure of the burner, and by pointing to a pipe on another live video (see Tani Plate 3), the graph is displayed that shows the amount of fuel running through the pipe. Furthermore, users can get a more detailed video or a related video of an object just by pointing to it on a video image without troublesome remote manipulation of cameras. For example, when users point to a part of the boiler (see Tani Plate 4-1), which is a window for monitoring status inside the boiler, the codes linked to that part are executed, and the camera is remotely controlled to zoom in on this window (see Tani Plate 4-2). Pointing to this window again while pressing another button on the mouse in the zoomed video image causes the video image to be changed to one being taken by another camera monitoring the flame inside the boiler through the window (see Tani Plate 4-3).

This technique is similar to that using buttons on bit-mapped images employed in many hypermedia systems (e.g. [1]). The significant difference is that the former allows users to use real objects in real space as retrieval cues instead of graphical objects in virtual space on the screen. Real-world objects can be better retrieval cues, especially for occasional users, than graphical objects, because the latter might have gaps between what they look like and what they really represent, which real-world objects in a video image do not have. Such gaps can make learning and operation difficult.

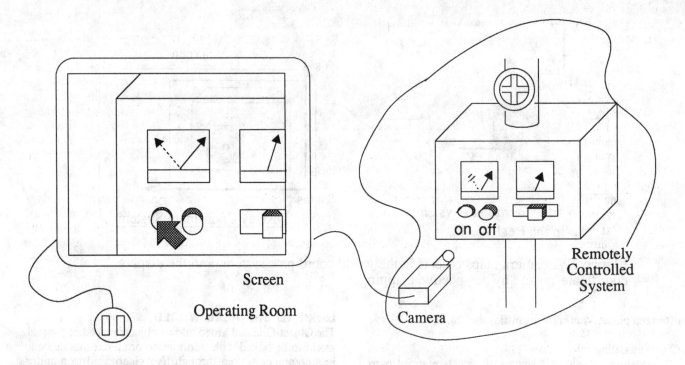

Figure 3. A schematic diagram of remote manipulation through live video.

Furthermore, this technique allows users who have actually seen the place where the objects are located to use their knowledge of spatiality, that is, their memory map of where objects are, to aid in information retrieval, as Bolt [2] has argued is the role of spatiality in managing and retrieving information. Video images taken by cameras retain spatial arrangement of objects in real 3D space. On the other hand, when graphics are used to represent real space, the spatial arrangement is often distorted to allow accommodation in a relatively small and 2D screen. This distortion might be an obstacle to using a mental schema of where objects are in real space.

DIRECT MANIPULATION OF REAL-WORLD OBJECTS

The Object-Oriented Video allows users to manipulate devices placed in a remotely-controlled system by direct manipulation techniques, such as clicking or dragging on the screen through live video. Figure 3 shows a schematic diagram of remote manipulation through video. Machines at a remote place are imaged by a video camera and displayed on the screen in an operating room. Those machines may have control devices (such as knobs and push buttons) that can be directly manipulated by hand and remotely controlled from the operating room by using the actuators that mechanically move the control devices. For example, when users move the pointer onto the knob of a slider on a live video image and drag the pointer (see Tani Plate 5), the actuator of the slider moves the knob, so that users see the knob following the pointer, which gives them the feeling of directly manipulating the knob. Users also see a push button pressed down by the actuator when they click a push

button on a live video.

An advantage of this direct manipulation technique through live video is that real spatial context conveyed by video helps users to intuitively understand or easily remember the functions of control devices. For example, when users see a button on a motor in a video image, they intuitively grasp the relationship between the button and the motor. Graphical user interfaces for remotely-controlled systems tend to omit such a spatial context of the systems to get efficient space utilization of the screen, requiring only graphical control devices to be arranged on the screen without their nearby machines.

Another advantage of this technique is that users can see real visual feedback as a result of their manipulation through live video images on which they are operating. For example, when users see smoke rise up from the motor whose button they have just clicked, they immediately recognize that something was done wrongly.

OBJECT-ORIENTED GRAPHIC OVERLAYS

Another effective technique that the Object-Oriented Video can support is to overlay graphics based on positions and structures of objects in a video image. This object-oriented overlaying has been effectively used in HyperPlant (1) to provide an alternative direct manipulation technique for remote manipulation discussed above, called virtual control devices that are graphical user interface tools, such as buttons and sliders, overlaid on or around objects controlled by them, and (2) to visualize data or information related to objects, which, for example, allows users to see the inner status of an object that cannot be seen through usual video images, (3) to enhance live video, such as highlighting an object.

Virtual control devices are used for controlling machines instead of real control devices because not all machines have control devices that can be manipulated both by hand and remotely through actuators as discussed in the previous section. Tani Plate 6 shows an example of a virtual control device, a graphical slider that is displayed near a pipe in a live video image. Its proximity to that pipe suggests to users that this slider controls the amount of fuel running through the pipe. Major advantages of virtual control devices come from their proximity to what is actually controlled by them, which allows users to use the real spatial context discussed above and thereby understand or remember intuitively what virtual control devices control. This proximity also allows users to get real visual feedback through live video while manipulating the virtual control devices. If users see something wrong happening such as a fuel leak from the pipe, they can immediately stop manipulating the graphical slider. Screen layouts where graphical interaction tools and live video are displayed on different views make it difficult for users to simultaneously see what they are doing and what is going on as a result, although most current plant control centers use such layouts.

We can see objects externally through usual cameras, but not internally. For example, a fuel leak might be seen at a pipe, but not the amount of fuel running through the pipe. In plants or other remotely-controlled systems, users monitor the internal status of objects through graphics that show data acquired with various sensors. Such graphics, however, are displayed in different views from the ones displaying live video showing the external status of objects. Such layouts make it difficult to monitor the external and internal statuses of objects simultaneously. The object-oriented overlaying technique enables the integration of external and internal views of objects. Tani Plate 6 shows simple graphics overlaid on a pipe that indicate the amount of fuel running through the pipe. The color of the graphics is changed when users manipulate the slider displayed near the pipe to change the amount of fuel.

Although video images are good at conveying reality and atmosphere, they can sometimes be too detailed to intuitively find their important features because of lack of abstraction, while graphics are suitable for abstract and symbolized representation, which can be used for complementing video images. For example, simple graphics are used for highlighting an object that is being manipulated (see Tani Plates 2 - 6)

Emerging technology for blending graphics with video images in real time, such as hardware support for α-channel compositing [5], provides more natural integration of graphics and video than simple graphic overlay, which can refine the object-oriented overlaying technique discussed above, especially the integration of the external and internal

views of objects.

Overlaying graphics on video are not new techniques. Such techniques are often seen on television and are also applied to user interfaces of various systems, but most do not use object-oriented overlays. For example, Movie Map [7] overlays graphical interaction tools for driving through a town built using videodiscs, such as buttons for stopping or changing direction, onto the video image of the town. These graphical interaction tools, however, do not relate to the content of the video image and their display is not based on objects in the video image.

Some recent interactive video systems use graphic overlays for showing internal states of objects, such as a schematic overlay of a fetus onto video images of a pregnant woman's abdomen to teach student nurses the correct position of the fetus [9]. But these techniques can be used only for recorded video images whose content can be known in advance, not for live video images whose content is generally unknown in advance. The Object-Oriented Video described in this paper provides a systematic framework for overlaying graphics based on objects in live video images, which allows an integrated view for monitoring the external and internal states of objects in the real world. This integrated view is especially useful for monitoring statuses changing every moment.

CONCLUSION

The Object-Oriented Video provides models of real-world objects monitored by cameras. These models enable users to interact with objects in live video, and this object-oriented interaction allows them to work on a task in real spatial context. This context helps users to intuitively grasp what they are doing and what is going on as the result of their operation. The real spatial context can be enhanced by overlaying graphics based on the object models, such as virtual control devices, the internal status of an object, and outlining an object to highlight it.

Although objects with which the Object-Oriented Video allows interactions are limited to those whose movement is controlled, there are many potential applications of the Object-Oriented Video. For example, a system for collaborative work might provide a shared studio equipped with remotely controllable instruments like audio mixers. The Object-Oriented Video allows people in other rooms to operate an audio mixer of the shared studio through live video, while listening to the edited sound and collaborating with people in the studio.

HyperPlant, the prototype system we have developed, provides a simple tool set for defining object models. This tool set basically requires users to draw the outlines of objects manually by tracing them on video images, which might be time-consuming and troublesome. The task of acquiring the object models could be avoided or aided by using image processing technologies, especially scene-analysis techniques (e.g. [4]), and this remains a topic for future work.

ACKNOWLEDGEMENTS

We would like to thank Carol Kikuchi for her proof-reading and the three CHI'92 reviewers for their encouraging comments.

REFERENCES

1. Apple Computer, Inc. Macintosh HyperCard User's Guide. 1989.

2. Bolt, R.A. The human interface. Lifetime Learning Publications, Belmont, California, 1984.

3. Clark, S.L., Steventon, J., and Masiello, R.D. Full-graphics man-machine interface for power system control centers. IEEE Computer Applications in Power (July 1988), 27-32.

4. Fischler, M.A., and Firschein, O., eds. Readings in computer vision. Morgan Kaufmann Publishers, Inc., Los Altos, California, 1987.

5. Foley, J. D. et al. Computer graphics - Principles and practice. Addison-Wesley, Reading, Massachusetts, 1990.

6. Laffra, C. Object oriented methods for graphics. In Course Notes C22 "Object and constraint paradigms for graphics" of SIGGRAPH '91 (Las Vegas, Nevada, July 28 - August 2). ACM, New York, 1991.

7. Lippman, A. Movie-Maps: An application of the optical videodisc to computer graphics. SIGGRAPH'80 Conference Proceedings (Seattle, Washington, July 14 - 18 1980). Computer Graphics 14, 3 (July, 1980), 32-42.

8. Mackay, W.E., and Davenport, G. Virtual video editing in interactive multimedia applications. Communications of the acm 32, 7 (July 1989), 802-810.

9. McMillan, T. Interactive video bolsters. Computer Graphics World 13, 5 (May 1990), 44-52, PennWell Publishing Company, Westford, Massachusetts.

10. Norman, D.A., and Draper, S.W. User centered system design. Lawrence Erlbaum Associates, Inc, Hillsdale, New Jersey, 1986.

11. Potmesil, M., and Chakravarty, I. Synthetic image generation with a lens and aperture camera model. ACM Trans. on Graphics 1, 2 (April 1982), 85-108.

12. Ripley, G.D. DVI - A digital multimedia technology. Communications of the acm 32, 7 (July 1989), 811-822.

13. Seyfert, G.A., and Liu, K.C. Full graphic operator's consoles for power control center applications. IFAC Symposium on Power Sytems and Power Plant Control (1989), 763-767.

14. Shneiderman, B. Direct manipulation: A step beyond programming languages. IEEE Computer 16, 8 (August 1983) 57-69.

LIVEBOARD: A LARGE INTERACTIVE DISPLAY SUPPORTING GROUP MEETINGS, PRESENTATIONS AND REMOTE COLLABORATION

Scott Elrod, Richard Bruce, Rich Gold, David Goldberg, Frank Halasz, William Janssen, David Lee, Kim McCall, Elin Pedersen, Ken Pier, John Tang* and Brent Welch

Xerox Palo Alto Research Center
3333 Coyote Hill Road
Palo Alto, CA 94304
elrod@parc.xerox.com, (415)812-4224

ABSTRACT

This paper describes the Liveboard, a large interactive display system. With nearly one million pixels and an accurate, multi-state, cordless pen, the Liveboard provides a basis for research on user interfaces for group meetings, presentations and remote collaboration. We describe the underlying hardware and software of the Liveboard, along with several software applications that have been developed. In describing the system, we point out the design rationale that was used to make various choices. We present the results of an informal survey of Liveboard users, and describe some of the improvements that have been made in response to user feedback. We conclude with several general observations about the use of large public interactive displays.

KEYWORDS: interactive display, large-area display, cordless stylus, collaboration, group work, gestural interface.

INTRODUCTION

An integral part of most meetings is a central display or drawing surface which serves as a medium for presenting and capturing ideas. Examples include slides and viewgraphs projected onto a screen, whiteboards and flip-charts.

Recent work on computer-supported meeting environments [6,4,2] has recognized the importance of a central display surface. Meeting rooms such as Colab [6], Capture Lab [4] and Project Nick [2] all utilize one or more large displays as a major focus of the group work. For the most part, however, these displays function primarily to present information.

Drawing and recording ideas is usually accomplished with a keyboard and a mouse at a workstation adjacent to the large display. Although this configuration supports the interactive presentation and discussion of ideas, it still lacks the dynamic, direct interactivity of a whiteboard or flip-chart.

Recent work has explored the use of more directly interactive display surfaces. For example, VideoWhiteboard[7] used audio-video links to create a large-area interactive drawing surface that could be shared between remote locations. Commune [5] examined the use of a stylus-based computational sketchpad to support shared drawing at a distance. Although the drawing surfaces in these systems are more directly interactive, the technologies are not suitable as the central display in a fully networked computer-supported meeting room.

The Liveboard system described in this paper is an attempt to build a directly interactive, stylus-based, large-area display for use in computer-supported meetings. While still falling short of the ultimate wall-sized, flat-panel, high-resolution display, prototype Liveboards have enabled us to begin to develop and evaluate user interfaces for group meetings, presentations and remote collaboration.

The Liveboard project fits into the broader scheme of ubiquitous computing for the workplace of the future [9]. Liveboards complement other personal computing devices (i.e. office workstations and portable sketchpads) by providing a shared workspace around which groups can collaborate.

*Current address of John Tang is: Sun Microsystems Laboratories, Inc, 2550 Garcia Avenue, Mountain View, CA 94043, Tang@eng.sun.com, (415) 336-1636.

Figure 1: The Liveboard in use.

As can be seen in Fig. 1, the current Liveboard is a large display housed in a wooden cabinet. The display surface (46 x 32 inches) is approximately the size of an office whiteboard and has nearly 1 million pixels. Two features of the system allow the display to be viewed comfortably at very close distances. First, the Liveboard image is projected from a digitally addressed liquid crystal display. As a result, the image does not exhibit any of the jittering and wavering often found in CRT-based projection systems. Second, the Liveboard incorporates a rear-projection screen which widely disperses the image and can be easily seen at oblique angles. The result is a crisp, stable image which can be viewed comfortably by a group of people standing around the Liveboard.

The Liveboard incorporates an accurate cordless pen, a feature which is particularly important for group meetings. Allowing participants to interact directly with the display provides a natural point of focus for meetings. By contrast, it is difficult to maintain the focus of a meeting when interaction with the central display is mediated by an adjacent keyboard. In addition, the cordless pen is easy to pass among participants. For these reasons, the pen is a particularly appropriate technology for group interaction around a large display surface.

The pen has four distinct states which are controlled by buttons on its body, and by a pressure-sensitive tip switch. Under software control, these states are used for drawing, to pop up menus, or to provide other means of input control.

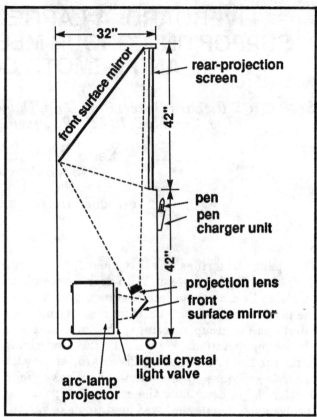

Figure 2: Optical and mechanical details.

The Liveboard is controlled by a high-performance workstation (Sun SPARCstation-2) and can run a large collection of UNIX-based software. Liveboards are fully networked, and can be used in a shared mode between remote locations.

SYSTEM HARDWARE: Display

The Liveboard image is produced by projecting a liquid crystal display (LCD) onto a rear-projection screen, as shown in the side view of Fig 2. The LCD's 1120 x 780 monochrome pixels are magnified to give an image that measures 46 x 32 inches and has a resolution of 25 lines per inch. The Liveboard optics can accommodate projected images with resolutions up to 50 lines per inch. In order to minimize the depth of the cabinet, the optical path is folded twice, as shown in Fig. 2. We found it necessary to exclusively use front surface mirrors in order to eliminate secondary reflection images. In order to make the image sufficiently bright, we chose a 600W arc-lamp overhead projector for the light source. This results in images which are bright enough (25-50 foot-lamberts) for use in a typical office or conference room.

Cordless Pen

The design of the Liveboard pens was driven by several requirements. They were to be cordless for ease of use and especially to avoid tangling when several pens were used simultaneously. They were to provide input at some distance from the board to allow for remote pointing and gestural input. Also, they were to provide the functionality of a three-button mouse so that they could be used with existing software. Human factors considerations dictated that the pens be as small and light as possible, and that the batteries be placed so that the weight was properly balanced.

Shown in Fig. 3 are functional details of the Liveboard pen. The pen emits a beam of optical radiation which is imaged onto a detector module located behind the screen near the LCD. After

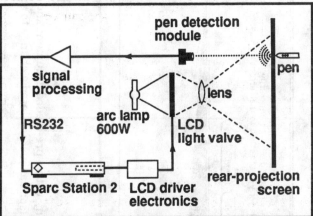

Figure 3: Functional diagram of optics and pen.

some signal-processing, the digitized pen position readings are sent through a serial port to the computer. The pen is capable of a marking accuracy of better than 1 mm, and produces 90 X-Y coordinate pairs per second.

Circuitry inside the pen allows for operation in four distinct states, one for cursor tracking and three that are controlled by the buttons on the body of the pen and by the pressure-sensitive tip switch. The front, middle and rear buttons on the pen body are configured to emulate the left, middle and right buttons of the standard mouse. The tip switch is redundantly mapped to the left mouse button.

In Fig. 4, a person is using the pen to pop up a menu by touching the tip to the screen. The pen can be used at distances of up to several feet from the screen, as can be seen in Fig. 5, where the user has depressed the front button to pop up a menu. The pen has rechargeable batteries, and charging

Figure 4: Popping up a menu by pressing the pen tip against the screen.

Figure 5: Operating the pen remotely to pop up a menu.

sockets are provided on the front of the Liveboard cabinet.

SYSTEM SOFTWARE: Pen Device Driver

In order to give the pen the widest possible applicability, we developed a custom software device driver. The driver serves to map readings from the pen detection electronics to genuine X-Y screen coordinates, and packages them in a form that can be readily integrated with window systems. With this device driver, the pen can be used as the pointing device in X windows (MIT X11R4 or XNeWS) or in SunView.

Walk-Up User Interface

The Liveboard is intended to be an information appliance with wide usage, rather than merely a large computer display. As such, it requires an

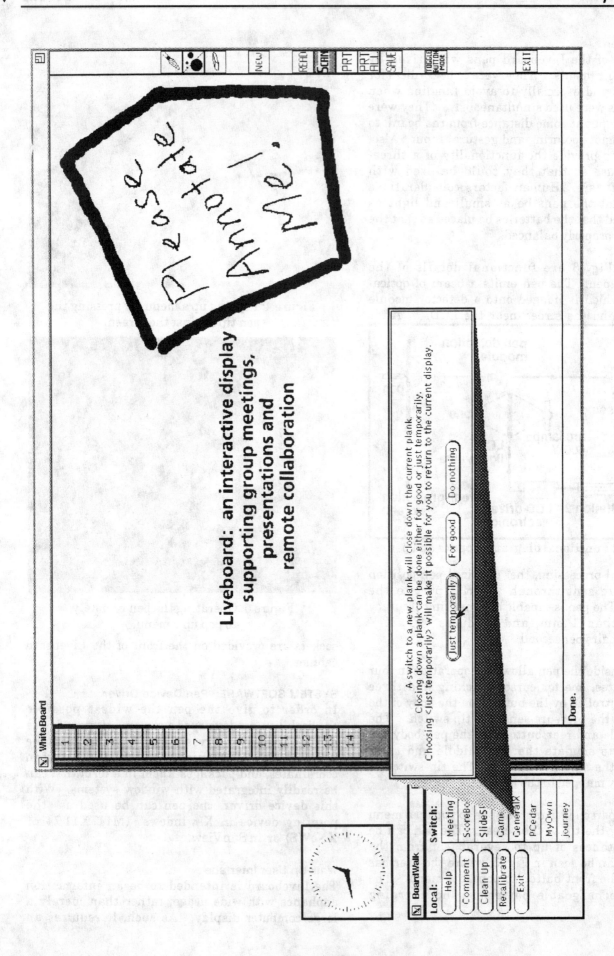

Fig. 6: The Whiteboard application, with a pre-loaded document and annotations made using the pen. The user has just initiated a change to another plank.

interface which the average meeting participant can use without knowing the intricacies of UNIX. Our solution to this requirement is a custom *walk-up* interface called the *BoardWalk*.

BoardWalk is implemented as a simple extension of the TWM window manager. It makes use of the basic mechanisms of the window manager, but hides the details with a layer of tailored environments, called *planks*. We chose not to use the well-known Rooms system [3] for this purpose because we believed that it was too powerful for novice users.

The BoardWalk control panel is shown in the lower left corner of Fig. 6. The control panel contains a list of planks that the user can choose among. The standard planks are:

1) *Meeting*--meeting tools, including a Whiteboard application, a text editor and a clock.
2) *Scoreboard*--a dynamic electronic bulletin board (under development [8].)
3) *SlideShow*--an application for versatile display of prepared slides.
4) *Games* ---what to do when the boss is away.
5) *General X*--a plain and unrestricted X/Unix environment.
5) *PCedar*--for applications written in PARC's PCedar [1] programming environment.

Choosing a plank automatically opens a set of applications. A dialogue box, shown in Fig. 6, asks whether the user wants to leave the current plank *for good*, or only *temporarily*. When the user logs in as *liveboard*, the Meeting plank comes up as the default environment.

In addition to the planks, there are utility functions like *Help*, *Comment*, *Clean up*, *Recalibrate* and *Exit*.

SOFTWARE APPLICATIONS: Whiteboard

One of the uses imagined for the Liveboard is as a meeting support tool, at which people can write down ideas and retrieve documents. Shown in Fig. 6 is *Whiteboard*, an application designed to support this use. The application provides whiteboard-like functionality, with an added flip-chart capability to handle multiple *sheets* that can be printed or saved for later use.

Whiteboard is a simple X11-based bitmap painting program. Features include a variable brush size and an eraser that can wipe out pixels. New sheets can be readily created by touching an icon with the pen. All sheets are remembered, and any sheet can be easily recalled. The sheets can be printed, or can be stored in a file and retrieved at a later time.

The Whiteboard program has been used both for taking notes at informal meetings, and for presentations. For meetings, two important features differentiate the Whiteboard program from conventional copy-boards. First, the meeting record can be stored and subsequently retrieved on any Liveboard. Having such a record has been found to be very useful in returning the collective attention of work groups to previous discussions. The Whiteboard has multiple sheets that can be rapidly switched, providing almost unlimited drawing space.

For presentations, people usually pre-load the Whiteboard with text or scanned images. With the Whiteboard, material is much more available than with conventional slides. One can circle important concepts while they are being discussed, draw connections between related ideas, and illustrate ideas as they are being explained. The final annotated version of the slides can be printed.

SlideShow

Another BoardWalk plank is for the SlideShow presentation tool, which combines the features of a slide projector and an overhead transparency projector. SlideShow presents a multi-page image file, encoded in a page description language such as PostScript, as a set of slides. The presenter, standing a few feet from the Liveboard, gestures with the pen at the SlideShow window. A sweeping gesture to the right is used to bring up the next slide, while vertical gestures are used for direct-manipulation scrolling. SlideShow also provides random access to slides via a gauge at the top of the window. Buttons can be tapped with the pen to adjust the scale of the displayed images. In Fig. 7, the user has chosen the *Fill* option (i.e. fill the SlideShow window) for the current slide, and has just gestured with the pen to bring up the next slide.

SlideShow uses a display graphics package with device-independent imaging, so scrolling, scaling and filling the screen are easily accomplished. Unlike conventional slides or overhead transparencies, each SlideShow slide may be individually scrolled and scaled for optimum viewing, or a common viewing transformation may be applied to all slides in a set. Finally, the presenter may use the pen to write directly on the slides.

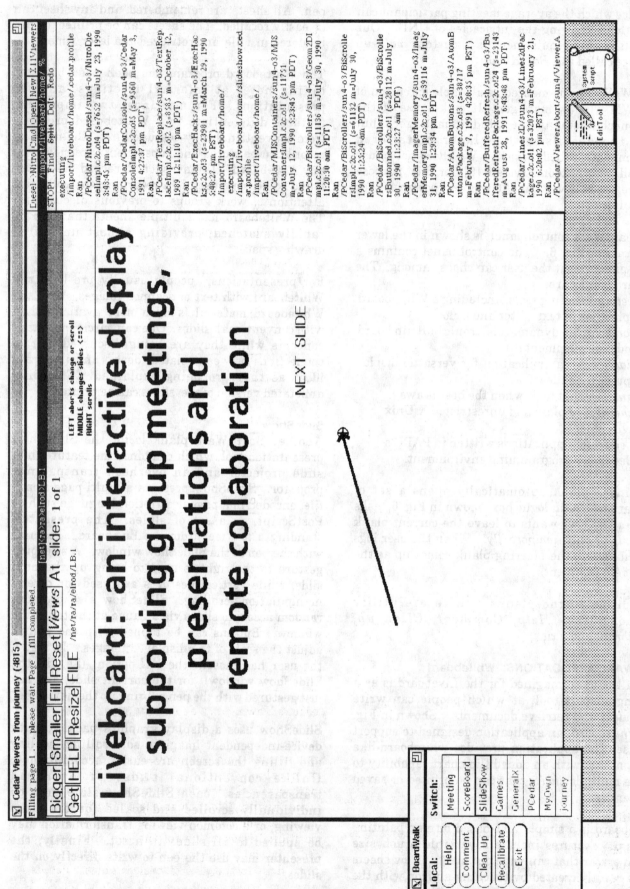

Fig. 7: The SlideShow presentation tool. The user has just made a sweeping gesture to the right to bring up the next slide.

SlideShow is motivated by the observation that default font sizes displayed on the Liveboard are generally too small to be easily viewed in meeting rooms. In addition, most editors do not provide bidirectional scrolling or scaling for presentation purposes. The SlideShow user interface is deliberately simple in an attempt to make it immediately available to novice users. After a few tries, people generally remember and use the gestures naturally.

LIVEBOARD USE: Informal Survey Results

Of the twelve prototype Liveboards that have been built, ten have been placed in conference rooms and open areas within PARC, while two have been sent to Xerox facilities overseas. During the year since they were installed, Liveboards have been used by diverse people for wide-ranging purposes: hardware researchers for meeting facilitation, managers for presentations, designers for remote collaboration, authors for collaborative writing of papers, and software developers for code reviews.

In order to better understand the situations in which Liveboards have been used, we conducted an informal survey of the PARC community. The survey consisted of an e-mail questionnaire sent out to everyone at PARC (250 researchers, managers and support personnel). The 60 respondents were self-selected, and while the survey was not conducted in a scientific manner, we believe that it raises important issues about the design of large, public, interactive display systems.

Table I summarizes the results of the survey. Perhaps most striking is the fact that while most respondents have used the Liveboard at least once, a significant number of those who have used it (34%) do not know how to turn it on. (This is despite the prominent display of an "ON" button on the front panel.) Users have reported general feelings of discomfort at the idea of walking up and just trying things. Some are intimidated by the size of the Liveboard, while others express fear of making a mistake and damaging it. Still others feel limited by their lack of UNIX knowledge.

Not surprisingly, the Liveboard is most often used for meeting facilitation (50% of respondents.) Of the different software applications that can be run on the Liveboard, the Whiteboard meeting tool is the oldest and most well publicized in the PARC community. In fact, it has had the favored status of being the default tool that comes up whenever the

Total number of respondents who:	Yes	No
1) know how to turn it on	32	16
2) have ever used one	46	3

Purposes for which respondents have used a Liveboard:	%Yes
1) in a meeting	50%
2) to randomly walk up and draw	48%
3) to show something to a friend	36%
4) to explain an idea	30%
5) in a presentation	26%
6) to write or look at code	18%
7) to write a paper	8%
8) to write a paper collaboratively	8%
9) for remote communication	8%

Items needing improvement, ordered from most to least as indicated by respondents:
1) image quality
2) accuracy of pen
3) size of cabinet
4) feel of pen
5) shape of cabinet
6) color of image (i.e. add color)
7) add printer
8) add scanner

Table I: Results of informal survey taken one year after Liveboards were installed. (60 respondents)

BoardWalk is started. Other common uses are casual drawing and explaining ideas to others.

Above all else, people would like to have better image quality on the Liveboard. While the number of pixels is high (1 million), there are still perceptible jaggies that degrade the appearance of handwriting. Next in importance to users is the accuracy of the pen. People are troubled by positional inaccuracies of the pen that can result from optical parallax in the screen and from long-term drift in the detection electronics. People are also concerned about the way the pen feels. They are concerned both about its size and shape, but also about having a tip which feels "right" as it moves across the screen surface (i.e. uniform friction of the proper amount.)

RESPONSE TO SURVEY FEEDBACK

We have begun to take steps to address the concerns raised by Liveboard users. First, we have attempted to reduce the barrier that users feel in getting started at the Liveboard. The PARC security staff now turns on all Liveboards before people arrive at work in the morning. A software script has been implemented which automatically starts up the BoardWalk whenever the Liveboard is rebooted. The script includes a loop which automatically restores the machine to the Meeting plank of the BoardWalk whenever the Liveboard is not being actively used. The result is that the Liveboards are more reliably in a state of readiness, where they look like a clean whiteboard.

Steps have also been taken to reduce the parallax of the Liveboard pen, and to improve the feel of the pen tip on the surface of the screen. In addition, a simple four-point pen recalibration has been implemented which allows users to correct for long-term drift in pen accuracy.

GENERAL OBSERVATIONS: Input to a Large Screen

Only by observing the Liveboards in use have we realized the extent to which stylus input on a large screen is different from a mouse at a workstation. Before building the current Liveboard pen, we constructed several prototypes in an effort to understand the optimal size, shape and placement of buttons. Despite these efforts, we have observed that while people readily use the pen for drawing, they find the buttons awkward and tend to avoid using them.

Clearly, a usable multi-state stylus will require semantics that are more intuitive than the current Liveboard pen. On the other hand, our early experience suggests that with more carefully designed user interfaces, most functions could be implemented using only two states (i.e. tracking and screen contact.)

Another important difference between the pen and a mouse is that the act of putting the pen down frequently causes the cursor to move across the screen. This makes it difficult for the user to define an input focus and then move to the keyboard. We have partially alleviated this problem by using a click-to-type mode in our window manager. A more

satisfactory solution might be to separate the tracking feedback and focus point functions that are commonly combined in mouse-based software. The tracking cursor would still follow the pen, but explicit action would be required to specify a new focus point.

The fact that the Liveboard pen is cordless, operates from a distance and interacts directly with the screen allows for types of input that make no sense with a mouse. As an example, we have found ways to use natural gestures (i.e. sweeping motions up or down) to accomplish various functions in a slide presentation (i.e scrolling).

Large Interactive Displays vs Workstations

Unlike workstations, Liveboards are frequently used by a group, often with one person standing at the screen and a larger number of people seated in the room. For the person working at the Liveboard screen, the user interfaces of most workstations and notebook computers are inadequate. The Liveboard is large enough that fixed buttons can be difficult to locate, and awkward to reach. We believe that either gestural input, or some type of floating or movable menus or buttons will be required for such large screens. For those people seated in the room, the default font size is often too small for comfortable viewing. Arbitrary scaling and scrolling will be needed to accommodate groups of different sizes.

While users may tolerate the intricacies of UNIX in the privacy of their offices, we have found that in group settings, people are much less willing to take the time to solve software mysteries. Typically, they will give up on using the Liveboard, and revert to a conventional whiteboard if they encounter problems with the software. To be accepted in group settings, systems like the Liveboard must have robust, easy-to-use software.

On the other hand, one of the virtues of Liveboards is that they are fully networked and, like workstations, can draw on a rich and complex set of applications and document formats. Finding the compromise between these two requirements (having both ease of use and the full power of networked workstations) will be central focus of much of our future work.

ACKNOWLEDGEMENTS

Many people have made valuable contributions to the Liveboard project. On the hardware side, we would like to thank R. Bell, T. Fisli, J. Gasbarro, W.

Jackson, E. Richley, G. Sander, D. Steinmetz and F. Vest. For their software contributions, we are indebted to N. Adams, R. Allen, P. Dourish, D. MacDonald, D. Nichols, M. Theimer, M. Toho and P. Wellner. For their contributions to early use studies, we are grateful to S. Bly, S. Harrison, S. Irwin and S. Minneman. Finally, we would like to thank a number of others for their creative suggestions and support of the project: R. Bauer, R. Beach, E. Bier, D. Bobrow, W. Buxton, R. Flegal, R. Gold, A. Henderson, C. Kent, S. Kojima, M. Krueger, J. Mackinlay, C. Marshall, M. Molloy, T. Moran, G. Robertson, Z. Smith, M. Stefik, and M. Weiser.

REFERENCES

1. Atkinson, R., Demers, A., Hauser, C., Jacobi, C., Kessler, P., and Weiser, M., Experiences creating a portable Cedar. In Proceedings of the 1989 ACM SIGPLAN Conference on Programming Language Design and Implementation, Portland, OR (June 1989), SIGPLAN Notices 24, 7 (July 1989), 322-329.

2. Cook, P., Ellis, C., Graf, M., Rein, G., and Smith, T. Project Nick: Meetings Augmentation and Analysis. ACM Transactions on Office Information Systems 5, 2 (April 1987), 132-146.

3. Henderson, D. A. Jr., and Card, S. K. Rooms: The Use of Multiple Virtual Workspaces to Reduce Space Contention in a Window-Based Graphical User Interface. ACM Trans. on Graphics, 5, 3 (July 1986) 211-243.

4. Mantei, M., Capturing the Capture Lab Concepts: A Case Study in the Design of Computer Supported Meeting Environments. Proceedings of the Conference on Computer-Supported Cooperative Work (Portland, OR, September 1988), 257-270.

5. Minneman, S. L., and Bly, S. A. Managing a trois: a study of a multi-user drawing tool in distributed design work. Proceedings of the Conference on Computer Human Interaction (CHI), New Orleans, LA (April 1991), 217-224.

6. Stefik, M., Foster, G., Bobrow, D., Kahn, K., Lanning, S., and Suchman, L. Beyond the chalkboard: Computer support for collaboration and problem solving in meetings. Communications of the ACM 30, 1 (Jan. 1987), 32-47.

7. Tang, J. C., and Minneman, S. L. VideoWhiteboard: Video Shadows to Support Remote Collaboration. Proceedings of the Conference on Computer Human Interaction (CHI), New Orleans, LA (April 1991), 315-322.

8. Theimer, M., and Nichols, D. Private Communication.

9. Weiser, M. The Computer for the 21st Century. Sci. Amer. 265, 3 (Sept. 1991), 94-104.

INTERACTIVE CONSTRAINT-BASED SEARCH AND REPLACE

David Kurlander
Steven Feiner

Department of Computer Science
Columbia University
New York, NY 10027

E-Mail: {djk, feiner}@cs.columbia.edu

ABSTRACT

We describe enhancements to graphical search and replace that allow users to extend the capabilities of a graphical editor. Interactive constraint-based search and replace can search for objects that obey user-specified sets of constraints and automatically apply other constraints to modify these objects. We show how an interactive tool that employs this technique makes it possible for users to define sets of constraints graphically that modify existing illustrations or control the creation of new illustrations. The interface uses the same visual language as the editor and allows users to understand and create powerful rules without conventional programming. Rules can be saved and retrieved for use alone or in combination. Examples, generated with a working implementation, demonstrate applications to drawing beautification and transformation.

KEYWORDS: Constraint specification, interactive techniques, demonstrational techniques, editor extensibility, graphical editing.

INTRODUCTION

When repetitive changes must be made to a document, there are several approaches to consider. The changes can be performed by hand, which is tedious if there are many modifications to make or if they are complex to perform. Custom programs can be written to perform the changes automatically, but this requires programming skill, and familiarity with either the editor's programming interface or file format. Some editors, particularly text editors, allow macros to be defined by demonstration. These macros do

not however extend easily to domains, such as graphical editing, where it is difficult to assign an unambiguous meaning to each interaction.

As most users of text editors are keenly aware, another approach to making repetitive changes involves the use of search and replace. Previously we adapted this technique to the 2D graphical editing domain by building a utility called the MatchTool [8]. Using the MatchTool, we could search for all objects matching a set of graphical attributes, such as a particular fill color, line style, or shape, and change either these or a different set of attributes. However, there was a large class of search and replace operations that MatchTool could not perform. There was no way to search for a particular geometric relationship, because shape-based searches matched on the complete shape of the pattern. For example, MatchTool could search for triangles of a particular shape, but not all right triangles. Similarly, shape-based replacements would substitute the complete shape of the pattern without any way of preserving particular geometric relationships in the match.

By adding constraints to the search and replace specification we now have better control of which features are sought and modified. Many complex geometric transformations can be expressed using constraint-based search and replace. For example, the user can now search for all pairs of nearly connected segments in the scene, and make them connected, or search for connected Bezier curves and enforce tangent continuity between them. All text located in boxes can be automatically centered, or boxes can be automatically created and centered around existing text. Lines parallel within a chosen tolerance can be made parallel. These object transformations can be used, for example, to beautify roughly drawn scenes, and enforce other design decisions.

Several other systems use automatic constraint generation for scene beautification. Pavlidis and Van Wyk's illustration beautifier searches for certain relationships, such as nearly aligned lines or nearly coincident vertices, and enforces these relationships precisely [17]. Myers' Peridot, an interactive system for designing new interface widgets, uses a rule set to find particular relationships between pairs of scene objects and establish new constraints among them [13]. Our system differs from these in that the constraint rules can be defined by the system's users, thereby providing a powerful new form of editor extensibility [9]. Rules are defined by direct manipulation [19], using the same techniques that are used for editing ordinary scenes. Furthermore, users can view the constraint rules graphically, in the same visual language as the rest of the editor interface. As will be described later in this paper, simple demonstrational techniques [14] help in defining these rules.

The ability to create custom rules is particularly important, now that methods have been developed to allow the user to define new types of constraints with little or no programming. For example, Borning's ThingLab allows new constraint classes to be defined using graphical techniques [2], and several recent systems allow new constraints to be entered via spreadsheets [5][11][15]. If the system designers cannot foresee every constraint that may be necessary, they clearly cannot provide for every transformation rule based on these constraints.

Search and replace is also a particularly easy way to add constraints to similar sets of objects. Sutherland's Sketchpad [20] introduced instancing to facilitate the same task. Instancing, though an extremely useful technique with its own benefits, requires that the user know, prior to object creation, the types of constraints that will be used. Also, many instancing systems place objects in an explicit hierarchy, not allowing one object to be a member of two unrelated instances. Constraint-based search and replace has neither of these limitations.

Nelson's Juno, a two-view constraint-based graphical editor, allows constraints to be added either in a WYSIWYG view, or a program view, resulting in a procedure that can be parameterized and applied to other objects [16]. Our search and replace rules are implicit procedures that are specified through a direct manipulation interface. The procedures are parameterized through the search portion of the rule, which also specifies the criteria that an object must match to be a valid argument. When a replacement rule is to be applied many times, the search mechanism reduces the burden by finding appropriate argument sets automatically.

Constraint rules have been used by several researchers in human-computer interaction. Weitzman's Designer was supplied with a set of rules to enforce design goals [22]. Peridot's rules, written in Interlisp, infer geometric constraints among objects in an interface editor. Maulsby's MetaMouse graphical editor infers graphical procedures by demonstration [12]. Each program step is associated with a

set of preconditions and postconditions to be met, which can include "touch" constraints. Vander Zanden developed a method of specifying graphical applications using constraint grammars to isolate the visual display from the data structures [21].

We have implemented constraint-based search and replace as part of MatchTool 2, an application that works in conjunction with the graphics and interface editing modes of the Chimera editor [10]. Here we discuss the motivation, interface, and implementation of constraint-based search and replace. We introduce the capabilities of our system and its interface through a series of examples. Next we discuss the algorithm and implementation. The last section presents our conclusions and planned future work. All figures in this paper are working examples, generated by Chimera's PostScript output facility.

EXAMPLE 1: MAKING A NEARLY RIGHT ANGLE RIGHT

Suppose that we would like to specify that all pairs of connected lines *nearly* 90 degrees apart should be *precisely* 90 degrees apart. Figure 1 shows MatchTool 2's interface for doing this.

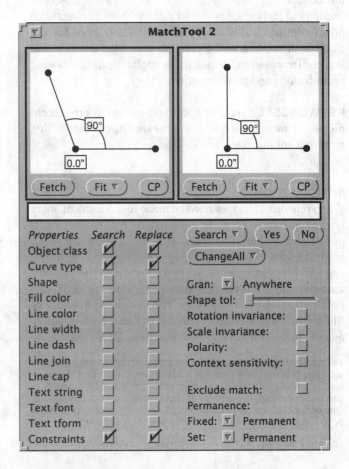

FIGURE 1. The MatchTool 2 interface.

At the top are two graphical editor panes in which objects can be drawn directly or fetched from any editor scene. The *Search Pane* on the left contains the search objects, and the *Replace Pane* on the right contains the replacement objects. Below these and to the left are two columns of checkboxes, the *Search* and *Replace Columns*. These specify which graphical properties of the objects in the Search and Replace Panes will be looked for or substituted into the match. Here we have selected "Object class", "Curve type" and "Constraints" from both the Search and Replace Columns. Starting at the middle right of the window is a set of buttons ("Search", "Yes", "No", and "ChangeAll") that invoke the search and replace operations.

When the "Constraints" box is checked in the Search Column, MatchTool 2 searches the scene for *relationships* expressed by the constraints in the Search Pane. The scene may contain constraints too, but the search ignores these. For example, there are two constraints in the Search Pane of Figure 1. The zero length distance constraint connects an endpoint of each line. It indicates that the MatchTool should look for two segments that touch at their endpoints. The 90 degree angle constraint between the two lines specifies that the lines matched must meet within a given tolerance of a right angle. Constraints are shown in these figures as they appear in the editor, and the display of individual constraints can be turned on and off from a constraint browser.

TOLERANCES BY EXAMPLE

We intend that the pattern should match all angles that are roughly 90 degrees, so we need a way to specify the tolerance of the search. We use a simple demonstrational technique. When system constraints are turned off, objects can be moved from their constrained positions. The user shows how far off a particular relation can be by demonstrating it on the search pattern. In the above example, the angle match will be 90 ± 20 degrees, since the angle drawn is 110 degrees, and the constraint specifies 90 degrees. To represent an asymmetric range (e.g. 90 +0 –20 degrees), we can simply convert it into a symmetric range about a different value (e.g. 80 ± 10 degrees). In the search specified by Figure 1, the distance constraint must be satisfied exactly since the endpoints are coincident in the Search Pane. We also provide an option that lets the user arrange the search pattern into several configurations, and takes the maximum deviation.

When we were first developing the system, we used Match-Tool 2's "Shape tolerance" slider for specifying constraint tolerances. The results were quite unsatisfactory because this control adjusted the tolerances of all the constraints simultaneously. Also, there was no visual clue relating how far off a constraint could be for a given position of the slider.

SEARCH AND REPLACE PARAMETERS

In the lower right hand corner of Figure 1, underneath the "ChangeAll" button, is a set of controls that affect how the search and replace is performed. Most of the parameters from the original MatchTool are still useful, but others have been added as well. The new controls appear at the bottom of Figure 1, starting with "Exclude match".

Match Exclusion

In the original MatchTool, scene objects that match the pattern are excluded from future matches. When dealing with constraints, this behavior is usually undesirable. For example, in our search for angles of nearly 90 degrees, we do not want to rule out other potential matches involving some of the same objects, since segments can participate in multiple angle relationships. When "Exclude match" is selected, scene objects can match at most one time in a single search. When it is not selected, scene objects can match multiple times; however to insure that the search will halt, no permutation of objects can match more than once.

Constraint Permanence

Just as constraints in the Search Pane indicate relationships to be sought, constraints in the Replace Pane specify relationships to be established in each match. To establish the relationship, MatchTool 2 applies copies of the replacement constraints to the match, and solves the system. Whether or not constraints remain in the scene after the match is a user option. The user has three choices: the constraints can be removed from the match immediately upon solving the replacement system, they can be removed after *all* the replacements have been made, or they can be made permanent. In the current example, it is important to choose one of the latter two options. A segment can participate in multiple angles, and if we delete the angle constraint immediately upon making a replacement, a subsequent application of constraints might destroy the established relationship. As will be discussed later, there are two different classes of constraints: *fixed constraints* and *set constraints*. The permanence of each class is controlled independently.

Before   (a)   After   (b)

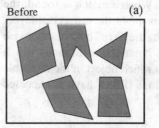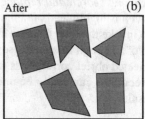

FIGURE 2. Application of the rule to make right angles out of nearly right angles. (a) The initial editor scene; (b) The modified scene.

With these parameters now set, we are ready to begin the search. First we place the software cursor in the editor scene shown in Figure 2(a), to indicate the window in which the search should occur. Then we press the "ChangeAll" button in the MatchTool 2 window. All of the 90 ± 20 degree angles become true right angles, as shown in Figure 2(b).

RULE SETS

Many constraint-based rules have wide applicability, so an archiving facility is important. Once search and replace rules have been defined, they can be saved in libraries, or *rule sets*. We have built a utility for manipulating rule sets, called the RuleTool, and its interface is shown in Figure 3.

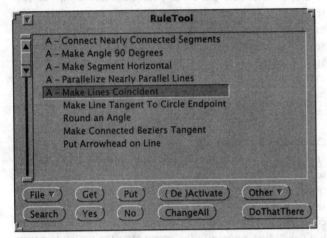

FIGURE 3. The RuleTool interface, a utility for building libraries of rules.

The RuleTool contains a scrolling list, in which rules are catalogued. Rules are initially defined through the Match-Tool 2 interface, but can be loaded into the RuleTool. Once in the RuleTool, a rule can be executed directly without using the MatchTool 2 window at all. A single rule can be selected and executed, or a set of activated rules can be executed in sequence in the order listed (activated rules are preceded with an "A"). The user can execute rules in the RuleTool as a post-process, after the illustration has been completed, or dynamically as objects are added or modified, in the manner of Peridot. We refer to the latter mode as *dynamic search and replace*. When a match is found, the match is highlighted, and the name of the rule is displayed. To invoke the rule, the user hits the "Yes" button, otherwise "No". Though in some cases it may be ambiguous which selected object corresponds to which object in the rule, rule executions can easily be undone if they have unexpected results.

Figure 4 shows the results of executing the activated rules of Figure 3 on a rough drawing of a house. Figure 4(a) is the initial drawing, and Figure 4(b) is the neatened version. The

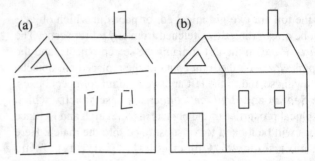

FIGURE 4. Renovating a house. (a) The original house; (b) The house after application of the activated rules in the rule set of Figure 3.

user explicitly accepted or rejected each of the matches. The results have the flavor of a simple version of Pavlidis and Wyk's drawing beautifier. In contrast, however, all of the rules used to neaten the drawing of the house were specified interactively, by the user, with constraint-based search and replace. These rules are simple rules and might have realistically been pre-coded by the implementer. In the next two examples we demonstrate more sophisticated tasks that introduce other capabilities of the system.

EXAMPLE 2: MAKING A LINE TANGENT TO A CIRCLE

As the Gargoyle graphical editor was being developed at Xerox PARC, several people proved their drafting prowess by constructing letters from the Roman alphabet, following the instructions described by Goines [4]. An example of this is included in [1]. These constructions consist of a small number of tasks that are repeated many times, some of which are difficult to perform or require some geometric knowledge. At the time, we tried our hand at one of these constructions, and felt that a macro facility would be extremely helpful, particularly since others had drawn the letters before us and presumably would have written the macros. One particular task that we found difficult was making a line tangent to a circle through a particular point. Here we show how this task can be encapsulated in a constraint-based search and replace rule.

We would like to find lines with one endpoint nearly tangent to a circle, and make that endpoint precisely tangent. The search pattern is given in Figure 5(a). Since our system currently has no tangency constraints, the user expresses the relationship with two constraints. The distance between the center of the circle and its other control point is constrained to be the same as that between the center of the circle and the near endpoint. This expresses that the endpoint lie on the circle. As shown in Figure 5, this distance constraint is represented in Chimera by a "D" connecting the two equi-length vectors. Also, the angle formed by the line's far endpoint, its near endpoint, and the center of the circle is constrained to be 90 degrees. (Actually, there are two lines tangent to a circle through a point, and we should be looking for –90 degree angles as well. After defining our rule we can easily copy it and modify it to catch the second case). Since we would like to match objects that nearly fulfill the given constraints, we manipulate the objects to show how much tolerance should be assigned to each constraint. Next, the objects in the Search Pane are selected and copied into the Replace Pane, shown in Figure 5(b).

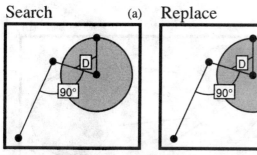

FIGURE 5. Search Pane (a) and initial Replace Pane (b) for line-endpoint and circle tangency.

One helpful test to find mistakes in the replacement specification is to invoke the constraint solver on the replacement pattern directly, and confirm that the objects adapt the desired configuration. The reason why this works is that typically the Search Pane is copied to the Replace Pane as an initial step, and the Search Pane contains a valid match. If the constraints already on these objects or subsequently added to them bring the match into the desired configuration, then they are fulfilling their job. The result of invoking the constraint solver is shown in Figure 6. Though the line has indeed become tangent to the circle at one endpoint, the result is not exactly what we had in mind. The circle expanded to meet the line, and both endpoints of the line moved as well. We would like to refine our specification to allow only the near endpoint of the line to move. To do this, we undo the last command (using Chimera's undo facility), putting the system back into its prior configuration, and specify additional constraints, as explained next.

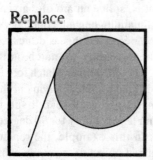

FIGURE 6. A test reveals a problem in the replacement specification.

FIXED CONSTRAINTS AND SET CONSTRAINTS

In this example there is a fundamental difference between the constraints already specified and those still to be added. The existing constraints specify relationships that must be changed in the match—two distances must be made equal and an angle must be set to 90 degrees. Additional constraints are needed to fix geometric relationships of the match at their *original* values. When we match a circle and line in the scene, we want to fix both the circle and the far endpoint of the line at their locations in the match, not their locations in the Replace Pane. We refer to the first type of constraint that *sets* geometric relationships to their values in the Replace Pane, as *set constraints*. Constraints that *fix* geometric attributes of the match at their original values are called *fixed constraints*.

At first thought it may not be clear why fixed constraints are necessary at all. One might think that only the geometric relationships explicitly expressed by set constraints in the Replace Pane should be changed in the match, and all other relationships should remain invariant. However, this is not possible—changing some relationships automatically results in others being changed as well. In the general case, it is impossible to make an endpoint of a line tangent to a circle, keeping the center of the circle, its radius, the other endpoint of the line, and the line's slope and length fixed. Given that some of these relationships must change, it is important to allow the user a choice of which.

Fundamentally, the difference between set and fixed constraints is the difference between checking and not checking an attribute in the Replace Column of the Match-Tool. During replacements, checked attributes come from the Replace Pane, and unchecked attributes come from the match. We considered adding entries to the Replace Column for constraints specified in the Replace Pane, and using checkboxes to specify the source of the constraint value. However this would clutter the interface. Instead, we have developed a simple demonstrational heuristic for determining whether the constraint should come from the match or the Replace Pane, without the user having to reason about it.

The heuristic requires that the Search Pane contents initially be copied into the Replace Pane, as is a common first step in specifying the replacement pattern. As a result, the Replace Pane contains a sample match. The user then adds constraints to this sample match, transforming it into a valid replacement. Conceptually, the user demonstrates the constraints to be added to all matches by adding constraints to this example.

We have two different interfaces for specifying constraints, either of which may be used in a MatchTool 2 pane or in an arbitrary scene. The user can select commands from the FIX menu to fix relationships at their current value, or alternatively they can specify a new value by using the SET menu and typing the new value into a text input widget. It is always easier to use FIX to make an existing relationship invariant, and it is usually simpler to use SET rather than manually enforcing the relationship and invoking FIX. MatchTool 2 keeps track of whether the user chooses FIX or SET and creates fixed or set constraints accordingly.

This heuristic works well, but occasionally the user does not take the path of least resistance or a relationship that we would like to enforce is coincidentally already satisfied in the sample. In these cases, the user may choose the wrong interface or forget to instantiate the constraint at all. To further test the constraint specification, constraint enforcement can be temporarily turned off, the Replace Pane objects manipulated into another sample match, and a Verification command executed. This command resets all fixed constraints to their values in the new configuration, and the constraint system is re-solved. If this second example reconfigures correctly, it is a good indication that the specification is correct. Fixed and set constraints are displayed differently in the Replace Pane (fixed constraints are marked by an asterisk), and the interface contains a command that converts between types.

We now return to the task of making the near endpoint of a line tangent to a circle, while moving only this endpoint. After selecting both control points of the circle and the far endpoint of the line, we select "Fix Location" from a menu. We now solve the system in the Replace Pane, and it reconfigures in the desired way, indicating the replacement specification is probably correct. When Chimera is given the sample scene of Figure 7(a), our rule makes all line endpoints that are nearly tangent to circles, truly tangent, resulting in the scene shown in Figure 7(b).

DO THAT THERE

While for certain editing tasks it is useful to keep rules such as line-circle tangency active, they can interfere at other times by matching too frequently if the tolerances are high, and by slowing down the editor. An extension to the current system that would allow tolerances to be scaled down without editing the rules would be helpful in the first case. Another approach is to keep all but the most necessary rules inactive, and require that the user explicitly invoke other rules on an as-needed basis.

We provide two new facilities for this. In both versions of the MatchTool, forward searches proceed from the position of the software cursor towards the bottom of the scene. A new "Do-That-There" command orders the search roughly radially outward from the cursor. The search is invoked using the rule selected in the RuleTool, and the MatchTool interface is circumvented entirely. As is the case with regu-

Before   (a)

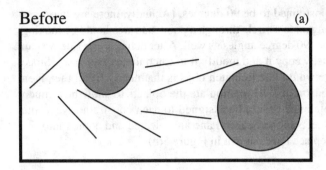

After   (b)

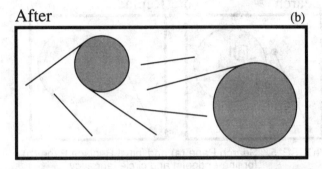

FIGURE 7. Applying the tangency rule. (a) a scene containing lines and circles; (b) nearly tangent lines made tangent.

lar MatchTool searches, the matches can be accepted or rejected with "Yes" and "No" buttons. Another option invokes a chosen rule only on selected objects, so for example, selected quadrilaterals can be transformed into rectangles by choosing the "Make Angle 90 Degrees" rule from the RuleTool, and invoking the RuleTool's "ChangeAll" button.

EXAMPLE 3: ROUNDING CORNERS

As we were developing the first MatchTool, we accumulated a list of editing tasks that would be facilitated by an ideal graphical search and replace utility, and evaluated our implementation by determining which tasks it could actually solve. A task suggested by Eric Bier was to "round" 90 degree corners, that is, splice an arc of a given radius into the angles while maintaining tangent continuity between the arc and the lines. We perceived this as difficult, because we thought it would be necessary to match on the shape of pieces of segments. Though neither MatchTool implementation can perform this kind of matching, in our third example we show how constraint-based search and replace can perform the rounding task not only for 90 degree angles, but for arbitrary ones. In this example, the replacement rule adds a new, constrained object to the scene, which is a type of replacement beyond the capabilities of other existing beautifiers.

Search (a)　Replace (b)　Replace (c)　Replace (d)

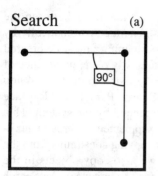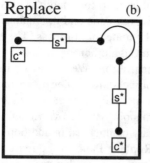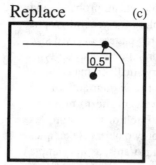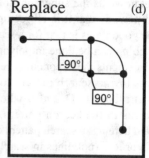

FIGURE 8. Rounding corners. (a) Search Pane; (b) Replace Pane after splicing in an arc, and adding fixed location and fixed slope constraints (labeled c* and s*, respectively); (c) Replace Pane after adding a 1/2 inch distance constraint on the arc's radius (the figure has been reduced); (d) Replace Pane after adding two more angle constraints.

The search pattern shown in Figure 8(a), matches on two segments, meeting at 90 degrees. Since the lines in the Search Pane are part of a single polyline, and we have chosen to search on "Object class", "Curve type", and "Constraints", MatchTool 2 will match only pairs of joined line segments that are part of the same polyline. We copy the Search Pane contents into the Replace Pane, and delete the angle constraint. The Replace Pane now contains a representative match that we will, step by step, transform into its replacement. Figure 8(b-d) shows the steps in this sequence.

First we fix the far endpoints at their current locations, since they should not move, and we fix the slopes of the line segments as well. We shorten the segments a bit, and splice in an arc, producing the pane shown in Figure 8(b).

A few additional constraints still must be added. Though the arc implicitly constrains both of its endpoints to be the same distance from its center, we still need to constrain its radius. Eventually we plan to allow numerical parameters for replacement rules, but in this example we set the radius to a constant of one half inch. This constraint is shown in Figure 8(c). Finally, we add two additional constraints to ensure tangency. The angle formed by the arc's center, the near endpoint of the top line, and the far endpoint, is set to –90 degrees, and the corresponding angle formed with the other line is set to 90 degrees. These final constraints are shown in

Figure 8(d) (Note that for each of these figures we have turned off the display of constraints not added by the step.).

The representative match has now been completely transformed into the desired replacement. After applying the rule to the "F" in Figure 9(a), the corners are correctly rounded, producing Figure 9(b).

The rule can easily be generalized to round all angles. In fact, the constraints added to the Replace Pane will already round any angle between 0 and 180 degrees, provided it can be rounded. We need only add a 90 degree tolerance to the search pattern, making the entire rule work for angles between 0 and 180 degrees. Given two lines that meet at an angle ABC, either this angle or its reverse, angle CBA, is between 0 and 180 degrees. Thus this search pattern will match any pair of connected lines, and the convex angles of the search pattern and the match will be aligned, which is important for the replacement. Applied to the "N" of Figure 10(a), the rule rounds all the angles, producing Figure 10(b).

FIGURE 10. Rounding arbitrary angles in an N. (a) The unrounded version; (b) After application of the generalized rule. (This figure has been reduced.)

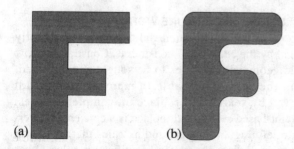

FIGURE 9. Rounding right angles in an F. (a) The unrounded version; (b) After application of our rounding rule. (This figure has been reduced.)

ALGORITHM

Objects in both the scene and the Search Pane can be viewed as nodes in a graph, with constraints linking the nodes. Therefore, matching the search pattern to the scene requires finding occurrences of one graph within another.

This is known as the subgraph isomorphism problem, and the bad news is that it is NP-complete for general graphs [3]. The good news is that for a search pattern of fixed size the matching can be done in polynomial time, and for typical replacements the exponent is very small. To match the n elements of the search pattern to the m elements of the scene, the cost is $O(cm^n)$, where c is the number of constraints in the search pattern. Each of the examples presented here has a search pattern of two objects (examples 1 and 2) or less (polylines in search patterns, as in example 3, count as single objects), so the costs are $O(m^2)$ and $O(m)$, respectively. For dynamic search and replace, when a single object is created or modified, the search proceeds even faster, since we know this object must participate in the match. In this case the exponent is reduced by one, and the search costs for the examples in this paper are linear or constant time.

Initially, objects in the Search Pane are placed in a list, and one by one each is matched against scene objects. If a match is found for an object, the search proceeds to the next element of the list. If no match can be found for a given object, the search backtracks and a different match is sought for the previous object. When matching a Search Pane object against scene objects, MatchTool 2 first verifies that the graphical attributes selected in the Search Column correspond, and then proceeds to examine relationships expressed by constraints. Only those constraints that reference the Search Pane object currently being matched, with no references to other unmatched objects, need to be considered at this step. As an optimization, constraints are pre-sorted according to when in the search process they can be tested.

Another technique accelerates the search by using the Search Pane constraints to isolate where in the scene matches might be found. For example, if the Search Pane contains two objects with a distance constraint between them, and a match has been found for the first object, then we can determine how far away the second match must be located in the scene (to the accuracy of the constraint tolerance). When matching the second object, we can immediately rule out objects whose bounding box does not intersect this region. Similarly, slope and angle constraints also narrow down the match's location, but the intersection calculations are more costly, so we currently do not use this information.

When a match is found that the user chooses to replace, the constraints of the objects in the Replace Pane are copied and applied to the match. This operation is somewhat tricky, since it requires a mapping between objects in the Replace Pane and the matched objects of the scene. We do this as a two step process: first we map the Replace Pane objects to those in the Search Pane, and then we map the Search Pane

objects to the match. The second mapping, between the Search Pane and the match, is generated automatically by the matching process. The first mapping must be created through other means and is done only once, in advance of searching. We have two mechanisms to do this. When objects are copied from the Search Pane to the Replace Pane, they are automatically mapped by the system. This mapping can be overridden or supplemented through auxiliary commands. In addition to copying constraints from the Replace Pane to the match, we also copy objects in the Replace Pane that are not mapped to objects in the Search Pane. This allows constraint-based replacements to add objects to the scene.

IMPLEMENTATION

MatchTool 2 and the RuleTool are both implemented as part of the Chimera editor. Chimera is written mainly in Lucid COMMON LISP (using the Common Lisp Object System), with a little C code thrown in for numerically intensive tasks and window system communications. It runs on Sun Workstations under the OpenWindows 3.0 window system. Chimera uses Levenberg-Marquadt iteration to solve systems of constraints [18], and can currently enforce about 10 different types of geometric relations.

The implementation of MatchTool 2 was greatly facilitated by the use of *generators*, which are objects that return the values of a sequence on an as-needed basis. Both the function and data for producing the next value are stored in the generator. The first MatchTool used a single generator for producing all matching orientations of one shape against another. It worked so well that in MatchTool 2 we use generators pervasively. MatchTool 2 has generators for matching sets of segments within an object, matching a single Search Pane object, matching the entire search pattern, and matching the activated rules of a ruleset. The abstractions provided by these generators made the program elegant and much easier to write. The code runs reasonably quickly. For example, the search and replace operations in Figure 7 take 0.11 seconds on a Sun Sparcstation 2 (28.5 MIPS), including the time spent solving constraints.

CONCLUSIONS AND FUTURE WORK

The power of graphical search and replace is significantly enhanced by the addition of constraints. Constraints allow specific geometric relations to be sought and enforced, making the rules applicable in many situations not addressed by search and replace on complete shapes. Constraint-based search and replace is a convenient interface for defining and understanding rules that transform drawings, including illustration beautification rules. Other systems have pre-coded beautification rules, so that existing rules can be understood only by reading documentation or using the system, and new rules can be defined only as programming enhancements. Constraint-based search and replace allows new rules to be defined by the user, making an additional kind of editor extensibility possible. Constraint-based search and replace can add new objects to a scene, constrained against existing objects, which extends the applications of the technique beyond simple beautification.

We are pleased with the interface for constraint-based search and replace specifications, though several important user options need to be added. In Peridot the search process is terminated when all of an object's degrees of freedom have been constrained. This is a very useful feature that we would like to add. However, the constraints that we use are multi-directional, and often non-unique (i.e., they may constrain a degree of freedom without uniquely determining it), so it is harder in Chimera to determine when this is the case. For example, in beautifying the house shown in Figure 4, our implementation prompts the user to accept or reject replacements, even if they add only *redundant constraints* (i.e. constraints already implied by other constraints in the scene). We are currently investigating methods for determining when a degree of freedom is already constrained.

These methods might also indicate if existing constraints conflict with another that we would like to add, and if so which. If there is a constraint conflict, MatchTool 2 should allow the option of either removing conflicting constraints and applying the new ones, or not performing the replacement at all. Currently we can determine only whether or not the augmented system can be solved by our editor. If it cannot, we print a message and the user can either undo the replacement or manually remove the unwanted constraints.

Recent research has dealt with merging rule-based techniques into direct manipulation systems [6][7]. Constraint-based search and replace is a direct manipulation technique for defining rules that govern the geometry and placement of graphical objects. Since direct manipulation interfaces represent data in terms of such objects, dynamic constraint-based search and replace might be useful for defining rules to control the behavior of these interfaces. For example, certain types of semantic snapping could be defined with this technique. We are interested in modifying constraint-based search and replace to make it useful for this task.

Rules in our system could be enhanced in a number of ways. Currently there is no mechanism for expressing the value of a replacement attribute relative to the match. For example, our system currently cannot search for all angles in a given range, and add 5 degrees to each. In addition, we would like to be able to control the permanence of constraints in the replacement pattern individually, and to assign them individual priorities if necessary. To improve the visual representation of rules we should display the tolerance of the Search Pane constraints, textually, in their labels.

Finally, we would like to improve our tools for archiving and merging multiple rule sets, add new kinds of constraints to our system, and allow numerical parameters to the search and replace rules.

ACKNOWLEDGMENTS
Eric Bier originally suggested the idea of graphical search and replace, and participated in the development of Match-Tool 1. Michael Elhadad's comments lead to an improved paper. This work was partially funded by a grant from IBM.

REFERENCES

1. Bier, E. A., and Stone, M. C. Snap-Dragging. Proceedings of SIGGRAPH '86 (Dallas, Texas, August 18-22, 1986) In *Computer Graphics 20*, 4 (August 1986). 233-240.

2. Borning, A. Graphically Defining New Building Blocks in ThingLab. *Human Computer Interaction 2*, 4. 1986. 269-295. Reprinted in *Visual Programming Environments: Paradigms and Systems*. Ephraim Glinert, ed. IEEE Computer Society Press, Los Alamitos, CA. 1990. 450-469.

3. Garey, M. R., and Johnson, D. S. *Computers and Intractability: A Guide to the Theory of NP-Completeness*. Freeman, San Francisco, CA. 1979.

4. Goines, D. L. *A Constructed Roman Alphabet*. David R. Godine, publisher. 306 Dartmouth St., Boston, MA 02116. 1982.

5. Hudson, S. E. An Enhanced Spreadsheet Model for User Interface Specification. Report TR 90-33. Univ. of Arizona. Computer Science. October 1990.

6. Hudson, S. E., and Yeatts, A. K. Smoothly Integrating Rule-Based Techniques into a Direct Manipulation Interface Builder. In Proceedings of UIST '91 (Hilton Head, SC, November 11-13). ACM, New York, 1991. 145-153.

7. Karsenty, S., Landay, J. A., and Weikart, C. Inferring Graphical Constraints with Rockit. Research Report. DEC Paris Research Laboratory. In preparation.

8. Kurlander, D., and Bier, E. A. Graphical Search and Replace. Proceedings of SIGGRAPH '88 (Atlanta, Georgia, August 1-5, 1988). In *Computer Graphics 22*, 4 (August 1988). 113-120.

9. Kurlander, D. Editor Extensibility: Domains and Mechanisms. Technical Report CUCS-516-89. Columbia University, Computer Science. May 1989.

10. Kurlander, D. *Graphical Editing by Example*. Ph.D. Thesis. Columbia University. Computer Science. In preparation.

11. Lewis, C. NoPumpG: Creating Interactive Graphics with Spreadsheet Machinery. In E. Glinert, *Visual Programming Environments: Paradigms and Systems*, IEEE Computer Society Press, Los Alamitos, CA. 526-546.

12. Maulsby, D. L., Witten, I. H., and Kittlitz, K. A. Metamouse: Specifying Graphical Procedures by Example. Proceedings of SIGGRAPH '89 (Boston, MA, July 31-August 4, 1989) In *Computer Graphics 23*, 4 (July 1989). 127-136.

13. Myers, B. A. *Creating User Interfaces by Demonstration*. Academic Press, Boston, 1988.

14. Myers, B. A. Demonstrational Interfaces: A Step Beyond Direct Manipulation. Technical Report CMU-CS-90-162. Carnegie Mellon University, School of Computer Science. August 1990.

15. Myers, B. A. Graphical Techniques in a Spreadsheet for Specifying User Interfaces. In CHI '91 Proceedings (New Orleans, LA, April 27-May 2, 1991). ACM, New York. 1991. 243-249.

16. Nelson, G. Juno, A Constraint-Based Graphics System. Proceedings of SIGGRAPH '85 (San Francisco, CA, July 22-26, 1985) In *Computer Graphics 19*, 3 (July 1985). 235-243.

17. Pavlidis, T. and Van Wyk, C. J. An Automatic Beautifier for Drawings and Illustrations. Proceedings of SIGGRAPH '85 (San Francisco, CA, July 22-26, 1985) In *Computer Graphics 19*, 3 (July 1985). 225-234.

18. Press, W. H., Flannery, B. P., Teukolsky, S. A., and Vetterling, W. T. *Numerical Recipes in C: The Art of Scientific Computing*. Cambridge University Press, Cambridge, 1988.

19. Shneiderman, B. Direct Manipulation: A Step Beyond Programming Languages. *IEEE Computer 16*, 8 (August 1983), 57-69.

20. Sutherland, I. E. Sketchpad: A Man-Machine Graphical Communication System. AFIPS Conference Proceedings, Spring Joint Computer Conference. 1963. 329-346.

21. Vander Zanden, B. T. Constraint Grammars—A New Model for Specifying Graphical Applications. In CHI '89 Proceedings (Austin TX, April 30-May 4, 1989). ACM, New York, 1989, 325-330.

22. Weitzman, L. DESIGNER: A Knowledge-Based Graphic Design Assistant. ICS Report 8609. University of California, San Diego. July 1986.

Dynamic Queries for Information Exploration:
An Implementation and Evaluation

Christopher Ahlberg*, Christopher Williamson, and Ben Shneiderman

Department of Computer Science
Human-Computer Interaction Laboratory
University of Maryland, College Park, MD 20742
ben@cs.umd.edu

Abstract

We designed, implemented and evaluated a new concept for direct manipulation of databases, called *dynamic queries*, that allows users to formulate queries with graphical widgets, such as sliders. By providing a graphical visualization of the database and search results, users can find trends and exceptions easily. Eighteen undergraduate chemistry students performed statistically significantly faster using a dynamic queries interface compared to two interfaces both providing form fill-in as input method, one with graphical visualization output and one with all-textual output. The interfaces were used to expore the periodic table of elements and search on their properties.

1. INTRODUCTION

Most database systems require the user to create and formulate a complex query, which presumes that the user is familiar with the logical structure of the database [4]. The queries on a database are usually expressed in high level query languages (such as SQL, QUEL). This works well for many applications, but it is not a fully satisfying way of finding data. For naïve users these systems are difficult to use and understand, and they require a long training period [3].

Clearly there is a need for easy to use, quick and powerful query methods for database retrieval. Direct manipulation has proved to be successful for other applications such as display editors, spreadsheets, computer aided design/manufacturing systems, computer games and graphical environments for operating systems such as the Apple Macintosh [8]. Direct manipulation interfaces support:

----

* *Current address: Dept of Comp. Sci., Chalmers Univ.*
S-412 96 Göteborg, Sweden

- Continuous visual representation of objects and actions of interest
- Physical actions or labelled button presses instead of complex syntax
- Rapid, incremental, reversible operations whose impact on the object of interest is immediately visible.
- Layered or spiral approach to learning that permits usage with minimal knowledge.

One of the great advantages of direct manipulation is that it places the task in the center of what users have to do. [7] describes it as "The user is able to apply intellect directly to the task; the tool itself seems to disappear". The success of direct manipulation can be understood in the context of the syntactic/semantic model which describes the different levels of understanding users have [8]. Objects of interest are displayed so that actions are directly in the high level semantic domain. Users do not need to decompose tasks into syntactically complex sequences. Thus each command is a comprehensible action in the problem domain whose effect is immediately visible. The closeness of the command action to the problem domain reduces user problem-solving load and stress.

For databases, there have been few attempts to use direct manipulation. Zloof describes a method of data manipulation based on the direct representations of the relations on the screen, Query-by-Example [10]. Zloof writes "a user dealing with 'simple' queries needs to study the system only to that point of complexity which is compatible with the level of sophistication required within the domain of those queries." Query-by-Example succeeds because novices can begin working with just a little training, yet there is ample power for the expert.

Another attempt to create a more user friendly query language is the PICASSO query language [3]. The authors state that the major contribution of PICASSO and graphical interface ROGUE is that users can pose complex queries using a mouse without knowing the details of the underlying database schema nor the details of first-order predicate calculus or algebra. The power of direct manipulation can be applied even further. Neither Query-by-Example nor PICASSO provide any visual display of actions. Query-by-Example relies on users entering values with a keyboard. Even though PICASSO supports input through mouse and menus, it requires users to perform a number of operations in each step. The combination of graphical input/output is not applied in either system.

A more desirable database interface:

- represents the query graphically,
- provides a visible limits on the query range,
- provides a graphical representation of the database and the query result,
- gives immediate feedback of the result after every query adjustment, and
- allows novice users to begin working with little training but still provides expert users with powerful features.

An interface utilizing dynamic queries possesses the above-mentioned properties [9].

In dynamic queries the query is represented by a number of widgets such as sliders [1] (figure 1). A slider consists of a label, a field indicating its current value, a slider bar with a drag box, and a value at each end of the slider bar indicating minimum and maximum values. Sliding the drag box with the mouse changes the slider value. Clicking on the slider bar increases or decreases the value one step at a time.

Figure 1. Slider from Open Look.

The database is represented on the screen in graphical form. This paper describes a program dealing with the chemical elements and accordingly the periodic table of elements was chosen as the representation. The result of the query can be highlighted by coloring, changing points of light, marking of regions, or blinking.

The combination of a graphical query and graphical output matches well the ideas of direct manipulation. The slider serves as a metaphor for the operation of entering a value for a field in the query - it provides a mental model [5] of the range. Changing the value is done by a physical action - sliding the drag box with a mouse - instead of entering the value by keyboard. By being able to slide the drag box back and forth and getting immediate updates of the query results, it is possible to do tens of queries in just a few seconds, i.e the operation is rapid. The operation is incremental and if the query result is not what users expected the operation is reversible by just sliding the drag box in the opposite direction. Error messages are not needed - there is no such thing as an 'illegal' operation.

The interaction between the database visualization and the query mechanism is important. The sliders have to be placed close to the visualization to reduce eye movement. The highlighting of elements should be in harmony with the coloring scheme of the slider. For example the color of the area to the left of the drag box on the slider bar is the same as the highlighted elements in the visualization, because the values to the left of the drag box are the values that satisfy the query.

The dynamic queries program used for the experiment is an educational program for the periodic table of elements. It allows users to set properties such as atomic number, atomic mass, electronegativity, etc. to highlight elements that satisfy the query displayed on the periodic table. This lets users explore how these properties interact with each other. Other interesting discoveries can be made regarding trends of properties in the periodic table - such as how electronegativity increases from the lower left corner to the upper right corner of the periodic table. Exceptions to trends can also be found easily, such as the two places in the periodic table where the atomic mass does not increase with atomic number.

2. EXPERIMENT
2.1 Introduction
This experiment compared three different interfaces for database query and visualization: a dynamic queries interface, a second interface (FG) providing graphical visualization output but using form fill-in as the input method [6] (Form fill-in - Graphical output) and a third interface (FT) also using a forms fill-in as input but providing output as a list of elements fulfilling the query (Form fill-in - Textual output). The alternative interfaces were chosen to find out which aspect of dynamic queries makes the major difference, the input by sliders allowing users to quickly browse through the database, or the output visualization providing an overview of the database. These were compared using three sets of matched questions.

2.2 Hypotheses
The primary hypothesis was that, because of the visualization of the periodic table in the dynamic queries and the FG interfaces, there would be a major difference compared to the FT interface. Performance results were measured as the time used for each question and the number of correct answers.

For questions asking subjects to find trends in the periodic table, the hypothesis was that the visualization of the periodic table in the dynamic queries and FG interfaces would make the major difference compared to the FT interface. But the ability to perform a large number of queries during a small period of time with the dynamic queries interface would make a difference favoring dynamic queries over FG.

2.3 Interfaces
All interfaces were built using the Developer's Guide user interface development package in the OpenWindows environment on a Sun Microsystems SparcStation 1+ workstation with a 17-inch color monitor and optical three button mouse.

2.3.1 Dynamic Queries interface

The dynamic queries interface (figure 2) provides a visualization of the query result. A periodic table showing the elements is displayed in 40-point Roman font. The elements that fulfill the criteria set by the user's latest query are highlighted by being displayed in red. The rest of the elements are displayed in light grey. Users perform queries by setting the values of six properties using sliders (figure 1). All interfaces included two other buttons, 'Max' and 'Min' that set the values of all input fields to the minimum or maximum value.

The query result is determined by ANDing all six sliders, so all the elements that have an atomic mass less than or equal to X AND an atomic number less than or equal to Y, etc., fulfill the criteria. The area to the left of the slider drag box is painted in red, corresponding to the red color of the highlighted elements in the visualization and thereby providing feedback about how elements are selected. The sliders are positioned under the periodic table, close to the visualization to minimize the distance users have to move their eyes. One direct manipulation feature in the dynamic queries interface was left out

for experimental purposes. It allows users to click on any element and thereby set the sliders to the values of the properties of that element.

2.3.2 FG interface

The FG interface (figure 3) provides users with the same visualization as the dynamic queries interface, but the query is composed by form fill-in. Instead of a slider, a numeric field allowing users to enter a value for that property by keyboard is provided. To the left of the numeric field the range of the criterion is given. If a value bigger than the upper bound is entered, the field is set to the upper bound.

The search is performed when users press the return key. The cursor indicating which numeric field is active stays in the same numeric field. Entering new values is done by either modifying the old one or deleting it and entering a new one. This is to provide an easy way to do the fine-tuning often needed when completing tasks. Users change the active field by using the up/down arrow keys. The left and right keys move the cursor inside the numeric field. The graphical output is exactly the same as in the dynamic queries interface.

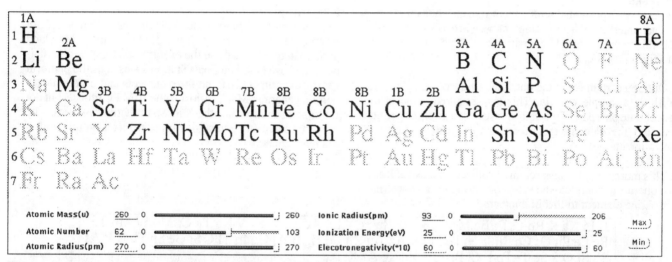

Figure 2. Dynamic Queries interface for the periodic table of elements

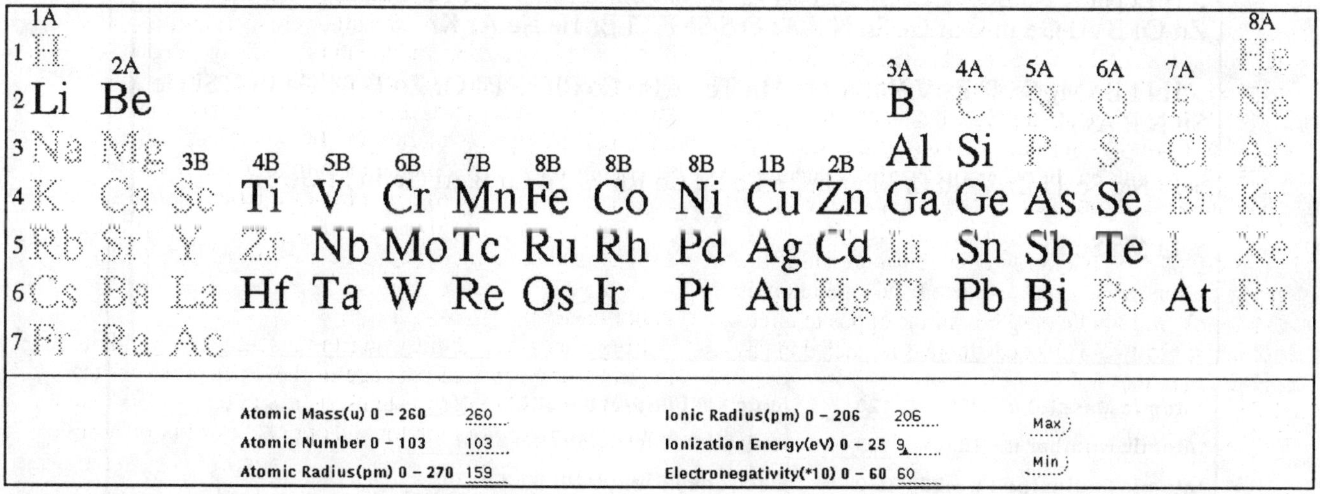

Figure 3. FG interface for periodic table

2.3.3 FT interface

The all textual interface (figure 4) provides exactly the same style of input as the FG interface but the output is given in an all textual manner. The elements that fulfill the criteria are listed in order of atomic number in a text window above the input fields. To be able to answer the questions, subjects were provided with a printed periodic table when using this interface.

2.4 Experimental variables

The independent variable in the experiment was the type of interface, with three treatments:

i. Dynamic Queries
ii. FG
iii FT

The dependent variables were:

i. Time to find answers
ii. Number of correct answers
iii. Subjective satisfaction

2.5 Tasks

Subjects were presented with a set of five matched questions for each interface. The questions, chosen in cooperation with a chemistry professor at University of Maryland, were divided into five categories:

1. Out of a certain set in the database, find a certain element fulfilling a simple criteria. This task required subjects to concentrate on a part of the database such as a group or period and find the element that, for example, had the highest ionization energy.

2. This more complex task required subjects to make at least two queries to complete the task; comparing the characteristics of one element to that of another.

3. Combine sliders/fields to get a subset of elements and find the element fulfilling a certain criteria in this set. This task required the set to examine to be formed by combining several criteria.

4. Find a trend for a property. The task requires subjects to create a mental picture of how a property changes through the database. This might be how atomic mass increases with atomic number.

5. Find an exception to a trend. This task asked subjects to find, from a given number of elements, the element that didn't follow 'normal behavior' .

2.6 Pilot Study Results

A pilot study of four subjects was conducted. It led to several changes in the experiment design. The initial manual timing procedure was changed to a computerized procedure. The instrument used for measuring subjective satisfaction was the Questionaire for User Interface Satisfaction (QUIS) [2], but shortened to 30 of the 72 original questions.

2.7 Participants

Eighteen undergraduate students, 9 females and 9 males, from summer session chemistry classes at University of Maryland participated voluntarily in the experiment. Only two participants had used the Sun SparcStation 1+ used as the platform for the experiment. All but three subjects had used a mouse before, generally Macintosh or some IBM PC mouse, but not the optical mouse that the Sun SparcStation 1+ uses. The subjects' chemistry education ranged from one to four undergraduate courses.

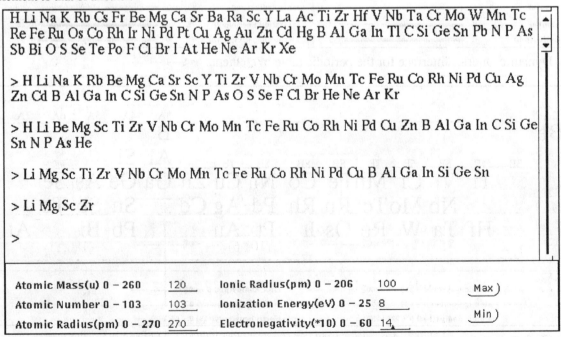

Figure 4. FT interface for periodic table

2.8 Procedures

A counterbalanced within-subjects design was used. The question sets were always given in the same order. Each session lasted an hour and consisted of four phases:

1. Introduction and training: Subjects were given a description of the purpose and procedures of the experiment and were also given training with the mouse and controls of the interfaces.

2. Practice tasks: Two practice tasks were given for each interface. During these tasks subjects were free to ask questions about both tasks and interface.

3. Timed tasks: For each interface five questions were given. Before answering each question the interface was set to the initial state. Subjects read the question, and were asked if they fully understood it. If so they pushed the Start button and started the query. This was to eliminate variations in subjects comprehension speed. When subjects found the answer they wrote it down and pushed the Done button.

4. Subjective evaluation: Subjects were asked to fill out a shortened QUIS-form after having completed each interface and to provide open commentary while answering questions.

Phases 2, 3 and 4 were repeated for each interface.

Administration

The experiment was run over a period of 12 days. Subjects were asked to work as quickly and accurately as possible. The experimenter sat next to the subject, presented questions and ensured that the subject initialized the query and followed the proper timing procedures.

3. RESULTS

Analysis of the timed tasks was done using an ANOVA with repeated measures for interface type. Observing the mean times to complete all tasks 1-5, shows a significant main effect, $F(2,34)=36.1$ $(p<0.001)$. Similarly a significant main effect was found for individual tasks 1,2,4 and 5, $F(2,34)=19.0$, 16.4, 21.4, 20.2 respectively $(p<0.001)$ and for task 3 $F(2,34)= 7.1$ $(p<0.005)$.

Tukey's post-hoc HSD analysis was used to determine which interface(s) was significantly faster. The dynamic queries interface had a significantly faster mean time for completing all tasks than both FG and FT interfaces, $(p<0.005)$ and $(p<0.001)$ respectively.

The time to complete each task is shown in Table 1. Figure 5 gives a bar chart of the same data.

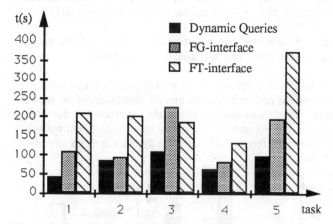

Figure 5. Mean time to complete each task

Timing Data For Each Task

	Dynamic Queries		FG		FT
1	40.6 (21.5)	◀ .05	108.8 (62.3)	◀ .001	210.2 (129.3)
2	87.3 (92.3)		91.5 (44.8)	◀ .001	200.8 (79.1)
3	111.0 (55.8)	◀ .005	225.2 (105.1)		187.8 (114.5)
4	60.4 (41.4)		81.4 (30.9)	◀ .001	126.8 (32.0)
5	95.9 (51.4)	◀ .05	202.5 (101.6)	◀ .001	367.9 (180.1)
Σ	412.0 (216.1)	◀ .005	709.5 (182.9)	◀ .001	1093.6 (336.3)

Table 1. Table showing mean time to complete each task. Variance is shown in parantheses. An arrow from one cell to another indicates significantly smaller time for the cell being pointed at. Significance level is given above arrow.

For task 1 the dynamic queries interface was significantly faster than the FG interface, (p<0.05) and the FG interface was significantly faster than the FT interface, (p<0.001). For task 2, no difference between dynamic queries and the FG interface was found, but both were significantly faster than the FT interface, (p<0.001).

For task 3 the dynamic queries interface was significantly faster than both FG and FT interfaces, (p<0.005) and (p<0.05) respectively, no significant difference between the FG and FT interfaces was found. Actually, the mean time for the FT interface was 37.4 seconds faster than the FG interface.

For task 4 both the dynamic queries and FG interfaces were faster than the FT interface, (p<0.001). Task 5 showed significantly faster mean time for the dynamic queries interface compared to the FG interface, (p<0.05) and the FG interface was significantly faster than the FT interface, (p<0.001).

Figure 6 shows the number of errors subjects made for each task and interface, out of a total of 18 questions.

For the QUIS, there was a statistically significant difference between the dynamic queries and FT interfaces for **all** questions. There was also a statistically significant difference between the FG and FT interfaces for all questions; but no significant differences between the dynamic queries and FG interfaces.

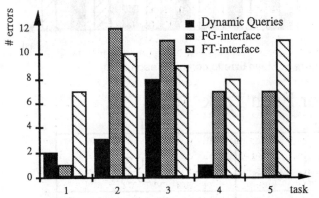

Figure 6. Table showing number of errors for each interface and task.

4. DISCUSSION

The hypothesis that the dynamic queries interface would perform better than both the FG interface and the FT interface was confirmed. Similarly the FG interface produced faster performance times than the FT interface. The major difference in mean performance times was between the dynamic queries and FG interfaces compared to the FT interface. This was also confirmed in participants' comments which indicated that the visualization is the most important part.

The lack of difference in performance between the dynamic queries and FG interfaces in task 2 and four was surprising. The results for task 2 can possibly be explained by the fact that it was similar to task 1, and therefore subjects learned how to apply a good strategy. For task 4 subjects already had an idea of what the answer should be from their coursework. The

range of the properties was limited and not too many values had to be checked to get a picture of the trend, therefore the slider did not make a big difference.

4.1 Timed tasks

Task 1: The dynamic queries interface performed significantly better than both the FG and FT interfaces. The correct answer could be found by adjusting the correct slider until either the first or the last element in the subset changed color. Using the FG interface or the FT interface required subjects to use some kind of binary search method to find the correct element since each query had to be typed-in, which accounts for the slower performance. Using the FT interface required users to locate the subset of the periodic table in question in the larger set retrieved from the database with the query, which accounts for the longer performance time using that interface.

Task 2: Surprisingly no difference in performance time were found between the dynamic queries interface and the FG interface. This can probably be explained by the fact that the task was similar to task 1, and subjects figured out a good strategy while solving task 1. Similarly to task 1, the FT interface performed poorly as participants had to locate the relevant subset of elements to be analyzed in the larger set.

Task 3: The dynamic queries interface performed significantly better than both the FG interface and the FT interface. No significant difference between the FG interface and the FT interface was found but the mean time for the FT interface was actually shorter than the mean time for the FG interface. The task required subjects to set two input fields to find a subset of elements and in this subset find one element that fulfilled a criteria. As the subsets were rather big the visualization of the dynamic queries and FG interfaces caused some problems. To see one element shifting color when moving the slider or entering values was found to be hard. The dynamic queries interface compensated for this by making it possible to quickly change the value. The FT interface performed better than the FG interface as it was possible to see the result of the latest queries on the screen. By comparing the line length of the current and the previous result subjects could easily find the correct element. The FG interface posed an interesting problem for subjects that were novice computer users. Trying to find which element was the first to change from red to gray, required them to enter values repeatedly. In doing this, novices had to look down at the keyboard, press <return> and before they had moved their eyes to the screen, the change had already taken place.

Trying to see which element changed color, subjects were found leaning backwards to get an overview. This problem is probably a result of two factors, the colors used and the width of the window. The colors were found to be good in the QUIS results, ~8 on the 1-9 scale, but maybe some better combination can be found.

Task 4: This task required subjects to find an overall trend in the database. The hypothesis that the visualization would make the major difference was confirmed. Finding a trend is greatly simplified by getting an overview of the database, which was reflected in the experiment results. But comparing the dynamic queries interface with the FG interface showed no difference which was not in line with our hypothesis. The reason for this is twofold, a lot of the students already had a general idea of the answer and only had to confirm it, and even if they did not know the answer they only had to type in a few values to find the solution using the FG interface.

Task 5: The dynamic queries interface performed significantly better than both the FG interface and the FT interface, this stemming from the two advantages of the dynamic queries interface, the visualization and the sliders. The visualization allowed subjects to see exceptions easily when they showed up on the screen and the sliders allowed subjects to quickly change the values to find the correct answer. This task was very hard to solve with the FT interface, as subjects didn't have any visualization and had to use the keyboard to enter the values.

4.2 Interface Characteristics

4.2.1 Dynamic Queries interface
Studying slider use revealed several interesting possibilities for improvements. Most subjects had never used the optical mouse before and had problems pointing accurately enough with it. This caused problems with the slider as the drag box was small. Similarly several subjects found it hard to click on the slider bar to "fine tune" the setting. Also the fine tuning feature caused problems as the mouse arrow moved to the end of the slider bar when users clicked on it. For experimental purposes, subjects were unable to type in a value for the slider setting, which several subjects did request. Moving the slider can cause confusion if you move it too fast, and several subjects were found clicking at the sides of the slider bar, to adjust the slider up/down one step at a time, when making big changes.

The interface was wide, ~14 inches, which many subjects found to be a problem. They were observed leaning backwards to get an overview of what was changing on the screen. This was in sharp contrast to the FT interface where subjects were observed to lean forward, put fingers on both screen and the provided periodic table to create some sort of mental model of what they saw. Although the colors used were found to be good by participants, question 3 asking for the largest element in a fairly large set of elements caused problems because it was difficult to see when one single change occurs in the graphical query result. This problem can be overcome by either highlighting elements that changed last or introducing a short "click" sound every time the graphical output changes.

4.2.2 FG interface
Using the keyboard proved to give participants several problems. Subjects invariably failed to remember that they had to delete the last number and forgot to move the cursor to reach another field. It should be noted that three subjects, having somewhat extreme problems with the mouse, stated their definite preference of the FG interface and felt they had more control using it.

Participants found it hard to know the range of the property they were manipulating, even though the range was given to the left of the field. Analogously participants found it hard to know when they reached the upper bound. With the slider it was easy to grasp both the range and the current value. The slider provides an intuition about which set is selected by painting the area to the left of the drag box red and vice-versa for the area to the right. This can not be done metaphorically with textual input, and accordingly subjects were found having trouble grasping which elements were selected.

4.2.3 FT interface
The FT interface performed very poorly compared to both the dynamic queries interface and the FG interface. This was also reflected in the user subjective evaluation (see section 4.3). This was to be expected but it was interesting to see how subjects reacted when the model of the periodic table was taken away, and they had to create one of their own. Using the FT interface, participants were found holding one hand pointing at the screen and the other on the provided printed periodic table, trying to interpret the query result.

4.3 Subjective Evaluation
The superior performance using dynamic queries compared to the FG interface was not reflected in the QUIS results. This is surprising as several QUIS questions addressed commands and ways of solving tasks.

Although it was not reflected in the QUIS results, subjects' delight was most obvious using the dynamic queries interface. They offered comments such as "The sliders are more fun than the key punch", "With the sliders you can watch the periodic table and see what changes color right before your eyes", "dynamic queries presented a more direct method of entering data for trial and error attempt", "You can play around more without worrying about messing it up".

Subjects having problems with the mouse stated for the FG interface: "You have more control over the numbers and you can read better what changes you have made." Some subjects using the dynamic queries interface asked: "Can I set the value directly instead of this guessing?" Participants were very critical of the FT interface, which also was reflected in the users subjective evaluation, the QUIS. But some positive responses were found, one subject stated "You can see what you have done before".

5. FUTURE RESEARCH
Further research about dynamic queries is needed. The sliders must be examined further:
- construct sliders giving ranges not bound to the minimum or maximum values by providing two drag boxes, and the issues of displaying such a range.
- select a set of sliders from a large set of properties, and
- select boolean combinations of sliders.

The visualization is equally important to examine. For example how to:
- find good visualizations for databases that do not have natural representations as a map.

- solve the problem of visualizations too large to fit into one screen, and
- find the best highlighting methods, such as colors, points of light, blinking, etc.

The last and maybe most important issue to examine is other applications of dynamic queries. How can direct manipulation of databases not consisting of well-formed ordinal data be implemented?

6. CONCLUSIONS

Results of this experiment suggest that direct manipulation can be applied to database queries with success. Results showed that visualization of the database and query result is the most important part of the dynamic queries, but that sliders direct manipulation of the query are also important.

For dynamic queries to be successfully implemented, several issues must be addressed. A good visualization must be found, such as a map, an organization chart, or a table, with good color combinations for highlighting. The control panel manipulating the query must be placed in a logical way to reduce eye and mouse movement. Sliders must be implemented so they are easy for novice users to use, i.e the drag box must be big enough and the slider must provide enough information without being cluttered. The search time must be immediate so that users feel in control and have a sense of causation.

7. ACKNOWLEDGEMENTS

We appreciate the support of Sun Microsystems, Inc. and NCR Corporation; as well as the comments from Rick Chimera, Holmes Liao and other members of the HCIL. Thanks also to Staffan Truvé and Dr Samuel O. Grim for help in constructing the tasks.

8. REFERENCES

1. *OPEN LOOK - GUI Functional Specification.* Sun Microsystems, Inc. Reading, MA, 1989.

2. Chin, J., Diehl, V., Norman, K. Development of an instrument measuring user satisfaction of the human-computer interface. *Proc. CHI'88 Human Factors in Comp. Systems Conf.*, ACM Press, pp. 213-218.

3. Kim H., Korth H, Silberschatz A. PICASSO: A Graphical Query Language, *Software - Practice and Experience 18*, 3 (March 1988), pp. 169-203.

4. Larsson, James A. A Visual Approach to Browsing in a Database Environment. *IEEE Computer 19*, 6 (June 1986), pp. 62-71.

5. Norman, Donald A. *The Psychology of Everyday Things*. Basic Books, Inc., New York, 1988.

6. Rowe, L.A. Fill-in-the-Form Programming. *Proc. 11th International on Very Large Databases*. ACM Press, 1985, pp. 394-403.

7. Rutkowski, Chris. An Introduction to the Human Applications Standard Computer Interface. *Byte 7* (Oct. 1982), pp. 291-310.

8. Shneiderman, Ben, Direct Manipulation: A step beyond programming languages, *IEEE Computer 16*, 8 (August 1983), pp. 57-69.

9. Williamson, C., Shneiderman, B. *The Dynamic HomeFinder: Evaluating Dyunamic Queries in a Real-Estate Information Exploration System*, University of Maryland CS-TR-2819, College Park, MD, 1992.

10. Zloof M. Query-by-Example. *Proc. National Computer Conference*, AFIPS Press, 1975, 431-437.

A 'Pile' Metaphor for Supporting
Casual Organization of Information

Richard Mander, Gitta Salomon and Yin Yin Wong

Human Interface Group, Advanced Technology
Apple Computer, Inc.
20525 Mariani Ave., MS 76-3H
Cupertino, California 95014
(408)996-1010

ABSTRACT

A user study was conducted to investigate how people deal with the flow of information in their workspaces. Subjects reported that, in an attempt to quickly and informally manage their information, they created piles of documents. Piles were seen as complementary to the folder filing system, which was used for more formal archiving. A new desktop interface element – the pile – was developed and prototyped through an iterative process. The design includes direct manipulation techniques and support for browsing, and goes beyond physical world functionality by providing system assistance for automatic pile construction and reorganization. Preliminary user tests indicate the design is promising and raise issues that will be addressed in future work.

KEYWORDS: interface design, design process, interactive systems, user observation, desktop metaphor, interface metaphors, pile metaphor, information visualization, information organization, end-user programming.

INTRODUCTION

As the amount of information users confront on their computers increases, tools to organize and manipulate this information become increasingly important.

Today's direct manipulation computer interfaces, such as the Macintosh® desktop interface [1], offer limited means of handling information. Users can manually place files within folders, organized in a rigid hierarchy. Users are responsible for appropriately filing all items; the system offers little assistance in this often tedious task. Recent enhancements, such as "aliases" [2], allow users to overcome a frequent problem, namely that an item belongs in more than one folder. However, the folder as the sole container type presents an impoverished set of possibilities.

The real world provides a rich array of organization systems. In the past, researchers have looked at how users find items in their physical offices [9]. We conducted a study to observe how users *organize* the large amounts of information they work with in their physical offices. Our study differed from previous work in that we looked at ways in which people use and interact with filing systems.

We were also interested in how people work with assistants when dealing with information.

By examining individuals' information management schemes, we were able to extract and extrapolate a number of interesting interface ideas for a graphical interface. Our intent was not simply to emulate physical world functionality – several investigators have argued against this procedure [3,6] – but rather to leverage users' knowledge to create an intuitive and powerful system that goes beyond physical world capabilities. Using this approach, we sought to construct a design which provides new functionality and enhances the user interface.

Like Malone [9], we found that users like to group items spatially and often prefer to deal with information by creating physical piles of paper, rather than immediately categorizing it into specific folders. Computer users are confronted with large amounts of information, but currently are only provided with a hierarchical filing system for managing it.

Therefore, we propose that incorporating 'piles' within a graphical user interface could provide a number of interesting possibilities. Users have difficulty deciding where to file a new item; piling requires less mental effort. Today's office assistants use piles as a way of suggesting categories to others; computerized agents might make use of them in the same way to convey a certain degree of imprecision in the suggested organization. Piles may also provide an appropriate representation for the results of information retrieval algorithms which are inherently inexact [13].

At least one system, BUSINESS [11], previously explored this interface metaphor as a construct within a text-based application programming language. For example, a user could initiate an action by typing an instruction such as "Empty the In Box onto the Work Pile." However, there was no graphical representation, and so the system could do little more than allow the user to issue programmatic commands using a subset of English.

This paper provides both specific design ideas and insight into our design process as it progressed from user interviews to design to testing. The first section describes findings from observing and interviewing office workers. In particular, we report why folders were not always appropriate and how and when users found piles useful. We then describe the interface designs inspired by these observations. In the third section, we report results from informal tests of these designs. In conclusion, we describe directions for future work.

USER INTERVIEWS

As part of our design process, we undertook a user study to find out how people deal with information in their physical workspaces. Studies of this kind are important in helping us understand the user's perspective. Our aim was to identify aspects of the real world work process which could offer insight into a new, more powerful interface.

Method

The study involved interviews with thirteen men and women in Marketing, Support, Human Resources, and Technical departments within Apple Computer, Inc. The interviews lasted between 30 and 60 minutes and were conducted in the participant's work area. All interviews were videotaped.

We asked people to describe the way information arrived in their work area, what they initially did with this information, where it went next, and how it was finally stored. Participants gave us a tour of their workspace to help us understand what purpose various cabinets, shelves, and storage devices served. We also took a small pile of documents with us and asked participants to judge what these documents were on the basis of their appearance. In this way, we could find out how they worked with completely unfamiliar information. Since we are interested in developing ways for the computer to help the user, we also asked people how they worked with assistants.

Findings

Our subjects used a variety of techniques – folders, file cabinets, file racks, piles, binders, card files, and bulletin boards – for managing the information in their offices. Since our primary concern in this paper is the uses of folders and piles, we'll focus on observations relevant to these items.

Uses for folders. File folders were used in several ways. As could be expected, items were placed in folders which were in turn placed in file cabinets as a means of archiving information not currently needed. Users applied a variety of organizations to their file cabinets, ranging from totally random arrangements to strict alphabetical and color coded systems.

Users were sometimes dissatisfied with using folders in this way, because they were required to make an explicit decision about how to categorize individual items. This was often especially difficult with new information. One user said "I'm not always as good at categorizing things as I would like...it's hard to get it right and I'm sort of a perfectionist, so I think that I should know exactly how I should do it...I like things in their place, but I can't figure out exactly what place."

One solution, identified by several users, would be to file the information in several places. However, even though copiers were near at hand, people did not choose to duplicate information in order to store it in more than one folder.

Folders were also used in informal ways. Many people mounted folders in racks, which enabled the folders to stand up. These folders were used for frequently accessed information – most often action items and items requiring regular maintenance, such as expense reports and things to read. Some users ordered or changed the orientation of the folders in their racks to make the most important or urgent information prominent. Folders were also used as a storage medium within piles, as a way to hold together a certain group of items. As one user commented, "...[I] folderize to keep things neat...there's no hierarchy in there, because building a hierarchy takes too much time."

Based on these observations, we inferred two things about the current folder-based interface offered on the Macintosh: the categorization problems are presumably amplified by the use of multiply nested folders, and support for more informal grouping techniques, such as racks, could be useful.

Piles: A less rigid categorization system. In addition to using folders, users grouped items into piles. For example, most workers kept information they needed in a specific working area. A common strategy was to create separate piles for each project and place them within the working area, at distances that reflected their urgency. Many workers also created piles for incoming information that they could not deal with immediately. The contents of users' piles was clearly not restricted to paper documents – we observed piles composed of various items such as books, folders, reports, binders, cassette tapes, video tapes, postcards, envelopes, magazines, journals, and boxes.

People used piles instead of hierarchical folders because they did not require detailed categorization and they could be more easily reordered than a folder and file system. For many workers, the pile was viewed as an entity that was subject to change. Users reported that over a period of time, items within a pile would often be reshuffled and broken down into several sub-piles, and an informal process of categorization would begin. We noted several approaches to separating material within piles: some users stacked materials at different angles, while some placed dividers within the pile.

To the outside observer, an office containing piles often appears disorganized. However, all of our participants had several piles in their workspace and in most cases, they knew what was in each pile and could tell us quite a lot about its history. Seemingly disordered piles were often sensible to the person who created them, because they developed through many interactions over a long period of time. For instance, many piles grew as newer items were added to the top, and workers could tell where things were by their date, since the stack was ordered chronologically.

Piles: self-revealing, browseable. Several users remarked that the outer appearance of their piles conveniently allowed them to recognize particular items. Our subjects were also able to make use of the appearance of previously unseen piles. We asked them to look at a small pile of unfamiliar materials which we took with us to the interview. By looking at the pile's outside form, they were able to infer quite a lot about its contents.

Consequently, we noted that piles facilitate browsing, and we observed four different browsing methods. In the *edge* browse method described above, people looked at the outside edges of the pile for clues about the items within. Information such as color, texture, and thickness was commonly used to judge the contents of a pile. In the *restack* method, people started at the top of the pile and dealt with each item in turn by lifting it off the pile, looking at it and then placing it somewhere other than back on the pile. In the *hinge* method, the items stayed in the pile, but the pile was hinged open at different points to display a single item. The final method was to *spread out* a pile and look at its contents in parallel.

<u>Assistance with information management</u>. Most participants did not have an assistant, but said they would welcome one. We asked those who did have assistants to describe how they worked together.

Assistants commonly took care of routine tasks, such as sorting mail into different categories. For people who had to deal with large amounts of information, their assistant acted as a filter, passing along urgent material and removing junk mail. Some assistants would reorganize the workspace and create a filing system in which information could be more easily organized. This usually happened in collaboration with the worker. Typically the assistant would suggest categories and discuss these with the worker before actually filing the material. The assistant would often not understand the technical content, but could scan through the materials looking for keywords that might help in the categorization task. Piles were often used by assistants to indicate potential categories. As one assistant remarked, "I'll go into his office and put [labels] on piles on his floor and he'll look at it and say 'no' or he'll say 'that's pretty good'."

FROM OBSERVATION TO DESIGN SKETCH
The next step in our process was to take our observations and develop a number of design sketches using Macro-Mind's Director™ application [8] which supports scripted interaction and animation. These design sketches illustrated particular interaction techniques and were used to facilitate group discussion about interaction possibilities and the technology necessary to support them. They centered around the development of a new organizational element – the pile – which would support informal groupings of items on the computer desktop. In addition, we extended the metaphor to include functionality which could only be provided by the existence of a computer. The design sketches created are described below.

<u>User-created piles</u>. One objective was to allow users to create piles of mixed content and multiple data types. Each item within a pile would be represented by a miniature depicting its first page and extent (see Figure 1a). We wanted to maintain the informal quality of physical piles by provid-

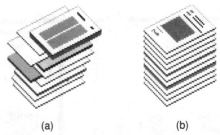

(a)   (b)

Figure 1. <u>Piles on the desktop</u>. In general, piles can contain various media, such as folders and individual documents. The pile in (a) was created by the user, and is consequently disheveled in appearance. In addition, the system can create piles for the user, based on rules explicitly stated by the user or developed through user-system collaboration. These piles have a neat appearance, as shown in (b), to indicate that there is a script, or set of rules, behind them.

ing direct manipulation techniques which resemble real world interactions. For example, a pile is created by overlapping two items; items are added to an existing pile by simply placing them on top (Figure 2). These user-created piles have a disheveled look.

<u>System-created piles</u>. In addition, we postulated that the system could create piles for a user. As shown in Figure 1 (b), these piles would have an orderly appearance. The system would assemble these piles using a script either developed through user-system collaboration, or explicitly written by the user. By creating and maintaining piles for the user, the system could serve as an office assistant.

How might this user-system collaboration work? Potentially, the user could supply sample documents as input for pile construction. By analyzing these documents, the system could offer various criteria for script construction. For example, the system could determine a document's unique terms and let the user select the specific terms to use as piling criteria. Additionally, the system might extract structural data, such as the "Re:" line in a mail message and ask the user if similar mail messages should be collected into the pile. Malone suggested a similar tact for automatic classification [9] and reported successful results in the Information Lens system [10]. As shown in Figure 3, our design provides a way for users to gradually learn to create scripts. As in the work of MacLean et al [7], we wanted to provide a natural way for users to approach "tailorability" of piles as a part of the system.

<u>Support for browsing</u>. We wanted to support some of the browsing techniques users applied in their physical offices.

Figure 2. <u>Adding a document to a pile</u>. If a document is positioned over an existing pile, the pile highlights to show that it can accept the new document. When the mouse button is released the document 'drops' onto the pile.

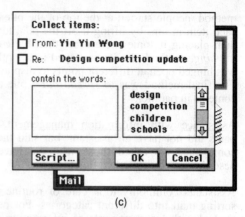

| (a) | (b) | (c) |

Figure 3. <u>Scripting a pile</u>. (a) depicts a mail area containing two scripted piles; one for important items, one for everything else. Over time, the criteria for 'important' may change. As shown, an item in the 'other' pile has been removed because the user desires that it, and items like it, now appear in the important pile. When this item is dropped onto the important pile, as shown in (b), the system queries the user to find out whether this action is a singular event or whether the pile's script should be modified. If the user chooses to modify the script, the system suggests criteria which could be used, as shown in (c). Alternatively, users can gain direct access to the scripting language and write their own criteria via the "Script..." button. Once the script is updated, items satisfying the new criteria visibly move to the 'important' pile.

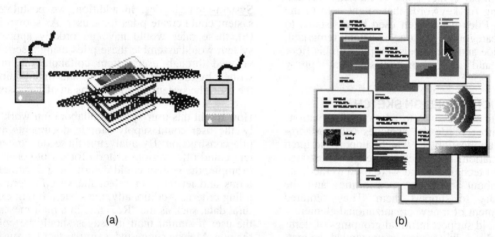

| (a) | (b) |

Figure 4. <u>Browsing by spreading out a pile</u>. Gesturing sideways with the mouse pointer, or with a finger in the case of a touch screen, causes the pile contents to spread out. Individual items can now be directly manipulated.

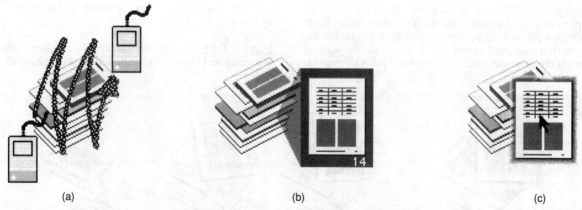

| (a) | (b) | (c) |

Figure 5. <u>Browsing while maintaining the pile's structure</u>. Gesturing vertically with the mouse pointer as shown in (a), or with a finger in the case of a touch screen, generates a 'viewing cone' (b) that contains a minature version of the first page of the item under the pointer. This viewing cone will follow the vertical position of the pointer; the miniature changes as the pointer moves over each item. The user can move through the pages of an item in the viewing cone by using the left and right cursor keys on the keyboard. When an item is visible in the viewing cone, it can be selected by clicking the mouse button. The item then appears next to the pile on the desktop, as shown in (c).

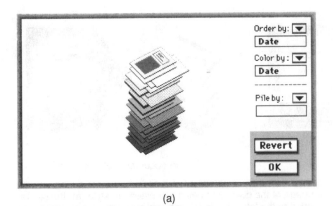
(a)

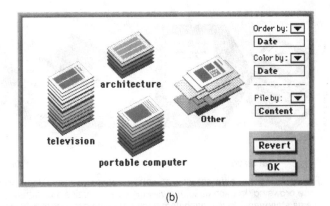
(b)

Figure 6. <u>Visualizing a pile's contents</u>. The pile shown is within a 'visualizing environment' that allows the user to select and visualize several criteria. Criteria can be mapped to the pile's order, the color of the items within the pile, or the way a pile is broken into sub-piles. In (a) the pile is both ordered and colored by date. In (b) the user chose to 'pile by' content. Therefore, the system separated the original pile into four content-based piles. Three are labeled with specific terms suggested by the system (e.g. "architecture"), appear neat and are now scripted to maintain similar content. The remaining disheveled pile, "other," contains items which did not fit into any of the other three piles.

By virtue of using miniatures of the actual documents, we offered edge browsing capabilities. In addition, we explored gestural inputs as a way to invoke other browsing methods. For example, a horizontal gesture would spread out a pile so that miniatures of each item's first page were visible (Figure 4). A vertical up-and-down movement over a pile would allow users to browse a pile using a 'viewing cone' (Figure 5). When an item was visible in the viewing cone, the user could move through miniature representations of its pages by using the cursor keys on the keyboard. In the design sketches, a mouse was used to create the gestures, but we thought that these interaction techniques would be particularly well-suited to a touch screen display.

<u>Managing piles</u>. In physical offices, the user is confronted with many pile management tasks, such as re-piling and sub-piling when a particular pile becomes unwieldy or specific information must be retrieved. We wanted the system to act as a collaborator in dealing with these issues, and therefore designed a 'visualizing environment' which would help users understand the contents of piles. As shown in Figure 6, a user might choose to emphasize certain criteria in a pile by using order, color or sub-piles. A user can elect to view combinations of criteria simultaneously. For example, the user could choose that items in a pile be ordered by date. The user might also request that the items in a pile be color coded according to their data type. Additionally, the user might have the system suggest subject-based sub-piles, by choosing the "pile by content" option. The sub-piles deemed useful could be moved out of the visualization area for use on the desktop.

TESTING USER'S EXPECTATIONS OF PILES
The design sketches raised interest amongst our colleagues and were the focal point for discussions. However, since the sketches were 'hard-wired,' we did not know if the interaction techniques were usable and of value to end-users. Consequently, we undertook a user test of the interaction techniques.

We constructed a suite of prototypes in Director that supported the interactivity we wished to test. We hoped to gauge people's expectations about the inclusion of piles on the desktop. Our method was informal, resembling the type of testing described in [4,12], in order to provide us with quick results that could be used in design iteration.

Method
Five men and five women in nontechnical positions at Apple Computer were individually tested in approximately one hour sessions. The subjects were asked to think aloud [5] while working through 5 tasks, and the sessions were videotaped. The first two tasks compared two different pile models. In the third task, users explored methods of initiating pile browsing. Task four allowed users to indicate preferences between three different viewing cone representations. In the final task, users were asked to locate items within a pile. At the conclusion of the test, users were informally asked for their comments and general impressions concerning piles.

<u>Piling models</u>. Two different models for a pile were compared: a "document-centered" model and a "pile-centered" model. Possible ordering effects were avoided by varying the presentation of these two models across users.

In the "document-centered" task, the pile was represented as a collection of individual items. The user was presented with a series of colored rectangles within a white screen area. These rectangles were intended to represent files on a desktop. The rectangles could be selected and moved with the mouse. When one rectangle was placed over another rectangle, both would fall back to create a disheveled pile. Additional documents could be added to an existing pile by moving them over the pile and releasing the mouse. Documents could be removed by individually selecting them via any visible region and dragging them away from the pile. The pile itself could not be moved as a unit.

In the "pile-centered" task, piles were created in the same way, except that the pile acted more like a Macintosh folder – a single entity containing a collection of documents. When one document 'rectangle' was moved over another rectangle, the latter would highlight to indicate a pile would be formed if the mouse button was released. Subsequent documents moved to the pile would automatically drop onto the top of the pile. The pile itself, as opposed to independent documents, could then be dragged around the desktop by mouse-clicking on any part of it.

<u>Initiating browsing</u>. In this task, participants tried out different ways of initiating pile browsing. They compared double-clicking and the horizontal gesture (shown in Figure

(a) stationary   (b) side shift   (c) document pull-out

Figure 7. <u>Test of different viewing cone representations.</u> Users were presented with three different ways a pile could react during viewing cone browsing. In each case, the viewing cone contains a miniature of the first page of the document being examined. In style (a), the pile remains stationary. In (b), each item above the item being currently viewed is moved to the left side. In (c), the item currently being viewed temporarily moves out of the pile and to the right. Users preferred methods (b) and (c).

4) as ways to spread out a pile's contents. They also compared double-clicking and vertical gesturing (Figure 5) for initiating browsing with the view cone.

<u>Viewing cone representations</u>. In this task, participants were presented with three different visual representations of the viewing cone (see Figure 7). All were initiated by the same interaction – a single mouse click on the pile – but the order of presentation was varied for each user. When users settled on a preferable representation, they were shown how to use the keyboard to examine a miniature document's pages while it was within the viewing cone. Users were shown which key would move the document forward one page, and which would move it backwards.

<u>Finding items within a pile</u>. In this task, participants were asked to use the viewing cone and paging ability to locate specific pages within documents in the pile. First they were asked to locate a picture of a hand on a mouse, for which they were shown a real report illustration as a stimulus. Then they were asked to locate three separate items within the pile: a colored bar graph, a map of North America which was contained in an Atlas document, and a document containing bullet point text. Users were not timed – this part of the test was aimed at determining if pile browsing was, in general, qualitatively suitable to users for locating information.

Results

<u>Piling models</u>. Although each user had a clear preference for one of our methods of pile creation ("pile-centered" or "document-centered"), neither method was judged to be clearly superior. In the "document-centered" model, users liked the ability to grab an individual document within a pile. A problem with this model was that users were not sure how to move a pile as a unit, since selecting any part of the pile led to moving an individual item rather than the pile as a whole. In the "pile-centered" model, users liked the way the system automatically aligned the items in the pile, the ability to move a pile as a unit, and the highlighting that indicated a pile was ready to accept an item. A problem with this model was the difficulty of selecting an individual item within the pile.

Most users also expected that any desktop item could be added to a pile. This led to discussion of what would happen if a document was placed on top of an isolated folder; users were unsure whether the item would go into the folder or if a new pile would be created. Most users thought that, based on their previous Macintosh experience, the item would go into the folder. This raises questions about how the pile metaphor fits into the current Macintosh desktop metaphor.

Most users asked for features generally available in desktop systems, but which were not present in the testing prototypes. For example, they wanted to be able to add a selected group of items to a pile, name piles, apply ordering schemes based on date, size, name, and kind, and control where a document was placed within a pile.

Since users liked and disliked certain features of each model, new design work will be undertaken to create models that both embody users' preferences and are internally consistent. Further testing of these new models will be conducted.

<u>Initiating browsing</u>. Subjects tried using both gestures and mouse double-clicks to spread out a pile and also to obtain the viewing cone. In both cases, 9 out of the 10 participants preferred the double-click method. They found it faster and more Macintosh-like, which was not unexpected given that the subjects were all accustomed to the Macintosh. However, users also felt that the gestures were non-intuitive and somewhat ambiguous, and that the piles might be spread out accidentally while moving the cursor around on the screen. The gestures were originally intended for use on a touch screen and most participants said that using a finger on the screen for the gesture might be more intuitive than using a mouse. This needs to be confirmed in a test with a touch screen. Note that we did not ask users *which* of the browsing methods they would want initiated by the double-click action; we only ascertained that they preferred double-clicking over gesturing.

In general, users thought they would make use of the 'spread out' view. Since all items were visible at once, it supported recognition and comparison. A few users expressed interest in viewing a grid layout rather than the overlapping one used in our testing prototype. While in this view, most users expected to both be able to act on individual items in standard ways, and move the documents as a group. In addition to the miniature representation of each item, many users requested that other information such as name, date, and kind be made available, and that the system provide representations which would specifically help the user differentiate similar items.

<u>Viewing cone representations</u>. Of the three viewing cone-designs, the stationary pile version (Figure 7a) was rejected by all 10 users. All thought it was difficult to gauge where they were within the pile. Four users preferred the 'side shift' style (Figure 7b), 5 preferred the 'document pull-out' style (Figure 7c), and 1 user was undecided between these latter two designs. Both of the preferred designs clearly provided a view of an item's location in the pile, in addition to a representation shown within the viewing cone. Although it was not implemented in theprototype, once users had an item visible in the cone they often tried to grab it by either releasing and then quickly clicking the mouse, or by attempting to drag it from the pile.

Most users liked the viewing cone as a browsing method. It made it possible for them to identify items by their miniature representation without disturbing the pile's state. Users also liked the ability to view any page of an individual item, although not all were pleased with using the cursor keys on the keyboard to cause this action. Page numbering information (e.g. '1 of 10') was found valuable while paging through the document, because it indicated the relative size of each item, as well as position within an item. One user desired random access to any page via selection of its number from the keyboard. A few users expressed interest in being able to target the viewing cone at any item on the desktop – a single document, a folder – and not just items in piles.

During the tests we noted a potential problem with the viewing cone implementation – users might need to depress the mouse button for a long time while browsing, which could lead to repetitive stress injury. A possible solution is to invoke the cone whenever the user clicks on a pile, thereby alleviating the need for the mouse button to be continuously depressed. This would also allow the user to click the mouse button again to select an item for removal from the pile while the viewing cone was active.

<u>Finding items within the pile</u>. We showed the subjects a physical version of a report and identified a specific illustration which we wanted them to find within a pile on the computer desktop. Users were asked to use the viewing cone and cursor keys to examine items in the pile. All of the users were able to find the illustration within a reasonable amount of time. As mentioned earlier, we were not concerned with timing information, but rather with the feasibility of the viewing cone for this task.

Since the picture was within a report which was bound in a green-edged cover, several users recognized the document within the pile by its clearly visible green spine. A common strategy was to subsequently move through the document's miniature pages, looking for a small colored image in the top right corner of a page. Only one user took advantage of the page numbers on the miniature representations to identify the page. A few users did not expect the document on the computer to have the green spine that was present on the physical report because they perceived it to be an addition which the system could not have known about. These users' strategy was to start at the top of the pile and systematically look through every item, page by page, to find the picture.

We also asked the subjects to find a colored bar graph, a map of the North American continent within an atlas, and

some bullet point text. Only some of the users found the items, and with some difficulty. Many users felt they would do better with their own information and their difficulty was due to a lack of familiarity with the material in the pile. Several users discussed ways they would like the system to help them in such a situation. They commonly wanted the ability to search for specific data types, names, keywords, and other identifiers.

From this feedback, we inferred that it might be useful to give the user control over the information presented in the viewing cone. For instance, when searching for a graph, the user could select data type 'graph' as the search criteria, thereby causing the viewing cone to display only pages containing graph data types. This could be a powerful way to search, since it would enable the user to tailor the view according to current needs.

<u>General discussion</u>. At the end of the test, we asked users how they would use piles, and how the system might assist them. In general, users were receptive to the idea of having the system help them with their routine tasks, such as sorting incoming mail. Most users reported having between two and five mail systems, fax, and voice mail. They liked the idea of receiving all incoming information in a pile which could be accessed with the viewing cone. Within such a pile, they would want the system to prioritize items using characteristics such as sender, topic, content keywords, date, and urgency. We anticipate these priorities could be learned by the system over a period of time by watching the user interact with incoming information.

FUTURE WORK:
FROM DESIGN SKETCH TO IMPLEMENTATION
There are many areas in which this work can proceed. A few of our current directions are described below.

Improving Designs and Working with Familiar Data
We plan to further explore the appropriate model for a pile – and how to possibly combine users' expectations about its document-centeredness vs. pile-centeredness – by iterating on our previous Director prototypes.

In addition, we intend to build prototypes that incorporate items of relevance to the individual being tested. The informal tests described above involved fabricated data that was unfamiliar to our subjects. In order to continue refining our designs, we need to construct prototypes that will allow subjects to interactively use piles for their own information over an extended period of time. An extension to the current Finder interface that would allow users to create and work with piles alongside folders would provide an excellent opportunity to further these designs. However, it may prove more feasible to undertake the next round of iteration by addressing a limited domain, such as a mail system.

Browsing by Other Criteria
The current design allows users to browse the contents of piles by viewing miniature representations of each item. While users found this feature useful in the tests, they also expressed interest in accessing other representations. We are currently exploring the types of "browse by..." criteria the system might offer. For example, users might want to selectively emphasize some data type during browsing, as in the case of 'show me all the documents containing movies within this pile.' When confronted with unfamiliar

data, users might want to browse by textual abstract, since a miniature visual representation might not provide insight into an unknown item's content.

Technology to Support Pile Interactions

The interface designs described in this paper were primarily inspired by observations with users, and not necessarily by existing technology. At the time of design, we were unsure if information retrieval techniques could adequately support some of the interactions, such as pile scripting-by-example or sub-pile creation. Consequently, we initiated a collaborative research effort with the Information Retrieval Team within Apple Computer's Advanced Technology Group.

Some preliminary work in implementing low level support for pile functionality has been undertaken. Current research is focussing on a clustering technique that would automatically create sub-piles. For example, a user could supply the system with a pile of documents, and based on the content of the documents within that pile, the system would suggest and describe suitable sub-piles.

As this work progresses, we plan to adapt our designs to reflect the technology that can be realized.

ACKNOWLEDGEMENTS

We would like to thank Dan Rose and Tim Oren for exploring information retrieval systems that will support sub-piling and other pile management operations; Stephanie Houde for creating the Director prototypes used in testing; Penny Bauersfeld and Leo Degen for their participation in early design sessions; and Tom Erickson for input on the user study design and feedback on the various drafts of this paper.

BIBLIOGRAPHY

[1] Apple Computer, Inc. *Human Interface Guidelines: The Apple Desktop Interface*. Addison-Wesley Publishing Company, Inc., Reading, MA, 1987.

[2] Apple Computer, Inc. *Inside Macintosh, Volume VI*. Addison-Wesley Publishing Company, Inc., Reading, MA, 1991.

[3] Cole, I. Human aspects of office filing: Implications for the electronic office *Proceedings of the Human Factors Society, 26th Annual Meeting*, Seattle, Washington. 1982.

[4] Gomoll, K. Some Techniques for Observing Users *The Art of Human-Computer Interface Design* (ed. Brenda Laurel) Addison-Wesley Publishing Company, Inc., Reading, MA. 1990. pp. 85-90.

[5] Ericsson, K.A. and Simon, H. A. *Protocol analysis*. Cambridge, Massachusetts: MIT Press. 1984.

[6] Lansdale, M. The psychology of personal information management. *Applied Ergonomics*, 55, (1988), pp. 55-66.

[7] MacLean, A., Carter, K., Lovstrand, L. and Moran, T. User-Tailorable Systems: Pressing the Issues with Buttons. In *Proceedings of CHI 1990 (Seattle, Washington, April 1-5, 1990)* ACM, New York, 1990. pp. 175-182.

[8] MacroMind, Inc. *Director™ 2.0*. April 1990.

[9] Malone, T. W. How do People Organize Their Desks? Implications for the Design of Office Information Systems. *ACM Transactions on Office Information Systems*, 1,1, (January 1983), pp. 99-112.

[10] Malone, T. W., Grant, K.R., Turbak, F.A., Brobst, S.A. and Cohen, M.D. Intelligent Information-Sharing Systems. *Communications of the ACM*, 30, 5, (May 1987), pp. 390-402.

[11] Miller, P., Tetelbaum, S. and Webb, K. BUSINESS – an end-user oriented application development language. *SIGMOD Record*, 12, 1, (October 1981), pp. 38-69

[12] Nielsen, J. Usability Engineering at a Discount. In G. Salvendy and M.J. Smith (Eds.), *Designing and Using Human-Computer Interfaces and Knowledge Based Systems*. Amsterdam: Elsevier. 1989.

[13] van Rijsbergen, C.J. *Information Retrieval. (2nd. Ed.)* Butterworths, London, England. 1983.

HCI Standards on Trial: You be the Jury

Moderators: *Jaclyn R. Schrier*
              American Institutes for Research
              Bedford, MA
              (617) 275-0800
              xt.jrs@forsythe.stanford.edu

              Evelyn L. Williams, Ph.D.
              Hewlett-Packard Corporation
              Fort Collins, CO
              (303) 229-4024
              elw@hpfcla.fc.hp.com

Panelists: *Kevin S. MacDonell,* Apple Computer Inc., Cupertino, CA
              Larry A. Peterson, US ARMY HEL, Aberdeen Proving Ground, MD
              Paulien F. Strijland, Apple Computer Inc., Cupertino, CA
              Anna M. Wichansky, Ph.D., Silicon Graphics, Inc., Mountain View, CA
              James R. Williams, Ph.D., Bell Communications Research, Piscataway, NJ

INTRODUCTION

The European Committee for Standardization (CEN) directive 90/270/EEC of May 29, 1990, requires all employers within the EEC to purchase and use only those software products that comply with a series of user interface standards including ISO 9241, *Ergonomic requirements for office work with visual display terminals (VDTs)*. The CEN directive takes effect on January 1, 1993, and allows European employers five years to make sure that all computer products in use comply with the appropriate standards. Although many previous user-oriented standards have concerned hardware aspects of computer systems, the standards in question legislate software interface design requirements. All software products marketed within the EEC will need to comply with these standards, regardless of where the software products were developed. This panel will discuss these standards and how they will influence the work of the CHI community. The session will focus on a standard devoted to *Menus* (ISO 9241-14), a component common to most user interfaces. This particular document falls under the CEN directive, has already passed the first vote of the ISO member nations, and is considered well on its way to becoming an official CEN requirement.

The panel session will be staged as a courtroom trial in which four "witnesses" will respond to questions from the "prosecution" and "defense." The witnesses will discuss the benefits and drawbacks of the standard from the perspective of a: 1) consumer, 2) software engineer, 3) human factors expert, and 4) internationalization specialist. The prosecution and the defense will ask the witnesses questions to explore the positive and negative effects of the standard. The audience will be asked to judge whether the standard is "guilty" or "not guilty" of being detrimental to the state of user interface design.

ISO 9241 STANDARD SUMMARY

James R. Williams, of Bell Communications Research, is the primary author of ISO 9241-14, Menu Dialogues.

Part 14 (menu dialogues) is one part of the multi-part ISO standard 9241, *Ergonomic requirements for office work with visual display terminals (VDTs)*. As indicated by its title, ISO 9241 covers the ergonomics of VDT use and concerns both hardware and software aspects. It should be noted that the European Communities take ergonomic standards seriously and, through Council Directive 90/270/EEC, the European standards organization (CEN) plans to implement the standards in the 9241 series through appropriate legislation. The EEC directive essentially requires employers within the EEC to purchase and use only those hardware and software products that comply with CEN standards. For example, the menus in a software product would have to comply with ISO 9241, Part 14 to be sold in Europe. Although Part 14 is the first of the software parts to be distributed as a Draft International Standard (DIS), the other dialogue parts (command dialogues, form-filling dialogues, direct manipulation dialogues, etc.) are expected to follow the same approach and structure.

The Menu dialogues part consists of a number of conditional requirements and recommendations for the design of menus. Conditional requirements are requirements which must be met only within the specific context for which they are relevant (e.g., particular kinds of users, tasks, environments, technology). The following guideline from Part 14 illustrates this conditional approach: "If particular options have great importance or need to be considered first, these options should be placed first in the group." The conformance approach in Part 14 is a two-step process (i.e., applicability is determined, then compliance). It should be noted that only the applicability step is mandatory. If the guideline is found to be applicable, then meeting the guideline would be a requirement. The previous example guideline would only be mandatory if there were options that had great importance or needed to be considered first.

Part 14 is organized into the following sections: introduction, scope, definitions, sections containing conditional requirements and recommendations concerning the design of menus (menu-structure, navigation, option selection and execution, and menu presentation) and a section describing how conformance is determined. Each conditional requirement/recommendation lists relevant dialogue design principles, examples (when appropriate), and the relevant methods for determining both applicability and compliance. In Section 6.1 of Part 14, *Option accessibility and discrimination*, for example, conditional requirements and recommendations are provided for displaying and highlighting options and option designators under various task conditions. Topics include continual versus on demand display, available and unavailable options, selection defaults, titling, multiple option selection, and option designators.

CONSUMER PERSPECTIVE

Larry A. Peterson is Team Leader of the Intelligent Machine Interface Team of the Combat Support Division of the U.S. Army Human Engineering Laboratory.

These remarks are made from the perspective of a Department of Defense "procurement" official. Computers have moved relentlessly forward from the offices of the MIS people to the operator consoles of the tank commanders and soldiers at the front line level. In a very significant part of the environment in which my customers work, the time available in which decisions must be correctly made is very short and the cost of human error is potentially very high. The human-computer interface is the medium through which my customers and their systems interact, and the need for a consistent and easy to use interface is emerging as a critical path item for the designer of military equipment.

Having an objective standard for HCI design would positively affect our ability to procure equipment that was not only internally consistent in terms of operability, but - if the HCI standards can be agreed on by the industry as a whole - consistent across several types of equipment and different systems. This consistency would significantly reduce our massive annual training (and re-training) costs. Again, remember my perspective is that many of my customers are only going to be with my "company" for a few years, so the less of that time spent in training the better.

Of the current products available, the Apple Macintosh 'environment' seems to be the most consistent and compliant with the overall intent of the HCI standards approach. I would strongly support the application of a consistent approach within each program (i.e. in terms of consistency to the user of how to find help, exit a program, close a window, etc.) so that some basic 'navigational' and operational skills could be taught independently of a specific application.

SOFTWARE ENGINEERING PERSPECTIVE

Kevin S. MacDonell is a software engineer with Apple Computer where he is responsible for the Macintosh Menu and Dialog Managers.

In general, I believe that good menu design is a product of experience, testing, and applicability to a particular task. Thus, it may be difficult to legislate all but the most rudimentary features of good menu interface design. What I consider a menu and how I use menus is substantially different than the way this standard talks about them. This standard is completely alien to how I, as a software engineer, think about menus in terms of availability, names, selection, category, etc. The terminology leaves the interpretation of the standard up to the reader. If the reader makes a liberal interpretation, products can easily meet the standard. If the terms used for various interface components vary widely, then compliance will be difficult to determine. A standards evaluator will be required to determine if products comply with the standard.

Many software engineers today develop their user interfaces using toolkits that allow higher level programming. These toolkits take a number of the decisions about menu selection, highlighting, etc. out of the hands of the developer. The compliance of applications developed using toolkits will be partially dependent on the underlying toolkit for the GUI.

If the underlying toolkit is not compliant, it could be prohibitively expensive to become compliant. Thousands of applications used by millions of people are using menus based on the built-in menu facility. Changing this facility to become compliant with the ISO standard potentially means that all of these applications will stop working or will work incorrectly (with the possible loss of data). The costs to the application developers to update every one of the user interfaces to new ISO compliant software would be prohibitive.

Looking at menus separately is too myopic to be useful - you need to consider the synergy of the set of user interface elements (windows, menus, dialogs, controls). What is important is that applications work and do the job and are easy to use. Compliance to a standard will not make bad software good. Badly designed programs don't gain much market acceptance.

VisiCalc (the original spreadsheet program) might not have complied with any standard at all. However, the idea was so important that spreadsheets have become a fundamental application across all computer platforms. A bad implementation of a good idea may be thwarted by endeavoring to force it to be compliant. This is not what the computer industry needs. Innovation and differentiation are the fertile soil in which new ideas sprout. Bad ideas are naturally stopped by virtue of the way the industry develops. Good ideas are embraced and refined to a high state of utility. The standard, in order not to impede the creativity process, would need to be so general as to be useless. A better approach would be guidelines of the principles of good design, and a survey of good and bad things to do, and why they were that way.

HUMAN FACTORS PERSPECTIVE

Anna M. Wichansky is the manager of the Human Factors Group and Laboratory at Silicon Graphics Computer Systems.

As a human factors specialist, I consider the ISO 9241-14 working draft as a partial list of requirements for minimum usability of menu dialogues. The standard encourages application of consistency, task orientation, and other principles of user-oriented design, given a text or graphical user interface based on early 1980's technology. Software developed for these types of platforms would probably be more usable if it complied with the standard, although compliance would not automatically guarantee usability. Software applications of the 1990's include high resolution color graphics, 3D, multimedia user interfaces. Compliance with standards for text, typing, cursors, and other vestiges of old technology is less critical.

Standards compliance activities would initially require more human factors staff than currently exist in my group. There are approximately 90 items that require compliance checks for Part 14 alone. Usability testing and task analysis are two major methodologies to check compliance, which takes time and specialized expertise to perform. User interface developers and software testers could also participate by applying design checklists for the standards which could be verified by inspection.

Prior knowledge of standards may improve the general user interface quality of software being developed, especially for those products which human factors engineers do not cover. However, designing *to* the standard is not an appropriate method of developing new software if improvements in ease of use is the ultimate goal. In order to reach new markets, a complete breakthrough in user interface paradigms is needed, to make computers as accessible and fun to use as consumer products. This will not be achievable by designing to standards based on older, less user-friendly technologies.

INTERNATIONALIZATION PERSPECTIVE

Paulien F. Strijland is a manager in the Macintosh Human Interface group at Apple Computer where she deals with internationalization issues

Although ISO is an international committee for standardization, most countries represented are European. In my experience the Japanese are the only regular attenders that use a script system that is different from ours. As a result, the fact that a standard is worked on by ISO doesn't always mean that international issues get addressed. In this particular case the general principles that underlie most guidelines are generally applicable, but the specific examples are not. This means that it will be a lot more difficult to know what to do to comply with the standard when developing for a non-roman script system.

The standard refers to user needs only in a very generic way. It assumes one kind of user, and is not specific about the level of experience of users, their culture, or their language. For example, it is stated that "the availability of individual options, the category to which they belong, their names, and the means to select them, always should be evident to the user." The way to accomplish this may be different for different users. As a result, systems could become inconsistent between different countries or even between different user groups (for example business versus home users). The examples that are given for syntax are difficult to translate in some languages.

To address globalization, many of the examples should be taken out, or provided in multiple ways (in addition to the left to right examples). Although in principle it is possible to read left to right examples and do a translation in your mind, it makes interpreting the standard very difficult. If I am developing a product specifically for the Arabic market, reading a standard that is focussed on roman languages will not make me feel very comfortable about the whole thing. There are many issues that deal with tradeoffs that need to be made in how the software gets written (flexibility is a key issue), consistency across countries versus optimization for one country, etc. The standard doesn't give any insights into what these tradeoffs are and how to make decisions.

As a final statement, I'd like to raise the issue of guidelines versus rules. This standard contains mainly (if not only) guidelines worded as "should" statements. It is easy to foresee how a procurer would interpret these statements as "shall" statements because otherwise there wouldn't be anything to comply with. As soon as that happens, it will be a big issue to judge conformance. The standard is full of statements that require things to be done in "a meaningful way" or "any acceptable" way, etc. This cannot be tested objectively. At the same time, most guidelines cannot be made into "shall" statements because they are too specific to certain situations, and all require tradeoffs to be made. In my opinion that leaves us with a very "unstandard" kind of standard.

PROSECUTION SUMMARY

Evelyn L. Williams manages a Human Factors group at Hewlett-Packard, where she supports software products for the workstation market. She has been a member of the Human Factors Society Human-Computer Interaction Standards Committee for six years.

Due to the loose nature of the standard, there are many different ways of meeting its requirements. Therefore, the interfaces developed to be in compliance with the standard may not be "standardized" or "consistent." The lack of consistency may minimize or eliminate any learning or productivity for the consumer. Compliance with the standard will not guarantee usability.

Application developers may have no control over their ability to meet the standard. The application developer can attempt to be compliant by changing all aspects of the user interface that they control. However, they still may not be compliant. If the GUI toolkit for the platform on which they are developing is not compliant with the standard, applications automatically will not be compliant.

Even if we assume that the user interface standard will help improve user interfaces and minimize learning for end-users, it is likely to be costly. Consumers will have to pay for the cost of software development companies hiring standards evaluators to determine that the standard is met. They will have to pay for modifications that will need to be made to applications and to underlying GUI toolkits in order for the software to become compliant.

Over time, the data in this standard will become dated, giving the standard the potential to interfere with progress in user interface design. New interfaces based on different technologies may be superior to ones based on this standard but may be kept off the market due to their failure to comply with the standard.

DEFENSE SUMMARY
Jaclyn R. Schrier designs and evaluates software user interfaces for the American Institutes for Research, a consulting firm. She has been a member of the Human Factors Society Human-Computer Interaction Standards Committee since 1988.

This menu design standard (ISO 9241-14) offers many benefits for software end-users and software designers, as well as for the firms that develop and use software products. The guidelines that appear in the standard are based on extensive human performance research and were approved by a large international committee of human factors experts as sound principles of good user interface design. Because the standard was developed with a "conditional" approach to conformance, a software product need only comply with those guidelines that are relevant to the particular users, tasks, environment, and technologies of a given software product. This approach of tailoring a product to specific users, tasks, environments, and technologies will give software development firms strong motivation to tailor products to meet the diverse needs of an international market.

Compliance with the standard will result in the development of menu structures that are easier to learn and use. This will improve efficiency and reduce stress for the end-users of software products that comply with the standard. Software designers and human factors experts who use the standard will be able to work more efficiently as they spend less time discussing, debating, and evaluating various menu design alternatives.

Finally, the standard offers benefits for firms that develop and use software products. As software designers use the standard to develop products more efficiently, the costs associated with product development will be reduced. As software products that comply with the standard will be easier to learn and use, employee training costs will be reduced.

The Ircam Signal Processing Workstation Prototyping Environment

M. De Cecco, E. Lindeman, M. Puckette

IRCAM - Centre Georges-Pompidou
31 rue Saint Merri
F 75004 Paris
tel: +33-(1)- 42771233
email: dececco@ircam.fr

ABSTRACT

This demo show the prototyping environment of the Ircam Signal Processing Workstation. The environment is oriented toward rapid prototyping of DSP and Musical applications.

KEYWORDS

Graphic programming, rapid prototyping, real-time systems, computer music, digital signal processing.

SUMMARY

The IRCAM Signal Processing Workstation (ISPW) project begun in August 1988 involving eight to ten engineers. The intention is to provide a system which is well adapted to both real-time signal processing and event processing especially for musical applications.

The system uses the NeXT machine as host computer. We have developed a high-speed general purpose multiprocessor configured as plugin boards for the NeXT cube. The board, designed at IRCAM, uses two Intel i860 processors for number crunching and a 560001 for I/O. Three boards can be plugged into a NeXT cube for a total of 6 i860's.

We have developed a real-time operating system called CPOS/FTS which is designed to support real-time signal processing and event processing (MIDI, etc.) in a unified way A number of tools have been designed to support rapid prototyping of graphical applications for the ISPW. Among those which we will be demonstrating are Max and Animal.

MAX

Max is a graphic programming language suited to real-time applications. MAX is an editor for message-based data-flow like systems, with extensions for defining and handling real-time event and signal processing. Max runs on the ISPW in a distributed fashion: the user interface runs on the Next machine; the functional kernel--called FTS--runs on the ISPW i860 multiprocessor as a collection of tasks under CPOS.

Using Max, one can interconnect signal generators and filters, build custom controller modules and simulation units, all from a core collection of signal processing objects.

ANIMAL

Animal is an objected oriented programming environment with the usual notions of class, method, and instance. A class is defined in Animal by designing its graphic representation(s). These representations then serve as interfaces for creating and manipulating networks of "live" instances of classes. Animal provides for persistent storage on disk of instance networks, and for reusable libraries of classes, graphic representations, and instances.

Animal is intended as a tool for building "fine-grained" graphic real-time application applications, and in general, any application requiring visualization and interaction with large structured parameter spaces. Animal and MAX share a common object oriented data base implemented on the multi-processor.

By interacting through this database Max can serve as the "scripting language" for Animal applications, allowing the user to define graphic Max "methods" for Animal defined classes.

Animal and MAX share a common object oriented data base implemented on the multi-processor. The two tools allow the implementation of entire applications without writing a line of C code, working exclusively in a graphic programming environment; the developement times are lowered considerably with respect to standard UNIX programming.

THE DEMOSTRATION

The planned demostration will show a working application built with Animal and MAX (a musical sampling synthetizer). We will then rebuild a substantial part of the application using the graphical programming environment..This demonstration shows the advantages of the emphasis on rapid prototyping, by programming live a working prototype of a non-trivial real-time application.

From the point of view of the research comunity, besides the effectiviness of the tool, Animal presents an interesting paradigm for building interfaces: an interface is seen as a set of representations of objects belonging to an Object Oriented data network; the Class structure of the network itself is built by drawing representations of class instances using both a graphical and "programming by example" paradigm.

COMMERCIAL STATUS

The ISPW i860 multiprocessor board is currently manufactured and distributed by Ariel Corp. (Highland Park,

New Jersey). Included in the release and supported directly by Ariel is the CPOS operating system and a complete development environment (C compiler, assembler, linker, debugger, ANSI library) based on GNU (Free Software Foundation) tools.

Additional commercial applications and tools (optimizing compilers, math libraries) are available through Ariel Corp. Max, and Animal, as well as other ISPW applications, are available free from an FTP site at Stanford University. As a convenience these applications are made available on distribution disks delivered with the system.

A different version of Max is available from Opcode Systems as a commercial application running on the Macintosh.

THE AUTHORS

Maurizio De Cecco; in Ircam since September 90, working onAnimal and on other IMW applications; previously, he worked in industrial research Projects with several Italian companies in User Interface and Knowledge Representation.

Eric Lindemann; at IRCAM since 1988 as manager of the ISPW project. Wrote and conceived of first prototype of Animal as well as designing the i860 board for the ISPW. Previously worked for various companies involved with audio production and computer music.

Miller Puckette; the author of Max, received a B.S. from MIT in 1980 and a Ph.D. from Harvard in 1986, both in mathematics. Before joining the research staff at IRCAM, he was a Research Scientist at the MIT Media.

BUILDING USER INTERFACES INTERACTIVELY USING PRE- AND POSTCONDITIONS

Martin R. Frank, J.J. "Hans" de Graaff, Daniel F. Gieskens and James D. Foley

Graphics, Visualization and Usability Center
College of Computing, Georgia Institute of Technology
Atlanta, Georgia 30332-0280
(404) 853-0672, {martin,graaff,daniel,foley}@cc.gatech.edu

ABSTRACT
A tool is presented which allows graphic layout of a user interface integrated with specification of behavior using pre- and postconditions.

KEYWORDS
User Interface Management Systems. Graphical User Interface Builders. Dialogue Sequencing.

INTRODUCTION
Development of user interfaces has traditionally been a tedious process, especially constructing non-textual interfaces using a textual programming language. Interface builders were developed to interactively design user interfaces. The Developer's Guide for the OPEN LOOK Graphical User Interface[3] is one of them. Like other builders, this tool is limited to specifying the appearance - not the functionality - of an interface. We have extended the Developer's Guide with a simple and powerful way to specify functionality.

METHODOLOGY
Pre- and postconditions are associated with widgets (sliders, buttons, ...). A widget has two preconditions - one for controlling widget visibility and one for controlling widget enablement. The postconditions describe how the state of the interface changes when the widget has been activated (e.g. a button pressed). The interface and application share a global state, the *blackboard*. Both can access predicates on the blackboard. They communicate by using predicate names. If either the application or the interface make changes to the blackboard the other component will be notified of the change. An application may have several different interfaces provided that the alternative interfaces use the same predicate names.

Postconditions of widgets can contain calls to a UNIX™ shell script defining application functionality. If all application functionality is contained in this shell script then there is no difference between the interpreted application in run mode and the compiled application (other than execution speed). However, the shell script method is not general enough to cover all possible interfaces (e.g. direct manipulation in an application window), so the designer is free to add code. Even in this case our tool assists in separating the interface and application provided that the programmer uses the blackboard mechanism in the intended way.

The description of user interface behavior through pre- and postconditions is used to automatically generate context-sensitive help. For example, help is given on why a certain command is disabled by examining which of the enabling preconditions are false. The system translates the missing preconditions into human-readable form using a forms-based approach and displays the help text in a pop-up window.

EXAMPLE
Let us go through the steps of designing a simple user interface to a hypothetical device consisting of two buttons, labeled "On" and "Off". The desired functionality is that these buttons are mutually exclusive, so that only one of them is enabled at any time.

First we create a base window and two buttons by dragging them from a palette. We use property sheets to enter the pre- and postconditions. The predicate *status(Device,On)* denotes that the device controlled by the interface is on, and that *status(Device,Off)* denotes that it is off. Thus the precondition for enabling the "On" button is that the device is off, in our notation *status(Device,Off)*. The postcondition of pressing the "On" button is that *status(Device,Off)* is taken off the blackboard and *status(Device,On)* is placed there instead. We enter equivalent conditions for the "Off" button. Finally we specify that the initial status of the device is off by specifying that *status(Device,Off)* is put on the blackboard at start-up time. Seven lines of text are required to specify the dynamics of this particular interface.

We can then immediately verify that we achieved the desired behavior by switching from "Build" to "Run" mode. A debugging window pops up that shows which predicates are currently on the blackboard and the interface we designed is now "alive": only one of the buttons is enabled and clicking on the enabled button will enable the other one. Moving the cursor over the disabled "Off" button and pressing the help

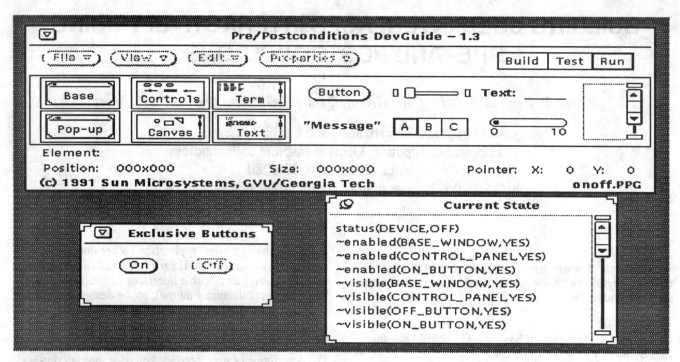

Figure 1: The Example Interface in Run Mode

key pops up the message "The button Off is disabled because the Status of the Device is Off".

In the figure the Developer's Guide is shown in "Run" mode. One of the buttons is greyed out as desired and the blackboard is shown. The tilde (~) before some of the predicates denotes that they are automatically generated system predicates controlling the visibility and enablement of interface objects. The other predicates are designer-defined and are used to communicate between interface and application or to control sequencing. Here, the current state is that the device is off (the first predicate). Both buttons, their control panel and the base window are visible (the last four predicates). Only the "On" button, the control panel and the base window are enabled.

EXTENSIONS

The help facility will be extended so that help is given not only on why a widget is disabled but also on how to *enable* it. This is done in two steps. First, the system finds out which predicates are missing for the precondition of the disabled command to evaluate to true. Second, it finds out which commands or command sequences would set these predicates by examining the postconditions. This search recursively extends over several levels through backchaining.This form of help has already been implemented in the framework of the User Interface Design Environment [1], but has not been integrated with this tool so far.

We will add a graphical front-end tool that can generate some of the typical pre- and postconditions automatically. The tool will translate graphical connections between user interface objects into corresponding pre- and postconditions.

This will make designing interfaces with our system more comfortable. However, we do not intend to hide the underlying pre- and postcondition engine from the designer since there are many constraints which cannot easily be expressed in a graphical way.

CONCLUSIONS

Relieving user interface designers from the burden of low-level programming is bound to boost productivity. While we have not conducted formal studies on the usage of our enhanced Developer's Guide versus the original and C or C++ to add functionality, we noticed that we ourselves started to experiment with a variety of interfaces and interface alternatives simply because our tool makes it so simple - and fun!

ACKNOWLEDGEMENTS

Partial funding was provided by Sun Microsystems' Collaborative Research Program and by National Science Foundation #IRI-8813179.

REFERENCES

[1] Foley, J., W. Kim, S. Kovacevic, and K. Murray, "Defining Interfaces at a High Level of Abstraction", IEEE Software, (6)1, January 1989, pp. 25-32.

[2] Gieskens, D., and J. Foley, "Controlling User Interface Objects Through Pre- and Postconditions" in Proceedings of CHI'92, Monterey, CA, May 1992.

[3] Sun Microsystems, Inc., "Open Windows Developer's Guide 1.1, Reference Manual", Part No. 800-5380-10, Revision A, of June 1990.

Formal Videos Program

CHI '92 Formal Video Program

The next section of the proceedings contains abstracts of the thirteen videos that are part of the CHI'92 Formal Video Program. Many aspects of human-computer interaction can best be presented using a videotape presentation. Therefore, videos are an important part of the CHI'92 conference. Submissions for the video program are judged by the video review committee, and only the best videos are presented. The Formal Video Program at CHI'92 is two hours long. When reading the abstracts, please keep in mind that you can get a much better idea of how the systems work by watching the accompanying video.

In addition to the Formal Videos, this year there are two Special Video Programs containing Graphic Design Videos and Future Scenario Videos. The Graphic Design Videos allow graphic designers, industrial designers, and design firms to show off their best human-computer interface designs. Future Scenarios show ideas about what human-computer interfaces may be like in five or ten years, or more. Abstracts for these Special Videos will be available at the conference and they are on the pamphlets that come with the videotapes.

The videos are for sale at the conference, and you can also purchase them from SIGGRAPH. The CHI'92 Formal Video Program is published as SIGGRAPH Video Review numbers 76 and 77, and the Special Video Program (containing the graphic design and future scenarios) is SIGGRAPH Video Review numbers 78 and 79. Tapes from the video programs of all previous SIGCHI conferences, as well as special CHI programs such as "All the Widgets," are also available.

For More Information

on acquiring these videotapes, contact:

SVR Order Department
c/o First Priority
PO Box 576
Itasca, IL 60143-0576
(800) 523-5503 or from outside the U.S.
+1 -708-250-0807
FAX: +1-708- 250-0038

FORMAL VIDEOS

MMM: The Multi-Device Multi-User Multi-Editor

Eric A. Bier[†], Steve Freeman[‡], and Ken Pier[†]

[†]Xerox PARC, 3333 Coyote Hill Road, Palo Alto, CA 94304
(415) 812-4000, bier.parc@xerox.com, pier.parc@xerox.com

[‡]Darwin College, Silver Street, Cambridge, England CB3 9EU
011-44-223-335-660, smgf@computer-lab.cambridge.ac.uk

EXTENDED ABSTRACT

Shared Editing on a Single Screen

We are interested in the software architecture and user interface needed to build multi-user editors that are convenient to use. While most previous multi-user editors assume that each user has a networked workstation, we are also interested in cases where editors are shared on a *single* workstation with multiple pointing devices. For example, we wish to support scenarios such as the following:

(1)   Users collaborating on the same workstation screen. For example, two programmers working together at a workstation may both desire input devices.

(2)   Several people sharing a computer with a blackboard-sized display, writing directly with a stylus or controlling it from hand-held computers.

(3)   People sharing a hand-held computer by passing it back and forth.

The Multi-Device Multi-User Multi-Editor (MMM) is a set of toy editors that support simultaneous real-time collaboration with fine-grained sharing including simultaneous access to the same text string or graphical object. A mouse can be registered with a user and will work with that user's defaults and preferences (such as insertion points, modes, current colors and mouse parameters) until registered with another user. Registration is fast enough that users can pass devices back and forth during a session. Users can alternately collaborate tightly or work separately. MMM editors can be nested inside of each other on the screen. Users can edit in the same or different editors simultaneously.

MMM is related to several previous systems, including SharedARK [Smith89], ShrEdit [Olson90a], and other group editors [Olson90b].

The Software and Environment

MMM's object-oriented architecture is described in a recent paper [Bier91]. It is implemented in the Cedar programming language and environment. Cedar runs on top of SunOS, a

Unix[TM]-compatible operating system. This video was shot from the screen of a SUN Microsystems SPARCstation 2.

The User Interface

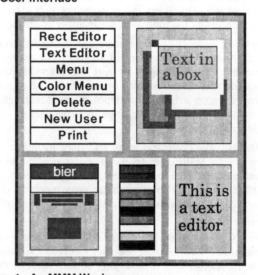

Figure 1. An MMM Workspace.

MMM's user interface consists of three visible components: *Home areas* provide iconic representations of users. *Editors* allow users to view and modify document media. *Menus* provide buttons that users can press to invoke commands. Figure 1 shows a complete MMM workspace, including (clockwise from lower right): a text editor, a color menu, a home area for user "bier", a command menu, and a rectangle editor (containing a nested text editor). Below, we describe how home areas, editors, and menus are used to support multi-user editing.

Claiming Devices. Users associate input devices with themselves by clicking on a home area (e.g., the rectangle labeled "bier" in figure 1) with the cursor of a particular mouse. The cursor's color changes to that user's color. Additional users can register using additional home areas.

MMM Editors. MMM includes a rectangle editor and a text editor. These editors can be customized to individual users and used by multiple users at once. For example, in the rectangle editor, several users can create rectangles of different colors, drag and stretch different rectangles or jointly stretch a rectangle by grabbing it at opposite corners (see figure 2). Similarly, in the text editor, one user can type text, while the other user repositions the new text.

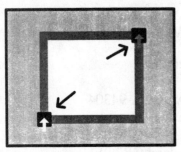

Figure 2. Two users stretching a rectangle.

Selections and Feedback. A user's identifying color is used to highlight selected objects. A selected rectangle draws a highlight square in one corner if selected by one user, two corners if selected by two users, and so on up to four users. If selected by more than four users, the rectangle shows the colors of the last four users who selected it. The border of an editor changes color when a user selects that editor. Multi-colored borders are used if several users select the editor. Selected text fragments are underlined in the selecting user's color. Fragments selected by multiple users are multiply underlined.

Users can select multiple objects at once, and the selections of one user can overlap the selections of another. For example, one user can recolor rectangles or text while another user drags some of them. Likewise, two or more users can recolor overlapping character strings or overlapping sets of rectangles. The last user to apply the color change to a character or rectangle determines its final color.

Shared Menus. The command menu and color menu can be applied to objects at different levels. For instance, the same Delete button can be used to delete text, rectangles, editors, or even itself. Similarly, the color menu can color objects at different levels. Several users can use the command or color menu at the same time.

Multi-Level Collaboration. Users can edit at different levels at the same time. For instance, one user can resize an editor window while another user is modifying objects inside of that window. Likewise, one user can select from a menu that another user is moving.

New Users. A new user can join a session by having existing users create a new home area.

Per-Editor Modes. Each editor remembers what each user is doing *in that editor.* For example, a user may create blue italic text in one editor and red plain text in another. The user can go back and forth between editors and each editor remembers its state. As feedback, the current modes in each user's currently selected editor are displayed in that user's home area. For text editors, this feedback consists of an example string in the current font.

Swapping the Keyboard. In our system, there is only one keyboard, which is passed back and forth. A picture of a keyboard is displayed in the home area of the user who currently owns it. Another user takes the keyboard by clicking on this picture. Keyboard input is placed at the insertion point of the user who owns the keyboard.

Conclusion

MMM is an experimental software architecture supporting multi-user editors and a set of user interface techniques for editors that can be shared synchronously. Our prototype assumes that the users are sharing a single screen. However, we believe that both the architecture and the user interface techniques can also be applied to editors shared over a network.

From our experiences, we draw these conclusions about the user interface of shared editors:

(1)   The home area is effective as a quick way to register a pointing device with a user and as a place in which to display per-user feedback.

(2)   Where possible, users should be able to work at different document levels at once, without interfering.

(3)   Using color to associate feedback with particular users allows the use of traditional shapes and sizes of feedback, such as underlines in the text editor and control point highlighting in the rectangle editor. However, this technique is less effective on black and white displays or with color-vision-impaired users.

(4)   Allowing menus to be shared among users and among editors simplifies the interface and conserves screen space.

In the future, we plan to use the MMM framework to build a set of practical applications that support cooperative work, giving us a chance to see how well MMM performs when editor complexity increases and actual user demands are placed on the system. We also plan to use MMM to develop user interfaces that allow a single user to edit by pointing with both hands at once, using either trackballs, touch-sensitive displays, electronic pens, or a combination.

Acknowledgments

We thank our reviewers for comments that lead to a shorter, clearer tape. We thank Jennifer Ernst and Theron Thompson for production talents that included not only fine camera and editing work but for noticing software problems and helping to reword the script. We also thank Polle Zellweger for helpful comments on this abstract. Finally, we thank Xerox for supporting all stages of this work.

References

[Bier91]   Eric A. Bier and Steve Freeman. MMM: A user interface architecture for shared editors on a single screen. In *Proceedings of the UIST'91 Symposium on User Interface Software and Technology* (South Carolina, November). ACM Press, 1991, pages 79-86.

[Olson90a]   Gary M. Olson. *Technology Support for Collaborative Workgroups.* Annual progress report for 1989-90 to the National Science Foundation, Grant #IRI-8902930, University of Michigan, June 1990.

[Olson90b]   Judith S. Olson, Gary M. Olson, Lisbeth A. Mack, and Pierre Wellner. Concurrent editing: the group's interface. In *Proceedings of Interact '90—The IFIP TC 13 Third International Conference on Human-Computer Interaction* (Cambridge, UK, August), 1990, pages 835-840.

[Smith89]   Randall B. Smith, Tim O'Shea, Claire O'Malley, Eileen Scanlon, and Josie Taylor. Preliminary experiments with a distributed, multi-media, problem solving environment. In *Proceedings of the First European Conference on Computer Supported Cooperative Work* (Gatwick, UK) 1989, pages 19-34.

GO FISH! A MULTI-USER GAME
IN THE RENDEZVOUS SYSTEM

Steven L. Rohall, John F. Patterson, and Ralph D. Hill

Bellcore
445 South Street
Morristown, NJ 07962-1910

(201) 829-5203
slr@thumper.bellcore.com

ABSTRACT

The Rendezvous™ System is an infrastructure for building multi-user, synchronous applications. Multi-user, synchronous applications are those that are designed to be
used by several people simultaneously. Examples of such
applications range from collaborative debugging of
software to multi-party contract negotiations to games for
several players. This videotape shows a demonstration of
one multi-user application we have built. The application
is a card table that allows up to four people to play any
card game they wish. On the tape, you will see several
rounds of a game of fish. This game, though simple,
serves to highlight four key capabilities that an infrastructure for building multi-user applications must support.
These are: 1) support for separate, customized views for
each user of the same underlying data, 2) support for public data (i.e., data shown to all users) as well as private
data (i.e., data shown only to a particular user), 3) support
for access control among users so that certain data is only
accessible to some users, and 4) support for the direct
manipulation of data objects on the users' displays. We
believe that the ability for people to communicate with
one another in the structured manner of multi-user applications offers an enormous opportunity for people to
enrich the way they work, learn, and play. Many sorts of
multi-user applications are possible and research into
infrastructures like the Rendezvous System may some day
allow for the rapid production of these types of systems.
For more information, please see the suggested readings.

SUGGESTED READINGS

Hill, R.D., The Abstraction-Link-View Paradigm: Using
Constraints to Connect User Interfaces to Applications,
*Proceedings of CHI'92, the Conference on Human Fac-
tors in Computing Systems*, (Monterey, CA, May 3-7,
1992), ACM Press, elsewhere in this volume.

Hill, R.D., Languages for the Construction of Multi-User
Multi-Media Synchronous (MUMMS) Applications, in
Languages for Developing User Interfaces, B. Myers
(Ed.), Boston: Jones and Bartlett, 1992.

Hill, R.D., A 2-D Graphics System for Multi-User
Interactive Graphics Based on Objects and Constraints, in
Advances in Object-Oriented Graphics, E. Blake and P.
Wisskirchen (Eds.), Berlin: Springer-Verlag, 1991.

Patterson, J.F., Comparing the Programming Demands of
Single-User and Multi-User Applications, *Proceedings of
UIST'91, the ACM Symposium on User Interface Software
and Technology*, (Hilton Head, SC, November 11-13,
1991), ACM Press, pp. 87-94.

Patterson, J.F., Hill, R.D., Rohall, S.L., and Meeks, W.S.,
Rendezvous: An Architecture for Synchronous Multi-User
Applications, *Proceedings of CSCW'90, the Conference
on Computer-Supported Cooperative Work*, (Los Angeles,
CA, October 7-10, 1990), ACM Press, pp. 317-328.

May 3 - 7, 1992

A Case Study of a Multimedia
Co-working Task and the Resulting Interface Design of a
Collaborative Communication Tool

Amanda Ropa

Amanda Ropa Design
P.O. Box 695
Palo Alto, California 94302
tel: (415) 325-3753
aropa@well.sf.ca.us

Bengt Ahlström

IPLab Interaction and Presentation Lab
Department of Computing Science
Royal Institute of Technology
S-100 44 Stockholm, Sweden
tel: +46 8 7909106
bahl@nada.kth.se

ABSTRACT
The Video Viewer is a communication tool that allows two
users to share video information across a network. The
design of this tool was based on the results of a case study
involving two multimedia, collaborative workstations
situated in two separate rooms. Users performed several
tasks collaboratively using different media in an
unstructured environment (i.e. there were four monitors to
increase screen space and there was no specific interface for
guidance). This video outlines the case study, the
preliminary case study results and how these results effected
the interface design of the Video Viewer.

CASE STUDY PLATFORM
The platform for the study consisted of three Macintosh
computers: one for each workstation and one for shared
access. Each workstation had four monitors representing
different forms of interaction. One monitor displayed the
user's private desktop, another the shared desktop. In
addition, each workstation had a monitor to display an
overhead area where documents could be broadcast to the
other user. In this overhead area, three windows represent
input from three video sources: a camera to broadcast a face
image to the other user, a camera to broadcast images of 3-
D objects or documents, and a window for CD-ROM or
videodisc input.

CASE STUDY SUMMARY
The experimental case study involved three pairs of users
and three different tasks, each lasting one week. For that
week, users would treat their workstation as their office.
The first task was to create a text document together about
this collaborative project. The second task was to create
overhead slides using text and graphics and the third task
was to create a multimedia presentation using all media
available, including video. These were tasks the users
needed to accomplish as part of their regular work duties.
Results from these tasks were gathered via observations,
interviewing, a logging system that tracked mouse activity
and video recording.

Some of the initial study results were first that users relied
most heavily on audio communication to accomplish all
three tasks. This may have been due to the difficulty in
establishing eye contact resulting from the camera's
position and/or to the fact that the users all knew each other
well and could easily talk face to face outside the study.
The ability to see the other user's face appeared important
only when the focus was on discussion or for checking
communication status. The camera for viewing 3-D objects
and documents proved very valuable to incorporate elements
not in the computer environment. Also, users seemed to
transfer their real-world social protocols into this
environment, for example in giving author precedence in
editing or in asking permission to move a window. An
unexpected outcome was that users also used the system for
social interactions, for example for sharing music. In all
three tasks, users were able to focus on both audio and
visual elements at the same time but were only able to
focus on one visual element at a time.

VIDEO VIEWER DESIGN GOALS
The unstructured environment of the case study exemplified
by the increased screen space and the lack of a specific
collaborative interface, allowed us to observe how users
handled "raw" media in a collaborative situation. The
results have provided insights into how to provide users
with a structure that specifically handles their needs in such
an environment. The Video Viewer is a first attempt in
providing an interface structure to handle the sharing of
video on a one monitor system, based on the case study
results.

The main design objectives for the Video Viewer were first,
to provide tools for operating video sources such as
cameras or videodisc players within the interface. In the
system created for the study, users had to manually operate
these video sources. Second, the Video Viewer should be a
tool accessible from any application so that users can use
this tool while working on a document, for example.
Third, the Video Viewer should be straight forward and very
easy to use.

TOOL DESCRIPTION

The Video Viewer was designed with the metaphor of user-defined viewing channels based on the user's own video sources. For example, the prototype provides three channels. The user could have all three channels represent three different videodisc players available in that user's office or ascribe one channel to represent videodisc control, one channel to represent a video and audio connection to a colleague, and one channel to represent the images from a document or overhead camera. When the user clicks on one of these channels, the tools to control that device become available. This metaphor is based on the case study results that revealed that users usually concentrate visually on one item at a time whereas their audio concentration can exist simultaneously with many visual stimuli. The Video Viewer therefore, allows users a voice channel that exists across all video channels but the users can only see one video channel at a time. Changing channels involves only one mouse click.

The function of the Video Viewer is to allow two users to share video information with each other. Control of the video source remains with whichever user owns the hardware. So, for example, if user 1 owns a videodisc player and wants to show user 2 some videodisc images, it would not be necessary for user 2 to own a videodisc player. User 2 would simply receive the video images from user 1's player over the network. Users can record conferencing sessions or record videoclips to be shown later. These recordings would be stored in a compressed video file. In addition to the voice channel there is also audio control for each of the video devices allowing users to converse while listening to audio from a video source.

The Video Viewer functions as a device used for simultaneous communication. Therefore, when two users connect to each other via the Video Viewer, it is important first to know who is requesting the connection and secondly, it is important to provide the receiving viewer with the option of ignoring or granting the connection request quickly and easily. Furthermore, the connection request should not disrupt the receiving user's current activities on the computer. In order to accomplish these goals a small unobtrusive connection window is seen on the receiving user's screen that shows who is requesting the connection and gives the option of granting or ignoring the request. If ignored, the requesting user can leave a message in a multimedia mailbox. If granted, the Video Viewer automatically appears on the receiving user's screen.

In this design, the social protocol involved in sharing information is left with the user. The study detailed above revealed that despite system configurations, users define their own methods of social interaction. It was felt that the design of the Video Viewer should allow users maximum flexibility in defining these social protocols therefore the Video Viewer provides very little formal social protocol structure. The only social protocol structure imbedded in the Video Viewer is to keep each user aware of all activities occurring within the tool. For example, when a user is receiving images from another user, the receiving user has information about what kinds of images he/she is receiving (videodisc, videotape, CD ROM) and where these images are coming from (sender's address). Furthermore, if one user is recording a session, the other user is also made aware of this recording.

CONCLUSIONS

The study provided important insights into how people use different media when collaborating. The Video Viewer is one tool designed based on these insights and represents a next step in defining a structure for electronic collaboration tools. Perhaps the most revealing outcome of this study is that electronic collaboration has the potential to revolutionize the way people work and as collaborative tools develop and users embark on a learning curve of these new ways of working, interfaces need to work hand in hand with user studies to provide the best possible future work environments.

ACKNOWLEDGEMENTS

This study was performed at the Swedish National Defense Research Establishment as a part of the Swedish research program MULTIG, a collaborative research program on distributed multimedia applications in a multi-gigabit per second network.

REFERENCES

1. Buxton, B. & Moran, T. (1990). Europarc's integrated interactive intermedia facility: Early experiences in multi-user interfaces and applications, S. Gibbs & A.A. Verrijn-Stuart (Eds.), Elsevier Science Publisher, North Holland.

2. Heath, Christian & Luff, Paul. (1991). Disembodied conduct: communication through video in a multi-media office environment. *CHI'91 Conference Proceedings*, April, New Orleans, LA, 99-103.

3. Ishii, Hiroshi.(1990). TeamWorkstation: Towards a seamless shared workspace. *Proc. CSCW'90 Conference on Computer-SupportedCooperative Work*, October, Los Angeles, CA, 13-27.

4. Mantei M. Marilyn, Baecker M. Ronald, Abigail J. Sellen, Buxton, A.S. William, Milligan, Thomas,Wellman, Barry. (1991). Experiences in the use of media space. *CHI'91 Conference Proceedings*, April, New Orleans, LA, 203-207.

5. MultiG: A Collaborative Research Program on Distributed Multimedia Applications in a Multi-Gigabit per Second Network. (1990). *Proceedings from the 1st MultiG workshop*, Stockholm, Sweden.

USING SPATIAL CUES TO IMPROVE VIDEOCONFERENCING

Abigail Sellen* and Bill Buxton
Computer Systems Research Institute
University of Toronto
Toronto, Ontario
Canada M5S 1A1

John Arnott,
Arnott Design Group
33 Davies Ave.
Toronto, Ontario
Canada M4M 2A9

Figure 1. A user is seated in front of three Hydra units. Each Hydra unit contains a video monitor, camera, and loudspeaker.

INTRODUCTION

In this video we describe and demonstrate Hydra, a prototype system for supporting four-way videoconferencing. The design is intended to build as

---

*Abigail Sellen is now at Rank Xerox Cambridge EuroPARC, and the MRC Applied Psychology Unit, Cambridge, UK.

much as possible upon existing skills used in face-to-face discussions.

A conventional approach to multiparty videoconferencing is to support a four way meeting using a Picture-in-a-Picture (PIP) device. In this approach, each remote participant's image is placed in one quadrant of the screen of a single monitor. This common view is then distributed to each person. In addition, the audio from each participant is combined, and all voices emanate from a single loudspeaker.

Because each participant has a single monitor, camera, and loudspeaker, PIP videoconferences are limited in their support of participants' ability to:

- establish eye contact with other participants;

- be aware of who, if anyone, is visually attending to them;

- selectively listen to different, parallel conversations;

- make side comments to other participants;

- hold parallel conversations.

Hydra, on the other hand, is intended to preserve the unique personal space that participants occupy in face-to-face meetings. In simulating a 4-way round table meeting, the place that would otherwise be occupied by a remote participant is held by a Hydra unit as shown in Figure 1. Each Hydra unit consists of a camera, monitor, and speaker. Hydra units are, in effect, "video surrogates" for the participants, occupying the physical space that would be held by people, if they were physically present. The technique used is similar to that of Fields (1983), although it was developed independently.

The result of this technique is that each participant is presented with a unique view of each remote participant, and that view and its accompanying voice emanates from a distinct location in space. The net effect is that conversational acts such as gaze and head turning are preserved because each participant occupies a distinct place on the desktop.

The fact that each participant is represented by a separate camera/monitor pair means that gazing toward someone is effectively conveyed. In other words, when person A turns to look at person B, B is able to see A turn to look towards B's camera. The spatial separation between camera and monitor is small enough to maintain the illusion of mutual gaze or eye contact. Looking away and gazing at someone else is also conveyed, and the direction of head turning indicates who is being looked at. Furthermore, because the voices come from distinct locations, one is able to selectively attend to different speakers who may be speaking simultaneously.

The ways in which the design of Hydra affects behaviour is currently being investigated experimentally. The first of these analyses appears in these proceedings (see the paper by Sellen). Preliminary analysis of the data indicates that Hydra is successful in supporting selective attention both visually and auditorily. In addition, the data show that Hydra does make aside and parallel conversations possible.

A key aspect of the success of the design of Hydra is the contribution of industrial design. We describe and illustrate this process. We also show one office with three prototypes designed by the Arnott Design Group,

and contrast that with a room equipped with standard video equipment.

ACKNOWLEDGMENTS
This work was undertaken as part of the *Ontario Telepresence Project*. It has been sponsored by the Arnott Design Group, the Information Technology Research Centre of Ontario, Xerox PARC, IBM Canada's Laboratory Centre for Advanced Studies (Toronto), Apple Computer's Human Interface Group, and the Natural and Engineering Science Research Council of Canada. This support is gratefully acknowledged.

REFERENCES
Buxton, W. and Sellen, A. (1991). *Interfaces for multiparty videoconferencing*. Unpublished paper. Dynamic Graphics Project, Dept. of Computer Science, University of Toronto: Toronto, Canada.

Fields, C.I. (1983). Virtual space teleconference system. *United States Patent 4,400,724*, August 23, 1983.

Sellen, A.J. (1992). *Speech patterns in video-mediated conversations*. In these proceedings.

MULTI-MODAL NATURAL DIALOGUE

Kristinn R. Thorisson   *David B. Koons*   *Richard A. Bolt*

The Media Laboratory
Massachusetts Institute of Technology
20 Ames Street, E15-404
Cambridge, MA 01239
kris@media-lab.media.mit.edu

INTRODUCTION

When people communicate with each other they use a wealth of interaction techniques. The multitudes of gestures, intonation, facial expressions, and gaze set the context for the spoken word, and are usually essential in human interaction [1, 5].

The Advanced Human Interface Group at the MIT Media Laboratory is exploring how the three modes of speech, gestures, and gaze can be combined at the interface to allow people to use their natural communication skills in interacting with the computer [2, 3]. The work is aimed at widening the means to communicate with computers and to make computing power available to the widest range of people.

The prototype system we have designed allows a person to interact in real-time with a graphics display by pointing, looking, asking questions, and issuing commands. The system responds with graphical manipulations and spoken answers to the user's requests.

INPUT TECHNOLOGIES
Speech
A head worn, noise-cancelling microphone feeds the speech to an AT 386 computer with hardware and software that allow for discrete word recognition. The recognized words are in turn sent to one of two host computers (Figure 2).

Hand
The VPL Dataglove™ gives information about finger posture of the user. The position and attitude of the hand is given by a magnetic sensor on the back of the hand. Pointing gestures are recognized on a host computer by a template-matching algorithm. Once a gesture has been recognized, a 3-dimensional vector extending out of the hand is intersected with the screen to find point of reference.

Eye
To analyze the user's looking behavior we use a head mounted, corneal reflection eye tracker. The user looks through a half-silvered mirror; an infrared LED light shines from above and lights up the eye. An infrared-sensitive camera picks up the reflection from the eye off the mirror

and sends the resulting TV signal to an AT 286 computer for image processing. The resulting eye data is analyzed into *fixations*, *saccades*, and *blinks*.

Position of the head is found by using a magnetic sensor attached to the eye tracker. Fixations are sent to the host computer along with the user's head position during each fixation. These data are then combined to arrive at the user's point-of-gaze on a graphics screen (see Figure 1).

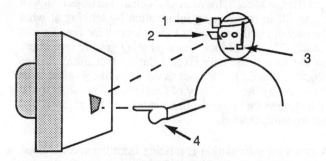

Figure 1.
An eye tracker (1=camera, 2=half-silvered mirror), microphone (3), and glove (4) allow the user to refer to objects on the screen by pointing, speaking, and looking.

SYSTEM DESCRIPTION
The system running on the two host computers has two basic components: an object-oriented map, with icons representing airplanes, trucks, helicopters, fire-fighting crews, and fire locations. The map is maintained by a graphics manager that keeps track of the position of all its icons, as well as their color, class, and name tag.

The second part of the system is a collection of modules called the *Agent*. The Agent can request information from the map manager about the layout of objects, and integrate it with the user's multi-modal requests. The Agent can thus arrive at an appropriate response for any request that the user issues. In the current version, the actions a user can perform are: *Move* an object to a new location, *delete* an object, *name* an object, *create* an object, and *request information* about the objects.

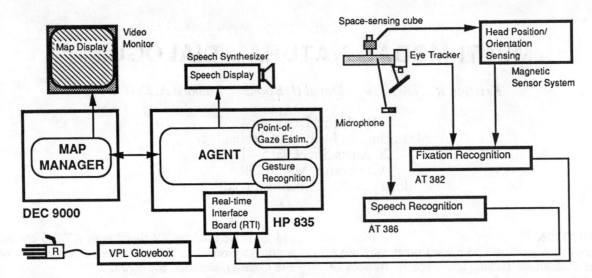

Figure 2.
System configuration, data links, and software modules.

Resolving Missing Information

Whenever the Agent receives a request that is under specified in speech, for example "delete *that* object," it will try to fill in the missing information by looking at what the user did in the two other modes around the time he said "that." The Agent looks for a pointing gesture and where on the screen the user fixated during that time. If one object is clearly singled out as the most likely referent, as indicated by the proximity of fixations and pointing to the object, then that object will be chosen as the referent and subsequently deleted.

When vital information is missing from the speech input, and the Agent cannot find a referent based on either hand or eye it will ask the user for further specifications.

Resolving Multiple Reference

The Agent can reason about relations between objects. This allows a user to say "delete the truck south of that fire." A reference is made to two objects, but one is derived by the location of the other.

"Move" commands involve two references; one to an object and one to a new location, as in "move *that helicopter* to *there*." The system can successfully deal with a continuous input of such commands by looking at the time that actions occurred and comparing it to the time that the user utters the important words of the phrase (in this case "that helicopter" and "there").

FUTURE DIRECTIONS

By allowing for multi-modal interaction, people can use their social skills in interacting with the computer. We will be looking at further ways to make such interaction possible; giving the computer a greater sense of two-handed gestures as they occur naturally in 3-dimensional space, and the role of gaze in communication.

Other tasks include giving the Agent a memory, a greater understanding of spatial relationships, and a face that can glance back at the user [4].

ACKNOWLEDGEMENTS

The authors acknowledge the contributions of graduate students Brent C.J. Britton and Edward Herranz, assistants David L. Berger, Michael P. Johnson, Mathew Kaminski, Brian Lawrence, and Christopher Wren, and research affiliate Masaru Sugai, NEC, Japan.

This research was supported by the Defence Advanced Research Projects Agency under Rome Laboratories, contract F30602-89-C-0022.

REFERENCES

1. Argyle, M. & Cook, M. *Gaze and Mutual Gaze*. Cambridge University Press, Cambridge, England, 1975.

2. Bolt, R. A. *The Human Interface*. Lifetime Learning Publications, Belmont, CA, 1984.

3. Bolt, R. A. The Integrated Multi-Modal Interface. In *Transactions of the Institute of Electronics, Information, and Communication Engineers* (Japan), (Nov. Vol. J70-D, No. 11, 1987), pp. 2017-2025.

4. Britton, Brent C.J. *Enhancing Computer-Human Interaction With Animated Facial Expressions*. Unpublished Master's Thesis, Massachusetts Institute of Technology, Cambridge, Massachusetts, 1991.

5. Nespoulous, J-L, & Lecours, A. R. Gestures: Nature and Function. In *The Biological foundations of Gestures: Motor and Semiotic Aspects*, J-L. Nespoulous, P. Perron, & A. Roch (eds.). Lawrence Erlbaum Associates, Hillsdale, NJ, 1986, pp. 49-62.

Wordspotting for Voice Editing and Audio Indexing

Lynn Wilcox[†], Ian Smith[‡], and Marcia Bush[†]

[†]Xerox PARC
3333 Coyote Hill Road
Palo Alto, CA 94304
(415) 812-4217
wilcox.parc@xerox.com

[‡]Multimedia Computing Group
Georgia Institute of Technology

ABSTRACT

Wordspotting

Wordspotting is the ability to locate a keyword or phrase in the context of fluent speech. The location of the keyword or phrase is identified, without the need to recognize the non-keyword speech. Thus wordspotting differs from isolated word recognition [2], in which words to be recognized must be spoken in isolation, and continuous speech recognition [1], in which each word in the continuous stream must be recognized.

Wordspotting is useful in tasks such as editing of voice audio and indexing into stored audio files. In voice editing, wordspotting is used to automatically find the boundaries of keywords or phrases for substitutions, deletions or insertions. This is in contrast to more traditional audio editors [3,4], in which boundaries for editing must be set manually, typically by trial and error using a visual display of the speech signal coupled with audio playback. Wordspotting also provides indexing by keywords into long audio files, thus allowing retrieval of specific information without the need to listen to the entire recording.

The wordspotter described here is incorporated into an audio editor, which is a tool for general purpose audio display and manipulation. The editor is implemented on a Sun SPARCstation and uses the X window system. It provides a visual display of the audio, a number of playback options, and the usual editing operations such as cutting and pasting. Editing operations are performed on selected regions of the audio, which are obtained either manually or by using the wordspotter.

The audio editor displays the time waveform of the audio in a scrollable window, as shown in Figure 1. Magnification is provided by a zoom capability. The editor allows playback of selected portions of the audio, for example, the playback of a portion of the audio containing a keyword located by the wordspotter. This allows easy verification of the wordspotter's selection. It also allows playback in a region surrounding the selected area, so that context can be provided. In addition, it allows playback between consecutive repetitions of a keyword as identified by the wordspotter. A time scale modification feature [7] allows playback of the audio at twice the normal speed, without the usual pitch distortions associated with such rate increases.

The wordspotter is speaker dependent, and requires an initial training for each talker. This training is performed on a segment of recorded speech, either the audio document for which indexing and editing is required, or an arbitrary segment of the talker's speech. When wordspotting is to be performed, the talker simply speaks the keyword or phrase to be located. Alternately, a keyword can be manually excised from the recorded document for use in further editing or indexing. There is no restriction on the number of keywords. There are no linguistic assumptions, so the system is multi-lingual.

The wordspotter is based on hidden Markov models, a statistical technique commonly used in speech recognition [6]. During the initial training phase, a set of acoustic units is learned which are used to model the speech of a talker. These acoustic units are obtained by unsupervised clustering, or vector quantization [5], of an arbitrary segment of the talker's speech. No attempt is made to correlate these acoustic units with the theoretical phonetic units often used to describe speech (e.g. the phonetic pronunciation found in a dictionary). Rather, the sequence of acoustic units describing a keyword is determined from the actual utterance of the keyword by the talker. Statistical techniques are used to model expected variations in other pronunciations of the keyword by the same talker. More details on the system can be found in [8].

Application Scenarios For Wordspotting

The video contains three application scenarios for the wordspotting-based audio editor. In the first, a librarian uses the system to fill out an audio form letter, which is then sent as voice mail. The form letter (in Italian) is an overdue book notice. Keywords in the audio form letter represent blanks to be filled in. To fill in the form, the librarian brings up the wordspotting panel by selecting the "WordSpot" option in the audio editor. The wordspotting panel is shown in Figure 2. She selects the "Record" option and speaks the required keyword, then initiates wordspotting using the "WordSpot" button. The "Number of Occurrences" field indicates the number of instances of the keyword found, in this case one. The "Next" button is used to select the next instance of the keyword, which is then highlighted in the audio editor window, as seen in Figure 1. She can play the selected region to verify the occurrence the keyword. Using the replace option in the audio editor, she speaks the correct information, thus replacing the keyword.

The second application is voice editing of a prerecorded newscast (in French). The newscaster uses the audio editor to review his newscasts before broadcasting. Wordspotting allows him to find the location of his mistakes without having to listen to the broadcast several times. The wordspotter is not limited to speech; in this example laughter is found and removed from the newscast.

In the third application, an administrative assistant uses the audio editor to index into dictation (in English). Wordspotting allows her to position the audio playback to the desired location. For example, she can locate portions where E-mail transcription is required. In addition, wordspotting allows her to set markers to control the playback for aide in transcription. She uses this capability by wordspotting on the keyword "paragraph". The playback option can then be set to stop between consecutive instances of the keyword.

References

[1] J.M. Baker. Large Vocabulary, Speaker Adaptive Continuous Speech Recognition Research Overview at Dragon Systems. In Proceedings of Eurospeech 91 (Genova, Italy, September 24-26). ESCA, 1991, pp. 29-32.

[2] Dragon Dictate User Manual, Dragon Systems, Inc. Newton, MA. 1990.

[3] Waves+, Entropic Research Laboratory, Inc. Washington, DC. 1991.

[4] Farallon MacRecorder User's Guide, Farallon Computing, Inc. Emeryville, CA. 1990.

[5] R.M. Gray. Vector Quantization. IEEE ASSP Magazine (April 1984) 4-29.

[6] L.R. Rabiner. A Tutorial on Hidden Markov Models and Selected Applications in Speech Recognition. Proceedings of the IEEE 77, 2 (February 1989) 257-285.

[7] S. Roucos, A.M. Wilgus. High Quality Time-Scale Modification for Speech. In Proceedings of Int. Conf. Acoustics, Speech and Signal Processing (Tampa, FL, March) IEEE, 1985. pp. 493-496.

[8] L.D. Wilcox, M.A. Bush. HMM-based Wordspotting for Voice Editing and Indexing. In Proceedings of Eurospeech 91 (Genova, Italy, September 24-26). ESCA, 1991, pp. 25-28.

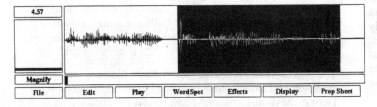

Figure 1. User interface to the audio editor. The speech signal is displayed in a scrollable window. The highlighted region represents an instance of the keyword selected by the wordspotter.

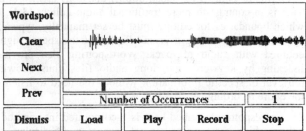

Figure 2. User interface to the wordspotter. The "Number of Occurrences" field indicates the number of instances of the keyword found by the wordspotter. The "Next" button is used to select and highlight the next instance of the keyword in the audio editor.

Coupling Application Design and User Interface Design

Mark H. Gray
College of Computing, Georgia Institute of Technology
Atlanta, GA 30332-0280, *email:* vatavian@cc.gatech.edu

Dennis J.M.J. de Baar
Faculty of Technical Mathematics and Informatics, Delft University of Technology,
Binnenwatersloot 3, 2611 BJ Delft, The Netherlands, *email*: winfddb@duticai.tudelft.nl

James D. Foley
College of Computing, Georgia Institute of Technology
Atlanta, GA 30332-0280, *email:*foley@cc.gatech.edu

Kevin Mullet
Human Interface Engineering Group, SunSoft, Inc.
2550 Garcia Ave. MS-MTV225 Mountain View, CA, *email:* mullet@eng.sun.com

ABSTRACT

Building an interactive application involves the design of both a data model and a graphical user interface (GUI) to represent that model to the user. These two design activities are typically approached as separate tasks and are frequently undertaken by different individuals or groups. Our approach eliminates redundant specification work by generating an interface directly from the data model itself. An inference engine using style rules for selecting and placing GUI controls (i.e., widgets) is integrated with an interface design tool to generate a user interface definition. This approach allows a single data model to be mapped onto multiple GUI's by substituting the appropriate rule set and thus represents a first step toward a GUI-independent run-time layout facility.

KEYWORDS: User Interface Software, Automatic User Interface Design, Data Models

INTRODUCTION

An early step in the design of an interactive application is the definition of the application's data model. In an object-oriented design, the data model consists of an object class hierarchy in which each object has an associated set of attributes and methods. Single or multiple inheritance is typically used to avoid repetitive specification of shared methods and attributes. The attributes and methods of an object are either internal or external. Internal attributes and methods are meant for use within the application and are not exposed in the user interface. External attributes and methods are represented in the user interface as standard interaction objects such as buttons, settings, or sliders (hereafter referred to as "controls") or as data manipulated directly by the user.

The external attributes and methods of the data model must be mapped onto a set of controls in the target GUI. These controls must then be divided among one or more application windows and arranged to fit within the available space while maintaining the organizational characteristics required for clear communication and aesthetic quality. Guidelines for control selection and arrangement are provided by GUI-specific style guides such as the OPEN LOOK GUI Application Style Guidelines [Sun90b], the OSF/Motif Style Guide [OSF90], the Apple Human Interface Guidelines [Appl87] and the CUA Style Guide [IBM87]. These documents provide high-level rules and principles that help to maximize consistency across applications in the respective GUI's.

A number of commercially-available software tools provide a GUI interface to the GUI design task. *GUI builders* such as Devguide [Sun90a], Interface Builder [NeXT90], and Interface Architect [Hewl90] present the designer with standard user interface components that can be dragged onto the work surface and arranged using direct manipulation. Each of these tools can be used to generate source code or executables for a particular configuration of GUI components, but all rely on the skill and knowledge of the user interface designer to create the desired configuration themselves by manually selecting the appropriate controls and specifying their locations within the parent window. This limitation means that the interface designer is required to repeatedly perform three tasks that are at least potentially unnecessary:

(1) Access details of the data model, either from documentation or from (the designer's) memory.

(2) Access and apply GUI-specific control selection rules that determine how each element of the data model is mapped onto a particular control in the target GUI.

(3) Access and apply GUI-specific layout rules governing the placement of each control in the target GUI.

To create a property window, for example, the designer must know the attributes (properties) of the object represented by that property window, decide on a particular GUI component to use for each attribute, and arrange the components within a window according to the layout conventions established by the target GUI.

Automatic generation of window and menu layouts from information already present in the application data model can relieve the application designer of unnecessary work while providing an opportunity to automatically apply style rules.

TRANSFORMING DATA OBJECTS INTO INTERACTION OBJECTS

In the current system, objects from the application data model are used as input to an automatic control selection and layout facility. An inference engine uses the actions and attributes of the data objects to generate a set of interaction objects in a direct manipulation interface design environment, which instantiates the interaction objects using a GUI toolkit and produces a textual specification describing the GUI components and their locations within one or more windows.

Following the selection of specific interaction objects, a set of layout rules determines the location of each object. The layout rules implement a set of high-level graphic design conventions addressing the size, spacing, and alignment of individual controls.

REFERENCES

de Baar, Foley, and Mullet "Coupling Application Design and User Interface Design," in this proceedings.

[Appl87]   Apple Computer, Inc. *Human Interface Guidelines: The Apple Desktop Interface.* Reading, MA: Addison-Wesley, 1987.

[Beek90]   Beekman, W.H.R. *D2m2edit*, Master's Thesis, Delft University of Technology, The Netherlands, July 1990.

[Besh88]   Beshers, C. and S. Feiner, "Scope: Automated Generation of Graphical Interfaces," *Proc. of the ACM SIGGRAPH Symposium on User Interface Software and Technology*, Banff, Alberta, Canada, October 1988, pp. 76-85.

[Fole88]   Foley, J.D., C. Gibbs, W. Kim, S. Kovacevic, L. Moran, P. Sukaviriya, "A Knowledge-Based User Interface Management System," *Human Factors in Computing Systems, CHI'88 Conference Proceedings*, Washington DC, May 1988, pp. 67-72.

[Fole91]   Foley, J.D., W. C. Kim, S. Kovacevic, and K. Murray, "UIDE - An intelligent User Interface Design Environment," in Sullivan, J and S. Tyler (eds.), *Architectures for Intelligent Interfaces: Elements and Prototypes*, Addison-Wesley, Reading, MA, 1991.

[Hew90]   Hewlett-Packard Company, *HP Interface Architect Developer's Guide*, Hewlett-Packard Company, Corvallis, Oregon, October 1990.

[IBM87]   IBM Corporation. *System Application Architecture, Common Access Panel Design and User Interaction.* SC26-4351-0. December 1987.

[NeXT90]   NeXT Computer Inc., *NeXTstep Concepts*, Redwood City, CA: NeXT Computer, Inc., pp. 8-1 to 8-53.

[Olsen89]   Olsen, D. "A programming Language Basis for User Interface Management," *Human Factors in Computing Systems, CHI'89 Conference Proceedings*, Austin, Texas, May 1989, pp. 171-176.

[OSF90]   Open Software Foundation. *OSF/Motif Style Guide*, Revision 1.0, OSF 11 Cambridge Center, Cambridge, MA 02142, ISBN 0-13-640491-X, 1990.

[Sun90a]   Sun Microsystems, Inc. and AT&T, *OPEN LOOK* GUI *Application Style Guidelines*. Addison-Wesley, Reading, MA, 1990.

[Sun90b]   Sun Microsystems, Inc., *Open Windows Developer's Guide 1.1, Reference Manual*, Part No. 800-5380-10, Revision A, June 1990.

[Wiec89]   Wiecha, C., W. Bennett, S. Boies, and J. Gould, "Generating Highly Interactive User Interfaces," *Human Factors in Computing Systems, CHI'89 Conference Proceedings*, Austin, Texas, May 1989, pp. 277-282.

[Zand90]   Zanden, B. Vander and B.A. Myers, "Automatic, Look-and-Feel Independent Dialog Creation for graphical User Interfaces," *Human Factors in Computing Systems, CHI'90 Conference Proceedings*, Seattle, Washington, April 1990, pp. 27-34.

COMBINING GESTURES AND DIRECT MANIPULATION

Dean Rubine

Information Technology Center
School of Computer Science
Carnegie Mellon University
Pittsburgh, PA
412-268-3650
Rubine@andrew.cmu.edu

INTRODUCTION

A gesture, as the term is used here, is a handmade mark used to give a command to a computer. The attributes of the gesture (its location, size, extent, orientation, and dynamic properties) can be mapped to parameters of the command. An operation, operands, and parameters can all be communicated simultaneously with a single, intuitive, easily drawn gesture. This makes gesturing an attractive interaction technique.

Typically, a gestural interaction is completed (e.g. the stylus is lifted) before the the gesture is classified, its attributes computed, and the intended command performed. There is no opportunity for the interactive manipulation of parameters in the presence of application feedback that is typical of drag operations in direct manipulation interfaces. This lack of continuous feedback during the interaction makes the use of gestures awkward for tasks that require such feedback.

The video presents a *two-phase* interaction technique that combines gesture and direct manipulation. A two-phase interaction begins with a gesture, which is recognized during the interaction (e.g. while the stylus is still touching the writing surface). After recognition, the application is informed and the interaction continues, allowing the user to manipulate parameters interactively. The result is a powerful interaction which combines the advantages of gesturing and direct manipulation.

EXAMPLE 1: GDP

GDP is a mouse-based drawing program that utilizes the two-phase interaction to create, copy, move, rotate, scale, delete, and group lines, rectangles, ellipses, and text. For example, the create-line gesture consists of positioning the mouse, pressing the button and making the gesture (a straight segment). The user stops moving the mouse (while continuing to press the mouse button) and the gesture is recognized. A line is created, one endpoint of which is placed at the start of the gesture, the other endpoint at the current mouse location. The user drags around the latter endpoint (rubberbanding) until the mouse button is released. The other creation gestures work similarly, utilizing the starting point of the gesture as one parameter and interactive dragging to determine another.

The gestures that operate on existing objects (move, copy, rotate-scale, group, and delete) work similarly. The copy gesture begins on an object. After it is recognized (and the mouse button is still being pressed) a copy of the object appears and may be dragged. The start of the rotate-scale gesture determines the object to be rotated as well as the center of rotation; after it is recognized the user drags a point on the object interactively rotating and scaling the object. The group gesture collects together all objects encircled by the gesture into a single composite object; after recognition, additional objects may be added to the group by touching them with the mouse cursor until the mouse button is released.

All the gestures in GDP are single strokes. While this restricts the possible gestures, it has the important property that the user holds the mouse button down during the entire two-phase interaction, releasing the button only at the end. Thus the physical tension and relaxation of the interaction correlates nicely with the mental tension and relaxation involved in performing a primitive task in the application.

Though not shown in the video, it is possible to tie other gestural attributes to application parameters in GDP. For example, one version uses the length of the create-line gesture to determine the thickness of the resulting line and the orientation of the create-rectangle gesture to determine the initial orientation of the rectangle.

EXAMPLE 2: EAGER RECOGNITION

Example 1 illustrated the two-phase interaction in which the user makes the gesture, stops moving the mouse while holding the mouse button, the gesture is recognized, and direct manipulation begins. The mouse must remain still for an interval of time (one-quarter second by default) before recognition occurs. In some contexts, forcing the user to stop is awkward. For example, using a gesture to turn a knob would involve making the turn-knob gesture (which would presumably be the beginning of a natural turn motion of the knob), stopping, and then resuming the knob turning, this time with application feedback.

It seems desirable to have the gesture recognized as soon as enough of it has been seen to do so unambiguously. This is the goal of *eager recognition*. Thus the user would begin the turn the knob, the knob-turning gesture would be recognized, and then the knob would start to turn. No stopping or other explicit indication of the end of the gesture is necessary. What begins as a gesture smoothly becomes a direct-manipulation interaction.

The second example shows GDP with eager recognition enabled. Since the create-rectangle gesture, an 'L', is the only expected gesture that begins with a downward stroke, it is recognized almost immediately, a rectangle created, and direct manipulation of its corner begins. The copy gesture, a 'C', works similarly: as soon as the curvature of the 'C' is apparent, the gesture is recognized, the object is copied, and the copy is dragged. The line gesture, a straight segment, is not eagerly recognized. This is because the system recognizes that the gesture in progress may also be a move gesture, an arrow drawn with a single stroke. Thus the line gesture is only recognized when the mouse motion stops, as in the non-eager GDP. The rotate-scale and delete gestures are eagerly recognized.

EXAMPLE 3: GSCORE

GSCORE is an editor for musical scores which uses gestures and the two-phase interaction. For example, after the time-signature gesture is recognized, the x and y coordinates of the mouse interactively control the numerator and denominator of the time signature. GSCORE has separate gestures for whole notes, half notes, quarter notes, eighth notes and sixteenth notes (actually, there are two gestures for each except whole notes, one for upward stems, and one for downward stems). While it would be possible to have a single note gesture and then interactively control the duration and stem direction of the note, having separate gestures appears to result in faster interactions. It is possible to edit the set of gestures and their meanings (at runtime) to try out various interfaces, so the two approaches may be compared.

The video shows how a new gesture is added to GSCORE. Gestures are associated with classes of views on the screen (e.g. a note responds to a different set of gestures than a staff), so the user first clicks to examine the set of gestures associated with a particular view. Adding a new gesture involves pressing the "new class" button and then entering fifteen examples of the new gesture. There is a click-and-drag interface to an Objective-C interpreter through which the semantics of the gesture are specified. The new gesture may be tried immediately. Although not shown, it is possible to evaluate the new classifier by testing all the training examples. This evaluation indicates when a new gesture is mistaken for an existing gesture (or vice versa), indicating that the new gesture needs to be redesigned to look different.

EXAMPLE 4: MULTIPLE FINGER GESTURES

The two-phase interaction may be used with multi-finger input. The video shows MDP, a version of the drawing program that uses a Sensor Frame as a multi-finger input device. The mouse gestures of GDP are mapped to single-finger gestures in MDP. After the gesture is recognized, additional fingers may be brought into the sensing plane of the Sensor Frame to control additional parameters. For example, after recognizing create-line, the first finger rubberbands one endpoint of the new line (as in GDP), and additional fingers control the line's color and thickness.

Multiple finger gestures are also recognized. The training of the undo gesture is shown, and later the use of undo is demonstrated. The two-phase interaction allows the amount of "undoing" to be determined interactively after the gesture is recognized. Also interesting is the two finger rotate-scale-translate gesture. After recognition, each of the two fingers attaches to a point on the object. By spreading the fingers apart or moving the fingers closer together the object can be scaled, by changing the orientation of the fingers the object can be rotated, and by moving the two fingers in parallel the object can be translated. It is seen that multiple finger interaction allows for the intuitive manipulation of many parameters simultaneously.

CONCLUSION

The purpose of the video is to demonstrate the two-phase interaction technique, in which gesture and direct-manipulation are combined. While previously described in print [1, 2, 3], the video shows the dynamic aspects of the interaction in ways that print cannot. In particular, it shows how the two-phase interaction is applicable in two applications, a drawing program and a score editor, and for both single-pointer and multiple-pointer input devices. Eager recognition, a technique for smoothing the transition between the gesture and the direct manipulation phases of the interaction, is also shown. While the video demonstrates the potential of combining gesture and direct manipulation, user testing is needed to determine if this potential can be realized.

REFERENCES

[1] RUBINE, D. Integrating gesture recognition and direct manipulation. In *Proceedings of the Summer '91 USENIX Technical Conference* (June 1991), USENIX Association, pp. 281–298.

[2] RUBINE, D. Specifying gestures by example. *Computer Graphics 25*, 4 (July 1991), 329–337.

[3] RUBINE, D. *The Automatic Recognition of Gestures.* PhD thesis, School of Computer Science, Carnegie Mellon University, CMU-CS-91-202, 1991.

BRIAR:
A CONSTRAINT-BASED DRAWING PROGRAM

Michael Gleicher
School of Computer Science
Carnegie Mellon University
Pittsburgh, PA 15213-3890
USA

gleicher@cs.cmu.edu

CR Categories: I.3.6 Interaction techniques.

Additional Keywords: constraints, drawing, direct manipulation, Snap-Dragging.

Geometric relationships between parts are an important element in drawings. From the earliest days of interactive systems[5], the benefits of using constraints to explicitly represent these relationships have been known. Although many have discussed the value of constraints, constraint-based approaches have not been successful in practical systems.

In contrast to the failure of constraints, direct manipulation systems have been successful for geometric modeling tasks. Users control the geometry of objects by interactively grabbing and pulling them, with continuous update providing feedback. Such systems employ snapping techniques, such as grids, to aid in establishing relationships, but these relationships are immediately forgotten. They are neither explicitly represented nor automatically preserved. It is the user's job to maintain them during subsequent editing.

The *Briar*[1] drawing program combines the two approaches: snapping techniques establish relationships and constraint techniques maintain them during subsequent dragging. *Briar's* approach distinguishes the problem of establishing relationships from that of maintaining them during subsequent editing. This separation allows us to skirt several difficult issues in constraint-based systems. Integration with direct manipulation techniques addresses issues in solving, specifying, debugging, displaying and editing constraints.

BRIAR'S INTERFACE

Briar uses a set of techniques called *Snap-Dragging*[1] to aid users in establishing relationships in a drawing. Gravity

---

[1]It is called *Briar* because, like the plant it is named for, things stick together inside it.

snaps the drawing cursor to interesting locations in the drawing. In Snap-Dragging, the cursor snaps to objects, but has a preference for interesting points such as vertices, centers, and intersections. *Briar's* feedback mechanisms show the state of snapping by lighting up the object snapped to and changing the cursor shape depending on whether the cursor is snapped to a point or to an edge. When there are multiple objects to snap to, cycling selects among them.

Snap-Dragging also provides alignment objects, special objects which are not part of the drawing *per se*, but exist only to be snapped to. Alignment objects are placed automatically at interesting points in the drawing by the system. They allow a wide variety of relationships to be established by snapping.

Most systems that provide snapping quickly forget about snapping operations as soon as they are completed. However, *Briar* provides the user with the option of making these relationships into persistent constraints which are maintained during subsequent editing. The snapping operation is augmented to specify constraints in addition to positions, with little or no additional work by the user.

When a snapping operation occurs, *Briar* acknowledges it by showing the newly established relationship to the user. The user has the opportunity to accept the new relationship, transforming it into a persistent constraint. To make the constraint creation process more transparent, the default can be to accept new constraints.[2]

There are two basic snapping operations: snapping the cursor to a line or curve, or snapping the cursor to a point, such as a vertex. These operations correspond to *Briar's* two basic constraints, "point-on-object" and "points-coincident" respectively. Combining these basic constraints with alignment objects permits a wide range of relationships to be enforced. Symbols for the basic constraints, an empty square and a filled diamond, combine with alignment objects to form a visual language for displaying the constraints.

Briar permits users to directly manipulate the drawing subject to the constraints imposed on it. Objects are dragged, as

---

[2]Although we provide an "accident-prone" mode where acceptance is not the default, we find that it is seldom used.

they are in other direct manipulation drawing programs, except that relationships can be maintained among them. This allows the drawing process to be incremental: each new relationship added to a drawing does not disturb previously established ones.

Editing constraints has been problematic for constraint-based systems. Not only must a user specify how to delete or modify a constraint, but they must also figure out which constraints to alter. Briar addresses both these issues. Users edit constraints by refering to the desired effects on objects, not the constraints themselves. Instead of pointing at constraints, users directly manipulate objects to show how they are to move. For example, constraint maintenance can be disabled so objects move freely. Constraints which are broken are clearly noted to the user. When maintenance is restarted, violated constraints are removed. A variant is a "rip" command which allows the user to pull part of an object free from its constraints.

DRAWING WITH CONSTRAINTS

By incorporating techniques of direct manipulation drawing programs, *Briar* is able to address many of the difficult issues in employing constraints. Users need only use constraints where convenient; other attributes of the drawing can be specified by direct manipulation. Direct manipulation of a drawing subject to constraints provides a method for exploring the range of configurations of an underconstrained model. The continuous motion during dragging can make it easier to understand complex behaviors of constrained models.

Previous constraint-based systems have used constraint satisfaction to transform a model from an arbitrary configuration to one where the constraints are satisfied. However, *Briar* separates the tasks of initially establishing relationships in drawings from that of maintaining them during subsequent editing. Constraint techniques are reserved for relationships that are established by snapping. *Briar* never needs to solve constraint satisfaction problems from arbitrary initial configurations. Not only does this mean *Briar* avoids the issue of performing this difficult task, but it also avoids the issues of presenting the transformations between configurations to the user and dealing with inconsistent models.

Briar's augmented Snap-Dragging has advantages as a method for specifying constraints. It lets the user specify constraints in addition to positions with little or no extra effort. By providing an initial configuration, augmented snapping assures that the constraints are not inconsistent, since at least this one solution exists. A wide variety of relationships can be specified without a similarly wide variety of constraint creation commands.

THE VIDEO

The accompanying video demonstrates *Briar*. Segments describe the basic features, beginning with snapping and continuing on to show how augmented snapping specifies constraints and how alignment objects are used to specify other relationships. The equilateral triangle example, taken from

[1], shows how quickly constrained models can be created with snap-dragging. Other segments demonstrate how constraints are used to aid in manipulation and are deleted. The example of a V-Engine shows how easily a constrained model can be assembled. The subsequent example shows some of *Briar's* special features for drawing and animating planar mechanisms. The segment on grouping shows how *Briar* is able to mix standard drawing program features with constraints.

More information on Briar can be found in references [2] and [3]. The former discusses how *Briar* addresses the issues in building constraint-based systems, while the latter provides more details about *Briar's* interface. The techniques to support constrained dragging in *Briar* are similar to those discussed in [4].

Acknowledgments

This research was funded in part by Apple Computer, a fellowship from the Schlumberger Foundation, and an equipment grant from Silicon Graphics. I would like to thank Andy Witkin for his assistance throughout this project. I would also like to thank Will Welch, Brad Myers, Francesmary Modugno and Virginia Peck for their helpful criticisms of the video and Peter Weyhrauch for his help with the audio.

REFERENCES

[1] Eric Bier and Maureen Stone. Snap-dragging. *Computer Graphics*, 20(4):233–240, 1986.

[2] Michael Gleicher. Integrating constraints and direct manipulation. In *Proceedings of the 1992 Symposium on Interactive 3D Graphics*, March 1992.

[3] Michael Gleicher and Andrew Witkin. Creating and manipulating constrained models. Technical Report CMU-CS-91-125, School of Computer Science, Carnegie Mellon University, April 1991.

[4] Michael Gleicher and Andrew Witkin. Differential manipulation. *Graphics Interface*, pages 61–67, June 1991.

[5] Ivan Sutherland. *Sketchpad: A Man Machine Graphical Communication System*. PhD thesis, Massachusetts Institute of Technology, January 1963.

AN INTRODUCTION TO ZEUS:
AUDIOVISUALIZATION OF SOME ELEMENTARY
SEQUENTIAL AND PARALLEL SORTING ALGORITHMS

Marc H. Brown

DEC Systems Research Center
130 Lytton Ave.
Palo Alto, CA 94301
mhb@src.dec.com

INTRODUCTION

Algorithm animation is a powerful technique for exploring a program's behavior that has proven to be helpful in a number of contexts, especially in teaching computer science courses and in designing and analyzing algorithms.

Systems for algorithm animation provide facilities for users to view and interact with an animation of an algorithm, and for programmers to develop such animations. For a user, there are ways to control the data given to an algorithm, the ensemble of active views, and the execution of the algorithm. For a programmer, producing an animation of an algorithm becomes almost as easy as producing a textual trace of it.

The Zeus algorithm animation system [2] follows the "classical" approach for animating algorithms (specified in high-level procedural languages), pioneered in BALSA [4]. Briefly, the approach is as follows: An algorithm is annotated with "interesting events" that identify its fundamental operations that are to be displayed. Events can have parameters, which typically identify program data. Each view controls some screen real estate and is notified when an event happens in the algorithm. A view is responsible for updating its graphical (or auditory) display appropriately based on the event. Views can also propagate information from the user back to the algorithm. The Zeus system is noteworthy for its use of objects, strong-typing, parallelism, and graphical development of views.

This videotape concentrates on novel techniques for algorithm animation, not on the specifics of the Zeus system. The Zeus system allowed us — and encouraged us — to explore these new techniques, but the techniques illustrated in the videotape are applicable to any algorithm animation. The novel areas are the use of color and especially sound, the animation of parallel algorithms, and the ways a user can give data to a program.

WHAT TO NOTICE: COLOR

The videotape illustrates three of the most fundamental uses we have made of color:

Color unites multiple views. When multiple views show different aspects of the same data structure, or different representations of logically related objects, an application can create a smoother, more harmonious picture by painting corresponding features with the same colors in all the views. This point is particularly obvious in the views of Parallel Quicksort, where color in all views shows the part of the array each thread is working on.

Color reveals an algorithm's state. Color gives an extra dimension for state display—one can encode information in both the shape and the color of objects. Moreover, color allows denser presentation of information: fewer pixels are needed to make a color change visible than to make a change in the shape of an object visible. For instance, in the Quicksort Partition Tree view, red and blue are used to distinguish active subfiles being processed from inactive ones.

Color highlights areas of interest. For instance, in the Selection sort animation, yellow is used to highlight the smallest element seen so far during each pass through the array, and a gray overlay to highlight the current comparison.

WHAT TO NOTICE: SOUND

We strongly concur with Gaver that "auditory displays have the potential to convey information that is difficult or awkward to display graphically. Sound can provide information about events that may not be visually attended, and about events that are obscured or difficult to visualize. Auditory information can be redundant with visual information, so that the strengths of each mode can be exploited. In addition, using sound can help reduce the visual clutter of current graphic interfaces by providing an alternative means for information presentation" [5].

The specific ways we have used sound are as follows:

Audio reinforces visual views. Our first foray into using audio, and perhaps its most obvious use, was simply to reinforce what was being displayed visually. For example, in the sorting animation, each comparison or movement of an element produces a tone whose pitch is linearly related to the element's value.

Audio conveys patterns. It became immediately obvious to us in "hearing" the sorting animation that sorting algorithms produce auditory signatures just as distinctive as the visual patterns of moving sticks or dots. It is possible for people to hear relationships in data that are never seen or displayed (and vice versa). Because sound intrinsically depends on the passage of time to be perceived, it is not surprising that sound is very effective for displaying dynamic phenomena, such as running algorithms.

Patterns become especially distinctive and informative when different instruments are used to convey different aspects of a program.

Audio replaces visual views. We've used audio views to replace what can easily be displayed in a visual view in order to allow the user to focus full visual attention on other visual views. For example, in the Parallel Quicksort algorithm, the audio view produces a tone whose pitch rises with the number of active threads (virtual processors). This number could easily be printed textually, or graphically displayed as a bar chart. However, because the user receives the thread information through a non-visual channel, he can focus full visual attention on the primary views of the algorithm at work.

WHAT TO NOTICE: PARALLELISM

The videotape illustrates two fundamental uses of parallelism. (Keep in mind that because Zeus runs on a 4-processor workstation, multiple threads do in fact run in parallel; parallelism is real, not simulated.)

First, all views are updated in parallel each time the algorithm generates an interesting event. That is, when the algorithm signals an event (by invoking a Zeus procedure, passing to it the name of the event and the parameters), a thread is forked for each view. Each view updates itself in its own thread (perhaps even forking more threads). The call in the algorithm to generate an event is suspended until all threads have completed, indicating that all views have completed their updating for the algorithm event.

Second, the algorithms themselves may be intrinsically parallel. Zeus does not synchronize the threads of the algorithm in any way; when a thread generates an event, that event is processed (with views being updated in parallel) with no regard to other events that may be underway in other threads.

WHAT TO NOTICE: USER INPUT

The videotape shows three ways to give information to the algorithm. The most common technique is to fill out an algorithm-specific data form. A second method is to use a control panel view (provided as a view by Zeus) to cause an event to happen with specific parameters. The event may flow from the algorithm to views, or may flow to the algorithm. Finally, one can interact directly in an algorithm-specific view.

It's relevant to mention that the idea of giving data to an algorithm by gesturing in views led to the development of FormsEdit, a multi-view editor for building user interfaces in FormsVBT [1]. A videotape of FormsEdit was part of the CHI '90 video program.

ACKNOWLEDGMENTS

A detailed discussion on the use of color and sound in algorithm animation was prepared with John Hershberger [3].

REFERENCES

[1] Gideon Avrahami, Kenneth P. Brooks, and Marc H. Brown. A two-view approach to constructing user interfaces. *Computer Graphics*, 23(3):137–146, July 1989.

[2] Marc H. Brown. Zeus: A system for algorithm animation and multi-view editing. In *Proc. 1991 IEEE Workshop on Visual Languages*, October 1991.

[3] Marc H. Brown and John Hershberger. Color and sound in algorithm animation. Research Report 76a, DEC Systems Research Center, 130 Lytton Ave., Palo Alto, CA, September 1991. A preliminary version appeared in the *Proc. 1991 IEEE Workshop on Visual Languages*, October 1991.

[4] Marc H. Brown and Robert Sedgewick. A system for algorithm animation. *Computer Graphics*, 18(3):177–186, 1984.

[5] William W. Gaver. The SonicFinder: An interface that uses auditory icons. *Human-Computer Interaction*, 4(1), 1989.

POINTING AND VISUALIZATION

William C. Hill and James D. Hollan

Computer Graphics and Interactive Media Research Group
Bellcore, 445 South Street, Morristown, NJ 07962-1910

Email: willhill@bellcore.com, hollan@bellcore.com

ABSTRACT

The nature of visualizations and the social uses to which they are put rely heavily on pointing behavior. In the context of a switched telephone network visualization, this tape illustrates novel task-specific pointing facilities.

Keywords: Pointing, visualization, graphical user interface, visual attention, interface mechanisms.

INTRODUCTION

The accepted wisdom of what tools and skills are required to produce visualization excellence is undergoing redefinition in order to incorporate, among other changes, new *pointing facilities*. These facilities are enabled for the first time by the controlled dynamics that computational graphics offer. The facilities wbecame visibleill be in demand because they will allow users to express complex task-specific pointing intentions.

Broadly construed, pointing involves directing visual attention. Pointing with your index finger is a simple example. Just turning your head to look may point if it directs the visual attention of others. Using a laser-pointer during a presentation is another common example. But so is explaining travel directions with maps over the phone by verbally directing the visual attention of another to specific map locations. Theatrical lighting is a more complex form of pointing. For example, the synchronous dimming of one spotlight and brightening of another serves to direct audience attention. So too, the many and varied ways film directors direct visual attention around movie scenes serve as sophisticated examples. In the realm of human computer interfaces pointing is almost synonymous with using the mouse. Normally the mouse is used to direct the flow of control but during demonstration users employ the cursor to direct others' visual attention. As should be clear from these examples, pointing mechanisms vary widely and are often central to effective communication.

Rarely are graphics employed for strictly private individual purposes. More commonly, through meetings, presentations, publications, and mass media, graphics are employed as social instruments, shared among individuals and groups. Social use of graphics is the norm. Empirical observation shows that the social use of graphics relies heavily on pointing behaviors, often in coordination with speech or text. The paradigmatic example is a presenter pointing at presentation graphics before a live audience but there are many other social situations where graphics serve as shared interaction-organizing artifacts. Visualizations are such social graphics and as expected, if you just look, the amount of pointing by hand, mouse and cursor, narrative reference, and embedded visual technique during their use is enormous. Thus, from an empirical point of view, pointing is fundamental to visualization.

For understanding the existing practice of pointing as the ground upon which to build more effective pointing facilities, three observations are paramount. First, pointing behaviors commonly realize intents more complex than *look here*. By analyzing pointing performances captured on videotape we have produced a preliminary taxonomy of such complex pointing intents. Because pointing behaviors realize complex intents, the simplistic assertion that a mouse and cursor handle the majority of interactive pointing needs is suspect. Second, graphical resources for pointing differ according to medium and situation. This amounts to saying we should expect and prepare for task-specific pointing techniques. Third, by reifying pointing behaviors and bringing them into the graphics themselves, computational techniques radically alter what pointing can be.

TASK-SPECIFIC POINTING IN VISUALIZATION

In the realm of visualization, the narrative use of graphics almost always involves pointing. Good visualizations, for example, are rich with the interplay of beautiful and subtle pointing. Choices of lighting, materials, highlights, textures, point of view, size, transparency, cutouts, arrows, motion blur, eye-catching movement, time dilation, edge-pushing, burnout, to name only a few, are mechanisms employed to direct visual attention. Fast rendering speeds, double-buffering, 3D geometry, and texture mapping techniques now common to current visualization efforts extend the power of graphic transformation and provide new ways for expressing pointing intentions that employ the preattentive powers of human vision. Until recently, these methods have been unavailable.

But not every use of graphic technique is pointing. Otherwise pointing would mean nothing more than graphic technique and that is not the case. Although most graphic techniques may be employed to point, in any given image only a few serve pointing intent. Only if you can remove the pointing and *still have the image* do you have pointing. The kind of pointing we are discussing is *separable*, *removable*, and *temporary*. Thus, in practice, on separate occasions, a presenter, having conceived particular communicative purposes relevant to distinct audiences, will point at the same image in different ways tailored to those purposes.

Our example concerns the visualization of switched telephone network activity, in particular the performance of digital signals on fiber optic cables connecting mobile telephone transceiver sites to a central telephone switching office. These digital signals run at 45 Mb/second but are subject to transient errors of various types. Special monitoring hardware collects error data so that performance can be examined to attempt to find predictive patterns. However, depending on the number of signals, number of error parameters per signal, and the frequency of collection one frequently confronts an overwhelming volume of data. One such collection effort with which we are involved collects over 100,000 error parameters per day.

We have built a visualization of these data for digital signal experts. They are interested in improving the quality of digital service so that one might be able to guarantee that transient errors will not occur more often than once in, say, 10^{-8} clock cycles or some other suitably low level. The users of our visualization are concerned, among other things, with seeing error threshold breaking in the context of previous patterns of errors. That is to say, they want to see what is going on with the errors in periods preceding that in which particular thresholds are broken.

Their goal is to detect error signatures predictive of future threshold breaking. In terms of visualization, this means we wanted to direct their attention at the occurrence of threshold-breaking events but in a way that also highlights potentially relevant subthreshold error data. The visualization technique we developed serves as an example of task-specific pointing. We refer to the pointing intention as *threshold-breaking in context*.

The threshold-breaking in context pointing intention is served by a variably-transparent movable neutral grey cutting plane to represent the current threshold as set by the user. The transparent grey plane creates a contrast luminance between errors that exceed the threshold and those under the threshold. Within the dynamic scene, this creates a *popout effect* [1] in which the eye is effortlessly drawn specifically to the threshold-breaking errors. Transparency handles the other part of the pointing intention --- not to occlude error activity under the threshold. Subthreshold activity can still be discerned and users can manipulate a transparency control to get more or less visual stimulation from subthreshold activity. Users of this prototype system have found this technique effective. Essentially, the technique enables users to state a myriad of threshold-related questions graphically.

The intent of our video is to draw attention to the importance of pointing, construed broadly, but implemented narrowly to substitute easy visual tasks for otherwise difficult ones as they arise naturally in a real task. We think this kind of task-specific pointing will play an increasing role in future graphical interfaces and in the wider use of dynamic graphics. Techniques for exploiting computational graphics to express complex pointing intentions are just beginning to be explored. How to effectively use them is challenging, particularly for new types of applications. For example, computer supported cooperative work applications raise a variety of issues resulting from the existence of multiple points of view and the complex nature of shared tasks.

ACKNOWLEDGMENT

The authors would like to acknowledge the assistance of Larry Stead in the making of this video tape.

REFERENCES

1. Triesman, A. Features and Objects: The Fourteenth Bartlett Memorial Lecture. *The Quarterly Journal of Experimental Psychology*, 40A(2), 203-237, 1988.

TOUCHSCREEN TOGGLE DESIGN

Catherine Plaisant

Human-Computer Interaction Laboratory
Center for Automation Research
University of Maryland
College Park, MD 20742

Tel. (301) 405-2768
plaisant@cs.umd.edu

Daniel Wallace*

Vitro Corporation
Advanced Technology Dept.
14000 Georgia Avenue
Silver Spring, MD 20906

Tel. (301) 231-2041
dfw@at1147.vitro.com

INTRODUCTION

This video describes and compares six different touchscreen based toggle switches to be used by novice or occasional users to control two state (on/off) devices in a touchscreen environment.

Computer based toggle switches can be very confusing. The most common problem encountered is the confusion between state indication and possible action label; does the label ON indicates the state of the device or does it indicate the resulting state when the toggle is activated? Another common problem comes from the difficulty of deciding what to do to change the state of the device. The design needs to signal to the user the appropriate activity necessary to perform the desired action. For example, Valk showed that users were confused by a design which showed a slider switch where only touches on the end of the slider were permitted, but "sliding" was not possible [5].

Computers allow designers to design many new types of "soft" toggle switches by providing an easy way to create and modify the appearance and behavior (or look and feel) of the controls. It is no longer necessary to select a control from a catalog, but unfortunately the lessons from traditional control design [1,2] are often ignored. This additional freedom brought a new wave of inadequate toggle designs (Figure 1).

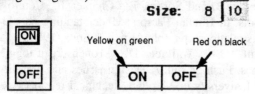

Figure 1 - Examples of ambiguous toggles we found in existing systems.

* This work was done while Daniel Wallace was a graduate student in the Psychology Dept. of the Univ. of Maryland.

The project had a practical orientation since this work was conducted in collaboration with Custom Command Systems Inc. which specializes in the development and marketing of integrated entertainment, security, and climate control systems for homes and offices. Their focus is on providing state-of-the-art systems that are easy for the home owner to use. The control of these systems is afforded through a touchscreen interface. Users see the screen flushmounted into the wall or the cabinetry. Our goal was to select a usability-tested/error-free toggle and to better understand some of the problems and issues involved in the design of controls for a touchscreen environment.

The color, graphical screen displays are implemented under MS-DOS in VGA mode. The touchscreen used returns a continuous flow of coordinates allowing the dragging of objects, the identification of sliding motion and the use of a lift-off strategy for selection [4].

DESCRIPTION OF THE TOGGLES

A requirement imposed by our particular application was to design toggles allowing lists of devices or options to be presented on the screen. This limited us to horizontal toggles (Figure 2) to increase the number of possible toggles and labels per page.

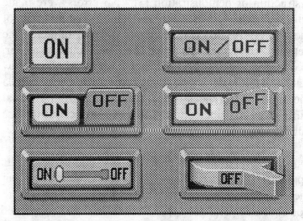

Figure 2: The six toggles: one-button, "words", two-button, rocker, slider and lever. In the tested application users did see several lines of devices names with the corresponding toggles on the side (only one type of toggle is used at a time).

• *One-button toggle* (Pushbutton): The main problem with pushbuttons is that their identification as a toggle (and not a simple indicator) might not be obvious; users may not realize that they can change the state by touching it. Once recognized as a toggle the pushbutton has the advantage of being graphically simple and uncluttered and its size can be reduced if necessary [4].

• *"Words" toggle:* When the device is ON the ON-label is on a bright green background, when OFF the OFF-label is on a bright green background (this design simulated the existing implementation in Custom Command's system).

• *Two-button toggle:* When the device is ON the ON side is depressed and the ON-label is on a buttercup yellow background while the OFF-label is gray like the button itself. The advantage of this toggle is that it allows the design of very similar controls having 3 or more states.

• *Rocker toggle:* This toggle only differs from the two-button by its graphical appearance which is less "busy" than the two-button toggle.

• *Slider toggle:* In this toggle a sliding/dragging movement is required to change the position of the yellow pointer from one side of the toggle to the other. A simple three step animation shows the movement of the pointer along the slide. If the device is ON the pointer is on the ON side. Users can then grab the pointer and slide it to the other side. If the finger is released before reaching the other side the pointer springs back to its previous position.

• *Lever toggle:* Same "behavior" as the slider. Only the graphical appearance is different.

The video shows other aspects of the prototypes (such as highlighting, animation, sound effects, etc.) which are very important but described with difficulties in such an abstract as this.

USABILITY TESTING

Fifteen undergraduate students used every toggles without instruction or demonstration [3]. No errors were made when subjects were asked to determine the current state of the toggles. A fairly consistent rank ordering of preference between the toggles was found (from one-button to rocker, two-button, "words", slider and lever). Although few statistical differences were found at the a priori level of 0.05 the mean differences were sizable. Large individual differences contributed to the lack of statistical difference between toggles.

Our interpretation was that the one-button design is appreciated for its simplicity (but of course users know that they were dealing with toggles and the pushbuttons were not confused with labels). The rocker was appreciated probably because the required movement on the screen matched the action on a real rocker. Its graphic is also simpler and more appealing than the two-button and word toggles.

The toggles that are pushed seemed to be preferred over the toggles that slide. A possible explanation is that sliding is a more complex task than simply touching, but we also noticed that sliders are more difficult to implement than buttons! The usability test brought to light many imperfections in our two sliding toggles (e.g.: because of its strong perspective the lever toggle was often touched too low - this bias has to be corrected; the slider pointer should be larger, and the lever or pointer should highlight when touched to signify that the user now has control over it). Even if several subjects first attempted to touch the extremities of the toggle before trying to slide the lever or pointer we observed that all subjects (spontaneously or after one trial) used sliding motions successfully to manipulate the sliding toggles. Even if sliders were not preferred, the fact that users used them correctly is encouraging since many other controls can be designed using sliding motions. Another advantage of the sliding movement is that it is less likely to be done inadvertently therefore making the toggle very secure (the finger has to land on and lift off the right locations). This advantage can be pushed further and controls can be designed to be very secure by requiring more complex gestures (e.g. a U or W shape slider can be used for a 2 or 3 setting control respectively).

The evaluation of the toggles showed some important differences in personal preferences. Every toggle had at least one unconditional fan. Only the one-button and rocker received all positive or neutral comments. Therefore toggles are good candidates for user customization. If one toggle had to be recommended as a potential "always acceptable toggle" (the vanilla ice-cream of toggles), the rocker implementation is probably the best bet.

REFERENCES

1. Chapanis, A. and Kinkade R. Design of controls, Chapter 8 in Human Engineering Guide to Equipment Design, Sponsored by Joint Army-Navy-Air Force Steering Committee, John Wiley & Sons (1972).

2. Kantowitz, B. and Sorkin, R. Chapter 10: Controls and tools, in Human Factors: Understanding people-systems relationships, John Wiley & Sons (1983).

3. Plaisant, C. , Wallace D. Touchscreen toggle Switches: Push or slide? Design issues and usability study. University of Maryland technical report CAR-TR-521, CS-TR-2557 (Nov. 1990).

4. Sears, A., Plaisant, C. and Shneiderman, B., A new era for high-precision touchscreens. To appear in Hartson, R. and Hix, D. ed., Advances in Human-Computer Interaction, Vol.3, Ablex Publ., NJ (1992).

5. Valk A. M. An experiment to study touchscreen "button" design, Proceeding of the Human Factors Society, 29, 127-131 (1985).

Dynamic Queries:
Database Searching by Direct Manipulation

Ben Shneiderman, Christopher Williamson, and Christopher Ahlberg

Computer Science Department and Center for Automation Research
Human-Computer Interaction Laboratory
University of Maryland, College Park, MD 20742
ben@cs.umd.edu

INTRODUCTION

This video explores the application of direct manipulation to information exploration. Specifically, it introduces the idea of a dynamic query, which empowers the user to search a database of information in the task domain while requiring minimal syntax or computer knowledge. Key features that separate a dynamic query from current information retreival systems are its direct manipulative nature, providing immediate search feedback with object interaction, and a harmonious display of the query and results in a graphical environment appropriate for the task domain [3].

A slider serves as a metaphor for the operation of entering a value for a field in the query - it provides a mental model [2] of the range. Changing the value is done by a physical action - sliding the drag box with a mouse - instead of entering the value by keyboard. By being able to slide the drag box back and forth and getting immediate updates of the query results, it is possible to do dozens of queries in just a few seconds. The operation is incremental and if the query result is not what users expected the operation is reversible by simply sliding the slider back. Error messages are not needed - there is no such thing as an 'illegal' operation or incorrect syntax.

The results of the query are displayed in a graphical format near the sliders. The interaction between the visualization and the query mechanism is important. The sliders have to be placed close to the visualization to reduce eye movement. The highlighting of elements should be in harmony with the coloring scheme of the slider. The color of the area to the left of the drag box on the slider bar is the same as the highlighted elements in the visualization, because the values to the left of the drag box are the values that satisfy the query.

APPLICATION: PERIODIC TABLE

The first application of dynamic queries explored was an educational program for the periodic table of elements. Designed by Christopher Ahlberg on the Sun SparcStation 1+, it allows users to set properties such as atomic number, atomic mass, electronegativity, etc. to highlight a certain number of elements in the periodic table (Figure 1). This lets users explore how these properties interact with each other. Other interesting discoveries can be made regarding trends of properties in the periodic table - such as how electronegativity increases from the lower left corner to the upper right corner of the periodic table and to find exceptions to trends.

A user study was conducted on this interface and subjects were found to perform statistically significantly faster with the dynamic queries interface than with the form fill-in interface [1]. The subjects also showed a statistically significant preference for the dynamic queries interface over the other two interfaces.

This application also demonstrates the power of dynamic queries to find trends and exceptions in a database. The causality, incrementability, and the display's graphical nature make exceptions more apparent. Since most users have excellent visual discrimination and many people look for exceptions in a database (such as finding the cheap home in a nice neighborhood, or the weak part in an automobile), dynamic queries can help the user find them.

Finally, this application demonstrates a form of Query-by-Example [4], we call Query-by-Instance, whereby the user may select an item in the graphical display and initialize the slider's settings to the properties of that element. This can be very helpful for those who are not familiar with the values of the properties, but can specify that they wish to find elements with similar properties to that of a known element. The user can then manipulate the sliders to widen the range of specific properties from those of the specified instance.

APPLICATION: DYNAMIC HOMEFINDER

The second application of dynamic queries explored was a practical public-access program for helping users find a Williamson on the IBM PC utilizing a touchscreen, it allows users to set properties with sliders such as proximity to work or school, number of bedrooms, cost, and services such as fireplaces and air conditioning (Figure 2). A map of the area is displayed beside these sliders with points of light designating individual homes that meet the properties specified. More specific information on a home could then be retrieved by selecting that home on the touchscreen.

This application shows that a relatively complex searching specification for a home can be designed using dynamic queries such that it is suitable for first-time users and public-access systems. Further, the proximity specification allows the user to specify geographically the area and distance in which they are looking for a home. This simple area specification is rarely offered on current real estate searching systems. The trends, although less apparent than in the periodic table application, are still visible such as cost and type of homes in given neighborhoods. One of the classic problems with information retrieval is narrowing the results of the search. With typical command-line interfaces, it is too easy for a user to specify a query which fails to find anything. They modify their previous query, this time getting back too much information - the user is forced to guess values to narrow their results. Dynamic queries help to overcome this all-or-nothing problem: users can easily fine-tune their search based on previous results. If the desired results fail to turn up enough hits, or too many, the user can simply fine-tune the sliders on one or more attributes until the desired number of hits is achieved.

This application dramatically demonstrates the feeling of causality conveyed to the user. The direct manipulative qualities of incrementability, reversibility, and smooth graphical feedback encourage the user to explore the database, freely manipulating the properties without fear of syntax errors or of getting lost.

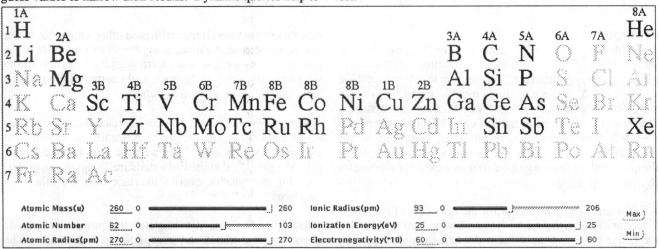

Figure 1. Application: Periodic Table of Elements

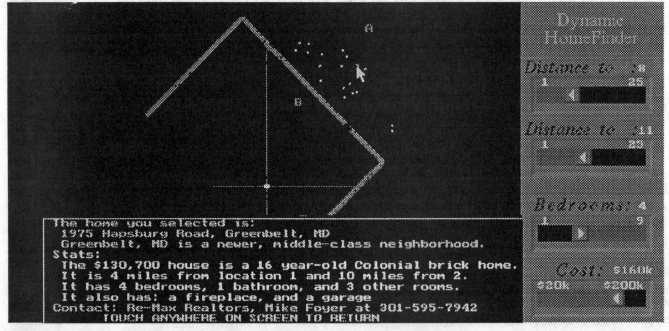

Figure 2. Application: Close-up of Dynamic HomeFinder

REFERENCES

1. Ahlberg, C., Williamson, C., and Shneiderman, B. Dynamic Queries for Information Exploration: An Implementation and Evaluation. *Proc. ACM CHI '92.*

2. Shneiderman, Ben, Direct Manipulation: A step beyond programming languages. IEEE Computer. 16, 8 (August 1983), pp. 57-69.

3. Williamson, C. and Shneiderman, B. *The Dynamic HomeFinder: Evaluating Dynamic Queries in a Real-Estate Information Exploration System.* CS-TR-2819, College Park, MD, 1991.

4. Zloof M. Query-by-Example. National Computer Conference, AFIPS Press,1975, pp. 431-437.

Doctoral Consortium

James D. Foley, Chair
Georgia Institute of Technology

Lin Brown, *Sun Microsystems, Inc.*

Gerhard Fischer, *University of Colorado*

David Kieras, *University of Michigan*

Michael Harrison, *University of York*

Incremental Change in the Development of Expertise
Wai On Lee
MRC Applied Psychology Unit

Advisor: Phil Barnard

The research examines skill development in using computer systems. The approach adopted examines expertise by focusing on the cognitive changes that occur within skill development over time. The thesis encompasses two strands of empirical enquiry: the development of performance and knowledge utilization. In the first strand, a study was carried out to examine the relationship between skill development, action slips, and feedback. It was found that action slips remained persistent even after extensive practice on a task and a dynamic form of feedback was able to significantly reduce action slips than a static type of feedback. Whilst in the second strand, the effective utilization of system functionality was examined. A model of function utilization provided the hypothesis for a study comparing advice of two types: Function Revelation (FR), and Problem Reformulation (PR). It was shown that advice of the FR type, typically associated with "Intelligent support systems", did not enable users to make effective use of functions in later tasks, where as a PR type of advice, which enables the proper identification of the main difficulty with the task and the formulation of the retrieval description for the appropriate function, enabled users to make effective use of newly discovered functions.

Group Communication and Performance: An Experimental Assessment of the Impacts of Technology Support in Groups
Marianne N. Størrosten
The University of Michigan

Advisor: Judith S. Olson

Research on group support systems (GSS) provides evidence that, in general, computer technology can and does impact the quality of the group product. However, researchers do not fully understand how groups interact, how this influences the quality of what they do, and how technology of different design might affect different aspects of group behavior.

This dissertation addresses these problems by studying the consequences of computer support for teams working on unstructured, high-level design problems in face-to-face group settings. An experimental study is underway to examine differences in group communication and the quality of the outcome of groups using a group editor (one which allows all to see and edit the same document at the same time) compared to groups using conventional meeting tools.

Communication in Design
Diane H. Sonnenwald
Rutgers University

Advisor: Nicholas J. Belkin

Information systems coexist with, and ideally support, patterns of work activities, social groups, and personal beliefs. Thus, information systems designers, developers, and users, with their own group and individual perspectives need to interact so that they can come to a working understanding of how the information system will coexist with, and support, users. This is fundamentally a communicative process, and, therefore, the goal of this dissertation is to develop a descriptive design model that accounts for communication among participants. A preliminary model, based on a content analysis of two design case histories, will be elaborated

on through an empirical investigation that includes participant observation, unstructured interviews, sociometric surveys, artifact collection, and critical incident methods. The dissertation provides an opportunity to study the evolution of intra- and intergroup communication among multiple groups doing cooperative, complex design tasks that require specialized knowledge and involve decision making and conflict resolution over a period of time. An ultimate research goal is to influence communication in, and the quality of, design.

Supporting Exploration in Human-Computer Interaction
John Rieman
University of Colorado

Advisor: Clayton Lewis

Mainstream research in human-computer interaction has focused on situations where users have well-defined tasks or goals. A different form of interaction occurs when a user decides to explore the functionality of a system with no clear goal in mind. The user's motivation may be to gain knowledge for future use, or to solve an ill-structured problem such as "make an attractive graphic", or simply to satisfy curiosity. These exploratory episodes are an opportunity to acquire advanced computer skills.

How can a computer system support exploratory behavior? My research looks at two sides of this question. First, it investigates exploration in an abstract sense: what is involved in exploring an action space, what are the difficulties, and what makes a structure of actions more or less explorable? Second, it investigates the cognitive behavior of computer users in exploratory situations, collecting empirical data and considering that data in a theoretical framework.

DOCTORAL CONSORTIUM

System Delay and User Strategy Selection: From Performance Models to Engineering Models

Steven L. Teal
Carnegie Mellon University

Advisor: Alexander Rudnicky

This thesis attempts to develop a predictive, zero-parameter engineering model that characterizes the relationship between system delay and user performance. Strategy selection is hypothesized to be based on a cost function that combines two factors: (1) the effort required to synchronize input with system availability and (2) the accuracy level afforded. Experimental results indicate that users, seeking to minimize effort and maximize accuracy, choose among three strategies: automatic performance, pacing, and monitoring. These findings provide a systematic account of the influence of system delay on user performance, based on adaptive strategy choice driven by cost.

The GOMS Model Methodology and Minimalist Instruction: An Evaluation of Two Methods for Generating Procedural Instructions

Richard Gong
University of Michigan

Advisor: David Kieras

Well-designed documentation and on-line help can significantly contribute to improving the computing skill of novice and occasional users. However, relatively little research has been conducted to determine how help content should be specified to most effectively aid users. This research seeks to compare the relative effectiveness of two research-based approaches in designing a help system for the popular Macintosh application HyperCard. The Minimalist Instruction approach (Carroll, 1990) encourages users to infer the proper methods for accomplishing specific goals while the GOMS Model Methodology (Kieras, 1988) directly presents step-by-step procedures to the user based on the GOMS Model of the task environment. It is hypothesized that each approach will demonstrate unique costs and benefits depending upon the task situation of the user. It is also hypothesized that the results of this research will suggest specific guidelines for the application of each approach.

Delivering Case-Based Information in Integrated, Knowledge-Based Design Environments

Kumiyo Nakakoji
University of Colorado

Advisor: Gerhard Fischer

Integrated, domain-oriented, knowledge-based design environments that support co-evolution of problem specification and solution construction empower designers by providing them with useful information, or "knowledge" about the domain. The dissertation research is to investigate a knowledge delivery mechanism for such design environments, called CASEDELIVERER, which delivers case-based information relevant to designers task at hand. The mechanism allows designers to exploit the information, a source of accumulated design experiences, that provides designers with possible solutions, warns of possible failures, and provides them with justification in terms of their task at hand, even when designers do not perceive their information needs or the existence of potentially useful information. The synergy of the integrated design environments enables CASE-DELIVERER to partially identify the designers task at hand from a combination of a partial specification and construction. The relevance between the case-based information and the identified task is inferred using rules that are dynamically derived from an argumentation component in the environments.

Widget Level Models of Human-Computer Interaction: Applying Simple Task Descriptions to Design and Evaluation

Andrew Sears
University of Maryland

Advisor: Ben Shneiderman

Many methods have been developed to assist both designers and evaluators of user interfaces. These methods typically require either very little or very detailed information concerning the tasks to be performed. This research focuses on demonstrating the potential benefits of a simple task description. Three parts of the design and evaluation process are emphasized:

• selection of widgets and organization of information within widgets,
• arrangement of widgets on an individual screen,
• placement of and movement between dynamic

objects including dialog boxes and windows. First, the impact of task description on widget selection and organization of information within the widgets was considered. Buttons, pop-up scrolling lists, and scrolling text lists were considered for the task of selecting one item from a set. Next a metric, Layout Appropriateness, was developed to analyze the appropriateness of a widget layout given a simple task description. Finally, the effects of window placement, relative the cursor and original screen, on user performance were investigated. This research will result in guidelines and metrics that should benefit both interface designers and evaluators.

Theoretically Guided Semi-Automatic Routine protocol Analysis

Frank Ritter
Carnegie Mellon University

Advisor: Allen Newell

Verbal protocol analysis has been hindered in the past by the lack of a strong cognitive theory to guide the coding and implement the analysis, and manual coding and analysis, which have limited the available analyses and data set size that can be approached. Soar/PA is a set of semi-automatic general tools to do protocol analysis in a routine way that addresses these problems. It is theoretically guided: the coding of segments in Soar/PA is guided by and results in a running cognitive model in Soar, a unified theory of cognition. Soar/PA is integrated with Soar. This helps automate the coding and provide built-in analysis such as cognitive operation counts. Soar/PA also provides tools to manipulate and manage models. It will be demonstrated first by duplicating existing analyses and then by analyzing a total of approximately 30 subjects on example tasks.

Organization Design Viewed as a Group Process Technology

Gail Louise Rein
The University of Texas at Austin

Advisor: Andrew B. Whinston

The dissertation is concerned in particular with the design of organizations. The focus is on a design process that potentially involves all members of the organization and those significantly associated with the organization (e.g., stakeholders, bond holders, union members, consultants, regulators, and customers). As such we are concerned with designed not an individual product, but a whole system, an environment. The design produces change not only in the organization (the thing being designed), but also in the people in the organization and in the organizations and the people with which the organization interacts.

This pervasiveness of change, in essence, forces the design process to be a continuous, ongoing activity. An organization is an open system, a system that affects and is affected by its environment (Constantine, 1986). The continuous nature of the design process leads to the next assumption of the dissertation: repetitive activities are prime candidates for technology support.

The dissertation describes a prototype technology that supports organization design as a group process. The technology consists of two tightly interconnected pieces: (1) an interactive, multi-user, graphical editor for generating process descriptions, and (2) an associated group process for using the editor to design organizations, which is expressed in the modeling language supported by the editor.
The significant resulting artifact from the dissertation is GPOD, a set of Role Interaction Net scripts that describes a group process of organization design. GPOD specifies a meta-process for organization design that incorporates elements reported in case studies of successful, large-scale, organization change. The GPOD process description is considerably more explicit than any of the organization design and change processes described in the literature. It is sufficiently detailed that it could serve as a practical guide to an organization design process in the real world.

The use of the GPOD scripts within a coordination system is also described in detail.

Principled Auditory Feedback
Robert Vermilyer
University of Washington

Advisor: Alan Borning

Environments with complex information displays often overburden the user's perceptual system by directing all information to one channel: vision. The goal of this research is to develop design recommendations for the increased use of richer auditory feedback. The design recommendations for principled auditory feedback will be based upon prior psychoacoustical research, a taxonomy that categorizes events (using criteria such as urgency, completedness, and number of other processes

affected), and empirical studies of the discriminability of sounds and the associability of sounds to concepts. The design recommendations will address the issues of how to compose auditory feedback using the various dimensions of sound (amplitude, frequency, and duration), the constraints of different environments, and when to use auditory feedback to complement or replace visual feedback. The effect on performance of using principled auditory feedback will be empirically evaluated.

Tools for Debugging Constraint Hierarchies
Michael Sannella
The Ohio State University

Advisor: Gary Perlman

Constraint-based systems have been applied to many problems in computer graphics, including two-dimensional layout and user interface construction. Constraint hierarchies specifying both requirements and preferences as constraints have proven particularly useful for controlling interactive user interfaces. However, large constraint hierarchies with multiple strength levels can be difficult to understand and debug. This research will focus on creating better tools for examining and manipulating constraint hierarchies. One particular area that will be explored is the use of data visualization techniques to display the behavior of individual constraints within a constraint hierarchy, and the interactions between constraints. This research will also investigate debugging techniques for several distinct types of constraint hierarchies, including hierarchies of error-measuring constraints and data-flow constraints. These techniques will be examined and compared in an attempt to discover general concepts that can be used when constructing debugging tools for other constraint-based systems.

The Dynamics of Group Authoring: Implications for the Design of Computer Support for Distributed Collaborative Authoring
Levi L. Beck
University of Sussex

Advisor: Mike Sharples

Collaborative authoring is an activity engaged in by many writers whether they are professional or not. This project has a theory-driven approach to developing computer support for collaborative writing, advocating a thorough understanding of the process of co-authoring as

the basis for developing computer support systems. An approach to studying the dynamics of this process through the analyses of non-task focussed aspects has been developed. It is hypothesized that this approach provides insights into (some of) the dynamics which serve as coordinating pivots for the work in a co-authoring group, thereby providing useful pointers to what kinds of tools might support this aspect of collaborative writing when co-authors are geographically distributed. The conceptual framework is presented together with preliminary results from applying it to both quantitative and qualitative data.

Specifying Temporal Behavior in Multimedia Documents
M. Cecelia Buchanan
University of Washington

Advisors: John Zahorian, Polle Zellweger

I have designed and implemented a system for creating, editing, and displaying multimedia documents. It uses an improved multimedia document model that maintains information about the events of interest in media items and the temporal synchronization constraints among those events. Authors specify synchronization constraints by explicitly relating the occurrence of important events in one media item to those in another, rather than relating all events to a timeline. The system has several advantages over existing multimedia document editors. First, the ability to specify relationships directly between media items simplifies the process of creating and modifying documents. Second, asynchronous information can be included, allowing more expressive documents to be constructed. Third, the system automatically constructs a schedule for displaying a document, freeing the author from this task. Finally, because synchronization constraints record the author's intentions and because the system creates schedules automatically, maintenance of documents throughout their life cycles is easier.

Interactive Experience

A Mi Abuelita: A Day of the Dead Shrine
Lucia Grossberger
Women's Caucus for Art

Day of the Dead is celebrated in Mexico and in some parts of South America as a day when families and friends gather to remember their dead. This shrine installation is dedicated to the memory of the artist's grandmother, Modesta.

The installation first acquaints participants with the concept of celebrating, rather than mourning, the death of someone who lived a full and happy life, including a hypertext exploration of Modesta's life. The second part of the installation uses a computer to place the participants' image in a Day of the Dead shrine. This image changes to a death mask unexpectedly, causing the participant to confront the possibility of his or her own death and perhaps accept that only when we confront and accept death can we truly live.

A Gallery of Interactive Art
Douglas MacLeod and the Media Arts Department
The Banff Centre for the Arts

Three installations have been designed to allow the audience to create and modify artworks by interacting with a variety of input and display devices.

The Voice in the Machine
In this piece, a play of nature and technology is mediated by the users' vocal input. Soundscapes evocative of the ancient division of the cosmos into air, fire, water and earth reside as samples that are placed into 3D motion by MAX programs. Vocal sounds made by users are analyzed and processed, they both merge into and transform the soundscapes. Complementary visual scenes of natural environments are accessed from laser disk by MAX, subject to the same voice-controlled interaction.

The AB Box
The AB Box is an audio-installation project that makes sounds by itself, creating its own audio

environment. The installation is composed of a number of interconnected, sound-producing objects and seven chairs with touch-sensitive armrests. Together participants will have to learn new ways of acting in and on this environment with the sounds being the result of their cooperative, rather than individual actions.

Drumming up a Building
In this piece, audience members use various percussion devices and musical controllers to create three dimensional shapes in AutoCAD. Each device controls a different architectural element. MAX is used to interpret the MIDI information from these devices which is sent to AutoCAD as input.

Interactive Imagination
Dorothy Shamonsky
New York University

This installation describes by example how graphics can be used in the interface. Inspired by works such as Edward Tufte's "Envisioning Information," it presents a collection of interactive examples and ideas, including a tongue-in-cheek Name the Icon game.

This installation tries to create a structure to draw participants' attention to, and enhance visual literacy in, interface design.

Is Anyone There?
Stephen Wilson
San Francisco State University

This installation appropriates the often intrusive computer-based telemarketing technology and uses it to involve people who do not traditionally participate in the art world in an event that probes the diversity of life in the city. It explores such issues as the commoditization of art, computer mediated voice telephone communication, and conversations with computer-simulated characters. For one week a computer telemarketing device made hourly calls to selected pay telephones in San Francisco,

engaged whoever answered in conversations about life in the city, and digitally stored the conversations. The locations were chosen based on socioeconomic diversity and their significance to the life of the city. The computer used intelligent response programming to engage passers-by curious enough to answer a ringing pay phone, and digitally recorded the conversations. Topics included the lives of those who answered and their perceptions of their immediate environment. Video was used to capture representative images of the phones' locations and of the people who typically inhabit the space.

The installation allows participants to interactively explore the city by using this bank of stored sound and digital Quicktime video to selectively call up recorded responses and images. An interactive hypermedia program encourages viewers to devise strategies for exploring the information. Digital video of the phone locales accompanies the recordings, and digitally manipulated images become metaphors for information about the recorded calls. Viewers use their voice to move among the spots and to indicate their strategies of exploration.

It's a Scream
Gitta Salomon, Ian Small, I. Kenneth Miller
Apple Computer, Inc.

Leo Degan
Utrecht School of the Arts

This installation presents an interactive room that can accommodate several simultaneous participants. Audio input from participants is used to drive a large-screen projection of point-of-view movies of scenes such as motorbike racing or bungee jumping. The volume of sound produced by participants will be used to effect realtime semantic control of the movies. Louder sounds may increase the level of apparent danger presented or the direction of navigation in the movie. If more people participate and a higher volume level is achieved, additional levels of control become possible.

INTERACTIVE EXPERIENCE

The movie display is controlled using QuickTime™ and HyperCard™. Custom audio software, coupled with a sensing device, tracks volume level to a great degree of accuracy.

The Streams of a Story

I. Kenneth Miller
Apple Computer, Inc.

Participants are presented with a large rock containing a computer screen showing video water. Faces and other graphic elements float by in the stream and wink, encouraging interaction. When touched, the faces give information. Participants can get more information on that topic by continuing to touch the face. The computer tracks the topics of interest to the user and presents more faces with information on those topics.

The premise of this installation is that the user can do no wrong. To this end, the entire screen is active, whether a graphic element is present or not; the installation responds through sound and video to every touch.

TPTV

Abbe Don
In Context

Mark Petrakis
pARTy Science

Nick West
Media 360

Mitchell Yawitz
Apple Computer, Inc.

TPTV is a provocative, open-ended multimedia system designed to engage users in a dialog about contemporary political and social issues. The installation features animated broadsides inspired by Jerry Mander's recent book "In the Absence of the Sacred: The Failure of Technology and the Survival of the Indian Nations" which explores the impact of technology on society and the environment as it offers possible solutions to keep us from destroying the planet.

Users appear in a live video window in the upper right hand corner of the screen. At any point, they can record a response to either the animated broadsides or the responses of previous users. The TPTV system was built in HyperCard, calling on Apple Computer's new

QuickTime software and a RasterOps video board to capture responses through a video camera. Users can review their contributions instantaneously. As the system is used, the resulting movies create a virtual roundtable discussion available for others to view and participate.

TPTV is displayed inside a teepee structure with slides projected onto it. This set design approach extends the interface from the computer to the surrounding environment as it creates an immersive experience and an atmosphere for reflection.

Virtual Acoustic Environments

Dr. Elizabeth M. Wenzel
NASA Ames Research Center

Scott H. Foster
Crystal River Engineering, Inc.

The Virtual Acoustic Environments installation is a realtime interactive simulation of several virtual sound sources that appear to be located at distinct locations within a simple room. You can experience how sound quality generated by a Convolvotron is affected by the manipulation of the environment such as expanding the virtual walls or changing the absorption characteristics of the walls, ceiling, and floor surfaces. You, as the architect or recording engineer, can design an artificial listening space and explore the acoustic consequences of your design, creating a new orchestral arrangement with a live spatial mix of the individual musical, speech or sound effects tracks. In a simulation of acoustical CAD/CAM in the design studio of the future, you control the environmental parameters of your design while viewing the space using the BOOM viewer with real-time, stereoscopic computer graphics.

The installation illustrates a completely new development in the capabilities of 3D audio systems; previously, because of their computational complexity, only free-field or rooms without echoes have been simulated interactively in real time. This installation simulates the direct path to each sound source plus six first-order reflections, one from the floor, the ceiling, and each of the walls, using four Convolvotrons to render to the four virtual sound sources.

Just as a movie with sound is much more compelling and informationally rich than a silent film, computer interfaces can be enhanced by an appropriate three-

dimensional sound track to the task at hand. Applications include acoustic environments for architectural design, music recording, and entertainment; air traffic control and cockpit displays for aviation; enhanced communications systems; applications involving encoded sound, such as the acoustic visualization of multi-dimensional data and alternative interfaces for the blind; and telepresence environments, including advanced teleconferencing, shared electronic workspaces, and monitoring telerobotic activities in hazardous situations.

The Virtual Museum

Sally Ann Applin, Dean Blackketter, Eric Chen, Eric Hoffert, Gavin Miller, Libby Patterson, Steve Rubin, Derrick Yim
Apple Computer, Inc.

The Virtual Museum is an electronic museum for the creation and display of a large variety of media objects which convey the key ideas in a scientific or artistic discipline. The idea of a virtual museum actually originated in the Renaissance, and was called a kunsthammer, or knowledge warehouse. The idea at that time was to display a painting that contained miniature versions of a large number of objects. Museum visitors could then order any object seen in the painting, and an elaborate system of elevators would be used to bring objects out of a basement warehouse.

Four or five centuries later, we have designed a digital kunsthammer, or virtual museum. Various new technologies have been used to produce a museum where visitors can move at will from room to room and select any exhibit that they want to see and learn more about. Visitors can now digitally order the objects seen within the artwork for themselves, without elaborate elevators or large warehouses. Once an exhibit is selected, the visitor is shown a screen designed to imitate the experience of standing in front of an actual museum exhibit, complete with frames and a textual description.

Specific exhibits and museum rooms are accessed by selecting objects within each 3D movie. Although there is a button-activated floor plan so that visitors can travel from room to room without walking, the visitor must select an object from within the 3D movie to go to a specific exhibit.

Interactive Performance

High Wire - The CHI'92 Interactive Performance

CHI this year is about "striking a balance" between the many forces that shape user interface design. If CHI is about balance, then the Interactive Performance is the high wire - where balance is critical to success. This year's show includes work by some of the most innovative interface designers in the world: those who work with, or as, artists. Each act features a skilled practitioner of an ancient art: storytelling, clowning, music, or dance.

Dana Atchley
storyteller/author
San Francisco, CA

Atchley tells stories using video, music and slides under centralized computer control. His stories come from experience as wide as the horizon.

Digital Media
sound, imagery
Santa Cruz, CA

Using a variety of state of the art computers and projectors, this group creates an ever-changing context for the rest of the show.

Derique McGee
"one man band"
San Francisco, CA

McGee's body and hands control Sibyl, a percussion-triggered music generator. His skill as a clown pushes this tool to its limits.

Don Ritter
designer/composer
Montreal, Quebec

Trevor Tureski
percussionist/composer
Banff, Alberta

Tureski's percussion is translated (by Ritter's "Orpheus") into a series of animations composed of pre-rendered video frames.

Leslie-Ann Coles
dancer/composer
Toronto, Ontario

David Rokeby
designer/composer
Toronto, Ontario

Coles' every motion is translated (by Rokeby's "Very Nervous System") into sound. She plays empty space as if it were an instrument.

Chris Van Raalte
dancer/designer
San Francisco, CA

A skilled dancer, Van Raalte uses wireless MIDI controllers to muscularly control sound in real time.

Mark "Spoonman" Petrakis
host/director
San Francisco, CA

Petrakis is director of Cobra Lounge Melto-o-Media, a collaborative visual performance group, and a partner in pARTy/SCIENCE, an art/tech events company.

INTERACTIVE PERFORMANCE

Posters

Designing For Use
Chair: Michael Atwood, *NYNEX Corporation*

Knowledge Structure and Subject Access
Kay A. Flowers, Nancy J. Cooke
Rice University

**Personalized Information Delivery:
An Analysis of Filtering Methods**
Peter W. Foltz, *University of Colorado*
Susan T. Dumais, *Bellcore*

**IRMail: A Minimal Interface for a
Retrieval System**
Peter W. Foltz, *University of Colorado*

**Strategy for Managing Metaphor
Mismatching**
Makoto Hirose
*Institute for Personalized Information
Environment*

**The Electronic Scrapbook: Knowledge
Representation and Interface Design for
Desktop Video**
Amy Bruckman, *MIT Media Laboratory*

**"Why Can't I Adjust My Refrigerator's
Temperature?" or "What's Wrong With My
Mental Model?"**
Sharon A. Davison, Marc M. Sebrechts
The Catholic University of America

**A Self-Promoting and Explanatory Audio
Control Panel**
John de Vet, Kees van Deemter, Hans Kemp,
Jack Gerrissen
Institute for Perception Research

Home Networks - The Race DCPN Project
Martin Maguire, Gordon Allison, Stephen Hirst,
Kate Howey, *The HUSAT Research Institute*

**IBC Systems and Services Usability
Engineering - The Race Issue Project**
Gordon Allison, Anne Clarke
The HUSAT Research Institute

**Specialized Methods Do Not Always
Increase Efficiency**
Catherine A. Ashworth, *University of Colorado*

**A Comparison of Direct-Manipulation,
Selection, and Data-Entry Techniques for
Re-ordering Fields in a Table**
Thomas S. Tullis, Marianne L. Kodimer
Canon Information Systems

**Does the User Interface Make Interruptions
Disruptive? A Study of Interface Style and
Form of Interruption**
Nancy A. Storch
Lawrence Livermore National Laboratory

**Computer-Based Workstation Design
Evaluations**
Mihriban Whitmore, Robert P. Wilmington,
Randy B. Morris, Ann M. Aldridge
Lockheed Engineering and Science Company
Dean G. Jensen, *NASA-Johnson Space Center*

**Interface Development for Individuals with
Mild Learning Disabilities from Traumatic
Brain Injury**
Elliot Cole, Parto Dehdashti
Institute for Cognitive Prosthetics

**Eloquent Video Expressions (ELVES):
A Communication System Design for People
with Linguistic or Neurological Limitations**
Hilarie Nickerson, *Molecular Design Limited*

**Realtime Graphical Display of Intonation
for SpeechTraining**
Dik J. Hermes, Gerard W. G. Spaai,
Arent Storm
Institute for Perception Research

Helping Users, Programmers, and Designers
Chair: Deborah Boehm-Davis
George Mason University

**On-Line Help: Are We Tossing the Users a
Life Saver or an Anchor?**
A. Brady Farrand, Susan J. Wolfe
Tandem Computers

An Active Task Manual
Rodney Ruddock, *University of Guelph*

**Evaluation Criterion for Computer-Based
Training Courseware**
G. Patterson, T. J. Anderson, F. C. Monds
University of Ulster

Automated Expert Advisor Interfaces
Kevin O'Brien
Lockheed Engineering Science Co.
Evan M. Feldman, *Rice University*
Marianne Rudisill, *NASA-Johnson Space Center*

**Tutorial: A Tool for Teaching Graphics
Programming**
Michael J. Papper, Michael A. Gigante
Royal Melbourne Institute of Technology

**Design Strategies in Object-Oriented
Programming and Expertise**
Françoise Détienne, *Institut National de
Recherche en Informatique ot Automatique*

**Comparing Procedural and Object-Oriented
Design**
Adrienne Lee, Nancy Pennington
University of Colorado
Scott Wolff, *U S WEST Advanced Technologies*

Participatory Video Prototyping
Emilie Young, Russell Greenlee
U S WEST Advanced Technologies

SUIT: The Simple User Interface Toolkit
Randy Pausch, Robert DeLine, Matthew
Conway
University of Virginia

POSTERS

Agentsheets: A Tool for Building Visual Programming Environments
Alex Repenning, Tamara Sumner
University of Colorado

Iterative Design of a Voice Dialog Design Environment
Tamara Sumner, Susan Davies, Peter G. Polson
University of Colorado
Andreas C. Lemke, *GMD-IPSI*

User Interfaces for Distributed Control Systems: The Hyperface UIMS
R. Polillo, *Etnoteam Spa*

Designing Graphical User Interfaces by Direct Composition
Matthias Schneider-Hufschmidt, Thomas Kühme
Siemens Corporate Research and Development

Taxonomy of Participatory Design Practices: A Participatory Poster
Michael J. Muller, Daniel M. Wildman,
Ellen A.White, *Bellcore*

Developing a Design Method: Task Analyses in User Interface Design
Mathilde M. Bekker, Arnold P.O.S. Vermeeren
Delft University of Technology

Determining `Characteristic Interactions' for Early Prototyping
Raghu Kolli, Arnold P.O.S. Vermeeren
Delft University of Technology

Using the Cognitive Walkthrough in Iterative Design
Marita Franzke, *University of Colorado*

Usability Testing: Is the Whole Test Greater than the Sum of its Parts
Alice Y. K. Wong, Adriane M. Donkers,
Richard F. Dillon, Jo W. Tombaugh
Carleton University

Improving Team Performance
Chair: J. Bryan Lewis
IBM T.J. Watson Research Center

TelePICTIVE Groupware for Collaborative GUI Design
John G. Smith, David S. Miller, Michael J. Muller
Bellcore

The Design of the Conversation Board
Tom Brinck, Louis M. Gomez, *Bellcore*

GROUPKIT: A Groupware Toolkit
Mark Roseman, Saul Greenberg
University of Calgary

Collection and Analysis of Data About Group Processes in Computer Supported Meetings
Mark Carter, James D. Herbsleb, Robin Lampert,
Gary M. Olson, Judith S. Olson, Henry H. Rueter,
Marianne Størrosten, *University of Michigan*

The Introduction of GDSS in Bulgaria
Terri L. Griffith, Gregory B. Northcraft
Northwestern University
Mark A. Fuller, *University of Arizona*

An Empirical Examination of Software-Mediated Information Exchange and Communication Richness
Gary J. Cook, Severin V. Grabski
Michigan State University

The Evolution of Linking Facilities in OISE's CSILE System
Sheryl Brock, Aron Kwok, Alan Rosenthal,
Peter Rowley, Jim Hewitt
Ontario Institute for Studies in Education

Designs to Encourage Discourse in the OISE CSILE System
Jim Hewitt
Ontario Institute for Studies in Education

An Interface Design for Learning Spelling Through Integrated Intentional Spell-Checking
Douglas R. Ward, Esther L. Tiessen
Ontario Institute for Studies in Education

Introducing the Suitware Project
Thomas Kühme, Uwe Malinowski,
Matthias Schneider-Hufschmidt, Hartmut Dieterich
Siemens Corporate Research and Development

Who Adapts What in HCI?
Manfred Langen, Gerd Hornung
Siemens Corporate Research and Development

The Utility of Various Windowing Capabilities for Single-Task and Multi-Task Environments
Kritina L. Holden, Michael R. O'Neal
Lockheed Engineering & Science Co.

Developing an Error Prevention Methodology Based on Cognitive Error Models
Kristin J. Bruno, Linda L. Welz, Josef Sherif
Jet Propulsion Laboratory

Modeling System Evolution: A Means of Cutting Through Obstacles to Desirable Change to Large Business (Information) Systems, Their Many Computer-Human Interfaces, and User/Operator Responsibilities
Richard I. Anderson, *Consultant*

The Xerox Work Practices Project
Pam Barrett, Francoise Brun-Cottan, Jean Giacomi,
Ruediger W. Knodt, Denise McLaughlin, Andrea
Mosher, Susan L. Saunders, Patricia S. Wall,
James B. Williams, Nancy B. Williamson
Xerox Corporation
Jeanette Blomberg, *Xerox PARC*

Designing the Ins and the Outs
Chair: Alonso Vera, *Carnegie Mellon University*

User Acceptance of Computer Applications with Speech, Handwriting and Keyboard Input Devices
Mary J. LaLomia, *IBM Corporation*

Of Mice and Children
Maria Milenkovic, Roland Alo, *IBM Corporation*

The Multi-Modal Integrative Mouse - A Mouse with Tactile Display
Motoyuki Akamatsu, Sigeru Sato
Industrial Products Research Institute

Contextual Motor Feedback in Cursor Control
Reinder Haakma
Institute for Perception Research

"Finger-Pointer": A Glove Free Interface
Masaaki Fukumoto, Kenji Mase,
Yasuhito Suenaga
NTT Human Interface Laboratories

A Graphic Object Manipulation System Using Hand Gestures
Takeshi Onishi, Haruo Takemura, Fumio Kishino
ATR Communication Systems Research Laboratories

HyperMark: Issuing Commands by Drawing Marks in HyperCard
Gordon Kurtenbach, Thomas Baudel
University of Toronto

Remote Manipulation Interfaces: The Case of a Telepathology Workstation
Catherine Plaisant, David A. Carr
University of Maryland

DispLayers: Multi-Layer Display Technique to Enhance Selective Looking of Overlaid Image
Minoru Kobayashi, Hiroshi Ishii
NTT Human Interface Laboratories

Design Techniques for Scientific Visualization
Colleen Bushell
University of Illinois at Urbana-Champaign

An Image Synthesizing Method Based on Human Motion Recognition from Stereo Images
Hirofumi Ishii, Kenji Mochizuki, Fumio Kishino
ATR Communication Systems Research Laboratories

Voice-Reactive Facial Expression Graphics Feedback for Improved Human-to-Machine Speech Input
Tomio Watanabe, *Yamagata University*

Integrating Animation with Interfaces
Stephane Chatty, *CENA*
Michael Beaudouin-Lafon, *LRI*

Research Symposium

CHI'92 Research Symposium

Organizers:
John M. Carroll,

IBM T.J. Watson Research Center

Jonathan Grudin, *University of California, Irvine*

James Hollan, *Bell Communications Research*

David Kieras, *University of Michigan*

Ben Shneiderman, *University of Maryland*

The CHI'92 Research Symposium was held on the Friday and Saturday immediately prior to the CHI conference itself. The underlying idea was to provide an intense and informal forum for CHI researchers to meet and discuss their current and proposed projects, an occasion to try out new ideas and to engage in extended give-and-take with colleagues. We particularly wanted to encourage participants to take risks, to talk programmatically, to conjecture, and to search.

We received fifty submissions for the Symposium, and invited several additional senior researchers to serve as discussants. We divided the two days into four generous "megasessions". The first session sought to make sense of the research programmes that have typified research in human-computer interaction in recent years. The second session focused on design as something we need to understand better but which also provides opportunities for us to better pursue established research concerns in problem-solving, collaboration, and the nature of work. The third session focused on vision-based interaction. The fourth session opened a discussion of what research programmes will guide us in the future.

Abstracts Submitted to the Symposium:

Using Formal Methods for the Specification of User Interfaces
Gregory D. Abowd

Language and Technical Artifacts
Phil Agre

Integrating Complementary Inputs to Design: The Role of Design Space Analysis
Victoria Bellotti, Allan MacLean

On the Use of Task and Domain Modeling for Intelligent User Interface Design
Hans Brunner

Making History by Telling Stories
John M. Carroll

Supporting Skills of the Hand and Eye
Kathleen Carter

Research in Human-Computer Interaction at Rice University
Nancy J. Cooke

Embodying Concepts in Design Notations
Alan Dix

Human Computer Interaction Research-Going Beyond the City Walls Again
Gerhard Fischer

Top Level Editing vs. Top Level Information Retrieval: Scale in Information Manipulation
George W. Furnas

Taking an Ecological Approach to Design
William W. Gaver

The Weak Science of Human-Computer Interaction
Saul Greenberg, Harold Thimbleby

Two HCI Research Communities
Jonathan Grudin

Simulating Opportunistic Design to Derive Principles for Interactive Design
Raymonde Guindon

Object-Centered Integration History: Read wear, Edit Wear, Menu Wear...
William C. Hill, James D. Hollan

Towards an Informational Physics Perspective for Interface Design
Jim Hollan, Will Hill

Cognitive Bug Rumblers
Andrew Howes, Richard M. Young

Design Rationale: A Design Method or a Research Technique?
Peter Johnson

Facilitation of Partnership in HCI Design
John Karat, John Bennett

Artifact as Product: Theory-Nexus Meets Real-World Design
Wendy A. Kellogg, Clare-Marie Karat

Misadventures with Mental Models or the Triumph of the Rote
David Kieras

A Process Model of Display-Based Human-Computer Interaction
Muneo Kitajima, Peter G. Polson

Interacting in Time
Andreas Lemke

RESEARCH SYMPOSIUM

Short Talks

Good Graphics!
Application of graphic design
Chair: Suzanne Watzman
Watzman Information Design

Maintaining Legibility, Structure, and Style of Information Layout in Dynamic Display Environments
Grace Colby, *MIT Media Laboratory*

Minimalism in Graphics
Douglas J. Gillan, Edward Richman, Michael Neary, *University of Idaho*

Audio Cues for Graphic Design
Solange Karsent
Digital Equipment Corporation
James A. Landay, *Carnegie Mellon University*
Chris Weikart, *Digital Equipment Corporation*

Three-Dimensional Algorithm Animation
John T. Stasko, Joseph F. Wehrli
Georgia Institute of Technology

Programming with Characters
Michael Travers, Marc Davis
MIT Media Laboratory

Rough and Ready Prototypes: Lessons from Graphic Design
Yin Yin Wong, *Apple Computer, Inc.*

Audio Video and Beyond...
Series of tools and architectures which open up new domains
Chair: Randy Pausch, *University of Virginia*

Digitized Speech's Serial Position Effect
G. Michael Barnes
California State University, Northridge

Semi-Structured Display of Telephone Conversations
Debby Hindus, Chris Schmandt
MIT Media Laboratory

3-D Video Modeling
Henry Holtzman, *MIT Media Laboratory*

Salient Stills
Laura Teodosio, Walter Bender
MIT Media Laboratory

Bioelectric Input Devices, An Example: BIOLINK
François Aubin, *Biolinka Inc.*
Jean-Marc Robert
Ecole Polytechnique de Montréal

Physically-Grounded Interface Architecture for Human-Robot Cooperation
Yasushi Nakauchi, Kenji Kawasugi, Yuichiro Anzai
Keio University

Make it Work!
Papers study work in context, ranging from applications of GOMS to positioning of touch screens to groupware
Chair: Ellen White, *Bellcore*

Overcoming Touchscreen User Fatigue by Workplace Design
Bengt Ahlström
Interaction and Presentation Laboratory
Sören Lenman
Ecolé Polytechnique de Montréal
Thomas Marmolin
National Defence Research Establishment

Natural Dialog in a Time-Sensitive Setting, A Study of Telephone Operators
Debbie Lawrence, Shelly Dews
NYNEX Science and Technology, Inc.

Accuracy of MHP/GOMS Predictions for the Task of Issuing Recurrent Commands
Alison Lee, *University of Toronto*

Can Mental Models Be Considered Harmful?
Victor Kaptelinin
Institute of General and Educational Psychology

Virtual Open Office: Supporting Effective "Open" Contact
Jin Li, Marilyn M. Mantei
University of Toronto

Rules of Thumb for Designing Effective External Aids
Henry B. Strub
University of California, San Diego

The Electronic Receptionist: A Knowledge-Based Approach to Personal Communications
Warren S. Gifford, David L. Turock, *Bellcore*

WeMet: Progress Report on a Pen-based Meeting Support Tool
Catherine G. Wolf, James R. Rhyne
IBM T.J. Watson Research Center

In Search of a Method...
Chair: Kate Ehrlich, *Sun Microsystems, Inc.*

Ideal: A Tool to Enable User-Centered Design
Stacey Ashlund, Deborah Hix
Virginia Polytechnic Institute & State University

A Seeded Design Environment for Service Creation
Anders Morch, Bart Burns
NYNEX Science and Technology, Inc.
Jonathan Ostwald, *University of Colorado*

The MUSiC Methodology for Usability Measurement
Nigel Bevan, *National Physical Laboratory*

What is Gained and Lost When Using Usability Methods Other Than Empirical Testing
Heather Desurvire, Jim Kondziela, Michael E. Atwood
NYNEX Science and Technology, Inc.

Observer Accuracy in Usability Testing: The Effects of Obviousness and Prior Knowledge of Usability Problems
Adriane M. Donkers, Jo W. Tombaugh, Richard F. Dillon, *Carleton University*

Reliability of Severity Estimates for Usability Problems Found by Heuristic Evaluation
Jakob Nielsen, *Bellcore*

SHORT TALKS

Special Interest Groups

Midyear Meeting of the Human Factors Society's Computer Systems Technical Group
Organizer:
Martha Crosby, *University of Hawaii*

User Interface Standards: Update for 1992
Organizer:
Pat Billingsley , *Interactive Technologies*

Interfaces for Persons with Disabilities
Organizer:
David L. Jaffe, *Palo Alto VA Medical Center*

GUI Styleguides for Fun and Profit
Organizers:
Robert W. Root, *Bellcore*
Kathy Uyeda, *Symantec Corporation*

Visual Design
Organizer:
Suzanne Watzman, *Watzman Information Design*

Recognition-Based Interfaces: Dealing with Errors
Organizers:
Catherine G. Wolf, James R. Rhyne
IBM T.J. Watson Research Center

Usability Labs in the 90's
Organizers:
Kay Chalupnik, *IDS*
Janice James, *American Airlines*
Judith Ramey, *University of Washington*

Issues in Multi-disciplinary Team Software Development
Organizers:
Gary Anderson, *Boeing*
Carol Taylor, *Sakson and Taylor*
Beth Meyer, *NCR*
Sharon Kasper, *Boeing*

Current HCI Research Concerns for Speech Recognition
Organizer:
David Leip, *University of Guelph*

Making Human Factors Work in Organisations
Organizer:
Bronwen Taylor, *HUSAT*

Using TAE Plus: A Graphical User Interface Development Tool
Organizer:
Martha R. Szczur
NASA/Goddard Space Flight Center

The Garnet User Interface Development Environment
Organizer:
Brad A. Myers, *Carnegie Mellon University*

Providing Education and Promoting Technical Vitality in Usability in the '90s
Organizers:
Deborah A. Zucker, Fran L. Phillips,
Emily B. Ellenbogen, *IBM*

Usability Foresight
Organizer:
Alan Happ, *IBM*

Non-Productivity HyperCard Stacks
Organizer:
Mike Mosher

Artists Using Science and Technology
Organizer:
Eleanor Kent

Methodology for User Centred Systems Design: Preliminary Meeting of Prospective IFIP TC 13.x Working Group.
Organizers:
Alistair Sutcliffe
Michael Tauber, *University Paderborn*
Jack Carroll, *IBM T.J. Watson Research Center*

Lessons Learned from Teaching HCI
Organizer:
Jean Gasen, *Virginia Commonwealth University*

SPECIAL INTEREST GROUPS

Tutorials

Designing Graphical Interfaces in the Real World
Annette Wagner, Bruce "Tog" Tognazzini
SunSoft, Inc.

Virtual Reality and Highly Interactive Three Dimensional User Interfaces
Mark Green, Chris Shaw, *University of Alberta*
Randy Pausch, *University of Virginia*

Computer Supported Meeting Environments
Marilyn Mantei, *University of Toronto*

Multimedia and Multimodal User Interface Design
Meera Blattner, *University of California, Davis,* and *Lawrence Livermore National Laboratory*

Contextual Design: Using Contextual Inquiry for System Development
Karen Holtzblatt, Sandra Jones
Digital Equipment Corporation

Early Design Methodology for Usable Products and Documentation
Stephanie Rosenbaum, *Tec-Ed, Inc.*
Judith Ramey, *University of Washington*
Judee Humburg, *Hewlett-Packard Company*
Anne Seeley, *Aldus Corporation*

Introduction to Cognitive Psychology
John Jonides, *University of Michigan*

Applying the Task-Artifact Framework to HCI Design
John M. Carroll, Mary Beth Rosson,
Mark K. Singley
IBM T. J. Watson Research Center

Film Craft in User Interface Design
Chuck Clanton, Frank Iannella, Emilie Young,
Aratar

Successful Hypertext Projects
Robert J. Glushko, *Hypertext Engineering*

Conversational Paradigms in User Interfaces
Debby Hindus, *MIT Media Laboratory*
Susan Brennan, *State University of New York, Stony Brook*

Introduction and Overview of Human-Computer Interaction
Keith Butler, *Boeing Computer Services*
D. Austin Henderson, *Xerox*
Robert J. K. Jacob, *Naval Research Laboratory*
Bonnie E. John, *Carnegie Mellon University*

Teaching User Interface Development
Gary Perlman, *Ohio State University*

Presenting Information Visually: Graphic Design Principles for User Interface Designers
Suzanne Watzman, *Watzman Information Design*

Copyright Protection for Software and User Interfaces
Pamela Samuelson, *University of Pittsburgh*

Building Collaborative Interfaces
Alan Wexelblat, *Electric Blue Lighting and Art*

A Practical Introduction to Experimental Design in CHI Research
Jo W. Tombaugh, Richard F. Dillon
Carleton University

Games and Other Techniques for Group Design of User Interfaces
Michael J. Muller, Daniel M. Wildman,
Ellen A. White, *Bellcore*

GOMS Analyses for Parallel Activities
Bonnie E. John, *Carnegie Mellon University*
Waye D. Gray, *Fordham University*

New Interaction Media
Robert J.K. Jacob, *Naval Research Laboratory*
Barry Arons, Walter Bender, *MIT Media Laboratory*
Scott S. Fisher, *Telepresence Research*

Sequential Experimentation Techniques for Evaluating Computer-Human Interactions
Robert C. Williges, Beverly H. Williges
Virginia Polytechnic Institute and State University

A Cost-Effective Technique for Refining the Usability of Prototype Systems
Andrew Monk, Peter Wright, *University of York*
Lora Davenport, *Information Dimensions Inc.*
Cognitive Walkthroughs: A Method for Theory-Based Evaluation of User Interfaces
Clayton Lewis, Peter G. Polson
University of Colorado

Designing Interactive Applications
William Newman, Mik Lamming
Rank Xerox EuroPARC

Innovating Interfaces: Concept Creation and Visualization
Shelley Evenson, John Rheinfrank,
Duncan Sutherland, Kate Welker, Wendie Wulff
Fitch RichardsonSmith

Product Usability Survival Techniques
Jared M. Spool, *User Interface Engineering*

Practical Techniques for User-Centered IT Product Specification
Bronwen Taylor, Neil Waddell
HUSAT Research Institute UK

Participatory Design
Morten Kyng, *Aarhus University, Denmark*
Joan Greenbaum
*La Guardia Community College,
City University of New York*

TUTORIALS

**Computer Supported Cooperative Work
and Groupware**
Steven Poltrock, *Boeing Computer-Services*
Jonathan Grudin, *University of California, Irvine*

**Automating the Design of Effective Graphics for
Intelligent User Interfaces**
Steven Feiner, *Columbia University*
Jock Mackinlay, *Xerox PARC*
Joe Marks, *Digital Equipment Corporation*

**Interactive Learning Environments: Where They've
Come From and Where They're Going**
Elliott Soloway, *University of Michigan*

GUI Designs: An Art History Perspective
Lori Marchak, *TASC*

**Cost-Benefit and Business Case Analysis of
Usability Engineering**
Clare-Marie Karat
IBM T. J. Watson Research Center

Icon Design
Paulien Strijland, *Apple Computer, Inc.*

**Interface Builder and Object-Oriented Design in
the NeXTstep Environment**
Michael K. Mahoney
California State University, Long Beach

**Walking the Wire: Balanced Design for
Computer-Human Interaction**
George Casaday, Sandra Jones
Digital Equipment Corporation
Eliot Tarlin, *Apple Computer , Inc.*

**Strategies for Encouraging Successful Adoption of
Group Communication Technologies**
Susan Ehrlich Rudman
U S WEST Advanced Technologies
Ellen Francik, *Pacific Bell*

Workshops

Usability Inspection Methods
Robert Mack, *IBM T.J. Watson Research Center*
Jakob Nielsen, *Bellcore*

Cross-Cultural Perspectives on Human-Computer Interaction
John Thomas, *NYNEX Science & Technology, Inc.*
Wendy Kellogg, *IBM T.J. Watson Research Center*
Jonathan Grudin, *University of California at Irvine*

Advances in Computer-Human Interaction in Complex Systems
William Hefley, *Carnegie Mellon University*
Steven Jacobs, *TRW*
Christine Mitchell, *Georgia Institute of Technology*

End-User Programming
Wayne Gray, *Fordham University*
James Spohrer, *Apple Computer, Inc.*
T.R.G. Green, *MRC Applied Psychology Unit*

Exploratory Sequential Data Analysis: Traditions, Techniques and Tools
Penelope Sanderson
University of Illinois, Urbana-Champaign
Carolanne Fisher, *MAYA Design Group*

Skills Needed By User-Centered Designers in Real Software Development Environments
Tom Dayton, *Bellcore*

Lessons Learned From Teaching HCI: Challenges, Innovations and Visions
Jean Gasen, *Virginia Commonwealth University*
Tom Carey, *University of Guelph*
Gary Strong, *Drexel University*
Bill Verplank, *IDEO*
Peter Aiken, *George Mason University*

WORKSHOPS

Authors Index

Color Plates

Color Plates appear alphabetically by
first author on the following pages.

COLOR PLATES

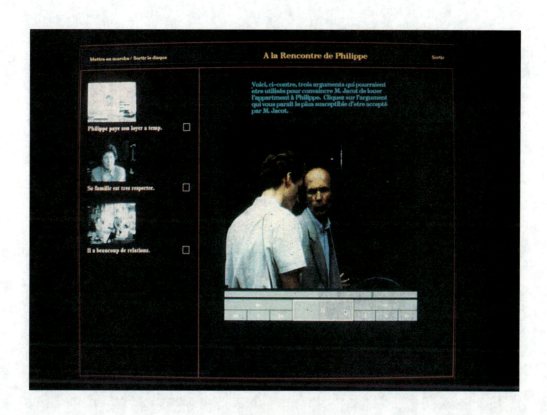

Adelson, Plate 1

Adelson, Plate 2

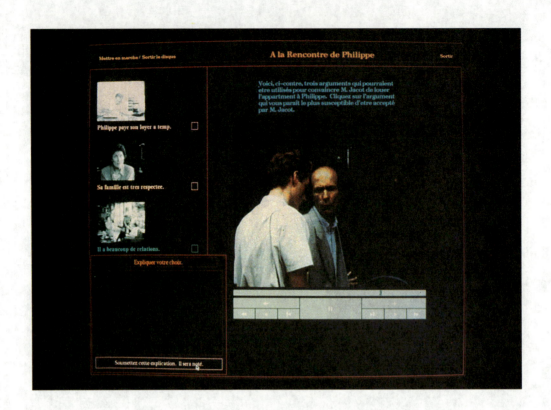

Adelson, Plate 3

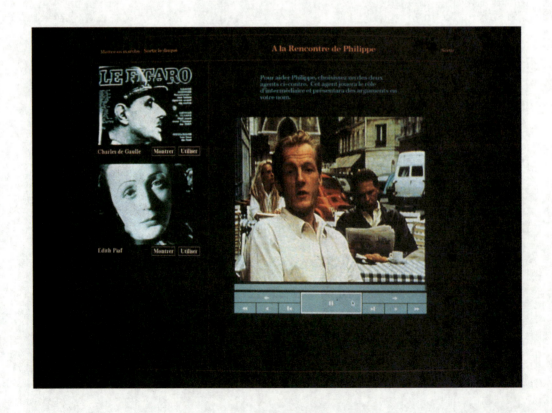

Adelson, Plate 4

Adelson, Plate 5

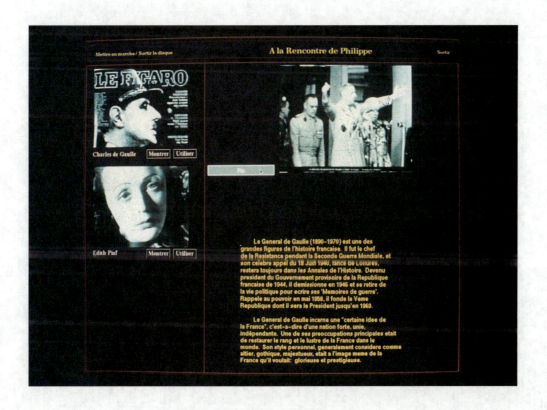

Adelson, Plate 6

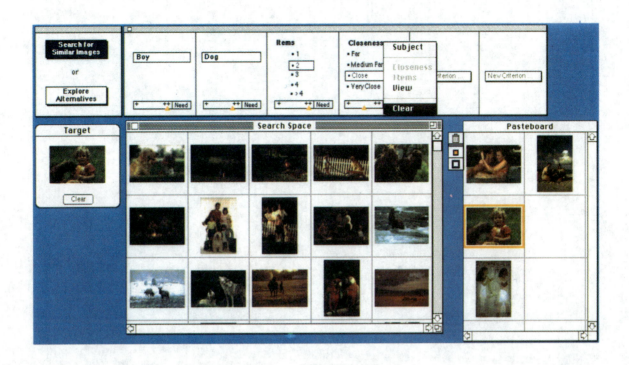

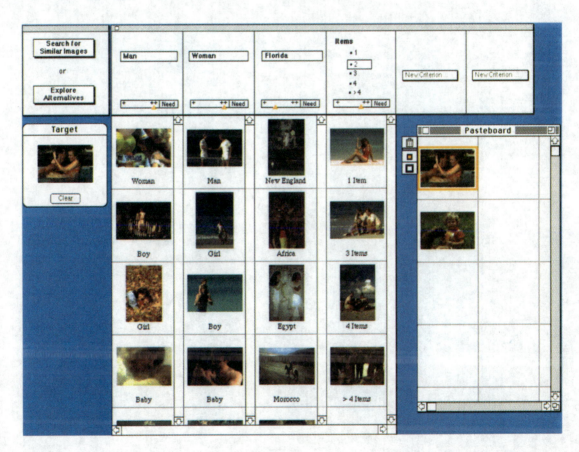

Garber, Plate 1

Ishii and Kobayashi, Plate 1

Ishii and Kobayashi, Plate 2

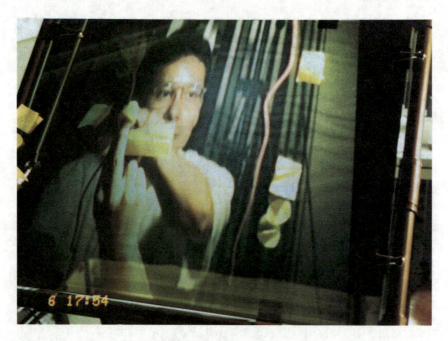

Ishii and Kobayashi, Plate 3

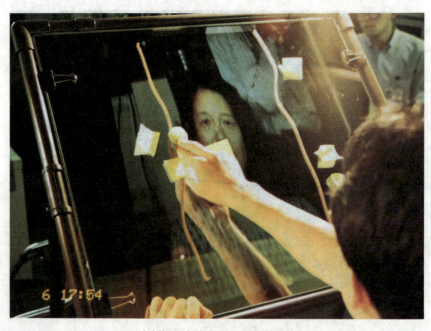

Ishii and Kobayashi, Plate 4

Koons, Plate 1: The CSEM's August 1991 *Cover*, the base of the CSEM's structural tree.

Koons, Plate 3: *Departments* Screen, 8/91. Users liked the graphic design of this screen, but misintepreted the term "Departments".

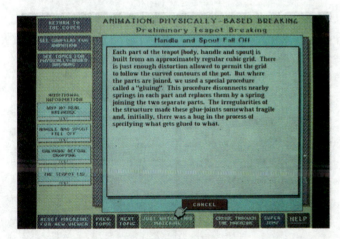

Koons, Plate 5: An all-text *sidebar*. The sidebar information (surrounded by blue border) was overlaid on the topic to which it related.

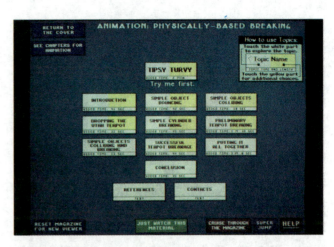

Koons, Plate 2: An *topics screen* for the article "Animation: Physically-Based Breaking". This design didn't clearly convey the article's structure.

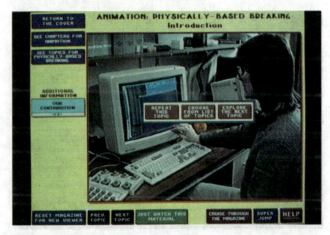

Koons, Plate 4: The first *topic* in the "Animation: Physically-Based Breaking" Article, "Introduction". Here the video has finished and the user is offered a choice of navigational buttons in the middle of the video window.

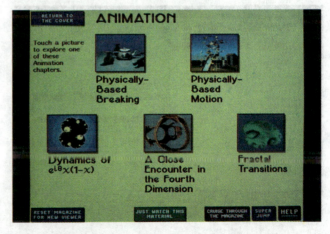

Koons, Plate 6: The "Animation" article contained so much material it was further divided into *chapters*.

Koons, Plate 7: *Cruise* was our first try at offering the user the ability to "flip through" the CSEM.

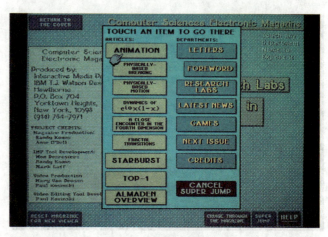

Koons, Plate 8: *Super Jump* was used like a table of contents in the 8/91 CSEM, but didn't provide enough information to be truly useful to users.

Koons, Plate 9: *Contents Page,* one of the most important elements in the re-designed CSEM.

Koons, Plate 10: The CSEM's *re-designed Cover* still has the familiar masthead, but offers quick access to the Contents page.

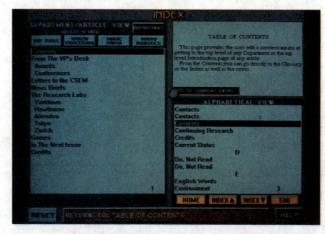

Koons, Plate 11: *Index* gives users a familiar means of accessing information in the re-designed CSEM.

Koons, Plate 12: *Page* layout in the re-designed CSEM is simpler and easier to use. VCR-like controls have been added, and buttons display reverse-color when touched.

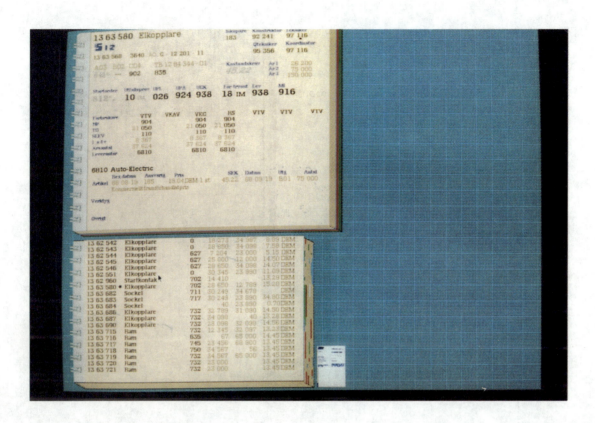

Nygren, Lind, Johnson, Sandblad, Plate1. An example of a user-interface where filled-in data creates an interpretable pattern. The bottom-pad contains an index of about 400 articles (an article = a detail necessary for car manufacturing). Every article have a fixed position on the page so that the frequent user will be able to create a memory-picture of "where" the articles are. The top-pad gives overview information about one article selected from the bottom pad. Character and position codes have been used for expressing relevant information.

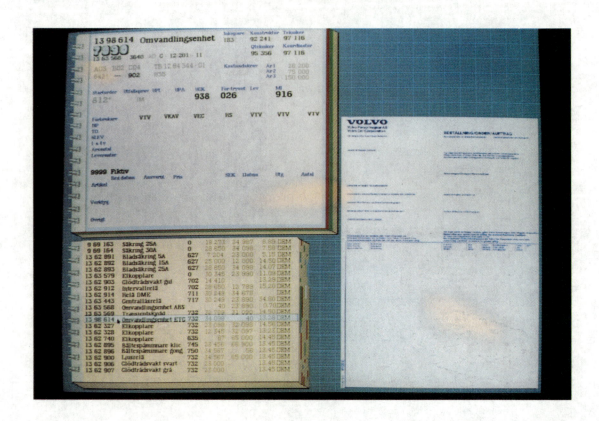

Nygren, Lind, Johnson, Sandblad, Plate 2. The thickness of a pad gives approximate knowledge about the number of pages. Colour-coding of the articles means that an overview of the distribution of articles on different projects can be seen in the colour-pattern on the side of the pad. There is enough screen-space left for work sheets, for instance an order form.

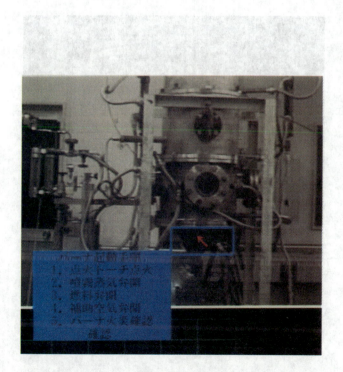

Editor for
defining
actions

Drawn models of
objects

Drawing tools

Tani Plate1

A tool set for defining simple 2D models of objects.

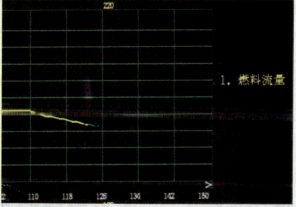

Tani Plate 2

Pointing to the burner causes it to be highlighted by
the blue rectangle and the document on its ignition
procedure also shows up.

Tani Plate 3

The graph shows the amount of fuel running through the
pipe pointed to by the user and highlighted by the blue
rectangle in the video image.

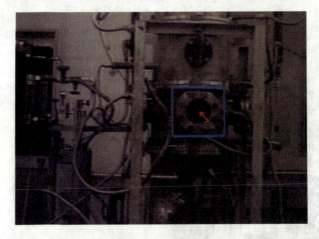

Tani Plate 4-1

Pointing to the window of the boiler causes it to be highlighted by the blue rectangle.

Tani Plate 5

The knob of the slider is dragged on the video image.

Tani Plate 4-2

The window pointed to is zoomed in on and then pointed again.

Tani Plate 6

An example of virtual control devices and graphic overlays that show the internal states which cannot be seen through cameras.

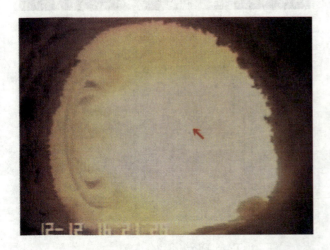

Tani Plate 4-3

The video image is switched to one taken through the window by a camera monitoring the flame inside the boiler.

Topic Guides

We are including topic guides as an experiment this year, to provide you with more information about the papers and panels than just their titles and authors. With the help of the authors and the Program Committee, each of the papers and panels has been categorized. These topic guides are not to be considered definitive or comprehensive. The chart below designates which papers were reviewed and categorized as work that relates predominantly to Theory, Methodology, and Concepts (T), or Practice and Experience (P). In addition, one or more of the following topic areas has been assigned:

e evaluation and testing	i implementation	s standards	u user interface design
g group work	p psychology of use	t tool development	

Tuesday, May 5, 2:00 - 3:30pm Pg. 18-19

Title	T/P	e	g	i	p	s	t	u
Edit Wear and Read Wear	T		g					u
The Computer Sciences Electronic Magazine: Translating from Paper to ...	P	e						u
Hypertext or Book: Which is Better for Answering Questions?	T	e			p			
Realizing a Video Environment: EuroPARC's RAVE System	T		g				t	
Evaluating Video as a Technology for Informal Communication	P	e	g					
Speech Patterns in Video-Mediated Conversations	T		g				t	u
PANEL: Anthropomorphism: From Eliza to Terminator 2	T				p			

Tuesday, May 5, 4:00 - 5:30pm

Title	T/P	e	g	i	p	s	t	u
An Interface for Interactive Spatial Reasoning and Visualization	T						t	u
Graphical Fisheye Views of Graphs	T			i				u
A Magnifier Tool for Video Data	T							u
A Research Program to Assess User Perceptions of Group Work Support	P		g					
Gardeners and Gurus: Patterns of Cooperation Among CAD Users	P		g					
Beyond Being There	T		g					
Evaluating Two Aspects of Direct Manipulation in Advanced Cockpits	T	e			p			u
Iterative Design of an Interface for Easy 3-D Direct Manipulation	T						t	u
Computing for Users with Special Needs and Models of CHI	T	e			p			u
PANEL: Designing Usable Systems Under Real-World Constraints. . .	P							u

Wednesday, May 6, 8:30 - 10:00 am Pg. 22-23

Title	T/P	e	g	i	p	s	t	u
The Art of Search: A Study of Art Directors	P				p			u
Browser-Soar: A Computational Model of a Highly Interactive Task	T				p			
Towards Task Models for Embedded Information Retrieval	T				p			
Knowledge-Based Evaluation as Design Support for Graphical User...	T	e					t	u
Controlling User Interface Objects Through Pre- and Postconditions	T			i			t	
Survey on User Interface Programming	P			i			t	
Orderable Dimensions of Visual Texture For Data Display...	T	e			p			
The Perceptual Structure of Multidimensional Input Device Selection	I	e			p			
Extending Fitts' Law to Two-Dimensional Tasks	T	e			p			
PANEL: When TVs are Computers are TVs	T							u

Wednesday, May 6, 10:30 am - 12:00 pm

Title	T/P	e	g	i	p	s	t	u
The Art of the Obvious	T	e			p			u
A Computational Model of Skilled Use of Graphical User Interfaces	T				p			
A GOMS Analysis of a Graphic, Machine-Paced, Highly Interactive ...	T				p			
Coupling Application Design and User Interface Design	T			i			t	u
Workspaces: An Architecture for Editing Collections of Objects	T			i			t	
Selectors: Going Beyond User-Interface Widgets	T			i			t	
PANEL: Interfaces for Consumer Products: "How to Camouflage the ...	P							u

Wednesday, May 6, 1:30 - 3:00 pm

Title	T/P	e	g	i	p	s	t	u
A Performance Model of System Delay and User Strategy Selection	T				p			u
The Précis of Project Ernestine or An Overview of a Validation of GOMS	T	e			p			u
Method Engineering: From Data to Model to Practice	T				p			u
The Decoupled Simulation Model for Virtual Reality Systems	T			i			t	
Interactive Simulation in a Multi-Person Virtual World	P		g	i				

Title	T/P	e	g	i	p	s	t	u
The Abstraction-Link-View Paradigm: Using Constraints to Connect...	T		g	i			t	
Grace Meets the "Real World": Tutoring COBOL as a Second Language	P	e			p			
Evocative Agents and Multi-Media Interface Design	T	e			p			
Graphic StoryWriter: An Interactive Environment for Emergent Storytelling	P	e			p		t	
PANEL: Toward a More Humane Keyboard	P							u

Wednesday, May 6, 3:30 - 5:30pm

Title	T/P	e	g	i	p	s	t	u
Finding Usability Problems Through Heuristic Evaluation	T	e						u
Applying Cognitive Walkthroughs to More Complex User Interfaces...	T	e						u
The Cognitive Jogthrough: A Fast-Paced User Interface Evaluation...	P	e						u
Comparison of Empirical Testing and Walkthrough Methods in User ...	T	e						u
One Dimensional Motion Tailoring for the Disabled: A User Study	T				p			u
Working with Audio: Integrating Personal Tape Recorders and Desktop ...	T							u
Skip and Scan: Cleaning up Telephone Interfaces	T	e		i	p			u
PANEL: Designing Collaborative, Knowledge-Building Environments for...	T+P	e						u

Wednesday, May 6, 5:30 - 7:30 pm

Title	T/P	e	g	i	p	s	t	u
Sci-Fi at CHI: Cyberpunk Novelists Predict Future User Interfaces	T							u

Thursday, May 7, 8:30 - 10:00 am Pg. 24-25

Title	T/P	e	g	i	p	s	t	u
Participatory Design of a Portable Torque-Feedback Device	P			i				
User Centred Development of a General Practice Medical Workstation ...	P			i				
Retrospective on a Year of Participatory Design using the PICTIVE...	P						t	u
Evolving Task Oriented Systems	P			i				u
A Visit to a Very Small Database: Lessons From Managing the Review ...	P			i				u
Designing Theory-Based Systems: A Case Study	P	e						u
Towards a Model of Cognitive Process in Logical Design: Comparing ...	T	e			p			u
Oriented Requirements and Design of DesignVision, An Object Oriented ...	T			i				u
Facilitating the Exploration of Interface Design Alternatives: Tho ...	T						t	u
PANEL: Collaborating in the World of Interactive Media	P		g					

Thursday, May 7, 10:30 am - 12:00 pm

Title	T/P	e	g	i	p	s	t	u
Clearboard: A Seamless Medium for Shared Drawing and Conversation...	T		g				t	
Spatial Workspace Collaboration: A Sharedview Video Support System ...	T		g				t	
Portholes: Supporting Awareness in a Distributed Work Group	T		g				t	
A Method for (Recruiting) Methods: Facilitating Human Factors Input to...	T	e						u
Teaching Experienced Developers to Design Graphical User Interfaces	P							u
Integrating Human Factors on a Large Scale: "Product Usability...	P	e						u
PANEL: In Search of the Ideal Prototype	T							u

Thursday, May 7, 1:30 -3:00 pm

Title	T/P	e	g	i	p	s	t	u
A Desk Supporting Computer-Based Interaction with Paper Documents	T			i				u
Object-Oriented Video: Interaction with Real-World Objects Through Live...	T			i				u
Liveboard: A Large Interactive Display Supporting Group Meetings...	T		g	i				u
Interactive Constraint-Based Search and Replace	T			i			t	u
Dynamic Queries for Information Exploration: An Implementation and...	T	e		i				u
A 'Pile' Metaphor for Supporting Casual Organization of Information	T			i	p			u
PANEL: HCI Standards on Trial: You be the Jury	P					s		

ACM SIGCHI
MEMBERSHIP APPLICATION

Scope The scope of SIGCHI consists of the study of the human-computer interaction and includes research and development efforts leading to the design and evaluation of user interfaces. The focus of SIGCHI is on how people communicate and interact with computer systems. SIGCHI serves as a forum for the exchange of ideas among computer scientists, human factors scientists, psychologists, social scientists, systems designers and end users.

Membership Includes
- Subscription to SIGCHI Bulletin (quarterly).
- CHI Conference Proceedings.

Topics Human factors in the interaction process; monitoring and evaluating the computer-human interface; methods, techniques and components of the user interface; cognitive functions involved in the interactive process; interaction between hardware, software, the task and the user; and promoting and understanding of the relationship between studies of user psychology and technology of computing and systems design.

Please check the appropriate membership dues box below.

To add SIGCHI to ACM Membership
- ☐ Adding SIGCHI to ACM Membership $25.00
- ☐ Adding SIGCHI to ACM Student Membership $10.00

ACM Membership #_____

Membership Note: If you are an ACM Member, send no money now. SIGCHI can be added to your current membership period at no cost. You will be billed when your membership is renewed. You will receive only those issues of the newsletter that are published from the time you join SIGCHI until your membership expires. (Current ACM members need only provide their membership number above)

To Join or Subscribe To SIGCHI
- ☐ SIG Membership only (non-ACM) .... $ 47.00
- ☐ Subscription to SIGCHI Bulletin only .... $ 45.00

To Join ACM and/or SIGCHI
- ☐ ACM Associate Member Dues .... $ 75.00
- ☐ ACM Associate Dues + SIGCHI $100.00
- ☐ ACM Student Member Dues .... $ 22.00
- ☐ ACM Student Dues + SIGCHI .... $ 32.00

ACM Associate and Student Member Dues includes a complimentary subscription to the monthly *Communications of the ACM.* For Voting Member privileges contact Member Services at address below.

Overseas Air Options ☐ Partial Air.........................$16.00 ☐ FullAir........................$50.00

ACM Purposes: To advance the sciences and arts of information processing; to promote the free interchange of information processing among computing specialists and the public; and to develop and maintain the integrity and competence of individuals engaged in the practice of information processing.

As an ACM member, I subscribe to the purposes of ACM: _____
Signature

☐ *Information about ACM and SIGCHI membership? Please provide your name and address below.*

Name (please print)_____ E-Mail_____

Mailing Address_____ Phone_____

City_____ State or Province_____ Country/ZipCode_____

Form of Payment ☐ Check(payable to ACM) ☐ Money Order ☐ Amex ☐ Mastercard ☐ Visa

If paying by credit card: Card#_____ Card Expiration Date_____

Signature_____

If you have any questions about ACM and/or SIGCHI membership contact:
ACM Member Service Department, Phone: 212-869-7440, E-mail: ACMHELP@ACMVM.BITNET, Fax:212-944-1318
Mail to: Association for Computing Machinery, P.O. Box 12114, Church Street Station, NY, NY 10257